More Resources Online

For additional help for writing about literature and links to other on-line writing resources, visit the Experience Literature Web site at:
www.smpcollege.com/experience_literature.

SEVENTH EDITION

LITERATURE
READING AND WRITING
THE HUMAN EXPERIENCE

RICHARD ABCARIAN AND MARVIN KLOTZ
California State University, Northridge, Emeriti

with PETER RICHARDSON
University of North Texas

St. Martin's Press
New York

Sponsoring editor: Donna Erickson
Development editor: Kristin Bowen
Managing editor: Erica T. Appel
Project editor: Harold Chester
Production supervisor: Scott Lavelle
Art director and cover design: Lucy Krikorian

Library of Congress Catalog Card Number: 97-65206

Manufactured in the United States of America.

3 2 1 0 9
f e d c b

For information, write:
St. Martin's Press, Inc.
175 Fifth Avenue
New York, NY 10010

ISBN: 0-312-15311-2

To Joan and Debra

Love: a word properly applied to our delight in particular kinds of food; sometimes metaphorically spoken of the favorite objects of all our appetites.

—Henry Fielding

CONTENTS

Innocence and Experience   58

For Thinking and Writing   60

Conformity and Rebellion *310*

For Thinking and Writing 312

Love and Hate   *944*

For Thinking and Writing   946

The Presence of Death   1150

POETRY   1256

Poetry and Fine Art   *1353*

ALTERNATE TABLE OF CONTENTS

arranged by genre*

*Within each genre, authors are listed chronologically by date of birth.

POETRY

DRAMA

ESSAYS

ART

PREFACE

Since publication of the first edition of *Literature* in 1973, we have been governed by a belief that the first task of an introductory anthology of literature is to engage the reader's interest, to make the experience of literature an immediate and exciting one. Thus, we have selected works not primarily because they illustrate critical definitions or lend themselves to a particular approach, but because we find them exciting and believe that students will, too. In this seventh edition we've added a new subtitle, *Reading and Writing the Human Experience,* to reflect the goals of the new edition: to connect students to literature by inviting them to participate in the conversation, to talk back to the works through writing.

The seventh edition of *Literature* was therefore developed to better serve the goals of the second-term course in composition with a focus on writing about literature. With two new introductory chapters on responding to and writing about literature, written by Peter Richardson of the University of North Texas, combined with strengthened apparatus throughout the anthology, *Literature* now offers all the support needed to teach any writing about literature or introduction to literature course. Selections have also been chosen to emphasize conflict and expose students to various styles and points of view, thereby encouraging students to articulate their own responses.

NEW TO THIS EDITION

Introductory Chapters on the Reading and Writing Process Designed to prepare students to write and argue about literature, the seventh edition includes two new introductory chapters on reading and writing about literature written by Peter Richardson. "Responding to Literature" helps students improve their critical reading and thinking skills with each of the four genres — fiction, poetry, drama, and essays. It also includes guidelines for interpreting literary works. The second chapter, "Writing about Literature," includes a brief overview of the writing process, as well as specific guidelines for writing explications, comparison/contrast essays, and other commonly assigned essays. This chapter also covers MLA documentation guidelines and provides some advice on working with sources.

Coverage of the Literary Essay The seventh edition of *Literature* now includes the literary essay as a fourth genre, along with fiction, poetry, and drama. Twenty-one classic and contemporary selections highlight the essay as literature and offer models for composition.

A Fifth Theme on Culture and Identity The works in a new section, Culture and Identity, reveal how culture powerfully shapes identity. These selections also reveal the tension and conflict generated by interacting cultures and allow readers to step outside the bounds and bonds of their own culture.

A Full-Color Portfolio of Art and Poetry A new 16-page color section adds stimulus for the imagination and new possibilities for writing. This section contains fourteen full-color plates alongside poems inspired by the art. Questions designed to help students "read" the images as texts draw students to make connections as they enter the dialog between poetry and painting.

Exciting New Selections New selections in the seventh edition, chosen to appeal to students, include 10 stories, 52 poems, and 9 plays, along with 21 literary essays. New selections include fiction by Chinua Achebe, Sandra Cisneros, and Tim O'Brien; poems by Charles Bukowski, Li-Young Lee, Marge Piercy, and Pablo Neruda; essays by Joan Didion, Mark Twain, and Martin Luther King Jr.; and class-tested dramatic favorites such as Ibsen's *A Doll's House,* Arthur Miller's *Death of a Salesman,* along with newer works such as August Wilson's *Two Trains Running.*

Thought-Provoking Apparatus throughout the Book Introductory essays begin each thematic part preparing students for the complex issues they are likely to encounter in the works that follow. The introductions include pre-reading questions that challenge students to reflect on their own experiences and spark classroom discussion. Each part concludes with newly expanded Questions and Writing Topics encouraging students to connect their experience of the literature with their own lives.

To provide the groundwork for discussion and debate, we now include four new types of questions following many selections. For Analysis questions promote critical reading and thinking by asking students to do a close reading of the text, examining the embedded issues and content. Making Connections questions engage students by encouraging them to consider the work in light of their own experiences as well as to discover links among the readings. On Style questions focus on the intricacy and power of the writer's use of language, while introducing students to the basic elements of literature, now with cross references to entries in the glossary set in bold type. Writing Topics include suggestions for brief, in-class activities and ideas for full-length essays.

Multimedia Resources for Teaching Literature and Writing
The Experience Literature Web Site at *www.smpcollege.com/experience _literature* links students and instructors to a wide variety of literary reference sources, including sites devoted to some of the authors included in the anthology. The Web site also provides instructors with additional teaching tips

and gives students additional background on critical approaches, as well as help with research and composition.

A *Poetry Audio Cassette* offers students a deeper experience of poetry, with a collection of forty classic and contemporary works from the text, by well-known readers as well as by the poets themselves.

The St. Martin's Video Library provides instructors with selected full-length feature film versions of selected works, including classic performances of *Othello, The Glass Menagerie, A Rose for Emily,* and *"MASTER HAROLD" . . . and the Boys,* among others.

Robert Frost: Poems, Life, Legacy CD-ROM, an in-depth guide, includes searchable text of Frost's poetry and biography, 90 minutes of audio of Frost reading 69 of his finest poems, over 1,500 pages of literary criticism and biography, and a new documentary film narrated by Richard Wilbur.

The *Instructor's Manual* is thoroughly revised and updated, now with a spiral binding for ease of use. Full of teaching ideas for each selection, the manual also includes additional thematic connections and writing topics.

ACKNOWLEDGMENTS

Many people at St. Martin's Press made valuable contributions to this textbook. We wish to acknowledge the efforts of Donna Erickson, Sandy Schechter, Patricia Phelan, Erica Appel, Scott Lavelle, Lucy Krikorian, Patricia McFadden, Susan Kaprov, John Sisson, Charles Cavaliere, Tonya Strong, Jason Noe, Griff Hansbury, and, of course, Sam. We are especially grateful to our Development Editor, Kristin Bowen, and our Project Editor, Harold Chester, for guiding this long, complex book through so many perils.

We thank Gary Miller down at the Venice Beach Paddle Tennis courts for insisting on Charles Bukowski.

We especially wish to thank Márgara Auerbach, our friend and colleague in Buenos Aires, Argentina, for giving us the benefit of her wide knowledge of American literature, North and South.

As well, we are grateful for the advice we received from those who reviewed for the seventh edition: Jed Allen, Phoenix College; Kathleen Anderson-Wyman, Idaho State University; Roger C. Arpin, Southeast Missouri State University; Carolyn Baker, San Antonio College; Jamie Barlowe, University of Toledo; Tim Barnes, Portland Community College; Mary Baron, University of North Florida; David A. Boxwell, United States Air Force Academy; James L. Brown, Kansas City Kansas Community College; Elizabeth Coughlin, Depaul University; Carol A. Cross, Cantonsville Community College; Michael R. Cross, Tulsa Community College, Metro Campus; Norma Cruz-Gonzalez, San Antonio College; David A. Boxwell, United States Air Force Academy; Cathy Della Penta, Mesa Community College; Irene R. Fairley, Northeastern University; Michael Fleming, University of San Francisco; Jane F. Friedmann, Northern Virginia Community College; Vaughn Hamilton,

Wharton County Junior College; Joan E. Hellman, Catonsville Community College; Nancy Kennedy, Edmonds Community College; W. David LeNoir, Western Kentucky University; Michele Frucht Levy, Xavier University of Louisiana; Cecilia Macheski, LaGuardia Community College; Susan Murray-Moore, Kent State University; Karen Lea Nead, Vincennes University; Shirley F. Nelson, Chattanooga State Technical Community College; Allene M. Parker, Idaho State University; Carolyn Sue Poor, Wharton County Junior College; Dale Salwak, Citrus College; Norman A. Spencer, Nassau Community College; Dean Stover, Gateway Community College; and Robert Zeller, Southeast Missouri State University.

Richard Abcarian
Marvin Klotz

SEVENTH EDITION

LITERATURE

READING AND WRITING
THE HUMAN EXPERIENCE

Responding to Literature

WHY WE READ LITERATURE

The word *literature* means different things to different people. To some, it suggests imaginative works of exceptional quality. To others, it refers to written works that have held up to repeated readings by various audiences over time. To still others, literature simply refers to what gets taught in schools and colleges, regardless of the reasons for their inclusion in the curriculum. How readers think about literature and assess literary value varies over time and even from person to person.

Although there isn't a universally accepted definition of literature and the standards of literary value change over time, there is a surprising amount of agreement about which works are most important to read and study. Together, these works are said to make up the literary *canon*. Over the last thirty years, the canon has changed significantly. In particular, previously ignored authors and works have been read intensively, with the result that the canon has been expanded and diversified. Just as our sense of which works deserve study has changed, so too have our ideas about how these works should be interpreted. Indeed, some critics have argued that literary works prove their worth in part by repaying various kinds of interpretative efforts over time.

Most readers would agree that works of literature distinguish themselves from other kinds of writing by a particular kind of attention to language. That is, in addition to treating some aspect of human experience imaginatively, many works call attention to their own linguistic virtuosity. This attention to language alters the usual relationship between the written word and the world. Much of the writing we do for school or work, for example, is meant to refer to the world as we know it, and language is a means to that end. Writing a lab report for your introductory biology class might require you to clearly describe and draw conclusions about an experiment you conducted. The language you choose for a lab report must be appropriate to your purpose (to accurately describe or summarize) and your audience (an instructor or your classmates). In contrast, literature evokes imaginative worlds through the self-conscious and stylized arrangement of words that tell a story. The story can be made up or true, but because literary works use words to create possible worlds, language itself is on display to a far greater degree than in many "everyday" kinds of writing.

Although literature has other goals besides telling a story and creating possible worlds, the relationship between a masterpiece and real life can be complex. This is because our sense of reality depends in part on our language and imagination, the very faculties that literature exercises so thoroughly.

In some sense, reality is related to the verbal universe we inherit, occupy, and construct for ourselves. What literature does is shape and maintain that part of the verbal universe most concerned with imagination and new possibilities.

Reading literature is not always an easy pleasure; it is not like enjoying a tasty meal or relaxing in a hot bath. On the contrary, literature makes significant linguistic, intellectual, moral, and emotional demands. Only if the reader attempts to meet these demands do works begin to yield their pleasures. The pleasures derived from literature are proportional to the energy we expended to achieve them.

Though reading literature is not terribly useful in the sense that it does not in and of itself improve the reader in financial or social ways, it does not follow that literature—or the pleasure readers take in it—has no value. If reading literature is in any way practical over and above its capacity to give pleasure, that practicality consists not in its immediate usefulness but in its ability to teach us new ways to read, think, imagine, feel, and make sense of our experience.

When a work of literature pleases, when it moves its reader, he or she has responded to the author's carefully created world. The pleasure, the emotional commitment, the human response in the reader are not the results of analysis. The reader has not registered in some mental adding machine the several details that establish character, the manipulation of the point of view, the plot, the theme, the style. The reader has recognized and accepted the world of the author and has been delighted (or saddened or angered) by what happens in it.

This anthology presents four literary *genres:* fiction, poetry, drama, and essays. If you have been in a video store, you have encountered genres. Just as films can be organized into groups (drama, comedy, western, horror, and so on), works of literature can be sorted into categories. Each genre contains sub-genres; for example, poems may be classified as ballads, odes, sonnets, and epics. These genres are associated with certain conventions, or widely used devices or techniques that shape our expectations—and therefore our reading experiences—in significant ways. For example, we bring different expectations to mysteries or romances than we do to comic books or epic poems; these expectations, in turn, affect our responses to these works.

These expectations are important not only because they shape our responses but because authors take account of them in various ways. In certain kinds of writing, for example, authors mainly strive to satisfy audience expectations. A good portion of the sitcoms on television and the novels we see in drug stores fall into this category. The pleasure we derive from these shows and books is produced by slight variations on familiar plots and themes. More complex literary works, however, often challenge, subvert, or play against the expectations readers bring to them, asking us to review, reconsider, or reject our expectations. Literature of exceptional power may even transform your ideas about "real life."

While authors respond to familiar stories and readers' expectations, authors also respond to other influences. Many authors acknowledge that their work is shaped by other writers and the literature that has spoken to them most directly and powerfully. Authors frequently write about what happens around them and thereby express historically situated ideas, feelings, and values. In placing literary works in their historical context, we can better understand how past cultures differ from our own. The more we know about ancient Greece, for example, the more differences we can cite between Sophocles' world and ours. On balance, the similarities between different cultures—that is, the aspects of human experience that tend to persist over time and space—are often as remarkable as the differences. These similarities make a thematic approach to literature possible. The themes of innocence and experience, conformity and rebellion, culture and identity, love and hate, and the presence of death are not specific to any one society, even if the unique expressions of those themes finally are.

READING ACTIVELY AND THINKING CRITICALLY

As you read, you are also preparing to write about literature. This process compels you to discover and come to terms with your own response to a work. Every element in a literary work has been deliberately incorporated by the author—the description of setting, the events that constitute the plot, the dialogue, the imagery. One can perceive only a few things simultaneously and can hardly respond to everything contained in a well-wrought literary work all at once.

Reading with a Pen in Hand

To get at the meaning of a work, it is important, after first reading it straight through, to go back and reread it. You may want to highlight things that seem significant in this first reading, but to really get at what a writer is saying and to form your own response, you must reread and annotate as you go. As you read all of the works in this anthology, keep a pen in hand, underlining or highlighting interesting or confusing passages. Circle and look up unfamiliar words or references and jot down your dictionary's definitions. Annotate in the margins, recording first impressions that you may want to remember after this first reading. Highlight things you think are noteworthy, images that seem memorable, or anything else you like or dislike. As you begin to gather ideas for possible essay topics, these initial comments will become useful avenues to explore.

Thinking Critically to Form a Response

After reading a story, a reader likely thinks back, makes adjustments, and reflects on the significance of things before reaching the emotional and intellectual experience we refer to as *response*. Though there is no exact correspondence between "writer's purpose" and "reader's response," any attempt to write about literature is, in one way or another, an attempt to discover and describe that correspondence. In other words, whatever the assignment, your fundamental task is to provide the answers to two questions: "How do I respond to this piece? How has the author brought about my response?"

Your first reading of a literary work gives an overall view of the work, a sense of the plot and other essential elements—it may even just be for pleasure. As you reread a work, adding new annotations and getting additional insights into a work, you engage in your own critical reading, beginning to articulate your response.

Adopting a critical stance toward a work should involve scrutiny of the author's beliefs about human experience and his or her methods. But thinking critically also involves questioning your own assumptions about a work. For example, what does a story mean to you, and what evidence from the story did you choose to support your analysis? As you develop a working thesis, test the evidence you use. Is there any evidence in the story that points to different conclusions than the ones you draw? Are the reasons for your interpretation good ones? To be effective, it is important to scrutinize your argument, to determine whether your readers will find it persuasive and your supporting evidence convincing.

READING FICTION

Like other literary genres, fiction creates imaginary worlds. Unlike other sorts of literature, however, novels and short stories do so primarily by telling stories in prose, with realistic characters in actual physical environments, and with sustained attention to descriptive detail.

Works of fiction *narrate,* or tell stories. Of course, narrative is not specific to fiction or to any other literary genre; in fact, it pervades almost every aspect of our daily lives. We learn very early on how to recognize and tell stories, and we rely heavily on narrative to organize and make sense of our experience. For example, when we study history, we mostly study stories of various events. Likewise, an astronomer's account of the universe's origins may take the shape of a narrative. Even in our sleep, we tell ourselves stories in the form of dreams. It is impossible to imagine our lives without these narratives; in fact, every culture uses them to order, frame, and make sense of lived experience. Narrative fiction is not meant to recount actual events, of course, though it may refer to such events or include references to real persons. Rather than relate actual experiences, fiction uses narrative to shape imaginary ones.

Works of fiction, however, cannot be reduced to their narrative events any more than paintings can be replaced by diagrams. In such summaries the realism associated with these works, a realism produced by the careful description of characters, settings, and actions, is lost. By inventing, developing, and amassing descriptive details, works of fiction create the illusion of full, authentic, and realistic reports of human experience. Although not all works of fiction strive to imitate reality in this way, many do. This imitation of reality makes it easy for readers to suspend disbelief, or to enter the imaginary world of the novel or short story.

The Methods of Fiction

In order to reflect on the methods of fiction—tone, plot, theme, characterization, and point of view—let us explore in detail one story, James Joyce's "Araby" (p. 81).

Tone   One of the things most readers of short stories first respond to in a work of fiction is its *tone*. Because it is like an aura or atmosphere, tone is difficult to talk about. It can be defined as an author's implicit attitude toward the characters, places, and events in the story. Tone depends for its substance on delicate emotional responses to language and situation. Notice how a distinct tone is established in the opening lines of "Araby."

> North Richmond Street, being blind, was a quiet street except at the hour when the Christian Brothers' School set the boys free. An uninhabited house of two storeys stood at the blind end, detached from its neighbours in a square ground. The other houses of the street, conscious of decent lives within them, gazed at one another with brown imperturbable faces.

Is this scene cheerful? Vital and active? Should we expect this story to celebrate the joys of growing up in Dublin? Negative responses to these questions arise from the tone of the opening description. Notice, for example, that the dead-end street is "blind"; that the school is said to "set the boys free," which makes it sound like a prison; that the uninhabited house is "detached from its neighbours"; and that the other houses, personified, gaze at one another with "brown, imperturbable faces"—*brown* being a nondescript color, and *imperturbable* reinforcing the still, lifeless, somber quality of the passage as a whole.

Setting   Unlike novels, short stories usually work themselves out in a restricted geographical *setting,* in a single place, and within a rather short period of time. Any consideration of setting should include the time when a story takes place and the social situation set in the story, as well as the physical location of the events. In "Araby," the dreary details of Dublin, where the boy lives, are significantly described in the story's very first lines.

Plot   In "Araby," the *plot,* or the connected sequence of narrative events, may be simply stated. A young boy who lives in a drab but respectable neighborhood develops a crush on his playmate's sister. She asks him if he intends to go to a charity fair that she cannot attend. He resolves to go and purchase a gift for her. He is tormented by the late and drunken arrival of his uncle, who has promised him the money he needs. When the boy finally arrives at the bazaar, he is disappointed by the difference between his expectation and the actuality of the almost deserted fair. He perceives some minor events, overhears some minor conversation, and the climax occurs when he confronts the darkened fair and the banal expression of sexual attraction between two gentlemen and a young woman. This sequence of events prompts the boy to see himself "as a creature driven and derided by vanity."

Theme   This tiny stretch of experience out of the boy's life introduces him to an awareness of the differences between imagination and reality, between his romantic infatuation and the vulgar reality all about him. The *theme* of "Araby" emerges from the drab setting and mundane events of the story as a general statement about an intensely idealized and childish love, the shattering recognition of the false sentimentality that occasions it, and the enveloping vulgarity of adult life. By detailing a few events from one boy's life, the story illuminates the painful loss of innocence we all endure. In this case, the protagonist experiences what Joyce called an *epiphany,* or sudden flash of recognition, that signals the awareness of a set of moral complexities in a world that once seemed uncomplicated and predictable.

Characterization   Certainly theme is a centrally important aspect of prose fiction, but "good" themes do not necessarily ensure good stories. It would not be difficult to write a wretched story with the same theme as "Araby." Instinctively we know the difference between good stories and bad stories. Good stories, to begin with, are interesting; they present characters you care about; however fantastic, they are yet somehow plausible; they project a moral world you recognize. One of the obvious differences between short stories and novels is that story writers develop characters rapidly and limit the number of developed characters. Many stories have only one fleshed character; the other characters are frequently two-dimensional projections or even stereotypes. Rarely does a short story have more than three developed characters. One feature that distinguishes "Araby" from less successful stories with the same theme is its *characterization,* or the process by which the characters are rendered to make them seem real to the reader. The more we think about characterization, however, the more we realize that it cannot be separated from the other elements of fiction; that is, it depends heavily on tone, plot, theme, setting, and so on. It is part of the boy's character, for example, that he lives in a brown imperturbable house on North Richmond Street, that he does the things he does (which constitute the plot of the story), and that he learns about what he does (which is the theme). Much of this characterization in "Araby" emerges from Joyce's rich and suggestive style. Consider how the boy's character is revealed in the following paragraph.

> Her image accompanied me even in places the most hostile to romance. On Saturday evenings when my aunt went marketing I had to go to carry some of the parcels. We walked through the flaring streets, jostled by drunken men and bargaining women, amid the curses of labourers, the shrill litanies of shop-boys who stood on guard by the barrels of pigs' cheeks, the nasal chanting of street-singers, who sang a *come-all-you* about O'Donovan Rossa, or a ballad about the troubles in our native land. These noises converged in a single sensation of life for me: I

imagined that I bore my chalice safely through a throng of foes. Her name sprang to my lips at moments in strange prayers and praises which I myself did not understand. My eyes were often full of tears (I could not tell why) and at times a flood from my heart seemed to pour itself out into my bosom. I thought little of the future. I did not know whether I would ever speak to her or not or, if I spoke to her, how I could tell her of my confused adoration. But my body was like a harp and her words and gestures were like fingers running upon the wires.

In this passage, character is revealed through *diction,* or choice of words. By using the words *litanies, prayers,* and *adoration,* the narrator draws heavily from the distinctive vocabulary of the Roman Catholic Church. (The reference to the harp also reinforces the religious tone of the passage.) The *chalice* and *throng of foes* are related to this tradition as well; a chalice is a cup for the consecrated wine of the Eucharist, and throngs of foes often confronted the Christian martyrs whose deeds are immortalized in religious literature. At the same time, however, these last two phrases call up the world of chivalric romance, which is alluded to in the first line of the paragraph. The narrator's diction casts his awakening sexuality in the mold of high romance on the one hand and Christian devotion on the other. This sense of holy chivalry (reinforced by the reference to the priest who owned a chivalric novel) stands in sharp contrast to the humdrum experience of carrying groceries home from the market.

Point of View   The diction also raises important questions about the speaker. Who is narrating this story and what is he like? Is he reliable or unreliable? How can we judge? Such questions bring into play another element of fiction, *point of view.* "Araby" is a first-person narrative; that is, the story is told from the perspective of a *narrator* who speaks in the first person (*I, we, my, our*).

A standard alternative is third-person narration, where the speaker does not appear as a character in the story. Third-person narration allows the narrator to report characters' thoughts and feelings, which is to say that it allows for omniscient, or all-knowing, narration.

A less frequently employed point of view is that of the second person, in which the author presents the action from the perspective of a character identified as *you.* For example, "You ask the clerk for change; he gives you four quarters. You go outside and wait for the bus." (For an example of a story using second-person narration, see Pam Houston's "How to Talk to a Hunter," p. 988.)

Authors' decisions about point of view create powerful narrative effects. Throughout "Araby" we sense a gap between the boy's sensibility and that of the more mature narrator, who refers at various times to his "innumerable follies" and "foolish blood." That is, we see the events of "Araby" from the boy's perspective, even though the language is that of an adult. The gap between the boy's knowledge and the narrator's creates *irony.*

There may be more than one level of irony at work in a story. When the narrator calls himself "a creature driven and derided by vanity," whose eyes "burned with anguish and anger," this overstatement is known as *verbal irony*. Some critics have maintained that the romanticized language of the epiphany itself invites an ironical reading, which is to say that we readers may know something about the narrator that he does not know himself, that he idealizes disenchantment as fervently as the boy idealized romance and religion. In short, Joyce may be using *dramatic irony,* encouraging the reader to see things about the first-person narrator that he does not see about himself. Both kinds of irony hinge on differing levels of knowledge and the author's skillful manipulation of narrative perspective.

We often speak of character, setting, plot, theme, and style as separate aspects of a story in order to break down a complex narrative into more manageable parts. But it is important to understand that this analytic process of separating various elements is something we have done to the story—the story (if it is a good one) is an integrated whole. The more closely we examine the separate elements, the clearer it becomes that each is integrally related to the others.

In "Araby," Joyce employs the methods of fiction to create a world based on 1895 Dublin and Irish middle-class society. The success or failure of the story depends on Joyce's ability to render that world convincingly and our willingness to enter it imaginatively. We must not refuse to engage that world because the characters do not act as we would have them or because none of those events actually happened. Henry James urged that the author must be allowed his or her *donnée,* his or her "given." When we grant this, the act of reading fiction provides us with much more pleasure and emotional insight.

Exploring Fiction

Here are some questions you might ask when you are faced with the task of reading or writing about fiction. Your answers to these questions will help you begin brainstorming, to overcome the awful whiteness of the empty page.

1. From what point of view is the story told? Can you speculate on the appropriateness of that point of view? If a story is told from the point of view of a first-person narrator who participates in the action, what significant changes would occur if it were told from the point of view of an omniscient author? And, of course, vice versa. Keep in mind that first-person narrators do not know what other characters think. On the other hand, omniscient narrators know everything about the lives of the characters. How would the story you are writing about be changed if the viewpoint were changed?

2. Who are the principal characters in the story? (There will rarely be more than three in a short story—the other characters will often be portrayed sketchily; sometimes they are even stereotypes.) What functions do the minor characters serve? Do any of the characters change during the course of the story? How, and why?

3. What is the plot of the story? Do the events that constitute the plot emerge logically from the nature of the characters and circumstances, or are the plot elements coincidental and arbitrary?

4. What is the setting of the story? Does the setting play an important role in the story, or is it simply the place where things happen? What might the consequences of some other setting be for the effectiveness of the story?

5. What is the tone of the story? Read the first several paragraphs of the story to see how the tone is established. Does the tone change with events, or remain fixed? How does the tone contribute to the effect of the story?

6. Do you find ambiguities in the story? That is, can you interpret some element of the story in more than one way? Does that ambiguity result in confusion, or does it add to the complexity of the story?

7. Does the story seem to support or attack your own political and moral positions?

8. When was the story written? Bring your knowledge of history and contemporary events to bear on your reading of the story. Does the story clarify, enhance, or contradict your understanding of history?

9. What is the theme of the story? This, finally, is often the most significant question to answer. All the elements of fiction—tone, setting, plot, theme, characterization, point of view—have been marshaled to project a theme—the moral proposition the author wishes to advance. When you write about a work, resist the tendency to do the easiest thing—retell the plot, incident by incident. You must work instead to understand the devices the author uses to convey his or her theme, and, in your essay, reveal that understanding.

READING POETRY

Reading poetry is unlike the other reading you do. In order to get the sounds and meaning of a poem, it is best to start by reading it aloud. Some poems are straightforward, requiring little analysis; others are more dense and complex. Try reading this poem by Whitman out loud.

Walt Whitman   [1819–1892]

When I Heard the Learn'd Astronomer   1865

When I heard the learn'd astronomer,
When the proofs, the figures, were ranged in columns before me,
When I was shown the charts and diagrams, to add, divide, and measure
   them,
When I sitting heard the astronomer where he lectured with much
   applause in the lecture-room,
How soon unaccountable I became tired and sick,

Till rising and gliding out I wander'd off by myself,
In the mystical moist night-air, and from time to time,
Look'd up in perfect silence at the stars.

The distinction implicit in Walt Whitman's poem between the mind (intellectual knowledge) and the heart (emotion and feelings) is very old, but still a useful one. All of us have no doubt felt at some time that the overexercise of the mind interfered with our capacity to feel. Compelled to analyze, dissect, categorize, and classify, we finally yearn for the simple and "mindless" pleasure of unanalytical enjoyment. But the distinction between the mind and the heart cannot be pushed too far before it breaks down. Understanding the elements of poetry will certainly deepen the pleasure a poem can give you.

Poems have to be read with the greatest possible intensity but without any sense of urgency. This kind of relaxed but complete mindfulness is, as critic Northrop Frye notes, a kind of "meditation"; it requires that readers slow down, pay attention, and allow the language of the poem to work.

Word Choice

Once you have listened to the poem, what should you pay attention to next? Start with the words that make up the poem. *Where* a poem arrives is inseparable from *how* it arrives. Everything must be right in a poem, every word. Consider the following sonnet by William Shakespeare, paying close attention to the individual words that make up the poem.

When forty winters shall besiege thy brow,
And dig deep trenches in thy beauty's field,
Thy youth's proud livery so gazed on now,
Will be a tattered weed of small worth held:
Then being asked, where all thy beauty lies,
Where all the treasure of thy lusty days;
To say within thine own deep-sunken eyes,
Were an all-eating shame, and thriftless praise.
How much more praise deserved thy beauty's use,
If thou couldst answer 'This fair child of mine
Shall sum my count and make my old excuse'
Proving his beauty by succession thine.
    This were to be new made when thou art old,
    And see thy blood warm when thou feel'st it cold.

First consider the words and phrases whose *denotations,* or dictionary definitions, are unclear. The dictionary tells us that *livery* is the costume or insignia worn by retainers of a feudal lord. We know that a weed is an undesirable plant, of course, but *weed* can also refer to a garment, especially one that represents mourning. *Thriftless* means wasteful, and *to sum a count* means to present a balanced audit. In most of your everyday reading, you are already used to encountering unfamiliar words and phrases, figuring out their meanings from the contexts in which they occur. Reading poetry requires even more scrupulous attention to language, however, and treating unusual words and phrases with care is worthwhile.

Figurative Language

Having gained a working knowledge of the sonnet's words and phrases, we can begin to make out what this speaker is saying: he is asking someone to consider the prospect of aging and to preserve or pass on his beauty by fathering a child. So far, so good. But there are still some questions. What about the words and phrases whose meanings seem clear enough but whose significance seems to go beyond their dictionary definitions? For example, why does the speaker use the word *besiege,* a military term for surrounding with aggressive intent, to describe what forty winters will do to the man's brow? The word is an example of *figurative language,* or nonliteral language that achieves some special effect. In the first line of the sonnet, the speaker uses a *metaphor,* or a figure of speech that compares two dissimilar things; aging is compared to war. The metaphor is elaborated in the second line, in which wrinkles are implicitly compared to trenches dug on the battlefield.

Figurative language allows us—and the poet—to transcend the confinement of the literal and the vagueness of the abstract through the use of *imagery.* The world is revealed to us through our senses—sight, sound, taste, touch, and smell. Through imagery, the poet creates a recognizable world by drawing on this fund of common experiences. Bad poetry is often bad because the imagery is stale ("golden sunset," "the smiling sun," "the rolling sea") or so skimpy that the poem dissolves into vague and meaningless abstraction.

The difference between good and bad poetry often turns on the skill with which imagery (or other figurative language) is used. When Robert Frost in his poem "Birches" (p. 140) compares life to "a pathless wood" (line 44), the image strikes us as natural and appropriate (the comparison of life to a path or road is a common one, as is a wood or forest to a state of moral bewilderment).

The sonnet contains other examples of figurative language. When the speaker says that those trenches will be dug by forty winters he uses *personification,* attributing human qualities to nonhuman things (such as winters). The word *weed* also merits attention because it performs double duty; it refers to the ragged costume of a retainer, but it also retains its botanical sense by resonating with the "field" in the second line. Notice, too, this word's *connotations,* or suggestive meanings, that supplement its literal or denotative meaning. *Weed* has a negative connotation insofar as it refers to an undesirable plant; it also has a somber connotation insofar as it refers to garments that betoken mourning. Because this poem addresses the matter of aging and death, these connotations make the image of the tattered weed especially evocative.

After the fourth line, the military metaphor gives way to beauty, as a treasure imagined sunken in the eyes of the aging man. The speaker notes that the man will earn no praise for either hoarding the treasure of his beauty or devouring it wastefully. In effect, these lines chastise the man for simultaneously being a miser and a glutton. The speaker then contrasts that criticism with the praise the man will attract if he fathers a child. At this point the speaker uses an accounting metaphor, in which the child is said to sum the man's count, or render a complete list of assets, and justify his life in the face of old age. The financial metaphor suggests that fathering a child is a kind of investment, which is preferable to unproductive hoarding or selfish consumption.

Simile is closely related to metaphor. But where metaphor says that one thing is another, simile says that one thing is like another, as in Burns's "O My Luve's like a red, red rose" and Frost's "life is too much like a pathless wood." The distinction between simile and metaphor, while easy enough to make technically, is often difficult to distinguish in terms of effect. Frost establishes a comparison between life and a pathless wood and keeps the two even more fully separated by adding the qualifier "too much." Burns's simile maintains the same separation and, in addition, because it occurs in the opening line of the poem, eliminates any possible confusion the reader might experience if the line were, "O My Luve is a red, red rose." You can test the difference in effect by changing a metaphor into a simile or a simile into a metaphor to see if the meaning is in any way altered.

Allusion to other literary works, persons, places, or events enables poets to call up associations and contexts that complicate and enrich their poems. Whether these allusions are obvious or subtle, they draw on knowledge shared by the poet and the reader. For example, critics have read lines five through twelve of Shakespeare's sonnet as an allusion to the biblical parable of the talents (Matthew 25:14–30), in which a servant who buries money given to him by his master is chastised for not investing it. Like the parable, this sonnet suggests that burying treasure—which, in this poem, means beauty—is unworthy. The allusion intensifies the sonnet by producing a sympathetic vibration between the poem and the Bible.

A *symbol*, in its broadest sense, is anything that stands for something else. In this sense, most words are symbolic: the word *tree* stands for an object in the real world. When we speak of a symbol in a literary work, however, we mean something more precise. In poetry, a symbol is an object or event that suggests more than itself. It is one of the most common and powerful devices available to the poet, for it allows him or her to convey economically and simply a wide range of meanings.

It is useful to distinguish between two kinds of symbols, *public symbols* and *contextual symbols*. Public symbols are those objects or events that history has invested with rich meanings and associations, for example, national flags or religious objects such as the cross. William Butler Yeats uses such a symbol in his poem "Sailing to Byzantium" (p. 1270) drawing upon the celebrated and enduring art of the ancient Byzantine Empire as a symbol of timelessness.

In contrast to public symbols, contextual symbols are objects or events that are symbolic by virtue of the poet's handling of them in a particular work—that is, by virtue of the context. Consider, for example, the opening lines of Robert Frost's "After Apple-Picking" (p. 1272):

My long two-pointed ladder's sticking through a tree
Toward heaven still,
And there's a barrel that I didn't fill
Beside it, and there may be two or three
Apples I didn't pick upon some bough.

The apple tree is a literal tree, but as one reads through the poem, it becomes clear that the apple tree symbolizes the speaker's life, with a wide range of possible meanings (do the few apples he hasn't picked symbolize the hopes, dreams, aspirations that even the fullest life cannot satisfy?). Contextual symbols by their very nature tend to present more difficulties than public symbols, because recognizing them depends on a sensitivity to everything else in the poem.

The Music of Poetry

In order to consider the *music* of poetry, which most poets consider at least as important as its sense, we can use a variety of terms to describe the music, or sound patterns in poetry. Of these, *rhyme* is the best known. There is a regular pattern of end rhyme in Shakespeare's sonnet: *brow/now, lies/eyes, days/praise,* and so on. *Alliteration,* or the repetition of a consonant, is also heard within some of the lines: "besiege thy *brow*," "*dig deep* trenches," "*W*ill be a tattered *weed* of small *worth* held." Alliteration is frequently used to underscore key words and ideas.

Rhythm, created by the relationship between stressed and unstressed syllables, is another way poets can convey meaning. The pattern formed when the lines of a poem follow a recurrent or similar rhythm is the poem's *meter.* The smallest repeated unit in this pattern is called a *foot.* Looking at the first line of Shakespeare's sonnet, we see that the foot consists of an *iamb,* or an unstressed syllable followed by a stressed one:

When forty winters shall besiege thy brow.

Because the line consists of five *iambs,* or sets of unstressed syllables followed by stressed ones, it is called *iambic pentameter.* (If the line had four iambic feet, it would be in iambic tetrameter; if six, iambic hexameter, and so on.) The rest of the lines do not follow this pattern slavishly; instead, we see skillful variations beginning with the second line, in which consecutive syllables (*dig* and *deep*) are stressed.

Other metrical feet include the *trochee, anapest, dactyl,* and *spondee* (all of which are defined in the "Glossary of Literary Terms"); but such terms are the tools of literary study and not its object. Perhaps the most important thing to remember about meter is that it should not be mistaken for the actual rhythm of the poem. Instead, it is best thought of as a kind of ideal rhythm that the poem can play against. Just as genre suggests certain characteristics, meter suggests certain patterns that invite expectations that may or may not be satisfied. Much of the poet's art consists in crafting variations of sound and rhythm to create specific effects.

Some of these effects are illustrated nicely in the following passage from Alexander Pope's "An Essay on Criticism," in which the definitions of bad and good verse are ingeniously supported by the music of the lines.

> These[1] equal syllables alone require,
> Though oft the ear the open vowels tire;
> While expletives their feeble aid do join;
> And ten low words oft creep in one dull line;
> While they ring round the same unvaried chimes,
> With sure returns of still expected rhymes;
> Where 'er you find "the cooling western breeze,"
> In the next line, it "whispers through the trees";
> If crystal streams "with pleasing murmurs creep,"
> The reader's threatened (not in vain) with "sleep";
> Then, at the last and only couplet fraught
> With some unmeaning thing they call a thought,
> A needless Alexandrine[2] ends the song
> That, like a wounded snake, drags its slow length along.
>
> · · · · ·
>
> True ease in writing comes from art, not chance,
> As those move easiest who have learned to dance.
> 'Tis not enough no harshness gives offense,
> The sound must seem an echo to the sense:
> Soft is the strain when Zephyr gently blows,
> And the smooth stream in smoother numbers flows;
> But when loud surges lash the sounding shore,
> The hoarse, rough verse should like the torrent roar:
> When Ajax[3] strives some rock's vast weight to throw,
> The line too labors, and the words move slow;
> Not so, when swift Camilla[4] scours the plain,
> Flies o'er the unbending corn, and skims along the main.

When the speaker condemns the use of ten monosyllables, the line contains ten monosyllables: "And ten low words oft creep in one dull line." When he speaks of the wind, the line is rich in hissing sounds that imitate that wind. When he speaks of Ajax striving, clusters of consonants and stressed syllables combine to slow the line; when he speaks of Camilla's swiftness, the final consonants and initial sounds form liaisons that can be pronounced swiftly.

[1] Bad poets.
[2] Twelve-syllable line.
[3] A Greek warrior celebrated for his strength.
[4] A swift-footed queen in Virgil's *Aeneid*.

Consider also the following opening lines of Wilfred Owen's poem "Dulce et Decorum Est" (p. 1279). (The title is Latin for "[It] is sweet and fitting," which alludes to an ancient Roman adage that it is sweet and fitting to die for one's country.) The lines describe a company of battle-weary World War I soldiers trudging toward their camp and rest.

> Bent double, like old beggars under sacks,
> Knock-kneed, coughing like hags, we cursed through sludge.

These lines are dominated by harsh, explosive, and alliterating consonant sounds (*b, d, k, g*) that manage to reinforce the ungainly and indecorous images in these lines. In particular, the first two syllables of each line are heavily stressed, which serves to slow the reading. While the poem ultimately develops a prevailing meter, the irregular rhythms of these opening lines imitate a weary, stumbling march.

Analysis of this sort can illuminate and enrich our understanding of poetry, but it does not exhaust the significance of a poem. As Dylan Thomas once remarked,

> You can tear a poem apart to see what makes it technically tick and say to yourself when the works are laid out before you—the vowels, the consonants, the rhymes, and rhythms—"Yes, this is it. This is why the poem moves me so. It is because of the craftsmanship." But you're back where you began. The best craftsmanship always leaves holes and gaps in the works of the poem so that something that is not in the poem can creep, crawl, flash, or thunder in.

A truly fine poem not only repays attention to its formal features but also points beyond its technique to something more sensuous and less domesticated.

Exploring Poetry

Here are some questions you might ask when you are faced with the task of reading and writing about poetry.

1. Who is the speaker? What does the poem reveal about the speaker's character? In some poems the speaker may be nothing more than a voice meditating on a theme, while in others the speaker takes on a specific personality. For example, the speaker in Shelley's "Ozymandias" (p. 1264) is a voice meditating on the transitoriness of all things; except for the views expressed in the poem, we know nothing about the speaker's character. The same might be said of the speaker in Hopkins's "Spring and Fall To a Young Child" (p. 136) but with this important exception: we know that he is older than Margaret and therefore has a wisdom she does not.

2. Is the speaker addressing a particular person? If so, who is that person, and why is the speaker interested in him or her? Many poems, like "Ozymandias," are addressed to no one in particular and therefore to anyone, any reader. Others, such as Donne's "A Valediction: Forbidding Mourning" (p. 1000), while addressed to a specific person, reveal nothing about that person because the focus of the poem is on the speaker's feelings and attitudes. In a dramatic monologue (see "Glossary of Literary Terms"), the speaker usually addresses a silent auditor. The identity of the auditor will be important to the poem.

3. Does the poem have a setting? Is the poem occasioned by a particular event? The answer to these questions will often be "no" for lyric poems, such as Frost's "Fire and Ice" (p. 1008). It will always be "yes" if the poem is a dramatic monologue or a poem that tells or implies a story, such as Tennyson's "Ulysses" (p. 434) and Lowell's "Patterns" (p. 716).

4. Is the theme of the poem stated directly or indirectly? Some poems, such as Frost's "Provide, Provide" (p. 142) and Owen's "Dulce et Decorum Est" (p. 1279), use language in a fairly straightforward and literal way and state the theme, often in the final lines. Others may conclude with a statement of the theme that is more difficult to apprehend because it is made with figurative language and symbols. This difference will be readily apparent if you compare the final lines of the Frost and Owen poems mentioned above with, say, the final stanzas of Stevens's "Sunday Morning" (p. 422).

5. From what perspective (or point of view) is the speaker describing specific events? Is the speaker recounting events of the past or events that are occurring in the present? If past events are being recalled, what present meaning do they have for the speaker? These questions are particularly appropriate to the works in the section "Innocence and Experience," many of which contrast an early innocence with adult experience.

6. Does a close examination of the figurative language (see "Glossary of Literary Terms") of the poem reveal any patterns? Yeats's "Sailing to Byzantium" (p. 1270) may begin to open up to you once you recognize the pattern of bird imagery. Likewise, Thomas's attitude toward his childhood in "Fern Hill" (p. 145) will be clearer if you detect the pattern of biblical imagery that associates childhood with Adam and Eve before the Fall.

7. What is the structure of the poem? Since narrative poems, those that tell stories, reveal a high degree of selectivity, it is useful to ask why the poet has focused on particular details and left out others. Analyzing the structure of a nonnarrative or lyric poem can be more difficult because it does not contain an obvious series of chronologically related events. The structure of Thomas's "Fern Hill," for example, is based in part on a description of perhaps a day and a half in the speaker's life as a child. But more significant in terms of its structure is the speaker's realization that the immortality he felt as a child was merely a stage in the inexorable movement of life toward death. The structure of the poem, therefore, will be revealed through an analysis of patterns of images (biblical, color, day and night, dark and light) that embody the theme. To take another example, Marvell's "To His Coy Mistress" (p. 1002) is divided into three verse paragraphs, the opening words of each ("Had we . . . ," "But . . . ," "Now therefore . . . ,") suggesting a logically constructed argument.

8. What do sound and meter (see "Glossary of Literary Terms") contribute to the poem? Alexander Pope said that in good poetry "the sound must seem an echo to the sense," a statement that is sometimes easier to agree with than to demonstrate. For sample analyses of the music of poetry, see the section on music (p. 13).

9. What was your response to the poem on first reading? Did your response change after study of the poem or class discussions about it?

READING DRAMA

Drama is fundamentally different from other literary forms. Unlike fiction, for example, most plays are designed to be performed in public, not read in private. The public nature of drama is reflected in the words we use to discuss it. The word *drama* itself is derived from the Greek word for action, deed, or performance, and *theater* derives from the Greek word for sight or contemplation. By their nature, plays are more spectacular than poems or works of fiction. Directors and their staffs pay great attention to costuming, set design, lighting, and stage movement; the reader, who doesn't experience these elements, must imagine the action on the basis of words alone. Dramatists use words as starting points for, rather than realizations of, their artistic visions.

Although plays typically lack narration and description—they are designed to show, not tell—they can be considered in terms of plot, setting, theme, character, and irony. Indeed, these notions are even more important in drama than in fiction, where narrative style and point of view carry great weight, or in poetry, where diction and imagery are central.

As much as possible, the way to read a play is to imagine that you are its director. In this role you will concern yourself with creating the set and the lighting. You will see people dressed so that their clothes give support to their words. You will think about timing—how long between events and speeches—and blocking—how the characters move as they interact on stage. Perhaps the best way to confront the literature of the stage, to respond most fully to what is there, is to attempt to produce some scenes in class or after class. If possible, attend the rehearsals of plays in production on the campus. Nothing will provide better insight into the complexities of the theater than attending a rehearsal where the problems are encountered and solved.

As an exercise, read the opening speeches of any of the plays in this anthology and make decisions. How should the lines be spoken (quietly, angrily, haltingly)? What should the characters do as they speak (remain stationary, look in some direction, traverse the stage)? How should the stage be lit (partially, brightly, in some color that contributes to the mood of the dialogue and action)? What should the characters who are not speaking do? What possibilities exist for conveying appropriate signals solely through gesture and facial expression—signals not contained in the words you read?

Stages and Staging

Although staging is more important to spectators than to readers, some knowledge of staging history can enrich your reading of a play. For example, it helps to know that in the Greek theater of Dionysius in Athens (p. 19) there was no scene shifting. In *Antigonê* (p. 460), which was staged in an open-air amphitheater seating about 14,000 people, actors entered from the *skene,* or a fixed stage house, which might have had painted panels to suggest a scene. Consequently, the Palace of Creon is the fixed backdrop for all of *Antigonê.* Important events, especially violent ones, occur offstage, and the audience learns of these events from a messenger, who comes on stage to describe them. This convention was partly a matter of taste, but the conditions of the Greek stage also prevented Sophocles from moving the action to another scene. Later dramatists, writing for a more flexible stage and a more intimate theater, exploited the dramatic possibilities of such violence.

The vast outdoor theater imposed restrictions on acting style. Facial expressions played no role in the actor's craft; in fact, the actors wore large masks, which were probably equipped with some sort of megaphone to amplify speech. As a result, it was difficult to modulate speech to create subtle effects, and the speeches were probably delivered in formal, declamatory style. In addition to these limitations, the Athenian government made available only three principal actors, all male, as the cast (excluding the chorus) for each play. Consequently, there were never more than three players on stage at once, and the roles were designed so that each actor could take several parts, each signified by a different mask.

Shakespeare's stage was altogether different from Sophocles'. Although both theaters were open-air, the enclosure around the Elizabethan stage was much smaller than the Greek amphitheater, and the theater's capacity was limited to between 2,000 and 3,000 spectators. As in classical drama, men played all the roles, but they no longer wore masks. The stage protruded into the audience, allowing for more intimacy and a greater range of speech, gesture, and expression (p. 20). Even so, and despite Hamlet's advice to the troupe "to hold as 't were, the mirror up to nature," Shakespearean tragedy did not lend itself to a modern realistic style. Those great speeches are written in verse; they frequently are meant to augment the meager set design with verbal imagery; and they are much denser in texture, image, and import than is ordinary speech. Most of the important action was played out on the uncurtained main platform, jutting into the audience and surrounded on three sides by spectators. The swiftly moving scenes followed each other without interruption, doubtless using different areas of the stage to signify different locations. There was some sort of terrace or balcony one story above the main stage, and there was an area at the back of the main protruding stage that could be curtained off when not in use. Although Shakespeare's plays are usually divided into five separate acts in printed versions, they were played straight through, without intermission, much like a modern motion picture. These

The Dionysius Theatre in Athens

Interior of the Swan Theatre, London, 1596

characteristics distinguish the Shakespearean stage from the familiar realism of most contemporary theater.

Much current theater uses a *box stage*, essentially a box with one wall removed so that the audience can see into the playing area. The box stage lends

Hypothetical reconstruction of the interior of the Globe Theatre in the days of Shakespeare

itself to realistic settings. It can be easily furnished to look like a room; or, if outdoor scenes are required, painted backdrops and angled sets provide perspective. Shortly after the introduction of the box stage, the possibilities for scenic design produced great set designers and increasingly sophisticated stage machinery. These new possibilities, in turn, freed the dramatist from the physical limitations imposed by earlier stages.

By the late-nineteenth century, the versatility of the box stage enabled playwrights such as Henrik Ibsen to write detailed stage settings for the various locations in which the drama unfolds. Further, the furnishing of the stage in Ibsen's plays sometimes functions symbolically to visually reinforce the claustrophobic quality of the bourgeois life depicted in his plays. Later dramatists have relied on realistic settings to convey meaning and to serve symbolic functions. The modern production may take place in a theater that is simply a large empty room (with provisions for technical flexibility in the matter of lighting) that can be rearranged to suit the requirements of specific productions. This ideal of a "theater space" that can be freely manipulated has become increasingly attractive since it frees the dramatist and the performance from limitations built into permanent stage design.

The Elements of Drama

Characters   Most plays consist of narratives with plots, settings, themes, characters, and irony. However, plays have no narrators as such. The story un-

A seventeenth-century French box stage

folds before our eyes without the intervention of an authorial voice or point of view. Because we have no narrator to tell us what a character is thinking, we usually infer such things based on action or dialogue. *Characterization,* in plays as in fiction, is revealed by what characters do, say, and by what other characters say or reveal. Sometimes we are offered a glimpse into a character's consciousness in the form of a *soliloquy,* in which an actor speaks his or her thoughts aloud.

Dramatic Irony   *Dramatic irony* allows the audience to know more than the characters do about their own circumstances, *hearing more* than do the characters who speak. Shakespeare's *Othello* (p.1041) provides an excellent illustration of the uses of dramatic irony. At the end of Act II, Cassio, who has lost his position as Othello's lieutenant, asks Iago for advice on how to regain favor. Iago, who, unknown to Cassio, had engineered Cassio's disgrace, advises him to ask Desdemona, Othello's adored wife, to intervene. Actually this is good advice; ordinarily the tactic would succeed, so much does Othello love his wife and wish to please her. But Iago explains, in a soliloquy to the audience, that he is laying groundwork for the ruin of all the objects of his envy and hatred—Cassio, Desdemona, and Othello:

> . . . for while this honest fool
> Plies Desdemona to repair his fortunes,
> And she for him pleads strongly to the Moor,
> I'll pour this pestilence into his ear
> That she repeals him for her body's lust;
> And, by how much she strives to do him good,
> She shall undo her credit with the Moor,
> So will I turn virtue into pitch,
> And out of her goodness make the net
> That shall enmesh them all.

Of course Desdemona, Cassio, and Othello are ignorant of Iago's enmity. Worse, all of them consider Iago a loyal friend. But the audience knows Iago's design, and that knowledge provides the chilling dramatic irony of Act III, scene 3.

When Cassio asks for Desdemona's help, she immediately consents, declaring, "I'll intermingle every thing he does / With Cassio's suit." At this, the audience, knowing what it does, grows a little uneasy. As Iago and Othello come on stage, Cassio, understandably ill at ease, leaves at the approach of the commander who has stripped him of his rank, thus providing Iago with a magnificent tactical advantage. And as Cassio leaves, Iago utters an exclamation and four simple words:

> Ha! I like not that.

These words do not mean much either to Othello or Desdemona. But they are for the audience the intensely anticipated first drop of poison. Othello hasn't heard clearly:

> What dost thou say?

Maybe it will all pass, and Iago's clever design will fail. But what a hiss of held breath the audience expels when Iago replies:

> Nothing, my lord: or if—I know not what.

And Othello is hooked:

> Was that not Cassio parted from my wife?

The bait taken, Iago begins to play his line:

> Cassio, my lord? No, sure, I cannot think it,
> That he would steal away, so guilty-like,
> Seeing you coming.

And from this point on in the scene, Iago cleverly and cautiously leads Othello. He assumes the role of Cassio's great friend—reluctant to say anything that might cast suspicion on him. But he is also the "friend" of Othello and cannot keep silent in his suspicions. So "honest" Iago, apparently full of sympathy and kindness, skillfully brings the trusting Othello to emotional chaos. And every word they exchange is doubly meaningful to the audience, which perceives Othello led on the descent into a horrible jealousy by his "friend." The scene ends with Othello visibly shaken and convinced of Desdemona's faithlessness and Cassio's perfidy:

> Damn her, lewd minx! O, damn her!
> Come, go with me apart; I will withdraw,
> To furnish me with some swift means of death
> For the fair devil. Now art thou my lieutenant.

To which Iago replies:

> I am your own for ever.

All the emotional tautness in the audience results from irony, from knowing what the victims do not know. But dramatic irony is the special tool of the dramatist, well suited to produce an electric tension in a live audience that watches and overhears the action onstage.

Plot and Conflict   Plays often portray oppositions between characters or groups, or even between two aspects of a character's personality; this opposition often takes the form of a *conflict* that drives the plot. Sometimes a single conflict has many dimensions. In *Antigonê,* for example—when the young, female protagonist challenges the aging king's refusal to allow her brother the customary burial rights—the conflict between Creon and Antigonê can be viewed as a conflict between man and woman, between age and youth, between the state and the family, between the living and the dead, and between mortals and gods.

Understanding the methods of drama can help us analyze a play and its various effects. But such analysis only gestures at the emotional experience produced by successful drama. More than other forms of literature, plays give physical expression to the social and psychological conflicts that define us individually and collectively. As in *Antigonê,* a play may torment its audience by imposing on a courageous character a duty that will end in tragic death. Or, as in Susan Glaspell's *Trifles* (p. 551), a play may mock prevalent attitudes and compel its audience to reexamine their values. By giving expression to human impulses and conflicts, plays enact our most persistent concerns with the greatest possible intensity.

Exploring Drama
Here are some questions you might ask when you are faced with the task of reading or writing about drama.

1. How does the play begin? Is the exposition presented dramatically through the interaction among characters, or novelistically through long, less realistic, speeches that convey a lot of information, or through some device such as the reading of long letters or lengthy reports delivered by a messenger?

2. How does the information conveyed in exposition (which may occur at various moments throughout the play) establish the basis for dramatic irony? That is, what is the role of the ironic response generated in an audience when it knows more than do the characters? For example, because we know that Iago is a villain in Shakespeare's *Othello,* we hear an ironic dimension in his speeches that the characters do not hear, and that irony is the source of much tension in the audience.

3. Who are the principal characters, and how are the distinctive qualities of each dramatically conveyed? How do they change as the play proceeds? Are they sympathetic? What function do the minor characters serve? A paper that thoughtfully assesses the role of minor characters can often succeed better than the attempt to analyze the major figures who may embody too much complexity to deal with in 1,000 words.

4. Where is the play set? Does it matter that it is set there? Why? Does the setting play some significant role in the drama, or is it merely a place, any place?

5. What is the central conflict in the play? How is it resolved? Is the resolution satisfying?

6. Do you need to know something of the historical circumstances out of which the play emerged, or something of the life of the author in order to appreciate the play fully? If so, how does the information enhance your understanding?

7. Since plays are usually written to be performed rather than read, what visual and auditory elements of the play are significant to your response? If you are reading a text, place yourself in the position of the director and the actors in order to respond to this aspect of drama.

8. What is the play's theme? How does the dramatic action embody that theme?

READING ESSAYS

Essays differ from fiction in that they generally do not create imaginary worlds inhabited by fictional characters. We know, for example, through media accounts and the testimony of his friends, that Martin Luther King Jr. was indeed jailed in Birmingham, Alabama, where he wrote his famous argument for social justice, "Letter from Birmingham Jail" (p. 643). And, although we cannot independently verify that George Orwell actually shot an elephant, or that Richard Selzer is describing a real patient, their works exhibit the formal nonfictional qualities of the essay rather than the imagined world of the short story.

Writers turn to the essay form when they wish to confront their readers directly with an idea, a problem (often with a proposed solution), an illuminating experience, an important definition, or some flaw (or virtue) in the social system. Usually, the essay is relatively short, and almost always it embodies the writer's personal viewpoint. And although the essay may share many elements with other literary forms, it generally speaks with the voice of a real person about the real world. The term *essay* derives from the French verb *essayer*, "try," "attempt." That verb, in turn, derives from the Latin verb *exigere*, "weigh out," "examine."

While the French term calls attention to the personal perspective that characterizes the essay, the Latin verb suggests another dimension. The essay not only examines personal experiences but also explores and clarifies ideas, argues for or against a position. Thus, "The American Way of Death" (p. 933) is obviously the title of an essay. The title, however, suggests that the essay will be less personal and more analytical, perhaps even argumentative.

As you read an essay, you need to ask yourself, "What is the central argument or idea?" Sometimes the answer is obvious. "The American Way of Death" attacks extravagant funerals fostered by the undertaker industry. The essay, if successful, will change—or, perhaps, reinforce—the reader's attitudes toward death rituals.

Some essays address instead the inner lives of their readers. John Donne's "Meditation XVII" (p. 1333), for example, does not attack or justify anything. Rather, it insists that we be aware of our mortality; that awareness might well alter our behavior, our interaction with or perception of the people around us.

Types of Essays

In first-year composition, you may have read and written narrative, descriptive, expository, and argumentative essays. While reviewing the characteristics of each of these types, keep in mind that in the real world, essays, more interested in effectiveness than in purity of form, frequently combine features of different formal types.

Narrative Essays   Narrative essays recount a sequence of related events and are often autobiographical. But those events are chosen because they suggest or illustrate some truth or insight. In "Shooting an Elephant" (p. 924), for example, George Orwell narrates an episode from his life that led him to an important insight about imperialism. In "Rage" (p. 937), James Baldwin uses an episode from his life to show how a frustrating powerlessness can lead to self-destructive behavior. In these narrative essays, the writers discover in their own experiences the evidence for generalizations about themselves and their societies.

Descriptive Essays   Descriptive essays depict in words sensory observations—they evoke in the reader's imagination the sights and sounds, perhaps even the smells, that transport him or her to such places as Joan Didion's Death Valley or Lars Eighner's dumpster. Sometimes, the writer is satisfied simply to create a lifelike evocation of some engaging object or landscape; but Didion and Eighner use their descriptions as vehicles for expressing ideas about morality and poverty. The descriptive essay, like the narrative essay, often addresses complex issues that trouble our lives—but it does so by appealing primarily to sensory awareness—sight, sound, touch, taste, smell—rather than to intellect. The power of description is so great that narrative and expository essays often use lengthy descriptive passages to communicate forcefully.

Expository Essays   Expository essays attempt to explain and elucidate, to organize and provide information. Often they embody an extended definition of a complex conception such as love or patriotism. Or expository essays may describe a process—how to do something. This book's coverage of essays, for example, is clearly not narrative, because it doesn't depend for its form on a chronological sequence of meaningful events. It is not descriptive in the pure sense of that type, because it does not depend on conveying sensory impressions. It is, in fact, expository. It acquaints its readers with the techniques and types of essays and provides some tips to help students read essays both analytically and pleasurably. This discussion used a number of rhetorical strategies that you may recognize from other writing courses. We *classify* essays by type; we *compare and contrast* them; we use *definition;* we give *examples* to make a point; we imply that there is a *cause and effect* relationship between what readers bring to an essay and the pleasure they derive from it. Similarly, the essayists represented in this book use a variety of such rhetorical strategies to achieve their aims.

Argumentative Essays   Although Orwell's "Shooting an Elephant" can be categorized as a narrative essay, we might reasonably assert that it is also argumentative, because it is designed to convince readers that imperialism is as destructive to the oppressors as to the oppressed. The argumentative essay wishes to persuade its readers. Thus, it usually deals with controversial ideas; it marshals arguments and evidence to support a view; it anticipates and answers opposing arguments. Martin Luther King Jr. accomplishes all these ends in his "Letter from Birmingham Jail." So does Jonathan Swift in "A Modest Proposal" (p. 628), with an approach complicated by his reliance on irony and satire.

Analyzing the Essay

The Thesis   The best way to begin analyzing an essay is to ask, what is the point of this piece of writing; what is the author trying to show, attack, defend, or prove? If you can answer that question satisfactorily and succinctly, then the analysis of the essay's elements (that is, its rhetorical strategies, its structure, style, tone, and language) becomes easier. Lewis Thomas's "The

Iks" (p. 930) is a very short and relatively simple essay, and the author clearly states the thesis when he says, "Nations have themselves become too frightening to think about, but we might learn some things by watching [the Iks]." On the other hand, a much more complex and ambitious essay such as Virginia Woolf's "What if Shakespeare Had Had a Sister?" (p. 916) does not yield up its thesis quite so easily. We might say that Woolf's examination of the historical record leads her to argue that women did not write during the Elizabethan period because literary talent could not flourish in a social system that made women the ill-educated property of men. This formulation of the essay's thesis, as you will see when you read the essay, leaves a good deal out—notably the exhortation to action with which Woolf concludes the piece.

Structure and Detail   Read carefully the first and last paragraphs of a number of essays. Note the writers' strategy for engaging you at the outset with an irresistible proposition.

> In Moulmein, in Lower Burma, I was hated by large numbers of people—the only time in my life that I have been important enough for this to happen to me.

> If I speak in tongues of men and of angels, but have not love, I am a noisy gong or a clanging cymbal.

> I spy on my patients.

These opening sentences are startling, hooking readers so that they will eagerly read on to find out what it was that made the writer so hated in Burma, why love is so important, why the doctor spies on his patients. You will find that the opening lines of most well-wrought essays instantly capture your attention.

Endings, too, are critical. And if you examine the concluding lines of any of the essays in this collection, you will find forceful assertions that focus the matter that precedes them to sharp intensity. Essayists, unsurprisingly, systematically use gripping beginnings and forceful endings.

What comes between those beginnings and endings are often abstract issues—the nature of love, the inevitability of death, the evils of imperialism. Though such abstractions do significantly influence our lives, as subject matter for reading they seem impersonal and distant. Reading about great ideas becomes a sort of academic task, relegated to some intellectual sphere, separate from the pain and passion of our own humanity. The accomplished essay writer, however, entices us to confront such issues by converting abstract ideas into concrete and illustrative detail.

For example, George Orwell points out early in "Shooting an Elephant" that the "anti-European feeling was very bitter" in British-controlled Burma. But he immediately moves from the abstraction of "anti-European feeling" to "if a European woman went through the bazaars alone somebody would probably spit betel juice over her dress" and "when a nimble Burman tripped me up on the football field and the referee (another Burman) looked the other way, the crowd yelled with hideous laughter." The tiny bits of hateful experience, because they are physical and concrete, powerfully reinforce the abstract assertion about "anti-European feeling" that lies at the center of Orwell's essay, and the narrative account of the speaker's behavior in front of the mob culminates in an illuminating insight—"I perceived in this moment that when the white man turns tyrant it is his own freedom that he destroys." The large generality emerges from deeply felt personal experience.

In "The Discus Thrower" (p. 1340), Richard Selzer spies on his terminally ill patient who has in a sense become a "discus thrower." How, after all, can a writer, trying to deal with the inevitability of death, convey the intense pain and emotional agony of a dying person? Selzer's patient concretizes that pain and agony in a simple repetitive act:

> In time the man reaches to find the rim of the tray, then on to find the dome of the covered dish. He lifts off the cover and places it on the stand. He fingers across the plate until he probes the eggs. He lifts the plate in both hands, sets it on the palm of his right hand, centers it, balances it. He hefts it up and down slightly, getting the feel of it. Abruptly, he draws back his right arm as far as he can.
>
> There is the crack of the plate breaking against the wall at the foot of his bed and the small wet sound of the scrambled eggs dropping to the floor.
>
> And then he laughs. It is a sound you have never heard.

Can you imagine any objective and clinical description of the anguish and rage of a dying person that would convey the feeling more effectively than the concrete details of this understated anecdote?

Style and Tone   The word *style* refers to all the writing skills that contribute to the effect of any piece of literature. And *tone*—the attitude conveyed by the language a writer chooses—is a particularly significant aspect of writing style. As an illustration of the effect of tone, consider these opening lines of two essays—Martin Luther King Jr.'s "Letter from Birmingham Jail" and William Saroyan's "Five Ripe Pears."

> While confined here in the Birmingham city jail, I came across your recent statement calling my present activities "unwise and untimely." Seldom do I pause to answer criticism of my work and ideas. If I sought to answer all the criticisms that cross my desk, my secretaries would have little time for anything other than such correspondence in the course of the day, and I would have no time for constructive work. But since I feel that you are men of genuine good will and that your criticisms are sincerely set forth, I want to try to answer your statement in what I hope will be patient and reasonable terms.

> If old man Pollard is still alive I hope he reads this because I want him to know I am not a thief and never have been. Instead of making up a lie, which I could have done, I told the truth and got a licking. I don't care about the licking because I got a lot of them in grammar school. They were part of my education. Some of them I deserved and some I didn't. The licking Mr. Pollard gave me I didn't deserve, and I am going to tell him why. I couldn't tell him that day because I didn't know how to explain what I knew.

Both first-person accounts use provocative openings, immediately hooking the reader. King's tone, however, is formal; his grave rhythm ("Seldom do I pause . . .") and diction ("If I sought to answer . . .") recall a certain kind of well-known oratory. Consider his mature and studied word choices: *confined, statement, correspondence, constructive, sincerely, patient, reasonable.*

Saroyan's tone, in his first-person account, is personal and informal. He uses slang (*licking*) and contractions (*don't, didn't*). Most of his verbs are active. Although a reminiscing adult describes the event, the writer creates the voice of a child by using simple grammar and a kind of artless repetition, as well as a child's vocabulary.

The tone a writer creates contributes substantially to the message he or she conveys. Jonathan Swift might have written a sound, academic essay about the economic diseases of Ireland and how to cure them—but his invention of the speaker of "A Modest Proposal," who ironically and sardonically proposes the establishment of a human-baby meat-exporting industry, jars the readers in ways no scholarly essay could. The outraged tone of Jessica Mitford's "The American Way of Death" comically reinforces her attack on greedy undertakers. The high seriousness of Donne's tone in "Meditation XVII" perfectly suits his contemplation of the relationship among the living, the dying, and the dead.

Style is a more difficult quality to define than tone. Dictionaries will tell you that style is both "a manner of expression in language" and "excellence in expression." Certainly it is easier to distinguish between various *manners* of expression than it is to describe just what constitutes *excellence* in expression. For example, the manners of expression of John Donne in "Meditation XVII," of Richard Selzer in "The Discus Thrower," of Jessica Mitford in "The American Way of Death" clearly differ. The first muses about death in a style characterized by formality and complex extended images. The second achieves informality with a style characterized by short direct sentences and understatement. The essay's figurative language describes the dying patient rather than the nature of death. The third uses the breezy style of a muckraking journalist, replete with contemptuous asides and sardonic exclamations.

Nonetheless, we can describe the excellence of each style. Donne, an Anglican priest, meditates on the community of all living humans and the promise of eternal life in the face of physical death. He creates a remarkable image when he argues that "all mankind is of one author." Not so remarkable, you might argue; God is often called the "author of mankind." But Donne insists on the figurative quality of God as author and the intimate relationship among all people when he adds that all humankind "is one volume." Then he extends this metaphor by arguing that "when one man dies, one chapter is not torn out of the book, but translated into a better language." The daring image is further extended. "God," Donne tells us, "employs several translators; some pieces are translated by age, some by sickness, some by war, some by justice." By alluding to the actual making of a book by the bookbinder, Donne elaborates on the central image and reestablishes the idea of community—"God's hand is in every translation, and his hand shall bind up all our scattered leaves again for that library where every book shall lie open to one another." Surely, this magnificent figurative characterization of death (regardless of your personal beliefs) exhibits stylistic excellence.

Richard Selzer also deals with death.

> From the doorway of Room 542 the man in the bed seems deeply tanned. Blue eyes and close-cropped white hair give him the appearance of vigor and good health. But I know that his skin is not brown from the sun. It is rusted, rather, in the last stage of containing the vile repose within. And the blue eyes are frosted, looking inward like the windows of a snowbound cottage. This man is blind.

Here you see a very different style. Whereas Donne's sentences are long and move with the rolling cadence of oratory, Selzer's are terse and direct. Selzer's metaphors and similes characterize the ugliness of dying. The man's skin is not tanned by the sun; it is "rusted." His sightless eyes are frosted "like the windows of a snowbound cottage." These images, together with the artful simplicity of Selzer's short, halting sentences, powerfully convey the degradation and the impotence of the dying. Here again, style plays a significant role.

Jessica Mitford's attack on the American funeral industry begins:

> O Death, where is thy sting? O grave, where is thy victory? Where, indeed. Many a badly stung survivor, faced with the aftermath of some relative's funeral, has ruefully concluded that the victory has been won hands down by a funeral establishment—in disastrously unequal battle.

This essay opens with a quote from Paul's Letter to the Corinthians—certainly a sober and exalted allusion. But immediately, the tone turns sardonic with the question "Where indeed?" And the writer compounds the sarcasm by extending the biblical metaphor that compares death with a painful bee-sting to the equally painful experience of the "stung" survivor who has been conned into enormous expenditure by a funeral establishment. Her breezy style juxtaposes the ancient biblical promise of a spiritual victory over death with the crass modern reality—the only victor, nowadays, is the greedy funeral director. The perception is "rueful," and the victory "has been won hands down" in an encounter characterized as a "disastrously unequal battle." Mitford's language, playing off the high seriousness of the biblical quotation, stylistically advances her purpose by introducing a note of mockery. Certainly her argument gains force from the pervasive sardonic tone that characterizes her style.

Three different writers, all discussing some aspect of death, exhibit three distinctive manners of expression and three distinctive varieties of excellence—in short, three distinctive styles.

Your principal concern, when reading an essay, must always be to discover the essay's central thesis. What does the writer wish you to understand about his or her experience, the world, or yourself? Once you have understood the essay's thesis, you can enhance your understanding by examining the means the author used to convey it and, perhaps, recognize techniques that will enhance the quality of your own writing. To that end, you ought to examine the essay's structure and the rhetorical strategies that shape it. How does it begin and end? What type is it—narrative, descriptive, expository, argumentative? How do rhetorical strategies—definition, cause and effect, classification, exemplification, comparison and contrast—function to serve the author's purposes? Then, analyze the sources of the essay's effectiveness by closely analyzing the language of the essay. Watch writers energize abstract ideas with details and moving experience; consider the uses of figurative language—the metaphors and similes that create both physical and emotional landscapes in the prose; respond to the tone of voice and the stylistic choices that create it. When you have done all this successfully, when you have discovered not only *what* the author has said, but also *how* the author moved you to his or her point of view—then you will have understood the essay.

Exploring Essays

Here are some questions you might ask when you are faced with the task of reading and writing about essays.

1. What is the author's thesis (or unifying idea)? What evidence or arguments does the author advance to support the thesis? Is the thesis convincing? If not, why not? Does the author rely on any basic but unstated assumptions?

2. What is the author's tone? Select for analysis a passage you consider illustrative of the author's tone. Does the author maintain that tone consistently throughout the essay?

3. How would you characterize the author's style? For example, are the syntax, length of sentences, and diction elevated and formal or familiar and informal?

4. What rhetorical strategies does the author use? For example, can you identify the effective use of narration, description, classification, comparison and contrast, analogy, cause and effect, or definition? Note that one of these rhetorical strategies may constitute the unifying idea of the essay and the means of structuring it. Jessica Mitford's "The American Way of Death" is an essay in definition that effectively uses comparison and contrast and analogy.

5. What are the major divisions in the essay, and how are they set off? Are the transitions between the divisions effective and easy to follow?

6. Analyze the author's opening paragraph. Is it effective in gaining the reader's attention? Does it clearly state the essay's thesis? If it does not, at what point does the author's thesis and purpose become clear?

Writing About Literature

If reading literature offers a way to listen to the outrageously alive voices of the past, writing about literature affords the opportunity to respond to these voices. Sometimes your responses are just a jumble of vague impressions. Classroom discussion can help to clarify your thoughts, but the best ideas do not usually come together until you sit down and do some writing. The act of composition often generates a line of thinking. Writing about literature is an invitation to organize your impressions and to check those impressions against the work that prompted them. When you accept this invitation, you undertake a process that helps make sense of the literary work and helps you understand your reactions to it.

GETTING IDEAS: KEEPING A JOURNAL, ASKING GOOD QUESTIONS

As you know from your own experience, complete essays do not pop into a writer's head immediately after reading a work of literature. The process starts with an impression here, a fragment there, or a question about something that catches your attention. For this reason, many instructors will ask you to keep a journal, or a day-by-day collection of responses to reading assignments. Whether or not you are required to do so, recording your responses to literature is a good idea for several reasons. First, it helps you prepare for and contribute to class discussions, which often lead to new ways of understanding a work. Second, it limbers up your writing muscles, especially when you write regularly. Third, written responses are especially helpful when you are asked to generate your own essay topics. By committing a few words to paper, you begin a process that will eventually lead to a finished essay.

Often the best ideas for paper topics begin as questions or as responses that can be turned into questions. In reading James Joyce's "Araby," for example, you may notice that the narrator makes a big deal out of carrying the groceries home. This observation can be converted into a question: "Why the big deal about carrying the groceries home?" Or, to focus the question a bit, "Why and how does the boy idealize these everyday situations?" Note that these questions do not lead to a single irrefutable answer. Good literature cheerfully resists final, definitive interpretations. When you write responses to literature, a more modest and realistic goal is to pose a good question, answer it clearly, and support the answer with evidence from the work.

While it is important to clear up basic questions—for example, what a word or phrase means, or who did what, or how the characters are related to one another—successful papers usually take up questions that are less easily settled. For example, you would probably not want to ask whether or not Creon made mistakes of judgment in *Antigonê,* or whether the tragedy could have been avoided if he had acted otherwise. Questions such as these do not lend themselves to sustained discussion. Questions of personal taste are not immediately useful for the same reason; if you say you like a particular work, there is little anyone can say to the contrary. Sometimes such assertions can be usefully converted, especially if you begin to ask why you like or dislike a work. In general, however, you should strive to explore open-ended interpretative and thematic questions rather than rehash the facts or declare personal preferences.

Establishing a Working Thesis A careful discussion of a work identifies and analyzes related details, which is why it is important to highlight remarkable passages as you read. For example, you may be struck by the peculiar line uttered by Creon after Antigonê defies him: "Who is the man here, / She or I, if this crime goes unpunished?" This line prompts the question, "How does Creon understand manhood?" At first these lines suggest that Creon cannot separate his ideas about manhood from his ideas about justice. This preliminary answer can serve as a working *thesis,* or major claim. The next step is to reread *Antigonê* and ask whether any other details in the work support the claim, and, if not, whether the thesis needs refining to accommodate those details.

DRAFTING THE ESSAY

It is important to start writing even if you are unsure about the exact shape or direction of the argument since frequently your ideas develop and become more focused as you proceed. In working through a draft, for example, you may become more interested in Creon's ideas about manhood, especially his sense that masculinity is something that can be won (by Antigonê) or lost (by himself) depending on the outcome of the conflict. As you write your first draft and your thoughts evolve, you may wish to try a new thesis, perhaps that Creon's decisions have more to do with gender than with the ideals of good governance he proclaims in his first speech. Here again do not feel that all the details must be worked out before you begin writing. The main thing is to get started, and to do so without a lot of self-criticism.

Once the draft is done and you have a clear idea of your thesis and the passages in the work that best support it, you can begin to shape and refine the essay. In doing so, pay special attention to the introductory paragraph, which should introduce the topic and lead directly to a clear, arguable thesis. While there is no sure-fire formula for a first paragraph, some strategies are better than others. Be on the lookout for the following types of opening sentences.

> Ever since the dawn of time, people have been interested in the principles of good governance.

> Gender is an important issue for many people.

This kind of throat-clearing generalization is common and even helpful at the draft stage, but it gets the essay off to a slow start. If the central claim is that Creon's decisions have more to do with ideas about gender than with his stated principles of governance, a direct approach is more effective:

> Creon's first speech in <u>Antigonê</u> articulates the principles by which he intends to govern Thebes. These principles, including his view that private friendships should not be set above the public welfare, seem reasonable, especially in light of the bloody civil war that immediately preceded his ascension to the throne. As the drama unfolds, however, Creon's decisions seem to reflect considerations quite different from those articulated in his opening speech. In particular, his actions seem motivated more by his attitudes about gender, especially his fear that Antigonê will unman him, than by his concern for the welfare of Thebes.

Note that this opening paragraph introduces the topic and moves directly toward an explicit and arguable claim. By doing so, it lets the reader know where the paper is going. Just as important, it lets the writer know the same thing. That is, once a clear thesis is in place, both writer and reader can use it as a kind of road map for the rest of the essay.

Supporting Your Thesis   The body of the essay will be devoted to supporting the thesis. The best way to establish a claim is to cite and analyze carefully selected passages from the text that relate directly to it. The following paragraph focuses on lines that support the sample claim directly:

> At several points in the play, Creon calls attention to the fact that Antigonê is a woman. To him, this fact compounds the seriousness of her crime, for he sees their conflict as a battle in the war between the sexes:

> We keep the laws then, and the lawmakers,
>
> And no woman shall seduce us. If we must lose,
>
> Let's lose to a man, at least! Is a woman stronger
>
> than we? (3.46-48)
>
> As these lines indicate, Creon sees the situation in
>
> terms of winning and losing, and he is especially
>
> averse to the idea of losing to a woman.

The first part of the paragraph tells the reader what to look for in the cited lines, and the subsequent analysis underscores their relevance to the overall argument clearly and convincingly.

If you offer a claim, support it with an analysis of the relevant passages, and consider different interpretations of those passages, you have completed the main task in much writing about literature. Concluding paragraphs can move toward closure by reviewing the claim and its significance, which you should be careful not to overstate. In the essay on *Antigonê*, for example, it would not be effective to conclude by claiming that gender is the sole source of contention between the main characters, or by making sweeping statements about Athenian society. Your readers will find your claims more convincing if you do not exaggerate their importance.

REVISING THE ESSAY

After you've completed your draft, it is time to look at the essay more critically, paying special attention to stylistic revision. Reread your draft with an eye for grammatical, spelling, and other usage problems. Reading your essay aloud, or asking someone else to read it, will help you catch many of these problems. Revision is most effective if begun well before the paper is due. Your essay will be more effective if you start writing early so that there is time to review your decisions, to get feedback from others, and to revise accordingly. Getting feedback is an especially valuable part of the revision process. Because you cannot always anticipate audience reaction, a preliminary reading by a friend, a teaching assistant, a tutor, or an instructor can highlight the areas that need attention or additional revision.

The basic guidelines for good style are not mysterious; in fact, you use them every day in conversation. In conversation and in writing, we all rely heavily on cooperation to make sense of exchanges, and a polished practical style makes cooperation easier. Writers develop such a style by acknowledging that readers expect the same things that listeners expect in conversation: clarity, relevance, and proportion. If you listen to someone who is not clear, who cannot stay on the topic, or who offers too much or too little information, you will quickly lose interest in the conversation. So it is with writing; writers need to be clear, to stay on the topic, to give information appropriately. In fact, this attention to audience and appropriateness may be even more important in writing than in conversation because writing does not permit the nonverbal communication and immediate feedback that are part of conversation. As writers, we have to anticipate the absent reader's response; in effect, we have to imagine both halves of a virtual conversation.

Begin with your essay's thesis: is it clear? Obscurity or tentativeness on page one usually means problems later in the essay, so make sure your thesis is crystal clear. Second, is the evidence you present relevant to the claim? While it is tempting and sometimes productive to go off on tangents while drafting a paper, in the final essay, if the evidence doesn't fit the claim, tinker with the claim or look for better evidence. Finally, ask yourself if the general proportions of your essay are suitable. A five-page paper should not use three of those pages to introduce the topic or recount a work's plot. If the essay is too short, the trouble might be an unarguable thesis or insufficient attention to the evidence. If it is running too long, eliminate or compress the parts that do not bear directly on the main claim or limit the claim to something more manageable.

Editing Your Draft

After you have revised your draft for meaning and purpose, edit it carefully, paying close attention to specific sentences and paragraphs. These guidelines will help you focus on some common trouble spots.

Selecting Verbs   Many stylistic problems result from poor verb selection. Consider the main verb in the following sentence:

```
Three conflicts, all of which play crucial roles in the

plot, are evident in Antigonê.
```

If we take away this sentence's trimmings, the core assertion is that three conflicts are evident. Notice that nothing actually happens in this sentence. To stir things up, borrow the verb *play* from another part of the sentence:

```
Three conflicts play crucial roles in the plot of

Antigonê.
```

The revision is better, but the sentence can be made even more concise using *drive*:

```
Three conflicts drive the plot of Antigonê.
```

This sentence better satisfies the goals of clarity, relevance, and proportion. The revised version is clearer than the original, an effect that is rarely lost on an audience. It also permits a more direct move to the topic, namely, the conflicts. Finally, in an economical seven words rather than a verbose fifteen, it neither belabors nor omits anything of importance in the first sentence.

In addition to dulling a sentence, poor verb choice, especially use of *be* verbs, often produces wordiness and unnecessary abstraction:

```
There was opposition to the law among the citizens of
Thebes.
```

Editing out the *be* verb (*was*) and converting the abstract noun *opposition* into a verb makes the sentence more active:

```
The citizens of Thebes opposed the law.
```

This clearer sentence lets the verb do the major work. Of course, a good verb does not always present itself as an abstract noun in an early draft; in those cases it often pays to consult a thesaurus or a dictionary to find just the right word. Search your draft for weak verbs and insignificant words in sentences that begin "There is," "There are," "It is." Often, a few words later, a "that," "which," or "who" will appear. Simplify your sentences by revising to use strong verbs to sharpen your style immediately.

Finally, look for passive constructions (the ball *was thrown*) and replace them with active verbs. For example, change "The essay was read by the class" to "The class read the essay."

Eliminating Unnecessary Modifiers When choosing or revising a verb, you are also choosing the sentence elements that necessarily accompany it. These other sentence elements are called *complements* because they complete the meaning of the verb. In the following sentences the complements are underlined:

```
Creon governed Thebes.
The boy idealized his situation.
```

Creon cannot just govern; he has to govern something. Likewise, *his situation* completes the meaning of the verb *idealized*. Almost everything else added to these sentences will be *modifiers,* additional elements that will modify, rather than complete, the meanings of the sentences. A writer can add any number of modifiers to a sentence:

```
Creon governed Thebes with an iron hand, self-
ishly, and without due regard for the traditional
claims of kinship and religion.
```

From a grammatical standpoint, these modifiers are optional; eliminate them and the sentence still expresses a complete thought. Of course, the fact that you can eliminate them does not mean that you should; sometimes modifiers are the most significant parts of a sentence. Unnecessary modifiers, however, can make your writing heavy and murky:

> <u>Basically</u>, the Greeks invented <u>a rather innovative</u>
> <u>and distinctive form of government known as</u> democracy.

Eliminating the modifiers, and making a few other snips, results in the following:

> The Greeks invented democracy.

The clearer sentence does not lose much in the way of content. Of course, you can always use modifiers for nuance or emphasis; but you must ruthlessly trim unnecessary modifiers from wordy, unclear sentences.

Making Connections   After reviewing your essay for sentence-level concerns, make sure your sentences and paragraphs are firmly linked. Forging these links can take time, but the benefits are significant. When readers have to guess at the relationship between one sentence and the next, they will not understand your meaning. Making connections keeps you focused as well; by linking each sentence to the ones around it, you make your paragraphs flow and give them clearer direction.

Make connections explicit by using transitional phrases such as *however, although, likewise, for example, therefore,* and so on. Note in this sample opening paragraph how the underlined transitional phrases indicate the relationships between the sentences:

> In his first speech in <u>Antigonê</u>, Creon articulates
> the principles by which he intends to govern Thebes.
> These principles, including his view that private
> friendships should not be set above the public welfare,
> strike the reader as reasonable, especially in light of
> the bloody civil war that immediately preceded his as-
> cension to the throne. As the drama unfolds, <u>however</u>,
> the basis for Creon's decisions seem to reflect consid-
> erations quite different from those articulated in his
> opening speech. <u>In particular</u>, his actions seem moti-
> vated more by his attitudes about gender, especially
> his fear that Antigonê will unman him, than by his con-
> cern for the welfare of Thebes.

The appearance of *however* halfway through the paragraph signals the contrast between Creon's principles and his attitudes toward gender. The transitional phrase *in particular* in the next sentence signals that we are narrowing the preceding point and focusing our discussion. Experienced readers look for such transitional phrases that suggest an interpretive path through an argument.

Note also that the second sentence of the paragraph repeats a key word from the first one (*principles*). This repetition helps keep the spotlight on Creon's ideals, an important notion in the paragraph. By repeating key terms, sometimes with slight variation, you can illuminate the main idea of a paragraph clearly and intensively.

After checking for explicit connections within paragraphs, make sure that the progression of ideas from one paragraph to another is clear. Here again, transitional phrases are useful. A simple transition such as *nevertheless, furthermore,* or *on the other hand* is often adequate. Sometimes the entire opening sentence of a paragraph may provide the transition, including keywords, pronouns, or other references to the previous paragraph.

SOME COMMON WRITING ASSIGNMENTS

In many literature courses, assigned essays tend to fall into one of three modes—explication, analysis, and comparison and contrast—or some combination of these. Familiarity with all three will help you not only with your own papers, but also with exams and other in-class writing.

Explication

In explication, you examine a work in much detail: line by line, stanza by stanza, scene by scene, explaining each part as fully as you can and showing how the author's techniques produce your response. An explication is essentially a demonstration of your thorough understanding of a work.

Here is a sample essay that explicates a relatively difficult poem, Dylan Thomas's "Do Not Go Gentle into That Good Night." (p. 1285).

> Dylan Thomas's villanelle "Do Not Go Gentle into
> That Good Night" is addressed to his aged father. The
> poem is remarkable in a number of ways, most notably in
> that contrary to most common poetic treatments of the
> inevitability of death, which argue for serenity or
> celebrate the peace that death provides, this poem
> urges resistance and rage in the face of death. It jus-
> tifies that unusual attitude by describing the rage and
> resistance to death of four kinds of men, all of whom

can summon up the image of a complete and satisfying life that is denied to them by death.

The first tercet of the intricately rhymed villanelle opens with an arresting line. The adjective gentle appears where we would expect the adverb gently. The strange diction suggests that gentle may describe both the going (i.e., gently dying) and the person (i.e., gentleman) who confronts death. Further, the speaker characterizes "night," here clearly a figure for death, as "good." Yet in the next line, the speaker urges that the aged should violently resist death, characterized as the "close of day" and "the dying of the light." In effect, the first three lines argue that however good death may be, the aged should refuse to die gently, should passionately rave and rage against death.

In the second tercet, the speaker turns to a description of the way the first of four types of men confronts death (which is figuratively defined through-out the poem as "that good night" and "the dying of the light"). These are the "wise men," the scholars, the philosophers, those who understand the inevitability of death, men who "know dark is right." But they do not acquiesce in death "because their words had forked no lightning," because their published wisdom failed to bring them to that sense of completeness and fulfill-ment that can accept death. Therefore, wise as they are, they reject the theoretical "rightness" of death and refuse to "go gentle."

The second sort of men--"good men," the moralists, the social reformers, those who attempt to better the world through action as the wise men attempt to better it through "words"--also rage against death. Their

deeds are, after all, "frail." With sea imagery, the
speaker suggests that these men might have accomplished
fine and fertile things--their deeds "might have danced
in a green bay." But with the "last wave" gone, they
see only the frailty, the impermanence of their acts,
and so they, too, rage against the death that deprives
them of the opportunity to leave a meaningful legacy.

The "wild men," the poets who "sang" the
loveliness and vitality of nature, also learn as they
approach death that the sensuous joys of human existence wane. As the life-giving sun moves toward dusk,
as death approaches, their singing turns to grieving,
and they refuse to surrender gently, to leave willingly
the warmth, pleasure, and beauty that life can give.

Finally, with a pun suggestive of death, the
"grave men," those who go through life with such high
seriousness as never to experience gaiety and pleasure,
see all the joyous possibilities that they were blind
to in life. And they, too, rage against the dying of a
light that they had never properly seen before.

The speaker then calls upon his aged father to
join these men raging against death. Only in this
final stanza do we discover that the entire poem is
addressed to the speaker's father and that, despite the
generalized statements about old age and the focus upon
types of men, the poem is a personal lyric. The edge of
death becomes a "sad height," the summit of wisdom and
experience old age attains includes the sad knowledge
of life's failure to satisfy the vision we all pursue.
The depth and complexity of the speaker's sadness is
startlingly given in the second line when he calls upon
his father to both curse and bless him. These opposites

```
richly suggest several related possibilities. Curse me

for not living up to your expectations. Curse me for

remaining alive as you die. Bless me with forgiveness

for my failings. Bless me for teaching you to rage

against death. And the curses and blessings are

contained in the "fierce tears"--fierce because you

will burn and rave and rage against death. As the poem

closes by bringing together the two powerful refrains,

the speaker himself seems to rage because his father's

death will cut off a relationship that is incomplete.
```

This explication deals with the entire poem by coming to grips with each element in it.

You can learn a great deal about the technique of drama by selecting a short, self-contained scene and writing a careful description of it. The length of plays will probably require that you focus on a single segment—a scene, for example—rather than the entire play. This method of explication will force you to confront every speech and stage direction and to come to some conclusion regarding its function. Why is the set furnished as it is? Why does a character speak the words he or she does or remain silent? What do we learn of characters from the interchanges among them? Assume that everything that occurs in the play, whether on the printed page or on the stage, is put there for a purpose. Seek to discover the purpose, and you will, at the same time, discover the peculiar nature of drama.

Fiction, too, can be treated effectively in a formal explication. As with drama, it will be necessary to limit the text—you will not be able to explicate a 10-page story in a 1,000-word essay. Choose a key passage—a half page that reflects the form and content of the overall story, if possible. Often the first half page of a story, where the author, like the playwright, must supply information to the reader, will make a fine text for an explication. Although the explication will deal principally with only an excerpt, feel free to range across the story and show how the introductory material foreshadows what is to come. Or, perhaps, you can explicate the climax of the story—the half page that most pointedly establishes the story's theme—and subject it to a close line-by-line reading that illuminates the whole story.

Analysis

Breaking a literary work down into its elements is only the first step in literary analysis. When you are assigned an analysis essay, you are expected to focus on one of the elements that contributes to the complex compound of a work. This process requires that you extricate the element you plan to explore from the other elements that you can identify, study this element—not only in isolation but also in relation to the other elements and the work as a whole—and, using the insights you have gained from your special perspective, make an informed statement about it.

This process may sound complicated, but if you approach it methodically, each stage follows naturally from the stage that precedes it. If, for example, you are to write an analysis essay on characterization in *Othello,* you would begin by thinking about each character in the play. You would then select the character whose development you would like to explore and reread carefully those speeches that help to establish his or her substance. Exploring a character's development in this way involves a good deal of explication: in order to identify the "building blocks" that Shakespeare uses to create a three-dimensional role, you must comb very carefully through that character's speeches and actions. You must also be sensitive to the ways in which other characters respond to these speeches and actions. When you have completed this investigation, you will probably have a good understanding of why you intuitively responded to the character as you did when you first read the play. You will also probably be prepared to make a statement about the character's development: "From a realistic perspective, it is hard to believe that a man of Othello's position could be so gullible; however, Shakespeare develops the role with such craft that we accept the Moor as flesh and blood." At this point, you have moved from the broad *subject* "characterization in *Othello*" to a *thesis,* a statement that you must prove. As you formulate your thesis, think of it as a position that you intend to *argue* for with a reader you need to persuade. This approach is useful in any essay that requires a thesis, where you move beyond simple explication and commit yourself to a stand. Note that our sample thesis is *argumentative* on two counts; "characterization in *Othello*" is not remotely argumentative. Further, you have more than enough material to write a well-documented essay of 1,000 words supporting your proposition; you cannot write a well-documented 1,000-word essay on the general subject of characterization in *Othello* without being superficial.

You may be one among the many writers who find it difficult to find a starting point. For example, you have been assigned an analysis essay on a very broad subject, such as "imagery in love poetry." A few poems come to mind, but you don't know where to begin. You read these poems and underline all the images that you can find. You look at these images over and over, finding no relation among them. You read some more poems, again underlining the images, but you still do not have even the germ of a thesis.

The technique of freewriting might help to overcome your block. You have read and reread the work you intend to write about. Now, put the assignment temporarily out of your mind and start writing about one or two of the poems without organizing your ideas, without trying to reach a point. Write down what you like about a poem, what you dislike about it, what sort of person the speaker is, which images seemed striking to you—anything at all about the work. If you do this for perhaps ten minutes, you will probably discover that you are voicing opinions. Pick one that interests you or seems the most promising to explore.

There are a few variations on the basic form of the analysis assignment. Your instructor might narrow the subject in a specific assignment: analyze the development of Othello's character in Act I. This sort of assignment limits the amount of text that you will have to study but the process from this point on is no different from the process that you would employ addressing a broader subject. Sometimes instructors will supply you with a thesis, and you will have to work backward from the thesis to find supporting material. Again, careful analysis of the text is required. The problem you will have to address when writing an analytical essay remains the same regardless of the literary genre you are asked to discuss. You must find an arguable thesis that deals with the sources of your response to the work.

Suppose your instructor has made the following assignment: write an analysis of Harlan Ellison's story, " 'Repent, Harlequin!' Said the Ticktockman," in which you discuss the theme of the story in terms of the characters and the setting. Now consider the following opening (taken from a student paper):

> " 'Repent, Harlequin!' Said the Ticktockman" is a story depicting a society in which time governs one's life. The setting is the United States, the time approximately A.D. 2400 somewhere in the heart of the country. Business deals, work shifts, and school lessons are started and finished with exacting precision. Tardiness is intolerable as this would hinder the system. In a society of order, precision, and punctuality, there is no room for likes, dislikes, scruples, or morals. Thus, personalities in people no longer exist. As these "personless" people know no good or bad, they very happily follow in the course of activities that their society has dictated.

At the outset, can you locate a thesis statement? The only sentences that would seem to qualify are the last three in the paragraph. But notice that, although those sentences are not unreasonable responses to the story, they do not establish a thesis that is *responsive to the assignment.* Because the assignment calls for a discussion of theme in terms of character and setting, there should be a thesis statement about the way in which character and setting embody the theme. Here is another opening paragraph on the same assignment (also taken from a student paper):

> Harlan Ellison's " 'Repent, Harlequin!' Said the Ticktockman" opens with a quotation from Thoreau's es-

```
say "Civil Disobedience," which establishes the story's
theme. Thoreau's observations about three varieties of
men, those who serve the state as machines, those who
serve it with their heads, and those who serve it with
their consciences, are dramatized in Ellison's story,
which takes place about 400 years in the future in a
setting characterized by machinelike order. The inter-
action among the three characters, each of whom repre-
sents one of Thoreau's types, results in a telling
restatement of his observation that "heroes, patriots,
martyrs, reformers in the great sense, and men . . .
necessarily resist [the state] and . . . are commonly
treated as enemies by it."
```

Compare the two opening paragraphs sentence by sentence for their re-
sponsiveness to the assignment. The first sentence of the first opening does
not refer to the theme of the story (or to its setting or characterization). In the
second sentence, the discussion of the setting ignores the most important aspect—that the story is set in a machine- and time-dominated future. The last
three sentences deal obliquely with character, but they are imprecise and do
not establish a thesis. The second opening, on the other hand, immediately
states the theme of the story. It goes on to emphasize the relevant aspects of
the futuristic setting and then refers to the three characters that animate the
story in terms of their reactions to the setting. The last sentence addresses the
assignment directly and also serves as a thesis statement for the paper. It
states the proposition that will be developed and supported in the rest of the
paper. The reader of the second opening will expect the next paragraph of
the paper to discuss the setting of the story and subsequent paragraphs to
discuss the response to the setting of the three principal characters.

   The middles of essays are largely determined by their opening paragraphs.
However long the middle of any essay may be, each of its paragraphs ought
to be responsive to some explicit statement made at the beginning of the essay. Note that it is practically impossible to predict what the paragraph following the first opening will address. Here is the first half of that next
paragraph as the first student wrote it.

```
     The Harlequin is a man in the society with no
sense of time. His having a personality enables him to
have a sense of moral values and a mind of his own. The
Harlequin thinks that it is obscene and wrong to let
```

```
time totally govern the lives of people. So, he sets
out to disrupt the time schedule with ridiculous antics
such as showering people with jelly beans in order to
try to break up the military fashion in which they are
used to doing things.
```

The paragraph then goes on to discuss the Ticktockman, the capture and brainwashing of the Harlequin, and the resulting lateness of the Ticktockman.

Note that nothing in the opening of this student's paper prepared readers for the introduction of the Harlequin. In fact, the opening concluded rather inaccurately that the people within the story "happily follow in the course of activities that their society has dictated." Hence, the description of the Harlequin in the second paragraph is wholly unexpected. Further, because the student has not dealt with the theme of the story (as the assignment asked), the comments about the Harlequin's antics remain disconnected from any clear purpose. They are essentially devoted to what teachers constantly warn against: a mere plot summary. The student has obviously begun to write before she has analyzed the story sufficiently to understand its theme. With further thought, the student would have perceived that the central thematic issue is resistance to an oppressive state—the issue stated in the epigraph from Thoreau. On the other hand, because the second opening makes that thematic point clearly, we can expect it to be followed by a discussion of the environment (that is, the setting) in which the action occurs. Here is such a paragraph taken from the second student's paper:

```
Ellison creates a society that reflects one
possible future development of the modern American pas-
sion for productivity and efficiency. The setting is in
perfect keeping with the time-conscious people who in-
habit the city. It is pictured as a neat, colorless,
and mechanized city. No mention is made of nature:
grass, flowers, trees, and birds do not appear. The
buildings are in a "Mondrian arrangement," stark and
geometrical. The cold steel sidewalks, slowstrips, and
expresstrips move with precision. Like a chorus line,
people move in unison to board the movers without a
wasted motion. Doors close silently and lock themselves
automatically. An ideal efficiency so dominates the so-
```

cial system that any "wasted time" is deducted from the
life of an inefficient citizen.

Once the setting has been established, to attend to the assignment, a
writer should turn to the characters, linking those characters to thematic
considerations, beginning with a short transitional paragraph that shapes the
remainder of the middle of the essay:

> Into this smoothly functioning but coldly mecha-
> nized society, Ellison introduces three characters:
> Pretty Alice, one of Thoreau's machinelike creatures;
> the Ticktockman, one of those who "serve the state
> chiefly with their heads, and, as they rarely make any
> moral distinctions, they are as likely to serve the
> devil without intending it, as God"; and Everett C.
> Marm, the Harlequin, whose conscience forces him to
> resist the oppressive state.

The reader will now expect a paragraph devoted to each of the three characters:

> Pretty Alice is, probably, very pretty. (Everett
> didn't fall in love with her brains.) In the brief sec-
> tion in which we meet her, we find her hopelessly ordi-
> nary in her attitudes. She is upset that Marm finds it
> necessary to go about "annoying people." She finds him
> ridiculous and wishes only that he would stay home, as
> other people do. Clearly, she has no understanding of
> what Everett is struggling against. Though her anger
> finally leads her to betray him, Everett himself can't
> believe that she has done so. His own loyal and under-
> standing nature colors his view of her so thoroughly
> that he cannot imagine the treachery that must have
> been so simple and satisfying for Pretty Alice, whose
> only desire is to be like everybody else.
>
> The Ticktockman is more complex. He sees himself

as a servant of the state, and he performs his duties
with resolution and competence. He skillfully supports
a System he has never questioned. The System exists; it
must be good. His conscience is simply not involved in
the performance of his duty. He is one of those who
follows orders and expects others to follow orders. As
a result, the behavior of the Harlequin is more than
just an irritant or a rebellion against authority. It
is unnerving. The Ticktockman wishes to understand that
behavior, and with Everett's time-card in his hand, he
muses that he has the name of "what he is . . . not who
he is. . . . Before I can exercise proper revocation, I
have to know who this what is." And when he confronts
Everett, he does not just liquidate him. He insists
that Everett repent. He tries to convince Everett that
the System is sound, and when he cannot win the
argument, he dutifully reconditions Everett, since he
is, after all, more interested in justifying the System
than in destroying its enemies. It is easy to see this
man as a competent servant of the devil who thinks he
is serving God.

But only Everett C. Marm truly serves the state,
because his conscience requires him to resist. He is
certainly not physically heroic. His very name suggests
weak conformity. Though he loves his Pretty Alice, he
cannot resign from the rebellious campaign on which his
conscience insists. So, without violence, and mainly
with the weapon of laughter, he attacks the mechanical
precision of the System and succeeds in breaking it
down simply by making people late. He is himself, as
Pretty Alice points out, always late, and the delays
that his antics produce seriously threaten the well-
being of the smooth but mindless System he hates. He is

```
captured and refuses, even then, to submit and so his
personality is destroyed by the authorities that fear
him. The Ticktockman is too strong for him.
```

An appropriate ending emerges naturally from this student's treatment of the assignment. Having established that the story presents characters who deal in different ways with the oppressive quality of life in a time- and machine-obsessed society, the student concludes with a comment on the author's criticisms of such a society:

```
    Harlequin is defeated, but Ellison, finally, leaves
us with an optimistic note. The idea of rebellion
against the System will linger in the minds of others.
There will be more Harlequins and more disruption of
this System. Many rebels will be defeated, but any
System that suppresses individualism will give birth to
resistance. And Harlequin's defeat is by no means to-
tal. The story ends with the Ticktockman himself
arriving for work three minutes late.
```

Comparison and Contrast

An essay in comparison and contrast, showing how two works are similar to and different from one another, almost always starts with a recognition of similarities, often of subject matter. While it is possible to compare *any* two works, the best comparison and contrast essays emerge from the analysis of two works similar enough to illuminate each other (most comparison and contrast assignments involve two works of the same genre). Two works about love, or death, or conformity, or innocence, or identity give you something to begin with. But two random poems about the same subject may be so dissimilar in other ways that writing a comparison and contrast essay about them would be very difficult. In the case of Dickinson's "Apparently with no surprise" and Frost's "Design," both are about death, and they both use remarkably similar events as the occasion for the poem. Starting with these similarities, you would soon find yourself noting the contrasts (in tone, for example, and theme) between nineteenth-century and twentieth-century views of the nature of God.

Before you begin writing your paper, you ought to have clearly in mind the points of comparison and contrast you wish to discuss and the order in which you can most effectively discuss them. You will need to give careful thought to the best way to organize your paper. As a general rule, it is best to avoid dividing the essay into separate discussions of each work. That method tends to produce two separate, loosely joined analysis essays. The successful comparison and contrast essay treats some point of similarity or contrast between the two works, then moves on to succeeding points, and ends with an evaluation of the comparative merits of the works.

Like any essay that goes beyond simple explication, comparison and contrast essays require theses. However, a comparison and contrast thesis is generally not difficult to formulate: you must identify the works under consideration and summarize briefly your reasons for making the comparison.

Here is a student paper that compares and contrasts Dylan Thomas's "Do Not Go Gentle into That Good Night" with the poetic response it triggered from a poet with different views.

> Dylan Thomas's "Do Not Go Gentle into That Good Night" and Catherine Davis's "After a Time" demand comparison: Davis's poem was written in deliberate response to Thomas's. Davis assumes the reader's familiarity with "Do Not Go Gentle...," which she uses to articulate her contrasting ideas. "After a Time," although it is a literary work in its own right, might even be thought of as serious parody--perhaps the greatest compliment one writer can pay another.
>
> "Do Not Go Gentle into That Good Night" was written by a young man of thirty-eight who addresses it to his old and ailing father. Perhaps because Thomas had very little of his own self-destructive life left as he was composing this piece, he seems to have more insight into the subject of death than most people of his age. He advocates raging and fighting against it, not giving in and accepting it.
>
> "After a Time" was written by Davis at about the same age and is addressed to no one in particular. Davis has a different philosophy about death. She "answers" Thomas's poem and presents her differing views using the same poetic form--a villanelle. Evidently, she felt it necessary to present a contrasting point of view eight years after Thomas's death.
>
> While "Do Not Go Gentle..." protests and rages

against death, Davis's poem suggests a quiet resignation and acquiescence. She seems to feel that raging
against death is useless and profitless. She argues
that we will eventually become tame, anyway, after the
raging is done.

Thomas talks about different types of men and why
they rage against death. "Wise men" desire immortality.
They rage against death occurring before they've made
their mark on history. "Good men" lament the frailty
of their deeds. Given more time, they might have accomplished great things. "Wild men" regret their constant
hedonistic pursuits. With more time they could prove
their worth. "Grave men" are quite the opposite and
regret they never took time for the pleasures in life.
Now it is too late. They rage against death because
they are not ready for it.

His father's death is painful to Thomas because he
sees himself lying in that bed; his father's dying
reminds him of his own inevitable death. The passion of
the last stanza, in which the poet asks his father to
bless and curse him, suggests that he has doubts about
his relationship with his father. He may feel that he
has not been a good enough son. He put off doing things
with and for his father because he always felt there
would be time later. Now time has run out and he feels
cheated.

Catherine Davis advocates a calm submission, a
peaceful acquiescence. She feels raging is useless and
says that those of us who rage will finally "go tame /
When what we have we can no longer use." When she says
"One more thing lost is one thing less to lose," the
reader can come to terms with the loss of different
aspects of the mind and body, such as strength,

eyesight, hearing, and intellect. Once one of these is lost, it's one thing less to worry about losing. After a time, everything will be lost, and we'll accept that, too, because we'll be ready for it.

Thomas's imagery is vivid and powerful. His various men not only rage and rave, they <u>burn</u>. Their words "forked no lightning," their deeds might have "danced in a green bay," they "sang the sun in flight," and they see that "blind eyes could blaze like meteors." Davis's images are quiet and generally abstract, without much sensory suggestiveness, as in "things lost," a "reassuring ruse," and "all losses are the same." Her most powerful image--"And we go stripped at last the way we came"--makes its point with none of the excitement of Thomas's rage. And yet, I prefer the quiet intelligence of Davis to the high energy of Thomas.

"And we go stripped at last the way we came" can give strange comfort and solace to those of us who always envied those in high places. People are not all created equal at birth, not by a long shot. But we will all be equal when we die. All wealth, power, and trappings will be left behind and we will all ulti-mately be equal. So why rage? It won't do us any good.

SOME MATTERS OF FORM

After you have worked hard to draft and revise an essay that readers can follow easily, take care not to undermine your work with an illegible or disorganized presentation. A consistent, well documented essay allows readers to focus on your argument rather than on your document.

Titles

The first word and all main words of titles are capitalized. Ordinarily (unless they are the first or last word), articles (*a, an,* and *the*), prepositions (*in, on, of, with, about,* and so on), conjunctions (*and, but, or,* and so on) and the *to* in an infinitive ("A Good Man Is Hard to Find") are not capitalized.

The titles of short stories, poems, articles, essays, songs, and parts of larger collections, are enclosed in quotation marks.

The titles of plays, books, movies, periodicals, operas, television series, recordings, paintings, and newspapers are italicized. If you are not writing with a word processor that produces italic type, use underlining.

The title you give your own essay is neither placed in quotation marks nor underlined. However, the title of a literary work used as a part of your title would be either placed in quotation marks or italicized depending on the type of work it is.

Quotations

Quotation marks indicate you are transcribing someone else's words; those words must, therefore, be *exactly* as they appear in your source.

As a general rule, quotations of not more than four lines of prose or two lines of poetry are placed between quotation marks and incorporated in your own text:

> Near the end of "Young Goodman Brown," the narrator
>
> asks, "Had Goodman Brown fallen asleep in the forest
>
> and only dreamed a wild dream of a witch-meeting?" (16).

If you are quoting two lines of verse in your text, indicate the division between lines with a slash. Leave a space before and after the slash:

> Prufrock hears the dilettantish talk in a room where
>
> "the women come and go / Talking of Michelangelo."

Longer quotations are indented ten spaces from the left margin and are double-spaced. They are not enclosed in quotation marks, since the indention signals a quotation.

If you insert anything into a quotation—even a word—the inserted material must be placed within brackets. If you wish to omit some material from a passage in quotation marks, use ellipses (three spaced periods: . . .) to indicate the omission. When an ellipsis occurs between complete sentences or at the end of a sentence, a fourth period, indicating the end of the sentence, should be inserted. No space precedes the first period.

Here is an example of a full quotation from an original source:

> As one critic puts it, "Richard Wright, like Dostoevsky
>
> before him, sends his hero underground to discover the
>
> truth about the upper world, a world that has forced
>
> him to confess to a crime he has not committed."

Here is the quotation with insertion and omissions:

> As one critic puts it, "Richard Wright . . . sends his
> hero [Fred Daniels] underground to discover the truth
> about the upper world. . . ."

Use a full line of spaced periods to indicate the omission of a line or more of poetry:

> For I have known them all already, known them all--
> Have known the evenings, mornings, afternoons,
> I have measured out my life with coffee spoons;
> . . . .
> And I have known the eyes already, known them all--
> The eyes that fix you in a formulated phrase.

Periods and commas are placed *inside* quotation marks:

> In "The Lesson," the narrator describes Miss Moore as
> someone "who always looked like she was going to
> church, though she never did."

Other punctuation marks go outside the quotation marks unless they are part of the material being quoted.

For poetry quotations, provide the line number or numbers in parentheses immediately following the quotation:

> With ironic detachment, Prufrock declares that he is
> "no prophet" (83).

Documentation

You must acknowledge sources for the ideas you paraphrase or summarize, and material you quote. Such acknowledgments are extremely important, for even an unintentional failure to give formal credit to others for their words or ideas can leave you open to an accusation of plagiarism—that is, the presentation of someone else's ideas as our own.

In the body of your essay, use parenthetical citations to document those works which you quote, paraphrase, or summarize. Then, on the last page of your paper list all the works you used to write your essay. If you use other kinds of sources not listed here, consult *MLA Handbook for Writers of Research Papers,* fourth edition (1995).

This whimsical paragraph demonstrates the use of parenthetical citations.

> Leslie Fielder's view of the relationship between Jim and Huck (669-70) uses a method often discussed by other critics (Abcarian and Klotz 1375-76). Cooper's 1971 study (180) raises similar issues, although such methods are not useful when dealing with such a line as "North Richmond Street, being blind, was a quiet street except at the hour when the Christian Brothers' School set the boys free" (Joyce, "Araby" 81). But when Joyce refers to the weather (Dubliners 224), the issue becomes clouded.

The first citation gives only the page reference, which is all that is necessary because the author's name is given in the text and only one work by that author appears in the list of works cited. The second citation gives the editors' names and thus identifies the work being cited. It then indicates the appropriate pages. The third citation, because the author's name is mentioned in the text, gives only a page reference. The fourth citation must provide the author's name *and* the work cited, because two works by the same author appear in the list of works cited. The last citation, because it refers to an author with two works in the list of works cited, gives the name of the work and the page where the reference can be found.

In short, your parenthetical acknowledgment should contain (1) the *minimum* information required to lead the reader to the appropriate work in the list of works cited and (2) the location within the work to which you refer. The main thing to remember about citations is that the object is to give credit whenever it is due and to enable your reader to go directly to your sources as quickly and easily as possible.

Works Cited

Abcarian, Richard, and Marvin Klotz, eds. Literature: Reading and Writing the Human Experience. 7th ed. New York: St. Martin's, 1998.

Cooper, Wendy. Hair, Sex, Society, Symbolism. New York: Stein, 1971.

Fiedler, Leslie. "Come Back to the Raft Ag'in, Huck Honey." Partisan Review 15 (1948): 664-71.

```
     Joyce, James. "Araby." Literature: Reading and

Writing the Human Experience. 7th ed. Ed. Richard

Abcarian and Marvin Klotz. New York: St. Martin's,

1998. 81-5

     ---. Dubliners. Ed. Robert Scholes and A. Walton

Litz. New York: Penguin, 1976.
```

The first of these citations is for this book. Note that the first editor's name is presented surname first, but the second is presented with the surname last. The second entry illustrates the form for citing a book with one author. The third gives the form for an article published in a periodical (note that the title of the article is in quotes and the title of the journal is underlined). The fourth entry shows how to cite a work included in an anthology. The fifth citation, because it is by the same author as the fourth, begins with three hyphens in place of the author's name.

A CHECKLIST FOR WRITING ABOUT LITERATURE

1. Start early. You will need time for thinking, reading, writing, and revising, not to mention for breaks between steps.

2. Read carefully, annotating the work and keeping separate notes as you go along. Respond to the work as a whole or to any part of it: write about what you like, what you don't like, or anything else that makes an impression on you. Use the guidelines on pp. 8, 15, 23, and 31 for prompts to keep in mind as you read fiction, poetry, drama, and essays.

3. To develop an essay topic, review your responses to the work in writing and identify one that can be explored in a paper of the assigned length. Frame a question that can lead to an arguable claim and sustained discussion. For suggestions, see the guidelines on pp. 8, 15, 23, and 31.

4. Reread the work with your question in mind, picking out passages that speak directly to it, annotating as you read.

5. Begin writing, even if your claim, or thesis, is not completely clear in your mind. Do not worry about form so much as getting some ideas down on paper. If preparing an outline helps you organize your thoughts, do that. Try to articulate a thesis early on, and use the rest of the draft to support it.

6. Take a break for at least a few hours. Then return to the draft and revise it. Again, don't worry about fine points, but make sure your thesis is clear and that the evidence you cite supports it. If necessary, rewrite the thesis or reconsider the evidence. Make sure each paragraph relates to the main claim and contains details or examples that support it.

7. If time allows, take another break, for a few days. Then pick up the draft as if you had never seen it before. Putting yourself in the reader's place, clarify ambiguous passages, eliminate whatever is irrelevant, and make sure you provide adequate evidence to support your claims.

8. Review your verb choices to edit out as many passive constructions and *be* verbs as possible. Eliminate unnecessary modifiers and wordy sequences of prepositional phrases. Check the transitions both within and between paragraphs to be sure they're clear and in logical order. (See advice on pp. 36–39 for specific suggestions for revising these elements of your essay.)

9. Read your essay aloud. Ask a friend, classmate, or instructor to read your draft. Better yet, ask someone else to read the essay aloud. Listening to your writing will help you identify grammatical errors and unclear passages to revise.

10. Check to be sure you've fully documented your sources, making certain all quotations, summaries, and paraphrases are properly credited and that your reader can check your citations. Proofread the final copy carefully, reading with an eye for errors in spelling or punctuation, omitted words, and other flaws that might distract your reader.

Innocence and
Experience

Child in a Straw Hat, 1886 by Mary Cassatt.

Humans strive to give order and meaning to their lives, to reduce the mystery and unpredictability that constantly threaten them. Life is infinitely more complex and surprising than we imagine, and the categories we establish to give it order and meaning are, for the most part, "momentary stays against confusion." At any time, the equilibrium of our lives, the comfortable image of ourselves and the world around us, may be disrupted suddenly by something new, forcing us into painful reevaluation. These disruptions create pain, anxiety, and terror but also wisdom and awareness.

The works in this section deal generally with the movement of a central character from moral simplicities and certainties into a more complex and problematic world. Though these works frequently deal with awareness, even wisdom, their central figures rarely act decisively. The main character or protagonist is more often a passive figure who learns the difference between the ideal world he or she imagines and the injurious real world. If the protagonist survives the ordeal, he or she often becomes a better human— better able to wrest some satisfaction from a bleak and threatening world. Many of the works here deal with the passage from childhood to adulthood, from a time of simplicities and certainties that give way to the complexities and uncertainties of adult life.

Almost universally, innocence is associated with childhood and youth, as experience is with age. We teach the young about an ideal world, without explaining that it has not yet been and may never be achieved. As innocents, children are terribly vulnerable to falsehood, to intrusive sexuality, and to the machinations of the wicked, who often triumph.

But the terms *innocence* and *experience* range widely in meaning, and that range is reflected here. Innocence may be defined almost biologically, as illustrated by the sexual innocence of the young boy in Frank O'Connor's "My Oedipus Complex." Innocence may be social—the innocence of Brown in Nathaniel Hawthorne's "Young Goodman Brown." Or innocence may be seen as the child's ignorance of his or her own mortality, as in Gerard Manley Hopkins's "Spring and Fall" and Dylan Thomas's "Fern Hill." In such works as Sophocles' *Oedipus Rex* and Robert Browning's "My Last Duchess," one discovers the tragic and violent consequences of an innocence that is blind.

The contrast between what we thought in our youth and what we have come to know, painfully, as adults stands as an emblem of the passage from innocence to experience. Yet, all of us remain, to one degree or another, innocent throughout life, since we never, except with death, stop learning from experience. Looked at in this way, experience is the ceaseless assault life makes upon our innocence, moving us to a greater wisdom about ourselves and the world around us.

FOR THINKING AND WRITING

As you read the selections in this section, consider the following questions. You may want to write out your thoughts informally in a journal or notebook as a way of preparing to respond to the selections, or you may wish to make one of these questions the basis for a formal essay.

1. Innocence is often associated with childhood, and responsibility with adulthood. Were you happier or more contented as a preteen than you are now? Why? Which particular aspects of your childhood do you remember with pleasure? Which with pain? Do you look forward to the future with pleasurable anticipation or with dread? Why?

2. Do you know any adults who seem to be innocents? On what do you base your judgment? Do you know any preteens who seem to be particularly "adult" in their behavior (beyond politeness and good manners—they may, for example, have to cope with severe family difficulties)? On what do you base your judgment?

3. Most of you have spent your lives under the authority of others, such as parents, teachers, and employers. How do you deal with authorities you resent? Do you look forward to exercising authority over others (your own children, your own students, employees under your supervision)? How will your experiences affect your behavior as an authority figure?

4. How does the growth from innocence to experience affect one's sexual behavior? Social behavior? Political behavior?

Innocence and Experience

Fiction

Nathaniel Hawthorne   [1804–1864]

Young Goodman Brown   1846

Young Goodman[1] Brown came forth at sunset into the street at Salem village; but put his head back, after crossing the threshold, to exchange a parting kiss with his young wife. And Faith, as the wife was aptly named, thrust her own pretty head into the street, letting the wind play with the pink ribbons of her cap while she called to Goodman Brown.

"Dearest heart," whispered she, softly and rather sadly, when her lips were close to his ear, "prithee put off your journey until sunrise and sleep in your own bed to-night. A lone woman is troubled with such dreams and such thoughts that she's afeared of herself sometimes. Pray tarry with me this night, dear husband, of all nights in the year."

"My love and my Faith," replied young Goodman Brown, "of all nights in the year, this one night must I tarry away from thee. My journey, as thou callest it, forth and back again, must needs be done 'twixt now and sunrise. What, my sweet, pretty wife, dost thou doubt me already, and we but three months married?"

"Then God bless you!" said Faith, with the pink ribbons; "and may you find all well when you come back."

"Amen!" cried Goodman Brown. "Say thy prayers, dear Faith, and go to bed at dusk, and no harm will come to thee."   5

So they parted; and the young man pursued his way until, being about to turn the corner by the meeting-house, he looked back and saw the head of Faith still peeping after him with a melancholy air, in spite of her pink ribbons.

"Poor little Faith!" thought he, for his heart smote him. "What a wretch am I to leave her on such an errand! She talks of dreams, too. Methought as she spoke there was trouble in her face, as if a dream had warned her what work is

[1] Equivalent to *Mr.*, a title given to a man below the rank of gentleman.

61

to be done to-night. But no, no; 'twould kill her to think it. Well, she's a blessed angel on earth; and after this one night I'll cling to her skirts and follow her to heaven."

With this excellent resolve for the future, Goodman Brown felt himself justified in making more haste on his present evil purpose. He had taken a dreary road, darkened by all the gloomiest trees of the forest, which barely stood aside to let the narrow path creep through, and closed immediately behind. It was all as lonely as could be; and there is this peculiarity in such a solitude, that the traveller knows not who may be concealed by the innumerable trunks and the thick boughs overhead; so that with lonely footsteps he may yet be passing through an unseen multitude.

"There may be a devilish Indian behind every tree," said Goodman Brown to himself; and he glanced fearfully behind him as he added, "What if the devil himself should be at my very elbow!"

His head being turned back, he passed a crook of the road, and, looking forward again, beheld the figure of a man, in grave and decent attire, seated at the foot of an old tree. He arose at Goodman Brown's approach and walked onward side by side with him.

"You are late, Goodman Brown," said he. "The clock of the Old South[2] was striking as I came through Boston, and that is full fifteen minutes agone."

"Faith kept me back a while," replied the young man, with a tremor in his voice, caused by the sudden appearance of his companion, though not wholly unexpected.

It was now deep dusk in the forest, and deepest in that part of it where these two were journeying. As nearly as could be discerned, the second traveller was about fifty years old, apparently in the same rank of life as Goodman Brown, and bearing a considerable resemblance to him, though perhaps more in expression than features. Still they might have been taken for father and son. And yet, though the elder person was as simply clad as the younger, and as simple in manner too, he had an indescribable air of one who knew the world, and who would not have felt abashed at the governor's dinner table or in King William's[3] court, were it possible that his affairs should call him thither. But the only thing about him that could be fixed upon as remarkable was his staff, which bore the likeness of a great black snake, so curiously wrought that it might almost be seen to twist and wriggle itself like a living serpent. This, of course, must have been an ocular deception, assisted by the uncertain light.

"Come, Goodman Brown," cried his fellow-traveller, "this is a dull pace for the beginning of a journey. Take my staff, if you are so soon weary."

"Friend," said the other, exchanging his slow pace for a full stop, "having kept covenant by meeting thee here, it is my purpose now to return whence I came. I have scruples touching the matter thou wot'st of."

10

15

[2] A church in Boston.
[3] Ruler of England from 1689 to 1702.

"Sayest thou so?" replied he of the serpent, smiling apart. "Let us walk on, nevertheless, reasoning as we go; and if I convince thee not thou shalt turn back. We are but a little way in the forest yet."

"Too far! too far!" exclaimed the goodman, unconsciously resuming his walk. "My father never went into the woods on such an errand, nor his father before him. We have been a race of honest men and good Christians since the days of the martyrs;[4] and shall I be the first of the name of Brown that ever took this path and kept—"

"Such company, thou wouldst say," observed the elder person, interpreting his pause. "Well said, Goodman Brown! I have been as well acquainted with your family as with ever a one among the Puritans; and that's no trifle to say. I helped your grandfather, the constable, when he lashed the Quaker woman so smartly through the streets of Salem; and it was I that brought your father a pitch-pine knot, kindled at my own hearth, to set fire to an Indian village, in King Philip's war.[5] They were my good friends, both; and many a pleasant walk have we had along this path, and returned merrily after midnight. I would fain be friends with you for their sake."

"If it be as thou sayest," replied Goodman Brown, "I marvel they never spoke of these matters; or, verily, I marvel not, seeing that the least rumor of the sort would have driven them from New England. We are a people of prayer, and good works to boot, and abide no such wickedness."

"Wickedness or not," said the traveller, with the twisted staff, "I have a very general acquaintance here in New England. The deacons of many a church have drunk the communion wine with me; the selectmen of divers towns make me their chairman; and a majority of the Great and General Court[6] are firm supporters of my interest. The governor and I, too—But these are state secrets."

"Can this be so?" cried Goodman Brown, with a stare of amazement at his undisturbed companion. "Howbeit, I have nothing to do with the governor and council; they have their own ways, and are no rule for a simple husbandman[7] like me. But, were I to go on with thee, how should I meet the eye of that good old man, our minister, at Salem village? Oh, his voice would make me tremble both Sabbath day and lecture day."

Thus far the elder traveller had listened with due gravity; but now burst into a fit of irrepressible mirth, shaking himself so violently that his snake-like staff actually seemed to wriggle in sympathy.

"Ha! ha! ha!" shouted he again and again; then composing himself, "Well, go on, Goodman Brown, go on; but, prithee, don't kill me with laughing."

"Well, then, to end the matter at once," said Goodman Brown, considerably

[4] A reference to the persecution of Protestants in England by the Catholic monarch Mary Tudor (1553–1558).

[5] War waged (1675–1676) against the colonists of New England by the Indian chief Metacomset, also known as "King Philip."

[6] The Puritan legislature.

[7] An ordinary person.

nettled, "there is my wife, Faith. It would break her dear little heart; and I'd rather break my own."

"Nay, if that be the case," answered the other, "e'en go thy ways, Goodman   25
Brown. I would not for twenty old women like the one hobbling before us that Faith should come to any harm."

As he spoke he pointed his staff at a female figure on the path, in whom Goodman Brown recognized a very pious and exemplary dame, who had taught him his catechism in youth, and was still his moral and spiritual adviser, jointly with the minister and Deacon Gookin.

"A marvel, truly, that Goody[8] Cloyse should be so far in the wilderness at nightfall," said he. "But with your leave, friend, I shall take a cut through the woods until we have left this Christian woman behind. Being a stranger to you, she might ask whom I was consorting with and whither I was going."

"Be it so," said his fellow-traveller. "Betake you to the woods, and let me keep the path."

Accordingly the young man turned aside, but took care to watch his companion, who advanced softly along the road until he had come within a staff's length of the old dame. She, meanwhile, was making the best of her way, with singular speed for so aged a woman, and mumbling some indistinct words—a prayer, doubtless—as she went. The traveller put forth his staff and touched her withered neck with what seemed the serpent's tail.

"The devil!" screamed the pious old lady.   30

"Then Goody Cloyse knows her old friend?" observed the traveller, confronting her and leaning on his writhing stick.

"Ah, forsooth, and is it your worship indeed?" cried the good dame. "Yea, truly is it, and in the very image of my old gossip, Goodman Brown, the grandfather of the silly fellow that now is. But—would your worship believe it?—my broomstick hath strangely disappeared, stolen, as I suspect, by that unhanged witch, Goody Cory, and that, too, when I was all anointed with the juice of smallage and cinquefoil and wolf's bane"[9]—

"Mingled with fine wheat and the fat of a new-born babe," said the shape of old Goodman Brown.

"Ah, your worship knows the recipe," cried the old lady, cackling aloud. "So, as I was saying, being all ready for the meeting, and no horse to ride on, I made up my mind to foot it; for they tell me there is a nice young man to be taken into communion to-night. But now your good worship will lend me your arm, and we shall be there in a twinkling."

"That can hardly be," answered her friend. "I may not spare you my arm,   35
Goody Cloyse; but here is my staff, if you will."

So saying, he threw it down at her feet, where, perhaps, it assumed life, being one of the rods which its owner had formerly lent to the Egyptian magi.[10] Of

---

[8] A polite title for a wife of humble rank.
[9] All these plants were associated with magic and witchcraft.
[10] Allusion to the biblical magicians who turned their rods into serpents (Exodus 7:11–12).

this fact, however, Goodman Brown could not take cognizance. He had cast up his eyes in astonishment, and, looking down again, beheld neither Goody Cloyse nor the serpentine staff, but his fellow-traveller alone, who waited for him as calmly as if nothing had happened.

"That old woman taught me my catechism," said the young man; and there was a world of meaning in this simple comment.

They continued to walk onward, while the elder traveller exhorted his companion to make good speed and persevere in the path, discoursing so aptly that his arguments seemed rather to spring up in the bosom of his auditor than to be suggested by himself. As they went, he plucked a branch of maple to serve for a walking stick, and began to strip it of the twigs and little boughs, which were wet with evening dew. The moment his fingers touched them they became strangely withered and dried up as with a week's sunshine. Thus the pair proceeded, at a good free pace, until suddenly, in a gloomy hollow of the road, Goodman Brown sat himself down on the stump of a tree and refused to go any farther.

"Friend," said he, stubbornly, "my mind is made up. Not another step will I budge on this errand. What if a wretched old woman do choose to go to the devil when I thought she was going to heaven: is that any reason why I should quit my dear Faith and go after her?"

"You will think better of this by and by," said his acquaintance, composedly. "Sit here and rest yourself a while; and when you feel like moving again, there is my staff to help you along."

40

Without more words, he threw his companion the maple stick, and was as speedily out of sight as if he had vanished into the deepening gloom. The young man sat a few moments by the roadside, applauding himself greatly, and thinking with how clear a conscience he should meet the minister in his morning walk, nor shrink from the eye of good old Deacon Gookin. And what calm sleep would be his that very night, which was to have been spent so wickedly, but so purely and sweetly now, in the arms of Faith! Amidst these pleasant and praiseworthy meditations, Goodman Brown heard the tramp of horses along the road, and deemed it advisable to conceal himself within the verge of the forest, conscious of the guilty purpose that had brought him thither, though now so happily turned from it.

On came the hoof tramps and the voices of the riders, two grave old voices, conversing soberly as they drew near. These mingled sounds appeared to pass along the road, within a few yards of the young man's hiding-place; but, owing doubtless to the depth of the gloom at that particular spot, neither the travellers nor their steeds were visible. Though their figures brushed the small boughs by the wayside, it could not be seen that they intercepted, even for a moment, the faint gleam from the strip of bright sky athwart which they must have passed. Goodman Brown alternately crouched and stood on tiptoe, pulling aside the branches and thrusting forth his head as far as he durst without discerning so much as a shadow. It vexed him the more, because he could have sworn, were such a thing possible, that he recognized the voices of the minister and Deacon

Gookin, jogging along quietly, as they were wont to do, when bound to some ordination or ecclesiastical council. While yet within hearing, one of the riders
stopped to pluck a switch.

"Of the two, reverend sir," said the voice like the deacon's, "I had rather miss
an ordination dinner than to-night's meeting. They tell me that some of our
community are to be here from Falmouth[11] and beyond, and others from Connecticut and Rhode Island, besides several of the Indian powwows,[12] who, after
their fashion, know almost as much deviltry as the best of us. Moreover, there is
a goodly young woman to be taken into communion."

"Mighty well, Deacon Gookin!" replied the solemn old tones of the minister.
"Spur up, or we shall be late. Nothing can be done, you know, until I get on the
ground."

The hoofs clattered again; and the voices, talking so strangely in the empty   45
air, passed on through the forest, where no church had ever been gathered, nor
solitary Christian prayed. Whither, then, could these holy men be journeying so
deep into the heathen wilderness? Young Goodman Brown caught hold of a
tree for support, being ready to sink down on the ground, faint and overbur-
dened with the heavy sickness of his heart. He looked up to the sky, doubting
whether there really was a heaven above him. Yet there was the blue arch, and
the stars brightening in it.

"With heaven above and Faith below, I will yet stand firm against the devil!"
cried Goodman Brown.

While he still gazed upward into the deep arch of the firmament and had
lifted his hands to pray, a cloud, though no wind was stirring, hurried across the
zenith and hid the brightening stars. The blue sky was still visible, except directly overhead, where this black mass of cloud was sweeping swiftly northward.
Aloft in the air, as if from the depths of the cloud, came a confused and doubtful sound of voices. Once the listener fancied that he could distinguish the accents of towns-people of his own, men and women, both pious and ungodly,
many of whom he had met at the communion table, and had seen others rioting
at the tavern. The next moment, so indistinct were the sounds, he doubted
whether he had heard aught but the murmur of the old forest, whispering without a wind. Then came a stronger swell of those familiar tones, heard daily in
the sunshine at Salem village, but never until now from a cloud of night. There
was one voice, of a young woman, uttering lamentations, yet with an uncertain
sorrow, and entreating for some favor, which, perhaps, it would grieve her to obtain; and all the unseen multitude, both saints and sinners, seemed to encourage her onward.

"Faith!" shouted Goodman Brown, in a voice of agony and desperation; and
the echoes of the forest mocked him, crying, "Faith! Faith!" as if bewildered
wretches were seeking her all through the wilderness.

The cry of grief, rage, and terror was yet piercing the night, when the un-

[11] A town near Salem, Massachusetts.
[12] Medicine men.

happy husband held his breath for a response. There was a scream, drowned immediately in a louder murmur of voices, fading into far-off laughter, as the dark cloud swept away, leaving the clear and silent sky above Goodman Brown. But something fluttered lightly down through the air and caught on the branch of a tree. The young man seized it, and beheld a pink ribbon.

"My Faith is gone!" cried he, after one stupefied moment. "There is no good on earth; and sin is but a name. Come, devil; for to thee is this world given." 50

And, maddened with despair, so that he laughed loud and long, did Goodman Brown grasp his staff and set forth again, at such a rate that he seemed to fly along the forest path rather than to walk or run. The road grew wilder and drearier and more faintly traced, and vanished at length, leaving him in the heart of the dark wilderness, still rushing onward with the instinct that guides mortal man to evil. The whole forest was peopled with frightful sounds—the creaking of the trees, the howling of wild beasts, and the yell of Indians; while sometimes the wind tolled like a distant church bell, and sometimes gave a broad roar around the traveller, as if all Nature were laughing him to scorn. But he was himself the chief horror of the scene, and shrank not from its other horrors.

"Ha! ha! ha!" roared Goodman Brown when the wind laughed at him. "Let us hear which will laugh loudest. Think not to frighten me with your deviltry. Come witch, come wizard, come Indian powwow, come devil himself, and here comes Goodman Brown. You may as well fear him as he fear you."

In truth, all through the haunted forest there could be nothing more frightful than the figure of Goodman Brown. On he flew among the black pines, brandishing his staff with frenzied gestures, now giving vent to an inspiration of horrid blasphemy, and now shouting forth such laughter as set all the echoes of the forest laughing like demons around him. The fiend in his own shape is less hideous than when he rages in the breast of man. Thus sped the demoniac on his course, until, quivering among the trees, he saw a red light before him, as when the felled trunks and branches of a clearing have been set on fire, and throw up their lurid blaze against the sky, at the hour of midnight. He paused, in a lull of the tempest that had driven him onward, and heard the swell of what seemed a hymn, rolling solemnly from a distance with the weight of many voices. He knew the tune; it was a familiar one in the choir of the village meeting-house. The verse died heavily away, and was lengthened by a chorus, not of human voices, but of all the sounds of the benighted wilderness pealing in awful harmony together. Goodman Brown cried out, and his cry was lost to his own ear by its unison with the cry of the desert.

In the interval of silence he stole forward until the light glared full upon his eyes. At one extremity of an open space, hemmed in by the dark wall of the forest, arose a rock, bearing some rude, natural resemblance either to an altar or a pulpit, and surrounded by four blazing pines, their tops aflame, their stems untouched, like candles at an evening meeting. The mass of foliage that had overgrown the summit of the rock was all on fire, blazing high into the night and fitfully illuminating the whole field. Each pendent twig and leafy festoon was in a blaze. As the red light arose and fell, a numerous congregation alternately shone forth, then disappeared in shadow, and again grew, as it were, out of the darkness, peopling the heart of the solitary woods at once.

"A grave and dark-clad company," quoth Goodman Brown.   55

In truth they were such. Among them, quivering to and fro between gloom and splendor, appeared faces that would be seen next day at the council board of the province, and others which, Sabbath after Sabbath, looked devoutly heavenward, and benignantly over the crowded pews, from the holiest pulpits in the land. Some affirm that the lady of the governor was there. At least there were high dames well known to her, and wives of honored husbands, and widows, a great multitude, and ancient maidens, all of excellent repute, and fair young girls, who trembled lest their mothers should espy them. Either the sudden gleams of light flashing over the obscure field bedazzled Goodman Brown, or he recognized a score of the church members of Salem village famous for their especial sanctity. Good old Deacon Gookin had arrived, and waited at the skirts of that venerable saint, his revered pastor. But, irreverently consorting with these grave, reputable, and pious people, these elders of the church, these chaste dames and dewy virgins, there were men of dissolute lives and women of spotted fame, wretches given over to all mean and filthy vice, and suspected even of horrid crimes. It was strange to see that the good shrank not from the wicked, nor were the sinners abashed by the saints. Scattered also among their pale-faced enemies were the Indian priests, or powwows, who had often scared their native forest with more hideous incantations than any known to English witchcraft.

"But where is Faith?" thought Goodman Brown; and, as hope came into his heart, he trembled.

Another verse of the hymn arose, a slow and mournful strain, such as the pious love, but joined to words which expressed all that our nature can conceive of sin, and darkly hinted at far more. Unfathomable to mere mortals is the lore of fiends. Verse after verse was sung; and still the chorus of the desert swelled between like the deepest tone of a mighty organ; and with the final peal of that dreadful anthem there came a sound, as if the roaring wind, the rushing streams, the howling beasts, and every other voice of the unconcerted wilderness were mingling and according with the voice of guilty man in homage to the prince of all. The four blazing pines threw up a loftier flame, and obscurely discovered shapes and visages of horror on the smoke wreaths above the impious assembly. At the same moment the fire on the rock shot redly forth and formed a glowing arch above its base, where now appeared a figure. With reverence be it spoken, the figure bore no slight similitude, both in garb and manner, to some grave divine of the New England churches.

"Bring forth the converts!" cried a voice that echoed through the field and rolled into the forest.

At the word, Goodman Brown stepped forth from the shadow of the trees   60
and approached the congregation, with whom he felt a loathful brotherhood by the sympathy of all that was wicked in his heart. He could have well-nigh sworn that the shape of his own dead father beckoned him to advance, looking down-

ward from a smoke wreath, while a woman, with dim features of despair, threw out her hand to warn him back. Was it his mother? But he had no power to retreat one step, nor to resist, even in thought, when the minister and good old Deacon Gookin seized his arms and led him to the blazing rock. Thither came also the slender form of a veiled female, led between Goody Cloyse, that pious teacher of the catechism, and Martha Carrier,[13] who had received the devil's promise to be queen of hell. A rampant hag was she. And there stood the proselytes beneath the canopy of fire.

"Welcome, my children," said the dark figure, "to the communion of your race. Ye have found thus young your nature and your destiny. My children, look behind you!"

They turned; and flashing forth, as it were, in a sheet of flame, the fiend worshippers were seen; the smile of welcome gleamed darkly on every visage.

"There," resumed the sable form, "are all whom ye have reverenced from youth. Ye deemed them holier than yourselves, and shrank from your own sin, contrasting it with their lives of righteousness and prayerful aspirations heavenward. Yet here are they all in my worshipping assembly. This night it shall be granted you to know their secret deeds: how hoary-bearded elders of the church have whispered wanton words to the young maids of their households; how many a woman, eager for widows' weeds, has given her husband a drink at bedtime and let him sleep his last sleep in her bosom; how beardless youths have made haste to inherit their fathers' wealth; and how fair damsels—blush not, sweet ones—have dug little graves in the garden, and bidden me, the sole guest, to an infant's funeral. By the sympathy of your human hearts for sin ye shall scent out all the places—whether in church, bed-chamber, street, field, or forest—where crime has been committed, and shall exult to behold the whole earth one stain of guilt, one mighty blood spot. Far more than this. It shall be yours to penetrate, in every bosom, the deep mystery of sin, the fountain of all wicked arts, and which inexhaustibly supplies more evil impulses than human power—than my power at its utmost—can make manifest in deeds. And now, my children, look upon each other."

They did so; and, by the blaze of the hell-kindled torches, the wretched man beheld his Faith, and the wife her husband, trembling before that unhallowed altar.

"Lo, there ye stand, my children," said the figure, in a deep and solemn tone, almost sad with its despairing awfulness, as if his once angelic nature could yet mourn for our miserable race. "Depending upon one another's hearts, ye had still hoped that virtue were not all a dream. Now are ye undeceived. Evil is the nature of mankind. Evil must be your only happiness. Welcome again, my children, to the communion of your race."

"Welcome," repeated the fiend worshippers, in one cry of despair and triumph.

And there they stood, the only pair, as it seemed, who were yet hesitating on

65

---

[13] One of the women hanged in Salem in 1697 for witchcraft.

the verge of wickedness in this dark world. A basin was hollowed, naturally, in the rock. Did it contain water, reddened by the lurid light? or was it blood? or, perchance, a liquid flame? Herein did the shape of evil dip his hand and prepare to lay the mark of baptism upon their foreheads, that they might be partakers of the mystery of sin, more conscious of the secret guilt of others, both in deed and thought, than they could now be of their own. The husband cast one look at his pale wife, and Faith at him. What polluted wretches would the next glance show them to each other, shuddering alike at what they disclosed and what they saw!

"Faith! Faith!" cried the husband, "look up to heaven, and resist the wicked one."

Whether Faith obeyed he knew not. Hardly had he spoken when he found himself amid calm night and solitude, listening to a roar of the wind which died heavily away through the forest. He staggered against the rock, and felt it chill and damp; while a hanging twig, that had been all on fire, besprinkled his cheek with the coldest dew.

The next morning young Goodman Brown came slowly into the street of Salem village, staring around him like a bewildered man. The good old minister was taking a walk along the graveyard to get an appetite for breakfast and meditate his sermon, and bestowed a blessing, as he passed, on Goodman Brown. He shrank from the venerable saint as if to avoid an anathema. Old Deacon Gookin was at domestic worship, and the holy words of his prayer were heard through the open window. "What God doth the wizard pray to?" quoth Goodman Brown. Goody Cloyse, that excellent old Christian, stood in the early sunshine at her own lattice, catechizing a little girl who had brought her a pint of morning's milk. Goodman Brown snatched away the child as from the grasp of the fiend himself. Turning the corner by the meeting-house, he spied the head of Faith, with the pink ribbons, gazing anxiously forth, and bursting into such joy at sight of him that she skipped along the street and almost kissed her husband before the whole village. But Goodman Brown looked sternly and sadly into her face, and passed on without a greeting.

Had Goodman Brown fallen asleep in the forest and only dreamed a wild dream of a witch-meeting?

Be it so if you will; but, alas! it was a dream of evil omen for young Goodman Brown. A stern, a sad, a darkly meditative, a distrustful, if not a desperate man did he become from the night of that fearful dream. On the Sabbath day, when the congregation were singing a holy psalm, he could not listen because an anthem of sin rushed loudly upon his ear and drowned all the blessed strain. When the minister spoke from the pulpit with power and fervid eloquence, and, with his hand on the open Bible, of the sacred truths of our religion, and of saint-like lives and triumphant deaths, and of future bliss or misery unutterable, then did Goodman Brown turn pale, dreading lest the roof should thunder down upon the gray blasphemer and his hearers. Often, awakening suddenly at midnight, he shrank from the bosom of Faith; and at morning or eventide, when the family knelt down at prayer, he scowled and muttered to himself, and gazed sternly at his wife, and turned away. And when he had lived long, and was borne to his grave a hoary corpse, followed by Faith, an aged woman, and children and grandchildren, a goodly procession, besides neighbors not a few, they carved no hopeful verse upon his tombstone, for his dying hour was gloom.

For Analysis

1. At the end of the story, the narrator asks, "Had Goodman Brown fallen asleep in the forest and only dreamed a wild dream of a witch-meeting?" Why, instead of answering the questions, does he say, "Be it so if you will . . ."? **2.** Examine the seemingly supernatural events Brown experiences as he penetrates ever deeper into the forest. Can the reader determine whether or not those events are really taking place? If not, what purpose does the ambiguity serve? **3.** What attitude does this story express toward the church of Puritan New England? **4.** What purpose do Faith's pink ribbons serve? **5.** What is the "guilty purpose" (par. 41) that has drawn Brown to the forest?

On Style

1. How would you characterize the **setting** of this story? **2.** What elements of the story can be described as **allegorical** or **symbolic**?

Making Connections

1. Both this story and Melville's "Bartleby the Scrivener" (p. 313) deal with protagonists who withdraw from life. What similarities and differences do you find in the reasons for their withdrawal, the ways in which they withdraw, and the consequences of their withdrawal? **2.** Both Hawthorne's "Young Goodman Brown" and Ellison's " 'Repent Harlequin!' Said the Ticktockman" (p. 395) rely upon fantasy. What advantages does the use of fantasy give the authors?

Writing Topics

1. Write an essay in which you argue for or against the proposition that the "truth" Brown discovers during the night in the forest justifies his gloom and withdrawal. **2.** Write out a paraphrase of Satan's sermon.

Stephen Crane   [1871–1900]

The Bride Comes to Yellow Sky   1898

I

The great Pullman was whirling onward with such dignity of motion that a glance from the window seemed simply to prove that the plains of Texas were pouring eastward. Vast flats of green grass, dull-hued space of mesquit and cactus, little groups of frame houses, woods of light and tender trees, all were sweeping into the east, sweeping over the horizon, a precipice.

A newly married pair had boarded this coach at San Antonio. The man's face was reddened from many days in the wind and sun, and a direct result of his new black clothes was that his brick-colored hands were constantly performing in a most conscious fashion. From time to time he looked down respectfully at his attire. He sat with a hand on each knee, like a man waiting in a barber's shop. The glances he devoted to other passengers were furtive and shy.

The bride was not pretty, nor was she very young. She wore a dress of blue cashmere, with small reservations of velvet here and there, and with steel buttons abounding. She continually twisted her head to regard her puff sleeves, very stiff, straight, and high. They embarrassed her. It was quite apparent that she had cooked, and that she expected to cook, dutifully. The blushes caused by the careless scrutiny of some passengers as she had entered the car were strange to see upon this plain, under-class countenance, which was drawn in placid, almost emotionless lines.

They were evidently very happy. "Ever been in a parlour-car before?" he asked, smiling with delight.

"No," she answered; "I never was. It's fine, ain't it?"

"Great! And then after a while we'll go forward to the diner, and get a big layout. Finest meal in the world. Charge a dollar."

"Oh, do they?" cried the bride. "Charge a dollar? Why, that's too much—for us—ain't it, Jack?"

"Not this trip, anyhow," he answered bravely. "We're going to go the whole thing."

Later he explained to her about the trains. "You see, it's a thousand miles from one end of Texas to the other; and this train runs right across it, and never stops but four times." He had the pride of an owner. He pointed out to her the dazzling fittings of the coach; and in truth her eyes opened wider as she contemplated the sea-green figured velvet, the shining brass, silver, and glass, the wood that gleamed as darkly brilliant as the surface of a pool of oil. At one end

5

72

a bronze figure sturdily held a support for a separated chamber, and at convenient places on the ceiling were frescos in olive and silver.

To the minds of the pair, their surroundings reflected the glory of their marriage that morning in San Antonio; this was the environment of their new estate; and the man's face in particular beamed with an elation that made him appear ridiculous to the negro porter. This individual at times surveyed them from afar with an amused and superior grin. On other occasions he bullied them with skill in ways that did not make it exactly plain to them that they were being bullied. He subtly used all the manners of the most unconquerable kind of snobbery. He oppressed them; but of this oppression they had small knowledge, and they speedily forgot that infrequently a number of travellers covered them with stares of derisive enjoyment. Historically there was supposed to be something infinitely humorous in their situation.

"We are due in Yellow Sky at 3:42," he said, looking tenderly into her eyes.

"Oh, are we?" she said, as if she had not been aware of it. To evince surprise at her husband's statement was part of her wifely amiability. She took from a pocket a little silver watch; and as she held it before her, and stared at it with a frown of attention, the new husband's face shone.

"I bought it in San Anton' from a friend of mine," he told her gleefully.

"It's seventeen minutes past twelve," she said, looking up at him with a kind of shy and clumsy coquetry. A passenger, noting this play, grew excessively sardonic, and winked at himself in one of the numerous mirrors.

At last they went to the dining-car. Two rows of negro waiters, in glowing white suits, surveyed their entrance with the interest, and also the equanimity, of men who had been forewarned. The pair fell to the lot of a waiter who happened to feel pleasure in steering them through their meal. He viewed them with the manner of a fatherly pilot, his countenance radiant with benevolence. The patronage, entwined with the ordinary deference, was not plain to them. And yet, as they returned to their coach, they showed in their faces a sense of escape.

To the left, miles down a long purple slope, was a little ribbon of mist where moved the keening Rio Grande. The train was approaching it at an angle, and the apex was Yellow Sky. Presently it was apparent that, as the distance from Yellow Sky grew shorter, the husband became commensurately restless. His brick-red hands were more insistent in their prominence. Occasionally he was even rather absent-minded and far-away when the bride leaned forward and addressed him.

As a matter of truth, Jack Potter was beginning to find the shadow of a deed weigh upon him like a leaden slab. He, the town marshal of Yellow Sky, a man known, liked, and feared in his corner, a prominent person, had gone to San Antonio to meet a girl he believed he loved, and there, after the usual prayers, had actually induced her to marry him, without consulting Yellow Sky for any part of the transaction. He was now bringing his bride before an innocent and unsuspecting community.

Of course people in Yellow Sky married as it pleased them, in accordance with a general custom; but such was Potter's thought of his duty to his friends, or of their idea of his duty, or of an unspoken form which does not control men in these matters, that he felt he was heinous. He had committed an extraordinary crime. Face to face with this girl in San Antonio, and spurred by his sharp impulse, he had gone headlong over all the social hedges. At San Antonio he was like a man hidden in the dark. A knife to sever any friendly duty, any form, was easy to his hand in that remote city. But the hour of Yellow Sky—the hour of daylight—was approaching.

He knew full well that his marriage was an important thing to his town. It could only be exceeded by the burning of the new hotel. His friends could not forgive him. Frequently he had reflected on the advisability of telling them by telegraph, but a new cowardice had been upon him. He feared to do it. And now the train was hurrying him toward a scene of amazement, glee, and reproach. He glanced out of the window at the line of haze swinging slowly in toward the train.

Yellow Sky had a kind of brass band, which played painfully, to the delight of the populace. He laughed without heart as he thought of it. If the citizens could dream of his prospective arrival with his bride, they would parade the band at the station and escort them, amid cheers and laughing congratulations, to his adobe home.

He resolved that he would use all the devices of speed and plainscraft in making the journey from the station to his house. Once within that safe citadel, he could issue some sort of vocal bulletin, and then not go among the citizens until they had time to wear off a little of their enthusiasm.

The bride looked anxiously at him. "What's worrying you, Jack?"

He laughed again. "I'm not worrying, girl; I'm only thinking of Yellow Sky."

She flushed in comprehension.

A sense of mutual guilt invaded their minds and developed a finer tenderness. They looked at each other with eyes softly aglow. But Potter often laughed the same nervous laugh; the flush upon the bride's face seemed quite permanent.

The traitor to the feelings of Yellow Sky narrowly watched the speeding landscape. "We're nearly there," he said.

Presently the porter came and announced the proximity of Potter's home. He held a brush in his hand, and, with all his airy superiority gone, he brushed Potter's new clothes as the latter slowly turned this way and that way. Potter fumbled out a coin and gave it to the porter, as he had seen others do. It was a heavy and muscle-bound business, as that of a man shoeing his first horse.

The porter took their bag, and as the train began to slow they moved forward to the hooded platform of the car. Presently the two engines and their string of coaches rushed into the station of Yellow Sky.

"They have to take water here," said Potter, from a constricted throat and in mournful cadence, as one announcing death. Before the train stopped his eye had swept the length of the platform, and he was glad and astonished to see there was none upon it but the station-agent, who, with a slightly hurried and anxious air, was walking toward the water-tanks. When the train had halted, the porter alighted first, and placed in position a little temporary step.

"Come on, girl," said Potter, hoarsely. As he helped her down they each laughed on a false note. He took the bag from the negro, and bade his wife cling to his arm. As they slunk rapidly away, his hang-dog glance perceived that they were unloading the two trunks, and also that the station-agent, far ahead near the baggage-car, had turned and was running toward him, making gestures. He laughed, and groaned as he laughed, when he noted the first effect of his marital bliss upon Yellow Sky. He gripped his wife's arm firmly to his side, and they fled. Behind them the porter stood, chuckling fatuously.

II

The California express on the Southern Railway was due at Yellow Sky in twenty-one minutes. There were six men at the bar of the Weary Gentleman saloon. One was a drummer who talked a great deal and rapidly; three were Texans who did not care to talk at that time; and two were Mexican sheep-herders, who did not talk as a general practice in the Weary Gentleman saloon. The barkeeper's dog lay on the board walk that crossed in front of the door. His head was on his paws, and he glanced drowsily here and there with the constant vigilance of a dog that is kicked on occasion. Across the sandy street were some vivid green grass-plots, so wonderful in appearance, amid the sands that burned near them in a blazing sun, that they caused a doubt in the mind. They exactly resembled the grass mats used to represent lawns on the stage. At the cooler end of the railway station, a man without a coat sat in a tilted chair and smoked his pipe. The fresh-cut bank of the Rio Grande circled near the town, and there could be seen beyond it a great plum-coloured plain of mesquit.

Save for the busy drummer and his companions in the saloon, Yellow Sky was dozing. The new-comer leaned gracefully upon the bar, and recited many tales with the confidence of a bard who has come upon a new field.

"—and at the moment that the old man fell downstairs with the bureau in his arms, the old woman was coming up with two scuttles of coal, and of course—"

The drummer's tale was interrupted by a young man who suddenly appeared in the open door. He cried: "Scratchy Wilson's drunk, and has turned loose with both hands." The two Mexicans at once set down their glasses and faded out of the rear entrance of the saloon.

The drummer, innocent and jocular, answered: "All right, old man. S'pose he has? Come in and have a drink, anyhow." 35

But the information had made such an obvious cleft in every skull in the room that the drummer was obliged to see its importance. All had become instantly solemn. "Say," said he, mystified, "what is this?" His three companions made the introductory gesture of eloquent speech; but the young man at the door forestalled them.

"It means, my friend," he answered, as he came into the saloon, "that for the next two hours this town won't be a health resort."

The barkeeper went to the door, and locked and barred it; reaching out of the window, he pulled in heavy wooden shutters, and barred them. Immediately a solemn, chapel-like gloom was upon the place. The drummer was looking from one to another.

"But, say," he cried, "what is this, anyhow? You don't mean there is going to be a gun-fight?"

"Don't know whether there'll be a fight or not," answered one man, grimly; 40 "but there'll be some shootin'—some good shootin'."

The young man who had warned them waved his hand. "Oh, there'll be a fight fast enough, if any one wants it. Anybody can get a fight out there in the street. There's a fight just waiting."

The drummer seemed to be swayed between the interest of a foreigner and a perception of personal danger.

"What did you say his name was?" he asked.

"Scratchy Wilson," they answered in chorus.

"And will he kill anybody? What are you going to do? Does this happen of- 45 ten? Does he rampage around like this once a week or so? Can he break in that door?"

"No; he can't break down that door," replied the barkeeper. "He's tried it three times. But when he comes you'd better lay down on the floor, stranger. He's dead sure to shoot at it, and a bullet may come through."

Thereafter the drummer kept a strict eye upon the door. The time had not yet called for him to hug the floor, but, as a minor precaution, he sidled near the wall. "Will he kill anybody?" he said again.

The men laughed low and scornfully at the question.

"He's out to shoot, and he's out for trouble. Don't see any good in experi-mentin' with him."

"But what do you do in a case like this? What do you do?" 50

A man responded: "Why, he and Jack Potter—"

"But," in chorus the other men interrupted, "Jack Potter's in San Anton'."

"Well, who is he? What's he got to do with it?"

"Oh, he's the town marshal. He goes out and fights Scratchy when he gets on one of these tears."

"Wow!" said the drummer, mopping his brow. "Nice job he's got." 55

The voices had toned away to mere whisperings. The drummer wished to ask further questions, which were born of an increasing anxiety and bewilderment; but when he attempted them, the men merely looked at him in irritation and motioned him to remain silent. A tense waiting hush was upon them. In the deep shadows of the room their eyes shone as they listened for sounds from the street. One man made three gestures at the barkeeper; and the latter, moving like a ghost, handed him a glass and a bottle. The man poured a full glass of whisky, and set down the bottle noiselessly. He gulped the whisky in a swallow, and turned again toward the door in immovable silence. The drummer saw that the barkeeper, without a sound, had taken a Winchester from beneath the bar. Later he saw this individual beckoning to him, so he tiptoed across the room.

"You better come with me back of the bar."

"No thanks," said the drummer, perspiring; "I'd rather be where I can make a break for the back door."

Whereupon the man of bottles made a kindly but peremptory gesture. The drummer obeyed it, and, finding himself seated on a box with his head below the level of the bar, balm was laid upon his soul at sight of various zinc and copper fittings that bore a resemblance to armour-plate. The barkeeper took a seat comfortably upon an adjacent box.

"You see," he whispered, "this here Scratchy Wilson is a wonder with a gun—   60
a perfect wonder; and when he goes on the war-trail, we hunt our holes—naturally. He's about the last one of the old gang that used to hang out along the river here. He's a terror when he's drunk. When he's sober he's all right—kind of simple—wouldn't hurt a fly—nicest fellow in town. But when he's drunk—whoo!"

There were periods of stillness. "I wish Jack Potter was back from San Anton'," said the barkeeper. "He shot Wilson up once—in the leg—and he would sail in and pull out the kinks in this thing."

Presently they heard from a distance the sound of a shot, followed by three wild yowls. It instantly removed a bond from the men in the darkened saloon. There was a shuffling of feet. They looked at each other. "Here he comes," they said.

III

A man in a maroon-coloured flannel shirt, which had been purchased for purposes of decoration, and made principally by some Jewish women on the East Side of New York, rounded a corner and walked into the middle of the main street of Yellow Sky. In either hand the man held a long, heavy, blue-black revolver. Often he yelled, and these cries rang through a semblance of a deserted village, shrilly flying over the roofs in a volume that seemed to have no relation to the ordinary vocal strength of a man. It was as if the surrounding stillness formed the arch of a tomb over him. These cries of ferocious challenge rang against walls of silence. And his boots had red tops with gilded imprints, of the kind beloved in winter by little sledding boys on the hillsides of New England.

The man's face flamed in a rage begot of whisky. His eyes, rolling, and yet keen for ambush, hunted the still doorways and windows. He walked with the creeping movement of the midnight cat. As it occurred to him, he roared menacing information. The long revolvers in his hands were as easy as straws; they were moved with an electric swiftness. The little fingers of each hand played sometimes in a musician's way. Plain from the low collar of the shirt, the cords of his neck straightened and sank, straightened and sank, as passion moved him. The only sounds were his terrible invitations. The calm adobes preserved their demeanor at the passing of this small thing in the middle of the street.

There was no offer of fight—no offer of fight. The man called to the sky.   65
There were no attractions. He bellowed and fumed and swayed his revolvers here and everywhere.

The dog of the barkeeper of the Weary Gentleman saloon had not appreciated the advance of events. He yet lay dozing in front of his master's door. At sight of the dog, the man paused and raised his revolver humorously. At sight of the man, the dog sprang up and walked diagonally away, with a sullen head, and growling. The man yelled, and the dog broke into a gallop. As it was about to enter an alley, there was a loud noise, a whistling, and something spat the ground directly before it. The dog screamed, and, wheeling in terror, galloped headlong in a new direction. Again there was a noise, a whistling, and sand was kicked viciously before it. Fear-stricken, the dog turned and flurried like an animal in a pen. The man stood laughing, his weapons at his hips.

Ultimately the man was attracted by the closed door of the Weary Gentleman saloon. He went to it and, hammering with a revolver, demanded drink.

The door remaining imperturbable, he picked a bit of paper from the walk, and nailed it to the framework with a knife. He then turned his back contemptuously upon this popular resort and, walking to the opposite side of the street and spinning there on his heel quickly and lithely, fired at the bit of paper. He missed it by a half-inch. He swore at himself, and went away. Later he comfortably fusilladed the windows of his most intimate friend. The man was playing with this town; it was a toy for him.

But still there was no offer of fight. The name of Jack Potter, his ancient antagonist, entered his mind, and he concluded that it would be a glad thing if he should go to Potter's house and by bombardment induce him to come out and fight. He moved in the direction of his desire, chanting Apache scalp-music.

When he arrived at it, Potter's house presented the same still front as had the   70
other adobes. Taking up a strategic position, the man howled a challenge. But this house regarded him as might a great stone god. It gave no sign. After a decent wait, the man howled further challenges, mingling with them wonderful epithets.

Presently there came the spectacle of a man churning himself into deepest rage over the immobility of a house. He fumed at it as the winter wind attacks a prairie cabin in the North. To the distance there should have gone the sound of a tumult like the fighting of two hundred Mexicans. As necessity bade him, he paused for breath or to reload his revolvers.

IV

Potter and his bride walked sheepishly and with speed. Sometimes they laughed together shamefacedly and low.

"Next corner, dear," he said finally.

They put forth the efforts of a pair walking bowed against a strong wind. Potter was about to raise a finger to point the first appearance of the new home when, as they circled the corner, they came face to face with a man in a marooncoloured shirt, who was feverishly pushing cartridges into a large revolver. Upon the instant the man dropped his revolver to the ground and, like lightning, whipped another from its holster. The second weapon was aimed at the bridegroom's chest.

There was a silence. Potter's mouth seemed to be merely a grave for his   75
tongue. He exhibited an instinct to at once loosen his arm from the woman's

grip, and he dropped the bag to the sand. As for the bride, her face had gone as yellow as old cloth. She was a slave to hideous rites, gazing at the apparitional snake.

The two men faced each other at a distance of three paces. He of the revolver smiled with a new and quiet ferocity.

"Tried to sneak up on me," he said. "Tried to sneak up on me!" His eyes grew more baleful. As Potter made a slight movement, the man thrust his revolver venomously forward. "No, don't you do it, Jack Potter. Don't you move a finger toward a gun just yet. Don't you move an eyelash. The time has come for me to settle with you, and I'm goin' to do it my own way, and loaf along with no interferin'. So if you don't want a gun bent on you, just mind what I tell you."

Potter looked at his enemy. "I ain't got a gun on me, Scratchy," he said. "Honest, I ain't." He was stiffening and steadying, but yet somewhere at the back of his mind a vision of the Pullman floated: the sea-green figured velvet, the shining brass, silver, and glass, the wood that gleamed as darkly brilliant as the surface of a pool of oil—all the glory of marriage, the environment of the new estate. "You know I fight when it comes to fighting, Scratchy Wilson; but I ain't got a gun on me. You'll have to do all the shootin' yourself."

His enemy's face went livid. He stepped forward, and lashed his weapon to and fro before Potter's chest. "Don't you tell me you ain't got no gun on you, you whelp. Don't tell me no lie like that. There ain't a man in Texas ever seen you without no gun. Don't take me for no kid." His eyes blazed with light, and his throat worked like a pump.

"I ain't takin' you for no kid," answered Potter. His heels had not moved an inch backward. "I'm takin' you for a damn fool. I tell you I ain't got a gun, and I ain't. If you're goin' to shoot me up, you better begin now; you'll never get a chance like this again." 80

So much enforced reasoning had told on Wilson's rage; he was calmer. "If you ain't got a gun, why ain't you got a gun?" he sneered. "Been to Sunday-school?"

"I ain't got a gun because I've just come from San Anton' with my wife. I'm married," said Potter. "And if I'd thought there was going to be any galoots like you prowling around when I brought my wife home, I'd had a gun, and don't you forget it."

"Married!" said Scratchy, not at all comprehending.

"Yes, married. I'm married," said Potter, distinctly.

"Married?" said Scratchy. Seemingly for the first time, he saw the drooping, 85 drowning woman at the other man's side. "No!" he said. He was like a creature allowed a glimpse of another world. He moved a pace backward, and his arm, with the revolver, dropped to his side. "Is this the lady?" he asked.

"Yes; this is the lady," answered Potter.

There was another period of silence.

"Well," said Wilson at last, slowly, "I s'pose it's all off now."

"It's all off if you say so, Scratchy. You know I didn't make the trouble." Potter lifted his valise.

"Well, I 'low it's off, Jack," said Wilson. He was looking at the ground. "Married!" He was not a student of chivalry; it was merely that in the presence of this foreign condition he was a simple child of the earlier plains. He picked up his starboard revolver, and, placing both weapons in their holsters, he went away. His feet made funnel-shaped tracks in the heavy sand.   90

For Analysis

1. Explain how the opening paragraph establishes the **tone** and **theme** of the story. **2.** Is it a weakness in the story that despite its title, Jack Potter's bride is not a developed or individualized character? Explain. **3.** Scratchy is described in the final paragraph as "a simple child of the earlier plains." What does this mean? Was Potter ever a simple child of the earlier plains? **4.** Early in the story we read that ". . . Jack Potter was beginning to find the shadow of a deed weigh upon him like a leaden slab. He, the town marshal of Yellow Sky, a man known, liked, and feared in his corner, a prominent person, had gone to San Antonio to meet a girl he believed he loved, and there, after the usual prayers, had actually induced her to marry him, without consulting Yellow Sky for any part of the transaction. He was now bringing his bride before an innocent and unsuspecting community" (par. 17). Jack Potter, like any adult, has the right to marry. How do you account for his feelings as described in this passage? **5.** A "drummer" is a traveling salesman. What effect does his presence have on the myth of the West? **6.** Characterize Scratchy's behavior. How does it relate to the myth of the West preserved in films and Western novels? Why is Scratchy disconsolate at the end?

On Style

1. Analyze Crane's **metaphors** and **images**. What functions do they serve? **2.** What is the narrator's attitude toward the story he is telling?

Making Connections

1. Contrast this story, which seems to be about the end of a tradition, with Alice Walker's "Everyday Use" (p. 693), which seems to be about preserving a tradition. **2.** In what ways is Scratchy's innocence similar to or different from the innocence of Hulga in O'Connor's "Good Country People" (p. 99) and of the young waiter in Hemingway's "A Clean, Well-Lighted Place" (p. 86)?

Writing Topics

1. Write a brief paragraph speculating on how the description of Scratchy's shirt at the beginning of Part III, especially the detail that it was made "by some Jewish women on the East Side of New York" (par. 63), relates to the theme of the story. **2.** Describe the source of your own views about the "old West" and explain how Crane makes use of such stereotypes to achieve comic effects.

James Joyce   [1882–1941]

Araby   1914

Nmorth Richmond Street, being blind, was a quiet street except at the hour when the Christian Brothers' School set the boys free. An uninhabited house of two storeys stood at the blind end, detached from its neighbours in a square ground. The other houses of the street, conscious of decent lives within them, gazed at one another with brown imperturbable faces.

The former tenant of our house, a priest, had died in the back drawing-room. Air, musty from having been long enclosed, hung in all the rooms, and the waste room behind the kitchen was littered with old useless papers. Among these I found a few paper-covered books, the pages of which were curled and damp: *The Abbot*, by Walter Scott, *The Devout Communicant* and *The Memoirs of Vidocq*. I liked the last best because its leaves were yellow. The wild garden behind the house contained a central apple-tree and a few straggling bushes under one of which I found the late tenant's rusty bicycle pump. He had been a very charitable priest; in his will he had left all his money to institutions and the furniture of his house to his sister.

When the short days of winter came dusk fell before we had well eaten our dinners. When we met in the street the houses had grown sombre. The space of sky above us was the colour of ever-changing violet and towards it the lamps of the street lifted their feeble lanterns. The cold air stung us and we played till our bodies glowed. Our shouts echoed in the silent street. The career of our play brought us through the dark muddy lanes behind the houses where we ran the gauntlet of the rough tribes from the cottages, to the back doors of the dark dripping gardens where odours arose from the ashpits, to the dark odorous stables where a coachman smoothed and combed the horse or shook music from the buckled harness. When we returned to the street light from the kitchen windows had filled the areas. If my uncle was seen turning the corner we hid in the shadow until we had seen him safely housed. Or if Mangan's sister came out on the doorstep to call her brother in to his tea we watched her from our shadow peer up and down the street. We waited to see whether she would remain or go in and, if she remained, we left our shadow and walked up to Mangan's steps resignedly. She was waiting for us, her figure defined by the light from the half-opened door. Her brother always teased her before he obeyed and I stood by the railings looking at her. Her dress swung as she moved her body and the soft rope of her hair tossed from side to side.

Every morning I lay on the floor in the front parlour watching her door. The blind was pulled down to within an inch of the sash so that I could not be seen.

When she came out on the doorstep my heart leaped. I ran to the hall, seized my books and followed her. I kept her brown figure always in my eye and, when we came near the point at which our ways diverged, I quickened my pace and passed her. This happened morning after morning. I had never spoken to her, except for a few casual words, and yet her name was like a summons to all my foolish blood.

Her image accompanied me even in places the most hostile to romance. On Saturday evenings when my aunt went marketing I had to go to carry some of the parcels. We walked through the flaring streets, jostled by drunken men and bargaining women, amid the curses of labourers, the shrill litanies of shop-boys who stood on guard by the barrels of pigs' cheeks, the nasal chanting of street-singers, who sang a *come-all-you*[1] about O'Donovan Rossa, or a ballad about the troubles in our native land. These noises converged in a single sensation of life for me: I imagined that I bore my chalice safely through a throng of foes. Her name sprang to my lips at moments in strange prayers and praises which I myself did not understand. My eyes were often full of tears (I could not tell why) and at times a flood from my heart seemed to pour itself out into my bosom. I thought little of the future. I did not know whether I would ever speak to her or not or, if I spoke to her, how I could tell her of my confused adoration. But my body was like a harp and her words and gestures were like fingers running upon the wires.

One evening I went into the back drawing-room in which the priest had died. It was a dark rainy evening and there was no sound in the house. Through one of the broken panes I heard the rain impinge upon the earth, the fine incessant needles of water playing in the sodden beds. Some distant lamp or lighted window gleamed below me. I was thankful that I could see so little. All my senses seemed to desire to veil themselves and, feeling that I was about to slip from them, I pressed the palms of my hands together until they trembled, murmuring: *"O love! O love!"* many times.

At last she spoke to me. When she addressed the first words to me I was so confused that I did not know what to answer. She asked me was I going to *Araby.* I forgot whether I answered yes or no. It would be a splendid bazaar, she said she would love to go.

"And why can't you?" I asked.

While she spoke she turned a silver bracelet round and round her wrist. She could not go, she said, because there would be a retreat that week in her convent. Her brother and two other boys were fighting for their caps and I was alone at the railings. She held one of the spikes, bowing her head towards me. The light from the lamp opposite our door caught the white curve of her neck, lit her hair that rested there and, falling, lit up the hand upon the railing. It fell over one side of her dress and caught the white border of a petticoat, just visible as she stood at ease.

"It's well for you," she said.

[1] A street ballad beginning with these words. This one is about Jeremiah Donovan, a nineteenth-century Irish nationalist popularly known as O'Donovan Rossa.

"If I go," I said, "I will bring you something."

What innumerable follies laid waste my waking and sleeping thoughts after that evening! I wished to annihilate the tedious intervening days. I chafed against the work of school. At night in my bedroom and by day in the classroom her image came between me and the page I strove to read. The syllables of the word *Araby* were called to me through the silence in which my soul luxuriated and cast an Eastern enchantment over me. I asked for leave to go to the bazaar on Saturday night. My aunt was surprised and hoped it was not some Freemason affair. I answered few questions in class. I watched my master's face pass from amiability to sternness; he hoped I was not beginning to idle. I could not call my wandering thoughts together. I had hardly any patience with the serious work of life which, now that it stood between me and my desire, seemed to me child's play, ugly monotonous child's play.

On Saturday morning I reminded my uncle that I wished to go to the bazaar in the evening. He was fussing at the hallstand, looking for the hat-brush, and answered me curtly:

"Yes, boy, I know."

As he was in the hall I could not go into the front parlour and lie at the window. I left the house in bad humour and walked slowly towards the school. The air was pitilessly raw and already my heart misgave me.

When I came home to dinner my uncle had not yet been home. Still it was early. I sat staring at the clock for some time and, when its ticking began to irritate me, I left the room. I mounted the staircase and gained the upper part of the house. The high cold empty gloomy rooms liberated me and I went from room to room singing. From the front window I saw my companions playing below in the street. Their cries reached me weakened and indistinct and, leaning my forehead against the cool glass, I looked over at the dark house where she lived. I may have stood there for an hour, seeing nothing but the brown-clad figure cast by my imagination, touched discreetly by the lamplight at the curved neck, at the hand upon the railings and at the border below the dress.

When I came downstairs again I found Mrs. Mercer sitting at the fire. She was an old garrulous woman, a pawnbroker's widow, who collected used stamps for some pious purpose. I had to endure the gossip of the tea-table. The meal was prolonged beyond an hour and still my uncle did not come. Mrs. Mercer stood up to go: she was sorry she couldn't wait any longer, but it was after eight o'clock and she did not like to be out late, as the night air was bad for her. When she had gone I began to walk up and down the room, clenching my fists. My aunt said:

"I'm afraid you may put off your bazaar for this night of Our Lord."

At nine o'clock I heard my uncle's latchkey in the hall door. I heard him talking to himself and heard the hallstand rocking when it had received the weight of his overcoat. I could interpret these signs. When he was midway through his dinner I asked him to give me the money to go to the bazaar. He had forgotten.

"The people are in bed and after their first sleep now," he said.

I did not smile. My aunt said to him energetically:

"Can't you give him the money and let him go? You've kept him late enough as it is."

My uncle said he was very sorry he had forgotten. He said he believed in the old saying: "All work and no play makes Jack a dull boy." He asked me where I was going and, when I had told him a second time he asked me did I know *The Arab's Farewell to His Steed*. When I left the kitchen he was about to recite the opening lines of the piece to my aunt.

I held a florin tightly in my hand as I strode down Buckingham Street towards the station. The sight of the streets thronged with buyers and glaring with gas recalled to me the purpose of my journey. I took my seat in a third-class carriage of a deserted train. After an intolerable delay the train moved out of the station slowly. It crept onward among ruinous houses and over the twinkling river. At Westland Row Station a crowd of people pressed to the carriage doors; but the porters moved them back, saying that it was a special train for the bazaar. I remained alone in the bare carriage. In a few minutes the train drew up beside an improvised wooden platform. I passed out on to the road and saw by the lighted dial of a clock that it was ten minutes to ten. In front of me was a large building which displayed the magical name.

I could not find any sixpenny entrance and, fearing that the bazaar would be   25
closed, I passed in quickly through a turnstile, handing a shilling to a weary-looking man. I found myself in a big hall girdled at half its height by a gallery. Nearly all the stalls were closed and the greater part of the hall was in darkness. I recognised a silence like that which pervades a church after a service. I walked into the centre of the bazaar timidly. A few people were gathered about the stalls which were still open. Before a curtain, over which the words *Café Chantant* were written in coloured lamps, two men were counting money on a salver. I listened to the fall of the coins.

Remembering with difficulty why I had come I went over to one of the stalls and examined porcelain vases and flowered tea-sets. At the door of the stall a young lady was talking and laughing with two young gentlemen. I remarked their English accents and listened vaguely to their conversation.

"O, I never said such a thing!"

"O, but you did!"

"O, but I didn't!"

"Didn't she say that?"   30

"Yes. I heard her."

"O, there's a . . . fib!"

Observing me the young lady came over and asked me did I wish to buy anything. The tone of her voice was not encouraging; she seemed to have spoken to me out of a sense of duty. I looked humbly at the great jars that stood like Eastern guards at either side of the dark entrance to the stall and murmured:

"No, thank you."

The young lady changed the position of one of the vases and went back to the   35
two young men. They began to talk of the same subject. Once or twice the young lady glanced at me over her shoulder.

I lingered before her stall, though I knew my stay was useless, to make my interest in her wares seem the more real. Then I turned away slowly and walked down the middle of the bazaar. I allowed the two pennies to fall against the sixpence in my pocket. I heard a voice call from one end of the gallery that the light was out. The upper part of the hall was now completely dark.

Gazing up into the darkness I saw myself as a creature driven and derided by vanity; and my eyes burned with anguish and anger.

For Analysis

1. Reread the opening paragraph. How does it set the tone for the story? **2.** What do we learn about the narrator from his comment (par. 2) that he liked *The Memoirs of Vidocq* best "because its leaves were yellow"? **3.** What does Mangan's sister represent to the narrator? **4.** Why does the dialogue the narrator overhears at the bazaar trigger the climax of the story and the insight described in the final paragraph?

On Style

1. What does the **tone** of this story, particularly its lack of humor, tell us about the kind of significance the adult narrator attaches to this childhood experience? **2.** Carefully examine the language of paragraph 5. What stylistic devices allow the narrator to transform a simple shopping trip into a chivalric romance?

Making Connections

1. Compare the use of the first-person **point of view** in this story with the first-person point of view in Frank O'Connor's "My Oedipus Complex" (p. 90). **2.** Describe an experience that led you to the realization that you were not acting out of the selfless motives you had thought you were.

Writing Topic

Write a page describing a romantic infatuation you experienced when you were younger that blinded you to the reality of the person you adored.

Ernest Hemingway [1899–1961]

A Clean, Well-Lighted Place 1933

It was late and everyone had left the café except an old man who sat in the shadow the leaves of the tree made against the electric light. In the day time the street was dusty, but at night the dew settled the dust and the old man liked to sit late because he was deaf and now at night it was quiet and he felt the difference. The two waiters inside the café knew that the old man was a little drunk, and while he was a good client they knew that if he became too drunk he would leave without paying, so they kept watch on him.

"Last week he tried to commit suicide," one waiter said.

"Why?"

"He was in despair."

"What about?" 5

"Nothing."

"How do you know it was nothing?"

"He has plenty of money."

They sat together at a table that was close against the wall near the door of the café and looked at the terrace where the tables were all empty except where the old man sat in the shadow of the leaves of the tree that moved slightly in the wind. A girl and a soldier went by in the street. The street light shone on the brass number on his collar. The girl wore no head covering and hurried beside him.

"The guard will pick him up," one waiter said. 10

"What does it matter if he gets what he's after?"

"He had better get off the street now. The guard will get him. They went by five minutes ago."

The old man sitting in the shadow rapped on his saucer with his glass. The younger waiter went over to him.

"What do you want?"

The old man looked at him. "Another brandy," he said. 15

"You'll be drunk," the waiter said. The old man looked at him. The waiter went away.

"He'll stay all night," he said to his colleague. "I'm sleepy now. I never get into bed before three o'clock. He should have killed himself last week."

The waiter took the brandy bottle and another saucer from the counter inside the café and marched out to the old man's table. He put down the saucer and poured the glass full of brandy.

"You should have killed yourself last week," he said to the deaf man. The old man motioned with his finger. "A little more," he said. The waiter poured on into the glass so that the brandy slopped over and ran down the stem into the top saucer of the pile. "Thank you," the old man said. The waiter took the bottle back inside the café. He sat down at the table with his colleague again.

"He's drunk now," he said. 20

"He's drunk every night."

"What did he want to kill himself for?"

"How should I know."

"How did he do it?"

"He hung himself with a rope." 25

"Who cut him down?"

"His niece."

"Why did they do it?"

"Fear for his soul."

"How much money has he got?" 30

"He's got plenty."

"He must be eighty years old."

"Anyway I should say he was eighty."

"I wish he would go home. I never get to bed before three o'clock. What kind of hour is that to go to bed?"

"He stays up because he likes it." 35

"He's lonely. I'm not lonely. I have a wife waiting in bed for me."

"He had a wife once too."

"A wife would be no good to him now."

"You can't tell. He might be better with a wife."

"His niece looks after him." 40

"I know. You said she cut him down."

"I wouldn't want to be that old. An old man is a nasty thing."

"Not always. This old man is clean. He drinks without spilling. Even now, drunk. Look at him."

"I don't want to look at him. I wish he would go home. He has no regard for those who must work."

The old man looked from his glass across the square, then over at the waiters. 45

"Another brandy," he said, pointing to his glass. The waiter who was in a hurry came over.

"Finished," he said, speaking with that omission of syntax stupid people employ when talking to drunken people or foreigners. "No more tonight. Close now."

"Another," said the old man.

"No. Finished." The waiter wiped the edge of the table with a towel and shook his head.

The old man stood up, slowly counted the saucers, took a leather coin purse 50 from his pocket and paid for the drinks, leaving half a peseta tip.

The waiter watched him go down the street, a very old man walking unsteadily but with dignity.

"Why didn't you let him stay and drink?" the unhurried waiter asked. They were putting up the shutters. "It is not half-past two."

"I want to go home to bed."

"What is an hour?"

"More to me than to him." 55

"An hour is the same."

"You talk like an old man yourself. He can buy a bottle and drink at home."

"It's not the same."

"No, it is not," agreed the waiter with a wife. He did not wish to be unjust. He was only in a hurry.

"And you? You have no fear of going home before your usual hour?" 60

"Are you trying to insult me?"

"No, hombre, only to make a joke."

"No," the waiter who was in a hurry said, rising from pulling down the metal shutters. "I have confidence. I am all confidence."

"You have youth, confidence, and a job," the older waiter said. "You have everything."

"And what do you lack?" 65

"Everything but work."

"You have everything I have."

"No. I have never had confidence and I am not young."

"Come on. Stop talking nonsense and lock up."

"I am of those who like to stay late at the café," the older waiter said. "With 70 all those who do not want to go to bed. With all those who need a light for the night."

"I want to go home and into bed."

"We are of two different kinds," the older waiter said. He was now dressed to go home. "It is not only a question of youth and confidence although those things are very beautiful. Each night I am reluctant to close up because there may be some one who needs the café."

"Hombre, there are bodegas open all night long."

"You do not understand. This is a clean and pleasant café. It is well lighted. The light is very good and also, now, there are shadows of the leaves."

"Good night," said the younger waiter. 75

"Good night," the other said. Turning off the electric light he continued the conversation with himself. It is the light of course but it is necessary that the place be clean and pleasant. You do not want music. Certainly you do not want music. Nor can you stand before a bar with dignity although that is all that is provided for these hours. What did he fear? It was not fear or dread. It was a nothing that he knew too well. It was all a nothing and a man was nothing too. It was only that and light was all it needed and a certain cleanness and order. Some lived in it and never felt it but he knew it was nada y pues nada y pues nada.[1] Our nada who art in nada, nada be thy name thy kingdom nada thy will be nada in nada as it is in nada. Give us this nada our daily nada and nada us our nada as we nada our nadas and nada us not into nada but deliver us from nada;

---

[1] Nothing, and then nothing, and then nothing.

pues nada. Hail nothing full of nothing, nothing is with thee. He smiled and stood before a bar with a shining steam pressure coffee machine.

"What's yours?" asked the barman.

"Nada."

"Otro loco más,"[2] said the barman and turned away.

"A little cup," said the waiter.   80

The barman poured it for him.

"The light is very bright and pleasant but the bar is unpolished," the waiter said.

The barman looked at him but did not answer. It was too late at night for conversation.

"You want another copita?" the barman asked.

"No, thank you," said the waiter and went out. He disliked bars and bodegas.   85
A clean, well-lighted café was a very different thing. Now, without thinking further, he would go home to his room. He would lie in the bed and finally, with daylight, he would go to sleep. After all, he said to himself, it is probably only insomnia. Many must have it.

For Analysis

1. How does the first dialogue between the two waiters establish the differences between them? **2.** What bearing do the waiters' two different views toward the old man have on the **theme** of the story? Is the difference in age between them relevant to the theme? Explain. **3.** How does the setting contribute to the story's theme? **4.** Explain the meaning of the story's title. **5.** What arguments could be made that this is a religious story?

On Style

Hemingway relies heavily on **dialogue** in this story. How effective is this use of dialogue?

Making Connections

1. What thematic similarities do you find between this story and Hawthorne's "Young Goodman Brown" (p. 61), Melville's "Bartleby the Scrivener" (p. 313), and Art Spiegelman's "Prisoner on the Hell Planet" (p. 1242)? **2.** Compare and contrast the meaning of *nada* in this story and Hulga's belief in "nothing" in O'Connor's "Good Country People" (p. 99).

Writing Topic

Write an essay on the connection between the **parody** of the Lord's Prayer (par. 76) and the title of the story.

---

[2] Another crazy one.

Frank O'Connor [1903–1966]

My Oedipus Complex 1950

Father was in the army all through the war—the first war, I mean—so, up to the age of five, I never saw much of him, and what I saw did not worry me. Sometimes I woke and there was a big figure in khaki peering down at me in the candlelight. Sometimes in the early morning I heard the slamming of the front door and the clatter of nailed boots down the cobbles of the lane. These were Father's entrances and exits. Like Santa Claus he came and went mysteriously.

In fact, I rather liked his visits, though it was an uncomfortable squeeze between Mother and him when I got into the big bed in the early morning. He smoked, which gave him a pleasant musty smell, and shaved, an operation of astounding interest. Each time he left a trail of souvenirs—model tanks and Gurkha knives with handles made of bullet cases, and German helmets and cap badges and button-sticks, and all sorts of military equipment—carefully stowed away in a long box on top of the wardrobe, in case they ever came in handy. There was a bit of the magpie about Father; he expected everything to come in handy. When his back was turned, Mother let me get a chair and rummage through his treasures. She didn't seem to think so highly of them as he did.

The war was the most peaceful period of my life. The window of my attic faced southeast. My mother had curtained it, but that had small effect. I always woke with the first light and, with all the responsibilities of the previous day melted, feeling myself rather like the sun, ready to illumine and rejoice. Life never seemed so simple and clear and full of possibilities as then. I put my feet out from under the clothes—I called them Mrs. Left and Mrs. Right—and invented dramatic situations for them in which they discussed the problems of the day. At least Mrs. Right did; she was very demonstrative, but I hadn't the same control of Mrs. Left, so she mostly contented herself with nodding agreement.

They discussed what Mother and I should do during the day, what Santa Claus should give a fellow for Christmas, and what steps should be taken to brighten the home. There was that little matter of the baby, for instance. Mother and I could never agree about that. Ours was the only house in the terrace without a new baby, and Mother said we couldn't afford one till Father came back from the war because they cost seventeen and six. That showed how simple she was. The Geneys up the road had a baby, and everyone knew they couldn't afford seventeen and six. It was probably a cheap baby, and Mother wanted something really good, but I felt she was too exclusive. The Geneys' baby would have done us fine.

Having settled my plans for the day, I got up, put a chair under the attic window, 5

90

and lifted the frame high enough to stick out my head. The window overlooked the front gardens of the terrace behind ours, and beyond these it looked over a deep valley to the tall, red-brick houses terraced up the opposite hillside, which were all still in shadow, while those at our side of the valley were all lit up, though with long strange shadows that made them seem unfamiliar; rigid and painted.

After that I went into Mother's room and climbed into the big bed. She woke and I began to tell her of my schemes. By this time, though I never seem to have noticed it, I was petrified in my nightshirt, and I thawed as I talked until, the last frost melted, I fell asleep beside her and woke again only when I heard her below in the kitchen, making the breakfast.

After breakfast we went into town; heard Mass at St. Augustine's and said a prayer for Father, and did the shopping. If the afternoon was fine we either went for a walk in the country or a visit to Mother's great friend in the convent, Mother St. Dominic. Mother had them all praying for Father, and every night, going to bed, I asked God to send him back safe from the war to us. Little, indeed, did I know what I was praying for!

One morning, I got into the big bed, and there, sure enough, was Father in his usual Santa Claus manner, but later, instead of uniform, he put on his best blue suit, and Mother was as pleased as anything. I saw nothing to be pleased about, because, out of uniform, Father was altogether less interesting, but she only beamed, and explained that our prayers had been answered, and off we went to Mass to thank God for having brought Father safely home.

The irony of it! That very day when he came in to dinner he took off his boots and put on his slippers, donned the dirty old cap he wore about the house to save him from colds, crossed his legs, and began to talk gravely to Mother, who looked anxious. Naturally, I disliked her looking anxious, because it destroyed her good looks, so I interrupted him.

"Just a moment, Larry!" she said gently.   10

This was only what she said when we had boring visitors, so I attached no importance to it and went on talking.

"Do be quiet, Larry!" she said impatiently. "Don't you hear me talking to Daddy?"

This was the first time I had heard those ominous words, "talking to Daddy," and I couldn't help feeling that if this was how God answered prayers, he couldn't listen to them very attentively.

"Why are you talking to Daddy?" I asked with as great a show of indifference as I could muster.

"Because Daddy and I have business to discuss. Now, don't interrupt again!"   15

In the afternoon, at Mother's request, Father took me for a walk. This time we went into town instead of out to the country, and I thought at first, in my usual optimistic way, that it might be an improvement. It was nothing of the sort. Father and I had quite different notions of a walk in town. He had no proper interest in trams, ships, and horses, and the only thing that seemed to divert him was talking to fellows as old as himself. When I wanted to stop he simply went on, dragging me behind him by the hand; when he wanted to stop I had no alternative but to do the same. I noticed that it seemed to be a sign that he wanted to stop for a long time whenever he leaned against a wall. The second time I saw him do it I got wild. He seemed to be settling himself forever. I pulled him by the coat and trousers, but, unlike Mother who, if you were too persistent, got into a wax and said: "Larry, if you don't behave yourself, I'll give you a good slap," Father had an extraordinary capacity for amiable inattention. I sized him up and wondered would I cry, but he seemed to be too remote to be annoyed even by that. Really, it was like going for a walk with a mountain! He either ignored the wrenching and pummeling entirely, or else glanced down with a grin of amusement from his peak. I had never met anyone so absorbed in himself as he seemed.

At teatime, "talking to Daddy" began again, complicated this time by the fact that he had an evening paper, and every few minutes he put it down and told Mother something new out of it. I felt this was foul play. Man for man, I was prepared to compete with him any time for Mother's attention, but when he had it all made up for him by other people it left me no chance. Several times I tried to change the subject without success.

"You must be quiet while Daddy is reading, Larry," Mother said impatiently.

It was clear that she either genuinely liked talking to Father better than talking to me, or else that he had some terrible hold on her which made her afraid to admit the truth.

"Mummy," I said that night when she was tucking me up, "do you think if I prayed hard God would send Daddy back to the war?" [20]

She seemed to think about that for a moment.

"No, dear," she said with a smile. "I don't think he would."

"Why wouldn't he, Mummy?"

"Because there isn't a war any longer, dear."

"But, Mummy, couldn't God make another war, if he liked?" [25]

"He wouldn't like to, dear. It's not God who makes wars, but bad people."

"Oh!" I said.

I was disappointed about that. I began to think that God wasn't quite what he was cracked up to be.

Next morning I woke at my usual hour, feeling like a bottle of champagne. I put out my feet and invented a long conversation in which Mrs. Right talked of the trouble she had with her own father till she put him in the Home. I didn't quite know what the Home was but it sounded the right place for Father. Then I got my chair and stuck my head out of the attic window. Dawn was just breaking, with a guilty air that made me feel I had caught it in the act. My head bursting with stories and schemes, I stumbled in next door, and in the half-darkness scrambled into the big bed. There was no room at Mother's side so I had to get between her and Father. For the time being I had forgotten about him, and for several minutes I sat bolt upright, racking my brains to know what I could do with him. He was taking up more than his fair share of the bed, and I couldn't get comfortable, so I gave him several kicks that made him grunt and stretch.

He made room all right, though. Mother waked and felt for me. I settled back comfortably in the warmth of the bed with my thumb in my mouth.

"Mummy!" I hummed, loudly and contentedly.

"Ssh! dear," she whispered. "Don't wake Daddy!"

This was a new development, which threatened to be even more serious than "talking to Daddy." Life without my early-morning conferences was unthinkable.

"Why?" I asked severely.

"Because poor Daddy is tired."

This seemed to me a quite inadequate reason, and I was sickened by the sentimentality of her "poor Daddy." I never liked that sort of gush; it always struck me as insincere.

"Oh!" I said lightly. Then in my most winning tone: "Do you know where I want to go with you today, Mummy?"

"No, dear," she sighed.

"I want to go down the Glen and fish for thornybacks with my new net, and then I want to go out to the Fox and Hounds, and—"

"Don't-wake-Daddy!" she hissed angrily, clapping her hand across my mouth.

But it was too late. He was awake, or nearly so. He grunted and reached for the matches. Then he stared incredulously at his watch.

"Like a cup of tea, dear?" asked Mother in a meek, hushed voice I had never heard her use before. It sounded almost as though she were afraid.

"Tea?" he exclaimed indignantly. "Do you know what the time is?"

"And after that I want to go up the Rathcooney Road," I said loudly, afraid I'd forget something in all those interruptions.

"Go to sleep at once, Larry!" she said sharply.

I began to snivel. I couldn't concentrate, the way that pair went on, and smothering my early-morning schemes was like burying a family from the cradle.

Father said nothing, but lit his pipe and sucked it, looking out into the shadows without minding Mother or me. I knew he was mad. Every time I made a remark Mother hushed me irritably. I was mortified. I felt it wasn't fair; there was even something sinister in it. Every time I had pointed out to her the waste of making two beds when we could both sleep in one, she had told me it was healthier like that, and now here was this man, this stranger, sleeping with her without the least regard for her health!

He got up early and made tea, but though he brought Mother a cup he brought none for me.

"Mummy," I shouted, "I want a cup of tea, too."

"Yes, dear," she said patiently. "You can drink from Mummy's saucer."

That settled it. Either Father or I would have to leave the house. I didn't want to drink from Mother's saucer; I wanted to be treated as an equal in my own home, so, just to spite her, I drank it all and left none for her. She took that quietly, too.

But that night when she was putting me to bed she said gently: "Larry, I want you to promise me something."

"What is it?" I asked.

"Not to come in and disturb poor Daddy in the morning. Promise?"

"Poor Daddy" again! I was becoming suspicious of everything involving that quite impossible man.

"Why?" I asked.   55

"Because poor Daddy is worried and tired and he doesn't sleep well."

"Why doesn't he, Mummy?"

"Well, you know, don't you, that while he was at the war Mummy got the pennies from the Post Office?"

"From Miss MacCarthy?"

"That's right. But now, you see, Miss MacCarthy hasn't any more pennies, so   60
Daddy must go out and find us some. You know what would happen if he couldn't?"

"No," I said, "tell us."

"Well, I think we might have to go out and beg for them like the poor old woman on Fridays. We wouldn't like that, would we?"

"No," I agreed. "We wouldn't."

"So you'll promise not to come in and wake him?"

"Promise."   65

Mind you, I meant that. I knew pennies were a serious matter, and I was all against having to go out and beg like the old woman on Fridays. Mother laid out all my toys in a complete ring round the bed so that, whatever way I got out, I was bound to fall over one of them.

When I woke I remembered my promise all right. I got up and sat on the floor and played—for hours, it seemed to me. Then I got my chair and looked out the attic window for more hours. I wished it was time for Father to wake; I wished someone would make me a cup of tea. I didn't feel in the least like the sun; instead, I was bored and so very, very cold! I simply longed for the warmth and depth of the big featherbed.

At last I could stand it no longer. I went into the next room. As there was still no room at Mother's side I climbed over her and she woke with a start.

"Larry," she whispered, gripping my arm very tightly, "what did you promise?"

"But I did, Mummy," I wailed, caught in the very act. "I was quiet for ever so   70
long."

"Oh, dear, and you're perished!" she said sadly, feeling me all over. "Now, if I let you stay will you promise not to talk?"

"But I want to talk, Mummy," I wailed.

"That has nothing to do with it," she said with a firmness that was new to me. "Daddy wants to sleep. Now, do you understand that?"

I understood it only too well. I wanted to talk, he wanted to sleep—whose house was it, anyway?

"Mummy," I said with equal firmness, "I think it would be healthier for   75
Daddy to sleep in his own bed."

That seemed to stagger her, because she said nothing for a while.

"Now, once for all," she went on, "you're to be perfectly quiet or go back to
your own bed. Which is it to be?"

The injustice of it got me down. I had convicted her out of her own mouth of
inconsistency and unreasonableness, and she hadn't even attempted to reply.
Full of spite, I gave Father a kick, which she didn't notice but which made him
grunt and open his eyes in alarm.

"What time is it?" he asked in a panic-stricken voice, not looking at Mother
but the door, as if he saw someone there.

"It's early yet," she replied soothingly. "It's only the child. Go to sleep   80
again. . . . Now, Larry," she added, getting out of bed, "you've wakened Daddy
and you must go back."

This time, for all her quiet air, I knew she meant it, and knew that my principal rights and privileges were as good as lost unless I asserted them at once. As
she lifted me, I gave a screech, enough to wake the dead, not to mind Father.
He groaned.

"That damn child! Doesn't he ever sleep?"

"It's only a habit, dear," she said quietly, though I could see she was vexed.

"Well, it's time he got out of it," shouted Father, beginning to heave in the
bed. He suddenly gathered all the bedclothes about him, turned to the wall, and
then looked back over his shoulder with nothing showing, only two small, spiteful, dark eyes. The man looked very wicked.

To open the bedroom door, Mother had to let me down, and I broke free and   85
dashed for the farthest corner, screeching. Father sat bolt upright in bed.

"Shut up, you little puppy!" he said in a choking voice.

I was so astonished that I stopped screeching. Never, never had anyone spoken to me in that tone before. I looked at him incredulously and saw his face
convulsed with rage. It was only then that I fully realized how God had codded
me, listening to my prayers for the safe return of this monster.

"Shut up, you!" I bawled, beside myself.

"What's that you said?" shouted Father, making a wild leap out of bed.

"Mick, Mick!" cried Mother. "Don't you see the child isn't used to you?"   90

"I see he's better fed than taught," snarled Father, waving his arms wildly.
"He wants his bottom smacked."

All his previous shouting was as nothing to these obscene words referring to
my person. They really made my blood boil.

"Smack your own!" I screamed hysterically. "Smack your own! Shut up!
Shut up!"

At this he lost his patience and let fly at me. He did it with the lack of conviction you'd expect of a man under Mother's horrified eyes, and it ended up as a
mere tap, but the sheer indignity of being struck at all by a stranger, a total
stranger who had cajoled his way back from the war into our big bed as a result

of my innocent intercession, made me completely dotty. I shrieked and shrieked, and danced in my bare feet, and Father, looking awkward and hairy in nothing but a short grey army shirt, glared down at me like a mountain out for murder. I think it must have been then that I realized he was jealous too. And there stood Mother in her nightdress, looking as if her heart was broken between us. I hoped she felt as she looked. It seemed to me that she deserved it all.

From that morning out my life was a hell. Father and I were enemies, open   95
and avowed. We conducted a series of skirmishes against one another, he trying to steal my time with Mother and I his. When she was sitting on my bed, telling me a story, he took to looking for some pair of old boots which he alleged he had left behind him at the beginning of the war. While he talked to Mother I played loudly with my toys to show my total lack of concern. He created a terrible scene one evening when he came in from work and found me at his box, play-ing with his regimental badges, Gurkha knives and button-sticks. Mother got up and took the box from me.

"You mustn't play with Daddy's toys unless he lets you, Larry," she said se-verely. "Daddy doesn't play with yours."

For some reason Father looked at her as if she had struck him and then turned away with a scowl.

"Those are not toys," he growled, taking down the box again to see had I lifted anything. "Some of those curios are very rare and valuable."

But as time went on I saw more and more how he managed to alienate Mother and me. What made it worse was that I couldn't grasp his method or see what attraction he had for Mother. In every possible way he was less winning than I. He had a common accent and made noises at his tea. I thought for a while that it might be the newspapers she was interested in, so I made up bits of news of my own to read to her. Then I thought it might be the smoking, which I personally thought attractive, and took his pipes and went round the house dribbling into them till he caught me. I even made noises at my tea, but Mother only told me I was disgusting. It all seemed to hinge round that unhealthy habit of sleeping together, so I made a point of dropping into their bedroom and nos-ing round, talking to myself, so that they wouldn't know I was watching them, but they were never up to anything that I could see. In the end it beat me. It seemed to depend on being grown-up and giving people rings, and I realized I'd have to wait.

But at the same time I wanted him to see that I was only waiting, not giving   100
up the fight. One evening when he was being particularly obnoxious, chattering away well above my head, I let him have it.

"Mummy," I said, "do you know what I'm going to do when I grow up?"

"No, dear," she replied. "What?"

"I'm going to marry you," I said quietly.

Father gave a great guffaw out of him, but he didn't take me in. I knew it must only be pretense. And Mother, in spite of everything, was pleased. I felt she was probably relieved to know that one day Father's hold on her would be broken.

"Won't that be nice?" she said with a smile.

"It'll be very nice," I said confidentially. "Because we're going to have lots and lots of babies."

"That's right, dear," she said placidly. "I think we'll have one soon, and then you'll have plenty of company."

I was no end pleased about that because it showed that in spite of the way she gave in to Father she still considered my wishes. Besides, it would put the Geneys in their place.

It didn't turn out like that, though. To begin with, she was very preoccupied—I supposed about where she would get the seventeen and six—and though Father took to staying out late in the evenings it did me no particular good. She stopped taking me for walks, became as touchy as blazes, and smacked me for nothing at all. Sometimes I wished I'd never mentioned the confounded baby—I seemed to have a genius for bringing calamity on myself.

And calamity it was! Sonny arrived in the most appalling hullabaloo—even that much he couldn't do without a fuss—and from the first moment I disliked him. He was a difficult child—so far as I was concerned he was always difficult—and demanded far too much attention. Mother was simply silly about him, and couldn't see when he was only showing off. As company he was worse than useless. He slept all day, and I had to go round the house on tiptoe to avoid waking him. It wasn't any longer a question of not waking Father. The slogan now was "Don't-wake-Sonny!" I couldn't understand why the child wouldn't sleep at the proper time, so whenever Mother's back was turned I woke him. Sometimes to keep him awake I pinched him as well. Mother caught me at it one day and gave me a most unmerciful flaking.

One evening, when Father was coming from work, I was playing trains in the front garden. I let on not to notice him; instead, I pretended to be talking to myself, and said in a loud voice: "If another bloody baby comes into this house, I'm going out."

Father stopped dead and looked at me over his shoulder.

"What's that you said?" he asked sternly.

"I was only talking to myself," I replied, trying to conceal my panic. "It's private."

He turned and went in without a word. Mind you, I intended it as a solemn warning, but its effect was quite different. Father started being quite nice to me. I could understand that, of course. Mother was quite sickening about Sonny. Even at mealtimes she'd get up and gawk at him in the cradle with an idiotic smile, and tell Father to do the same. He was always polite about it, but he looked so puzzled you could see he didn't know what she was talking about. He complained of the way Sonny cried at night, but she only got cross and said that Sonny never cried except when there was something up with him—which was a flaming lie, because Sonny never had anything up with him, and only cried for

105

110

115

attention. It was really painful to see how simple-minded she was. Father wasn't attractive, but he had a fine intelligence. He saw through Sonny, and now he knew that I saw through him as well.

One night I woke with a start. There was someone beside me in the bed. For one wild moment I felt sure it must be Mother, having come to her senses and left Father for good, but then I heard Sonny in convulsions in the next room, and Mother saying: "There! There! There!" and I knew it wasn't she. It was Father. He was lying beside me, wide awake, breathing hard and apparently as mad as hell.

After a while it came to me what he was mad about. It was his turn now. After turning me out of the big bed, he had been turned out himself. Mother had no consideration now for anyone but that poisonous pup, Sonny. I couldn't help feeling sorry for Father. I had been through it all myself, and even at that age I was magnanimous. I began to stroke him down and say: "There! There!" He wasn't exactly responsive.

"Aren't you asleep either?" he snarled.

"Ah, come on and put your arm around us, can't you?" I said, and he did, in a sort of way. Gingerly, I suppose, is how you'd describe it. He was very bony but better than nothing.

At Christmas he went out of his way to buy me a really nice model railway. 120

For Analysis

1. Is the story narrated from the **point of view** of a young child or an adult? Explain. **2.** What does the title allude to? **3.** Examine the phrases that refer to or evoke the narrator's father in the opening paragraph. How are they appropriate to the story the narrator is about to tell? **4.** Whom do you find the most sympathetic character? Explain.

On Style

How does the author create the comic **tone** of this story?

Making Connections

Compare the use of the first-person narrator in this story, in Toni Cade Bambara's "The Lesson" (p. 115), and in Sandra Cisneros's "The House on Mango Street" (p. 122).

Writing Topic

Analyze the use of **irony** as a comic device in this story.

Flannery O'Connor   [1925–1964]

Good Country People   1955

B esides the neutral expression that she wore when she was alone, Mrs. Freeman had two others, forward and reverse, that she used for all her human dealings. Her forward expression was steady and driving like the advance of a heavy truck. Her eyes never swerved to left or right but turned as the story turned as if they followed a yellow line down the center of it. She seldom used the other expression because it was not often necessary for her to retract a statement, but when she did, her face came to a complete stop, there was an almost imperceptible movement of her black eyes, during which they seemed to be receding, and then the observer would see that Mrs. Freeman, though she might stand there as real as several grain sacks thrown on top of each other, was no longer there in spirit. As for getting anything across to her when this was the case, Mrs. Hopewell had given it up. She might talk her head off. Mrs. Freeman could never be brought to admit herself wrong on any point. She would stand there and if she could be brought to say anything, it was something like, "Well, I wouldn't of said it was and I wouldn't of said it wasn't," or letting her gaze range over the top kitchen shelf where there was an assortment of dusty bottles, she might remark, "I see you ain't ate many of them figs you put up last summer."

They carried on their most important business in the kitchen at breakfast. Every morning Mrs. Hopewell got up at seven o'clock and lit her gas heater and Joy's. Joy was her daughter, a large blonde girl who had an artificial leg. Mrs. Hopewell thought of her as a child though she was thirty-two years old and highly educated. Joy would get up while her mother was eating and lumber into the bathroom and slam the door, and before long, Mrs. Freeman would arrive at the back door. Joy would hear her mother call, "Come on in," and then they would talk for a while in low voices that were indistinguishable in the bathroom. By the time Joy came in, they had usually finished the weather report and were on one or the other of Mrs. Freeman's daughters, Glynese or Carramae. Joy called them Glycerin and Caramel. Glynese, a redhead, was eighteen and had many admirers; Carramae, a blonde, was only fifteen but already married and pregnant. She could not keep anything on her stomach. Every morning Mrs. Freeman told Mrs. Hopewell how many times she had vomited since the last report.

Mrs. Hopewell liked to tell people that Glynese and Carramae were two of the finest girls she knew and that Mrs. Freeman was a *lady* and that she was never ashamed to take her anywhere or introduce her to anybody they might meet. Then she would tell how she had happened to hire the Freemans in the first place and how they were a godsend to her and how she had had them four years. The reason for her keeping them so long was that they were not trash. They were good country people. She had telephoned the man whose name they had given as a reference and he had told her that Mr. Freeman was a good farmer but that his wife was the nosiest woman ever to walk the earth. "She's got to be into everything," the man said. "If she don't get there before the dust settles, you can bet she's dead, that's all. She'll want to know all your business. I can stand him real good," he had said, "but me nor my wife neither could have stood that woman one more minute on this place." That had put Mrs. Hopewell off for a few days.

She had hired them in the end because there were no other applicants but she had made up her mind beforehand exactly how she would handle the woman. Since she was the type who had to be into everything, then, Mrs. Hopewell had decided, she would not only let her be into everything, she would *see* to it that she was into everything—she would give her the responsibility of everything, she would put her in charge. Mrs. Hopewell had no bad qualities of her own but she was able to use other people's in such a constructive way that she never felt the lack. She had hired the Freemans and she had kept them four years.

Nothing is perfect. This was one of Mrs. Hopewell's favorite sayings. Another 5 was: that is life! And still another, the most important, was: well, other people have their opinions too. She would make these statements, usually at the table, in a tone of gentle insistence as if no one held them but her, and the large hulking Joy, whose constant outrage had obliterated every expression from her face, would stare just a little to the side of her, her eyes icy blue, with the look of someone who has achieved blindness by an act of will and means to keep it.

When Mrs. Hopewell said to Mrs. Freeman that life was like that, Mrs. Freeman would say, "I always said so myself." Nothing had been arrived at by anyone that had not first been arrived at by her. She was quicker than Mr. Freeman. When Mrs. Hopewell said to her after they had been on the place a while, "You know, you're the wheel behind the wheel," and winked, Mrs. Freeman had said, "I know it. I've always been quick. It's some that are quicker than others."

"Everybody is different," Mrs. Hopewell said.

"Yes, most people is," Mrs. Freeman said.

"It takes all kinds to make the world."

"I always said it did myself." 10

The girl was used to this kind of dialogue for breakfast and more of it for dinner; sometimes they had it for supper too. When they had no guest they ate in the kitchen because that was easier. Mrs. Freeman always managed to arrive at some point during the meal and to watch them finish it. She would stand in the doorway if it were summer but in the winter she would stand with one elbow on top of the refrigerator and look down on them, or she would stand by the gas heater, lifting the back of her skirt slightly. Occasionally she would stand against the wall and roll her head from side to side. At no time was she in any hurry to leave. All this was very trying on Mrs. Hopewell but she was a woman of great patience. She realized that nothing is perfect and that in the Freemans she had good country people and that if, in this day and age, you get good country people, you had better hang onto them.

She had had plenty of experience with trash. Before the Freemans she had averaged one tenant family a year. The wives of these farmers were not the kind you would want to be around you for very long. Mrs. Hopewell, who had divorced her husband long ago, needed someone to walk over the fields with her; and when Joy had to be impressed for these services, her remarks were usually so ugly and her face so glum that Mrs. Hopewell would say, "If you can't come pleasantly, I don't want you at all," to which the girl, standing square and rigid-shouldered with her neck thrust slightly forward, would reply, "If you want me, here I am—LIKE I AM."

Mrs. Hopewell excused this attitude because of the leg (which had been shot off in a hunting accident when Joy was ten). It was hard for Mrs. Hopewell to realize that her child was thirty-two now and that for more than twenty years she had had only one leg. She thought of her still as a child because it tore her heart to think instead of the poor stout girl in her thirties who had never danced a step or had any *normal* good times. Her name was really Joy but as soon as she was twenty-one and away from home, she had had it legally changed. Mrs. Hopewell was certain that she had thought and thought until she had hit upon the ugliest name in any language. Then she had gone and had the beautiful name, Joy, changed without telling her mother until after she had done it. Her legal name was Hulga.

When Mrs. Hopewell thought the name, Hulga, she thought of the broad blank hull of a battleship. She would not use it. She continued to call her Joy to which the girl responded but in a purely mechanical way.

Hulga had learned to tolerate Mrs. Freeman, who saved her from taking walks with her mother. Even Glynese and Carramae were useful when they occupied attention that might otherwise have been directed at her. At first she had thought she could not stand Mrs. Freeman for she had found that it was not possible to be rude to her. Mrs. Freeman would take on strange resentments and for days together she would be sullen but the source of her displeasure was always obscure; a direct attack, a positive leer, blatant ugliness to her face—these never touched her. And without warning one day, she began calling her Hulga.

She did not call her that in front of Mrs. Hopewell who would have been incensed but when she and the girl happened to be out of the house together, she would say something and add the name Hulga to the end of it, and the big spectacled Joy-Hulga would scowl and redden as if her privacy had been intruded upon. She considered the name her personal affair. She had arrived at it first purely on the basis of its ugly sound and then the full genius of its fitness had struck her. She had a vision of the name working like the ugly sweating Vulcan who stayed in the furnace and to whom, presumably, the goddess had to come when called. She saw it as the name of her highest creative act. One of her major triumphs was that her mother had not been able to turn her dust into Joy, but the greater one was that she had been able to turn it herself into Hulga. However, Mrs. Freeman's relish for using the name only irritated her. It was as if Mrs. Freeman's beady steel-pointed eyes had penetrated far enough behind her face to reach some secret fact. Something about her seemed to fascinate Mrs. Freeman and then one day Hulga realized that it was the artificial leg. Mrs. Freeman had a special fondness for the details of secret infections, hidden deformities, assaults upon children. Of diseases, she preferred the lingering or incurable. Hulga had heard Mrs. Hopewell give her the details of the hunting accident, how the leg had been literally blasted off, how she had never lost consciousness. Mrs. Freeman could listen to it any time as if it had happened an hour ago.

When Hulga stumped into the kitchen in the morning (she could walk without making the awful noise but she made it—Mrs. Hopewell was certain—because it was ugly-sounding), she glanced at them and did not speak. Mrs. Hopewell would be in her red kimono with her hair tied around her head in rags. She would be sitting at the table, finishing her breakfast and Mrs. Freeman would be hanging by her elbow outward from the refrigerator, looking down at the table. Hulga always put her eggs on the stove to boil and then stood over them with her arms folded, and Mrs. Hopewell would look at her—a kind of indirect gaze divided between her and Mrs. Freeman—and would think that if she would only keep herself up a little, she wouldn't be so bad looking. There was nothing wrong with her face that a pleasant expression wouldn't help. Mrs. Hopewell said that people who looked on the bright side of things would be beautiful even if they were not.

Whenever she looked at Joy this way, she could not help but feel that it would have been better if the child had not taken the Ph.D. It had certainly not brought her out any and now that she had it, there was no more excuse for her to go to school again. Mrs. Hopewell thought it was nice for girls to go to school to have a good time but Joy had "gone through." Anyhow, she would not have been strong enough to go again. The doctors had told Mrs. Hopewell that with the best of care, Joy might see forty-five. She had a weak heart. Joy had made it plain that if it had not been for this condition, she would be far from these red hills and good country people. She would be in a university lecturing to people who knew what she was talking about. And Mrs. Hopewell could very well picture her there, looking like a scarecrow and lecturing to more of the same. Here she went about all day in a six-year-old skirt and a yellow sweat shirt with a faded cowboy on a horse embossed on it. She thought this was funny; Mrs. Hopewell thought it was idiotic and showed simply that she was still a child. She was brilliant but she didn't have a grain of sense. It seemed to Mrs. Hopewell that every year she grew less like other people and more like herself—bloated, rude, and squint-eyed. And she said such strange things! To her own mother she had said—without warning, without excuse, standing up in the middle of a meal with her face purple and her mouth half full—"Woman! do you ever look inside? Do you ever look inside and see what you are *not*? God!" she had cried sinking down again and staring at her plate, "Malebranche was right: we are not our own light. We are not our own light!" Mrs. Hopewell had no idea to this day what brought that on. She had only made the remark, hoping Joy would take it in, that a smile never hurt anyone.

The girl had taken the Ph.D. in philosophy and this left Mrs. Hopewell at a complete loss. You could say, "My daughter is a nurse," or "My daughter is a school teacher," or even, "My daughter is a chemical engineer." You could not say, "My daughter is a philosopher." That was something that had ended with the Greeks and Romans. All day Joy sat on her deck in a deep chair, reading. Sometimes she went for walks but she didn't like dogs or cats or birds or flowers or nature or nice young men. She looked at nice young men as if she could smell their stupidity.

One day Mrs. Hopewell had picked up one of the books the girl had just put 20 down and opening it at random, she read, "Science, on the other hand, has to assert its soberness and seriousness afresh and declare that it is concerned solely with what-is. Nothing—how can it be for science anything but a horror and a phantasm? If science is right, then one thing stands firm: science wishes to know nothing of nothing. Such is after all the strictly scientific approach to Nothing. We know it by wishing to know nothing of Nothing." These words had been underlined with a blue pencil and they worked on Mrs. Hopewell like some evil incantation in gibberish. She shut the book quickly and went out of the room as if she were having a chill.

This morning when the girl came in, Mrs. Freeman was on Carramae. "She thrown up four times after supper," she said, "and was up twict in the night after three o'clock. Yesterday she didn't do nothing but ramble in the bureau drawer. All she did. Stand up there and see what she could run up on."

"She's got to eat," Mrs. Hopewell muttered, sipping her coffee, while she watched Joy's back at the stove. She was wondering what the child had said to the Bible salesman. She could not imagine what kind of a conversation she could possibly have had with him.

He was a tall gaunt hatless youth who had called yesterday to sell them a Bible. He had appeared at the door, carrying a large black suitcase that weighted him so heavily on one side that he had to brace himself against the door facing. He seemed on the point of collapse but he said in a cheerful voice, "Good morning, Mrs. Cedars!" and set the suitcase down on the mat. He was not a bad-looking young man though he had on a bright blue suit and yellow socks that were not pulled up far enough. He had prominent face bones and a streak of sticky-looking brown hair falling across his forehead.

"I'm Mrs. Hopewell," she said.

"Oh!" he said, pretending to look puzzled but with his eyes sparkling, "I saw 25 it said 'The Cedars,' on the mailbox so I thought you was Mrs. Cedars!" and he burst out in a pleasant laugh. He picked up the satchel and under cover of a pant, he fell forward into her hall. It was rather as if the suitcase had moved first, jerking him after it. "Mrs. Hopewell!" he said and grabbed her hand. "I hope you are well!" and he laughed again and then all at once his face sobered completely. He paused and gave her a straight earnest look and said, "Lady, I've come to speak of serious things."

"Well, come in," she muttered, none too pleased because her dinner was almost ready. He came into the parlor and sat down on the edge of a straight chair and put the suitcase between his feet and glanced around the room as if he were sizing her up by it. Her silver gleamed on the two sideboards; she decided he had never been in a room as elegant as this.

"Mrs. Hopewell," he began, using her name in a way that sounded almost intimate, "I know you believe in Chrustian service."

"Well yes," she murmured.

"I know," he said and paused, looking very wise with his head cocked on one side, "that you're a good woman. Friends have told me."

Mrs. Hopewell never liked to be taken for a fool. "What are you selling?" she asked. 30

"Bibles," the young man said and his eye raced around the room before he added, "I see you have no family Bible in your parlor, I see that is the one lack you got!"

Mrs. Hopewell could not say, "My daughter is an atheist and won't let me keep the Bible in the parlor." She said, stiffening slightly, "I keep my Bible by my bedside." This was not the truth. It was in the attic somewhere.

"Lady," he said, "the word of God ought to be in the parlor."

"Well, I think that's a matter of taste," she began. "I think . . ."

"Lady," he said, "for a Chrustian, the word of God ought to be in every room 35 in the house besides in his heart. I know you're a Chrustian because I can see it in every line of your face."

She stood up and said, "Well, young man, I don't want to buy a Bible and I smell my dinner burning."

He didn't get up. He began to twist his hands and looking down at them, he said softly, "Well lady, I'll tell you the truth—not many people want to buy one nowadays and besides, I know I'm real simple. I don't know how to say a thing but to say it. I'm just a country boy." He glanced up into her unfriendly face. "People like you don't like to fool with country people like me!"

"Why!" she cried, "good country people are the salt of the earth! Besides, we all have different ways of doing, it takes all kinds to make the world go 'round. That's life!"

"You said a mouthful," he said.

"Why, I think there aren't enough good country people in the world!" she 40 said, stirred. "I think that's what's wrong with it!"

His face had brightened. "I didn't inraduce myself," he said. "I'm Manley Pointer from out in the country around Willohobie, not even from a place, just from near a place."

"You wait a minute," she said. "I have to see about my dinner." She went out to the kitchen and found Joy standing near the door where she had been listening.

"Get rid of the salt of the earth," she said, "and let's eat."

Mrs. Hopewell gave her a pained look and turned the heat down under the vegetables. "*I can't be rude to anybody,*" she murmured and went back into the parlor.

He had opened the suitcase and was sitting with a Bible on each knee. 45

"You might as well put those up," she told him. "I don't want one."

"I appreciate your honesty," he said. "You don't see any more real honest people unless you go way out in the country."

"I know," she said, "real genuine folks!" Through the crack in the door she heard a groan.

"I guess a lot of boys come telling you they're working their way through college," he said, "but I'm not going to tell you that. Somehow," he said, "I don't want to go to college. I want to devote my life to Chrustian service. See," he said, lowering his voice, "I got this heart condition. I may not live long. When you know it's something wrong with you and you may not live long, well then, lady . . ." He paused, with his mouth open, and stared at her.

He and Joy had the same condition! She knew that her eyes were filling with 50 tears but she collected herself quickly and murmured, "Won't you stay for dinner? We'd love to have you!" and was sorry the instant she heard herself say it.

"Yes mam," he said in an abashed voice. "I would sher love to do that!"

Joy had given him one look on being introduced to him and then throughout the meal had not glanced at him again. He had addressed several remarks to her, which she pretended not to hear. Mrs. Hopewell could not understand deliberate rudeness, although she lived with it, and she felt she had always to overflow with hospitality to make up for Joy's lack of courtesy. She urged him to talk about himself and he did. He said he was the seventh child of twelve and that his father had been crushed under a tree when he himself was eight years old. He had been crushed very badly, in fact, almost cut in two and was practically not recognizable. His mother had got along the best she could by hard working and she had always seen that her children went to Sunday School and that they read the Bible every evening. He was now nineteen years old and he had been selling Bibles for four months. In that time he had sold seventy-seven Bibles and had the promise of two more sales. He wanted to become a missionary because he thought that was the way you could do most for people. "He who losest his life shall find it," he said simply and he was so sincere, so genuine and earnest that Mrs. Hopewell would not for the world have smiled. He prevented his peas from sliding onto the table by blocking them with a piece of bread which he later cleaned his plate with. She could see Joy observing sidewise how he handled his knife and fork and she saw too that every few minutes, the boy would dart a keen appraising glance at the girl as if he were trying to attract her attention.

After dinner Joy cleared the dishes off the table and disappeared and Mrs. Hopewell was left to talk with him. He told her again about his childhood and his father's accident and about various things that had happened to him. Every five minutes or so she would stifle a yawn. He sat for two hours until finally she told him she must go because she had an appointment in town. He packed his Bibles and thanked her and prepared to leave, but in the doorway he stopped and wrung her hand and said that not on any of his trips had he met a lady as nice as her and he asked if he could come again. She had said she would always be happy to see him.

Joy had been standing in the road, apparently looking at something in the distance, when he came down the steps toward her, bent to the side with his heavy valise. He stopped where she was standing and confronted her directly. Mrs. Hopewell could not hear what he said but she trembled to think what Joy would say to him. She could see that after a minute Joy said something and that then the boy began to speak again, making an excited gesture with his free hand. After a minute Joy said something else at which the boy began to speak once more. Then to her amazement, Mrs. Hopewell saw the two of them walk off together, toward the gate. Joy had walked all the way to the gate with him and Mrs. Hopewell could not imagine what they had said to each other, and she had not yet dared to ask.

Mrs. Freeman was insisting upon her attention. She had moved from the refrigerator to the heater so that Mrs. Hopewell had to turn and face her in order to seem to be listening. "Glynese gone out with Harvey Hill again last night," she said. "She had this sty."

"Hill," Mrs. Hopewell said absently, "is that the one who works in the garage?"

"Nome, he's the one that goes to chiropracter school," Mrs. Freeman said. "She had this sty. Been had it two days. So she says when he brought her in the other night he says, 'Lemme get rid of that sty for you,' and she says, 'How?' and he says, 'You just lay yourself down acrost the seat of that car and I'll show you.' So she done it and he popped her neck. Kept on a-popping it several times until she made him quit. This morning," Mrs. Freeman said, "she ain't got no sty. She ain't got no traces of a sty."

"I never heard of that before," Mrs. Hopewell said.

"He ast her to marry him before the Ordinary," Mrs. Freeman went on, "and she told him she wasn't going to be married in no *office*."

"Well, Glynese is a fine girl," Mrs. Hopewell said. "Glynese and Carramae are both fine girls."

"Carramae said when her and Lyman was married Lyman said it sure felt sacred to him. She said he said he wouldn't take five hundred dollars for being married by a preacher."

"How much would he take?" the girl asked from the stove.

"He said he wouldn't take five hundred dollars," Mrs. Freeman repeated.

"Well we all have work to do," Mrs. Hopewell said.

"Lyman said it just felt more sacred to him," Mrs. Freeman said. "The doctor wants Carramae to eat prunes. Says instead of medicine. Says them cramps is coming from pressure. You know where I think it is?"

"She'll be better in a few weeks," Mrs. Hopewell said.

"In the tube," Mrs. Freeman said. "Else she wouldn't be as sick as she is."

Hulga had cracked her two eggs into a saucer and was bringing them to the table along with a cup of coffee that she had filled too full. She sat down carefully and began to eat, meaning to keep Mrs. Freeman there by questions if for any reason she showed an inclination to leave. She could perceive her mother's eye on her. The first roundabout question would be about the Bible salesman and she did not wish to bring it on. "How did he pop her neck?" she asked.

Mrs. Freeman went into a description of how he had popped her neck. She said he owned a '55 Mercury but that Glynese said she would rather marry a man with only a '36 Plymouth who would be married by a preacher. The girl asked what if he had a '32 Plymouth and Mrs. Freeman said what Glynese had said was a '36 Plymouth.

Mrs. Hopewell said there were not many girls with Glynese's common sense. 70 She said what she admired in those girls was their common sense. She said that reminded her that they had a nice visitor yesterday, a young man selling Bibles. "Lord," she said, "he bored me to death but he was so sincere and genuine I couldn't be rude to him. He was just good country people, you know," she said, "—just the salt of the earth."

"I seen him walk up," Mrs. Freeman said, "and then later—I seen him walk off," and Hulga could feel the slight shift in her voice, the slight insinuation, that he had not walked off alone, had he? Her face remained expressionless but the color rose into her neck and she seemed to swallow it down with the next spoonful of egg. Mrs. Freeman was looking at her as if they had a secret together.

"Well, it takes all kinds of people to make the world go 'round," Mrs. Hopewell said. "It's very good we aren't all alike."

"Some people are more alike than others," Mrs. Freeman said.

Hulga got up and stumped, with about twice the noise that was necessary, into her room and locked the door. She was to meet the Bible salesman at ten o'clock at the gate. She had thought about it half the night. She had started thinking of it as a great joke and then she had begun to see profound implications in it. She had lain in bed imagining dialogues for them that were insane on the surface but that reached below to depths that no Bible salesman would be aware of. Their conversation yesterday had been of this kind.

He had stopped in front of her and had simply stood there. His face was bony 75 and sweaty and bright, with a little pointed nose in the center of it, and his look was different from what it had been at the dinner table. He was gazing at her with open curiosity, with fascination, like a child watching a new fantastic animal at the zoo, and he was breathing as if he had run a great distance to reach her. His gaze seemed somehow familiar but she could not think where she had been regarded with it before. For almost a minute he didn't say anything. Then on what seemed an insuck of breath, he whispered, "You ever ate a chicken that was two days old?"

The girl looked at him stonily. He might have just put this question up for consideration at the meeting of a philosophical association. "Yes," she presently replied as if she had considered it from all angles.

"It must have been mighty small!" he said triumphantly and shook all over with little nervous giggles, getting very red in the face, and subsiding finally into his gaze of complete admiration, while the girl's expression remained exactly the same.

"How old are you?" he asked softly.

She waited some time before she answered. Then in a flat voice she said, "Seventeen."

His smiles came in succession like waves breaking on the surface of a little   80
lake. "I see you got a wooden leg," he said. "I think you're real brave. I think you're real sweet."

The girl stood blank and solid and silent.

"Walk to the gate with me," he said. "You're a brave sweet little thing and I liked you the minute I seen you walk in the door."

Hulga began to move forward.

"What's your name?" he asked, smiling down on the top of her head.

"Hulga," she said.   85

"Hulga," he murmured, "Hulga. Hulga. I never heard of anybody name Hulga before. You're shy, aren't you, Hulga?" he asked.

She nodded, watching his large red hand on the handle of the giant valise.

"I like girls that wear glasses," he said. "I think a lot. I'm not like these people that a serious thought don't ever enter their heads. It's because I may die."

"I may die too," she said suddenly and looked up at him. His eyes were very small and brown, glittering feverishly.

"Listen," he said, "don't you think some people was meant to meet on ac-   90
count of what all they got in common and all? Like they both think serious thoughts and all?" He shifted the valise to his other hand so that the hand nearest her was free. He caught hold of her elbow and shook it a little. "I don't work on Saturday," he said. "I like to walk in the woods and see what Mother Nature is wearing. O'er the hills and far away. Pic-nics and things. Couldn't we go on a pic-nic tomorrow? Say yes, Hulga," he said and gave her a dying look as if he felt his insides about to drop out of him. He had even seemed to sway slightly toward her.

During the night she had imagined that she seduced him. She imagined that the two of them walked on the place until they came to the storage barn beyond the two back fields and there, she imagined, that things came to such a pass that she very easily seduced him and that then, of course, she had to reckon with his remorse. True genius can get an idea across even to an inferior mind. She imagined that she took his remorse in hand and changed it into a deeper understanding of life. She took all his shame away and turned it into something useful.

She set off for the gate at exactly ten o'clock, escaping without drawing Mrs. Hopewell's attention. She didn't take anything to eat, forgetting that food is usually taken on a picnic. She wore a pair of slacks and a dirty white shirt, and as an afterthought, she had put some Vapex on the collar of it since she did not own any perfume. When she reached the gate no one was there.

She looked up and down the empty highway and had the furious feeling that she had been tricked, that he had only meant to make her walk to the gate after the idea of him. Then suddenly he stood up, very tall, from behind a bush on the opposite embankment. Smiling, he lifted his hat which was new and wide-brimmed. He had not worn it yesterday and she wondered if he had bought it for the occasion. It was toast-colored with a red and white band around it and was slightly too large for him. He stepped from behind the bush still carrying the black valise. He had on the same suit and the same yellow socks sucked down in his shoes from walking. He crossed the highway and said, "I knew you'd come!"

The girl wondered acidly how he had known this. She pointed to the valise and asked, "Why did you bring your Bibles?"

He took her elbow, smiling down on her as if he could not stop. "You can never tell when you'll need the word of God, Hulga," he said. She had a moment in which she doubted that this was actually happening and then they began to climb the embankment. They went down into the pasture toward the woods. The boy walked lightly by her side, bouncing on his toes. The valise did not seem to be heavy today; he even swung it. They crossed half the pasture without saying anything and then, putting his hand easily on the small of her back, he asked softly, "Where does your wooden leg join on?"

She turned an ugly red and glared at him and for an instant the boy looked abashed. "I didn't mean you no harm," he said. "I only meant you're so brave and all. I guess God takes care of you."

"No," she said, looking forward and walking fast, "I don't even believe in God."

At this he stopped and whistled. "No!" he exclaimed as if he were too astonished to say anything else.

She walked on and in a second he was bouncing at her side, fanning with his hat. "That's very unusual for a girl," he remarked, watching her out of the corner of his eye. When they reached the edge of the wood, he put his hand on her back again and drew her against him without a word and kissed her heavily.

The kiss, which had more pressure than feeling behind it, produced that extra surge of adrenalin in the girl that enables one to carry a packed trunk out of a burning house, but in her, the power went at once to the brain. Even before he released her, her mind, clear and detached and ironic anyway, was regarding him from a great distance, with amusement but with pity. She had never been kissed before and she was pleased to discover that it was an unexceptional experience and all a matter of the mind's control. Some people might enjoy drain water if they were told it was vodka. When the boy, looking expectant but uncertain, pushed her gently away, she turned and walked on, saying nothing as if such business, for her, were common enough.

He came along panting at her side, trying to help her when he saw a root that she might trip over. He caught and held back the long swaying blades of thorn vine until she had passed beyond them. She led the way and he came breathing heavily behind her. Then they came out on a sunlit hillside, sloping softly into another one a little smaller. Beyond, they could see the rusted top of the old barn where the extra hay was stored.

The hill was sprinkled with small pink weeds. "Then you ain't saved?" he asked suddenly, stopping.

The girl smiled. It was the first time she had smiled at him at all. "In my economy," she said, "I'm saved and you are damned but I told you I didn't believe in God."

Nothing seemed to destroy the boy's look of admiration. He gazed at her now as if the fantastic animal at the zoo had put its paw through the bars and given him a loving poke. She thought he looked as if he wanted to kiss her again and she walked on before he had the chance.

"Ain't there somewheres we can sit down sometime?" he murmured, his voice softening toward the end of the sentence. 105

"In that barn," she said.

They made for it rapidly as if it might slide away like a train. It was a large two-story barn, cool and dark inside. The boy pointed up the ladder that led into the loft and said, "It's too bad we can't go up there."

"Why can't we?" she asked.

"Yer leg," he said reverently.

The girl gave him a contemptuous look and putting both hands on the ladder, she climbed it while he stood below, apparently awestruck. She pulled herself expertly through the opening and then looked down at him and said, "Well, come on if you're coming," and he began to climb the ladder, awkwardly bringing the suitcase with him. 110

"We won't need the Bible," she observed.

"You never can tell," he said, panting. After he had got into the loft, he was a few seconds catching his breath. She had sat down in a pile of straw. A wide sheath of sunlight, filled with dust particles, slanted over her. She lay back against a bale, her face turned away, looking out the front opening of the barn where hay was thrown from a wagon into the loft. The two pink-speckled hillsides lay back against a dark ridge of woods. The sky was cloudless and cold blue. The boy dropped down by her side and put one arm under her and the other over her and began methodically kissing her face, making little noises like a fish. He did not remove his hat but it was pushed far enough back not to interfere. When her glasses got in his way, he took them off of her and slipped them into his pocket.

The girl at first did not return any of the kisses but presently she began to and after she had put several on his cheek, she reached his lips and remained there, kissing him again and again as if she were trying to draw all the breath out of him. His breath was clear and sweet like a child's and the kisses were sticky like a child's. He mumbled about loving her and about knowing when he first seen her that he loved her, but the mumbling was like the sleepy fretting of a child being put to sleep by his mother. Her mind, throughout this, never stopped or lost itself for a second to her feelings. "You ain't said you love me none," he whispered finally, pulling back from her. "You got to say that."

She looked away from him off into the hollow sky and then down at a black ridge and then down farther into what appeared to be two green swelling lakes.

She didn't realize he had taken her glasses but this landscape could not seem exceptional to her for she seldom paid any close attention to her surroundings.

"You got to say it," he repeated. "You got to say you love me." 115

She was always careful how she committed herself. "In a sense," she began, "if you use the word loosely, you might say that. But it's not a word I use. I don't have illusions. I'm one of those people who see *through* to nothing."

The boy was frowning. "You got to say it. I said it and you got to say it," he said.

The girl looked at him almost tenderly. "You poor baby," she murmured. "It's just as well you don't understand," and she pulled him by the neck, face-down, against her. "We are all damned," she said, "but some of us have taken off our blindfolds and see that there's nothing to see. It's a kind of salvation."

The boy's astonished eyes looked blankly through the ends of her hair. "Okay," he almost whined, "but do you love me or don'tcher?"

"Yes," she said and added, "in a sense. But I must tell you something. There 120 mustn't be anything dishonest between us." She lifted his head and looked him in the eye. "I am thirty years old," she said. "I have a number of degrees."

The boy's look was irritated but dogged. "I don't care," he said. "I don't care a thing about what all you done. I just want to know if you love me or don'tcher?" and he caught her to him and wildly planted her face with kisses until she said, "Yes, yes."

"Okay then," he said, letting her go. "Prove it."

She smiled, looking dreamily out on the shifty landscape. She had seduced him without even making up her mind to try. "How?" she asked, feeling that he should be delayed a little.

He leaned over and put his lips to her ear. "Show me where your wooden leg joins on," he whispered.

The girl uttered a sharp little cry and her face instantly drained of color. The 125 obscenity of the suggestion was not what shocked her. As a child she had sometimes been subject to feelings of shame but education had removed the last traces of that as a good surgeon scrapes for cancer; she would no more have felt it over what he was asking than she would have believed in his Bible. But she was as sensitive about the artificial leg as a peacock about his tail. No one ever touched it but her. She took care of it as someone else would his soul, in private and almost with her own eyes turned away. "No," she said.

"I known it," he muttered, sitting up. "You're just playing me for a sucker."

"Oh no no!" she cried. "It joins on at the knee. Only at the knee. Why do you want to see it?"

The boy gave her a long penetrating look. "Because," he said, "it's what makes you different. You ain't like nobody else."

She sat staring at him. There was nothing about her face or her round freezing-blue eyes to indicate that this had moved her; but she felt as if her heart had stopped and left her mind to pump her blood. She decided that for the first time in her life she was face to face with real innocence. This boy, with an instinct that came from beyond wisdom, had touched the truth about her.

When after a minute, she said in a low hoarse high voice, "All right," it was like surrendering to him completely. It was like losing her own life and finding it again, miraculously, in his.

Very gently he began to roll the slack leg up. The artificial limb, in a white 130 sock and brown flat shoe, was bound in a heavy material like canvas and ended in an ugly jointure where it was attached to the stump. The boy's face and his voice were entirely reverent as he uncovered it and said, "Now show me how to take it off and on."

She took it off for him and put it back on again and then he took it off himself, handling it as tenderly as if it were a real one. "See!" he said with a delighted child's face. "Now I can do it myself!"

"Put it back on," she said. She was thinking that she would run away with him and that every night he would take the leg off and every morning put it back on again. "Put it back on," she said.

"Not yet," he murmured, setting it on its foot out of her reach. "Leave it off for a while. You got me instead."

She gave a little cry of alarm but he pushed her down and began to kiss her again. Without the leg she felt entirely dependent on him. Her brain seemed to have stopped thinking altogether and to be about some other function that it was not very good at. Different expressions raced back and forth over her face. Every now and then the boy, his eyes like two steel spikes, would glance behind him where the leg stood. Finally she pushed him off and said, "Put it back on me now."

"Wait," he said. He leaned the other way and pulled the valise toward him 135 and opened it. It had a pale blue spotted lining and there were only two Bibles in it. He took one of these out and opened the cover of it. It was hollow and contained a pocket flask of whiskey, a pack of cards, and a small blue box with printing on it. He laid these out in front of her one at a time in an evenly spaced row, like one presenting offerings at the shrine of a goddess. He put the blue box in her hand. THIS PRODUCT TO BE USED ONLY FOR THE PREVENTION OF DISEASE, she read, and dropped it. The boy was unscrewing the top of the flask. He stopped and pointed, with a smile, to the deck of cards. It was not an ordinary deck but one with an obscene picture on the back of each card. "Take a swig," he said, offering her the bottle first. He held it in front of her, but like one mesmerized, she did not move.

Her voice when she spoke had an almost pleading sound. "Aren't you," she murmured, "aren't you just good country people?"

The boy cocked his head. He looked as if he were just beginning to understand that she might be trying to insult him. "Yeah," he said, curling his lip slightly, "but it ain't held me back none. I'm as good as you any day in the week."

"Give me my leg," she said.

He pushed it farther away with his foot. "Come on now, let's begin to have us a good time," he said coaxingly. "We ain't got to know one another good yet."

"Give me my leg!" she screamed and tried to lunge for it but he pushed her 140 down easily.

"What's the matter with you all of a sudden?" he asked, frowning as he screwed the top on the flask and put it quickly inside the Bible. "You just a while ago said you didn't believe in nothing. I thought you was some girl!"

Her face was almost purple. "You're a Christian!" she hissed. "You're a fine Christian! You're just like them all—say one thing and do another. You're a perfect Christian, you're . . ."

The boy's mouth was set angrily. "I hope you don't think," he said in a lofty indignant tone, "that I believe in that crap! I may sell Bibles but I know which end is up and I wasn't born yesterday and I know where I'm going!"

"Give me my leg!" she screeched. He jumped up so quickly that she barely saw him sweep the cards and the blue box back into the Bible and throw the Bible into the valise. She saw him grab the leg and then she saw it for an instant slanted forlornly across the inside of the suitcase with a Bible at either side of its opposite ends. He slammed the lid shut and snatched up the valise and swung it down the hole and then stepped through himself.

When all of him had passed but his head, he turned and regarded her with a look that no longer had any admiration in it. "I've gotten a lot of interesting things," he said. "One time I got a woman's glass eye this way. And you needn't to think you'll catch me because Pointer ain't really my name. I use a different name at every house I call at and don't stay nowhere long. And I'll tell you another thing, Hulga," he said, using the name as if he didn't think much of it, "you ain't so smart. I been believing in nothing ever since I was born!" and then the toast-colored hat disappeared down the hole and the girl was left, sitting on the straw in the dusty sunlight. When she turned her churning face toward the opening, she saw his blue figure struggling successfully over the green speckled lake.

Mrs. Hopewell and Mrs. Freeman, who were in the back pasture, digging up onions, saw him emerge a little later from the woods and head across the meadow toward the highway. "Why, that looks like that nice dull young man that tried to sell me a Bible yesterday," Mrs. Hopewell said, squinting. "He must have been selling them to the Negroes back in there. He was so simple," she said, "but I guess the world would be better off if we were all that simple."

Mrs. Freeman's gaze drove forward and just touched him before he disappeared under the hill. Then she returned her attention to the evil-smelling onion shoot she was lifting from the ground. "Some can't be that simple," she said. "I know I never could."

For Analysis

1. Why does Joy feel that changing her name to Hulga is "her highest creative act"? **2.** Examine the appropriateness of the names of the characters. **3.** In what ways do Mrs. Freeman's descriptions of her daughters Glynese and Carramae contribute to the **theme** of the story? **4.** Does Mrs. Hopewell's character in any way help to explain her daughter's character? Explain. **5.** Briefly describe the central conflict in this story and the manner in which it is resolved. **6.** Is the title **ironic**? Explain. **7.** Does the story have any admirable characters or heroes in the conventional sense? Explain. **8.** Why does Hulga agree to meet with Manley Pointer? Does her experience with him confirm her cynical philosophy of "nothing"? Explain. **9.** What is Manley Pointer's motive for humiliating Hulga?

On Style
Analyze the use of **irony** in this story.

Making Connections
Compare and contrast the meaning of Hulga's belief in "nothing" in this story and "nada" in Hemingway's "A Clean, Well-Lighted Place" (p. 86).

Writing Topic
The story begins and ends with a dialogue between Mrs. Hopewell and Mrs. Freeman. Write an essay showing how these two dialogues appropriately frame the story of Hulga and Manley Pointer.

Toni Cade Bambara   [1939–1995]

The Lesson   1972

Back in the days when everyone was old and stupid or young and foolish and me and Sugar were the only ones just right, this lady moved on our block with nappy hair and proper speech and no makeup. And quite naturally we laughed at her, laughed the way we did at the junk man who went about his business like he was some big-time president and his sorry-ass horse his secretary. And we kinda hated her too, hated the way we did the winos who cluttered up our parks and pissed on our handball walls and stank up our hallways and stairs so you couldn't halfway play hide-and-seek without a goddamn gas mask. Miss Moore was her name. The only woman on the block with no first name. And she was black as hell, cept for her feet, which were fish-white and spooky. And she was always planning these boring-ass things for us to do, us being my cousin, mostly, who lived on the block cause we all moved North the same time and to the same apartment then spread out gradual to breathe. And our parents would yank our heads into some kinda shape and crisp up our clothes so we'd be presentable for travel with Miss Moore, who always looked like she was going to church, though she never did. Which is just one of the things the grownups talked about when they talked behind her back like a dog. But when she came calling with some sachet she'd sewed up or some gingerbread she'd made or some book, why then they'd all be too embarrassed to turn her down and we'd get handed over all spruced up. She'd been to college and said it was only right that she should take responsibility for the young ones' education, and she not even related by marriage or blood. So they'd go for it. Specially Aunt Gretchen. She was the main gofer in the family. You got some old dumb shit foolishness you want somebody to go for, you send for Aunt Gretchen. She been screwed into the go-along for so long, it's a blood-deep natural thing with her. Which is how she got saddled with me and Sugar and Junior in the first place while our mothers were in a la-de-da apartment up the block having a good ole time.

So this one day Miss Moore rounds us all up at the mailbox and it's puredee hot and she's knockin herself out about arithmetic. And school suppose to let up in summer I heard, but she don't never let up. And the starch in my pinafore scratching the shit outta me and I'm really hating this nappy-head bitch and her goddamn college degree. I'd much rather go to the pool or to the show where it's cool. So me and Sugar leaning on the mailbox being surly, which is a Miss Moore word. And Flyboy checking out what everybody brought for lunch. And Fat Butt already wasting his peanut-butter-and-jelly sandwich like the pig he is. And Junebug punchin on Q.T.'s arm for potato chips. And Rosie Giraffe shifting from one hip to the other waiting for somebody to step on her foot or ask her if she from Georgia so she can kick ass, preferably Mercedes'. And Miss Moore asking us do we know what money is, like we a bunch of retards. I mean real money, she say, like it's only poker chips or monopoly papers we lay on the grocer. So right away I'm tired of this and say so. And would much rather snatch Sugar and go to the Sunset and terrorize the West Indian kids and take their hair ribbons and their money too. And Miss Moore files that remark away for next week's lesson on brotherhood, I can tell. And finally I say we oughta get to the subway cause it's cooler and besides we might meet some cute boys. Sugar done swiped her mama's lipstick, so we ready.

So we heading down the street and she's boring us silly about what things cost and what our parents make and how much goes for rent and how money ain't divided up right in this country. And then she gets to the part about we all poor and live in the slums, which I don't feature. And I'm ready to speak on that, but she steps out in the street and hails two cabs just like that. Then she hustles half the crew in with her and hands me a five-dollar bill and tells me to calculate 10 percent tip for the driver. And we're off. Me and Sugar and Junebug and Flyboy hangin out the window and hollering to everybody, putting lipstick on each other cause Flyboy a faggot anyway, and making farts with our sweaty armpits. But I'm mostly trying to figure how to spend this money. But they all fascinated with the meter ticking and Junebug starts laying bets as to how much it'll read when Flyboy can't hold his breath no more. Then Sugar lays bets as to how much it'll be when we get there. So I'm stuck. Don't nobody want to go for my plan, which is to jump out at the next light and run off to the first bar-b-que we can find. Then the driver tells us to get the hell out cause we there already. And the meter reads eighty-five cents. And I'm stalling to figure out the tip and Sugar say give him a dime. And I decide he don't need it bad as I do, so later for him. But then he tries to take off with Junebug foot still in the door so we talk about his mama something ferocious. Then we check out that we on Fifth Avenue and everybody dressed up in stockings. One lady in a fur coat, hot as it is. White folks crazy.

"This is the place," Miss Moore say, presenting it to us in the voice she uses at the museum. "Let's look in the windows before we go in."

"Can we steal?" Sugar asks very serious like she's getting the ground rules 5 squared away before she plays. "I beg your pardon," say Miss Moore, and we fall out. So she leads us around the windows of the toy store and me and Sugar screamin, "This is mine, that's mine, I gotta have that, that was made for me, I was born for that," till Big Butt drowns us out.

"Hey, I'm goin to buy that there."

"That there? You don't even know what it is, stupid."

"I do so," he say punchin on Rosie Giraffe. "It's a microscope."

"Whatcha gonna do with a microscope, fool?"

"Look at things." 10

"Like what, Ronald?" ask Miss Moore. And Big Butt ain't got the first notion. So here go Miss Moore gabbing about the thousands of bacteria in a drop of water and the somethinorother in a speck of blood and the million and one living things in the air around us is invisible to the naked eye. And what she say that for? Junebug go to town on that "naked" and we rolling. Then Miss Moore ask what it cost. So we all jam into the window smudgin it up and the price tag say $300. So then she ask how long'd take for Big Butt and Junebug to save up their allowances. "Too long," I say. "Yeh," adds Sugar, "outgrown it by that time." And Miss Moore say no, you never outgrow learning instruments. "Why, even medical students and interns and," blah, blah, blah. And we ready to choke Big Butt for bringing it up in the first damn place.

"This here costs four hundred eighty dollars," say Rosie Giraffe. So we pile up all over her to see what she pointin out. My eyes tell me it's a chunk of glass cracked with something heavy, and different-color inks dripped into the splits, then the whole thing put into a oven or something. But for $480 it don't make sense.

"That's a paperweight made of semi-precious stones fused together under tremendous pressure," she explains slowly, with her hands doing the mining and all the factory work.

"So what's a paperweight?" asks Rosie Giraffe.

"To weigh paper with, dumbbell," say Flyboy, the wise man from the East.   15

"Not exactly," say Miss Moore, which is what she say when you warm or way off too. "It's to weigh paper down so it won't scatter and make your desk untidy." So right away me and Sugar curtsy to each other and then to Mercedes who is more the tidy type.

"We don't keep paper on top of the desk in my class," say Junebug, figuring Miss Moore crazy or lyin one.

"At home, then," she say. "Don't you have a calendar and pencil case and a blotter and a letter-opener on your desk at home where you do your homework?" And she know damn well what our homes look like cause she nosys around in them every chance she gets.

"I don't even have a desk," say Junebug. "Do we?"

"No. And I don't get no homework neither," says Big Butt.   20

"And I don't even have a home," say Flyboy like he do at school to keep the white folks off his back and sorry for him. Send this poor kid to camp posters, is his specialty.

"I do," says Mercedes. "I have a box of stationery on my desk and a picture of my cat. My godmother bought the stationery and the desk. There's a big rose on each sheet and the envelopes smell like roses."

"Who wants to know about your smelly-ass stationery," say Rosie Giraffe fore I can get my two cents in.

"It's important to have a work area all your own so that . . ."

"Will you look at this sailboat, please," say Flyboy, cuttin her off and pointin   25 to the thing like it was his. So once again we tumble all over each other to gaze at this magnificent thing in the toy store which is just big enough to maybe sail two kittens across the pond if you strap them to the posts tight. We all start reciting the price tag like we in assembly. "Handcrafted sailboat of fiberglass at one thousand one hundred ninety-five dollars."

"Unbelievable," I hear myself say and am really stunned. I read it again for myself just in case the group recitation put me in a trance. Same thing. For some reason this pisses me off. We look at Miss Moore and she lookin at us, waiting for I dunno what.

"Who'd pay all that when you can buy a sailboat set for a quarter at Pop's, a tube of glue for a dime, and a ball of string for eight cents? It must have a mo- tor and a whole lot else besides," I say. "My sailboat cost me about fifty cents."

"But will it take water?" say Mercedes with her smart ass.

"Took mine to Alley Pond Park once," say Flyboy. "String broke. Lost it. Pity."

"Sailed mine in Central Park and it keeled over and sank. Had to ask my fa- ther for another dollar."

"And you got the strap," laugh Big Butt. "The jerk didn't even have a string on it. My old man wailed on his behind."

Little Q.T. was staring hard at the sailboat and you could see he wanted it bad. But he too little and somebody'd just take it from him. So what the hell. "This boat for kids, Miss Moore?"

"Parents silly to buy something like that just to get all broke up," say Rosie Giraffe.

"That much money it should last forever," I figure.

"My father'd buy it for me if I wanted it."

"Your father, my ass," say Rosie Giraffe getting a chance to finally push Mercedes.

"Must be rich people shop here," say Q.T.

"You are a very bright boy," say Flyboy. "What was your first clue?" And he rap him on the head with the back of his knuckles, since Q.T. the only one he could get away with. Though Q.T. liable to come up behind you years later and get his licks in when you half expect it.

"What I want to know is," I says to Miss Moore though I never talk to her, I wouldn't give the bitch that satisfaction, "is how much a real boat costs? I figure a thousand'd get you a yacht any day."

"Why don't you check that out," she says, "and report back to the group?" Which really pains my ass. If you gonna mess up a perfectly good swim day least you could do is have some answers. "Let's go in," she say like she got something up her sleeve. Only she don't lead the way. So me and Sugar turn the corner to where the entrance is, but when we get there I kinda hang back. Not that I'm scared, what's there to be afraid of, just a toy store. But I feel funny, shame. But what I got to be shamed about? Got as much right to go in as anybody. But somehow I can't seem to get hold of the door, so I step away for Sugar to lead. But she hangs back too. And I look at her and she looks at me and this is ridicu- lous. I mean, damn, I have never ever been shy about doing nothing or going nowhere. But then Mercedes steps up and then Rosie Giraffe and Big Butt crowd in behind and shove, and next thing we all stuffed into the doorway with only Mercedes squeezing past us, smoothing out her jumper and walking right down the aisle. Then the rest of us tumble in like a glued-together jigsaw done all wrong. And people lookin at us. And it's like the time me and Sugar crashed into the Catholic church on a dare. But once we got in there and everything so hushed and holy and the candles and the bowin and the handkerchiefs on all the drooping heads, I just couldn't go through with the plan. Which was for me to run up to the altar and do a tap dance while Sugar played the nose flute and messed around in the holy water. And Sugar kept givin me the elbow. Then later teased me so bad I tied her up in the shower and turned it on and locked her in. And she'd be there till this day if Aunt Gretchen hadn't finally figured I was lyin about the boarder takin a shower.

Same thing in the store. We all walkin on tiptoe and hardly touchin the games and puzzles and things. And I watched Miss Moore who is steady watchin us like she waitin for a sign. Like Mama Drewery watches the sky and sniffs the air and takes note of just how much slant is in the bird formation. Then me and Sugar bump smack into each other, so busy gazing at the toys, 'specially the sailboat. But we don't laugh and go into our fat-lady bump-stomach routine. We just stare at that price tag. Then Sugar run a finger over the whole boat. And I'm jealous and want to hit her. Maybe not her, but I sure want to punch somebody in the mouth.

"Watcha bring us here for, Miss Moore?"

"You sound angry, Sylvia. Are you mad about something?" Givin me one of them grins like she tellin a grown-up joke that never turns out to be funny. And she's lookin very closely at me like maybe she planning to do my portrait from memory. I'm mad, but I won't give her that satisfaction. So I slouch around the store bein very bored and say, "Let's go."

Me and Sugar at the back of the train watchin the tracks whizzin by large then small then gettin gobbled up in the dark. I'm thinkin about this tricky toy I saw in the store. A clown that somersaults on a bar then does chin-ups just cause you yank lightly at his leg. Cost $35. I could see me askin my mother for a $35 birthday clown. "You wanna who that costs what?" she'd say, cocking her head to the side to get a better view of the hole in my head. Thirty-five dollars could buy new bunk beds for Junior and Gretchen's boy. Thirty-five dollars and the whole household could go visit Granddaddy Nelson in the country. Thirty-five dollars would pay for the rent and the piano bill too. Who are these people that spend that much for performing clowns and $1000 for toy sailboats? What kinda work they do and how they live and how come we ain't in on it? Where we are is who we are, Miss Moore always pointin out. But it don't necessarily have to be that way, she always adds then waits for somebody to say that poor people have to wake up and demand their share of the pie and don't none of us know what kind of pie she talking about in the first damn place. But she ain't so smart cause I still got her four dollars from the taxi and she sure ain't gettin it. Messin up my day with this shit. Sugar nudges me in my pocket and winks.

Miss Moore lines us up in front of the mailbox where we started from, seem like years ago, and I got a headache for thinkin so hard. And we lean all over each other so we can hold up under the draggy-ass lecture she always finishes us   45 off with at the end before we thank her for borin us to tears. But she just looks at us like she readin tea leaves. Finally she say, "Well, what did you think of F. A. O. Schwarz?"

Rosie Giraffe mumbles, "White folks crazy."

"I'd like to go there again when I get my birthday money," says Mercedes, and we shove her out the pack so she has to lean on the mailbox by herself.

"I'd like a shower. Tiring day," say Flyboy.

Then Sugar surprises me by sayin, "You know, Miss Moore, I don't think all of us here put together eat in a year what that sailboat costs." And Miss Moore lights up like somebody goosed her. "And?" she say, urging Sugar on. Only I'm standin on her foot so she don't continue.

"Imagine for a minute what kind of society it is in which some people can 50 spend on a toy what it would cost to feed a family of six or seven. What do you think?"

"I think," say Sugar pushing me off her feet like she never done before, cause I whip her ass in a minute, "that this is not much of a democracy if you ask me. Equal chance to pursue happiness means an equal crack at the dough, don't it?" Miss Moore is besides herself and I am disgusted with Sugar's treachery. So I stand on her foot one more time to see if she'll shove me. She shuts up, and Miss Moore looks at me, sorrowfully I'm thinkin. And somethin weird is goin on, I can feel it in my chest.

"Anybody else learn anything today?" lookin dead at me. I walk away and Sugar has to run to catch up and don't even seem to notice when I shrug her arm off my shoulder.

"Well, we got four dollars anyway," she says.

"Uh hunh."

"We could go to Hascombs and get half a chocolate layer and then go to the 55 Sunset and still have plenty money for potato chips and ice cream sodas."

"Un hunh."

"Race you to Hascombs," she say.

We start down the block and she gets ahead which is O.K. by me cause I'm going to the West End and then over to the Drive to think this day through. She can run if she want to and even run faster. But ain't nobody gonna beat me at nuthin.

For Analysis

1. What are Sylvia's outstanding traits? How are they reflected in her language and in her description of her neighborhood? **2.** How is Sylvia's character revealed through her relationship with Sugar? **3.** Describe the lesson Miss Moore tries to teach the children by taking them to visit F. A. O. Schwarz. **4.** How is Sylvia's assessment of Miss Moore at the beginning of the story borne out by the ending? **5.** What evidence is there that Sylvia has been changed by the experience?

On Style

Analyze Bambara's use of language to create the sense of a young, bright narrator rambling aimlessly when in fact the story is carefully structured.

Making Connections

1. Compare and contrast the use of the first-person narrator in this story, in Frank O'Connor's "My Oedipus Complex" (p. 90), and in Sandra Cisneros's "The House on Mango Street" (p. 122). **2.** This story and William Saroyan's essay "Five Ripe Pears" (p. 290) deal with a child whose sense of justice is offended. What differences and similarities do you find in the source of the distress and the way the distress is resolved?

Writing Topic

Write an essay arguing for or against the proposition that the story ends optimistically.

Sandra Cisneros   [b. 1954]

The House on Mango Street   1983

We didn't always live on Mango Street. Before that we lived on Loomis on the third floor, and before that we lived on Keeler. Before Keeler it was Paulina, and before that I can't remember. But what I remember most is moving a lot. Each time it seemed there'd be one more of us. By the time we got to Mango Street we were six—Mama, Papa, Carlos, Kiki, my sister Nenny and me.

The house on Mango Street is ours and we don't have to pay rent to anybody or share the yard with the people downstairs or be careful not to make too much noise and there isn't a landlord banging on the ceiling with a broom. But even so, it's not the house we'd thought we'd get.

We had to leave the flat on Loomis quick. The water pipes broke and the landlord wouldn't fix them because the house was too old. We had to leave fast. We were using the washroom next door and carrying water over in empty milk gallons. That's why Mama and Papa looked for a house, and that's why we moved into the house on Mango Street, far away, on the other side of town.

They always told us that one day we would move into a house, a real house that would be ours for always so we wouldn't have to move each year. And our house would have running water and pipes that worked. And inside it would have real stairs, not hallway stairs, but stairs inside like the houses on T.V. And we'd have a basement and at least three washrooms so when we took a bath we didn't have to tell everybody. Our house would be white with trees around it, a great big yard and grass growing without a fence. This was the house Papa talked about when he held a lottery ticket and this was the house Mama dreamed up in the stories she told us before we went to bed.

But the house on Mango Street is not the way they told it at all. It's small and   5
red with tight little steps in front and windows so small you'd think they were holding their breath. Bricks are crumbling in places, and the front door is so swollen you have to push hard to get in. There is no front yard, only four little elms the city planted by the curb. Out back is a small garage for the car we don't own yet and a small yard that looks smaller between the two buildings on either side. There are stairs in our house, but they're ordinary hallway stairs, and the house has only one washroom, very small. Everybody has to share a bedroom— Mama and Papa, Carlos and Kiki, me and Nenny.

Once when we were living on Loomis, a nun from my school passed by and saw me playing out front. The laundromat downstairs had been boarded up because it had been robbed two days before and the owner had painted on the wood YES WE'RE OPEN so as not to lose business.

Where do you live? she asked.

There, I said pointing up to the third floor.

You live *there?*

There. I had to look to where she pointed—the third floor, the paint peeling, 10
wooden bars Papa had nailed on the windows so we wouldn't fall out. You live
there? The way she said it made me feel like nothing. *There.* I lived *there.* I
nodded.

I knew then I had to have a house. A real house. One I could point to. But this
isn't it. The house on Mango Street isn't it. For the time being, Mama said.
Temporary, said Papa. But I know how those things go.

For Analysis

1. Why did the family have to leave the flat on Loomis Street so fast? **2.** What does the
Loomis house represent to the speaker? **3.** What is the significance of the nun's comment on the speaker's house (par. 9)? **4.** Describe the speaker's feelings about the
move to Mango Street. **5.** Would you describe the narrator's family as healthy and
happy? Explain. **6.** How would you characterize the **tone** of the final paragraph?

On Style

1. What effect does Cisneros achieve by using the present tense in paragraphs 2 and
5? **2.** How might this story differ if it were told by an **omniscient** rather than a **first-
person narrator**?

Making Connections

Compare the house in this story with the pears in William Saroyan's essay "Five Ripe
Pears" (p. 290) as symbols.

Writing Topics

1. Write a personal essay that is organized, like Cisneros's story, around some place
or object (home, neighborhood, toy) or person (parent, sibling, friend, teacher) that
symbolized important emotions and meanings for your life at the time. **2.** Describe
the effects of moving to different homes during your childhood. **3.** The narrator
yearns for what she calls "a real house. One I could point to." Write an essay describing your own experience of living in what you did not consider a "real house."

Poetry

<u>William Blake</u> [1757–1827]

The Chimney Sweeper 1789

When my mother died I was very young,
And my Father sold me while yet my tongue
Could scarcely cry " 'weep! 'weep! 'weep! 'weep!"
So your chimneys I sweep, and in soot I sleep.

There's little Tom Dacre, who cried when his head,
That curled like a lamb's back, was shaved: so I said,
"Hush, Tom! never mind it, for when your head's bare
You know that the soot cannot spoil your white hair."

And so he was quiet and that very night
As Tom was a-sleeping, he had such a sight!   10
That thousands of sweepers, Dick, Joe, Ned, and Jack,
Were all of them locked up in coffins of black.

And by came an Angel who had a bright key,
And he opened the coffins and set them all free;
Then down a green plain leaping, laughing, they run,
And wash in a river, and shine in the Sun.

Then naked and white, all their bags left behind,
They rise upon clouds and sport in the wind;
And the Angel told Tom, if he'd be a good boy,
He'd have God for his father, and never want joy.   20

And so Tom awoke; and we rose in the dark,
And got with our bags and our brushes to work.
Though the morning was cold, Tom was happy and warm;
So if all do their duty they need not fear harm.

The Tyger   1794

Tyger! Tyger! burning bright
In the forests of the night,
What immortal hand or eye
Could frame thy fearful symmetry?

In what distant deeps or skies
Burnt the fire of thine eyes?
On what wings dare he aspire?
What the hand dare seize the fire?

And what shoulder, & what art,
Could twist the sinews of thy heart?   10
And when thy heart began to beat,
What dread hand? & what dread feet?

What the hammer? what the chain?
In what furnace was thy brain?
What the anvil? what dread grasp
Dare its deadly terrors clasp?

When the stars threw down their spears,
And water'd heaven with their tears,
Did he smile his work to see?
Did he who made the Lamb make thee?   20

Tyger! Tyger! burning bright
In the forests of the night,
What immortal hand or eye
Dare frame thy fearful symmetry?

The Garden of Love   1793

I went to the Garden of Love,
And saw what I never had seen:
A Chapel was built in the midst,
Where I used to play on the green.

And the gates of this Chapel were shut,
And "Thou shalt not" writ over the door;
So I turn'd to the Garden of Love,
That so many sweet flowers bore,

And I saw it was filled with graves,
And tomb-stones where flowers should be: 10
And Priests in black gowns were walking their rounds,
And binding with briars my joys & desires.

For Analysis

1. What meanings does the word *love* have in this poem? **2.** What is Blake's judgment on established religion? **3.** Explain the meaning of *Chapel* (l. 3) and of *briars* (l. 12). **4.** Examine the engraving of "The Garden of Love" reproduced on p. 1355. How does Blake's representation of the poem along with his use of images affect your understanding?

Writing Topic

Read the definition of **irony** in the glossary of literary terms. Write an essay in which you distinguish between the types of irony used in "The Chimney Sweeper" and "The Garden of Love."

London   1794

I wander through each chartered[1] street,
Near where the chartered Thames does flow
And mark in every face I meet
Marks of weakness, marks of woe.

In every cry of every man,
In every infant's cry of fear,
In every voice; in every ban,
The mind-forged manacles I hear:

How the chimney-sweeper's cry
Every blackening church appalls,   10
And the hapless soldier's sigh
Runs in blood down palace-walls.

But most, through midnight streets I hear
How the youthful harlot's curse
Blasts the new-born infant's tear,
And blights with plagues the marriage-hearse.

London
  [1] Preempted by the state and leased out under royal patent.

William Wordsworth [1770–1850]

Lines[1] 1798

*Composed a Few Miles above Tintern Abbey
on Revisiting the Banks of the Wye
during a Tour. July 13, 1798*

Five years have passed;[2] five summers, with the length
Of five long winters! and again I hear
These waters, rolling from their mountain-springs
With a soft inland murmur. Once again
Do I behold these steep and lofty cliffs,
That on a wild secluded scene impress
Thoughts of more deep seclusion; and connect
The landscape with the quiet of the sky.
The day is come when I again repose
Here, under this dark sycamore, and view   10
These plots of cottage ground, these orchard tufts,
Which at this season, with their unripe fruits,
Are clad in one green hue, and lose themselves
'Mid groves and copses. Once again I see
These hedgerows, hardly hedgerows, little lines
Of sportive wood run wild; these pastoral farms,
Green to the very door; and wreaths of smoke
Sent up, in silence, from among the trees!
With some uncertain notice, as might seem
Of vagrant dwellers in the houseless woods,   20
Or of some Hermit's cave, where by his fire
The Hermit sits alone.

                  These beauteous forms,
Through a long absence, have not been to me
As is a landscape to a blind man's eye;
But oft, in lonely rooms, and 'mid the din
Of towns and cities, I have owed to them
In hours of weariness, sensations sweet,
Felt in the blood, and felt along the heart;

[1] Wordsworth wrote this poem during a four- or five-day walking tour through the Wye valley with his sister Dorothy.
[2] The poet had visited the region on a solitary walking tour in August of 1793 when he was twenty-three years old.

And passing even into my purer mind,
With tranquil restoration—feelings too   30
Of unremembered pleasure; such, perhaps,
As have no slight or trivial influence
On that best portion of a good man's life,
His little, nameless, unremembered, acts
Of kindness and of love. Nor less, I trust,
To them I may have owed another gift,
Of aspect more sublime; that blessed mood,
In which the burthen of the mystery,
In which the heavy and the weary weight
Of all this unintelligible world,   40
Is lightened—that serene and blessed mood,
In which the affections gently lead us on—
Until, the breath of this corporeal frame
And even the motion of our human blood
Almost suspended, we are laid asleep
In body, and become a living soul;
While with an eye made quiet by the power
Of harmony, and the deep power of joy,
We see into the life of things

                    If this
Be but a vain belief, yet, oh! how oft—   50
In darkness and amid the many shapes
Of joyless daylight; when the fretful stir
Unprofitable, and the fever of the world,
Have hung upon the beatings of my heart—
How oft, in spirit, have I turned to thee,
O sylvan Wye! thou wanderer through the woods,
How often has my spirit turned to thee!

    And now, with gleams of half-extinguished thought
With many recognitions dim and faint,
And somewhat of a sad perplexity,   60
The picture of the mind revives again;
While here I stand, not only with the sense
Of present pleasure, but with pleasing thoughts
That in this moment there is life and food
For future years. And so I dare to hope,
Though changed, no doubt, from what I was when first
I came among these hills; when like a roe
I bounded o'er the mountains, by the sides
Of the deep rivers, and the lonely streams,

Wherever nature led—more like a man 70
Flying from something that he dreads than one
Who sought the thing he loved. For nature then
(The coarser pleasures of my boyish days,
And their glad animal movements all gone by)
To me was all in all.—I cannot paint
What then I was. The sounding cataract
Haunted me like a passion; the tall rock,
The mountain, and the deep and gloomy wood,
Their colors and their forms, were then to me
An appetite; a feeling and a love, 80
That had no need of a remoter charm,
By thought supplied, nor any interest
Unborrowed from the eye.—That time is past,
And all its aching joys are now no more,
And all its dizzy raptures. Not for this
Faint[3] I, nor mourn nor murmur; other gifts
Have followed; for such loss, I would believe,
Abundant recompense. For I have learned
To look on nature, not as in the hour
Of thoughtless youth; but hearing oftentimes 90
The still, sad music of humanity,
Nor harsh nor grating, though of ample power
To chasten and subdue. And I have felt
A presence that disturbs me with the joy
Of elevated thoughts; a sense sublime
Of something far more deeply interfused,
Whose dwelling is the light of setting suns,
And the round ocean and the living air,
And the blue sky, and in the mind of man:
A motion and a spirit, that impels 100
All thinking things, all objects of all thought,
And rolls through all things. Therefore am I still
A lover of the meadows and the woods,
And mountains; and of all that we behold
From this green earth; of all the mighty world
Of eye, and ear—both what they half create,
And what perceive; well pleased to recognize
In nature and the language of the sense
The anchor of my purest thoughts, the nurse,
The guide, the guardian of my heart, and soul 110
Of all my moral being.

[3] Lose heart.

Nor perchance,
If I were not thus taught, should I the more
Suffer my genial spirits to decay:
For thou art with me here upon the banks
Of this fair river; thou my dearest Friend,[4]
My dear, dear Friend; and in thy voice I catch
The language of my former heart, and read
My former pleasures in the shooting lights
Of thy wild eyes. Oh! yet a little while
May I behold in thee what I was once,   120
My dear, dear Sister! and this prayer I make,
Knowing that Nature never did betray
The heart that loved her; 'tis her privilege,
Through all the years of this our life, to lead
From joy to joy: for she can so inform
The mind that is within us, so impress
With quietness and beauty, and so feed
With lofty thoughts, that neither evil tongues,
Rash judgments, nor the sneers of selfish men,
Nor greetings where no kindness is, nor all   130
The dreary intercourse of daily life,
Shall e'er prevail against us, or disturb
Our cheerful faith, that all which we behold
Is full of blessings. Therefore let the moon
Shine on thee in thy solitary walk;
And let the misty mountain winds be free
To blow against thee: and, in after years,
When these wild ecstasies shall be matured
Into a sober pleasure; when thy mind
Shall be a mansion for all lovely forms,   140
Thy memory be as a dwelling place
For all sweet sounds and harmonies; oh! then,
If solitude, or fear, or pain, or grief
Should be thy portion, with what healing thoughts
Of tender joy wilt thou remember me,
And these my exhortations! Nor, perchance—
If I should be where I no more can hear
Thy voice, nor catch from thy wild eyes these gleams
Of past existence[5]—wilt thou then forget
That on the banks of this delightful stream   150
We stood together; and that I, so long
A worshiper of Nature, hither came

---

[4] The poet addresses his sister Dorothy.
[5] I.e., the poet's past experience. Note lines 116–19.

Unwearied in that service; rather say
With warmer love—oh! with far deeper zeal
Of holier love. Nor wilt thou then forget,
That after many wanderings, many years
Of absence, these steep woods and lofty cliffs,
And this green pastoral landscape, were to me
More dear, both for themselves and for thy sake!

For Analysis

1. In this poem the poet distinguishes between two important periods in his life: the first is described in lines 65–83, and the second is described in lines 83–111. How does he characterize these two periods? **2.** The poem describes a visit to a familiar scene of the poet's youth and includes a meditation upon the changes that have occurred. Are the changes in the poet, the scene itself, or both?

Writing Topic

Discuss the ways in which the poet contrasts the city and the countryside.

John Keats [1795–1821]

On First Looking into Chapman's Homer[1] 1816

Much have I travelled in the realms of gold,
And many goodly states and kingdoms seen:
Round many western islands have I been
Which bards in fealty to Apollo[2] hold.
Oft of one wide expanse had I been told
That deep-browed Homer ruled as his demesne;°   realm
Yet did I never breathe its pure serene°   clear air
Till I heard Chapman speak out loud and bold:
Then felt I like some watcher of the skies
When a new planet swims into his ken;   10
Or like stout Cortez[3] when with eagle eyes
He stared at the Pacific—and all his men

On First Looking into Chapman's Homer
    [1] George Chapman published translations of *The Iliad* (1611) and *The Odyssey* (1616).
    [2] The god of poetry.
    [3] Keats mistakenly attributes the discovery of the Pacific Ocean by Europeans to Hernando Cortez (1485–1547), the Spanish conqueror of Mexico. Vasco Nuñez de Balboa (1475–1519) first saw the Pacific from a mountain located in eastern Panama.

Looked at each other with a wild surmise—
   Silent, upon a peak in Darien.

Robert Browning   [1812–1889]

My Last Duchess   1842

FERRARA

That's my last Duchess painted on the wall,
Looking as if she were alive. I call
That piece a wonder, now: Frà Pandolf's[1] hands
Worked busily a day, and there she stands.
Will't please you sit and look at her? I said
"Frà Pandolf" by design, for never read
Strangers like you that pictured countenance,
The depth and passion of its earnest glance,
But to myself they turned (since none puts by
The curtain I have drawn for you, but I)   10
And seemed as they would ask me, if they durst,
How such a glance came there; so, not the first
Are you to turn and ask thus. Sir, 'twas not
Her husband's presence only, called that spot
Of joy into the Duchess' cheek: perhaps
Frà Pandolf chanced to say "Her mantle laps
Over my lady's wrist too much," or "Paint
Must never hope to reproduce the faint
Half-flush that dies along her throat": such stuff
Was courtesy, she thought, and cause enough   20
For calling up that spot of joy. She had
A heart—how shall I say?—too soon made glad,
Too easily impressed; she liked whate'er
She looked on, and her looks went everywhere.
Sir, 'twas all one! My favor at her breast,
The dropping of the daylight in the West,

My Last Duchess
   [1] Frà Pandolf and Claus of Innsbruck (who is mentioned in the last line) are fictitious artists.

The bough of cherries some officious fool
Broke in the orchard for her, the white mule
She rode with round the terrace—all and each
Would draw from her alike the approving speech,   30
Or blush, at least. She thanked men—good! but thanked
Somehow—I know not how—as if she ranked
My gift of a nine-hundred-years-old name
With anybody's gift. Who'd stoop to blame
This sort of trifling? Even had you skill
In speech—which I have not—to make your will
Quite clear to such an one, and say, "Just this
Or that in you disgusts me; here you miss,
Or there exceed the mark"—and if she let
Herself be lessoned° so, nor plainly set   taught
Her wits to yours, forsooth, and made excuse,
—E'en then would be some stooping; and I choose
Never to stoop. Oh sir, she smiled, no doubt,
Whene'er I passed her; but who passed without
Much the same smile? This grew; I gave commands;
Then all smiles stopped together. There she stands
As if alive. Will't please you rise? We'll meet
The company below, then. I repeat,
The Count your master's known munificence°   generosity
Is ample warrant that no just pretense   50
Of mine for dowry will be disallowed;
Though his fair daughter's self, as I avowed
At starting, is my object. Nay, we'll go
Together down, sir. Notice Neptune, though,
Taming a sea-horse, thought a rarity,
Which Claus of Innsbruck cast in bronze for me!

For Analysis

1. To whom is the Duke speaking, and what is the occasion? **2.** What does a comparison between the Duke's feelings about his artworks and his feelings about his last Duchess reveal about his character? **3.** What became of the Duke's last Duchess?

On Style

Does this poem rely upon **irony**? Explain.

Writing Topic

Write an essay in which you argue that the reader is or is not meant to sympathize with the Duke's characterization of his wife.

Emily Dickinson   [1830–1886]

I felt a Funeral, in my Brain   1861

I felt a Funeral, in my Brain,
And Mourners to and fro
Kept treading—treading—till it seemed
That Sense was breaking through—

And when they all were seated,
A Service, like a Drum—
Kept beating—beating—till I thought
My Mind was going numb—

And then I heard them lift a Box
And creak across my Soul   10
With those same Boots of Lead, again,
Then Space—began to toll,

As all the Heavens were a Bell,
And Being, but an Ear,
And I, and Silence, some strange Race
Wrecked, solitary, here—

And then a Plank in Reason, broke,
And I dropped down, and down—
And hit a World, at every plunge,
And Finished knowing—then—   20

Thomas Hardy   [1840–1928]

Hap   1898

If but some vengeful god would call to me
From up the sky, and laugh: "Thou suffering thing,
Know that thy sorrow is my ecstasy,
That thy love's loss is my hate's profiting!"

Then would I bear it, clench myself, and die,
Steeled by the sense of ire unmerited;
Half-eased in that a Powerfuller than I
Had willed and meted me the tears I shed.

But not so. How arrives it joy lies slain,
And why unblooms the best hope ever sown?   10
—Crass Casualty° obstructs the sun and rain,   chance
And dicing Time for gladness casts a moan. . . .
These purblind Doomsters[1] had as readily strown
Blisses about my pilgrimage as pain.

The Ruined Maid   1902

"O 'Melia, my dear, this does everything crown!
Who could have supposed I should meet you in Town?
And whence such fair garments, such prosperi-ty?"
"O didn't you know I'd been ruined?" said she.

"You left us in tatters, without shoes or socks,
Tired of digging potatoes, and spudding up docks;°   digging herbs
And now you've gay bracelets and bright feathers three!"
"Yes: that's how we dress when we're ruined," said she.

"At home in the barton° you said 'thee' and 'thou,'   farmyard
And 'thik oon,' and 'theäs oon,' and 't'other'; but now   10
Your talking quite fits 'ee for high compa-ny!"
"Some polish is gained with one's ruin," said she.

"Your hands were like paws then, your face blue and bleak
But now I'm bewitched by your delicate cheek,
And your little gloves fit as on any la-dy!"
"We never do work when we're ruined," said she.

"You used to call home-life a hag-ridden dream,
And you'd sigh, and you'd sock; but at present you seem
To know not of megrims° or melancho-ly!"   sick headaches
"True. One's pretty lively when ruined," said she.   20

Hap
  [1] Those who decide one's fate.

"I wish I had feathers, a fine sweeping gown,
And a delicate face, and could strut about Town!"
"My dear—a raw country girl, such as you be,
Cannot quite expect that. You ain't ruined," said she.

Gerard Manley Hopkins [1844–1889]

Spring and Fall 1880
To a Young Child

Márgarét, áre you gríeving
Over Goldengrove unleaving?°   losing leaves
Leáves, líke the things of man, you
With your fresh thoughts care for, can you?
Áh! ás the heart grows older
It will come to such sights colder
By and by, nor spare a sigh
Though worlds of wanwood leafmeal[1] lie;
And yet you wíll weep and know why.
Now no matter, child, the name: 10
Sórrow's spríngs áre the same.
Nor mouth had, no nor mind, expressed
What heart heard of, ghost° guessed: soul
It ís the blight man was born for,
It is Margaret you mourn for.

For Analysis
1. In this poem Margaret grieves over the passing of spring and the coming of fall.
What does the coming of fall symbolize? 2. Why, when Margaret grows older, will
she not sigh over the coming of fall? 3. What are "Sorrow's springs" (l. 11)?

Spring and Fall
   [1] Pale woods littered with mouldering leaves.

A. E. Housman [1859–1936]

When I Was One-and-Twenty 1896

When I was one-and-twenty
    I heard a wise man say,
"Give crowns and pounds and guineas
    But not your heart away;
Give pearls away and rubies
    But keep your fancy free."
But I was one-and-twenty,
    No use to talk to me.

When I was one-and-twenty
    I heard him say again,   10
"The heart out of the bosom
    Was never given in vain;
'Tis paid with sighs a plenty
    And sold for endless rue."
And I am two-and-twenty,
    And oh, 'tis true, 'tis true.

Terence, This Is Stupid Stuff[1] 1896

  "Terence, this is stupid stuff:
You eat your victuals fast enough;
There can't be much amiss, 'tis clear,
To see the rate you drink your beer.
But oh, good Lord, the verse you make,
It gives a chap the bellyache.
The cow, the old cow, she is dead;
It sleeps well, the hornéd head:
We poor lads, 'tis our turn now

Terence, This Is Stupid Stuff
  [1] Housman originally titled the volume in which this poem appeared *The Poems of Terence Hearsay.* Terence was a Roman satiric playwright.

To hear such tunes as killed the cow.   10
Pretty friendship 'tis to rhyme
Your friends to death before their time
Moping melancholy mad:
Come, pipe a tune to dance to, lad."

   Why, if 'tis dancing you would be,
There's brisker pipes than poetry.
Say, for what were hopyards meant,
Or why was Burton built on Trent?[2]
Oh many a peer of England brews
Livelier liquor than the Muse,   20
And malt does more than Milton can
To justify God's ways to man.[3]
Ale, man, ale's the stuff to drink
For fellows whom it hurts to think:
Look into the pewter pot
To see the world as the world's not.
And faith, 'tis pleasant till 'tis past:
The mischief is that 'twill not last.
Oh I have been to Ludlow fair
And left my necktie God knows where,   30
And carried halfway home, or near,
Pints and quarts of Ludlow beer:
Then the world seemed none so bad,
And I myself a sterling lad;
And down in lovely muck I've lain,
Happy till I woke again.
Then I saw the morning sky:
Heigho, the tale was all a lie;
The world, it was the old world yet,
I was I, my things were wet,   40
And nothing now remained to do
But begin the game anew.

   Therefore, since the world has still
Much good, but much less good than ill,
And while the sun and moon endure
Luck's a chance, but trouble's sure,

---

[2] The river Trent provides water for the town's brewing industry.
[3] In the invocation to *Paradise Lost*, Milton declares that his epic will "justify the ways of God to men."

I'd face it as a wise man would,
And train for ill and not for good.
'Tis true the stuff I bring for sale
Is not so brisk a brew as ale: 50
Out of a stem that scored the hand
I wrung it in a weary land.
But take it: if the smack is sour,
The better for the embittered hour;
It should do good to heart and head
When your soul is in my soul's stead;
And I will friend you, if I may,
In the dark and cloudy day.

    There was a king reigned in the East:
There, when kings will sit to feast,
They get their fill before they think   60
With poisoned meat and poisoned drink.
He gathered all that springs to birth
From the many-venomed earth;
First a little, thence to more,
He sampled all her killing store;
And easy, smiling, seasoned sound,
Sate the king when healths went round.
They put arsenic in his meat
And stared aghast to watch him eat;   70
They poured strychnine in his cup
And shook to see him drink it up:
They shook, they stared as white's their shirt:
Them it was their poison hurt.
—I tell the tale that I heard told.
Mithridates, he died old.[4]

For Analysis

1. What does the speaker of the first fourteen lines object to in Terence's poetry?
2. What is Terence's response to the criticism of his verse? What function of true poetry is implied by his comparison of bad poetry with liquor?

Writing Topic

How does the story of Mithridates (ll. 59–76) illustrate the theme of the poem?

---

[4] Mithridates, the King of Pontus (in Asia Minor), reputedly immunized himself against poisons by administering to himself gradually increasing doses.

William Butler Yeats [1865–1939]

Leda and the Swan[1]   1928

A sudden blow: the great wings beating still
Above the staggering girl, her thighs caressed
By the dark webs, her nape caught in his bill,
He holds her helpless breast upon his breast.

How can those terrified vague fingers push
The feathered glory from her loosening thighs?
And how can body, laid in that white rush,
But feel the strange heart beating where it lies?

A shudder in the loins engenders there
The broken wall, the burning roof and tower   10
And Agamemnon dead.
                              Being so caught up,
So mastered by the brute blood of the air,
Did she put on his knowledge with his power
Before the indifferent beak could let her drop?

Robert Frost   [1874–1963]

Birches   1916

When I see birches bend to left and right
Across the lines of straighter darker trees,
I like to think some boy's been swinging them.
But swinging doesn't bend them down to stay
As ice-storms do. Often you must have seen them
Loaded with ice a sunny winter morning
After a rain. They click upon themselves
As the breeze rises, and turn many-colored

Leda and the Swan
   [1] In Greek myth, Zeus, in the form of a swan, rapes Leda. As a consequence, Helen and Clytemnestra are born. Each sister marries the king of a city-state; Helen marries Menelaus and Clytemnestra marries Agamemnon. Helen, the most beautiful woman on earth, elopes with Paris, a prince of Troy, an act that precipitates the Trojan War in which Agamemnon commands the combined Greek armies. The war ends with the destruction of Troy. Agamemnon, when he returns to his home, is murdered by his unfaithful wife.

140

As the stir cracks and crazes their enamel.
Soon the sun's warmth makes them shed crystal shells 10
Shattering and avalanching on the snow-crust—
Such heaps of broken glass to sweep away
You'd think the inner dome of heaven had fallen.
They are dragged to the withered bracken by the load,
And they seem not to break; though once they are bowed
So low for long, they never right themselves:
You may see their trunks arching in the woods
Years afterwards, trailing their leaves on the ground
Like girls on hands and knees that throw their hair
Before them over their heads to dry in the sun. 20
But I was going to say when Truth broke in
With all her matter-of-fact about the ice-storm
I should prefer to have some boy bend them
As he went out and in to fetch the cows—
Some boy too far from town to learn baseball,
Whose only play was what he found himself,
Summer or winter, and could play alone.
One by one he subdued his father's trees
By riding them down over and over again
Until he took the stiffness out of them, 30
And not one but hung limp, not one was left
For him to conquer. He learned all there was
To learn about not launching out too soon
And so not carrying the tree away
Clear to the ground. He always kept his poise
To the top branches, climbing carefully
With the same pains you use to fill a cup
Up to the brim, and even above the brim.
Then he flung outward, feet first, with a swish,
Kicking his way down through the air to the ground. 40
So was I once myself a swinger of birches.
And so I dream of going back to be.
It's when I'm weary of considerations,
And life is too much like a pathless wood
Where your face burns and tickles with the cobwebs
Broken across it, and one eye is weeping
From a twig's having lashed across it open.
I'd like to get away from earth awhile
And then come back to it and begin over.
May no fate willfully misunderstand me 50
And half grant what I wish and snatch me away
Not to return. Earth's the right place for love:
I don't know where it's likely to go better.

I'd like to go by climbing a birch tree,
And climb black branches up a snow-white trunk
Toward heaven, till the tree could bear no more,
But dipped its top and set me down again.
That would be good both going and coming back.
One could do worse than be a swinger of birches.

Provide, Provide   1936

The witch that came (the withered hag)
To wash the steps with pail and rag,
Was once the beauty Abishag,[1]

The picture pride of Hollywood.
Too many fall from great and good
For you to doubt the likelihood.

Die early and avoid the fate.
Or if predestined to die late,
Make up your mind to die in state.

Make the whole stock exchange your own!   10
If need be occupy a throne,
Where nobody can call *you* crone.

Some have relied on what they knew;
Others on being simply true.
What worked for them might work for you.

No memory of having starred
Atones for later disregard,
Or keeps the end from being hard.

Better to go down dignified
With boughten friendship at your side   20
Than none at all. Provide, provide!

Provide, Provide
   [1] "Now King David was old and advanced in years; and although they covered him with clothes, he could not get warm. Therefore his servants said to him, 'Let a young maiden be sought for my lord the king, and let her wait upon the king, and be his nurse; let her lie in your bosom, that my lord the king may be warm.' So they sought for a beautiful maiden throughout all the territory of Israel, and found Abishag, the Shunammite, and brought her to the king. The maiden was very beautiful. . . ."—I Kings 1:1–4.

Robert Francis [1901–1987]

Pitcher 1960

His art is eccentricity, his aim
How not to hit the mark he seems to aim at,

His passion how to avoid the obvious,
His technique how to vary the avoidance.

The others throw to be comprehended. He
Throws to be a moment misunderstood.

Yet not too much. Not errant, arrant, wild,
But every seeming aberration willed.

Not to, yet still, still to communicate
Making the batter understand too late.   10

For Analysis
1. The poem describes the art of the baseball pitcher. But the description is an extended metaphor for the art of the poet. Is the pitcher described accurately? **2.** Is the analogy between pitcher and poet apt? Explain.

Writing Topic
Select any poem you have read, and write an essay on how it exhibits some of the characteristics of poetry as defined in this poem.

Stevie Smith [1902–1971]

To Carry the Child 1966

To carry the child into adult life
Is good? I say it is not,
To carry the child into adult life
Is to be handicapped.

The child in adult life is defenceless
And if he is grown-up, knows it,
And the grown-up looks at the childish part
And despises it.

The child, too, despises the clever grown-up,
The man-of-the-world, the frozen,   10
For the child has the tears alive on his cheek
And the man has none of them.

As the child has colours, and the man sees no
Colours or anything,
Being easy only in things of the mind,
The child is easy in feeling.

Easy in feeling, easily excessive
And in excess powerful,
For instance, if you do not speak to the child
He will make trouble.   20

You would say a man had the upper hand
Of the child, if a child survive,
But I say the child has fingers of strength
To strangle the man alive.

Oh! it is not happy, it is never happy,
To carry the child into adulthood,
Let the children lie down before full growth
And die in their infanthood
And be guilty of no man's blood.

But oh the poor child, the poor child, what can he do,   30
Trapped in a grown-up carapace,
But peer outside of his prison room
With the eye of an anarchist?

Not Waving but Drowning   1972

Nobody heard him, the dead man,
But still he lay moaning:
I was much further out than you thought
And not waving but drowning.

Poor chap, he always loved larking
And now he's dead
It must have been too cold for him his heart gave way,
They said.

Oh, no no no, it was too cold always
(Still the dead one lay moaning)   10
I was much too far out all my life
And not waving but drowning.

For Analysis

1. Explain the **paradox** in the first and last stanzas, where the speaker describes someone dead as moaning. Who do you suppose the *you* of line 3 is? And the *they* of line
8? **2.** Explain the meaning of line 7. Can it be interpreted in more than one way? Explain. **3.** Explain the meanings of *drowning*. **4.** The only thing we learn about the
dead man is that "he always loved larking." Why is this detail significant? What kind
of man do you think he was? **5.** Does the speaker know more about the dead man
than his friends did? Explain.

Writing Topics

1. Write an essay describing how you or someone you know suffered the experience
of "not waving but drowning." **2.** Write an essay describing how you came to the realization that someone close to you was not the person you thought he or she was.

Dylan Thomas [1914–1953]

Fern Hill 1946

Now as I was young and easy under the apple boughs
About the lilting house and happy as the grass was green,
    The night above the dingle° starry,   small wooded valley
        Time let me hail and climb
    Golden in the heydays of his eyes,
And honored among wagons I was prince of the apple towns
And once below a time I lordly had the trees and leaves
        Trail with daisies and barley
    Down the rivers of the windfall light.

And as I was green and carefree, famous among the barns   10
About the happy yard and singing as the farm was home,
    In the sun that is young once only,
        Time let me play and be
    Golden in the mercy of his means,
And green and golden I was huntsman and herdsman, the calves
Sang to my horn, the foxes on the hills barked clear and cold,
        And the sabbath rang slowly
    In the pebbles of the holy streams.

All the sun long it was running, it was lovely, the hay
Fields high as the house, the tunes from the chimneys, it was air   20
    And playing, lovely and watery
        And fire green as grass.
    And nightly under the simple stars
As I rode to sleep the owls were bearing the farm away,
All the moon long I heard, blessed among stables, the nightjars[1]
    Flying with the ricks, and the horses
        Flashing into the dark.

And then to awake, and the farm, like a wanderer white
With the dew, come back, the cock on his shoulder: it was all
    Shining, it was Adam and maiden,   30
        The sky gathered again
    And the sun grew round that very day.
So it must have been after the birth of the simple light
In the first, spinning place, the spellbound horses walking warm
    Out of the whinnying green stable
        On to the fields of praise.

And honored among foxes and pheasants by the gay house
Under the new made clouds and happy as the heart was long,
    In the sun born over and over,
        I ran my heedless ways,   40
    My wishes raced through the house high hay
And nothing I cared, at my sky blue trades, that time allows
In all his tuneful turning so few and such morning songs
    Before the children green and golden
        Follow him out of grace.

Nothing I cared, in the lamb white days, that time would take me
Up to the swallow thronged loft by the shadow of my hand,
    In the moon that is always rising,
        Nor that riding to sleep
    I should hear him fly with the high fields   50
And wake to the farm forever fled from the childless land.
Oh as I was young and easy in the mercy of his means,
        Time held me green and dying
    Though I sang in my chains like the sea.

[1] Nightjars are harsh-sounding nocturnal birds.

For Analysis

1. What emotional impact does the color imagery in the poem provide? **2.** Trace the behavior of "time" in the poem. **3.** Fairy tales often begin with the words "once upon a time." Why does Thomas alter that formula in line 7? **4.** Explain the **paradox** in line 53.

Writing Topics

1. Lines 17–18, 30, and 45–46 incorporate religious language and biblical allusion. How do those allusions clarify the poet's vision of his childhood? **2.** Compare this poem with Gerard Manley Hopkins's "Spring and Fall."

Lawrence Ferlinghetti [b. 1919]

Constantly Risking Absurdity 1958

<blockquote>

Constantly risking absurdity
     and death
  whenever he performs
     above the heads
       of his audience
 the poet like an acrobat
    climbs on rime
     to a high wire of his own making
and balancing on eyebeams
     above a sea of faces   10
  paces his way
    to the other side of day
 performing entrechats[1]
    and sleight-of-foot tricks
and other high theatrics
    and all without mistaking
  any thing
    for what it may not be

 For he's the super realist
     who must perforce perceive 20
  taut truth
    before the taking of each stance or step

</blockquote>

---

[1] In ballet, a leap straight upward in which the dancer repeatedly crosses her legs or strikes her heels together.

in his supposed advance
                toward that still higher perch
where Beauty stands and waits
             with gravity
                  to start her death-defying leap

And he
        a little charleychaplin[2] man
              who may or may not catch   30
     her fair eternal form
            spreadeagled in the empty air
      of existence

Philip Larkin   [1922–1985]

This Be the Verse   1974

They fuck you up, your mum and dad.
  They may not mean to, but they do.
They fill you with the faults they had
  And add some extra, just for you.

But they were fucked up in their turn
  By fools in old-style hats and coats,
Who half the time were soppy-stern
  And half at one another's throats.

Man hands on misery to man.
  It deepens like a coastal shelf.   10
Get out as early as you can,
  And don't have any kids yourself.

Constantly Risking Absurdity
[2] Charles Spencer Chaplin (1889–1977) was cinema's most celebrated comedian of the silent film era. His trademark was the mustachioed Little Tramp, whose pathos and comedy were accompanied by extraordinary acrobatic skills.

Anthony Hecht [b. 1923]

"More Light! More Light!"[1] 1961
For Heinrich Blücher and Hannah Arendt[2]

Composed in the Tower[3] before his execution
These moving verses, and being brought at that time
Painfully to the stake, submitted, declaring thus:
"I implore my God to witness that I have made no crime."

Nor was he forsaken of courage, but the death was horrible,
The sack of gunpowder failing to ignite.
His legs were blistered sticks on which the black sap
Bubbled and burst as he howled for the Kindly Light.

And that was but one, and by no means one of the worst;
Permitted at least his pitiful dignity;   10
And such as were by made prayers in the name of Christ,
That shall judge all men, for his soul's tranquillity.

We move now to outside a German wood
Three men are there commanded to dig a hole
In which the two Jews are ordered to lie down
And be buried by the third, who is a Pole.

Not light from the shrine at Weimar[4] beyond the hill
Nor light from heaven appeared. But he did refuse.
A Lüger[5] settled back deeply in its glove.
He was ordered to change places with the Jews.   20

Much casual death had drained away their souls.
The thick dirt mounted toward the quivering chin.
When only the head was exposed the order came
To dig him out again and to get back in.

---

[1] These were the last words of the German poet Johann Wolfgang von Goethe (1749–1832).

[2] Husband and wife who emigrated to the United States from Germany in 1941. Hannah Arendt wrote extensively on political totalitarianism.

[3] The Tower of London was used as a prison for eminent political prisoners. What follows is an account of a priest's execution for the crime of heresy. The punishment was death by fire, and often a sack of gunpowder was placed at the condemned's neck to shorten the agony.

[4] Goethe spent most of his life in Weimar, and his humanistic achievements are honored there in the Goethe National Museum. The event recounted here occurred at Buchenwald, a German concentration camp north of Weimar.

[5] A German automatic pistol.

No light, no light in the blue Polish eye.
When he finished a riding boot packed down the earth.
The Lüger hovered lightly in its glove.
He was shot in the belly and in three hours bled to death.

No prayers or incense rose up in those hours
Which grew to be years, and every day came mute   30
Ghosts from the ovens, sifting through crisp air,
And settled upon his eyes in a black soot.

For Analysis

1. What relationship does the event (which occurred in sixteenth-century England) recounted in the first two stanzas of the poem bear to the event recounted in the last five stanzas? **2.** What **irony** do you find in the title of the poem and the use of the word *light* in lines 8, 17, 18, and 25? How would you define *light* in each case? Can you imagine yourself in the place of the three prisoners in line 14? What would you do?

Alastair Reid   [b. 1926]

Curiosity   1959

may have killed the cat; more likely
the cat was just unlucky, or else curious
to see what death was like, having no cause
to go on licking paws, or fathering
litter on litter of kittens, predictably.

Nevertheless, to be curious
is dangerous enough. To distrust
what is always said, what seems,
to ask odd questions, interfere in dreams,
leave home, smell rats, have hunches   10
does not endear him to those doggy circles
where well-smelt baskets, suitable wives, good lunches
are the order of things and where prevails
much wagging of incurious heads and tails.

Face it. Curiosity
will not cause him to die—
only lack of it will.
Never to want to see
the other side of the hill,

or that improbable country   20
where living is an idyll
(although a probable hell)
would kill us all.
Only the curious
have, if they live, a tale
worth telling at all.

     Dogs say he loves too much, is irresponsible,
is changeable, marries too many wives,
deserts his children, chills all dinner tables
with tales of his nine lives.   30
Well, he is lucky. Let him be
nine-lived and contradictory,
curious enough to change, prepared to pay
the cat price, which is to die
and die again and again,
each time with no less pain.
A cat minority of one
is all that can be counted on
to tell the truth. And what he has to tell
on each return from hell   40
is this: that dying is what the living do,
that dying is what the loving do,
and that dead dogs are those who do not know
that hell is where, to live, they have to go.

W. D. Snodgrass   [b. 1926]

April Inventory   1959

The green catalpa tree has turned
All white; the cherry blooms once more.
In one whole year I haven't learned
A blessed thing they pay you for.
The blossoms snow down in my hair;
The trees and I will soon be bare.

The trees have more than I to spare.
The sleek, expensive girls I teach,
Younger and pinker every year,

Bloom gradually out of reach.   10
The pear tree lets its petals drop
Like dandruff on a tabletop.

The girls have grown so young by now
I have to nudge myself to stare.
This year they smile and mind me how
My teeth are falling with my hair.
In thirty years I may not get
Younger, shrewder, or out of debt.

The tenth time, just a year ago,
I made myself a little list   20
Of all the things I'd ought to know;
Then told my parents, analyst,
And everyone who's trusted me
I'd be substantial, presently.

I haven't read one book about
A book or memorized one plot.
Or found a mind I did not doubt.
I learned one date. And then forgot.
And one by one the solid scholars
Get the degrees, the jobs, the dollars.   30

And smile above their starchy collars.
I taught my classes Whitehead's notions;
One lovely girl, a song of Mahler's.
Lacking a source-book or promotions,
I showed one child the colors of
A luna moth and how to love.

I taught myself to name my name,
To bark back, loosen love and crying;
To ease my woman so she came,
To ease an old man who was dying.   40
I have not learned how often I
Can win, can love, but choose to die.

I have not learned there is a lie
Love shall be blonder, slimmer, younger;
That my equivocating eye
Loves only by my body's hunger;
That I have poems, true to feel,
Or that the lovely world is real.

While scholars speak authority
And wear their ulcers on their sleeves,   50
My eyes in spectacles shall see
These trees procure and spend their leaves.
There is a value underneath
The gold and silver in my teeth.

Though trees turn bare and girls turn wives,
We shall afford our costly seasons;
There is a gentleness survives
That will outspeak and has its reasons.
There is a loveliness exists,
Preserves us. Not for specialists.   60

For Analysis
1. What do the words "I have not learned" (ll. 41, 43) mean in the context of the poem? **2.** In what way does the **tone** of the first four stanzas differ from the tone of the last two? **3.** What is the meaning of *specialists* in the last line? **4.** What is the speaker's conception of teaching?

Writing Topic
Explicate the final stanza of this poem. Is it an appropriate conclusion? Explain.

X. J. Kennedy [b. 1929]

First Confession 1961

Blood thudded in my ears. I scuffed,
   Steps stubborn, to the telltale booth
Beyond whose curtained portal coughed
   The robed repositor of truth.

The slat shot back. The universe
   Bowed down his cratered dome to hear
Enumerated my each curse,
   The sip snitched from my old man's beer.

My sloth pride envy lechery,
   The dime held back from Peter's Pence   10
With which I'd bribed my girl to pee
   That I might spy her instruments.

Hovering scale-pans when I'd done
    Settled their balance slow as silt
While in the restless dark I burned
    Bright as a brimstone in my guilt

Until as one feeds birds he doled
    Seven Our Fathers and a Hail
Which I to double-scrub my soul
    Intoned twice at the altar rail   20

Where Sunday in seraphic light
    I knelt, as full of grace as most,
And stuck my tongue out at the priest:
    A fresh roost for the Holy Ghost.

A Visit from St. Sigmund 1993

    Freud is just an old Santa Claus.
        —Margaret Mead[1]

'Twas the night before Christmas, when all through each kid
Not an Ego was stirring, not even an Id.
The hangups were hung by the chimney with care
In hopes that St. Sigmund Freud soon would be there.
The children in scream class had knocked off their screams,
Letting Jungian archetypes dance through their dreams,
And Mamma with her bra off and I on her lap
Had just snuggled down when a vast thunderclap
Boomed and from my unconscious arose such a chatter
As Baptist John's teeth made on Salome's platter.   10
Away from my darling I flew like a flash,
Tore straight to the bathroom and threw up, and—*smash!*
Through the windowpane hurtled and bounced on the floor
A big brick—holy smoke, it was hard to ignore.
As I heard further thunderclaps—lo and behold—
Came a little psychiatrist eighty years old.
He drove a wheeled couch pulled by five fat psychoses

A Visit from St. Sigmund
  [1] Margaret Mead (1901–1978). American anthropologist.

And the gleam in his eye might induce a hypnosis.
Like subliminal meanings his coursers they came
And, consulting his notebook, he called them by name: 20
"Now Schizo, now Fetish, now Fear of Castration!
On Paranoia! on Penis-fixation!
Ach, yes, that big brick through your glass I should mention:
Just a simple device to compel your attention.
You need, boy, to be in an analyst's power:
You talk, I take notes—fifty schillings an hour."
A bag full of symbols he'd slung on his back;
He looked smug as a junk-peddler laden with smack
Or a shrewd politician soliciting votes
And his chinbeard was stiff as a starched billygoat's.   30
Then laying one finger aside of his nose,
He chortled, "What means this? Mein Gott, I suppose
There's a meaning in fingers, in candles and wicks,
In mouseholes und doughnut holes, steeples und sticks.
You see, it's the imminent prospect of sex
That makes all us humans run round till we're wrecks,
Und each innocent infant since people began
Wants to bed with his momma und kill his old man;
So never you fear that you're sick as a swine—
Your hangups are every sane person's und mine.   40
Even Hamlet was hot for his mom—there's the rub;
Even Oedipus Clubfoot was one of the club.
Hmmm, that's humor unconscious." He gave me rib-pokes
And for almost two hours explained phallic jokes.
Then he sprang to his couch, to his crew gave a nod,
And away they all flew like the concept of God.
In the worst of my dreams I can hear him shout still,
"Merry Christmas to all! In the mail comes my bill."

For Analysis
1. Why might Margaret Mead equate Freud with Santa Claus? How does the poem establish and develop that equation? **2.** How many elements of Freudian theory do you recognize in the poem?

Writing Topic
Write an essay discussing why Sigmund Freud is an appropriate figure for a **parody** that elevates him to sainthood.

Peter Meinke   [b. 1932]

Advice to My Son   1965
—for Tim

The trick is, to live your days
as if each one may be your last
(for they go fast, and young men lose their lives
in strange and unimaginable ways)
but at the same time, plan long range
(for they go slow: if you survive
the shattered windshield and the bursting shell
you will arrive
at our approximation here below
of heaven or hell).   10

To be specific, between the peony and the rose
plant squash and spinach, turnips and tomatoes;
beauty is nectar
and nectar, in a desert, saves—
but the stomach craves stronger sustenance
than the honied vine.
Therefore, marry a pretty girl
after seeing her mother;
speak truth to one man,
work with another;   20
and always serve bread with your wine.

But, son,
always serve wine.

For Analysis
1. Explain how the advice of lines 17–21 is logically related to the preceding lines.
2. What do the final two lines tell the reader about the speaker?

Writing Topic
The advice of the first stanza seems contradictory. In what ways does the second stanza attempt to resolve the contradiction or explain "The trick" (l. 1)? What do the various plants and the bread and wine symbolize?

156

Robert Mezey [b. 1935]

My Mother 1970

My mother writes from Trenton,
a comedian to the bone
but underneath, serious
and all heart. "Honey," she says,
"be a mensch[1] and Mary too,
it's no good to worry, you
are doing the best you can
your Dad and everyone
thinks you turned out very well
as long as you pay your bills   10
nobody can say a word
you can tell them to drop dead
so save a dollar it can't
hurt—remember Frank you went
to highschool with? he still lives
with his wife's mother, his wife
works while he writes his books and
did he ever sell a one
the four kids run around naked
36 and he's never had,   20
you'll forgive my expression
even a pot to piss in
or a window to throw it,
such a smart boy he couldn't
read the footprints on the wall
honey you think you know all
the answers you don't, please try
to put some money away
believe me it wouldn't hurt
artist shmartist life's too short   30
for that kind of, forgive me,
horseshit, I know what you want
better than you, all that counts
is to make a good living
and the best of everything,
as Sholem Aleichem said
he was a great writer did

[1] Man, in the sense of "human being."

you ever read his books dear,
you should make what he makes a year
anyway he says some place   40
Poverty is no disgrace
but it's no honor either
that's what I say,
                love,
                    Mother"

June Jordan   [b. 1936]

Memo: 1980

When I hear some woman say she
has finally decided you can spend time with
other women, I wonder what she means: Her
mother? My mother?
I've always despised my woman friends. Even
if they introduced me to a man I found
attractive I have never let them become
what you could call my intimates. Why
should I? Men are the ones with the money and
the big way with waiters and the passkey   10
to excitement in strange places of real
danger and the power to make things happen
like babies or war and all these great ideas
about mass magazines for members of the weaker sex
who need permission
to eat potatoes or a doctor's opinion on orgasm after death
or the latest word on what the female
executive should do, after hours, wearing
what. They must be morons: women!
Don't you think?   20
I guess you could say
I'm stuck in my ways
as
That Cosmopolitan Girl.

For Analysis
1. Explain the title. **2.** What do the first three lines mean? Why would a woman feel
she *can't* spend time with other women? **3.** Does this poem accurately describe the
power relations in our society? Explain. **4.** Describe the **tone** of this poem.

Writing Topic
Examine a few issues of *Cosmopolitan* magazine to show how it inspired this poem.

Eric Ormsby   [b. 1941]

Adages of a Grandmother   1992

Grandmother said to me, "Keep thyself
unspotted from the world." She spoke in quotes.
I got the feeling that she had rehearsed
all her admonitions as a child,
for when she issued them to me she grew
solemn and theatrical. I knew
she tasted in her words some sweet,
indissoluble flavor of the past; but even more,
as though at eighty-five or eighty-six
she stood still in the parlor of her recitation—   10
a plain, studious girl with long, brown braids
(I have the portraits of her as a child)—
and spoke her lessons for approving guests.
Such touches of girlishness accompanied
her adages. And then she gave me dimes
for so many lines of Shakespeare memorized.
For "The quality of mercy . . ." I was paid
a quarter, and at tea I gave her guests
a dollar's worth of Shakespeare with their toast.
"All the world's a stage," she reminded me.   20

Only armed with an adage might I sally forth.
"A foolish son's his mother's grief," she thought.
The world was scriptural and stratified.
It held raw veins of wisdom in its side,
like the Appalachians when we journeyed north.
She sat in the front seat of the Buick, hairnet drawn
over her white hair coiled in a dignified bun,
her straw, beflowered hat alert and prim.
From the back seat I'd study her, my grim
grandmother, with her dictatorial   30
chin, her gold-rimmed spectacles ablaze with all
the glory of the common highway where
field daisies spoke to her in doctrinaire
confidential accents of the master plan
confided to grandmothers by the Son of Man.

Wisdom was talismanic and opaque—
could be carried in a child's small fist
like the personal pebble I fished out of the lake.
And whenever I stepped outside she kissed
my head and armed me with a similitude.   40
Beyond the screen door, past the windowsill,
the bright earth rang with providence until
even the wise ants at my shoe tips moved
in dark amazements of exactitude,
and the small dusty sparrows swooped innumerably.

I write this on the sun porch of the house
where she lay, an invalid, in her last years.
And I'm abashed to realize I blamed
her stiffness and her stubborn uprightness
for much that happened to me afterward.   50
Now I look through the window where she looked
and see the sunlight on the windowsill
and wonder what it signifies,
for now I barely recognize
her world outside, as though sunlight effaced
not only human features but their memory.
Her adages are all scattered in my head
(*Neither a borrower, nor a lender be*),
and I cannot think for thinking of the dead
(*Go to the ant, thou sluggard;*   60
consider her ways, and be wise);
I cannot read the world now with her eyes
(*Sit, Jessica. Look how the floor of heaven*
is thick inlaid with patines of bright gold).
And I, who used to blame her so,
rummage in my pockets for
a nickel's worth of wisdom for my kids.

For Analysis
1. What were the speaker's feelings about his grandmother when he was a child?
2. Explain the meaning of lines 23 and 24. **3.** Discuss the use of **irony** in this poem.
4. How does the speaker finally come to judge his grandmother? Do the final three
lines constitute a tribute to his grandmother?

Writing Topic
Write an essay contrasting your feelings toward a relative when you were a child with
your present feelings. Explain how the change occurred.

Molly Peacock [b. 1947]

Our Room 1984

I tell the children in school sometimes
why I hate alcoholics: my father was one.
"Alcohol" and "disease" I use, and shun
the word "drunk" or even "drinking," since one time
the kids burst out laughing when I told them.
I felt as though they were laughing at me.
I waited for them, wounded, remembering how I imagined they'd howl at me
when I was in grade 5. Acting drunk
is a guaranteed screamer, especially   10
for boys. I'm quiet when I sort the junk
of my childhood for them, quiet so we
will all be quiet, and they can ask what
questions they have to and tell about what
happened to them, too. The classroom becomes
oddly lonely when we talk about our homes.

For Analysis

1. The implication of line 6 is that the children were laughing not at the speaker but at something else. What might that have been? **2.** Describe the speaker's attitude toward her classmates. **3.** Explain the title.

Writing Topic

Have you ever experienced shame about your family? Describe what it was that caused the shame, your feelings at the time, and your present feelings about it.

Katherine McAlpine [b. 1948]

Plus C'est la Même Chose[1] 1994

*Lines Written upon Chaperoning the
Seventh Grade Dance*

When did these little girls turn into women?
Lip-glossed and groomed, alarmingly possessed
of polish, poise and, in some cases, breasts,

Plus C'est la Même Chose
    [1] The title comes from the French expression *plus ça change, plus c'est la même chose,* which means "the more things change, the more they remain the same."

they're clustered at one corner of the gym in
elaborate indifference to the boys,
who, at the other end, convene with cables,
adjusting speakers, tuners and turntables
to make the optimum amount of noise.
If nobody plans to dance, what's this dance for?
Finally the boys all gather in formation,   10
tentatively begin a group migration
across the fearsome distance of the floor—
and then retreat, noticing no one's there.
The girls have gone, en masse, to fix their hair.

For Analysis
1. What is the **tone** of this sonnet? Point to specific elements to support your response. **2.** Explain the title. **3.** Explain the appropriateness of "elaborate indifference"
(l. 5), "gather in formation" (l. 10), and "migration" (l. 11).

Writing Topic
Write an essay in which you use one of the following as a thesis statement: (1) the poem
embodies a traditional, sexist view of gender differences, or (2) the poem describes,
without making a judgment, the culturally determined differences between males and
females. If you disagree with both of these statements, formulate your own.

<u>Lawrence Kearney</u> [b. 1948]

Father Answers His Adversaries 1980

It's early March, Eisenhower still
president, & Mother's heating up supper
for the third time tonight.
We're at the table doing homework,
& she tells us Father's next in line
for foreman, that today he'll know for sure.
He's three hours late.

Half past eight the Chevy
screeches into the carport.
For a minute, nothing.   10
Then the sudden slam, & the thump downstairs
to the basement. Beneath our feet
Father lays into the workbench
with a sledgehammer—the jam jars

of nails, of screws, of nuts & bolts
he'd taken years to sort out
exploding against the wall.

Later, sheepish, he comes up,
slumps in his seat & asks for supper.
And when Mother brings his plate   20
& he looks up at her
& she takes his head on her breast,
he blushes, turns away, & spits out
that final, weary-mouthed answer
to all of it—General Motors & the bosses
& the union pimps & the punched-out Johnnies,
every yes-man goddam ass-lick
who'd ever been jumped to foreman
over him—*aah, crap's like cream,*
it rises.   30

For Analysis

1. How would you characterize the family? Happy? Unhappy? Close-knit? Explain.
2. Why do you suppose the father did not get the job as foreman? **3.** Why is the father described as "sheepish" (l. 18)? Why does he blush (l. 23)? **4.** Put into your own words the father's answer to his adversaries.

Writing Topic

Write an essay describing someone you know who was unfairly passed over for a promotion (or fired from a job). Did he or she feel the same bitterness and helplessness as the father in this poem? What became of the person?

Katharyn Howd Machan   [b. 1952]

Hazel Tells LaVerne   1976

last night
im cleanin out my
howard johnsons ladies room
when all of a sudden
up pops this frog
musta come from the sewer
swimmin aroun an tryin ta
climb up the sida the bowl
so i goes ta flushm down

but sohelpmegod he starts talkin   10
bout a golden ball
an how i can be a princess
me a princess
well my mouth drops
all the way to the floor
an he says
kiss me just kiss me
once on the nose
well i screams
ya little green pervert   20
an i hitsm with my mop
an has ta flush
the toilet down three times
me
a princess

For Analysis
1. How would you describe Hazel? **2.** What does Hazel's language tell us about her?
3. Would the use of punctuation change the poem in any way?

Writing Topic
Write an analysis of this poem's humor.

Sandra Cisneros   [b. 1954]

My Wicked Wicked Ways   1987

This is my father.
See? He is young.
He looks like Errol Flynn.[1]
He is wearing a hat
that tips over one eye,
a suit that fits him good,
and baggy pants.
He is also wearing
those awful shoes,
the two-toned ones   10
my mother hates.

My Wicked Wicked Ways
   [1] Errol Flynn (1909–1959) was a handsome leading man in many Hollywood movies during the
1940s.

Here is my mother.
She is not crying.
She cannot look into the lens
because the sun is bright.
The woman,
the one my father knows,
is not here.
She does not come till later.

My mother will get very mad.   20
Her face will turn red
and she will throw one shoe.
My father will say nothing.
After a while everyone
will forget it.
Years and years will pass.
My mother will stop mentioning it.

This is me she is carrying.
I am a baby.
She does not know   30
I will turn out bad.

For Analysis
1. Why does the speaker tell us that her mother "is not crying"? **2.** What will the speaker's mother "get very mad" about? **3.** What is the connection between the last four lines and the rest of the poem?

Writing Topic
Discuss the meaning of the final line of the poem. What does the speaker mean by *bad*?

Drama

Sophocles   [496?–406 B.C.]

Oedipus Rex[1]   ca. 429 B.C.

PERSONS REPRESENTED

Oedipus	**Messenger**
A Priest	**Shepherd of Laïos**
Creon	**Second Messenger**
Teiresias	**Chorus of Theban Elders**
Iocastê	

Scene

Before the palace of Oedipus, King of Thebes. A central door and two lateral doors open onto a platform which runs the length of the facade. On the platform, right and left, are altars; and three steps lead down into the "orchestra," or chorus-ground. At the beginning of the action these steps are crowded by suppliants who have brought branches and chaplets of olive leaves and who lie in various attitudes of despair. Oedipus enters.

Prologue

Oedipus.   My children, generations of the living
   In the line of Kadmos,[2] nursed at his ancient hearth:
   Why have you strewn yourselves before these altars
   In supplication, with your boughs and garlands?
   The breath of incense rises from the city
   With a sound of prayer and lamentation.

---

[1] An English version by Dudley Fitts and Robert Fitzgerald.   [2] The legendary founder of Thebes.

Children,
I would not have you speak through messengers,
And therefore I have come myself to hear you—
I, Oedipus, who bear the famous name.
[*To a Priest.*] You, there, since you are eldest in the company,   10
Speak for them all, tell me what preys upon you,
Whether you come in dread, or crave some blessing:
Tell me, and never doubt that I will help you
In every way I can; I should be heartless
Were I not moved to find you suppliant here.

Priest.   Great Oedipus, O powerful King of Thebes!
You see how all the ages of our people
Cling to your altar steps: here are boys
Who can barely stand alone, and here are priests
By weight of age, as I am a priest of God,   20
And young men chosen from those yet unmarried;
As for the others, all that multitude,
They wait with olive chaplets in the squares,
At the two shrines of Pallas,³ and where Apollo⁴
Speaks in the glowing embers.

Your own eyes
Must tell you: Thebes is in her extremity
And can not lift her head from the surge of death.
A rust consumes the buds and fruits of the earth;
The herds are sick; children die unborn,
And labor is vain. The god of plague and pyre   30
Raids like detestable lightning through the city,
And all the house of Kadmos is laid waste,
All emptied, and all darkened: Death alone
Battens upon the misery of Thebes.

You are not one of the immortal gods, we know;
Yet we have come to you to make our prayer
As to the man of all men best in adversity
And wisest in the ways of God. You saved us
From the Sphinx,⁵ that flinty singer, and the tribute
We paid to her so long; yet you were never   40
Better informed than we, nor could we teach you:
It was some god breathed in you to set us free.
Therefore, O mighty King, we turn to you:

³ Athena, goddess of wisdom.   ⁴ God of sunlight, medicine, and prophecy.   ⁵ A winged
monster, with a woman's head and breasts and a lion's body, that destroyed those who failed to answer her riddle: "What walks on four feet in the morning, two at noon, and three in the evening?"
When the young Oedipus correctly answered, "Man" ("three" alluding to a cane in old age), the
Sphinx killed herself, and the plague ended.

Find us our safety, find us a remedy,
Whether by counsel of the gods or men.
A king of wisdom tested in the past
Can act in a time of troubles, and act well.
Noblest of men, restore
Life to your city! Think how all men call you
Liberator for your triumph long ago;   50
Ah, when your years of kingship are remembered,
Let them not say *We rose, but later fell*—
Keep the State from going down in the storm!
Once, years ago, with happy augury,
You brought us fortune; be the same again!
No man questions your power to rule the land:
But rule over men, not over a dead city!
Ships are only hulls, citadels are nothing,
When no life moves in the empty passageways.

Oedipus.   Poor children! You may be sure I know   60
All that you longed for in your coming here.
I know that you are deathly sick; and yet,
Sick as you are, not one is as sick as I.
Each of you suffers in himself alone
His anguish, not another's; but my spirit
Groans for the city, for myself, for you.

I was not sleeping, you are not waking me.
No, I have been in tears for a long while
And in my restless thought walked many ways.
In all my search, I found one helpful course,   70
And that I have taken: I have sent Creon,
Son of Menoikeus, brother of the Queen,
To Delphi, Apollo's place of revelation,
To learn there, if he can,
What act or pledge of mine may save the city.
I have counted the days, and now, this very day,
I am troubled, for he has overstayed his time.
What is he doing? He has been gone too long.
Yet whenever he comes back, I should do ill
To scant whatever hint the god may give.   80

Priest.   It is a timely promise. At this instant
They tell me Creon is here.

Oedipus.   O Lord Apollo!
May his news be fair as his face is radiant!

Priest.   It could not be otherwise: he is crowned with bay,
The chaplet is thick with berries.

Oedipus.   We shall soon know;
He is near enough to hear us now.

[*Enter Creon.*]

                              O Prince:
Brother: son of Menoikeus:
What answer do you bring us from the god?
Creon.   It is favorable. I can tell you, great afflictions
Will turn out well, if they are taken well.   90
Oedipus.   What was the oracle? These vague words
Leave me still hanging between hope and fear.
Creon.   Is it your pleasure to hear me with all these
Gathered around us? I am prepared to speak,
But should we not go in?
Oedipus.   Let them all hear it.
It is for them I suffer, more than for myself.
Creon.   Then I will tell you what I heard at Delphi.

In plain words
The god commands us to expel from the land of Thebes
An old defilement that it seems we shelter.   100
It is a deathly thing, beyond expiation.
We must not let it feed upon us longer.
Oedipus.   What defilement? How shall we rid ourselves of it?
Creon.   By exile or death, blood for blood. It was
Murder that brought the plague-wind on the city.
Oedipus.   Murder of whom? Surely the god has named him?
Creon.   My lord: long ago Laïos was our king,
Before you came to govern us.
Oedipus.   I know;
I learned of him from others; I never saw him.
Creon.   He was murdered; and Apollo commands us now   110
To take revenge upon whoever killed him.
Oedipus.   Upon whom? Where are they? Where shall we find a clue
To solve that crime, after so many years?
Creon.   Here in this land, he said.
                              If we make enquiry,
We may touch things that otherwise escape us.
Oedipus.   Tell me: Was Laïos murdered in his house,
Or in the fields, or in some foreign country?
Creon.   He said he planned to make a pilgrimage.
He did not come home again.
Oedipus.   And was there no one,

No witness, no companion, to tell what happened? 120
Creon. They were all killed but one, and he got away
So frightened that he could remember one thing only.
Oedipus. What was that one thing? One may be the key
To everything, if we resolve to use it.
Creon. He said that a band of highwaymen attacked them,
Outnumbered them, and overwhelmed the King.
Oedipus. Strange, that a highwayman should be so daring—
Unless some faction here bribed him to do it.
Creon. We thought of that. But after Laïos' death
New troubles arose and we had no avenger. 130
Oedipus. What troubles could prevent your hunting down the killers?
Creon. The riddling Sphinx's song
Made us deaf to all mysteries but her own.
Oedipus. Then once more I must bring what is dark to light.
It is most fitting that Apollo shows,
As you do, this compunction for the dead.
You shall see how I stand by you, as I should,
To avenge the city and the city's god,
And not as though it were for some distant friend,
But for my own sake, to be rid of evil. 140
Whoever killed King Laïos might—who knows?—
Decide at any moment to kill me as well.
By avenging the murdered king I protect myself.
Come, then, my children: leave the altar steps,
Lift up your olive boughs!
                              One of you go
And summon the people of Kadmos to gather here.
I will do all that I can; you may tell them that.

[*Exit a page.*]

So, with the help of God,
We shall be saved—or else indeed we are lost.
Priest. Let us rise, children. It was for this we came, 150
And now the King has promised it himself.
Phoibos[6] has sent us an oracle; may he descend
Himself to save us and drive out the plague.

[*Exeunt Oedipus and Creon into the palace by the central door. The Priest and the suppliants disperse R and L. After a short pause the Chorus enters the orchestra.*]

---

[6] Phoebus Apollo, god of the sun.

Párodos[7]

Chorus.   What is God singing in his profound   [*Strophe 1*]
  Delphi of gold and shadow?
  What oracle for Thebes, the sunwhipped city?
  Fear unjoints me, the roots of my heart tremble.
  Now I remember, O Healer, your power, and wonder;
  Will you send doom like a sudden cloud, or weave it
  Like nightfall of the past?
  Speak, speak to us, issue of holy sound:
  Dearest to our expectancy: be tender!

  Let me pray to Athenê, the immortal daughter of Zeus,   [*Antistrophe 1*]
  And to Artemis her sister
  Who keeps her famous throne in the market ring,
  And to Apollo, bowman at the far butts of heaven—

  O gods, descend! Like three streams leap against
  The fires of our grief, the fires of darkness;
  Be swift to bring us rest!

  As in the old time from the brilliant house
  Of air you stepped to save us, come again!

  Now our afflictions have no end,   [*Strophe 2*]
  Now all our stricken host lies down   20
  And no man fights off death with his mind;

  The noble plowland bears no grain,
  And groaning mothers can not bear—

  See, how our lives like birds take wing,
  Like sparks that fly when a fire soars,
  To the shore of the god of evening.

  The plague burns on, it is pitiless,   [*Antistrophe 2*]
  Though pallid children laden with death
  Lie unwept in the stony ways,

---

[7] The *Párodos* is the ode sung by the Chorus as it entered the theater and moved down the aisles to the playing area. The *strophe*, in Greek tragedy, is the unit of verse the Chorus chanted as it moved to the left in a dance rhythm. The Chorus sang the *antistrophe* as it moved to the right and the *epode* while standing still.

And old gray women by every path   30
Flock to the strand about the altars
There to strike their breasts and cry
Worship of Phoibos in wailing prayers:
Be kind, God's golden child!

There are no swords in this attack by fire,   [*Strophe 3*]
No shields, but we are ringed with cries.
Send the besieger plunging from our homes
Into the vast sea-room of the Atlantic
Or into the waves that foam eastward of Thrace—
For the day ravages what the night spares—   40

Destroy our enemy, lord of the thunder!
Let him be riven by lightning from heaven!

Phoibus Apollo, stretch the sun's bowstring,   [*Antistrophe 3*]
That golden cord, until it sing for us,
Flashing arrows in heaven!
    Artemis, Huntress
Race with flaring lights upon our mountains!

O scarlet god, O golden-banded brow,
O Theban Bacchos in a storm of Maenads,[8]

[*Enter Oedipus, C.*]

Whirl upon Death, that all the Undying hate!
Come with blinding cressets, come in joy!   50

Scene I

Oedipus. Is this your prayer? It may be answered. Come,
 Listen to me, act as the crisis demands,
 And you shall have relief from all these evils.
 Until now I was a stranger to this tale,
 As I had been a stranger to the crime.
 Could I track down the murderer without a clue?
 But now, friends,

---

[8] Bacchos is the god of wine and revelry, hence scarlet-faced. The Maenads were Bacchos' female attendants.

As one who became a citizen after the murder,
I make this proclamation to all Thebans:
If any man knows by whose hand Laïos, son of Labdakos,   10
Met his death, I direct that man to tell me everything,
No matter what he fears for having so long withheld it.
Let it stand as promised that no further trouble
Will come to him, but he may leave the land in safety.

Moreover: If anyone knows the murderer to be foreign,
Let him not keep silent: he shall have his reward from me.
However, if he does conceal it, if any man
Fearing for his friend or for himself disobeys this edict,
Hear what I propose to do:

I solemnly forbid the people of this country,   20
Where power and throne are mine, ever to receive that man
Or speak to him, no matter who he is, or let him
Join in sacrifice, lustration, or in prayer.
I decree that he be driven from every house,
Being, as he is, corruption itself to us: the Delphic
Voice of Zeus has pronounced this revelation.
Thus I associate myself with the oracle
And take the side of the murdered king.

As for the criminal, I pray to God—
Whether it be a lurking thief, or one of a number—   30
I pray that that man's life be consumed in evil and wretchedness.
And as for me, this curse applies no less
If it should turn out that the culprit is my guest here,
Sharing my hearth.
                    You have heard the penalty.
I lay it on you now to attend to this
For my sake, for Apollo's, for the sick
Sterile city that heaven has abandoned.
Suppose the oracle had given you no command:
Should this defilement go uncleansed for ever?
You should have found the murderer: your king,   40
A noble king, had been destroyed!
                    Now I,
Having the power that he held before me,
Having his bed, begetting children there
Upon his wife, as he would have, had he lived—
Their son would have been my children's brother,
If Laïos had had luck in fatherhood!
(But surely ill luck rushed upon his reign)—

I say I take the son's part, just as though
I were his son, to press the fight for him
And see it won! I'll find the hand that brought   50
Death to Labdakos' and Polydoros' child,
Heir of Kadmos' and Agenor's line.
And as for those who fail me,
May the gods deny them the fruit of the earth,
Fruit of the womb, and may they rot utterly!
Let them be wretched as we are wretched, and worse!

For you, for loyal Thebans, and for all
Who find my actions right, I pray the favor
Of justice, and of all the immortal gods.
Choragos.[9]   Since I am under oath, my lord, I swear   60
I did not do the murder. I can not name
The murderer. Might not the oracle
That has ordained the search tell where to find him?
Oedipus.   An honest question. But no man in the world
Can make the gods do more than the gods will.
Choragos.   There is one last expedient—
Oedipus.   Tell me what it is.
Though it seem slight, you must not hold it back.
Choragos.   A lord clairvoyant to the lord Apollo,
As we all know, is the skilled Teiresias.
One might learn much about this from him, Oedipus.   70
Oedipus.   I am not wasting time:
Creon spoke of this, and I have sent for him—
Twice, in fact; it is strange that he is not here.
Choragos.   The other matter—that old report—seems useless.
Oedipus.   Tell me. I am interested in all reports.
Choragos.   The King was said to have been killed by highwaymen.
Oedipus.   I know. But we have no witnesses to that.
Choragos.   If the killer can feel a particle of dread,
Your curse will bring him out of hiding!
Oedipus.   No.
The man who dared that act will fear no curse.   80

[*Enter the blind seer Teiresias, led by a page.*]

Choragos.   But there is one man who may detect the criminal.
This is Teiresias, this is the holy prophet
In whom, alone of all men, truth was born.
Oedipus.   Teiresias: seer: student of mysteries,

---

[9] Choragos is the leader of the Chorus.

Of all that's taught and all that no man tells,
Secrets of Heaven and secrets of the earth:
Blind though you are, you know the city lies
Sick with plague; and from this plague, my lord,
We find that you alone can guard or save us.

Possibly you did not hear the messengers?   90
Apollo, when we sent to him,
Sent us back word that this great pestilence
Would lift, but only if we established clearly
The identity of those who murdered Laïos.
They must be killed or exiled.
                              Can you use
Birdflight or any art of divination
To purify yourself, and Thebes, and me
From this contagion? We are in your hands.
There is no fairer duty
Than that of helping others in distress.   100
Teiresias.   How dreadful knowledge of the truth can be
When there's no help in truth! I knew this well,
But did not act on it: else I should not have come.
Oedipus.   What is troubling you? Why are your eyes so cold?
Teiresias.   Let me go home. Bear your own fate, and I'll
Bear mine. It is better so: trust what I say.
Oedipus.   What you say is ungracious and unhelpful
To your native country. Do not refuse to speak.
Teiresias.   When it comes to speech, your own is neither temperate
Nor opportune. I wish to be more prudent.   110
Oedipus.   In God's name, we all beg you—
Teiresias.   You are all ignorant.
No; I will never tell you what I know.
Now it is my misery; then, it would be yours.
Oedipus.   What! You do know something, and will not tell us?
You would betray us all and wreck the State?
Teiresias.   I do not intend to torture myself, or you.
Why persist in asking? You will not persuade me.
Oedipus.   What a wicked old man you are! You'd try a stone's
Patience! Out with it! Have you no feeling at all?
Teiresias.   You call me unfeeling. If you could only see   120
The nature of your own feelings . . .
Oedipus.   Why,
Who would not feel as I do? Who could endure
Your arrogance toward the city?
Teiresias.   What does it matter!
Whether I speak or not, it is bound to come.

Oedipus.   Then, if "it" is bound to come, you are bound to tell me.
Teiresias.   No, I will not go on. Rage as you please.
Oedipus.   Rage? Why not!
                              And I'll tell you what I think:
    You planned it, you had it done, you all but
    Killed him with your own hands: if you had eyes,
    I'd say the crime was yours, and yours alone.   130
Teiresias.   So? I charge you, then,
    Abide by the proclamation you have made:
    From this day forth
    Never speak again to these men or to me;
    You yourself are the pollution of this country.
Oedipus.   You dare say that! Can you possibly think you have
    Some way of going free, after such insolence?
Teiresias.   I have gone free. It is the truth sustains me.
Oedipus.   Who taught you shamelessness? It was not your craft.
Teiresias.   You did. You made me speak. I did not want to.   140
Oedipus.   Speak what? Let me hear it again more clearly.
Teiresias.   Was it not clear before? Are you tempting me?
Oedipus.   I did not understand it. Say it again.
Teiresias.   I say that you are the murderer whom you seek.
Oedipus.   Now twice you have spat out infamy! You'll pay for it!
Teiresias.   Would you care for more? Do you wish to be really angry?
Oedipus.   Say what you will. Whatever you say is worthless.
Teiresias.   I say you live in hideous shame with those
    Most dear to you. You can not see the evil.
Oedipus.   It seems you can go on mouthing like this for ever.   150
Teiresias.   I can, if there is power in truth.
Oedipus.   There is:
    But not for you, not for you,
    You sightless, witless, senseless, mad old man!
Teiresias.   You are the madman. There is no one here
    Who will not curse you soon, as you curse me.
Oedipus.   You child of endless night! You can not hurt me
    Or any other man who sees the sun.
Teiresias.   True: it is not from me your fate will come.
    That lies within Apollo's competence,
    As it is his concern.
Oedipus.   Tell me: 160
    Are you speaking for Creon or for yourself?
Teiresias.   Creon is no threat. You weave your own doom.
Oedipus.   Wealth, power, craft of statesmanship!
    Kingly position, everywhere admired!
    What savage envy is stored up against these,
    If Creon, whom I trusted, Creon my friend,

For this great office which the city once
Put in my hands unsought—if for this power
Creon desires in secret to destroy me!

He has brought this decrepit fortune-teller, this   170
Collector of dirty pennies, this prophet fraud—
Why, he is no more clairvoyant than I am!
                                        Tell us:
Has your mystic mummery ever approached the truth?
When that hellcat the Sphinx was performing here,
What help were you to these people?
Her magic was not for the first man who came along:
It demanded a real exorcist. Your birds—
What good were they? or the gods, for the matter of that?
But I came by,
Oedipus, the simple man, who knows nothing—   180
I thought it out for myself, no birds helped me!
And this is the man you think you can destroy,
That you may be close to Creon when he's king!
Well, you and your friend Creon, it seems to me,
Will suffer most. If you were not an old man,
You would have paid already for your plot.
Choragos.   We can not see that his words or yours
Have been spoken except in anger, Oedipus,
And of anger we have no need. How can God's will
Be accomplished best? That is what most concerns us.   190
Teiresias.   You are a king. But where argument's concerned
I am your man, as much a king as you.
I am not your servant, but Apollo's.
I have no need of Creon to speak for me.

Listen to me. You mock my blindness, do you?
But I say that you, with both your eyes, are blind:
You can not see the wretchedness of your life,
Nor in whose house you live, no, nor with whom.
Who are your father and mother? Can you tell me?
You do not even know the blind wrongs   200
That you have done them, on earth and in the world below.
But the double lash of your parents' curse will whip you
Out of this land some day, with only night
Upon your precious eyes.
Your cries then—where will they not be heard?
What fastness of Kithairon[10] will not echo them?

---

[10] A mountain range near Thebes where the infant Oedipus was left to die.

And that bridal-descant of yours—you'll know it then,
The song they sang when you came here to Thebes
And found your misguided berthing.
All this, and more, that you can not guess at now,   210
Will bring you to yourself among your children.

Be angry, then. Curse Creon. Curse my words.
I tell you, no man that walks upon the earth
Shall be rooted out more horribly than you.
Oedipus.   Am I to bear this from him?—Damnation
Take you! Out of this place! Out of my sight!
Teiresias.   I would not have come at all if you had not asked me.
Oedipus.   Could I have told that you'd talk nonsense, that
You'd come here to make a fool of yourself, and of me?
Teiresias.   A fool? Your parents thought me sane enough.   220
Oedipus.   My parents again!—Wait: who were my parents?
Teiresias.   This day will give you a father, and break your heart.
Oedipus.   Your infantile riddles! Your damned abracadabra!
Teiresias.   You were a great man once at solving riddles.
Oedipus.   Mock me with that if you like; you will find it true.
Teiresias.   It was true enough. It brought about your ruin.
Oedipus.   But if it saved this town?
Teiresias [*to the page*].   Boy, give me your hand.
Oedipus.   Yes, boy; lead him away.
                                         While you are here
We can do nothing. Go; leave us in peace.
Teiresias.   I will go when I have said what I have to say.   230
How can you hurt me? And I tell you again:
The man you have been looking for all this time,
The damned man, the murderer of Laïos,
That man is in Thebes. To your mind he is foreignborn,
But it will soon be shown that he is a Theban,
A revelation that will fail to please.
                                         A blind man,
Who has his eyes now; a penniless man, who is rich now;
And he will go tapping the strange earth with his staff;
To the children with whom he lives now he will be
Brother and father—the very same; to her   240
Who bore him, son and husband—the very same
Who came to his father's bed, wet with his father's blood.
Enough. Go think that over.
If later you find error in what I have said,
You may say that I have no skill in prophecy.

[*Exit Teiresias, led by his page. Oedipus goes into the palace.*]

Ode I

Chorus.   The Delphic stone of prophecies   [*Strophe 1*]
   Remembers ancient regicide
   And a still bloody hand.
   That killer's hour of flight has come.
   He must be stronger than riderless
   Coursers of untiring wind,
   For the son of Zeus[11] armed with his father's thunder
   Leaps in lightning after him;
   And the Furies follow him, the sad Furies.[12]

   Holy Parnassos' peak of snow   [*Antistrophe 1*]
   Flashes and blinds that secret man,
   That all shall hunt him down:
   Though he may roam the forest shade
   Like a bull gone wild from pasture
   To rage through glooms of stone.
   Doom comes down on him; flight will not avail him;
   For the world's heart calls him desolate,
   And the immortal Furies follow, for ever follow.

   But now a wilder thing is heard   [*Strophe 2*]
   From the old man skilled at hearing Fate in the wingbeat of a bird.   20
   Bewildered as a blown bird, my soul hovers and can not find
   Foothold in this debate, or any reason or rest of mind.
   But no man ever brought—none can bring
   Proof of strife between Thebes' royal house,
   Labdakos' line, and the son of Polybos;[13]
   And never until now has any man brought word
   Of Laïos' dark death staining Oedipus the King.

   Divine Zeus and Apollo hold   [*Antistrophe 2*]
   Perfect intelligence alone of all tales ever told;
   And well though this diviner works, he works in his own night;   30
   No man can judge that rough unknown or trust in second sight,
   For wisdom changes hands among the wise.
   Shall I believe my great lord criminal
   At a raging word that a blind old man let fall?
   I saw him, when the carrion woman faced him of old,
   Prove his heroic mind! These evil words are lies.

---

[11] I.e., Apollo (see note 3).   [12] The goddesses of divine vengeance.   [13] Labdakos was an early king of Thebes and an ancestor of Oedipus. Oedipus is mistakenly referred to as the son of Polybus.

Scene II

Creon.   Men of Thebes:
I am told that heavy accusations
Have been brought against me by King Oedipus.

I am not the kind of man to bear this tamely.

If in these present difficulties
He holds me accountable for any harm to him
Through anything I have said or done—why, then,
I do not value life in this dishonor.
It is not as though this rumor touched upon
Some private indiscretion. The matter is grave.   10
The fact is that I am being called disloyal
To the State, to my fellow citizens, to my friends.
Choragos.   He may have spoken in anger, not from his mind.
Creon.   But did you not hear him say I was the one
Who seduced the old prophet into lying?
Choragos.   The thing was said; I do not know how seriously.
Creon.   But you were watching him! Were his eyes steady?
Did he look like a man in his right mind?
Choragos.   I do not know.
I can not judge the behavior of great men.
But here is the King himself.

[*Enter Oedipus.*]

Oedipus.   So you dared come back.   20
Why? How brazen of you to come to my house,
You murderer!
                    Do you think I do not know
That you plotted to kill me, plotted to steal my throne?
Tell me, in God's name: am I coward, a fool,
That you should dream you could accomplish this?
A fool who could not see your slippery game?
A coward, not to fight back when I saw it?
You are the fool, Creon, are you not? hoping
Without support or friends to get a throne?
Thrones may be won or bought: you could do neither.   30
Creon.   Now listen to me. You have talked; let me talk, too.
You can not judge unless you know the facts.
Oedipus.   You speak well: there is one fact; but I find it hard
To learn from the deadliest enemy I have.

Creon.   That above all I must dispute with you.
Oedipus.   That above all I will not hear you deny.
Creon.   If you think there is anything good in being stubborn
    Against all reason, then I say you are wrong.
Oedipus.   If you think a man can sin against his own kind
    And not be punished for it, I say you are mad.   40
Creon.   I agree. But tell me: what have I done to you?
Oedipus.   You advised me to send for that wizard, did you not?
Creon.   I did. I should do it again.
Oedipus.   Very well. Now tell me:
    How long has it been since Laïos—
Creon.   What of Laïos?
Oedipus.   Since he vanished in that onset by the road?
Creon.   It was long ago, a long time.
Oedipus.   And this prophet,
    Was he practicing here then?
Creon.   He was; and with honor, as now.
Oedipus.   Did he speak of me at that time?
Creon.   He never did;
    At least, not when I was present.
Oedipus.   But . . . the enquiry?
    I suppose you held one?
Creon.   We did, but we learned nothing.   50
Oedipus.   Why did the prophet not speak against me then?
Creon.   I do not know; and I am the kind of man
    Who holds his tongue when he has no facts to go on.
Oedipus.   There's one fact that you know, and you could tell it.
Creon.   What fact is that? If I know it, you shall have it.
Oedipus.   If he were not involved with you, he could not say
    That it was I who murdered Laïos.
Creon.   If he says that, you are the one that knows it!—
    But now it is my turn to question you.
Oedipus.   Put your questions. I am no murderer.   60
Creon.   First then: You married my sister?
Oedipus.   I married your sister.
Creon.   And you rule the kingdom equally with her?
Oedipus.   Everything that she wants she has from me.
Creon.   And I am the third, equal to both of you?
Oedipus.   That is why I call you a bad friend.
Creon.   No. Reason it out, as I have done.
    Think of this first. Would any sane man prefer
    Power, with all a king's anxieties,
    To that same power and the grace of sleep?
    Certainly not I.   70
    I have never longed for the king's power—only his rights.

Would any wise man differ from me in this?
As matters stand, I have my way in everything
With your consent, and no responsibilities.
If I were king, I should be a slave to policy.

How could I desire a scepter more
Than what is now mine—untroubled influence?
No, I have not gone mad; I need no honors,
Except those with the perquisites I have now.
I am welcome everywhere; every man salutes me,   80
And those who want your favor seek my ear,
Since I know how to manage what they ask.
Should I exchange this ease for that anxiety?
Besides, no sober mind is treasonable.
I hate anarchy
And never would deal with any man who likes it.

Test what I have said. Go to the priestess
At Delphi, ask if I quoted her correctly.
And as for this other thing: if I am found
Guilty of treason with Teiresias,   90
Then sentence me to death! You have my word
It is a sentence I should cast my vote for—
But not without evidence!
                           You do wrong
When you take good men for bad, bad men for good.
A true friend thrown aside—why, life itself
Is not more precious!
                           In time you will know this well:
For time, and time alone, will show the just man,
Though scoundrels are discovered in a day.
Choragos.   This is well said, and a prudent man would ponder it.
Judgments too quickly formed are dangerous.   100
Oedipus.   But is he not quick in his duplicity?
And shall I not be quick to parry him?
Would you have me stand still, hold my peace, and let
This man win everything, through my inaction?
Creon.   And you want—what is it, then? To banish me?
Oedipus.   No, not exile. It is your death I want,
So that all the world may see what treason means.
Creon.   You will persist, then? You will not believe me?
Oedipus.   How can I believe you?
Creon.   Then you are a fool.
Oedipus.   To save myself?

Creon.   In justice, think of me.   110
Oedipus.   You are evil incarnate.
Creon.   But suppose that you are wrong?
Oedipus.   Still I must rule.
Creon.   But not if you rule badly.
Oedipus.   O city, city!
Creon.   It is my city, too!
Choragos.   Now, my lords, be still. I see the Queen,
  Iocastê, coming from her palace chambers;
  And it is time she came, for the sake of you both.
  This dreadful quarrel can be resolved through her.   120

[*Enter Iocastê.*]

Iocastê.   Poor foolish men, what wicked din is this?
  With Thebes sick to death, is it not shameful
  That you should rake some private quarrel up?
  [*To Oedipus.*] Come into the house.
                         —And you, Creon, go now:
  Let us have no more of this tumult over nothing.
Creon.   Nothing? No, sister: what your husband plans for me
  Is one of two great evils: exile or death.
Oedipus.   He is right.
                    Why, woman I have caught him squarely
  Plotting against my life.
Creon.   No! Let me die
  Accurst if ever I have wished you harm!
Iocastê.   Ah, believe it, Oedipus!
  In the name of the gods, respect this oath of his
  For my sake, for the sake of these people here!   130

Choragos.   Open your mind to her my lord. Be ruled by her,   [*Strophe 1*]
  I beg you!
Oedipus.   What would you have me do?
Choragos.   Respect Creon's word. He has never spoken like a fool,
  And now he has sworn an oath.
Oedipus.   You know what you ask?
Choragos.   I do.
Oedipus.   Speak on, then.
Choragos.   A friend so sworn should not be baited so,
  In blind malice, and without final proof.
Oedipus.   You are aware, I hope, that what you say
  Means death for me, or exile at the least.

Choragos. No, I swear by Helios,[14] first in Heaven! [*Strophe 2*]
  May I die friendless and accurst, 140
  The worst of deaths, if ever I meant that!
    It is the withering fields
      That hurt my sick heart:
    Must we bear all these ills,
      And now your bad blood as well?
Oedipus. Then let him go. And let me die, if I must,
  Or be driven by him in shame from the land of Thebes.
  It is your unhappiness, and not his talk,
  That touches me.
              As for him—
  Wherever he is, I will hate him as long as I live. 150
Creon. Ugly in yielding, as you were ugly in rage!
  Natures like yours chiefly torment themselves.
Oedipus. Can you not go? Can you not leave me?
Creon.   I can.
  You do not know me; but the city knows me,
  And in its eyes I am just, if not in yours.

[*Exit Creon.*]

Choragos. Lady Iocastê, did you not ask the King to go [*Antistrophe 1*]
  to his chambers?
Iocastê. First tell me what has happened.
Choragos. There was suspicion without evidence; yet it rankled
  As even false charges will.
Iocastê.   On both sides?
Choragos.   On both.
Iocastê.   But what was said?
Choragos. Oh let it rest, let it be done with! 160
  Have we not suffered enough?
Oedipus. You see to what your decency has brought you:
  You have made difficulties where my heart saw none.

Choragos. Oedipus, it is not once only I have told you— [*Antistrophe 2*]
  You must know I should count myself unwise
  To the point of madness, should I now forsake you—
    You, under whose hand,
      In the storm of another time,
    Our dear land sailed out free.
      But now stand fast at the helm! 170

---

[14] The sun god.

Iocastê.   In God's name, Oedipus, inform your wife as well:
  Why are you so set in this hard anger?
Oedipus.   I will tell you, for none of these men deserves
  My confidence as you do. It is Creon's work,
  His treachery, his plotting against me.
Iocastê.   Go on, if you can make this clear to me.
Oedipus.   He charges me with the murder of Laïos.
Iocastê.   Has he some knowledge? Or does he speak from hearsay?
Oedipus.   He would not commit himself to such a charge,
  But he has brought in that damnable soothsayer   180
  To tell his story.
Iocastê.   Set your mind at rest.
  If it is a question of soothsayers, I tell you
  That you will find no man whose craft gives knowledge
  Of the unknowable.
                    Here is my proof:

An oracle was reported to Laïos once
(I will not say from Phoibos himself, but from
His appointed ministers, at any rate)
That his doom would be death at the hands of his own son—
His son, born of his flesh and of mine!

Now, you remember the story: Laïos was killed   190
By marauding strangers where three highways meet;
But his child had not been three days in this world
Before the King had pierced the baby's ankles
And left him to die on a lonely mountainside.

Thus, Apollo never caused that child
To kill his father, and it was not Laïos' fate
To die at the hands of his son, as he had feared.
This is what prophets and prophecies are worth!
Have no dread of them.
                  It is God himself
Who can show us what he wills, in his own way.   200
Oedipus.   How strange a shadowy memory crossed my mind,
  Just now while you were speaking; it chilled my heart.
Iocastê.   What do you mean? What memory do you speak of?
Oedipus.   If I understand you, Laïos was killed
  At a place where three roads meet.
Iocastê.   So it was said;
  We have no later story.
Oedipus.   Where did it happen?

Iocastê.   Phokis, it is called: at a place where the Theban Way
   Divides into the roads towards Delphi and Daulia.
Oedipus.   When?
Iocastê.   We had the news not long before you came
   And proved the right to your succession here.   210
Oedipus.   Ah, what net has God been weaving for me?
Iocastê.   Oedipus! Why does this trouble you?
Oedipus.   Do not ask me yet.
   First, tell me how Laïos looked, and tell me
   How old he was.
Iocastê.   He was tall, his hair just touched
   With white; his form was not unlike your own.
Oedipus.   I think that I myself may be accurst
   By my own ignorant edict.
Iocastê.   You speak strangely.
   It makes me tremble to look at you, my King.
Oedipus.   I am not sure that the blind man can not see.
   But I should know better if you were to tell me—   220
Iocastê.   Anything—though I dread to hear you ask it.
Oedipus.   Was the King lightly escorted, or did he ride
   With a large company, as a ruler should?
Iocastê.   There were five men with him in all: one was a herald;
   And a single chariot, which he was driving.
Oedipus.   Alas, that makes it plain enough!
                                    But who—
   Who told you how it happened?
Iocastê.   A household servant,
   The only one to escape.
Oedipus.   And is he still
   A servant of ours?
Iocastê.   No; for when he came back at last
   And found you enthroned in the place of the dead king,   230
   He came to me, touched my hand with his, and begged
   That I would send him away to the frontier district
   Where only the shepherds go—
   As far away from the city as I could send him.
   I granted his prayer; for although the man was a slave,
   He had earned more than this favor at my hands.
Oedipus.   Can he be called back quickly?
Iocastê.   Easily.
   But why?
Oedipus.   I have taken too much upon myself
   Without enquiry; therefore I wish to consult him.

Iocastê.   Then he shall come.
But am I not one also   240
To whom you might confide these fears of yours?
Oedipus.   That is your right; it will not be denied you,
    Now least of all; for I have reached a pitch
    Of wild foreboding. Is there anyone
    To whom I should sooner speak?
    Polybos of Corinth is my father.
    My mother is a Dorian: Meropê.
    I grew up chief among the men of Corinth
    Until a strange thing happened—
    Not worth my passion, it may be, but strange.   250

    At a feast, a drunken man maundering in his cups
    Cries out that I am not my father's son!

    I contained myself that night, though I felt anger
    And a sinking heart. The next day I visited
    My father and mother, and questioned them. They stormed,
    Calling it all the slanderous rant of a fool;
    And this relieved me. Yet the suspicion
    Remained always aching in my mind;
    I knew there was talk; I could not rest;
    And finally, saying nothing to my parents,   260
    I went to the shrine at Delphi.
    The god dismissed my question without reply;
    He spoke of other things.
Some were clear,
    Full of wretchedness, dreadful, unbearable:
    As, that I should lie with my own mother, breed
    Children from whom all men would turn their eyes;
    And that I should be my father's murderer.

    I heard all this, and fled. And from that day
    Corinth to me was only in the stars
    Descending in that quarter of the sky,   270
    As I wandered farther and farther on my way
    To a land where I should never see the evil
    Sung by the oracle. And I came to this country
    Where, so you say, King Laïos was killed.

    I will tell you all that happened there, my lady.

There were three highways
Coming together at a place I passed;
And there a herald came towards me, and a chariot
Drawn by horses, with a man such as you describe
Seated in it. The groom leading the horses   280
Forced me off the road at his lord's command;
But as this charioteer lurched over towards me
I struck him in my rage. The old man saw me
And brought his double goad down upon my head
As I came abreast.
                    He was paid back, and more!
Swinging my club in this right hand I knocked him
Out of his car, and he rolled on the ground.
                              I killed him.

I killed them all.
Now if that stranger and Laïos were—kin,
Where is a man more miserable than I?   290
More hated by the gods? Citizen and alien alike
Must never shelter me or speak to me—
I must be shunned by all.
                    And I myself
Pronounced this malediction upon myself!

Think of it: I have touched you with these hands,
These hands that killed your husband. What defilement!

Am I all evil, then? It must be so,
Since I must flee from Thebes, yet never again
See my own countrymen, my own country,
For fear of joining my mother in marriage   300
And killing Polybos, my father.
                         Ah,
If I was created so, born to this fate,
Who could deny the savagery of God?

O holy majesty of heavenly powers!
May I never see that day! Never!
Rather let me vanish from the race of men
Than know the abomination destined me!
Choragos.   We too, my lord, have felt dismay at this.
   But there is hope: you have yet to hear the shepherd.
Oedipus.   Indeed, I fear no other hope is left me.   310
Iocastê.   What do you hope from him when he comes?

Oedipus.   This much:
   If his account of the murder tallies with yours,
   Then I am cleared.
Iocastê.   What was it that I said
   Of such importance?
Oedipus.   Why, "marauders," you said,
   Killed the King, according to this man's story.
   If he maintains that still, if there were several,
   Clearly the guilt is not mine: I was alone.
   But if he says one man, singlehanded, did it,
   Then the evidence all points to me.
Iocastê.   You may be sure that he said there were several;   320
   And can he call back that story now? He can not.
   The whole city heard it as plainly as I.
   But suppose he alters some detail of it:
   He can not ever show that Laïos' death
   Fulfilled the oracle: For Apollo said
   My child was doomed to kill him; and my child—
   Poor baby!—it was my child that died first.

   No. From now on, where oracles are concerned,
   I would not waste a second thought on any.
Oedipus.   You may be right.
                      But come: let someone go   330
   For the shepherd at once. This matter must be settled.
Iocastê.   I will send for him.
   I would not wish to cross you in anything.
   And surely not in this.—Let us go in.

[*Exeunt into the palace.*]

Ode II

Chorus.   Let me be reverent in the ways of right,   [*Strophe 1*]
   Lowly the paths I journey on;
   Let all my words and actions keep
   The laws of the pure universe
   From highest Heaven handed down.
   For Heaven is their bright nurse,
   Those generations of the realms of light;

Ah, never of mortal kind were they begot,
Nor are they slaves of memory, lost in sleep:
Their Father is greater than Time, and ages not.   10

The tyrant is a child of Pride   [*Antistrophe 1*]
Who drinks from his great sickening cup
Recklessness and vanity,
Until from his high crest headlong
He plummets to the dust of hope.
That strong man is not strong.
But let no fair ambition be denied;
May God protect the wrestler for the State
In government, in comely policy,
Who will fear God, and on His ordinance wait.   20

Haughtiness and the high hand of disdain   [*Strophe 2*]
Tempt and outrage God's holy law;
And any mortal who dares hold
No immortal Power in awe
Will be caught up in a net of pain:
The price for which his levity is sold.
Let each man take due earnings, then,
And keep his hands from holy things,
And from blasphemy stand apart—
Else the crackling blast of heaven   30
Blows on his head, and on his desperate heart;
Though fools will honor impious men,
In their cities no tragic poet sings.

Shall we lose faith in Delphi's obscurities,   [*Antistrophe 2*]
We who have heard the world's core
Discredited, and the sacred wood
Of Zeus at Elis praised no more?
The deeds and the strange prophecies
Must make a pattern yet to be understood.
Zeus, if indeed you are lord of all,   40
Throned in light over night and day,
Mirror this in your endless mind:
Our masters call the oracle
Words on the wind, and the Delphic vision blind!
Their hearts no longer know Apollo,
And reverence for the gods has died away.

Scene III

[*Enter Iocastê.*]

Iocastê.   Princes of Thebes, it has occurred to me
   To visit the altars of the gods, bearing
   These branches as a suppliant, and this incense.
   Our King is not himself: his noble soul
   Is overwrought with fantasies of dread,
   Else he would consider
   The new prophecies in the light of the old.
   He will listen to any voice that speaks disaster,
   And my advice goes for nothing.

[*She approaches the altar, R.*]

                              To you, then, Apollo,
   Lycean lord, since you are nearest, I turn in prayer.   10
   Receive these offerings, and grant us deliverance
   From defilement. Our hearts are heavy with fear
   When we see our leader distracted, as helpless sailors
   Are terrified by the confusion of their helmsman.

[*Enter Messenger.*]

Messenger.   Friends, no doubt you can direct me:
   Where shall I find the house of Oedipus,
   Or, better still, where is the King himself?
Choragos.   It is this very place, stranger; he is inside.
   This is his wife and mother of his children.
Messenger.   I wish her happiness in a happy house,   20
   Blest in all the fulfillment of her marriage.
Iocastê.   I wish as much for you: your courtesy
   Deserves a like good fortune. But now, tell me:
   Why have you come? What have you to say to us?
Messenger.   Good news, my lady, for your house and your husband.
Iocastê.   What news? Who sent you here?
Messenger.   I am from Corinth.
   The news I bring ought to mean joy for you,
   Though it may be you will find some grief in it.
Iocastê.   What is it? How can it touch us in both ways?
Messenger.   The people of Corinth, they say,   30
   Intend to call Oedipus to be their king.
Iocastê.   But old Polybos—is he not reigning still?

Messenger.   No. Death holds him in his sepulchre.

Iocastê.   What are you saying? Polybos is dead?

Messenger.   If I am not telling the truth, may I die myself.

Iocastê [*to a maidservant*].   Go in, go quickly; tell this to your master.
O riddlers of God's will, where are you now!
This was the man whom Oedipus, long ago,
Feared so, fled so, in dread of destroying him—
But it was another fate by which he died.   40

[*Enter Oedipus, C.*]

Oedipus.   Dearest Iocastê, why have you sent for me?

Iocastê.   Listen to what this man says, and then tell me
What has become of the solemn prophecies.

Oedipus.   Who is this man? What is his news for me?

Iocastê.   He has come from Corinth to announce your father's death!

Oedipus.   Is it true, stranger? Tell me in your own words.

Messenger.   I can not say it more clearly: the King is dead.

Oedipus.   Was it by treason? Or by an attack of illness?

Messenger.   A little thing brings old men to their rest.

Oedipus.   It was sickness, then?

Messenger.   Yes, and his many years.   50

Oedipus.   Ah!
Why should a man respect the Pythian hearth,[15] or
Give heed to the birds that jangle above his head?
They prophesied that I should kill Polybos,
Kill my own father; but he is dead and buried,
And I am here—I never touched him, never,
Unless he died of grief for my departure,
And thus, in a sense, through me. No. Polybos
Has packed the oracles off with him underground.
They are empty words.

Iocastê.   Had I not told you so?   60

Oedipus.   You had; it was my faint heart that betrayed me.

Iocastê.   From now on never think of those things again.

Oedipus.   And yet—must I not fear my mother's bed?

Iocastê.   Why should anyone in this world be afraid,
Since Fate rules us and nothing can be foreseen?
A man should live only for the present day.

Have no more fear of sleeping with your mother:
How many men, in dreams, have lain with their mothers!
No reasonable man is troubled by such things.

---

[15] Delphi, where Apollo spoke through an oracle.

Oedipus.   That is true; only—   70
  If only my mother were not still alive!
  But she is alive. I can not help my dread.
Iocastê.   Yet this news of your father's death is wonderful.
Oedipus.   Wonderful. But I fear the living woman.
Messenger.   Tell me, who is this woman that you fear?
Oedipus.   It is Meropê, man; the wife of King Polybos.
Messenger.   Meropê? Why should you be afraid of her?
Oedipus.   An oracle of the gods, a dreadful saying.
Messenger.   Can you tell me about it or are you sworn to silence?
Oedipus.   I can tell you, and I will.   80
  Apollo said through his prophet that I was the man
  Who should marry his own mother, shed his father's blood
  With his own hands. And so, for all these years
  I have kept clear of Corinth, and no harm has come—
  Though it would have been sweet to see my parents again.
Messenger.   And is this the fear that drove you out of Corinth?
Oedipus.   Would you have me kill my father?
Messenger.   As for that
  You must be reassured by the news I gave you.
Oedipus.   If you could reassure me, I would reward you.
Messenger.   I had that in mind, I will confess: I thought   90
  I could count on you when you returned to Corinth.
Oedipus.   No: I will never go near my parents again.
Messenger.   Ah, son, you still do not know what you are doing—
Oedipus.   What do you mean? In the name of God tell me!
Messenger.   —If these are your reasons for not going home.
Oedipus.   I tell you, I fear the oracle may come true.
Messenger.   And guilt may come upon you through your parents?
Oedipus.   That is the dread that is always in my heart.
Messenger.   Can you not see that all your fears are groundless?
Oedipus.   How can you say that? They are my parents, surely?   100
Messenger.   Polybos was not your father.
Oedipus.   Not my father?
Messenger.   No more your father than the man speaking to you.
Oedipus.   But you are nothing to me!
Messenger.   Neither was he.
Oedipus.   Then why did he call me son?
Messenger.   I will tell you:
  Long ago he had you from my hands, as a gift.
Oedipus.   Then how could he love me so, if I was not his?
Messenger.   He had no children, and his heart turned to you.
Oedipus.   What of you? Did you buy me? Did you find me by chance?
Messenger.   I came upon you in the crooked pass of Kithairon.
Oedipus.   And what were you doing there?

Messenger.   Tending my flocks.   110

Oedipus.   A wandering shepherd?

Messenger.   But your savior, son, that day.

Oedipus.   From what did you save me?

Messenger.   Your ankles should tell you that.

Oedipus.   Ah, stranger, why do you speak of that childhood pain?

Messenger.   I cut the bonds that tied your ankles together.

Oedipus.   I have had the mark as long as I can remember.

Messenger.   That was why you were given the name you bear.[16]

Oedipus.   God! Was it my father or my mother who did it?
   Tell me!

Messenger.   I do not know. The man who gave you to me
   Can tell you better than I.   120

Oedipus.   It was not you that found me, but another?

Messenger.   It was another shepherd gave you to me.

Oedipus.   Who was he? Can you tell me who he was?

Messenger.   I think he was said to be one of Laïos' people.

Oedipus.   You mean the Laïos who was king here years ago?

Messenger.   Yes; King Laïos; and the man was one of his herdsmen.

Oedipus.   Is he still alive? Can I see him?

Messenger.   These men here
   Know best about such things.

Oedipus.   Does anyone here
   Know this shepherd that he is talking about?
   Have you seen him in the fields, or in the town?   130
   If you have, tell me. It is time things were made plain.

Choragos.   I think the man he means is that same shepherd
   You have already asked to see. Iocastê perhaps
   Could tell you something.

Oedipus.   Do you know anything
   About him, Lady? Is he the man we have summoned?
   Is that the man this shepherd means?

Iocastê.   Why think of him?
   Forget this herdsman. Forget it all.
   This talk is a waste of time.

Oedipus.   How can you say that?
   When the clues to my true birth are in my hands?

Iocastê.   For God's love, let us have no more questioning!   140
   Is your life nothing to you?
   My own is pain enough for me to bear.

Oedipus.   You need not worry. Suppose my mother a slave,
   And born of slaves: no baseness can touch you.

Iocastê.   Listen to me, I beg you: do not do this thing!

---

[16] *Oedipus* literally means "swollen-foot."

Oedipus.   I will not listen; the truth must be made known.
Iocastê.   Everything that I say is for your own good!
Oedipus.   My own good
   Snaps my patience, then; I want none of it.
Iocastê.   You are fatally wrong! May you never learn who you are!
Oedipus.   Go, one of you, and bring the shepherd here.   150
   Let us leave this woman to brag of her royal name.
Iocastê.   Ah, miserable!
   That is the only word I have for you now.
   That is the only word I can ever have.

[*Exit into the palace.*]

Choragos.   Why has she left us, Oedipus? Why has she gone
   In such a passion of sorrow? I fear this silence:
   Something dreadful may come of it.
Oedipus.   Let it come!
   However base my birth, I must know about it.
   The Queen, like a woman, is perhaps ashamed
   To think of my low origin. But I   160
   Am a child of Luck; I can not be dishonored.
   Luck is my mother; the passing months, my brothers,
   Have seen me rich and poor.
                           If this is so,
   How could I wish that I were someone else?
   How could I not be glad to know my birth?

Ode III

Chorus.   If ever the coming time were known   [*Strophe*]
   To my heart's pondering,
   Kithairon, now by Heaven I see the torches
   At the festival of the next full moon,
   And see the dance, and hear the choir sing
   A grace to your gentle shade:
   Mountain where Oedipus was found,
   O mountain guard of a noble race!
   May the god who heals us lend his aid,
   And let that glory come to pass   10
   For our king's cradling-ground.

   Of the nymphs that flower beyond the years,   [*Antistrophe*]
   Who bore you, royal child,

To Pan of the hills or the timberline Apollo,
Cold in delight where the upland clears,
Or Hermês for whom Kyllenê's heights are piled?[17]
Or flushed as evening cloud,
Great Dionysos, roamer of mountains,
He—was it he who found you there,
And caught you up in his own proud   20
Arms from the sweet god-ravisher
Who laughed by the Muses' fountains?

Scene IV

Oedipus.   Sirs: though I do not know the man,
  I think I see him coming, this shepherd we want:
  He is old, like our friend here, and the men
  Bringing him seem to be servants of my house.
  But you can tell, if you have ever seen him.

[*Enter Shepherd escorted by servants.*]

Choragos.   I know him, he was Laïos' man. You can trust him.
Oedipus.   Tell me first, you from Corinth: is this the shepherd
  We were discussing?
Messenger.   This is the very man.
Oedipus [*to Shepherd*].   Come here. No, look at me. You must answer
  Everything I ask. You belonged to Laïos?   10
Shepherd.   Yes: born his slave, brought up in his house.
Oedipus.   Tell me what kind of work did you do for him?
Shepherd.   I was a shepherd of his, most of my life.
Oedipus.   Where mainly did you go for pasturage?
Shepherd.   Sometimes Kithairon, sometimes the hills near-by.
Oedipus.   Do you remember ever seeing this man out there?
Shepherd.   What would he be doing there? This man?
Oedipus.   This man standing here. Have you ever seen him before?
Shepherd.   No. At least, not to my recollection.
Messenger.   And that is not strange, my lord. But I'll refresh   20
  His memory: he must remember when we two
  Spent three whole seasons together, March to September,
  On Kithairon or thereabouts. He had two flocks;

---

[17] Hermês, the herald of the Olympian gods, was born on the mountain of Kyllenê.

I had one. Each autumn I'd drive mine home
And he would go back with his to Laïos' sheepfold.—
Is this not true, just as I have described it?

Shepherd. True, yes; but it was all so long ago.

Messenger. Well, then: do you remember, back in those days
That you gave me a baby boy to bring up as my own?

Shepherd. What if I did? What are you trying to say? 30

Messenger. King Oedipus was once that little child.

Shepherd. Damn you, hold your tongue!

Oedipus. No more of that!
It is your tongue needs watching, not this man's.

Shepherd. My King, my Master, what is it I have done wrong?

Oedipus. You have not answered his question about the boy.

Shepherd. He does not know . . . He is only making trouble . . .

Oedipus. Come, speak plainly, or it will go hard with you.

Shepherd. In God's name, do not torture an old man!

Oedipus. Come here, one of you; bind his arms behind him.

Shepherd. Unhappy king! What more do you wish to learn? 40

Oedipus. Did you give this man the child he speaks of?

Shepherd. I did.
And I would to God I had died that very day.

Oedipus. You will die now unless you speak the truth.

Shepherd. Yet if I speak the truth, I am worse than dead.

Oedipus. Very well; since you insist on delaying—

Shepherd. No! I have told you already that I gave him the boy.

Oedipus. Where did you get him? From your house? From somewhere else?

Shepherd. Not from mine, no. A man gave him to me.

Oedipus. Is that man here? Do you know whose slave he was?

Shepherd. For God's love, my King, do not ask me any more! 50

Oedipus. You are a dead man if I have to ask you again.

Shepherd. Then . . . Then the child was from the palace of Laïos.

Oedipus. A slave child? or a child of his own line?

Shepherd. Ah, I am on the brink of dreadful speech!

Oedipus. And I of dreadful hearing. Yet I must hear.

Shepherd. If you must be told, then . . .
They said it was Laïos' child,
But it is your wife who can tell you about that.

Oedipus. My wife!—Did she give it to you?

Shepherd. My lord, she did.

Oedipus. Do you know why?

Shepherd. I was told to get rid of it.

Oedipus. An unspeakable mother!

Shepherd. There had been prophecies . . . 60

Oedipus. Tell me.

Shepherd.   It was said that the boy would kill his own father.
Oedipus.   Then why did you give him over to this old man?
Shepherd.   I pitied the baby, my King,
And I thought that this man would take him far away
To his own country.
                        He saved him—but for what a fate!
For if you are what this man says you are,
No man living is more wretched than Oedipus.
Oedipus.   Ah God!
It was true!
            All the prophecies!
                        —Now,
O Light, may I look on you for the last time!   70
I, Oedipus,
Oedipus, damned in his birth, in his marriage damned,
Damned in the blood he shed with his own hand!

[*He rushes into the palace.*]

Ode IV

Chorus.   Alas for the seed of men.   [*Strophe 1*]

What measure shall I give these generations
That breathe on the void and are void
And exist and do not exist?

Who bears more weight of joy
Than mass of sunlight shifting in images,
Or who shall make his thought stay on
That down time drifts away?

Your splendor is all fallen.

O naked brow of wrath and tears,   10
O change of Oedipus!
I who saw your days call no man blest—
Your great days like ghosts gone.

That mind was a strong bow.   [*Antistrophe 1*]

Deep, how deep you drew it then, hard archer,

At a dim fearful range,
And brought dear glory down!

You overcame the stranger—
The virgin with her hooking lion claws—
And though death sang, stood like a tower   20
To make pale Thebes take heart.

Fortress against our sorrow!

Divine king, giver of laws,
Majestic Oedipus!
No prince in Thebes had ever such renown,
No prince won such grace of power.

And now of all men ever known   [*Strophe 2*]
Most pitiful is this man's story:
His fortunes are most changed, his state
Fallen to a low slave's   30
Ground under bitter fate.

O Oedipus, most royal one!
The great door that expelled you to the light
Gave at night—ah, gave night to your glory:
As to the father, to the fathering son.

All understood too late.

How could that queen whom Laïos won,
The garden that he harrowed at his height,
Be silent when that act was done?

But all eyes fail before time's eye,   [*Antistrophe 2*]
All actions come to justice there
Though never willed, though far down the deep past,
Your bed, your dread sirings,
Are brought to book at last.

Child by Laïos doomed to die,
Then doomed to lose that fortunate little death,
Would God you never took breath in this air
That with my wailing lips I take to cry:

For I weep the world's outcast.

I was blind, and now I can tell why: 50
Asleep, for you had given ease of breath
To Thebes, while the false years went by.

Exodos

[*Enter, from the palace, Second Messenger.*]

Second Messenger.   Elders of Thebes, most honored in this land,
What horrors are yours to see and hear, what weight
Of sorrow to be endured, if, true to your birth,
You venerate the line of Labdakos!
I think neither Istros nor Phasis, those great rivers,
Could purify this place of the corruption
It shelters now, or soon must bring to light—
Evil not done unconsciously, but willed.

The greatest griefs are those we cause ourselves.
Choragos.   Surely, friend, we have grief enough already;   10
What new sorrow do you mean?
Second Messenger.   The Queen is dead.
Choragos.   Iocastê? Dead? But at whose hand?
Second Messenger.   Her own.
The full horror of what happened you can not know,
For you did not see it; but I, who did, will tell you
As clearly as I can how she met her death.

When she had left us,
In passionate silence, passing through the court,
She ran to her apartment in the house,
Her hair clutched by the fingers of both hands.

She closed the doors behind her; then, by that bed   20
Where long ago the fatal son was conceived—
The son who should bring about his father's death—
We heard her call upon Laïos, dead so many years,
And heard her wail for the double fruit of her marriage,
A husband by her husband, children by her child.

Exactly how she died I do not know:
For Oedipus burst in moaning and would not let us
Keep vigil to the end: it was by him

As he stormed about the room that our eyes were caught.
From one to another of us he went, begging a sword,   30
Cursing the wife who was not his wife, the mother
Whose womb had carried his own children and himself.
I do not know: it was none of us aided him,
But surely one of the gods was in control!
For with a dreadful cry
He hurled his weight, as though wrenched out of himself,
At the twin doors: the bolts gave, and he rushed in.
And there we saw her hanging, her body swaying
From the cruel cord she had noosed about her neck.
A great sob broke from him, heartbreaking to hear,   40
As he loosed the rope and lowered her to the ground.

I would blot out from my mind what happened next!
For the King ripped from her gown the golden brooches
That were her ornament, and raised them, and plunged them down
Straight into his own eyeballs, crying, "No more,
No more shall you look on the misery about me,
The horrors of my own doing! Too long have you known
The faces of those whom I should never have seen,
Too long been blind to those for whom I was searching!
From this hour, go in darkness!" And as he spoke,   50
He struck at his eyes—not once, but many times;
And the blood spattered his beard,
Bursting from his ruined sockets like red hail.

So from the unhappiness of two this evil has sprung,
A curse on the man and woman alike. The old
Happiness of the house of Labdakos
Was happiness enough: where is it today?
It is all wailing and ruin, disgrace, death—all
The misery of mankind that has a name—
And it is wholly and for ever theirs.   60
Choragos.   Is he in agony still? Is there no rest for him?
Second Messenger.   He is calling for someone to lead him to the gates
So that all the children of Kadmos may look upon
His father's murderer, his mother's—no,
I can not say it!
                And then he will leave Thebes,
Self-exiled, in order that the curse
Which he himself pronounced may depart from the house.
He is weak, and there is none to lead him,
So terrible is his suffering.
                But you will see:

Look, the doors are opening; in a moment 70
You will see a thing that would crush a heart of stone.

[*The central door is opened; Oedipus, blinded, is led in.*]

Choragos.   Dreadful indeed for men to see.
Never have my own eyes
Looked on a sight so full of fear.

Oedipus!
What madness came upon you, what daemon
Leaped on your life with heavier
Punishment than a mortal man can bear?
No: I can not even
Look at you, poor ruined one. 80
And I would speak, question, ponder,
If I were able. No.
You make me shudder.
Oedipus.   God. God.
Is there a sorrow greater?
Where shall I find harbor in this world?
My voice is hurled far on a dark wind.
What has God done to me?
Choragos.   Too terrible to think of, or to see.

Oedipus.   O cloud of night,   [*Strophe 1*]
Never to be turned away: night coming on,
I can not tell how: night like a shroud!

My fair winds brought me here.
                         Oh God. Again
The pain of the spikes where I had sight,
The flooding pain
Of memory, never to be gouged out.
Choragos.   This is not strange.
You suffer it all twice over, remorse in pain,
Pain in remorse.

Oedipus.   Ah dear friend   [*Antistrophe 1*]
Are you faithful even yet, you alone?
Are you still standing near me, will you stay here,
Patient, to care for the blind?
                         The blind man!
Yet even blind I know who it is attends me,
By the voice's tone—
Though my new darkness hide the comforter.

Choragos. Oh fearful act!
  What god was it drove you to rake black
  Night across your eyes?
Oedipus. Apollo. Apollo. Dear   *[Strophe 2]*
  Children, the god was Apollo.
  He brought my sick, sick fate upon me.
  But the blinding hand was my own!
  How could I bear to see
  When all my sight was horror everywhere?
Choragos. Everywhere; that is true.
Oedipus. And now what is left?
  Images? Love? A greeting even,
  Sweet to the senses? Is there anything?
  Ah no, friends: lead me away.   120
  Lead me away from Thebes.
                     Lead the great wreck
  And hell of Oedipus, whom the gods hate.
Choragos. Your fate is clear, you are not blind to that.
  Would God you had never found it out!

Oedipus. Death take the man who unbound   *[Antistrophe 2]*
  My feet on that hillside
  And delivered me from death to life! What life?
  If only I had died,
  This weight of monstrous doom
  Could not have dragged me and my darlings down.   130
Choragos. I would have wished the same.
Oedipus. Oh never to have come here
  With my father's blood upon me! Never
  To have been the man they call his mother's husband!
  Oh accurst! Oh child of evil,
  To have entered that wretched bed—
                         the selfsame one!
  More primal than sin itself, this fell to me.
Choragos. I do not know how I can answer you.
  You were better dead than alive and blind.
Oedipus. Do not counsel me any more. This punishment   140
  That I have laid upon myself is just.
  If I had eyes,
  I do not know how I could bear the sight
  Of my father, when I came to the house of Death,
  Or my mother: for I have sinned against them both
  So vilely that I could not make my peace
  By strangling my own life.
                 Or do you think my children,
  Born as they were born, would be sweet to my eyes?

Ah never, never! Nor this town with its high walls,
Nor the holy images of the gods.
For I, 150
Thrice miserable!—Oedipus, noblest of all the line
Of Kadmos, have condemned myself to enjoy
These things no more, by my own malediction
Expelling that man whom the gods declared
To be a defilement in the house of Laïos.
After exposing the rankness of my own guilt,
How could I look men frankly in the eyes?
No, I swear it,
If I could have stifled my hearing at its source,
I would have done it and made all this body 160
A tight cell of misery, blank to light and sound:
So I should have been safe in a dark agony
Beyond all recollection.
Ah Kithairon!
Why did you shelter me? When I was cast upon you,
Why did I not die? Then I should never
Have shown the world my execrable birth.

Ah Polybos! Corinth, city that I believed
The ancient seat of my ancestors: how fair
I seemed, your child! And all the while this evil
Was cancerous within me!
For I am sick 170
In my daily life, sick in my origin.

O three roads, dark ravine, woodland and way
Where three roads met: you, drinking my father's blood,
My own blood, spilled by my own hand: can you remember
The unspeakable things I did there, and the things
I went on from there to do?
O marriage, marriage!
The act that engendered me, and again the act
Performed by the son in the same bed—
Ah, the net
Of incest, mingling fathers, brothers, sons,
With brides, wives, mothers; the last evil 180
That can be known by men: no tongue can say
How evil!
No. For the love of God, conceal me
Somewhere far from Thebes; or kill me; or hurl me
Into the sea, away from men's eyes for ever.
Come, lead me. You need not fear to touch me.
Of all men, I alone can bear this guilt.

[*Enter Creon.*]

Choragos.   We are not the ones to decide; but Creon here
  May fitly judge of what you ask. He only
  Is left to protect the city in your place.
Oedipus.   Alas, how can I speak to him? What right have I   190
  To beg his courtesy whom I have deeply wronged?
Creon.   I have not come to mock you, Oedipus,
  Or to reproach you, either.
  [*To attendants.*]   —You, standing there:
  If you have lost all respect for man's dignity,
  At least respect the flame of Lord Helios:
  Do not allow this pollution to show itself
  Openly here, an affront to the earth
  And Heaven's rain and the light of day. No, take him
  Into the house as quickly as you can.
  For it is proper   200
  That only the close kindred see his grief.
Oedipus.   I pray you in God's name, since your courtesy
  Ignores my dark expectation, visiting
  With mercy this man of all men most execrable:
  Give me what I ask—for your good, not for mine.
Creon.   And what is it that you would have me do?
Oedipus.   Drive me out of this country as quickly as may be
  To a place where no human voice can ever greet me.
Creon.   I should have done that before now—only,
  God's will had not been wholly revealed to me.   210
Oedipus.   But his command is plain: the parricide
  Must be destroyed. I am that evil man.
Creon.   That is the sense of it, yes; but as things are,
  We had best discover clearly what is to be done.
Oedipus.   You would learn more about a man like me?
Creon.   You are ready now to listen to the god.
Oedipus.   I will listen. But it is to you
  That I must turn for help. I beg you, hear me.

  The woman in there—
  Give her whatever funeral you think proper: 220
  She is your sister.
                —But let me go, Creon!
  Let me purge my father's Thebes of the pollution
  Of my living here, and go out to the wild hills,
  To Kithairon, that has won such fame with me,
  The tomb my mother and father appointed for me,
  And let me die there, as they willed I should.
  And yet I know

Death will not ever come to me through sickness
Or in any natural way: I have been preserved
For some unthinkable fate. But let that be.   230
As for my sons, you need not care for them.
They are men, they will find some way to live.
But my poor daughters, who have shared my table,
Who never before have been parted from their father—
Take care of them, Creon; do this for me.
And will you let me touch them with my hands
A last time, and let us weep together?
Be kind, my lord,
Great prince, be kind!
                   Could I but touch them,
They would be mine again, as when I had my eyes.   240

[*Enter Antigone and Ismene, attended.*]

Ah, God!
Is it my dearest children I hear weeping?
Has Creon pitied me and sent my daughters?
Creon.   Yes, Oedipus: I knew that they were dear to you
In the old days, and know you must love them still.
Oedipus.   May God bless you for this—and be a friendlier
Guardian to you than he has been to me!

Children, where are you?
Come quickly to my hands: they are your brother's—
Hands that have brought your father's once clear eyes   250
To this way of seeing—
                   Ah dearest ones,
I had neither sight nor knowledge then, your father
By the woman who was the source of his own life!
And I weep for you—having no strength to see you—,
I weep for you when I think of the bitterness
That men will visit upon you all your lives.
What homes, what festivals can you attend
Without being forced to depart again in tears?

And when you come to marriageable age,
Where is the man, my daughters, who would dare   260
Risk the bane that lies on all my children?
Is there any evil wanting? Your father killed
His father; sowed the womb of her who bore him;
Engendered you at the fount of his own existence!
That is what they will say of you.

Then whom
Can you ever marry? There are no bridegrooms for you,
And your lives must wither away in sterile dreaming.
O Creon, son of Menoikeus!
You are the only father my daughters have,
Since we, their parents, are both of us gone for ever.   270
They are your own blood: you will not let them
Fall into beggary and loneliness;
You will keep them from the miseries that are mine!
Take pity on them; see, they are only children,
Friendless except for you. Promise me this,
Great Prince, and give me your hand in token of it.

[*Creon clasps his right hand.*]

Children:
I could say much, if you could understand me,
But as it is, I have only this prayer for you:
Live where you can, be as happy as you can—   280
Happier, please God, than God has made your father!
Creon.   Enough. You have wept enough. Now go within.
Oedipus.   I must; but it is hard.
Creon.   Time eases all things.
Oedipus.   But you must promise—
Creon.   Say what you desire.
Oedipus.   Send me from Thebes!
Creon.   God grant that I may!
Oedipus.   But since God hates me . . .
Creon.   No, he will grant your wish.
Oedipus.   You promise?
Creon.   I can not speak beyond my knowledge.
Oedipus.   Then lead me in.
Creon.   Come now, and leave your children.
Oedipus.   No! Do not take them from me!
Creon.   Think no longer
That you are in command here, but rather think   290
How, when you were, you served your own destruction.

[*Exeunt into the house all but the Chorus; the Choragos chants directly to the
audience.*]

Choragos.   Men of Thebes: look upon Oedipus.

This is the king who solved the famous riddle
And towered up, most powerful of men.

No mortal eyes but looked on him with envy,
Yet in the end ruin swept over him.
Let every man in mankind's frailty
Consider his last day; and let none
Presume on his good fortune until he find
Life, at his death, a memory without pain.   300

For Analysis

1. How does the Prologue establish the mood and theme of the play? What aspects of Oedipus's character are revealed there? **2.** Sophocles' audience knew the Oedipus story as others, for instance, know the story of the Buddha, of the crucifixion of Jesus, or of Allah. What literary devices does Sophocles use nonetheless to create suspense and interest in the outcome of the action? **3.** What is the nature of the conflict in the play? Who or what is the antagonist who opposes Oedipus, the protagonist? **4.** A classic **tragedy** tells the story of a noble and heroic protagonist who is brought down by arrogance and pride. What evidence do you find that Oedipus suffers from these frailties? **5.** Teiresias is one of many figures in legend and literature whose wisdom and spirituality is somehow connected with blindness. Speculate on what the connection might be based on. **5.** What function does the Exodos serve?

On Style

1. Discuss the role of the chorus in the dramatic development and creation of suspense in the play. **2.** The play embodies a pattern of figurative and literal **allusions** to darkness and light, to vision and blindness. How does that figurative language function, and what relationship does it bear to Oedipus's self-inflicted punishment? **3.** Analyze the use of **dramatic irony** in this play.

Making Connections

1. Compare Oedipus and Shakespeare's Othello (p. 1041) as classic tragic protagonists. **2.** Examine Creon's role in both this play and Sophocles' *Antigonê* (p. 460) and describe how his character changes. **3.** While Oedipus is a king, a man of great power and high station, and Willy Loman, in Arthur Miller's *Death of a Salesman* (p. 746), is an ordinary man and a seeming failure, what connection might be made between the two protagonists?

Writing Topics

1. In the Exodos, Oedipus declares that Apollo "brought my sick, sick fate upon me. / But the blinding hand was my own!" (ll. 112–13) and "This punishment / That I have laid upon myself is just" (ll. 140–41); later he declares, ". . . the parricide / Must be destroyed. I am that evil man" (ll. 211–12). How can Oedipus's acceptance of responsibility for his fate be reconciled with the fact that his fate was divinely ordained? Consider a similar paradox in Christian theology, which holds that God is all-knowing and has foreknowledge and yet humans exercise free will and thus are responsible for their acts. **2.** Analyze Scene IV, the shortest of the four scenes, as the climax of the play, bringing together all the threads of the drama.

Tennessee Williams [1911–1983]

The Glass Menagerie 1945

nobody, not even the rain, has such small hands
> —E. E. Cummings

LIST OF CHARACTERS

Amanda Wingfield, *the mother. A little woman of great but confused vitality clinging frantically to another time and place. Her characterization must be carefully created, not copied from type. She is not paranoiac, but her life is paranoia. There is much to admire in Amanda, and as much to love and pity as there is to laugh at. Certainly she has endurance and a kind of heroism, and though her foolishness makes her unwittingly cruel at times, there is tenderness in her slight person.*

Laura Wingfield, *her daughter. Amanda, having failed to establish contact with reality, continues to live vitally in her illusions, but Laura's situation is even graver. A childhood illness has left her crippled, one leg slightly shorter than the other, and held in a brace. This defect need not be more than suggested on the stage. Stemming from this, Laura's separation increases till she is like a piece of her own glass collection, too exquisitely fragile to move from the shelf.*

Tom Wingfield, *her son. And the narrator of the play. A poet with a job in a warehouse. His nature is not remorseless, but to escape from a trap he has to act without pity.*

Jim O'Connor, *the gentleman caller. A nice, ordinary, young man.*

Scene. *An alley in St. Louis.*
Part I. *Preparation for a Gentleman Caller.*
Part II. *The Gentleman Calls.*
Time. *Now and the Past.*

Scene I

The Wingfield apartment is in the rear of the building, one of those vast hivelike conglomerations of cellular living-units that flower as warty growths in over-crowded urban centers of lower middle-class population and are symptomatic of the impulse of this largest and fundamentally enslaved section of American society to avoid fluidity and differentiation and to exist and function as one inter-fused mass of automatism.

The apartment faces an alley and is entered by a fire-escape, a structure whose name is a touch of accidental poetic truth, for all of these huge buildings are always burning with the slow and implacable fires of human desperation. The fire-escape is included in the set—that is, the landing of it and steps descending from it.

The scene is memory and is therefore nonrealistic. Memory takes a lot of poetic license. It omits some details; others are exaggerated, according to the emotional value of the articles it touches, for memory is seated predominantly in the heart. The interior is therefore rather dim and poetic.

At the rise of the curtain, the audience is faced with the dark, grim rear wall of the Wingfield tenement. This building, which runs parallel to the footlights, is flanked on both sides by dark, narrow alleys which run into murky canyons of tangled clotheslines, garbage cans, and the sinister latticework of neighboring fire-escapes. It is up and down these side alleys that exterior entrances and exits are made, during the play. At the end of Tom's opening commentary, the dark tenement wall slowly reveals (by means of a transparency) the interior of the ground floor Wingfield apartment.

Downstage is the living room, which also serves as a sleeping room for Laura, the sofa unfolding to make her bed. Upstage, center, and divided by a wide arch or second proscenium with transparent faded portieres (or second curtain), is the dining room. In an old-fashioned what-not in the living room are seen scores of transparent glass animals. A blown-up photograph of the father hangs on the wall of the living room, facing the audience, to the left of the archway. It is the face of a very handsome young man in a doughboy's First World War cap. He is gallantly smiling, ineluctably smiling, as if to say, "I will be smiling forever."

The audience hears and sees the opening scene in the dining room through both the transparent fourth wall of the building and the transparent gauze portieres of the dining-room arch. It is during this revealing scene that the fourth wall slowly ascends, out of sight. This transparent exterior wall is not brought down again until the very end of the play, during Tom's final speech.

The narrator is an undisguised convention of the play. He takes whatever license with dramatic convention as is convenient to his purposes.

Tom enters dressed as a merchant sailor from alley, stage left, and strolls across the front of the stage to the fire-escape. There he stops and lights a cigarette. He addresses the audience.

Tom.   Yes, I have tricks in my pocket, I have things up my sleeve. But I am the opposite of a stage magician. He gives you illusion that has the appearance of truth. I give you truth in the pleasant disguise of illusion. To begin with, I turn back time. I reverse it to that quaint period, the thirties, when the huge middle class of America was matriculating in a school for the blind. Their eyes had failed them, or they had failed their eyes, and so they were having their fingers pressed forcibly down on the fiery Braille alphabet of a dissolving economy. In Spain there was revolution. Here there was only shouting and confusion. In Spain there was Guernica.[1] Here there were disturbances

---

[1] A town in northern Spain without military significance that was destroyed in 1937 by German bombers supporting Francisco Franco's fascists during the Spanish Civil War.

of labor, sometimes pretty violent, in otherwise peaceful cities such as Chicago, Cleveland, Saint Louis. . . . This is the social background of the play.

(Music.)

The play is memory. Being a memory play, it is dimly lighted, it is sentimental, it is not realistic. In memory everything seems to happen to music. That explains the fiddle in the wings. I am the narrator of the play, and also a character in it. The other characters are my mother, Amanda, my sister, Laura, and a gentleman caller who appears in the final scenes. He is the most realistic character in the play, being an emissary from a world of reality that we were somehow set apart from. But since I have a poet's weakness for symbols, I am using this character also as a symbol; he is the long delayed but always expected something that we live for. There is a fifth character in the play who doesn't appear except in this larger-than-life photograph over the mantel. This is our father who left us a long time ago. He was a telephone man who fell in love with long distances; he gave up his job with the telephone company and skipped the light fantastic out of town. . . . The last we heard of him was a picture post-card from Mazatlán, on the Pacific coast of Mexico, containing a message of two words—"Hello—Good-bye!" and no address. I think the rest of the play will explain itself. . . .

Amanda's voice becomes audible through the portieres.
(Legend on screen: "Où sont les neiges."[2])
He divides the portieres and enters the upstage area.
Amanda and Laura are seated at a drop-leaf table. Eating is indicated by gestures without food or utensils. Amanda faces the audience.
Tom and Laura are seated in profile.
The interior has lit up softly and through the scrim we see Amanda and Laura seated at the table in the upstage area.

Amanda *(calling).*   Tom?
Tom.   Yes, Mother.
Amanda.   We can't say grace until you come to the table!
Tom.   Coming, Mother. *(He bows slightly and withdraws, reappearing a few moments later in his place at the table.)*
Amanda *(to her son).*   Honey, don't *push* with your *fingers.* If you have to push with something, the thing to push with is a crust of bread. And chew—chew! Animals have sections in their stomachs which enable them to digest food without mastication, but human beings are supposed to chew their food before they swallow it down. Eat food leisurely, son, and really enjoy it. A well-cooked meal has lots of delicate flavors that have to be held in the mouth for appreciation. So chew your food and give your salivary glands a chance to function!

---

[2] From a famous medieval ballad by François Villon (1431–?). The complete line generates a wistful nostalgia by asking, "Where are the snows of yesteryear?"

Tom deliberately lays his imaginary fork down and pushes his chair back from the table.

Tom. I haven't enjoyed one bite of this dinner because of your constant directions on how to eat it. It's you that makes me rush through meals with your hawklike attention to every bite I take. Sickening—spoils my appetite—all this discussion of animals' secretion—salivary glands—mastication!

Amanda *(lightly).* Temperament like a Metropolitan star! *(He rises and crosses downstage.)* You're not excused from the table.

Tom. I am getting a cigarette.

Amanda. You smoke too much.

Laura rises.

Laura. I'll bring in the blanc mange.

He remains standing with his cigarette by the portieres during the following.

Amanda *(rising).* No, sister, no, sister—you be the lady this time and I'll be the darky.

Laura. I'm already up.

Amanda. Resume your seat, little sister—I want you to stay fresh and pretty—for gentlemen callers!

Laura. I'm not expecting any gentlemen callers.

Amanda *(crossing out to kitchenette. Airily).* Sometimes they come when they are least expected! Why, I remember one Sunday afternoon in Blue Mountain—*(Enters kitchenette.)*

Tom. I know what's coming!

Laura. Yes. But let her tell it.

Tom. Again?

Laura. She loves to tell it.

Amanda returns with bowl of dessert.

Amanda. One Sunday afternoon in Blue Mountain—your mother received—*seventeen!*—gentlemen callers! Why, sometimes there weren't chairs enough to accommodate them all. We had to send the nigger over to bring in folding chairs from the parish house.

Tom *(remaining at portieres).* How did you entertain those gentlemen callers?

Amanda. I understood the art of conversation!

Tom. I bet you could talk.

Amanda. Girls in those days *knew* how to talk, I can tell you.

Tom. Yes?

(Image: Amanda as a girl on a porch greeting callers.)

Amanda.   They knew how to entertain their gentlemen callers. It wasn't enough for a girl to be possessed of a pretty face and a graceful figure—although I wasn't slighted in either respect. She also needed to have a nimble wit and a tongue to meet all occasions.

Tom.   What did you talk about?

Amanda.   Things of importance going on in the world! Never anything coarse or common or vulgar. *(She addresses Tom as though he were seated in the vacant chair at the table though he remains by portieres. He plays this scene as though he held the book.)* My callers were gentlemen—all! Among my callers were some of the most prominent young planters of the Mississippi Delta—planters and sons of planters!

Tom motions for music and a spot of light on Amanda.
Her eyes lift, her face glows, her voice becomes rich and elegiac.
(Screen legend: "Où sont les neiges.")

There was young Champ Laughlin who later became vice-president of the Delta Planters Bank. Hadley Stevenson who was drowned in Moon Lake and left his widow one hundred and fifty thousand in Government bonds. There were the Cutrere brothers, Wesley and Bates. Bates was one of my bright particular beaux! He got in a quarrel with that wild Wainright boy. They shot it out on the floor of Moon Lake Casino. Bates was shot through the stomach. Died in the ambulance on his way to Memphis. His widow was also well-provided for, came into eight or ten thousand acres, that's all. She married him on the rebound—never loved her—carried my picture on him the night he died! And there was that boy that every girl in the Delta had set her cap for! That beautiful, brilliant young Fitzhugh boy from Green County!

Tom.   What did he leave his widow?

Amanda.   He never married! Gracious, you talk as though all of my old admirers had turned up their toes to the daisies!

Tom.   Isn't this the first you mentioned that still survives?

Amanda.   That Fitzhugh boy went North and made a fortune—came to be known as the Wolf of Wall Street! He had the Midas touch, whatever he touched turned to gold! And I could have been Mrs. Duncan J. Fitzhugh, mind you! But—I picked your *father!*

Laura *(rising).*   Mother, let me clear the table.

Amanda.   No dear, you go in front and study your typewriter chart. Or practice your shorthand a little. Stay fresh and pretty!—It's almost time for our gentlemen callers to start arriving. *(She flounces girlishly toward the kitchenette.)* How many do you suppose we're going to entertain this afternoon?

Tom throws down the paper and jumps up with a groan.

Laura (*alone in the dining room*).   I don't believe we're going to receive any, Mother.

Amanda (*reappearing, airily*).   What? No one—not one? You must be joking! (*Laura nervously echoes her laugh. She slips in a fugitive manner through the half-open portieres and draws them gently behind her. A shaft of very clear light is thrown on her face against the faded tapestry of the curtains.*) (*Music: "The Glass Menagerie" under faintly.*) (*Lightly.*) Not one gentleman caller? It can't be true! There must be a flood, there must have been a tornado!

Laura.   It isn't a flood, it's not a tornado, Mother. I'm just not popular like you were in Blue Mountain. . . . (*Tom utters another groan. Laura glances at him with a faint, apologetic smile. Her voice catching a little.*) Mother's afraid I'm going to be an old maid.

(*The scene dims out with "Glass Menagerie" music.*)

Scene II

"Laura, Haven't You Ever Liked Some Boy?"

On the dark stage the screen is lighted with the image of blue roses.
    Gradually Laura's figure becomes apparent and the screen goes out.
    The music subsides.
    Laura is seated in the delicate ivory chair at the small clawfoot table.
    She wears a dress of soft violet material for a kimono—her hair tied back from her forehead with a ribbon.
    She is washing and polishing her collection of glass.
    Amanda appears on the fire-escape steps. At the sound of her ascent, Laura catches her breath, thrusts the bowl of ornaments away, and seats herself stiffly before the diagram of the typewriter keyboard as though it held her spellbound. Something has happened to Amanda. It is written in her face as she climbs to the landing: a look that is grim and hopeless and a little absurd.
    She has on one of those cheap or imitation velvety-looking cloth coats with imitation fur collar. Her hat is five or six years old, one of those dreadful cloche hats that were worn in the late twenties, and she is clasping an enormous black patent-leather pocketbook with nickel clasp and initials. This is her full-dress outfit, the one she usually wears to the D.A.R.[3]
    Before entering she looks through the door.
    She purses her lips, opens her eyes wide, rolls them upward, and shakes her head.

---

[3] Daughters of the American Revolution—an exclusive society of women who can trace their ancestry to the American patriots who fought in the Revolutionary War.

Then she slowly lets herself in the door. Seeing her mother's expression Laura touches her lips with a nervous gesture.

Laura. Hello, Mother, I was—(*She makes a nervous gesture toward the chart on the wall. Amanda leans against the shut door and stares at Laura with a martyred look.*)

Amanda. Deception? Deception? (*She slowly removes her hat and gloves, continuing the swift suffering stare. She lets the hat and gloves fall on the floor—a bit of acting.*)

Laura (*shakily*). How was the D.A.R. meeting? (*Amanda slowly opens her purse and removes a dainty white handkerchief, which she shakes out delicately and delicately touches to her lips and nostrils.*) Didn't you go to the D.A.R. meeting, Mother?

Amanda (*faintly, almost inaudibly*). —No.—No. (*Then more forcibly.*) I did not have the strength—to go to the D.A.R. In fact, I did not have the courage! I wanted to find a hole in the ground and hide myself in it forever! (*She crosses slowly to the wall and removes the diagram of the typewriter keyboard. She holds it in front of her for a second, staring at it sweetly and sorrowfully—then bites her lips and tears it in two pieces.*)

Laura (*faintly*). Why did you do that, Mother? (*Amanda repeats the same procedure with the chart of the Gregg Alphabet.[4]*) Why are you—

Amanda. Why? Why? How old are you, Laura?

Laura. Mother, you know my age.

Amanda. I thought that you were an adult; it seems that I was mistaken. (*She crosses slowly to the sofa and sinks down and stares at Laura.*)

Laura. Please don't stare at me, Mother.

Amanda closes her eyes and lowers her head. Count ten.

Amanda. What are we going to do, what is going to become of us, what is the future?

Count ten.

Laura. Has something happened, Mother? (*Amanda draws a long breath and takes out the handkerchief again. Dabbing process.*) Mother, has—something happened?

Amanda. I'll be all right in a minute. I'm just bewildered—(*count five*)—by life. . . .

Laura. Mother, I wish that you would tell me what's happened.

Amanda. As you know, I was supposed to be inducted into my office at the D.A.R. this afternoon. (*Image: A swarm of typewriters.*) But I stopped off at

---

[4] Shorthand symbols created by John Robert Gregg, designed to allow secretaries to take dictation rapidly.

Rubicam's Business College to speak to your teachers about your having a cold and ask them what progress they thought you were making down there.

Laura. Oh. . . .

Amanda. I went to the typing instructor and introduced myself as your mother. She didn't know who you were. Wingfield, she said. We don't have any such student enrolled at the school! I assured her she did, that you had been going to classes since early in January. "I wonder," she said, "if you could be talking about that terribly shy little girl who dropped out of school after only a few days' attendance?" "No," I said, "Laura, my daughter, has been going to school every day for the past six weeks!" "Excuse me," she said. She took the attendance book out and there was your name, unmistakably printed, and all the dates you were absent until they decided that you had dropped out of school. I still said, "No, there must have been some mistake! There must have been some mix-up in the records!" And she said, "No—I remember her perfectly now. Her hand shook so that she couldn't hit the right keys! The first time we gave a speed-test, she broke down completely—was sick at the stomach and almost had to be carried into the wash-room! After that morning she never showed up any more. We phoned the house but never got any answer"—while I was working at Famous and Barr, I suppose, demonstrating those—Oh! I felt so weak I could barely keep on my feet. I had to sit down while they got me a glass of water! Fifty dollars' tuition, all of our plans—my hopes and ambitions for you—just gone up the spout, just gone up the spout like that. *(Laura draws a long breath and gets awkwardly to her feet. She crosses to the Victrola, and winds it up.)* What are you doing?

Laura. Oh! *(She releases the handle and returns to her seat.)*

Amanda. Laura, where have you been going when you've gone out pretending that you were going to business college?

Laura. I've just been going out walking.

Amanda. That's not true.

Laura. It is. I just went walking.

Amanda. Walking? Walking? In winter? Deliberately courting pneumonia in that light coat? Where did you walk to, Laura?

Laura. It was the lesser of two evils, Mother. *(Image: Winter scene in park.)* I couldn't go back up. I—threw up—on the floor!

Amanda. From half past seven till after five every day you mean to tell me you walked around in the park, because you wanted to make me think that you were still going to Rubicam's Business College?

Laura. It wasn't as bad as it sounds. I went inside places to get warmed up.

Amanda. Inside where?

Laura. I went in the art museum and the bird-houses at the Zoo. I visited the penguins every day! Sometimes I did without lunch and went to the movies. Lately I've been spending most of my afternoons in the Jewel-box, that big glass house where they raise the tropical flowers.

Amanda.   You did all this to deceive me, just for the deception? *(Laura looks down.)* Why?

Laura.   Mother, when you're disappointed, you get that awful suffering look on your face, like the picture of Jesus' mother in the museum!

Amanda.   Hush!

Laura.   I couldn't face it.

Pause. A whisper of strings.
(Legend: "The Crust of Humility.")

Amanda *(hopelessly fingering the huge pocketbook).*   So what are we going to do the rest of our lives? Stay home and watch the parades go by? Amuse ourselves with the glass menagerie, darling? Eternally play those worn-out phonograph records your father left as a painful reminder of him? We won't have a business career—we've given that up because it gave us nervous indigestion! *(Laughs wearily.)* What is there left but dependency all our lives? I know so well what becomes of unmarried women who aren't prepared to occupy a position. I've seen such pitiful cases in the South—barely tolerated spinsters living upon the grudging patronage of sister's husband or brother's wife!—stuck away in some little mousetrap of a room—encouraged by one in-law to visit another—little birdlike women without any nest—eating the crust of humility all their life! Is that the future that we've mapped out for ourselves? I swear it's the only alternative I can think of! It isn't a very pleasant alternative, is it? Of course—some girls *do marry. (Laura twists her hands nervously.)* Haven't you ever liked some boy?

Laura.   Yes. I liked one once. *(Rises.)* I came across his picture a while ago.

Amanda *(with some interest).*   He gave you his picture?

Laura.   No, it's in the year-book.

Amanda *(disappointed).*   Oh—a high-school boy.

(Screen image: Jim as a high-school hero bearing a silver cup.)

Laura.   Yes. His name was Jim. *(Laura lifts the heavy annual from the claw-foot table.)* Here he is in *The Pirates of Penzance.*

Amanda *(absently).*   The what?

Laura.   The operetta the senior class put on. He had a wonderful voice and we sat across the aisle from each other Mondays, Wednesdays, and Fridays in the Aud. Here he is with the silver cup for debating! See his grin?

Amanda *(absently).*   He must have had a jolly disposition.

Laura.   He used to call me—Blue Roses.

(Image: Blue roses.)

Amanda. Why did he call you such a name as that?

Laura. When I had that attack of pleurosis—he asked me what was the matter when I came back. I said pleurosis—he thought that I said Blue Roses! So that's what he always called me after that. Whenever he saw me, he'd holler, "Hello, Blue Roses!" I didn't care for the girl that he went out with. Emily Meisenbach. Emily was the best-dressed girl at Soldan. She never struck me, though, as being sincere. . . . It says in the Personal Section—they're engaged. That's—six years ago! They must be married by now.

Amanda. Girls that aren't cut out for business careers usually wind up married to some nice man. (*Gets up with a spark of revival.*) Sister, that's what you'll do!

Laura utters a startled, doubtful laugh. She reaches quickly for a piece of glass.

Laura. But, Mother—

Amanda. Yes? (*Crossing to photograph.*)

Laura (*in a tone of frightened apology*). I'm—crippled!

(*Image: Screen.*)

Amanda. Nonsense! Laura, I've told you never, never to use that word. Why, you're not crippled, you just have a little defect—hardly noticeable, even! When people have some slight disadvantage like that, they cultivate other things to make up for it—develop charm—and vivacity—and—*charm!* That's all you have to do! (*She turns again to the photograph.*) One thing your father had *plenty of*—was *charm!*

Tom motions to the fiddle in the wings.
(*The scene fades out with music.*)

Scene III

(*Legend on the screen: "After the Fiasco—"*)
Tom speaks from the fire-escape landing.

Tom. After the fiasco at Rubicam's Business College, the idea of getting a gentleman caller for Laura began to play a more important part in Mother's calculations. It became an obsession. Like some archetype of the universal unconscious, the image of the gentleman caller haunted our small apartment. . . . (*Image: Young man at door with flowers.*) An evening at home rarely passed without some allusion to this image, this specter, this hope. . . . Even when he wasn't mentioned, his presence hung in Mother's preoccupied look and in my sister's frightened, apologetic manner—hung like a sentence passed upon the Wingfields! Mother was a woman of action as well as words. She began to take logical steps in the planned direction. Late that winter and in the early spring—realizing that extra money would be needed to properly feather the nest and plume the bird—she conducted a vigorous campaign on the telephone, roping in subscribers to one of those magazines for matrons called *The Home-maker's Companion,* the type of journal that features the serialized sublimations of ladies of letters who think in terms of delicate cuplike breasts, slim, tapering waists, rich, creamy thighs, eyes like wood-smoke in autumn, fingers that soothe and caress like strains of music, bodies as powerful as Etruscan sculpture.

(*Screen image:* Glamour *magazine cover.*)
Amanda enters with phone on long extension cord. She is spotted in the dim stage.

Amanda.   Ida Scott? This is Amanda Wingfield! We *missed* you at the D.A.R. last Monday! I said to myself: She's probably suffering with that sinus condition! How is that sinus condition? Horrors! Heaven have mercy!—You're a Christian martyr, yes, that's what you are, a Christian martyr! Well, I just now happened to notice that your subscription to the *Companion's* about to expire! Yes, it expires with the next issue, honey!—just when that wonderful new serial by Bessie Mae Hopper is getting off to such an exciting start. Oh, honey, it's something that you can't miss! You remember how *Gone with the Wind* took everybody by storm? You simply couldn't go out if you hadn't read it. All everybody *talked* was Scarlett O'Hara. Well, this is a book that critics already compare to *Gone with the Wind.* It's the *Gone with the Wind* of the post–World War generation!—What?—Burning?—Oh, honey, don't let them burn, go take a look in the oven and I'll hold the wire! Heavens—I think she's hung up!

(*Dim out.*)
    (*Legend on screen: "You think I'm in love with Continental Shoemakers?"*)
    Before the stage is lighted, the violent voices of Tom and Amanda are heard. They are quarreling behind the portieres. In front of them stands Laura with clenched hands and panicky expression.
    A clear pool of light on her figure throughout this scene.

Tom.   What in Christ's name am I—
Amanda (*shrilly*).   Don't you use that—
Tom.   Supposed to do!
Amanda.   Expression! Not in my—
Tom.   Ohhh!

Amanda. Presence! Have you gone out of your senses?

Tom. I have, that's true, *driven* out!

Amanda. What is the matter with you, you—big—big—IDIOT!

Tom. Look—I've got *no thing,* no single thing—

Amanda. Lower your voice!

Tom. In my life here that I can call my own! Everything is—

Amanda. Stop that shouting!

Tom. Yesterday you confiscated my books! You had the nerve to—

Amanda. I took that horrible novel back to the library—yes! That hideous book by that insane Mr. Lawrence.[5] *(Tom laughs wildly.)* I cannot control the output of diseased minds or people who cater to them—*(Tom laughs still more wildly.)* BUT I WON'T ALLOW SUCH FILTH BROUGHT INTO MY HOUSE! No, no, no, no, no!

Tom. House, house! Who pays rent on it, who makes a slave of himself to—

Amanda *(fairly screeching).* Don't you DARE to—

Tom. No, no, *I* mustn't say things! *I've* got to just—

Amanda. Let me tell you—

Tom. I don't want to hear any more! *(He tears the portieres open. The upstage area is lit with a turgid smoky red glow.)*

Amanda's hair is in metal curlers and she wears a very old bathrobe, much too large for her slight figure, a relic of the faithless Mr. Wingfield.

An upright typewriter and a wild disarray of manuscripts are on the drop-leaf table. The quarrel was probably precipitated by Amanda's interruption of his creative labor. A chair lying overthrown on the floor.

Their gesticulating shadows are cast on the ceiling by the fiery glow.

Amanda. You *will* hear more, you—

Tom. No, I won't hear more, I'm going out!

Amanda. You come right back in—

Tom. Out, out, out! Because I'm—

Amanda. Come back here, Tom Wingfield! I'm not through talking to you!

Tom. Oh, go—

Laura *(desperately).* Tom!

Amanda. You're going to listen, and no more insolence from you! I'm at the end of my patience! *(He comes back toward her.)*

Tom. What do you think I'm at? Aren't I supposed to have any patience to reach the end of, Mother? I know, I know. It seems unimportant to you, what I'm *doing*—what I *want* to do—having a little *difference* between them! You don't think that—

Amanda. I think you've been doing things that you're ashamed of. That's why you act like this. I don't believe that you go every night to the movies. Nobody

---

[5] D. H. Lawrence (1885–1930), a controversial English novelist who startled readers with the frank sexuality depicted in his work.

goes to the movies night after night. Nobody in their right minds goes to the movies as often as you pretend to. People don't go to the movies at nearly midnight, and movies don't let out at two A.M. Come in stumbling. Muttering to yourself like a maniac! You get three hours' sleep and then go to work. Oh, I can picture the way you're doing down there. Moping, doping, because you're in no condition.

Tom (*wildly*).   No, I'm in no condition!

Amanda.   What right have you got to jeopardize your job? Jeopardize the security of us all? How do you think we'd manage if you were—

Tom.   Listen! You think I'm crazy *about* the *warehouse!* (*He bends fiercely toward her slight figure.*) You think I'm in love with the Continental Shoemakers? You think I want to spend fifty-five *years* down there in that—*celotex interior!* with—*fluorescent—tubes!* Look! I'd rather somebody picked up a crowbar and battered out my brains—than go back mornings! I *go!* Every time you come in yelling that God damn *"Rise and Shine!" "Rise and Shine!"* I say to myself "How *lucky dead* people are!" But I get up. I *go!* For sixty-five dollars a month I give up all that I dream of doing and being *ever!* And you say self—*self's* all I ever think of. Why, listen, if self is what I thought of, Mother, I'd be where he is—! (*Pointing to father's picture.*) As far as the system of transportation reaches! (*He starts past her. She grabs his arm.*) Don't grab at me, Mother!

Amanda.   Where are you going?

Tom.   I'm going to the *movies!*

Amanda.   I don't believe that lie!

Tom (*crouching toward her, overtowering her tiny figure. She backs away, gasping*).   I'm going to opium dens! Yes, opium dens, dens of vice and criminals' hang-outs, Mother. I've joined the Hogan gang, I'm a hired assassin, I carry a tommy-gun in a violin case! I run a string of cat-houses in the Valley! They call me Killer, Killer Wingfield, I'm leading a double-life, a simple, honest warehouse worker by day, by night a dynamic *czar* of the *underworld, Mother.* I go to gambling casinos, I spin away fortunes on the roulette table! I wear a patch over one eye and a false mustache, sometimes I put on green whiskers. On those occasions they call me—*El Diablo!*[6] Oh, I could tell you things to make you sleepless! My enemies plan to dynamite this place. They're going to blow us all sky-high some night! I'll be glad, very happy, and so will you! You'll go up, up on a broomstick, over Blue Mountain with seventeen gentlemen callers! You ugly—babbling old—*witch.* . . . (*He goes through a series of violent, clumsy movements, seizing his overcoat, lunging to the door, pulling it fiercely open. The women watch him, aghast. His arm catches in the sleeve of the coat as he struggles to pull it on. For a moment he is pinioned by the bulky garment. With an outraged groan he tears the coat off again, splitting the shoulders of it, and hurls it across the room. It strikes*

---

[6] The devil.

against the shelf of Laura's glass collection, there is a tinkle of shattering glass. Laura cries out as if wounded.)

(Music legend: "The Glass Menagerie.")

Laura *(shrilly).*   My glass!—menagerie. . . . *(She covers her face and turns away.)*

But Amanda is still stunned and stupefied by the "ugly witch" so that she barely notices this occurrence. Now she recovers her speech.

Amanda *(in an awful voice).*   I won't speak to you—until you apologize! *(She crosses through portieres and draws them together behind her. Tom is left with Laura. Laura clings weakly to the mantel with her face averted. Tom stares at her stupidly for a moment. Then he crosses to shelf. Drops awkwardly to his knees to collect the fallen glass, glancing at Laura as if he would speak but couldn't.)*

"The Glass Menagerie" music steals in as the scene dims out.

Scene IV

The interior is dark. Faint light in the alley.
   A deep-voiced bell in a church is tolling the hour of five as the scene commences.
   Tom appears at the top of the alley. After each solemn boom of the bell in the tower, he shakes a little noise-maker or rattle as if to express the tiny spasm of man in contrast to the sustained power and dignity of the Almighty. This and the unsteadiness of his advance make it evident that he has been drinking.
   As he climbs the few steps to the fire-escape landing light steals up inside. Laura appears in night-dress, observing Tom's empty bed in the front room.
   Tom fishes in his pockets for the door-key, removing a motley assortment of articles in the search, including a perfect shower of movie-ticket stubs and an empty bottle. At last he finds the key, but just as he is about to insert it, it slips from his fingers. He strikes a match and crouches below the door.

Tom *(bitterly).*   One crack—and it falls through!

Laura opens the door.

Laura.   Tom! Tom, what are you doing?
Tom.   Looking for a door-key.
Laura.   Where have you been all this time?

Tom.   I have been to the movies.

Laura.   All this time at the movies?

Tom.   There was a very long program. There was a Garbo picture and a Mickey Mouse and a travelogue and a newsreel and a preview of coming attractions. And there was an organ solo and a collection for the milk-fund—simultaneously—which ended up in a terrible fight between a fat lady and an usher!

Laura (*innocently*).   Did you have to stay through everything?

Tom.   Of course! And, oh, I forgot! There was a big stage show! The headliner on this stage show was Malvolio the Magician. He performed wonderful tricks, many of them, such as pouring water back and forth between pitchers. First it turned to wine and then it turned to beer and then it turned to whiskey. I know it was whiskey it finally turned into because he needed some-body to come up out of the audience to help him, and I came up—both shows! It was Kentucky Straight Bourbon. A very generous fellow, he gave souvenirs. (*He pulls from his back pocket a shimmering rainbow-colored scarf.*) He gave me this. This is his magic scarf. You can have it, Laura. You wave it over a canary cage and you get a bowl of gold-fish. You wave it over the gold-fish bowl and they fly away canaries. . . . But the wonderfullest trick of all was the coffin trick. We nailed him into a coffin and he got out of the coffin without removing one nail. (*He has come inside.*) There is a trick that would come in handy for me—get me out of this 2 by 4 situation! (*Flops onto bed and starts removing shoes.*)

Laura.   Tom—Shhh!

Tom.   What you shushing me for?

Laura.   You'll wake up Mother.

Tom.   Goody, goody! Pay 'er back for all those "Rise an' Shines." (*Lies down, groaning.*) You know it don't take much intelligence to get yourself into a nailed-up coffin, Laura. But who in hell ever got himself out of one without removing one nail?

As if in answer, the father's grinning photograph lights up.
   (*Scene dims out.*)
   Immediately following: The church bell is heard striking six. At the sixth stroke the alarm clock goes off in Amanda's room, and after a few moments we hear her calling: "Rise and Shine! Rise and Shine! Laura, go tell your brother to rise and shine!"

Tom (*sitting up slowly*).   I'll rise—but I won't shine.

The light increases.

Amanda.   Laura, tell your brother his coffee is ready.

Laura slips into front room.

Laura. Tom! it's nearly seven. Don't make Mother nervous. (*He stares at her stupidly. Beseechingly.*) Tom, speak to Mother this morning. Make up with her, apologize, speak to her!

Tom. She won't to me. It's her that started not speaking.

Laura. If you just say you're sorry she'll start speaking.

Tom. Her not speaking—is that such a tragedy?

Laura. Please—please!

Amanda (*calling from kitchenette*). Laura, are you going to do what I asked you to do, or do I have to get dressed and go out myself?

Laura. Going, going—soon as I get on my coat! (*She pulls on a shapeless felt hat with nervous, jerky movement, pleadingly glancing at Tom. Rushes awkwardly for coat. The coat is one of Amanda's, inaccurately made-over, the sleeves too short for Laura.*) Butter and what else?

Amanda (*entering upstage*). Just butter. Tell them to charge it.

Laura. Mother, they make such faces when I do that.

Amanda. Sticks and stones may break my bones, but the expression on Mr. Garfinkel's face won't harm us! Tell your brother his coffee is getting cold.

Laura (*at door*). Do what I asked you, will you, will you, Tom?

He looks sullenly away.

Amanda. Laura, go now or just don't go at all!

Laura (*rushing out*). Going—going! (*A second later she cries out. Tom springs up and crosses to the door. Amanda rushes anxiously in. Tom opens the door.*)

Tom. Laura?

Laura. I'm all right. I slipped, but I'm all right.

Amanda (*peering anxiously after her*). If anyone breaks a leg on those fire-escape steps, the landlord ought to be sued for every cent he possesses! (*She shuts door. Remembers she isn't speaking and returns to other room.*)

As Tom enters listlessly for his coffee, she turns her back to him and stands rigidly facing the window on the gloomy gray vault of the areaway. Its light on her face with its aged but childish features is cruelly sharp, satirical as a Daumier[7] print.

(Music under: "Ave Maria.")

Tom glances sheepishly but sullenly at her averted figure and slumps at the table. The coffee is scalding hot; he sips it and gasps and spits it back in the cup. At his gasp, Amanda catches her breath and half turns. Then catches herself and turns back to window.

Tom blows on his coffee, glancing sidewise at his mother. She clears her

---

[7] Honoré Daumier (1808–1879), French painter and satirical caricaturist of French middle-class society.

throat. Tom clears his. He starts to rise. Sinks back down again, scratches his head, clears his throat again. Amanda coughs. Tom raises his cup in both hands to blow on it, his eyes staring over the rim of it at his mother for several moments. Then he slowly sets the cup down and awkwardly and hesitantly rises from the chair.

Tom *(hoarsely)*.   Mother. I—I apologize. Mother. *(Amanda draws a quick, shuddering breath. Her face works grotesquely. She breaks into childlike tears.)* I'm sorry for what I said, for everything that I said, I didn't mean it.

Amanda *(sobbingly)*.   My devotion has made me a witch and so I make myself hateful to my children!

Tom.   No, you *don't.*

Amanda.   I worry so much, don't sleep, it makes me nervous!

Tom *(gently)*.   I understand that.

Amanda.   I've had to put up a solitary battle all these years. But you're my right-hand bower! Don't fall down, don't fail!

Tom *(gently)*.   I try, Mother.

Amanda *(with great enthusiasm)*.   Try and you will SUCCEED! *(The notion makes her breathless.)* Why, you—you're just *full* of natural endowments! Both of my children—they're *unusual* children! Don't you think I know it? I'm so—*proud!* Happy and—feel I've—so much to be thankful for but— Promise me one thing, son!

Tom.   What, Mother?

Amanda.   Promise, son, you'll—never be a drunkard!

Tom *(turns to her grinning)*.   I will never be a drunkard, Mother.

Amanda.   That's what frightened me so, that you'd be drinking! Eat a bowl of Purina!

Tom.   Just coffee, Mother.

Amanda.   Shredded wheat biscuit?

Tom.   No. No, Mother, just coffee.

Amanda.   You can't put in a day's work on an empty stomach. You've got ten minutes—don't gulp! Drinking too-hot liquids makes cancer of the stomach. . . . Put cream in.

Tom.   No, thank you.

Amanda.   To cool it.

Tom.   No! No, thank you, I want it black.

Amanda.   I know, but it's not good for you. We have to do all that we can to build ourselves up. In these trying times we live in, all that we have to cling to is—each other. . . . That's why it's so important to—Tom, I—I sent out your sister so I could discuss something with you. If you hadn't spoken I would have spoken to you. *(Sits down.)*

Tom *(gently)*.   What is it, Mother, that you want to discuss?

Amanda.   Laura!

Tom puts his cup down slowly.

(Legend on screen: "Laura.")
(Music: "The Glass Menagerie.")

Tom. —Oh.—Laura . . .

Amanda *(touching his sleeve).* You know how Laura is. So quiet but—still water runs deep! She notices things and I think she—broods about them. *(Tom looks up.)* A few days ago I came in and she was crying.

Tom. What about?

Amanda. You.

Tom. Me?

Amanda. She has an idea that you're not happy here.

Tom. What gave her that idea?

Amanda. What gives her any idea? However, you do act strangely. I—I'm not criticizing, understand *that!* I know your ambitions do not lie in the warehouse, that like everybody in the whole wide world—you've had to—make sacrifices, but—Tom—Tom—life's not easy, it calls for—Spartan endurance! There's so many things in my heart that I cannot describe to you! I've never told you but I—*loved* your father. . . .

Tom *(gently).* I know that, Mother.

Amanda. And you—when I see you taking after his ways! Staying out late—and—well, you *had* been drinking the night you were in that—terrifying condition! Laura says that you hate the apartment and that you go out nights to get away from it! Is that true, Tom?

Tom. No. You say there's so much in your heart that you can't describe to me. That's true of me, too. There's so much in my heart that I can't describe to *you!* So let's respect each other's—

Amanda. But, why—*why*, Tom—are you always so *restless?* Where do you go to, nights?

Tom. I—go to the movies.

Amanda. Why do you go to the movies so much, Tom?

Tom. I go to the movies because—I like adventure. Adventure is something I don't have much of at work, so I go to the movies.

Amanda. But, Tom, you go to the movies *entirely too much!*

Tom. I like a lot of adventure.

Amanda looks baffled, then hurt. As the familiar inquisition resumes he becomes hard and impatient again. Amanda slips back into her querulous attitude toward him.

(Image on screen: Sailing vessel with Jolly Roger.)

Amanda. Most young men find adventure in their careers.

Tom. Then most young men are not employed in a warehouse.

Amanda. The world is full of young men employed in warehouses and offices and factories.

Tom. Do all of them find adventure in their careers?

Amanda. They do or they do without it! Not everybody has a craze for adventure.

Tom. Man is by instinct a lover, a hunter, a fighter, and none of those instincts are given much play at the warehouse!

Amanda. Man is by instinct! Don't quote instinct to me! Instinct is something that people have got away from! It belongs to animals! Christian adults don't want it!

Tom. What do Christian adults want, then, Mother?

Amanda. Superior things! Things of the mind and the spirit! Only animals have to satisfy instincts! Surely your aims are somewhat higher than theirs! Than monkeys—pigs—

Tom. I reckon they're not.

Amanda. You're joking. However, that isn't what I wanted to discuss.

Tom (*rising*). I haven't much time.

Amanda (*pushing his shoulders*). Sit down.

Tom. You want me to punch in red[8] at the warehouse, Mother?

Amanda. You have five minutes. I want to talk about Laura.

(*Legend: "Plans and Provisions."*)

Tom. All right! What about Laura?

Amanda. We have to be making plans and provisions for her. She's older than you, two years, and nothing has happened. She just drifts along doing nothing. It frightens me terribly how she just drifts along.

Tom. I guess she's the type that people call home girls.

Amanda. There's no such type, and if there is, it's a pity! That is unless the home is hers, with a husband!

Tom. What?

Amanda. Oh, I can see the handwriting on the wall as plain as I see the nose in front of my face! It's terrifying! More and more you remind me of your father! He was out all hours without explanation—Then *left! Good-bye!* And me with the bag to hold. I saw that letter you got from the Merchant Marine. I know what you're dreaming of. I'm not standing here blindfolded. Very well, then. Then *do* it! But not till there's somebody to take your place.

Tom. What do you mean?

Amanda. I mean that as soon as Laura has got somebody to take care of her, married, a home of her own, independent—why, then you'll be free to go wherever you please, on land, on sea, whichever way the wind blows! But until that time you've got to look out for your sister. I don't say me because I'm old and don't matter! I say for your sister because she's young and dependent.

---

[8] Be late for work.

I put her in business college—a dismal failure! Frightened her so it made her sick to her stomach. I took her over to the Young People's League at the church. Another fiasco. She spoke to nobody, nobody spoke to her. Now all she does is fool with those pieces of glass and play those worn-out records. What kind of a life is that for a girl to lead!

Tom. What can I do about it?

Amanda. Overcome selfishness! Self, self, self is all that you ever think of! *(Tom springs up and crosses to get his coat. It is ugly and bulky. He pulls on a cap with earmuffs.)* Where is your muffler? Put your wool muffler on! *(He snatches it angrily from the closet and tosses it around his neck and pulls both ends tight.)* Tom! I haven't said what I had in mind to ask you.

Tom. I'm too late to—

Amanda *(catching his arms—very importunately. Then shyly.)* Down at the warehouse, aren't there some—nice young men?

Tom. No!

Amanda. There *must* be—*some*.

Tom. Mother—

Gesture.

Amanda. Find out one that's clean-living—doesn't drink and—ask him out for sister!

Tom. What?

Amanda. For *sister!* To *meet!* Get *acquainted!*

Tom *(stamping to door).* Oh, my go-osh!

Amanda. Will you? *(He opens door. Imploringly.)* Will you? *(He starts down.)* Will you? *Will* you, dear?

Tom *(calling back).* YES!

Amanda closes the door hesitantly and with a troubled but faintly hopeful expression.
(Screen image: Glamour *magazine cover.)*
Spot Amanda at phone.

Amanda. Ella Cartwright? This is Amanda Wingfield! How are you, honey? How is that kidney condition? *(Count five.)* Horrors! *(Count five.)* You're a Christian martyr, yes, honey, that's what you are, a Christian martyr! Well, I just happened to notice in my little red book that your subscription to the *Companion* has just run out! I knew that you wouldn't want to miss out on the wonderful serial starting in this new issue. It's by Bessie Mae Hopper, the first thing she's written since *Honeymoon for Three.* Wasn't that a strange and interesting story? Well, this one is even lovelier, I believe. It has a sophisticated society background. It's all about the horsey set on Long Island!

(Fade out.)

Scene V

(Legend on screen: "Annunciation.") Fade with music.

It is early dusk of a spring evening. Supper has just been finished in the Wing-field apartment. Amanda and Laura in light colored dresses are removing dishes from the table, in the upstage area, which is shadowy, their movements formalized almost as a dance or ritual, their moving forms as pale and silent as moths.

Tom, in white shirt and trousers, rises from the table and crosses toward the fire-escape.

Amanda *(as he passes her).* Son, will you do me a favor?

Tom. What?

Amanda. Comb your hair! You look so pretty when your hair is combed! *(Tom slouches on sofa with evening paper. Enormous caption "Franco Triumphs."*[9]*)* There is only one respect in which I would like you to emulate your father.

Tom. What respect is that?

Amanda. The care he always took of his appearance. He never allowed himself to look untidy. *(He throws down the paper and crosses to fire-escape.)* Where are you going?

Tom. I'm going out to smoke.

Amanda. You smoke too much. A pack a day at fifteen cents a pack. How much would that amount to in a month? Thirty times fifteen is how much, Tom? Figure it out and you will be astounded at what you could save. Enough to give you a night-school course in accounting at Washington U! Just think what a wonderful thing that would be for you, son!

Tom is unmoved by the thought.

Tom. I'd rather smoke. *(He steps out on landing, letting the screen door slam.)*

Amanda *(sharply).* I know! That's the tragedy of it. . . . *(Alone, she turns to look at her husband's picture.)*

(Dance music: "All the World Is Waiting for the Sunrise!")

Tom *(to the audience).* Across the alley from us was the Paradise Dance Hall. On evenings in spring the windows and doors were open and the music came outdoors. Sometimes the lights were turned out except for a large glass sphere that hung from the ceiling. It would turn slowly about and filter the dusk with delicate rainbow colors. Then the orchestra played a waltz or a tango, something that had a slow and sensuous rhythm. Couples would come outside, to the relative privacy of the alley. You could see them kissing behind

---

[9] General Francisco Franco led fascist Spanish rebels, aided by Nazi Germany, in a civil war against Loyalists to the Spanish throne, aided by the Soviet Union. Franco's forces triumphed in 1939.

ash-pits and telephone poles. This was the compensation for lives that passed like mine, without any change or adventure. Adventure and change were imminent in this year. They were waiting around the corner for all these kids. Suspended in the mist over the Berchtesgaden,[10] caught in the folds of Chamberlain's[11] umbrella—In Spain there was Guernica! But here there was only hot swing music and liquor, dance halls, bars, and movies, and sex that hung in the gloom like a chandelier and flooded the world with brief, deceptive rainbows. . . . All the world was waiting for bombardments!

Amanda turns from the picture and comes outside.

Amanda *(sighing).* A fire-escape landing's a poor excuse for a porch. *(She spreads a newspaper on a step and sits down, gracefully and demurely as if she were settling into a swing on a Mississippi veranda.)* What are you looking at?
Tom. The moon.
Amanda. Is there a moon this evening?
Tom. It's rising over Garfinkel's Delicatessen.
Amanda. So it is! A little silver slipper of a moon. Have you made a wish on it yet?
Tom. Um-hum.
Amanda. What did you wish for?
Tom. That's a secret.
Amanda. A secret, huh? Well, I won't tell mine either. I will be just as mysterious as you.
Tom. I bet I can guess what yours is.
Amanda. Is my head so transparent?
Tom. You're not a sphinx.
Amanda. No, I don't have secrets. I'll tell you what I wished for on the moon. Success and happiness for my precious children! I wish for that whenever there's a moon, and when there isn't a moon, I wish for it, too.
Tom. I thought perhaps you wished for a gentleman caller.
Amanda. Why do you say that?
Tom. Don't you remember asking me to fetch one?
Amanda. I remember suggesting that it would be nice for your sister if you brought home some nice young man from the warehouse. I think I've made that suggestion more than once.
Tom. Yes, you have made it repeatedly.
Amanda. Well?

---

[10] The location of Hitler's mountain resort in Bavaria.
[11] Neville Chamberlain (1869–1940), famous for carrying an umbrella, and infamous for appeasing Hitler in an attempt to avoid war..

Tom.   We are going to have one.
Amanda.   *What?*
Tom.   A gentleman caller!

(The Annunciation is celebrated with music.)
Amanda rises.
(Image on screen: Caller with bouquet.)

Amanda.   You mean you have asked some nice young man to come over?
Tom.   Yep. I've asked him to dinner.
Amanda.   You really did?
Tom.   I did!
Amanda.   You did, and did he—*accept?*
Tom.   He did!
Amanda.   Well, well—well, well! That's—lovely!
Tom.   I thought that you would be pleased.
Amanda.   It's definite, then?
Tom.   Very definite.
Amanda.   Soon?
Tom.   Very soon.
Amanda.   For heaven's sake, stop putting on and tell me some things, will you?
Tom.   What things do you want me to tell you?
Amanda.   Naturally I would like to know when he's *coming!*
Tom.   He's coming tomorrow.
Amanda.   *Tomorrow?*
Tom.   Yep. Tomorrow.
Amanda.   But, Tom!
Tom.   Yes, Mother?
Amanda.   Tomorrow gives me no time!
Tom.   Time for what?
Amanda.   Preparations! Why didn't you phone me at once, as soon as you asked him, the minute that he accepted? Then, don't you see, I could have been getting ready!
Tom.   You don't have to make any fuss.
Amanda.   Oh, Tom, Tom, Tom, of course I have to make a fuss! I want things nice, not sloppy! Not thrown together. I'll certainly have to do some fast thinking, won't I?
Tom.   I don't see why you have to think at all.
Amanda.   You just don't know. We can't have a gentleman caller in a pig-sty! All my wedding silver has to be polished, the monogrammed table linen ought to be laundered! The windows have to be washed and fresh curtains put up. And how about clothes? We have to *wear* something, don't we?

Tom. Mother, this boy is no one to make a fuss over!

Amanda. Do you realize he's the first young man we've introduced to your sister? It's terrible, dreadful, disgraceful that poor little sister has never received a single gentleman caller! Tom, come inside! *(She opens the screen door.)*

Tom. What for?

Amanda. I want to ask you some things.

Tom. If you're going to make such a fuss, I'll call it off, I'll tell him not to come.

Amanda. You certainly won't do anything of the kind. Nothing offends people worse than broken engagements. It simply means I'll have to work like a Turk! We won't be brilliant, but we'll pass inspection. Come on inside. *(Tom follows, groaning.)* Sit down.

Tom. Any particular place you would like me to sit?

Amanda. Thank heavens I've got that new sofa! I'm also making payments on a floor lamp I'll have sent out! And put the chintz covers on, they'll brighten things up! Of course I'd hoped to have these walls re-papered. . . . What is the young man's name?

Tom. His name is O'Connor.

Amanda. That, of course, means fish—tomorrow is Friday! I'll have that salmon loaf—with Durkee's dressing! What does he do? He works at the warehouse?

Tom. Of course! How else would I—

Amanda. Tom, he—doesn't drink?

Tom. Why do you ask me that?

Amanda. Your father *did!*

Tom. Don't get started on that!

Amanda. He *does* drink, then?

Tom. Not that I know of!

Amanda. Make sure, be certain! The last thing I want for my daughter's a boy who drinks!

Tom. Aren't you being a little premature? Mr. O'Connor has not yet appeared on the scene!

Amanda. But will tomorrow. To meet your sister, and what do I know about his character? Nothing! Old maids are better off than wives of drunkards!

Tom. Oh, my God!

Amanda. Be still!

Tom *(leaning forward to whisper).* Lots of fellows meet girls whom they don't marry!

Amanda. Oh, talk sensibly, Tom—and don't be sarcastic! *(She has gotten a hairbrush.)*

Tom. What are you doing?

Amanda. I'm brushing that cow-lick down! What is this young man's position at the warehouse?

Tom (*submitting grimly to the brush and the interrogation*). This young man's
position is that of a shipping clerk, Mother.

Amanda. Sounds to me like a fairly responsible job, the sort of a job *you*
would be in if you just had more *get-up*. What is his salary? Have you got any
idea?

Tom. I would judge it to be approximately eighty-five dollars a month.

Amanda. Well—not princely, but—

Tom. Twenty more than I make.

Amanda. Yes, how well I know! But for a family man, eighty-five dollars a
month is not much more than you can just get by on. . . .

Tom. Yes, but Mr. O'Connor is not a family man.

Amanda. He might be, mightn't he? Some time in the future?

Tom. I see. Plans and provisions.

Amanda. You are the only young man that I know of who ignores the fact that
the future becomes the present, the present the past, and the past turns into
everlasting regret if you don't plan for it!

Tom. I will think that over and see what I can make of it.

Amanda. Don't be supercilious with your mother! Tell me some more about
this—what do you call him?

Tom. James D. O'Connor. The D. is for Delaney.

Amanda. Irish on *both* sides! *Gracious!* And doesn't drink?

Tom. Shall I call him up and ask him right this minute?

Amanda. The only way to find out about those things is to make discreet inquiries at the proper moment. When I was a girl in Blue Mountain and it was
suspected that a young man drank, the girl whose attentions he had been receiving, if any girl *was,* would sometimes speak to the minister of his church,
or rather her father would if her father was living, and sort of feel him out on
the young man's character. That is the way such things are discreetly handled
to keep a young woman from making a tragic mistake!

Tom. Then how did you happen to make a tragic mistake?

Amanda. That innocent look of your father's had everyone fooled! He
smiled—the world was *enchanted!* No girl can do worse than put herself at
the mercy of a handsome appearance! I hope that Mr. O'Connor is not too
good-looking.

Tom. No, he's not too good-looking. He's covered with freckles and hasn't too
much of a nose.

Amanda. He's not right-down homely, though?

Tom. Not right-down homely. Just medium homely, I'd say.

Amanda. Character's what to look for in a man.

Tom. That's what I've always said, Mother.

Amanda. You've never said anything of the kind and I suspect you would
never give it a thought.

Tom. Don't be suspicious of me.

Amanda. At least I hope he's the type that's up and coming.

Tom.   I think he really goes in for self-improvement.

Amanda.   What reason have you to think so?

Tom.   He goes to night school.

Amanda *(beaming).*   Splendid! What does he do, I mean study?

Tom.   Radio engineering and public speaking!

Amanda.   Then he has visions of being advanced in the world! Any young man who studies public speaking is aiming to have an executive job some day! And radio engineering? A thing for the future! Both of these facts are very illuminating. Those are the sort of things that a mother should know concerning any young man who comes to call on her daughter. Seriously or—not.

Tom.   One little warning. He doesn't know about Laura. I didn't let on that we had dark ulterior motives. I just said, why don't you come have dinner with us? He said okay and that was the whole conversation.

Amanda.   I bet it was! You're eloquent as an oyster. However, he'll know about Laura when he gets here. When he sees how lovely and sweet and pretty she is, he'll thank his lucky stars he was asked to dinner.

Tom.   Mother, you mustn't expect too much of Laura.

Amanda.   What do you mean?

Tom.   Laura seems all those things to you and me because she's ours and we love her. We don't even notice she's crippled any more.

Amanda.   Don't say crippled! You know that I never allow that word to be used!

Tom.   But face facts, Mother. She is and—that's not all—

Amanda.   What do you mean "not all"?

Tom.   Laura is very different from other girls.

Amanda.   I think the difference is all to her advantage.

Tom.   Not quite all—in the eyes of others—strangers—she's terribly shy and lives in a world of her own and those things make her seem a little peculiar to people outside the house.

Amanda.   Don't say peculiar.

Tom.   Face the facts. She is.

(The dance-hall music changes to a tango that has a minor and somewhat ominous tone.)

Amanda.   In what way is she peculiar—may I ask?

Tom *(gently).*   She lives in a world of her own—a world of—little glass ornaments, Mother. . . . *(Gets up. Amanda remains holding brush, looking at him, troubled.)* She plays old phonograph records and—that's about all—*(He glances at himself in the mirror and crosses to door.)*

Amanda *(sharply).*   Where are you going?

Tom.   I'm going to the movies. *(Out screen door.)*

Amanda.   Not to the movies, every night to the movies! *(Follows quickly to screen door.)* I don't believe you always go to the movies! *(He is gone. Amanda

*looks worriedly after him for a moment. Then vitality and optimism return
and she turns from the door. Crossing to portieres.)* Laura! Laura! *(Laura answers from kitchenette.)*

Laura. Yes, Mother.

Amanda. Let those dishes go and come in front! *(Laura appears with dish
towel. Gaily.)* Laura, come here and make a wish on the moon!

Laura *(entering).* Moon—moon?

Amanda. A little silver slipper of a moon. Look over your left shoulder,
Laura, and make a wish! *(Laura looks faintly puzzled as if called out of sleep.
Amanda seizes her shoulders and turns her at angle by the door.)* Now! Now,
darling, *wish!*

Laura. What shall I wish for, Mother?

Amanda *(her voice trembling and her eyes suddenly filling with tears).* Happiness! Good Fortune!

The violin rises and the stage dims out.

Scene VI

(Image: High-school hero.)

Tom. And so the following evening I brought Jim home to dinner. I had
known Jim slightly in high school. In high school Jim was a hero. He had
tremendous Irish good nature and vitality with the scrubbed and polished
look of white chinaware. He seemed to move in a continual spotlight. He was
a star in basketball, captain of the debating club, president of the senior class
and the glee club and he sang the male lead in the annual light operas. He
was always running or bounding, never just walking. He seemed always at the
point of defeating the law of gravity. He was shooting with such velocity
through his adolescence that you would logically expect him to arrive at nothing short of the White House by the time he was thirty. But Jim apparently
ran into more interference after his graduation from Soldan. His speed had
definitely slowed. Six years after he left high school he was holding a job that
wasn't much better than mine.

(Image: Clerk.)

He was the only one at the warehouse with whom I was on friendly terms. I
was valuable to him as someone who could remember his former glory, who
had seen him win basketball games and the silver cup in debating. He knew of
my secret practice of retiring to a cabinet of the washroom to work on poems
when business was slack in the warehouse. He called me Shakespeare. And

while the other boys in the warehouse regarded me with suspicious hostility, Jim took a humorous attitude toward me. Gradually his attitude affected the others, their hostility wore off, and they also began to smile at me as people smile at an oddly fashioned dog who trots across their paths at some distance.

I knew that Jim and Laura had known each other at Soldan, and I had heard Laura speak admiringly of his voice. I didn't know if Jim remembered her or not. In high school Laura had been as unobtrusive as Jim had been astonishing. If he did remember Laura, it was not as my sister, for when I asked him to dinner, he grinned and said, "You know, Shakespeare, I never thought of you as having folks!"

He was about to discover that I did. . . .

(Light upstage.)

(Legend on screen: "The Accent of a Coming Foot.")

Friday evening. It is about five o'clock of a late spring evening which comes "scattering poems in the sky."

A delicate lemony light is in the Wingfield apartment.

Amanda has worked like a Turk in preparation for the gentleman caller. The results are astonishing. The new floor lamp with its rose-silk shade is in place, a colored paper lantern conceals the broken light fixture in the ceiling, new billowing white curtains are at the windows, chintz covers are on chairs and sofa, a pair of new sofa pillows make their initial appearance.

Open boxes and tissue paper are scattered on the floor.

Laura stands in the middle with lifted arms while Amanda crouches before her, adjusting the hem of the new dress, devout and ritualistic. The dress is colored and designed by memory. The arrangement of Laura's hair is changed; it is softer and more becoming. A fragile, unearthly prettiness has come out in Laura: she is like a piece of translucent glass touched by light, given a momentary radiance, not actual, not lasting.

Amanda *(impatiently).* Why are you trembling?
Laura. Mother, you've made me so nervous!
Amanda. How have I made you nervous?
Laura. By all this fuss! You make it seem so important!
Amanda. I don't understand you, Laura. You couldn't be satisfied with just sitting home, and yet whenever I try to arrange something for you, you seem to resist it. *(She gets up.)* Now take a look at yourself. No, wait! Wait just a moment—I have an idea!
Laura. What is it now?

Amanda produces two powder puffs which she wraps in handkerchiefs and stuffs in Laura's bosom.

Laura. Mother, what are you doing?
Amanda. They call them "Gay Deceivers"!

Laura.   I won't wear them!

Amanda.   You will!

Laura.   Why should I?

Amanda.   Because, to be painfully honest, your chest is flat.

Laura.   You make it seem like we were setting a trap.

Amanda.   All pretty girls are a trap, a pretty trap, and men expect them to be. (*Legend: "A Pretty Trap."*) Now look at yourself, young lady. This is the prettiest you will ever be! I've got to fix myself now! You're going to be surprised by your mother's appearance! (*She crosses through portieres, humming gaily.*)

Laura moves slowly to the long mirror and stares solemnly at herself.

A wind blows the white curtains inward in a slow, graceful motion and with a faint, sorrowful sighing.

Amanda (*off stage*).   It isn't dark enough yet. (*She turns slowly before the mirror with a troubled look.*)

(*Legend on screen: "This Is My Sister: Celebrate Her with Strings!" Music.*)

Amanda (*laughing, off*).   I'm going to show you something. I'm going to make a spectacular appearance!

Laura.   What is it, Mother?

Amanda.   Possess your soul in patience—you will see! Something I've resurrected from that old trunk! Styles haven't changed so terribly much after all. . . . (*She parts the portieres.*) Now just look at your mother! (*She wears a girlish frock of yellowed voile with a blue silk sash. She carries a bunch of jonquils—the legend of her youth is nearly revived. Feverishly.*) This is the dress in which I led the cotillion. Won the cakewalk twice at Sunset Hill, wore one spring to the Governor's ball in Jackson! See how I sashayed around the ballroom, Laura? (*She raises her skirt and does a mincing step around the room.*) I wore it on Sundays for my gentlemen callers! I had it on the day I met your father—I had malaria fever all that spring. The change of climate from East Tennessee to the Delta—weakened resistance—I had a little temperature all the time—not enough to be serious—just enough to make me restless and giddy! Invitations poured in—parties all over the Delta!—"Stay in bed," said Mother, "you have fever!"—but I just wouldn't.—I took quinine but kept on going, going!—Evenings, dances!—Afternoons, long, long rides! Picnics— lovely!—So lovely, that country in May.—All lacy with dogwood, literally flooded with jonquils!—That was the spring I had the craze for jonquils. Jonquils became an absolute obsession. Mother said, "Honey, there's no more room for jonquils." And still I kept bringing in more jonquils. Whenever, wherever I saw them, I'd say, "Stop! Stop! I see jonquils!" I made the young men help me gather the jonquils! It was a joke, Amanda and her jonquils! Finally there were no more vases to hold them, every available space was filled with jonquils. No vases to hold them? All right, I'll hold them myself! And then I—(*She stops in front of the picture.*) (*Music.*) met your father! Malaria fever and jonquils and then—this—boy. . . . (*She switches on the rose-colored lamp.*) I hope they get here before it starts to rain. (*She crosses upstage and places the jonquils in bowl on table.*) I gave your brother a little extra change so he and Mr. O'Connor could take the service car home.

Laura (*with altered look*). What did you say his name was?

Amanda. O'Connor.

Laura. What is his first name?

Amanda. I don't remember. Oh, yes, I do. It was—Jim!

Laura sways slightly and catches hold of a chair.
(*Legend on screen: "Not Jim!"*)

Laura (*faintly*) Not—Jim!

Amanda. Yes, that was it, it was Jim! I've never known a Jim that wasn't nice!

(*Music: Ominous.*)

Laura. Are you sure his name is Jim O'Connor?

Amanda. Yes. Why?

Laura. Is he the one that Tom used to know in high school?

Amanda. He didn't say so. I think he just got to know him at the warehouse.

Laura. There was a Jim O'Connor we both knew in high school—(*Then, with effort.*) If that is the one that Tom is bringing to dinner—you'll have to excuse me, I won't come to the table.

Amanda. What sort of nonsense is this?

Laura. You asked me once if I'd ever liked a boy. Don't you remember I showed you this boy's picture?

Amanda. You mean the boy you showed me in the year-book?

Laura. Yes, that boy.

Amanda. Laura, Laura, were you in love with that boy?

Laura. I don't know, Mother. All I know is I couldn't sit at the table if it was him!

Amanda. It won't be him! It isn't the least bit likely. But whether it is or not, you will come to the table. You will not be excused.

Laura. I'll have to be, Mother.

Amanda. I don't intend to humor your silliness, Laura. I've had too much from you and your brother, both! So just sit down and compose yourself till they come. Tom has forgotten his key so you'll have to let them in, when they arrive.

Laura (*panicky*). Oh, Mother—*you* answer the door!

Amanda (*lightly*). I'll be in the kitchen—busy!

Laura. Oh, Mother, please answer the door, don't make me do it!

Amanda *(crossing into kitchenette).*   I've got to fix the dressing for the salmon. Fuss, fuss—silliness!—over a gentleman caller!

Door swings shut. Laura is left alone.
   (Legend: "Terror!")
   She utters a low moan and turns off the lamp—sits stiffly on the edge of the sofa, knotting her fingers together.
   (Legend on screen: "The Opening of a Door!")
   Tom and Jim appear on the fire-escape steps and climb to landing. Hearing their approach, Laura rises with a panicky gesture. She retreats to the portieres.
   The doorbell. Laura catches her breath and touches her throat. Low drums.

Amanda *(calling).*   Laura, sweetheart! The door!

Laura stares at it without moving.

Jim.   I think we just beat the rain.
Tom.   Uh-huh. *(He rings again, nervously. Jim whistles and fishes for a cigarette.)*
Amanda *(very, very gaily).*   Laura, that is your brother and Mr. O'Connor! Will you let them in, darling?

Laura crosses toward kitchenette door.

Laura *(breathlessly).*   Mother—you go to the door!

Amanda steps out of kitchenette and stares furiously at Laura. She points imperiously at the door.

Laura.   Please, please!
Amanda *(in a fierce whisper).*   What is the matter with you, you silly thing?
Laura *(desperately).*   Please, you answer it, *please!*
Amanda.   I told you I wasn't going to humor you, Laura. Why have you chosen this moment to lose your mind?
Laura.   Please, please, please, you go!
Amanda.   You'll have to go to the door because I can't!
Laura *(despairingly).*   I can't either!
Amanda.   Why?
Laura.   I'm *sick!*
Amanda.   I'm sick, too—of your nonsense! Why can't you and your brother be normal people? Fantastic whims and behavior! *(Tom gives a long ring.)* Preposterous goings on! Can you give me one reason—*(Calls out lyrically.)*—why should you be afraid to open a door? Now you answer it, Laura!

Laura.   Oh, oh, oh . . . (*She returns through the portieres. Darts to the Victrola and winds it frantically and turns it on.*)
Amanda.   Laura Wingfield, you march right to that door!
Laura.   Yes—yes, Mother!

A faraway, scratchy rendition of "Dardanella" softens the air and gives her strength to move through it. She slips to the door and draws it cautiously open. Tom enters with the caller, Jim O'Connor.

Tom.   Laura, this is Jim. Jim, this is my sister, Laura.
Jim (*stepping inside*).   I didn't know that Shakespeare had a sister!
Laura (*retreating stiff and trembling from the door*).   How—how do you do?
Jim (*heartily extending his hand*).   Okay!

Laura touches it hesitantly with hers.

Jim.   Your hand's *cold*, Laura!
Laura.   Yes, well—I've been playing the Victrola . . .
Jim.   Must have been playing classical music on it! You ought to play a little hot swing music to warm you up!
Laura.   Excuse me—I haven't finished playing the Victrola . . .

She turns awkwardly and hurries into the front room. She pauses a second by the Victrola. Then catches her breath and darts through the portieres like a frightened deer.

Jim (*grinning*).   What was the matter?
Tom.   Oh—with Laura? Laura is—terribly shy.
Jim.   Shy, huh? It's unusual to meet a shy girl nowadays. I don't believe you ever mentioned you had a sister.
Tom.   Well, now you know. I have one. Here is the *Post Dispatch*. You want a piece of it?
Jim.   Uh-huh.
Tom.   What piece? The comics?
Jim.   Sports! (*Glances at it.*) Ole Dizzy Dean is on his bad behavior.
Tom (*disinterest*).   Yeah? (*Lights cigarette and crosses back to fire-escape door.*)
Jim.   Where are *you* going?
Tom.   I'm going out on the terrace.
Jim (*goes after him*).   You know, Shakespeare—I'm going to sell you a bill of goods!
Tom.   What goods?
Jim.   A course I'm taking.
Tom.   Huh?
Jim.   In public speaking! You and me, we're not the warehouse type.

Tom. Thanks—that's good news. But what has public speaking got to do with it?

Jim. It fits you for—executive positions!

Tom. Awww.

Jim. I tell you it's done a helluva lot for me.

(Image: Executive at desk.)

Tom. In what respect?

Jim. In every! Ask yourself what is the difference between you an' me and men in the office down front? Brains?—No!—Ability?—No! Then what? Just one little thing—

Tom. What is that one little thing?

Jim. Primarily it amounts to—social poise! Being able to square up to people and hold your own on any social level!

Amanda *(off stage).* Tom?

Tom. Yes, Mother?

Amanda. Is that you and Mr. O'Connor?

Tom. Yes, Mother.

Amanda. Well, you just make yourselves comfortable in there.

Tom. Yes, Mother.

Amanda. Ask Mr. O'Connor if he would like to wash his hands.

Jim. Aw—no—no—thank you—I took care of that at the warehouse. Tom—

Tom. Yes?

Jim. Mr. Mendoza was speaking to me about you.

Tom. Favorably?

Jim. What do you think?

Tom. Well—

Jim. You're going to be out of a job if you don't wake up.

Tom. I am waking up—

Jim. You show no signs.

Tom. The signs are interior.

(Image on screen: The sailing vessel with Jolly Roger again.)

Tom. I'm planning to change. *(He leans over the rail speaking with quiet exhilaration. The incandescent marquees and signs of the first-run movie houses light his face from across the alley. He looks like a voyager.)* I'm right at the point of committing myself to a future that doesn't include the warehouse and Mr. Mendoza or even a night-school course in public speaking.

Jim. What are you gassing about?

Tom. I'm tired of the movies.

Jim. Movies!

Tom. Yes, movies! Look at them—*(A wave toward the marvels of Grand Avenue.)* All of those glamorous people—having adventures—hogging it all, gobbling the whole thing up! You know what happens? People go to the *movies* instead of *moving!* Hollywood characters are supposed to have all the adventures for everybody in America, while everybody in America sits in a dark room and watches them have them! Yes, until there's a war. That's when adventure becomes available to the masses! *Everyone's* dish, not only Gable's! Then the people in the dark room come out of the dark room to have some adventures themselves—Goody, goody—It's our turn now, to go to the South Sea Island—to make a safari—to be exotic, far-off—But I'm not patient. I don't want to wait till then. I'm tired of the *movies* and I am *about* to *move!*

Jim *(incredulously).* Move?

Tom. Yes.

Jim. When?

Tom. Soon!

Jim. Where? Where?

(Theme three: Music seems to answer the question, while Tom thinks it over. He searches among his pockets.)

Tom. I'm starting to boil inside. I know I seem dreamy, but inside—well, I'm boiling! Whenever I pick up a shoe, I shudder a little thinking how short life is and what I am doing!—Whatever that means. I know it doesn't mean shoes—except as something to wear on a traveler's feet! *(Finds paper.)* Look—

Jim. What?

Tom. I'm a member.

Jim *(reading).* The Union of Merchant Seamen.

Tom. I paid my dues this month, instead of the light bill.

Jim. You will regret it when they turn the lights off.

Tom. I won't be here.

Jim. How about your mother?

Tom. I'm like my father. The bastard son of a bastard! See how he grins? And he's been absent going on sixteen years!

Jim. You're just talking, you drip. How does your mother feel about it?

Tom. Shhh—Here comes Mother! Mother is not acquainted with my plans!

Amanda *(enters portieres).* Where are you all?

Tom. On the terrace, Mother.

They start inside. She advances to them. Tom is distinctly shocked at her appearance. Even Jim blinks a little. He is making his first contact with girlish Southern vivacity and in spite of the night-school course in public speaking is somewhat thrown off the beam by the unexpected outlay of social charm.

Certain responses are attempted by Jim but are swept aside by Amanda's gay laughter and chatter. Tom is embarrassed but after the first shock Jim reacts very warmly. Grins and chuckles, is altogether won over.

(Image: Amanda as a girl.)

Amanda (*coyly smiling, shaking her girlish ringlets*).   Well, well, well, so this is Mr. O'Connor. Introductions entirely unnecessary. I've heard so much about you from my boy. I finally said to him, Tom—good gracious!—why don't you bring this paragon to supper? I'd like to meet this nice young man at the warehouse!—Instead of just hearing him sing your praises so much! I don't know why my son is so stand-offish—that's not Southern behavior! Let's sit down and—I think we could stand a little more air in here! Tom, leave the door open. I felt a nice fresh breeze a moment ago. Where has it gone? Mmm, so warm already! And not quite summer, even. We're going to burn up when summer really gets started. However, we're having—we're having a very light supper. I think light things are better fo' this time of year. The same as light clothes are. Light clothes an' light food are what warm weather calls fo'. You know our blood gets so thick during th' winter—it takes a while fo' us to *adjust* ou'selves!—when the season changes. . . . It's come so quick this year. I wasn't prepared. All of a sudden—heavens! Already summer!—I ran to the trunk an' pulled out this light dress—Terribly old! Historical almost! But feels so good—so good an' co-ol, y'know. . . .

Tom.   Mother—

Amanda.   Yes, honey?

Tom.   How about—supper?

Amanda.   Honey, you go ask Sister if supper is ready! You know that Sister is in full charge of supper! Tell her you hungry boys are waiting for it. (*To Jim.*) Have you met Laura?

Jim.   She—

Amanda.   Let you in? Oh, good, you've met already! It's rare for a girl as sweet an' pretty as Laura to be domestic! But Laura is, thank heavens, not only pretty but also very domestic. I'm not at all. I never was a bit. I never could make a thing but angel-food cake. Well, in the South we had so many servants. Gone, gone, gone. All vestiges of gracious living! Gone completely! I wasn't prepared for what the future brought me. All of my gentlemen callers were sons of planters and so of course I assumed that I would be married to one and raise my family on a large piece of land with plenty of servants. But man proposes—and woman accepts the proposal!—To vary that old, old saying a little bit—I married no planter! I married a man who worked for the telephone company!—that gallantly smiling gentleman over there! (*Points to the picture.*) A telephone man who—fell in love with long distance!—Now he travels and I don't even know where!—But what am I going on for about my—tribulations! Tell me yours—I hope you don't have any! Tom?

Tom (*returning*).   Yes, Mother?

Amanda.   Is supper nearly ready?

Tom.   It looks to me like supper is on the table.

Amanda.   Let me look—(*She rises prettily and looks through portieres.*) Oh, lovely—But where is Sister?

Tom.   Laura is not feeling well and she says that she thinks she'd better not come to the table.

Amanda. What?—Nonsense!—Laura? Oh, Laura!

Laura (*off stage, faintly*). Yes, Mother.

Amanda. You really must come to the table. We won't be seated until you come to the table! Come in, Mr. O'Connor. You sit over there and I'll— Laura? Laura Wingfield! You're keeping us waiting, honey! We can't say grace until you come to the table!

The back door is pushed weakly open and Laura comes in. She is obviously quite faint, her lips trembling, her eyes wide and staring. She moves unsteadily toward the table.

(Legend: "Terror!")

Outside a summer storm is coming abruptly. The white curtains billow inward at the windows and there is a sorrowful murmur and deep blue dusk.

Laura suddenly stumbles—She catches at a chair with a faint moan.

Tom. Laura!

Amanda. Laura! *(There is a clap of thunder.)* *(Legend: "Ah!")* *(Despairingly.)* Why, Laura, you *are* sick, darling! Tom, help your sister into the living room, dear! Sit in the living room, Laura—rest on the sofa. Well! *(To the gentleman caller.)* Standing over the hot stove made her ill!—I told her that it was just too warm this evening, but—*(Tom comes back in. Laura is on the sofa.)* Is Laura all right now?

Tom. Yes.

Amanda. What *is* that? Rain? A nice cool rain has come up! *(She gives the gentleman caller a frightened look.)* I think we may—have grace—now . . . *(Tom looks at her stupidly.)* Tom, honey—you say grace!

Tom. Oh . . . "For these and all thy mercies—" *(They bow their heads, Amanda stealing a nervous glance at Jim. In the living room Laura, stretched on the sofa, clenches her hand to her lips, to hold back a shuddering sob.)* God's Holy Name be praised—

(The scene dims out.)

Scene VII

A Souvenir

Half an hour later. Dinner is just being finished in the upstage area, which is concealed by the drawn portieres.

As the curtain rises Laura is still huddled upon the sofa, her feet drawn under her, her head resting on a pale blue pillow, her eyes wide and mysteriously watchful. The new floor lamp with its shade of rose-colored silk gives a soft, be-

coming light to her face, bringing out the fragile, unearthly prettiness which usually escapes attention. There is a steady murmur of rain, but it is slackening and stops soon after the scene begins; the air outside becomes pale and luminous as the moon breaks out.

A moment after the curtain rises, the lights in both rooms flicker and go out.

Jim. Hey, there, Mr. Light Bulb!

Amanda laughs nervously.
(Legend: "Suspension of a Public Service.")

Amanda. Where was Moses when the lights went out? Ha-ha. Do you know the answer to that one, Mr. O'Connor?
Jim. No, Ma'am, what's the answer?
Amanda. In the dark! (*Jim laughs appreciatively.*) Everybody sit still. I'll light the candles. Isn't it lucky we have them on the table? Where's a match? Which of you gentlemen can provide a match?
Jim. Here.
Amanda. Thank you, sir.
Jim. Not at all, Ma'am!
Amanda. I guess the fuse has burnt out. Mr. O'Connor, can you tell a burnt-out fuse? I know I can't and Tom is a total loss when it comes to mechanics. (*Sound: Getting up: Voices recede a little to kitchenette.*) Oh, be careful you don't bump into something. We don't want our gentleman caller to break his neck. Now wouldn't that be a fine howdy-do?
Jim. Ha-ha! Where is the fuse-box?
Amanda. Right here next to the stove. Can you see anything?
Jim. Just a minute.
Amanda. Isn't electricity a mysterious thing? Wasn't it Benjamin Franklin who tied a key to a kite? We live in such a mysterious universe, don't we? Some people say that science clears up all the mysteries for us. In my opinion it only creates more! Have you found it yet?
Jim. No, Ma'am. All these fuses look okay to me.
Amanda. Tom!
Tom. Yes, Mother?
Amanda. That light bill I gave you several days ago. The one I told you we got the notices about?
Tom. Oh.—Yeah.

(Legend: "Ha!")

Amanda. You didn't neglect to pay it by any chance?
Tom. Why, I—
Amanda. Didn't! I might have known it!

Jim.   Shakespeare probably wrote a poem on that light bill, Mrs. Wingfield.

Amanda.   I might have known better than to trust him with it! There's such a high price for negligence in this world!

Jim.   Maybe the poem will win a ten-dollar prize.

Amanda.   We'll just have to spend the remainder of the evening in the nineteenth century, before Mr. Edison made the Mazda lamp!

Jim.   Candlelight is my favorite kind of light.

Amanda.   That shows you're romantic! But that's no excuse for Tom. Well, we got through dinner. Very considerate of them to let us get through dinner before they plunged us into everlasting darkness, wasn't it, Mr. O'Connor?

Jim.   Ha-ha!

Amanda.   Tom, as a penalty for your carelessness you can help me with the dishes.

Jim.   Let me give you a hand.

Amanda.   Indeed you will not!

Jim.   I ought to be good for something.

Amanda.   Good for something? (*Her tone is rhapsodic.*) You? Why, Mr. O'Connor, nobody, *nobody's* given me this much entertainment in years—as you have!

Jim.   Aw, now, Mrs. Wingfield!

Amanda.   I'm not exaggerating, not one bit! But Sister is all by her lonesome. You go keep her company in the parlor! I'll give you this lovely old candelabrum that used to be on the altar at the church of the Heavenly Rest. It was melted a little out of shape when the church burnt down. Lightning struck it one spring. Gypsy Jones was holding a revival at the time and he intimated that the church was destroyed because the Episcopalians gave card parties.

Jim.   Ha-ha.

Amanda.   And how about coaxing Sister to drink a little wine? I think it would be good for her! Can you carry both at once?

Jim.   Sure. I'm Superman!

Amanda.   Now, Thomas, get into this apron!

The door of kitchenette swings closed on Amanda's gay laughter; the flickering light approaches the portieres.

Laura sits up nervously as he enters. Her speech at first is low and breathless from the almost intolerable strain of being alone with a stranger.

(Legend: "I Don't Suppose You Remember Me at All!")

In her first speeches in this scene, before Jim's warmth overcomes her paralyzing shyness, Laura's voice is thin and breathless as though she has run up a steep flight of stairs.

Jim's attitude is gently humorous. In playing this scene it should be stressed that while the incident is apparently unimportant, it is to Laura the climax of her secret life.

Jim. Hello, there, Laura.

Laura *(faintly).* Hello. *(She clears her throat.)*

Jim. How are you feeling now? Better?

Laura. Yes. Yes, thank you.

Jim. This is for you. A little dandelion wine. *(He extends it toward her with extravagant gallantry.)*

Laura. Thank you.

Jim. Drink it—but don't get drunk! *(He laughs heartily. Laura takes the glass uncertainly; laughs shyly.)* Where shall I set the candles?

Laura. Oh—oh, anywhere . . .

Jim. How about here on the floor? Any objections?

Laura. No.

Jim. I'll spread a newspaper under to catch the drippings. I like to sit on the floor. Mind if I do?

Laura. Oh, no.

Jim. Give me a pillow?

Laura. What?

Jim. A pillow!

Laura. Oh . . . *(Hands him one quickly.)*

Jim. How about you? Don't you like to sit on the floor?

Laura. Oh—yes.

Jim. Why don't you, then?

Laura. I—will.

Jim. Take a pillow! *(Laura does. Sits on the other side of the candelabrum. Jim crosses his legs and smiles engagingly at her.)* I can't hardly see you sitting way over there.

Laura. I can—see you.

Jim. I know, but that's not fair, I'm in the limelight. *(Laura moves her pillow closer.)* Good! Now I can see you! Comfortable?

Laura. Yes.

Jim. So am I. Comfortable as a cow. Will you have some gum?

Laura. No, thank you.

Jim. I think that I will indulge, with your permission. *(Musingly unwraps it and holds it up.)* Think of the fortune made by the guy that invented the first piece of chewing gum. Amazing, huh? The Wrigley Building is one of the sights of Chicago.—I saw it summer before last when I went up to the Century of Progress. Did you take in the Century of Progress?

Laura. No, I didn't.

Jim. Well, it was quite a wonderful exposition. What impressed me most was the Hall of Science. Gives you an idea of what the future will be in America, even more wonderful than the present time is! *(Pause. Smiling at her.)* Your brother tells me you're shy. Is that right, Laura?

Laura. I—don't know.

Jim. I judge you to be an old-fashioned type of girl. Well, I think that's a pretty good type to be. Hope you don't think I'm being too personal—do you?

Laura (*hastily, out of embarrassment*). I believe I *will* take a piece of gum, if you—don't mind. (*Clearing her throat.*) Mr. O'Connor, have you—kept up with your singing?

Jim. Singing? Me?

Laura. Yes. I remember what a beautiful voice you had.

Jim. When did you hear me sing?

(*Voice off stage in the pause.*)

Voice (*off stage*). 　O blow, ye winds, heigh-ho,
　　　　　　　　A-roving I will go!
　　　　　　　　I'm off to my love
　　　　　　　　With a boxing glove—
　　　　　　　　Ten thousand miles away!

Jim. You say you've heard me sing?

Laura. Oh, yes! Yes, very often . . . I—don't suppose you remember me—at all?

Jim (*smiling doubtfully*). You know I have an idea I've seen you before. I had that idea soon as you opened the door. It seemed almost like I was about to remember your name. But the name that I started to call you—wasn't a name! And so I stopped myself before I said it.

Laura. Wasn't it—Blue Roses?

Jim (*springs up, grinning*). Blue Roses! My gosh, yes—Blue Roses! That's what I had on my tongue when you opened the door! Isn't it funny what tricks your memory plays? I didn't connect you with the high school somehow or other. But that's where it was; it was high school. I didn't even know you were Shakespeare's sister! Gosh, I'm sorry.

Laura. I didn't expect you to. You—barely knew me!

Jim. But we did have a speaking acquaintance, huh?

Laura. Yes, we—spoke to each other.

Jim. When did you recognize me?

Laura. Oh, right away!

Jim. Soon as I came in the door?

Laura. When I heard your name I thought it was probably you. I knew that Tom used to know you a little in high school. So when you came in the door—Well, then I was—sure.

Jim. Why didn't you *say* something, then?

Laura (*breathlessly*). I didn't know what to say, I was—too surprised!

Jim. For goodness' sakes! You know, this sure is funny!

Laura. Yes! Yes, isn't it, though . . .

Jim. Didn't we have a class in something together?

Laura. Yes, we did.

Jim. What class was that?

Laura. It was—singing—Chorus!

Jim. Aw!

Laura. I sat across the aisle from you in the Aud.

Jim. Aw.

Laura. Mondays, Wednesdays, and Fridays.

Jim. Now I remember—you always came in late.

Laura. Yes, it was so hard for me, getting upstairs. I had that brace on my leg—it clumped so loud!

Jim. I never heard any clumping.

Laura (*wincing in the recollection*). To me it sounded like—thunder!

Jim. Well, well, well. I never even noticed.

Laura. And everybody was seated before I came in. I had to walk in front of all those people. My seat was in the back row. I had to go clumping all the way up the aisle with everyone watching!

Jim. You shouldn't have been self-conscious.

Laura. I know, but I was. It was always such a relief when the singing started.

Jim. Aw, yes, I've placed you now! I used to call you Blue Roses. How was it that I got started calling you that?

Laura. I was out of school a little while with pleurosis. When I came back you asked me what was the matter. I said I had pleurosis—you thought I said Blue Roses. That's what you always called me after that!

Jim. I hope you didn't mind.

Laura. Oh, no—I liked it. You see, I wasn't acquainted with many— people. . . .

Jim. As I remember you sort of stuck by yourself.

Laura. I—I—never had much luck at—making friends.

Jim. I don't see why you wouldn't.

Laura. Well, I—started out badly.

Jim. You mean being—

Laura. Yes, it sort of—stood between me—

Jim. You shouldn't have let it!

Laura. I know, but it did, and—

Jim. You were shy with people!

Laura. I tried not to be but never could—

Jim. Overcome it?

Laura. No, I—I never could!

Jim. I guess being shy is something you have to work out of kind of gradually.

Laura (*sorrowfully*). Yes—I guess it—

Jim. Takes time!

Laura. Yes—

Jim. People are not so dreadful when you know them. That's what you have to remember! And everybody has problems, not just you, but practically everybody has got some problems. You think of yourself as having the only problems, as being the only one who is disappointed. But just look around you and you will see lots of people as disappointed as you are. For instance, I hoped when I was going to high school that I would be further along at this time, six years later, than I am now—You remember that wonderful write-up I had in *The Torch?*

Laura. Yes! *(She rises and crosses to table.)*

Jim. It said I was bound to succeed in anything I went into! *(Laura returns with the annual.)* Holy Jeez! *The Torch! (He accepts it reverently. They smile across it with mutual wonder. Laura crouches beside him and they begin to turn through it. Laura's shyness is dissolving in his warmth.)*

Laura. Here you are in *Pirates of Penzance!*

Jim *(wistfully).* I sang the baritone lead in that operetta.

Laura *(rapidly).* So—*beautifully!*

Jim *(protesting).* Aw—

Laura. Yes, yes—beautifully—beautifully!

Jim. You heard me?

Laura. All three times!

Jim. No!

Laura. Yes!

Jim. All three performances?

Laura *(looking down).* Yes.

Jim. Why?

Laura. I—wanted to ask you to—autograph my program.

Jim. Why didn't you ask me to?

Laura. You were always surrounded by your own friends so much that I never had a chance to.

Jim. You should have just—

Laura. Well, I—thought you might think I was—

Jim. Thought I might think you was—what?

Laura. Oh—

Jim *(with reflective relish).* I was beleaguered by females in those days.

Laura. You were terribly popular!

Jim. Yeah—

Laura. You had such a—friendly way—

Jim. I was spoiled in high school.

Laura. Everybody—liked you!

Jim. Including you?

Laura. I—yes, I—I did, too—*(She gently closes the book in her lap.)*

Jim. Well, well, well!—Give me that program, Laura. *(She hands it to him. He signs it with a flourish.)* There you are—better late than never!

Laura. Oh, I—what a—surprise!

Jim. My signature isn't worth very much right now. But some day—maybe—it will increase in value! Being disappointed is one thing and being discouraged is something else. I am disappointed but I'm not discouraged. I'm twenty-three years old. How old are you?

Laura. I'll be twenty-four in June.

Jim. That's not old age.

Laura. No, but—

Jim. You finished high school?

Laura *(with difficulty).* I didn't go back.

Jim. You mean you dropped out?

Laura. I made bad grades in my final examinations. *(She rises and replaces the book and the program. Her voice strained.)* How is—Emily Meisenbach getting along?

Jim. Oh, that kraut-head!

Laura. Why do you call her that?

Jim. That's what she was.

Laura. You're not still—going with her?

Jim. I never see her.

Laura. It said in the Personal Section that you were—engaged!

Jim. I know, but I wasn't impressed by that—propaganda!

Laura. It wasn't—the truth?

Jim. Only in Emily's optimistic opinion!

Laura. Oh—

(Legend: "What Have You Done since High School?")

Jim lights a cigarette and leans indolently back on his elbows smiling at Laura with a warmth and charm which light her inwardly with altar candles. She remains by the table and turns in her hands a piece of glass to cover her tumult.

Jim *(after several reflective puffs on a cigarette).* What have you done since high school? *(She seems not to hear him.)* Huh? *(Laura looks up.)* I said what have you done since high school, Laura?

Laura. Nothing much.

Jim. You must have been doing something these six long years.

Laura. Yes.

Jim. Well, then, such as what?

Laura. I took a business course at business college—

Jim. How did that work out?

Laura. Well, not very—well—I had to drop out, it gave me—indigestion—

Jim laughs gently.

Jim. What are you doing now?

Laura. I don't do anything—much. Oh, please don't think I sit around doing nothing! My glass collection takes up a good deal of my time. Glass is something you have to take good care of.

Jim. What did you say—about glass?

Laura. Collection I said—I have one—*(She clears her throat and turns away again, acutely shy.)*

Jim *(abruptly)*.   You know what I judge to be the trouble with you? Inferiority complex! Know what that is? That's what they call it when someone low-rates himself! I understand it because I had it, too. Although my case was not so aggravated as yours seems to be. I had it until I took up public speaking, developed my voice, and learned that I had an aptitude for science. Before that time I never thought of myself as being outstanding in any way whatsoever! Now I've never made a regular study of it, but I have a friend who says I can analyze people better than doctors that make a profession of it. I don't claim that to be necessarily true, but I can sure guess a person's psychology, Laura! *(Takes out his gum.)* Excuse me, Laura. I always take it out when the flavor is gone. I'll use this scrap of paper to wrap it in. I know how it is to get it stuck on a shoe. Yep—that's what I judge to be your principal trouble. A lack of confidence in yourself as a person. You don't have the proper amount of faith in yourself. I'm basing that fact on a number of your remarks and also on certain observations I've made. For instance that clumping you thought was so awful in high school. You say that you even dreaded to walk into class. You see what you did? You dropped out of school, you gave up an education because of a clump, which as far as I know was practically nonexistent! A little physical defect is what you have. Hardly noticeable even! Magnified thousands of times by imagination! You know what my strong advice to you is? Think of yourself as *superior* in some way!

Laura.   In what way would I think?

Jim.   Why, man alive, Laura! Just look about you a little. What do you see? A world full of common people! All of 'em born and all of 'em going to die! Which of them has one-tenth of your good points! Or mine! Or anyone else's, as far as that goes—Gosh! Everybody excels in some one thing. Some in many! *(Unconsciously glances at himself in the mirror.)* All you've got to do is discover in *what!* Take me, for instance. *(He adjusts his tie at the mirror.)* My interest happened to lie in electrodynamics. I'm taking a course in radio engineering at night school, Laura, on top of a fairly responsible job at the warehouse. I'm taking that course and studying public speaking.

Laura.   Ohhhh.

Jim.   Because I believe in the future of television! *(Turning back to her.)* I wish to be ready to go up right along with it. Therefore I'm planning to get in on the ground floor. In fact, I've already made the right connections and all that remains is for the industry itself to get under way! Full steam—*(His eyes are starry.)* Knowledge—Zzzzzp! Money—Zzzzzzp!—Power! That's the cycle democracy is built on! *(His attitude is convincingly dynamic. Laura stares at him, even her shyness eclipsed in her absolute wonder. He suddenly grins.)* I guess you think I think a lot of myself!

Laura.   No—o-o-o, I—

Jim.   Now how about you? Isn't there something you take more interest in than anything else?

Laura.   Well, I do—as I said—have my—glass collection—

A peal of girlish laughter from the kitchen.

Jim. I'm not right sure I know what you're talking about. What kind of glass is it?

Laura. Little articles of it, they're ornaments mostly! Most of them are little animals made out of glass, the tiniest little animals in the world. Mother calls them a glass menagerie! Here's an example of one, if you'd like to see it! This one is one of the oldest. It's nearly thirteen. *(He stretches out his hand.)* *(Music: "The Glass Menagerie.")* Oh, be careful—if you breathe, it breaks!

Jim. I'd better not take it. I'm pretty clumsy with things.

Laura. Go on, I trust you with him! *(Places it in his palm.)* There now— you're holding him gently! Hold him over the light, he loves the light! You see how the light shines through him?

Jim. It sure does shine!

Laura. I shouldn't be partial, but he is my favorite one.

Jim. What kind of thing is this one supposed to be?

Laura. Haven't you noticed the single horn on his forehead?

Jim. A unicorn, huh?

Laura. Mmm-hmmm!

Jim. Unicorns, aren't they extinct in the modern world?

Laura. I know!

Jim. Poor little fellow, he must feel sort of lonesome.

Laura *(smiling)*. Well, if he does he doesn't complain about it. He stays on a shelf with some horses that don't have horns and all of them seem to get along nicely together.

Jim. How do you know?

Laura *(lightly)*. I haven't heard any arguments among them!

Jim *(grinning)*. No arguments, huh? Well, that's a pretty good sign! Where shall I set him?

Laura. Put him on the table. They all like a change of scenery once in a while!

Jim *(stretching)*. Well, well, well, well—Look how big my shadow is when I stretch!

Laura. Oh, oh, yes—it stretches across the ceiling!

Jim *(crossing to door)*. I think it's stopped raining. *(Opens fire-escape door.)* Where does the music come from?

Laura. From the Paradise Dance Hall across the alley.

Jim. How about cutting the rug a little, Miss Wingfield?

Laura. Oh, I—

Jim. Or is your program filled up? Let me have a look at it. *(Grasps imaginary card.)* Why, every dance is taken! I'll have to scratch some out. *(Waltz music: "La Golondrina.")* Ahhh, a waltz! *(He executes some sweeping turns by himself then holds his arms toward Laura.)*

Laura *(breathlessly)*. I—can't dance!

Jim. There you go, that inferiority stuff!

Laura.   I've never danced in my life!

Jim.   Come on, try!

Laura.   Oh, but I'd step on you!

Jim.   I'm not made out of glass.

Laura.   How—how—how do we start?

Jim.   Just leave it to me. You hold your arms out a little.

Laura.   Like this?

Jim.   A little bit higher. Right. Now don't tighten up, that's the main thing about it—relax.

Laura (*laughing breathlessly*).   It's hard not to.

Jim.   Okay.

Laura.   I'm afraid you can't budge me.

Jim.   What do you bet I can't? (*He swings her into motion.*)

Laura.   Goodness, yes, you can!

Jim.   Let yourself go, now, Laura, just let yourself go.

Laura.   I'm—

Jim.   Come on!

Laura.   Trying.

Jim.   Not so stiff—Easy does it!

Laura.   I know but I'm—

Jim.   Loosen th' backbone! There now, that's a lot better.

Laura.   Am I?

Jim.   Lots, lots better! (*He moves her about the room in a clumsy waltz.*)

Laura.   Oh, my!

Jim.   Ha-ha!

Laura.   Goodness, yes you can!

Jim.   Ha-ha-ha! (*They suddenly bump into the table. Jim stops.*) What did we hit on?

Laura.   Table.

Jim.   Did something fall off it? I think—

Laura.   Yes.

Jim.   I hope it wasn't the little glass horse with the horn!

Laura.   Yes.

Jim.   Aw, aw, aw. Is it broken?

Laura.   Now it is just like all the other horses.

Jim.   It's lost its—

Laura.   Horn! It doesn't matter. Maybe it's a blessing in disguise.

Jim.   You'll never forgive me. I bet that that was your favorite piece of glass.

Laura.   I don't have favorites much. It's no tragedy, Freckles. Glass breaks so easily. No matter how careful you are. The traffic jars the shelves and things fall off them.

Jim.   Still I'm awfully sorry that I was the cause.

Laura (*smiling*).   I'll just imagine he had an operation. The horn was removed to make him feel less—freakish! (*They both laugh.*) Now he will feel more at home with the other horses, the ones that don't have horns . . .

Jim.   Ha-ha, that's very funny! *(Suddenly serious.)* I'm glad to see that you have a sense of humor. You know—you're—well—very different! Surprisingly different from anyone else I know! *(His voice becomes soft and hesitant with a genuine feeling.)* Do you mind me telling you that? *(Laura is abashed beyond speech.)* You make me feel sort of—I don't know how to put it! I'm usually pretty good at expressing things, but—This is something that I don't know how to say! *(Laura touches her throat and clears it—turns the broken unicorn in her hands.) (Even softer.)* Has anyone ever told you that you were pretty?

Pause: Music.

   (Laura looks up slowly, with wonder, and shakes her head.) Well, you are! In a very different way from anyone else. And all the nicer because of the difference, too. *(His voice becomes low and husky. Laura turns away, nearly faint with the novelty of her emotions.)* I wish that you were my sister. I'd teach you to have some confidence in yourself. The different people are not like other people, but being different is nothing to be ashamed of. Because other people are not such wonderful people. They're one hundred times one thousand. You're one times one! They walk all over the earth. You just stay here. They're common as—weeds, but—you—well, you're—*Blue Roses!*

(Image on screen: Blue Roses.)
(Music changes.)

Laura.   But blue is wrong for—roses . . .
Jim.   It's right for you—You're—pretty!
Laura.   In what respect am I pretty?
Jim.   In all respects—believe me! Your eyes—your hair—are pretty! Your hands are pretty! *(He catches hold of her hand.)* You think I'm making this up because I'm invited to dinner and have to be nice. Oh, I could do that! I could put on an act for you, Laura, and say lots of things without being very sincere. But this time I am. I'm talking to you sincerely. I happened to notice you had this inferiority complex that keeps you from feeling comfortable with people. Somebody needs to build your confidence up and make you proud instead of shy and turning away and—blushing—Somebody ought to—ought to—*kiss* you, Laura! *(His hand slips slowly up her arm to her shoulder.) (Music swells tumultuously.) (He suddenly turns her about and kisses her on the lips. When he releases her Laura sinks on the sofa with a bright, dazed look. Jim backs away and fishes in his pocket for a cigarette.) (Legend on screen: "Souvenir.")* Stumble-john! *(He lights the cigarette, avoiding her look. There is a peal of girlish laughter from Amanda in the kitchen. Laura slowly raises and opens her hand. It still contains the little broken glass animal. She looks at it with a tender, bewildered expression.)* Stumble-john! I shouldn't have done that— That was way off the beam. You don't smoke, do you? *(She looks up, smiling,*

not hearing the question. He sits beside her a little gingerly. She looks at him speechlessly—waiting. He coughs decorously and moves a little farther aside as he considers the situation and senses her feelings, dimly, with perturbation. Gently.) Would you—care for a—mint? *(She doesn't seem to hear him but her look grows brighter even.)* Peppermint—Life Saver? My pocket's a regular drug store—wherever I go . . . *(He pops a mint in his mouth. Then gulps and decides to make a clean breast of it. He speaks slowly and gingerly.)* Laura, you know, if I had a sister like you, I'd do the same thing as Tom. I'd bring out fellows—introduce her to them. The right type of boys of a type to—appreciate her. Only—well—he made a mistake about me. Maybe I've got no call to be saying this. That may not have been the idea in having me over. But what if it was? There's nothing wrong about that. The only trouble is that in my case—I'm not in a situation to—do the right thing. I can't take down your number and say I'll phone. I can't call up next week and—ask for a date. I thought I had better explain the situation in case you misunderstood it and— hurt your feelings. . . . *(Pause. Slowly, very slowly, Laura's look changes, her eyes returning slowly from his to the ornament in her palm.)*

Amanda utters another gay laugh in the kitchen.

Laura *(faintly).* You—won't—call again?

Jim. No, Laura, I can't. *(He rises from the sofa.)* As I was just explaining, I've—got strings on me, Laura, I've—been going steady! I go out all the time with a girl named Betty. She's a home-girl like you, and Catholic, and Irish, and in a great many ways we—get along fine. I met her last summer on a moonlight boat trip up the river to Alton, on the *Majestic.* Well—right away from the start it was—love! *(Legend: Love!) (Laura sways slightly forward and grips the arm of the sofa. He fails to notice, now enrapt in his own comfortable being.)* Being in love has made a new man of me! *(Leaning stiffly forward, clutching the arm of the sofa, Laura struggles visibly with her storm. But Jim is oblivious, she is a long way off.)* The power of love is really pretty tremendous! Love is something that—changes the whole world, Laura! *(The storm abates a little and Laura leans back. He notices her again.)* It happened that Betty's aunt took sick, she got a wire and had to go to Centralia. So Tom—when he asked me to dinner—I naturally just accepted the invitation, not knowing that you—that he—that I—*(He stops awkwardly.)* Huh—I'm a stumble-john! *(He flops back on the sofa. The holy candles in the altar of Laura's face have been snuffed out! There is a look of almost infinite desolation. Jim glances at her uneasily.)* I wish that you would—say something. *(She bites her lip which was trembling and then bravely smiles. She opens her hand again on the broken glass ornament. Then she gently takes his hand and raises it level with her own. She carefully places the unicorn in the palm of his hand, then pushes his fingers closed upon it.)* What are you—doing that for? You want me to have him?—Laura? *(She nods.)* What for?

Laura. A—souvenir . . .

She rises unsteadily and crouches beside the Victrola to wind it up.
    (Legend on screen: "Things Have a Way of Turning Out So Badly.")
    (Or image: "Gentleman caller waving good-bye!—Gaily.")
    At this moment Amanda rushes brightly back in the front room. She bears a pitcher of fruit punch in an old-fashioned cut-glass pitcher and a plate of macaroons. The plate has a gold border and poppies painted on it.

Amanda.   Well, well, well! Isn't the air delightful after the shower? I've made you children a little liquid refreshment. *(Turns gaily to the gentleman caller.)* Jim, do you know that song about lemonade?

"Lemonade, lemonade
Made in the shade and stirred with a spade—
Good enough for any old maid!"

Jim *(uneasily).*   Ha-ha! No—I never heard it.
Amanda.   Why, Laura! You look so serious!
Jim.   We were having a serious conversation.
Amanda.   Good! Now you're better acquainted!
Jim *(uncertainly).*   Ha-ha! Yes.
Amanda.   You modern young people are much more serious-minded than my generation. I was so gay as a girl!
Jim.   You haven't changed, Mrs. Wingfield.
Amanda.   Tonight I'm rejuvenated! The gaiety of the occasion, Mr. O'Connor! *(She tosses her head with a peal of laughter. Spills lemonade.)* Oooo! I'm baptizing myself!
Jim.   Here—let me—
Amanda *(setting the pitcher down).*   There now. I discovered we had some maraschino cherries. I dumped them in, juice and all!
Jim.   You shouldn't have gone to that trouble, Mrs. Wingfield.
Amanda.   Trouble, trouble? Why it was loads of fun! Didn't you hear me cutting up in the kitchen? I bet your ears were burning! I told Tom how outdone with him I was for keeping you to himself so long a time! He should have brought you over much, much sooner! Well, now that you've found your way, I want you to be a very frequent caller! Not just occasional but all the time. Oh, we're going to have a lot of gay times together! I see them coming! Mmm, just breathe that air! So fresh, and the moon's so pretty! I'll skip back out—I know where my place is when young folks are having a—serious conversation!
Jim.   Oh, don't go out, Mrs. Wingfield. The fact of the matter is I've got to be going.
Amanda.   Going, now? You're joking! Why, it's only the shank of the evening, Mr. O'Connor!
Jim.   Well, you know how it is.
Amanda.   You mean you're a young workingman and have to keep workingmen's hours. We'll let you off early tonight. But only on the condition that

next time you stay later. What's the best night for you? Isn't Saturday night the best night for you workingmen?

Jim. I have a couple of time-clocks to punch, Mrs. Wingfield. One at morning, another one at night!

Amanda. My, but you *are* ambitious! You work at night, too?

Jim. No, Ma'am, not work but—Betty! (*He crosses deliberately to pick up his hat. The band at the Paradise Dance Hall goes into a tender waltz.*)

Amanda. Betty? Betty? Who's—Betty! (*There is an ominous cracking sound in the sky.*)

Jim. Oh, just a girl. The girl I go steady with! (*He smiles charmingly. The sky falls.*)

(*Legend: "The Sky Falls."*)

Amanda (*a long-drawn exhalation*). Ohhhh . . . Is it a serious romance, Mr. O'Connor?

Jim. We're going to be married the second Sunday in June.

Amanda. Ohhhh—how nice! Tom didn't mention that you were engaged to be married.

Jim. The cat's not out of the bag at the warehouse yet. You know how they are. They call you Romeo and stuff like that. (*He stops at the oval mirror to put on his hat. He carefully shapes the brim and the crown to give a discreetly dashing effect.*) It's been a wonderful evening, Mrs. Wingfield. I guess this is what they mean by Southern hospitality.

Amanda. It really wasn't anything at all.

Jim. I hope it don't seem like I'm rushing off. But I promised Betty I'd pick her up at the Wabash depot, an' by the time I get my jalopy down there her train'll be in. Some women are pretty upset if you keep 'em waiting.

Amanda. Yes, I know—The tyranny of women! (*Extends her hand.*) Goodbye, Mr. O'Connor. I wish you luck—and happiness—and success! All three of them, and so does Laura—Don't you, Laura?

Laura. Yes!

Jim (*taking her hand*). Good-bye, Laura. I'm certainly going to treasure that souvenir. And don't you forget the good advice I gave you. (*Raises his voice to a cheery shout.*) So long, Shakespeare! Thanks again, ladies—Good night!

He grins and ducks jauntily out.

Still bravely grimacing, Amanda closes the door on the gentleman caller. Then she turns back to the room with a puzzled expression. She and Laura don't dare to face each other. Laura crouches beside the Victrola to wind it.

Amanda (*faintly*). Things have a way of turning out so badly. I don't believe that I would play the Victrola. Well, well—well—Our gentleman caller was engaged to be married! Tom!

Tom (*from back*). Yes, Mother?

Amanda. Come in here a minute. I want to tell you something awfully funny.

Tom (*enters with macaroon and a glass of the lemonade*). Has the gentleman caller gotten away already?

Amanda. The gentleman caller has made an early departure. What a wonderful joke you played on us!

Tom. How do you mean?

Amanda. You didn't mention that he was engaged to be married.

Tom. Jim? Engaged?

Amanda. That's what he just informed us.

Tom. I'll be jiggered! I didn't know about that.

Amanda. That seems very peculiar.

Tom. What's peculiar about it?

Amanda. Didn't you call him your best friend down at the warehouse?

Tom. He is, but how did I know?

Amanda. It seems extremely peculiar that you wouldn't know your best friend was going to be married!

Tom. The warehouse is where I work, not where I know things about people!

Amanda. You don't know things anywhere! You live in a dream; you manufacture illusions! (*He crosses to door.*) Where are you going?

Tom. I'm going to the movies.

Amanda. That's right, now that you've had us make such fools of ourselves. The effort, the preparations, all the expense! The new floor lamp, the rug, the clothes for Laura! All for what? To entertain some other girl's fiancé! Go to the movies, go! Don't think about us, a mother deserted, an unmarried sister who's crippled and has no job! Don't let anything interfere with your selfish pleasure! Just go, go, go—to the movies!

Tom. All right, I will! The more you shout about my selfishness to me the quicker I'll go, and I won't go to the movies!

Amanda. Go, then! Then go to the moon—you selfish dreamer!

Tom smashes his glass on the floor. He plunges out on the fire-escape, slamming the door. Laura screams—cut by door.

Dance-hall music up. Tom goes to the rail and grips it desperately, lifting his face in the chill white moonlight penetrating the narrow abyss of the alley.

(Legend on screen: "And So Good-Bye . . .")

Tom's closing speech is timed with the interior pantomime. The interior scene is played as though viewed through sound-proof glass. Amanda appears to be making a comforting speech to Laura who is huddled upon the sofa. Now that we cannot hear the mother's speech, her silliness is gone and she has dignity and tragic beauty. Laura's dark hair hides her face until at the end of the speech she lifts it to smile at her mother. Amanda's gestures are slow and graceful, almost dancelike, as she comforts the daughter. At the end of her speech she glances a moment at the father's picture—then withdraws through the portieres. At close of Tom's speech, Laura blows out the candles, ending the play.

Tom.   I didn't go to the moon, I went much further—for time is the longest distance between two places—Not long after that I was fired for writing a poem on the lid of a shoe-box. I left Saint Louis. I descended the steps of this fire-escape for a last time and followed, from then on, in my father's footsteps, attempting to find in motion what was lost in space—I traveled around a great deal. The cities swept about me like dead leaves, leaves that were brightly colored but torn away from the branches. I would have stopped, but I was pursued by something. It always came upon me unawares, taking me altogether by surprise. Perhaps it was a familiar bit of music. Perhaps it was only a piece of transparent glass—Perhaps I am walking along a street at night, in some strange city, before I have found companions. I pass the lighted window of a shop where perfume is sold. The window is filled with pieces of colored glass, tiny transparent bottles in delicate colors, like bits of a shattered rainbow. Then all at once my sister touches my shoulder. I turn around and look into her eyes. . . . Oh, Laura, Laura, I tried to leave you behind me, but I am more faithful than I intended to be! I reach for a cigarette, I cross the street, I run into the movies or a bar, I buy a drink, I speak to the nearest stranger—anything that can blow your candles out! *(Laura bends over the candles)*—for nowadays the world is lit by lightning! Blow out your candles, Laura—and so good-bye . . .

She blows the candles out.
(The scene dissolves.)

For Analysis

1. Who is the central character in the play? Explain. **2.** What does the glass menagerie symbolize? Specifically, what does the unicorn symbolize? Why does Laura give the unicorn, after its horn has broken off, to Jim? **3.** In his address at the start of the play, Tom tells the audience that Jim "is the most realistic character in the play . . . an emissary from a world of reality that we were somehow set apart from." What is the world of reality Jim represents? Is Tom paying him a compliment? **4.** In his opening address, Tom sketches in "the social background of the play." How does this background help us to understand the Wingfield family? **5.** Although she has refused to accept the characterization from Tom, in her final words Amanda refers to Laura as crippled. Why? **6.** Is Tom's escape as complete as his father's seems to have been? Explain. **7.** Explain why you do or do not find effective the device of projecting images and titles on a screen above the stage.

On Style

1. How does the fact that the play is presented as Tom's memory shape its structure and meaning? **2.** Are the nonrealistic techniques effective and appropriate to the **theme** of the play?

Making Connections

1. In what ways is Tom's function in this play similar to the function of the chorus in Sophocles' *Oedipus Rex* (p. 166)? In what ways is it different? **2.** Compare the use of nonrealistic devices in this play and in Arthur Miller's *Death of a Salesman* (p. 746). Do you find one or the other of the plays more successful in employing these devices?

Writing Topic

Are we meant to admire Amanda for holding her family together under very difficult circumstances or to condemn her for her destructive illusions? In this connection, explain the statement in the final stage direction: "Now that we cannot hear the mother's speech, her silliness is gone and she has dignity and tragic beauty."

Alice Childress [1920–1994]

Wine in the Wilderness 1969

CHARACTERS

Bill Jameson, *an artist aged thirty-three*

Oldtimer, *an old roustabout character in his sixties*

Sonny-man, *a writer aged twenty-seven*

Cynthia, *a social worker aged twenty-five, Sonny-man's wife*

Tommy, *a woman factory worker aged thirty*

Time: *The summer of 1964. Night of a riot.*

Place: *Harlem, New York City, New York, U.S.A.*

Scene: *A one room apartment in a Harlem Tenement. It used to be a three room apartment but the tenant has broken out walls and is half finished with a redecorating job. The place is now only partly reminiscent of its past tawdry days, plaster broken away and lathing exposed right next to a new brick-faced portion of wall. The kitchen is now a part of the room. There is a three-quarter bed covered with an African throw, a screen is placed at the foot of the bed to insure privacy when needed. The room is obviously black dominated—pieces of sculpture, wall hangings, paintings. An artist's easel is standing with a drapery thrown across it so the empty canvas beneath it is hidden. Two other canvases the same size are next to it; they too are covered and conceal paintings. The place is in a beautiful, rather artistic state of disorder. The room also reflects an interest in other darker peoples of the world . . . a Chinese incense-burner Buddha, an American Indian feathered war helmet, a Mexican serape, a Japanese fan, a West Indian travel poster. There is a kitchen table, chairs, floor cushions, a couple of box crates, books, bookcases, plenty of artist's materials. There is a small raised platform for model posing. On the platform is a backless chair. The tail end of a riot is going on out in the street. Noise and screaming can be heard in the distance . . . running feet, voices shouting over loudspeakers.*

Offstage voices. Offa the street! Into your homes! Clear the street! [*The whine of a bullet is heard.*] Cover the roof! It's from the roof! [*Bill is seated on the floor with his back to the wall, drawing on a large sketch pad with charcoal pencil. He is very absorbed in his task but flinches as he hears the bullet sound, ducks and shields his head with upraised hand . . . then resumes sketching. The telephone rings, he reaches for phone with caution, pulls it toward him by the cord in order to avoid going near window or standing up.*]

Bill. Hello? Yeah, my phone is on. How the hell I'm gonna be talkin' to you if it's not on? [*Sound of glass breaking in the distance.*] I could lose my damn life answerin' the phone. Sonny-man, what the hell you callin' me up for! I thought you and Cynthia might be downstairs dead. I banged on the floor and hollered down the air-shaft, no answer. No stuff! Thought yall was dead. I'm sittin' here drawin' a picture in your memory. In a bar! Yall sittin' in a bar? See there, you done blew the picture that's in your memory . . . No kiddin', they wouldn't let you in the block? Man, they can't keep you outta your own house. Found? You found who? Model? What model? Yeah, yeah, thanks, . . . but I like to find my own models. No! Don't bring nobody up here in the middle of a riot . . . Hey, Sonny-man! Hey! [*Sound of yelling and rushing footsteps in the hall.*]

Woman's voice [*offstage*]. Damnit, Bernice! The riot is over! What you hidin' in the hall for? I'm in the house, your father's in the house, . . . and you out there hidin' in the hall!

Girl's voice [*offstage*]. The house might burn down!

Bill. Sonny-man, I can't hear you!

Woman's voice [*offstage*]. If it do burn down, what the hell you gon' do, run off and leave us to burn up by ourself? The riot is over. The police say it's over! Get back in the house!

[*Sound of running feet and a knock on the door.*]

Bill. They say it's over. Man, they oughta let you on your own block, in your own house . . . Yeah, we still standin', this seventy-year-old house got guts. Thank you, yeah, thanks but I like to pick my own models. You drunk? Can't you hear when I say not to . . . Okay, all right, bring her . . . [*Frantic knocking at the door.*] I gotta go. Yeah, yeah, bring her. I gotta go . . . [*Hangs up phone and opens the door for Oldtimer. The old man is carrying a haul of loot . . . two or three bottles of liquor, a ham, a salami and a suit with price tags attached.*] What's this! Oh, no, no, no, Oldtimer, not here . . . [*Faint sound of a police whistle.*] The police after you? What you bring that stuff in here for?

Oldtimer [*runs past Bill to center as he looks for a place to hide the loot*]. No, no, they not really after me but . . . I was in the basement so I could stash this stuff, . . . but a fella told me they pokin' round down there . . . in the back yard pokin' round . . . the police doin' a lotta pokin' round.

Bill. If the cops are searchin' why you wanna dump your troubles on me?

Oldtimer. I don't wanna go to jail. I'm too old to go to jail. What we gonna do?

Bill. We can throw it the hell outta the window. Didn't you think of just throwin' it away and not worry 'bout jail?

Oldtimer. I can't do it. It's like . . . I'm Oldtimer but my hands and arms is somebody else that I don' know-a-tall. [*Bill pulls stuff out of Oldtimer's arms and places loot on the kitchen table. Oldtimer's arms fall to his sides.*] Thank you, son.

Bill.   Stealin' ain't worth a bullet through your brain, is it? You wanna get shot down and drown in your own blood, . . . for what? A suit, a bottle of whiskey? Gonna throw your life away for a damn ham?

Oldtimer.   But I ain' really stole nothin', Bill, 'cause I ain' no thief. Them others, . . . they smash the windows, they run in the stores and grab and all. Me, I pick up what they left scatter in the street. Things they drop . . . things they trample underfoot. What's in the street ain' like stealin'. This is leavin's. What I'm gon' do if the police come?

Bill [*starts to gather the things in the tablecloth that is on the table*].   I'll throw it out the air-shaft window.

Oldtimer [*places himself squarely in front of the air-shaft window*].   I be damn. Uh-uh, can't let you do it, Bill-Boy. [*Grabs the liquor and holds on.*]

Bill [*wraps the suit, the ham and the salami in the tablecloth and ties the ends together in a knot*].   Just for now, then you can go down and get it later.

Oldtimer [*getting belligerent*].   I say I ain' gon' let you do it.

Bill.   Sonny-man calls this "The people's revolution." A revolution should not be looting and stealing. Revolutions are for liberation. [*Oldtimer won't budge from before the window.*] Okay, man, you win, it's all yours. [*Walks away from Oldtimer and prepares his easel for sketching.*]

Oldtimer.   Don't be mad with me. Bill-Boy, I couldn't help myself.

Bill [*at peace with the old man*].   No hard feelin's.

Oldtimer [*as he uncorks bottle*].   I don't blame you for bein' fed up with us, . . . fella like you oughta be fed up with your people sometime. Hey, Billy, let's you and me have a little taste together.

Bill.   Yeah, why not.

Oldtimer [*at table pouring drinks.*]   You mustn't be too hard on me. You see, you talented, you got somethin' on the ball, you gonna make it on past these white folk, . . . but not me, Billy-boy, it's too late in the day for that. Time, time, time, . . . time done put me down. Father Time is a bad white cat. Whatcha been paintin' and drawin' lately? You can paint me again if you wanta, . . . no charge. Paint me 'cause that might be the only way I get to stay in the world after I'm dead and gone. Somebody'll look up at your paintin' and say, . . . "Who's that?" And you say, . . . "That's Oldtimer." [*Bill joins Oldtimer at table and takes one of the drinks.*] Well, here's lookin' at you and goin' down me. [*Gulps drink down.*]

Bill [*raising his glass*].   Your health, Oldtimer.

Oldtimer.   My day we didn't have all this grants and scholarship like now. Whatcha been doin'?

Bill.   I'm working on the third part of a triptych.

Oldtimer.   A what tick?

Bill.   A triptych.

Oldtimer.   Hot-damn, that calls for another drink. Here's to the trip-tick. Down the hatch. What is one-a-those?

Bill.   It's three paintings that make one work . . . three paintings that make one subject.

Oldtimer.   Goes together like a new outfit . . . hat, shoes and suit.

Bill.   Right. The title of my triptych is . . . "Wine In The Wilderness" . . . Three canvases on black womanhood. . . .

Oldtimer [*eyes light up*].   Are they naked pitchers?

Bill [*crosses to paintings*].   No, all fully clothed.

Oldtimer [*wishing it was a naked picture*].   Man, ain' nothin' dirty 'bout naked pitchers. That's art. What you call artistic.

Bill.   Right, right, right, but these are with clothes. That can be artistic too. [*Uncovers one of the canvases and reveals painting of a charming little girl in Sunday dress and hair ribbon.*] I call her . . . "Black girlhood."

Oldtimer.   Awwwww, that's innocence! Don't know what it's all about. Ain't that the little child that live right down the street? Yeah. That call for another drink.

Bill.   Slow down, Oldtimer, wait till you see this. [*Covers the painting of the little girl, then uncovers another canvas and reveals a beautiful woman, deep mahogany complexion, she is cold but utter perfection, draped in startling colors of African material, very "Vogue" looking. She wears a golden head-dress sparkling with brilliants and sequins applied over the paint.*] There she is . . . "Wine In The Wilderness" . . . Mother Africa, regal, black womanhood in her noblest form.

Oldtimer.   Hot damn. I'd die for her, no stuff, . . . oh, man. "Wine In The Wilderness."

Bill.   Once, a long time ago, a poet named Omar[1] told us what a paradise life could be if a man had a loaf of bread, a jug of wine and . . . a woman singing to him in the wilderness. She is the woman, she is the bread, she is the wine, she is the singing. This Abyssinian maiden[2] is paradise, . . . perfect black womanhood.

Oldtimer [*pours for Bill and himself*].   To our Abyssinian maiden.

Bill.   She's the Sudan, the Congo River, the Egyptian Pyramids . . . Her thighs are African Mahogany . . . she speaks and her words pour forth sparkling clear as the waters . . . Victoria Falls.

Oldtimer.   Ow! Victoria Falls! She got a pretty name.

Bill [*covers her up again*].   Victoria Falls is a waterfall not her name. Now, here's the one that calls for a drink. [*Snatches cover from the empty canvas.*]

Oldtimer [*stunned by the empty canvas*].   Your . . . your pitcher is gone.

Bill.   Not gone . . . she's not painted yet. This will be the third part of the trip-tych. This is the unfinished third of "Wine In The Wilderness." She's gonna be the kinda chick that is grass roots, . . . no, not grass roots, . . . I mean she's underneath the grass roots. The lost woman, . . . what the society has made out of our women. She's as far from my African queen as a woman can get and still be female, she's as close to the bottom as you can get without crackin' up . . . she's ignorant, unfeminine, coarse, rude . . . vulgar . . . a poor, dumb chick

---

[1] Omar Khayyám (ca. 1048–1123) was a Persian poet whose most famous work, the *Rubáiyát*, celebrates the sensuous pleasures of life.   [2] Abyssinia (now Ethiopia) was a kingdom in Africa.

that's had her behind kicked until it's numb . . . and the sad part is . . . she ain't
together, you know . . . there's no hope for her.

Oldtimer. Oh, man, you talkin 'bout my first wife.

Bill. A chick that ain' fit for nothin' but to . . . to . . . just pass her by.

Oldtimer. Yeah, later for her. When you see her, cross over to the other side
of the street.

Bill. If you had to sum her up in one word it would be nothin'!

Oldtimer [*roars with laughter*]. That call for a double!

Bill [*beginning to slightly feel the drinks. He covers the canvas again*]. Yeah,
that's a double! The kinda woman that grates on your damn nerves. And
Sonny-man just called to say he found her runnin' round in the middle-a this
riot. Sonny-man say she's the real thing from underneath them grass roots. A
back-country chick right outta the wilds of Mississippi, . . . but she ain't never
been near there. Born in Harlem, raised right here in Harlem, . . . but back
country. Got the picture?

Oldtimer [*full of laughter*]. When . . . when . . . when she get here let's us
stomp her to death.

Bill. Not till after I paint her. Gonna put her right here on this canvas. [*Pats
the canvas, walks in a strut around the table.*] When she gets put down on
canvas, . . . then triptych will be finished.

Oldtimer [*joins him in the strut*]. Trip-tick will be finish . . . trip-tick will be
finish . . .

Bill. Then "Wine In The Wilderness" will go up against the wall to improve
the view of some post office . . . or some library . . . or maybe a bank . . . and
I'll win a prize . . . and the queen, my black queen will look down from the
wall so the messed up chicks in the neighborhood can see what a woman
oughta be . . . and the innocent child on one side of her and the messed up
chick on the other side of her . . . MY STATEMENT.

Oldtimer [*turning the strut into a dance*]. Wine in the wilderness . . . up
against the wall . . . wine in the wilderness . . . up against the wall . . .

Woman from upstairs apt [*offstage*]. What's the matter! The house on fire?

Bill [*calls upstairs through the air-shaft window*]. No, baby! We down here
paintin' pictures! [*Sound of police siren in distance.*]

Woman from upstairs apt [*offstage*]. So much-a damn noise! Cut out the
noise! [*To her husband hysterically.*] Percy! Percy! You hear a police siren!
Percy! That a fire engine?!

Bill. Another messed up chick. [*Gets a rope and ties it to Oldtimer's bundle.*]
Got an idea. We'll tie the rope to the bundle, . . . then . . . [*Lowers bundle out
of window.*] lower the bundle outta the window . . . and tie it to this nail here
behind the curtain. Now! Nobody can find it except you and me . . . Cops
come, there's no loot. [*Ties rope to nail under curtain.*]

Oldtimer. Yeah, yeah, loot long gone 'til I want it. [*Makes sure window knot
is secure.*] It'll be swingin' in the breeze free and easy. [*There is knocking on
the door.*]

Sonny-man. Open up! Open up! Sonny-man and company.

Bill [*putting finishing touches on securing knot to nail*].   Wait, wait, hold on. . . .

Sonny-man.   And-a here we come! [*Pushes the door open. Enters room with his wife, Cynthia, and Tommy. Sonny-man is in high spirits. He is in his late twenties; his wife, Cynthia, is a bit younger. She wears her hair in a natural style; her clothing is tweedy and in good, quiet taste. Sonny-man is wearing slacks and a dashiki over a shirt. Tommy is dressed in a mismatched skirt and sweater, wearing a wig that is not comical, but is wiggy looking. She has the habit of smoothing it every once in a while, patting to make sure it's in place. She wears sneakers and bobby sox, carries a brown paper sack.*]

Cynthia.   You didn't think it was locked, did you?

Bill.   Door not locked? [*Looking over Tommy.*]

Tommy.   You oughta run him outta town, pushin' open people's door.

Bill.   Come right on in.

Sonny-man [*standing behind Tommy and pointing down at her to draw Bill's attention*].   Yes, sireeeeee.

Cynthia.   Bill, meet a friend-a ours . . . This is Miss Tommy Fields. Tommy, meet a friend-a ours . . . this is Bill Jameson . . . Bill, Tommy.

Bill.   Tommy, if I may call you that . . .

Tommy [*likes him very much*].   Help yourself, Bill. It's a pleasure. Bill Jameson, well, all right.

Bill.   The pleasure is all mine. Another friend-a ours. Oldtimer.

Tommy [*with respect and warmth*].   How are you, Mr. Timer?

Bill [*laughs along with others, Oldtimer included*].   What you call him, baby?

Tommy.   Mr. Timer, . . . ain't that what you say? [*They all laugh expansively.*]

Bill.   No, sugar pie, that's not his name, . . . we just say . . . "Oldtimer," that's what everybody call him. . . .

Oldtimer.   Yeah, they all call me that . . . everybody say that . . . Oldtimer.

Tommy.   That's cute, . . . but what's your name?

Bill.   His name is . . . er . . . er . . . What is your name?

Sonny-man.   Dog-bite, what's your name, man? [*There is a significant moment of self-consciousness as Cynthia, Sonny-man and Bill realize they don't know Oldtimer's name.*]

Oldtimer.   Well, it's . . . Edmond L. Matthews.

Tommy.   Edmond *L.* Matthews. What's the L for?

Oldtimer.   Lorenzo, . . . Edmond Lorenzo Matthews.

Bill and Sonny-man.   Edmond Lorenzo Matthews.

Tommy.   Pleased to meetcha, Mr. Matthews.

Oldtimer.   Nobody call me that in a long, long time.

Tommy.   I'll call you Oldtimer like the rest but I like to know who I'm meetin'. [*Oldtimer gives her a chair.*] There you go. He's a gentleman too. Bet you can tell my feet hurt. I got one corn, . . . and that one is enough. Oh, it'll ask you for somethin'. [*General laughter. Bill indicates to Sonny-man that Tommy seems right. Cynthia and Oldtimer take seats near Tommy.*]

Bill.   You rest yourself, baby, er . . . er . . . Tommy. You did say Tommy.

Tommy. I cut it to Tommy . . . Tommy-Marie, I use both of 'em sometime.

Bill. How 'bout some refreshment?

Sonny-man. Yeah, how 'bout that. [*Pouring drinks.*]

Tommy. Don't yall carry me too fast, now.

Bill [*indicating liquor bottles*]. I got what you see and also some wine . . . couple-a cans-a beer.

Tommy. I'll take the wine.

Bill. Yeah, I knew it.

Tommy. Don't wanta start nothin' I can't keep up. [*Oldtimer slaps his thigh with pleasure.*]

Bill. That's all right, baby, you just a wine-o.

Tommy. You the one that's got the wine, not me.

Bill. I use it for cookin'.

Tommy. You like to get loaded while you cook? [*Oldtimer is having a ball.*]

Bill [*as he pours wine for Tommy*]. Oh, baby, you too much.

Oldtimer [*admiring Tommy*]. Oh, Lord, I wish, I wish, I wish I was young again.

Tommy [*flirtatiously*]. Lively as you are, . . . I don't know what we'd do with you if you got any younger.

Oldtimer. Oh, hush now!

Sonny-man [*whispering to Bill and pouring drinks*]. Didn't I tell you! Know what I'm talkin' about. You dig? All the elements, man.

Tommy [*worried about what the whispering means*]. Let's get somethin' straight. I didn't come bustin' in on the party . . . I was asked. If you married and any wives or girlfriends round here . . . I'm innocent. Don't wanna get shot at, or jumped on. 'Cause I wasn't doin' a thing but mindin' my business! . . . [*Saying the last in loud tones to be heard in other rooms.*]

Oldtimer. Jus' us here, that's all.

Bill. I'm single, baby. Nobody wants a poor artist.

Cynthia. Oh, honey, we wouldn't walk you into a jealous wife or girlfriend.

Tommy. You paint all-a these pitchers? [*Bill and Sonny-man hand out drinks.*]

Bill. Just about. Your health, baby, to you.

Tommy [*lifts her wine glass*]. All right, and I got one for you. . . . Like my grampaw used-ta say, . . . Here's to the men's collars and the women's skirts, . . . may they never meet. [*General laughter.*]

Oldtimer. But they ain't got far to go before they do.

Tommy [*suddenly remembers her troubles*]. Niggers, niggers . . . niggers, . . . I'm sick-a niggers, ain't you? A nigger will mess up everytime . . . Lemmie tell you what the niggers done . . .

Bill. Tommy, baby, we don't use that word around here. We can talk about each other a little better than that.

Cynthia. Oh, she doesn't mean it.

Tommy. What must I say?

Bill. Try Afro-Americans.

Tommy. Well, . . . the Afro-Americans burnt down my house.

Oldtimer. Oh, no they didn't!

Tommy. Oh, yes they did . . . it's almost burn down. Then the firemen nailed up my door . . . the door to my room, nailed up shut tight with all I got in the world.

Oldtimer. Shame, what a shame.

Tommy. A *damn* shame. My clothes . . . Everything gone. This riot blew my life. All I got is gone like it never was.

Oldtimer. I know it.

Tommy. My transistor radio . . . that's gone.

Cynthia. Ah, gee.

Tommy. The transistor . . . and a brand new pair-a shoes I never had on one time . . . [*Raises her right hand.*] If I never move, that's the truth . . . new shoes gone.

Oldtimer. Child, when hard luck fall it just keep fallin'.

Tommy. And in my top dresser drawer I got a my-on-ase jar with forty-one dollars in it. The fireman would not let me in to get it . . . And it was a Afro-American fireman, don'tcha know.

Oldtimer. And you ain't got no place to stay. [*Bill is studying her for portrait possibilities.*]

Tommy [*rises and walks around room*]. That's a lie. I always got some place to go. I don't wanta boast but I ain't never been no place that I can't go back the second time. Woman I use to work for say . . . "Tommy, any time, any time you want a sleep-in place you come right here to me." . . . And that's Park Avenue, my own private bath and T.V. set. . . . But I don't want that . . . so I make it on out here to the dress factory. I got friends . . . not a lot of 'em . . . but a few *good* ones. I call my friend—girl and her mother . . . they say . . . "Tommy, you come here, bring yourself over here." So Tommy got a roof with no sweat. [*Looks at torn walls.*] Looks like the Afro-Americans got to you too. Breakin' up, breakin' down, . . . that's all they know.

Bill. No, Tommy, . . . I'm redecorating the place . . .

Tommy. You mean you did this to yourself?

Cynthia. It's gonna be wild . . . brick-face walls . . . wall to wall carpet.

Sonny-man. She was breakin' up everybody in the bar . . . had us all laughin' . . . crackin' us up. In the middle of a riot . . . she's gassin' everybody!

Tommy. No need to cry. It's sad enough. They hollerin' whitey, whitey . . . but who they burn out? Me.

Bill. The brothers and sisters are tired, weary of the endless get-no-where struggle.

Tommy. I'm standin' there in the bar . . . tellin' like it is . . . next thing I know they talkin' 'bout bringin' me to meet you. But you know what I say? Can't nobody pick nobody for nobody else. It don't work. And I'm standin' there in a mismatch skirt and top and these sneaker-shoes. I just went to put my dresses in the cleaner . . . Oh, Lord, wonder if they burn down the cleaner. Well, no matter, when I got back it was all over . . . They went in the grocery store, rip out the shelves, pull out all the groceries . . . the hams . . . the . . . the . . . the can goods . . . everything . . . and then set fire . . . Now who you think live over the grocery? Me, that's who. I don't even go to the store lookin' this way . . . but this would be the time, when . . . folks got a fella they want me to meet.

Bill [*suddenly self-conscious*].   Tommy, they thought . . . they thought I'd like to paint you . . . that's why they asked you over.

Tommy [*pleased by the thought but she can't understand it*].   Paint me? For what? If he was gonna paint somebody seems to me it'd be one of the pretty girls they show in the beer ads. They even got colored on television now, . . . brushin' their teeth and smokin' cigarettes, . . . some of the prettiest girls in the world. He could get them, . . . couldn't you?

Bill.   Sonny-man and Cynthia were right. I want to paint you.

Tommy [*suspiciously*].   Naked, with no clothes on?

Bill.   No, baby, dressed just as you are now.

Oldtimer.   Wearin' clothes is also art.

Tommy.   In the cleaner I got a white dress with a orlon sweater to match it, maybe I can get it out tomorrow and pose in that. [*Cynthia, Oldtimer and Sonny-man are eager for her to agree.*]

Bill.   No, I will paint you today, Tommy, just as you are, holding your brown paper bag.

Tommy.   Mmmmmm, me holdin' the damn bag, I don't know 'bout that.

Bill.   Look at it this way, tonight has been a tragedy.

Tommy.   Sure in hell has.

Bill.   And so I must paint you tonight, . . . Tommy in her moment of tragedy.

Tommy.   I'm tired.

Bill.   Damn, baby, all you have to do is sit there and rest.

Tommy.   I'm hungry.

Sonny-man.   While you're posin' Cynthia can run down to our house and fix you some eggs.

Cynthia [*gives her husband a weary look*].   Oh, Sonny, that's such a lovely idea.

Sonny-man.   Thank you, darlin', I'm in there, . . . on the beam.

Tommy [*ill at ease about posing*].   I don't want no eggs. I'm goin' to find me some Chinese food.

Bill.   I'll go. If you promise to stay here and let me paint you, . . . I'll get you anything you want.

Tommy [*brightening up*].   Anything I want. Now, how he sound? All right, you comin' on mighty strong there. "Anything you want." When last you heard somebody say that? . . . I'm warnin' you, now, . . . I'm free, single and disengage, . . . so you better watch yourself.

Bill [*keeping her away from ideas of romance*].   Now this is the way the program will go down. First I'll feed you, then I'll paint you.

Tommy.   Okay, I'm game, I'm a good sport. First off, I want me some Chinese food.

Cynthia.   Order up, Tommy, the treat's on him.

Tommy. How come it is you never been married? All these girls runnin' round Harlem lookin' for husbands. [*To Cynthia.*] I don't blame 'em, 'cause I'm lookin' for somebody myself.

Bill. I've been married, married and divorced, she divorced me, Tommy, so maybe I'm not much of a catch.

Tommy. Look at it this-a-way. Some folks got bad taste. That woman had bad taste. [*All laugh except Bill who pours another drink.*] Watch it, Bill, you gonna rust the linin' of your stomach. Ain't this a shame? The riot done wipe me out and I'm sittin' here havin' me a ball. Sittin' here ballin'! [*As Bill refills her glass.*] Hold it, that's enough. Likker ain' my problem.

Oldtimer. I'm havin' me a good time.

Tommy. Know what I say 'bout divorce. [*Slaps her hands together in a final gesture.*] Anybody don' wantcha, . . . later, let 'em go. That's bad taste for you.

Bill. Tommy, I don't wanta ever get married again. It's me and my work, I'm not gettin' serious about anybody. . . .

Tommy. He's spellin' at me, now. Nigger . . . I mean Afro-American . . . I ain' ask you nothin'. You hinkty, I'm hinkty too. I'm independent as a hog on ice, . . . and a hog on ice is dead, cold, well-preserved . . . and don't need a mother-grabbin' thing. [*All laugh heartily except Bill and Cynthia.*] I know models get paid. I ain' no square but this is a special night and so this one'll be on the house. Show you my heart's in the right place.

Bill. I'll be glad to pay you, baby.

Tommy. You don't really like me, do you? That's all right, sometime it happen that way. You can't pick for *nobody*. Friends get to matchin' up friends and they mess up everytime. Cynthia and Sonny-man done messed up.

Bill. I like you just fine and I'm glad and grateful that you came.

Tommy. Good enough. [*Extends her hand. They slap hands together.*] You 'n me friends?

Bill. Friends, baby, friends. [*Putting rock record on.*]

Tommy [*trying out the model stand*]. Okay. Dad! Let's see 'bout this *anything I want* jive. Want me a bucket-a Egg Foo Yong, and you get you a shrimp-fry rice, we split that and each have some-a both. Make him give you the soy sauce, the hot mustard and the duck sauce too.

Bill. Anything else, baby?

Tommy. Since you ask, yes. If your money hold out, get me a double order egg roll. And a half order of the sweet and sour spare ribs.

Bill [*to Oldtimer and Sonny-man*]. Come on, come on. I need some strong men to help me bring back your order, baby.

Tommy [*going into her dance . . . simply standing and going through some boo-ga-loo motions*]. Better go get it 'fore I think up some more to go 'long with it. [*The men laugh and vanish out of the door. Steps heard descending stairs.*] Turn that off. [*Cynthia turns off the record player.*] How could I forget your name, good as you been to me this day. Thank you. Cynthia, thank you. I *like* him. Oh, I *like* him. But I don't wanta push him too fast. Oh, I got to play these cards right.

Cynthia [*a bit uncomfortable*].   Oh, Honey, . . . Tommy, you don't want a poor artist.

Tommy.   Tommy's not lookin' for a meal ticket. I been doin' for myself all my life. It takes two to make it in this high-price world. A black man see a hard way to go. The both of you gotta pull together. That way you accomplish.

Cynthia.   I'm a social worker . . . and I see so many broken homes. Some of these men! Tommy, don't be in a rush about the marriage thing.

Tommy.   Keep it to yourself, . . . but I was thirty my last birthday and haven't ever been married. I coulda been. Oh, yes, indeed, coulda been. But I don't want any and everybody. What I want with a no-good piece-a nothin'? I'll never forget what the Reverend Martin Luther King said . . . "I have a dream." I liked him sayin' it 'cause truer words have never been spoke. [*Straightening the room.*] I have a dream, too. Mine is to find a man who'll treat me just half-way decent . . . just to meet me half-way is all I ask, to smile, be kind to me. Somebody in my corner. Not to wake up by myself in the mornin' and face this world all alone.

Cynthia.   About Bill, it's best not to ever count on anything, anything at all, Tommy.

Tommy [*this remark bothers her for a split second but she shakes it off*].   Of course, Cynthia, that's one of the foremost rules of life. Don't count on *nothin'!*

Cynthia.   Right, don't be too quick to put your trust in these men.

Tommy.   You put your trust in one and got yourself a husband.

Cynthia.   Well, yes, but what I mean is . . . Oh, you know. A man is a man and Bill is also an artist and his work comes before all else and there are other factors . . .

Tommy [*sits facing Cynthia*].   What's wrong with me?

Cynthia.   I don't know what you mean.

Tommy.   Yes you do. You tryin' to tell me I'm aimin' too high by lookin' at Bill.

Cynthia.   Oh, no, my dear.

Tommy.   Out there in the street, in the bar, you and your husband were so sure that he'd *like* me and want to paint my picture.

Cynthia.   But he does want to paint you, he's very eager to . . .

Tommy.   But why? Somethin' don't fit right.

Cynthia [*feeling sorry for Tommy*].   If you don't want to do it, just leave and that'll be that.

Tommy.   Walk out while he's buyin' me what I ask for, spendin' his money on me? That'd be too dirty. [*Looks at books. Takes one from shelf.*] Books, books, books everywhere. "Afro-American History." I like that. What's wrong with me, Cynthia? Tell me, I won't get mad with you, I swear. If there's somethin' wrong that I can change, I'm ready to do it. Eighth grade, that's all I had of school. You a social worker, I know that means college. I come from poor people. [*Examining the book in her hand.*] Talkin' 'bout poverty this and poverty that and studyin' it. When you in it you don' be studyin' 'bout it. Cynthia, I remember my mother tyin' up her stockin's with strips-a rag 'cause she didn't have no garters. When I get home from school she'd say, . . . "Nothin' much here to eat." Nothin' much might be grits, or bread and coffee. I got sick-a all that, got me a job. Later for school.

Cynthia. The Matriarchal Society.

Tommy. What's that?

Cynthia. A Matriarchal Society is one in which the women rule . . . the women have the power . . . the women head the house.

Tommy. We didn't have nothin' to rule over, not a pot nor a window. And my papa picked hisself up and run off with some finger-poppin' woman and we never hear another word 'til ten, twelve years later when a undertaker call up and ask if Mama wanta come claim his body. And don'tcha know, mama went on over and claim it. A woman need a man to claim, even if it's a dead one. What's wrong with me? Be honest.

Cynthia. You're a fine person . . .

Tommy. Go on, I can take it.

Cynthia. You're too brash. You're too used to looking out for yourself. It makes us lose our femininity . . . It makes us hard . . . it makes us seem very hard. We do for ourselves too much.

Tommy. If I don't, who's gonna do for me?

Cynthia. You have to let the black man have his manhood again. You have to give it back, Tommy.

Tommy. I didn't take it from him, how I'm gonna give it back? What else is the matter with me? You had school, I didn't. I respect that.

Cynthia. Yes, I've had it, the degree and the whole bit. For a time I thought I was about to move into another world, the so-called "integrated" world, a place where knowledge and know-how could set you free and open all the doors, but that's a lie. I turned away from that idea. The first thing I did was give up dating white fellas.

Tommy. I never had none to give up. I'm not soundin' on you. White folks nothin' happens when I look at 'em. I don't hate 'em, don't love 'em . . . just nothin' shakes a-tall. The dullest people in the world. The way they talk . . . "Oh, hooty, hooty, hoo" . . . Break it down for me to A, B, C's. That Bill . . . I like him, with his black, uppity, high-handed ways. What do you do to get a man you want? A social worker oughta tell you things like that.

Cynthia. Don't chase him . . . at least don't let it look that way. Let him pursue you.

Tommy. What if he won't? Men don't chase me much, not the kind I like.

Cynthia [*rattles off instructions glibly*]. Let him do the talking. Learn to listen. Stay in the background a little. Ask his opinion . . . "What do you think, Bill?"

Tommy. Mmmmm, "Oh, hooty, hooty, hoo."

Cynthia. But why count on him? There are lots of other nice guys.

Tommy. You don't think he'd go for me, do you?

Cynthia [*trying to be diplomatic*]. Perhaps you're not really his type.

Tommy. Maybe not, but he's mine. I'm so lonesome . . . I'm *lonesome* . . . I want somebody to love. Somebody to say . . . "That's all right," when the world treats me mean.

Cynthia.   Tommy, I think you're too good for Bill.

Tommy.   I don't wanta hear that. The last man that told me I was too good for him . . . was tryin' to get away. He's good enough for me. [*Straightening room.*]

Cynthia.   Leave the room alone. What we need is a little more sex appeal and a little less washing, cooking and ironing. [*Tommy puts down the room straightening.*] One more thing . . . do you have to wear that wig?

Tommy [*a little sensitive*].   I like how your hair looks. But some of the naturals I don't like. Can see all the lint caught up in the hair like it hasn't been combed since know not when. You a Muslim?[3]

Cynthia.   No.

Tommy.   I'm just sick-a hair, hair, hair. Do it this way, don't do it, leave it natural, straighten it, process, no process. I get sick-a hair and talkin' 'bout it and foolin' with it. That's why I wear the wig.

Cynthia.   I'm sure your own must be just as nice or nicer than that.

Tommy.   It oughta be. I only paid nineteen ninety-five for this.

Cynthia.   You ought to go back to usin' your own.

Tommy [*tensely*].   I'll be givin' that some thought.

Cynthia.   You're pretty nice people just as you are. Soften up, Tommy. You might surprise yourself.

Tommy.   I'm listenin'.

Cynthia.   Expect more. Learn to let men open doors for you . . .

Tommy.   What if I'm standin' there and they don't open it?

Cynthia [*trying to level with her*].   You're a fine person. He wants to paint you, that's all. He's doing a kind of mural thing and we thought he would enjoy painting you. I'd hate to see you expecting more out of the situation than what's there.

Tommy.   Forget it, sweetie-pie, don' nothin' happen that's not suppose to. [*Sound of laughter in the hall. Bill, Oldtimer and Sonny-man enter.*]

Bill.   No Chinese restaurant left, baby! It's wiped out. Gone with the revolution.

Sonny-man [*to Cynthia*].   Baby, let's move, split the scene, get on with it, time for home.

Bill.   The revolution is here. Whatta you do with her? You paint her!

Sonny-man.   You write her . . . you write the revolution. I'm gonna write the revolution into a novel nine hundred pages long.

Bill.   Dance it! Sing it! "Down in the cornfield Hear dat mournful sound . . . [*Sonny-man and Oldtimer harmonize.*] Dear old Massa am-a sleepin' A-sleepin' in the cold, cold ground." Now for "Wine In The Wilderness!" Triptych will be finished.

Cynthia [*in Bill's face*].   "Wine In The Wilderness," huh? Exploitation!

Sonny-man.   Upstairs, all out, come on, Oldtimer. Folks can't create in a crowd. Cynthia, move it, baby.

---

[3] The Black Muslim movement in the United States, established in the 1930s, embraces a strict moral and ethical code of personal conduct and family values.

Oldtimer [*starting toward the window*].   My things! I got a package.

Sonny-man [*heads him off*].   Up and out. You don't have to go home, but you have to get outta here. Happy paintin', yall. [*One backward look and they are all gone.*]

Bill.   Whatta night, whatta night, whatta night, baby. It will be painted, written, sung and discussed for generations.

Tommy [*notices nothing that looks like Chinese food; he is carrying a small bag and a container*].   Where's the Foo-Yong?

Bill.   They blew the restaurant, baby. All I could get was a couple-a franks and a orange drink from the stand.

Tommy [*tersely*].   You brought me a frank-footer? That's what you think-a me, a frank-footer?

Bill.   Nothin' to do with what I think. Place is closed.

Tommy [*quietly surly*].   This is the damn City-a New York, any hour on the clock they sellin' the chicken in the basket, barbecue ribs, pizza pie, hot pastrami samitches; and you brought me a frank-footer?

Bill.   Baby, don't break bad over somethin' to eat. The smart set, the jet, the beautiful people, kings and queens eat frankfurters.

Tommy.   If a queen sent you out to buy her a bucket-a Foo Yong, you wouldn't come back with no lonely-ass frank-footer.

Bill.   Kill me 'bout it, baby! Go 'head and shoot me six times. That's the trouble with our women, yall always got your mind on food.

Tommy.   Is that our trouble? [*Laughs.*] Maybe you right. Only two things to do. Either eat the frankfooter or walk on outta here. You got any mustard?

Bill [*gets mustard from the refrigerator*].   Let's face it, our folks are not together. The brothers and sisters have busted up Harlem . . . no plan, no nothin'. There's your black revolution, heads whipped, hospital full and we still in the same old bag.

Tommy [*seated at the kitchen table*].   Maybe what everybody need is somebody like you, who know how things oughta go, to get on out there and start some action.

Bill.   You still mad about the frankfurter?

Tommy.   No. I keep seein' pitchers of what was in my room and how it all must be spoiled now. [*Sips the orange drink.*] A orange never been near this. Well, it's cold. [*Looking at an incense burner.*] What's that?

Bill.   An incense burner, was given to me by the Chinese guy, Richard Lee. I'm sorry they blew his restaurant.

Tommy.   Does it help you to catch the number?

Bill.   No, baby, I just burn incense sometime.

Tommy.   For what?

Bill.   Just 'cause I feel like it. Baby, ain't you used to nothin'?

Tommy.   Ain't used to burnin' incent for nothin'.

Bill [*laughs*].   Burnin' what?

Tommy.   That stuff.

Bill.   What did you call it?

Tommy. Incent.

Bill. It's not incent, baby. It's incense.

Tommy. Like the sense you got in your head. In-sense. Thank you. You're a very correctable person, ain't you?

Bill. Let's put you on canvas.

Tommy [*stubbornly*]. I have to eat first.

Bill. That's another thing 'bout black women, they wanta eat 'fore they do anything else. Tommy. . . . Tommy, . . . I bet your name is Thomasina. You look like a Thomasina.

Tommy. You could sit there and guess till your eyes pop out and you never would guess my first name. You might could guess the middle name but not the first one.

Bill. Tell it to me.

Tommy. My name is Tomorrow.

Bill. How's that?

Tommy. Tomorrow, . . . like yesterday and *tomorrow,* and the middle name is just plain Marie. That's what my father name me. Tomorrow Marie. My mother say he thought it had a pretty sound.

Bill. Crazy! I never met a girl named Tomorrow.

Tommy. They got to callin' me Tommy for short, so I stick with that. Tomorrow Marie, . . . Sound like a promise that can never happen.

Bill [*straightens chair on stand; he is very eager to start painting*]. That's what Shakespeare said, . . . "Tomorrow and tomorrow and tomorrow." Tomorrow, you will be on this canvas.

Tommy [*still uneasy about being painted*]. What's the hurry? Rome wasn't built in a day, . . . that's another saying.

Bill. If I finish in time, I'll enter you in the exhibition.

Tommy [*loses interest in the food. Examines the room. Looks at portrait on the wall*]. He looks like somebody I know or maybe saw before.

Bill. That's Frederick Douglass.[4] A man who used to be a slave. He escaped and spent his life trying to make us all free. He was a great man.

Tommy. Thank you, Mr. Douglass. Who's the light colored man? [*Indicates a frame next to the Douglass.*]

Bill. He's white. That's John Brown.[5] They killed him for tryin' to shoot the country outta the slavery bag. He dug us, you know. Old John said, "Hell no, slavery must go."

Tommy. I heard all about him. Some folks say he was crazy.

Bill. If he had been shootin' at *us* they wouldn't have called him a nut.

Tommy. School wasn't a great part-a my life.

---

[4] Frederick Douglass (1817–1895) recounted his life in his celebrated autobiography, *Narrative of the Life of Frederick Douglass, an American Slave* (1845). After his escape from slavery, he devoted himself to the abolitionist cause.   [5] John Brown (1800–1859) and his followers captured the U.S. armory at Harper's Ferry, Virginia, in 1859, with the intention of establishing a base from which to free slaves by armed force. The insurrection was quickly quelled and Brown was hanged.

Bill. If it was you wouldn't-a found out too much 'bout black history 'cause the books full-a nothin' but whitey, . . . all except the white ones who dug us, . . . they not there either. Tell me, . . . who was Elijah Lovejoy?[6]

Tommy. Elijah Lovejoy, . . . Mmmmmmm. I don't know. Have anything to do with the Bible?

Bill. No, that's another white fella, . . . Elijah had a printin' press and the main thing he printed was "Slavery got to go." Well the man moved in on him, smashed his press time after time . . . but he kept puttin' it back together and doin' his thing. So, one final day, they came in a mob and burned him to death.

Tommy [*blows her nose with sympathy as she fights tears*]. That's dirty.

Bill [*as Tommy glances at titles in book case*]. Who was Monroe Trotter?[7]

Tommy. Was he white?

Bill. No, soul brother. Spent his years tryin' to make it all right. Who was Harriet Tubman?[8]

Tommy. I heard-a her. But don't put me through no test, Billy. [*Moving around studying pictures and books.*] This room is full-a things I don't know nothin' about. How'll I get to know?

Bill. Read, go to the library, book stores, ask somebody.

Tommy. Okay, I'm askin'. Teach me things.

Bill. Aw, baby, why torment yourself? Trouble with our women, . . . they all wanta be great brains. Leave somethin' for a man to do.

Tommy [*eager to impress him*]. What you think-a Martin Luther King?

Bill. A great guy. But it's too late in the day for the singin' and prayin' now.

Tommy. What about Malcolm X?[9]

Bill. Great cat . . . but there again . . . Where's the program?

Tommy. What about Adam Powell?[10] I voted for him. That's one thing 'bout me. I vote. Maybe if everybody vote for the right people . . .

Bill. The ballot box. It would take me all my life to straighten you on that hype.

Tommy. I got the time.

Bill. You gonna wind up with a king size headache. The Matriarchy gotta go. Yall throw them suppers together, keep your husband happy, raise the kids.

Tommy. I don't have a husband. Course, that could be fixed. [*Leaving the unspoken proposal hanging in the air.*]

Bill. You know the greatest thing you could do for your people? Sit up there and let me put you down on canvas.

[6] Elijah Parish Lovejoy (1802–1837), editor of an abolitionist newspaper in Alton, Illinois, was murdered trying to defend the presses on which his paper was printed from the attacks of pro-slavery extremists. [7] Monroe Trotter (1872–1934) was a newspaper editor and civil rights activist. [8] Harriet Tubman (1820–1913), after escaping from slavery, became active in the Underground Railroad, which led slaves to freedom. [9] Malcolm Little (1925–1965) became a Black Muslim while in prison and assumed the name Malcolm X, becoming an important leader in his adopted religion. He was assassinated in 1965. [10] Adam Clayton Powell, Jr. (1908–1972) served in Congress for many years as a representative from Harlem.

Tommy. Bein' married and havin' a family might be good for your people as a race, but I was thinkin' 'bout myself a little.

Bill. Forget yourself sometime, sugar. On that canvas you'll be givin' and givin' and givin' . . . That's where you can do your thing best. What you stallin' for?

Tommy [*returns to table and sits in chair*]. I . . . I don't want to pose in this outfit.

Bill [*patience is wearing thin*]. Why, baby, why?

Tommy. I don't feel proud-a myself in this.

Bill. Art, baby, we are talkin' art. Whatcha want . . . Ribbons? Lace? False eyelashes?

Tommy. No, just my white dress with the orlon sweater, . . . or anything but this what I'm wearin'. You oughta see me in that dress with my pink linen shoes. Oh, hell, the shoes are gone. I forgot 'bout the fire . . .

Bill. Oh, stop fightin' me! Another thing . . . our women don't know a damn thing 'bout bein' feminine. *Give in* sometime. It won't kill you. You tellin' me how to paint? Maybe you oughta hang out your shingle and give art lessons! You too damn opinionated. You gonna pose or you not gonna pose? Say somethin'!

Tommy. You makin' me nervous! Hollerin' at me. My mama never holler at me. Hollerin'.

Bill. But I'll soon be too tired to pick up the brush, baby.

Tommy [*eye catches picture of white woman on the wall*]. That's a white woman! Bet you never hollered at her and I bet she's your girlfriend . . . too, and when she posed for her pitcher I bet yall was laughin' . . . and you didn't buy her no frankfooter!

Bill [*feels a bit smug about his male prowess*]. Awww, come on, cut that out, baby. That's a little blonde, blue-eyed chick who used to pose for me. That ain't where it's at. This is a new day, the deal is goin' down different. This is the black moment, doll. Black, black, black is bee-yoo-tee-full. Got it? *Black is beautiful.*

Tommy. Then how come it is that I don't *feel* beautiful when you *talk* to me?!!

Bill. That's your hang-up, not mine. You supposed to stretch forth your wings like Ethiopia, shake off them chains that been holdin' you down. Langston Hughes[11] said let 'em see how beautiful you are. But you determined not to ever be beautiful. Okay, that's what makes you Tommy.

Tommy. Do you have a girlfriend? And who is she?

Bill [*now enjoying himself to the utmost*]. Naw, naw, naw, doll. I *know* people, but none-a this "tie-you-up-and-I-own-you" jive. I ain't mistreatin' nobody and there's enough-a me to go around. That's another thing with our women, . . . they wanta *latch* on. Learn to play it by ear, roll with the punches, cut down on some-a this "got-you-to-the-grave" kinda relationship. Was today

---

[11] Langston Hughes (1902–1967), one of the great modern writers, was a central figure in the Harlem Renaissance of the 1920s and 1930s, a period which saw a great outpouring of creativity by black writers.

all right? Good, be glad, . . . take what's at hand because tomorrow never comes, it's always today. [*She begins to cry.*] Awwww, I didn't mean it that way . . . I forgot your name. [*He brushes her tears away.*] You act like I belong to you. You're jealous of a picture?

Tommy. That's how women are, always studyin' each other and wonderin' how they look up 'gainst the next person.

Bill [*a bit smug*]. That's human nature. Whatcha call healthy competition.

Tommy. You think she's pretty?

Bill. She was, perhaps still is. Long, silky hair. She could sit on her hair.

Tommy [*with bitter arrogance*]. Doesn't *everybody?*

Bill. You got a head like a rock and gonna have the last word if it kills you. Baby, I bet you could knock out Muhammad Ali in the first round, then rare back and scream like Tarzan . . . "Now, I am the greatest!" [*He is very close to her and is amazed to feel a great sense of physical attraction.*] What we arguin' 'bout? [*Looks her over as she looks away. He suddenly wants to put the conversation on a more intimate level. His eye is on the bed.*] Maybe tomorrow would be a better time for paintin'. Wanna freshen up, take a bath, baby? Water's nice 'n hot.

Tommy [*knows the sound and turns to check on the look; notices him watching the bed; starts weeping*]. No, I don't! Nigger!

Bill. Was that nice? What the hell, let's paint the picture. Or are you gonna hold that back too?

Tommy. I'm posin'. Shall I take off the wig?

Bill. No, it's a part of your image, ain't it? You must have a reason for wearin' it. [*Tommy snatches up her orange drink and sits in the model's chair.*]

Tommy [*with defiance*]. Yes, I wear it 'cause you and those like you go for long, silky hair, and this is the only way I can have some without burnin' my mother-grabbin' brains out. Got it? [*She accidentally knocks over container of orange drink into her lap.*] Hell, I can't wear this. I'm soaked through. I'm not gonna catch no double pneumonia sittin' up here wringin' wet while you paint and holler at me.

Bill. Bitch!

Tommy. You must be talkin' 'bout your mama!

Bill. Shut up! Aw, shut-up! [*Phone rings. He finds an African throw-cloth and hands it to her.*] Put this on. Relax, don't go way mad, and all the rest-a that jazz. Change, will you? I apologize. I'm sorry. [*He picks up phone.*] Hello, survivor of a riot speaking. Who's calling? [*Tommy retires behind the screen with the throw. During the conversation she undresses and wraps the throw around her. We see Tommy and Bill but they can't see each other.*] Sure, told you not to worry. I'll be ready for the exhibit. If you don't dig it, don't show it. Not time for you to see it yet. Yeah, yeah, next week. You just make sure your exhibition room is big enough to hold the crowds that's gonna congregate to see this fine chick I got here. [*This perks Tommy's ears up.*] You oughta see her. The finest black woman in the world . . . No, . . . the finest *any* woman in the world . . . This gorgeous satin chick is . . . is . . . black velvet moonlight . . .

an ebony queen of the universe . . . [*Tommy can hardly believe her ears.*] One look at her and you go back to Spice Islands . . . She's Mother Africa . . . You flip, double flip. She has come through everything that has been put on her . . . [*He unveils the gorgeous woman he has painted . . . "Wine In The Wilderness." Tommy believes he is talking about her.*] Regal . . . grand . . . magnificent, fantastic . . . You would vote her the woman you'd most like to meet on a desert island, or around the corner from anywhere. She's here with me now . . . and I don't know if I want to show her to you or anybody else . . . I'm beginnin' to have this deep attachment . . . She sparkles, man, Harriet Tubman, Queen of the Nile . . . sweetheart, wife, mother, sister, friend . . . The night . . . a black diamond . . . A dark, beautiful dream . . . A cloud with a silvery lining . . . Her wrath is a storm over the Bahamas. "Wine In The Wilderness" . . . The memory of Africa . . . The *now* of things . . . but best of all and most important . . . She's tomorrow . . . she's my tomorrow . . . [*Tommy is dressed in the African wrap. She is suddenly awakened to the feeling of being loved and admired. She removes the wig and fluffs her hair. Her hair under the wig must not be an accurate, well-cut Afro . . . but should be rather attractive natural hair. She studies herself in a mirror. We see her taller, more relaxed and sure of herself. Perhaps braided hair will go well with Afro robe.*] Aw, man, later. You don't believe in nothin'! [*He covers "Wine In The Wilderness." Is now in a glowing mood.*] Baby, whenever you ready. [*She emerges from behind the screen. Dressed in the wrap, sans wig. He is astounded.*] Baby, what . . . ? Where . . . where's the wig?

Tommy. I don't think I want to wear it, Bill.

Bill. That is very becoming . . . the drape thing.

Tommy. Thank you.

Bill. I don't know what to say.

Tommy. It's time to paint. [*Steps up on the model stand and sits in the chair. She is now a queen, relaxed and smiling her appreciation for his past speech to the art dealer. Her feet are bare.*]

Bill [*mystified by the change in her; tries to do a charcoal sketch*]. It is quite late.

Tommy. Makes me no difference if it's all right with you.

Bill [*wants to create the other image*]. Could you put the wig back on?

Tommy. You don't really like wigs, do you?

Bill. Well, no.

Tommy. Then let's have things the way you like.

Bill [*has no answer for this. He makes a haphazard line or two as he tries to remember the other image*]. Tell me something about yourself, . . . anything.

Tommy [*now on sure ground*]. I was born in Baltimore, Maryland, and raised here in Harlem. My favorite flower is "Four O'clocks," that's a bush flower. My wearin' flower, corsage flower, is pink roses. My mama raised me, mostly by herself, God rest the dead. Mama belonged to "The Eastern Star." Her father was a "Mason." If a man in the family is a "Mason" any woman related to him can be an "Eastern Star." My grandfather was a member of "The Prince

Hall Lodge." I had a uncle who was an "Elk," . . . a member of "The Improved Benevolent Protective Order of Elks of the World": "The Henry Lincoln Johnson Lodge." You know, the white "Elks" are called "The Benevolent Protective Order of Elks" but the black "Elks" are called "The *Improved* Benevolent Protective Order of Elks of the World." That's because the black "Elks" got the copyright first but the white "Elks" took us to court about it to keep us from usin' the name. Over fifteen hundred black folk went to jail for wearin' the "Elk" emblem on their coat lapel. Years ago, . . . that's what you call history.

Bill.   I didn't know about that.

Tommy.   Oh, it's understandable. Only way I heard 'bout John Brown was because the black "Elks" bought his farmhouse where he trained his men to attack the government.

Bill.   The black "Elks" bought the John Brown Farm? What did they do with it?

Tommy.   They built a outdoor theatre and put a perpetual light in his memory, . . . and they buildin' cottages there, one named for each state in the union and . . .

Bill.   How do you know about it?

Tommy.   Well, our "Elks" helped my cousin go through school with a scholarship. She won a speaking contest and wrote a composition titled "Onward and Upward, O, My Race." That's how she won the scholarship. Coreen knows all that Elk history.

Bill [*seeing her with new eyes*].   Tell me some more about you, Tomorrow Marie. I bet you go to church.

Tommy.   Not much as I used to. Early in life I pledged myself in the A.M.E. Zion Church.

Bill [*studying her face, seeing her for the first time*].   A.M.E.

Tommy.   A.M.E. That's African Methodist Episcopal. We split off from the white Methodist Episcopal and started our own in the year Seventeen hundred and ninety-six. We built our first buildin' in the year 1800. How 'bout that?

Bill.   That right?

Tommy.   Oh, I'm just showin' off. I taught Sunday School for two years and you had to know the history of A.M.E. Zion . . . or else you couldn't teach. My great, great grandparents was slaves.

Bill.   Guess everybody's was.

Tommy.   Mine was slaves in a place called Sweetwater Springs, Virginia. We tried to look it up one time but somebody at church told us that Sweetwater Springs had become a part of Norfolk . . . so we didn't carry it any further . . . As it would be a expense to have a lawyer trace your people.

Bill [*throws charcoal pencil across room*].   No good! It won't work! I can't work anymore.

Tommy.   Take a rest. Tell me about you.

Bill [*sits on bed*].   Everybody in my family worked for the post office. They bought a home in Jamaica, Long Island. Everybody on that block bought an aluminum screen door with a duck on it, . . . or was it a swan? I guess that makes my favorite flower crab grass and hedges. I have a lot of bad dreams. [*Tommy massages his temples and the back of his neck.*] A dream like suffocating, dying of suffocation. The worst kinda dream. People are standing in a weird looking art gallery, they're looking and laughing at everything I've ever done. My work begins to fade off the canvas, right before my eyes. Everything I've ever done is laughed away.

Tommy.   Don't be so hard on yourself. If I was smart as you I'd wake up singin' every mornin'. [*There is the sound of thunder. He kisses her.*] When it thunders that's the angels in heaven playin' with their hoops, rollin' their hoops and bicycle wheels in the rain. My Mama told me that.

Bill.   I'm glad you're here. Black is beautiful, you're beautiful, A.M.E. Zion, Elks, pink roses, bush flower, . . . blooming out of the slavery of Sweetwater Springs, Virginia.

Tommy.   I'm gonna take a bath and let the riot and the hell of living go down the drain with the bath water.

Bill.   Tommy, Tommy, Tomorrow Marie, let's save each other, let's be kind and good to each other while it rains and the angels roll those hoops and bicycle wheels. [*They embrace. The sound of rain.*]

[*Music in as lights come down. As lights fade down to darkness, music comes in louder. There is a flash of lightning. We see Tommy and Bill in each other's arms. It is very dark. Music up louder, then softer and down to very soft. Music is mixed with the sound of rain beating against the window. Music slowly fades as gray light of dawn shows at window. Lights go up gradually. The bed is rumpled and empty. Bill is in the bathroom. Tommy is at the stove turning off the coffee pot. She sets table with cups and saucers, spoons. Tommy's hair is natural; she wears another throw draped around her. She sings and hums a snatch of a joyous spiritual.*]

Tommy.   "Great day, Great day, the world's on fire, Great day . . ." [*Calling out to Bill who is in bath.*] Honey, I found the coffee, and it's ready. Nothin' here to go with it but a cucumber and a Uneeda biscuit.

Bill [*offstage; joyous yell from offstage*].   Tomorrow and tomorrow and tomorrow! Good mornin', Tomorrow!

Tommy [*more to herself than to Bill*].   "Tomorrow and tomorrow." That's Shakespeare. [*Calls to Bill.*] You say that was Shakespeare?

Bill [*offstage*].   Right, baby, right!

Tommy.   I bet Shakespeare was black! You know how we love poetry. That's what give him away. I bet he was passin'. [*Laughs.*]

Bill [*offstage*].   Just you wait, one hundred years from now all the honkys gonna claim our poets just like they stole our blues. They gonna try to steal Paul Laurence Dunbar and LeRoi and Margaret Walker.[12]

---

[12] Paul Laurence Dunbar (1872–1906), LeRoi Jones (Imamu Amiri Baraka, b. 1934), and Margaret Walker (b. 1915) are black writers.

Tommy [*to herself*].　God moves in a mysterious way, even in the middle of a riot. [*A knock on the door.*] Great day, great day the world's on fire . . . [*Opens the door. Oldtimer enters. He is soaking wet. He does not recognize her right away.*]

Oldtimer.　'Scuse me, I must be in the wrong place.

Tommy [*patting her hair*].　This is me. Come on in, Edmond Lorenzo Matthews. I took off my hair-piece. This is me.

Oldtimer [*very distracted and worried*].　Well, howdy-do and good mornin'. [*He has had a hard night of drinking and sleeplessness.*] Where Bill-boy? It pourin' down some rain out there. [*Makes his way to the window.*]

Tommy.　What's the matter?

Oldtimer [*raises the window and starts pulling in the cord, the cord is weightless and he realizes there is nothing on the end of it*].　No, no, it can't be. Where is it? It's gone! [*Looks out the window.*]

Tommy.　You gonna catch your death. You wringin' wet.

Oldtimer.　Yall take my things in? It was a bag-a loot. A suit and some odds and ends. It was my loot. Yall took it in?

Tommy.　No. [*Realizes his desperation. She calls to Bill through the closed bathroom door.*] Did you take in any loot that was outside the window?

Bill [*offstage*].　No.

Tommy.　He said "no."

Oldtimer [*yells out window*].　Thieves, . . . dirty thieves . . . lotta good it'll do you . . .

Tommy [*leads him to a chair, dries his head with a towel*].　Get outta the wet things. You smell just like a whiskey still. Why don't you take care of yourself. [*Dries off his hands.*]

Oldtimer.　Drinkin' with the boys. Likker was everywhere all night long.

Tommy.　You got to be better than this.

Oldtimer.　Everything I ever put my hand and mind to do, it turn out wrong . . . Nothin' but mistakes . . . When you don' know, you don' know. I don't know nothin'. I'm ignorant.

Tommy.　Hush that talk . . . You know lotsa things, everybody does. [*Helps him remove wet coat.*]

Oldtimer.　Thanks. How's the trip-tick?

Tommy.　The what?

Oldtimer.　*Trip-tick.* That's a paintin'.

Tommy.　See there, you know more about art than I do. What's a trip-tick? Have some coffee and explain me a trip-tick.

Oldtimer [*proud of his knowledge*].　Well, I tell you, . . . a trip-tick is a paintin' that's in three parts . . . but they all belong together to be looked at all at once. Now . . . this is the first one . . . a little innocent girl . . . [*Unveils picture.*]

Tommy.　She's sweet.

Oldtimer.　And this is "Wine In The Wilderness" . . . The Queen of the Universe . . . the finest chick in the world.

Tommy [*Tommy is thoughtful as he unveils the second picture*].　That's not me.

Oldtimer. No, you gonna be this here last one. The worst gal in town. A messed-up chick that—that—[*He unveils the third canvas and is face to face with the almost blank canvas, then realizes what he has said. He turns to see the stricken look on Tommy's face.*]

Tommy. The messed-up chick, *that's* why they brought me here, ain't it? That's why he wanted to paint me! Say it!

Oldtimer. No, I'm lyin'. I didn't mean it. It's the society that messed her up. Awwwwww, Tommy, don't look that-a-way. It's art, . . . it's only art . . . He couldn't mean you . . . it's art . . . [*The door opens. Cynthia and Sonny-man enter.*]

Sonny-man. Anybody want a ride down . . . down . . . down . . . downtown? What's wrong? Excuse me . . . [*Starts back out.*]

Tommy [*blocking the exit to Cynthia and Sonny-man*]. No, come on in. Stay with it . . . "Brother" . . . "Sister." Tell 'em what a trip-tick is, Oldtimer.

Cynthia [*very ashamed*]. Oh, no.

Tommy. You don't have to tell 'em. They already know. The messed-up chick! How come you didn't pose for that, my sister? The messed-up chick lost her home last night, . . . burnt out with no place to go. You and Sonny-man gave me comfort, you cheered me up and took me in . . . *took me in!*

Cynthia. Tommy, we didn't know you, we didn't mean . . .

Tommy. It's all right! I was lost but now I'm found! Yeah, the blind can see! [*She dashes behind the screen and puts on her clothing, sweater, skirt, etc.*]

Oldtimer [*goes to bathroom door*]. Billy, come out!

Sonny-man. Billy, step out here, please! [*Bill enters shirtless, wearing dungarees.*] Oldtimer let it out 'bout the triptych.

Bill. The rest of you move on.

Tommy [*looking out from behind screen*]. No, don't go a step. You brought me here, see me out!

Bill. Tommy, let me explain it to you.

Tommy [*coming out from behind screen*]. I gotta check out my apartment and my clothes and money. Cynthia, . . . I can't wait for anybody to open the door or look out for me and all that kinda crap you talk. A bunch-a liars!

Bill. Oldtimer, why you . . .

Tommy. Leave him the hell alone. He ain't said nothin' that ain't so!

Sonny-man. Explain to the sister that some mistakes have been made.

Bill. Mistakes have been made, baby. The mistakes were yesterday, this is to-day . . .

Tommy. Yeah, and I'm Tomorrow, remember? Trouble is I was Tommin' to you, to all of you, . . . "Oh, maybe they gon' like me." . . . I was your fool, thinkin' writers and painters know more'n me, that maybe a little bit of you would rub off on me.

Cynthia. We are wrong. I knew it yesterday. Tommy, I told you not to expect anything out of this . . . this arrangement.

Bill. This is a relationship, not an arrangement.

Sonny-man. Cynthia, I tell you all the time, keep outta other people's business. What the hell you got to do with who's gonna get what outta what? You and Oldtimer, yakkin' and yakkin'. [*To Oldtimer.*] Man, your mouth gonna kill you.

Bill. It's me and Tommy. Clear the room.

Tommy. Better not, I'll kill him! The "black people" this and the "Afro-American" . . . that . . . You ain't got no use for none-a us. Oldtimer, you their fool too. Till I got here they didn't even know your damn name. There's something inside-a me that says I ain' suppose to let *nobody* play me cheap. Don't care how much they know! [*She sweeps some of the books to the floor.*]

Bill. Don't you have any forgiveness in you? Would I be beggin' you if I didn't care? Can't you be generous enough . . .

Tommy. Nigger, I been too damn generous with you, already. All-a these people know I wasn't down here all night posin' for no pitcher, nigger!

Bill. Cut that out, Tommy, and you not going anywhere!

Tommy. You wanna bet? Nigger!

Bill. Okay, you called it, baby, I did act like a low, degraded person . . .

Tommy [*combing out her wig with her fingers while holding it*]. Didn't call you no low, degraded person. Nigger! [*To Cynthia who is handing her a comb.*] "Do you have to wear a wig?" Yes! To soften the blow when yall go upside-a my head with a baseball bat. [*Going back to taunting Bill and ignoring Cynthia's comb.*] Nigger!

Bill. That's enough-a that. You right and you're wrong too.

Tommy. Ain't a-one-a us you like that's alive and walkin' by you on the street . . . you don't like flesh and blood niggers.

Bill. Call me that, baby, but don't call yourself. That what you think of yourself?

Tommy. If a black somebody is in a history book, or printed on a pitcher, or drawed on a paintin', . . . or if they're a statue, . . . dead, and outta the way, and can't talk back, then you dig 'em and full-a so much-a damn admiration and talk 'bout "our" history. But when you run into us livin' and breathin' ones, with the life's blood still pumpin' through us, . . . then you comin' on 'bout how we ain' never together. You hate us, that's what! *You hate black me!*

Bill [*stung to the heart, confused and saddened by the half truth which applies to himself*]. I never hated you, I never will, no matter what you or any of the rest of you do to *make* me hate you. I won't! Hell, woman, why do you say that! Why would I hate you??

Tommy. Maybe I look too much like the mother that gave birth to you. Like the Ma and Pa that worked in the post office to buy you a house and a screen door with a damn duck on it. And you so ungrateful you didn't even like it.

Bill. No, I didn't, baby. I don't like screen doors with ducks on 'em.

Tommy. You didn't like who was livin' behind them screen doors. Phoney Nigger!

Bill. That's all! Damnit! don't go there no more!

Tommy.   Hit me, so I can tear this place down and scream bloody murder.

Bill [*somewhere between laughter and tears*].   Looka here, baby, I'm willin' to say I'm wrong, even in fronta the room fulla people . . .

Tommy [*through clenched teeth*].   Nigger.

Sonny-man.   The sister is upset.

Tommy.   And you stop callin' me "the" sister, . . . if you feelin' so brotherly why don't you say "my" sister? Ain't no we-ness in your talk. "The" Afro-American, "the" black man, there's no we-ness in you. Who you think you are?

Sonny-man.   I was talkin' in general er . . . *my* sister, 'bout the masses.

Tommy.   There he go again. "The" masses. Tryin' to make out like we pitiful and you got it made. You the masses your damn self and don't even know it. [*Another angry look at Bill.*] Nigger.

Bill [*pulls dictionary from shelf*].   Let's get this ignorant "nigger" talk squared away. You can stand some education.

Tommy.   You *treat* me like a nigger, that's what. I'd rather be called one than treated that way.

Bill [*questions Tommy*].   What is a nigger? [*Talks as he is trying to find word.*] A nigger is a low, degraded person, *any* low degraded person. I learned that from my teacher in the fifth grade.

Tommy.   Fifth grade is a liar! Don't pull that dictionary crap on me.

Bill [*pointing to the book*].   Webster's New World Dictionary of the American Language, College Edition.

Tommy.   I don't need to find out what no college white folks say nigger is.

Bill.   I'm tellin' you it's a low, degraded person. Listen. [*Reads from the book.*] Nigger, N-i-g-g-e-r, . . . a Negro . . . A member of any dark-skinned people . . . Damn. [*Amazed by dictionary description.*]

Sonny-man.   Brother Malcolm *said* that's what they meant, . . . nigger is a Negro, Negro is a nigger.

Bill [*slowly finishing his reading*].   A vulgar, offensive term of hostility and contempt. Well, so much for the fifth grade teacher.

Sonny-man.   No, they do not call low, degraded white folks niggers. Come to think of it, did you ever hear whitey call Hitler a nigger? Now if some whitey digs us, . . . the others might call him a nigger-*lover*, but they don't call him no nigger.

Oldtimer.   No, they don't.

Tommy [*near tears*].   When they say "nigger," just dry-long-so, they mean educated you and uneducated me. They hate you and call you "nigger," I called you "nigger" but I love you. [*There is dead silence in the room for a split second.*]

Sonny-man [*trying to establish peace*].   There you go. There you go.

Cynthia [*cautioning Sonny-man*].   Now is not the time to talk, darlin'.

Bill.   You love me? Tommy, that's the greatest compliment you could . . .

Tommy [*sorry she said it*].   You must be runnin' a fever, nigger, I ain' said nothin' 'bout lovin' you.

Bill [*in a great mood*].   You did, yes, you did.

Tommy.   Well, you didn't say it to *me*.

Bill.   Oh, Tommy, . . .

Tommy [*cuts him off abruptly*].   And don't you dare say it now. I'm tellin' you, . . . it ain't to be said now. [*Checks through her paper bag to see if she has everything. Starts to put on the wig, changes her mind, holds it to end of scene. Turns to the others in the room.*] Oldtimer, . . . my brothers and my sister.

Oldtimer.   I wish I was a thousand miles away. I'm so sorry. [*He sits at the foot of the model stand.*]

Tommy.   I don't stay mad, it's here today and gone tomorrow. I'm sorry your feelin's got hurt, . . . but when I'm hurt I turn and hurt back. Somewhere, in the middle of last night, I thought the old me was gone, . . . lost forever, and gladly. But today was flippin' time, so back I flipped. Now it's "turn the other cheek" time. If I can go through life other-cheekin' the white folk, . . . guess yall can be other-cheeked too. But I'm goin' back to the nitty-gritty crowd, where the talk is we-ness and us-ness. I hate to do it but I have to thank you 'cause I'm walkin' out with much more than I brought in. [*Goes over and looks at the queen in the "Wine In The Wilderness" painting.*] Tomorrow Marie had such a lovely yesterday. [*Bill takes her hand, she gently removes it from his grasp.*] Bill, I don't have to wait for anybody's by-your-leave to be a "Wine In The Wilderness" woman. I can be if I wanta, . . . and I *am*. I am. I am. I'm not the one you made up and painted, the very pretty lady who can't talk back, . . . but I'm "Wine In The Wilderness" . . . alive and kickin', me . . . Tomorrow Marie, cussin' and fightin' and lookin' out for my damn self 'cause ain' nobody else 'round to do it, don'tcha know. And, Cynthia, if my hair is straight, or if it's natural, or if I wear a wig, or take it off, . . . that's all right; because wigs . . . shoes . . . hats . . . bags . . . and even this . . . [*She picks up the African throw she wore a few moments before . . . fingers it.*] They're just what you call . . . access . . . [*Fishing for the word.*] . . . like what you wear with your Easter outfit . . .

Cynthia.   Accessories.

Tommy.   Thank you, my sister. Accessories. Somethin' you add on or take off. The real thing is takin' place on the inside . . . that's where the action is. That's "Wine In The Wilderness," . . . a woman that's a real one and a good one. And yall just better believe I'm it. [*She proceeds to the door.*]

Bill.   Tommy. [*She turns. He takes the beautiful queen, "Wine In The Wilderness" from the easel.*] She's not it at all, Tommy. This chick on the canvas, . . . nothin' but accessories, a dream I drummed up outta the junk room of my mind. [*Places the "queen" to one side.*] You are and . . . [*Points to Oldtimer*] . . . Edmond Lorenzo Matthews . . . the real beautiful people, . . . Cynthia . . .

Cynthia [*bewildered and unbelieving*].   Who? Me?

Bill.   Yeah, honey, you and Sonny-man, don't know how beautiful you are. [*Indicates the other side of model stand.*] Sit there.

Sonny-man [*places cushions on the floor at the foot of the model stand*].   Just sit here and be my beautiful self. [*To Cynthia.*] Turn on, baby, we gonna get our picture took. [*Cynthia smiles.*]

Bill.   Now there's Oldtimer, the guy who was here before there were scholarships and grants and stuff like that, the guy they kept outta the schools, the man the factories wouldn't hire, the union wouldn't let him join . . .

Sonny-man.   Yeah, yeah, rap to me. Where you goin' with it, man? Rap on.

Bill.   I'm makin' a triptych.

Sonny-man.   Make it, man.

Bill [*indicating Cynthia and Sonny-man*].   On the other side, Young Man and Woman, workin' together to do our thing.

Tommy [*quietly*].   I'm goin' now.

Bill.   But you belong up there in the center, "Wine In The Wilderness" . . . that's who you are. [*Moves the canvas of "the little girl" and places a sketch pad on the easel.*] The nightmare, about all that I've done disappearing before my eyes. It was a good nightmare. I was painting in the dark, all head and no heart. I couldn't see until you came, baby. [*To Cynthia, Sonny-man and Oldtimer.*] Look at Tomorrow. She came through the biggest riot of all, . . . somethin' called "Slavery," and she's even comin' through the "now" scene, . . . folks laughin' at her, even her own folks laughin' at her. And look *how* . . . with her head high like she's poppin' her fingers at the world. [*Takes up charcoal pencil and tears old page off sketch pad so he can make a fresh drawing.*] Aw, let me put it down, Tommy. "Wine In The Wilderness," you gotta let me put it down so all the little boys and girls can look up and see you on the wall. And you know what they're gonna say? "Hey, don't she look like somebody we know?" [*Tommy slowly returns and takes her seat on the stand. Tommy is holding the wig in her lap. Her hands are very graceful looking against the texture of the wig.*] And they'll be right, you're somebody they know . . . [*He is sketching hastily. There is a sound of thunder and the patter of rain.*] Yeah, roll them hoops and bicycle wheels. [*Music in low. Music up higher as Bill continues to sketch.*]

For Analysis

1. What thematic relevance does the riot have to the main action of the play? **2.** What do the three paintings in Bill's projected triptych tell us about his view of African American history? **3.** What is Bill's attitude toward black women? In this connection, contrast his attitude toward the women he is painting and the real woman, Cynthia. **4.** What significance is there to the fact that Bill, Sonny-man, and Cynthia do not know Oldtimer's real name? **5.** Does the play say anything about the way blacks should deal with white racism? Does the play focus on white racism? Explain. **6.** Why does Tommy feel betrayed at the end of the play? **7.** Does the play conclude on a hopeful note? Explain.

On Style

Characterize the speech patterns of each character. What function does the difference in diction serve? Is there any relationship between a character's diction and his or her moral standing in the play? Explain.

Making Connections

Contrast the play's treatment of the impact of racism on African Americans with the way it is treated in one of the following works: James Alan McPherson's *A Loaf of Bread* (p. 405) or August Wilson's *Two Trains Running* (p. 565).

Writing Topic

Write an essay arguing for or against the proposition that the play is as much about class differences as it is about racism.

Essays

William Saroyan   [1908–1981]

Five Ripe Pears   1936

If old man Pollard is still alive I hope he reads this because I want him to know I am not a thief and never have been. Instead of making up a lie, which I could have done, I told the truth and got a licking. I don't care about the licking because I got a lot of them in grammar school. They were part of my education. Some of them I deserved and some I didn't. The licking Mr. Pollard gave me I didn't deserve, and I am going to tell him why. I couldn't tell him that day because I didn't know how to explain what I knew.

It was about spring pears.

The trees grew in a yard protected by a spike fence, but some of the branches grew beyond the fence. I was six, but logical. A fence, I reasoned, can protect only that which it encloses.

Therefore, I said, the pears growing on the branches beyond the fence are mine—if I can reach them.

It happened during school recess. The trees were two blocks from the school.   5

I told the Jewish boy, Isaacs, that I was going to the trees, and he said it was stealing. This meant nothing, or it meant that he was afraid to go with me. I did not bother at the time to investigate what it meant, and went running out of the school grounds, down the street.

I reached the trees breathless but alert and smiling. The pears were fat and ready. The sun was warm. The moment was a moment of numerous clarities, air, body, and mind.

Among the leaves I watched the pears, fat and yellow and red, full of the stuff of life, from the sun, and I wanted. It was a thing they could not speak about in the second grade.

The pears were mine if I could reach them, but I couldn't. It was almost enough to see them, but I had been looking at them for weeks. I had seen the trees when they had been bare of leaf. I had seen the coming of leaves and the

290

coming of blossoms. I had seen the blossoms fall away before the pressure of the hard green shapes of unripe pears.

Now the pears were ripe and ready, and I was ready. 10

But it was not to eat. It was not to steal. It was to know: *the pear.* Of life—the sum of it—which *could* decay.

I was determined to get them, and remain innocent.

Afterwards, when they made a thief of me, I weakened and almost believed I *was* a thief, but it was not so.

A misfortune of youth is that it is speechless when it has most to say, and a fault of maturity is that it is garrulous when it has forgotten where to begin or what language to use. Oh, we have been well educated in error, all right. We at least know that we have forgotten.

I couldn't reach the pears, so I tried leaping. At first I leaped with the idea of 15 reaching a branch and lowering it, but after I had leaped two or three times I leaped because it was fun to do so.

I was leaping when I heard the school bell ring, and I remember the ringing sickened me because I knew I was going to be late. A moment afterwards, though, I thought nothing of being late, having as justification both the ripe pears and my discovery of leaping.

I believed it was a reasonable bargain.

I didn't stop to think they would ask me questions, and I wouldn't have the words with which to answer them accurately.

I got five pears by using a dead tree twig. There were many more to have, but I chose only five, those that were most ready. One I ate. Four I took to class, arriving ten minutes late.

A sensible man is no less naïve at six than at sixty, but few men are sensible. 20 Four pears I took to class, showing them as the reason for lateness.

This caused an instantaneous misunderstanding, and I knew I was being taken for a thief. I had nothing to say because I did have the pears. They were both the evidence of theft and the proof of innocence. I was amazed to discover that to Miss Larkin they were only the evidence.

She was severe and said many things. I understood only that she was angry and inclined toward the opinion that I should be punished. The details are blurred, but I remember sitting in the school office, feeling somewhat a thief, waiting for Mr. Pollard to put in an appearance.

The pears were on his table. They were cheerless and I was frightened.

There was nothing else to do: I ate a pear. It was sweet, sweeter than the one I had eaten by the tree. The core remained in my hand, lingering there in a foolish way.

I ate also the core, keeping in my hand only a number of seeds. These I pock- 25 eted, thinking of growing pear-trees of my own.

One pear followed another because I was frightened and disliked feeling a thief.

The Principal of the school came at last. His coming was like the coming of doom, and when he coughed I thought the whole world shook. He coughed a number of times, looked at me severely a number of times, and then said: I hear you have been stealing pears. Where are they?

I imagined he wanted to eat a pear, so I felt ashamed of myself because I had none to give him, but I suppose he took it the other way around and believed I was ashamed because I was a thief who had been caught.

I could see him taking advantage of my shame, and I knew I would be punished.

It was not pleasant, either, to hear him say that I had stolen the pears. I ate them, I said.   30

You *ate* the pears? he said. It seemed to me that he was angry.

Nevertheless, I said: Yes, sir.

How many pears? he said.

Four, I said.

You *stole* four pears, he said, and then *ate* them?   35

No, sir, I said. Five. One I ate by the tree.

Everything was misunderstood, but all I could do was answer questions in a way that would justify his punishing me, which he did.

I cried for all I was worth, because it seemed very strange to me that no one could even faintly understand why I had picked the five ripe pears.

I know Miss Larkin is dead, but if old man Pollard is still alive I hope he reads this because I want him to know that I did *not* steal the pears, I created them, and took four to class because I wanted others to see them. No hard feelings, Mr. Pollard, but I thought I ought to tell you how it really was with me that day.

For Analysis

1. Why has this event lingered in the author's memory for so many years? **2.** Why does the author insist that taking the pears was not stealing? **3.** Explain what the author means when he declares that the pears "were both the evidence of theft and the proof of innocence" (par. 21). **4.** In what sense has the author "created" the pears, as he claims in the final paragraph?

On Style

1. How effective is Saroyan's device of addressing Mr. Pollard directly? Pay particular attention to the final sentence of the story. **2.** Numerous short paragraphs beginning with "I" dominate this essay. What effect does this stylistic device have on the reader's response?

Making Connections

1. Compare and contrast the pears in this essay and the house in Sandra Cisneros's "The House on Mango Street" (p. 122) as **symbols**. **2.** This essay and Toni Cade Bambara's story "The Lesson" (p. 115) deal with a child whose sense of justice is offended. What differences and similarities do you find in the source of each child's distress and the way it is resolved? **3.** Compare this essay with Frank O'Connor's "My Oedipus Complex" (p. 90) in their portrayals of young protagonists who feel betrayed by the adult world. Describe the nature of the betrayal and the success each protagonist has in dealing with it.

Writing Topic

Describe a childhood experience where the adult world judged you harshly or punished you for what in your mind was an innocent act.

Joan Didion [b. 1934]

On Morality 1965

As it happens I am in Death Valley, in a room at the Enterprise Motel and Trailer Park, and it is July, and it is hot. In fact it is 119°. I cannot seem to make the air conditioner work, but there is a small refrigerator, and I can wrap ice cubes in a towel and hold them against the small of my back. With the help of the ice cubes I have been trying to think, because *The American Scholar*[1] asked me to, in some abstract way about "morality," a word I distrust more every day, but my mind veers inflexibly toward the particular.

Here are some particulars. At midnight last night, on the road in from Las Vegas to Death Valley Junction, a car hit a shoulder and turned over. The driver, very young and apparently drunk, was killed instantly. His girl was found alive but bleeding internally, deep in shock. I talked this afternoon to the nurse who had driven the girl to the nearest doctor, 185 miles across the floor of the Valley and three ranges of lethal mountain road. The nurse explained that her husband, a talc miner, had stayed on the highway with the boy's body until the coroner could get over the mountains from Bishop, at dawn today. "You can't just leave a body on the highway," she said. "It's immoral."

It was one instance in which I did not distrust the word, because she meant something quite specific. She meant that if a body is left alone for even a few minutes on the desert, the coyotes close in and eat the flesh. Whether or not a corpse is torn apart by coyotes may seem only a sentimental consideration, but of course it is more: one of the promises we make to one another is that we will try to retrieve our casualties, try not to abandon our dead to the coyotes. If we have been taught to keep our promises—if, in the simplest terms, our upbringing is good enough—we stay with the body, or have bad dreams.

I am talking, of course, about the kind of social code that is sometimes called, usually pejoratively, "wagon-train morality." In fact that is precisely what it is. For better or worse, we are what we learned as children: my own childhood was illuminated by graphic litanies of the grief awaiting those who failed in their loyalties to each other. The Donner-Reed Party,[2] starving in the Sierra snows, all the ephemera of civilization gone save that one vestigial taboo, the provision that no one should eat his own blood kin. The Jayhawkers, who quarreled and

---

[1] A general interest journal published by the Phi Beta Kappa Society.

[2] A group of eighty-seven people who tried to cross the mountains into California during the stormy winter of 1846. The forty-seven who survived the ordeal ate the flesh of those who died.

separated not far from where I am tonight. Some of them died in the Funerals[3] and some of them died down near Badwater and most of the rest of them died in the Panamints. A woman who got through gave the Valley its name. Some might say that the Jayhawkers were killed by the desert summer, and the Donner Party by the mountain winter, by circumstances beyond control; we were taught instead that they had somewhere abdicated their responsibilities, somehow breached their primary loyalties, or they would not have found themselves helpless in the mountain winter or the desert summer, would not have given way to acrimony, would not have deserted one another, would not have *failed.* In brief, we heard such stories as cautionary tales, and they still suggest the only kind of "morality" that seems to me to have any but the most potentially mendacious meaning.

You are quite possibly impatient with me by now; I am talking, you want to say, about a "morality" so primitive that it scarcely deserves the name, a code that has as its point only survival, not the attainment of the ideal good. Exactly. Particularly out here tonight, in this country so ominous and terrible that to live in it is to live with antimatter, it is difficult to believe that "the good" is a knowable quantity. Let me tell you what it is like out here tonight. Stories travel at night on the desert. Someone gets in his pickup and drives a couple of hundred miles for a beer, and he carries news of what is happening, back wherever he came from. Then he drives another hundred miles for another beer, and passes along stories from the last place as well as from the one before; it is a network kept alive by people whose instincts tell them that if they do not keep moving at night on the desert they will lose all reason. Here is a story that is going around the desert tonight: over across the Nevada line, sheriff's deputies are diving in some underground pools, trying to retrieve a couple of bodies known to be in the hole. The widow of one of the drowned boys is over there; she is eighteen, and pregnant, and is said not to leave the hole. The divers go down and come up, and she just stands there and stares into the water. They have been diving for ten days but have found no bottom to the caves, no bodies and no trace of them, only the black 90° water going down and down and down, and a single translucent fish, not classified. The story tonight is that one of the divers has been hauled up incoherent, out of his head, shouting—until they got him out of there so that the widow could not hear—about water that got hotter instead of cooler as he went down, about light flickering through the water, about magma, about underground nuclear testing.

That is the tone stories take out here, and there are quite a few of them tonight. And it is more than the stories alone. Across the road at the Faith Community Church a couple of dozen old people, come here to live in trailers and die in the sun, are holding a prayer sing. I cannot hear them and do not want to. What I can hear are occasional coyotes and a constant chorus of "Baby the Rain

5

---

[3] The Funerals and the Panamints are mountain ranges close to Death Valley.

Must Fall" from the jukebox in the Snake Room next door, and if I were also to hear those dying voices, those Midwestern voices drawn to this lunar country for some unimaginable atavistic rites, *rock of ages cleft for me,* I think I would lose my own reason. Every now and then I imagine I hear a rattlesnake, but my husband says that it is a faucet, a paper rustling, the wind. Then he stands by a window, and plays a flashlight over the dry wash outside.

What does it mean? It means nothing manageable. There is some sinister hysteria in the air out here tonight, some hint of the monstrous perversion to which any human idea can come. "I followed my own conscience." "I did what I thought was right." How many madmen have said it and meant it? How many murderers? Klaus Fuchs said it, and the men who committed the Mountain Meadows Massacre said it, and Alfred Rosenberg[4] said it. And, as we are rotely and rather presumptuously reminded by those who would say it now, Jesus said it. Maybe we have all said it, and maybe we have been wrong. Except on that most primitive level—our loyalties to those we love—what could be more arrogant than to claim the primacy of personal conscience? ("Tell me," a rabbi asked Daniel Bell when he said, as a child, that he did not believe in God. "Do you think God cares?") At least some of the time, the world appears to me as a painting by Hieronymus Bosch;[5] were I to follow my conscience then, it would lead me out onto the desert with Marion Faye, out to where he stood in *The Deer Park*[6] looking east to Los Alamos and praying, as if for rain, that it would happen: "*. . . let it come and clear the rot and the stench and the stink, let it come for all of everywhere, just so it comes and the world stands clear in the white dead dawn.*"

Of course you will say that I do not have the right, even if I had the power, to inflict that unreasonable conscience upon you; nor do I want you to inflict your conscience, however reasonable, however enlightened, upon me. ("We must be aware of the dangers which lie in our most generous wishes," Lionel Trilling[7] once wrote. "Some paradox of our nature leads us, when once we have made our fellow men the objects of our enlightened interest, to go on to make them the objects of our pity, then of our wisdom, ultimately of our coercion.") That the ethic of conscience is intrinsically insidious seems scarcely a revelatory point, but it is one raised with increasing infrequency; even those who do raise

---

[4] Klaus Fuchs fled Germany to the United States, where he worked on the development of the atomic bomb during World War II. He moved to Great Britain to assume an important position at the British atomic energy center. He was convicted and imprisoned for providing atomic energy secrets to the Soviet Union. The Mountain Meadows Massacre occurred in September 1857 in Utah. A group of 130–140 emigrants heading for California were attacked by Indians incited and joined by Mormons angry at the treatment they had received during their earlier trek across the continent. All but seventeen children were massacred. Alfred Rosenberg was a Nazi leader often called "The Grand Inquisitor of the Third Reich." He was hanged for war crimes in 1946.

[5] Hieronymus Bosch (1450?–1516), a Dutch painter of fantastic and hellish images.

[6] A novel by Norman Mailer.

[7] Lionel Trilling (1905–1975), an eminent critic of literature and modern culture.

it tend to *segue* with troubling readiness into the quite contradictory position that the ethic of conscience is dangerous when it is "wrong," and admirable when it is "right."

You see I want to be quite obstinate about insisting that we have no way of knowing—beyond that fundamental loyalty to the social code—what is "right" and what is "wrong," what is "good" and what "evil." I dwell so upon this because the most disturbing aspect of "morality" seems to me to be the frequency with which the word now appears; in the press, on television, in the most perfunctory kinds of conversation. Questions of straightforward power (or survival) politics, questions of quite indifferent public policy, questions of almost anything: they are all assigned these factitious moral burdens. There is something facile going on, some self-indulgence at work. Of course we would all like to "believe" in something, like to assuage our private guilts in public causes, like to lose our tiresome selves; like, perhaps, to transform the white flag of defeat at home into the brave white banner of battle away from home. And of course it is all right to do that; that is how, immemorially, things have gotten done. But I think it is all right only so long as we do not delude ourselves about what we are doing, and why. It is all right only so long as we remember that all the *ad hoc* committees, all the picket lines, all the brave signatures in *The New York Times*, all the tools of agitprop straight across the spectrum, do not confer upon anyone any *ipso facto* virtue. It is all right only so long as we recognize that the end may or may not be expedient, may or may not be a good idea, but in any case has nothing to do with "morality." Because when we start deceiving ourselves into thinking not that we want something or need something, not that it is a pragmatic necessity for us to have it, but that it is a *moral imperative* that we have it, then is when we join the fashionable madmen, and then is when the thin whine of hysteria is heard in the land, and then is when we are in bad trouble. And I suspect we are already there.

For Analysis
1. What instances of "wagon-train" or "primitive" morality does Didion cite? How would you characterize that morality? Why is Didion comfortable with that sort of morality? **2.** Why is Didion pleased that the music from a jukebox drowns out the singing of the prayer meeting near the motel (par. 6)? How does her identification of the musical pieces contribute to the argument of this essay? **3.** What is the point of her including the speech from *The Deer Park* (par. 7)? **4.** What names and, by implication, events does Didion use to illustrate some possibilities of abstract morality? **5.** What role does the quotation from Lionel Trilling (par. 8) play in the essay?

On Style
This essay examines an abstraction—morality. Comment on the author's use of concrete illustrations to illuminate abstract ideas.

Making Connections
Didion says in paragraph 4 that "we are what we learned as children." Are your own moral values reflections of what you learned as a child, or did those values change as you grew older? Explain.

Writing Topic

Focusing on the next-to-last sentence of this piece, write an essay in which you distinguish between *needs, wants,* and *pragmatic necessities* on one hand and *moral imperatives* on the other. Give examples of each, and suggest the relationship each bears to some meaning of the word *morality.* Conclude with your own judgment on the usefulness or necessity of moral imperatives.

Lars Eighner [b. 1948]

On Dumpster Diving[1] 1993

Long before I began Dumpster diving I was impressed with Dumpsters, enough so that I wrote the Merriam-Webster research service to discover what I could about the word *Dumpster*. I learned from them that it is a proprietary word belonging to the Dempster Dumpster company. Since then I have dutifully capitalized the word, although it was lowercased in almost all the citations Merriam-Webster photocopied for me. Dempster's word is too apt. I have never heard these things called anything but Dumpsters. I do not know anyone who knows the generic name for these objects. From time to time I have heard a wino or hobo give some corrupted credit to the original and call them Dipsy Dumpsters.

I began Dumpster diving about a year before I became homeless.

I prefer the word *scavenging* and use the word *scrounging* when I mean to be obscure. I have heard people, evidently meaning to be polite, use the word *foraging*, but I prefer to reserve that word for gathering nuts and berries and such, which I do also according to the season and the opportunity. *Dumpster diving* seems to me to be a little too cute and, in my case, inaccurate because I lack the athletic ability to lower myself into the Dumpsters as the true divers do, much to their increased profit.

I like the frankness of the word *scavenging*, which I can hardly think of without picturing a big black snail on an aquarium wall. I live from the refuse of others. I am a scavenger. I think it a sound and honorable niche, although if I could I would naturally prefer to live the comfortable consumer life, perhaps—and only perhaps—as a slightly less wasteful consumer, owing to what I have learned as a scavenger.

While Lizbeth[2] and I were still living in the shack on Avenue B as my savings ran out, I put almost all my sporadic income into rent. The necessities of daily life I began to extract from Dumpsters. Yes, we ate from them. Except for jeans, all my clothes came from Dumpsters. Boom boxes, candles, bedding, toilet paper, a virgin male love doll, medicine, books, a typewriter, dishes, furnishings, and change, sometimes amounting to many dollars—I acquired many things from the Dumpsters.

I have learned much as a scavenger. I mean to put some of what I have

---

[1] This chapter was composed while the author was homeless. The present tense has been preserved [Eighner's note].

[2] The author's dog, apparently a Labrador mix.

learned down here, beginning with the practical art of Dumpster diving and proceeding to the abstract.

What is safe to eat?

After all, the finding of objects is becoming something of an urban art. Even respectable employed people will sometimes find something tempting sticking out of a Dumpster or standing beside one. Quite a number of people, not all of them of the bohemian type, are willing to brag that they found this or that piece in the trash. But eating from Dumpsters is what separates the dilettanti from the professionals. Eating safely from the Dumpsters involves three principles: using the senses and common sense to evaluate the condition of the found materials, knowing the Dumpsters of a given area and checking them regularly, and seeking always to answer the question "Why was this discarded?"

Perhaps everyone who has a kitchen and a regular supply of groceries has, at one time or another, made a sandwich and eaten half of it before discovering mold on the bread or got a mouthful of milk before realizing the milk had turned. Nothing of the sort is likely to happen to a Dumpster diver because he is constantly reminded that most food is discarded for a reason. Yet a lot of perfectly good food can be found in Dumpsters.

Canned goods, for example, turn up fairly often in the Dumpsters I frequent. 10 All except the most phobic people would be willing to eat from a can, even if it came from a Dumpster. Canned goods are among the safest of foods to be found in Dumpsters but are not utterly foolproof.

Although very rare with modern canning methods, botulism is a possibility. Most other forms of food poisoning seldom do lasting harm to a healthy person, but botulism is almost certainly fatal and often the first symptom is death. Except for carbonated beverages, all canned goods should contain a slight vacuum and suck air when first punctured. Bulging, rusty, and dented cans and cans that spew when punctured should be avoided, especially when the contents are not very acidic or syrupy.

Heat can break down the botulin, but this requires much more cooking than most people do to canned goods. To the extent that botulism occurs at all, of course, it can occur in cans on pantry shelves as well as in cans from Dumpsters. Need I say that home-canned goods are simply too risky to be recommended.

From time to time one of my companions, aware of the source of my provisions, will ask, "Do you think these crackers are really safe to eat?" For some reason it is most often the crackers they ask about.

This question has always made me angry. Of course I would not offer my companion anything I had doubts about. But more than that, I wonder why he cannot evaluate the condition of the crackers for himself. I have no special knowledge and I have been wrong before. Since he knows where the food comes from, it seems to me he ought to assume some of the responsibility for deciding what he will put in his mouth. For myself I have few qualms about dry foods such as crackers, cookies, cereal, chips, and pasta if they are free of visible contaminates and still dry and crisp. Most often such things are found in the original packaging, which is not so much a positive sign as it is the absence of a negative one.

Raw fruits and vegetables with intact skins seem perfectly safe to me, exclud- 15 ing of course the obviously rotten. Many are discarded for minor imperfections that can be pared away. Leafy vegetables, grapes, cauliflower, broccoli, and similar things may be contaminated by liquids and may be impractical to wash.

Candy, especially hard candy, is usually safe if it has not drawn ants. Chocolate is often discarded only because it has become discolored as the cocoa butter de-emulsified. Candying, after all, is one method of food preservation because pathogens do not like very sugary substances.

All of these foods might be found in any Dumpster and can be evaluated with some confidence largely on the basis of appearance. Beyond these are foods that cannot be correctly evaluated without additional information.

I began scavenging by pulling pizzas out of the Dumpster behind a pizza delivery shop. In general, prepared food requires caution, but in this case I knew when the shop closed and went to the Dumpster as soon as the last of the help left.

Such shops often get prank orders; both the orders and the products made to fill them are called *bogus*. Because help seldom stays long at these places, pizzas are often made with the wrong topping, refused on delivery for being cold, or baked incorrectly. The products to be discarded are boxed up because inventory is kept by counting boxes: A boxed pizza can be written off; an unboxed pizza does not exist.

I never placed a bogus order to increase the supply of pizzas and I believe no 20 one else was scavenging in this Dumpster. But the people in the shop became suspicious and began to retain their garbage in the shop overnight. While it lasted I had a steady supply of fresh, sometimes warm pizza. Because I knew the Dumpster I knew the source of the pizza, and because I visited the Dumpster regularly I knew what was fresh and what was yesterday's.

The area I frequent is inhabited by many affluent college students. I am not here by chance; the Dumpsters in this area are very rich. Students throw out many good things, including food. In particular they tend to throw everything out when they move at the end of a semester, before and after breaks, and around midterm, when many of them despair of college. So I find it advantageous to keep an eye on the academic calendar.

Students throw food away around breaks because they do not know whether it has spoiled or will spoil before they return. A typical discard is a half jar of peanut butter. In fact, nonorganic peanut butter does not require refrigeration and is unlikely to spoil in any reasonable time. The student does not know that, and since it is Daddy's money, the student decides not to take a chance. Opened containers require caution and some attention to the question "Why was this discarded?" But in the case of discards from student apartments, the answer may be that the item was thrown out through carelessness, ignorance, or wastefulness. This can sometimes be deduced when the item is found with many others, including some that are obviously perfectly good.

Some students, and others, approach defrosting a freezer by chucking out the whole lot. Not only do the circumstances of such a find tell the story, but also the mass of frozen goods stays cold for a long time and items may be found still frozen or freshly thawed.

Yogurt, cheese, and sour cream are items that are often thrown out while they are still good. Occasionally I find a cheese with a spot of mold, which of course I pare off, and because it is obvious why such a cheese was discarded, I treat it with less suspicion than an apparently perfect cheese found in similar circumstances. Yogurt is often discarded, still sealed, only because the expiration date on the carton had passed. This is one of my favorite finds because yogurt will keep for several days, even in warm weather.

Students throw out canned goods and staples at the end of semesters and when they give up college at midterm. Drugs, pornography, spirits, and the like are often discarded when parents are expected—Dad's Day, for example. And spirits also turn up after big party weekends, presumably discarded by the newly reformed. Wine and spirits, of course, keep perfectly well even once opened, but the same cannot be said of beer. 25

My test for carbonated soft drinks is whether they still fizz vigorously. Many juices or other beverages are too acidic or too syrupy to cause much concern, provided they are not visibly contaminated. I have discovered nasty molds in vegetable juices, even when the product was found under its original seal; I recommend that such products be decanted slowly into a clear glass. Liquids always require some care. One hot day I found a large jug of Pat O'Brien's Hurricane mix. The jug had been opened but was still ice cold. I drank three large glasses before it became apparent to me that someone had added the rum to the mix, and not a little rum. I never tasted the rum, and by the time I began to feel the effects I had already ingested a very large quantity of the beverage. Some divers would have considered this a boon, but being suddenly intoxicated in a public place in the early afternoon is not my idea of a good time.

I have heard of people maliciously contaminating discarded food and even handouts, but mostly I have heard of this from people with vivid imaginations who have had no experience with the Dumpsters themselves. Just before the pizza shop stopped discarding its garbage at night, jalapeños began showing up on most of the thrown-out pizzas. If indeed this was meant to discourage me, it was a wasted effort because I am a native Texan.

For myself, I avoid game, poultry, pork, and egg-based foods, whether I find them raw or cooked. I seldom have the means to cook what I find, but when I do I avail myself of plentiful supplies of beef, which is often in very good condition. I suppose fish becomes disagreeable before it becomes dangerous. Lizbeth is happy to have any such thing that is past its prime and, in fact, does not recognize fish as food until it is quite strong.

Home leftovers, as opposed to surpluses from restaurants, are very often bad. Evidently, especially among students, there is a common type of personality that carefully wraps up even the smallest leftover and shoves it into the back of the refrigerator for six months or so before discarding it. Characteristic of this

type are the reused jars and margarine tubs to which the remains are committed. I avoid ethnic foods I am unfamiliar with. If I do not know what it is supposed to look like when it is good, I cannot be certain I will be able to tell if it is
bad.

No matter how careful I am I still get dysentery at least once a month, oftener   30
in warm weather. I do not want to paint too romantic a picture. Dumpster diving has serious drawbacks as a way of life.

I learned to scavenge gradually, on my own. Since then I have initiated several companions into the trade. I have learned that there is a predictable series
of stages a person goes through in learning to scavenge.

At first the new scavenger is filled with disgust and self-loathing. He is
ashamed of being seen and may lurk around, trying to duck behind things, or he
may try to dive at night. (In fact, most people instinctively look away from a
scavenger. By skulking around, the novice calls attention to himself and arouses
suspicion. Diving at night is ineffective and needlessly messy.)

Every grain of rice seems to be a maggot. Everything seems to stink. He can
wipe the egg yolk off the found can, but he cannot erase from his mind the
stigma of eating garbage.

That stage passes with experience. The scavenger finds a pair of running
shoes that fit and look and smell brand-new. He finds a pocket calculator in perfect working order. He finds pristine ice cream, still frozen, more than he can
eat or keep. He begins to understand: People throw away perfectly good stuff, a
lot of perfectly good stuff.

At this stage, Dumpster shyness begins to dissipate. The diver, after all, has   35
the last laugh. He is finding all manner of good things that are his for the taking.
Those who disparage his profession are the fools, not he.

He may begin to hang on to some perfectly good things for which he has neither a use nor a market. Then he begins to take note of the things that are not
perfectly good but are nearly so. He mates a Walkman with broken earphones
and one that is missing a battery cover. He picks up things that he can repair.

At this stage he may become lost and never recover. Dumpsters are full of
things of some potential value to someone and also of things that never have
much intrinsic value but are interesting. All the Dumpster divers I have known
come to the point of trying to acquire everything they touch. Why not take it,
they reason, since it is all free? This is, of course, hopeless. Most divers come to
realize that they must restrict themselves to items of relatively immediate utility. But in some cases the diver simply cannot control himself. I have met several of these pack-rat types. Their ideas of the values of various pieces of junk
verge on the psychotic. Every bit of glass may be a diamond, they think, and all
that glisters, gold.

I tend to gain weight when I am scavenging. Partly this is because I always
find far more pizza and doughnuts than water-packed tuna, nonfat yogurt, and
fresh vegetables. Also I have not developed much faith in the reliability of
Dumpsters as a food source, although it has been proven to me many times. I
tend to eat as if I have no idea where my next meal is coming from. But mostly

I just hate to see food go to waste and so I eat much more than I should. Something like this drives the obsession to collect junk.

As for collecting objects, I usually restrict myself to collecting one kind of small object at a time, such as pocket calculators, sunglasses, or campaign buttons. To live on the street I must anticipate my needs to a certain extent: I must pick up and save warm bedding I find in August because it will not be found in Dumpsters in November. As I have no access to health care, I often hoard essential drugs, such as antibiotics and antihistamines. (This course can be recommended only to those with some grounding in pharmacology. Antibiotics, for example, even when indicated are worse than useless if taken in insufficient amounts.) But even if I had a home with extensive storage space, I could not save everything that might be valuable in some contingency.

I have proprietary feelings about my Dumpsters. As I have mentioned, it is no accident that I scavenge from ones where good finds are common. But my limited experience with Dumpsters in other areas suggests to me that even in poorer areas, Dumpsters, if attended with sufficient diligence, can be made to yield a livelihood. The rich students discard perfectly good kiwifruit; poorer people discard perfectly good apples. Slacks and polo shirts are found in the one place; jeans and T-shirts in the other. The population of competitors rather than the affluence of the dumpers most affects the feasibility of survival by scavenging. The large number of competitors is what puts me off the idea of trying to scavenge in places like Los Angeles. 40

Curiously, I do not mind my direct competition, other scavengers, so much as I hate the can scroungers.

People scrounge cans because they have to have a little cash. I have tried scrounging cans with an able-bodied companion. Afoot a can scrounger simply cannot make more than a few dollars a day. One can extract the necessities of life from the Dumpsters directly with far less effort than would be required to accumulate the equivalent value in cans. (These observations may not hold in places with container redemption laws.)

Can scroungers, then, are people who must have small amounts of cash. These are drug addicts and winos, mostly the latter because the amounts of cash are so small. Spirits and drugs do, like all other commodities, turn up in Dumpsters and the scavenger will from time to time have a half bottle of a rather good wine with his dinner. But the wino cannot survive on these occasional finds; he must have his daily dose to stave off the DTs. All the cans he can carry will buy about three bottles of Wild Irish Rose.

I do not begrudge them the cans, but can scroungers tend to tear up the Dumpsters, mixing the contents and littering the area. They become so specialized that they can see only cans. They earn my contempt by passing up change, canned goods, and readily hockable items.

There are precious few courtesies among scavengers. But it is common practice to set aside surplus items: pairs of shoes, clothing, canned goods, and such. A true scavenger hates to see good stuff go to waste, and what he cannot use he leaves in good condition in plain sight. 45

Can scroungers lay waste to everything in their path and will stir one of a pair of good shoes to the bottom of a Dumpster, to be lost or ruined in the muck. Can scroungers will even go through individual garbage cans, something I have never seen a scavenger do.

Individual garbage cans are set out on the public easement only on garbage days. On other days going through them requires trespassing close to a dwelling. Going through individual garbage cans without scattering litter is almost impossible. Litter is likely to reduce the public's tolerance of scavenging. Individual cans are simply not as productive as Dumpsters; people in houses and duplexes do not move so often and for some reason do not tend to discard as much useful material. Moreover, the time required to go through one garbage can that serves one household is not much less than the time required to go through a Dumpster that contains the refuse of twenty apartments.

But my strongest reservation about going through individual garbage cans is that this seems to me a very personal kind of invasion to which I would object if I were a householder. Although many things in Dumpsters are obviously meant never to come to light, a Dumpster is somehow less personal.

I avoid trying to draw conclusions about the people who dump in the Dumpsters I frequent. I think it would be unethical to do so, although I know many people will find the idea of scavenger ethics too funny for words.

Dumpsters contain bank statements, correspondence, and other documents, 50 just as anyone might expect. But there are also less obvious sources of information. Pill bottles, for example. The labels bear the name of the patient, the name of the doctor, and the name of the drug. AIDS drugs and antipsychotic medicines, to name but two groups, are specific and are seldom prescribed for any other disorders. The plastic compacts for birth-control pills usually have complete label information.

Despite all this sensitive information, I have had only one apartment resident object to my going through the Dumpster. In that case it turned out the resident was a university athlete who was taking bets and who was afraid I would turn up his wager slips.

Occasionally a find tells a story. I once found a small paper bag containing some unused condoms, several partial tubes of flavored sexual lubricants, a partially used compact of birth-control pills, and the torn pieces of a picture of a young man. Clearly she was through with him and planning to give up sex altogether.

Dumpster things are often sad—abandoned teddy bears, shredded wedding books, despaired-of sales kits. I find many pets lying in state in Dumpsters. Although I hope to get off the streets so Lizbeth can have a long and comfortable old age, I know this hope is not very realistic. So I suppose when her time comes she too will go into a Dumpster. I will have no better place for her. And after all, it is fitting, since for most of her life her livelihood has come from the Dumpster. When she finds something I think is safe that has been spilled from a Dumpster, I let her have it. She already knows the route around the best ones. I like to think that if she survives me she will have a chance of evading the dog catcher and of finding her sustenance on the route.

Silly vanities also come to rest in the Dumpsters. I am a rather accomplished needleworker. I get a lot of material from the Dumpsters. Evidently sorority girls, hoping to impress someone, perhaps themselves, with their mastery of a womanly art, buy a lot of embroider-by-number kits, work a few stitches horribly, and eventually discard the whole mess. I pull out their stitches, turn the canvas over, and work an original design. Do not think I refrain from chuckling as I make gifts from these kits.

I find diaries and journals. I have often thought of compiling a book of literary found objects. And perhaps I will one day. But what I find is hopelessly commonplace and bad without being, even unconsciously, camp. College students also discard their papers. I am horrified to discover the kind of paper that now merits an A in an undergraduate course. I am grateful, however, for the number of good books and magazines the students throw out. 55

In the area I know best I have never discovered vermin in the Dumpsters, but there are two kinds of kitty surprise. One is alley cats whom I meet as they leap, claws first, out of Dumpsters. This is especially thrilling when I have Lizbeth in tow. The other kind of kitty surprise is a plastic garbage bag filled with some ponderous, amorphous mass. This always proves to be used cat litter.

City bees harvest doughnut glaze and this makes the Dumpster at the doughnut shop more interesting. My faith in the instinctive wisdom of animals is always shaken whenever I see Lizbeth attempt to catch a bee in her mouth, which she does whenever bees are present. Evidently some birds find Dumpsters profitable, for birdie surprise is almost as common as kitty surprise of the first kind. In hunting season all kinds of small game turn up in Dumpsters, some of it, sadly, not entirely dead. Curiously, summer and winter, maggots are uncommon.

The worst of the living and near-living hazards of the Dumpsters are the fire ants. The food they claim is not much of a loss, but they are vicious and aggressive. It is very easy to brush against some surface of the Dumpster and pick up half a dozen or more fire ants, usually in some sensitive area such as the underarm. One advantage of bringing Lizbeth along as I make Dumpster rounds is that, for obvious reasons, she is very alert to ground-based fire ants. When Lizbeth recognizes a fire-ant infestation around our feet, she does the Dance of the Zillion Fire Ants. I have learned not to ignore this warning from Lizbeth, whether I perceive the tiny ants or not, but to remove ourselves at Lizbeth's first pas de bourrée.[3] All the more so because the ants are the worst in the summer months when I wear flip-flops if I have them. (Perhaps someone will misunderstand this. Lizbeth does the Dance of the Zillion Fire Ants when she recognizes more fire ants than she cares to eat, not when she is being bitten. Since I have learned to react promptly, she does not get bitten at all. It is the isolated patrol of fire ants that falls in Lizbeth's range that deserves pity. She finds them quite tasty.)

By far the best way to go through a Dumpster is to lower yourself into it. Most of the good stuff tends to settle at the bottom because it is usually weightier

---

[3] A ballet dance step.

than the rubbish. My more athletic companions have often demonstrated to me that they can extract much good material from a Dumpster I have already been over.

To those psychologically or physically unprepared to enter a Dumpster, I recommend a stout stick, preferably with some barb or hook at one end. The hook can be used to grab plastic garbage bags. When I find canned goods or other objects loose at the bottom of a Dumpster, I lower a bag into it, roll the desired object into the bag, and then hoist the bag out—a procedure more easily described than executed. Much Dumpster diving is a matter of experience for which nothing will do except practice.

Dumpster diving is outdoor work, often surprisingly pleasant. It is not entirely predictable; things of interest turn up every day and some days there are finds of great value. I am always very pleased when I can turn up exactly the thing I most wanted to find. Yet in spite of the element of chance, scavenging more than most other pursuits tends to yield returns in some proportion to the effort and intelligence brought to bear. It is very sweet to turn up a few dollars in change from a Dumpster that has just been gone over by a wino.

The land is now covered with cities. The cities are full of Dumpsters. If a member of the canine race is able to know what it is doing, then Lizbeth knows that when we go around to the Dumpsters, we are hunting. I think of scavenging as a modern form of self-reliance. In any event, after having survived nearly ten years of government service, where everything is geared to the lowest common denominator, I find it refreshing to have work that rewards initiative and effort. Certainly I would be happy to have a sinecure again, but I am no longer heartbroken that I left one.

I find from the experience of scavenging two rather deep lessons. The first is to take what you can use and let the rest go by. I have come to think that there is no value in the abstract. A thing I cannot use or make useful, perhaps by trading, has no value however rare or fine it may be. I mean useful in a broad sense—some art I would find useful and some otherwise.

I was shocked to realize that some things are not worth acquiring, but now I think it is so. Some material things are white elephants that eat up the possessor's substance. The second lesson is the transience of material being. This has not quite converted me to a dualist, but it has made some headway in that direction. I do not suppose that ideas are immortal, but certainly mental things are longer lived than other material things.

Once I was the sort of person who invests objects with sentimental value. Now I no longer have those objects, but I have the sentiments yet.

Many times in our travels I have lost everything but the clothes I was wearing and Lizbeth. The things I find in Dumpsters, the love letters and rag dolls of so many lives, remind me of this lesson. Now I hardly pick up a thing without envisioning the time I will cast it aside. This I think is a healthy state of mind. Almost everything I have now has already been cast out at least once, proving that what I own is valueless to someone.

Anyway, I find my desire to grab for the gaudy bauble has been largely sated.

I think this is an attitude I share with the very wealthy—we both know there is plenty more where what we have came from. Between us are the rat-race millions who nightly scavenge the cable channels looking for they know not what.

I am sorry for them.

For Analysis

1. What purpose does the opening paragraph serve? **2.** What kind of reader is the author writing for? **3.** Do Eighner's comments about students ring true? **4.** What, in your opinion, are the writer's outstanding personality traits? **5.** What is your reaction to the conclusion of the essay, particularly the final sentence?

On Style

1. How would you characterize the **tone** of this essay? **2.** In paragraph 6, Eighner explains that his essay will begin with the practical and move to the abstract. Is this an effective organizational principle? Explain.

Making Connections

1. Describe how Eighner's essay altered your views about homelessness and Dumpster diving. **2.** What similarities do you find between Eighner and Fred Daniels, the protagonist of Richard Wright's story "The Man Who Lived Underground" (p. 351)?

Writing Topics

1. Use the following comment from a review in the *New Yorker* magazine as the basis for an analysis of the tone and style of Eighner's essay: "Part of the fascination of reading Eighner comes from the cleavage between his stately, slightly fussbudget diction and the indignity of his circumstances." **2.** Discuss Eighner's essay in terms of Henry David Thoreau's assertion in *Walden* that "a man is rich in proportion to the number of things which he can afford to let alone."

Innocence and Experience _____

Questions and Writing Topics

1. What support do the works in this section provide for Thomas Gray's well-known observation that "where ignorance is bliss, / 'Tis folly to be wise"? **Writing Topic:** Use Gray's observation as the basis for an analysis of Flannery O'Connor's "Good Country People" or Toni Cade Bambara's "The Lesson."

2. In poems such as William Blake's "The Garden of Love," William Wordsworth's "Lines Composed a Few Miles above Tintern Abbey," Robert Frost's "Birches," and Stevie Smith's "To Carry the Child," growing up is seen as a growing away from a kind of truth and reality; in other poems, such as Gerard Manley Hopkins's "Spring and Fall" and Dylan Thomas's "Fern Hill," growing up is seen as growing into truth and reality. Do these two groups of poems embody contradictory and mutually exclusive conceptions of childhood? Explain. **Writing Topic:** Select one poem from each of these two groups, and contrast the conception of childhood embodied in each.

3. An eighteenth-century novelist wrote: "Oh Innocence, how glorious and happy a portion art thou to the breast that possesses thee! Thou fearest neither the eyes nor the tongues of men. Truth, the most powerful of all things, is thy strongest friend; and the brighter the light is in which thou art displayed, the more it discovers thy transcendent beauties." Which works in this section support this assessment of innocence? Which works contradict it? How would you characterize the relationship between "truth" and "innocence" in the fiction, drama, and the essays presented here? **Writing Topic:** Use this observation as the basis for an analysis of Saroyan's "Five Ripe Pears" (p. 290) or Childress's *Wine in the Wilderness* (p. 262).

4. A certain arrogance is associated with the innocence of Oedipus in Sophocles' *Oedipus Rex* and Brown in Hawthorne's "Young Goodman Brown." On what is their arrogance based, and how is it modified? **Writing Topic:** Contrast the nature and the consequences of the central characters' arrogance in these works.

5. James Joyce's "Araby" and Frank O'Connor's "My Oedipus Complex" deal with some aspect of sexuality as a force that moves the protagonist from innocence toward experience. How does the recognition of sexuality function in each of the stories? **Writing Topic:** Discuss the relationship between sexuality and innocence in these stories.

6. Which poems in this section depend largely on irony for their force? Can you suggest why irony is a useful device in literature that portrays innocence and experience? **Writing Topics:** a. Show how Sophocles uses irony in *Oedipus Rex* to advance the plot and create suspense. b. Write an analysis of the function of irony in Blake's "The Garden of Love" and Hardy's "The Ruined Maid."

7. Some authors treat the passage from innocence to experience as comedy, while others treat it more seriously, even as tragedy. Do you find one or the other treatment more satisfying? Explain. **Writing Topic:** Select one short story and show how the author achieves either a comic or serious tone.

Conformity and Rebellion

The Fall from Terrestrial Paradise, from the Sistine Chapel, 1509–10
by Michelangelo.

The works in this section, "Conformity and Rebellion," feature a tension usually due to the clash between two well-articulated positions in which the rebel, on principle, confronts and struggles with established authority. Central in these works are powerful external forces—the state, the church, tradition—which sometimes can be obeyed only at the expense of conscience and humanity. At the most general level, these works confront a dilemma older than Antigonê's Thebes: the very organizations men and women establish to protect and nurture the individual often demand—on pain of economic ruin, social ostracism, even spiritual or physical death—that individuals violate their most deeply cherished beliefs. In these works, some individuals refuse such a demand and translate their awareness of a hostile social order into action against it. In *Antigonê,* the issue is drawn with utter clarity: Antigonê must obey either the state (Creon) or the gods. In *A Doll's House,* Nora realizes that dehumanization is too high a price to pay for domestic tranquillity. On a different note, in "Bartleby the Scrivener," Bartleby's "preference" not to obey his employer results in a crisis of passive resistance.

Many of the works in this section, particularly the poems, do not treat the theme of conformity and rebellion quite so explicitly and dramatically. Some, like Emily Dickinson's "She rose to His Requirement," reveal the painful injustice of certain traditional values; others, like W. H. Auden's "The Unknown Citizen," tell us that the price exacted for total conformity to the industrial superstate is spiritual death. In "Easter 1916," William Butler Yeats meditates upon the awesome meaning of the lives and deaths of political revolutionaries, and in "Harlem," Langston Hughes warns that an inflexible and constricting social order will generate explosion.

While in many of the works, the individual is caught up in a crisis that forces him or her into rebellion, in other works the focus may be on the individual's failure to move from awareness into action. For example, the portrait of Auden's unknown citizen affirms the necessity for rebellion by rendering so effectively the hollow life of mindless conformity.

Although diverse in treatment and technique, all the works in this section are about individuals struggling with complex sets of external forces that regulate and define their lives. As social beings, these individuals may recognize that they must be controlled for some larger good; yet they are aware that established social power is often abusive. The institution at its best can act as a conserving force, keeping in check the individual's disruptive impulse to abandon and destroy, without cause, old ways and ideas. At its worst, the power of social institutions is self-serving. It is up to the individual to judge whether power is being abused. Because the power of the individual is often negligible beside that of abusive social forces, it is not surprising that many artists find a fundamental human dignity in the resistance of the individual to organized society. One of humanity's ancient and profound recognitions, after all, is that the impulse of a Creon is always to make unknown citizens of us all.

FOR THINKING AND WRITING

Before you begin reading the selections in "Conformity and Rebellion," consider the following questions. Write out your thoughts informally in a reading journal, if you are keeping one, as a way of preparing to respond to the selections. Or you may wish to make one of these questions the basis for a formal essay.

1. How would you define *conformity?* What forms of rebellion are possible for a person in your situation? Do you perceive yourself as a conformist? A rebel? Some combination of the two? Explain.

2. How would you define *sanity?* Based on your own definition, do you know an insane person? What form does that insanity take? Do you agree or disagree with Emily Dickinson's assertion that "Much Madness is divinest Sense"? Explain.

3. Discuss this proposition: Governments routinely engage in behavior that would cause an individual to be imprisoned or institutionalized.

4. Freewrite an extended response to each of the following questions: Is war sane? Should one obey an "unjust" law? Should one be guided absolutely by religious principles?

Fiction

Herman Melville [1819–1891]

Bartleby the Scrivener 1853
A Story of Wall Street

I am a rather elderly man. The nature of my avocations, for the last thirty years, has brought me into more than ordinary contact with what would seem an interesting and somewhat singular set of men, of whom, as yet, nothing, that I know of, has ever been written—I mean, the law-copyists, or scriveners. I have known very many of them, professionally and privately, and, if I pleased, could relate divers histories, at which good-natured gentlemen might smile, and sentimental souls might weep. But I waive the biographies of all other scriveners, for a few passages in the life of Bartleby, who was a scrivener, the strangest I ever saw, or heard of. While, of other law-copyists, I might write the complete life, of Bartleby nothing of that sort can be done. I believe that no materials exist for a full and satisfactory biography of this man. It is an irreparable loss to literature. Bartleby was one of those beings of whom nothing is ascertainable, except from the original sources, and, in his case, those are very small. What my own astonished eyes saw of Bartleby, *that* is all I know of him, except, indeed, one vague report, which will appear in the sequel.

Ere introducing the scrivener, as he first appeared to me, it is fit I make some mention of myself, my employees, my business, my chambers, and general surroundings; because some such description is indispensable to an adequate understanding of the chief character about to be presented. Imprimis: I am a man who, from his youth upwards, has been filled with a profound conviction that the easiest way of life is the best. Hence, though I belong to a profession proverbially energetic and nervous, even to turbulence, at times, yet nothing of that sort have I ever suffered to invade my peace. I am one of those unambitious lawyers who never addresses a jury, or in any way draws down public applause; but, in the cool tranquillity of a snug retreat, do a snug business among rich men's bonds, and mortgages, and title-deeds. All who know me, consider me an

313

eminently *safe* man. The late John Jacob Astor,[1] a personage little given to poetic enthusiasm, had no hesitation in pronouncing my first grand point to be
prudence; my next, method. I do not speak it in vanity, but simply record the
fact, that I was not unemployed in my profession by the late John Jacob Astor; a
name which, I admit, I love to repeat; for it hath a rounded and orbicular sound
to it, and rings like unto bullion. I will freely add, that I was not insensible to the
late John Jacob Astor's good opinion.

Some time prior to the period at which this little history begins, my avocations had been largely increased. The good old office, now extinct in the State of
New York, of a Master in Chancery,[2] had been conferred upon me. It was not a
very arduous office, but very pleasantly remunerative. I seldom lose my temper;
much more seldom indulge in dangerous indignation at wrongs and outrages;
but, I must be permitted to be rash here, and declare that I consider the sudden
and violent abrogation of the office of Master in Chancery, by the new Constitution, as a—premature act; inasmuch as I had counted upon a lifelease of the
profits, whereas I only received those of a few short years. But this is by the way.

My chambers were up stairs, at No. ——— Wall Street. At one end, they
looked upon the white wall of the interior of a spacious sky-light shaft, penetrating the building from top to bottom.

This view might have been considered rather tame than otherwise, deficient   5
in what landscape painters call "life." But, if so, the view from the other end of
my chambers offered, at least, a contrast, if nothing more. In that direction, my
windows commanded an unobstructed view of a lofty brick wall, black by age
and everlasting shade; which wall required no spyglass to bring out its lurking
beauties, but, for the benefit of all near-sighted spectators, was pushed up to
within ten feet of my window panes. Owing to the great height of the surrounding buildings, and my chambers being on the second floor, the interval between
this wall and mine not a little resembled a huge square cistern.

At the period just preceding the advent of Bartleby, I had two persons as
copyists in my employment, and a promising lad as an office-boy. First, Turkey;
second, Nippers; third, Ginger Nut. These may seem names, the like of which
are not usually found in the Directory. In truth, they were nicknames, mutually conferred upon each other by my three clerks, and were deemed expres-
sive of their respective persons or characters. Turkey was a short, pursy
Englishman, of about my own age—that is, somewhere not far from sixty. In
the morning, one might say, his face was of a fine florid hue, but after twelve
o'clock, meridian—his dinner hour—it blazed like a grate full of Christmas
coals; and continued blazing—but, as it were, with a gradual wane—till six
o'clock P.M., or thereabouts; after which, I saw no more of the proprietor of the
face, which, gaining its meridian with the sun, seemed to set with it, to rise,
culminate, and decline the following day, with the like regularity and undimin-

---

[1] A poor immigrant who rose to become one of the great business tycoons of the nineteenth
century.
[2] Courts of Chancery often adjudicated business disputes.

ished glory. There are many singular coincidences I have known in the course of my life, not the least among which was the fact, that, exactly when Turkey displayed his fullest beams from his red and radiant countenance, just then, too, at that critical moment, began the daily period when I considered his business capacities as seriously disturbed for the remainder of the twenty-four hours. Not that he was absolutely idle, or averse to business, then; far from it. The difficulty was, he was apt to be altogether too energetic. There was a strange, inflamed, flurried, flighty recklessness of activity about him. He would be incautious in dipping his pen into his inkstand. All his blots upon my documents were dropped there after twelve o'clock meridian. Indeed, not only would he be reckless, and sadly given to making blots in the afternoon, but, some days, he went further, and was rather noisy. At such times, too, his face flamed with augmented blazonry, as if cannel coal had been heaped on anthracite. He made an unpleasant racket with his chair; spilled his sand-box; in mending his pens, impatiently split them all to pieces, and threw them on the floor in a sudden passion; stood up, and leaned over his table, boxing his papers about in a most indecorous manner, very sad to behold in an elderly man like him. Nevertheless, as he was in many ways a most valuable person to me, and all the time before twelve o'clock meridian, was the quickest, steadiest creature, too, accomplishing a great deal of work in a style not easily to be matched—for these reasons, I was willing to overlook his eccentricities, though, indeed, occasionally, I remonstrated with him. I did this very gently, however, because, though the civilest, nay, the blandest and most reverential of men in the morning, yet, in the afternoon, he was disposed, upon provocation, to be slightly rash with his tongue—in fact, insolent. Now, valuing his morning services as I did, and resolved not to lose them—yet, at the same time, made uncomfortable by his inflamed ways after twelve o'clock—and being a man of peace, unwilling by my admonitions to call forth unseemly retorts from him, I took upon me, one Saturday noon (he was always worse on Saturdays) to hint to him, very kindly, that, perhaps, now that he was growing old, it might be well to abridge his labors; in short, he need not come to my chambers after twelve o'clock, but, dinner over, had best go home to his lodgings, and rest himself till tea-time. But no; he insisted upon his afternoon devotions. His countenance became intolerably fervid, as he oratorically assured me—gesticulating with a long ruler at the other end of the room—that if his services in the morning were useful, how indispensable, then, in the afternoon?

"With submission, sir," said Turkey, on this occasion, "I consider myself your right-hand man. In the morning I but marshal and deploy my columns; but in the afternoon I put myself at their head, and gallantly charge the foe, thus"—and he made a violent thrust with the ruler.

"But the blots, Turkey," intimated I.

"True; but, with submission, sir, behold these hairs! I am getting old. Surely, sir, a blot or two of a warm afternoon is not to be severely urged against gray hairs. Old age—even if it blot the page—is honorable. With submission, sir, we *both* are getting old."

This appeal to my fellow-feeling was hardly to be resisted. At all events, I saw   10
that go he would not. So, I made up my mind to let him stay, resolving, nevertheless, to see to it that, during the afternoon, he had to do with my less important papers.

Nippers, the second on my list, was a whiskered, sallow, and, upon the whole,
rather piratical-looking young man, of about five and twenty. I always deemed
him the victim of two evil powers—ambition and indigestion. The ambition was
evinced by a certain impatience of the duties of a mere copyist, an unwar-
rantable usurpation of strictly professional affairs, such as the original drawing
up of legal documents. The indigestion seemed betokened in an occasional nervous testiness and grinning irritability, causing the teeth to audibly grind together over mistakes committed in copying; unnecessary maledictions, hissed,
rather than spoken, in the heat of business; and especially by a continual discontent with the height of the table where he worked. Though of a very ingenious, mechanical turn, Nippers could never get this table to suit him. He put
chips under it, blocks of various sorts, bits of pasteboard, and at last went so far
as to attempt an exquisite adjustment, by final pieces of folded blotting-paper.
But no invention would answer. If, for the sake of easing his back, he brought
the table-lid at a sharp angle well up towards his chin, and wrote there like a
man using the steep roof of a Dutch house for his desk, then he declared that it
stopped the circulation in his arms. If now he lowered the table to his waist-
bands, and stooped over it in writing, then there was a sore aching in his back.
In short, the truth of the matter was, Nippers knew not what he wanted. Or, if
he wanted anything, it was to be rid of a scrivener's table altogether. Among the
manifestations of his diseased ambition was a fondness he had for receiving visits from certain ambiguous-looking fellows in seedy coats, whom he called his
clients. Indeed, I was aware that not only was he, at times, considerable of a
ward-politician, but he occasionally did a little business at the Justices' courts,
and was not unknown on the steps of the Tombs.[3] I have good reason to believe,
however, that one individual who called upon him at my chambers, and who,
with a grand air, he insisted was his client, was no other than a dun, and the alleged title-deed, a bill. But, with all his failings, and the annoyances he caused
me, Nippers, like his compatriot Turkey, was a very useful man to me; wrote a
neat, swift hand; and, when he chose, was not deficient in a gentlemanly sort of
deportment. Added to this, he always dressed in a gentlemanly sort of way; and
so, incidentally, reflected credit upon my chambers. Whereas, with respect to
Turkey, I had much ado to keep him from being a reproach to me. His clothes
were apt to look oily, and smell of eating houses. He wore his pantaloons very
loose and baggy in summer. His coats were execrable, his hat not to be handled.
But while the hat was a thing of indifference to me, inasmuch as his natural civility and deference, as a dependent Englishman, always led him to doff it the
moment he entered the room, yet his coat was another matter. Concerning his

[3] A prison in New York City.

coats, I reasoned with him; but with no effect. The truth was, I suppose, that a man with so small an income could not afford to sport such a lustrous face and a lustrous coat at one and the same time. As Nippers once observed, Turkey's money went chiefly for red ink. One winter day, I presented Turkey with a highly respectable-looking coat of my own—a padded gray coat, of a most comfortable warmth, and which buttoned straight up from the knee to the neck. I thought Turkey would appreciate the favor, and abate his rashness and obstreperousness of afternoons. But no; I verily believe that buttoning himself up in so downy and blanket-like a coat had a pernicious effect upon him—upon the same principle that too much oats are bad for horses. In fact, precisely as a rash, restive horse is said to feel his oats, so Turkey felt his coat. It made him insolent. He was a man whom prosperity harmed.

Though, concerning the self-indulgent habits of Turkey, I had my own private surmises, yet, touching Nippers, I was well persuaded that, whatever might be his faults in other respects, he was, at least, a temperate young man. But, indeed, nature herself seemed to have been his vintner, and, at his birth, charged him so thoroughly with an irritable, brandy-like disposition, that all subsequent potations were needless. When I consider how, amid the stillness of my chambers, Nippers would sometimes impatiently rise from his seat, and stooping over his table, spread his arms wide apart, seize the whole desk, and move it, and jerk it, with a grim, grinding motion on the floor, as if the table were a perverse voluntary agent and vexing him, I plainly perceive that, for Nippers, brandy-and-water were altogether superfluous.

It was fortunate for me that, owing to its peculiar cause—indigestion—the irritability and consequent nervousness of Nippers were mainly observable in the morning, while in the afternoon he was comparatively mild. So that, Turkey's paroxysms only coming on about twelve o'clock, I never had to do with their eccentricities at one time. Their fits relieved each other, like guards. When Nippers's was on, Turkey's was off; and *vice versa*. This was a good natural arrangement, under the circumstances.

Ginger Nut, the third on my list, was a lad, some twelve years old. His father was a car-man, ambitious of seeing his son on the bench instead of a cart, before he died. So he sent him to my office, as student at law, errand-boy, cleaner and sweeper, at the rate of one dollar a week. He had a little desk to himself; but he did not use it much. Upon inspection, the drawer exhibited a great array of shells of various sorts of nuts. Indeed, to this quick-witted youth, the whole noble science of the law was contained in a nutshell. Not the least among the employments of Ginger Nut, as well as one which he discharged with the most alacrity, was his duty as cake and apple purveyor for Turkey and Nippers. Copying law-papers being proverbially a dry, husky sort of business, my two scriveners were fain to moisten their mouths very often with Spitzenbergs,[4] to be had at the numerous stalls nigh the Custom House and Post Office. Also, they sent

---

[4] A variety of apple.

Ginger Nut very frequently for that peculiar cake—small, flat, round, and very spicy—after which he had been named by them. Of a cold morning, when business was but dull, Turkey would gobble up scores of these cakes, as if they were mere wafers—indeed, they sell them at the rate of six or eight for a penny—the scrape of his pen blending with the crunching of the crisp particles in his mouth. Rashest of all the fiery afternoon blunders and flurried rashnesses of Turkey, was his once moistening a ginger-cake between his lips, and clapping it on to a mortgage, for a seal. I came within an ace of dismissing him then. But he mollified me by making an oriental bow, and saying—

"With submission, sir, it was generous of me to find you in stationery on my own account."   15

Now my original business—that of a conveyancer and title hunter, and drawer-up of recondite documents of all sorts—was considerably increased by receiving the master's office. There was now great work for scriveners. Not only must I push the clerks already with me, but I must have additional help.

In answer to my advertisement, a motionless young man one morning stood upon my office threshold, the door being open, for it was summer. I can see that figure now—pallidly neat, pitiably respectable, incurably forlorn! It was Bartleby.

After a few words touching his qualifications, I engaged him, glad to have among my corps of copyists a man of so singularly sedate an aspect, which I thought might operate beneficially upon the flighty temper of Turkey, and the fiery one of Nippers.

I should have stated before that ground-glass folding-doors divided my premises into two parts, one of which was occupied by my scriveners, the other by myself. According to my humor, I threw open these doors, or closed them. I resolved to assign Bartleby a corner by the folding-doors, but on my side of them, so as to have this quiet man within easy call, in case any trifling thing was to be done. I placed his desk close up to a small side-window in that part of the room, a window which originally had afforded a lateral view of certain grimy backyards and bricks, but which, owing to subsequent erections, commanded at present no view at all, though it gave some light. Within three feet of the panes was a wall, and the light came down from far above, between two lofty buildings, as from a very small opening in a dome. Still further to a satisfactory arrangement, I procured a high green folding screen, which might entirely isolate Bartleby from my sight, though not remove him from my voice. And thus, in a manner, privacy and society were conjoined.

At first, Bartleby did an extraordinary quantity of writing. As if long famishing   20
for something to copy, he seemed to gorge himself on my documents. There was no pause for digestion. He ran a day and night line, copying by sun-light and by candle-light. I should have been quite delighted with his application, had he been cheerfully industrious. But he wrote on silently, palely, mechanically.

It is, of course, an indispensable part of a scrivener's business to verify the accuracy of his copy, word by word. Where there are two or more scriveners in an office, they assist each other in this examination, one reading from the copy, the other holding the original. It is a very dull, wearisome, and lethargic affair. I can readily imagine that, to some sanguine temperaments, it would be altogether intolerable. For example, I cannot credit that the mettlesome poet, Byron, would have contentedly sat down with Bartleby to examine a law document of, say five hundred pages, closely written in a crimpy hand.

Now and then, in the haste of business, it had been my habit to assist in comparing some brief document myself, calling Turkey or Nippers for this purpose. One object I had, in placing Bartleby so handy to me behind the screen, was to avail myself of his services on such trivial occasions. It was on the third day, I think, of his being with me, and before any necessity had arisen for having his own writing examined, that, being much hurried to complete a small affair I had in hand, I abruptly called to Bartleby. In my haste and natural expectancy of instant compliance, I sat with my head bent over the original on my desk, and my right hand sideways, and somewhat nervously extended with the copy, so that, immediately upon emerging from his retreat, Bartleby might snatch it and proceed to business without the least delay.

In this very attitude did I sit when I called to him, rapidly stating what it was I wanted him to do—namely, to examine a small paper with me. Imagine my surprise, nay, my consternation, when, without moving from his privacy, Bartleby, in a singularly mild, firm voice, replied, "I would prefer not to."

I sat awhile in perfect silence, rallying my stunned faculties. Immediately it occurred to me that my ears had deceived me, or Bartleby had entirely misunderstood my meaning. I repeated my request in the clearest tone I could assume; but in quite as clear a one came the previous reply, "I would prefer not to."

"Prefer not to," echoed I, rising in high excitement, and crossing the room with a stride. "What do you mean? Are you moon-struck? I want you to help me compare this sheet here—take it," and I thrust it towards him.   25

"I would prefer not to," said he.

I looked at him steadfastly. His face was leanly composed; his gray eye dimly calm. Not a wrinkle of agitation rippled him. Had there been the least uneasiness, anger, impatience, or impertinence in his manner; in other words, had there been any thing ordinarily human about him, doubtless I should have violently dismissed him from the premises. But as it was, I should have as soon thought of turning my pale plaster-of-paris bust of Cicero out of doors. I stood gazing at him awhile, as he went on with his own writing, and then reseated myself at my desk. This is very strange, thought I. What had one best do? But my business hurried me. I concluded to forget the matter for the present, reserving it for my future leisure. So calling Nippers from the other room, the paper was speedily examined.

A few days after this, Bartleby concluded four lengthy documents, being quadruplicates of a week's testimony taken before me in my High Court of Chancery. It became necessary to examine them. It was an important suit, and great accuracy was imperative. Having all things arranged, I called Turkey, Nippers, and Ginger Nut from the next room, meaning to place the four copies in the hands of my four clerks, while I should read from the original. Accordingly, Turkey, Nippers, and Ginger Nut had taken their seats in a row, each with his document in his hand, when I called to Bartleby to join this interesting group.

"Bartleby! quick, I am waiting."

I heard a slow scrape of his chair legs on the uncarpeted floor, and soon he appeared standing at the entrance of his hermitage. 30

"What is wanted?" said he, mildly.

"The copies, the copies," said I, hurriedly. "We are going to examine them. There—" and I held towards him the fourth quadruplicate.

"I would prefer not to," he said, and gently disappeared behind the screen.

For a few moments I was turned into a pillar of salt, standing at the head of my seated column of clerks. Recovering myself, I advanced towards the screen, and demanded the reason for such extraordinary conduct.

"*Why* do you refuse?" 35

"I would prefer not to."

With any other man I should have flown outright into a dreadful passion, scorned all further words, and thrust him ignominiously from my presence. But there was something about Bartleby that not only strangely disarmed me, but in a wonderful manner, touched and disconcerted me. I began to reason with him.

"These are your own copies we are about to examine. It is labor saving to you, because one examination will answer for your four papers. It is common usage. Every copyist is bound to help examine his copy. Is it not so? Will you not speak? Answer!"

"I prefer not to," he replied in a flutelike tone. It seemed to me that, while I had been addressing him, he carefully revolved every statement that I made; fully comprehended the meaning; could not gainsay the irresistible conclusion; but, at the same time, some paramount consideration prevailed with him to reply as he did.

"You are decided, then, not to comply with my request—a request made according to common usage and common sense?" 40

He briefly gave me to understand, that on that point my judgment was sound. Yes: his decision was irreversible.

It is not seldom the case that, when a man is browbeaten in some unprecedented and violently unreasonable way, he begins to stagger in his own plainest faith. He begins, as it were, vaguely to surmise that, wonderful as it may be, all the justice and all the reason is on the other side. Accordingly, if any disinterested persons are present, he turns to them for some reinforcement of his own faltering mind.

"Turkey," said I, "what do you think of this? Am I not right?"

"With submission, sir," said Turkey, in his blandest tone, "I think that you are."

"Nippers," said I, "what do *you* think of it?" 45

"I think I should kick him out of the office."

(The reader, of nice perceptions, will here perceive that, it being morning, Turkey's answer is couched in polite and tranquil terms, but Nippers replies in ill-tempered ones. Or, to repeat a previous sentence, Nippers's ugly mood was on duty, and Turkey's off.)

"Ginger Nut," said I, willing to enlist the smallest suffrage in my behalf, "what do *you* think of it?"

"I think, sir, he's a little *luny*," replied Ginger Nut, with a grin.

"You hear what they say," said I, turning towards the screen, "come forth and do your duty." 50

But he vouchsafed no reply. I pondered a moment in sore perplexity. But once more business hurried me. I determined again to postpone the consideration of this dilemma to my future leisure. With a little trouble we made out to examine the papers without Bartleby, though at every page or two Turkey deferentially dropped his opinion, that this proceeding was quite out of the common; while Nippers, twitching in his chair with a dyspeptic nervousness, ground out, between his set teeth, occasional hissing maledictions against the stubborn oaf behind the screen. And for his (Nippers's) part, this was the first and the last time he would do another man's business without pay.

Meanwhile Bartleby sat in his hermitage, oblivious to everything but his own peculiar business there.

Some days passed, the scrivener being employed upon another lengthy work. His late remarkable conduct led me to regard his ways narrowly. I observed that he never went to dinner; indeed, that he never went anywhere. As yet I had never, of my personal knowledge, known him to be outside of my office. He was a perpetual sentry in the corner. At about eleven o'clock though, in the morning, I noticed that Ginger Nut would advance toward the opening in Bartleby's screen, as if silently beckoned thither by a gesture invisible to me where I sat. The boy would then leave the office, jingling a few pence, and reappear with a handful of ginger-nuts, which he delivered in the hermitage, receiving two of the cakes for his trouble.

He lives, then, on ginger-nuts, thought I; never eats a dinner, properly speaking; he must be a vegetarian, then; but no; he never eats even vegetables; he eats nothing but ginger-nuts. My mind then ran on in reveries concerning the probable effects upon the human constitution of living entirely on ginger-nuts. Ginger-nuts are so called, because they contain ginger as one of their peculiar constituents, and the final flavoring one. Now, what was ginger? A hot, spicy thing. Was Bartleby hot and spicy? Not at all. Ginger, then, had no effect upon Bartleby. Probably he preferred it should have none.

Nothing so aggravates an earnest person as a passive resistance. If the individual so resisted be of a not inhumane temper, and the resisting one perfectly harmless in his passivity, then, in the better moods of the former, he will endeavor charitably to construe to his imagination what proves impossible to be solved by his judgment. Even so, for the most part, I regarded Bartleby and his ways. Poor fellow! thought I, he means no mischief; it is plain he intends no insolence; his aspect sufficiently evinces that his eccentricities are involuntary. He is useful to me. I can get along with him. If I turn him away, the chances are he will fall in with some less-indulgent employer, and then he will be rudely 55 treated, and perhaps driven forth miserably to starve. Yes. Here I can cheaply purchase a delicious self-approval. To befriend Bartleby; to humor him in his strange willfulness, will cost me little or nothing, while I lay up in my soul what will eventually prove a sweet morsel for my conscience. But this mood was not invariable with me. The passiveness of Bartleby sometimes irritated me. I felt strangely goaded on to encounter him in new opposition—to elicit some angry spark from him answerable to my own. But, indeed, I might as well have es-sayed to strike fire with my knuckles against a bit of Windsor soap. But one af-ternoon the evil impulse in me mastered me, and the following little scene ensued:

"Bartleby," said I, "when those papers are all copied, I will compare them with you."

"I would prefer not to."

"How? Surely you do not mean to persist in that mulish vagary?"

No answer.

I threw open the folding-doors near by, and, turning upon Turkey and Nip-   60
pers, exclaimed:

"Bartleby a second time says, he won't examine his papers. What do you think of it, Turkey?"

It was afternoon, be it remembered. Turkey sat glowing like a brass boiler; his bald head steaming; his hands reeling among his blotted papers.

"Think of it?" roared Turkey; "I think I'll just step behind his screen, and black his eyes for him!"

So saying, Turkey rose to his feet and threw his arms into a pugilistic position. He was hurrying away to make good his promise, when I detained him, alarmed at the effect of incautiously rousing Turkey's combativeness after dinner.

"Sit down, Turkey," said I, "and hear what Nippers has to say. What do you   65
think of it, Nippers? Would I not be justified in immediately dismissing Bartleby?"

"Excuse me, that is for you to decide, sir. I think his conduct quite unusual, and, indeed, unjust, as regards Turkey and myself. But it may only be a passing whim."

"Ah," exclaimed I, "you have strangely changed your mind, then—you speak very gently of him now."

"All beer," cried Turkey; "gentleness is effects of beer—Nippers and I dined together to-day. You see how gentle I am, sir. Shall I go and black his eyes?"

"You refer to Bartleby, I suppose. No, not to-day, Turkey," I replied; "pray, put up your fists."

I closed the doors, and again advanced towards Bartleby. I felt additional in-   70
centives tempting me to my fate. I burned to be rebelled against again. I re-membered that Bartleby never left the office.

"Bartleby," said I, "Ginger Nut is away; just step around to the post office, won't you? (it was but a three minutes' walk), and see if there is anything for me."

"I would prefer not to."

"You *will* not?"

"I *prefer* not."

I staggered to my desk, and sat there in a deep study. My blind inveteracy re- 75
turned. Was there any other thing in which I could procure myself to be ignominiously repulsed by this lean, penniless wight?—my hired clerk? What added
thing is there, perfectly reasonable, that he will be sure to refuse to do?
"Bartleby!"

No answer.

"Bartleby," in a louder tone.

No answer.

"Bartleby," I roared.

Like a very ghost, agreeably to the laws of magical invocation, at the third 80
summons, he appeared at the entrance of his hermitage.

"Go to the next room, and tell Nippers to come to me."

"I prefer not to," he respectfully and slowly said and mildly disappeared.

"Very good, Bartleby," said I, in a quiet sort of serenely-severe, self-possessed
tone, intimating the unalterable purpose of some terrible retribution very close
at hand. At the moment I half intended something of the kind. But upon the
whole, as it was drawing towards my dinner-hour, I thought it best to put on my
hat and walk home for the day, suffering much from perplexity and distress of
mind.

Shall I acknowledge it? The conclusion of this whole business was, that it
soon became a fixed fact of my chambers, that a pale young scrivener, by the
name of Bartleby, had a desk there; that he copied for me at the usual rate of
four cents a folio (one hundred words); but he was permanently exempt from
examining the work done by him, that duty being transferred to Turkey and
Nippers, out of compliment, doubtless, to their superior acuteness; moreover,
said Bartleby was never, on any account, to be dispatched on the most trivial errand of any sort; and that even if entreated to take upon him such a matter, it
was generally understood that he would "prefer not to"—in other words, he
would refuse point blank.

As days passed on, I became considerably reconciled to Bartleby. His steadi- 85
ness, his freedom from all dissipation, his incessant industry (except when he
chose to throw himself into a standing revery behind his screen), his great stillness, his unalterableness of demeanor under all circumstances, made him a
valuable acquisition. One prime thing was this—*he was always there*—first in
the morning, continually through the day, and the last at night. I had a singular
confidence in his honesty. I felt my most precious papers perfectly safe in his
hands. Sometimes, to be sure, I could not, for the very soul of me, avoid falling
into sudden spasmodic passions with him. For it was exceeding difficult to bear
in mind all the time those strange peculiarities, privileges, and unheard of ex-
emptions, forming the tacit stipulations on Bartleby's part under which he remained in my office. Now and then, in the eagerness of dispatching pressing
business, I would inadvertently summon Bartleby, in a short, rapid tone, to put
his finger, say, on the incipient tie of a bit of red tape with which I was about

compressing some papers. Of course, from behind the screen the usual answer, "I prefer not to," was sure to come; and then, how could a human creature, with the common infirmities of our nature, refrain from bitterly exclaiming upon such perverseness—such unreasonableness? However, every added repulse of this sort which I received only tended to lessen the probability of my repeating the inadvertence.

Here it must be said, that according to the custom of most legal gentlemen occupying chambers in densely-populated law buildings, there were several keys to my door. One was kept by a woman residing in the attic, which person weekly scrubbed and daily swept and dusted my apartments. Another was kept by Turkey for convenience sake. The third I sometimes carried in my own pocket. The fourth I knew not who had.

Now, one Sunday morning I happened to go to Trinity Church, to hear a celebrated preacher, and finding myself rather early on the ground I thought I would walk round to my chambers for a while. Luckily I had my key with me; but upon applying it to the lock, I found it resisted by something inserted from the inside. Quite surprised, I called out; when to my consternation a key was turned from within; and thrusting his lean visage at me, and holding the door ajar, the apparition of Bartleby appeared, in his shirt sleeves, and otherwise in a strangely tattered *déshabillé,* saying quietly that he was sorry, but he was deeply engaged just then, and—preferred not admitting me at present. In a brief word or two, he moreover added, that perhaps I had better walk around the block two or three times, and by that time he would probably have concluded his affairs.

Now, the utterly unsurmised appearance of Bartleby, tenanting my law-chambers of a Sunday morning, with his cadaverously gentlemanly *nonchalance,* yet withal firm and self-possessed, had such a strange effect upon me, that incontinently I slunk away from my own door, and did as desired. But not without sundry twinges of impotent rebellion against the mild effrontery of this unaccountable scrivener. Indeed, it was his wonderful mildness chiefly, which not only disarmed me, but unmanned me as it were. For I consider that one, for the time, is somehow unmanned when he tranquilly permits his hired clerk to dictate to him, and order him away from his own premises. Furthermore, I was full of uneasiness as to what Bartleby could possibly be doing in my office in his shirt sleeves, and in an otherwise dismantled condition of a Sunday morning. Was anything amiss going on? Nay, that was out of the question. It was not to be thought of for a moment that Bartleby was an immoral person. But what could he be doing there?—copying? Nay again, whatever might be his eccentricities, Bartleby was an eminently decorous person. He would be the last man to sit down to his desk in any state approaching to nudity. Besides, it was Sunday; and there was something about Bartleby that forbade the supposition that he would by any secular occupation violate the proprieties of the day.

Nevertheless, my mind was not pacified; and full of a restless curiosity, at last I returned to the door. Without hindrance I inserted my key, opened it, and entered. Bartleby was not to be seen. I looked round anxiously, peeped behind his screen; but it was very plain that he was gone. Upon more closely examining the place, I surmised that for an indefinite period Bartleby must have eaten, dressed, and slept in my office, and that, too, without plate, mirror, or bed. The cushioned seat of a rickety old sofa in one corner bore the faint impress of a lean, reclining form. Rolled away under his desk, I found a blanket; under the empty grate, a blacking box and brush; on a chair, a tin basin, with soap and a ragged towel; in a newspaper a few crumbs of ginger-nuts and a morsel of cheese. Yes, thought I, it is evident enough that Bartleby has been making his home here, keeping bachelor's hall all by himself. Immediately then the thought came sweeping across me, what miserable friendlessness and loneliness are here revealed! His poverty is great; but his solitude, how horrible! Think of it. Of a Sunday, Wall Street is deserted as Petra;[5] and every night of every day it is an emptiness. This building, too, which of week-days hums with industry and life, at nightfall echoes with sheer vacancy, and all through Sunday is forlorn. And here Bartleby makes his home; sole spectator of a solitude which he has seen all populous—a sort of innocent and transformed Marius brooding among the ruins of Carthage![6]

For the first time in my life a feeling of over-powering stinging melancholy seized me. Before, I had never experienced aught but a not unpleasing sadness. The bond of a common humanity now drew me irresistibly to gloom. A fraternal melancholy! For both I and Bartleby were sons of Adam. I remembered the bright silks and sparkling faces I had seen that day, in gala trim, swan-like sailing down the Mississippi of Broadway; and I contrasted them with the pallid copyist, and thought to myself, Ah, happiness courts the light, so we deem the world is gay; but misery hides aloof, so we deem that misery there is none. These sad fancyings—chimeras, doubtless, of a sick and silly brain—led on to other and more special thoughts, concerning the eccentricities of Bartleby. Presentiments of strange discoveries hovered round me. The scrivener's pale form appeared to me laid out, among uncaring strangers, in its shivering winding sheet. 90

Suddenly I was attracted by Bartleby's closed desk, the key in open sight left in the lock.

I mean no mischief, seek the gratification of no heartless curiosity, thought I; besides, the desk is mine, and its contents, too, so I will make bold to look within. Everything was methodically arranged, the papers smoothly placed. The pigeon holes were deep, and removing the files of documents, I groped into their recesses. Presently I felt something there, and dragged it out. It was an old bandanna handkerchief, heavy and knotted. I opened it, and saw it was a saving's bank.

I now recalled all the quiet mysteries which I had noted in the man. I remembered that he never spoke but to answer; that, though at intervals he had considerable time to himself, yet I had never seen him reading—no, not even a

[5] A city in Palestine found by explorers in 1812. It had been deserted and lost for centuries.
[6] Gaius Marius (155–86 B.C.), a plebeian general who was forced to flee from Rome. Nineteenth-century democratic literature sometimes pictured him old and alone among the ruins of Carthage.

newspaper; that for long periods he would stand looking out, at his pale window behind the screen, upon the dead brick wall; I was quite sure he never visited any refectory or eating house; while his pale face clearly indicated that he never drank beer like Turkey; or tea and coffee even, like other men; that he never went anywhere in particular that I could learn; never went out for a walk, unless, indeed, that was the case at present; that he had declined telling who he was, or whence he came, or whether he had any relatives in the world; that though so thin and pale, he never complained of ill health. And more than all, I remembered a certain unconscious air of pallid—how shall I call it?—of pallid haughtiness, say, or rather an austere reserve about him, which had positively awed me into my tame compliance with his eccentricities, when I had feared to ask him to do the slightest incidental thing for me, even though I might know, from his long-continued motionlessness, that behind his screen he must be standing in one of those dead-wall reveries of his.

Revolving all these things, and coupling them with the recently discovered fact, that he made my office his constant abiding place and home, and not forgetful of his morbid moodiness; revolving all these things, a prudential feeling began to steal over me. My first emotions had been those of pure melancholy and sincerest pity; but just in proportion as the forlornness of Bartleby grew and grew to my imagination, did that same melancholy merge into fear, that pity into repulsion. So true it is, and so terrible, too, that up to a certain point the thought or sight of misery enlists our best affections; but, in certain special cases, beyond that point it does not. They err who would assert that invariably this is owing to the inherent selfishness of the human heart. It rather proceeds from a certain hopelessness of remedying excessive and organic ill. To a sensitive being, pity is not seldom pain. And when at last it is perceived that such pity cannot lead to effectual succor, common sense bids the soul be rid of it. What I saw that morning persuaded me that the scrivener was the victim of innate and incurable disorder. I might give alms to his body; but his body did not pain him; it was his soul that suffered, and his soul I could not reach.

I did not accomplish the purpose of going to Trinity Church that morning. Somehow, the things I had seen disqualified me for the time from churchgoing. I walked homeward, thinking what I would do with Bartleby. Finally, I resolved upon this—I would put certain calm questions to him the next morning, touching his history, etc., and if he declined to answer them openly and unreservedly (and I supposed he would prefer not), then to give him a twenty dollar bill over and above whatever I might owe him, and tell him his services were no longer required; but that if in any other way I could assist him, I would be happy to do so, especially if he desired to return to his native place, wherever that might be, I would willingly help to defray the expenses. Moreover, if, after reaching home, he found himself at any time in want of aid, a letter from him would be sure of a reply.

The next morning came.

"Bartleby," said I, gently calling to him behind his screen.

No reply.

"Bartleby," said I, in a still gentler tone, "come here; I am not going to ask you to do anything you would prefer not to do—I simply wish to speak to you."

Upon this he noiselessly slid into view. 100

"Will you tell me, Bartleby, where you were born?"

"I would prefer not to."

"Will you tell me *anything* about yourself?"

"I would prefer not to."

"But what reasonable objection can you have to speak to me? I feel friendly 105 towards you."

He did not look at me while I spoke, but kept his glance fixed upon my bust of Cicero, which, as I then sat, was directly behind me, some six inches above my head.

"What is your answer, Bartleby," said I, after waiting a considerable time for a reply, during which his countenance remained immovable, only there was the faintest conceivable tremor of the white attenuated mouth.

"At present I prefer to give no answer," he said, and retired into his hermitage.

It was rather weak in me I confess, but his manner, on this occasion, nettled me. Not only did there seem to lurk in it a certain calm disdain, but his perverseness seemed ungrateful, considering the undeniable good usage and indulgence he had received from me.

Again I sat ruminating what I should do. Mortified as I was at his behavior, 110 and resolved as I had been to dismiss him when I entered my office, nevertheless I strangely felt something superstitious knocking at my heart, and forbidding me to carry out my purpose, and denouncing me for a villain if I dared to breathe one bitter word against this forlornest of mankind. At last, familiarly drawing my chair behind his screen, I sat down and said: "Bartleby, never mind, then, about revealing your history; but let me entreat you, as a friend, to comply as far as may be with the usages of this office. Say now, you will help to examine papers to-morrow or next day: in short, say now, that in a day or two you will begin to be a little reasonable—say so, Bartleby."

"At present I would prefer not to be a little reasonable," was his mildly cadaverous reply.

Just then the folding-doors opened, and Nippers approached. He seemed suffering from an unusually bad night's rest, induced by severer indigestion than common. He overheard those final words of Bartleby.

"*Prefer not*, eh?" gritted Nippers—"I'd *prefer* him, if I were you, sir," addressing me—"I'd *prefer* him; I'd give him preferences, the stubborn mule! What is it, sir, pray, that he *prefers* not to do now?"

Bartleby moved not a limb.

"Mr. Nippers," said I, "I'd prefer that you would withdraw for the present." 115

Somehow, of late, I had got into the way of involuntarily using this word "prefer" upon all sorts of not exactly suitable occasions. And I trembled to think that my contact with the scrivener had already and seriously affected me in a mental way. And what further and deeper aberration might it not yet produce? This apprehension had not been without efficacy in determining me to summary measures.

As Nippers, looking very sour and sulky, was departing, Turkey blandly and deferentially approached.

"With submission, sir," said he, "yesterday I was thinking about Bartleby here, and I think that if he would but prefer to take a quart of good ale every day, it would do much towards mending him, and enabling him to assist in examining his papers."

"So you have got the word, too," said I, slightly excited.

"With submission, what word, sir," asked Turkey, respectfully crowding himself into the contracted space behind the screen, and by so doing, making me jostle the scrivener. "What word, sir?"   120

"I would prefer to be left alone here," said Bartleby, as if offended at being mobbed in his privacy.

"*That's* the word, Turkey," said I—"*that's* it."

"Oh, *prefer?* oh yes—queer word. I never use it myself. But, sir, as I was saying, if he would but prefer—"

"Turkey," interrupted I, "you will please withdraw."

"Oh certainly, sir, if you prefer that I should."   125

As he opened the folding-door to retire, Nippers at his desk caught a glimpse of me, and asked whether I would prefer to have a certain paper copied on blue paper or white. He did not in the least roguishly accent the word prefer. It was plain that it involuntarily rolled from his tongue. I thought to myself, surely I must get rid of a demented man, who already has in some degree turned the tongues, if not the heads of myself and clerks. But I thought it prudent not to break the dismission at once.

The next day I noticed that Bartleby did nothing but stand at his window in his dead-wall revery. Upon asking him why he did not write, he said that he had decided upon doing no more writing.

"Why, how now? What next?" exclaimed I, "do no more writing?"

"No more."

"And what is the reason?"   130

"Do you not see the reason for yourself?" he indifferently replied.

I looked steadfastly at him, and perceived that his eyes looked dull and glazed. Instantly it occurred to me, that his unexampled diligence in copying by his dim window for the first few weeks of his stay with me might have temporarily impaired his vision.

I was touched. I said something in condolence with him. I hinted that of course he did wisely in abstaining from writing for a while; and urged him to embrace that opportunity of taking wholesome exercise in the open air. This, however, he did not do. A few days after this, my other clerks being absent, and being in a great hurry to dispatch certain letters by the mail, I thought that, having nothing else earthly to do, Bartleby would surely be less inflexible than usual, and carry these letters to the post office. But he blankly declined. So, much to my inconvenience, I went myself.

Still added days went by. Whether Bartleby's eyes improved or not, I could not say. To all appearance, I thought they did. But when I asked him if they did, he vouchsafed no answer. At all events, he would do no copying. At last, in reply to my urgings, he informed me that he had permanently given up copying.

"What!" exclaimed I; "suppose your eyes should get entirely well—better than ever before—would you not copy then?"   135

"I have given up copying," he answered, and slid aside.

He remained as ever, a fixture in my chamber. Nay—if that were possible—he became still more of a fixture than before. What was to be done? He would do nothing in the office; why should he stay there? In plain fact, he had now become a millstone to me, not only useless as a necklace, but afflictive to bear. Yet I was sorry for him. I speak less than truth when I say that, on his own account, he occasioned me uneasiness. If he would but have named a single relative or friend, I would instantly have written, and urged their taking the poor fellow away to some convenient retreat. But he seemed alone, absolutely alone in the universe. A bit of wreck in the mid-Atlantic. At length, necessities connected with my business tyrannized over all other considerations. Decently as I could, I told Bartleby that in six days time he must unconditionally leave the office. I warned him to take measures, in the interval, for procuring some other abode. I offered to assist him in this endeavor, if he himself would but take the first step towards a removal. "And when you finally quit me, Bartleby," added I, "I shall see that you go not away entirely unprovided. Six days from this hour, remember."

At the expiration of that period, I peeped behind the screen, and lo! Bartleby was there.

I buttoned up my coat, balanced myself; advanced slowly towards him, touched his shoulder, and said, "The time has come; you must quit this place; I am sorry for you; here is money; but you must go."

"I would prefer not," he replied, with his back still towards me.   140

"You *must*."

He remained silent.

Now I had an unbounded confidence in this man's common honesty. He had frequently restored to me sixpences and shillings carelessly dropped upon the floor, for I am apt to be very reckless in such shirt-button affairs. The proceeding, then, which followed will not be deemed extraordinary.

"Bartleby," said I, "I owe you twelve dollars on account; here are thirty-two, the odd twenty are yours—Will you take it?" and I handed the bills towards him.

But he made no motion.   145

"I will leave them here, then," putting them under a weight on the table. Then taking my hat and cane and going to the door, I tranquilly turned and added—"After you have removed your things from these offices, Bartleby, you will of course lock the door—since every one is now gone for the day but you—and if you please, slip your key underneath the mat, so that I may have it in the morning. I shall not see you again; so good-by to you. If, hereafter, in your new place of abode, I can be of any service to you, do not fail to advise me by letter. Good-by, Bartleby, and fare you well."

But he answered not a word; like the last column of some ruined temple, he remained standing mute and solitary in the middle of the otherwise deserted room.

As I walked home in a pensive mood, my vanity got the better of my pity. I could not but highly plume myself on my masterly management in getting rid of Bartleby. Masterly I call it, and such it must appear to any dispassionate thinker. The beauty of my procedure seemed to consist in its perfect quietness. There was no vulgar bullying, no bravado of any sort, no choleric hectoring, and striding to and fro across the apartment, jerking out vehement commands for Bartleby to bundle himself off with his beggarly traps. Nothing of the kind. Without loudly bidding Bartleby depart—as an inferior genius might have done—I *assumed* the ground that depart he must; and upon that assumption built all I had to say. The more I thought over my procedure, the more I was charmed with it. Nevertheless, next morning, upon awakening, I had my doubts—I had somehow slept off the fumes of vanity. One of the coolest and wisest hours a man has, is just after he awakes in the morning. My procedure seemed as sagacious as ever—but only in theory. How it would prove in practice—there was the rub. It was truly a beautiful thought to have assumed Bartleby's departure; but, after all, that assumption was simply my own, and none of Bartleby's. The great point was, not whether I had assumed that he would quit me, but whether he would prefer to do so. He was more a man of preferences than assumptions.

After breakfast, I walked down town, arguing the probabilities *pro* and *con.* One moment I thought it would prove a miserable failure, and Bartleby would be found all alive at my office as usual; the next moment it seemed certain that I should find his chair empty. And so I kept veering about. At the corner of Broadway and Canal Street, I saw quite an excited group of people standing in earnest conversation.

"I'll take odds he doesn't," said a voice as I passed.

"Doesn't go?—done!" said I; "put up your money."

I was instinctively putting my hand in my pocket to produce my own, when I remembered that this was an election day. The words I had overheard bore no reference to Bartleby, but to the success or non-success of some candidate for the mayoralty. In my intent frame of mind, I had, as it were, imagined that all Broadway shared in my excitement, and were debating the same question with me. I passed on, very thankful that the uproar of the street screened my momentary absent-mindedness.

As I had intended, I was earlier than usual at my office door. I stood listening for a moment. All was still. He must be gone. I tried the knob. The door was locked. Yes, my procedure had worked to a charm; he indeed must be vanished. Yet a certain melancholy mixed with this: I was almost sorry for my brilliant success. I was fumbling under the door mat for the key, which Bartleby was to have left there for me, when accidentally my knee knocked against a panel, producing a summoning sound, and in response a voice came to me from within—"Not yet; I am occupied."

It was Bartleby.

150

I was thunderstruck. For an instant I stood like the man who, pipe in mouth, was killed one cloudless afternoon long ago in Virginia, by summer lightning; at his own warm open window he was killed, and remained leaning out there upon the dreamy afternoon, till some one touched him, when he fell.

"Not gone!" I murmured at last. But again obeying that wondrous ascendancy which the inscrutable scrivener had over me, and from which ascendancy, for all my chafing, I could not completely escape, I slowly went down stairs and out into the street, and while walking round the block, considered what I should next do in this unheard-of perplexity. Turn the man out by an actual thrusting I could not; to drive him away by calling him hard names would not do; calling in the police was an unpleasant idea; and yet, permit him to enjoy his cadaverous triumph over me—this, too, I could not think of. What was to be done? or, if nothing could be done, was there anything further that I could *assume* in the matter? Yes, as before I had prospectively assumed that Bartleby would depart, so now I might retrospectively assume that departed he was. In the legitimate carrying out of this assumption, I might enter my office in a great hurry, and pretending not to see Bartleby at all, walk straight against him as if he were air. Such a proceeding would in a singular degree have the appearance of a home-thrust. It was hardly possible that Bartleby could withstand such an application of the doctrine of assumption. But upon second thoughts the success of the plan seemed rather dubious. I resolved to argue the matter over with him again.

"Bartleby," said I, entering the office, with a quietly severe expression, "I am seriously displeased. I am pained, Bartleby. I had thought better of you. I had imagined you of such a gentlemanly organization, that in any delicate dilemma a slight hint would suffice—in short, an assumption. But it appears I am de-ceived. Why," I added, unaffectedly starting, "you have not even touched that money yet," pointing to it, just where I had left it the evening previous.

He answered nothing.

"Will you, or will you not, quit me?" I now demanded in a sudden passion, ad-vancing close to him.

"I would prefer *not* to quit you," he replied, gently emphasizing the *not*.

"What earthly right have you to stay here? Do you pay any rent? Do you pay my taxes? Or is this property yours?"

He answered nothing.

"Are you ready to go on and write now? Are your eyes recovered? Could you copy a small paper for me this morning? or help examine a few lines? or step round to the post office? In a word, will you do anything at all, to give a coloring to your refusal to depart the premises?"

He silently retired into his hermitage.

I was now in such a state of nervous resentment that I thought it but prudent to check myself at present from further demonstrations. Bartleby and I were alone. I remembered the tragedy of the unfortunate Adams and the still more unfortunate Colt in the solitary office of the latter; and how poor Colt, being dreadfully incensed by Adams, and imprudently permitting himself to get wildly excited, was at unawares hurried into his fatal act—an act which certainly

no man could possibly deplore more than the actor himself.[7] Often it had occurred to me in my ponderings upon the subject that had that altercation taken
place in the public street, or at a private residence, it would not have terminated
as it did. It was the circumstance of being alone in a solitary office, up stairs, of
a building entirely unhallowed by humanizing domestic associations—an uncarpeted office, doubtless, of a dusty, haggard sort of appearance—this it must
have been, which greatly helped to enhance the irritable desperation of the
hapless Colt.

But when this old Adam of resentment rose in me and tempted me concerning Bartleby, I grappled him and threw him. How? Why, simply by recalling the
divine injunction: "A new commandment give I unto you, that ye love one another." Yes, this it was that saved me. Aside from higher considerations, charity
often operates as a vastly wise and prudent principle—a great safeguard to its
possessor. Men have committed murder for jealousy's sake, and anger's sake,
and hatred's sake, and selfishness' sake, and spiritual pride's sake; but no man,
that ever I heard of, ever committed a diabolical murder for sweet charity's
sake. Mere self-interest, then, if no better motive can be enlisted, should, especially with high-tempered men, prompt all beings to charity and philanthropy.
At any rate, upon the occasion in question, I strove to drown my exasperated
feelings towards the scrivener by benevolently construing his conduct. Poor fellow, poor fellow! thought I, he don't mean anything; and besides, he has seen
hard times, and ought to be indulged.

I endeavored, also, immediately to occupy myself, and at the same time to
comfort my despondency. I tried to fancy, that in the course of the morning, at
such time as might prove agreeable to him, Bartleby, of his own free accord,
would emerge from his hermitage and take up some decided line of march in
the direction of the door. But no. Half-past twelve o'clock came; Turkey began
to glow in the face, overturn his inkstand, and become generally obstreperous;
Nippers abated down into quietude and courtesy; Ginger Nut munched his
noon apple; and Bartleby remained standing at his window in one of his pro-
foundest dead-wall reveries. Will it be credited? Ought I to acknowledge it?
That afternoon I left the office without saying one further word to him.

Some days now passed, during which, at leisure intervals I looked a little into
"Edwards on the Will," and "Priestley on Necessity."[8] Under the circumstances,
those books induced a salutary feeling. Gradually I slid into the persuasion that
these troubles of mine, touching the scrivener, had been all predestinated from
eternity, and Bartleby was billeted upon me for some mysterious purpose of an
all-wise Providence, which it was not for a mere mortal like me to fathom. Yes,
Bartleby, stay there behind your screen, thought I; I shall persecute you no
more; you are harmless and noiseless as any of these old chairs; in short, I never
feel so private as when I know you are here. At last I see it, I feel it; I penetrate

---

[7] A sensational homicide case in which Colt murdered Adams in a fit of passion.
[8] Jonathan Edwards (1703–1758), American theologian, and Joseph Priestley (1733–1804), English clergyman and chemist, both held that a person's life was predetermined.

to the predestinated purpose of my life. I am content. Others may have loftier parts to enact; but my mission in this world, Bartleby, is to furnish you with office-room for such period as you may see fit to remain.

I believe that this wise and blessed frame of mind would have continued with me, had it not been for the unsolicited and uncharitable remarks obtruded upon me by my professional friends who visited the rooms. But thus it often is, that the constant friction of illiberal minds wears out at last the best resolves of the more generous. Though to be sure, when I reflected upon it, it was not strange that people entering my office should be struck by the peculiar aspect of the unaccountable Bartleby, and so be tempted to throw out some sinister observations concerning him. Sometimes an attorney, having business with me, and calling at my office, and finding no one but the scrivener there, would undertake to obtain some sort of precise information from him touching my whereabouts; but without heeding his idle talk, Bartleby would remain standing immovable in the middle of the room. So after contemplating him in that position for a time, the attorney would depart, no wiser than he came.

Also, when a reference was going on, and the room full of lawyers and witnesses, and business driving fast, some deeply-occupied legal gentleman present, seeing Bartleby wholly unemployed, would request him to run round to his (the legal gentleman's) office and fetch some papers for him. Thereupon, Bartleby would tranquilly decline, and yet remain idle as before. Then the lawyer would give a great stare, and turn to me. And what could I say? At last I was made aware that all through the circle of my professional acquaintance, a whisper of wonder was running round, having reference to the strange creature I kept at my office. This worried me very much. And as the idea came upon me of his possibly turning out a long-lived man, and keep occupying my chambers, and denying my authority; and perplexing my visitors; and scandalizing my professional reputation; and casting a general gloom over the premises; keeping soul and body together to the last upon his savings (for doubtless he spent but half a dime a day), and in the end perhaps outlive me, and claim possession of my office by right of his perpetual occupancy: as all these dark anticipations crowded upon me more and more, and my friends continually intruded their relentless remarks upon the apparition in my room; a great change was wrought in me. I resolved to gather all my faculties together, and forever rid me of this intolerable incubus. [170]

Ere revolving any complicated project, however, adapted to this end, I first simply suggested to Bartleby the propriety of his permanent departure. In a calm and serious tone, I commended the idea to his careful and mature consideration. But, having taken three days to meditate upon it, he apprised me, that his original determination remained the same; in short, that he still preferred to abide with me.

What shall I do? I now said to myself, buttoning up my coat to the last button. What shall I do? what ought I to do? what does conscience say I *should* do with this man, or, rather, ghost. Rid myself of him, I must; go, he shall. But how? You will not thrust him, the poor, pale, passive mortal—you will not thrust such a helpless creature out of your door? you will not dishonor yourself by such cruelty? No, I will not, I cannot do that. Rather would I let him live and die here, and then mason up his remains in the wall. What, then, will you do? For all your coaxing, he will not budge. Bribes he leaves under your own paper-weight on your table; in short, it is quite plain that he prefers to cling to you.

Then something severe, something unusual must be done. What! surely you will not have him collared by a constable, and commit his innocent pallor to the common jail? And upon what ground could you procure such a thing to be done?—a vagrant, is he? What! he a vagrant, a wanderer, who refuses to budge? It is because he will *not* be a vagrant, then, that you seek to count him *as* a vagrant. That is too absurd. No visible means of support: there I have him. Wrong again: for indubitably he *does* support himself, and that is the only unanswerable proof that any man can show of his possessing the means so to do. No more, then. Since he will not quit me, I must quit him. I will change my offices; I will move elsewhere, and give him fair notice, that if I find him in my new premises I will then proceed against him as a common trespasser.

Acting accordingly, next day I thus addressed him: "I find these chambers too far from the City Hall; the air is unwholesome. In a word, I propose to remove my offices next week, and shall no longer require your services. I tell you this now, in order that you may seek another place."

He made no reply, and nothing more was said. 175

On the appointed day I engaged carts and men, proceeded to my chambers, and, having but little furniture, everything was removed in a few hours. Throughout, the scrivener remained standing behind the screen, which I directed to be removed the last thing. It was withdrawn; and, being folded up like a huge folio, left him the motionless occupant of a naked room. I stood in the entry watching him a moment, while something from within me upbraided me.

I re-entered, with my hand in my pocket—and—and my heart in my mouth.

"Good-by, Bartleby; I am going—good-by, and God some way bless you; and take that," slipping something in his hand. But it dropped upon the floor, and then—strange to say—I tore myself from him whom I had so longed to be rid of.

Established in my new quarters, for a day or two I kept the door locked, and started at every footfall in the passages. When I returned to my rooms, after any little absence, I would pause at the threshold for an instant, and attentively listen, ere applying my key. But these fears were needless. Bartleby never came nigh me.

I thought all was going well, when a perturbed-looking stranger visited 180 me, inquiring whether I was the person who had recently occupied rooms at No. ———Wall Street.

Full of forebodings, I replied that I was.

"Then, sir," said the stranger, who proved a lawyer, "you are responsible for the man you left there. He refuses to do any copying; he refuses to do anything; he says he prefers not to; and he refuses to quit the premises."

"I am very sorry, sir," said I, with assumed tranquillity, but an inward tremor, "but, really, the man you allude to is nothing to me—he is no relation or apprentice of mine, that you should hold me responsible for him."

"In mercy's name, who is he?"

"I certainly cannot inform you. I know nothing about him. Formerly I employed him as a copyist; but he has done nothing for me now for some time past."

"I shall settle him, then—good morning, sir."

Several days passed, and I heard nothing more; and, though I often felt a charitable prompting to call at the place and see poor Bartleby, yet a certain squeamishness, of I know not what, withheld me.

All is over with him, by this time, thought I, at last, when, through another week, no further intelligence reached me. But, coming to my room the day after, I found several persons waiting at my door in a high state of nervous excitement.

"That's the man—here he comes," cried the foremost one, whom I recognized as the lawyer who had previously called upon me alone.

"You must take him away, sir, at once," cried a portly person among them, advancing upon me, and whom I knew to be the landlord of No. —— Wall Street. "These gentlemen, my tenants, cannot stand it any longer; Mr. B——," pointing to the lawyer, "has turned him out of his room, and he now persists in haunting the building generally, sitting upon the banisters of the stairs by day, and sleeping in the entry by night. Everybody is concerned; clients are leaving the offices; some fears are entertained of a mob; something you must do, and that without delay."

Aghast at this torrent, I fell back before it, and would fain have locked myself in my new quarters. In vain I persisted that Bartleby was nothing to me—no more than to any one else. In vain—I was the last person known to have anything to do with him, and they held me to the terrible account. Fearful, then, of being exposed in the papers (as one person present obscurely threatened), I considered the matter, and, at length, said, that if the lawyer would give me a confidential interview with the scrivener, in his (the lawyer's) own room, I would, that afternoon, strive my best to rid them of the nuisance they complained of.

Going up stairs to my old haunt, there was Bartleby silently sitting upon the banister at the landing.

"What are you doing here, Bartleby?" said I.

"Sitting upon the banister," he mildly replied.

I motioned him into the lawyer's room, who then left us.

"Bartleby," said I, "are you aware that you are the cause of great tribulation to me, by persisting in occupying the entry after being dismissed from the office?"

No answer.

"Now one of two things must take place. Either you must do something, or something must be done to you. Now what sort of business would you like to engage in? Would you like to re-engage in copying for some one?"

"No; I would prefer not to make any change."

"Would you like a clerkship in a dry-goods store?"   200

"There is too much confinement about that. No, I would not like a clerkship; but I am not particular."

"Too much confinement," I cried, "why, you keep yourself confined all the time!"

"I would prefer not to take a clerkship," he rejoined, as if to settle that little item at once.

"How would a bar-tender's business suit you? There is no trying of the eyesight in that."

"I would not like it at all; though, as I said before, I am not particular."   205

His unwonted wordiness inspirited me. I returned to the charge.

"Well, then, would you like to travel through the country collecting bills for the merchants? That would improve your health."

"No, I would prefer to be doing something else."

"How, then, would going as a companion to Europe, to entertain some young gentleman with your conversation—how would that suit you?"

"Not at all. It does not strike me that there is anything definite about that. I   210
like to be stationary. But I am not particular."

"Stationary you shall be, then," I cried, now losing all patience, and, for the first time in all my exasperating connection with him, fairly flying into a passion. "If you do not go away from these premises before night, I shall feel bound—indeed, I *am* bound—to—to—to quit the premises myself!" I rather absurdly concluded, knowing not with what possible threat to try to frighten his immobility into compliance. Despairing of all further efforts, I was precipitately leaving him, when a final thought occurred to me—one which had not been wholly unindulged before.

"Bartleby," said I, in the kindest tone I could assume under such exciting circumstances, "will you go home with me now—not to my office, but my dwelling—and remain there till we can conclude upon some convenient arrangement for you at our leisure? Come, let us start now, right away."

"No: at present I would prefer not to make any change at all."

I answered nothing; but, effectually dodging every one by the suddenness and rapidity of my flight, rushed from the building, ran up Wall Street towards Broadway, and, jumping into the first omnibus, was soon removed from pursuit. As soon as tranquillity returned, I distinctly perceived that I had now done all that I possibly could, both in respect to the demands of the landlord and his tenants, and with regard to my own desire and sense of duty, to benefit Bartleby, and shield him from rude persecution. I now strove to be entirely care-free and quiescent; and my conscience justified me in the attempt; though, indeed, it was not so successful as I could have wished. So fearful was I of being again hunted out by the incensed landlord and his exasperated tenants, that, surrendering my business to Nippers, for a few days, I drove about the upper part of the town and through the suburbs, in my rockaway; crossed over to Jersey City and Hoboken, and paid fugitive visits to Manhattanville and Astoria. In fact, I almost lived in my rockaway for the time.

When again I entered my office, lo, a note from the landlord lay upon the   215
desk. I opened it with trembling hands. It informed me that the writer had sent
to the police, and had Bartleby removed to the Tombs as a vagrant. Moreover,
since I knew more about him than any one else, he wished me to appear at that
place, and make a suitable statement of the facts. These tidings had a conflict-
ing effect upon me. At first I was indignant; but, at last, almost approved. The
landlord's energetic, summary disposition, had led him to adopt a procedure
which I do not think I would have decided upon myself; and yet, as a last resort,
under such peculiar circumstances, it seemed the only plan.

As I afterwards learned, the poor scrivener, when told that he must be conducted to the Tombs, offered not the slightest obstacle, but, in his pale, unmoving way, silently acquiesced.

Some of the compassionate and curious by-standers joined the party; and
headed by one of the constables arm in arm with Bartleby, the silent procession
filed its way through all the noise, and heat, and joy of the roaring thoroughfares
at noon.

The same day I received the note, I went to the Tombs, or, to speak
more properly, the Halls of Justice. Seeking the right officer, I stated the purpose of my call, and was informed that the individual I described was, indeed,
within. I then assured the functionary that Bartleby was a perfectly honest
man, and greatly to be compassionated, however unaccountably eccentric. I
narrated all I knew, and closed by suggesting the idea of letting him remain in
as indulgent confinement as possible, till something less harsh might be
done—though, indeed, I hardly knew what. At all events, if nothing else could
be decided upon, the alms-house must receive him. I then begged to have an
interview.

Being under no disgraceful charge, and quite serene and harmless in all his
ways, they had permitted him freely to wander about the prison, and, especially,
in the inclosed grass-platted yards thereof. And so I found him there, standing
all alone in the quietest of the yards, his face towards a high wall, while all
around, from the narrow slits of the jail windows, I thought I saw peering out
upon him the eyes of murderers and thieves.

"Bartleby!"   220

"I know you," he said, without looking round—"and I want nothing to say to
you."

"It was not I that brought you here, Bartleby," said I, keenly pained at his implied suspicion. "And to you, this should not be so vile a place. Nothing re-
proachful attaches to you by being here. And see, it is not so sad a place as one
might think. Look, there is the sky, and here is the grass."

"I know where I am," he replied, but would say nothing more, and so I left
him.

As I entered the corridor again, a broad meat-like man, in an apron, accosted
me, and, jerking his thumb over his shoulder, said—"Is that your friend?"

"Yes."   225

"Does he want to starve? If he does, let him live on the prison fare, that's all."

"Who are you?" asked I, not knowing what to make of such an unofficially speaking person in such a place.

"I am the grub-man. Such gentlemen as have friends here, hire me to provide them with something good to eat."

"Is this so?" said I, turning to the turnkey.

He said it was. 230

"Well, then," said I, slipping some silver into the grub-man's hands (for so they called him), "I want you to give particular attention to my friend there; let him have the best dinner you can get. And you must be as polite to him as possible."

"Introduce me, will you?" said the grub-man, looking at me with an expression which seemed to say he was all impatience for an opportunity to give a specimen of his breeding.

Thinking it would prove of benefit to the scrivener, I acquiesced; and, asking the grub-man his name, went up with him to Bartleby.

"Bartleby, this is a friend; you will find him very useful to you."

"Your sarvant, sir, your sarvant," said the grub-man, making a low salutation 235 behind his apron. "Hope you find it pleasant here, sir; nice grounds—cool apartments—hope you'll stay with us some time—try to make it agreeable. What will you have for dinner to-day?"

"I prefer not to dine to-day," said Bartleby, turning away. "It would disagree with me; I am unused to dinners." So saying, he slowly moved to the other side of the inclosure, and took up a position fronting the deadwall.

"How's this?" said the grub-man, addressing me with a stare of astonishment. "He's odd, ain't he?"

"I think he is a little deranged," said I, sadly.

"Deranged? deranged is it? Well, now, upon my word, I thought that friend of yourn was a gentleman forger; they are always pale and genteel-like, them forgers. I can't help pity 'em—can't help it, sir. Did you know Monroe Edwards?" he added, touchingly, and paused. Then, laying his hand piteously on my shoulder, sighed, "he died of consumption at Sing-Sing.[9] So you weren't acquainted with Monroe?"

"No, I was never socially acquainted with any forgers. But I cannot stop 240 longer. Look to my friend yonder. You will not lose by it. I will see you again."

Some few days after this, I again obtained admission to the Tombs, and went through the corridors in quest of Bartleby; but without finding him.

"I saw him coming from his cell not long ago," said a turnkey, "may be he's gone to loiter in the yards."

So I went in that direction.

"Are you looking for the silent man?" said another turnkey, passing me. "Yonder he lies—sleeping in the yard there. 'Tis not twenty minutes since I saw him lie down."

The yard was entirely quiet. It was not accessible to the common prisoners. 245

---

[9] The state prison near Ossining, New York.

The surrounding walls of amazing thickness, kept off all sounds behind them. The Egyptian character of the masonry weighed upon me with its gloom. But a soft imprisoned turf grew under foot. The heart of the eternal pyramids, it seemed, wherein, by some strange magic, through the clefts, grass-seed, dropped by birds, had sprung.

Strangely huddled at the base of the wall, his knees drawn up, and lying on his side, his head touching the cold stones, I saw the wasted Bartleby. But nothing stirred. I paused; then went close up to him; stooped over, and saw that his dim eyes were open; otherwise he seemed profoundly sleeping. Something prompted me to touch him. I felt his hand, when a tingling shiver ran up my arm and down my spine to my feet.

The round face of the grub-man peered upon me now. "His dinner is ready. Won't he dine to-day, either? Or does he live without dining?"

"Lives without dining," said I, and closed the eyes.

"Eh!—He's asleep, ain't he?"

"With kings and counselors," murmured I.   250

There would seem little need for proceeding further in this history. Imagination will readily supply the meagre recital of poor Bartleby's interment. But, ere parting with the reader, let me say, that if this little narrative has sufficiently interested him, to awaken curiosity as to who Bartleby was, and what manner of life he led prior to the present narrator's making his acquaintance, I can only reply, that in such curiosity I fully share, but am wholly unable to gratify it. Yet here I hardly know whether I should divulge one little item of rumor, which came to my ear a few months after the scrivener's decease. Upon what basis it rested, I could never ascertain; and hence, how true it is I cannot now tell. But, inasmuch as this vague report has not been without a certain suggestive interest to me, however said, it may prove the same with some others; and so I will briefly mention it. The report was this: that Bartleby had been a subordinate clerk in the Dead Letter[10] Office at Washington, from which he had been suddenly removed by a change in the administration. When I think over this rumor, hardly can I express the emotions which seize me. Dead letters! does it not sound like dead men? Conceive a man by nature and misfortune prone to a pallid hopelessness, can any business seem more fitted to heighten it than that of continually handling these dead letters, and assorting them for the flames? For by the cart-load they are annually burned. Some times from out the folded paper the pale clerk takes a ring—the finger it was meant for, perhaps, moulders in the grave; a bank-note sent in swiftest charity—he whom it would relieve, nor eats nor hungers any more; pardon for those who died despairing; hope for those who died unhoping; good tidings for those who died stifled by unrelieved calamities. On errands of life, these letters speed to death.

Ah, Bartleby! Ah, humanity!

---

[10] A letter that is undeliverable because it lacks a correct address and unreturned to the sender.

For Analysis

1. Draw up a list of a half dozen adjectives that describe the narrator. Would the narrator agree that these adjectives are accurate? **2.** What is it about Bartleby that so intrigues and fascinates the narrator? Why does the narrator continue to feel a moral obligation to an employee who refuses to work and curtly rejects kind offers of help? **3.** What thematic function do Turkey and Nippers serve? **4.** As the narrator congratulates himself on the cleverness of his scheme to dismiss Bartleby, he becomes fascinated with his "assumptions" about how Bartleby will behave. Examine the passage (par. 149–56) and show how it advances the narrator's growing awareness of what Bartleby represents. **5.** Readers differ as to whether this is the story of Bartleby or the lawyer-narrator. What is your view? **6.** Would it be fair to describe Bartleby as a rebel without a cause, as a young man who refuses to participate in a comfortable and well-ordered business world but fails to offer any alternative way of life? Write a paragraph or two explaining why or why not.

On Style

1. Identify the humor in this somber story and discuss its sources. **2.** Suppose that Melville had given us some biographical information that would help explain Bartleby's character, say a hideous childhood of abuse and neglect. Would that make this a better story? Explain.

Making Connections

What comparisons and contrasts can be drawn between Bartleby's form of rebellion and Fred Daniels's rebellion in Wright's "The Man Who Lived Underground" (p. 351)?

Writing Topics

1. About midway through the story (par. 87–94), the narrator discovers that Bartleby has been living in the law offices and is profoundly moved when his eyes fall on the scrivener's worldly possessions. Reread those paragraphs and write an analysis showing how they describe the narrator's growing awareness of who Bartleby is. **2.** With his final utterance, "Ah, Bartleby! Ah, humanity!" the narrator apparently penetrates the mystery of the silent scrivener. The comment suggests that the narrator sees Bartleby as a representative of humanity. In what sense might the narrator have come to see Bartleby in this light? **3.** Why does Melville allow the narrator (and the reader) to discover so little about Bartleby and the causes of his behavior? All we learn of Bartleby's past is related in the next-to-last paragraph. What clues does this paragraph give us to the narrator's fascination with Bartleby?

Luigi Pirandello   [1867–1936]

War[1]   1918

The passengers who had left Rome by the night express had had to stop until dawn at the small station of Fabriano in order to continue their journey by the small old-fashioned "local" joining the main line with Sulmona.

At dawn, in a stuffy and smoky second-class carriage in which five people had already spent the night, a bulky woman in deep mourning was hoisted in—almost like a shapeless bundle. Behind her—puffing and moaning, followed her husband—a tiny man, thin and weakly, his face death-white, his eyes small and bright and looking shy and uneasy.

Having at last taken a seat he politely thanked the passengers who had helped his wife and who had made room for her; then he turned round to the woman trying to pull down the collar of her coat and politely enquired:

"Are you all right, dear?"

The wife, instead of answering, pulled up her collar again to her eyes, so as to   5
hide her face.

"Nasty world," muttered the husband with a sad smile.

And he felt it his duty to explain to his travelling companions that the poor woman was to be pitied for the war was taking away from her her only son, a boy of twenty to whom both had devoted their entire life, even breaking up their home at Sulmona to follow him to Rome where he had to go as a student, then allowing him to volunteer for war with an assurance, however, that at least for six months he would not be sent to the front and now, all of a sudden, receiving a wire saying that he was due to leave in three days' time and asking them to go and see him off.

The woman under the big coat was twisting and wriggling, at times growling like a wild animal, feeling certain that all those explanations would not have aroused even a shadow of sympathy from those people who—most likely—were in the same plight as herself. One of them, who had been listening with particular attention, said:

"You should thank God that your son is only leaving now for the front. Mine has been sent there the first day of the war. He has already come back twice wounded and been sent back again to the front."

"What about me? I have two sons and three nephews at the front," said an-   10
other passenger.

"Maybe, but in our case it is our *only* son," ventured the husband.

[1] Translated by Michele Pettinati.

341

"What difference can it make? You may spoil your only son with excessive attentions, but you cannot love him more than you would all your other children if you had any. Paternal love is not like bread that can be broken into pieces and split amongst the children in equal shares. A father gives *all* his love to each one of his children without discrimination, whether it be one or ten, and if I am suffering now for my two sons, I am not suffering half for each of them but double. . . ."

"True . . . true . . ." sighed the embarrassed husband, "but suppose (of course we all hope it will never be your case) a father has two sons at the front and he loses one of them, there is still one left to console him . . . while . . ."

"Yes," answered the other, getting cross, "a son left to console him but also a son left for whom he must survive, while in the case of the father of an only son if the son dies the father can die too and put an end to his distress. Which of the two positions is the worse? Don't you see how my case would be worse than yours?"

"Nonsense," interrupted another traveller, a fat, red-faced man with blood-shot eyes of the palest grey.   15

He was panting. From his bulging eyes seemed to spurt inner violence of an uncontrolled vitality which his weakened body could hardly contain.

"Nonsense," he repeated, trying to cover his mouth with his hand so as to hide the two missing front teeth. "Nonsense. Do we give life to our children for our own benefit?"

The other travellers stared at him in distress. The one who had had his son at the front since the first day of the war sighed: "You are right. Our children do not belong to us, they belong to the Country. . . ."

"Bosh," retorted the fat traveller. "Do we think of the Country when we give life to our children? Our sons are born because . . . well, because they must be born and when they come to life they take our own life with them. This is the truth. We belong to them but they never belong to us. And when they reach twenty they are exactly what we were at their age. We too had a father and mother, but there were so many other things as well . . . girls, cigarettes, illusions, new ties . . . and the Country, of course, whose call we would have answered—when we were twenty—even if father and mother had said no. Now, at our age, the love of our Country is still great, of course, but stronger than it is the love for our children. Is there any one of us here who wouldn't gladly take his son's place at the front if he could?"

There was a silence all round, everybody nodding as to approve.   20

"Why then," continued the fat man, "shouldn't we consider the feelings of our children when they are twenty? Isn't it *natural* that at their age they should consider the love for their Country (I am speaking of decent boys, of course) even greater than the love for us? Isn't it *natural* that it should be so, as after all they must look upon us as upon old boys who cannot move any more and must stay at home? If Country exists, if Country is a natural necessity like bread, of which each of us must eat in order not to die of hunger, somebody must go to defend it. And our sons go, when they are twenty, and they don't want tears, because if they die, they die inflamed and happy (I am speaking, of course, of decent boys). Now, if one dies young and happy, without having the ugly sides of life, the boredom of it, the pettiness, the bitterness of disillusion . . . what more can we ask for him? Everyone should stop crying: everyone should laugh, as I do . . . or at least thank God—as I do—because my son, before dying, sent me a message saying that he was dying satisfied at having ended his life in the best way he could have wished. That is why, as you see, I do not even wear mourning. . . ."

He shook his light fawn coat as to show it; his livid lip over his missing teeth was trembling, his eyes were watery and motionless and soon after he ended with a shrill laugh which might well have been a sob.

"Quite so . . . quite so . . ." agreed the others.

The woman who, bundled in a corner under her coat, had been sitting and listening had—for the last three months—tried to find in the words of her husband and her friends something to console her in her deep sorrow, something that might show her how a mother should resign herself to send her son not even to death but to a probable danger of life. Yet not a word had she found amongst the many which had been said . . . and her grief had been greater in seeing that nobody—as she thought—could share her feelings.

But now the words of the traveller amazed and almost stunned her. She suddenly realized that it wasn't the others who were wrong and could not understand her but herself who could not rise up to the same height of those fathers and mothers willing to resign themselves, without crying, not only to the departure of their sons but even to their death.

She lifted her head, she bent over from her corner trying to listen with great attention to the details which the fat man was giving to his companions about the way his son had fallen as a hero, for his King and his Country, happy and without regrets. It seemed to her that she had stumbled into a world she had never dreamt of, a world so far unknown to her and she was so pleased to hear everyone joining in congratulating that brave father who could so stoically speak of his child's death.

Then suddenly, just as if she had heard nothing of what had been said and almost as if waking up from a dream, she turned to the old man, asking him:

"Then . . . is your son really dead?"

Everybody stared at her. The old man, too, turned to look at her, fixing his great, bulging, horribly watery light grey eyes, deep in her face. For some little time he tried to answer, but words failed him. He looked and looked at her, almost as if only then—at that silly, incongruous question—he had suddenly realized at last that his son was really dead . . . gone for ever . . . for ever. His face contracted, became horribly distorted, then he snatched in haste a handkerchief from his pocket and, to the amazement of everyone, broke into harrowing, heart-rending, uncontrollable sobs.

For Analysis

1. Is this an antiwar story? Explain. **2.** The publication date (1918) and the setting make clear that Pirandello is writing about World War I. How would your response to the story be different if there had been some discussion among the characters of the issues at stake in the war? **3.** What are the passengers trying to establish in the opening dialogue about their children? **4.** Why is the mother in such awe of the fat man?

On Style

1. Reread the story, pinpointing the places the author makes use of **irony. 2.** While the subject matter and theme of this story and of James Joyce's "Araby" (p. 81) are very different, compare them for their similarities in structure, the way in which both narratives move from beginning to middle to end in a roughly similar way.

Making Connections

1. Compare and contrast the statement about war made in this story with Wilfred Owen's in the poem "Dulce et Decorum Est" (p. 1279). **2.** What similarities do you find between the fat man in this story and Iván Ilých in "The Death of Iván Ilých" (p. 1165) as they confront death as an abstraction and as a reality?

Writing Topic

Write an essay analyzing why the mother's question at the end of the story has such a devastating effect on the fat man, "that brave father who could so stoically speak of his child's death" (par. 26).

James Thurber   [1894–1961]

The Greatest Man in the World   1935

Looking back on it now, from the vantage point of 1950, one can only marvel that it hadn't happened long before it did. The United States of America had been, ever since Kitty Hawk, blindly constructing the elaborate petard by which, sooner or later, it must be hoist. It was inevitable that some day there would come roaring out of the skies a national hero of insufficient intelligence, background, and character successfully to endure the mounting orgies of glory prepared for aviators who stayed up a long time or flew a great distance. Both Lindbergh and Byrd, fortunately for national decorum and international amity, had been gentlemen; so had our other famous aviators. They wore their laurels gracefully, withstood the awful weather of publicity, married excellent women, usually of fine family, and quietly retired to private life and the enjoyment of their varying fortunes. No untoward incidents, on a worldwide scale, marred the perfection of their conduct on the perilous heights of fame. The exception to the rule was, however, bound to occur and it did, in July, 1937, when Jack ("Pal") Smurch, erstwhile mechanics' helper in a small garage in Westfield, Iowa, flew a second-hand, single-motored Bresthaven Dragon-Fly III monoplane all the way around the world, without stopping.

Never before in the history of aviation had such a flight as Smurch's ever been dreamed of. No one had even taken seriously the weird floating auxiliary gas tanks, invention of the mad New Hampshire professor of astronomy, Dr. Charles Lewis Gresham, upon which Smurch placed full reliance. When the garage worker, a slightly built, surly, unprepossessing young man of twenty-two, appeared at Roosevelt Field in early July, 1937, slowly chewing a great quid of scrap tobacco, and announced "Nobody ain't seen no flyin' yet," the newspapers touched briefly and satirically upon his projected twenty-five-thousand-mile flight. Aeronautical and automotive experts dismissed the idea curtly, implying that it was a hoax, a publicity stunt. The rusty, battered, second-hand plane wouldn't go. The Gresham auxiliary tanks wouldn't work. It was simply a cheap joke.

Smurch, however, after calling on a girl in Brooklyn who worked in the flap-folding department of a large paper-box factory, a girl whom he later described as his "sweet patootie," climbed nonchalantly into his ridiculous plane at dawn of the memorable seventh of July, 1937, spat a curve of tobacco juice into the still air, and took off, carrying with him only a gallon of bootleg gin and six pounds of salami.

When the garage boy thundered out over the ocean the papers were forced to record, in all seriousness, that a mad, unknown young man—his name was variously misspelled—had actually set out upon a preposterous attempt to span the world in a rickety, one-engined contraption, trusting to the long-distance refueling device of a crazy schoolmaster. When, nine days later, without having stopped once, the tiny plane appeared above San Francisco Bay, headed for New York, spluttering and choking, to be sure, but still magnificently and miraculously aloft, the headlines, which long since had crowded everything else off the front page—even the shooting of the Governor of Illinois by the Vileti gang—swelled to unprecedented size, and the news stories began to run to twenty-five and thirty columns. It was noticeable, however, that the accounts of the epoch-making flight touched rather lightly upon the aviator himself. This was not because facts about the hero as a man were too meagre, but because they were too complete.

Reporters, who had been rushed out to Iowa when Smurch's plane was first   5
sighted over the little French coast town of Serly-le-Mar, to dig up the story of the great man's life, had promptly discovered that the story of his life could not be printed. His mother, a sullen short-order cook in a shack restaurant on the edge of a tourists' camping ground near Westfield, met all enquiries as to her son with an angry, "Ah, the hell with him; I hope he drowns." His father appeared to be in jail somewhere for stealing spotlights and laprobes from tourists' automobiles; his younger brother, a weak-minded lad, had but recently escaped from the Preston, Iowa, Reformatory and was already wanted in several Western towns for the theft of money-order blanks from post offices. These alarming discoveries were still piling up at the very time that Pal Smurch, the greatest hero of the twentieth century, blear-eyed, dead for sleep, half-starved, was piloting his crazy junk-heap high above the region in which the lamentable story of his private life was being unearthed, headed for New York under greater glory than any man of his time had ever known.

The necessity for printing some account in the papers of the young man's career and personality had led to a remarkable predicament. It was of course impossible to reveal the facts, for a tremendous popular feeling in favor of the young hero had sprung up, like a grass fire, when he was halfway across Europe on his flight around the globe. He was, therefore, described as a modest chap, taciturn, blond, popular with his friends, popular with girls. The only available snapshot of Smurch, taken at the wheel of a phony automobile in a cheap photo studio at an amusement park, was touched up so that the little vulgarian looked quite handsome. His twisted leer was smoothed into a pleasant smile. The truth was, in this way, kept from the youth's ecstatic compatriots; they did not dream that the Smurch family was despised and feared by its neighbors in the obscure Iowa town, nor that the hero himself, because of numerous unsavory exploits, had come to be regarded in Westfield as a nuisance and a menace. He had, the reporters discovered, once knifed the principal of his high school—not mortally, to be sure, but he had knifed him; and on another occasion, surprised in the act of stealing an altar-cloth from a church, he had bashed the sacristan over the head with a pot of Easter lilies; for each of these offences he had served a sentence in the reformatory.

Inwardly, the authorities, both in New York and in Washington, prayed that an understanding Providence might, however awful such a thing seemed, bring disaster to the rusty, battered plane and its illustrious pilot, whose unheard-of flight had aroused the civilized world to hosannas of hysterical praise. The authorities were convinced that the character of the renowned aviator was such that the limelight of adulation was bound to reveal him to all the world, as a congenital hooligan mentally and morally unequipped to cope with his own prodigious fame. "I trust," said the Secretary of State, at one of many secret Cabinet meetings called to consider the national dilemma, "I trust that his mother's prayer will be answered," by which he referred to Mrs. Emma Smurch's wish that her son might be drowned. It was, however, too late for that—Smurch had leaped the Atlantic and then the Pacific as if they were millponds. At three minutes after two o'clock in the afternoon of 17 July, 1937, the garage boy brought his idiotic plane into Roosevelt Field for a perfect three-point landing.

It had, of course, been out of the question to arrange a modest little reception for the greatest flier in the history of the world. He was received at Roosevelt Field with such elaborate and pretentious ceremonies as rocked the world. Fortunately, however, the worn and spent hero promptly swooned, had to be removed bodily from his plane, and was spirited from the field without having opened his mouth once. Thus he did not jeopardize the dignity of this first reception, a reception illumined by the presence of the Secretaries of War and the Navy, Mayor Michael J. Moriarity of New York, the Premier of Canada, Governors Fanniman, Groves, McFeely, and Critchfield, and a brilliant array of European diplomats. Smurch did not, in fact, come to in time to take part in the gigantic hullabaloo arranged at City Hall for the next day. He was rushed to a secluded nursing home and confined to bed. It was nine days before he was able to get up, or to be more exact, before he was permitted to get up. Meanwhile the greatest minds in the country, in solemn assembly, had arranged a secret conference of city, state and government officials, which Smurch was to attend for the purpose of being instructed in the ethics and behavior of heroism.

On the day that the little mechanic was finally allowed to get up and dress and, for the first time in two weeks, took a great chew of tobacco, he was permitted to receive the newspapermen—this by way of testing him out. Smurch did not wait for questions. "Youse guys," he said—and the *Times* man winced— "youse guys can tell the cock-eyed world dat I put it over on Lindbergh, see? Yes—an' made an ass o' them two frogs." The "two frogs" was a reference to a pair of gallant French fliers who, in attempting a flight only halfway round the world, had, two weeks before, unhappily been lost at sea. The *Times* man was bold enough, at this point, to sketch out for Smurch the accepted formula for interviews in cases of this kind; he explained that there should be no arrogant statements belittling the achievements of other heroes, particularly heroes of foreign nations. "Ah, the hell with that," said Smurch. "I did it, see? I did it, an' I'm talkin' about it." And he did talk about it.

None of this extraordinary interview was, of course, printed. On the contrary, the newspapers, already under the disciplined direction of a secret directorate created for the occasion and composed of statesmen and editors, gave out to a panting and restless world that "Jacky," as he had been arbitrarily nicknamed, would consent to say only that he was very happy and that anyone could have done what he did. "My achievement has been, I fear, slightly exaggerated," the *Times* man's article had him protest, with a modest smile. These newspaper stories were kept from the hero, a restriction which did not serve to abate the rising malevolence of his temper. The situation was, indeed, extremely grave, for Pal Smurch was, as he kept insisting, "rarin' to go." He could not much longer be kept from a nation clamorous to lionize him. It was the most desperate crisis the United States of America had faced since the sinking of the *Lusitania.*

On the afternoon of the twenty-seventh of July, Smurch was spirited away to a conference-room in which were gathered mayors, governors, government officials, behaviorist psychologists, and editors. He gave them each a limp, moist paw and a brief unlovely grin. "Hah ya?" he said. When Smurch was seated, the Mayor of New York arose and, with obvious pessimism, attempted to explain what he must say and how he must act when presented to the world, ending his talk with a high tribute to the hero's courage and integrity. The Mayor was followed by Governor Fanniman of New York, who, after a touching declaration of faith, introduced Cameron Spottiswood, Second Secretary of the American Embassy in Paris, the gentleman selected to coach Smurch in the amenities of public ceremonies. Sitting in a chair, with a soiled yellow tie in his hand and his shirt open at the throat, unshaved, smoking a rolled cigarette, Jack Smurch listened with a leer on his lips. "I get ya, I get ya," he cut in nastily. "Ya want me to ack like a softy, huh? Ya want me to ack like that—baby-faced Lindbergh, huh? Well, nuts to that, see?" Everyone took in his breath sharply; it was a sigh and a hiss. "Mr. Lindbergh," began a United States Senator, purple with rage, "and Mr. Byrd—" Smurch, who was paring his nails with a jackknife, cut in again. "Byrd!" he exclaimed. "Aw fa God's sake, dat big—" Somebody shut off his blasphemies with a sharp word. A newcomer had entered the room. Everyone stood up, except Smurch, who, still busy with his nails, did not even glance up. "Mr. Smurch," said someone sternly, "the President of the United States!" It had been thought that the presence of the Chief Executive might have a chastening effect upon the young hero, and the former had been, thanks to the remarkable co-operation of the press, secretly brought to the obscure conference-room.

A great, painful silence fell. Smurch looked up, waved a hand at the President. "How ya comin'?" he asked, and began rolling a fresh cigarette. The silence deepened. Someone coughed in a strained way. "Geez, it's hot, ain't it?" said Smurch. He loosened two more shirt buttons, revealing a hairy chest and the tattooed word "Sadie" enclosed in a stenciled heart. The great and important men in the room, faced by the most serious crisis in recent American history, exchanged worried frowns. Nobody seemed to know how to proceed.

"Come awn, come awn," said Smurch. "Let's get the hell out of here! When do I start cuttin' in on de parties, huh? And what's they goin' to be *in* it?" He rubbed a thumb and a forefinger together meaningly. "Money!" exclaimed a state senator, shocked, pale. "Yeh, money," said Pal, flipping his cigarette out of a window, "an' big money." He began rolling a fresh cigarette. "Big money," he repeated, frowning over the rice paper. He tilted back in his chair, and leered at each gentleman, separately, the leer of an animal that knows its power, the leer of a leopard loose in a bird-and-dog shop. "Aw, fa God's sake, let's get some place where it's cooler," he said. "I been cooped up plenty for three weeks!"

Smurch stood up and walked over to an open window, where he stood staring down into the street, nine floors below. The faint shouting of newsboys floated up to him. He made out his name. "Hot dog!" he cried, grinning, ecstatic. He leaned out over the sill. "You tell 'em, babies!" he shouted down. "Hot diggity dog!" In the tense little knot of men standing behind him, a quick, mad impulse flared up. An unspoken word of appeal, of command, seemed to ring through the room. Yet it was deadly silent. Charles K. L. Brand, secretary to the Mayor of New York City, happened to be standing nearest Smurch; he looked inquiringly at the President of the United States. The President, pale, grim, nodded shortly. Brand, a tall, powerfully built man, once a tackle at Rutgers, stepped forward, seized the greatest man in the world by his left shoulder and the seat of his pants, and pushed him out of the window.

"My God, he's fallen out the window!" cried a quick-witted editor.

"Get me out of here!" cried the President. Several men sprang to his side and 15 he was hurriedly escorted out of a door toward a side-entrance to the building. The editor of the Associated Press took charge, being used to such things. Crisply he ordered certain men to leave, others to stay; quickly he outlined a story which all the papers were to agree on, sent two men to the street to handle that end of the tragedy, commanded a Senator to sob and two Congressmen to go to pieces nervously. In a word, he skillfully set the stage for the gigantic task that was to follow, the task of breaking to a grief-stricken world the sad story of the untimely, accidental death of its most illustrious and spectacular figure.

The funeral was, as you know, the most elaborate, the finest, the solemnest, and the saddest ever held in the United States of America. The monument in Arlington Cemetery, with its clean white shaft of marble and the simple device of a tiny plane carved on its base, is a place for pilgrims, in deep reverence, to visit. The nations of the world paid lofty tributes to little Jacky Smurch, America's greatest hero. At a given hour there were two minutes of silence throughout the nation. Even the inhabitants of the small, bewildered town of Westfield, Iowa, observed this touching ceremony; agents of the Department of Justice saw to that. One of them was especially assigned to stand grimly in the doorway of a little shack restaurant on the edge of the tourists' camping ground just outside the town. There, under his stern scrutiny, Mrs. Emma Smurch bowed her head above two hamburger steaks sizzling on her grill—bowed her head and turned away, so that the Secret Service man could not see the twisted, strangely familiar, leer on her lips.

For Analysis

1. In what respects is Smurch a typical American hero? In what respects is he not?
2. Could it be argued that Jack Smurch is a distinctively modern hero? How does he compare to heroes of earlier eras? **3.** What connotations does the name "Smurch" evoke? **4.** Why does the government feel compelled to get rid of Smurch?

On Style

How does the contrast between the formal, rather elevated narrative style and the subject of the story, Jack ("Pal") Smurch, help create the comic **tone**?

Making Connections

1. Compare Smurch and Jack Potter in Stephen Crane's "The Bride Comes to Yellow Sky" (p. 72) as heroes. **2.** Compare Everett C. Marm in Ellison's " 'Repent, Harlequin!' Said the Ticktockman" (p. 395) and Pal Smurch as heroes. Which do you find more admirable and heroic? In what ways are the names they bear appropriate?

Writing Topics

1. Use Thurber's story as the basis for a discussion of the nature and responsibilities of heroes in America. **2.** Write an essay arguing for or against the assertion that in contrast to the America Thurber writes about in this story, a Pal Smurch today would not represent a public and official problem.

Richard Wright   [1908–1960]

The Man Who Lived Underground   1944

I've got to hide, he told himself. His chest heaved as he waited, crouching in a dark corner of the vestibule. He was tired of running and dodging. Either he had to find a place to hide, or he had to surrender. A police car swished by through the rain, its siren rising sharply. They're looking for me all over . . . He crept to the door and squinted through the fogged plate glass. He stiffened as the siren rose and died in the distance. Yes, he had to hide, but where? He gritted his teeth. Then a sudden movement in the street caught his attention. A throng of tiny columns of water snaked into the air from the perforations of a manhole cover. The columns stopped abruptly, as though the perforations had become clogged; a gray spout of sewer water jutted up from underground and lifted the circular metal cover, juggled it for a moment, then let it fall with a clang.

He hatched a tentative plan: he would wait until the siren sounded far off, then he would go out. He smoked and waited, tense. At last the siren gave him his signal; it wailed, dying, going away from him. He stepped to the sidewalk, then paused and looked curiously at the open manhole, half expecting the cover to leap up again. He went to the center of the street and stooped and peered into the hole, but could see nothing. Water rustled in the black depths.

He started with terror; the siren sounded so near that he had the idea that he had been dreaming and had awakened to find the car upon him. He dropped instinctively to his knees and his hands grasped the rim of the manhole. The siren seemed to hoot directly above him and with a wild gasp of exertion he snatched the cover far enough off to admit his body. He swung his legs over the opening and lowered himself into watery darkness. He hung for an eternal moment to the rim by his finger tips, then he felt rough metal prongs and at once, he knew that sewer workmen used these ridges to lower themselves into manholes. Fist over fist, he let his body sink until he could feel no more prongs. He swayed in dank space; the siren seemed to howl at the very rim of the manhole. He dropped and was washed violently into an ocean of warm, leaping water. His head was battered against a wall and he wondered if this were death. Frenziedly his fingers clawed and sank into a crevice. He steadied himself and measured the strength of the current with his own muscular tension. He stood slowly in water that dashed past his knees with fearful velocity.

He heard a prolonged scream of brakes and the siren broke off. Oh, God! They had found him! Looming above his head in the rain a white face hovered over the hole. "How did this damn thing get off?" he heard a policeman ask. He saw the steel cover move slowly until the hole looked like a quarter moon turned black.

351

"Give me a hand here," someone called. The cover clanged into place, muffling the sights and sounds of the upper world. Knee-deep in the pulsing current, he breathed with aching chest, filling his lungs with the hot stench of yeasty rot.

From the perforations of the manhole cover, delicate lances of hazy violet sifted down and wove a mottled pattern upon the surface of the streaking current. His lips parted as a car swept past along the wet pavement overhead, its heavy rumble soon dying out, like the hum of a plane speeding through a dense cloud. He had never thought that cars could sound like that; everything seemed strange and unreal under here. He stood in darkness for a long time, knee-deep in rustling water, musing.

The odor of rot had become so general that he no longer smelled it. He got his cigarettes, but discovered that his matches were wet. He searched and found a dry folder in the pocket of his shirt and managed to strike one; it flared weirdly in the wet gloom, glowing greenishly, turning red, orange, then yellow. He lit a crumpled cigarette; then, by the flickering light of the match, he looked for support so that he would not have to keep his muscles flexed against the pouring water. His pupils narrowed and he saw to either side of him two steaming walls that rose and curved inward some six feet above his head to form a dripping, mouse-colored dome. The bottom of the sewer was a sloping V-trough. To the left, the sewer vanished in ashen fog. To the right was a deep down-curve into which water plunged.

He saw now that had he not regained his feet in time, he would have been swept to death, or had he entered any other manhole he would have probably drowned. Above the rush of the current he heard sharper juttings of water; tiny streams were spewing into the sewer from smaller conduits. The match died; he struck another and saw a mass of debris sweep past him and clog the throat of the down-curve. At once the water began rising rapidly. Could he climb out before he drowned? A long hiss sounded and the debris was sucked from sight; the current lowered. He understood now what had made the water toss the manhole cover; the down-curve had become temporarily obstructed and the perforations had become clogged.

He was in danger; he might slide into a down-curve; he might wander with a lighted match into a pocket of gas and blow himself up; or he might contract some horrible disease . . . Though he wanted to leave, an irrational impulse held him rooted. To the left, the convex ceiling swooped to a height of less than five feet. With cigarette slanting from pursed lips, he waded with taut muscles, his feet sloshing over the slimy bottom, his shoes sinking into spongy slop, the slate-colored water cracking in creamy foam against his knees. Pressing flat his left palm against the lowered ceiling, he struck another match and saw a metal pole nestling in a niche of the wall. Yes, some sewer workman had left it. He reached for it, then jerked his head away as a whisper of scurrying life whisked past and was still. He held the match close and saw a huge rat, wet with slime, blinking beady eyes and baring tiny fangs. The light blinded the rat and the frizzled head moved aimlessly. He grabbed the pole and let it fly against the rat's soft body; there was shrill piping and the grizzly body splashed into the dun-colored water and was snatched out of sight, spinning in the scuttling stream.

He swallowed and pushed on, following the curve of the misty cavern, sounding the water with the pole. By the faint light of another manhole cover he saw, amid loose wet brick, a hole with walls of damp earth leading into blackness. Gingerly he poked the pole into it; it was hollow and went beyond the length of the pole. He shoved the pole before him, hoisted himself upward, got to his hands and knees, and crawled. After a few yards he paused, struck to wonderment by the silence; it seemed that he had traveled a million miles away from the world. As he inched forward again he could sense the bottom of the dirt tunnel becoming dry and lowering slightly. Slowly he rose and to his astonishment he stood erect. He could not hear the rustling of the water now and he felt confoundingly alone, yet lured by the darkness and silence.

He crept a long way, then stopped, curious, afraid. He put his right foot forward and it dangled in space; he drew back in fear. He thrust the pole outward and it swung in emptiness. He trembled, imagining the earth crumbling and burying him alive. He scratched a match and saw that the dirt floor sheered away steeply and widened into a sort of cave some five feet below him. An old sewer, he muttered. He cocked his head, hearing a feathery cadence which he could not identify. The match ceased to burn.

Using the pole as a kind of ladder, he slid down and stood in darkness. The air was a little fresher and he could still hear vague noises. Where was he? He felt suddenly that someone was standing near him and he turned sharply, but there was only darkness. He poked cautiously and felt a brick wall; he followed it and the strange sounds grew louder. He ought to get out of here. This was crazy. He could not remain here for any length of time; there was no food and no place to sleep. But the faint sounds tantalized him; they were strange but familiar. Was it a motor? A baby crying? Music? A siren? He groped on, and the sounds came so clearly that he could feel the pitch and timbre of human voices. Yes, singing! That was it! He listened with open mouth. It was a church service. Enchanted, he groped toward the waves of melody.

Jesus, take me to your home above
And fold me in the bosom of Thy love . . .

The singing was on the other side of the brick wall. Excited, he wanted to watch the service without being seen. Whose church was it? He knew most of the churches in this area aboveground, but the singing sounded too strange and detached for him to guess. He looked to the left, to the right, down to the black dirt, then upward and was startled to see a bright sliver of light slicing the darkness like the blade of a razor. He struck one of his two remaining matches and saw rusty pipes running along an old concrete ceiling. Photographically he located the exact position of the pipes in his mind. The match flame sank and he sprang upward; his hands clutched a pipe. He swung his legs and tossed his body onto the bed of pipes and they creaked, swaying up and down; he thought that the tier was about to crash, but nothing happened. He edged to the crevice and saw a segment of black men and women, dressed in white robes, singing, holding tattered songbooks in their black palms. His first impulse was to laugh, but he checked himself.

What was he doing? He was crushed with a sense of guilt. Would God strike him dead for that? The singing swept on and he shook his head, disagreeing in spite of himself. They oughtn't to do that, he thought. But he could think of no reason *why* they should not do it. Just singing with the air of the sewer blowing in on them . . . He felt that he was gazing upon something abysmally obscene, yet he could not bring himself to leave.

After a long time he grew numb and dropped to the dirt. Pain throbbed in his legs and a deeper pain, induced by the sight of those black people groveling and begging for something they could never get, churned in him. A vague conviction made him feel that those people should stand unrepentant and yield no quarter in singing and praying, yet *he* had run away from the police, had pleaded with them to believe in *his* innocence. He shook his head, bewildered.

How long had he been down here? He did not know. This was a new kind of living for him; the intensity of feelings he had experienced when looking at the church people sing made him certain that he had been down here a long time, but his mind told him that the time must have been short. In this darkness the only notion he had of time was when a match flared and measured time by its fleeting light. He groped back through the hole toward the sewer and the waves of song subsided and finally he could not hear them at all. He came to where the earth hole ended and he heard the noise of the current and time lived again for him, measuring the moments by the wash of the water.

The rain must have slackened, for the flow of water had lessened and came only to his ankles. Ought he to go up into the streets and take his chances on hiding somewhere else? But they would surely catch him. The mere thought of dodging and running again from the police made him tense. No, he would stay and plot how to elude them. But what could he do down here? He walked forward into the sewer and came to another manhole cover; he stood beneath it, debating. Fine pencils of gold spilled suddenly from the little circles in the manhole cover and trembled on the surface of the current. Yes, street lamps . . . It must be night . . .

He went forward for about a quarter of an hour, wading aimlessly, poking the pole carefully before him. Then he stopped, his eyes fixed and intent. What's that? A strangely familiar image attracted and repelled him. Lit by the yellow stems from another manhole cover was a tiny nude body of a baby snagged by debris and half-submerged in water. Thinking that the baby was alive, he moved impulsively to save it, but his roused feelings told him that it was dead, cold, nothing, the same nothingness he had felt while watching the men and women singing in the church. Water blossomed about the tiny legs, the tiny arms, the tiny head, and rushed onward. The eyes were closed, as though in sleep; the fists were clenched, as though in protest; and the mouth gaped black in a soundless cry.

He straightened and drew in his breath, feeling that he had been staring for all eternity at the ripples of veined water skimming impersonally over the shriveled limbs. He felt as condemned as when the policemen had accused him. Involuntarily he lifted his hand to brush the vision away, but his arm fell listlessly to his side. Then he acted; he closed his eyes and reached forward slowly with the soggy shoe of his right foot and shoved the dead baby from where it had

been lodged. He kept his eyes closed, seeing the little body twisting in the current as it floated from sight. He opened his eyes, shivered, placed his knuckles
in the sockets, hearing the water speed in the somber shadows.

He tramped on, sensing at times a sudden quickening in the current as he
passed some conduit whose waters were swelling the stream that slid by his feet.
A few minutes later he was standing under another manhole cover, listening to
the faint rumble of noises aboveground. Streetcars and trucks, he mused. He
looked down and saw a stagnant pool of gray-green sludge; at intervals a balloon
pocket rose from the scum, glistening a bluish-purple, and burst. Then another.
He turned, shook his head, and tramped back to the dirt cave by the church, his
lips quivering.

Back in the cave, he sat and leaned his back against a dirt wall. His body was   20
trembling slightly. Finally his senses quieted and he slept. When he awakened
he felt stiff and cold. He had to leave this foul place, but leaving meant facing
those policemen who had wrongly accused him. No he could not go back aboveground. He remembered the beating they had given him and how he had
signed his name to a confession, a confession which he had not even read. He
had been too tired when they had shouted at him, demanding that he sign his
name; he had signed it to end his pain.

He stood and groped about in the darkness. The church singing had stopped.
How long had he slept? He did not know. But he felt refreshed and hungry. He
doubled his fist nervously, realizing that he could not make a decision. As he
walked about he stumbled over an old rusty iron pipe. He picked it up and felt
a jagged edge. Yes, there was a brick wall and he could dig into it. What would
he find? Smiling, he groped to the brick wall, sat, and began digging idly into
damp cement. I can't make any noise, he cautioned himself. As time passed he
grew thirsty, but there was no water. He had to kill time or go aboveground. The
cement came out of the wall easily; he extracted four bricks and felt a soft draft
blowing into his face. He stopped, afraid. What was beyond? He waited a long
time and nothing happened; then he began digging again, soundlessly, slowly;
he enlarged the hole and crawled through into a dark room and collided with
another wall. He felt his way to the right; the wall ended and his fingers toyed in
space, like the antennae of an insect.

He fumbled on and his feet struck something hollow, like wood. What's this?
He felt with his fingers. Steps . . . He stooped and pulled off his shoes and
mounted the stairs and saw a yellow chink of light shining and heard a low voice
speaking. He placed his eye to a keyhole and saw the nude waxen figure of a man
stretched out upon a white table. The voice, low-pitched and vibrant, mumbled
indistinguishable words, neither rising nor falling. He craned his neck and
squinted to see the man who was talking, but he could not locate him. Above the
naked figure was suspended a huge glass container filled with a bloodred liquid
from which a white rubber tube dangled. He crouched closer to the door and saw
the tip end of a black object lined with pink satin. A coffin, he breathed. This is
an undertaker's establishment . . . A fine-spun lace of ice covered his body and he
shuddered. A throaty chuckle sounded in the depths of the yellow room.

He turned to leave. Three steps down it occurred to him that a light switch should be nearby; he felt along the wall, found an electric button, pressed it, and a blinding glare smote his pupils so hard that he was sightless, defenseless. His pupils contracted and he wrinkled his nostrils at a peculiar odor. At once he knew that he had been dimly aware of this odor in the darkness, but the light had brought it sharply to his attention. Some kind of stuff they use to embalm, he thought. He went down the steps and saw piles of lumber, coffins, and a long workbench. In one corner was a tool chest. Yes, he could use tools, could tunnel through walls with them. He lifted the lid of the chest and saw nails, a hammer, a crowbar, a screwdriver, a light bulb, and a long length of electric wire. Good! He would lug these back to his cave.

He was about to hoist the chest to his shoulders when he discovered a door behind the furnace. Where did it lead? He tried to open it and found it securely bolted. Using the crowbar so as to make no sound, he pried the door open; it swung on creaking hinges, outward. Fresh air came to his face and he caught the faint roar of faraway sound. Easy now, he told himself. He widened the door and a lump of coal rattled toward him. A coalbin . . . Evidently the door led into another basement. The roaring noise was louder, but he could not identify it. Where was he? He groped slowly over the coal pile, then ranged in darkness over a gritty floor. The roaring noise seemed to come from above him, then below. His fingers followed a wall until he touched a wooden ridge. A door, he breathed.

The noise died to a low pitch; he felt his skin prickle. It seemed that he was playing a game with an unseen person whose intelligence outstripped his. He put his ear to the flat surface of the door. Yes, voices . . . Was this a prize fight stadium? The sound of the voices came near and sharp, but he could not tell if they were joyous or despairing. He twisted the knob until he heard a soft click and felt the springy weight of the door swinging toward him. He was afraid to open it, yet captured by curiosity and wonder. He jerked the door wide and saw on the far side of the basement a furnace glowing red. Ten feet away was still another door, half ajar. He crossed and peered through the door into an empty, high-ceilinged corridor that terminated in a dark complex of shadow. The belling voices rolled about him and his eagerness mounted. He stepped into the corridor and the voices swelled louder. He crept on and came to a narrow stairway leading circularly upward; there was no question but that he was going to ascend those stairs.

Mounting the spiraled staircase, he heard the voices roll in a steady wave, then leap to crescendo, only to die away, but always remaining audible. Ahead of him glowed red letters: E—X—I—T. At the top of the steps he paused in front of a black curtain that fluttered uncertainly. He parted the folds and looked into a convex depth that gleamed with clusters of shimmering lights. Sprawled below him was a stretch of human faces, tilted upward, chanting, whistling, screaming, laughing. Dangling before the faces, high upon a screen of silver, were jerking shadows. A movie, he said with slow laughter breaking from his lips.

He stood in a box in the reserved section of a movie house and the impulse

25

he had had to tell the people in the church to stop their singing seized him. These people were laughing at their lives, he thought with amazement. They were shouting and yelling at the animated shadows of themselves. His compassion fired his imagination and he stepped out of the box, walked out upon thin air, walked on down to the audience; and, hovering in the air just above them, he stretched out his hand to touch them . . . His tension snapped and he found himself back in the box, looking down into the sea of faces. No; it could not be done; he could not awaken them. He sighed. Yes, these people were children, sleeping in their living, awake in their dying.

He turned away, parted the black curtain, and looked out. He saw no one. He started down the white stone steps and when he reached the bottom he saw a man in trim blue uniform coming toward him. So used had he become to being underground that he thought that he could walk past the man, as though he were a ghost. But the man stopped. And he stopped.

"Looking for the men's room, sir?" the man asked, and without waiting for an answer, he turned and pointed. "This way, sir. The first door to your right."

He watched the man turn and walk up the steps and go out of sight. Then he laughed. What a funny fellow! He went back to the basement and stood in the red darkness, watching the glowing embers in the furnace. He went to the sink and turned the faucet and the water flowed in a smooth silent stream that looked like a spout of blood. He brushed the mad image from his mind and began to wash his hands leisurely, looking about for the usual bar of soap. He found one and rubbed it in his palms until a rich lather bloomed in his cupped fingers, like a scarlet sponge. He scrubbed and rinsed his hands meticulously, then hunted for a towel; there was none. He shut off the water, pulled off his shirt, dried his hands on it; when he put it on again he was grateful for the cool dampness that came to his skin. 30

Yes, he was thirsty; he turned on the faucet again, bowled his fingers and when the water bubbled over the brim of his cupped palms, he drank in long, slow swallows. His bladder grew tight; he shut off the water, faced the wall, bent his head, and watched a red stream strike the floor. His nostrils wrinkled against acrid wisps of vapor; though he had tramped in the waters of the sewer, he stepped back from the wall so that his shoes, wet with sewer slime, would not touch his urine.

He heard footsteps and crawled quickly into the coalbin. Lumps rattled noisily. The footsteps came into the basement and stopped. Who was it? Had someone heard him and come down to investigate? He waited, crouching, sweating. For a long time there was silence, then he heard the clang of metal and a brighter glow lit the room. Somebody's tending the furnace, he thought. Footsteps came closer and he stiffened. Looming before him was a white face lined with coal dust, the face of an old man with watery blue eyes. Highlights spotted his gaunt cheekbones, and he held a huge shovel. There was a screechy scrape of metal against stone, and the old man lifted a shovelful of coal and went from sight.

The room dimmed momentarily, then a yellow glare came as coal flared at the furnace door. Six times the old man came to the bin and went to the furnace with shovels of coal, but not once did he lift his eyes. Finally he dropped the shovel, mopped his face with a dirty handkerchief, and sighed: "Wheeew!" He turned slowly and trudged out of the basement, his footsteps dying away.

He stood, and lumps of coal clattered down the pile. He stepped from the bin and was startled to see the shadowy outline of an electric bulb hanging above his head. Why had not the old man turned it on? Oh, yes . . . He understood. The old man had worked here for so long that he had no need for light; he had learned a way of seeing in his dark world, like those sightless worms that inch along underground by a sense of touch.

His eyes fell upon a lunch pail and he was afraid to hope that it was full. He   35
picked it up; it was heavy. He opened it. *Sandwiches!* He looked guiltily around; he was alone. He searched farther and found a folder of matches and a half-empty tin of tobacco; he put them eagerly into his pocket and clicked off the light. With the lunch pail under his arm, he went through the door, groped over the pile of coal, and stood again in the lighted basement of the undertaking establishment. I've got to get those tools, he told himself. And turn off that light. He tiptoed back up the steps and switched off the light; the invisible voice still droned on behind the door. He crept down and, seeing with his fingers, opened the lunch pail and tore off a piece of paper bag and brought out the tin and spilled grains of tobacco into the makeshift concave. He rolled it and wet it with spittle, then inserted one end into his mouth and lit it: he sucked smoke that bit his lungs. The nicotine reached his brain, went out along his arms to his finger tips, down to his stomach, and over all the tired nerves of his body.

He carted the tools to the hole he had made in the wall. Would the noise of the falling chest betray him? But he would have to take a chance; he had to have those tools. He lifted the chest and shoved it; it hit the dirt on the other side of the wall with a loud clatter. He waited, listening; nothing happened. Head first, he slithered through and stood in the cave. He grinned, filled with a cunning idea. Yes, he would now go back into the basement of the undertaking establishment and crouch behind the coal pile and dig another hole. Sure! Fumbling, he opened the tool chest and extracted a crowbar, a screwdriver, and a hammer; he fastened them securely about his person.

With another lumpish cigarette in his flexed lips, he crawled back through the hole and over the coal pile and sat, facing the brick wall. He jabbed with the crowbar and the cement sheered away; quicker than he thought, a brick came loose. He worked an hour; the other bricks did not come easily. He sighed, weak from effort. I ought to rest a little, he thought. I'm hungry. He felt his way back to the cave and stumbled along the wall till he came to the tool chest. He sat upon it, opened the lunch pail, and took out two thick sandwiches. He smelled them. Pork chops . . . His mouth watered. He closed his eyes and devoured a sandwich, savoring the smooth rye bread and juicy meat. He ate rapidly, gulping down lumpy mouthfuls that made him long for water. He ate the other sandwich and found an apple and gobbled that up too, sucking the core till the last trace of flavor was drained from it. Then, like a dog, he ground the meat bones with his teeth, enjoying the salty, tangy marrow. He finished and stretched out full length on the ground and went to sleep. . . .

. . . His body was washed by cold water that gradually turned warm and he was buoyed upon a stream and swept out to sea where waves rolled gently and suddenly he found himself walking upon the water how strange and delightful to walk upon the water and he came upon a nude woman holding a nude baby in her arms and the woman was sinking into the water holding the baby above her head and screaming *help* and he ran over the water to the woman and he reached her just before she went down and he took the baby from her hands and stood watching the breaking bubbles where the woman sank and he called *lady* and still no answer yes dive down there and rescue that woman but he could not take this baby with him and he stooped and laid the baby tenderly upon the surface of the water expecting it to sink but it floated and he leaped into the water and held his breath and strained his eyes to see through the gloomy volume of water but there was no woman and he opened his mouth and called *lady* and the water bubbled and his chest ached and his arms were tired but he could not see the woman and he called again *lady lady* and his feet touched sand at the bottom of the sea and his chest felt as though it would burst and he bent his knees and propelled himself upward and water rushed past him and his head bobbed out and he breathed deeply and looked around where was the baby the baby was gone and he rushed over the water looking for the baby calling *where is it* and the empty sky and sea threw back his voice *where is it* and he began to doubt that he could stand upon the water and then he was sinking and as he struggled the water rushed him downward spinning dizzily and he opened his mouth to call for help and water surged into his lungs and he choked . . .

He groaned and leaped erect in the dark, his eyes wide. The images of terror that thronged his brain would not let him sleep. He rose, made sure that the tools were hitched to his belt, and groped his way to the coal pile and found the rectangular gap from which he had taken the bricks. He took out the crowbar and hacked. Then dread paralyzed him. How long had he slept? Was it day or night now? He had to be careful. Someone might hear him if it were day. He hewed softly for hours at the cement, working silently. Faintly quivering in the air above him was the dim sound of yelling voices. Crazy people, he muttered. They're still there in that movie . . .

Having rested, he found the digging much easier. He soon had a dozen bricks out. His spirits rose. He took out another brick and his fingers fluttered in space. Good! What lay ahead of him? Another basement? He made the hole larger, climbed through, walked over an uneven floor and felt a metal surface. He lighted a match and saw that he was standing behind a furnace in a basement; before him, on the far side of the room, was a door. He crossed and opened it; it was full of odds and ends. Daylight spilled from a window above his head.

Then he was aware of a soft, continuous tapping. What was it? A clock? No, it was louder than a clock and more irregular. He placed an old empty box beneath the window, stood upon it, and looked into an areaway. He eased the window up and crawled through; the sound of the tapping came clearly now. He glanced about; he was alone. Then he looked upward at a series of window ledges. The tapping identified itself. That's a typewriter, he said to himself. It seemed to be coming from just above. He grasped the ridges of a rain pipe and lifted himself upward; through a half-inch opening of window he saw a doorknob about three feet away. No, it was not a doorknob; it was a small circular disk made of stainless steel with many fine markings upon it. He held his breath; an eerie white hand, seemingly detached from its arm, touched the metal knob and whirled it, first to the left, then to the right. It's a safe! . . . Suddenly he could see the dial no more; a huge metal door swung slowly toward him and he was looking into a safe filled with green wads of paper money, rows of coins wrapped in brown paper, and glass jars and boxes of various sizes. His heart quickened. Good Lord! The white hand went in and out of the safe, taking wads of bills and cylinders of coins. The hand vanished and he heard the muffled click of the big door as it closed. Only the steel dial was visible now. The typewriter still tapped in his ears, but he could not see it. He blinked, wondering if what he had seen was real. There was more money in that safe than he had seen in all his life.

As he clung to the rain pipe, a daring idea came to him and he pulled the screwdriver from his belt. If the white hand twirled that dial again, he would be able to see how far to left and right it spun and he would have the combination! His blood tingled. I can scratch the numbers right here, he thought. Holding the pipe with one hand, he made the sharp edge of the screwdriver bite into the brick wall. Yes, he could do it. Now, he was set. Now, he had a reason for staying here in the underground. He waited for a long time, but the white hand did not return. Goddamn! Had he been more alert, he could have counted the twirls and he would have had the combination. He got down and stood in the areaway, sunk in reflection.

How could he get into that room? He climbed back into the basement and saw wooden steps leading upward. Was that the room where the safe stood? Fearing that the dial was now being twirled, he clambered through the window, hoisted himself up the rain pipe, and peered; he saw only the naked gleam of the steel dial. He got down and doubled his fists. Well, he would explore the basement. He returned to the basement room and mounted the steps to the door and squinted through the keyhole; all was dark, but the tapping was still somewhere near, still faint and directionless. He pushed the door in; along one wall of a room was a table piled with radios and electrical equipment. A radio shop, he muttered.

Well, he could rig up a radio in his cave. He found a sack, slid the radio into it, and slung it across his back. Closing the door, he went down the steps and stood again in the basement, disappointed. He had not solved the problem of the steel dial and he was irked. He set the radio on the floor and again hoisted himself through the window and up the rain pipe and squinted; the metal door was swinging shut. Goddamn! He's worked the combination again. If I had been patient, I'd have had it! How could he get into that room? He *had* to get into it. He could jimmy the window, but it would be much better if he could get in without any traces. To the right of him, he calculated, should be the basement of the building that held the safe; therefore, if he dug a hole right *here,* he ought to reach his goal.

He began a quiet scraping; it was hard work, for the bricks were not damp. 45 He eventually got one out and lowered it softly to the floor. He had to be careful; perhaps people were beyond this wall. He extracted a second layer of brick and found still another. He gritted his teeth, ready to quit. I'll dig one more, he resolved. When the next brick came out he felt air blowing into his face. He waited to be challenged, but nothing happened.

He enlarged the hole and pulled himself through and stood in quiet darkness. He scratched a match to flame and saw steps; he mounted and peered through a keyhole; Darkness . . . He strained to hear the typewriter, but there was only silence. Maybe the office had closed? He twisted the knob and swung the door in; a frigid blast made him shiver. In the shadows before him were halves and quarters of hogs and lambs and steers hanging from metal hooks on the low ceiling, red meat encased in folds of cold white fat. Fronting him was frost-coated glass from behind which came indistinguishable sounds. The odor of fresh raw meat sickened him and he backed away. A meat market, he whispered.

He ducked his head, suddenly blinded by light. He narrowed his eyes; the red-white rows of meat were drenched in yellow glare. A man wearing a crimson spotted jacket came in and took down a bloody meat cleaver. He eased the door to, holding it ajar just enough to watch the man, hoping that the darkness in which he stood would keep him from being seen. The man took down a hunk of steer and placed it upon a bloody wooden block and bent forward and whacked with the cleaver. The man's face was hard, square, grim; a jet of mustache smudged his upper lip and a glistening cowlick of hair fell over his left eye. Each time he lifted the cleaver and brought it down upon the meat, he let out a short, deep-chested grunt. After he had cut the meat, he wiped blood off the wooden block with a sticky wad of gunny sack and hung the cleaver upon a hook. His face was proud as he placed the chunk of meat in the crook of his elbow and left.

The door slammed and the light went off; once more he stood in shadow. His tension ebbed. From behind the frosted glass he heard the man's voice: "Forty-eight cents a pound, ma'am." He shuddered, feeling that there was something he had to do. But what? He stared fixedly at the cleaver, then he sneezed and was terrified for fear that the man had heard him. But the door did not open. He took down the cleaver and examined the sharp edge smeared with cold blood. Behind the ice-coated glass a cash register rang with a vibrating, musical tinkle.

Absent-mindedly holding the meat cleaver, he rubbed the glass with his thumb and cleared a spot that enabled him to see into the front of the store. The shop was empty, save for the man who was now putting on his hat and coat. Beyond the front window a wan sun shone in the streets; people passed and now and then a fragment of laughter or the whir of a speeding auto came to him. He peered closer and saw on the right counter of the shop a mosquito netting covering pears, grapes, lemons, oranges, bananas, peaches, and plums. His stomach contracted.

The man clicked out the light and he gritted his teeth, muttering, Don't lock the icebox door . . . The man went through the door of the shop and locked it from the outside. Thank God! Now, he would eat some more! He waited, trembling. The sun died and its rays lingered on in the sky, turning the streets to dusk. He opened the door and stepped inside the shop. In reverse letters across the front window was: NICK'S FRUITS AND MEATS. He laughed, picked up a soft ripe yellow pear and bit into it; juice squirted; his mouth ached as his saliva glands reacted to the acid of the fruit. He ate three pears, gobbled six bananas, and made away with several oranges, taking a bite out of their tops and holding them to his lips and squeezing them as he hungrily sucked the juice.

He found a faucet, turned it on, laid the cleaver aside, pursed his lips under the stream until his stomach felt about to burst. He straightened and belched, feeling satisfied for the first time since he had been underground. He sat upon the floor, rolled and lit a cigarette, his bloodshot eyes squinting against the film of drifting smoke. He watched a patch of sky turn red, then purple; night fell and he lit another cigarette, brooding. Some part of him was trying to remember the world he had left, and another part of him did not want to remember it. Sprawling before him in his mind was his wife, Mrs. Wooten for whom he worked, the three policemen who had picked him up . . . He possessed them now more completely than he had ever possessed them when he had lived aboveground. How this had come about he could not say, but he had no desire to go back to them. He laughed, crushed the cigarette, and stood up.

He went to the front door and gazed out. Emotionally he hovered between the world aboveground and the world underground. He longed to go out, but sober judgment urged him to remain here. Then impulsively he pried the lock loose with one swift twist of the crowbar; the door swung outward. Through the twilight he saw a white man and a white woman coming toward him. He held himself tense, waiting for them to pass; but they came directly to the door and confronted him.

"I want to buy a pound of grapes," the woman said.

Terrified, he stepped back into the store. The white man stood to one side and the woman entered.

"Give me a pound of dark ones," the woman said.

The white man came slowly forward, blinking his eyes.

"Where's Nick?" the man asked.

"Were you just closing?" the woman asked.

"Yes, ma'am," he mumbled. For a second he did not breathe, then he mumbled again: "Yes, ma'am."

"I'm sorry," the woman said.

The street lamps came on, lighting the store somewhat. Ought he run? But that would raise an alarm. He moved slowly, dreamily, to a counter and lifted up a bunch of grapes and showed them to the woman.

"Fine," the woman said. "But isn't that more than a pound?"

He did not answer. The man was staring at him intently.

"Put them in a bag for me," the woman said, fumbling with her purse.

"Yes, ma'am." 65

He saw a pile of paper bags under a narrow ledge; he opened one and put the grapes in.

"Thanks," the woman said, taking the bag and placing a dime in his dark palm.

"Where's Nick?" the man asked again. "At supper?"

"Sir? Yes, sir," he breathed.

They left the store and he stood trembling in the doorway. When they were out of sight, he burst out laughing and crying. A trolley car rolled noisily past and he controlled himself quickly. He flung the dime to the pavement with a gesture of contempt and stepped into the warm night air. A few shy stars trembled above him. The look of things was beautiful, yet he felt a lurking threat. He went to an unattended newsstand and looked at a stack of papers. He saw a headline: HUNT NEGRO FOR MURDER. 70

He felt that someone had slipped up on him from behind and was stripping off his clothes; he looked about wildly, went quickly back into the store, picked up the meat cleaver where he had left it near the sink, then made his way through the icebox to the basement. He stood for a long time, breathing heavily. They know I didn't do anything, he muttered. But how could he prove it? He had signed a confession. Though innocent, he felt guilty, condemned. He struck a match and held it near the steel blade, fascinated and repelled by the dried blotches of blood. Then his fingers gripped the handle of the cleaver with all the strength of his body, he wanted to fling the cleaver from him, but he could not. The match flame wavered and fled; he struggled through the hole and put the cleaver in the sack with the radio. He was determined to keep it for what purpose he did not know.

He was about to leave when he remembered the safe. Where was it? He wanted to give up, but felt that he ought to make one more try. Opposite the last hole he had dug, he tunneled again, plying the crowbar. Once he was so exhausted that he lay on the concrete floor and panted. Finally he made another hole. He wriggled through and his nostrils filled with the fresh smell of coal. He struck a match; yes, the usual steps led upward. He tiptoed to a door and eased it open. A fair-haired white girl stood in front of a steel cabinet, her blue eyes wide upon him. She turned chalky and gave a high-pitched scream. He bounded down the steps and raced to his hole and clambered through, replacing the bricks with nervous haste. He paused, hearing loud voices.

"What's the matter, Alice?"

"A man . . ."

"What man? Where?" 75

"A man was at that door . . ."

"Oh, nonsense!"

"He was looking at me through the door!"

"Aw, you're dreaming."

"I *did* see a man!" 80

The girl was crying now.

"There's nobody here."

Another man's voice sounded.

"What is it, Bob?"

"Alice says she saw a man in here, in that door!" 85

"Let's take a look."

He waited, poised for flight. Footsteps descended the stairs.

"There's nobody down here."

"The window's locked."

"And there's no door." 90

"You ought to fire that dame."

"Oh, I don't know. Women are that way."

"She's too hysterical."

The men laughed. Footsteps sounded again on the stairs. A door slammed. He sighed, relieved that he had escaped. But he had not done what he had set out to do; his glimpse of the room had been too brief to determine if the safe was there. He had to know. Boldly he groped through the hole once more; he reached the steps and pulled off his shoes and tiptoed up and peered through the keyhole. His head accidentally touched the door and it swung silently in a fraction of an inch; he saw the girl bent over the cabinet, her back to him. Beyond her was the safe. He crept back down the steps, thinking exultingly: I found it!

Now he had to get the combination. Even if the window in the areaway was 95 locked and bolted, he could gain entrance when the office closed. He scoured through the holes he had dug and stood again in the basement where he had left the radio and the cleaver. Again he crawled out of the window and lifted himself up the rain pipe and peered. The steel dial showed lonely and bright, reflecting the yellow glow of an unseen light. Resigned to a long wait, he sat and leaned against the wall. From far off came the faint sounds of life aboveground; once he looked with a baffled expression at the dark sky. Frequently he rose and climbed the pipe to see the white hand spin the dial, but nothing happened. He bit his lip with impatience. It was not the money that was luring him, but the mere fact that he could get it with impunity. Was the hand now twirling the dial? He rose and looked, but the white hand was not in sight.

Perhaps it would be better to watch continuously? Yes; he clung to the pipe and watched the dial until his eyes thickened with tears. Exhausted, he stood again in the areaway. He heard a door being shut and he clawed up the pipe and looked. He jerked tense as a vague figure passed in front of him. He stared unblinkingly, hugging the pipe with one hand and holding the screwdriver with the

RICHARD WRIGHT • 365

other, ready to etch the combination upon the wall. His ears caught: *Dong* . . . *Dong* . . . *Dong* . . . *Dong* . . . *Dong* . . . *Dong* . . . *Dong.* . . . Seven o'clock, he whispered. Maybe they were closing now? What kind of a store would be open as late as this? he wondered. Did anyone live in the rear? Was there a night watchman? Perhaps the safe was *already* locked for the night! Goddamn! While he had been eating in that shop, they had locked up everything . . . Then, just as he was about to give up, the white hand touched the dial and turned it once to the right and stopped at six. With quivering fingers, he etched 1—R—6 upon the brick wall with the tip of the screwdriver. The hand twisted the dial twice to the left and stopped at two, and he engraved 2—L—2 upon the wall. The dial was spun four times to the right and stopped at six again: he wrote 4—R—6. The dial rotated three times to the left and was centered straight up and down; he wrote 3—L—0. The door swung open and again he saw the piles of green money and the rows of wrapped coins. I got it, he said grimly.

Then he was stone still, astonished. There were two hands now. A right hand lifted a wad of green bills and deftly slipped it up the sleeve of the left arm. The hands trembled; again the right hand slipped a packet of bills up the left sleeve. He's stealing he said to himself. He grew indignant, as if the money belonged to him. Though *he* had planned to steal the money, he despised and pitied the man. He felt that his stealing the money and the man's stealing were two entirely different things. He wanted to steal the money merely for the sensation involved in getting it, and he had no intention whatever of spending a penny of it; but he knew that the man who was now stealing it was going to spend it, perhaps for pleasure. The huge steel door closed with a soft click.

Though angry, he was somewhat satisfied. The office would close soon. I'll clean the place out, he mused. He imagined the entire office staff cringing with fear; the police would question everyone for a crime they had not committed, just as they had questioned him. And they would have no idea of how the money had been stolen until they discovered the holes he had tunneled in the walls of the basements. He lowered himself and laughed mischievously, with the abandoned glee of an adolescent.

He flattened himself against the wall as the window above him closed with a rasping sound. He looked; somebody was bolting the window securely with a metal screen. That won't help you, he snickered to himself. He clung to the rain pipe until the yellow light in the office went out. He went back into the basement, picked up the sack containing the radio and cleaver, and crawled through the two holes he had dug and groped his way into the basement of the building that held the safe. He moved in slow motion, breathing softly. Be careful now, he told himself. There might be a night watchman . . . In his memory was the combination written in bold white characters as upon a blackboard. Eel-like he squeezed through the last hole and crept up the steps and put his hand on the knob and pushed the door in about three inches. Then his courage ebbed; his imagination wove dangers for him.

Perhaps the night watchman was waiting in there, ready to shoot. He dangled his cap on a forefinger and poked it past the jamb of the door. If anyone fired,   100 they would hit his cap; but nothing happened. He widened the door, holding the crowbar high above his head, ready to beat off an assailant. He stood like that for five minutes; the rumble of a streetcar brought him to himself. He entered the room. Moonlight floated in from a side window. He confronted the safe, then checked himself. Better take a look around first . . . He stepped about and found a closed door. Was the night watchman in there? He opened it and saw a washbowl, a faucet, and a commode. To the left was still another door that opened into a huge dark room that seemed empty; on the far side of that room he made out the shadow of still another door. Nobody's here, he told himself.

He turned back to the safe and fingered the dial; it spun with ease. He laughed and twirled it just for fun. Get to work, he told himself. He turned the dial to the figures he saw on the blackboard of his memory; it was so easy that he felt that the safe had not been locked at all. The heavy door eased loose and he caught hold of the handle and pulled hard, but the door swung open with a slow momentum of its own. Breathless, he gaped at wads of green bills, rows of wrapped coins, curious glass jars full of white pellets, and many oblong green metal boxes. He glanced guiltily over his shoulder; it seemed impossible that someone should not call to him to stop.

They'll be surprised in the morning, he thought. He opened the top of the sack and lifted a wad of compactly tied bills; the money was crisp and new. He admired the smooth, cleancut edges. The fellows in Washington sure know how to make this stuff, he mused. He rubbed the money with his fingers, as though expecting it to reveal hidden qualities. He lifted the wad to his nose and smelled the fresh odor of ink. Just like any other paper, he mumbled. He dropped the wad into the sack and picked up another. Holding the bag, he thought and laughed.

There was in him no sense of possessiveness; he was intrigued with the form and color of the money, with the manifold reactions which he knew that men aboveground held toward it. The sack was one-third full when it occurred to him to examine the denominations of the bills; without realizing it, he had put many wads of one-dollar bills into the sack. Aw, nuts, he said in disgust. Take the big ones . . . He dumped the one-dollar bills onto the floor and swept all the hundred-dollar bills he could find into the sack, then he raked in rolls of coins with crooked fingers.

He walked to a desk upon which sat a typewriter, the same machine which the blond girl had used. He was fascinated by it; never in his life had he used one of them. It was a queer instrument of business, something beyond the rim of his life. Whenever he had been in an office where a girl was typing, he had almost always spoken in whispers. Remembering vaguely what he had seen others do, he inserted a sheet of paper into the machine; it went in lopsided and he did not know how to straighten it. Spelling in a soft diffident voice, he pecked out his name on the keys: *freddaniels.* He looked at it and laughed. He would learn to type correctly one of these days.

Yes, he would take the typewriter too. He lifted the machine and placed it atop the bulk of money in the sack. He did not feel that he was stealing, for the

105

cleaver, the radio, the money, and the typewriter were all on the same level of value, all meant the same thing to him. They were the serious toys of the men who lived in the dead world of sunshine and rain he had left, the world that had condemned him, branded him guilty.

But what kind of a place is this? he wondered. What was in that dark room to his rear? He felt for his matches and found that he had only one left. He leaned the sack against the safe and groped forward into the room, encountering smooth, metallic objects that felt like machines. Baffled, he touched a wall and tried vainly to locate an electric switch. Well, he *had* to strike his last match. He knelt and struck it, cupping the flame near the floor with his palms. The place seemed to be a factory, with benches and tables. There were bulbs with green shades spaced about the tables; he turned on a light and twisted it low so that the glare was limited. He saw a half-filled packet of cigarettes and appropriated it. There were stools at the benches and he concluded that men worked here at some trade. He wandered and found a few half-used folders of matches. If only he could find more cigarettes! But there were none.

But what kind of a place was this? On a bench he saw a pad of paper captioned: PEER'S—MANUFACTURING JEWELERS. His lips formed an "O," then he snapped off the light and ran back to the safe and lifted one of the glass jars and stared at the tiny white pellets. Gingerly he picked up one and found that it was wrapped in tissue paper. He peeled the paper and saw a glittering stone that looked like glass, glinting white and blue sparks. Diamonds, he breathed.

Roughly he tore the paper from the pellets and soon his palm quivered with precious fire. Trembling, he took all four glass jars from the safe and put them into the sack. He grabbed one of the metal boxes, shook it, and heard a tinny rattle. He pried off the lid with the screwdriver. Rings! Hundreds of them . . . Were they worth anything? He scooped up a handful and jets of fire shot fitfully from the stones. These are diamonds too, he said. He pried open another box. Watches! A chorus of soft, metallic ticking filled his ears. For a moment he could not move, then he dumped all the boxes into the sack.

He shut the safe door, then stood looking around, anxious not to overlook anything. Oh! He had seen a door in the room where the machines were. What was in there? More valuables? He re-entered the room, crossed the floor, and stood undecided before the door. He finally caught hold of the knob and pushed the door in; the room beyond was dark. He advanced cautiously inside and ran his fingers along the wall for the usual switch, then he was stark still. *Something had moved in the room!* What was it? Ought he to creep out, taking the rings and diamonds and money? Why risk what he already had? He waited and the ensuing silence gave him confidence to explore further. Dare he strike a match? Would not a match flame make him a good target? He tensed again as he heard a faint sigh; he was now convinced that there was something alive near him, something that lived and breathed. On tiptoe he felt slowly along the wall, hoping that he would not collide with anything. Luck was with him; he found the light switch.

No; don't turn the light on . . . Then suddenly he realized that he did not 110
know in what direction the door was. Goddamn! He had to turn the light on or
strike a match. He fingered the switch for a long time, then thought of an idea.
He knelt upon the floor, reached his arm up to the switch and flicked the button, hoping that if anyone shot, the bullet would go above his head. The moment the light came on he narrowed his eyes to see quickly. He sucked in his
breath and his body gave a violent twitch and was still. In front of him, so close
that it made him want to bound up and scream, was a human face.

He was afraid to move lest he touch the man. If the man had opened his eyes
at that moment, there was no telling what he might have done. The man—long
and rawboned—was stretched out on his back upon a little cot, sleeping in his
clothes, his head cushioned by a dirty pillow; his face, clouded by a dark stubble
of beard, looked straight up to the ceiling. The man sighed, and he grew tense
to defend himself; the man mumbled and turned his face away from the light.
I've got to turn off that light, he thought. Just as he was about to rise, he saw a
gun and cartridge belt on the floor at the man's side. Yes, he would take the gun
and cartridge belt, not to use them, but just to keep them, as one takes a memento from a country fair. He picked them up and was about to click off the
light when his eyes fell upon a photograph perched upon a chair near the man's
head; it was the picture of a woman, smiling, shown against a background of
open fields; at the woman's side were two young children, a boy and a girl. He
smiled indulgently; he could send a bullet into that man's brain and time would
be over for him. . . .

He clicked off the light and crept silently back into the room where the safe
stood; he fastened the cartridge belt about him and adjusted the holster at his
right hip. He strutted about the room on tiptoe, lolling his head nonchalantly,
then paused, abruptly pulled the gun, and pointed it with grim face toward an
imaginary foe. "Boom!" he whispered fiercely. Then he bent forward with silent
laughter. That's just like they do it in the movies, he said.

He contemplated his loot for a long time, then got a towel from the washroom and tied the sack securely. When he looked up he was momentarily frightened by his shadow looming on the wall before him. He lifted the sack, dragged
it down the basement steps, lugged it across the basement, gasping for breath.
After he had struggled through the hole, he clumsily replaced the bricks, then
tussled with the sack until he got it to the cave. He stood in the dark, wet with
sweat, brooding about the diamonds, the rings, the watches, the money; he remembered the singing in the church, the people yelling in the movie, the dead
baby, the nude man stretched out upon the white table . . . He saw these items
hovering before his eyes and felt that some dim meaning linked them together,
that some magical relationship made them kin. He stared with vacant eyes, convinced that all of these images, with their tongueless reality, were striving to tell
him something . . .

Later, seeing with his fingers, he untied the sack and set each item neatly
upon the dirt floor. Exploring, he took the bulb, the socket, and the wire out of
the tool chest; he was elated to find a double socket at one end of the wire. He

crammed the stuff into his pockets and hoisted himself upon the rusty pipes and squinted into the church; it was dim and empty. Somewhere in this wall were live electric wires; but where? He lowered himself, groped and tapped the wall with the butt of the screwdriver, listening vainly for hollow sounds. I'll just take a chance and dig, he said.

For an hour he tried to dislodge a brick, and when he struck a match, he found that he had dug a depth of only an inch! No use in digging here, he sighed. By the flickering light of a match, he looked upward, then lowered his eyes, only to glance up again, startled. Directly above his head, beyond the pipes, was a wealth of electric wiring. I'll be damned, he snickered.

He got an old dull knife from the chest and, seeing again with his fingers, separated the two strands of wire and cut away the insulation. Twice he received a slight shock. He scraped the wiring clean and managed to join the two twin ends, then screwed in the bulb. The sudden illumination blinded him and he shut his lids to kill the pain in his eyeballs. I've got that much done, he thought jubilantly.

He placed the bulb on the dirt floor and the light cast a blatant glare on the bleak clay walls. Next he plugged one end of the wire that dangled from the radio into the light socket and bent down and switched on the button; almost at once there was the harsh sound of static, but no words or music. Why won't it work? he wondered. Had he damaged the mechanism in any way? Maybe it needed grounding? Yes . . . He rummaged in the tool chest and found another length of wire, fastened it to the ground of the radio, and then tied the opposite end to a pipe. Rising and growing distinct, a slow strain of music entranced him with its measured sound. He sat upon the chest, deliriously happy.

Later he searched again in the chest and found a half-gallon can of glue; he opened it and smelled a sharp odor. Then he recalled that he had not even looked at the money. He took a wad of green bills and weighed it in his palm, then broke the seal and held one of the bills up to the light and studied it closely. *The United States of America will pay to the bearer on demand one hundred dollars,* he read in slow speech; then: *This note is legal tender for all debts, public and private . . .* He broke into a musing laugh, feeling that he was reading of the doings of people who lived on some far-off planet. He turned the bill over and saw on the other side of it a delicately beautiful building gleaming with paint and set amidst green grass. He had no desire whatever to count the money; it was what it stood for—the various currents of life swirling above-ground—that captivated him. Next he opened the rolls of coins and let them slide from their paper wrappings to the ground; the bright, new gleaming pennies and nickels and dimes piled high at his feet, a glowing mound of shimmering copper and silver. He sifted them through his fingers, listening to their tinkle as they struck the conical heap.

Oh, yes! He had forgotten. He would now write his name on the typewriter. He inserted a piece of paper and poised his fingers to write. But what was his name? He stared, trying to remember. He stood and glared about the dirt cave, his name on the tip of his lips. But it would not come to him. Why was he here?

115

Yes, he had been running away from the police. But why? His mind was blank. He bit his lips and sat again, feeling a vague terror. But why worry? He laughed, then pecked slowly: *itwasalonghotday.* He was determined to type the sentence without making any mistakes. How did one make capital letters? He experimented and luckily discovered how to lock the machine for capital letters and then shift it back to lower case. Next he discovered how to make spaces, then he wrote neatly and correctly: *It was a long hot day.* Just why he selected that sentence he did not know; it was merely the ritual of performing the thing that appealed to him. He took the sheet out of the machine and looked around with stiff neck and hard eyes and spoke to an imaginary person:

"Yes, I'll have the contracts ready tomorrow." 120

He laughed. That's just the way they talk, he said. He grew weary of the game and pushed the machine aside. His eyes fell upon the can of glue, and a mischievous idea bloomed in him, filling him with nervous eagerness. He leaped up and opened the can of glue, then broke the seals on all the wads of money. I'm going to have some wallpaper, he said with a luxurious, physical laugh that made him bend at the knees. He took the towel with which he had tied the sack and balled it into a swab and dipped it into the can of glue and dabbed glue onto the wall; then he pasted one green bill by the side of another. He stepped back and cocked his head. Jesus! That's funny . . . He slapped his thighs and guffawed. He had triumphed over the world aboveground! He was free! If only people could see this! He wanted to run from this cave and yell his discovery to the world.

He swabbed all the dirt walls of the cave and pasted them with green bills; when he had finished the walls blazed with a yellow-green fire. Yes, this room would be his hide-out; between him and the world that had branded him guilty would stand this mocking symbol. He had not stolen the money; he had simply picked it up, just as a man would pick up firewood in a forest. And that was how the world aboveground now seemed to him, a wild forest filled with death.

The walls of money finally palled on him and he looked about for new interests to feed his emotions. The cleaver! He drove a nail into the wall and hung the bloody cleaver upon it. Still another idea welled up. He pried open the metal boxes and lined them side by side on the dirt floor. He grinned at the gold and fire. From one box he lifted up a fistful of ticking gold watches and dangled them by their gleaming chains. He stared with an idle smile, then began to wind them up; he did not attempt to set them at any given hour, for there was no time for him now. He took a fistful of nails and drove them into the papered walls and hung the watches upon them, letting them swing down by their glittering chains, trembling and ticking busily against the backdrop of green with the lemon sheen of the electric light shining upon the metal watch casings, converting the golden disks into blobs of liquid yellow. Hardly had he hung up the last watch than the idea extended itself; he took more nails from the chest and drove them into the green paper and took the boxes of rings and went from nail to nail and hung up the golden bands. The blue and white sparks from the stones filled the cave with brittle laughter, as though enjoying his hilarious secret. People certainly can do some funny things, he said to himself.

He sat upon the tool chest, alternately laughing and shaking his head soberly.

Hours later he became conscious of the gun sagging at his hip and he pulled it from the holster. He had seen men fire guns in movies, but somehow his life had never led him into contact with firearms. A desire to feel the sensation others felt in firing came over him. But someone might hear . . . Well, what if they did? They would not know where the shot had come from. Not in their wildest notions would they think that it had come from under the streets! He tightened his fingers on the trigger; there was a deafening report and it seemed that the entire underground had caved in upon his eardrums; and in the same instant there flashed an orange-blue spurt of flame that died quickly but lingered on as a vivid after-image. He smelled the acrid stench of burnt powder filling his lungs and he dropped the gun abruptly.

The intensity of his feelings died and he hung the gun and cartridge belt upon the wall. Next he lifted the jars of diamonds and turned them bottom upward, dumping the white pellets upon the ground. One by one he picked them up and peeled the tissue paper from them and piled them in a neat heap. He wiped his sweaty hands on his trousers, lit a cigarette, and commenced playing another game. He imagined that he was a rich man who lived aboveground in the obscene sunshine and he was strolling through a park of a summer morning, smiling, nodding to his neighbors, sucking an after-breakfast cigar. Many times he crossed the floor of the cave, avoiding the diamonds with his feet, yet subtly gauging his footsteps so that his shoes, wet with sewer slime, would strike the diamonds at some undetermined moment. After twenty minutes of sauntering, his right foot smashed into the heap and diamonds lay scattered in all directions, glinting with a million tiny chuckles of icy laughter. Oh, shucks, he mumbled in mock regret, intrigued by the damage he had wrought. He continued walking, ignoring the brittle fire. He felt that he had a glorious victory locked in his heart.

He stooped and flung the diamonds more evenly over the floor and they showered rich sparks, collaborating with him. He went over the floor and trampled the stones just deeply enough for them to be faintly visible, as though they were set deliberately in the prongs of a thousand rings. A ghostly light bathed the cave. He sat on the chest and frowned. Maybe *any*thing's right, he mumbled. Yes, if the world as men had made it was right, then anything else was right, any act a man took to satisfy himself, murder, theft, torture.

He straightened with a start. What was happening to him? He was drawn to these crazy thoughts, yet they made him feel vaguely guilty. He would stretch out upon the ground, then get up; he would want to crawl again through the holes he had dug, but would restrain himself; he would think of going up into the streets, but fear would hold him still. He stood in the middle of the cave, surrounded by green walls and a laughing floor, trembling. He was going to do something, but what? Yes, he was afraid of himself, afraid of doing some nameless thing.

To control himself, he turned on the radio. A melancholy piece of music rose. Brooding over the diamonds on the floor was like looking up into a sky full of restless stars; then the illusion turned into its opposite: he was high up in the air looking down at the twinkling lights of a sprawling city. The music ended and a man recited news events. In the same attitude in which he had contemplated the city,

125

so now, as he heard the cultivated tone, he looked down upon land and sea as men fought, as cities were razed, as planes scattered death upon open towns, as long lines of trenches wavered and broke. He heard the names of generals and the names of mountains and the names of countries and the names and numbers of divisions that were in action on different battle fronts. He saw black smoke billowing from the stacks of warships as they neared each other over wastes of water and he heard their huge thunder as red-hot shells screamed across the surface of night seas. He saw hundreds of planes wheeling and droning in the sky and heard the clatter of machine guns as they fought each other and he saw planes falling in plumes of smoke and a blaze of fire. He saw steel tanks rumbling across fields of ripe wheat to meet other tanks and there was a loud clang of steel as numberless tanks collided. He saw troops with fixed bayonets charging in waves against other troops who held fixed bayonets and men groaned as steel ripped into their bodies and they went down to die . . . The voice of the radio faded and he was staring at the diamonds on the floor at his feet.

He shut off the radio, fighting an irrational compulsion to act. He walked aimlessly about the cave, touching the walls with his finger tips. Suddenly he stood still. *What was the matter with him?* Yes, he knew . . . It was these walls; these crazy walls were filling him with a wild urge to climb out into the dark sunshine aboveground. Quickly he doused the light to banish the shouting walls, then sat again upon the tool chest. Yes, he was trapped. His muscles were flexed taut and sweat ran down his face. He knew now that he could not stay here and he could not go out. He lit a cigarette with shaking fingers; the match flame revealed the green-papered walls with militant distinctness; the purple on the gun barrel glinted like a threat; the meat cleaver brooded with its eloquent splotches of blood; the mound of silver and copper smoldered angrily; the diamonds winked at him from the floor, and the gold watches ticked and trembled, crowning time the king of consciousness, defining the limits of living . . . The match blaze died and he bolted from where he stood and collided brutally with the nails upon the walls. The spell was broken. He shuddered, feeling that, in spite of his fear, sooner or later he would go up into that dead sunshine and somehow say something to somebody about all this.

He sat again upon the tool chest. Fatigue weighed upon his forehead and eyes. Minutes passed and he relaxed. He dozed, but his imagination was alert. He saw himself rising, wading again in the sweeping water of the sewer; he came to a manhole and climbed out and was amazed to discover that he hoisted himself into a room filled with armed policemen who were watching him intently. He jumped awake in the dark; he had not moved. He sighed, closed his eyes, and slept again; this time his imagination designed a scheme of protection for him. His dreaming made him feel that he was standing in a room watching over his own nude body lying stiff and cold upon a white table. At the far end of the room he saw a crowd of people huddled in a corner, afraid of his body. Though lying dead upon the table, he was standing in some mysterious way at his side, warding off the people, guarding his body, and laughing to himself as he observed the situation. They're scared of me, he thought.

130

He awakened with a start, leaped to his feet, and stood in the center of the black cave. It was a full minute before he moved again. He hovered between sleeping and waking, unprotected, a prey of wild fears. He could neither see nor hear. One part of him was asleep; his blood coursed slowly and his flesh was numb. On the other hand he was roused to a strange, high pitch of tension. He lifted his fingers to his face, as though about to weep. Gradually his hands lowered and he struck a match, looking about, expecting to see a door through which he could walk to safety; but there was no door, only the green walls and the moving floor. The match flame died and it was dark again.

Five minutes later he was still standing when the thought came to him that he had been asleep. Yes . . . But he was not yet fully awake; he was still queerly blind and deaf. How long had he slept? Where was he? Then suddenly he recalled the green-papered walls of the cave and in the same instant he heard loud singing coming from the church beyond the wall. Yes, they woke me up, he muttered. He hoisted himself and lay atop the bed of pipes and brought his face to the narrow slit. Men and women stood here and there between pews. A song ended and a young black girl tossed back her head and closed her eyes and broke plaintively into another hymn:

Glad, glad, glad, oh, so glad
I got Jesus in my soul . . .

Those few words were all she sang, but what her words did not say, her emotions said as she repeated the lines, varying the mood and tempo, making her tone express meanings which her conscious mind did not know. Another woman melted her voice with the girl's, and then an old man's voice merged with that of the two women. Soon the entire congregation was singing:

Glad, glad, glad, oh, so glad
I got Jesus in my soul . . .

They're wrong, he whispered in the lyric darkness. He felt that their search for a happiness they could never find made them feel that they had committed some dreadful offense which they could not remember or understand. He was now in possession of the feeling that had gripped him when he had first come into the underground. It came to him in a series of questions: Why was this sense of guilt so seemingly innate, so easy to come by, to think, to feel, so verily physical? It seemed that when one felt this guilt one was retracing in one's feelings a faint pattern designed long before; it seemed that one was always trying to remember a gigantic shock that had left a haunting impression upon one's body which one could not forget or shake off, but which had been forgotten by the conscious mind, creating in one's life a state of eternal anxiety.

He had to tear himself away from this; he got down from the pipes. His 135 nerves were so taut that he seemed to feel his brain pushing through his skull. He felt that he had to do something, but he could not figure out what it was. Yet he knew that if he stood here until he made up his mind, he would never move. He crawled through the hole he had made in the brick wall and the exertion afforded him respite from tension. When he entered the basement of the radio store, he stopped in fear, hearing loud voices.

"Come on, boy! Tell us what you did with the radio!"

"Mister, I didn't steal the radio! I swear!"

He heard a dull thumping sound and he imagined a boy being struck violently.

"Please, mister!"

"Did you take it to a pawn shop?"   140

"No, sir! I didn't steal the radio! I got a radio at home," the boy's voice pleaded hysterically. "Go to my home and look!"

There came to his ears the sound of another blow. It was so funny that he had to clap his hand over his mouth to keep from laughing out loud. They're beating some poor boy, he whispered to himself, shaking his head. He felt a sort of distant pity for the boy and wondered if he ought to bring back the radio and leave it in the basement. No. Perhaps it was a good thing that they were beating the boy; perhaps the beating would bring to the boy's attention, for the first time in his life, the secret of his existence, the guilt that he could never get rid of.

Smiling, he scampered over a coal pile and stood again in the basement of the building where he had stolen the money and jewelry. He lifted himself into the areaway, climbed the rain pipe, and squinted through a two-inch opening of window. The guilty familiarity of what he saw made his muscles tighten. Framed before him in a bright tableau of daylight was the night watchman sitting upon the edge of a chair, stripped to the waist, his head sagging forward, his eyes red and puffy. The watchman's face and shoulders were stippled with red and black welts. Back of the watchman stood the safe, the steel door wide open showing the empty vault. Yes, they think he did it, he mused.

Footsteps sounded in the room and a man in a blue suit passed in front of him, then another, then still another. Policemen, he breathed. Yes, they were trying to make the watchman confess, just as they had once made him confess to a crime he had not done. He stared into the room, trying to recall something. Oh . . . Those were the same policemen who had beaten him, had made him sign that paper when he had been too tired and sick to care. Now, they were doing the same thing to the watchman. His heart pounded as he saw one of the policemen shake a finger into the watchman's face.

"Why don't you admit it's an inside job, Thompson?" the policeman said.   145

"I've told you all I know," the watchman mumbled through swollen lips.

"But nobody was here but you!" the policeman shouted.

"I was sleeping," the watchman said. "It was wrong, but I was sleeping all that night!"

"Stop telling us that lie!"

"It's the truth!"   150

"When did you get the combination?"

"I don't know how to open the safe," the watchman said.

He clung to the rain pipe, tense; he wanted to laugh, but he controlled himself. He felt a great sense of power; yes, he could go back to the cave, rip the money off the walls, pick up the diamonds and rings, and bring them here and write a note, telling them where to look for their foolish toys. No . . . What good would that do? It was not worth the effort. The watchman was guilty; although he was not guilty of the crime of which he had been accused, he was guilty, had always been guilty. The only thing that worried him was that the man who had been really stealing was not being accused. But he consoled himself: they'll catch him sometime during his life.

He saw one of the policemen slap the watchman across the mouth.

"Come clean, you bastard!"   155

"I've told you all I know," the watchman mumbled like a child.

One of the police went to the rear of the watchman's chair and jerked it from under him; the watchman pitched forward upon his face.

"Get up!" a policeman said.

Trembling, the watchman pulled himself up and sat limply again in the chair.

"Now, are you going to talk?"   160

"I've told you all I know," the watchman gasped.

"Where did you hide the stuff?"

"I didn't take it!"

"Thompson, your brains are in your feet," one of the policemen said. "We're going to string you up and get them back into your skull."

He watched the policemen clamp handcuffs on the watchman's wrists and   165
ankles; then they lifted the watchman and swung him upside-down and hoisted his feet to the edge of a door. The watchman hung, head down, his eyes bulging. They're crazy, he whispered to himself as he clung to the ridges of the pipe.

"You going to talk?" a policeman shouted into the watchman's ear.

He heard the watchman groan.

"We'll let you hang there till you talk, see?"

He saw the watchman close his eyes.

"Let's take 'im down. He passed out," a policeman said.   170

He grinned as he watched them take the body down and dump it carelessly upon the floor. The policemen took off the handcuffs.

"Let 'im come to. Let's get a smoke," a policeman said.

The three policemen left the scope of his vision. A door slammed. He had an impulse to yell to the watchman that he could escape through the hole in the basement and live with him in the cave. But he wouldn't understand, he told himself. After a moment he saw the watchman rise and stand, swaying from weakness. He stumbled across the room to a desk, opened a drawer, and took out a gun. He's going to kill himself, he thought, intent, eager, detached, yearning to see the end of the man's actions. As the watchman stared vaguely about he lifted the gun to his temple; he stood like that for some minutes, biting his lips until a line of blood etched its way down a corner of his chin. No, he oughtn't do that, he said to himself in a mood of pity.

"Don't!" he half whispered and half yelled.

The watchman looked wildly about; he had heard him. But it did not help;   175 there was a loud report and the watchman's head jerked violently and he fell like a log and lay prone, the gun clattering over the floor.

The three policemen came running into the room with drawn guns. One of the policemen knelt and rolled the watchman's body over and stared at a ragged, scarlet hole in the temple.

"Our hunch was right," the kneeling policeman said. "He was guilty, all right."

"Well, this ends the case," another policeman said.

"He knew he was licked," the third one said with grim satisfaction.

He eased down the rain pipe, crawled back through the holes he had made, and went back into his cave. A fever burned in his bones. He had to act, yet he was afraid. His eyes stared in the darkness as though propped open by invisible hands, as though they had become lidless. His muscles were rigid and he stood for what seemed to him a thousand years.   180

When he moved again his actions were informed with precision, his muscular system reinforced from a reservoir of energy. He crawled through the hole of earth, dropped into the gray sewer current, and sloshed ahead. When his right foot went forward at a street intersection, he fell backward and shot down into water. In a spasm of terror his right hand grabbed the concrete ledge of a down-curve and he felt the streaking water tugging violently at his body. The current reached his neck and for a moment he was still. He knew if he moved clumsily he would be sucked under. He held onto the ledge with both hands and slowly pulled himself up. He sighed, standing once more in the sweeping water, thankful that he had missed death.

He waded on through sludge, moving with care, until he came to a web of light sifting down from a manhole cover. He saw steel hooks running up the side of the sewer wall; he caught hold and lifted himself and put his shoulder to the cover and moved it an inch. A crash of sound came to him as he looked into a hot glare of sunshine through which blurred shapes moved. Fear scalded him and he dropped back into the pallid current and stood paralyzed in the shadows. A heavy car rumbled past overhead, jarring the pavement, warning him to stay in his world of dark light, knocking the cover back into place with an imperious clang.

He did not know how much fear he felt, for fear claimed him completely; yet it was not a fear of the police or of people, but a cold dread at the thought of the actions he knew he would perform if he went out into that cruel sunshine. His mind said no; his body said yes; and his mind could not understand his feelings. A low whine broke from him and he was in the act of uncoiling. He climbed upward and heard the faint honking of auto horns. Like a frantic cat clutching a rag, he clung to the steel prongs and heaved his shoulder against the cover and pushed it off halfway. For a split second his eyes were drowned in the terror of yellow light and he was in a deeper darkness than he had ever known in the underground.

Partly out of the hole, he blinked, regaining enough sight to make out meaningful forms. An odd thing was happening: No one was rushing forward to challenge him. He had imagined the moment of his emergence as a desperate tussle with men who wanted to cart him off to be killed; instead, life froze about him as the traffic stopped. He pushed the cover aside, stood, swaying in a world so fragile that he expected it to collapse and drop him into some deep void. But no- body seemed to pay him heed. The cars were now swerving to shun him and the gaping hole.

"Why in hell don't you put up a red light, dummy?" a raucous voice yelled.   185

He understood; they thought that he was a sewer workman. He walked toward the sidewalk, weaving unsteadily through the moving traffic.

"Look where you're going, nigger!"

"That's right! Stay there and get killed!"

"You blind, you bastard?"

"Go home and sleep your drunk off!"   190

A policeman stood at the curb, looking in the opposite direction. When he passed the policeman, he feared that he would be grabbed, but nothing hap- pened. Where was he? Was this real? He wanted to look about to get his bear- ings, but felt that something awful would happen to him if he did. He wandered into a spacious doorway of a store that sold men's clothing and saw his reflection in a long mirror: his cheekbones protruded from a hairy black face; his greasy cap was perched askew upon his head and his eyes were red and glassy. His shirt and trousers were caked with mud and hung loosely. His hands were gummed with a black stickiness. He threw back his head and laughed so loudly that passers-by stopped and stared.

He ambled on down the sidewalk, not having the merest notion of where he was going. Yet, sleeping within him, was the drive to go somewhere and say something to somebody. Half an hour later his ears caught the sound of spirited singing.

> The Lamb, the Lamb, the Lamb
>   I hear thy voice a-calling
> The Lamb, the Lamb, the Lamb
>   I feel thy grace a-falling

A church! he exclaimed. He broke into a run and came to brick steps leading downward to a subbasement. This is it! The church into which he had peered. Yes, he was going in and tell them. What? He did not know; but, once face to face with them, he would think of what to say. Must be Sunday, he mused. He ran down the steps and jerked the door open; the church was crowded and a deluge of song swept over him.

> The Lamb, the Lamb, the Lamb
>   Tell me again your story
> The Lamb, the Lamb, the Lamb
>   Flood my soul with your glory

He stared at the singing faces with a trembling smile.

"Say!" he shouted.   195

Many turned to look at him, but the song rolled on. His arm was jerked violently.

"I'm sorry, Brother, but you can't do that in here," a man said.

"But, mister!"

"You can't act rowdy in God's house," the man said.

"He's filthy," another man said.　　　　　　　　　　　　　　　　　　200

"But I want to tell 'em," he said loudly.

"He stinks," someone muttered.

The song had stopped, but at once another one began.

> Oh, wondrous sight upon the cross
> *Vision sweet and divine*
> Oh, wondrous sight upon the cross
> *Full of such love sublime*

He attempted to twist away, but other hands grabbed him and rushed him into the doorway.

"Let me alone!" he screamed, struggling.　　　　　　　　　　　　205

"Get out!"

"He's drunk," somebody said. "He ought to be ashamed!"

"He acts crazy!"

He felt that he was failing and he grew frantic.

"But, mister, let me tell—"　　　　　　　　　　　　　　　　210

"Get away from this door, or I'll call the police!"

He stared, his trembling smile fading in a sense of wonderment.

"The police," he repeated vacantly.

"Now, get!"

He was pushed toward the brick steps and the door banged shut. The waves　215
of song came.

> Oh, wondrous sight, wondrous sight
> *Lift my heavy heart above*
> Oh, wondrous sight, wondrous sight
> *Fill my weary soul with love*

He was smiling again now. Yes, the police . . . That was it! Why had he not thought of it before? The idea had been deep down in him, and only now did it assume supreme importance. He looked up and saw a street sign: COURT STREET—HARTSDALE AVENUE. He turned and walked northward, his mind filled with the image of the police station. Yes, that was where they had beaten him, accused him, and had made him sign a confession of his guilt. He would go there and clear up everything, make a statement. What statement? He did not know. He was the statement, and since it was all so clear to him, surely he would be able to make it clear to others.

He came to the corner of Hartsdale Avenue and turned westward. Yeah, there's the station . . . A policeman came down the steps and walked past him without a glance. He mounted the stone steps and went through the door, paused; he was in a hallway where several policemen were standing, talking, smoking. One turned to him.

"What do you want, boy?"

He looked at the policeman and laughed.

"What in hell are you laughing about?" the policeman asked.   220

He stopped laughing and stared. His whole being was full of what he wanted to say to them, but he could not say it.

"Are you looking for the Desk Sergeant?"

"Yes, sir," he said quickly; then: "Oh, no, sir."

"Well, make up your mind, now."

Four policemen grouped themselves around him.   225

"I'm looking for the men," he said.

"What men?"

Peculiarly, at that moment he could not remember the names of the policemen; he recalled their beating him, the confession he had signed, and how he had run away from them. He saw the cave next to the church, the money on the walls, the gun, the rings, the cleaver, the watches, and the diamonds on the floor.

"They brought me here," he began.

"When?"   230

His mind flew back over the blur of the time lived in the underground blackness. He had no idea of how much time had elapsed, but the intensity of what had happened to him told him that it could not have transpired in a short space of time, yet his mind told him that time must have been brief.

"It was a long time ago." He spoke like a child relating a dimly remembered dream. "It was a long time," he repeated, following the promptings of his emotions. "They beat me . . . I was scared . . . I ran away."

A policeman raised a finger to his temple and made a derisive circle.

"Nuts," the policeman said.

"Do you know what place this is, boy?"   235

"Yes, sir. The police station," he answered sturdily, almost proudly.

"Well, who do you want to see?"

"The men," he said again, feeling that surely they knew the men. "You know the men," he said in a hurt tone.

"What's your name?"

He opened his lips to answer and no words came. He had forgotten. But what   240
did it matter if he had? It was not important.

"Where do you live?"

Where did he live? It had been so long ago since he had lived up here in this strange world that he felt it was foolish even to try to remember. Then for a moment the old mood that had dominated him in the underground surged back. He leaned forward and spoke eagerly.

"They said I killed the woman."

"What woman?" a policeman asked.

"And I signed a paper that said I was guilty," he went on, ignoring their ques-   245
tions. "Then I ran off . . ."

"Did you run off from an institution?"

"No, sir," he said, blinking and shaking his head. "I came from under the ground. I pushed off the manhole cover and climbed out . . ."

"All right, now," a policeman said, placing an arm about his shoulder. "We'll send you to the psycho and you'll be taken care of."

"Maybe he's a Fifth Columnist!"[1] a policeman shouted.

There was laughter and, despite his anxiety, he joined in. But the laughter lasted so long that it irked him.   250

"I got to find those men," he protested mildly.

"Say, boy, what have you been drinking?"

"Water," he said. "I got some water in a basement."

"Were the men you ran away from dressed in white, boy?"

"No, sir," he said brightly. "They were men like you."   255

An elderly policeman caught hold of his arm.

"Try and think hard. Where did they pick you up?"

He knotted his brows in an effort to remember, but he was blank inside. The policeman stood before him demanding logical answers and he could no longer think with his mind; he thought with his feelings and no words came.

"I was guilty," he said. "Oh, no, sir. I wasn't then, I mean, mister!"

"Aw, talk sense. Now, where did they pick you up?"   260

He felt challenged and his mind began reconstructing events in reverse; his feelings ranged back over the long hours and he saw the cave, the sewer, the bloody room where it was said that a woman had been killed.

"Oh, yes, sir," he said, smiling. "I was coming from Mrs. Wooten's."

"Who is she?"

"I work for her."

"Where does she live?"   265

"Next door to Mrs. Peabody, the woman who was killed."

The policemen were very quiet now, looking at him intently.

"What do you know about Mrs. Peabody's death, boy?"

"Nothing, sir. But they said I killed her. But it doesn't make any difference, I'm guilty!"

"What are you talking about, boy?"   270

His smile faded and he was possessed with memories of the underground; he saw the cave next to the church and his lips moved to speak. But how could he say it? The distance between what he felt and what these men meant was vast. Something told him, as he stood there looking into their faces, that he would never be able to tell them, that they would never believe him if he told them.

"All the people I saw was guilty," he began slowly.

"Aw, nuts," a policeman muttered.

"Say," another policeman said, "that Peabody woman was killed over on Winewood. That's Number Ten's beat."

"Where's Number Ten?" a policeman asked.   275

[1] A member of a subversive organization aiding the enemy from within his own country.

"Upstairs in the swing room," someone answered.

"Take this boy up, Sam," a policeman ordered.

"O.K. Come along, boy."

An elderly policeman caught hold of his arm and led him up a flight of wooden stairs, down a long hall, and to a door.

"Squad Ten!" the policeman called through the door. 280

"What?" a gruff voice answered.

"Someone to see you!"

"About what?"

The old policeman pushed the door in and then shoved him into the room.

He stared, his lips open, his heart barely beating. Before him were the three 285 policemen who had picked him up and had beaten him to extract the confession. They were seated about a small table, playing cards. The air was blue with smoke and sunshine poured through a high window, lighting up fantastic smoke shapes. He saw one of the policemen look up; the policeman's face was tired and a cigarette drooped limply from one corner of his mouth and both of his fat, puffy eyes were squinting and his hands gripped his cards.

"Lawson!" the man exclaimed.

The moment the man's name sounded he remembered the names of all of them: Lawson, Murphy, and Johnson. How simple it was. He waited, smiling, wondering how they would react when they knew that he had come back.

"Looking for me?" the man who had been called Lawson mumbled, sorting his cards. "For what?"

So far only Murphy, the red-headed one, had recognized him.

"Don't you-all remember me?" he blurted, running to the table. 290

All three of the policemen were looking at him now. Lawson, who seemed the leader, jumped to his feet.

"Where in hell have you been?"

"Do you know 'im, Lawson?" the old policeman asked.

"Huh?" Lawson frowned. "Oh, yes. I'll handle 'im." The old policeman left the room and Lawson crossed to the door and turned the key in the lock. "Come here, boy," he ordered in a cold tone.

He did not move; he looked from face to face. Yes, he would tell them about 295 his cave.

"He looks batty to me," Johnson said, the one who had not spoken before.

"Why in hell did you come back here?" Lawson said.

"I—I just didn't want to run away no more," he said. "I'm all right, now." He paused; the men's attitude puzzled him.

"You've been hiding, huh?" Lawson asked in a tone that denoted that he had not heard his previous words. "You told us you were sick, and when we left you in the room, you jumped out of the window and ran away."

Panic filled him. Yes, they were indifferent to what he would say! They were 300 waiting for him to speak and they would laugh at him. He had to rescue himself from this bog; he had to force the reality of himself upon them.

"Mister, I took a sackful of money and pasted it on the walls . . ." he began.

"I'll be damned," Lawson said.

"Listen," said Murphy, "let me tell you something for your own good. We don't want you, see? You're free, free as air. Now go home and forget it. It was all a mistake. We caught the guy who did the Peabody job. He wasn't colored at all. He was an Eyetalian."

"Shut up!" Lawson yelled. "Have you no sense!"

"But I want to tell 'im," Murphy said.   305

"We can't let this crazy fool go," Lawson exploded. "He acts nuts, but this may be a stunt . . ."

"I was down in the basement," he began in a childlike tone, as though re-peating a lesson learned by heart; "and I went into a movie . . ." His voice failed. He was getting ahead of his story. First, he ought to tell them about the singing in the church, but what words could he use? He looked at them appealingly. "I went into a shop and took a sackful of money and diamonds and watches and rings . . . I didn't steal 'em, I'll give 'em all back. I just took 'em to play with . . ." He paused, stunned by their disbelieving eyes.

Lawson lit a cigarette and looked at him coldly.

"What did you do with the money?" he asked in a quiet, waiting voice.

"I pasted the hundred-dollar bills on the walls."   310

"What walls?" Lawson asked.

"The walls of the dirt room," he said, smiling, "the room next to the church. I hung up the rings and the watches and I stamped the diamonds into the dirt . . ." He saw that they were not understanding what he was saying. He grew frantic to make them believe, his voice tumbled on eagerly. "I saw a dead baby and a dead man . . ."

"Aw, you're nuts," Lawson snarled, shoving him into a chair.

"But mister . . ."

"Johnson, where's the paper he signed?" Lawson asked.   315

"What paper?"

"The confession, fool!"

Johnson pulled out his billfold and extracted a crumpled piece of paper.

"Yes, sir, mister," he said, stretching forth his hand. "That's the paper I signed . . ."

Lawson slapped him and he would have toppled had his chair not struck a   320
wall behind him. Lawson scratched a match and held the paper over the flame; the confession burned down to Lawson's finger tips.

He stared, thunderstruck; the sun of the underground was fleeting and the terrible darkness of the day stood before him. They did not believe him, but he *had* to make them believe him!

"But mister . . ."

"It's going to be all right, boy," Lawson said with a quiet, soothing laugh. "I've burned your confession, see? You didn't sign anything." Lawson came close to him with the black ashes in his palm. "You don't remember a thing about this, do you?"

"Don't you-all be scared of me," he pleaded, sensing their uneasiness. "I'll sign another paper, if you want me to. I'll show you the cave."

"What's your game, boy?" Lawson asked suddenly.   325
"What are you trying to find out?" Johnson asked.
"Who sent you here?" Murphy demanded.
"Nobody sent me, mister," he said. "I just want to show you the room . . ."
"Aw, he's plumb bats," Murphy said. "Let's ship 'im to the psycho."
"No," Lawson said. "He's playing a game and I wish to God I knew what it   330
was."

There flashed through his mind a definite way to make them believe him; he
rose from the chair with nervous excitement.

"Mister, I saw the night watchman blow his brains out because you accused
him of stealing," he told them. "But he didn't steal the money and diamonds. I
took 'em."

Tigerishly Lawson grabbed his collar and lifted him bodily.

"Who told you about that?"

"Don't get excited, Lawson," Johnson said. "He read about it in the papers."   335
Lawson flung him away.

"He couldn't have," Lawson said, pulling papers from his pocket. "I haven't
turned in the reports yet."

"Then how *did* he find out?" Murphy asked.

"Let's get out of here," Lawson said with quick resolution. "Listen, boy, we're
going to take you to a nice, quiet place, see?"

"Yes, sir," he said. "And I'll show you the underground."   340

"Goddamn," Lawson muttered, fastening the gun at his hip. He narrowed his
eyes at Johnson and Murphy. "Listen," he spoke just above a whisper, "say nothing about this, you hear?"

"O.K.," Johnson said.

"Sure," Murphy said.

Lawson unlocked the door and Johnson and Murphy led him down the stairs.
The hallway was crowded with policemen.

"What have you got there, Lawson?"   345
"What did he do, Lawson?"
"He's psycho, ain't he, Lawson?"

Lawson did not answer; Johnson and Murphy led him to the car parked at the
curb, pushed him into the back seat. Lawson got behind the steering wheel and
the car rolled forward.

"What's up, Lawson?" Murphy asked.

"Listen," Lawson began slowly, "we tell the papers that he spilled about the   350
Peabody job, then he escapes. The Wop is caught and we tell the papers that we
steered them wrong to trap the real guy, see? Now this dope shows up and acts
nuts. If we let him go, he'll squeal that we framed him, see?"

"I'm all right, mister," he said, feeling Murphy's and Johnson's arms locked
rigidly into his. "I'm guilty . . . I'll show you everything in the underground. I
laughed and laughed . . ."

"Shut that fool up!" Lawson ordered.

Johnson tapped him across the head with a blackjack and he fell back against
the seat cushion, dazed.

"Yes, sir," he mumbled. "I'm all right."

The car sped along Hartsdale Avenue, then swung onto Pine Street and 355 rolled to State Street, then turned south. It slowed to a stop, turned in the middle of a block, and headed north again.

"You're going around in circles, Lawson," Murphy said.

Lawson did not answer; he was hunched over the steering wheel. Finally he pulled the car to a stop at a curb.

"Say, boy, tell us the truth," Lawson asked quietly. "Where did you hide?"

"I didn't hide, mister."

The three policemen were staring at him now; he felt that for the first time 360 they were willing to understand him.

"Then what happened?"

"Mister, when I looked through all of those holes and saw how people were living, I loved 'em . . ."

"Cut out that crazy talk!" Lawson snapped. "Who sent you back here?"

"Nobody, mister."

"Maybe he's talking straight," Johnson ventured. 365

"All right," Lawson said. "Nobody hid you. Now, tell us *where* you hid."

"I went underground . . ."

"What goddamn underground do you keep talking about?"

"I just went . . ." He paused and looked into the street, then pointed to a manhole cover. "I went down in there and stayed."

"In the *sewer*?" 370

"Yes, sir."

The policemen burst into a sudden laugh and ended quickly. Lawson swung the car around and drove to Woodside Avenue; he brought the car to a stop in front of a tall apartment building.

"What're we going to do, Lawson?" Murphy asked.

"I'm taking him up to my place," Lawson said. "We've got to wait until night. There's nothing we can do now."

They took him out of the car and led him into a vestibule. 375

"Take the steps," Lawson muttered.

They led him up four flights of stairs and into the living room of a small apartment. Johnson and Murphy let go of his arms and he stood uncertainly in the middle of the room.

"Now, listen, boy," Lawson began, "forget those wild lies you've been telling us. Where did you hide?"

"I just went underground, like I told you."

The room rocked with laughter. Lawson went to a cabinet and got a bottle of 380 whiskey; he placed glasses for Johnson and Murphy. The three of them drank.

He felt that he could not explain himself to them. He tried to muster all the sprawling images that floated in him; the images stood out sharply in his mind, but he could not make them have the meaning for others that they had for him. He felt so helpless that he began to cry.

"He's nuts, all right," Johnson said. "All nuts cry like that."

Murphy crossed the room and slapped him.

"Stop that raving!"

A sense of excitement flooded him; he ran to Murphy and grabbed his arm.   385

"Let me show you the cave," he said. "Come on, and you'll see!"

Before he knew it a sharp blow had clipped him on the chin; darkness covered his eyes. He dimly felt himself being lifted and laid out on the sofa. He heard low voices and struggled to rise, but hard hands held him down. His brain was clearing now. He pulled to a sitting posture and stared with glazed eyes. It had grown dark. How long had he been out?

"Say, boy," Lawson said soothingly, "will you show us the underground?"

His eyes shone and his heart swelled with gratitude. Lawson believed him! He rose, glad; he grabbed Lawson's arm, making the policeman spill whiskey from the glass to his shirt.

"Take it easy, goddammit," Lawson said.   390

"Yes, sir."

"O.K. We'll take you down. But you'd better be telling us the truth, you hear?"

He clapped his hands in wild joy.

"I'll show you everything!"

He had triumphed at last! He would now do what he had felt was compelling   395
him all along. At last he would be free of his burden.

"Take 'im down," Lawson ordered.

They led him down to the vestibule; when he reached the sidewalk he saw that it was night and a fine rain was falling.

"It's just like when I went down," he told them.

"What?" Lawson asked.

"The rain," he said, sweeping his arm in a wide arc. "It was raining when I   400
went down. The rain made the water rise and lift the cover off."

"Cut it out," Lawson snapped.

They did not believe him now, but they would. A mood of high selflessness throbbed in him. He could barely contain his rising spirits. They would see what he had seen; they would feel what he had felt. He would lead them through all the holes he had dug and . . . He wanted to make a hymn, prance about in physical ecstasy, throw his arm about the policemen in fellowship.

"Get into the car," Lawson ordered.

He climbed in and Johnson and Murphy sat at either side of him; Lawson slid behind the steering wheel and started the motor.

"Now, tell us where to go," Lawson said.   405

"It's right around the corner from where the lady was killed," he said.

The car rolled slowly and he closed his eyes, remembering the song he had heard in the church, the song that had wrought him to such a high pitch of terror and pity. He sang softly, lolling his head:

Glad, glad, glad, oh, so glad
I got Jesus in my soul . . .

"Mister," he said, stopping his song, "you ought to see how funny the rings look on the wall." He giggled. "I fired a pistol, too. Just once, to see how it felt."

"What do you suppose he's suffering from?" Johnson asked.

"Delusions of grandeur, maybe," Murphy said. 410

"Maybe it's because he lives in a white man's world," Lawson said.

"Say, boy, what did you eat down there?" Murphy asked, prodding Johnson anticipatorily with his elbow.

"Pears, oranges, bananas, and pork chops," he said.

The car filled with laughter.

"You didn't eat any watermelon?" Lawson asked, smiling. 415

"No, sir," he answered calmly. "I didn't see any."

The three policemen roared harder and louder.

"Boy, you're sure some case," Murphy said, shaking his head in wonder.

The car pulled to a curb.

"All right, boy," Lawson said. "Tell us where to go." 420

He peered through the rain and saw where he had gone down. The streets, save for a few dim lamps glowing softly through the rain, were dark and empty.

"Right there, mister," he said, pointing.

"Come on; let's take a look," Lawson said.

"Well, suppose he did hide down there," Johnson said, "what is that supposed to prove?"

"I don't believe he hid down there," Murphy said. 425

"It won't hurt to look," Lawson said. "Leave things to me."

Lawson got out of the car and looked up and down the street.

He was eager to show them the cave now. If he could show them what he had seen, then they would feel what he had felt and they in turn would show it to others and those others would feel as they had felt, and soon everybody would be governed by the same impulse of pity.

"Take 'im out," Lawson ordered.

Johnson and Murphy opened the door and pushed him out; he stood trem- 430
bling in the rain, smiling. Again Lawson looked up and down the street; no one was in sight. The rain came down hard, slanting like black wires across the wind-swept air.

"All right," Lawson said. "Show us."

He walked to the center of the street, stopped and inserted a finger in one of the tiny holes of the cover and tugged, but he was too weak to budge it.

"Did you really go down in there, boy?" Lawson asked; there was a doubt in his voice.

"Yes, sir. Just a minute. I'll show you."

"Help 'im get that damn thing off," Lawson said. 435

Johnson stepped forward and lifted the cover; it clanged against the wet pavement. The hole gaped round and black.

"I went down in there," he announced with pride.

Lawson gazed at him for a long time without speaking, then he reached his right hand to his holster and drew his gun.

"Mister, I got a gun just like that down there," he said, laughing, and looking into Lawson's face. "I fired it once then hung it on the wall. I'll show you."

"Show us how you went down," Lawson said quietly.   440

"I'll go down first, mister, and then you-all can come after me, hear?" he spoke like a little boy playing a game.

"Sure, sure," Lawson said soothingly. "Go ahead. We'll come."

He looked brightly at the policemen; he was bursting with happiness. He bent down and placed his hands on the rim of the hole and sat on the edge, his feet dangling into watery darkness. He heard the familiar drone of the gray current. He lowered his body and hung for a moment by his fingers, then he went downward on the steel prongs, hand over hand, until he reached the last rung. He dropped and his feet hit the water and he felt the stiff current trying to suck him away. He balanced himself quickly and looked back upward at the policemen.

"Come on, you-all!" he yelled, casting his voice above the rustling at his feet.

The vague forms that towered above him in the rain did not move. He   445
laughed, feeling that they doubted him. But, once they saw the things he had done, they would never doubt again.

"Come on! The cave isn't far!" he yelled. "But be careful when your feet hit the water, because the current's pretty rough down here!"

Lawson still held the gun. Murphy and Johnson looked at Lawson quizzically.

"What are we going to do, Lawson?" Murphy asked.

"We are not going to follow that crazy nigger down into that sewer, are we?" Johnson asked.

"Come on, you-all!" he begged in a shout.   450

He saw Lawson raise the gun and point it directly at him. Lawson's face twitched, as though he were hesitating.

Then there was a thunderous report and a streak of fire ripped through his chest. He was hurled into the water, flat on his back. He looked in amazement at the blurred white faces above him. They shot me, he said to himself. The water flowed past him, blossoming in foam about his arms, his legs, and his head. His jaw sagged and his mouth gaped soundless. A vast pain gripped his head and gradually squeezed out consciousness. As from a great distance he heard hollow voices.

"What did you shoot him for, Lawson?"

"I had to."

"Why?"   455

"You've got to shoot his kind. They'd wreck things."

As though in a deep dream, he heard a metallic clank; they had replaced the manhole cover, shutting out forever the sound of wind and rain. From overhead came the muffled roar of a powerful motor and the swish of a speeding car. He felt the strong tide pushing him slowly into the middle of the sewer, turning him about. For a split second there hovered before his eyes the glittering cave, the shouting walls, and the laughing floor . . . Then his mouth was full of thick, bitter water. The current spun him around. He sighed and closed his eyes, a whirling object rushing alone in the darkness, veering, tossing, lost in the heart of the earth.

For Analysis

1. What attitude toward religion is expressed in this story? What evidence can you find that points to this attitude? **2.** Before taking the typewriter, Daniels pecks out his name (par. 104) but can't remember it later when he tries again (par. 119). What does his inability to remember his name suggest about what is happening to him? **3.** Why does Daniels decorate his hideaway with the money instead of using it to escape? **4.** What significance do you find in the fact that Daniels tries to communicate his joyous feelings at a church and a police station? What is it that he wants to communicate? **5.** The police officer who kills Daniels sees him as a dangerous rebel, as the kind who would "wreck things." What do you suppose the policeman means? **6.** What significance do Fred Daniels's two dreams (par. 38 and 126–30) have in this story?

On Style

Why do you suppose Wright chose to tell the story from the third-person **point of view** rather than the first-person?

Making Connections

1. Fred Daniels journeys underground and Young Goodman Brown journeys in the forest in Hawthorne's story (p. 61). Compare and contrast the nature of each journey and the discoveries each **protagonist** makes.

Writing Topic

Fred Daniels goes underground to escape punishment for a crime he did not commit. He is a black man, and the underground becomes an appropriate metaphor for the position white America has accorded blacks. The underground is more than a place of escape for him, however; it is a place where he comes to understand what the society he lives in, black and white, is about. How do episodes such as Daniels's discovery of the dead baby, his reactions to the funeral parlor, the movie house, the meat market, and the black church contribute to this understanding?

Ursula K. Le Guin [b. 1929]

The Ones Who Walk Away from Omelas 1974

With a clamor of bells that set the swallows soaring, the Festival of Summer came to the city Omelas, bright-towered by the sea. The rigging of the boats in harbor sparkled with flags. In the streets between houses with red roofs and painted walls, between old moss-grown gardens and under avenues of trees, past great parks and public buildings, processions moved. Some were decorous: old people in long stiff robes of mauve and grey, grave master work-men, quiet, merry women carrying their babies and chatting as they walked. In other streets the music beat faster, a shimmering of gong and tambourine, and the people went dancing, the procession was a dance. Children dodged in and out, their high calls rising like the swallows' crossing flights over the music and the singing. All the processions wound towards the north side of the city, where on the great water-meadow called the Green Fields boys and girls, naked in the bright air, with mud-stained feet and ankles and long, lithe arms, exer-cised their restive horses before the race. The horses wore no gear at all but a halter without bit. Their manes were braided with streamers of silver, gold, and green. They flared their nostrils and pranced and boasted to one another; they were vastly excited, the horse being the only animal who has adopted our cere-monies as his own. Far off to the north and west the mountains stood up half en-circling Omelas on her bay. The air of morning was so clear that the snow still crowning the Eighteen Peaks burned with white-gold fire across the miles of sunlit air, under the dark blue of the sky. There was just enough wind to make the banners that marked the racecourse snap and flutter now and then. In the silence of the broad green meadows one could hear the music winding through the city streets, farther and nearer and ever approaching, a cheerful faint sweet-ness of the air that from time to time trembled and gathered together and broke out into the great joyous clanging of the bells.

Joyous! How is one to tell about joy? How describe the citizens of Omelas?

They were not simple folk, you see, though they were happy. But we do not say the words of cheer much any more. All smiles have become archaic. Given a description such as this one tends to make certain assumptions. Given a de-scription such as this one tends to look next for the King, mounted on a splen-did stallion and surrounded by his noble knights, or perhaps in a golden litter borne by great-muscled slaves. But there was no king. They did not use swords, or keep slaves. They were not barbarians. I do not know the rules and laws of their society, but I suspect that they were singularly few. As they did without monarchy and slavery, so they also got on without the stock exchange, the advertisement, the secret police, and the bomb. Yet I repeat that these were not simple folk, not dulcet shepherds, noble savages, bland utopians. They were not less complex than us. The trouble is that we have a bad habit, encouraged by pedants and sophisticates, of considering happiness as something rather stupid. Only pain is intellectual, only evil interesting. This is the treason of the artist: a refusal to admit the banality of evil and the terrible boredom of pain. If you can't lick 'em, join 'em. If it hurts, repeat it. But to praise despair is to condemn delight, to embrace violence is to lose hold of everything else. We have almost lost hold; we can no longer describe a happy man, nor make any celebration of joy. How can I tell you about the people of Omelas? They were not naïve and happy children—though their children were, in fact, happy. They were mature, intelligent, passionate adults whose lives were not wretched. O miracle! but I wish I could describe it better. I wish I could convince you. Omelas sounds in my words like a city in a fairy tale, long ago and far away, once upon a time. Perhaps it would be best if you imagined it as your own fancy bids, assuming it will rise to the occasion, for certainly I cannot suit you all. For instance, how about technology? I think that there would be no cars or helicopters in and above the streets; this follows from the fact that the people of Omelas are happy people. Happiness is based on a just discrimination of what is necessary, what is neither necessary nor destructive, and what is destructive. In the middle category, however—that of the unnecessary but undestructive, that of comfort, luxury, exuberance, etc.—they could perfectly well have central heating, subway trains, washing machines, and all kinds of marvelous devices not yet invented here, floating light-sources, fuelless power, a cure for the common cold. Or they could have none of that: it doesn't matter. As you like it. I incline to think that people from towns up and down the coast have been coming in to Omelas during the last days before the Festival on very fast little trains and double-decker trams, and that the train station of Omelas is actually the handsomest building in town, though plainer than the magnificent Farmers' Market. But even granted trains, I fear that Omelas so far strikes some of you as goody-goody. Smiles, bells, parades, horses, bleh. If so, please add an orgy. If an orgy would help, don't hesitate. Let us not, however, have temples from which issue beautiful nude priests and priestesses already half in ecstasy and ready to copulate with any man or woman, lover or stranger, who desires union with the deep godhead of the blood, although that was my first idea. But really it would be better not to have any temples in Omelas—at least, not manned temples. Religion yes, clergy no. Surely the beautiful nudes can just wander about, offering themselves like divine soufflés to the hunger of the needy and the rapture of the flesh. Let them join the processions. Let tambourines be struck above the copulations, and the glory of desire be proclaimed upon the gongs, and (a not unimportant point) let the offspring of these delightful rituals be beloved and looked after by all. One thing I know there is none of in Omelas is guilt. But what else should there be? I thought at first there were no drugs, but that is puritanical. For those who like it, the faint insistent sweetness of *drooz* may perfume the ways of the city, *drooz* which first brings a great lightness and brilliance to the mind and limbs, and then after some hours a dreamy languor, and wonderful visions at last of the very arcana and inmost secrets of the Universe, as well as exciting the pleasure of sex beyond all belief; and it is not habit-forming. For more modest tastes I think there ought to be beer. What else, what else belongs in the joyous city? The sense of victory, surely, the celebration of courage. But as we did without clergy, let us do without soldiers. The joy built upon successful slaughter is not the right kind of joy; it will not do; it is fearful and it is trivial. A boundless and generous contentment, a magnanimous triumph felt not against some outer enemy but in communion with the finest and fairest in the souls of all men everywhere and the splendor of the world's summer: this is what swells the hearts of the people of Omelas, and the victory they celebrate is that of life. I really don't think many of them need to take *drooz*.

Most of the processions have reached the Green Fields by now. A marvelous smell of cooking goes forth from the red and blue tents of the provisioners. The faces of small children are amiably sticky; in the benign grey beard of a man a couple of crumbs of rich pastry are entangled. The youths and girls have mounted their horses and are beginning to group around the starting line of the course. An old woman, small, fat, and laughing, is passing out flowers from a basket, and tall young men wear her flowers in their shining hair. A child of nine or ten sits at the edge of the crowd, alone, playing on a wooden flute. People pause to listen, and they smile, but they do not speak to him, for he never ceases playing and never sees them, his dark eyes wholly rapt in the sweet, thin magic of the tune.

He finishes, and slowly lowers his hands holding the wooden flute.   5

As if that little private silence were the signal, all at once a trumpet sounds from the pavilion near the starting line: imperious, melancholy, piercing. The horses rear on their slender legs, and some of them neigh in answer. Sober-faced, the young riders stroke the horses' necks and soothe them, whispering, "Quiet, quiet, there my beauty, my hope. . . ." They begin to form in rank along the starting line. The crowds along the racecourse are like a field of grass and flowers in the wind. The Festival of Summer has begun.

Do you believe? Do you accept the festival, the city, the joy? No? Then let me describe one more thing.

In a basement under one of the beautiful public buildings of Omelas, or perhaps in the cellar of one of its spacious private homes, there is a room. It has one locked door, and no window. A little light seeps in dustily between cracks in the boards, secondhand from a cobwebbed window somewhere across the cellar. In one corner of the little room a couple of mops, with stiff, clotted, foul-smelling heads, stand near a rusty bucket. The floor is dirt, a little damp to the touch, as cellar dirt usually is. The room is about three paces long and two wide: a mere broom closet or disused tool room. In the room a child is sitting. It could be a boy or a girl. It looks about six, but actually is nearly ten. It is feeble-minded. Perhaps it was born defective, or perhaps it has become imbecile through fear, malnutrition, and neglect. It picks its nose and occasionally fumbles vaguely with its toes or genitals, as it sits hunched in the corner farthest from the bucket and the two mops. It is afraid of the mops. It finds them horrible. It shuts its eyes, but it knows the mops are still standing there; and the door is locked; and nobody will come. The door is always locked; and nobody ever comes, except that sometimes—the child has no understanding of time or interval—sometimes the door rattles terribly and opens, and a person, or several people, are there. One of them may come in and kick the child to make it stand up. The others never come close, but peer in at it with frightened, disgusted eyes. The food bowl and the water jug are hastily filled, the door is locked, the eyes disappear. The people at the door never say anything, but the child, who has not always lived in the tool room, and can remember sunlight and its mother's voice, sometimes speaks. "I will be good," it says. "Please let me out. I will be good!" They never answer. The child used to scream for help at night, and cry a good deal, but now it only makes a kind of whining, "eh-haa, eh-haa," and it speaks less and less often. It is so thin there are no calves to its legs; its belly protrudes; it lives on a half-bowl of corn meal and grease a day. It is naked. Its buttocks and thighs are a mass of festered sores, as it sits in its own excrement continually.

They all know it is there, all the people of Omelas. Some of them have come to see it, others are content merely to know it is there. They all know that it has to be there. Some of them understand why, and some do not, but all understand that their happiness, the beauty of their city, the tenderness of their friendships, the health of their children, the wisdom of their scholars, the skill of their makers, even the abundance of their harvest and the kindly weathers of their skies, depend wholly on this child's abominable misery.

This is usually explained to children when they are between eight and twelve, 10 whenever they seem capable of understanding; and most of those who come to see the child are young people, though often enough an adult comes, or comes back, to see the child. No matter how well the matter has been explained to them, these young spectators are always shocked and sickened at the sight. They feel disgust, which they had thought themselves superior to. They feel anger, outrage, impotence, despite all the explanations. They would like to do something for the child. But there is nothing they can do. If the child were brought up into the sunlight out of that vile place, if it were cleaned and fed and comforted, that would be a good thing, indeed; but if it were done, in that day and hour all the prosperity and beauty and delight of Omelas would wither and be destroyed. Those are the terms. To exchange all the goodness and grace of every life in Omelas for that single, small improvement: to throw away the happiness of thousands for the chance of the happiness of one: that would be to let guilt within the walls indeed.

The terms are strict and absolute; there may not even be a kind word spoken to the child.

Often the young people go home in tears, or in a tearless rage, when they have seen the child and faced this terrible paradox. They may brood over it for weeks or years. But as time goes on they begin to realize that even if the child could be released, it would not get much good of its freedom: a little vague plea-sure of warmth and food, no doubt, but little more. It is too degraded and im-becile to know any real joy. It has been afraid too long ever to be free of fear. Its habits are too uncouth for it to respond to humane treatment. Indeed, after so long it would probably be wretched without walls about it to protect it, and darkness for its eyes, and its own excrement to sit in. Their tears at the bitter in-justice dry when they begin to perceive the terrible justice of reality, and to ac-cept it. Yet it is their tears and anger, the trying of their generosity and the acceptance of their helplessness, which are perhaps the true source of the splendor of their lives. Theirs is no vapid, irresponsible happiness. They know that they, like the child, are not free. They know compassion. It is the existence of the child, and their knowledge of its existence, that makes possible the nobil-ity of their architecture, the poignancy of their music, the profundity of their science. It is because of the child that they are so gentle with children. They know that if the wretched one were not there snivelling in the dark, the other one, the flute-player, could make no joyful music as the young riders line up in their beauty for the race in the sunlight of the first morning of summer.

Now do you believe in them? Are they not more credible? But there is one more thing to tell, and this is quite incredible.

At times one of the adolescent girls or boys who go to see the child does not go home to weep or rage, does not, in fact, go home at all. Sometimes also a man or woman much older falls silent for a day or two, and then leaves home. These people go out into the street, and walk down the street alone. They keep walk-ing, and walk straight out of the city of Omelas, through the beautiful gates. They keep walking across the farmlands of Omelas. Each one goes alone, youth or girl, man or woman. Night falls; the traveler must pass down village streets, between the houses with yellow-lit windows, and on out into the darkness of the fields. Each alone, they go west or north, towards the mountains. They go on. They leave Omelas, they walk ahead into the darkness, and they do not come back. The place they go towards is a place even less imaginable to most of us than the city of happiness. I cannot describe it at all. It is possible that it does not exist. But they seem to know where they are going, the ones who walk away from Omelas.

For Analysis

1. Who is the narrator? What are her feelings about Omelas, particularly about the misery of the child on which the happiness of the city depends? **2.** Does the narrator sympathize with those who walk away? Or with those who remain? Or is she am-bivalent? **3.** Is Omelas described in sufficient detail, or are there other things about the city you wish the author had included? **4.** Look up the dictionary definition of *utopia*. Does Omelas fit that definition? **5.** How would you describe the conflict in this story? Is there a **protagonist** and **antagonist**? Who are they?

On Style

Characterize the **tone** of this story.

Making Connections

1. This story, Hawthorne's "Young Goodman Brown" (p. 61), and Ellison's " 'Repent, Harlequin!' Said the Ticktockman" (p. 395) all rely on fantasy. What advantages does the use of fantasy give the authors? **2.** Do you find this story a compelling comment on human society, or is it too remote from reality to be believable? **3.** Compare the statement this story makes about the human spirit with that made in Ellison's " 'Repent, Harlequin!' Said the Ticktockman" (p. 395). Do the ones who walk away from Omelas share any of the attributes of the Harlequin?

Writing Topics

1. In paragraph 3, the narrator comments: "The trouble is that we have a bad habit, encouraged by pedants and sophisticates, of considering happiness as something rather stupid. Only pain is intellectual, only evil interesting. This is the treason of the artist: a refusal to admit the banality of evil and the terrible boredom of pain" (par. 3). Write an essay examining this statement. Are the narrator's claims persuasive? **2.** Is Le Guin's story, first published in 1975, still relevant? Why or why not?

Harlan Ellison [b. 1934]

"Repent, Harlequin!" Said the Ticktockman 1965

There are always those who ask, what is it all about? For those who need to ask, for those who need points sharply made, who need to know "where it's at," this:

> *The mass of men serve the state thus, not as men mainly, but as machines, with their bodies. They are the standing army, and the militia, jailors, constables, posse comitatus, etc. In most cases there is no free exercise whatever of the judgment or of the moral sense; but they put themselves on a level with wood and earth and stones; and wooden men can perhaps be manufactured that will serve the purpose as well. Such command no more respect than men of straw or a lump of dirt. They have the same sort of worth only as horses and dogs. Yet such as these even are commonly esteemed good citizens. Others—as most legislators, politicians, lawyers, ministers, and officeholders—serve the state chiefly with their heads; and, as they rarely make any moral distinctions, they are as likely to serve the Devil, without intending it, as God. A very few, as heroes, patriots, martyrs, reformers in the great sense, and men, serve the state with their consciences also, and so necessarily resist it for the most part; and they are commonly treated as enemies by it.*

Henry David Thoreau
CIVIL DISOBEDIENCE

That is the heart of it. Now begin in the middle, and later learn the beginning; the end will take care of itself.

But because it was the very world it was, the very world they had allowed it to *become*, for months his activities did not come to the alarmed attention of The Ones Who Kept The Machine Functioning Smoothly, the ones who poured the very best butter over the cams and mainsprings of the culture. Not until it had become obvious that somehow, someway, he had become a notoriety, a celebrity, perhaps even a hero for (what Officialdom inescapably tagged) "an emotionally disturbed segment of the populace," did they turn it over to the Ticktockman and his legal machinery. But by then, because it was the very world it was, and they had no way to predict he would happen—possibly a strain of disease long-defunct, now, suddenly, reborn in a system where immunity had been forgotten, had lapsed—he had been allowed to become too real. Now he had form and substance.

He had become a *personality*, something they had filtered out of the system many decades before. But there it was, and there *he* was, a very definitely imposing personality. In certain circles—middle-class circles—it was thought disgusting. Vulgar ostentation. Anarchistic. Shameful. In others, there was only sniggering: those strata where thought is subjugated to form and ritual, niceties, proprieties. But down below, ah, down below, where the people always needed their saints and sinners, their bread and circuses, their heroes and villains, he was considered a Bolivar; a Napoleon; a Robin Hood; a Dick Bong (Ace of Aces); a Jesus; a Jomo Kenyatta.

And at the top—where, like socially-attuned Shipwreck Kellys, every tremor   5
and vibration threatening to dislodge the wealthy, powerful and titled from their flagpoles—he was considered a menace; a heretic; a rebel; a disgrace; a peril. He was known down the line, to the very heart-meat core, but the important reactions were high above and far below. At the very top, at the very bottom.

So his file was turned over, along with his time-card and his cardioplate, to the office of the Ticktockman.

The Ticktockman: very much over six feet tall, often silent, a soft purring man when things went timewise. The Ticktockman.

Even in the cubicles of the hierarchy, where fear was generated, seldom suffered, he was called the Ticktockman. But no one called him that to his mask.

You don't call a man a hated name, not when that man, behind his mask, is capable of revoking the minutes, the hours, the days and nights, the years of your life. He was called the Master Timekeeper to his mask. It was safer that way.

"That is *what* he is," said the Ticktockman with genuine softness, "but not   10
who he is. This time-card I'm holding in my left hand has a name on it, but it is the name of *what* he is, not *who* he is. The cardioplate here in my right hand is also named, but not *whom* named, merely *what* named. Before I can exercise proper revocation, I have to know *who* this *what* is."

To his staff, all the ferrets, all the loggers, all the finks, all the commex, even the mineez, he said, "Who is this Harlequin?"

He was not purring smoothly. Timewise, it was jangle.

However, it *was* the longest speech they had ever heard him utter at one time, the staff, the ferrets, the loggers, the finks, the commex, but not the mineez, who usually weren't around to know, in any case. But even they scurried to find out.

Who is the Harlequin?

High above the third level of the city, he crouched on the humming   15
aluminum-frame platform of the air-boat (foof! air-boat, indeed! swizzleskid is what it was, with a tow-rack jerry-rigged) and he stared down at the neat Mondrian arrangement of the buildings.

Somewhere nearby, he could hear the metronomic left-right-left of the 2:47 PM shift, entering the Timkin roller-bearing plant in their sneakers. A minute later, precisely, he heard the softer right-left-right of the 5:00 AM formation, going home.

An elfin grin spread across his tanned features, and his dimples appeared for a moment. Then, scratching at his thatch of auburn hair, he shrugged within his motley, as though girding himself for what came next, and threw the joystick forward, and bent into the wind as the air-boat dropped. He skimmed over a slidewalk, purposely dropping a few feet to crease the tassels of the ladies of fashion, and—inserting thumbs in large ears—he stuck out his tongue, rolled his eyes and went wugga-wugga-wugga. It was a minor diversion. One pedestrian skittered and tumbled, sending parcels everywhichway, another wet herself, a third keeled slantwise and the walk was stopped automatically by the servitors till she could be resuscitated. It was a minor diversion.

Then he swirled away on a vagrant breeze, and was gone. Hi-ho.

As he rounded the cornice of the Time-Motion Study Building, he saw the shift, just boarding the slidewalk. With practiced motion and an absolute conservation of movement, they sidestepped up onto the slow-strip and (in a chorus line reminiscent of a Busby Berkeley film of the antediluvian 1930s) advanced across the strips ostrich-walking till they were lined up on the expresstrip.

Once more, in anticipation, the elfin grin spread, and there was a tooth miss-   20
ing back there on the left side. He dipped, skimmed, and swooped over them; and then, scrunching about on the air-boat, he released the holding pins that fastened shut the ends of the home-made pouring troughs that kept his cargo from dumping prematurely. And as he pulled the trough-pins, the air-boat slid over the factory workers and one hundred and fifty thousand dollars' worth of jelly beans cascaded down on the expresstrip.

Jelly beans! Millions and billions of purples and yellows and greens and licorice and grape and raspberry and mint and round and smooth and crunchy outside and soft-mealy inside and sugary and bouncing jouncing tumbling clittering clattering skittering fell on the heads and shoulders and hardhats and carapaces of the Timkin workers, tinkling on the slidewalk and bouncing away and rolling about underfoot and filling the sky on their way down with all the colors of joy and childhood and holidays, coming down in a steady rain, a solid wash, a torrent of color and sweetness out of the sky from above, and entering a universe of sanity and metronomic order with quite-mad coocoo newness. Jelly beans!

The shift workers howled and laughed and were pelted, and broke ranks, and the jelly beans managed to work their way into the mechanism of the slidewalks after which there was a hideous scraping as the sound of a million fingernails rasped down a quarter of a million blackboards, followed by a coughing and a sputtering, and then the slidewalks all stopped and everyone was dumped thisawayandthataway in a jackstraw tumble, still laughing and popping little jelly bean eggs of childish color into their mouths. It was a holiday, and a jollity, an absolute insanity, a giggle. But . . .

The shift was delayed seven minutes.

They did not get home for seven minutes.

The master schedule was thrown off by seven minutes.   25

Quotas were delayed by inoperative slidewalks for seven minutes.

He had tapped the first domino in the line, and one after another, like chik chik chik, the others had fallen.

The System had been seven minutes' worth of disrupted. It was a tiny matter, one hardly worthy of note, but in a society where the single driving force was order and unity and equality and promptness and clocklike precision and attention to the clock, reverence of the gods of the passage of time, it was a disaster of major importance.

So he was ordered to appear before the Ticktockman. It was broadcast across every channel of the communications web. He was ordered to be *there* at 7:00 dammit on time. And they waited, and they waited, but he didn't show up till almost ten-thirty, at which time he merely sang a little song about moonlight in a place no one had ever heard of, called Vermont, and vanished again. But they had all been waiting since seven, and it wrecked *hell* with their schedules. So the question remained: Who is the Harlequin?

But the *unasked* question (more important of the two) was: how did we get *into* this position, where a laughing, irresponsible japer of jabberwocky and jive could disrupt our entire economic and cultural life with a hundred and fifty thousand dollars' worth of jelly beans . . .

Jelly for God's sake *beans!* This is madness! Where did he get the money to buy a hundred and fifty thousand dollars' worth of jelly beans? (They knew it would have cost that much, because they had a team of Situation Analysts pulled off another assignment, and rushed to the slidewalk scene to sweep up and count the candies, and produce findings, which disrupted *their* schedules and threw their entire branch at least a day behind.) Jelly beans! Jelly . . . *beans?* Now wait a second—a second accounted for—no one has manufactured jelly beans for over a hundred years. Where did he get jelly beans?

That's another good question. More than likely it will never be answered to your complete satisfaction. But then, how many questions ever are?

The middle you know. Here is the beginning. How it starts:

A desk pad. Day for day, and turn each day. 9:00—open the mail. 9:45—appointment with planning commission board. 10:30—discuss installation progress charts with J.L. 11:45—pray for rain. 12:00—lunch. *And so it goes.*

"I'm sorry, Miss Grant, but the time for interviews was set at 2:30, and it's almost five now. I'm sorry you're late, but those are the rules. You'll have to wait till next year to submit application for this college again." *And so it goes.*

The 10:10 local stops at Cresthaven, Galesville, Tonawanda Junction, Selby and Farnhurst, but not at Indiana City, Lucasville and Colton, except on Sunday. The 10:35 express stops at Galesville, Selby and Indiana City, except on Sundays & Holidays, at which time it stops at . . . *and so it goes.*

"I couldn't wait, Fred. I had to be at Pierre Cartain's by 3:00, and you said you'd meet me under the clock in the terminal at 2:45, and you weren't there, so I had to go on. You're always late, Fred. If you'd been there, we could have sewed it up together, but as it was, well, I took the order alone . . ." *And so it goes.*

Dear Mr. and Mrs. Atterley: In reference to your son Gerold's constant tardiness, I am afraid we will have to suspend him from school unless some more reliable method can be instituted guaranteeing he will arrive at his classes on time. Granted he is an exemplary student, and his marks are high, his constant

30

35

flouting of the schedules of this school makes it impractical to maintain him in a system where the other children seem capable of getting where they are supposed to be on time *and so it goes.*

YOU CANNOT VOTE UNLESS YOU APPEAR AT 8:45 AM.

"I don't care if the script is *good,* I need it Thursday!"

CHECK-OUT TIME IS 2:00 PM.

"You got here late. The job's taken. Sorry."

YOUR SALARY HAS BEEN DOCKED FOR TWENTY MINUTES TIME LOST.

"God, what time is it, I've gotta run!"

And so it goes. And so it goes. And so it goes. And so it goes goes goes goes   45
goes tick tock tick tock tick tock and one day we no longer let time serve us, we serve time and we are slaves of the schedule, worshippers of the sun's passing, bound into a life predicated on restrictions because the system will not function if we don't keep the schedule tight.

Until it becomes more than a minor inconvenience to be late. It becomes a sin. Then a crime. Then a crime punishable by this:

EFFECTIVE 15 JULY 2389 12:00:00 midnight, the office of the Master Timekeeper will require all citizens to submit their time-cards and cardioplates for processing. In accordance with Statute 555–7-SGH-999 governing the revocation of time per capita, all cardioplates will be keyed to the individual holder and—

What they had done, was devise a method of curtailing the amount of life a person could have. If he was ten minutes late, he lost ten minutes of his life. An hour was proportionately worth more revocation. If someone was consistently tardy, he might find himself, on a Sunday night, receiving a communiqué from the Master Timekeeper that his time had run out, and he would be "turned off" at high noon on Monday, please straighten your affairs, sir, madame or bisex.

And so, by this simple scientific expedient (utilizing a scientific process held dearly secret by the Ticktockman's office) the System was maintained. It was the only expedient thing to do. It was, after all, patriotic. The schedules had to be met. After all, there *was* a war on!

But, wasn't there always?   50

"Now that is really disgusting," the Harlequin said, when Pretty Alice showed him the wanted poster. "Disgusting and *highly* improbable. After all, this isn't the Day of the Desperado. A *wanted* poster!"

"You know," Pretty Alice noted, "you speak with a great deal of inflection."

"I'm sorry," said the Harlequin, humbly.

"No need to be sorry. You're always saying 'I'm sorry.' You have such massive guilt, Everett, it's really very sad."

"I'm sorry," he said again, then pursed his lips so the dimples appeared mo-   55
mentarily. He hadn't wanted to say that at all. "I have to go out again. I have to *do* something."

Pretty Alice slammed her coffee-bulb down on the counter. "Oh for God's *sake*, Everett, can't you stay home just *one* night! Must you always be out in that ghastly clown suit, running around an*noy*ing people?"

"I'm—" He stopped, and clapped the jester's hat onto his auburn thatch with a tiny tingling of bells. He rose, rinsed out his coffee-bulb at the spray, and put it into the dryer for a moment. "I have to go."

She didn't answer. The faxbox was purring, and she pulled a sheet out, read it, threw it toward him on the counter. "It's about you. Of course. You're ridiculous."

He read it quickly. It said the Ticktockman was trying to locate him. He didn't care, he was going out to be late again. At the door, dredging for an exit line, he hurled back petulantly, "Well, *you* speak with inflection, *too!*"

Pretty Alice rolled her pretty eyes heavenward. "You're ridiculous." The Har- 60
lequin stalked out, slamming the door, which sighed shut softly, and locked itself.

There was a gentle knock, and Pretty Alice got up with an exhalation of exasperated breath, and opened the door. He stood there. "I'll be back about ten-thirty, okay?"

She pulled a rueful face. "Why do you tell me that? Why? You *know* you'll be late! You *know* it! You're *always* late, so why do you tell me these dumb things?" She closed the door.

On the other side, the Harlequin nodded to himself. *She's right. She's always right. I'll be late. I'm always late. Why* do *I tell her these dumb things?*

He shrugged again, and went off to be late once more.

He had fired off the firecracker rockets that said: I will attend the 115th an- 65
nual International Medical Association Invocation at 8:00 PM precisely. I do hope you will all be able to join me.

The words had burned in the sky, and of course the authorities were there, lying in wait for him. They assumed, naturally, that he would be late. He arrived twenty minutes early, while they were setting up the spiderwebs to trap and hold him. Blowing a large bullhorn, he frightened and unnerved them so, their own moisturized encirclement webs sucked closed, and they were hauled up, kicking and shrieking, high above the amphitheater's floor. The Harlequin laughed and laughed, and apologized profusely. The physicians, gathered in solemn conclave, roared with laughter, and accepted the Harlequin's apologies with exaggerated bowing and posturing, and a merry time was had by all, who thought the Harlequin was a regular foofaraw in fancy pants; all, that is, but the authorities, who had been sent out by the office of the Ticktockman; they hung there like so much dockside cargo, hauled up above the floor of the amphitheater in a most unseemly fashion.

(In another part of the same city where the Harlequin carried on his "activities," totally unrelated in every way to what concerns us here, save that it illustrates the Ticktockman's power and import, a man named Marshall Delahanty received his turn-off notice from the Ticktockman's office. His wife received the notification from the gray-suited minee who delivered it, with the traditional "look of sorrow" plastered hideously across his face. She knew what it was, even without unsealing it. It was a billet-doux of immediate recognition to everyone these days. She gasped, and held it as though it were a glass slide tinged with botulism, and prayed it was not for her. Let it be for Marsh, she thought, brutally, realistically, or one of the kids, but not for me, please dear God, not for me. And then she opened it, and it *was* for Marsh, and she was at one and the same time horrified and relieved. The next trooper in the line had caught the bullet. "Marshall," she screamed, "Marshall! Termination, Marshall! OhmiGod, Marshall, whattl we do, whattl we do, Marshall omigod-marshall . . ." and in their home that night was the sound of tearing paper and fear, and the stink of madness went up the flue and there was nothing, absolutely nothing they could do about it.

(But Marshall Delahanty tried to run. And early the next day, when turn-off time came, he was deep in the Canadian forest two hundred miles away, and the office of the Ticktockman blanked his cardioplate, and Marshall Delahanty keeled over, running, and his heart stopped, and the blood dried up on its way to his brain, and he was dead that's all. One light went out on the sector map in the office of the Master Timekeeper, while notification was entered for fax reproduction, and Georgette Delahanty's name was entered on the dole roles till she could remarry. Which is the end of the footnote, and all the point that need be made, except don't laugh, because that is what would happen to the Harlequin if ever the Ticktockman found out his real name. It isn't funny.)

The shopping level of the city was thronged with the Thursday-colors of the buyers. Women in canary yellow chitons and men in pseudo-Tyrolean outfits that were jade and leather and fit very tightly, save for the balloon pants.

When the Harlequin appeared on the still-being-constructed shell of the new Efficiency Shopping Center, his bullhorn to his elfishly-laughing lips, everyone pointed and stared, and he berated them: 70

"Why let them order you about? Why let them tell you to hurry and scurry like ants or maggots? Take your time! Saunter a while! Enjoy the sunshine, enjoy the breeze, let life carry you at your own pace! Don't be slaves of time, it's a helluva way to die, slowly, by degrees . . . down with the Ticktockman!"

Who's the nut? most of the shoppers wanted to know. Who's the nut oh wow I'm gonna be late I gotta run . . .

And the construction gang on the Shopping Center received an urgent order from the office of the Master Timekeeper that the dangerous criminal known as the Harlequin was atop their spire, and their aid was urgently needed in apprehending him. The work crew said no, they would lose time on their construction schedule, but the Ticktockman managed to pull the proper threads of governmental webbing, and they were told to cease work and catch that nitwit up there on the spire; up there with the bullhorn. So a dozen and more burly workers began climbing into their construction platforms, releasing the a-grav plates, and rising toward the Harlequin.

After the debacle (in which, through the Harlequin's attention to personal safety, no one was seriously injured), the workers tried to reassemble, and assault him again, but it was too late. He had vanished. It had attracted quite a crowd, however, and the shopping cycle was thrown off by hours, simply hours. The purchasing needs of the system were therefore falling behind, and so measures were taken to accelerate the cycle for the rest of the day, but it got bogged down and speeded up and they sold too many float-valves and not nearly enough wegglers, which meant that the popli ratio was off, which made it necessary to rush cases and cases of spoiling Smash-O to stores that usually needed a case only every three or four hours. The shipments were bollixed, the transshipments were misrouted, and in the end, even the swizzleskid industries felt it.

"Don't come back till you have him!" the Ticktockman said, very quietly, very   75
sincerely, extremely dangerously.

They used dogs. They used probes. They used cardioplate crossoffs. They used teepers. They used bribery. They used stiktytes. They used intimidation. They used torment. They used torture. They used finks. They used cops. They used search&seizure. They used fallaron. They used betterment incentive. They used fingerprints. They used the Bertillon system. They used cunning. They used guile. They used treachery. They used Raoul Mitgong, but he didn't help much. They used applied physics. They used techniques of criminology.

And what the hell: they caught him.

After all, his name was Everett C. Marm, and he wasn't much to begin with, except a man who had no sense of time.

"Repent, Harlequin!" said the Ticktockman.

"Get stuffed!" the Harlequin replied, sneering.   80

"You've been late a total of sixty-three years, five months, three weeks, two days, twelve hours, forty-one minutes, fifty-nine seconds, point oh three six one one one microseconds. You've used up everything you can, and more. I'm going to turn you off."

"Scare someone else. I'd rather be dead than live in a dumb world with a bogeyman like you."

"It's my job."

"You're full of it. You're a tyrant. You have no right to order people around and kill them if they show up late."

"You can't adjust. You can't fit in."   85

"Unstrap me, and I'll fit my fist into your mouth."

"You're a nonconformist."

"That didn't used to be a felony."

"It is now. Live in the world around you."

"I hate it. It's a terrible world."   90

"Not everyone thinks so. Most people enjoy order."

"I don't, and most of the people I know don't."

"That's not true. How do you think we caught you?"

"I'm not interested."

"A girl named Pretty Alice told us who you were."   95
"That's a lie."
"It's true. You unnerve her. She wants to belong; she wants to conform; I'm going to turn you off."
"Then do it already, and stop arguing with me."
"I'm not going to turn you off."
"You're an idiot!"   100
"Repent, Harlequin!" said the Ticktockman.
"Get stuffed."

So they sent him to Coventry. And in Coventry they worked him over. It was just like what they did to Winston Smith in NINETEEN EIGHTY-FOUR, which was a book none of them knew about, but the techniques are really quite ancient, and so they did it to Everett C. Marm; and one day, quite a long time later, the Harlequin appeared on the communications web, appearing elfin and dimpled and bright-eyed, and not at all brainwashed, and he said he had been wrong, that it was a good, a very good thing indeed, to belong, to be right on time hip-ho and away we go, and everyone stared up at him on the public screens that covered an entire city block, and they said to themselves, well, you see, he was just a nut after all, and if that's the way the system is run, then let's do it that way, because it doesn't pay to fight city hall, or in this case, the Ticktockman. So Everett C. Marm was destroyed, which was a loss, because of what Thoreau said earlier, but you can't make an omelet without breaking a few eggs, and in every revolution a few die who shouldn't, but they have to, because that's the way it happens, and if you make only a little change, then it seems to be worthwhile. Or, to make the point lucidly:

"Uh, excuse me, sir, I, uh, don't know how to uh, to uh, tell you this, but you were three minutes late. The schedule is a little, uh, bit off."
He grinned sheepishly.   105
"That's ridiculous!" murmured the Ticktockman behind his mask. "Check your watch." And then he went into his office, going *mrmee, mrmee, mrmee, mrmee.*

For Analysis
1. What are the connotations of the names Harlequin and Everett C. Marm? Is the contrast between the names similar to that between, say, Superman and Clark Kent? **2.** What is it about his society that drives Everett C. Marm to rebel? **3.** What is Pretty Alice's role in the story? **4.** Explain the final section of the story (par. 104–106). Has the Ticktockman triumphed?

On Style
1. Why does Ellison not present the events in **chronological order**? **2.** How would you characterize the prose **style** of this story? What effect is the author trying to achieve? Is he successful?

Making Connections

1. Compare the statement this story makes about the human spirit with that made in Le Guin's "The Ones Who Walk Away from Omelas." Does Everett C. Marm share any of the attributes of the ones who walk away from Omelas? **2.** Compare Everett C. Marm and "Pal" Smurch in James Thurber's story "The Greatest Man in the World" (p. 345) as heroes. Which do you find more admirable and heroic?

Writing Topic

Carefully read the passage taken from Henry David Thoreau's "Civil Disobedience" (par. 1). Write an essay explaining why you do or do not agree (in whole or in part) with Thoreau's view of "the state" and with his classification of citizens as those who serve the state with their "bodies," those who serve it with their "heads," and those who serve it with their "consciences." Where would you place Everett C. Marm?

James Alan McPherson   [b. 1943]

A Loaf of Bread   1979

It was one of those obscene situations, pedestrian to most people, but invested with meaning for a few poor folk whose lives are usually spent outside the imaginations of their fellow citizens. A grocer named Harold Green was caught red-handed selling to one group of people the very same goods he sold at lower prices at similar outlets in better neighborhoods. He had been doing this for many years, and at first he could not understand the outrage heaped upon him. He acted only from habit, he insisted, and had nothing personal against the people whom he served. They were his neighbors. Many of them he had carried on the cuff during hard times. Yet, through some mysterious access to a television station, the poor folk were now empowered to make grand denunciations of the grocer. Green's children now saw their father's business being picketed on the Monday evening news.

No one could question the fact that the grocer had been overcharging the people. On the news even the reporter grimaced distastefully while reading the statistics. His expression said, "It is my job to report the news, but sometimes even I must disassociate myself from it to protect my honor." This, at least, was the impression the grocer's children seemed to bring away from the television. Their father's name had not been mentioned, but there was a close-up of his store with angry black people and a few outraged whites marching in groups of three in front of it. There was also a close-up of his name. After seeing this, they were in no mood to watch cartoons. At the dinner table, disturbed by his children's silence, Harold Green felt compelled to say, "I am not a dishonest man." Then he felt ashamed. The children, a boy and his older sister, immediately left the table, leaving Green alone with his wife. "Ruth, I am not dishonest," he repeated to her.

Ruth Green did not say anything. She knew, and her husband did not, that the outraged people had also picketed the school attended by their children. They had threatened to return each day until Green lowered his prices. When they called her at home to report this, she had promised she would talk with him. Since she could not tell him this, she waited for an opening. She looked at her husband across the table.

"I did not make the world," Green began, recognizing at once the seriousness in her stare. "My father came to this country with nothing but his shirt. He was exploited for as long as he couldn't help himself. He did not protest or picket. He put himself in a position to play by the rules he had learned." He waited for his wife to answer, and when she did not, he tried again. "I did not make this world," he repeated. "I only make my way in it. Such people as these, they do

405

not know enough to not be exploited. If not me, there would be a Greek, a Chinaman, maybe an Arab or a smart one of their own kind. Believe me, I deal with them. There is something in their style that lacks the patience to run a concern such as mine. If I closed down, take my word on it, someone else would do what has to be done."

But Ruth Green was not thinking of his leaving. Her mind was on other matters. Her children had cried when they came home early from school. She had no special feeling for the people who picketed, but she did not like to see her children cry. She had kissed them generously, then sworn them to silence. "One day this week," she told her husband, "you will give free, for eight hours, anything your customers come in to buy. There will be no publicity, except what they spread by word of mouth. No matter what they say to you, no matter what they take, you will remain silent." She stared deeply into him for what she knew was there. "If you refuse, you have seen the last of your children and myself."

Her husband grunted. Then he leaned toward her. "I will not knuckle under," he said. "I will *not* give!"

"We shall see," his wife told him.

The black pickets, for the most part, had at first been frightened by the audacity of their undertaking. They were peasants whose minds had long before become resigned to their fate as victims. None of them, before now, had thought to challenge this. But now, when they watched themselves on television, they hardly recognized the faces they saw beneath the hoisted banners and placards. Instead of reflecting the meekness they all felt, the faces looked angry. The close-ups looked especially intimidating. Several of the first pickets, maids who worked in the suburbs, reported that their employers, seeing the activity on the afternoon news, had begun treating them with new respect. One woman, midway through the weather report, called around the neighborhood to disclose that her employer had that very day given her a new china plate for her meals. The paper plates, on which all previous meals had been served, had been thrown into the wastebasket. One recipient of this call, a middle-aged woman known for her bashfulness and humility, rejoined that her husband, a sheet-metal worker, had only a few hours before been called "Mister" by his supervisor, a white man with a passionate hatred of color. She added the tale of a neighbor down the street, a widow woman named Murphy, who had at first been reluctant to join the picket; this woman now was insisting it should be made a daily event. Such talk as this circulated among the people who had been instrumental in raising the issue. As news of their victory leaked into the ears of others who had not participated, they received all through the night calls from strangers requesting verification, offering advice, and vowing support. Such strangers listened and then volunteered stories about indignities inflicted on them by city officials, policemen, other grocers. In this way, over a period of hours, the community became even more incensed and restless than it had been at the time of the initial picket.

Soon the man who had set events in motion found himself a hero. His name was Nelson Reed, and all his adult life he had been employed as an assembly-line worker. He was a steady husband, the father of three children, and a deacon in the Baptist church. All his life he had trusted in God and gotten along. But now something in him capitulated to the reality that came suddenly into focus. "I was wrong," he told people who called him. "The onliest thing that matters in this world is *money.* And when was the last time you seen a picture of Jesus on a dollar bill?" This line, which he repeated over and over, caused a few callers to laugh nervously, but not without some affirmation that this was indeed the way things were. Many said they had known it all along. Others argued that although it was certainly true, it was one thing to live without money and quite another to live without faith. But still most callers laughed and said, "You right. You *know* I know you right. Ain't it the truth, though?" Only a few people, among them Nelson Reed's wife, said nothing and looked very sad.

Why they looked sad, however, they would not communicate. And anyone   10
observing their troubled faces would have to trust his own intuition. It is known that Reed's wife, Betty, measured all events against the fullness of her own experience. She was skeptical of everything. Brought to the church after a number of years of living openly with a jazz musician, she had embraced religion when she married Nelson Reed. But though she no longer believed completely in the world, she nonetheless had not fully embraced God. There was something in the nature of Christ's swift rise that had always bothered her, and something in the blood and vengeance of the Old Testament that was mellowing and refreshing. But she had never communicated these thoughts to anyone, especially her husband. Instead, she smiled vacantly while others professed leaps of faith, remained silent when friends spoke fiercely of their convictions. The presence of this vacuum in her contributed to her personal mystery; people said she was beautiful, although she was not outwardly so. Perhaps it was because she wished to protect this inner beauty that she did not smile now, and looked extremely sad, listening to her husband on the telephone.

Nelson Reed had no reason to be sad. He seemed to grow more energized and talkative as the days passed. He was invited by an alderman, on the Tuesday after the initial picket, to tell his story on a local television talk show. He sweated heavily under the hot white lights and attempted to be philosophical. "I notice," the host said to him, "that you are not angry at this exploitative treatment. What, Mr. Reed, is the source of your calm?" The assembly-line worker looked unabashedly into the camera and said, "I have always believed in *Justice* with a capital *J.* I was raised up from a baby believin' that God ain't gonna let nobody go *too* far. See, in *my* mind God is in charge of *all* the capital letters in the alphabet of this world. It say in the Scripture He is Alpha and Omega, the first and the last. He is just about the *onliest* capitalizer they is." Both Reed and the alderman laughed. "Now, when *men* start to capitalize, they gets *greedy.* They put a little *j* in *joy* and a littler one in *justice.* They raise up a big *G* in *Greed* and a big *E* in *Evil.* Well, soon as they commence to put a little *g* in *god,* you can expect some kind of reaction. The Savior will just raise up the *H* in *Hell* and go on from there. And that's just what I'm doin', giving these sharpies *HELL* with a big *H*." The talk show host laughed along with Nelson Reed and the alderman. After the taping they drank coffee in the back room of the studio and talked about the sad shape of the world.

Three days before he was to comply with his wife's request, Green, the grocer, saw this talk show on television while at home. The words of Nelson Reed sent a chill through him. Though Reed had attempted to be philosophical, Green did not perceive the statement in this light. Instead, he saw a vindictive-looking black man seated between an ambitious alderman and a smug talk-show host. He saw them chatting comfortably about the nature of evil. The cameraman had shot mostly close-ups, and Green could see the set in Nelson Reed's jaw. The color of Reed's face was maddening. When his children came into the den, the grocer was in a sweat. Before he could think, he had shouted at them and struck the button turning off the set. The two children rushed from the room screaming. Ruth Green ran in from the kitchen. She knew why he was upset because she had received a call about the show, but she said nothing and pretended ignorance. Her children's school had been picketed that day, as it had the day before. But both children were still forbidden to speak of this to their father.

"Where do they get so much power?" Green said to his wife. "Two days ago nobody would have cared. Now everywhere, even in my home, I am condemned as a rascal. And what do I own? An airline? A multinational? Half of South America? *No!* I own three stores, one of which happens to be in a certain neighborhood inhabited by people who cost me money to run it." He sighed and sat upright on the sofa, his chubby legs spread wide. "A cabdriver has a meter that clicks as he goes along. I pay extra for insurance, iron bars, pilfering by customers and employees. Nothing clicks. But when I add a little overhead to my prices, suddenly everything clicks. But for someone else. When was there last such a world?" He pressed the palms of both hands to his temples, suggesting a bombardment of brain-stinging sounds.

This gesture evoked no response from Ruth Green. She remained standing by the door, looking steadily at him. She said, "To protect yourself, I would not stock any more fresh cuts of meat in the store until after the giveaway on Saturday. Also, I would not tell it to the employees until after the first customer of the day has begun to check out. But I would urge you to hire several security guards to close the door promptly at seven-thirty, as is usual." She wanted to say much more than this, but did not. Instead she watched him. He was looking at the blank gray television screen, his palms still pressed against his ears. "In case you need to hear again," she continued in a weighty tone of voice, "I said two days ago, and I say again now, that if you fail to do this you will not see your children again for many years."

He twisted his head and looked up at her. "What is the color of these people?" he asked.   15

"Black," his wife said.

"And what is the name of my children?"

"Green."

The grocer smiled. "There is your answer," he told his wife. "Green is the only color I am interested in."

His wife did not smile. "Insufficient," she said.   20

"The world is mad!" he moaned. "But it is a point of sanity with me to not bend. I will not bend." He crossed his legs and pressed one hand firmly atop his knee. *"I will not bend,"* he said.

"We will see," his wife said.

Nelson Reed, after the television interview, became the acknowledged leader of the disgruntled neighbors. At first a number of them met in the kitchen at his house; then, as space was lacking for curious newcomers, a mass meeting was held on Thursday in an abandoned theater. His wife and three children sat in the front row. Behind them sat the widow Murphy, Lloyd Dukes, Tyrone Brown, Les Jones—those who had joined him on the first picket line. Behind these sat people who bought occasionally at the store, people who lived on the fringes of the neighborhood, people from other neighborhoods come to investigate the problem, and the merely curious. The middle rows were occupied by a few people from the suburbs, those who had seen the talk show and whose outrage at the grocer proved much more powerful than their fear of black people. In the rear of the theater crowded aging, old-style leftists, somber students, cynical young black men with angry grudges to explain with inarticulate gestures. Leaning against the walls, huddled near the doors at the rear, tape-recorder-bearing social scientists looked as detached and serene as bookies at the track. Here and there, in this diverse crowd, a politician stationed himself, pumping hands vigorously and pressing his palms gently against the shoulders of elderly people. Other visitors passed out leaflets, buttons, glossy color prints of men who promoted causes, the familiar and obscure. There was a hubbub of voices, a blend of the strident and the playful, the outraged and the reverent, lending an undercurrent of ominous energy to the assembly.

Nelson Reed spoke from a platform on the stage, standing before a yellowed, shredded screen that had once reflected the images of matinee idols. "I don't mind sayin' that I have always been a sucker," he told the crowd. "All my life I have been a sucker for the words of Jesus. Being a natural-born fool, I just ain't never had the *sense* to learn no better. Even right today, while the whole world is sayin' wrong is right and up is down, I'm so dumb I'm *still* steady believin' what is wrote in the Good Book. . . ."

From the audience, especially the front rows, came a chorus singing,   25 "Preach!"

"I have no doubt," he continued in a low baritone, "that it's true what is writ in the Good Book: 'The last shall be first and the first shall be last.' I don't know about y'all, but I have *always* been the last. I never wanted to be the first, but

sometimes it look like the world get so bad that them that's holdin' onto the tree
of life is the onliest ones left when God commence to blowin' dead leafs off the
branches."

"Now you preaching," someone called.

In the rear of the theater a white student shouted an awkward "Amen."

Nelson Reed began walking across the stage to occupy the major part of his
nervous energy. But to those in the audience, who now hung on his every word,
it looked as though he strutted. "All my life," he said, "I have claimed to be a
man without earnin' the right to call myself that. You know, the *average* man
ain't really a man. The average man is a *bootlicker.* In fact, the *average* man
would *run away* if he found hisself standing alone facin' down a adversary. I
have done that *too many a time* in my life! But *not no more.* Better to be *once*
was than *never* was a man. I will tell you tonight, there is somethin' *wrong* in being average. *I intend to stand up!* Now, if your average man that ain't really a
man stand up, two things gonna happen: *one,* he gon bust through all the
weights that been place on his head, and, *two,* he gon feel a lot of pain. But that
same hurt is what make things fall in place. That, and gettin' your hands on one
of these slick four-flushers tight enough so's you can squeeze him and say, 'No
more!' You do that, you g'on hurt some, but *you won't be average no more.* . . ."

"No *more!*" a few people in the front rows repeated.   30

"I say *no more!*" Nelson Reed shouted.

"No more! No more! No more!" The chant rustled through the crowd like the
rhythm of an autumn wind against a shedding tree.

Then people laughed and chattered in celebration.

As for the grocer, from the evening of the television interview he had begun
to make plans. Unknown to his wife, he cloistered himself several times with his
brother-in-law, an insurance salesman, and plotted a course. He had no intention of tossing steaks to the crowd. "And why should I, Tommy?" he asked his
wife's brother, a lean, bald-headed man named Thomas. "I don't cheat anyone.
I have never cheated anyone. The businesses I run are always on the up-and-up.
So why should I pay?"

"Quite so," the brother-in-law said, chewing an unlit cigarillo. "The world has   35
gone crazy. Next they will say that people in my business are responsible for
prolonging life. I have found that people who refuse to believe in death refuse
also to believe in the harshness of life. I sell well by saying that death is a long
happiness. I show people the realities of life and compare this to a funeral with
dignity, *and* the promise of a bundle for every loved one salted away. When they
look around hard at life, they usually buy."

"So?" asked Green. Thomas was a college graduate with a penchant for philosophy.

"So," Thomas answered. "You must fight to show these people the reality of
both your situation and theirs. How would it be if you visited one of their meetings and chalked out, on a blackboard, the dollars and cents of your operation?

Explain your overhead, your security fees, all the additional expenses. If you treat them with respect, they might understand."

Green frowned. "That I would never do," he said. "It would be admission of a certain guilt."

The brother-in-law smiled, but only with one corner of his mouth. "Then you have something to feel guilty about?" he asked.

The grocer frowned at him. *"Nothing!"* he said with great emphasis. 40

"So?" Thomas said.

This first meeting between the grocer and his brother-in-law took place on Thursday, in a crowded barroom.

At the second meeting, in a luncheonette, it was agreed that the grocer should speak privately with the leader of the group, Nelson Reed. The meeting at which this was agreed took place on Friday afternoon. After accepting this advice from Thomas, the grocer resigned himself to explain to Reed, in as finite detail as possible, the economic structure of his operation. He vowed to suppress no information. He would explain everything: inventories, markups, sale items, inflation, balance sheets, specialty items, overhead, and that mysterious item called profit. This last item, promising to be the most difficult to explain, Green and his brother-in-law debated over for several hours. They agreed first of all that a man should not work for free, then they agreed that it was unethical to ruthlessly exploit. From these parameters, they staked out an area between fifteen and forty percent, and agreed that someplace between these two borders lay an amount of return that could be called fair. This was easy, but then Thomas introduced the factor of circumstance. He questioned whether the fact that one serviced a risky area justified the earning of profits, closer to the forty-percent edge of the scale. Green was unsure. Thomas smiled. "Here is a case that will point out an analogy," he said, licking a cigarillo. "I read in the papers that a family wants to sell an electric stove. I call the home and the man says fifty dollars. I ask to come out and inspect the merchandise. When I arrive I see they are poor, have already bought a new stove that is connected, and are selling the old one for fifty dollars because they want it out of the place. The electric stove is in good condition, worth much more than fifty. But because I see what I see I offer forty-five."

Green, for some reason, wrote down this figure on the back of the sales slip for the coffee they were drinking.

The brother-in-law smiled. He chewed his cigarillo. "The man agrees to take 45 forty-five dollars, saying he has had no other calls. I look at the stove again and see a spot of rust. I say I will give him forty dollars. He agrees to this, on condition that I myself haul it away. I say I will haul it away if he comes down to thirty. You, of course, see where I am going."

The grocer nodded. "The circumstances of his situation, his need to get rid of the stove quickly, placed him in a position where he has little room to bargain?"

"Yes," Thomas answered. "So? Is it ethical, Harry?"

Harold Green frowned. He had never liked his brother-in-law, and now he thought the insurance agent was being crafty. "But," he answered, "this man does not *have* to sell! It is his choice whether to wait for other calls. It is not the fault of the buyer that the seller is in a hurry. It is the right of the buyer to get what he wants at the lowest price possible. That is the rule. That has *always* been the rule. And the reverse of it applies to the seller as well."

"Yes," Thomas said, sipping coffee from the Styrofoam cup. "But suppose that in addition to his hurry to sell, the owner was also of a weak soul. There are, after all, many such people." He smiled. "Suppose he placed no value on the money?"

"Then," Green answered, "your example is academic. Here we are not talk- 50 ing about real life. One man lives by the code, one man does not. Who is there free enough to make a judgment?" He laughed. "Now you see," he told his brother-in-law. "Much more than a few dollars are at stake. If this one buyer is to be condemned, then so are most people in the history of the world. An examination of history provides the only answer to your question. This code will be here tomorrow, long after the ones who do not honor it are not."

They argued fiercely late into the afternoon, the brother-in-law leaning heavily on his readings. When they parted, a little before five o'clock, nothing had been resolved.

Neither was much resolved during the meeting between Green and Nelson Reed. Reached at home by the grocer in the early evening, the leader of the group spoke coldly at first, but consented finally to meet his adversary at a nearby drugstore for coffee and a talk. They met at the lunch counter, shook hands awkwardly, and sat for a few minutes discussing the weather. Then the grocer pulled two gray ledgers from his briefcase. "You have for years come into my place," he told the man. "In my memory I have always treated you well. Now our relationship has come to this." He slid the books along the counter until they touched Nelson Reed's arm.

Reed opened the top book and flipped the thick green pages with his thumb. He did not examine the figures. "All I know," he said, "is over at your place a can of soup cost me fifty-five cents, and two miles away at your other store for white folks you chargin' thirty-nine cents." He said this with the calm authority of an outraged soul. A quality of condescension tinged with pity crept into his gaze.

The grocer drummed his fingers on the counter top. He twisted his head and looked away, toward shelves containing cosmetics, laxatives, toothpaste. His eyes lingered on a poster of a woman's apple-red lips and milk-white teeth. The rest of the face was missing.

"Ain't no use to hide," Nelson Reed said, as to a child. "*I* know you wrong, *you* 55 know you wrong, and before I finish, *everybody in this city* g'on know you wrong. God don't *like* ugly." He closed his eyes and gripped the cup of coffee. Then he swung his head suddenly and faced the grocer again. "Man, why you want to *do* people that way?" he asked. "We human, same as you."

"Before *God!*" Green exclaimed, looking squarely into the face of Nelson Reed. "Before God!" he said again. "*I am not an evil man!*" These last words sounded more like a moan as he tightened the muscles in his throat to lower the sound of his voice. He tossed his left shoulder as if adjusting the sleeve of his coat, or as if throwing off some unwanted weight. Then he peered along the counter top. No one was watching. At the end of the counter the waitress was scrubbing the coffee urn. "Look at these figures, please," he said to Reed.

The man did not drop his gaze. His eyes remained fixed on the grocer's face.

"All right," Green said. "Don't look. I'll tell you what is in these books, believe me if you want. I work twelve hours a day, one day off per week, running my business in three stores. I am not a wealthy person. In one place, in the area you call white, I get by barely by smiling lustily at old ladies, stocking gourmet stuff on the chance I will build a reputation as a quality store. The two clerks there cheat me; there is nothing I can do. In this business you must be friendly with everybody. The second place is on the other side of town, in a neighborhood as poor as this one. I get out there seldom. The profits are not worth the gas. I use the loss there as a write-off against some other properties," he paused. "Do you understand write-off?" he asked Nelson Reed.

"Naw," the man said.

Harold Green laughed. "What does it matter?" he said in a tone of voice intended for himself alone. "In this area I will admit I make a profit, but it is not so much as you think. But I do not make a profit here because the people are black. I make a profit because a profit is here to be made. I invest more here in window bars, theft losses, insurance, spoilage; I deserve to make more here than at the other places." He looked, almost imploringly, at the man seated next to him. "You don't accept this as the right of a man in business?" 60

Reed grunted. "Did the bear shit in the woods?" he said.

Again Green laughed. He gulped his coffee awkwardly, as if eager to go. Yet his motions slowed once he had set his coffee cup down on the blue plastic saucer. "Place yourself in *my* situation," he said, his voice high and tentative. "If *you* were running my store in this neighborhood, what would be *your* position? Say on a profit scale of fifteen to forty percent, at what point in between would you draw the line?"

Nelson Reed thought. He sipped his coffee and seemed to chew the liquid. "Fifteen to forty?" he repeated.

"Yes."

"I'm a churchgoin' man," he said. "Closer to fifteen than to forty." 65

"How close?"

Nelson Reed thought. "In church you tithe ten percent."

"In restaurants you tip fifteen," the grocer said quickly.

"All right," Reed said. "Over fifteen."

"How much over?" 70

Nelson Reed thought.

"Twenty, thirty, thirty-five?" Green chanted, leaning closer to Reed.

Still the man thought.

"Forty? Maybe even forty-five or fifty?" the grocer breathed in Reed's ear. "In the supermarkets, you know, they have more subtle ways of accomplishing such feats."

Reed slapped his coffee cup with the back of his right hand. The brown liq-   75
uid swirled across the counter top, wetting the books. *"Damn this!"* he shouted.

Startled, Green rose from his stool.

Nelson Reed was trembling. "I ain't *you,*" he said in a deep baritone. "I ain't
the *supermarket* neither. All I is is a poor man that works *too* hard to see his pay
slip through his fingers like rainwater. All I know is you done *cheat* me, you done
cheat everybody in the neighborhood, and we organized now to get some of it
back!" Then he stood and faced the grocer. "My daddy sharecropped down in
Mississippi and bought in the company store. He owed them twenty-three years
when he died. I paid off five of them years and then run away to up here. Now,
I'm a deacon in the Baptist church. I raised my kids the way my daddy raise me
and don't bother nobody. Now come to find out, after all my runnin', they done
lift that *same company store* up out of Mississippi and slip it down on us here!
Well, my daddy was a *fighter,* and if he hadn't owed all them years he would of
raise him some hell. Me, I'm steady my daddy's child, plus I got seniority in my
union. I'm a free man. Buddy, don't you know *I'm gonna raise me some hell!*"

Harold Green reached for a paper napkin to sop the coffee soaking into his
books.

Nelson Reed threw a dollar on top of the books and walked away.

"I *will not* do it!" Harold Green said to his wife that same evening. They were   80
in the bathroom of their home. Bending over the face bowl, she was washing
her hair with a towel draped around her neck. The grocer stood by the door,
looking in at her. "I will not bankrupt myself tomorrow," he said.

"I've been thinking about it, too," Ruth Green said, shaking her wet hair.
"You'll do it, Harry."

"Why should I?" he asked. "You won't leave. You know it was a bluff. I've
waited this long for you to calm down. Tomorrow is Saturday. This week has
been a hard one. Tonight let's be realistic."

"Of course you'll do it," Ruth Green said. She said it the way she would say
"Have some toast." She said. "You'll do it because you want to see your children
grow up."

"And for what other reason?" he asked.

She pulled the towel tighter around her neck. "Because you are at heart a   85
moral man."

He grinned painfully. "If I am, why should I have to prove it to *them?*"

"Not them," Ruth Green said, freezing her movements and looking in the
mirror. "Certainly not them. By no means them. They have absolutely nothing
to do with this."

"Who, then?" he asked, moving from the door into the room. "Who else
should I prove something to?"

His wife was crying. But her entire face was wet. The tears moved secretly
down her face.

"Who else?" Harold Green asked.   90

It was almost eleven P.M. and the children were in bed. They had also cried when they came home from school. Ruth Green said, "For yourself, Harry. For the love that lives inside your heart."

All night the grocer thought about this.

Nelson Reed also slept little that Friday night. When he returned home from the drugstore, he reported to his wife as much of the conversation as he could remember. At first he had joked about the exchange between himself and the grocer, but as more details returned to his conscious mind he grew solemn and then bitter. "He ask me to put myself in *his* place," Reed told his wife. "Can you imagine that kind of gumption? I never cheated nobody in my life. All my life I have lived on Bible principles. I am a deacon in the church. I have work all my life for other folks and I don't even own the house I live in." He paced up and down the kitchen, his big arms flapping loosely at his sides. Betty Reed sat at the table, watching. "This here's a low-down, ass-kicking world," he said. "I swear to God it is! All my life I have lived on principle and I ain't got a dime in the bank. Betty," he turned suddenly toward her, "don't you think I'm a fool?"

"Mr. Reed," she said. "Let's go on to bed."

But he would not go to bed. Instead, he took the fifth of bourbon from the   95
cabinet under the sink and poured himself a shot. His wife refused to join him. Reed drained the glass of whiskey, and then another, while he resumed pacing the kitchen floor. He slapped his hands against his sides. "*I* think I'm a fool," he said. "Ain't got a dime in the bank, ain't got a pot to *pee* in or a wall to pitch it over, and that there *cheat* ask me to put myself inside *his* shoes. Hell, I can't even *afford* the kind of shoes he wears." He stopped pacing and looked at his wife.

"Mr. Reed," she whispered, "tomorrow ain't a work day. Let's go to bed."

Nelson Reed laughed, the bitterness in his voice rattling his wife. "The *hell* I will!" he said.

He strode to the yellow telephone on the wall beside the sink and began to dial. The first call was to Lloyd Dukes, a neighbor two blocks away and a lieutenant in the organization. Dukes was not at home. The second call was to McElroy's Bar on the corner of Sixty-fifth and Carroll, where Stanley Harper, another of the lieutenants, worked as a bartender. It was Harper who spread the word, among those men at the bar, that the organization would picket the grocer's store the following morning. And all through the night, in the bedroom of their house, Betty Reed was awakened by telephone calls coming from Lester Jones, Nat Lucas, Mrs. Tyrone Brown, the widow-woman named Murphy, all coordinating the time when they would march in a group against the store owned by Harold Green. Betty Reed's heart beat loudly beneath the covers as she listened to the bitterness and rage in her husband's voice. On several occasions, hearing him declare himself a fool, she pressed the pillow against her eyes and cried.

The grocer opened later than usual this Saturday morning, but still it was early enough to make him one of the first walkers in the neighborhood. He parked his car one block from the store and strolled to work. There were no birds singing. The sky in this area was not blue. It was smog-smutted and gray, seeming on the verge of a light rain. The street, as always, was littered with cans, papers, bits of broken glass. As always the garbage cans overflowed. The morning breeze plastered a sheet of newspaper playfully around the sides of a rusted garbage can. For some reason, using his right foot, he loosened the paper and stood watching it slide into the street and down the block. The movement made him feel good. He whistled while unlocking the bars shielding the windows and door of his store. When he had unlocked the main door he stepped in quickly and threw a switch to the right of the jamb, before the shrill sound of the alarm could shatter his mood. Then he switched on the lights. Everything was as it had been the night before. He had already telephoned his two employees and given them the day off. He busied himself doing the usual things—hauling milk and vegetables from the cooler, putting cash in the till—not thinking about the silence of his wife, or the look in her eyes, only an hour before when he left home. He had determined, at some point while driving through the city, that today it would be business as usual. But he expected very few customers.

The first customer of the day was Mrs. Nelson Reed. She came in around 100 nine-thirty A.M. and wandered about the store. He watched her from the checkout counter. She seemed uncertain of what she wanted to buy. She kept glancing at him down the center aisle. His suspicions aroused, he said finally, "Yes, may I help you, Mrs. Reed?" His words caused her to jerk, as if some devious thought had been perceived going through her mind. She reached over quickly and lifted a loaf of whole wheat bread from the rack and walked with it to the counter. She looked at him and smiled. The smile was a broad, shy one, that rare kind of smile one sees on virgin girls when they first confess love to themselves. Betty Reed was a woman of about forty-five. For some reason he could not comprehend, this gesture touched him. When she pulled a dollar from her purse and laid it on the counter, an impulse, from no place he could locate with his mind, seized control of his tongue. "Free," he told Betty Reed. She paused, then pushed the dollar toward him with a firm and determined thrust of her arm. "Free," he heard himself saying strongly, his right palm spread and meeting her thrust with absolute force. She clutched the loaf of bread and walked out of his store.

The next customer, a little girl, arriving well after ten-thirty A.M., selected a candy bar from the rack beside the counter. "Free," Green said cheerfully. The little girl left the candy on the counter and ran out of the store.

At eleven-fifteen A.M. a wino came in looking desperate enough to sell his soul. The grocer watched him only for an instant. Then he went to the wine counter and selected a half-gallon of medium-grade red wine. He shoved the jug into the belly of the wino, the man's sour breath bathing his face. "Free," the grocer said. "But you must not drink it in here."

He felt good about the entire world, watching the wino through the window gulping the wine and looking guiltily around.

At eleven twenty-five A.M. the pickets arrived.

Two dozen people, men and women, young and old, crowded the pavement 105
in front of his store. Their signs, placards, and voices denounced him as a para-
site. The grocer laughed inside himself. He felt lighthearted and wild, like a
man drugged. He rushed to the meat counter and pulled a long roll of brown
wrapping paper from the rack, tearing it neatly with a quick shift of his body resembling a dance step practiced fervently in his youth. He laid the paper on the
chopping block and with the black-inked, felt-tipped marker scrawled, in giant
letters, the word FREE. This he took to the window and pasted in place with
many strands of Scotch tape. He was laughing wildly. "Free!" he shouted from
behind the brown paper. "Free! Free! Free! Free! Free! Free!" He rushed to
the door, pushed his head out, and screamed to the confused crowd, *"Free!"*
Then he ran back to the counter and stood behind it, like a soldier at attention.

They came in slowly.

Nelson Reed entered first, working his right foot across the dirty tile as if
tracking a squiggling worm. The others followed: Lloyd Dukes dragging a plac-
ard, Mr. and Mrs. Tyrone Brown, Stanley Harper walking with his fists
clenched, Lester Jones with three of his children, Nat Lucas looking sheepish
and detached, a clutch of winos, several bashful nuns, ironic-smiling teenagers
and a few students. Bringing up the rear was a bearded social scientist holding
a tape recorder to his chest. "Free!" the grocer screamed. He threw up his arms
in a gesture that embraced, or dismissed, the entire store. *"All free!"* he
shouted. He was grinning with the grace of a madman.

The winos began grabbing first. They stripped the shelf of wine in a matter of
seconds. Then they fled, dropping bottles on the tile in their wake. The others,
stepping quickly through this liquid, soon congealed it into a sticky, bloodlike
consistency. The young men went for the cigarettes and luncheon meats and
beer. One of them had the prescience to grab a sack from the counter, while the
others loaded their arms swiftly, hugging cartons and packages of cold cuts like
long-lost friends. The students joined them, less for greed than for the thrill of
the experience. The two nuns backed toward the door. As for the older people,
men and women, they stood at first as if stuck to the wine-smeared floor. Then
Stanley Harper, the bartender, shouted, "The man said *free,* y'all heard him."
He paused. "Didn't you say *free* now?" he called to the grocer.

"I said free," Harold Green answered, his temples pounding.

A cheer went up. The older people began grabbing, as if the secret lusts of a 110
lifetime had suddenly seized command of their arms and eyes. They grabbed
toilet tissue, cold cuts, pickles, sardines, boxes of raisins, boxes of starch, cans of
soup, tins of tuna fish and salmon, bottles of spices, cans of boned chicken, slippery cans of olive oil. Here a man, Lester Jones, burdened himself with several
heads of lettuce, while his wife, in another aisle, shouted for him to drop those
small items and concentrate on the gourmet section. She herself took imported
sardines, wheat crackers, bottles of candied pickles, herring, anchovies, imported olives, French wafers, an ancient, half-rusted can of paté, stocked, by
mistake, from the inventory of another store. Others packed their arms with de-
tergents, hams, chocolate-coated cereal, whole chickens with hanging asses,

wedges of bologna and salami like squashed footballs, chunks of cheeses, yellow and white, shriveled onions, and green peppers. Mrs. Tyrone Brown hung a curve of pepperoni around her neck and seemed to take on instant dignity, much like a person of noble birth in possession now of a long sought-after gem. Another woman, the widow Murphy, stuffed tomatoes into her bosom, holding a half-chewed lemon in her mouth. The more enterprising fought desperately over the three rusted shopping carts, and the victors wheeled these along the narrow aisles, sweeping into them bulk items—beer in six-packs, sacks of sugar, flour, glass bottles of syrup, toilet cleanser, sugar cookies, prune, apple and tomato juices—while others endeavored to snatch the carts from them. There were several fistfights and much cursing. The grocer, standing behind the counter, hummed and rang his cash register like a madman.

Nelson Reed, the first into the store, followed the nuns out, empty-handed.

In less than half an hour the others had stripped the store and vanished in many directions up and down the block. But still more people came, those late in hearing the news. And when they saw the shelves were bare, they cursed soberly and chased those few stragglers still bearing away goods. Soon only the grocer and the social scientist remained, the latter stationed at the door with his tape recorder sucking in leftover sounds. Then he, too, slipped away up the block.

By twelve-ten P.M. the grocer was leaning against the counter, trying to make his mind slow down. Not a man given to drink during work hours, he nonetheless took a swallow from a bottle of wine, a dusty bottle from beneath the wine shelf, somehow overlooked by the winos. Somewhat recovered, he was preparing to remember what he should do next when he glanced toward a figure at the door. Nelson Reed was standing there, watching him.

"All gone," Harold Green said. "My friend, Mr. Reed, there is no more." Still the man stood in the doorway, peering into the store.

The grocer waved his arms about the empty room. Not a display case had a single item standing. "All gone," he said again, as if addressing a stupid child. "There is nothing left to get. You, my friend, have come back too late for a second load. I am cleaned out." 115

Nelson Reed stepped into the store and strode toward the counter. He moved through wine-stained flour, lettuce leaves, red, green, and blue labels, bits and pieces of broken glass. He walked toward the counter.

"All day," the grocer laughed, not quite hysterically now, "all day long I have not made a single cent of profit. The entire day was a loss. This store, like the others, is *bleeding* me." He waved his arms about the room in a magnificent gesture of uncaring loss. "Now do you understand?" he said. "Now will you put yourself in my shoes? I have nothing here. Come, now, Mr. Reed, would it not be so bad a thing to walk in my shoes?"

"Mr. Green," Nelson Reed said coldly. "My wife bought a loaf of bread in here this mornin'. She forgot to pay you. I, myself, have come here to pay you your money."

"Oh," the grocer said.

"I think it was brown bread. Don't that cost more than white?" 120

The two men looked away from each other, but not at anything in the store.

"In my store, yes," Harold Green said. He rang the register with the most casual movement of his finger. The register read fifty-five cents.

Nelson Reed held out a dollar.

"And two cents tax," the grocer said.

The man held out the dollar. 125

"After all," Harold Green said. "We are all, after all, Mr. Reed, in debt to the government."

He rang the register again. It read fifty-seven cents.

Nelson Reed held out a dollar.

For Analysis

1. Is Harold Green an exploiter of the poor and ignorant or, as his wife declares, a "moral" man? **2.** Is Nelson Reed an opportunist or a man genuinely seeking to combat racism and exploitation? **3.** What does Green's conversation with his brother-in-law Thomas, particularly the part that includes the analogy about the family selling a stove (par. 43–51), contribute to the theme of the story? **4.** What does Green mean when he tells Reed, during their meeting in the drugstore, ". . . I do not make a profit here because the people are black. I make a profit because a profit is here to be made" (par. 60)? **5.** Does the scene in which the neighbors empty the store vindicate Green's position? **6.** Explain the significance of the title.

On Style

Why is the third person narrative **point of view** right for this story? How would the story be changed if it were told from the first-person point of view, if the narrator were Harold Green or Nelson Reed?

Making Connections

Contrast the treatment of racial injustice in this story, in Richard Wright's "The Man Who Lived Underground" (p. 351), and in Toni Cade Bambara's "The Lesson" (p. 115).

Writing Topics

1. Write an essay focusing on the conflict between Harold Green and Nelson Reed as a mirror of the larger struggle in American society for racial justice and equality. **2.** Argue for or against the proposition that this story has a single hero—Harold Green or Nelson Reed—whose position and actions are vindicated in the end.

Tim O'Brien   [b. 1946]

On the Rainy River   1990

This is one story I've never told before. Not to anyone. Not to my parents, not to my brother or sister, not even to my wife. To go into it, I've always thought, would only cause embarrassment for all of us, a sudden need to be elsewhere, which is the natural response to a confession. Even now, I'll admit, the story makes me squirm. For more than twenty years I've had to live with it, feeling the shame, trying to push it away, and so by this act of remembrance, by putting the facts down on paper, I'm hoping to relieve at least some of the pressure on my dreams. Still, it's a hard story to tell. All of us, I suppose, like to believe that in a moral emergency we will behave like the heroes of our youth, bravely and forthrightly, without thought of personal loss or discredit. Certainly that was my conviction back in the summer of 1968. Tim O'Brien: a secret hero. The Lone Ranger.[1] If the stakes ever became high enough—if the evil were evil enough, if the good were good enough—I would simply tap a secret reservoir of courage that had been accumulating inside me over the years. Courage, I seemed to think, comes to us in finite quantities, like an inheritance, and by being frugal and stashing it away and letting it earn interest, we steadily increase our moral capital in preparation for that day when the account must be drawn down. It was a comforting theory. It dispensed with all those bothersome little acts of daily courage; it offered hope and grace to the repetitive coward; it justified the past while amortizing the future.

In June of 1968, a month after graduating from Macalester College, I was drafted to fight a war I hated. I was twenty-one years old. Young, yes, and politically naive, but even so the American war in Vietnam seemed to me wrong. Certain blood was being shed for uncertain reasons. I saw no unity of purpose, no consensus on matters of philosophy or history or law. The very facts were shrouded in uncertainty: Was it a civil war? A war of national liberation or simple aggression? Who started it, and when, and why? What really happened to the USS *Maddox* on that dark night in the Gulf of Tonkin?[2] Was Ho Chi Minh[3] a Communist stooge, or a nationalist savior, or both, or neither? What

---

[1] The Lone Ranger was the hero of a popular 1940s film and radio serial.

[2] On August 7, 1964, the U.S. Congress passed the Gulf of Tonkin resolution, authorizing President Lyndon Johnson to escalate America's involvement in the Vietnam War in retaliation for an alleged North Vietnamese attack on an American destroyer engaged in electronic espionage in international waters. Whether the attack (as well as a second one two days later) and the events leading up to it happened as President Johnson claimed has been brought into serious doubt.

[3] Ho Chi Minh (1890–1969) was the first president of North Vietnam.

about the Geneva Accords?[4] What about SEATO[5] and the Cold War? What about dominoes?[6] America was divided on these and a thousand other issues, and the debate had spilled out across the floor of the United States Senate and into the streets, and smart men in pinstripes could not agree on even the most fundamental matters of public policy. The only certainty that summer was moral confusion. It was my view then, and still is, that you don't make war without knowing why. Knowledge, of course, is always imperfect, but it seemed to me that when a nation goes to war it must have reasonable confidence in the justice and imperative of its cause. You can't fix your mistakes. Once people are dead, you can't make them undead.

In any case those were my convictions, and back in college I had taken a modest stand against the war. Nothing radical, no hothead stuff, just ringing a few doorbells for Gene McCarthy,[7] composing a few tedious, uninspired editorials for the campus newspaper. Oddly, though, it was almost entirely an intellectual activity. I brought some energy to it, of course, but it was the energy that accompanies almost any abstract endeavor; I felt no personal danger; I felt no sense of an impending crisis in my life. Stupidly, with a kind of smug removal that I can't begin to fathom, I assumed that the problems of killing and dying did not fall within my special province.

The draft notice arrived on June 17, 1968. It was a humid afternoon, I remember, cloudy and very quiet, and I'd just come in from a round of golf. My mother and father were having lunch out in the kitchen. I remember opening up the letter, scanning the first few lines, feeling the blood go thick behind my eyes. I remember a sound in my head. It wasn't thinking, just a silent howl. A million things all at once—I was too *good* for this war. Too smart, too compassionate, too everything. It couldn't happen. I was above it. I had the world dicked—Phi Beta Kappa and summa cum laude and president of the student body and a full-ride scholarship for grad studies at Harvard. A mistake, maybe—a foul-up in the paperwork. I was no soldier. I hated Boy Scouts. I hated camping out. I hated dirt and tents and mosquitoes. The sight of blood made me queasy, and I couldn't tolerate authority, and I didn't know a rifle from a slingshot. I was a *liberal,* for Christ sake: If they needed fresh bodies, why not draft some back-to-the-stone-age hawk?[8] Or some dumb jingo in his hard hat

[4] The Geneva Accords grew out of the Geneva Conference of 1954 to settle the war between France and the Communist-backed Viet Minh in Indochina. They called for a cease-fire along the seventeenth parallel, effectively dividing Vietnam into two countries, the north dominated by the Communists, the south by the French.

[5] SEATO, an acronym for the Southeast Asia Treaty Organization, was a mutual defense alliance established in 1954 by the United States, Great Britain, France, Australia, New Zealand, Pakistan, Thailand, and the Philippines. It was dissolved in 1977.

[6] One of the justifications for American involvement in the Vietnam War was the so-called domino theory, which held that a Communist victory in South Vietnam would have a domino effect and lead to Communist victories in the entire region.

[7] Eugene McCarthy (b. 1916) campaigned in 1968 on an anti–Vietnam War platform for the Democratic nomination for president.

[8] During the era of the Vietnam War, those who supported the war were known as "hawks" (those who opposed it were known as "doves").

and Bomb Hanoi[9] button, or one of LBJ's[10] pretty daughters, or Westmore-land's[11] whole handsome family—nephews and nieces and baby grandson. There should be a law, I thought. If you support a war, if you think it's worth the price, that's fine, but you have to put your own precious fluids on the line. You have to head for the front and hook up with an infantry unit and help spill the blood. And you have to bring along your wife, or your kids, or your lover. A *law*, I thought.

I remember the rage in my stomach. Later it burned down to a smoldering self-pity, then to numbness. At dinner that night my father asked what my plans were.

"Nothing," I said. "Wait."

I spent the summer of 1968 working in an Armour meat-packing plant in my hometown of Worthington, Minnesota. The plant specialized in pork products, and for eight hours a day I stood on a quarter-mile assembly line—more prop-erly, a disassembly line—removing blood clots from the necks of dead pigs. My job title, I believe, was Declotter. After slaughter, the hogs were decapitated, split down the length of the belly, pried open, eviscerated, and strung up by the hind hocks on a high conveyer belt. Then gravity took over. By the time a car-cass reached my spot on the line, the fluids had mostly drained out, everything except for thick clots of blood in the neck and upper chest cavity. To remove the stuff, I used a kind of water gun. The machine was heavy, maybe eighty pounds, and was suspended from the ceiling by a heavy rubber cord. There was some bounce to it, an elastic up-and-down give, and the trick was to maneuver the gun with your whole body, not lifting with the arms, just letting the rubber cord do the work for you. At one end was a trigger; at the muzzle end was a small nozzle and a steel roller brush. As a carcass passed by, you'd lean forward and swing the gun up against the clots and squeeze the trigger, all in one motion, and the brush would whirl and water would come shooting out and you'd hear a quick splattering sound as the clots dissolved into a fine red mist. It was not pleasant work. Goggles were a necessity, and a rubber apron, but even so it was like standing for eight hours a day under a lukewarm blood-shower. At night I'd go home smelling of pig. It wouldn't go away. Even after a hot bath, scrubbing hard, the stink was always there—like old bacon, or sausage, a dense greasy pig-stink that soaked deep into my skin and hair. Among other things, I remember, it was tough getting dates that summer. I felt isolated; I spent a lot of time alone. And there was also that draft notice tucked away in my wallet.

In the evenings I'd sometimes borrow my father's car and drive aimlessly around town, feeling sorry for myself, thinking about the war and the pig factory

---

[9] The capital of Vietnam.

[10] Lyndon Baines Johnson (1908–1973), who became president in 1963 upon the assassination of President John F. Kennedy. Johnson's escalation of American involvement in the Vietnam War eroded his popularity and led to his decision not to run for reelection in 1968.

[11] General William Westmoreland (b. 1914) was appointed by President Johnson to head the Military Assistance Command in Vietnam. He enthusiastically supported the escalation of Ameri-can involvement in the war.

and how my life seemed to be collapsing toward slaughter. I felt paralyzed. All around me the options seemed to be narrowing, as if I were hurtling down a huge black funnel, the whole world squeezing in tight. There was no happy way out. The government had ended most graduate school deferments; the waiting lists for the National Guard and Reserves were impossibly long; my health was solid; I didn't qualify for CO[12] status—no religious grounds, no history as a pacifist. Moreover, I could not claim to be opposed to war as a matter of general principle. There were occasions, I believed, when a nation was justified in using military force to achieve its ends, to stop a Hitler[13] or some comparable evil, and I told myself that in such circumstances I would've willingly marched off to the battle. The problem, though, was that a draft board did not let you choose your war.

Beyond all this, or at the very center, was the raw fact of terror. I did not want to die. Not ever. But certainly not then, not there, not in a wrong war. Driving up Main Street, past the courthouse and the Ben Franklin store, I sometimes felt the fear spreading inside me like weeds. I imagined myself dead. I imagined myself doing things I could not do—charging an enemy position, taking aim at another human being.

At some point in mid-July I began thinking seriously about Canada. The border lay a few hundred miles north, an eight-hour drive. Both my conscience and my instincts were telling me to make a break for it, just take off and run like hell and never stop. In the beginning the idea seemed purely abstract, the word Canada printing itself out in my head; but after a time I could see particular shapes and images, the sorry details of my own future—a hotel room in Winnipeg, a battered old suitcase, my father's eyes as I tried to explain myself over the telephone. I could almost hear his voice, and my mother's. Run, I'd think. Then I'd think, Impossible. Then a second later I'd think, *Run*.

It was a kind of schizophrenia. A moral split. I couldn't make up my mind. I feared the war, yes, but I also feared exile. I was afraid of walking away from my own life, my friends and my family, my whole history, everything that mattered to me. I feared losing the respect of my parents. I feared the law. I feared ridicule and censure. My hometown was a conservative little spot on the prairie, a place where tradition counted, and it was easy to imagine people sitting around a table down at the old Gobbler Café on Main Street, coffee cups poised, the conversation slowly zeroing in on the young O'Brien kid, how the damned sissy had taken off for Canada. At night, when I couldn't sleep, I'd sometimes carry on fierce arguments with those people. I'd be screaming at them, telling them how much I detested their blind, thoughtless, automatic acquiescence to it all, their simple-minded patriotism, their prideful ignorance, their love-it-or-leave-it platitudes, how they were sending me off to fight a war they didn't understand and didn't want to understand. I held them responsible.

10

---

[12] Conscientious objector, a person who is allowed exemption from military service on the grounds of religious or humanitarian beliefs.

[13] Adolf Hitler (1889–1945) was chancellor of Germany (1933–1945) and head of the German Nazi party.

By God, yes, I *did*. All of them—I held them personally and individually responsible—the polyestered Kiwanis boys, the merchants and farmers, the pious churchgoers, the chatty housewives, the PTA and the Lions club and the Veterans of Foreign Wars and the fine upstanding gentry out at the country club. They didn't know Bao Dai[14] from the man in the moon. They didn't know history. They didn't know the first thing about Diem's[15] tyranny, or the nature of Vietnamese nationalism, or the long colonialism of the French—this was all too damned complicated, it required some reading—but no matter, it was a war to stop the Communists, plain and simple, which was how they liked things, and you were a treasonous pussy if you had second thoughts about killing or dying for plain and simple reasons.

I was bitter, sure. But it was so much more than that. The emotions went from outrage to terror to bewilderment to guilt to sorrow and then back again to outrage. I felt a sickness inside me. Real disease.

Most of this I've told before, or at least hinted at, but what I have never told is the full truth. How I cracked. How at work one morning, standing on the pig line, I felt something break open in my chest. I don't know what it was. I'll never know. But it was real, I know that much, it was a physical rupture—a cracking-leaking-popping feeling. I remember dropping my water gun. Quickly, almost without thought, I took off my apron and walked out of the plant and drove home. It was midmorning, I remember, and the house was empty. Down in my chest there was still that leaking sensation, something very warm and precious spilling out, and I was covered with blood and hog-stink, and for a long while I just concentrated on holding myself together. I remember taking a hot shower. I remember packing a suitcase and carrying it out to the kitchen, standing very still for a few minutes, looking carefully at the familiar objects all around me. The old chrome toaster, the telephone, the pink and white Formica on the kitchen counters. The room was full of bright sunshine. Everything sparkled. My house, I thought. My life. I'm not sure how long I stood there, but later I scribbled out a short note to my parents.

What it said, exactly, I don't recall now. Something vague. Taking off, will call, love Tim.

I drove north.

It's a blur now, as it was then, and all I remember is a sense of high velocity and the feel of the steering wheel in my hands. I was riding on adrenaline. A giddy feeling, in a way, except there was the dreamy edge of impossibility to it—like running a dead-end maze—no way out—it couldn't come to a happy conclusion and yet I was doing it anyway because it was all I could think of to do. It was pure flight, fast and mindless. I had no plan. Just hit the border at high

[14] Bao Dai (b. 1913) was the emperor of the French protectorate Annam, now part of Vietnam.
[15] Ngo Dinh Diem (1901–1963) became, with U.S. support, ruler of South Vietnam when the Geneva Accords divided the country in two. He was assassinated in 1963 during a military coup d'état.

speed and crash through and keep on running. Near dusk I passed through Bemidji, then turned northeast toward International Falls. I spent the night in the car behind a closed-down gas station a half mile from the border. In the morning, after gassing up, I headed straight west along the Rainy River, which separates Minnesota from Canada, and which for me separated one life from another. The land was mostly wilderness. Here and there I passed a motel or bait shop, but otherwise the country unfolded in great sweeps of pine and birch and sumac. Though it was still August, the air already had the smell of October, football season, piles of yellow-red leaves, everything crisp and clean. I remember a huge blue sky. Off to my right was the Rainy River, wide as a lake in places, and beyond the Rainy River was Canada.

For a while I just drove, not aiming at anything, then in the late morning I began looking for a place to lie low for a day or two. I was exhausted, and scared sick, and around noon I pulled into an old fishing resort called the Tip Top Lodge. Actually it was not a lodge at all, just eight or nine tiny yellow cabins clustered on a peninsula that jutted northward into the Rainy River. The place was in sorry shape. There was a dangerous wooden dock, an old minnow tank, a flimsy tar paper boathouse along the shore. The main building, which stood in a cluster of pines on high ground, seemed to lean heavily to one side, like a cripple, the roof sagging toward Canada. Briefly, I thought about turning around, just giving up, but then I got out of the car and walked up to the front porch.

The man who opened the door that day is the hero of my life. How do I say this without sounding sappy? Blurt it out—the man saved me. He offered exactly what I needed, without questions, without any words at all. He took me in. He was there at the critical time—a silent, watchful presence. Six days later, when it ended, I was unable to find a proper way to thank him, and I never have, and so, if nothing else, this story represents a small gesture of gratitude twenty years overdue.

Even after two decades I can close my eyes and return to that porch at the Tip Top Lodge. I can see the old guy staring at me. Elroy Berdahl: eighty-one years old, skinny and shrunken and mostly bald. He wore a flannel shirt and brown work pants. In one hand, I remember, he carried a green apple, a small paring knife in the other. His eyes had the bluish gray color of a razor blade, the same polished shine, and as he peered up at me I felt a strange sharpness, almost painful, a cutting sensation, as if his gaze were somehow slicing me open. In part, no doubt, it was my own sense of guilt, but even so I'm absolutely certain that the old man took one look and went right to the heart of things—a kid in trouble. When I asked for a room, Elroy made a little clicking sound with his tongue. He nodded, led me out to one of the cabins, and dropped a key in my hand. I remember smiling at him. I also remember wishing I hadn't. The old man shook his head as if to tell me it wasn't worth the bother.

"Dinner at five-thirty," he said. "You eat fish?"   20

"Anything," I said.

Elroy grunted and said, "I'll bet."

       ✿   ✿   ✿

We spent six days together at the Tip Top Lodge. Just the two of us. Tourist season was over, and there were no boats on the river, and the wilderness seemed to withdraw into a great permanent stillness. Over those six days Elroy Berdahl and I took most of our meals together. In the mornings we sometimes went out on long hikes into the woods, and at night we played Scrabble or listened to records or sat reading in front of his big stone fireplace. At times I felt the awkwardness of an intruder, but Elroy accepted me into his quiet routine without fuss or ceremony. He took my presence for granted, the same way he might've sheltered a stray cat—no wasted sighs or pity—and there was never any talk about it. Just the opposite. What I remember more than anything is the man's willful, almost ferocious silence. In all that time together, all those hours, he never asked the obvious questions: Why was I there? Why alone? Why so preoccupied? If Elroy was curious about any of this, he was careful never to put it into words.

My hunch, though, is that he already knew. At least the basics. After all, it was 1968, and guys were burning draft cards, and Canada was just a boat ride away. Elroy Berdahl was no hick. His bedroom, I remember, was cluttered with books and newspapers. He killed me at the Scrabble board, barely concentrating, and on those occasions when speech was necessary he had a way of compressing large thoughts into small, cryptic packets of language. One evening, just at sunset, he pointed up at an owl circling over the violet-lighted forest to the west.

"Hey, O'Brien," he said. "There's Jesus." 25

The man was sharp—he didn't miss much. Those razor eyes. Now and then he'd catch me staring out at the river, at the far shore, and I could almost hear the tumblers clicking in his head. Maybe I'm wrong, but I doubt it.

One thing for certain, he knew I was in desperate trouble. And he knew I couldn't talk about it. The wrong word—or even the right word—and I would've disappeared. I was wired and jittery. My skin felt too tight. After supper one evening I vomited and went back to my cabin and lay down for a few moments and then vomited again; another time, in the middle of the afternoon, I began sweating and couldn't shut it off. I went through whole days feeling dizzy with sorrow. I couldn't sleep; I couldn't lie still. At night I'd toss around in bed, half awake, half dreaming, imagining how I'd sneak down to the beach and quietly push one of the old man's boats out into the river and start paddling my way toward Canada. There were times when I thought I'd gone off the psychic edge. I couldn't tell up from down, I was just falling, and late in the night I'd lie there watching weird pictures spin through my head. Getting chased by the Border Patrol—helicopters and searchlights and barking dogs—I'd be crashing through the woods, I'd be down on my hands and knees—people shouting out my name—the law closing in on all sides—my hometown draft board and the FBI and the Royal Canadian Mounted Police. It all seemed crazy and impossible. Twenty-one years old, an ordinary kid with all the ordinary dreams and ambitions, and all I wanted was to live the life I was born to—a mainstream life—I loved baseball and hamburgers and cherry Cokes—and now I was off on the margins of exile, leaving my country forever, and it seemed so impossible and terrible and sad.

I'm not sure how I made it through those six days. Most of it I can't remember. On two or three afternoons, to pass some time, I helped Elroy get the place ready for winter, sweeping down the cabins and hauling in the boats, little chores that kept my body moving. The days were cool and bright. The nights were very dark. One morning the old man showed me how to split and stack firewood, and for several hours we just worked in silence out behind his house. At one point, I remember, Elroy put down his maul and looked at me for a long time, his lips drawn as if framing a difficult question, but then he shook his head and went back to work. The man's self-control was amazing. He never pried. He never put me in a position that required lies or denials. To an extent, I suppose, his reticence was typical of that part of Minnesota, where privacy still held value, and even if I'd been walking around with some horrible deformity—four arms and three heads—I'm sure the old man would've talked about everything except those extra arms and heads. Simple politeness was part of it. But even more than that, I think, the man understood that words were insufficient. The problem had gone beyond discussion. During that long summer I'd been over and over the various arguments, all the pros and cons, and it was no longer a question that could be decided by an act of pure reason. Intellect had come up against emotion. My conscience told me to run, but some irrational and powerful force was resisting, like a weight pushing me toward the war. What it came down to, stupidly, was a sense of shame. Hot, stupid shame. I did not want people to think badly of me. Not my parents, not my brother and sister, not even the folks down at the Gobbler Café. I was ashamed to be there at the Tip Top Lodge. I was ashamed of my conscience, ashamed to be doing the right thing.

Some of this Elroy must've understood. Not the details, of course, but the plain fact of crisis.

Although the old man never confronted me about it, there was one occasion   30
when he came close to forcing the whole thing out into the open. It was early evening, and we'd just finished supper, and over coffee and dessert I asked him about my bill, how much I owed so far. For a long while the old man squinted down at the tablecloth.

"Well, the basic rate," he said, "is fifty bucks a night. Not counting meals. This makes four nights, right?"

I nodded. I had three hundred and twelve dollars in my wallet.

Elroy kept his eyes on the tablecloth. "Now that's an on-season price. To be fair, I suppose we should knock it down a peg or two." He leaned back in his chair. "What's a reasonable number, you figure?"

"I don't know," I said. "Forty?"

"Forty's good. Forty a night. Then we tack on food—say another hundred?   35
Two hundred sixty total?"

"I guess."

He raised his eyebrows. "Too much?"

"No, that's fair. It's fine. Tomorrow, though . . . I think I'd better take off tomorrow."

Elroy shrugged and began clearing the table. For a time he fussed with the dishes, whistling to himself as if the subject had been settled. After a second he slapped his hands together.

"You know what we forgot?" he said. "We forgot wages. Those odd jobs you done. What we have to do, we have to figure out what your time's worth. Your last job—how much did you pull in an hour?"

"Not enough," I said.

"A bad one?"

"Yes. Pretty bad."

Slowly then, without intending any long sermon, I told him about my days at the pig plant. It began as a straight recitation of the facts, but before I could stop myself I was talking about the blood clots and the water gun and how the smell had soaked into my skin and how I couldn't wash it away. I went on for a long time. I told him about wild hogs squealing in my dreams, the sounds of butchery, slaughter-house sounds, and how I'd sometimes wake up with that greasy pig-stink in my throat.

When I was finished, Elroy nodded at me.

"Well, to be honest," he said, "when you first showed up here, I wondered about all that. The aroma, I mean. Smelled like you was awful damned fond of pork chops." The old man almost smiled. He made a snuffling sound, then sat down with a pencil and a piece of paper. "So what'd this crud job pay? Ten bucks an hour? Fifteen?"

"Less."

Elroy shook his head. "Let's make it fifteen. You put in twenty-five hours here, easy. That's three hundred seventy-five bucks total wages. We subtract the two hundred sixty for food and lodging, I will owe you a hundred and fifteen."

He took four fifties out of his shirt pocket and laid them on the table.

"Call it even," he said.

"No."

"Pick it up. Get yourself a haircut."

The money lay on the table for the rest of the evening. It was still there when I went back to my cabin. In the morning, though, I found an envelope tacked to my door. Inside were the four fifties and a two-word note that said EMERGENCY FUND.

The man knew.

Looking back after twenty years, I sometimes wonder if the events of that summer didn't happen in some other dimension, a place where your life exists before you've lived it, and where it goes afterward. None of it ever seemed real. During my time at the Tip Top Lodge I had the feeling that I'd slipped out of my own skin, hovering a few feet away while some poor yo-yo with my name and face tried to make his way toward a future he didn't understand and didn't want. Even now I can see myself as I was then. It's like watching an old home movie:

I'm young and tan and fit. I've got hair—lots of it. I don't smoke or drink. I'm wearing faded blue jeans and a white polo shirt. I can see myself sitting on Elroy Berdahl's dock near dusk one evening, the sky a bright shimmering pink, and I'm finishing up a letter to my parents that tells what I'm about to do and why I'm doing it and how sorry I am that I'd never found the courage to talk to them about it. I ask them not to be angry. I try to explain some of my feelings, but there aren't enough words, and so I just say that it's a thing that has to be done. At the end of the letter I talk about the vacations we used to take up in this north country, at a place called Whitefish Lake, and how the scenery here reminds me of those good times. I tell them I'm fine. I tell them I'll write again from Winnipeg or Montreal or wherever I end up.

On my last full day, the sixth day, the old man took me out fishing on the Rainy River. The afternoon was sunny and cold. A stiff breeze came in from the north, and I remember how the little fourteen-foot boat made sharp rocking motions as we pushed off from the dock. The current was fast. All around us, I remember, there was a vastness to the world, an unpeopled rawness, just the trees and the sky and the water reaching out toward nowhere. The air had the brittle scent of October.

For ten or fifteen minutes Elroy held a course upstream, the river choppy and silver-gray, then he turned straight north and put the engine on full throttle. I felt the bow lift beneath me. I remember the wind in my ears, the sound of the old outboard Evinrude. For a time I didn't pay attention to anything, just feeling the cold spray against my face, but then it occurred to me that at some point we must've passed into Canadian waters, across that dotted line between two different worlds, and I remember a sudden tightness in my chest as I looked up and watched the far shore come at me. This wasn't a daydream. It was tangible and real. As we came in toward land, Elroy cut the engine, letting the boat fishtail lightly about twenty yards off shore. The old man didn't look at me or speak. Bending down, he opened up his tackle box and busied himself with a bobber and a piece of wire leader, humming to himself, his eyes down.

It struck me then that he must've planned it. I'll never be certain, of course, but I think he meant to bring me up against the realities, to guide me across the river and to take me to the edge and to stand a kind of vigil as I chose a life for myself.

I remember staring at the old man, then at my hands, then at Canada. The shoreline was dense with brush and timber. I could see tiny red berries on the bushes. I could see a squirrel up in one of the birch trees, a big crow looking at me from a boulder along the river. That close—twenty yards—and I could see the delicate latticework of the leaves, the texture of the soil, the browned needles beneath the pines, the configurations of geology and human history. Twenty yards. I could've done it. I could've jumped and started swimming for my life. Inside me, in my chest, I felt a terrible squeezing pressure. Even now, as I write this, I can still feel that tightness. And I want you to feel it—the wind coming off the river, the waves, the silence, the wooded frontier. You're at the bow of a boat on the Rainy River. You're twenty-one years old, you're scared, and there's a hard squeezing pressure in your chest.

What would you do?

60

Would you jump? Would you feel pity for yourself? Would you think about your family and your childhood and your dreams and all you're leaving behind? Would it hurt? Would it feel like dying? Would you cry, as I did?

I tried to swallow it back. I tried to smile, except I was crying.

Now, perhaps, you can understand why I've never told this story before. It's not just the embarrassment of tears. That's part of it, no doubt, but what embarrasses me much more, and always will, is the paralysis that took my heart. A moral freeze: I couldn't decide, I couldn't act, I couldn't comport myself with even a pretense of modest human dignity.

All I could do was cry. Quietly, not bawling, just the chest-chokes.

At the rear of the boat Elroy Berdahl pretended not to notice. He held a fish-   65
ing rod in his hands, his head bowed to hide his eyes. He kept humming a soft, monotonous little tune. Everywhere, it seemed, in the trees and water and sky, a great worldwide sadness came pressing down on me, a crushing sorrow, sorrow like I had never known it before. And what was so sad, I realized, was that Canada had become a pitiful fantasy. Silly and hopeless. It was no longer a possibility. Right then, with the shore so close, I understood that I would not do what I should do. I would not swim away from my hometown and my country and my life. I would not be brave. That old image of myself as a hero, as a man of conscience and courage, all that was just a threadbare pipe dream. Bobbing there on the Rainy River, looking back at the Minnesota shore, I felt a sudden swell of helplessness come over me, a drowning sensation, as if I had toppled overboard and was being swept away by the silver waves. Chunks of my own history flashed by. I saw a seven-year-old boy in a white cowboy hat and a Lone Ranger mask and a pair of holstered six-shooters; I saw a twelve-year-old Little League shortstop pivoting to turn a double play; I saw a sixteen-year-old kid decked out for his first prom, looking spiffy in a white tux and a black bow tie, his hair cut short and flat, his shoes freshly polished. My whole life seemed to spill out into the river, swirling away from me, everything I had ever been or ever wanted to be. I couldn't get my breath; I couldn't stay afloat; I couldn't tell which way to swim. A hallucination, I suppose, but it was as real as anything I would ever feel. I saw my parents calling to me from the far shoreline. I saw my brother and sister, all the townsfolk, the mayor and the entire Chamber of Commerce and all my old teachers and girlfriends and high school buddies. Like some weird sporting event: everybody screaming from the sidelines, rooting me on—a loud stadium roar. Hotdogs and popcorn—stadium smells, stadium heat. A squad of cheerleaders did cartwheels along the banks of the Rainy River; they had megaphones and pompoms and smooth brown thighs. The crowd swayed left and right. A marching band played fight songs. All my aunts and uncles were there, and Abraham Lincoln, and Saint George, and a nine-year-old girl named Linda who had died of a brain tumor back in fifth grade, and several members of the United States Senate, and a blind poet scribbling notes, and LBJ, and

Huck Finn, and Abbie Hoffman,[16] and all the dead soldiers back from the grave, and the many thousands who were later to die—villagers with terrible burns, little kids without arms or legs—yes, and the Joint Chiefs of Staff were there, and a couple of popes, and a first lieutenant named Jimmy Cross, and the last surviving veteran of the American Civil War, and Jane Fonda dressed up as Barbarella,[17] and an old man sprawled beside a pigpen, and my grandfather, and Gary Cooper,[18] and a kind-faced woman carrying an umbrella and a copy of Plato's *Republic,* and a million ferocious citizens waving flags of all shapes and colors—people in hard hats, people in headbands—they were all whooping and chanting and urging me toward one shore or the other. I saw faces from my distant past and distant future. My wife was there. My unborn daughter waved at me, and my two sons hopped up and down, and a drill sergeant named Blyton sneered and shot up a finger and shook his head. There was a choir in bright purple robes. There was a cabbie from the Bronx. There was a slim young man I would one day kill with a hand grenade along a red clay trail outside the village of My Khe.

The little aluminum boat rocked softly beneath me. There was the wind and the sky.

I tried to will myself overboard.

I gripped the edge of the boat and leaned forward and thought, *Now.*

I did try. It just wasn't possible.

All those eyes on me—the town, the whole universe—and I couldn't risk the embarrassment. It was as if there were an audience to my life, that swirl of faces along the river, and in my head I could hear people screaming at me. Traitor! they yelled. Turncoat! Pussy! I felt myself blush. I couldn't tolerate it. I couldn't endure the mockery, or the disgrace, or the patriotic ridicule. Even in my imagination, the shore just twenty yards away, I couldn't make myself be brave. It had nothing to do with morality. Embarrassment, that's all it was.

And right then I submitted.

I would go to the war—I would kill and maybe die—because I was embarrassed not to.

That was the sad thing. And so I sat in the bow of the boat and cried.

It was loud now. Loud, hard crying.

Elroy Berdahl remained quiet. He kept fishing. He worked his line with the tips of his fingers, patiently, squinting out at his red and white bobber on the Rainy River. His eyes were flat and impassive. He didn't speak. He was simply there, like the river and the late-summer sun. And yet by his presence, his mute watchfulness, he made it real. He was the true audience. He was a witness, like God, or like the gods, who look on in absolute silence as we live our lives, as we make our choices or fail to make them.

---

[16] Abbie Hoffman (1936–1989) was a radical antiwar activist during the Vietnam War era.

[17] Jane Fonda (b. 1937), who was outspoken in her opposition to the Vietnam war, starred in the 1968 film *Barbarella.*

[18] Gary Cooper (1901–1961) was one of the most famous film stars of his day.

"Ain't biting," he said.

Then after a time the old man pulled in his line and turned the boat back toward Minnesota.

I don't remember saying goodbye. That last night we had dinner together, and I went to bed early, and in the morning Elroy fixed breakfast for me. When I told him I'd be leaving, the old man nodded as if he already knew. He looked down at the table and smiled.

At some point later in the morning it's possible that we shook hands—I just don't remember—but I do know that by the time I'd finished packing the old man had disappeared. Around noon, when I took my suitcase out to the car, I noticed that his old black pickup truck was no longer parked in front of the house. I went inside and waited for a while, but I felt a bone certainty that he wouldn't be back. In a way, I thought, it was appropriate. I washed up the breakfast dishes, left his two hundred dollars on the kitchen counter, got into the car, and drove south toward home.

The day was cloudy. I passed through towns with familiar names, through the 80 pine forests and down to the prairie, and then to Vietnam, where I was a soldier, and then home again. I survived, but it's not a happy ending. I was a coward. I went to the war.

For Analysis

1. This story is a chapter from O'Brien's novel *The Things They Carried,* a fictional memoir of the author's own experiences as a combat soldier in Vietnam. The volume is narrated by a character named "Tim O'Brien" (see the first paragraph), who the author states is not himself although he shares many other similarities with the author. Why would an author model a narrator so closely on his own experiences, give him the same name, and yet assert that the narrator is not himself? **2.** Why does the author describe his summer job at the meat-packing plant in such detail? **3.** The fourth section of the story ends with the narrator's comment, "The man knew" (par. 54). What is it that Elroy Berdahl knew?

On Style

1. Why does the author interrupt the chronological flow of the narrative in the sixth section (par. 65)? **2.** How does the author achieve **conflict** and suspense? Where do the climaxes occur in the narrative?

Making Connections

1. Compare the perspectives on war in "On the Rainy River" with Luigi Pirandello's in "War" (p. 341), Bertolt Brecht's in "War Has Been Given a Bad Name" (p. 446), and Wilfred Owen's in "Dulce et Decorum Est" (p. 1279). Are they all antiwar statements? Which do you find the most effective as an antiwar statement?

Writing Topics

1. Write an essay analyzing the importance of the setting in helping the narrator clarify his feelings and resolve his dilemma. **2.** Write an essay describing your experience with a "moral split," a situation in which you confronted conflict and confusion between what you wanted to do and family and social pressure to act otherwise.

Poetry

Su Tung-P'o   [1036–1101]

On the Birth of His Son   11th century

Families, when a child is born
Want it to be intelligent.
I, through intelligence,
Having wrecked my whole life,
Only hope the baby will prove
Ignorant and stupid.
Then he will crown a tranquil life
By becoming a Cabinet Minister.

For Analysis
1. How might one's life be wrecked "through intelligence"? **2.** What is the **theme** of this poem? Does the poet truly wish his son to grow up "ignorant and stupid"? Explain.

Writing Topic
Write an essay in which you show, through your own experience and knowledge, why you agree with Su Tung-P'o's implied judgment on government and politicians.

William Wordsworth   [1770–1850]

The World Is Too Much with Us   1807

The world is too much with us; late and soon,
Getting and spending, we lay waste our powers;
Little we see in Nature that is ours;
We have given our hearts away, a sordid boon!
This Sea that bares her bosom to the moon,
The winds that will be howling at all hours,
And are up-gathered now like sleeping flowers,
For this, for everything, we are out of tune;

433

It moves us not.—Great God! I'd rather be
A Pagan suckled in a creed outworn; 10
So might I, standing on this pleasant lea,
Have glimpses that would make me less forlorn;
Have sight of Proteus rising from the sea;
Or hear old Triton blow his wreathèd horn.[1]

For Analysis

1. What does "world" mean in line 1? **2.** What does Wordsworth complain of in the first four lines? **3.** In lines 4–8 Wordsworth tells us what we have lost; in the concluding lines he suggests a remedy. What is that remedy? What do Proteus and Triton symbolize?

Writing Topic

In what ways does Wordsworth's use of images both define what we have lost and suggest a remedy for this loss?

Alfred, Lord Tennyson [1809–1892]

Ulysses[1] 1833

It little profits that an idle king,
By this still hearth, among these barren crags,
Matched with an agéd wife, I mete and dole
Unequal laws unto a savage race,
That hoard, and sleep, and feed, and know not me.

    I cannot rest from travel; I will drink
Life to the lees. All times I have enjoyed
Greatly, have suffered greatly, both with those
That loved me, and alone; on shore, and when
Through scudding drifts the rainy Hyades[2] 10
Vexed the dim sea. I am become a name;
For always roaming with a hungry heart
Much have I seen and known—cities of men
And manners, climates, councils, governments,

The World . . .
[1] Proteus and Triton are both figures from Greek mythology. Proteus had the power to assume different forms; Triton was often represented blowing on a conch shell.

Ulysses
[1] Ulysses, according to Greek legend, was the king of Ithaca and a hero of the Trojan War. Tennyson represents him as eager to resume the life of travel and adventure.
[2] A group of stars in the constellation Taurus. According to Greek mythology, the rising of these stars with the sun foretold rain.

Myself not least, but honored of them all—
And drunk delight of battle with my peers,
Far on the ringing plains of windy Troy.
I am a part of all that I have met;
Yet all experience is an arch wherethrough
Gleams that untraveled world whose margin fades   20
Forever and forever when I move.
How dull it is to pause, to make an end,
To rust unburnished, not to shine in use!
As though to breathe were life. Life piled on life
Were all too little, and of one to me
Little remains; but every hour is saved
From that eternal silence, something more,
A bringer of new things; and vile it were
For some three suns to store and hoard myself,
And this gray spirit yearning in desire   30
To follow knowledge like a sinking star,
Beyond the utmost bound of human thought.

    This is my son, mine own Telemachus,
To whom I leave the scepter and the isle—
Well-loved of me, discerning to fulfill
This labor, by slow prudence to make mild
A rugged people, and through soft degrees
Subdue them to the useful and the good.
Most blameless is he, centered in the sphere
Of common duties, decent not to fail   40
In offices of tenderness, and pay
Meet° adoration to my household gods,   proper
When I am gone. He works his work, I mine.

    There lies the port; the vessel puffs her sail;
There gloom the dark, broad seas. My mariners,
Souls that have toiled, and wrought, and thought with me—
That ever with a frolic welcome took
The thunder and the sunshine, and opposed
Free hearts, free foreheads—you and I are old;
Old age hath yet his honor and his toil.   50
Death closes all; but something ere the end,
Some work of noble note, may yet be done,
Not unbecoming men that strove with Gods.
The lights begin to twinkle from the rocks;
The long day wanes; the slow moon climbs; the deep
Moans round with many voices. Come, my friends,
'Tis not too late to seek a newer world.
Push off, and sitting well in order smite

The sounding furrows; for my purpose holds
To sail beyond the sunset, and the baths   60
Of all the western stars, until I die.
It may be that the gulfs will wash us down;
It may be we shall touch the Happy Isles,[3]
And see the great Achilles, whom we knew.
Though much is taken, much abides; and though
We are not now that strength which in old days
Moved earth and heaven, that which we are, we are—
One equal temper of heroic hearts,
Made weak by time and fate, but strong in will
To strive, to seek, to find, and not to yield.   70

For Analysis

1. Is Ulysses' desire to abdicate his duties as king irresponsible? **2.** Contrast Ulysses with his son Telemachus as the latter is described in lines 33–43. Is Telemachus admirable? **3.** At the conclusion of the poem Ulysses is determined not to yield. Yield to what?

Emily Dickinson   [1830–1886]

Much Madness is divinest Sense—   1862

Much Madness is divinest Sense—
To a discerning Eye—
Much Sense—the starkest Madness—
'Tis the Majority
In this, as All, prevail—
Assent—and you are sane—
Demur—you're straightway dangerous—
And handled with a Chain—

She rose to His Requirement   ca. 1863

She rose to His Requirement—dropt
The Playthings of Her Life
To take the honorable Work
Of Woman, and of Wife—

Ulysses
[3] The Islands of the Blessed (also Elysium), thought to be in the far western oceans, where those favored by the gods, such as Achilles, enjoyed life after death.

If ought° She missed in Her new Day,   anything
Of Amplitude, or Awe—
Or first Prospective—Or the Gold
In using, wear away,

It lay unmentioned—as the Sea
Develope Pearl, and Weed,   10
But only to Himself—be known
The Fathoms they abide—

For Analysis

1. What are the "Playthings" referred to in line 2? **2.** Why does the poet refer to both "Woman" and "Wife" in line 4, since a wife is also a woman? **3.** Look up in your dictionary *amplitude, awe,* and *prospective,* and consider how these words help you to understand the woman's losses. **4.** What does "It" in the third stanza refer to? **5.** Why is the sea image at the end of the poem appropriate? What does the contrast between "Pearl" and "Weed" suggest? **6.** The last word of the poem, *abide,* has several meanings. Which of them are relevant to the meaning of the poem?

Making Connections

Compare and contrast the attitudes toward marriage in this poem and in Helen Sorrells's "From a Correct Address in a Suburb of a Major City" (p. 449).

Writing Topic

Write an essay describing a woman you know who gave up an important part of herself to be a wife.

Gerard Manley Hopkins   [1844–1889]

Thou Art Indeed Just, Lord   1889

*Justus quidem tu es, Domine, si disputem tecum: verumtamen
justa loquar ad te: Quare via impiorum prosperatur?* &c.[1]

Thou art indeed just, Lord, if I contend
With thee; but, sir, so what I plead is just.
Why do sinners' ways prosper? and why must
Disappointment all I endeavour end?
    Wert thou my enemy, O thou my friend,
How wouldst thou worse, I wonder, than thou dost
Defeat, thwart me? Oh, the sots and thralls of lust
Do in spare hours more thrive than I that spend,

Thou Art Indeed . . .
    [1] The first three lines of the poem translate the Latin epigraph.

Sir, life upon thy cause. See, banks and brakes
Now, leavèd how thick! lacèd they are again   10
With fretty chervil,° look, and fresh wind shakes   parsley
Them; birds build—but not I build; no, but strain,
Time's eunuch, and not breed one work that wakes.
Mine, O thou lord of life, send my roots rain.

For Analysis

1. How is the nature **imagery** used to indicate the speaker's plight? **2.** How would you characterize the poet's attitude toward God?

Writing Topic

Summarize the debate in this poem. What implications about divine justice emerge from the poet's questions in lines 3 and 4?

William Butler Yeats   [1865–1939]

Easter 1916¹   1916

I have met them at close of day
Coming with vivid faces
From counter or desk among grey
Eighteenth-century houses.
I have passed with a nod of the head
Or polite meaningless words,
Or have lingered awhile and said
Polite meaningless words,
And thought before I had done
Of a mocking tale or a gibe   10
To please a companion
Around the fire at the club,
Being certain that they and I
But lived where motley is worn:
All changed, changed utterly:
A terrible beauty is born.

Easter 1916
    ¹ On Easter Sunday of 1916, a group of Irish nationalists seized key points in Ireland, including the Dublin Post Office, from which they proclaimed an independent Irish Republic. At first, most Irishmen were indifferent to the nationalists' futile and heroic gesture, but as the rebellion was crushed and the leaders executed, they became heroes in their countrymen's eyes. Some of those leaders are alluded to in the second stanza and are named in lines 75 and 76.

That woman's days were spent
In ignorant good-will,
Her nights in argument
Until her voice grew shrill.   20
What voice more sweet than hers
When, young and beautiful,
She rode to harriers?
This man had kept a school
And rode our wingéd horse;[2]
This other his helper and friend
Was coming into his force;
He might have won fame in the end,
So sensitive his nature seemed,
So daring and sweet his thought.   30
This other man I had dreamed
A drunken, vainglorious lout.
He had done most bitter wrong
To some who are near my heart,
Yet I number him in the song;
He, too, has resigned his part
In the casual comedy;
He, too, has been changed in his turn,
Transformed utterly:
A terrible beauty is born.   40

Hearts with one purpose alone
Through summer and winter seem
Enchanted to a stone
To trouble the living stream.
The horse that comes from the road,
The rider, the birds that range
From cloud to tumbling cloud,
Minute by minute they change;
A shadow of cloud on the stream
Changes minute by minute;   50
A horse-hoof slides on the brim,
And a horse plashes within it;
The long-legged moor-hens dive,
And hens to moor-cocks call;
Minute by minute they live:
The stone's in the midst of all.

[2] In Greek mythology, a winged horse is associated with poetic inspiration.

Too long a sacrifice
Can make a stone of the heart.
O when may it suffice?
That is Heaven's part, our part   60
To murmur name upon name,
As a mother names her child
When sleep at last has come
On limbs that had run wild.
What is it but nightfall?
No, no, not night but death;
Was it needless death after all?
For England may keep faith
For all that is done and said.
We know their dream; enough   70
To know they dreamed and are dead;
And what if excess of love
Bewildered them till they died?
I write it out in a verse—
MacDonagh and MacBride
And Connolly and Pearse
Now and in time to be,
Wherever green is worn,
Are changed, changed utterly:
A terrible beauty is born.   80

For Analysis

1. What is "changed utterly," and in what sense can beauty be "terrible"? **2.** What does "they" in line 55 refer to? What does the "stone" in lines 43 and 56 symbolize? What is Yeats contrasting? **3.** How does the poet answer the question he asks in line 67?

Writing Topic

In the first stanza the attitude of the poet toward the people he is describing is indifferent, even contemptuous. How is that attitude modified in the rest of the poem?

Edwin Arlington Robinson   [1869–1935]

Miniver Cheevy   1910

Miniver Cheevy, child of scorn,
    Grew lean while he assailed the seasons;
He wept that he was ever born,
    And he had reasons.

Miniver loved the days of old
    When swords were bright and steeds were prancing;
The vision of a warrior bold
    Would set him dancing.

Miniver sighed for what was not,
    And dreamed, and rested from his labors;   10
He dreamed of Thebes and Camelot,
    And Priam's neighbors.[1]

Miniver mourned the ripe renown
    That made so many a name so fragrant,
He mourned Romance, now on the town,
    And Art, a vagrant.

Miniver loved the Medici,[2]
    Albeit he had never seen one;
He would have sinned incessantly
    Could he have been one.   20

Miniver cursed the commonplace
    And eyed a khaki suit with loathing;
He missed the medieval grace
    Of iron clothing.

Miniver scorned the gold he sought,
    But sore annoyed was he without it;
Miniver thought, and thought, and thought,
    And thought about it.

Miniver Cheevy, born too late,
    Scratched his head and kept on thinking;   30
Miniver coughed, and called it fate,
    And kept on drinking.

---

[1] Thebes was an ancient Greek city, famous in history and legend; Camelot was the site of the legendary King Arthur's court; Priam was king of Troy during the Trojan War.
[2] A family of bankers and statesmen, notorious for their cruelty, who ruled Florence for nearly two centuries during the Italian Renaissance.

Wallace Stevens   [1879–1955]

Sunday Morning   1923

I

Complacencies of the peignoir, and late
Coffee and oranges in a sunny chair,
And the green freedom of a cockatoo
Upon a rug mingle to dissipate
The holy hush of ancient sacrifice.
She dreams a little, and she feels the dark
Encroachment of that old catastrophe,
As a calm darkens among water-lights.
The pungent oranges and bright, green wings
Seem things in some procession of the dead,   10
Winding across wide water, without sound.
The day is like wide water, without sound,
Stilled for the passing of her dreaming feet
Over the seas, to silent Palestine,
Dominion of the blood and sepulchre.

II

Why should she give her bounty to the dead?
What is divinity if it can come
Only in silent shadows and in dreams?
Shall she not find in comforts of the sun,
In pungent fruit and bright, green wings, or else   20
In any balm or beauty of the earth,
Things to be cherished like the thought of heaven?
Divinity must live within herself:
Passions of rain, or moods in falling snow;
Grievings in loneliness, or unsubdued
Elations when the forest blooms; gusty
Emotions on wet roads on autumn nights;
All pleasures and all pains, remembering
The bough of summer and the winter branch.
These are the measures destined for her soul.   30

III

Jove in the clouds had his inhuman birth.[1]
No mother suckled him, no sweet land gave

---

[1] Jove is Jupiter, the principal god of the Romans, who, unlike Jesus, had an "inhuman birth."

442

Large-mannered motions to his mythy mind
He moved among us, as a muttering king,
Magnificent, would move among his hinds,°   farm servants
Until our blood, commingling, virginal,
With heaven, brought such requital to desire
The very hinds discerned it, in a star.
Shall our blood fail? Or shall it come to be
The blood of paradise? And shall the earth   40
Seem all of paradise that we shall know?
The sky will be much friendlier then than now,
A part of labor and a part of pain,
And next in glory to enduring love,
Not this dividing and indifferent blue.

IV

She says, "I am content when wakened birds,
Before they fly, test the reality
Of misty fields, by their sweet questionings;
But when the birds are gone, and their warm fields
Return no more, where, then, is paradise?"   50
There is not any haunt of prophecy,
Nor any old chimera[2] of the grave,
Neither the golden underground, nor isle
Melodious, where spirits gat them home,
Nor visionary south, nor cloudy palm
Remote on heaven's hill, that has endured
As April's green endures; or will endure
Like her remembrance of awakened birds,
Or her desire for June and evening, tipped
By the consummation of the swallow's wings.   60

V

She says, "But in contentment I still feel
The need of some imperishable bliss."
Death is the mother of beauty; hence from her,
Alone, shall come fulfilment to our dreams
And our desires. Although she strews the leaves
Of sure obliteration on our paths,
The path sick sorrow took, the many paths
Where triumph rang its brassy phrase, or love
Whispered a little out of tenderness,
She makes the willow shiver in the sun   70

[2] A monster with a lion's head, a goat's body, and a serpent's tail. Here an emblem for the belief in other worlds described in the following lines.

For maidens who were wont to sit and gaze
Upon the grass, relinquished to their feet.
She causes boys to pile new plums and pears
On disregarded plate. The maidens taste
And stray impassioned in the littering leaves.

VI

Is there no change of death in paradise?
Does ripe fruit never fall? Or do the boughs
Hang always heavy in that perfect sky,
Unchanging, yet so like our perishing earth,
With rivers like our own that seek for seas   80
They never find, the same receding shores
That never touch with inarticulate pang?
Why set the pear upon those river-banks
Or spice the shores with odors of the plum?
Alas, that they should wear our colors there,
The silken weavings of our afternoons,
And pick the strings of our insipid lutes!
Death is the mother of beauty, mystical,
Within whose burning bosom we devise
Our earthly mothers waiting, sleeplessly.   90

VII

Supple and turbulent, a ring of men
Shall chant in orgy on a summer morn
Their boisterous devotion to the sun,
Not as a god, but as a god might be,
Naked among them, like a savage source.
Their chant shall be a chant of paradise,
Out of their blood, returning to the sky;
And in their chant shall enter, voice by voice,
The windy lake wherein their lord delights,
The trees, like serafin, and echoing hills,   100
That choir among themselves long afterward.
They shall know well the heavenly fellowship
Of men that perish and of summer morn.
And whence they came and whither they shall go
The dew upon their feet shall manifest.

VIII

She hears, upon that water without sound,
A voice that cries, "The tomb in Palestine
Is not the porch of spirits lingering.

It is the grave of Jesus, where he lay."
We live in an old chaos of the sun, 110
Or old dependency of day and night,
Or island solitude, unsponsored, free,
Of that wide water, inescapable.
Deer walk upon our mountains, and the quail
Whistle about us their spontaneous cries;
Sweet berries ripen in the wilderness;
And, in the isolation of the sky,
At evening, casual flocks of pigeons make
Ambiguous undulations as they sink,
Downward to darkness, on extended wings. 120

For Analysis

1. In the opening stanza, the woman's enjoyment of a late Sunday morning breakfast in a relaxed and sensuous atmosphere is troubled by thoughts of what Sunday morning should mean to her. What are the thoughts that disturb her complacency? **2.** What does the speaker mean when he says, "Death is the mother of beauty" (ll. 63 and 88)? **3.** In stanza VI, what is the speaker's attitude toward the conventional Christian conception of paradise? **4.** Stanza VII presents the speaker's vision of an alternative religion. How does it differ from the paradise of stanza VI? **5.** In what ways does the cry of the voice in the final stanza (ll. 107–109) state the woman's dilemma? How do the lines about the pigeons at the end of the poem sum up the speaker's belief?

Writing Topic

This poem is, in a sense, a commentary by the speaker on the woman's desire for truth and certainty more enduring than the physical world can provide. Is the speaker sympathetic to her quest?

Claude McKay [1890–1948]

If We Must Die 1922

If we must die, let it not be like hogs
Hunted and penned in an inglorious spot,
While round us bark the mad and hungry dogs,
Making their mock at our accurséd lot.
If we must die, O let us nobly die,
So that our precious blood may not be shed
In vain; then even the monsters we defy
Shall be constrained to honor us though dead!
O kinsmen! we must meet the common foe!
Though far outnumbered let us show us brave, 10
And for their thousand blows deal one deathblow!

What though before us lies the open grave?
Like men we'll face the murderous, cowardly pack,
Pressed to the wall, dying, but fighting back!

Bertolt Brecht [1898–1956]

War Has Been Given a Bad Name[1] 1957

I am told that the best people have begun saying
How, from a moral point of view, the Second World War
Fell below the standard of the First. The Wehrmacht[2]
Allegedly deplores the methods by which the SS[3] effected
The extermination of certain peoples. The Ruhr industrialists[4]
Are said to regret the bloody manhunts
Which filled their mines and factories with slave workers. The intellectuals
So I heard, condemn industry's demand for slave workers
Likewise their unfair treatment. Even the bishops
Dissociate themselves from this way of waging war; in short the feeling   10
Prevails in every quarter that the Nazis did the Fatherland
A lamentably bad turn, and that war
While in itself natural and necessary, has, thanks to the
Unduly uninhibited and positively inhuman
Way in which it was conducted on this occasion, been
Discredited for some time to come.

For Analysis
1. Characterize the **tone** of this poem, including the title. How does the **diction** contribute to this tone? **2.** What is Brecht's attitude toward the "Wehrmacht" (l. 3), the "Ruhr industrialists" (l. 5), the "intellectuals" (l. 7), and the "bishops" (l. 9)? What do these groups have in common? **3.** What is the effect of the phrases "I am told" (l. 1) and "So I heard" (l. 8)?

Writing Topic
Compare and contrast the handling of the antiwar **theme** in this poem with Wilfred Owen's "Dulce et Decorum Est" (p. 1279).

War Has Been Given a Bad Name
  [1] Translated by John Willett.
  [2] The German armed forces.
  [3] Abbreviated form of the *Schutzstaffel*, the elite guard of the Nazi army.
  [4] One of Germany's most important industrial regions.

Langston Hughes   [1902–1967]

Harlem   1951

What happens to a dream deferred?

Does it dry up
like a raisin in the sun?
Or fester like a sore—
And then run?
Does it stink like rotten meat?
Or crust and sugar over—
like a syrupy sweet?

Maybe it just sags
like a heavy load.   10

Or does it explode?

Same in Blues   1951

I said to my baby,
Baby take it slow.
I can't, she said, I can't!
I got to go!

*There's a certain
amount of traveling
in a dream deferred.*

Lulu said to Leonard,
I want a diamond ring.
Leonard said to Lulu,   10
You won't get a goddam thing!

*A certain
amount of nothing
in a dream deferred.*

Daddy, daddy, daddy,
All I want is you.
You can have me, baby—
but my lovin' days is through.

447

A certain
amount of impotence   20
in a dream deferred.

Three parties
On my party line—
But that third party,
Lord, ain't mine!

There's liable
to be confusion
in a dream deferred.

From river to river
Uptown and down,   30
There's liable to be confusion
when a dream gets kicked around.

W. H. Auden   [1907–1973]

The Unknown Citizen   1940

(To JS/07/M/378
This Marble Monument
Is Erected by the State)

He was found by the Bureau of Statistics to be
One against whom there was no official complaint,
And all the reports on his conduct agree
That, in the modern sense of an old-fashioned word, he was a saint,
For in everything he did he served the Greater Community.
Except for the War till the day he retired
He worked in a factory and never got fired,
But satisfied his employers, Fudge Motors Inc.
Yet he wasn't a scab or odd in his views,
For his Union reports that he paid his dues,   10
(Our report on his Union shows it was sound)
And our Social Psychology workers found
That he was popular with his mates and liked a drink.
The Press are convinced that he bought a paper every day
And that his reactions to advertisements were normal in every way.
Policies taken out in his name prove that he was fully insured,

And his Health-card shows he was once in hospital but left it cured.
Both Producers Research and High-Grade Living declare
He was fully sensible to the advantages of the Installment Plan
And had everything necessary to the Modern Man,   20
A phonograph, radio, a car and a frigidaire.
Our researchers into Public Opinion are content
That he held the proper opinions for the time of year;
When there was peace, he was for peace; when there was war, he went.
He was married and added five children to the population,
Which our Eugenist says was the right number for a parent of his generation,
And our teachers report that he never interfered with their education.
Was he free? Was he happy? The question is absurd:
Had anything been wrong, we should certainly have heard.

Helen Sorrells   [b. 1908]

From a Correct Address in a Suburb of a Major City   1971

She wears her middle age like a cowled
gown, sleeved in it, folded high
at the breast,

charming, proper at cocktails
but the inner one raging
and how to hide her,

how to keep her leashed, contain
the heat of her, the soaring cry
never yet loosed,

demanding a chance before the years devour her,   10
before the marrow of her fine long legs
congeals and she

settles forever for this street, this house,
her face set to the world
sweet, sweet

above the shocked, astonished
hunger.

Muriel Rukeyser   [1913–1980]

Myth   1973

Long afterward, Oedipus, old and blinded, walked the
roads.[1]   He smelled a familiar smell.   It was
the Sphinx.   Oedipus said, "I want to ask one question.
Why didn't I recognize my mother?"   "You gave the
wrong answer," said the Sphinx.   "But that was what
made everything possible," said Oedipus.   "No," she said.
"When I asked, What walks on four legs in the morning,
two at noon, and three in the evening, you answered,
Man.   You didn't say anything about woman."
"When you say Man," said Oedipus, "you include women   10
too. Everyone knows that."   She said, "That's what
you think."

Dudley Randall   [b. 1914]

Ballad of Birmingham   1969

*(On the Bombing of a Church in Birmingham,
Alabama, 1963)*[1]

"Mother dear, may I go downtown
Instead of out to play,
And march the streets of Birmingham
In a Freedom March today?"

"No, baby, no, you may not go,
For the dogs are fierce and wild,
And clubs and hoses, guns and jails
Aren't good for a little child."

Myth
    [1] Oedipus became King of Thebes when he solved the riddle of the Sphinx quoted in the poem.
He blinded himself when he discovered that he had married his own mother.

Ballad of Birmingham
    [1] This poem commemorates the murder of four young African American girls when a bomb was
thrown into the Sixteenth Street Baptist Church in 1963, one of the early and most traumatic events
in the modern civil rights movement.

450

"But, mother, I won't be alone.
Other children will go with me,   10
And march the streets of Birmingham
To make our country free."

"No, baby, no, you may not go,
For I fear those guns will fire.
But you may go to church instead
And sing in the children's choir."

She has combed and brushed her night-dark hair,
And bathed rose petal sweet.
And drawn white gloves on her small brown hands,
And white shoes on her feet.   20

The mother smiled to know her child
Was in the sacred place,
But that smile was the last smile
To come upon her face.

For when she heard the explosion,
Her eyes grew wet and wild.
She raced through the streets of Birmingham
Calling for her child.

She clawed through bits of glass and brick,
Then lifted out a shoe.   30
"Oh, here's the shoe my baby wore,
But, baby, where are you?"

Lawrence Ferlinghetti   [b. 1919]

In Goya's Greatest Scenes   1958

In Goya's greatest scenes[1] we seem to see
                          the people of the world
        exactly at the moment when
               they first attained the title of
                      'suffering humanity'

In Goya's Greatest Scenes
[1] Francisco José de Goya (1746–1828), famous Spanish artist, celebrated for his representations of "suffering humanity."

They writhe upon the page
                  in a veritable rage
                            of adversity
Heaped up
          groaning with babies and bayonets   10
                          under cement skies
        in an abstract landscape of blasted trees
           bent statues bats wings and beaks
                slippery gibbets
          cadavers and carnivorous cocks
       and all the final hollering monsters
          of the
               'imagination of disaster'
       they are so bloody real
               it is as if they really still existed   20

And they do
        Only the landscape is changed

They still are ranged along the roads
        plagued by legionaires
                false windmills and demented roosters

They are the same people
               only further from home
   on freeways fifty lanes wide
          on a concrete continent
               spaced with bland billboards   30
           illustrating imbecile illusions of happiness
   The scene shows fewer tumbrils[2]
              but more maimed citizens
                    in painted cars
     and they have strange license plates
  and engines
        that devour America

For Analysis
1. To whom does the word "they" refer in line 26? **2.** What is responsible for the "suffering" of modern American "humanity"?

---

[2] Carts in which prisoners were conducted to the place of execution.

Charles Bukowski [1920–1994]

for marilyn m.[1] 1963

slipping keenly into bright ashes,
target of vanilla tears
your sure body lit candles for men
on dark nights,
and now your night is darker
than the candle's reach
and we will forget you, somewhat,
and it is not kind
but real bodies are nearer
and as the worms pant for your bones,   10
I would so like to tell you
that this happens to bears and elephants
to tyrants and heroes and ants
and frogs,
still, you brought us something,
some type of small victory,
and for this I say: good
and let us grieve no more;
like a flower dried and thrown away,
we forget, we remember,   20
we wait. child, child, child,
I raise my drink a full minute
and smile.

Richard Wilbur [b. 1921]

Museum Piece 1948

The good grey guardians of art
Patrol the halls on spongy shoes,
Impartially protective, though
Perhaps suspicious of Toulouse.[1]

for marilyn m.
    [1] Marilyn Monroe (1926–1962) became, during the 1950s, a celebrated movie star and America's foremost sex symbol.

Museum Piece
    [1] Henri de Toulouse-Lautrec (1864–1901), a French artist, celebrated for his paintings of the dancers, actresses, and prostitutes of Parisian nightlife.

Here dozes one against the wall,
Disposed upon a funeral chair.
A Degas[2] dancer pirouettes
Upon the parting of his hair.

See how she spins! The grace is there,
But strain as well is plain to see.   10
Degas loved the two together:
Beauty joined to energy.

Edgar Degas purchased once
A fine El Greco,[3] which he kept
Against the wall beside his bed
To hang his pants on while he slept.

For Analysis
1. Who are the guardians mentioned in the first stanza? Why are they described as "grey"? **2.** Explain the **image** of the second stanza. **3.** How does the anecdote of the final stanza embody the **theme** of the poem?

Writing Topic
Write an essay in which you compare and contrast this poem with W. H. Auden's "Musée des Beaux Arts" (p. 1283) as attempts to define the relationship between art and life.

Denise Levertov [b. 1923]

Protesters   1992

Living on the rim
of the raging cauldron, disasters

witnessed but
not suffered in the flesh.

The choice: to speak
or not to speak.
We spoke.

Museum Piece
[2] Edgar Degas (1834–1917), a French Impressionist who often painted ballet dancers.
[3] El Greco is the sobriquet of Doménikos Theotocópoulos (1541?–1614), a Greek-born Spanish painter.

Those of whom we spoke
had not that choice.

At every epicenter, beneath   10
roar and tumult,

enforced:
their silence.

Writing Topic
Write an essay about a decision you made to speak out even though you were not
personally involved in (or threatened by) the event or issue you were protesting.

Marge Piercy   [b. 1936]

Cats like angels   1980

Cats like angels are supposed to be thin;
pigs like cherubs are supposed to be fat.
People are mostly in between, a knob
of bone sticking out in the knee you might
like to pad, a dollop of flab hanging
over the belt. You punish yourself,
one of those rubber balls kids have
that come bouncing back off their own
paddles, rebounding on the same slab.
You want to be slender and seamless   10
as a bolt.
            When I was a girl
I loved spiny men with ascetic grimaces
all elbows and words and cartilage
ribbed like cast up fog-grey hulls,
faces to cut the eyes blind
on the glittering blade, chins
of Aegean prows bent on piracy.

Now I look for men whose easy bellies
show a love for the flesh and the table,   20
men who will come in the kitchen
and sit, who don't think peeling potatoes
makes their penis shrink; men with broad

fingers and purple figgy balls,
men with rumpled furrows and the slightly
messed look at ease of beds recently
well used.
       We are not all supposed
to look like undernourished fourteen year
old boys, no matter what the fashions   30
ordain. You are built to pull a cart,
to lift a heavy load and bear it,
to haul up the long slope, and so
am I, peasant bodies, earthy, solid
shapely dark glazed clay pots that can
stand on the fire. When we put our
bellies together we do not clatter
but bounce on the good upholstery.

For Analysis

1. The first two lines suggest that cats and angels are "supposed to be" thin and pigs and cherubs fat. Explain this statement. **2.** Describe the difference between the men the speaker loved when she was a girl and the men she now admires. **3.** Who is the "You" the speaker addresses in line 31?

Writing Topic

Write an essay describing how your view on some important personal matter (such as beauty, loyalty, honesty) changed over the course of time. Explain how you acquired your original view and why that view changed.

The low road   1980

What can they do
to you? Whatever they want.
They can set you up, they can
bust you, they can break
your fingers, they can
burn your brain with electricity,
blur you with drugs till you
can't walk, can't remember, they can
take your child, wall up
your lover. They can do anything   10
you can't stop them
from doing. How can you stop
them? Alone, you can fight,
you can refuse, you can
take what revenge you can
but they roll over you.

But two people fighting
back to back can cut through
a mob, a snake-dancing file
can break a cordon, an army
can meet an army.

20

Two people can keep each other
sane, can give support, conviction,
love, massage, hope, sex.
Three people are a delegation,
a committee, a wedge. With four
you can play bridge and start
an organization. With six
you can rent a whole house,
eat pie for dinner with no
seconds, and hold a fund raising party.
A dozen make a demonstration.
A hundred fill a hall.
A thousand have solidarity and your own newsletter;
ten thousand, power and your own paper;
a hundred thousand, your own media;
ten million, your own country.

30

It goes on one at a time,
it starts when you care
to act, it starts when you do
it again after they said no,
it starts when you say *We*
and know who you mean, and each
day you mean one more.

40

Nikki Giovanni   [b. 1943]

Dreams   1968

i used to dream militant
dreams of taking
over america to show
these white folks how it should be
done
i used to dream radical dreams
of blowing everyone away with my perceptive powers

of correct analysis
i even used to think i'd be the one
to stop the riot and negotiate the peace   10
then i awoke and dug
that if i dreamed natural
dreams of being a natural
woman doing what a woman
does when she's natural
i would have a revolution

Victor Hernández Cruz   [b. 1949]

Today Is a Day of Great Joy   1968

when they stop poems
in the mail & clap
their hands & dance to
them
when women become pregnant
by the side of poems
the strongest sounds making
the river go along

it is a great day

as poems fall down to   10

movie crowds in restaurants
in bars

when poems start to
knock down walls to
choke politicians
when poems scream &
begin to break the air

that is the time of
true poets that is
the time of greatness   20

a true poet aiming
poems & watching things
fall to the ground

it is a great day.

Writing Topic

Write an essay in which you argue for or against the proposition that one of the important and legitimate functions of poetry (or art in general) is to move people to direct social and political action.

Carolyn Forché [b. 1950]

The Colonel 1981

What you have heard is true. I was in his house. His wife carried a tray of coffee and sugar. His daughter filed her nails, his son went out for the night. There were daily papers, pet dogs, a pistol on the cushion beside him. The moon swung bare on its black cord over the house. On the television was a cop show. It was in English. Broken bottles were embedded in the walls round the house to scoop the kneecaps from a man's legs or cut his hands to lace. On the windows there were gratings like those in liquor stores. We had dinner, rack of lamb, good wine, a gold bell was on the table for calling the maid. The maid brought green mangoes, salt, a type of bread. I was asked how I enjoyed the country. There was a brief commercial in Spanish. His wife took everything   10
away. There was some talk then of how difficult it had become to govern. The parrot said hello on the terrace. The colonel told it to shut up, and pushed himself from the table. My friend said to me with his eyes: say nothing. The colonel returned with a sack used to bring groceries home. He spilled many human ears on the table. They were like dried peach halves. There is no other way to say this. He took one of them in his hands, shook it in our faces, dropped it into a water glass. It came alive there. I am tired of fooling around he said. As for the rights of anyone, tell your people they can go fuck themselves. He swept the ears to the floor with his arm and held the last of his wine in the air. Something for your poetry, no? he said. Some of the ears on the floor caught this scrap of   20
his voice. Some of the ears on the floor were pressed to the ground.

For Analysis

1. What is the occasion of this poem? Where is it set? How would you characterize the colonel's family? **2.** "There was some talk then of how difficult it had become to govern." Can you suggest why it had become difficult to govern? How does the colonel respond to these difficulties? **3.** What does the last sentence suggest? **4.** This piece is printed as if it were prose. Does it have any of the formal characteristics of a poem?

Drama

Sophocles   [496?–406 B.C.]

Antigonê   ca. 441 B.C.

CHARACTERS

Antigonê	**Teiresias**
Ismenê	**A Sentry**
Eurydicê	**A Messenger**
Creon	**Chorus**
Haimon	

Scene

Before the Palace of Creon, King of Thebes. A central double door, and two lateral doors. A platform extends the length of the façade, and from this platform three steps lead down into the "orchestra," or chorus-ground.

Time

Dawn of the day after the repulse of the Argive army from the assault on Thebes.

Prologue

[Antigonê and Ismenê enter from the central door of the Palace.]

Antigonê.   Ismenê, dear sister,
  You would think that we had already suffered enough

Antigonê: This English version is by Dudley Fitts and Robert Fitzgerald.

For the curse on Oedipus:[1]
I cannot imagine any grief
That you and I have not gone through. And now—
Have they told you of the new decree of our King Creon?
Ismenê.   I have heard nothing: I know
That two sisters lost two brothers, a double death
In a single hour; and I know that the Argive army
Fled in the night; but beyond this, nothing.   10
Antigonê.   I thought so. And that is why I wanted you
To come out here with me. There is something we must do.
Ismenê.   Why do you speak so strangely?
Antigonê.   Listen, Ismenê:
Creon buried our brother Eteoclês
With military honors, gave him a soldier's funeral,
And it was right that he should; but Polyneicês,
Who fought as bravely and died as miserably,—
They say that Creon has sworn
No one shall bury him, no one mourn for him,   20
But his body must lie in the fields, a sweet treasure
For carrion birds to find as they search for food.
That is what they say, and our good Creon is coming here
To announce it publicly; and the penalty—
Stoning to death in the public square!
                                        There it is,
And now you can prove what you are:
A true sister, or a traitor to your family.
Ismenê.   Antigonê, you are mad! What could I possibly do?
Antigonê.   You must decide whether you will help me or not.
Ismenê.   I do not understand you. Help you in what?   30
Antigonê.   Ismenê, I am going to bury him. Will you come?
Ismenê.   Bury him! You have just said the new law forbids it.
Antigonê.   He is my brother. And he is your brother, too.
Ismenê.   But think of the danger! Think what Creon will do!
Antigonê.   Creon is not strong enough to stand in my way.
Ismenê.   Ah sister!
Oedipus died, everyone hating him
For what his own search brought to light, his eyes
Ripped out by his own hand; and Iocastê died,
His mother and wife at once: she twisted the cords   40

---

[1]Oedipus, a former king of Thebes, unwittingly killed his father and married his own mother, Iocastê. By her he had four children, the sisters Antigonê and Ismenê and the brothers Polyneicês and Eteoclês. When Oedipus realized what he had done, he blinded himself and left Thebes. Eteoclês drove Polyneicês out of Thebes after a quarrel, but Polyneicês returned with an army and laid siege to Thebes. In the ensuing struggle, the brothers killed each other. Creon became king and, as a punishment, decreed that Polyneicês be denied the rites of burial.

That strangled her life; and our two brothers died,
Each killed by the other's sword. And we are left:
But oh, Antigonê,
Think how much more terrible than these
Our own death would be if we should go against Creon
And do what he has forbidden! We are only women,
We cannot fight with men, Antigonê!
The law is strong, we must give in to the law
In this thing, and in worse. I beg the Dead
To forgive me, but I am helpless: I must yield   50
To those in authority. And I think it is dangerous business
To be always meddling.

Antigonê.   If that is what you think,
I should not want you, even if you asked to come.
You have made your choice, you can be what you want to be.
But I will bury him; and if I must die,
I say that this crime is holy: I shall lie down
With him in death, and I shall be as dear
To him as he to me.
                    It is the dead,
Not the living, who make the longest demands:
We die for ever . . .
                    You may do as you like,   60
Since apparently the laws of the gods mean nothing to you.

Ismenê.   They mean a great deal to me; but I have no strength
To break laws that were made for the public good.

Antigonê.   That must be your excuse, I suppose. But as for me,
I will bury the brother I love.

Ismenê.   Antigonê,
I am so afraid for you!

Antigonê.   You need not be:
You have yourself to consider, after all.

Ismenê.   But no one must hear of this, you must tell no one!
I will keep it a secret, I promise!

Antigonê.   Oh tell it! Tell everyone!
Think how they'll hate you when it all comes out   70
If they learn that you knew about it all the time!

Ismenê.   So fiery! You should be cold with fear.

Antigonê.   Perhaps. But I am doing only what I must.

Ismenê.   But can you do it? I say that you cannot.

Antigonê.   Very well: when my strength gives out, I shall do no more.

Ismenê.   Impossible things should not be tried at all.

Antigonê.   Go away, Ismenê:
I shall be hating you soon, and the dead will too,
For your words are hateful. Leave me my foolish plan:

I am not afraid of the danger; if it means death, 80
    It will not be the worst of deaths—death without honor.
Ismenê.   Go then, if you feel you must.
    You are unwise,
    But a loyal friend indeed to those who love you.

[*Exit into the Palace. Antigonê goes off, L. Enter the Chorus.*]

Párodos²

Chorus.   Now the long blade of the sun, lying   [*Strophe 1*]
    Level east to west, touches with glory
    Thebes of the Seven Gates. Open, unlidded
    Eye of golden day! O marching light
    Across the eddy and rush of Dircê's stream,³
    Striking the white shields of the enemy
    Thrown headlong backward from the blaze of morning!
Choragos.⁴   Polyneicês their commander
    Roused them with windy phrases,
    He the wild eagle screaming   10
    Insults above our land,
    His wings their shields of snow,
    His crest their marshalled helms.

Chorus.   Against our seven gates in a yawning ring   [*Antistrophe 1*]
    The famished spears came onward in the night;
    But before his jaws were sated with our blood,
    Or pinefire took the garland of our towers,
    He was thrown back; and as he turned, great Thebes—
    No tender victim for his noisy power—
    Rose like a dragon behind him, shouting war.   20
Choragos.   For God hates utterly
    The bray of bragging tongues;
    And when he beheld their smiling,
    Their swagger of golden helms,
    The frown of his thunder blasted
    Their first man from our walls.

Chorus.   We heard his shout of triumph high in the air   [*Strophe 2*]
    Turn to a scream; far out in a flaming arc

---

² The *Párodos* is the ode sung by the Chorus as it entered the theater and moved down the aisles to the playing area. The *strophe*, in Greek tragedy, is the unit of verse the Chorus chanted as it moved to the left in a dance rhythm. The Chorus sang the *antistrophe* as it moved to the right, and the *epode* while standing still.   ³ A stream near Thebes.   ⁴ Choragos is the leader of the Chorus.

He fell with his windy torch, and the earth struck him.
And others storming in fury no less than his   30
Found shock of death in the dusty joy of battle.
Choragos.   Seven captains at seven gates
  Yielded their clanging arms to the god
  That bends the battle-line and breaks it.
  These two only, brothers in blood,
  Face to face in matchless rage,
  Mirroring each the other's death,
  Clashed in long combat.

Chorus.   But now in the beautiful morning of victory   [*Antistrophe 2*]
  Let Thebes of the many chariots sing for joy!   40
  With hearts for dancing we'll take leave of war:
  Our temples shall be sweet with hymns of praise,
  And the long night shall echo with our chorus.

Scene I

Choragos.   But now at last our new King is coming:
  Creon of Thebes, Menoikeus' son.
  In this auspicious dawn of his reign
  What are the new complexities
  That shifting Fate has woven for him?
  What is his counsel? Why has he summoned
  The old men to hear him?

[*Enter Creon from the Palace, C. He addresses the Chorus from the top step.*]

Creon.   Gentlemen: I have the honor to inform you that our Ship of State,
which recent storms have threatened to destroy, has come safely to harbor at
last, guided by the merciful wisdom of Heaven. I have summoned you here   10
this morning because I know that I can depend upon you: your devotion to
King Laïos was absolute; you never hesitated in your duty to our late ruler
Oedipus; and when Oedipus died, your loyalty was transferred to his children. Unfortunately, as you know, his two sons, the princes Eteoclês and
Polyneicês, have killed each other in battle; and I, as the next in blood, have
succeeded to the full power of the throne.
    I am aware, of course, that no Ruler can expect complete loyalty from his
subjects until he has been tested in office. Nevertheless, I say to you at the
very outset that I have nothing but contempt for the kind of Governor who is
afraid, for whatever reason, to follow the course that he knows is best for the   20

State; and as for the man who sets private friendship above the public welfare,—I have no use for him, either. I call God to witness that if I saw my country headed for ruin, I should not be afraid to speak out plainly; and I need hardly remind you that I would never have any dealings with an enemy of the people. No one values friendship more highly than I; but we must remember that friends made at the risk of wrecking our Ship are not real friends at all.

These are my principles, at any rate, and that is why I have made the following decision concerning the sons of Oedipus: Eteoclês, who died as a man should die, fighting for his country, is to be buried with full military honors, with all the ceremony that is usual when the greatest heroes die; but his brother Polyneicês, who broke his exile to come back with fire and sword against his native city and the shrines of his fathers' gods, whose one idea was to spill the blood of his blood and sell his own people into slavery— Polyneicês, I say, is to have no burial: no man is to touch him or say the least prayer for him; he shall lie on the plain, unburied; and the birds and the scavenging dogs can do with him whatever they like.   30

This is my command, and you can see the wisdom behind it. As long as I am King, no traitor is going to be honored with the loyal man. But whoever shows by word and deed that he is on the side of the State,—he shall have my respect while he is living and my reverence when he is dead.   40
Choragos.   If that is your will, Creon, son of Menoikeus,
You have the right to enforce it: we are yours.
Creon.   That is my will. Take care that you do your part.
Choragos.   We are old men: let the younger ones carry it out.
Creon.   I do not mean that: the sentries have been appointed.
Choragos.   Then what is it that you would have us do?
Creon.   You will give no support to whoever breaks this law.
Choragos.   Only a crazy man is in love with death!
Creon.   And death it is; yet money talks, and the wisest   50
Have sometimes been known to count a few coins too many.

[*Enter Sentry from L.*]

Sentry.   I'll not say that I'm out of breath from running, King, because every time I stopped to think about what I have to tell you, I felt like going back. And all the time a voice kept saying, "You fool, don't you know you're walking straight into trouble?"; and then another voice: "Yes, but if you let somebody else get the news to Creon first, it will be even worse than that for you!" But good sense won out, at least I hope it was good sense, and here I am with a story that makes no sense at all; but I'll tell it anyhow, because, as they say, what's going to happen's going to happen, and—
Creon.   Come to the point. What have you to say?   60
Sentry.   I did not do it. I did not see who did it. You must not punish me for what someone else has done.

Creon.   A comprehensive defense! More effective, perhaps,
  If I knew its purpose. Come: what is it?
Sentry.   A dreadful thing . . . I don't know how to put it—
Creon.   Out with it!
Sentry.   Well, then;
  The dead man—
                    Polyneicês—

[*Pause. The Sentry is overcome, fumbles for words. Creon waits impassively.*]

                    out there—   70
                                    someone,—

  New dust on the slimy flesh!

[*Pause. No sign from Creon.*]

  Someone has given it burial that way, and
  Gone . . .

[*Long pause. Creon finally speaks with deadly control.*]

Creon.   And the man who dared do this?
Sentry.   I swear I
  Do not know! You must believe me!
                                    Listen:
  The ground was dry, not a sign of digging, no,
  Not a wheeltrack in the dust, no trace of anyone.   80
  It was when they relieved us this morning: and one of them,
  The corporal, pointed to it.
                    There it was,
  The strangest—
                    Look:
  The body, just mounded over with light dust: you see?
  Not buried really, but as if they'd covered it
  Just enough for the ghost's peace. And no sign
  Of dogs or any wild animal that had been there.

  And then what a scene there was! Every man of us   90
  Accusing the other: we all proved the other man did it,
  We all had proof that we could not have done it.
  We were ready to take hot iron in our hands,
  Walk through fire, swear by all the gods,
  It was not I!
  I do not know who it was, but it was not I!

[*Creon's rage has been mounting steadily, but the Sentry is too intent upon his
story to notice it.*]

And then, when this came to nothing, someone said
A thing that silenced us and made us stare
Down at the ground: you had to be told the news,
And one of us had to do it! We threw the dice,   100
And the bad luck fell to me. So here I am,
No happier to be here than you are to have me:
Nobody likes the man who brings bad news.

Choragos.   I have been wondering, King: can it be that the gods have done
this?

Creon [*furiously*].   Stop!
Must you doddering wrecks
Go out of your heads entirely? "The gods!"
Intolerable!
The gods favor this corpse? Why? How had he served them?   110
Tried to loot their temples, burn their images,
Yes, and the whole State, and its laws with it!
Is it your senile opinion that the gods love to honor bad men?
A pious thought!—
                        No, from the very beginning
There have been those who have whispered together,
Stiff-necked anarchists, putting their heads together,
Scheming against me in alleys. These are the men,
And they have bribed my own guard to do this thing.
[*Sententiously.*] Money!   120
There's nothing in the world so demoralizing as money.
Down go your cities,
Homes gone, men gone, honest hearts corrupted,
Crookedness of all kinds, and all for money!
[*To Sentry.*]   But you—!
I swear by God and by the throne of God,
The man who has done this thing shall pay for it!
Find that man, bring him here to me, or your death
Will be the least of your problems: I'll string you up
Alive, and there will be certain ways to make you   130
Discover your employer before you die;
And the process may teach you a lesson you seem to have missed:
The dearest profit is sometimes all too dear:
That depends on the source. Do you understand me?
A fortune won is often misfortune.

Sentry.   King, may I speak?

Creon.   Your very voice distresses me.

Sentry.   Are you sure that it is my voice, and not your conscience?

Creon.   By God, he wants to analyze me now!

Sentry.   It is not what I say, but what has been done, that hurts you.   140

Creon.   You talk too much.

Sentry.   Maybe; but I've done nothing.

Creon. Sold your soul for some silver: that's all you've done.
Sentry. How dreadful it is when the right judge judges wrong!
Creon. Your figures of speech
    May entertain you now; but unless you bring me the man,
    You will get little profit from them in the end.

[*Exit Creon into the Palace.*]

Sentry. "Bring me the man"—!
    I'd like nothing better than bringing him the man!
    But bring him or not, you have seen the last of me here.   150
    At any rate, I am safe!

[*Exit Sentry.*]

Ode I

Chorus. Numberless are the world's wonders, but none   [*Strophe 1*]
    More wonderful than man; the stormgray sea
    Yields to his prows, the huge crests bear him high;
    Earth, holy and inexhaustible, is graven
    With shining furrows where his plows have gone
    Year after year, the timeless labor of stallions.

    The lightboned birds and beasts that cling to cover,   [*Antistrophe 1*]
    The lithe fish lighting their reaches of dim water,
    All are taken, tamed in the net of his mind;
    The lion on the hill, the wild horse windy-maned,   10
    Resign to him; and his blunt yoke has broken
    The sultry shoulders of the mountain bull.

    Words also, and thought as rapid as air,   [*Strophe 2*]
    He fashions to his good use; statecraft is his,
    And his the skill that deflects the arrows of snow,
    The spears of winter rain: from every wind
    He has made himself secure—from all but one:
    In the late wind of death he cannot stand.

    O clear intelligence, force beyond all measure!   [*Antistrophe 2*]
    O fate of man, working both good and evil!   20

When the laws are kept, how proudly his city stands!
When the laws are broken, what of his city then?
Never may the anarchic man find rest at my hearth,
Never be it said that my thoughts are his thoughts.

Scene II

[*Re-enter Sentry leading Antigonê.*]

Choragos.   What does this mean? Surely this captive woman
  Is the Princess, Antigonê. Why should she be taken?
Sentry.   Here is the one who did it! We caught her
  In the very act of burying him.—Where is Creon?
Choragos.   Just coming from the house.

[*Enter Creon, C.*]

Creon.   What has happened?
  Why have you come back so soon?
Sentry [*expansively*].   O King,
  A man should never be too sure of anything:
  I would have sworn
  That you'd not see me here again: your anger
  Frightened me so, and the things you threatened me with;   10
  But how could I tell then
  That I'd be able to solve the case so soon?
  No dice-throwing this time: I was only too glad to come!

  Here is this woman. She is the guilty one:
  We found her trying to bury him.
  Take her, then; question her; judge her as you will.
  I am through with the whole thing now, and glad of it.
Creon.   But this is Antigonê! Why have you brought her here?
Sentry.   She was burying him, I tell you!
Creon [*severely*].   Is this the truth?
Sentry.   I saw her with my own eyes. Can I say more?   20
Creon.   The details: come, tell me quickly!
Sentry.   It was like this:
  After those terrible threats of yours, King,
  We went back and brushed the dust away from the body.
  The flesh was soft by now, and stinking,

So we sat on a hill to windward and kept guard.
No napping this time! We kept each other awake.
But nothing happened until the white round sun
Whirled in the center of the round sky over us:
Then, suddenly,
A storm of dust roared up from the earth, and the sky   30
Went out, the plain vanished with all its trees
In the stinging dark. We closed our eyes and endured it.
The whirlwind lasted a long time, but it passed;
And then we looked, and there was Antigonê!
I have seen
A mother bird come back to a stripped nest, heard
Her crying bitterly a broken note or two
For the young ones stolen. Just so, when this girl
Found the bare corpse, and all her love's work wasted,
She wept, and cried on heaven to damn the hands   40
That had done this thing.
                              And then she brought more dust
And sprinkled wine three times for her brother's ghost.
We ran and took her at once. She was not afraid,
Not even when we charged her with what she had done.
She denied nothing.
                     And this was a comfort to me,
And some uneasiness: for it is a good thing
To escape from death, but it is no great pleasure
To bring death to a friend.
                              Yet I always say
There is nothing so comfortable as your own safe skin!
Creon [*slowly, dangerously*].   And you, Antigonê,   50
   You with your head hanging,—do you confess this thing?
Antigonê.   I do. I deny nothing.
Creon [*to Sentry*].   You may go.

[*Exit Sentry.*]

   [*To Antigonê.*] Tell me, tell me briefly:
   Had you heard my proclamation touching this matter?
Antigonê.   It was public. Could I help hearing it?
Creon.   And yet you dared defy the law.
Antigonê.   I dared.
   It was not God's proclamation. That final Justice
   That rules the world below makes no such laws.

   Your edict, King, was strong,
   But all your strength is weakness itself against   60
   The immortal unrecorded laws of God.

They are not merely now: they were, and shall be,
Operative for ever, beyond man utterly.

I knew I must die, even without your decree:
I am only mortal. And if I must die
Now, before it is my time to die,
Surely this is no hardship: can anyone
Living, as I live, with evil all about me,
Think Death less than a friend? This death of mine
Is of no importance; but if I had left my brother   70
Lying in death unburied, I should have suffered.
Now I do not.
          You smile at me. Ah Creon,
Think me a fool, if you like; but it may well be
That a fool convicts me of folly.
Choragos.   Like father, like daughter: both headstrong, deaf to reason!
She has never learned to yield.
Creon.   She has much to learn.
The inflexible heart breaks first, the toughest iron
Cracks first, and the wildest horses bend their necks
At the pull of the smallest curb.
                   Pride? In a slave?
This girl is guilty of a double insolence,   80
Breaking the given laws and boasting of it.
Who is the man here,
She or I, if this crime goes unpunished?
Sister's child, or more than sister's child,
Or closer yet in blood—she and her sister
Win bitter death for this!
[*To servants.*]   Go, some of you,
Arrest Ismenê. I accuse her equally.
Bring her: you will find her sniffling in the house there.

Her mind's a traitor: crimes kept in the dark
Cry for light, and the guardian brain shudders;   90
But how much worse than this
Is brazen boasting of barefaced anarchy!
Antigonê.   Creon, what more do you want than my death?
Creon.   Nothing.
That gives me everything.
Antigonê.   Then I beg you: kill me.
This talking is a great weariness: your words
Are distasteful to me, and I am sure that mine
Seem so to you. And yet they should not seem so:
I should have praise and honor for what I have done.
All these men here would praise me

Were their lips not frozen shut with fear of you.   100
[*Bitterly.*] Ah the good fortune of kings,
Licensed to say and do whatever they please!
Creon.   You are alone here in that opinion.
Antigonê.   No, they are with me. But they keep their tongues in leash.
Creon.   Maybe. But you are guilty, and they are not.
Antigonê.   There is no guilt in reverence for the dead.
Creon.   But Eteoclês—was he not your brother too?
Antigonê.   My brother too.
Creon.   And you insult his memory?
Antigonê [*softly*].   The dead man would not say that I insult it.
Creon.   He would: for you honor a traitor as much as him.   110
Antigonê.   His own brother, traitor or not, and equal in blood.
Creon.   He made war on his country. Eteoclês defended it.
Antigonê.   Nevertheless, there are honors due all the dead.
Creon.   But not the same for the wicked as for the just.
Antigonê.   Ah Creon, Creon,
Which of us can say what the gods hold wicked?
Creon.   An enemy is an enemy, even dead.
Antigonê.   It is my nature to join in love, not hate.
Creon [*finally losing patience*].   Go join them, then; if you must have your
    love,
Find it in hell!   120
Choragos.   But see, Ismenê comes:

[*Enter Ismenê, guarded.*]

Those tears are sisterly, the cloud
That shadows her eyes rains down gentle sorrow.
Creon.   You too, Ismenê,
Snake in my ordered house, sucking my blood
Stealthily—and all the time I never knew
That these two sisters were aiming at my throne!
                                        Ismenê,
Do you confess your share in this crime, or deny it?
Answer me.
Ismenê.   Yes, if she will let me say so. I am guilty.   130
Antigonê [*coldly*].   No, Ismenê. You have no right to say so.
You would not help me, and I will not have you help me.
Ismenê.   But now I know what you meant; and I am here
To join you, to take my share of punishment.
Antigonê.   The dead man and the gods who rule the dead
Know whose act this was. Words are not friends.
Ismenê.   Do you refuse me, Antigonê? I want to die with you:
I too have a duty that I must discharge to the dead.
Antigonê.   You shall not lessen my death by sharing it.

Ismenê.   What do I care for life when you are dead?   140
Antigonê.   Ask Creon. You're always hanging on his opinions.
Ismenê.   You are laughing at me. Why, Antigonê?
Antigonê.   It's a joyless laughter, Ismenê.
Ismenê.   But can I do nothing?
Antigonê.   Yes. Save yourself. I shall not envy you.
   There are those who will praise you; I shall have honor, too.
Ismenê.   But we are equally guilty!
Antigonê.   No more, Ismenê.
   You are alive, but I belong to Death.
Creon [*to the Chorus*].   Gentlemen, I beg you to observe these girls:
   One has just now lost her mind; the other,
   It seems, has never had a mind at all.   150
Ismenê.   Grief teaches the steadiest minds to waver, King.
Creon.   Yours certainly did, when you assumed guilt with the guilty!
Ismenê.   But how could I go on living without her?
Creon.   You are.
   She is already dead.
Ismenê.   But your own son's bride!
Creon.   There are places enough for him to push his plow.
   I want no wicked women for my sons!
Ismenê.   O dearest Haimon, how your father wrongs you!
Creon.   I've had enough of your childish talk of marriage!
Choragos.   Do you really intend to steal this girl from your son?
Creon.   No; Death will do that for me.
Choragos.   Then she must die?   160
Creon [*ironically*].   You dazzle me.
                              —But enough of this talk!
   [*To Guards.*] You there, take them away and guard them well:
   For they are but women, and even brave men run
   When they see Death coming.

[*Exeunt Ismenê, Antigonê, and Guards.*]

Ode II

Chorus.   Fortunate is the man who has never tasted   [*Strophe 1*]
      God's vengeance!
   Where once the anger of heaven has struck, that house is shaken
   For ever: damnation rises behind each child
   Like a wave cresting out of the black northeast,
   When the long darkness under sea roars up
   And bursts drumming death upon the windwhipped sand.

I have seen this gathering sorrow from time long past   [*Antistrophe 1*]
Loom upon Oedipus' children: generation from generation
Takes the compulsive rage of the enemy god.
So lately this last flower of Oedipus' line   10
Drank the sunlight! but now a passionate word
And a handful of dust have closed up all its beauty.

    What mortal arrogance   [*Strophe 2*]
    Transcends the wrath of Zeus?
Sleep cannot lull him, nor the effortless long months
Of the timeless gods: but he is young for ever,
And his house is the shining day of high Olympos.
    And that is and shall be,
    And all the past, is his.
No pride on earth is free of the curse of heaven.   20

    The straying dreams of men   [*Antistrophe 2*]
    May bring them ghosts of joy:
But as they drowse, the waking embers burn them;
Or they walk with fixed eyes, as blind men walk.
But the ancient wisdom speaks for our own time:
    Fate works most for woe
    With Folly's fairest show.
Man's little pleasure is the spring of sorrow.

Scene III

Choragos.   But here is Haimon, King, the last of all your sons.
  Is it grief for Antigonê that brings him here,
  And bitterness at being robbed of his bride?

[*Enter Haimon.*]

Creon.   We shall soon see, and no need of diviners.
                           —Son,
  You have heard my final judgment on that girl:
  Have you come here hating me, or have you come
  With deference and with love, whatever I do?
Haimon.   I am your son, father. You are my guide.
  You make things clear for me, and I obey you.
  No marriage means more to me than your continuing wisdom.   10
Creon.   Good. That is the way to behave: subordinate

Everything else, my son, to your father's will.
This is what a man prays for, that he may get
Sons attentive and dutiful in his house,
Each one hating his father's enemies,
Honoring his father's friends. But if his sons
Fail him, if they turn out unprofitably,
What has he fathered but trouble for himself
And amusement for the malicious?

So you are right

Not to lose your head over this woman.   20
Your pleasure with her would soon grow cold, Haimon,
And then you'd have a hellcat in bed and elsewhere.
Let her find her husband in Hell!
Of all the people in this city, only she
Has had contempt for my law and broken it.

Do you want me to show myself weak before the people?
Or to break my sworn word? No, and I will not.
The woman dies.
I suppose she'll plead "family ties." Well, let her.
If I permit my own family to rebel,   30
How shall I earn the world's obedience?
Show me the man who keeps his house in hand,
He's fit for public authority.

I'll have no dealings

With law-breakers, critics of the government:
Whoever is chosen to govern should be obeyed—
Must be obeyed, in all things, great and small,
Just and unjust! O Haimon,
The man who knows how to obey, and that man only,
Knows how to give commands when the time comes.
You can depend on him, no matter how fast   40
The spears come: he's a good soldier, he'll stick it out.
Anarchy, anarchy! Show me a greater evil!
This is why cities tumble and the great houses rain down,
This is what scatters armies!

No, no: good lives are made so by discipline.
We keep the laws then, and the lawmakers,
And no woman shall seduce us. If we must lose,
Let's lose to a man, at least! Is a woman stronger than we?
Choragos.   Unless time has rusted my wits,
What you say, King, is said with point and dignity.   50
Haimon [*boyishly earnest*].   Father:
Reason is God's crowning gift to man, and you are right

To warn me against losing mine. I cannot say—
I hope that I shall never want to say!—that you
Have reasoned badly. Yet there are other men
Who can reason, too; and their opinions might be helpful.
You are not in a position to know everything
That people say or do, or what they feel:
Your temper terrifies them—everyone
Will tell you only what you like to hear.   60
But I, at any rate, can listen; and I have heard them
Muttering and whispering in the dark about this girl.
They say no woman has ever, so unreasonably,
Died so shameful a death for a generous act:
"She covered her brother's body. Is this indecent?
She kept him from dogs and vultures. Is this a crime?
Death?—She should have all the honor that we can give her!"

This is the way they talk out there in the city.

You must believe me:
Nothing is closer to me than your happiness.   70
What could be closer? Must not any son
Value his father's fortune as his father does his?
I beg you, do not be unchangeable:
Do not believe that you alone can be right.
The man who thinks that,
The man who maintains that only he has the power
To reason correctly, the gift to speak, the soul—
A man like that, when you know him, turns out empty.
It is not reason never to yield to reason!

In flood time you can see how some trees bend
And because they bend, even their twigs are safe,   80
While stubborn trees are torn up, roots and all.
And the same thing happens in sailing:
Make your sheet fast, never slacken—and over you go,
Head over heels and under: and there's your voyage.
Forget you are angry! Let yourself be moved!
I know I am young; but please let me say this:
The ideal condition
Would be, I admit, that men should be right by instinct;
But since we are all too likely to go astray,   90
The reasonable thing is to learn from those who can teach.
Choragos.   You will do well to listen to him, King,
If what he says is sensible. And you, Haimon,
Must listen to your father.—Both speak well.

Creon.   You consider it right for a man of my years and experience
  To go to school to a boy?
Haimon.   It is not right
  If I am wrong. But if I am young, and right,
  What does my age matter?
Creon.   You think it right to stand up for an anarchist?
Haimon.   Not at all. I pay no respect to criminals.   100
Creon.   Then she is not a criminal?
Haimon.   The City would deny it, to a man.
Creon.   And the City proposes to teach me how to rule?
Haimon.   Ah. Who is it that's talking like a boy now?
Creon.   My voice is the one voice giving orders in this City!
Haimon.   It is no City if it takes orders from one voice.
Creon.   The State is the King!
Haimon.   Yes, if the State is a desert.

[*Pause.*]

Creon.   This boy, it seems, has sold out to a woman.
Haimon.   If you are a woman: my concern is only for you.
Creon.   So? Your "concern"! In a public brawl with your father!   110
Haimon.   How about you, in a public brawl with justice?
Creon.   With justice, when all that I do is within my rights?
Haimon.   You have no right to trample on God's right.
Creon [*completely out of control*].   Fool, adolescent fool! Taken in by a woman!
Haimon.   You'll never see me taken in by anything vile.
Creon.   Every word you say is for her!
Haimon [*quietly, darkly*].   And for you.
  And for me. And for the gods under the earth.
Creon.   You'll never marry her while she lives.
Haimon.   Then she must die.—But her death will cause another.
Creon.   Another?   120
  Have you lost your senses? Is this an open threat?
Haimon.   There is no threat in speaking to emptiness.
Creon.   I swear you'll regret this superior tone of yours!
  You are the empty one!
Haimon.   If you were not my father,
  I'd say you were perverse.
Creon.   You girlstruck fool, don't play at words with me!
Haimon.   I am sorry. You prefer silence.
Creon.   Now, by God—!
  I swear, by all the gods in heaven above us,
  You'll watch it, I swear you shall!
  [*To the servants.*]   Bring her out!

Bring the woman out! Let her die before his eyes!   130
Here, this instant, with her bridegroom beside her!
Haimon.   Not here, no; she will not die here, King.
And you will never see my face again.
Go on raving as long as you've a friend to endure you.

[*Exit Haimon.*]

Choragos.   Gone, gone.
Creon, a young man in a rage is dangerous!
Creon.   Let him do, or dream to do, more than a man can.
He shall not save these girls from death.
Choragos.   These girls?
You have sentenced them both?
Creon.   No, you are right.
I will not kill the one whose hands are clean.   140
Choragos.   But Antigonê?
Creon [*somberly*].   I will carry her far away
Out there in the wilderness, and lock her
Living in a vault of stone. She shall have food,
As the custom is, to absolve the State of her death.
And there let her pray to the gods of hell:
They are her only gods:
Perhaps they will show her an escape from death,
Or she may learn,
                  though late,   150
That piety shown the dead is pity in vain.

[*Exit Creon.*]

Ode III

Chorus.   Love, unconquerable   [*Strophe*]
Waster of rich men, keeper
Of warm lights and all-night vigil
In the soft face of a girl:
Sea-wanderer, forest-visitor!
Even the pure Immortals cannot escape you,
And mortal man, in his one day's dusk,
Trembles before your glory.

Surely you swerve upon ruin   [*Antistrophe*]
The just man's consenting heart,   10

As here you have made bright anger
Strike between father and son—
And none had conquered but Love!
A girl's glance working the will of heaven:
Pleasure to her alone who mocks us,
Merciless Aphroditê.[5]

Scene IV

Choragos [*as Antigonê enters guarded*].   But I can no longer stand in awe of
    this,
Nor, seeing what I see, keep back my tears.
Here is Antigonê, passing to that chamber
Where all find sleep at last.

Antigonê.   Look upon me, friends, and pity me   [*Strophe 1*]
Turning back at the night's edge to say
Good-by to the sun that shines for me no longer;
Now sleepy Death
Summons me down to Acheron,[6] that cold shore:
There is no bridesong there, nor any music.   10
Chorus.   Yet not unpraised, not without a kind of honor,
You walk at last into the underworld;
Untouched by sickness, broken by no sword.
What woman has ever found your way to death?
Antigonê.   How often I have heard the story of Niobê,[7]   [*Antistrophe 1*]
Tantalos' wretched daughter, how the stone
Clung fast about her, ivy-close: and they say
The rain falls endlessly
And sifting soft snow; her tears are never done.
I feel the loneliness of her death in mine.   20
Chorus.   But she was born of heaven, and you
Are woman, woman-born. If her death is yours,
A mortal woman's, is this not for you
Glory in our world and in the world beyond?

Antigonê.   You laugh at me. Ah, friends, friends,   [*Strophe 2*]
Can you not wait until I am dead? O Thebes,

---

   [5] Aphroditê is the goddess of love.   [6] A river of Hades.   [7] Niobê married an ancestor of
Oedipus named Amphion. Her fourteen children were killed by Apollo and Artemis after Niobê
boasted to their mother, Leto, that her children were superior to them. She wept incessantly and
was finally transformed into a rock on Mt. Sipylos, whose streams are her tears.

O men many-charioted, in love with Fortune,
Dear springs of Dircê, sacred Theban grove,
Be witnesses for me, denied all pity,
Unjustly judged! and think a word of love   30
For her whose path turns
Under dark earth, where there are no more tears.
Chorus.   You have passed beyond human daring and come at last
Into a place of stone where Justice sits.
I cannot tell
What shape of your father's guilt appears in this.

Antigonê.   You have touched it at last: that bridal bed   [*Antistrophe 2*]
Unspeakable, horror of son and mother mingling:
Their crime, infection of all our family!
O Oedipus, father and brother!   40
Your marriage strikes from the grave to murder mine.
I have been a stranger here in my own land:
All my life
The blasphemy of my birth has followed me.
Chorus.   Reverence is a virtue, but strength
Lives in established law: that must prevail.
You have made your choice,
Your death is the doing of your conscious hand.

Antigonê.   Then let me go, since all your words are bitter,   [*Epode*]
And the very light of the sun is cold to me.   50
Lead me to my vigil, where I must have
Neither love nor lamentation; no song, but silence.

[*Creon interrupts impatiently.*]

Creon.   If dirges and planned lamentations could put off death,
Men would be singing for ever.
[*To the servants.*]   Take her, go!
You know your orders: take her to the vault
And leave her alone there. And if she lives or dies,
That's her affair, not ours: our hands are clean.
Antigonê.   O tomb, vaulted bride-bed in eternal rock,
Soon I shall be with my own again
Where Persephonê[8] welcomes the thin ghosts underground: 60
And I shall see my father again, and you, mother,
And dearest Polyneicês—
                              dearest indeed

---

[8] Queen of Hades.

To me, since it was my hand
That washed him clean and poured the ritual wine:
And my reward is death before my time!

And yet, as men's hearts know, I have done no wrong,
I have not sinned before God. Or if I have,
I shall know the truth in death. But if the guilt
Lies upon Creon who judged me, then, I pray,
May his punishment equal my own.

Choragos.   O passionate heart,   70
  Unyielding, tormented still by the same winds!
Creon.   Her guards shall have good cause to regret their delaying.
Antigonê.   Ah! That voice is like the voice of death!
Creon.   I can give you no reason to think you are mistaken.
Antigonê.   Thebes, and you my fathers' gods,
  And rulers of Thebes, you see me now, the last
  Unhappy daughter of a line of kings,
  Your kings, led away to death. You will remember
  What things I suffer, and at what men's hands,
  Because I would not transgress the laws of heaven.   80
  [*To the guards, simply.*] Come: let us wait no longer.

[*Exit Antigonê, L., guarded.*]

Ode IV

Chorus.   All Danaê's[9] beauty was locked away   [*Strophe 1*]
  In a brazen cell where the sunlight could not come:
  A small room, still as any grave, enclosed her.
  Yet she was a princess too,
  And Zeus in a rain of gold poured love upon her.
  O child, child,
  No power in wealth or war
  Or tough sea-blackened ships
  Can prevail against untiring Destiny!

And Dryas' son[10] also, that furious king,   [*Antistrophe 1*]
  Bore the god's prisoning anger for his pride:
  Sealed up by Dionysos in deaf stone,

---

[9] Though Danaê, a beautiful princess of Argos, was confined by her father, Zeus visited her in the form of a shower of gold, and she gave birth to Perseus as a result.   [10] Lycurgus, King of Thrace, who was driven mad by Dionysos, the god of wine.

His madness died among echoes.
So at the last he learned what dreadful power
His tongue had mocked:
For he had profaned the revels,
And fired the wrath of the nine
Implacable Sisters[11] that love the sound of the flute.

And old men tell a half-remembered tale   *[Strophe 2]*
Of horror where a dark ledge splits the sea   20
And a double surf beats on the gray shores:
How a king's new woman,[12] sick
With hatred for the queen he had imprisoned,
Ripped out his two sons' eyes with her bloody hands
While grinning Arês[13] watched the shuttle plunge
Four times: four blind wounds crying for revenge,

Crying, tears and blood mingled.—Piteously born,   *[Antistrophe 2]*
Those sons whose mother was of heavenly birth!
Her father was the god of the North Wind
And she was cradled by gales,   30
She raced with young colts on the glittering hills
And walked untrammeled in the open light:
But in her marriage deathless Fate found means
To build a tomb like yours for all her joy.

Scene V

[*Enter blind Teiresias, led by a boy. The opening speeches of Teiresias should be in singsong contrast to the realistic lines of Creon.*]

Teiresias.   This is the way the blind man comes, Princes, Princes,
   Lock-step, two heads lit by the eyes of one.
Creon.   What new thing have you to tell us, old Teiresias?
Teiresias.   I have much to tell you: listen to the prophet, Creon.
Creon.   I am not aware that I have ever failed to listen.
Teiresias.   Then you have done wisely, King, and ruled well.
Creon.   I admit my debt to you. But what have you to say?
Teiresias.   This, Creon: you stand once more on the edge of fate.

---

[11] The Muses.   [12] The ode alludes to a story indicating the uselessness of high birth against implacable fate. The king's new woman is Eidothea, the second wife of King Phineus. Though Cleopatra, his first wife, was the daughter of Boreas, the north wind, and Phineus was descended from kings, yet Eidothea, out of hatred for Cleopatra, blinded her two sons.   [13] The god of war.

Creon.   What do you mean? Your words are a kind of dread.
Teiresias.   Listen, Creon: 10
    I was sitting in my chair of augury, at the place
    Where the birds gather about me. They were all a-chatter,
    As is their habit, when suddenly I heard
    A strange note in their jangling, a scream, a
    Whirring fury; I knew that they were fighting,
    Tearing each other, dying
    In a whirlwind of wings clashing. And I was afraid.
    I began the rites of burnt-offering at the altar,
    But Hephaistos[14] failed me: instead of bright flame,
    There was only the sputtering slime of the fat thigh-flesh   20
    Melting: the entrails dissolved in gray smoke;
    The bare bone burst from the welter. And no blaze!

    This was a sign from heaven. My boy described it,
    Seeing for me as I see for others.

    I tell you, Creon, you yourself have brought
    This new calamity upon us. Our hearths and altars
    Are stained with the corruption of dogs and carrion birds
    That glut themselves on the corpse of Oedipus' son.
    The gods are deaf when we pray to them, their fire
    Recoils from our offering, their birds of omen   30
    Have no cry of comfort, for they are gorged
    With the thick blood of the dead.
                    O my son,
    These are no trifles! Think: all men make mistakes,
    But a good man yields when he knows his course is wrong,
    And repairs the evil. The only crime is pride.

    Give in to the dead man, then: do not fight with a corpse—
    What glory is it to kill a man who is dead?
    Think, I beg you:
    It is for your own good that I speak as I do.
    You should be able to yield for your own good.   40
Creon.   It seems that prophets have made me their especial province.
    All my life long
    I have been a kind of butt for the dull arrows
    Of doddering fortune-tellers!
                 No, Teiresias:
    If your birds—if the great eagles of God himself
    Should carry him stinking bit by bit to heaven,
    I would not yield. I am not afraid of pollution:

[14] The god of fire.

No man can defile the gods.
Do what you will,

Go into business, make money, speculate
In India gold or that synthetic gold from Sardis,   50
Get rich otherwise than by my consent to bury him.
Teiresias, it is a sorry thing when a wise man
Sells his wisdom, lets out his words for hire!

Teiresias. Ah Creon! Is there no man left in the world—
Creon. To do what?—Come, let's have the aphorism!
Teiresias. No man who knows that wisdom outweighs any wealth?
Creon. As surely as bribes are baser than any baseness.
Teiresias. You are sick, Creon! You are deathly sick!
Creon. As you say: it is not my place to challenge a prophet.
Teiresias. Yet you have said my prophecy is for sale.   60
Creon. The generation of prophets has always loved gold.
Teiresias. The generation of kings has always loved brass.
Creon. You forget yourself! You are speaking to your King.
Teiresias. I know it. You are a king because of me.
Creon. You have a certain skill; but you have sold out.
Teiresias. King, you will drive me to words that—
Creon.   Say them, say them!
Only remember: I will not pay you for them.
Teiresias. No, you will find them too costly.
Creon.   No doubt. Speak:
Whatever you say, you will not change my will.
Teiresias. Then take this, and take it to heart!   70
The time is not far off when you shall pay back
Corpse for corpse, flesh of your own flesh.
You have thrust the child of this world into living night,
You have kept from the gods below the child that is theirs:
The one in a grave before her death, the other,
Dead, denied the grave. This is your crime:
And the Furies and the dark gods of Hell
Are swift with terrible punishment for you.

Do you want to buy me now, Creon?
Not many days,

And your house will be full of men and women weeping,   80
And curses will be hurled at you from far
Cities grieving for sons unburied, left to rot
Before the walls of Thebes.
These are my arrows, Creon: they are all for you.

[*To boy.*] But come, child: lead me home.
Let him waste his fine anger upon younger men.

Maybe he will learn at last
To control a wiser tongue in a better head.

[*Exit Teiresias.*]

Choragos.   The old man has gone, King, but his words
   Remain to plague us. I am old, too,   90
   But I cannot remember that he was ever false.
Creon.   That is true. . . . It troubles me.
   Oh it is hard to give in! but it is worse
   To risk everything for stubborn pride.
Choragos.   Creon: take my advice.
Creon.   What shall I do?
Choragos.   Go quickly: free Antigonê from her vault
   And build a tomb for the body of Polyneicês.
Creon.   You would have me do this?
Choragos.   Creon, yes!
   And it must be done at once: God moves
   Swiftly to cancel the folly of stubborn men.   100
Creon.   It is hard to deny the heart! But I
   Will do it: I will not fight with destiny.
Choragos.   You must go yourself, you cannot leave it to others.
Creon.   I will go.
                —Bring axes, servants:
   Come with me to the tomb. I buried her, I
   Will set her free.
                Oh quickly!
   My mind misgives—
   The laws of the gods are mighty, and a man must serve them
   To the last days of his life!

[*Exit Creon.*]

Paean[15]

Choragos.   God of many names   [*Strophe 1*]
Chorus.   O Iacchos[16]
                          son

---

[15] A hymn.   [16] Iacchos is a name for Dionysos. His mother was Sémelê, daughter of Kadmos, the founder of Thebes. His father was Zeus. The Maenads were priestesses of Dionysos who cry "evohé evohé."

of Kadmeian Sémelê
                 O born of the Thunder!
Guardian of the West
               Regent
of Eleusis's plain
             O Prince of maenad Thebes
and the Dragon Field by rippling Ismenos:[17]

Choragos.   God of many names   *[Antistrophe 1]*
Chorus.   the flame of torches
  flares on our hills
              the nymphs of Iacchos
  dance at the spring of Castalia:[18]
  from the vine-close mountain
                  come ah come in ivy:
  Evohé evohé! sings through the streets of Thebes   10

Choragos.   God of many names   *[Strophe 2]*
Chorus.   Iacchos of Thebes
  heavenly Child
             of Sémelê bride of the Thunderer!
  The shadow of plague is upon us:
                  come
  with clement feet
           oh come from Parnasos
  down the long slopes
             across the lamenting water

Choragos.   Iô Fire! Chorister of the throbbing stars!   *[Antistrophe 2]*
  O purest among the voices of the night!
  Thou son of God, blaze for us!
Chorus.   Come with choric rapture of circling Maenads
  Who cry *Iô Iacche!*
                God of many names!   20

---

[17] A river of Thebes, sacred to Apollo. Dragon Field refers to the legend that the ancestors of Thebes sprang from the dragon's teeth sown by Kadmos.   [18] A spring on Mt. Parnasos.

Exodos

[*Enter Messenger, L.*]

Messenger.   Men of the line of Kadmos, you who live
   Near Amphion's[19] citadel:
                              I cannot say
Of any condition of human life "This is fixed,
This is clearly good, or bad." Fate raises up,
And Fate casts down the happy and unhappy alike:
No man can foretell his Fate.
                         Take the case of Creon:
Creon was happy once, as I count happiness:
Victorious in battle, sole governor of the land,
Fortunate father of children nobly born.
And now it has all gone from him! Who can say   10
That a man is still alive when his life's joy fails?
He is a walking dead man. Grant him rich,
Let him live like a king in his great house:
If his pleasure is gone, I would not give
So much as the shadow of smoke for all he owns.
Choragos.   Your words hint at sorrow: what is your news for us?
Messenger.   They are dead. The living are guilty of their death.
Choragos.   Who is guilty? Who is dead? Speak!
Messenger.   Haimon.
   Haimon is dead; and the hand that killed him
   Is his own hand.
Choragos.   His father's? or his own?   20
Messenger.   His own, driven mad by the murder his father had done.
Choragos.   Teiresias, Teiresias, how clearly you saw it all!
Messenger.   This is my news: you must draw what conclusions you can from it.
Choragos.   But look: Eurydicê, our Queen:
   Has she overheard us?

[*Enter Eurydicê from the Palace, C.*]

Eurydicê.   I have heard something, friends:
   As I was unlocking the gate of Pallas'[20] shrine,
   For I needed her help today, I heard a voice
   Telling of some new sorrow. And I fainted
   There at the temple with all my maidens about me.   30

---

[19] A child of Zeus and Antiope. He is noted for building the walls of Thebes by charming the stones into place with a lyre.   [20] Pallas Athene, goddess of wisdom.

But speak again: whatever it is, I can bear it:
Grief and I are no strangers.
Messenger.   Dearest lady,
I will tell you plainly all that I have seen.
I shall not try to comfort you: what is the use,
Since comfort could lie only in what is not true?
The truth is always best.
                         I went with Creon
To the outer plain where Polyneicês was lying,
No friend to pity him, his body shredded by dogs.
We made our prayers in that place to Hecatê[21]
And Pluto,[22] that they would be merciful. And we bathed   40
The corpse with holy water, and we brought
Fresh-broken branches to burn what was left of it,
And upon the urn we heaped up a towering barrow
Of the earth of his own land.
                         When we were done, we ran
To the vault where Antigonê lay on her couch of stone.
One of the servants had gone ahead,
And while he was yet far off he heard a voice
Grieving within the chamber, and he came back
And told Creon. And as the King went closer,
The air was full of wailing, the words lost,   50
And he begged us to make all haste. "Am I a prophet?"
He said, weeping, "And must I walk this road,
The saddest of all that I have gone before?
My son's voice calls me on. Oh quickly, quickly!
Look through the crevice there, and tell me
If it is Haimon, or some deception of the gods!"

We obeyed; and in the cavern's farthest corner
We saw her lying:
She had made a noose of her fine linen veil
And hanged herself. Haimon lay beside her,   60
His arms about her waist, lamenting her,
His love lost under ground, crying out
That his father had stolen her away from him.

When Creon saw him the tears rushed to his eyes
And he called to him: "What have you done, child? Speak to me.
What are you thinking that makes your eyes so strange?
O my son, my son, I come to you on my knees!"

---

[21] Hecatê is often identified with Persephone, a goddess of Hades; generally Hecatê is a goddess of sorcery and witchcraft.   [22] King of Hades and brother of Zeus and Poseidon.

But Haimon spat in his face. He said not a word,
Staring—
        And suddenly drew his sword
And lunged. Creon shrank back, the blade missed; and the boy,   70
Desperate against himself, drove it half its length
Into his own side, and fell. And as he died
He gathered Antigonê close in his arms again,
Choking, his blood bright red on her white cheek.
And now he lies dead with the dead, and she is his
At last, his bride in the houses of the dead.

[*Exit Eurydicê into the Palace.*]

Choragos.   She has left us without a word. What can this mean?
Messenger.   It troubles me, too; yet she knows what is best,
Her grief is too great for public lamentation,
And doubtless she has gone to her chamber to weep   80
For her dead son, leading her maidens in his dirge.
Choragos.   It may be so: but I fear this deep silence.

[*Pause.*]

Messenger.   I will see what she is doing. I will go in.

[*Exit Messenger into the Palace.*]
[*Enter Creon with attendants, bearing Haimon's body.*]

Choragos.   But here is the King himself: oh look at him,
Bearing his own damnation in his arms.
Creon.   Nothing you say can touch me any more.
My own blind heart has brought me
From darkness to final darkness. Here you see
The father murdering, the murdered son—
And all my civic wisdom!   90
Haimon my son, so young to die,
I was the fool, not you; and you died for me.
Choragos.   That is the truth; but you were late in learning it.
Creon.   This truth is hard to bear. Surely a god
Has crushed me beneath the hugest weight of heaven,
And driven me headlong a barbaric way
To trample out the thing I held most dear.

The pains that men will take to come to pain!

[*Enter Messenger from the Palace.*]

Messenger. The burden you carry in your hands is heavy,
But it is not all: you will find more in your house.   100
Creon. What burden worse than this shall I find there?
Messenger. The Queen is dead.
Creon. O port of death, deaf world,
Is there no pity for me? And you, Angel of evil,
I was dead, and your words are death again.
Is it true, boy? Can it be true?
Is my wife dead? Has death bred death?
Messenger. You can see for yourself.

[*The doors are opened, and the body of Eurydicê is disclosed within.*]

Creon. Oh pity!
All true, all true, and more than I can bear!   110
O my wife, my son!
Messenger. She stood before the altar, and her heart
Welcomed the knife her own hand guided,
And a great cry burst from her lips for Megareus[23] dead,
And for Haimon dead, her sons; and her last breath
Was a curse for their father, the murderer of her sons,
And she fell, and the dark flowed in through her closing eyes.
Creon. O God, I am sick with fear.
Are there no swords here? Has no one a blow for me?
Messenger. Her curse is upon you for the deaths of both.   120
Creon. It is right that it should be. I alone am guilty.
I know it, and I say it. Lead me in,
Quickly, friends.
I have neither life nor substance. Lead me in.
Choragos. You are right, if there can be right in so much wrong.
The briefest way is best in a world of sorrow.
Creon. Let it come,
Let death come quickly, and be kind to me.
I would not ever see the sun again.
Choragos. All that will come when it will; but we, meanwhile,   130
Have much to do. Leave the future to itself.
Creon. All my heart was in that prayer!
Choragos. Then do not pray any more: the sky is deaf.
Creon. Lead me away. I have been rash and foolish.
I have killed my son and my wife.
I look for comfort; my comfort lies here dead.
Whatever my hands have touched has come to nothing.
Fate has brought all my pride to a thought of dust.

---

[23] Son of Creon who was killed in the attack on Thebes.

[*As Creon is being led into the house, the Choragos advances and speaks directly to the audience.*]

Choragos.   There is no happiness where there is no wisdom;
No wisdom but in submission to the gods.   140
Big words are always punished,
And proud men in old age learn to be wise.

For Analysis

1. Critics have divided over the question of whether Antigonê or Creon is the **protagonist** of the play. How does the answer to this question affect one's interpretation of the play? **2.** Show how the Prologue establishes the **mood** and **theme** of the play. What does it reveal about the characters of the two sisters? **3.** What evidence is there that Creon would treat Antigonê differently if she were a man? **4.** Does the character of Antigonê change in the course of the play? **5.** Does the action of the play prepare us for Creon's sudden realization that he has been wrong? **6.** Is there any justification for Antigonê's cold refusal to allow Ismenê to share her martyrdom? **7.** Speculate on why Sophocles never brings Haimon and Antigonê together.

On Style

1. How does the chorus contribute to the dramatic development and tension of the play? **2.** Analyze the use of **dramatic irony** in the play.

Making Connections

1. Examine Creon's role in both this play and in Sophocles' *Oedipus Rex* (p. 166), and describe how his character changes. **2.** What arguments used by Martin Luther King Jr., in "Letter from Birmingham Jail" (p. 643) echo Antigonê's arguments and actions?

Writing Topics

1. In a brief paragraph, summarize the **theme** of this play. **2.** Write a one-page essay using this play and Susan Glaspell's *Trifles* (p. 551) as the basis for defining poetic drama on the one hand and realistic drama on the other.

Henrik Ibsen   [1828–1906]

A Doll's House   1879

CHARACTERS

Torvald Helmer, a lawyer
Nora, his wife
Dr. Rank
Mrs. Linde
Krogstad

The Helmers' three small children
Anne, the children's nurse
A Maid
A Porter

Act I

SCENE.   *A room furnished comfortably and tastefully, but not extravagantly. At the back, a door to the right leads to the entrance hall, another to the left leads to Helmer's study. Between the doors stands a piano. In the middle of the left-hand wall is a door, and beyond it a window. Near the window are a round table, armchairs and a small sofa. In the right-hand wall, at the farther end, another door; and on the same side, nearer the footlights, a stove, two easy chairs and a rocking-chair; between the stove and the door, a small table. Engravings on the walls; a cabinet with china and other small objects; a small book-case with well-bound books. The floors are carpeted, and a fire burns in the stove. It is winter.*

A bell rings in the hall; shortly afterwards the door is heard to open. Enter Nora, humming a tune and in high spirits. She is in out-door dress and carries a number of parcels; these she lays on the table to the right. She leaves the outer door open after her, and through it is seen a Porter who is carrying a Christmas tree and a basket, which he gives to the Maid who has opened the door.

Nora.   Hide the Christmas tree carefully, Helen. Be sure the children do not see it till this evening, when it is dressed. *(To the Porter, taking out her purse.)* How much?

Porter.   Sixpence.

Nora.   There is a shilling. No, keep the change. *(The Porter thanks her, and goes out. Nora shuts the door. She is laughing to herself, as she takes off her hat and coat. She takes a packet of macaroons from her pocket and eats one or two; then goes cautiously to her husband's door and listens.)* Yes, he is in.

[*Still humming, she goes to the table on the right.*]

A Doll's House: translated by R. Farquharson Sharp.

Helmer (*calls out from his room*).   Is that my little lark twittering out there?

Nora (*busy opening some of the parcels*).   Yes, it is!

Helmer.   Is it my little squirrel bustling about?

Nora.   Yes!

Helmer.   When did my squirrel come home?

Nora.   Just now. (*Puts the bag of macaroons into her pocket and wipes her mouth.*) Come in here, Torvald, and see what I have bought.

Helmer.   Don't disturb me. (*A little later, he opens the door and looks into the room, pen in hand.*) Bought, did you say? All these things? Has my little spendthrift been wasting money again?

Nora.   Yes, but, Torvald, this year we really can let ourselves go a little. This is the first Christmas that we have not needed to economise.

Helmer.   Still, you know, we can't spend money recklessly.

Nora.   Yes, Torvald, we may be a wee bit more reckless now, mayn't we? Just a tiny wee bit! You are going to have a big salary and earn lots and lots of money.

Helmer.   Yes, after the New Year; but then it will be a whole quarter before the salary is due.

Nora.   Pooh! we can borrow till then.

Helmer.   Nora! (*Goes up to her and takes her playfully by the ear.*) The same little featherhead! Suppose, now, that I borrowed fifty pounds to-day, and you spent it all in the Christmas week, and then on New Year's Eve a slate fell on my head and killed me, and——

Nora (*putting her hands over his mouth*).   Oh! don't say such horrid things.

Helmer.   Still, suppose that happened,—what then?

Nora.   If that were to happen, I don't suppose I should care whether I owed money or not.

Helmer.   Yes, but what about the people who had lent it?

Nora.   They? Who would bother about them? I should not know who they were.

Helmer.   That is like a woman! But seriously, Nora, you know what I think about that. No debt, no borrowing. There can be no freedom or beauty about a home life that depends on borrowing and debt. We two have kept bravely on the straight road so far, and we will go on the same way for the short time longer that there need be any struggle.

Nora (*moving towards the stove*).   As you please, Torvald.

Helmer (*following her*).   Come, come, my little skylark must not droop her wings. What is this! Is my little squirrel out of temper? (*Taking out his purse.*) Nora, what do you think I have got here?

Nora (*turning round quickly*).   Money!

Helmer.   There you are. (*Gives her some money.*) Do you think I don't know what a lot is wanted for house-keeping at Christmas-time?

Nora (*counting*).   Ten shillings—a pound—two pounds! Thank you, thank you, Torvald; that will keep me going for a long time.

Helmer.   Indeed it must.

Nora. Yes, yes, it will. But come here and let me show you what I have bought. And all so cheap! Look, here is a new suit for Ivar, and a sword; and a horse and a trumpet for Bob; and a doll and dolly's bedstead for Emmy,— they are very plain, but anyway she will soon break them in pieces. And here are dress-lengths and handkerchiefs for the maids; old Anne ought really to have something better.

Helmer. And what is in this parcel?

Nora (*crying out*). No, no! you mustn't see that till this evening.

Helmer. Very well. But now tell me something reasonable that you would particularly like to have.

Nora. No, I really can't think of anything—unless, Torvald——

Helmer. Well?

Nora (*playing with his coat buttons, and without raising her eyes to his*). If you really want to give me something, you might—you might——

Helmer. Well, out with it!

Nora (*speaking quickly*). You might give me money, Torvald. Only just as much as you can afford; and then one of these days I will buy something with it.

Helmer. But, Nora——

Nora. Oh, do! dear Torvald; please, please do! Then I will wrap it up in beautiful gilt paper and hang it on the Christmas tree. Wouldn't that be fun?

Helmer. What are little people called that are always wasting money?

Nora. Spendthrifts—I know. Let us do as you suggest, Torvald, and then I shall have time to think what I am most in want of. That is a very sensible plan, isn't it?

Helmer (*smiling*). Indeed it is—that is to say, if you were really to save out of the money I give you, and then really buy something for yourself. But if you spend it all on the housekeeping and any number of unnecessary things, then I merely have to pay up again.

Nora. Oh but, Torvald——

Helmer. You can't deny it, my dear little Nora. (*Puts his arm round her waist.*) It's a sweet little spendthrift, but she uses up a deal of money. One would hardly believe how expensive such little persons are!

Nora. It's a shame to say that. I do really save all I can.

Helmer (*laughing*). That's very true,—all you can. But you can't save anything!

Nora (*smiling quietly and happily*). You haven't any idea how many expenses we skylarks and squirrels have, Torvald.

Helmer. You are an odd little soul. Very like your father. You always find some new way of wheedling money out of me, and, as soon as you have got it, it seems to melt in your hands. You never know where it has gone. Still, one must take you as you are. It is in the blood; for indeed it is true that you can inherit these things, Nora.

Nora. Ah, I wish I had inherited many of papa's qualities.

Helmer. And I would not wish you to be anything but just what you are, my sweet little skylark. But, do you know, it strikes me that you are looking rather—what shall I say—rather uneasy to-day?

Nora. Do I?

Helmer. You do, really. Look straight at me.

Nora (*looks at him*). Well?

Helmer (*wagging his finger at her*). Hasn't Miss Sweet-Tooth been breaking rules in town to-day?

Nora. No; what makes you think that?

Helmer. Hasn't she paid a visit to the confectioner's?

Nora. No, I assure you, Torvald——

Helmer. Not been nibbling sweets?

Nora. No, certainly not.

Helmer. Not even taken a bite at a macaroon or two?

Nora. No, Torvald, I assure you really——

Helmer. There, there, of course I was only joking.

Nora (*going to the table on the right*). I should not think of going against your wishes.

Helmer. No, I am sure of that! Besides, you gave me your word—— (*Going up to her.*) Keep your little Christmas secrets to yourself, my darling. They will all be revealed to-night when the Christmas tree is lit, no doubt.

Nora. Did you remember to invite Doctor Rank?

Helmer. No. But there is no need; as a matter of course he will come to dinner with us. However, I will ask him, when he comes in this morning. I have ordered some good wine. Nora, you can't think how I am looking forward to this evening.

Nora. So am I! And how the children will enjoy themselves, Torvald!

Helmer. It is splendid to feel that one has a perfectly safe appointment, and a big enough income. It's delightful to think of, isn't it?

Nora. It's wonderful!

Helmer. Do you remember last Christmas? For a full three weeks beforehand you shut yourself up every evening till long after midnight, making ornaments for the Christmas tree and all the other fine things that were to be a surprise to us. It was the dullest three weeks I ever spent!

Nora. I didn't find it dull.

Helmer (*smiling*). But there was precious little result, Nora.

Nora. Oh, you shouldn't tease me about that again. How could I help the cat's going in and tearing everything to pieces?

Helmer. Of course you couldn't, poor little girl. You had the best of intentions to please us all, and that's the main thing. But it is a good thing that our hard times are over.

Nora. Yes, it is really wonderful.

Helmer. This time I needn't sit here and be dull all alone, and you needn't ruin your dear eyes and your pretty little hands——

Nora *(clapping her hands).* No, Torvald, I needn't any longer, need I! It's wonderfully lovely to hear you say so! *(Taking his arm.)* Now I will tell you how I have been thinking we ought to arrange things, Torvald. As soon as Christmas is over—— *(A bell rings in the hall.)* There's the bell. *(She tidies the room a little.)* There's someone at the door. What a nuisance!

Helmer. If it is a caller, remember I am not at home.

Maid *(in the doorway).* A lady to see you, ma'am,—a stranger.

Nora. Ask her to come in.

Maid *(to Helmer).* The doctor came at the same time, sir.

Helmer. Did he go straight into my room?

Maid. Yes, sir.

[*Helmer goes into his room. The Maid ushers in Mrs. Linde, who is in traveling dress, and shuts the door.*]

Mrs. Linde *(in a dejected and timid voice).* How do you do, Nora?

Nora *(doubtfully).* How do you do——

Mrs. Linde. You don't recognise me, I suppose.

Nora. No, I don't know—yes, to be sure, I seem to—— *(Suddenly.)* Yes! Christine! Is it really you?

Mrs. Linde. Yes, it is I.

Nora. Christine! To think of my not recognising you! And yet how could I—— *(In a gentle voice.)* How you have altered, Christine!

Mrs. Linde. Yes, I have indeed. In nine, ten long years——

Nora. Is it so long since we met? I suppose it is. The last eight years have been a happy time for me, I can tell you. And so now you have come into the town, and have taken this long journey in winter—that was plucky of you.

Mrs. Linde. I arrived by steamer this morning.

Nora. To have some fun at Christmas-time, of course. How delightful! We will have such fun together! But take off your things. You are not cold, I hope. *(Helps her.)* Now we will sit down by the stove, and be cosy. No, take this arm-chair; I will sit here in the rocking-chair. *(Takes her hands.)* Now you look like your old self again; it was only the first moment—— You are a little paler, Christine, and perhaps a little thinner.

Mrs. Linde. And much, much older, Nora.

Nora. Perhaps a little older; very, very little; certainly not much. *(Stops suddenly and speaks seriously.)* What a thoughtless creature I am, chattering away like this. My poor, dear Christine, do forgive me.

Mrs. Linde. What do you mean, Nora?

Nora *(gently).* Poor Christine, you are a widow.

Mrs. Linde. Yes; it is three years ago now.

Nora. Yes, I knew; I saw it in the papers. I assure you, Christine, I meant ever so often to write to you at the time, but I always put it off and something always prevented me.

Mrs. Linde.   I quite understand, dear.

Nora.   It was very bad of me, Christine. Poor thing, how you must have suffered. And he left you nothing?

Mrs. Linde.   No.

Nora.   And no children?

Mrs. Linde.   No.

Nora.   Nothing at all, then?

Mrs. Linde.   Not even any sorrow or grief to live upon.

Nora (*looking incredulously at her*).   But, Christine, is that possible?

Mrs. Linde (*smiles sadly and strokes her hair*).   It sometimes happens, Nora.

Nora.   So you are quite alone. How dreadfully sad that must be. I have three lovely children. You can't see them just now, for they are out with their nurse. But now you must tell me all about it.

Mrs. Linde.   No, no; I want to hear you.

Nora.   No, you must begin. I mustn't be selfish to-day, to-day I must only think of your affairs. But there is one thing I must tell you. Do you know we have just had a great piece of good luck?

Mrs. Linde.   No, what is it?

Nora.   Just fancy, my husband has been made manager of the Bank!

Mrs. Linde.   Your husband? What good luck!

Nora.   Yes, tremendous! A barrister's profession is such an uncertain thing, especially if he won't undertake unsavoury cases; and naturally Torvald has never been willing to do that, and I quite agree with him. You may imagine how pleased we are! He is to take up his work in the Bank at the New Year, and then he will have a big salary and lots of commissions. For the future we can live quite differently—we can do just as we like. I feel so relieved and so happy, Christine! It will be splendid to have heaps of money and not need to have any anxiety, won't it?

Mrs. Linde.   Yes, anyhow I think it would be delightful to have what one needs.

Nora.   No, not only what one needs, but heaps and heaps of money.

Mrs. Linde (*smiling*).   Nora, Nora, haven't you learnt sense yet? In our schooldays you were a great spendthrift.

Nora (*laughing*).   Yes, that is what Torvald says now (*Wags her finger at her.*) But "Nora, Nora" is not so silly as you think. We have not been in a position for me to waste money. We have both had to work.

Mrs. Linde.   You too?

Nora.   Yes; odds and ends, needlework, crochet-work, embroidery, and that kind of thing. (*Dropping her voice.*) And other things as well. You know Torvald left his office when we were married? There was no prospect of promotion there, and he had to try and earn more than before. But during the first year he overworked himself dreadfully. You see, he had to make money every way he could, and he worked early and late; but he couldn't stand it, and fell dreadfully ill, and the doctors said it was necessary for him to go south.

Mrs. Linde.   You spent a whole year in Italy, didn't you?

Nora. Yes. It was no easy matter to get away, I can tell you. It was just after Ivar was born; but naturally we had to go. It was a wonderfully beautiful journey, and it saved Torvald's life. But it cost a tremendous lot of money, Christine.

Mrs. Linde. So I should think.

Nora. It cost about two hundred and fifty pounds. That's a lot, isn't it?

Mrs. Linde. Yes, and in emergencies like that it is lucky to have the money.

Nora. I ought to tell you that we had it from papa.

Mrs. Linde. Oh, I see. It was just about that time that he died, wasn't it?

Nora. Yes; and, just think of it, I couldn't go and nurse him. I was expecting little Ivar's birth every day and I had my poor sick Torvald to look after. My dear, kind father—I never saw him again, Christine. That was the saddest time I have known since our marriage.

Mrs. Linde. And your husband came back quite well?

Nora. As sound as a bell!

Mrs. Linde. But—the doctor?

Nora. What doctor?

Mrs. Linde. I thought your maid said the gentleman who arrived here just as I did was the doctor?

Nora. Yes, that was Doctor Rank, but he doesn't come here professionally. He is our greatest friend, and comes in at least once every day. No, Torvald has not had an hour's illness since then, and our children are strong and healthy and so am I. (*Jumps up and claps her hands.*) Christine! Christine! it's good to be alive and happy!—— But how horrid of me; I am talking of nothing but my own affairs. (*Sits on a stool near her, and rests her arms on her knees.*) You mustn't be angry with me. Tell me, is it really true that you did not love your husband? Why did you marry him?

Mrs. Linde. My mother was alive then, and was bedridden and helpless, and I had to provide for my two younger brothers; so I did not think I was justified in refusing his offer.

Nora. No, perhaps you were quite right. He was rich at that time, then?

Mrs. Linde. I believe he was quite well off. But his business was a precarious one; and, when he died, it all went to pieces and there was nothing left.

Nora. And then?——

Mrs. Linde. Well, I had to turn my hand to anything I could find—first a small shop, then a small school, and so on. The last three years have seemed like one long working-day, with no rest. Now it is at an end, Nora. My poor mother needs me no more, for she is gone; and the boys do not need me either; they have got situations and can shift for themselves.

Nora. What a relief you must feel it——

Mrs. Linde. No, indeed; I only feel my life unspeakably empty. No one to live for any more. (*Gets up restlessly.*) That was why I could not stand the life in my little backwater any longer. I hope it may be easier here to find something which will busy me and occupy my thoughts. If only I could have the good luck to get some regular work—office work of some kind——

Nora. But, Christine, that is so frightfully tiring, and you look tired out now. You had far better go away to some watering-place.

Mrs. Linde (*walking to the window*). I have no father to give me money for a journey, Nora.

Nora (*rising*). Oh, don't be angry with me.

Mrs. Linde (*going up to her*). It is you that must not be angry with me, dear. The worst of a position like mine is that it makes one so bitter. No one to work for, and yet obliged to be always on the look-out for chances. One must live, and so one becomes selfish. When you told me of the happy turn your fortunes have taken—you will hardly believe it—I was delighted not so much on your account as on my own.

Nora. How do you mean?—Oh, I understand. You mean that perhaps Torvald could get you something to do.

Mrs. Linde. Yes, that was what I was thinking of.

Nora. He must, Christine. Just leave it to me; I will broach the subject very cleverly—I will think of something that will please him very much. It will make me so happy to be of some use to you.

Mrs. Linde. How kind you are, Nora, to be so anxious to help me! It is doubly kind in you, for you know so little of the burdens and troubles of life.

Nora. I——? I know so little of them?

Mrs. Linde (*smiling*). My dear! Small household cares and that sort of thing!—You are a child, Nora.

Nora (*tosses her head and crosses the stage*). You ought not to be so superior.

Mrs. Linde. No?

Nora. You are just like the others. They all think that I am incapable of anything really serious——

Mrs. Linde. Come, come——

Nora. —that I have gone through nothing in this world of cares.

Mrs. Linde. But, my dear Nora, you have just told me all your troubles.

Nora. Pooh!—those were trifles. (*Lowering her voice.*) I have not told you the important thing.

Mrs. Linde. The important thing? What do you mean?

Nora. You look down upon me altogether, Christine—but you ought not to. You are proud, aren't you, of having worked so hard and so long for your mother?

Mrs. Linde. Indeed, I don't look down on any one. But it is true that I am both proud and glad to think that I was privileged to make the end of my mother's life almost free from care.

Nora. And you are proud to think of what you have done for your brothers.

Mrs. Linde. I think I have the right to be.

Nora. I think so, too. But now, listen to this; I too have something to be proud and glad of.

Mrs. Linde. I have no doubt you have. But what do you refer to?

Nora. Speak low. Suppose Torvald were to hear! He mustn't on any account—no one in the world must know, Christine, except you.

Mrs. Linde.   But what is it?

Nora.   Come here. (*Pulls her down on the sofa beside her.*) Now I will show you that I too have something to be proud and glad of. It was I who saved Torvald's life.

Mrs. Linde.   "Saved"? How?

Nora.   I told you about our trip to Italy. Torvald would never have recovered if he had not gone there——

Mrs. Linde.   Yes, but your father gave you the necessary funds.

Nora (*smiling*).   Yes, that is what Torvald and all the others think, but——

Mrs. Linde.   But——

Nora.   Papa didn't give us a shilling. It was I who procured the money.

Mrs. Linde.   You? All that large sum?

Nora.   Two hundred and fifty pounds. What do you think of that?

Mrs. Linde.   But, Nora, how could you possibly do it? Did you win a prize in the Lottery?

Nora (*contemptuously*).   In the Lottery? There would have been no credit in that.

Mrs. Linde.   But where did you get it from, then?

Nora (*humming and smiling with an air of mystery*).   Hm, hm! Aha!

Mrs. Linde.   Because you couldn't have borrowed it.

Nora.   Couldn't I? Why not?

Mrs. Linde.   No, a wife cannot borrow without her husband's consent.

Nora (*tossing her head*).   Oh, if it is a wife who has any head for business—a wife who has the wit to be a little bit clever——

Mrs. Linde.   I don't understand it at all, Nora.

Nora.   There is no need you should. I never said I had borrowed the money. I may have got it some other way. (*Lies back on the sofa.*) Perhaps I got it from some other admirer. When anyone is as attractive as I am——

Mrs. Linde.   You are a mad creature.

Nora.   Now, you know you're full of curiosity, Christine.

Mrs. Linde.   Listen to me, Nora dear. Haven't you been a little bit imprudent?

Nora (*sits up straight*).   Is it imprudent to save your husband's life?

Mrs. Linde.   It seems to me imprudent, without his knowledge, to——

Nora.   But it was absolutely necessary that he should not know! My goodness, can't you understand that? It was necessary he should have no idea what a dangerous condition he was in. It was to me that the doctors came and said that his life was in danger, and that the only thing to save him was to live in the south. Do you suppose I didn't try, first of all, to get what I wanted as if it were for myself? I told him how much I should love to travel abroad like other young wives; I tried tears and entreaties with him; I told him that he ought to remember the condition I was in, and that he ought to be kind and indulgent to me; I even hinted that he might raise a loan. That nearly made him angry, Christine. He said I was thoughtless, and that it was his duty as my husband not to indulge me in my whims and caprices—as I believe he called them. Very well I thought, you must be saved—and that was how I came to devise a way out of the difficulty——

Mrs. Linde. And did your husband never get to know from your father that the money had not come from him?

Nora. No, never. Papa died just at that time. I had meant to let him into the secret and beg him never to reveal it. But he was so ill then—alas, there never was any need to tell him.

Mrs. Linde. And since then have you never told your secret to your husband?

Nora. Good Heavens, no! How could you think so? A man who has such strong opinions about these things! And besides, how painful and humiliating it would be for Torvald, with his manly independence, to know that he owed me anything! It would upset our mutual relations altogether; our beautiful happy home would no longer be what it is now.

Mrs. Linde. Do you mean never to tell him about it?

Nora (*meditatively, and with a half smile*). Yes—some day, perhaps, after many years, when I am no longer as nice-looking as I am now. Don't laugh at me! I mean, of course, when Torvald is no longer as devoted to me as he is now; when my dancing and dressing-up and reciting have palled on him; then it may be a good thing to have something in reserve—— (*Breaking off.*) What nonsense! That time will never come. Now, what do you think of my great secret, Christine? Do you still think I am of no use? I can tell you, too, that this affair has caused me a lot of worry. It has been by no means easy for me to meet my engagements punctually. I may tell you that there is something that is called, in business, quarterly interest, and another thing called payment in instalments, and it is always so dreadfully difficult to manage them. I have had to save a little here and there, where I could, you understand. I have not been able to put aside much from my housekeeping money, for Torvald must have a good table. I couldn't let my children be shabbily dressed; I have felt obliged to use up all he gave me for them, the sweet little darlings!

Mrs. Linde. So it has all had to come out of your own necessaries of life, poor Nora?

Nora. Of course. Besides, I was the one responsible for it. Whenever Torvald has given me money for new dresses and such things, I have never spent more than half of it; I have always bought the simplest and cheapest things. Thank Heaven, any clothes look well on me, and so Torvald has never noticed it. But it was often very hard on me, Christine—because it is delightful to be really well dressed, isn't it?

Mrs. Linde. Quite so.

Nora. Well, then I have found other ways of earning money. Last winter I was lucky enough to get a lot of copying to do; so I locked myself up and sat writing every evening until quite late at night. Many a time I was desperately tired; but all the same it was a tremendous pleasure to sit there working and earning money. It was like being a man.

Mrs. Linde. How much have you been able to pay off in that way?

Nora. I can't tell you exactly. You see, it is very difficult to keep an account of a business matter of that kind. I only know that I have paid every penny that I could scrape together. Many a time I was at my wits' end. (*Smiles.*) Then I used to sit here and imagine that a rich old gentleman had fallen in love with me——

Mrs. Linde. What! Who was it?

Nora. Be quiet!—that he had died; and that when his will was opened it contained, written in big letters, the instruction: "The lovely Mrs. Nora Helmer is to have all I possess paid over to her at once in cash."

Mrs. Linde. But, my dear Nora—who could the man be?

Nora. Good gracious, can't you understand? There was no old gentleman at all; it was only something that I used to sit here and imagine, when I couldn't think of any way of procuring money. But it's all the same now; the tiresome old person can stay where he is, as far as I am concerned; I don't care about him or his will either, for I am free from care now. (*Jumps up.*) My goodness, it's delightful to think of, Christine! Free from care! To be able to be free from care, quite free from care; to be able to play and romp with the children; to be able to keep the house beautifully and have everything just as Torvald likes it! And, think of it, soon the spring will come and the big blue sky! Perhaps we shall be able to take a little trip—perhaps I shall see the sea again! Oh, it's a wonderful thing to be alive and be happy. (*A bell is heard in the hall.*)

Mrs. Linde (*rising*). There is the bell; perhaps I had better go.

Nora. No, don't go; no one will come in here; it is sure to be for Torvald.

Servant (*at the hall door*). Excuse me, ma'am—there is a gentleman to see the master, and as the doctor is with him——

Nora. Who is it?

Krogstad (*at the door*). It is I, Mrs. Helmer. (*Mrs. Linde starts, trembles, and turns to the window.*)

Nora (*takes a step towards him, and speaks in a strained, low voice*). You? What is it? What do you want to see my husband about?

Krogstad. Bank business—in a way. I have a small post in the Bank, and I hear your husband is to be our chief now——

Nora. Then it is——

Krogstad. Nothing but dry business matters, Mrs. Helmer; absolutely nothing else.

Nora. Be so good as to go into the study, then. (*She bows indifferently to him and shuts the door into the hall; then comes back and makes up the fire in the stove.*)

Mrs. Linde. Nora—who was that man?

Nora. A lawyer, of the name of Krogstad.

Mrs. Linde. Then it really was he.

Nora. Do you know the man?

Mrs. Linde. I used to—many years ago. At one time he was a solicitor's clerk in our town.

Nora.   Yes, he was.

Mrs. Linde.   He is greatly altered.

Nora.   He made a very unhappy marriage.

Mrs. Linde.   He is a widower now, isn't he?

Nora.   With several children. There now, it is burning up.

[*Shuts the door of the stove and moves the rocking-chair aside.*]

Mrs. Linde.   They say he carries on various kinds of business.

Nora.   Really! Perhaps he does; I don't know anything about it. But don't let us think of business; it is so tiresome.

Doctor Rank (*comes out of Helmer's study. Before he shuts the door he calls to him*).   No, my dear fellow, I won't disturb you; I would rather go into your wife for a little while. (*Shuts the door and sees Mrs. Linde.*) I beg your pardon; I am afraid I am disturbing you too.

Nora.   No, not at all. (*Introducing him.*) Doctor Rank, Mrs. Linde.

Rank.   I have often heard Mrs. Linde's name mentioned here. I think I passed you on the stairs when I arrived, Mrs. Linde?

Mrs. Linde.   Yes, I go up very slowly; I can't manage stairs well.

Rank.   Ah! some slight internal weakness?

Mrs. Linde.   No, the fact is I have been overworking myself.

Rank.   Nothing more than that? Then I suppose you have come to town to amuse yourself with our entertainments?

Mrs. Linde.   I have come to look for work.

Rank.   Is that a good cure for overwork?

Mrs. Linde.   One must live, Doctor Rank.

Rank.   Yes, the general opinion seems to be that it is necessary.

Nora.   Look here, Doctor Rank—you know you want to live.

Rank.   Certainly. However wretched I may feel, I want to prolong the agony as long as possible. All my patients are like that. And so are those who are morally diseased; one of them, and a bad case too, is at this very moment with Helmer——

Mrs. Linde (*sadly*).   Ah!

Nora.   Whom do you mean?

Rank.   A lawyer of the name of Krogstad, a fellow you don't know at all. He suffers from a diseased moral character, Mrs. Helmer; but even he began talking of its being highly important that he should live.

Nora.   Did he? What did he want to speak to Torvald about?

Rank.   I have no idea; I only heard that it was something about the Bank.

Nora.   I didn't know this—what's his name—Krogstad had anything to do with the Bank.

Rank.   Yes, he has some sort of appointment there. (*To Mrs. Linde.*) I don't know whether you find also in your part of the world that there are certain people who go zealously snuffing about to smell out moral corruption, and, as soon as they have found some, put the person concerned into some lucrative position where they can keep their eye on him. Healthy natures are left out in the cold.

Mrs. Linde.   Still I think the sick are those who most need taking care of.

Rank (*shrugging his shoulders*).   Yes, there you are. That is the sentiment that is turning Society into a sickhouse.

[*Nora, who has been absorbed in her thoughts, breaks out into smothered laughter and claps her hands.*]

Rank.   Why do you laugh at that? Have you any notion what Society really is?

Nora.   What do I care about tiresome Society? I am laughing at something quite different, something extremely amusing. Tell me, Doctor Rank, are all the people who are employed in the Bank dependent on Torvald now?

Rank.   Is that what you find so extremely amusing?

Nora (*smiling and humming*).   That's my affair! (*Walking about the room.*) It's perfectly glorious to think that we have—that Torvald has so much power over so many people. (*Takes the packet from her pocket.*) Doctor Rank, what do you say to a macaroon?

Rank.   What, macaroons? I thought they were forbidden here.

Nora.   Yes, but these are some Christine gave me.

Mrs. Linde.   What! I?—

Nora.   Oh, well, don't be alarmed! You couldn't know that Torvald had forbidden them. I must tell you that he is afraid they will spoil my teeth. But, bah!— once in a way—— That's so, isn't it, Doctor Rank? By your leave? (*Puts a macaroon into his mouth.*) You must have one too, Christine. And I shall have one, just a little one—or at most two. (*Walking about.*) I am tremendously happy. There is just one thing in the world now that I should dearly love to do.

Rank.   Well, what is that?

Nora.   It's something I should dearly love to say, if Torvald could hear me.

Rank.   Well, why can't you say it?

Nora.   No, I daren't; it's so shocking.

Mrs. Linde.   Shocking?

Rank.   Well, I should not advise you to say it. Still, with us you might. What is it you would so much like to say if Torvald could hear you?

Nora.   I should just love to say—Well, I'm damned!

Rank.   Are you mad?

Mrs. Linde.   Nora, dear——!

Rank.   Say it, here he is!

Nora (*hiding the packet*).   Hush! Hush! Hush!

[*Helmer comes out of his room, with his coat over his arm and his hat in his hand.*]

Nora.   Well, Torvald dear, have you got rid of him?

Helmer.   Yes, he has just gone.

Nora.   Let me introduce you—this is Christine, who has come to town.

Helmer.   Christine——? Excuse me, but I don't know——

Nora.   Mrs. Linde, dear; Christine Linde.

Helmer.   Of course. A school friend of my wife's, I presume?

Mrs. Linde.   Yes, we have known each other since then.

Nora.   And just think, she has taken a long journey in order to see you.

Helmer.   What do you mean?

Mrs. Linde.   No, really, I——

Nora.   Christine is tremendously clever at book-keeping, and she is frightfully anxious to work under some clever man, so as to perfect herself——

Helmer.   Very sensible, Mrs. Linde.

Nora.   And when she heard you had been appointed manager of the Bank— the news was telegraphed, you know—she travelled here as quick as she could, Torvald, I am sure you will be able to do something for Christine, for my sake, won't you?

Helmer.   Well, it is not altogether impossible. I presume you are a widow, Mrs. Linde?

Mrs. Linde.   Yes.

Helmer.   And have had some experience of book-keeping?

Mrs. Linde.   Yes, a fair amount.

Helmer.   Ah! well, it's very likely I may be able to find something for you——

Nora (clapping her hands).   What did I tell you? What did I tell you?

Helmer.   You have just come at a fortunate moment, Mrs. Linde.

Mrs. Linde.   How am I to thank you?

Helmer.   There is no need. (Puts on his coat.) But to-day you must excuse me——

Rank.   Wait a minute; I will come with you.

[Brings his fur coat from the hall and warms it at the fire.]

Nora.   Don't be long away, Torvald dear.

Helmer.   About an hour, not more.

Nora.   Are you going too, Christine?

Mrs. Linde (putting on her cloak).   Yes, I must go and look for a room.

Helmer.   Oh, well then, we can walk down the street together.

Nora (helping her).   What a pity it is we are so short of space here; I am afraid it is impossible for us——

Mrs. Linde.   Please don't think of it! Good-bye, Nora dear, and many thanks.

Nora.   Good-bye for the present. Of course you will come back this evening. And you too, Dr. Rank. What do you say? If you are well enough? Oh, you must be! Wrap yourself up well.

[They go to the door all talking together. Children's voices are heard on the stair-case.]

Nora. There they are. There they are! (*She runs to open the door. The Nurse comes in with the children.*) Come in! Come in! (*Stoops and kisses them.*) Oh, you sweet blessings! Look at them, Christine! Aren't they darlings?

Rank. Don't let us stand here in the draught.

Helmer. Come along, Mrs. Linde; the place will only be bearable for a mother now!

[*Rank, Helmer and Mrs. Linde go downstairs. The Nurse comes forward with the children; Nora shuts the hall door.*]

Nora. How fresh and well you look! Such red cheeks!—like apples and roses. (*The children all talk at once while she speaks to them.*) Have you had great fun? That's splendid! What, you pulled both Emmy and Bob along on the sledge?—both at once?—that *was* good. You are a clever boy, Ivar. Let me take her for a little, Anne. My sweet little baby doll! (*Takes the baby from the Maid and dances it up and down.*) Yes, yes, mother will dance with Bob too. What! Have you been snowballing? I wish I had been there too! No, no, I will take their things off, Anne; please let me do it, it is such fun. Go in now, you look half frozen. There is some hot coffee for you on the stove.

[*The Nurse goes into the room on the left. Nora takes off the children's things and throws them about, while they all talk to her at once.*]

Nora. Really! Did a big dog run after you? But it didn't bite you? No, dogs don't bite nice little dolly children. You mustn't look at the parcels, Ivar. What are they? Ah, I daresay you would like to know. No, no—it's something nasty! Come, let us have a game! What shall we play at? Hide and Seek? Yes, we'll play Hide and Seek. Bob shall hide first. Must I hide? Very well, I'll hide first.

[*She and the children laugh and shout, and romp in and out of the room; at last Nora hides under the table, the children rush in and look for her, but do not see her; they hear her smothered laughter, run to the table, lift up the cloth and find her. Shouts of laughter. She crawls forward and pretends to frighten them. Fresh laughter. Meanwhile there has been a knock at the hall door, but none of them has noticed it. The door is half opened, and Krogstad appears. He waits a little; the game goes on.*]

Krogstad. Excuse me, Mrs. Helmer.

Nora (*with a stifled cry, turns round and gets up on to her knees*). Ah! what do you want?

Krogstad. Excuse me, the outer door was ajar; I suppose someone forgot to shut it.

Nora (*rising*). My husband is out, Mr. Krogstad.

Krogstad. I know that.

Nora. What do you want here, then?

Krogstad. A word with you.

Nora. With me?— *(to the children, gently.)* Go in to nurse. What? No, the strange man won't do mother any harm. When he has gone we will have another game. *(She takes the children into the room on the left, and shuts the door after them.)* You want to speak to me?

Krogstad. Yes, I do.

Nora. To-day? It is not the first of the month yet.

Krogstad. No, it is Christmas Eve, and it will depend on yourself what sort of a Christmas you will spend.

Nora. What do you want? To-day it is absolutely impossible for me——

Krogstad. We won't talk about that till later on. This is something different. I presume you can give me a moment?

Nora. Yes—yes, I can—although——

Krogstad. Good. I was in Olsen's Restaurant and saw your husband going down the street——

Nora. Yes?

Krogstad. With a lady.

Nora. What then?

Krogstad. May I make so bold as to ask if it was a Mrs. Linde?

Nora. It was.

Krogstad. Just arrived in town?

Nora. Yes, to-day.

Krogstad. She is a great friend of yours, isn't she?

Nora. She is. But I don't see——

Krogstad. I knew her too, once upon a time.

Nora. I am aware of that.

Krogstad. Are you? So you know all about it; I thought as much. Then I can ask you, without beating about the bush—is Mrs. Linde to have an appointment in the Bank?

Nora. What right have you to question me, Mr. Krogstad?—You, one of my husband's subordinates! But since you ask, you shall know. Yes, Mrs. Linde *is* to have an appointment. And it was I who pleaded her cause, Mr. Krogstad, let me tell you that.

Krogstad. I was right in what I thought, then.

Nora *(walking up and down the stage).* Sometimes one has a tiny little bit of influence, I should hope. Because one is a woman, it does not necessarily follow that——. When anyone is in a subordinate position, Mr. Krogstad, they should really be careful to avoid offending anyone who—who——

Krogstad. Who has influence?

Nora. Exactly.

Krogstad *(changing his tone).* Mrs. Helmer, you will be so good as to use your influence on my behalf.

Nora. What? What do you mean?

Krogstad. You will be so kind as to see that I am allowed to keep my subordinate position in the Bank.

Nora. What do you mean by that? Who proposes to take your post away from you?

Krogstad. Oh, there is no necessity to keep up the pretence of ignorance. I can quite understand that your friend is not very anxious to expose herself to the chance of rubbing shoulders with me; and I quite understand, too, whom I have to thank for being turned off.

Nora. But I assure you——

Krogstad. Very likely; but, to come to the point, the time has come when I should advise you to use your influence to prevent that.

Nora. But, Mr. Krogstad, I *have* no influence.

Krogstad. Haven't you? I thought you said yourself just now——

Nora. Naturally I did not mean you to put that construction on it. I! What should make you think I have any influence of that kind with my husband?

Krogstad. Oh, I have known your husband from our student days. I don't suppose he is any more unassailable than other husbands.

Nora. If you speak slightingly of my husband, I shall turn you out of the house.

Krogstad. You are bold, Mrs. Helmer.

Nora. I am not afraid of you any longer. As soon as the New Year comes, I shall in a very short time be free of the whole thing.

Krogstad (*controlling himself*). Listen to me, Mrs. Helmer. If necessary, I am prepared to fight for my small post in the Bank as if I were fighting for my life.

Nora. So it seems.

Krogstad. It is not only for the sake of the money; indeed, that weighs least with me in the matter. There is another reason—well, I may as well tell you. My position is this. I daresay you know, like everybody else, that once, many years ago, I was guilty of an indiscretion.

Nora. I think I have heard something of the kind.

Krogstad. The matter never came into court; but every way seemed to be closed to me after that. So I took to the business that you know of. I had to do something; and, honestly, I don't think I've been one of the worst. But now I must cut myself free from all that. My sons are growing up; for their sake I must try and win back as much respect as I can in the town. This post in the Bank was like the first step up for me—and now your husband is going to kick me downstairs again into the mud.

Nora. But you must believe me, Mr. Krogstad; it is not in my power to help you at all.

Krogstad. Then it is because you haven't the will; but I have means to compel you.

Nora. You don't mean that you will tell my husband that I owe you money?

Krogstad. Hm!—suppose I were to tell him?

Nora. It would be perfectly infamous of you. (*Sobbing.*) To think of his learning my secret, which has been my joy and pride, in such an ugly, clumsy way—that he should learn it from you! And it would put me in a horribly disagreeable position——

Krogstad. Only disagreeable?

Nora (*impetuously*). Well, do it, then!—and it will be the worse for you. My husband will see for himself what a blackguard you are, and you certainly won't keep your post then.

Krogstad. I asked you if it was only a disagreeable scene at home that you were afraid of?

Nora. If my husband does get to know of it, of course he will at once pay you what is still owing, and we shall have nothing more to do with you.

Krogstad (*coming a step nearer*). Listen to me, Mrs. Helmer. Either you have a very bad memory or you know very little of business. I shall be obliged to remind you of a few details.

Nora. What do you mean?

Krogstad. When your husband was ill, you came to me to borrow two hundred and fifty pounds.

Nora. I didn't know anyone else to go to.

Krogstad. I promised to get you that amount——

Nora. Yes, and you did so.

Krogstad. I promised to get you that amount, on certain conditions. Your mind was so taken up with your husband's illness, and you were so anxious to get the money for your journey, that you seem to have paid no attention to the conditions of our bargain. Therefore it will not be amiss if I remind you of them. Now, I promised to get the money on the security of a bond which I signed.

Nora. Yes, and which I signed.

Krogstad. Good. But below your signature there were a few lines constituting your father a surety for the money; those lines your father should have signed.

Nora. Should? He did sign them.

Krogstad. I had left the date blank; that is to say your father should himself have inserted the date on which he signed the paper. Do you remember that?

Nora. Yes, I think I remember——

Krogstad. Then I gave you the bond to send by post to your father. Is that not so?

Nora. Yes.

Krogstad. And you naturally did so at once, because five or six days afterwards you brought me the bond with your father's signature. And then I gave you the money.

Nora. Well, haven't I been paying it off regularly?

Krogstad. Fairly so, yes. But—to come back to the matter in hand—that must have been a very trying time for you, Mrs. Helmer?

Nora. It was, indeed.

Krogstad. Your father was very ill, wasn't he?

Nora. He was very near his end.

Krogstad. And died soon afterwards?

Nora. Yes.

Krogstad.   Tell me, Mrs. Helmer, can you by any chance remember what day your father died?—on what day of the month, I mean.

Nora.   Papa died on the 29th of September.

Krogstad.   That is correct; I have ascertained it for myself. And, as that is so, there is a discrepancy *(taking a paper from his pocket)* which I cannot account for.

Nora.   What discrepancy? I don't know——

Krogstad.   The discrepancy consists, Mrs. Helmer, in the fact that your father signed this bond three days after his death.

Nora.   What do you mean? I don't understand——

Krogstad.   Your father died on the 29th of September. But, look here; your father has dated his signature the 2nd of October. It is a discrepancy, isn't it? *(Nora is silent.)* Can you explain it to me? *(Nora is still silent.)* It is a remarkable thing, too, that the words "2nd of October," as well as the year, are not written in your father's handwriting but in one that I think I know. Well, of course it can be explained; your father may have forgotten to date his signature, and someone else may have dated it haphazard before they knew of his death. There is no harm in that. It all depends on the signature of the name; and *that* is genuine, I suppose, Mrs. Helmer? It was your father himself who signed his name here?

Nora *(after a short pause, throws her head up and looks defiantly at him).*   No, it was not. It was I that wrote papa's name.

Krogstad.   Are you aware that is a dangerous confession?

Nora.   In what way? You shall have your money soon.

Krogstad.   Let me ask you a question; why did you not send the paper to your father?

Nora.   It was impossible; papa was so ill. If I had asked him for his signature, I should have had to tell him what the money was to be used for; and when he was so ill himself I couldn't tell him that my husband's life was in danger— it was impossible.

Krogstad.   It would have been better for you if you had given up your trip abroad.

Nora.   No, that was impossible. That trip was to save my husband's life; I couldn't give that up.

Krogstad.   But did it never occur to you that you were committing a fraud on me?

Nora.   I couldn't take that into account; I didn't trouble myself about you at all. I couldn't bear you, because you put so many heartless difficulties in my way, although you knew what a dangerous condition my husband was in.

Krogstad.   Mrs. Helmer, you evidently do not realise clearly what it is that you have been guilty of. But I can assure you that my one false step, which lost me all my reputation, was nothing more or nothing worse than what you have done.

Nora.   You? Do you ask me to believe that you were brave enough to run a risk to save your wife's life?

Krogstad.   The law cares nothing about motives.

Nora.   Then it must be a very foolish law.

Krogstad.   Foolish or not, it is the law by which you will be judged, if I produce this paper in court.

Nora.   I don't believe it. Is a daughter not to be allowed to spare her dying father anxiety and care? Is a wife not to be allowed to save her husband's life? I don't know much about law; but I am certain that there must be laws permitting such things as that. Have you no knowledge of such laws—you who are a lawyer? You must be a very poor lawyer, Mr. Krogstad.

Krogstad.   Maybe. But matters of business—such business as you and I have had together—do you think I don't understand that? Very well. Do as you please. But let me tell you this—if I lose my position a second time, you shall lose yours with me.

[*He bows, and goes out through the hall.*]

Nora (*appears buried in thought for a short time, then tosses her head*).   Nonsense! Trying to frighten me like that—I am not so silly as he thinks. (*Begins to busy herself putting the children's things in order.*) And yet——? No, it's impossible! I did it for love's sake.

The Children (*in the doorway on the left*).   Mother, the stranger man has gone out through the gate.

Nora.   Yes, dears, I know. But don't tell anyone about the stranger man. Do you hear? Not even papa.

Children.   No, mother; but will you come and play again?

Nora.   No, no,—not now.

Children.   But, mother, you promised us.

Nora.   Yes, but I can't now. Run away in; I have such a lot to do. Run away in, my sweet little darlings. (*She gets them into the room by degrees and shuts the door on them; then sits down on the sofa, takes up a piece of needlework and sews a few stitches, but soon stops.*) No! (*Throws down the work, gets up, goes to the hall door and calls out.*) Helen! bring the tree in. (*Goes to the table on the left, opens a drawer, and stops again.*) No, no! it is quite impossible!

Maid (*coming in with the tree*).   Where shall I put it, ma'am?

Nora.   Here, in the middle of the floor.

Maid.   Shall I get you anything else?

Nora.   No, thank you. I have all I want.

[*Exit Maid.*]

Nora (*begins dressing the tree*).   A candle here—and flowers here——. The horrible man! It's all nonsense—there's nothing wrong. The tree shall be splendid! I will do everything I can think of to please you, Torvald!—I will sing for you, dance for you—(*Helmer comes in with some papers under his arm.*) Oh! are you back already?

Helmer.   Yes. Has anyone been here?

Nora.   Here? No.

Helmer.   That is strange. I saw Krogstad going out of the gate.

Nora.   Did you? Oh yes, I forgot, Krogstad was here for a moment.

Helmer.   Nora, I can see from your manner that he has been here begging you to say a good word for him.

Nora.   Yes.

Helmer.   And you were to appear to do it of your own accord; you were to conceal from me the fact of his having been here; didn't he beg that of you too?

Nora.   Yes, Torvald, but——

Helmer.   Nora, Nora, and you would be a party to that sort of thing? To have any talk with a man like that, and give him any sort of promise? And to tell me a lie into the bargain?

Nora.   A lie——?

Helmer.   Didn't you tell me no one had been here? (*Shakes his finger at her.*) My little song-bird must never do that again. A song-bird must have a clean beak to chirp with—no false notes! (*Puts his arm round her waist.*) That is so, isn't it? Yes, I am sure it is. (*Lets her go.*) We will say no more about it. (*Sits down by the stove.*) How warm and snug it is here!

[*Turns over his papers.*]

Nora (*after a short pause, during which she busies herself with the Christmas tree*).   Torvald!

Helmer.   Yes.

Nora.   I am looking forward tremendously to the fancy dress ball at the Stenborgs' the day after to-morrow.

Helmer.   And I am tremendously curious to see what you are going to surprise me with.

Nora.   It was very silly of me to want to do that.

Helmer.   What do you mean?

Nora.   I can't hit upon anything that will do; everything I think of seems so silly and insignificant.

Helmer.   Does my little Nora acknowledge that at last?

Nora (*standing behind his chair with her arms on the back of it*).   Are you very busy, Torvald?

Helmer.   Well——

Nora.   What are all those papers?

Helmer.   Bank business.

Nora.   Already?

Helmer.   I have got authority from the retiring manager to undertake the necessary changes in the staff and in the rearrangement of the work; and I must make use of the Christmas week for that, so as to have everything in order for the new year.

Nora.   Then that was why this poor Krogstad——

Helmer.   Hm!

Nora *(leans against the back of his chair and strokes his hair).*   If you hadn't been so busy I should have asked you a tremendously big favour, Torvald.

Helmer.   What is that? Tell me.

Nora.   There is no one has such good taste as you. And I do so want to look nice at the fancy-dress ball. Torvald, couldn't you take me in hand and decide what I shall go as, and what sort of a dress I shall wear?

Helmer.   Aha! so my obstinate little woman is obliged to get someone to come to her rescue?

Nora.   Yes, Torvald, I can't get along a bit without your help.

Helmer.   Very well, I will think it over, we shall manage to hit upon something.

Nora.   That *is* nice of you. *(Goes to the Christmas tree. A short pause.)* How pretty the red flowers look——. But, tell me, was it really something very bad that this Krogstad was guilty of?

Helmer.   He forged someone's name. Have you any idea what that means?

Nora.   Isn't it possible that he was driven to do it by necessity?

Helmer.   Yes; or, as in so many cases, by imprudence. I am not so heartless as to condemn a man altogether because of a single false step of that kind.

Nora.   No you wouldn't, would you, Torvald?

Helmer.   Many a man has been able to retrieve his character, if he has openly confessed his fault and taken his punishment.

Nora.   Punishment——?

Helmer.   But Krogstad did nothing of that sort; he got himself out of it by a cunning trick, and that is why he has gone under altogether.

Nora.   But do you think it would——?

Helmer.   Just think how a guilty man like that has to lie and play the hypocrite with everyone, how he has to wear a mask in the presence of those near and dear to him, even before his own wife and children. And about the children—that is the most terrible part of it all, Nora.

Nora.   How?

Helmer.   Because such an atmosphere of lies infects and poisons the whole life of a home. Each breath the children take in such a house is full of the germs of evil.

Nora *(coming nearer him).*   Are you sure of that?

Helmer.   My dear, I have often seen it in the course of my life as a lawyer. Almost everyone who has gone to the bad early in life has had a deceitful mother.

Nora.   Why do you only say—mother?

Helmer.   It seems most commonly to be the mother's influence, though naturally a bad father's would have the same result. Every lawyer is familiar with the fact. This Krogstad, now, has been persistently poisoning his own children with lies and dissimulation; that is why I say he has lost all moral character. *(Holds out his hands to her.)* That is why my sweet little Nora must promise me not to plead his cause. Give me your hand on it. Come, come, what is this?

Give me your hand. There now, that's settled. I assure you it would be quite impossible for me to work with him; I literally feel physically ill when I am in the company of such people.

Nora *(takes her hand out of his and goes to the opposite side of the Christmas tree).*   How hot it is in here; and I have such a lot to do.

Helmer *(getting up and putting his papers in order).*   Yes, and I must try and read through some of these before dinner; and I must think about your costume, too. And it is just possible I may have something ready in gold paper to hang up on the tree. *(Puts his hand on her head.)* My precious little singing-bird!

[*He goes into his room and shuts the door after him.*]

Nora *(after a pause, whispers).*   No, no—it isn't true. It's impossible; it must be impossible.

[*The Nurse opens the door on the left.*]

Nurse.   The little ones are begging so hard to be allowed to come in to mamma.

Nora.   No, no, no! Don't let them come in to me! You stay with them, Anne.

Nurse.   Very well, ma'am.

[*Shuts the door.*]

Nora *(pale with terror).*   Deprave my little children? Poison my home? *(A short pause. Then she tosses her head.)* It's not true. It can't possibly be true.

Act II

THE SAME SCENE.   *The Christmas tree is in the corner by the piano, stripped of its ornaments and with burnt-down candle-ends on its dishevelled branches. Nora's cloak and hat are lying on the sofa. She is alone in the room, walking about uneasily. She stops by the sofa and takes up her cloak.*

Nora *(drops the cloak).*   Someone is coming now! *(Goes to the door and listens.)* No—it is no one. Of course, no one will come to-day, Christmas Day—nor tomorrow either. But, perhaps—*(Opens the door and looks out).* No, nothing in the letter-box; it is quite empty. *(Comes forward.)* What rubbish! of course he can't be in earnest about it. Such a thing couldn't happen; it is impossible—I have three little children.

[*Enter the Nurse from the room on the left, carrying a big cardboard box.*]

Nurse.   At last I have found the box with the fancy dress.

Nora.   Thanks; put it on the table.

Nurse *(doing so).*   But it is very much in want of mending.

Nora. I should like to tear it into a hundred thousand pieces.

Nurse. What an idea! It can easily be put in order—just a little patience.

Nora. Yes, I will go and get Mrs. Linde to come and help me with it.

Nurse. What, out again? In this horrible weather? You will catch cold, ma'am, and make yourself ill.

Nora. Well, worse than that might happen. How are the children?

Nurse. The poor little souls are playing with their Christmas presents, but——

Nora. Do they ask much for me?

Nurse. You see, they are so accustomed to have their mamma with them.

Nora. Yes, but, nurse, I shall not be able to be so much with them now as I was before.

Nurse. Oh well, young children easily get accustomed to anything.

Nora. Do you think so? Do you think they would forget their mother if she went away altogether?

Nurse. Good heavens!—went away altogether?

Nora. Nurse, I want you to tell me something I have often wondered about— how could you have the heart to put your own child out among strangers?

Nurse. I was obliged to, if I wanted to be little Nora's nurse.

Nora. Yes, but how could you be willing to do it?

Nurse. What, when I was going to get such a good place by it? A poor girl who has got into trouble should be glad to. Besides, that wicked man didn't do a single thing for me.

Nora. But I suppose your daughter has quite forgotten you.

Nurse. No, indeed she hasn't. She wrote to me when she was confirmed, and when she was married.

Nora (*putting her arms round her neck*). Dear old Anne, you were a good mother to me when I was little.

Nurse. Little Nora, poor dear, had no other mother but me.

Nora. And if my little ones had no other mother, I am sure you would—— What nonsense I am talking! (*Opens the box.*) Go in to them. Now I must——. You will see to-morrow how charming I shall look.

Nurse. I am sure there will be no one at the ball so charming as you, ma'am.

[*Goes into the room on the left.*]

Nora (*begins to unpack the box, but soon pushes it away from her*). If only I dared go out. If only no one would come. If only I could be sure nothing would happen here in the meantime. Stuff and nonsense! No one will come. Only I mustn't think about it. I will brush my muff. What lovely, lovely gloves! Out of my thoughts, out of my thoughts! One, two, three, four, five, six—— (*Screams.*) Ah! there is someone coming——

[*Makes a movement towards the door, but stands irresolute. Enter Mrs. Linde from the hall, where she has taken off her cloak and hat.*]

Nora.   Oh, it's you, Christine. There is no one else out there, is there? How good of you to come!

Mrs. Linde.   I heard you were up asking for me.

Nora.   Yes, I was passing by. As a matter of fact, it is something you could help me with. Let us sit down here on the sofa. Look here. To-morrow evening there is to be a fancy-dress ball at the Stenborgs', who live above us; and Torvald wants me to go as a Neapolitan fisher-girl, and dance the Tarantella that I learnt at Capri.

Mrs. Linde.   I see; you are going to keep up the character.

Nora.   Yes, Torvald wants me to. Look, here is the dress; Torvald had it made for me there, but now it is all so torn, and I haven't any idea——

Mrs. Linde.   We will easily put that right. It is only some of the trimming come unsewn here and there. Needle and thread? Now then, that's all we want.

Nora.   It *is* nice of you.

Mrs. Linde *(sewing)*.   So you are going to be dressed up to-morrow, Nora. I will tell you what—I shall come in for a moment and see you in your fine feathers. But I have completely forgotten to thank you for a delightful evening yesterday.

Nora *(gets up, and crosses the stage)*.   Well I don't think yesterday was as pleasant as usual. You ought to have come to town a little earlier, Christine. Certainly Torvald does understand how to make a house dainty and attractive.

Mrs. Linde.   And so do you, it seems to me; you are not your father's daughter for nothing. But tell me, is Doctor Rank always as depressed as he was yesterday?

Nora.   No; yesterday it was very noticeable. I must tell you that he suffers from a very dangerous disease. He has consumption of the spine, poor creature. His father was a horrible man who committed all sorts of excesses; and that is why his son was sickly from childhood, do you understand?

Mrs. Linde *(dropping her sewing)*.   But, my dearest Nora, how do you know anything about such things?

Nora *(walking about)*.   Pooh! When you have three children, you get visits now and then from—from married women, who know something of medical matters, and they talk about one thing and another.

Mrs. Linde *(goes on sewing. A short silence)*.   Does Doctor Rank come here every day?

Nora.   Every day regularly. He is Torvald's most intimate friend, and a great friend of mine too. He is just like one of the family.

Mrs. Linde.   But tell me this—is he perfectly sincere? I mean, isn't he the kind of man that is very anxious to make himself agreeable?

Nora.   Not in the least. What makes you think that?

Mrs. Linde.   When you introduced him to me yesterday, he declared he had often heard my name mentioned in this house; but afterwards I noticed that your husband hadn't the slightest idea who I was. So how could Doctor Rank——?

Nora.   That is quite right, Christine. Torvald is so absurdly fond of me that he wants me absolutely to himself, as he says. At first he used to seem almost jealous if I mentioned any of the dear folk at home, so naturally I gave up doing so. But I often talk about such things with Doctor Rank, because he likes hearing about them.

Mrs. Linde.   Listen to me, Nora. You are still very like a child in many things, and I am older than you in many ways and have a little more experience. Let me tell you this—you ought to make an end of it with Doctor Rank.

Nora.   What ought I to make an end of?

Mrs. Linde.   Of two things, I think. Yesterday you talked some nonsense about a rich admirer who was to leave you money——

Nora.   An admirer who doesn't exist, unfortunately! But what then?

Mrs. Linde.   Is Doctor Rank a man of means?

Nora.   Yes, he is.

Mrs. Linde.   And has no one to provide for?

Nora.   No, no one; but——

Mrs. Linde.   And comes here every day?

Nora.   Yes, I told you so.

Mrs. Linde.   But how can this well-bred man be so tactless?

Nora.   I don't understand you at all.

Mrs. Linde.   Don't prevaricate, Nora. Do you suppose I don't guess who lent you the two hundred and fifty pounds?

Nora.   Are you out of your senses? How can you think of such a thing! A friend of ours, who comes here every day! Do you realise what a horribly painful position that would be?

Mrs. Linde.   Then it really isn't he?

Nora.   No, certainly not. It would never have entered into my head for a moment. Besides, he had no money to lend then; he came into his money afterwards.

Mrs. Linde.   Well, I think that was lucky for you, my dear Nora.

Nora.   No, it would never have come into my head to ask Doctor Rank. Although I am quite sure that if I had asked him——

Mrs. Linde.   But of course you won't.

Nora.   Of course not. I have no reason to think it could possibly be necessary. But I am quite sure that if I told Doctor Rank——

Mrs. Linde.   Behind your husband's back?

Nora.   I must make an end of it with the other one, and that will be behind his back too. I *must* make an end of it with him.

Mrs. Linde.   Yes, that is what I told you yesterday, but——

Nora (*walking up and down*).   A man can put a thing like that straight much easier than a woman——

Mrs. Linde.   One's husband, yes.

Nora.   Nonsense! (*Standing still.*) When you pay off a debt you get your bond back, don't you?

Mrs. Linde.   Yes, as a matter of course.

Nora.   And can tear it into a hundred thousand pieces, and burn it up—the nasty dirty paper!

Mrs. Linde (*looks hard at her, lays down her sewing and gets up slowly*). Nora, you are concealing something from me.

Nora.   Do I look as if I were?

Mrs. Linde.   Something has happened to you since yesterday morning. Nora, what is it?

Nora (*going nearer to her*).   Christine! (*Listens.*) Hush! there's Torvald come home. Do you mind going in to the children for the present? Torvald can't bear to see dressmaking going on. Let Anne help you.

Mrs. Linde (*gathering some of the things together*).   Certainly—but I am not going away from here till we have had it out with one another.

[*She goes into the room on the left, as Helmer comes in from the hall.*]

Nora (*going up to Helmer*).   I have wanted you so much, Torvald dear.

Helmer.   Was that the dressmaker?

Nora.   No, it was Christine; she is helping me to put my dress in order. You will see I shall look quite smart.

Helmer.   Wasn't that a happy thought of mine, now?

Nora.   Splendid! But don't you think it is nice of me, too, to do as you wish?

Helmer.   Nice?—because you do as your husband wishes? Well, well, you little rogue, I am sure you did not mean it in that way. But I am not going to disturb you; you will want to be trying on your dress, I expect.

Nora.   I suppose you are going to work.

Helmer.   Yes. (*Shows her a bundle of papers.*) Look at that. I have just been into the bank.

[*Turns to go into his room.*]

Nora.   Torvald.

Helmer.   Yes.

Nora.   If your little squirrel were to ask you for something very, very prettily——?

Helmer.   What then?

Nora.   Would you do it?

Helmer.   I should like to hear what it is, first.

Nora.   Your squirrel would run about and do all her tricks if you would be nice, and do what she wants.

Helmer.   Speak plainly.

Nora.   Your skylark would chirp about in every room, with her song rising and falling——

Helmer. Well, my skylark does that anyhow.

Nora. I would play the fairy and dance for you in the moonlight, Torvald.

Helmer. Nora—you surely don't mean that request you made of me this morning?

Nora *(going near him).* Yes, Torvald, I beg you so earnestly——

Helmer. Have you really the courage to open up that question again?

Nora. Yes, dear, you *must* do as I ask; you *must* let Krogstad keep his post in the Bank.

Helmer. My dear Nora, it is his post that I have arranged Mrs. Linde shall have.

Nora. Yes, you have been awfully kind about that; but you could just as well dismiss some other clerk instead of Krogstad.

Helmer. This simply incredible obstinacy! Because you chose to give him a thoughtless promise that you would speak for him, I am expected to——

Nora. That isn't the reason, Torvald. It is for your own sake. This fellow writes in the most scurrilous newspapers; you have told me so yourself. He can do you an unspeakable amount of harm. I am frightened to death of him——

Helmer. Ah, I understand; it is recollections of the past that scare you.

Nora. What do you mean?

Helmer. Naturally you are thinking of your father.

Nora. Yes—yes, of course. Just recall to your mind what these malicious creatures wrote in the papers about papa, and how horribly they slandered him. I believe they would have procured his dismissal if the Department had not sent you over to inquire into it, and if you had not been so kindly disposed and helpful to him.

Helmer. My little Nora, there is an important difference between your father and me. Your father's reputation as a public official was not above suspicion. Mine is, and I hope it will continue to be so, as long as I hold my office.

Nora. You never can tell what mischief these men may contrive. We ought to be so well off, so snug and happy here in our peaceful home, and have no cares—you and I and the children, Torvald! That is why I beg of you so earnestly——

Helmer. And it is just by interceding for him that you make it impossible for me to keep him. It is already known at the Bank that I mean to dismiss Krogstad. Is it to get about now that the new manager has changed his mind at his wife's bidding——

Nora. And what if it did?

Helmer. Of course!—if only this obstinate little person can get her way! Do you suppose I am going to make myself ridiculous before my whole staff, to let people think that I am a man to be swayed by all sorts of outside influence? I should very soon feel the consequences of it, I can tell you! And besides, there is one thing that makes it quite impossible for me to have Krogstad in the Bank as long as I am manager.

Nora. Whatever is that?

Helmer. His moral failings I might perhaps have overlooked, if necessary——

Nora.   Yes, you could—couldn't you?

Helmer.   And I hear he is a good worker, too. But I knew him when we were boys. It was one of those rash friendships that so often prove an incubus in after life. I may as well tell you plainly, we were once on very intimate terms with one another. But this tactless fellow lays no restraint on himself when other people are present. On the contrary, he thinks it gives him the right to adopt a familiar tone with me, and every minute it is "I say, Helmer, old fellow!" and that sort of thing. I assure you it is extremely painful for me. He would make my position in the Bank intolerable.

Nora.   Torvald, I don't believe you mean that.

Helmer.   Don't you? Why not?

Nora.   Because it is such a narrow-minded way of looking at things.

Helmer.   What are you saying? Narrow-minded? Do you think I am narrow-minded?

Nora.   No, just the opposite, dear—and it is exactly for that reason.

Helmer.   It's the same thing. You say my point of view is narrow-minded, so I must be so too. Narrow-minded! Very well—I must put an end to this. (*Goes to the hall-door and calls.*) Helen!

Nora.   What are you going to do?

Helmer (*looking among his papers*).   Settle it. (*Enter Maid.*) Look here; take this letter and go downstairs with it at once. Find a messenger and tell him to deliver it, and be quick. The address is on it, and here is the money.

Maid.   Very well, sir.   [*Exit with the letter.*]

Helmer (*putting his papers together*).   Now then, little Miss Obstinate.

Nora (*breathlessly*).   Torvald—what was that letter?

Helmer.   Krogstad's dismissal.

Nora.   Call her back, Torvald! There is still time. Oh Torvald, call her back! Do it for my sake—for your own sake—for the children's sake! Do you hear me, Torvald? Call her back! You don't know what that letter can bring upon us.

Helmer.   It's too late.

Nora.   Yes, it's too late.

Helmer.   My dear Nora, I can forgive the anxiety you are in, although really it is an insult to me. It is, indeed. Isn't it an insult to think that I should be afraid of a starving quill-driver's vengeance? But I forgive you nevertheless, because it is such eloquent witness to your great love for me. (*Takes her in his arms.*) And that is as it should be, my darling Nora. Come what will, you may be sure I shall have both courage and strength if they be needed. You will see I am man enough to take everything upon myself.

Nora (*in a horror-stricken voice*).   What do you mean by that?

Helmer.   Everything, I say——

Nora (*recovering herself*).   You will never have to do that.

Helmer.   That's right. Well, we will share it, Nora, as man and wife should. That is how it shall be. (*Caressing her.*) Are you content now? There! there!—not these frightened dove's eyes! The whole thing is only the wildest fancy!—

Now, you must go and play through the Tarantella and practise with your tambourine. I shall go into the inner office and shut the door, and I shall hear nothing; you can make as much noise as you please. *(Turns back at the door.)* And when Rank comes, tell him where he will find me.

[*Nods to her, takes his papers and goes into his room, and shuts the door after him.*]

Nora *(bewildered with anxiety, stands as if rooted to the spot, and whispers).* He was capable of doing it. He will do it. He will do it in spite of everything.—No, not that! Never, never! Anything rather than that! Oh, for some help, some way out of it! *(The door-bell rings.)* Doctor Rank! Anything rather than that—anything, whatever it is!

[*She puts her hands over her face, pulls herself together, goes to the door and opens it. Rank is standing without, hanging up his coat. During the following dialogue it begins to grow dark.*]

Nora. Good-day, Doctor Rank. I knew your ring. But you mustn't go into Torvald now; I think he is busy with something.
Rank. And you?
Nora *(brings him in and shuts the door after him).* Oh, you know very well I always have time for you.
Rank. Thank you. I shall make use of as much of it as I can.
Nora. What do you mean by that? As much of it as you can?
Rank. Well, does that alarm you?
Nora. It was such a strange way of putting it. Is anything likely to happen?
Rank. Nothing but what I have long been prepared for. But certainly didn't expect it to happen so soon.
Nora *(gripping him by the arm).* What have you found out? Doctor Rank, you must tell me.
Rank *(sitting down by the stove).* It is all up with me. And it can't be helped.
Nora *(with a sigh of relief).* Is it about yourself?
Rank. Who else? It is no use lying to one's self. I am the most wretched of all my patients, Mrs. Helmer. Lately I have been taking stock of my internal economy. Bankrupt! Probably within a month I shall lie rotting in the churchyard.
Nora. What an ugly thing to say!
Rank. The thing itself is cursedly ugly, and the worst of it is that I shall have to face so much more that is ugly before that. I shall only make one more examination of myself; when I have done that, I shall know pretty certainly when it will be that the horrors of dissolution will begin. There is something I want to tell you. Helmer's refined nature gives him an unconquerable disgust at everything that is ugly; I won't have him in my sick-room.
Nora. Oh, but, Doctor Rank——

Rank. I won't have him there. Not on any account. I bar my door to him. As soon as I am quite certain that the worst has come, I shall send you my card with a black cross on it, and then you will know that the loathsome end has begun.

Nora. You are quite absurd to-day. And I wanted you so much to be in a really good humour.

Rank. With death stalking beside me?—To have to pay this penalty for another man's sin! Is there any justice in that? And in every single family, in one way or another, some such inexorable retribution is being exacted——

Nora *(putting her hands over her ears)*. Rubbish! Do talk of something cheerful.

Rank. Oh, it's a mere laughing matter, the whole thing. My poor innocent spine has to suffer for my father's youthful amusements.

Nora *(sitting at the table on the left)*. I suppose you mean that he was too partial to asparagus and pâté de foie gras, don't you.

Rank. Yes, and to truffles.

Nora. Truffles, yes. And oysters too, I suppose?

Rank. Oysters, of course, that goes without saying.

Nora. And heaps of port and champagne. It is sad that all these nice things should take their revenge on our bones.

Rank. Especially that they should revenge themselves on the unlucky bones of those who have not had the satisfaction of enjoying them.

Nora. Yes, that's the saddest part of it all.

Rank *(with a searching look at her)*. Hm!——

Nora *(after a short pause)*. Why did you smile?

Rank. No, it was you that laughed.

Nora. No, it was you that smiled, Doctor Rank!

Rank *(rising)*. You are a greater rascal than I thought.

Nora. I am in a silly mood to-day.

Rank. So it seems.

Nora *(putting her hands on his shoulders)*. Dear, dear Doctor Rank, death mustn't take you away from Torvald and me.

Rank. It is a loss you would easily recover from. Those who are gone are soon forgotten.

Nora *(looking at him anxiously)*. Do you believe that?

Rank. People form new ties, and then——

Nora. Who will form new ties?

Rank. Both you and Helmer, when I am gone. You yourself are already on the high road to it, I think. What did that Mrs. Linde want here last night?

Nora. Oho!—you don't mean to say you are jealous of poor Christine?

Rank. Yes, I am. She will be my successor in this house. When I am done for, this woman will—

Nora. Hush! don't speak so loud. She is in that room.

Rank. To-day again. There, you see.

Nora. She has only come to sew my dress for me. Bless my soul, how unreasonable you are! (*Sits down on the sofa.*) Be nice now, Doctor Rank, and tomorrow you will see how beautifully I shall dance, and you can imagine I am doing it all for you—and for Torvald too, of course. (*Takes various things out of the box.*) Doctor Rank, come and sit down here, and I will show you something.

Rank (*sitting down*). What is it?

Nora. Just look at those!

Rank. Silk stockings.

Nora. Flesh-coloured. Aren't they lovely? It is so dark here now, but tomorrow—. No, no, no! you must only look at the feet. Oh well, you may have leave to look at the legs too.

Rank. Hm!—

Nora. Why are you looking so critical? Don't you think they will fit me?

Rank. I have no means of forming an opinion about that.

Nora (*looks at him for a moment*). For shame! (*Hits him lightly on the ear with the stockings.*) That's to punish you. (*Folds them up again.*)

Rank. And what other nice things am I to be allowed to see?

Nora. Not a single thing more, for being so naughty. (*She looks among the things, humming to herself.*)

Rank (*after a short silence*). When I am sitting here, talking to you as intimately as this, I cannot imagine for a moment what would have become of me if I had never come into this house.

Nora (*smiling*). I believe you do feel thoroughly at home with us.

Rank (*in a lower voice, looking straight in front of him*). And to be obliged to leave it all——

Nora. Nonsense, you are not going to leave it.

Rank (*as before*). And not be able to leave behind one the slightest token of one's gratitude, scarcely even a fleeting regret—nothing but an empty place which the first comer can fill as well as any other.

Nora. And if I asked you now for a—? No!

Rank. For what?

Nora. For a big proof of your friendship——

Rank. Yes, yes!

Nora. I mean a tremendously big favour——

Rank. Would you really make me so happy for once?

Nora. Ah, but you don't know what it is yet.

Rank. No—but tell me.

Nora. I really can't, Doctor Rank. It is something out of all reason; it means advice, and help, and a favour——

Rank. The bigger a thing it is the better. I can't conceive what it is you mean. Do tell me. Haven't I your confidence?

Nora. More than anyone else. I know you are my truest and best friend, and so I will tell you what it is. Well, Doctor Rank, it is something you must help me to prevent. You know how devotedly, how inexpressibly deeply Torvald loves me; he would never for moment hesitate to give his life for me.

Rank *(leaning towards her).*   Nora—do you think he is the only one——?

Nora *(with a slight start).*   The only one—?

Rank.   The only one who would gladly give his life for your sake.

Nora *(sadly).*   Is that it?

Rank.   I was determined you should know it before I went away, and there will never be a better opportunity than this. Now you know it, Nora. And now you know, too, that you can trust me as you would trust no one else.

Nora *(rises, deliberately and quietly).*   Let me pass.

Rank *(makes room for her to pass him, but sits still).*   Nora!

Nora *(at the hall door).*   Helen, bring in the lamp. *(Goes over to the stove.)* Dear Doctor Rank, that was really horrid of you.

Rank.   To have loved you as much as anyone else does? Was that horrid?

Nora.   No, but to go and tell me so. There was really no need——

Rank.   What do you mean? Did you know—? *(Maid enters with lamp, puts it down on the table, and goes out.)* Nora—Mrs. Helmer—tell me, had you any idea of this?

Nora.   Oh, how do I know whether I had or whether I hadn't? I really can't tell you— To think you could be so clumsy, Doctor Rank! We were getting on so nicely.

Rank.   Well, at all events you know now that you can command me, body and soul. So won't you speak out?

Nora *(looking at him).*   After what happened?

Rank.   I beg you to let me know what it is.

Nora.   I can't tell you anything now.

Rank.   Yes, yes. You mustn't punish me in that way. Let me have permission to do for you whatever a man may do.

Nora.   You can do nothing for me now. Besides, I really don't need any help at all. You will find that the whole thing is merely fancy on my part. It really is so—of course it is! *(Sits down in the rocking-chair, and looks at him with a smile.)* You are a nice sort of man, Doctor Rank!—don't you feel ashamed of yourself, now the lamp has come?

Rank.   Not a bit. But perhaps I had better go—forever?

Nora.   No, indeed, you shall not. Of course you must come here just as before. You know very well Torvald can't do without you.

Rank.   Yes, but you?

Nora.   Oh, I am always tremendously pleased when you come.

Rank.   It is just that, that put me on the wrong track. You are a riddle to me. I have often thought that you would almost as soon be in my company as in Helmer's.

Nora.   Yes—you see there are some people one loves best, and others whom one would almost always rather have as companions.

Rank.   Yes, there is something in that.

Nora. When I was at home, of course I loved papa best. But I always thought it tremendous fun if I could steal down into the maids' room, because they never moralised at all, and talked to each other about such entertaining things.

Rank. I see—it is *their* place I have taken.

Nora (*jumping up and going to him*). Oh, dear, nice Doctor Rank, I never meant that at all. But surely you can understand that being with Torvald is a little like being with papa——

[*Enter Maid from the hall.*]

Maid. If you please, ma'am. (*Whispers and hands her a card.*)

Nora (*glancing at the card*). Oh! (*Puts it in her pocket.*)

Rank. Is there anything wrong?

Nora. No, no, not in the least. It is only something—it is my new dress——

Rank. What? Your dress is lying there.

Nora. Oh, yes, that one; but this is another. I ordered it. Torvald mustn't know about it——

Rank. Oho! Then that was the great secret.

Nora. Of course. Just go in to him; he is sitting in the inner room. Keep him as long as——

Rank. Make your mind easy; I won't let him escape. (*Goes into Helmer's room.*)

Nora (*to the Maid*). And he is standing waiting in the kitchen?

Maid. Yes; he came up the back stairs.

Nora. But didn't you tell him no one was in?

Maid. Yes, but it was no good.

Nora. He won't go away?

Maid. No; he says he won't until he has seen you, ma'am.

Nora. Well, let him come in—but quietly. Helen, you mustn't say anything about it to anyone. It is a surprise for my husband.

Maid. Yes ma'am, I quite understand. [*Exit.*]

Nora. This dreadful thing is going to happen! It will happen in spite of me! No, no, no, it can't happen—it shan't happen!

[*She bolts the door of Helmer's room. The Maid opens the hall door for Krogstad and shuts it after him. He is wearing a fur coat, high boots and a fur cap.*]

Nora (*advancing towards him*). Speak low—my husband is at home.

Krogstad. No matter about that.

Nora. What do you want of me?

Krogstad. An explanation of something.

Nora. Make haste then. What is it?

Krogstad. You know, I suppose, that I have got my dismissal.

Nora.   I couldn't prevent it, Mr. Krogstad. I fought as hard as I could on your side, but it was no good.

Krogstad.   Does your husband love you so little, then? He knows what I can expose you to, and yet he ventures——

Nora.   How can you suppose that he has any knowledge of the sort?

Krogstad.   I didn't suppose so at all. It would not be the least like our dear Torvald Helmer to show so much courage—

Nora.   Mr. Krogstad, a little respect for my husband, please.

Krogstad.   Certainly—all the respect he deserves. But since you have kept the matter so carefully to yourself, I make bold to suppose that you have a little clearer idea, than you had yesterday, of what it actually is that you have done?

Nora.   More than you could ever teach me.

Krogstad.   Yes, such a bad lawyer as I am.

Nora.   What is it you want of me?

Krogstad.   Only to see how you were, Mrs. Helmer. I have been thinking about you all day long. A mere cashier, a quill-driver, a—well, a man like me—even he has a little of what is called feeling, you know.

Nora.   Show it, then; think of my little children.

Krogstad.   Have you and your husband thought of mine? But never mind about that. I only wanted to tell you that you need not take this matter too seriously. In the first place there will be no accusation made on my part.

Nora.   No, of course not; I was sure of that.

Krogstad.   The whole thing can be arranged amicably; there is no reason why anyone should know anything about it. It will remain a secret between us three.

Nora.   My husband must never get to know anything about it.

Krogstad.   How will you be able to prevent it? Am I to understand that you can pay the balance that is owing?

Nora.   No, not just at present.

Krogstad.   Or perhaps that you have some expedient for raising the money soon?

Nora.   No expedient that I mean to make use of.

Krogstad.   Well, in any case, it would have been of no use to you now. If you stood there with ever so much money in your hand, I would never part with your bond.

Nora.   Tell me what purpose you mean to put it to.

Krogstad.   I shall only preserve it—keep it in my possession. No one who is not concerned in the matter shall have the slightest hint of it. So that if the thought of it has driven you to any desperate resolution——

Nora.   It has.

Krogstad.   If you had it in your mind to run away from your home——

Nora.   I had.

Krogstad.   Or even something worse——

Nora.   How could you know that?

Krogstad.   Give up the idea.

Nora. How did you know I had thought of *that?*

Krogstad. Most of us think of that at first. I did, too—but I hadn't the courage.

Nora (*faintly*). No more had I.

Krogstad (*in a tone of relief*). No, that's it, isn't it—you hadn't the courage either?

Nora. No, I haven't—I haven't.

Krogstad. Besides, it would have been a great piece of folly. Once the first storm at home is over—. I have a letter for your husband in my pocket.

Nora. Telling him everything?

Krogstad. In as lenient a manner as I possibly could.

Nora (*quickly*). He mustn't get the letter. Tear it up. I will find some means of getting money.

Krogstad. Excuse me, Mrs. Helmer, but I think I told you just now——

Nora. I am not speaking of what I owe you. Tell me what sum you are asking my husband for, and I will get the money.

Krogstad. I am not asking your husband for a penny.

Nora. What do you want, then?

Krogstad. I will tell you. I want to rehabilitate myself, Mrs. Helmer; I want to get on; and in that your husband must help me. For the last year and a half I have not had a hand in anything dishonourable, and all that time I have been struggling in most restricted circumstances. I was content to work my way up step by step. Now I am turned out, and I am not going to be satisfied with merely being taken into favour again. I want to get on, I tell you. I want to get into the Bank again, in a higher position. Your husband must make a place for me——

Nora. That he will never do!

Krogstad. He will; I know him; he dare not protest. And as soon as I am in there again with him, then you will see! Within a year I shall be the manager's right hand. It will be Nils Krogstad and not Torvald Helmer who manages the Bank.

Nora. That's a thing you will never see!

Krogstad. Do you mean that you will——?

Nora. I have courage enough for it now.

Krogstad. Oh, you can't frighten me. A fine, spoilt lady like you——

Nora. You will see, you will see.

Krogstad. Under the ice, perhaps? Down into the cold, coal-black water? And then, in the spring, to float up to the surface, all horrible and unrecognisable, with your hair fallen out——

Nora. You can't frighten me.

Krogstad. Nor you me. People don't do such things, Mrs. Helmer. Besides, what use would it be? I should have him completely in my power all the same.

Nora. Afterwards? When I am no longer——

Krogstad. Have you forgotten that it is I who have the keeping of your reputation? (*Nora stands speechlessly looking at him.*) Well, now, I have warned you. Do not do anything foolish. When Helmer has had my letter, I shall expect a message from him. And be sure you remember that it is your husband himself who has forced me into such ways as this again. I will never forgive him for that. Good-bye, Mrs. Helmer.   [*Exit through the hall.*]

Nora (*goes to the hall door, opens it slightly and listens*).   He is going. He is not putting the letter in the box. Oh no, no! that's impossible! (*Opens the door by degrees.*) He is going. He is standing outside. He is not going downstairs. Is he hesitating? Can he——

[A *letter drops into the box; then Krogstad's footsteps are heard, till they die away as he goes downstairs. Nora utters a stifled cry and runs across the room to the table by the sofa. A short pause.*]

Nora.   In the letter-box. (*Steals across to the hall door.*) There it lies—Torvald, Torvald, there is no hope for us now!

[*Mrs. Linde comes in from the room on the left carrying the dress.*]

Mrs. Linde.   There, I can't see anything more to mend now. Would you like to try it on——?

Nora (*in a hoarse whisper*).   Christine, come here.

Mrs. Linde (*throwing the dress down on the sofa*).   What is the matter with you? You look so agitated!

Nora.   Come here. Do you see that letter? There look—you can see it through the glass in the letter-box.

Mrs. Linde.   Yes, I see it.

Nora.   That letter is from Krogstad.

Mrs. Linde.   Nora—it was Krogstad who lent you the money!

Nora.   Yes, and now Torvald will know all about it.

Mrs. Linde.   Believe me, Nora, that's the best thing for both of you.

Nora.   You don't know all. I forged a name.

Mrs. Linde.   Good heavens——!

Nora.   I only want to say this to you, Christine—you must be my witness.

Mrs. Linde.   Your witness? What do you mean? What am I to—?

Nora.   If I should go out of my mind—and it might easily happen——

Mrs. Linde.   Nora!

Nora.   Or if anything else should happen to me—anything, for instance, that might prevent my being here—

Mrs. Linde.   Nora! Nora! you are quite out of your mind.

Nora.   And if it should happen that there were someone who wanted to take all the responsibility, all the blame, you understand——

Mrs. Linde.   Yes, yes—but how can you suppose—?

Nora.   Then you must be my witness, that it is not true, Christine. I am not out of my mind at all; I am in my right senses now, and I tell you no one else has known anything about it; I, and I alone, did the whole thing. Remember that.

Mrs. Linde.   I will, indeed. But I don't understand all this.

Nora. How should you understand it? A wonderful thing is going to happen.

Mrs. Linde. A wonderful thing?

Nora. Yes, a wonderful thing!—But it is so terrible, Christine; it *mustn't* happen, not for all the world.

Mrs. Linde. I will go at once and see Krogstad.

Nora. Don't go to him; he will do you some harm.

Mrs. Linde. There was a time when he would gladly do anything for my sake.

Nora. He?

Mrs. Linde. Where does he live?

Nora. How should I know—? Yes *(feeling in her pocket)* here is his card. But the letter, the letter——!

Helmer *(calls from his room, knocking at the door).* Nora!

Nora *(cries out anxiously).* Oh, what's that? What do you want?

Helmer. Don't be so frightened. We are not coming in; you have locked the door. Are you trying on your dress?

Nora. Yes, that's it. I look so nice, Torvald.

Mrs. Linde *(who has read the card).* I see he lives at the corner here.

Nora. Yes, but it's no use. It is hopeless. The letter is lying there in the box.

Mrs. Linde. And your husband keeps the key?

Nora. Yes, always.

Mrs. Linde. Krogstad must ask for his letter back unread, he must find some pretence——

Nora. But it is just at this time that Torvald generally——

Mrs. Linde. You must delay him. Go in to him in the meantime. I will come back as soon as I can.

[*She goes out hurriedly through the hall door.*]

Nora *(goes to Helmer's door, opens it and peeps in).* Torvald!

Helmer *(from the inner room).* Well? May I venture at last to come into my own room again? Come along, Rank, now you will see— *(Halting in the doorway.)* But what is this?

Nora. What is what, dear?

Helmer. Rank led me to expect a splendid transformation.

Rank *(in the doorway).* I understood so, but evidently I was mistaken.

Nora. Yes, nobody is to have the chance of admiring me in my dress until to-morrow.

Helmer. But, my dear Nora, you look so worn out. Have you been practising too much?

Nora. No, I have not practised at all.

Helmer. But you will need to—

Nora. Yes, indeed I shall, Torvald. But I can't get on a bit without you to help me; I have absolutely forgotten the whole thing.

Helmer. Oh, we will soon work it up again.

Nora.   Yes, help me, Torvald. Promise that you will! I am so nervous about it—all the people—. You must give yourself up to me entirely this evening. Not the tiniest bit of business—you mustn't even take a pen in your hand. Will you promise, Torvald dear?

Helmer.   I promise. This evening I will be wholly and absolutely at your service, you helpless little mortal. Ah, by the way, first of all I will just——

[*Goes towards the hall door.*]

Nora.   What are you going to do there?

Helmer.   Only see if any letters have come.

Nora.   No, no! don't do that, Torvald!

Helmer.   Why not?

Nora.   Torvald, please don't. There is nothing there.

Helmer.   Well, let me look. (*Turns to go to the letter-box. Nora at the piano, plays the first bars of the Tarantella. Helmer stops in the doorway.*) Aha!

Nora.   I can't dance to-morrow if I don't practise with you.

Helmer (*going up to her*).   Are you really so afraid of it, dear?

Nora.   Yes, so dreadfully afraid of it. Let me practise at once; there is time now, before we go to dinner. Sit down and play for me, Torvald dear; criticise me, and correct me as you play.

Helmer.   With great pleasure, if you wish me to.

[*Sits down at the piano.*]

Nora (*takes out of the box a tambourine and a long variegated shawl. She hastily drapes the shawl round her. Then she springs to the front of the stage and calls out*).   Now play for me! I am going to dance!

[*Helmer plays and Nora dances. Rank stands by the piano behind Helmer and looks on.*]

Helmer (*as he plays*).   Slower, slower!

Nora.   I can't do it any other way.

Helmer.   Not so violently, Nora!

Nora.   This is the way.

Helmer (*stops playing*).   No, no—that is not a bit right.

Nora (*laughing and swinging the tambourine*).   Didn't I tell you so?

Rank.   Let me play for her.

Helmer (*getting up*).   Yes, do. I can correct her better then.

[*Rank sits down at the piano and plays. Nora dances more and more wildly. Helmer has taken up a position beside the stove, and during her dance gives her frequent instructions. She does not seem to hear him; her hair comes down and falls over her shoulders; she pays no attention to it, but goes on dancing. Enter Mrs. Linde.*]

Mrs. Linde (*standing as if spell-bound in the doorway*).   Oh!——

Nora (*as she dances*).   Such fun, Christine!

Helmer.   My dear darling Nora, you are dancing as if your life depended on it.

Nora.   So it does.

Helmer.   Stop, Rank; this is sheer madness. Stop, I tell you! (*Rank stops playing, and Nora suddenly stands still. Helmer goes up to her.*) I could never have believed it. You have forgotten everything I taught you.

Nora (*throwing away the tambourine*).   There, you see.

Helmer.   You will want a lot of coaching.

Nora.   Yes, you see how much I need it. You must coach me up to the last minute. Promise me that, Torvald!

Helmer.   You can depend on me.

Nora.   You must not think of anything but me, either to-day or to-morrow; you mustn't open a single letter—not even open the letter-box——

Helmer.   Ah, you are still afraid of that fellow——

Nora.   Yes, indeed I am.

Helmer.   Nora, I can tell from your looks that there is a letter from him lying there.

Nora.   I don't know; I think there is; but you must not read anything of that kind now. Nothing horrid must come between us till this is all over.

Rank (*whispers to Helmer*).   You mustn't contradict her.

Helmer (*taking her in his arms*).   The child shall have her way. But to-morrow night, after you have danced——

Nora.   Then you will be free.

[*The Maid appears in the doorway to the right.*]

Maid.   Dinner is served, ma'am.

Nora.   We will have champagne, Helen.

Maid.   Very good, ma'am.   [*Exit.*]

Helmer.   Hullo!—are we going to have a banquet?

Nora.   Yes, a champagne banquet till the small hours. (*Calls out.*) And a few macaroons, Helen—lots, just for once!

Helmer.   Come, come, don't be so wild and nervous. Be my own little skylark, as you used.

Nora.   Yes, dear, I will. But go in now and you too, Doctor Rank. Christine, you must help me to do up my hair.

Rank (*whispers to Helmer as they go out*).   I suppose there is nothing—she is not expecting anything?

Helmer.   Far from it, my dear fellow; it is simply nothing more than this childish nervousness I was telling you of.

[*They go into the right-hand room.*]

Nora.   Well!

Mrs. Linde.   Gone out of town.

Nora. I could tell from your face.

Mrs. Linde. He is coming home to-morrow evening. I wrote a note for him.

Nora. You should have let it alone; you must prevent nothing. After all, it is splendid to be waiting for a wonderful thing to happen.

Mrs. Linde. What is it that you are waiting for?

Nora. Oh, you wouldn't understand. Go in to them, I will come in a moment. (*Mrs. Linde goes into the dining-room. Nora stands still for a little while, as if to compose herself. Then she looks at her watch.*) Five o'clock. Seven hours till midnight. Then the Tarantella will be over. Twenty-four and seven? Thirty-one hours to live.

Helmer (*from the doorway on the right*). Where's my little skylark?

Nora (*going to him with her arms outstretched*). Here she is!

Act III

THE SAME SCENE. *The table has been placed in the middle of the stage, with chairs round it. A lamp is burning on the table. The door into the hall stands open. Dance music is heard in the room above. Mrs. Linde is sitting at the table idly turning over the leaves of a book; she tries to read, but does not seem able to collect her thoughts. Every now and then she listens intently for a sound at the outer door.*

Mrs. Linde (*looking at her watch*). Not yet—and the time is nearly up. If only he does not—. (*Listens again.*) Ah, there he is. (*Goes into the hall and opens the outer door carefully. Light footsteps are heard on the stairs. She whispers.*) Come in. There is no one here.

Krogstad (*in the doorway*). I found a note from you at home. What does this mean?

Mrs. Linde. It is absolutely necessary that I should have a talk with you.

Krogstad. Really? And is it absolutely necessary that it should be here?

Mrs. Linde. It is impossible where I live; there is no private entrance to my rooms. Come in; we are quite alone. The maid is asleep, and the Helmers are at the dance upstairs.

Krogstad (*coming into the room*). Are the Helmers really at a dance to-night?

Mrs. Linde. Yes, why not?

Krogstad. Certainly—why not?

Mrs. Linde. Now, Nils, let us have a talk.

Krogstad. Can we two have anything to talk about?

Mrs. Linde. We have a great deal to talk about.

Krogstad. I shouldn't have thought so.

Mrs. Linde. No, you have never properly understood me.

Krogstad. Was there anything else to understand except what was obvious to all the world—a heartless woman jilts a man when a more lucrative chance turns up?

Mrs. Linde. Do you believe I am as absolutely heartless as all that? And do you believe that I did it with a light heart?

Krogstad. Didn't you?

Mrs. Linde. Nils, did you really think that?

Krogstad. If it were as you say, why did you write to me as you did at the time?

Mrs. Linde. I could do nothing else. As I had to break with you, it was my duty also to put an end to all that you felt for me.

Krogstad (*wringing his hands*). So that was it. And all this—only for the sake of money!

Mrs. Linde. You must not forget that I had a helpless mother and two little brothers. We couldn't wait for you, Nils; your prospects seemed hopeless then.

Krogstad. That may be so, but you had no right to throw me over for anyone else's sake.

Mrs. Linde. Indeed I don't know. Many a time did I ask myself if I had the right to do it.

Krogstad (*more gently*). When I lost you, it was as if all the solid ground went from under my feet. Look at me now—I am a shipwrecked man clinging to a bit of wreckage.

Mrs. Linde. But help may be near.

Krogstad. It *was* near; but then you came and stood in my way.

Mrs. Linde. Unintentionally, Nils. It was only to-day that I learnt it was your place I was going to take in the Bank.

Krogstad. I believe you, if you say so. But now that you know it, are you not going to give it up to me?

Mrs. Linde. No, because that would not benefit you in the least.

Krogstad. Oh, benefit, benefit—I would have done it whether or no.

Mrs. Linde. I have learnt to act prudently. Life, and hard, bitter necessity have taught me that.

Krogstad. And life has taught me not to believe in fine speeches.

Mrs. Linde. Then life has taught you something very reasonable. But deeds you must believe in?

Krogstad. What do you mean by that?

Mrs. Linde. You said you were like a shipwrecked man clinging to some wreckage.

Krogstad. I had good reason to say so.

Mrs. Linde. Well, I am like a shipwrecked woman clinging to some wreckage—no one to mourn for, no one to care for.

Krogstad. It was your own choice.

Mrs. Linde. There was no other choice—then.

Krogstad. Well, what now?

Mrs. Linde.   Nils, how would it be if we two shipwrecked people could join forces?

Krogstad.   What are you saying?

Mrs. Linde.   Two on the same piece of wreckage would stand a better chance than each on their own.

Krogstad.   Christine!

Mrs. Linde.   What do you suppose brought me to town?

Krogstad.   Do you mean that you gave me a thought?

Mrs. Linde.   I could not endure life without work. All my life, as long as I can remember, I have worked, and it has been my greatest and only pleasure. But now I am quite alone in the world—my life is so dreadfully empty and I feel so forsaken. There is not the least pleasure in working for one's self. Nils, give me someone and something to work for.

Krogstad.   I don't trust that. It is nothing but a woman's overstrained sense of generosity that prompts you to make such an offer of yourself.

Mrs. Linde.   Have you ever noticed anything of the sort in me?

Krogstad.   Could you really do it? Tell me—do you know all about my past life?

Mrs. Linde.   Yes.

Krogstad.   And do you know what they think of me here?

Mrs. Linde.   You seemed to me to imply that with me you might have been quite another man.

Krogstad.   I am certain of it.

Mrs. Linde.   Is it too late now?

Krogstad.   Christine, are you saying this deliberately? Yes, I am sure you are. I see it in your face. Have you really the courage then—?

Mrs. Linde.   I want to be a mother to someone, and your children need a mother. We two need each other. Nils, I have faith in your real character—I can dare anything together with you.

Krogstad (*grasps her hands*).   Thanks, thanks, Christine! Now I shall find a way to clear myself in the eyes of the world. Ah, but I forgot——

Mrs. Linde (*listening*).   Hush! The Tarantella! Go, go!

Krogstad.   Why? What is it?

Mrs. Linde.   Do you hear them up there? When that is over, we may expect them back.

Krogstad.   Yes, yes—I will go. But it is all no use. Of course you are not aware what steps I have taken in the matter of the Helmers.

Mrs. Linde.   Yes, I know all about that.

Krogstad.   And in spite of that have you the courage to—?

Mrs. Linde.   I understand very well to what lengths a man like you might be driven by despair.

Krogstad.   If I could only undo what I have done!

Mrs. Linde.   You cannot. Your letter is lying in the letter-box now.

Krogstad.   Are you sure of that?

Mrs. Linde.   Quite sure, but——

Krogstad (*with a searching look at her*).   Is that what it all means?—that you want to save your friend at my cost? Tell me frankly. Is that it?

Mrs. Linde.   Nils, a woman who has once sold herself for another's sake, doesn't do it a second time.

Krogstad.   I will ask for my letter back.

Mrs. Linde.   No, no.

Krogstad.   Yes, of course I will. I will wait here till Helmer comes; I will tell him he must give me my letter back—that it only concerns my dismissal—that he is not to read it——

Mrs. Linde.   No, Nils, you must not recall your letter.

Krogstad.   But, tell me, wasn't it for that very purpose that you asked me to meet you here?

Mrs. Linde.   In my first moment of fright, it was. But twenty-four hours have elapsed since then, and in that time I have witnessed incredible things in this house. Helmer must know all about it. This unhappy secret must be disclosed; they must have a complete understanding between them, which is impossible with all this concealment and falsehood going on.

Krogstad.   Very well, if you will take the responsibility. But there is one thing I can do in any case, and I shall do it at once.

Mrs. Linde (*listening*).   You must be quick and go! The dance is over; we are not safe a moment longer.

Krogstad.   I will wait for you below.

Mrs. Linde.   Yes, do. You must see me back to my door.

Krogstad.   I have never had such an amazing piece of good fortune in my life.

[*Goes out through the outer door. The door between the room and the hall remains open.*]

Mrs. Linde (*tidying up the room and laying her hat and cloak ready*).   What a difference! what a difference! Someone to work for and live for—a home to bring comfort into. That I will do, indeed. I wish they would be quick and come— (*Listens.*) Ah, there they are now. I must put on my things.

[*Takes up her hat and cloak. Helmer's and Nora's voices are heard outside; a key is turned, and Helmer brings Nora almost by force into the hall. She is in an Italian costume with a large black shawl round her; he is in evening dress and a black domino[1] which is flying open.*]

Nora (*hanging back in the doorway, and struggling with him.*)   No, no, no!—don't take me in. I want to go upstairs again; I don't want to leave so early.

Helmer.   But, my dearest Nora——

Nora.   Please, Torvald dear—please, *please*—only an hour more.

---

[1] A long loose hooded cloak.

Helmer. Not a single minute, my sweet Nora. You know that was our agreement. Come along into the room; you are catching cold standing there.

[*He brings her gently into the room, in spite of her resistance.*]

Mrs. Linde. Good evening.

Nora. Christine!

Helmer. You here, so late, Mrs. Linde?

Mrs. Linde. Yes, you must excuse me; I was so anxious to see Nora in her dress.

Nora. Have you been sitting here waiting for me?

Mrs. Linde. Yes, unfortunately I came too late, you had already gone upstairs; and I thought I couldn't go away again without having seen you.

Helmer (*taking off Nora's shawl*). Yes, take a good look at her. I think she is worth looking at. Isn't she charming, Mrs. Linde?

Mrs. Linde. Yes, indeed she is.

Helmer. Doesn't she look remarkably pretty? Everyone thought so at the dance. But she is terribly self-willed, this sweet little person. What are we to do with her? You will hardly believe that I had almost to bring her away by force.

Nora. Torvald, you will repent not having let me stay, even if it were only for half an hour.

Helmer. Listen to her, Mrs. Linde! She had danced her Tarantella, and it had been a tremendous success, as it deserved—although possibly the performance was a trifle too realistic—a little more so, I mean, than was strictly compatible with the limitations of art. But never mind about that! The chief thing is, she had made a success—she had made a tremendous success. Do you think I was going to let her remain there after that, and spoil the effect? No indeed! I took my charming little Capri maiden—my capricious little Capri maiden, I should say—on my arm; took one quick turn round the room; a curtsey on either side, and, as they say in novels, the beautiful apparition disappeared. An exit ought always to be effective, Mrs. Linde; but that is what I cannot make Nora understand. Pooh! this room is hot. (*Throws his domino on a chair and opens the door of his room.*) Hullo! it's dark in here. Oh, of course—excuse me——.

[*He goes in and lights some candles.*]

Nora (*in a hurried and breathless whisper*). Well?

Mrs. Linde (*in a low voice*). I have had a talk with him.

Nora. Yes, and——

Mrs. Linde. Nora, you must tell your husband all about it.

Nora (*in an expressionless voice*). I knew it.

Mrs. Linde. You have nothing to be afraid of as far as Krogstad is concerned; but you must tell him.

Nora.   I won't tell him.

Mrs. Linde.   Then the letter will.

Nora.   Thank you, Christine. Now I know what I must do. Hush——!

Helmer *(coming in again).*   Well, Mrs. Linde, have you admired her?

Mrs. Linde.   Yes, and now I will say good-night.

Helmer.   What, already? Is this yours, this knitting?

Mrs. Linde *(taking it).*   Yes, thank you, I have very nearly forgotten it.

Helmer.   So you knit?

Mrs. Linde.   Of course.

Helmer.   Do you know, you ought to embroider.

Mrs. Linde.   Really? Why?

Helmer.   Yes, it's far more becoming. Let me show you. You hold the embroidery thus in your left hand, and use the needle with the right—like this—with a long, easy sweep. Do you see?

Mrs. Linde.   Yes, perhaps——

Helmer.   But in the case of knitting—that can never be anything but ungraceful; look here—the arms close together, the knitting-needles going up and down—it has a sort of Chinese effect—. That was really excellent champagne they gave us.

Mrs. Linde.   Well,—good-night, Nora, and don't be self-willed any more.

Helmer.   That's right, Mrs. Linde.

Mrs. Linde.   Good-night, Mr. Helmer.

Helmer *(accompanying her to the door).*   Good-night, good-night. I hope you will get home all right. I should be very happy to—but you haven't any great distance to go. Good-night, good-night. *(She goes out; he shuts the door after her, and comes in again.)* Ah!—at last we have got rid of her. She is a frightful bore, that woman.

Nora.   Aren't you very tired, Torvald?

Helmer.   No, not in the least.

Nora.   Nor sleepy?

Helmer.   Not a bit. On the contrary, I feel extraordinarily lively. And you?— you really look both tired and sleepy.

Nora.   Yes, I am very tired. I want to go to sleep at once.

Helmer.   There, you see it was quite right of me not to let you stay there any longer.

Nora.   Everything you do is quite right, Torvald.

Helmer *(kissing her on the forehead).*   Now my little skylark is speaking reasonably. Did you notice what good spirits Rank was in this evening?

Nora.   Really? Was he? I didn't speak to him at all.

Helmer.   And I very little, but I have not for a long time seen him in such good form. *(Looks for a while at her and then goes nearer to her.)* It is delightful to be at home by ourselves again, to be all alone with you—you fascinating, charming little darling!

Nora.   Don't look at me like that, Torvald.

Helmer.   Why shouldn't I look at my dearest treasure?—at all the beauty that is mine, all my very own?

Nora (*going to the other side of the table*).   You mustn't say things like that to me to-night.

Helmer (*following her*).   You have still got the Tarantella in your blood, I see. And it makes you more captivating than ever. Listen—the guests are beginning to go now. (*In a lower voice.*) Nora—soon the whole house will be quiet.

Nora.   Yes, I hope so.

Helmer.   Yes, my own darling Nora. Do you know, when I am out at a party with you like this, why I speak so little to you, keep away from you, and only send a stolen glance in your direction now and then?—do you know why I do that? It is because I make believe to myself that we are secretly in love, and you are my secretly promised bride, and that no one suspects there is anything between us.

Nora.   Yes, yes—I know very well your thoughts are with me all the time.

Helmer.   And when we are leaving, and I am putting the shawl over your beautiful young shoulders—on your lovely neck—then I imagine that you are my young bride and that we have just come from the wedding, and I am bringing you for the first time into our home—to be alone with you for the first time—quite alone with my shy little darling! All this evening I have longed for nothing but you. When I watched the seductive figures of the Tarantella, my blood was on fire; I could endure it no longer, and that was why I brought you down so early——

Nora.   Go away, Torvald! You must let me go. I won't——

Helmer.   What's that? You're joking, my little Nora! You won't—you won't? Am I not your husband—?

[*A knock is heard at the outer door.*]

Nora (*starting*).   Did you hear——?

Helmer (*going into the hall*).   Who is it?

Rank (*outside*).   It is I. May I come in for a moment?

Helmer (*in a fretful whisper*).   Oh, what does he want now? (Aloud.) Wait a minute? (*Unlocks the door.*) Come, that's kind of you not to pass by our door.

Rank.   I thought I heard your voice, and felt as if I should like to look in. (*With a swift glance round.*) Ah, yes!—these dear familiar rooms. You are very happy and cosy in here, you two.

Helmer.   It seems to me that you looked after yourself pretty well upstairs too.

Rank.   Excellently. Why shouldn't I? Why shouldn't one enjoy everything in this world?—at any rate as much as one can, and as long as one can. The wine was capital——

Helmer.   Especially the champagne.

Rank.   So you noticed that too? It is almost incredible how much I managed to put away!

Nora.   Torvald drank a great deal of champagne tonight, too.

Rank. Did he?

Nora. Yes, and he is always in such good spirits afterwards.

Rank. Well, why should one not enjoy a merry evening after a well-spent day?

Helmer. Well spent? I am afraid I can't take credit for that.

Rank (*clapping him on the back*). But I can, you know!

Nora. Doctor Rank, you must have been occupied with some scientific investigation to-day.

Rank. Exactly.

Helmer. Just listen—little Nora talking about scientific investigations!

Nora. And may I congratulate you on the result?

Rank. Indeed you may.

Nora. Was it favourable, then?

Rank. The best possible, for both doctor and patient—certainty.

Nora (*quickly and searchingly*). Certainty?

Rank. Absolute certainty. So wasn't I entitled to make a merry evening of it after that?

Nora. Yes, you certainly were, Doctor Rank.

Helmer. I think so too, so long as you don't have to pay for it in the morning.

Rank. Oh well, one can't have anything in this life without paying for it.

Nora. Doctor Rank—are you fond of fancy-dress balls?

Rank. Yes, if there is a fine lot of pretty costumes.

Nora. Tell me—what shall we two wear at the next?

Helmer. Little featherbrain!—are you thinking of the next already?

Rank. We two? Yes, I can tell you. You shall go as a good fairy——

Helmer. Yes, but what do you suggest as an appropriate costume for that?

Rank. Let your wife go dressed just as she is in everyday life.

Helmer. That was really very prettily turned. But can't you tell us what you will be?

Rank. Yes, my dear friend, I have quite made up my mind about that.

Helmer. Well?

Rank. At the next fancy dress ball I shall be invisible.

Helmer. That's a good joke!

Rank. There is a big black hat—have you never heard of hats that make you invisible? If you put one on, no one can see you.

Helmer (*suppressing a smile*). Yes, you are quite right.

Rank. But I am clean forgetting what I came for. Helmer, give me a cigar—one of the dark Havanas.

Helmer. With the greatest pleasure.

[*Offers him his case.*]

Rank (*takes a cigar and cuts off the end*). Thanks.

Nora (*striking a match*). Let me give you a light.

Rank. Thank you. (*She holds the match for him to light his cigar.*) And now good-bye!

Helmer.   Good-bye, good-bye, dear old man!
Nora.   Sleep well, Doctor Rank.
Rank.   Thank you for that wish.
Nora.   Wish me the same.
Rank.   You? Well, if you want me to—sleep well! And thanks for the light.

[*He nods to them both and goes out.*]

Helmer (*in a subdued voice*).   He has drunk more than he ought.
Nora (*absently*).   Maybe. (*Helmer takes a bunch of keys out of his pocket and goes into the hall.*) Torvald! what are you going to do there?
Helmer.   Empty the letter-box; it is quite full; there will be no room to put the newspaper in to-morrow morning.
Nora.   Are you going to work to-night?
Helmer.   You know quite well I'm not. What is this? Some one has been at the lock.
Nora.   At the lock—?
Helmer.   Yes, someone has. What can it mean? I should never have thought the maid—. Here is a broken hairpin. Nora, it is one of yours.
Nora (*quickly*).   Then it must have been the children—
Helmer.   Then you must get them out of those ways. There, at last I have got it open. (*Takes out the contents of the letter-box, and calls to the kitchen.*) Helen!—Helen, put out the light over the front door. (*Goes back into the room and shuts the door into the hall. He holds out his hand full of letters.*) Look at that—look what a heap of them there are. (*Turning them over.*) What on earth is that?
Nora (*at the window*).   The letter—No! Torvald, no!
Helmer.   Two cards—of Rank's.
Nora.   Of Doctor Rank's?
Helmer (*looking at them*).   Doctor Rank. They were on the top. He must have put them in when he went out.
Nora.   Is there anything written on them?
Helmer.   There is a black cross over the name. Look there—what an uncomfortable idea! It looks as if he were announcing his own death.
Nora.   It is just what he is doing.
Helmer.   What? Do you know anything about it? Has he said anything to you?
Nora.   Yes. He told me that when the cards came it would be his leave-taking from us. He means to shut himself up and die.
Helmer.   My poor old friend. Certainly I knew we should not have him very long with us. But so soon! And so he hides himself away like a wounded animal.
Nora.   If it has to happen, it is best it should be without a word—don't you think so, Torvald?
Helmer (*walking up and down*).   He had so grown into our lives. I can't think

of him as having gone out of them. He, with his sufferings and his loneliness, was like a cloudy background to our sunlit happiness. Well, perhaps it is best so. For him, anyway. (*Standing still.*) And perhaps for us too, Nora. We two are thrown quite upon each other now. (*Puts his arms round her.*) My darling wife, I don't feel as if I could hold you tight enough. Do you know, Nora, I have often wished that you might be threatened by some great danger, so that I might risk my life's blood, and everything, for your sake.

Nora (*disengages herself, and says firmly and decidedly*).   Now you must read your letters, Torvald.

Helmer.   No, no; not to-night. I want to be with you, my darling wife.

Nora.   With the thought of your friend's death——

Helmer.   You are right, it has affected us both. Something ugly has come between us—the thought of the horrors of death. We must try and rid our minds of that. Until then—we will each go to our own room.

Nora (*hanging on his neck*).   Good-night, Torvald—Good-night!

Helmer (*kissing her on the forehead*).   Good-night, my little singing-bird. Sleep sound, Nora. Now I will read my letters through.

[*He takes his letters and goes into his room, shutting the door after him.*]

Nora (*gropes distractedly about, seizes Helmer's domino, throws it round her, while she says in quick, hoarse, spasmodic whispers*). Never to see him again. Never! Never! (*Puts her shawl over her head.*) Never to see my children again either—never again. Never! Never!—Ah! the icy, black water—the unfathomable depths—If only it were over! He has got it now—now he is reading it. Good-bye, Torvald and my children!

[*She is about to rush out through the hall, when Helmer opens his door hurriedly and stands with an open letter in his hand.*]

Helmer.   Nora!

Nora.   Ah!——

Helmer.   What is this? Do you know what is in this letter?

Nora.   Yes, I know. Let me go! Let me get out!

Helmer (*holding her back*).   Where are you going?

Nora (*trying to get free*).   You shan't save me, Torvald!

Helmer (*reeling*).   True? Is this true, what I read here? Horrible! No, no—it is impossible that it can be true.

Nora.   It is true. I have loved you above everything else in the world.

Helmer.   Oh, don't let us have any silly excuses.

Nora (*taking a step towards him*).   Torvald——!

Helmer.   Miserable creature—what have you done?

Nora.   Let me go. You shall not suffer for my sake. You shall not take it upon yourself.

Helmer. No tragedy airs, please. (*Locks the hall door.*) Here you shall stay and give me an explanation. Do you understand what you have done? Answer me? Do you understand what you have done?

Nora (*looks steadily at him and says with a growing look of coldness in her face*). Yes, now I am beginning to understand thoroughly.

Helmer (*walking about the room*). What a horrible awakening! All these eight years—she who was my joy and pride—a hypocrite, a liar—worse, worse—a criminal! The unutterable ugliness of it all! For shame! For shame! (*Nora is silent and looks steadily at him. He stops in front of her.*) I ought to have suspected that something of the sort would happen. I ought to have foreseen it. All your father's want of principle—be silent!—all your father's want of principle has come out in you. No religion, no morality, no sense of duty—. How I am punished for having winked at what he did! I did it for your sake, and this is how you repay me.

Nora. Yes, that's just it.

Helmer. Now you have destroyed all my happiness. You have ruined all my future. It is horrible to think of! I am in the power of an unscrupulous man; he can do what he likes with me, ask anything he likes of me, give me any orders he pleases—I dare not refuse. And I must sink to such miserable depths because of a thoughtless woman!

Nora. When I am out of the way, you will be free.

Helmer. No fine speeches, please. Your father had always plenty of those ready, too. What good would it be to me if you were out of the way, as you say? Not the slightest. He can make the affair known everywhere; and if he does, I may be falsely suspected of having been a party to your criminal action. Very likely people will think I was behind it all—that it was I who prompted you! And I have to thank you for all this—you whom I have cherished during the whole of our married life. Do you understand now what it is you have done for me?

Nora (*coldly and quietly*). Yes.

Helmer. It is so incredible that I can't take it in. But we must come to some understanding. Take off that shawl. Take it off, I tell you. I must try and appease him some way or another. The matter must be hushed up at any cost. And as for you and me, it must appear as if everything between us were just as before—but naturally only in the eyes of the world. You will still remain in my house, that is a matter of course. But I shall not allow you to bring up the children; I dare not trust them to you. To think that I should be obliged to say so to one whom I have loved so dearly, and whom I still——. No, that is all over. From this moment happiness is not the question; all that concerns us is to save the remains, the fragments, the appearance——

[*A ring is heard at the front-door bell.*]

Helmer (*with a start*). What is that? So late! Can the worst——? Can he——? Hide yourself, Nora. Say you are ill.

[*Nora stands motionless. Helmer goes and unlocks the hall door.*]

Maid (*half-dressed, comes to the door*).   A letter for the mistress.

Helmer.   Give it to me. (*Takes the letter, and shuts the door.*) Yes, it is from him. You shall not have it; I will read it myself.

Nora.   Yes, read it.

Helmer (*standing by the lamp*).   I scarcely have the courage to do it. It may mean ruin for both of us. No, I must know. (*Tears open the letter, runs his eye over a few lines, looks at a paper enclosed and gives a shout of joy.*) Nora! (*She looks at him questioningly.*) Nora!—No, I must read it once again——. Yes, it is true! I am saved! Nora, I am saved!

Nora.   And I?

Helmer.   You too, of course; we are both saved, both you and I. Look, he sends you your bond back. He says he regrets and repents—that a happy change in his life—never mind what he says! We are saved, Nora! No one can do anything to you. Oh, Nora, Nora!—no, first I must destroy these hateful things. Let me see——. (*Takes a look at the bond.*) No, no, I won't look at it. The whole thing shall be nothing but a bad dream to me. (*Tears up the bond and both letters, throws them all into the stove, and watches them burn.*) There—now it doesn't exist any longer. He says that since Christmas Eve you——. These must have been three dreadful days for you, Nora.

Nora.   I have fought a hard fight these three days.

Helmer.   And suffered agonies, and seen no way out but——. No, we won't call any of the horrors to mind. We will only shout with joy, and keep saying, "It's all over! It's all over!" Listen to me, Nora. You don't seem to realise that it is all over. What is this?—such a cold, set face! My poor little Nora, I quite understand; you don't feel as if you could believe that I have forgiven you. But it is true, Nora, I swear it; I have forgiven you everything. I know that what you did, you did out of love for me.

Nora.   That is true.

Helmer.   You have loved me as a wife ought to love her husband. Only you had not sufficient knowledge to judge of the means you used. But do you suppose you are any the less dear to me, because you don't understand how to act on your own responsibility? No, no; only lean on me; I will advise you and direct you. I should not be a man if this womanly helplessness did not just give you a double attractiveness in my eyes. You must not think any more about the hard things I said in my first moment of consternation, when I thought everything was going to overwhelm me. I have forgiven you, Nora; I swear to you I have forgiven you.

[*She goes out through the door to the right.*]

Helmer.   No, don't go——. (*Looks in.*) What are you doing in there?

Nora (*from within*).   Taking off my fancy dress.

Helmer (*standing at the open door*).   Yes, do. Try and calm yourself, and make your mind easy again, my frightened little singing-bird. Be at rest, and feel secure; I have broad wings to shelter you under. (*Walks up and down by the door.*) How warm and cosy our home is, Nora. Here is shelter for you; here I will protect you like a hunted dove that I have saved from a hawk's claws. I will bring peace to your poor beating heart. It will come, little by little, Nora, believe me. Tomorrow morning you will look upon it all quite differently; soon everything will be just as it was before. Very soon you won't need me to assure you that I have forgiven you; you will yourself feel the certainty that I have done so. Can you suppose I should ever think of such a thing as repudiating you, or even reproaching you? You have no idea what a true man's heart is like, Nora. There is something so indescribably sweet and satisfying, to a man, in the knowledge that he has forgiven his wife—forgiven her freely, and with all his heart. It seems as if that had made her, as it were, doubly his own; he has given her a new life, so to speak; and she has in a way become both wife and child to him. So you shall be for me after this, my little scared, helpless darling. Have no anxiety about anything, Nora; only be frank and open with me, and I will serve as will and conscience both to you——. What is this? Not gone to bed? Have you changed your things?

Nora (*in everyday dress*).   Yes, Torvald, I have changed my things now.

Helmer.   But what for?—so late as this.

Nora.   I shall not sleep to-night.

Helmer.   But, my dear Nora——

Nora (*looking at her watch*).   It is not so very late. Sit down here, Torvald. You and I have much to say to one another.

[*She sits down at one side of the table.*]

Helmer.   Nora—what is this?—this cold, set face?

Nora.   Sit down. It will take some time; I have a lot to talk over with you.

Helmer (*sits down at the opposite side of the table*).   You alarm me, Nora!— and I don't understand you.

Nora.   No, that is just it. You don't understand me, and I have never understood you either—before to-night. No, you mustn't interrupt me. You must simply listen to what I say. Torvald, this is a settling of accounts.

Helmer.   What do you mean by that?

Nora (*after a short silence*).   Isn't there one thing that strikes you as strange in our sitting here like this?

Helmer.   What is that?

Nora.   We have been married now eight years. Does it not occur to you that this is the first time we two, you and I, husband and wife, have had a serious conversation?

Helmer.   What do you mean by serious?

Nora.   In all these eight years—longer than that—from the very beginning of our acquaintance, we have never exchanged a word on any serious subject.

Helmer. Was it likely that I would be continually and for ever telling you about worries that you could not help me to bear?

Nora. I am not speaking about business matters. I say that we have never sat down in earnest together to try and get at the bottom of anything.

Helmer. But, dearest Nora, would it have been any good to you?

Nora. That is just it; you have never understood me. I have been greatly wronged, Torvald—first by papa and then by you.

Helmer. What! By us two—by us two, who have loved you better than any-one else in the world?

Nora (*shaking her head*). You have never loved me. You have only thought it pleasant to be in love with me.

Helmer. Nora, what do I hear you saying?

Nora. It is perfectly true, Torvald. When I was at home with papa, he told me his opinion about everything, and so I had the same opinions; and if I differed from him I concealed the fact, because he would not have liked it. He called me his doll-child, and he played with me just as I used to play with my dolls. And when I came to live with you——

Helmer. What sort of an expression is that to use about our marriage?

Nora (*undisturbed*). I mean that I was simply transferred from papa's hands into yours. You arranged everything according to your own taste, and so I got the same tastes as you—or else I pretended to, I am really not quite sure which—I think sometimes the one and sometimes the other. When I look back on it, it seems to me as if I had been living here like a poor woman—just from hand to mouth. I have existed merely to perform tricks for you, Torvald. But you would have it so. You and papa have committed a great sin against me. It is your fault that I have made nothing of my life.

Helmer. How unreasonable and how ungrateful you are, Nora! Have you not been happy here?

Nora. No, I have never been happy. I thought I was, but it has never really been so.

Helmer. Not—not happy!

Nora. No, only merry. And you have always been so kind to me. But our home has been nothing but a playroom. I have been your doll-wife, just as at home I was papa's doll-child; and here the children have been my dolls. I thought it great fun when you played with me, just as they thought it great fun when I played with them. That is what our marriage has been, Torvald.

Helmer. There is some truth in what you say—exaggerated and strained as your view of it is. But for the future it shall be different. Playtime shall be over, and lesson-time shall begin.

Nora. Whose lessons? Mine, or the children's?

Helmer. Both your and the children's, my darling Nora.

Nora. Alas, Torvald, you are not the man to educate me into being a proper wife for you.

Helmer. And you can say that!

Nora. And I—how am I fitted to bring up the children?

Helmer. Nora!

Nora. Didn't you say so yourself a little while ago—that you dare not trust me to bring them up?

Helmer. In a moment of anger! Why do you pay any heed to that?

Nora. Indeed, you were perfectly right. I am not fit for the task. There is another task I must undertake first. I must try and educate myself—you are not the man to help me in that. I must do that for myself. And that is why I am going to leave you now.

Helmer *(springing up).* What do you say?

Nora. I must stand quite alone, if I am to understand myself and everything about me. It is for that reason that I cannot remain with you any longer.

Helmer. Nora! Nora!

Nora. I am going away from here now, at once. I am sure Christine will take me in for the night——

Helmer. You are out of your mind! I won't allow it! I forbid you!

Nora. It is no use forbidding me anything any longer. I will take with me what belongs to myself. I will take nothing from you, either now or later.

Helmer. What sort of madness is this!

Nora. To-morrow I shall go home—I mean, to my old home. It will be easiest for me to find something to do there.

Helmer. You blind, foolish woman!

Nora. I must try and get some sense, Torvald.

Helmer. To desert your home, your husband and your children! And you don't consider what people will say!

Nora. I cannot consider that at all. I only know that it is necessary for me.

Helmer. It's shocking. This is how you would neglect your most sacred duties.

Nora. What do you consider my most sacred duties?

Helmer. Do I need to tell you that? Are they not your duties to your husband and your children?

Nora. I have other duties just as sacred.

Helmer. That you have not. What duties could those be?

Nora. Duties to myself.

Helmer. Before all else, you are a wife and a mother.

Nora. I don't believe that any longer. I believe that before all else I am a reasonable human being, just as you are—or, at all events, that I must try and become one. I know quite well, Torvald, that most people would think you right, and that views of that kind are to be found in books; but I can no longer content myself with what most people say, or with what is found in books. I must think over things for myself and get to understand them.

Helmer. Can you not understand your place in your own home? Have you not a reliable guide in such matters as that?—have you no religion?

Nora. I am afraid, Torvald, I do not exactly know what religion is.

Helmer. What are you saying?

Nora. I know nothing but what the clergyman said, when I went to be confirmed. He told us that religion was this, and that, and the other.

When I am away from all this, and am alone, I will look into that matter too. I will see if what the clergyman said is true, or at all events if it is true for me.

Helmer. This is unheard of in a girl of your age! But if religion cannot lead you aright, let me try and awaken your conscience. I suppose you have some moral sense? Or—answer me—am I to think you have none?

Nora. I assure you, Torvald, that is not an easy question to answer. I really don't know. The thing perplexes me altogether. I only know that you and I look at it in quite another light. I am learning, too, that the law is quite another thing from what I supposed; but I find it impossible to convince myself that the law is right. According to it a woman has no right to spare her old dying father, or to save her husband's life. I can't believe that.

Helmer. You talk like a child. You don't understand the conditions of the world in which you live.

Nora. No, I don't. But now I am going to try. I am going to see if I can make out who is right, the world or I.

Helmer. You are ill, Nora; you are delirious; I almost think you are out of your mind.

Nora. I have never felt my mind so clear and certain as to-night.

Helmer. And is it with a clear and certain mind that you forsake your husband and your children?

Nora. Yes, it is.

Helmer. Then there is only one possible explanation.

Nora. What is that?

Helmer. You do not love me any more.

Nora. No, that is just it.

Helmer. Nora!—and you can say that?

Nora. It gives me great pain, Torvald, for you have always been so kind to me, but I cannot help it. I do not love you any more.

Helmer (*regaining his composure*). Is that a clear and certain conviction too?

Nora. Yes, absolutely clear and certain. That is the reason why I will not stay here any longer.

Helmer. And can you tell me what I have done to forfeit your love?

Nora. Yes, indeed I can. It was to-night, when the wonderful thing did not happen; then I saw you were not the man I had thought you.

Helmer. Explain yourself better—I don't understand you.

Nora. I have waited so patiently for eight years; for, goodness knows, I knew very well that wonderful things don't happen every day. Then this horrible misfortune came upon me; and then I felt quite certain that the wonderful thing was going to happen at last. When Krogstad's letter was lying out there, never for a moment did I imagine that you would consent to accept this man's conditions. I was so absolutely certain that you would say to him: Publish the thing to the whole world. And when that was done——

Helmer. Yes, what then?—when I had exposed my wife to shame and disgrace?

Nora.   When that was done, I was so absolutely certain, you would come forward and take everything upon yourself, and say: I am the guilty one.

Helmer.   Nora——!

Nora.   You mean that I would never have accepted such a sacrifice on your part? No, of course not. But what would my assurances have been worth against yours? That was the wonderful thing which I hoped for and feared; and it was to prevent that, that I wanted to kill myself.

Helmer.   I would gladly work night and day for you, Nora—bear sorrow and want for your sake. But no man would sacrifice his honour for the one he loves.

Nora.   It is a thing hundreds of thousands of women have done.

Helmer.   Oh, you think and talk like a heedless child.

Nora.   Maybe. But you neither think nor talk like the man I could bind myself to. As soon as your fear was over—and it was not fear for what threatened me, but for what might happen to you—when the whole thing was past, as far as you were concerned it was exactly as if nothing at all had happened. Exactly as before, I was your little skylark, your doll, which you would in future treat with doubly gentle care, because it was so brittle and fragile. (*Getting up.*) Torvald—it was then it dawned upon me that for eight years I had been living here with a strange man, and had borne him three children——. Oh, I can't bear to think of it! I could tear myself into little bits!

Helmer (*sadly*).   I see, I see. An abyss has opened between us—there is no denying it. But, Nora, would it not be possible to fill it up?

Nora.   As I am now, I am no wife for you.

Helmer.   I have it in me to become a different man.

Nora.   Perhaps—if your doll is taken away from you.

Helmer.   But to part!—to part from you! No, no, Nora, I can't understand that idea.

Nora (*going out to the right*).   That makes it all the more certain that it must be done.

[*She comes back with her cloak and hat and a small bag which she puts on a chair by the table.*]

Helmer.   Nora, Nora, not now! Wait till to-morrow.

Nora (*putting on her cloak*).   I cannot spend the night in a strange man's room.

Helmer.   But can't we live here like brother and sister——?

Nora (*putting on her hat*).   You know very well that would not last long. (*Puts the shawl round her.*) Good-bye, Torvald. I won't see the little ones. I know they are in better hands than mine. As I am now, I can be of no use to them.

Helmer.   But some day, Nora—some day?

Nora.   How can I tell? I have no idea what is going to become of me.

Helmer.   But you are my wife, whatever becomes of you.

Nora.   Listen, Torvald. I have heard that when a wife deserts her husband's house, as I am doing now, he is legally freed from all obligations towards her.

In any case I set you free from all your obligations. You are not to feel yourself bound in the slightest way, any more than I shall. There must be perfect freedom on both sides. See here is your ring back. Give me mine.

Helmer. That too?

Nora. That too.

Helmer. Here it is.

Nora. That's right. Now it is all over. I have put the keys here. The maids know all about everything in the house—better than I do. To-morrow, after I have left her, Christine will come here and pack up my own things that I brought with me from home. I will have them sent after me.

Helmer. All over! All over!—Nora, shall you never think of me again?

Nora. I know I shall often think of you and the children and this house.

Helmer. May I write to you, Nora?

Nora. No—never. You must not do that.

Helmer. But at least let me send you——

Nora. Nothing—nothing——

Helmer. Let me help you if you are in want.

Nora. No. I can receive nothing from a stranger.

Helmer. Nora—can I never be anything more than a stranger to you?

Nora *(taking her bag)*. Ah, Torvald, the most wonderful thing of all would have to happen.

Helmer. Tell me what that would be!

Nora. Both you and I would have to be so changed that——. Oh, Torvald, I don't believe any longer in wonderful things happening.

Helmer. But I will believe in it. Tell me? So changed that——?

Nora. That our life together would be a real wedlock. Good-bye.

[*She goes out through the hall.*]

Helmer *(sinks down on a chair at the door and buries his face in his hands).* Nora! Nora! *(Looks round, and rises.)* Empty. She is gone. *(A hope flashes across his mind.)* The most wonderful thing of all——?

[*The sound of a door shutting is heard from below.*]

For Analysis

1. What evidence can you find to support the interpretation that this play is not only about the Helmers' marriage but also about the institution of marriage itself? **2.** What does the first meeting between Nora and Mrs. Linde tell us about Nora's character? **3.** On a number of occasions, Nora recalls her father. What relevance do these recollections have to the development of the **theme**? **4.** Is Krogstad presented as a conventional villain, or are we meant to sympathize with him? Explain. **5.** What function does Dr. Rank serve in the play? **6.** Examine the stage directions at the beginning of each act. In what ways do they contribute to and reflect the developing action? **7.** Acts I and II open with a dialogue between Nora and Torvald. What changes in

Nora does a comparison between the two dialogues reveal? **8.** At what point in the action, in your opinion, does Nora begin to understand the truth of her situation and to take responsibility for her life? **9.** Summarize the various arguments Torvald uses in his attempt to persuade Nora not to leave. **10.** Is the feminist theme of the play weakened by Ibsen's failure to suggest how Nora could conceivably make it on her own in such a patriarchal society? Explain.

On Style

1. Analyze and evaluate Ibsen's use of **exposition** in Act I. **2.** In the first two acts, Ibsen uses the impending party and the tarantella dance Nora is to perform to create suspense and dramatic tension. Discuss the way in which he achieves these effects.

Making Connections

1. What similar attitudes toward women do you find in this play, in Susan Glaspell's *Trifles* (p. 551), and August Wilson's *Two Trains Running* (p. 565)? **2.** Compare Nora and Antigonê in Sophocles' *Antigonê* (p. 460) as rebels against the constrictions of a patriarchal society. As part of this comparison, examine the similarities and differences between the arguments used by Creon and Torvald to dissuade Antigonê and Nora from their respective courses of action.

Writing Topics

1. Does the fact that Nora abandons her children undermine her otherwise heroic decision to walk out on a hollow marriage? For an 1880 German production, Ibsen— in response to public demand—provided an alternate ending in which Nora, after struggling with her conscience, decides that she cannot abandon her children. Do you think this is a better ending than the original one? **2.** How does the subplot involving the relationship between Mrs. Linde and Krogstad add force to the main plot of *A Doll's House*? **3.** Have you ever defied social pressure because the cost of conforming was too high? Describe the source of the pressure, the issues at stake, the consequences of your refusal. Since then, have you had second thoughts about your actions? **4.** Write a brief description of a marriage you are familiar with that endured only out of inertia or economic pressure or fear.

Susan Glaspell   [1882–1948]

Trifles   1916

CHARACTERS

George Henderson, county
   attorney
Henry Peters, sheriff

Lewis Hale, a neighboring farmer
Mrs. Peters
Mrs. Hale

SCENE

*The kitchen in the now abandoned farmhouse of John Wright, a gloomy
kitchen, and left without having been put in order—the walls covered with
a faded wall paper. Down right is a door leading to the parlor. On the right
wall above this door is a built-in kitchen cupboard with shelves in the upper
portion and drawers below. In the rear wall at right, up two steps is a door
opening onto stairs leading to the second floor. In the rear wall at left is a
door to the shed and from there to the outside. Between these two doors is an
old-fashioned black iron stove. Running along the left wall from the shed door
is an old iron sink and sink shelf, in which is set a hand pump. Downstage
of the sink is an uncurtained window. Near the window is an old wooden
rocker. Center stage is an unpainted wooden kitchen table with straight chairs
on either side. There is a small chair down right. Unwashed pans under the
sink, a loaf of bread outside the breadbox, a dish towel on the table—other
signs of incompleted work. At the rear the shed door opens and the Sheriff
comes in followed by the County Attorney and Hale. The Sheriff and Hale
are men in middle life, the County Attorney is a young man; all are much
bundled up and go at once to the stove. They are followed by the two women—
the Sheriff's wife, Mrs. Peters, first; she is a slightly wiry woman, with a
thin nervous face. Mrs. Hale is larger and would ordinarily be called more
comfortable looking, but she is disturbed now and looks fearfully about as she
enters. The women have come in slowly, and stand close together near the
door.*

County Attorney (*at stove rubbing his hands*).　This feels good. Come up to
   the fire, ladies.
Mrs. Peters (*after taking a step forward*).　I'm not—cold.
Sheriff (*unbuttoning his overcoat and stepping away from the stove to right of
   table as if to mark the beginning of official business*).　Now, Mr. Hale, before
   we move things about, you explain to Mr. Henderson just what you saw when
   you came here yesterday morning.
County Attorney (*crossing down to left of the table*).　By the way, has anything been moved? Are things just as you left them yesterday?

Sheriff *(looking about).*   It's just about the same. When it dropped below zero last night I thought I'd better send Frank out this morning to make a fire for us—*(sits right of center table)* no use getting pneumonia with a big case on, but I told him not to touch anything except the stove—and you know Frank.

County Attorney.   Somebody should have been left here yesterday.

Sheriff.   Oh—yesterday. When I had to send Frank to Morris Center for that man who went crazy—I want you to know I had my hands full yesterday. I knew you could get back from Omaha by today and as long as I went over everything here myself—

County Attorney.   Well, Mr. Hale, tell just what happened when you came here yesterday morning.

Hale *(crossing down to above table).*   Harry and I started to town with a load of potatoes. We came along the road from my place and as I got here I said, "I'm going to see if I can't get John Wright to go in with me on a party telephone." I spoke to Wright about it once before and he put me off, saying folks talked too much anyway, and all he asked was peace and quiet—I guess you know about how much he talked himself; but I thought maybe if I went to the house and talked about it before his wife, though I said to Harry that I didn't know as what his wife wanted made much difference to John———

County Attorney.   Let's talk about that later, Mr. Hale. I do want to talk about that, but tell now just what happened when you got to the house.

Hale.   I didn't hear or see anything; I knocked at the door, and still it was all quiet inside. I knew they must be up, it was past eight o'clock. So I knocked again, and I thought I heard somebody say, "Come in." I wasn't sure. I'm not sure yet, but I opened the door—this door *(indicating the door by which the two women are still standing)* and there in that rocker—*(pointing at it)* sat Mrs. Wright. *(They all look at the rocker down left.)*

County Attorney.   What—was she doing?

Hale.   She was rockin' back and forth. She had her apron in her hand and was kind of—pleating it.

County Attorney.   And how did she—look?

Hale.   Well, she looked queer.

County Attorney.   How do you mean—queer?

Hale.   Well, as if she didn't know what she was going to do next. And kind of done up.

County Attorney *(takes out notebook and pencil and sits left of center table).*   How did she seem to feel about your coming?

Hale.   Why, I don't think she minded—one way or another. She didn't pay much attention. I said, "How do, Mrs. Wright, it's cold, ain't it?" And she said, "Is it?"—and went on kind of pleating at her apron. Well, I was surprised; she didn't ask me to come up to the stove, or to set down, but just sat there, not even looking at me, so I said, "I want to see John." And then she—laughed. I guess you would call it a laugh. I thought of Harry and the team outside, so I said a little sharp: "Can't I see John?" "No," she says, kind o' dull like. "Ain't he home?" says I. "Yes," says she, "he's home." "Then why can't I see him?" I asked her, out of patience. " 'Cause he's dead," says she. "*Dead?*" says I. She just nodded her head, not getting a bit excited, but rockin' back and forth. "Why—where is he?" says I, not knowing what to say. She just pointed upstairs—like that. (*Himself pointing to the room above.*) I started for the stairs, with the idea of going up there. I walked from there to here—then I says, "Why, what did he die of?" "He died of a rope round his neck," says she, and just went on, pleatin' at her apron. Well, I went out and called Harry. I thought I might—need help. We went upstairs and there he was lyin'———

County Attorney. I think I'd rather have you go into that upstairs, where you can point it all out. Just go on now with the rest of the story.

Hale. Well, my first thought was to get that rope off. It looked . . . (*stops; his face twitches*) . . . but Harry, he went up to him, and he said, "No, he's dead all right, and we'd better not touch anything." So we went back downstairs. She was still sitting that same way. "Has anybody been notified?" I asked. "No," says she, unconcerned. "Who did this, Mrs. Wright?" said Harry. He said it businesslike—and she stopped pleatin' of her apron. "I don't know," she says. "You don't *know?*" says Harry. "No," says she. "Weren't you sleepin' in the bed with him?" says Harry. "Yes," says she, "but I was on the inside." "Somebody slipped a rope round his neck and strangled him and you didn't wake up?" says Harry. "I didn't wake up," she said after him. We must 'a' looked as if we didn't see how that could be, for after a minute she said, "I sleep sound." Harry was going to ask her more questions but I said maybe we ought to let her tell her story first to the coroner, or the sheriff, so Harry went fast as he could to Rivers' place, where there's a telephone.

County Attorney. And what did Mrs. Wright do when she knew that you had gone for the coroner?

Hale. She moved from the rocker to that chair over there (*pointing to a small chair in the down right corner*) and just sat there with her hands held together and looking down. I got a feeling that I ought to make some conversation, so I said I had come in to see if John wanted to put in a telephone, and at that she started to laugh, and then she stopped and looked at me—scared. (*The County Attorney, who has had his notebook out, makes a note.*) I dunno, maybe it wasn't scared. I wouldn't like to say it was. Soon Harry got back, and then Dr. Lloyd came and you, Mr. Peters, and so I guess that's all I know that you don't.

County Attorney (*rising and looking around*). I guess we'll go upstairs first—and then out to the barn and around there. (*To the Sheriff.*) You're convinced that there was nothing important here—nothing that would point to any motive?

Sheriff. Nothing here but kitchen things.

(*The County Attorney, after again looking around the kitchen, opens the door of a cupboard closet in right wall. He brings a small chair from right—gets on it and looks on a shelf. Pulls his hand away, sticky.*)

County Attorney.   Here's a nice mess. (*The women draw nearer up center.*)

Mrs. Peters (*to the other woman*).   Oh, her fruit; it did freeze. (*To the Lawyer.*) She worried about that when it turned so cold. She said the fire'd go out and her jars would break.

Sheriff (*rises*).   Well, can you beat the women! Held for murder and worryin' about her preserves.

County Attorney (*getting down from chair*).   I guess before we're through she may have something more serious than preserves to worry about. (*Crosses down right center.*)

Hale.   Well, women are used to worrying over trifles. (*The two women move a little closer together.*)

County Attorney (*with the gallantry of a young politician*).   And yet, for all their worries, what would we do without the ladies? (*The women do not unbend. He goes below the center table to the sink, takes a dipperful of water from the pail, and pouring it into a basin, washes his hands. While he is doing this the Sheriff and Hale cross to cupboard, which they inspect. The County Attorney starts to wipe his hands on the roller towel, turns it for a cleaner place.*) Dirty towels! (*Kicks his foot against the pans under the sink.*) Not much of a housekeeper, would you say, ladies?

Mrs. Hale (*stiffly*).   There's a great deal of work to be done on a farm.

County Attorney.   To be sure. And yet (*with a little bow to her*) I know there are some Dickson County farmhouses which do not have such roller towels.

(*He gives it a pull to expose its full length again.*)

Mrs. Hale.   Those towels get dirty awful quick. Men's hands aren't always as clean as they might be.

County Attorney.   Ah, loyal to your sex, I see. But you and Mrs. Wright were neighbors. I suppose you were friends, too.

Mrs. Hale (*shaking her head*).   I've not seen much of her of late years. I've not been in this house—it's more than a year.

County Attorney (*crossing to women up center*).   And why was that? You didn't like her?

Mrs. Hale.   I liked her all well enough. Farmers' wives have their hands full, Mr. Henderson. And then———

County Attorney.   Yes———?

Mrs. Hale (*looking about*).   It never seemed a very cheerful place.

County Attorney.   No—it's not cheerful. I shouldn't say she had the home-making instinct.

Mrs. Hale.   Well, I don't know as Wright had, either.

County Attorney.   You mean that they didn't get on very well?

Mrs. Hale.   No, I don't mean anything. But I don't think a place'd be any cheerfuller for John Wright's being in it.

County Attorney.   I'd like to talk more of that a little later. I want to get the lay of things upstairs now.

(He goes past the women to up right where steps lead to a stair door.)

Sheriff.   I suppose anything Mrs. Peters does'll be all right. She was to take in some clothes for her, you know, and a few little things. We left in such a hurry, yesterday.

County Attorney.   Yes, but I would like to see what you take, Mrs. Peters, and keep an eye out for anything that might be of use to us.

Mrs. Peters.   Yes, Mr. Henderson.

(The men leave by up right door to stairs. The women listen to the men's steps on the stairs, then look about the kitchen.)

Mrs. Hale *(crossing left to sink)*.   I'd hate to have men coming into my kitchen, snooping around and criticizing.

(She arranges the pans under sink which the Lawyer had shoved out of place.)

Mrs. Peters.   Of course it's no more than their duty.

(Crosses to cupboard up right.)

Mrs. Hale.   Duty's all right, but I guess that deputy sheriff that came out to make the fire might have got a little of this on. *(Gives the roller towel a pull.)* Wish I'd thought of that sooner. Seems mean to talk about her for not having things slicked up when she had to come away in such a hurry.

(Crosses right to Mrs. Peters at cupboard.)

Mrs. Peters *(who has been looking through cupboard, lifts one end of towel that covers a pan)*.   She had bread set.

(Stands still.)

Mrs. Hale *(eyes fixed on a loaf of bread beside the breadbox, which is on a low shelf of the cupboard)*.   She was going to put this in there. *(Picks up a loaf, abruptly drops it. In a manner of returning to familiar things.)* It's a shame about her fruit. I wonder if it's all gone. *(Gets up on the chair and looks.)* I think there's some here that's all right, Mrs. Peters. Yes—here; *(holding it toward the window)* this is cherries, too. *(Looking again.)* I declare I believe that's the only one. *(Gets down, jar in her hand. Goes to the sink and wipes it off on the outside.)* She'll feel awful bad after all her hard work in the hot weather. I remember the afternoon I put up my cherries last summer.

(She puts the jar on the big kitchen table, center of the room. With a sigh, is about to sit down in the rocking chair. Before she is seated realizes what chair it

is; with a slow look at it, steps back. The chair which she has touched rocks back and forth. Mrs. Peters moves to center table and they both watch the chair rock for a moment or two.)

Mrs. Peters *(shaking off the mood which the empty rocking chair has evoked. Now in a businesslike manner she speaks).* Well I must get those things from the front room closet. *(She goes to the door at the right but, after looking into the other room, steps back.)* You coming with me, Mrs. Hale? You could help me carry them. *(They go in the other room; reappear, Mrs. Peters carrying a dress, petticoat, and skirt, Mrs. Hale following with a pair of shoes.)* My, it's cold in there.

(She puts the clothes on the big table and hurries to the stove.)

Mrs. Hale *(right of center table examining the skirt).* Wright was close. I think maybe that's why she kept so much to herself. She didn't even belong to the Ladies' Aid. I suppose she felt she couldn't do her part, and then you don't enjoy things when you feel shabby. I heard she used to wear pretty clothes and be lively, when she was Minnie Foster, one of the town girls singing in the choir. But that—oh, that was thirty years ago. This all you want to take in?

Mrs. Peters. She said she wanted an apron. Funny thing to want, for there isn't much to get you dirty in jail, goodness knows. But I suppose just to make her feel more natural. *(Crosses to cupboard.)* She said they was in the top drawer in this cupboard. Yes, here. And then her little shawl that always hung behind the door. *(Opens stair door and looks.)* Yes, here it is.

(Quickly shuts door leading upstairs.)

Mrs. Hale *(abruptly moving toward her).* Mrs. Peters?
Mrs. Peters. Yes, Mrs. Hale?

(At up right door.)

Mrs. Hale. Do you think she did it?
Mrs. Peters *(in a frightened voice).* Oh, I don't know.
Mrs. Hale. Well, I don't think she did. Asking for an apron and her little shawl. Worrying about her fruit.
Mrs. Peters *(starts to speak, glances up, where footsteps are heard in the room above. In a low voice).* Mr. Peters says it looks bad for her. Mr. Henderson is awful sarcastic in a speech and he'll make fun of her sayin' she didn't wake up.
Mrs. Hale. Well, I guess John Wright didn't wake when they was slipping that rope under his neck.

Mrs. Peters (*crossing slowly to table and placing shawl and apron on table with other clothing*).   No, it's strange. It must have been done awful crafty and still. They say it was such a—funny way to kill a man, rigging it all up like that.

Mrs. Hale (*crossing to left of Mrs. Peters at table*).   That's just what Mr. Hale said. There was a gun in the house. He says that's what he can't understand.

Mrs. Peters.   Mr. Henderson said coming out that what was needed for the case was a motive; something to show anger, or—sudden feeling.

Mrs. Hale (*who is standing by the table*).   Well, I don't see any signs of anger around here. (*She puts her hand on the dish towel, which lies on the table, stands looking down at table, one-half of which is clean, the other half messy.*) It's wiped to here. (*Makes a move as if to finish work, then turns and looks at loaf of bread outside the breadbox. Drops towel. In that voice of coming back to familiar things.*) Wonder how they are finding things upstairs. (*Crossing below table to down right.*) I hope she had it a little more red-up[1] up there. You know, it seems kind of *sneaking*. Locking her up in town and then coming out here and trying to get her own house to turn against her!

Mrs. Peters.   But, Mrs. Hale, the law is the law.

Mrs. Hale.   I s'pose 'tis. (*Unbuttoning her coat.*) Better loosen up your things, Mrs. Peters. You won't feel them when you go out.

(*Mrs. Peters takes off her fur tippet, goes to hang it on chair back left of table, stands looking at the work basket on floor near down left window.*)

Mrs. Peters.   She was piecing a quilt.

(*She brings the large sewing basket to the center table and they look at the bright pieces, Mrs. Hale above the table and Mrs. Peters left of it.*)

Mrs. Hale.   It's a log cabin pattern. Pretty, isn't it? I wonder if she was goin' to quilt it or just knot it?

(*Footsteps have been heard coming down the stairs. The Sheriff enters followed by Hale and the County Attorney.*)

Sheriff.   They wonder if she was going to quilt it or just knot it!

(*The men laugh, the women look abashed.*)

County Attorney (*rubbing his hands over the stove*).   Frank's fire didn't do much up there, did it? Well, let's go out to the barn and get that cleared up.

(*The men go outside by up left door.*)

---

[1] A slang expression for "made attractive."

Mrs. Hale (*resentfully*).   I don't know as there's anything so strange, our takin' up our time with little things while we're waiting for them to get the evidence. (*She sits in chair right of table smoothing out a block with decision.*) I don't see as it's anything to laugh about.

Mrs. Peters (*apologetically*).   Of course they've got awful important things on their minds.

(*Pulls up a chair and joins Mrs. Hale at the left of the table.*)

Mrs. Hale (*examining another block*).   Mrs. Peters, look at this one. Here, this is the one she was working on, and look at the sewing! All the rest of it has been so nice and even. And look at this! It's all over the place! Why, it looks as if she didn't know what she was about!

(*After she has said this they look at each other, then start to glance back at the door. After an instant Mrs. Hale has pulled at a knot and ripped the sewing.*)

Mrs. Peters.   Oh, what are you doing, Mrs. Hale?

Mrs. Hale (*mildly*).   Just pulling out a stitch or two that's not sewed very good. (*Threading a needle.*) Bad sewing always made me fidgety.

Mrs. Peters (*with a glance at door, nervously*).   I don't think we ought to touch things.

Mrs. Hale.   I'll just finish up this end. (*Suddenly stopping and leaning forward.*) Mrs. Peters?

Mrs. Peters.   Yes, Mrs. Hale?

Mrs. Hale.   What do you suppose she was so nervous about?

Mrs. Peters.   Oh—I don't know. I don't know as she was nervous. I sometimes sew awful queer when I'm just tired. (*Mrs. Hale starts to say something, looks at Mrs. Peters, then goes on sewing.*) Well, I must get these things wrapped up. They may be through sooner than we think. (*Putting apron and other things together.*) I wonder where I can find a piece of paper, and string.

(*Rises.*)

Mrs. Hale.   In that cupboard, maybe.

Mrs. Peters (*crosses right looking in cupboard*).   Why, here's a bird-cage. (*Holds it up.*) Did she have a bird, Mrs. Hale?

Mrs. Hale.   Why, I don't know whether she did or not—I've not been here for so long. There was a man around last year selling canaries cheap, but I don't know as she took one; maybe she did. She used to sing real pretty herself.

Mrs. Peters (*glancing around*).   Seems funny to think of a bird here. But she must have had one, or why would she have a cage? I wonder what happened to it?

Mrs. Hale.   I s'pose maybe the cat got it.

Mrs. Peters.   No, she didn't have a cat. She's got that feeling some people have about cats—being afraid of them. My cat got in her room and she was real upset and asked me to take it out.

Mrs. Hale.   My sister Bessie was like that. Queer, ain't it?

Mrs. Peters (*examining the cage*).   Why, look at this door. It's broke. One hinge is pulled apart.

(*Takes a step down to Mrs. Hale's right.*)

Mrs. Hale (*looking too*).   Looks as if someone must have been rough with it.

Mrs. Peters.   Why, yes.

(*She brings the cage forward and puts it on the table.*)

Mrs. Hale (*glancing toward up left door*).   I wish if they're going to find any evidence they'd be about it. I don't like this place.

Mrs. Peters.   But I'm awful glad you came with me, Mrs. Hale. It would be lonesome for me sitting here alone.

Mrs. Hale.   It would, wouldn't it? (*Dropping her sewing.*) But I tell you what I do wish, Mrs. Peters. I wish I had come over sometimes when *she* was here. I—(*looking around the room*)—wish I had.

Mrs. Peters.   But of course you were awful busy, Mrs. Hale—your house and your children.

Mrs. Hale (*rises and crosses left*).   I could've come. I stayed away because it weren't cheerful—and that's why I ought to have come. I—(*looking out left window*)—I've never liked this place. Maybe because it's down in a hollow and you don't see the road. I dunno what it is, but it's a lonesome place and always was. I wish I had come over to see Minnie Foster sometimes. I can see now—

(*Shakes her head.*)

Mrs. Peters (*left of table and above it*).   Well, you mustn't reproach yourself, Mrs. Hale. Somehow we just don't see how it is with other folks until—something turns up.

Mrs. Hale.   Not having children makes less work—but it makes a quiet house, and Wright out to work all day, and no company when he did come in. (*Turning from window.*) Did you know John Wright, Mrs. Peters?

Mrs. Peters.   Not to know him; I've seen him in town. They say he was a good man.

Mrs. Hale.   Yes—good; he didn't drink, and kept his word as well as most, I guess, and paid his debts. But he was a hard man, Mrs. Peters. Just to pass the time of day with him—(*Shivers.*) Like a raw wind that gets to the bone.

(Pauses, her eye falling on the cage.) I should think she would 'a' wanted a bird. But what do you suppose went with it?

Mrs. Peters.   I don't know, unless it got sick and died.

(She reaches over and swings the broken door, swings it again, both women watch it.)

Mrs. Hale.   You weren't raised round here, were you? *(Mrs. Peters shakes her head.)* You didn't know—her?

Mrs. Peters.   Not till they brought her yesterday.

Mrs. Hale.   She—come to think of it, she was kind of like a bird herself—real sweet and pretty, but kind of timid and—fluttery. How—she—did—change. *(Silence: then as if struck by a happy thought and relieved to get back to everyday things. Crosses right above Mrs. Peters to cupboard, replaces small chair used to stand on to its original place down right.)* Tell you what, Mrs. Peters, why don't you take the quilt in with you? It might take up her mind.

Mrs. Peters.   Why, I think that's a real nice idea, Mrs. Hale. There couldn't possibly be any objection to it could there? Now, just what would I take? I wonder if her patches are in here—and her things.

(They look in the sewing basket.)

Mrs. Hale *(crosses to right of table)*.   Here's some red. I expect this has got sewing things in it. *(Brings out a fancy box.)* What a pretty box. Looks like something somebody would give you. Maybe her scissors are in here. *(Opens box. Suddenly puts her hand to her nose.)* Why————*(Mrs. Peters bends nearer, then turns her face away.)* There's something wrapped up in this piece of silk.

Mrs. Peters.   Why, this isn't her scissors.

Mrs. Hale *(lifting the silk)*.   Oh, Mrs. Peters—it's————

(Mrs. Peters bends closer.)

Mrs. Peters.   It's the bird.

Mrs. Hale.   But, Mrs. Peters—look at it! Its neck! Look at its neck! It's all— other side *to*.

Mrs. Peters.   Somebody—wrung—its—neck.

(Their eyes meet. A look of growing comprehension, of horror. Steps are heard outside. Mrs. Hale slips box under quilt pieces, and sinks into her chair. Enter Sheriff and County Attorney. Mrs. Peters steps down left and stands looking out of window.)

County Attorney *(as one turning from serious things to little pleasantries)*.   Well, ladies, have you decided whether she was going to quilt it or knot it?

(Crosses to center above table.)

Mrs. Peters.   We think she was going to—knot it.

(Sheriff crosses to right of stove, lifts stove lid, and glances at fire, then stands warming hands at stove.)

County Attorney.   Well, that's interesting, I'm sure. *(Seeing the bird-cage.)* Has the bird flown?
Mrs. Hale *(putting more quilt pieces over the box).*   We think the—cat got it.
County Attorney *(preoccupied).*   Is there a cat?

(Mrs. Hale glances in a quick covert way at Mrs. Peters.)

Mrs. Peters *(turning from window takes a step in).*   Well, not *now*. They're superstitious, you know. They leave.
County Attorney *(to Sheriff Peters, continuing an interrupted conversation).* No sign at all of anyone having come from the outside. Their own rope. Now let's go up again and go over it piece by piece. *(They start upstairs.)* It would have to have been someone who knew just the———

(Mrs. Peters sits down left of table. The two women sit there not looking at one another, but as if peering into something and at the same time holding back. When they talk now it is in the manner of feeling their way over strange ground, as if afraid of what they are saying, but as if they cannot help saying it.)

Mrs. Hale *(hesitatively and in hushed voice).*   She liked the bird. She was going to bury it in that pretty box.
Mrs. Peters *(in a whisper).*   When I was a girl—my kitten—there was a boy took a hatchet, and before my eyes—and before I could get there——— *(Covers her face an instant.)* If they hadn't held me back I would have— *(catches herself, looks upstairs where steps are heard, falters weakly)*—hurt him.
Mrs. Hale *(with a slow look around her).*   I wonder how it would seem never to have had any children around. *(Pause.)* No, Wright wouldn't like the bird—a thing that sang. She used to sing. He killed that, too.
Mrs. Peters *(moving uneasily).*   We don't know who killed the bird.
Mrs. Hale.   I knew John Wright.
Mrs. Peters.   It was an awful thing was done in this house that night, Mrs. Hale. Killing a man while he slept, slipping a rope around his neck that choked the life out of him.
Mrs. Hale.   His neck. Choked the life out of him.

(Her hand goes out and rests on the bird-cage.)

Mrs. Peters (*with rising voice*). We don't know who killed him. We don't know.

Mrs. Hale (*her own feeling not interrupted*). If there'd been years and years of nothing, then a bird to sing to you, it would be awful—still, after the bird was still.

Mrs. Peters (*something within her speaking*). I know what stillness is. When we homesteaded in Dakota, and my first baby died—after he was two years old, and me with no other then———

Mrs. Hale (*moving*). How soon do you suppose they'll be through looking for the evidence?

Mrs. Peters. I know what stillness is. (*Pulling herself back.*) The law has got to punish crime, Mrs. Hale.

Mrs. Hale (*not as if answering that*). I wish you'd seen Minnie Foster when she wore a white dress with blue ribbons and stood up there in the choir and sang. (*A look around the room.*) Oh, I *wish* I'd come over here once in a while! That was a crime! That was a crime! Who's going to punish that?

Mrs. Peters (*looking upstairs*). We mustn't—take on.

Mrs. Hale. I might have known she needed help! I know how things can be— for women. I tell you, it's queer, Mrs. Peters. We live close together and we live far apart. We all go through the same things—it's all just a different kind of the same thing. (*Brushes her eyes, noticing the jar of fruit, reaches out for it.*) If I was you I wouldn't tell her her fruit was gone. Tell her it *ain't*. Tell her it's all right. Take this in to prove it to her. She—she may never know whether it was broke or not.

Mrs. Peters (*takes the jar, looks about for something to wrap it in; takes petticoat from the clothes brought from the other room, very nervously begins winding this around the jar. In a false voice*). My, it's a good thing the men couldn't hear us. Wouldn't they just laugh! Getting all stirred up over a little thing like a—dead canary. As if that could have anything to do with—with— wouldn't they *laugh*!

(*The men are heard coming downstairs.*)

Mrs. Hale (*under her breath*). Maybe they would—maybe they wouldn't.

County Attorney. No, Peters, it's all perfectly clear except a reason for doing it. But you know juries when it comes to women. If there was some definite thing. (*Crosses slowly to above table. Sheriff crosses down right. Mrs. Hale and Mrs. Peters remain seated at either side of table.*) Something to show— something to make a story about—a thing that would connect up with this strange way of doing it———

(*The women's eyes meet for an instant. Enter Hale from outer door.*)

Hale (*remaining by door*). Well, I've got the team around. Pretty cold out there.

County Attorney. I'm going to stay awhile by myself. *(To the Sheriff.)* You can send Frank out for me, can't you? I want to go over everything. I'm not satisfied that we can't do better.

Sheriff. Do you want to see what Mrs. Peters is going to take in?

(The Lawyer picks up the apron, laughs.)

County Attorney. Oh, I guess they're not very dangerous things the ladies have picked out. *(Moves a few things about, disturbing the quilt pieces which cover the box. Steps back.)* No, Mrs. Peters doesn't need supervising. For that matter a sheriff's wife is married to the law. Ever think of it that way, Mrs. Peters?

Mrs. Peters. Not—just that way.

Sheriff *(chuckling).* Married to the law. *(Moves to down right door to the other room.)* I just want you to come in here a minute, George. We ought to take a look at these windows.

County Attorney *(scoffingly).* Oh, windows!

Sheriff. We'll be right out, Mr. Hale.

(Hale goes outside. The Sheriff follows the County Attorney into the room. Then Mrs. Hale rises, hands tight together, looking intensely at Mrs. Peters, whose eyes make a slow turn, finally meeting Mrs. Hale's. A moment Mrs. Hale holds her, then her own eyes point the way to where the box is concealed. Suddenly Mrs. Peters throws back quilt pieces and tries to put the box in the bag she is carrying. It is too big. She opens box, starts to take bird out, cannot touch it, goes to pieces, stands there helpless. Sound of a knob turning in the other room. Mrs. Hale snatches the box and puts it in the pocket of her big coat. Enter County Attorney and Sheriff, who remain down right.)

County Attorney *(crosses to up left door facetiously).* Well, Henry, at least we found out that she was not going to quilt it. She was going to—what is it you call it, ladies?

Mrs. Hale *(standing center below table facing front, her hand against her pocket).* We call it—knot it, Mr. Henderson.

Curtain.

For Analysis

1. What is the meaning of the title? Glaspell titled a short-story version of the play "A Jury of Her Peers." Is that a better title than *Trifles*? **2.** What are the major differences between Mrs. Hale and Mrs. Peters? **3.** At one point, Mrs. Peters tells Mrs. Hale a childhood story about a boy who killed her cat. Why is she reminded of this story? What does it tell us about her reaction to the Wrights' marriage? **4.** Which of the two women undergoes the most noticeable character development? **5.** In what ways do the relationships between the two couples—Mrs. Hale and Mrs. Peters, and Henry Peters and Lewis Hale—change by the end of the play? **6.** Do Henry Peters and Lewis Hale change in the course of the play? **7.** Why are the men unable to see the clues that become obvious to the women? **8.** Can you suggest why Mrs. Wright is the only one identified by her birth name?

On Style

1. What does Glaspell gain by **setting** this drama in rural (rather than urban) America? **2.** Are the bird cage and the quilt effective as **symbols**? **3.** Analyze the bird cage and quilt in this play and the tarantella dance and the party in Henrik Ibsen's *A Doll's House* (p. 492) as symbols that capture an important **theme** in each play.

Making Connections

1. What similarities in attitudes toward women do you find in this play, in Ibsen's *A Doll's House* (p. 492), in Alice Childress's *Wine in the Wilderness* (p. 262), and in August Wilson's *Two Trains Running* (p. 565)? **2.** Do you think it is fair to say that Mrs. Wright in this play and Laura in Tennessee Williams's *The Glass Menagerie* (p. 209) are people whose lives have been blighted by a patriarchal society that confines women to narrow, stereotypical roles?

Writing Topics

1. Show how the discussion of Minnie Wright's quilt embodies the major **themes** of *Trifles*. **2.** Argue for or against the proposition that Mrs. Hale and Mrs. Peters are morally obligated to tell the County Attorney what they know about the murder. **3.** Write a one-page essay using *Trifles* to define realistic drama and Sophocles' *Antigonê* (p. 460) as the basis for defining poetic drama.

August Wilson   [b. 1945]

Two Trains Running   1990
This one's for Judy

> *If the train don't hurry there's gonna be some walking done.*
> Traditional

The Setting

It is Pittsburgh, 1969. The action of the play takes place in a restaurant across the street from West's Funeral Home and Lutz's Meat Market. It is a small restaurant with four stools, a counter, and three booths lined against one wall. The menu is printed on a blackboard behind the counter.

Act I

Scene 1

(The lights come up on the restaurant. The menu reads
> *"Beans w/corn muffins 65 cents*
> *Chicken w/2 sides $2.45*
> *Meatloaf w/2 sides $2.35*
> *Sides—Collard greens*
> > *Mashed potatoes*
> > *Green beans*
> > *Macaroni & cheese*
> > *Potato salad"*

The winning number combination of the previous day, 651, is also written on the menu board. Wolf is in the telephone booth. He comes out, shuffles some papers, and starts to his seat at the counter when the phone rings. He answers it just as Memphis enters from the back carrying a newspaper. Memphis is a self-made man whose values of hard work, diligence, persistence, and honesty have been consistently challenged by the circumstances of his life. His greatest asset is his impeccable logic. Wolf, on the phone, writes something down.)

Wolf.   Wolf. . . . Eight sixty-four. Boxed for a dollar . . . Yeah, I got that.

Memphis. Hey, Wolf, I told you about that. You can't be tying up my phone with them numbers.[1]

Wolf. Seven thirty-one straight . . . for a dollar. Okay.

(He hangs up and exits the phone booth. He is a man who enjoys his notoriety and popularity as the community's numbers runner. While he manages to keep money in his pocket and a decent pair of shoes on his feet, his inability to find secure female companionship is the single failure that marks his life.)

Memphis. I told you about tying up my phone with them numbers. I don't want that in here.

Wolf. Who's trying to call you? Risa will tell you . . . ain't nobody trying to call you.

Memphis. My lawyer might be trying to call me.

Wolf. That's what happened to Harvey before he got them ten years. He sitting around waiting for his lawyer to call him. If I was him I would have been in Cleveland or Detroit. Naw, he wanna sit around and wait on his lawyer to call him.

Memphis. This a civil lawyer. There's more than one kind of lawyer. But you don't know nothing about that.

Wolf. I know there's different kinds of lawyers. The NAACP[2] got all kinds of lawyers. It don't do nobody no good.

(He calls out.)

Hey, Risa, give me some sugar.

Memphis. That's the second time this week that six fifty-one hit. I don't know the last time I can recall a number coming twice in the same week. That was L.D.'s number. If he was still living he'd be in big money.

Wolf. They had that six ninety-four come twice about a year ago. Milt hit for five dollars both times. Got mad cause he didn't have twenty dollars on it.

(He calls.)

Let me get some sugar, Risa.

(Risa enters from the back. Risa is a young woman who, in an attempt to define herself in terms other than her genitalia, has scarred her legs with a razor.)

---

[1] The numbers game is an illegal lottery. [2] The National Association for the Advancement of Colored People (NAACP), founded in 1910, is one of the oldest groups in the United States devoted to the cause of equality for African Americans.

Memphis.   I remember that. I had six ninety-six. I switched off to six ninety-two and it come back six ninety-four. I remember that. You talk about Milt being mad.

Risa.   I don't know why people waste their money playing numbers. Time you hit you just getting back what you put in.

Wolf.   It's the same thing as putting money in the bank. This way you might take out more than you put in . . . but Mellon ain't gonna let you do that. The numbers give you an opportunity. If it wasn't for the numbers all these niggers would be poor.

Memphis.   It wasn't till I hit the numbers eight or nine years ago that I got to the point where I could change my clothes every day. See, most of these niggers around here can't do that. The only way they can do that is to hit the numbers or get lucky in a crap game. The ones that working . . . the only way they can do anything is to wait on their income tax return. Half the time the government cheat them out of that.

Wolf.   You hear from your old lady, Memphis?

Memphis.   Don't bring up that woman to me. I ain't heard from her. I know where she at. She up her sister's house. She been up there two months since she left. Twenty-two years. I give her everything I had for twenty-two years. Naw . . . naw . . . I give her everything I had when I met her . . . then I give her everything I could get hold of for the next twenty-two years. And then when she was leaving . . . she wouldn't even shake my hand.

Wolf.   I know how that go. That's why I don't mess with these women but so far.

Memphis.   I ain't never left nobody in bad manners. I'm standing there trying to say, "May God bless you everywhere you go" . . . and she wouldn't even shake my hand.

Risa.   Maybe she didn't like the way you was treating her.

Memphis.   I treat that woman like she was a queen. Treat her like she made out of gold. Try to give her everything she want. She say "Baby, I want a car," she got a Cadillac. She want a TV . . . she got a color TV. It might take me a little while. Her wants might be too big for my pocket but I work it out and come up with something. I was working on the dishwasher when she walked out. I would have got her that but the plumbing got to be right. I'm talking to John D. about him fixing up the plumbing . . . and she got up and walked out the door. You talking about she tired of the way I treated her. I treated that woman like she was the Queen of Sheba.

Risa.   Maybe she don't see it like that. She had to leave for something.

Memphis.   I ain't done nothing but ask her to get up and make me some bread. And she got up and walked out the door. I know she don't expect me to make it myself. Got up and walked out the door! I went down there and saw her. Asked her what the matter was. She told me she was tired. Now, how you gonna get more tired than I am? I'm the one going out there wrestling with the world. She ain't got to do nothing but stay home and take care of the house. She got it nice. Talking about she tired. She wasn't too tired to make them four babies.

(*Holloway enters. Holloway is a man who all his life has voiced his outrage at injustice with little effect. His belief in the supernatural has enabled him to accept his inability to effect change and continue to pursue life with zest and vigor.*)

Holloway.   Hey, Wolf.

Wolf.   What's happening, Holloway?

Holloway.   The people lined up all the way up there past Webster to see Prophet Samuel. They was lined up there before the doors open. West ain't had a chance to open his door good before they was all tramping through there. They got a line all the way up past Webster. They done had two fellows get in a fight about gypping the line.

Wolf.   Where?

Holloway.   Just now as I was coming down. Man tried to slide in there beside somebody he knew and got in a fight about it.

Wolf.   I knew it was gonna be crowded. I didn't know they would be lined up.

Holloway.   Lined clear up to Webster. It take you an hour to get in there to see him.

Wolf.   They say how he died?

Memphis.   Ask Risa. She should know. She running up there giving the man her money.

Holloway.   They say he had a stroke.

Memphis.   I believe one of them old sandal-foot woman poisoned him. I wouldn't be a bit surprised. Got all them women walking around his house together . . . I wouldn't be a bit surprised if one of them didn't get jealous and poison him.

Holloway.   They over there now greeting the people and falling all over the place. All seven or eight of them. West can't wait to bury that nigger. One of them wanted to charge the people to see him, but West wouldn't have that over there. You think I'm lying, don't you? They had a little basket they put over there right by the casket. They was charging people a dollar to see him before West put a stop to it.

Memphis.   When they gonna bury him?

Wolf.   Tuesday. They say they gonna bury him Tuesday.

Holloway.   They gonna try and bury him Tuesday. West ain't gonna bury him until the people got a chance to see him.

Wolf.   They say he got hundred-dollar bills in the casket with him.

Holloway.   He got hundred-dollar bills . . . got diamonds on all his fingers. They got it roped off. You can't get within ten feet of the casket. He got gold and jewels and everything in there with him.

Wolf.   What . . . they supposed to bury him with all that money?

Memphis.   West ain't gonna bury that man with that money. West ain't no fool. You think he gonna put money and diamonds and all that gold in the ground? Half the time he don't even put the casket. Half the time he dump the body out and bring the casket back to sell it again. Bury somebody else in it.

Risa. West don't be doing that. That's against the law.

Holloway. West done buried four or five niggers in the same suit. How you think he got all that money?

Wolf. Who would you say had the most money—West or Prophet Samuel?

Holloway. Everybody know West got money. He get more business. More people dying than getting saved.

Wolf. Prophet Samuel got a lot of money. He right up there with West. He be cheating and fooling the people all these years.

Risa. He ain't done nothing but tell the truth. Most times people don't want to hear the truth. But Prophet Samuel say the truth ain't nothing to be afraid of. He say if you afraid of the truth to get back in the shadows cause you never will see the light.

Wolf. I ain't said all that. I just said he right up there with West when it comes to money. All them jewels and things he had. That big old white Cadillac. Seven or eight women. He was living a nice life.

Memphis. He ain't got nothing now. He ain't got as much as you got. And I don't believe he had as much money as West. West got money he ain't even counted.

Wolf. How much money would you say he got?

Holloway. West got a million dollars. Got it two or three times.

Memphis. And don't know how to spend it. Man living up over top of the funeral home—you'd think he'd have enough sense to buy him a house somewhere. He own every other building around here. Them that Hartzberger don't own. I got lucky and got hold to this piece of building and West got mad. I got it right out from under his nose and he ain't never forget that. All that property he own and had the nerve to get mad when I bought this. What make it so bad is he could have had it. He was talking to L.D. about buying the building from him. L.D. had his stroke and West figured he'd wait until he died and get it cheaper. I went over to the hospital to see him and we made the deal right there in the hospital about a week before he died. I got it for fifty-five hundred dollars. This is when I was walking around with four or five hundred dollars in my pocket every day. Used to carry a pistol and everything. Had me a .44. Had me one of them big .44s. Used to scare me to look at it. I give L.D. the fifty-five hundred in cash. I didn't find out till after he died that he owed twelve hundred dollars in back taxes . . . but I didn't care. I had seen a way for me to take off my pistol. I got my deed and went right home . . . took off my pistol and hung it up in the closet. West got mad when he found out L.D. sold me the building. He been trying to buy it from me ever since. He walked in the next day and offered me eight thousand dollars for it. That was a good price. But see . . . he didn't know it had come to mean more to me than that. I had found a way to live the rest of my life.

Wolf. When they gonna tear it down?

Holloway. You know how the city is. They been gonna tear this whole block down for the last twenty years.

Memphis. They told me to be downtown Tuesday. They liable to wait another twenty years before they tear it down, but I'm supposed to be down there Tuesday and find out how much they gonna give me.

Wolf. What you gonna do when they tear it down?

Memphis. Ain't nothing to do. Unless I do like West and go into the undertaking business. I can't go out there in Squirrel Hill and open up a restaurant. Ain't nothing gonna be left around here. Supermarket gone. Two drugstores. The five and ten. Doctor done moved out. Dentist done moved out. Shoe store gone. Ain't nothing gonna be left but these niggers killing one another. That don't never go out of style. West gonna get richer and everybody else gonna get poorer. At one time you couldn't get a seat in here. Had the jukebox working and everything. Time somebody get up somebody sit down before they could get out the door. People coming from everywhere. Everybody got to eat and everybody got to sleep. Some people don't have stoves. Some people don't have nobody to cook for them. Men whose wives done died and left them. Cook for them thirty years and lay down and die. Who's gonna cook for them now? Somebody got to do it. I order four cases of chicken on Friday and Sunday it's gone. Fry it up. Make a stew. Boil it. Add some dumplings. You couldn't charge more than a dollar. But then you didn't have to. It didn't cost you but a quarter. People used to come from all over. The man used to come twice a week to collect the jukebox. He making more money than I am. He pay seventy-five cents for the record and he make two hundred dollars off it. If it's a big hit he's liable to make four hundred. The record will take all the quarters you can give it. It don't never wear out. The chicken be gone by Sunday. It ain't nothing like that now. I'm lucky if I go through a case a chicken a week. That's alright. I'll take that. I ain't greedy. But if they wanna tear it down they gonna have to meet my price.

Wolf. They ought to give you a good price. That's what I hear . . . when the city buy something they give you a good price.

Memphis. They give white folks a good price. Most time that be who they buying it from. Well, they gonna give me just like they give them. I bought it eight years ago for fifty-five hundred dollars and I ain't taking a penny less than twenty-five thousand.

Wolf. You ought to be able to get that.

Memphis. Let me get a dollar on that seven sixty-four. If that come out that'll hold me till the city do their paperwork. If that come out I might buy me a new pair of shoes. I ain't going to be like West. West been wearing the same pair of shoes for three years. Got the heels all run over and everything. He do keep them shined. I'll say that for him. I ain't never seen him without his shoes shined.

Wolf. I ain't never seen him without them gloves. He wear them gloves everywhere. I believe he wear them to bed. I hear tell he got a wooden hand.

Holloway. West ain't got no wooden hand. He be touching them dead people . . . I'd wear gloves too.

Wolf.   He can take them off and wash his hands. He don't be touching them all the time. I ain't never seen him without them gloves. I ain't never seen him in nothing but black. Everything he wear is black. Black hat. Black suit. Black shoes. Black tie. The only thing he wear is that white shirt. Everything else is black.

Holloway.   That's what he supposed to wear. All undertakers wear black. What it look like if he showed up to bury somebody in a red suit? They supposed to wear black.

Wolf.   He do make them bodies look good. Make them look natural.

Memphis.   People kill me with that. How somebody dead gonna look natural?

Wolf.   That's what the people say. Say they look better than when they was living. That's why the people like West.

Holloway.   The people like West cause he get the cars there on time. He say he be there to pick you up at one o'clock . . . that's what time he come. He be real nice and polite—it's "No sir" and "Yes ma'am." "Watch your step." "Can I get you some water?" The people like that. You even act like you want to faint and West will be right there at your elbow.

Memphis.   He do all that after he got the money.

Holloway.   Quite naturally he gonna get the money first.

Memphis.   You go over there looking for a pine box and walk out with a five-thousand-dollar silver, satin-lined casket, guaranteed to be leak-proof. That's what get me. For an extra hundred dollars he give you a twenty-year guarantee that the casket ain't gonna leak and let the water seep in. Now how dumb can anybody get? You gonna dig up the casket twenty years later to see if it's leaking and go back and tell West and get your hundred dollars back? The first time it rain the water's liable to drown the corpse. You don't know. Yet you be surprised at the number of people come out of there talking about their twenty-year guarantee. Then if that ain't enough he charge you another hundred dollars to get a casket that lock. Like somebody gonna go down there and steal the body if it ain't locked up. Yet they come out of there clutching this little key he give them. West the only nigger I know who can cheat and rob the people and they be happy to see him. Calling him "Mr. West." "How you doing, Mr. West?" "Have a nice day, Mr. West." "Good to see you, Mr. West." He done cheated them out of four or five hundred dollars and they talking about "Have a nice day, Mr. West."

Wolf.   I don't want West to bury me. I'll go anywhere else. Charles. McTurner. Harris. I'll let anybody bury me but West. Hell, I'm liable to do like the white folks do and get cremated.

Memphis.   What you got against West?

Wolf.   I ain't got nothing against him. I just don't want him standing over me when I'm dead. I'd rather have a stranger standing over me.

Holloway.   You ain't gonna know nothing about it. What you care who be standing over top of you? You talk foolish. West don't care nothing about you. The last person West buried that he cared about was his wife. He don't care nothing about you. You just be another dead nigger to him. I doubt if West can tell one nigger from another. Man got four or five viewing rooms and don't have no trouble keeping somebody in all of them. I remember one time he had two niggers laid out in the hallway and one on the back porch. Most of them had welfare caskets, but West don't care cause the government pay on time. He might have to worry his money out of some of them other niggers, but the government pay quicker than the insurance companies.

Memphis.   Wasn't nothing but a pine box with some cloth stretched over it. That's what the welfare casket was.

Wolf.   They ain't changed. That's what they is now.

(Hambone enters. He is in his late forties. He is self-contained and in a world of his own. His mental condition has deteriorated to such a point that he can only say two phrases, and he repeats them idiotically over and over.)

Hambone.   He gonna give me my ham. He gonna give me my ham. I want my ham. He gonna give me my ham.

Risa.   Hambone, where you been? What I tell you? It don't matter whether you got any money or not . . . you come and get something to eat. You hear?

Hambone.   He gonna give me my ham. He gonna give me my ham.

Risa.   How you been? You been doing alright?

(Risa fixes him a bowl of beans and some corn bread. She sets it in front of him.)

Hambone.   He gonna give me my ham. He gonna give me my ham.

Risa.   You go on and eat. I got something for you.

(Risa exits into the back.)

Hambone.   He gonna give me my ham.

Memphis.   Alright, that's enough of that now!

Hambone *(under his breath).*   I want my ham. He gonna give me my ham.

(Risa comes out with a wool sport coat. She gives it to Hambone.)

Risa.   Here . . . put this on. It be cold out there sometimes at night. You button it up too.

Wolf.   Risa, you been over to see Prophet Samuel yet? I know you going over.

Risa.   I ain't going. I don't want to see him like that.

Memphis.   Risa been around here crying for two days. I tried to tell her the man got to die sometime.

Wolf.   Ain't nothing to it. Ain't nothing but a dead body laying up there.

Risa.   That's what I know. That's why I don't want to go.

Wolf.   Ain't nothing to be scared of. I done seen a whole bunch of dead niggers.

Memphis.   You around here following the man. Running up there giving the man your money, talking about Prophet Samuel this, Prophet Samuel that . . . and now you don't want to go pay your respect.

Wolf.   Risa . . . I'll go over with you any time you wanna go. Here . . . put that in the jukebox.

(He hands Risa two quarters.)

Risa.   It's broke.

Wolf.   I thought it was just fixed. Memphis, I thought you was gonna get you a new jukebox.

Memphis.   I told Zanelli to bring me a new one. That what he say he gonna do. He been saying that for the last year. *(Pause.)* Risa, get on back there and get that chicken ready, you ain't got time to be standing around.

(Risa exits into the back. Memphis takes his papers and goes to the booth.)

(Sterling enters. He is a young man of thirty. He wears a suit and a dress shirt without a tie, along with a straw hat that is out of style. He has been out of the penitentiary for one week and the suit is his prison issue. Sterling appears at times to be unbalanced, but it is a combination of his unorthodox logic and straightforward manner that makes him appear so.)

Memphis *(calling).*   Hey, Risa.

(Risa enters from the back.)

Risa.   What?

Memphis.   What you mean, "What?"? You see the man sitting there. Wait on him. That's what you here for.

Risa.   I was trying to clean the chicken.

Memphis.   The man want to eat now. He ain't thinking about you cleaning no chicken.

Risa.   We ain't got no chicken. And we ain't got no meat loaf. We ain't got no hamburger either. We just got beans and corn bread.

Memphis.   You got some hamburger back there.

Risa.   It's all frozen.

Memphis.   Well, take it out the freezer, thaw it out. Don't tell the man you ain't got none. Tell him you forgot to thaw it out.

Risa.   You want some beans?

Sterling.   That's all you got is beans? I don't want no beans. I been eating beans for five years. You got a great big sign out there say "restaurant" and you ain't got no food. Where your menu? You got a menu? What that say up there? Meat loaf with greens and mash potatoes. Give me some meat loaf. Some collard greens. You got all that sign out there say home-style cooking. Where the food at?

Memphis. You got to come back, I ain't went shopping yet. She have some chicken in a minute. Risa, go on back in there and get on that chicken. You been back there for a half hour and ain't even got the grease in the pan.

(to Sterling.)

She'll fry you up some chicken in a minute. She got the rice on.
Risa. I told you ain't but a half a box of rice.
Memphis. Well, cook that up. That's better than nothing.
Sterling. You ought to put a sign out there. Say "Gone shopping." Say, baby, give me a cup of coffee.
Memphis. Go on and give him some coffee and get on back to frying up that chicken before somebody else come in here.
Risa. You want cream?
Sterling. I like it black.

(Risa pours him a coffee.)

Oh, I know you. I know who you are.
Risa. Oh, yeah?
Sterling. You Rodney's sister. What happened? Where you get them hips from? You used to be a little skinny old thing. You don't remember me? Sterling Johnson. Used to be with Rodney all the time? You don't remember me? That's alright, I remember you.
Memphis. Risa, get on back there and get to work. You ain't got time to be standing around talking.
Sterling. This an old friend of mine. I knew her before you did. Her name is Clarissa Thomas. She got a brother named Rodney.
Memphis. I don't care how long you known her. She working now. She can't be standing around talking. She got things to do.
Sterling. Say, baby, if you get fired I can't take care of you. I'm trying to find a job myself. I just got out the penitentiary.
Risa. I ain't worried about getting fired.
Sterling. Where's Rodney staying? I kinda got out of touch with him.
Risa. He moved to Cleveland. He said he had to get out of Pittsburgh before he kill somebody.
Sterling. Me and him had some fun times together. You remember I used to come up to the house and eat all the time? That was you that was doing all the cooking. Rodney say, "Come on, man, my sister got something to eat." Then we used to come up there. You used to be skinny.
Risa. I wasn't all that skinny.
Sterling. I don't know how skinny you were but you sure grown up now. What's your phone number?
Risa. I ain't got none.
Sterling. Well, what's the address? If I can't walk I'll crawl up there.

Memphis. Risa, get on back there and get that chicken fried up so you can go get West his pie before he be over here.

Risa. I'm frying it!

(Risa exits into the back.)

Sterling *(almost to himself)*. Seem like to me if you come to work all the time and can't talk to nobody, then I don't know who would want that job. It's like being in school with somebody always telling you what to do.

(To Wolf.)

How you doing? I seen you down at Irv's.

Wolf. Yeah, I be down there sometimes.

Sterling. I just got out the penitentiary. I was down at Irv's yesterday. But I figure I hang out down there I'll be right back down the penitentiary. I don't want that. I'm trying to find a job. You know where I can get a job? Anybody know where I can get a job at?

Holloway. What kind of job you looking for?

Sterling. Any kind. I can do anything.

Wolf. Go up and see Hendricks. He got a construction company.

Sterling. That's who I was working for. He helped me get out the penitentiary. I work for him one week and he laid me off, say he ain't enough business to keep me working. He say he'd call me if he had any work for me.

Memphis. Go on over the steel mill. A big strong boy like you . . . if you ain't scared of work . . . they got work over there.

Sterling. That's what Hendricks told me. I went over to J&L Steel and they told me I got to join the union before I could work. I went down to the union and they told me I got to be working before I could join the union. They told me to go back to the steel mill and they'd put me on a waiting list. I went and asked my landlady if I could put her on a waiting list. She told me if I didn't give her twelve dollars by Friday I could wait on the street.

Holloway. You can go up to Boykins and see if he need anybody. You know Boykins up on Herron what got that junkyard? He always complaining he can't keep nobody. That's probably cause he don't pay nothing. But you can go up there and see him.

Sterling. I ain't got nothing to lose. I'll go up there. Thanks. Anybody want to buy a watch?

(He doesn't get any response.)

I carried it up to the pawnshop . . . he didn't want it either. It got seventeen jewels. That's what it say right here. I don't know what kind of jewels they are . . . they don't tell you that part. It's liable to be anything. You open it up it's liable to be diamonds and rubies, I don't know. I started to do that, but I didn't know if I could put it back together. You take something apart you should know how to put it back together. Seventeen jewels! And I can't get five dollars for it.

(To Wolf.)

I'll let you have it for three dollars.

Wolf.   I can't use it.

Sterling *(holding the watch out to Memphis and Holloway).*   Three dollars?

(He doesn't get a response.)

That's alright, I'm gonna keep it. I'm gonna keep it till it stop ticking. Whenever you see me I'm gonna have on this watch.

Wolf.   Well, let me get on and make my day. I'll see you all later. Hey, Risa . . . keep smiling, baby.

(Wolf exits.)

Sterling *(looking out the window).*   They got so many people lined up across the street I thought it was the surplus food line. I'm gonna go over and get in line with everybody else. Get my luck changed.

(To Holloway.)

You believe in luck? I was born with it. I was born with seven cents. My mama swallowed a nickel and two pennies and I come out with the nickel in one hand and the two pennies in the other. They say I was born with luck but they didn't say what kind. I think it was bad luck. What you think?

(Risa enters from the back.)
(To Risa.)

Say, baby, give me another cup of coffee.

(To Holloway.)

You been over there to see Prophet Samuel?

Holloway.   Yeah, I done seen him.

Sterling.   I was over there talking to one man he say if you rub his head you get good luck. One man found twenty dollars on the sidewalk on his way out. I'm going over there. Might go through the line twice. Have double luck. That might not even be enough the way things is going. Might have to go through there three times.

Holloway.   These niggers lining up over there to rub Prophet Samuel's head cause they think that's gonna make their hand itch and they gonna get some money. They don't know to go see Aunt Ester. Aunt Ester give you more than money. She make you right with yourself. You ain't got to go far. She live at eighteen thirty-nine Wylie. In the back. Go up there and you'll see a red door. Go up there and knock on that.

Hambone (*suddenly*). I want my ham. I want my ham.

Holloway. Aunt Ester got a power cause she got an understanding. Anybody live as long as she has is bound to have an understanding.

Hambone. He gonna give me my ham. I want my ham.

Sterling. Somebody got his ham.

(*To Hambone.*)

Who got your ham, man? Somebody took your ham?

Holloway. He talking about Lutz across the street. He painted his fence for him nine . . . almost ten years ago, and Lutz told him he'd give him a ham. After he painted the fence Lutz told him to take a chicken. He say he wanted his ham. Lutz told him to take a chicken or don't take nothing. So he wait over there every morning till Lutz come to open his store and he tell him he wants his ham. He ain't got it yet.

Memphis. That ain't how it went. Lutz told him if he painted his fence he'd give him a chicken. Told him if he do a good job he'd give him a ham. He think he did a good job and Lutz didn't. That's where he went wrong—letting Lutz decide what to pay him for his work. If you leave it like that, quite naturally he gonna say it ain't worth the higher price.

Hambone. He gonna give me my ham. He gonna give me my ham. I want my ham.

Memphis (*to Hambone*). Alright! I told you . . . That's enough of that!

Hambone (*to himself*). He gonna give me my ham. He gonna give me my ham.

Holloway. All he got to do is go see Aunt Ester. Aunt Ester could straighten him out. Don't care whatever your problem. She can straighten it out.

Sterling. You think she can help me find a job? I wanna open me up a nightclub.

Holloway. Whatever your problem is. It don't make no difference to Aunt Ester. She can help you with anything.

Sterling. Where she live at? What's that address again?

Holloway. Eighteen thirty-nine Wylie. In the back. Knock on the red door. You can't miss it. Don't care who answer. Just say you come to see Aunt Ester. You ain't got to tell them what you want to see her about. Just say, "I come to see Aunt Ester." You got to pay her, though. She won't take no money herself. She tell you to go down and throw it into the river. Say it'll come to her. She must be telling the truth, cause she don't want for nothing. She got some people there to take care of her and they don't want for nothing either.

Memphis. Ask her how old she is while you up there.

Holloway. She'll tell you. She don't try to hide it. And she don't care if you believe or not. She three hundred and twenty-two years old. She'll tell you.

Memphis. How the hell somebody gonna live to be three hundred and twenty-two years old, nigger? You talk like a fool.

Sterling. They lived that long in the Bible. I ain't surprised to hear that. Do she look like she come out the Bible?

Holloway. You got to go see what she look like for yourself. I'm just telling you she three hundred and twenty-two years old. Go on up there and see her. I go up to see her every once in a while. Get my soul washed. She don't do nothing but lay her hands on your head. But it's a feeling like you ain't never had before. Then everything in your life get real calm and peaceful.

Memphis. I'd rather believe if I rubbed Prophet Samuel's head I'd get rich. That make more sense to me than to talk about somebody being three hundred and twenty-two years old.

Holloway. She look like she five hundred. You be surprised when she say she ain't but three hundred and twenty-two. Don't ask me how she lived that long. I don't know. Look like death scared of her. Every time he come around her he just get up and get on away. Ask West about her. He'll tell you. He done went up there to see her. He been waiting to bury her since he saw her. Even told the people there in the house that he'd do it for free.

Memphis. I ain't seen her change nobody's luck. Every nigger I know got bad luck. If it was easy as that . . . hell, we'd all be rich.

Holloway. See? There you go talking about being rich. I ain't talking about that. I ain't said nothing about getting rich. I'm talking about getting your luck changed. You go up there with the wrong attitude and come out with worse luck than you had before. That's what the problem is now. Aunt Ester don't buy into that. She don't make people rich. You go up there talking about you wanna get rich and she won't have nothing to do with you. She send you to see Prophet Samuel . . . and you see how far that'll get you. Most people don't know Prophet Samuel went to see Aunt Ester. He wasn't always a prophet. He started out he was a reverend. Had him a truck, and he'd stand on the back of that truck . . . had him a loudspeaker, and he'd go out and preach the word of the gospel and sell barbecue on the side. Everybody knew Reverend Samuel. He even went out where the white folks lived and tried to preach to them. They seen him with that truck and thought he come out there to steal their furniture. Called the police on him. Many a time. He go on and pay his fifty-dollar fine for preaching without a permit and go on back out here.

They had him in big trouble one time. He had all his money going to his church and they arrested him for income-tax evasion. That's when he went to see Aunt Ester. He walked in there a reverend and walked out a prophet. I don't know what she told him. But he went down to see the mayor. Say if they arrested him they had to arrest Mellon too. Say God was gonna send a sign. The next day the stock market fell so fast they had to close it early. Mellon called the mayor and told him to drop the charges. The next day the stock market went right on back up there. Except for Gulf Oil, which Mellon owned. That went higher than it ever went before. Mellon was tickled pink. He sent Prophet Samuel a five-hundred-dollar donation and a brochure advertising his banking services. Had his picture taken with him and everything.

That's when Prophet Samuel went big. The police didn't bother him no more. Wouldn't even give him a parking ticket. If he hadn't started walking around in them robes going barefoot and whatnot . . . ain't no telling how big he would have got. A lot of people didn't like him wearing them robes . . . baptizing people in the river and all that kinda stuff.

Memphis. That's the damnedest thing I ever heard of.

Holloway. Don't take my word for it. Go on up there and see for yourself. Go knock on the door. You don't have to be scared.

Memphis. I ain't scared. What I got to be scared of? I just don't believe all that stuff.

Holloway. Ask West when you see him. Ask anybody that's been up there.

Sterling. You can ask me when I come back. Eighteen thirty-nine Wylie? In the back?

Holloway. Knock on the red door. Just say you come to see Aunt Ester. She'll straighten you out.

Sterling. Say, Risa, cook me up some chicken. I'll be back. I wanna eat what you been eating. See if I can get nice and healthy too.

(Sterling exits.)

Memphis. That boy ain't got good sense.

(The lights go down on the scene.)

Scene 2

(The lights come up on the restaurant. Wolf is looking out the window of the door. Memphis is at the end of the counter. Risa is in the back. "229" is written on the board.)

Wolf. Here he come now. Lutz coming down the street. Hambone standing there.

(Memphis comes around the corner of the counter and walks to the door and looks out.)

Memphis. What's Holloway doing?

Wolf. He watching him. He just standing there. He wanna hear what they say. Look at him . . . look at him. Look at Hambone.

Risa *(entering from the back).* What you all looking at?

Wolf. We watching Hambone. We want to see what he say to Lutz. Holloway went over there to stand on the corner. Hambone talking to Lutz now.

Memphis. That's the damnedest thing I ever seen.

(He walks back around the counter.)

Risa, you been here for a half an hour and ain't got the coffee on. What you doing back there? Get them grits cooked up. I told you put the bread in the refrigerator . . . keep it fresh.

Wolf.   Lutz going in his store. He turned his back to him and opening up his store. Holloway still standing there.

(Turning from the window.)

Lutz ought to go on and give him a ham.

Memphis.   Lutz ain't gonna give him no ham . . . cause he don't feel he owe him. I wouldn't give him one either.

Wolf.   After all this time it don't make no difference. He ought to go on and give him a ham. What difference do it make? It ain't like he ain't got none. Got a whole store full of hams.

Memphis.   What'd you do with that flour? Ain't even got the oven turned on. How you gonna cook biscuits without turning on the oven? Where the flour? I brought ten pound of flour in here yesterday.

Risa.   It's in the back.

Memphis.   Here's the sifter. Sift the baking soda and flour together. You ain't used this sifter in a month. And get on up to the bakery and get West his pie before he get over here.

Wolf.   I hear tell somebody tried to break in West's last night to steal Prophet Samuel's money and jewels. Set off the burglar alarm . . . woke West up.

(Holloway enters.)

Hey, Holloway, we was watching you. What Hambone say? We seen Lutz when he come down the street. What he say?

Holloway.   He told him he wanted his ham, that's all. Said, "I want my ham." Lutz told him, "Take a chicken," then he went on in his store. That was it. He ain't said nothing back to him. The only words exchanged was "I want my ham," and "Take a chicken."

Memphis.   I would just like to know . . . after nine and a half years . . . am I right, Holloway? . . . after nine and a half years . . . every day . . . I wish my arithmetic was right to tell you how many days that is . . . nine and a half years . . . every day . . . how . . . in his right mind . . . do he think Lutz is gonna give him his ham? You answer me that. That's all I want to know.

Wolf.   Anybody can see he ain't in his right mind.

Holloway.   I don't know. He might be more in his right mind than you are. He might have more sense than any of us.

Wolf.   Would you stand over there every morning for nine and a half years?

Holloway.   I ain't saying that. Naw . . . hell, no . . . I wouldn't stand over there for nine and a half years. But maybe I ain't got as much sense as he got.

Memphis.   You tell me how that make sense. You tell me what sense that make?

Holloway. Alright. I'll tell you. Now you take me or you. We ain't gonna do that. We gonna go ahead and forget about it. We might take a chicken. Then we gonna go home and cook that chicken. But how it gonna taste? It can't taste good to us. We gonna be eating just to be eating. How we gonna feel good about ourselves? Every time we even look at a chicken we gonna have a bad taste in our mouth. That chicken's gonna call up that taste. It's gonna make you feel ashamed. Even if it be walking around flapping its wings it's gonna remind us of that bad taste. We ain't gonna tell nobody about it. We don't want nobody to know. But you can't erase it. You got to carry it around with you. This fellow here . . . he say he don't want to carry it around with him. But he ain't willing to forget about it. He trying to put the shame on the other foot. He trying to shame Lutz into giving him his ham. And if Lutz ever break down and give it to him . . . he gonna have a big thing. He gonna have something he be proud to tell everybody. He gonna tell his grandkids if he have any. That's why I say he might have more sense than me and you. Cause he ain't willing to accept whatever the white man throw at him. It be easier. But he say he don't mind getting out of the bed in the morning to go at what's right. I don't believe you and me got that much sense.

Memphis. That's that old backward southern mentality. When I come up here they had to teach these niggers they didn't have to tip their hat to a white man. They walking around here tipping their hat, jumping off the sidewalk, talking about "Yessir, Captain," "How do, Major."

Wolf. How long you been up here, Memphis?

Memphis. I been up here since '36. They ran me out of Jackson in '31. I hung around Natchez for three or four years, then I come up here. I was born in Jackson. I used to farm down there. They ran me out in '31. Killed my mule and everything. One of these days I'm going back and get my land. I still got the deed.

Holloway. I got an uncle and a bunch of cousins down in Jackson.

Memphis. When I left out of Jackson I said I was gonna buy me a V-8 Ford and drive by Mr. Henry Ford's house and honk the horn. If anybody come to the window I was gonna wave. Then I was going out and buy me a 30.06, come on back to Jackson and drive up to Mr. Stovall's house and honk the horn. Only this time I wasn't waving. Only thing was, it took me thirteen years to get the Ford. Six years later I traded that in on a Cadillac. But I'm going back one of these days. I ain't even got to know the way. All I got to do is find my way down to the train depot. They got two trains running every day. I used to know the schedule. They might have changed it . . . but if they did, they got it posted up on the board.

Risa. The oven's on. I'm going to get the pie.

(Risa exits. Memphis watches after her.)

Memphis. A man would be happy to have a woman like that except she done ruined herself. She ain't right with herself . . . how she gonna be right with you? Anybody take a razor and cut up on herself ain't right. If she cut her legs she might cut your throat. That's the way I see it. Other than that, any man be glad to lay up next to that every night. Something ain't right with a woman don't want no man. That ain't natural. If she say she like women that be another thing. It ain't natural, but that be something else. But somebody that's all confused about herself and don't want nobody . . . I can't figure out where to put her.

Holloway. That's what the problem is . . . you trying to figure out where to put her. I know Risa. She one of them gals that matured quick. And every man that seen her since she was twelve years old think she ought to go lay up with them somewhere. She don't want that. She figure if she made her legs ugly that would force everybody to look at her and see what kind of personality she is.

Memphis. She a mixed-up personality. Anybody can see that. That plain to see. Who want a woman after she done that to herself? I don't want her. I don't know what she might do to me.

Holloway. They had her down there at Western Psych. They couldn't find nothing wrong with her. They tried every kind of counselor they could think of.

Wolf. She don't need no counselor. Ain't nothing wrong with Risa. All she need is a good man. Trust me, I know Risa.

Memphis. You don't know her like you want to know her. Don't nobody know her.

Wolf. I know Risa better than people think I do. That's what I'm trying to say. I know all she need is a man. Somebody to make her feel like a woman. She ain't had that in six years that I know of. Common sense say after six years she need a man. I see where that Sterling be eyeing her. He be after her. But he don't know Risa. He don't know her like I know her. Maybe he a better man than me. I don't know. But if I had to say, I don't think so. You want anything, Memphis?

Memphis. Give me a dollar on four twenty-one.

Wolf. Holloway?

Holloway. I'm gonna wait till I get me a good dream. I can't dream about nothing.

Wolf. I'll catch you all later.

(Wolf exits.)

Memphis. Hey, Holloway, you know what I just found out? You know who that boy is . . . that Sterling boy? I was talking to Hendricks. . . . That's the boy robbed that bank and was out spending the money ten minutes later. You remember that? Hendricks give him a job to help him get out and the boy worked one week and quit. See, Hendricks don't know . . . he don't know like I know. He trying to help him, but that boy don't wanna work.

Holloway. He say Hendricks laid him off. But I can't blame him if he did quit. Who wanna haul bricks on a construction site for a dollar and a quarter an hour? That ain't gonna help him. What's he gonna do with ten dollars a day?

Memphis. That be ten more than he got now. His grandaddy used to work for three dollars a day. He doing good!

Holloway. I ain't talking about that. Hell, his great-grandaddy used to work for nothing, for all that matter. I'm talking about he can make two or three hundred dollars a day gambling . . . if he get lucky. If he don't, somebody else will get it. That's all you got around here is niggers with somebody else's money in their pocket. And they don't do nothing but trade it off on each other. I got it today and you got it tomorrow. Until sooner or later as sure as the sun shine . . . somebody gonna take it and give it to the white man. The money go from you to me to you and then—bingo, it's gone. From him to you to me, then—bingo, it's gone. You give it to the white man. Pay your rent, pay your telephone, buy your groceries, see the doctor—bingo, it's gone. Just circulate it around till it find that hole, then—bingo. Like trying to haul sand in a bucket with a hole in it. Time you get where you going the bucket empty. That's why that ten dollars a day ain't gonna do him no good. A nigger with five hundred dollars in his pocket around here is a big man. But you go out there where they at . . . you go out to Squirrel Hill, they walking around there with five thousand dollars in their pocket trying to figure out how to make it into five hundred thousand.

Memphis. Ain't nothing wrong in saving your money and do like they do. These niggers just don't want to work. That boy don't want to work. He lazy.

Holloway. People kill me talking about niggers is lazy. Niggers is the most hard-working people in the world. Worked three hundred years for free. And didn't take no lunch hour. Now all of a sudden niggers is lazy. Don't know how to work. All of a sudden when they got to pay niggers, ain't no work for him to do. If it wasn't for you the white man would be poor. Every little bit he got he got standing on top of you. That's why he could reach so high. He give you three dollars a day for six months and he got him a railroad for the next hundred years. All you got is six months' worth of three dollars a day.

(Risa enters carrying a pie box.)

Now you can't even get that. Ain't no money in niggers working. Look out there on the street. If there was some money in it . . . if the white man could figure out a way to make some money by putting niggers to work . . . we'd all be working. He ain't building no more railroads. He got them. He ain't building no more highways. Somebody done already stuck the telephone poles in the ground. That's been done already. The white man ain't stacking no more niggers. You know what I'm talking about, stacking niggers, don't you? Well, here's how that go. If you ain't got nothing . . . you can go out here and get you a nigger. Then you got something, see. You got one nigger. If that one nigger get out there and plant something . . . get something out the ground . . . even if it ain't nothing but a bushel of potatoes . . . then you got one nigger and one bushel of potatoes. Then you take that bushel of potatoes and go get you another nigger. Then you got two niggers. Put them to work and you got two niggers and two bushels of potatoes. See, now you can go buy two more niggers. That's how you stack a nigger on top of a nigger. White folks got to stacking . . . and I'm talking about they stacked up some niggers! Stacked up close to fifty million niggers. If you stacked them on top of one another they make six or seven circles around the moon. It's lucky the boat didn't sink with all them niggers they had stacked up there. It take them two extra months to get here cause it ride so low in the water. They couldn't find you enough work back then. Now that they got to pay you they can't find you none. If this was different time wouldn't be nobody out there on the street. They'd all be in the cotton fields.

Memphis.   I still say that boy don't want to work.

(West enters. He is a widower in his early sixties. He is dressed all in black, except for a white shirt. He wears a pair of black gloves. Since his wife's death he has allowed his love of money to overshadow the other possibilities of life.)

Holloway.   Hey, West.
West.   Hey, Risa.
Risa.   How you doing, Mr. West?

(She puts his coffee in front of him and goes to get the pie.)

West.   Let me get a little bit of sugar here, Risa.
Memphis.   I see they lined up out there.
West.   Yeah, I finally got him laid out like they wanted and the people over there trying to rub his head. I got it roped off, but they duck right under the rope talking about they didn't see it.
Memphis.   I ain't been over there yet, but Holloway say they got all kind of jewels and hundred-dollar bills in the casket with him.
West.   I don't know how that got started. The man ain't got nothing but a couple of rings, that gold cross he wear, and two hundred-dollar bills. Got one in his breast pocket and one wrapped around his finger . . . tucked and glued in his hand.
Memphis.   You ain't glued the man's money in his hand.
West.   Yeah, I did. I done learned in this business. I can't tell you how many rings and watches and whatnot have disappeared.
Memphis.   I know you ain't gonna put that money in the ground.
West.   I'll bury anything with anybody. You be surprised what people want in the casket with them. I done buried people with Bibles, canes, crutches, guitars, radios, baby dolls. . . . One lady brought some tomatoes from her sister's

garden. She didn't just want me to put them in there. She wanted to tell me where to put them. That wouldn't have been so bad, but she kept changing her mind. People's something. They don't understand about dead folks. Dead folks don't know nothing. They don't know them tomatoes is in there with them. But the family know. That's who it's important to. It took me a while to figure that out. . . . But I don't mind putting anything in there with anybody as long as the casket close.

Memphis. Is you gonna put that money in the ground? That's what I wanna know.

West. Most times the family come and get the money before you close the casket. Take off their rings and everything else. I hate to even lay people out with jewelry . . . cause the family come and remind you every day that it ain't supposed to go in the ground.

Memphis. Holloway say they was over there taking up a collection. Say they was charging the people to see him.

West. I put a stop to that. I don't allow that kind of thing over there. I stopped them from doing that. What they say to you downtown there?

Memphis. I ain't went yet. I got to go down there tomorrow. I'm going down there and see what they offer me for it. I ain't taking a penny less than twenty-five thousand dollars.

West. They ain't gonna give you no twenty-five thousand dollars for this building. It ain't worth that. They look up what you paid for it and double that. That's one hundred percent profit. They figure anybody be satisfied with that. It's hard to argue against that. The lawyer can't even argue against that. They ain't gonna give you but ten . . . eleven thousand. Twelve at the most.

Memphis. I ain't taking a penny less than twenty-five thousand.

West. They ain't gonna give you no twenty-five thousand dollars on something they gonna tear down! I don't know how niggers think sometimes. Now, I told you I'd give you fifteen thousand dollars for it. Cash money. We can go down to the bank right now. Fifteen thousand dollars. Draw it right out in cash. You can get it any way you want. Hundreds. Twenties.

Memphis. Naw. Naw. I ain't taking a penny less than twenty-five thousand dollars.

West. You watch and see what I'm telling you. They gonna double what you paid for it. They ain't gonna give you no ten thousand dollars on top of that.

Memphis. Then they ain't getting my building. I figure that twenty-five thousand is cheap. They forcing me to move out . . . . close up my business . . . well, I figure they ought to pay something for that. I don't care what the building is worth or how much I bought it for.

West. They got the right of eminent domain. They don't care what you think. They can go anywhere in the city and take any piece of property they want. The city council done voted to take over these whole twelve blocks. They getting five this year and seven next year. They ain't gonna let you stand in their way. Talk to Philmore down the street. He sold me his place. He know the city wasn't gonna give him what it's worth.

Memphis.   Give me twenty-five thousand dollars and you can have it. Put it with your other property and go down there and get fifty for it.
West.   I told you I'd give you fifteen. It ain't worth no twenty-five. To me or nobody else.
Memphis.   I ain't taking a penny less than twenty-five thousand dollars.
West.   Alright. You gonna be surprised. Don't say I didn't warn you. Let me know if you change your mind. We can go right on down to the bank any time you want.

(West exits.)

Memphis.   You hear that, Holloway? The man own so much property around here the city gonna go broke trying to pay him for it and he trying to hustle me. Hell, if he offer me fifteen for it I know it's worth twenty-five. Might be able to get thirty.

(Sterling enters. He has a handful of flyers.)

Sterling.   How you all doing? Hey, Risa, let me get a cup of coffee.
Holloway.   Did you go up there to see Aunt Ester?
Sterling.   I went up there. Got a red door just like you say. I knocked on the door. I must have knocked on it about five minutes. I was getting ready to leave when a man opened the door. Big man. Must have been over seven feet tall. I told him I wanted to see Aunt Ester and he told me she was sick.
Holloway.   She get sick sometime. As you can imagine somebody three hundred and twenty-two years old is bound to get sick once in a while. But she ain't gonna die, I guarantee you that! You go on back up there next week.
Memphis.   Ain't nobody up there. I take that back . . . there might be somebody up there but she ain't no three hundred years old.
Holloway.   Three hundred and twenty-two. If you gonna tell it tell it right. Three hundred and twenty-two.

(Sterling hands a flyer to Memphis and Holloway.)

Sterling.   You all wanna go to this rally. They having a rally to celebrate Malcolm X's[3] birthday. It's right down there at the Savoy Ballroom.

(They read the flyers. Sterling hands one to Risa.)

Here you go, Risa.
Memphis.   Malcolm X is dead. Malcolm ain't having no more birthdays. Dead men don't have birthdays. I'd rather celebrate your birthday. I'll buy the cake,

---

[3] Malcolm Little (1925–1965), who became a Black Muslim while in prison and assumed the name Malcolm X, was an important leader in his adopted religion. He was assassinated in 1965.

a case of liquor, and we can have a party. I ain't going to no party for no dead man.

Holloway.   I remember when Malcolm didn't have but twelve followers. I remember when he come out to the Mosque there. I went out and saw him. He didn't have but twelve followers.

Sterling.   Why wasn't you number thirteen?

Memphis.   Where he gonna follow him to? The only place he was going was to the graveyard. Anybody could see that.

Holloway.   I didn't follow him cause I know where to find Aunt Ester. If she hadn't been there I don't know what I would have done.

Sterling.   I would have followed him. He the only one who told the truth. That's why they killed him.

Memphis.   Niggers killed Malcolm. Niggers killed Malcolm. When you want to talk about Malcolm, remember that first. Niggers killed Malcolm . . . and now they want to celebrate his birthday.

Holloway.   Malcolm got too big. People call him a saint. That's what the problem was. He got too big, and when you get that big ain't nothing else you could do. They killed all the saints. Saint Peter. Saint Paul. They killed them all. When you get to be a saint there ain't nothing else you can do but die. The people wouldn't have it any other way.

Memphis.   You right about that. They killed Martin.[4] If they did that to him you can imagine what they do to me or you. If they kill the sheep you know what they do to the wolf.

Sterling.   That's why they having the rally. They rallying for black power. Stop them from killing the sheep.

Memphis.   That's what half the problem is . . . these black power niggers. They got people confused. They don't know what they doing themselves. These niggers talking about freedom, justice, and equality and don't know what it mean. You born free. It's up to you to maintain it. You born with dignity and everything else. These niggers talking about freedom, but what you gonna do with it? Freedom is heavy. You got to put your shoulder to freedom. Put your shoulder to it and hope your back hold up. And if you around here looking for justice, you got a long wait. Ain't no justice. That's why they got that statue of her and got her blindfolded. Common sense would tell you if anybody need to see she do. There ain't no justice. Jesus Christ didn't get justice. What makes you think you gonna get it? That's just the nature of the world. These niggers talking about they want freedom, justice, and equality. Equal to what? Hell, I might be a better man than you. What I look like going around here talking about I want to be equal to you? I don't know how these niggers think sometimes. Talking about black power with their hands

---

[4] Martin Luther King Jr. (1929–1968), perhaps the most celebrated civil rights leader of the 1960s, rose to national and international prominence as the leader of the year-long bus boycott in Montgomery, Alabama, in 1955–1956. He was assassinated in 1968.

and their pockets empty. You can't do nothing without a gun. Not in this day and time. That's the only kind of power the white man understand. They think they gonna talk their way up on it. In order to talk your way you got to have something under the table. These niggers don't understand that. If I tell you to get out my yard and leave my apples alone, I can't talk you out. You sit up in the tree and laugh at me. But if you know I might come out with a shotgun . . . that be something different. You'd have to think twice about whether you wanted some apples.

These niggers around here talking about they black and beautiful. Sound like they trying to convince themselves. You got to think you ugly to run around shouting you beautiful. You don't hear me say that. Hell, I know I look nice. Got good manners and everything.

Sterling. Well, it say, "Come one, come all." You supposed to be there when it say that. But that's alright—if you don't go, it ain't gonna stop the show.

(Hambone enters.)

Hambone. He gonna give me my ham. He gonna give me my ham.
Memphis. Naw. Naw. Take that on out of here. Risa, don't give him nothing. Go on, take that somewhere else.
Hambone. He gonna give me my ham. He gonna give me my ham.
Memphis. I don't wanna hear that today. Go on out of here with that.
Risa. Here's your coffee, Hambone.
Memphis. I told you not to give him nothing.
Risa. He ain't bothering nobody.
Memphis. Let him take that somewhere else.

(Memphis comes around the counter, takes the coffee from Hambone, and throws it out.)

Risa. He ain't bothering nobody, Memphis. He just come in to get his coffee.
Hambone *(to Memphis).* He gonna give me my ham.
Memphis *(pushing Hambone toward the door).* Go on over there and get it.
Hambone. I want my ham!
Memphis *(at the door).* There he is. Go on over there.

(Hambone exits.)

Come in here running off at the mouth. I'm tired of hearing that.
Risa. He don't bother nobody.
Memphis. He bother me. Let him go on over there and get his ham. It ain't like Lutz hiding from him. That man crazy. He let Lutz drive him crazy. Well, go on over there with Lutz and tell *him.* Don't tell me. Man been around here ten years talking the same thing. I'm tired of hearing it.

(Memphis slams the restaurant door closed.)
(The lights go down on the scene.)

Scene 3

(The lights come up on the restaurant. Sterling sits at the counter eating a bowl of beans. The number is 460. Risa is in the back.)

Sterling.   Say, Risa, what you put in these beans? You must have stuck your finger in there or something. Give me another bowl. Give me a couple of them muffins too.

(Risa brings him a bowl of beans.)

I went up to see Boykins about a job. He say he don't need nobody. He told me to go over to the steel mill. He don't know they got a waiting list.
Risa.   Everybody got a waiting list.
Sterling.   I saw Hambone. I was trying to talk to him. We got us a thing going.
Risa.   Most people don't understand Hambone. That's cause they don't take the time. Most people think he can't understand nothing. But he understand everything what's going on around him. Most of the time he understand better than they do.
Sterling.   I seen Holloway a little while ago. He say he was going downtown to see about his social security. I didn't know he was that old. He say he was going down there and register.
Risa.   He used to paint houses. Sometime he still do that. Going up on people's roofs. I told him you'd never catch me going up there.
Sterling.   I wouldn't go up lessen it was flat on top. Then I wouldn't mind none. Where Memphis?
Risa.   He gone downtown to take care of his business. They gonna tear the building down.
Sterling.   That don't surprise me. Ain't nothing hardly around here no more no way. They done tore the orphanage down. I was born an orphan. My mama gave me away to Mrs. Johnson. She died and they put me in an orphanage. Down there at Toner Institute. I been on my own since I was eighteen. That's twelve years now. I made it pretty good so far. Except when I was in the penitentiary.
Risa.   What you go to jail for?
Sterling.   I robbed a bank. I was tired of waking up every day with no money. I figure a man supposed to have money sometime. Everybody else seem like they got it. Seem like I'm the only one ain't got no money. I figure I'd get my money where Mellon get his from. That was after Mr. Lewis at the orphanage died. I never would want him to know I would do something like that. After he died I got kinda desperate. I just kept getting deeper and deeper in a

hole. . . . Wolf say you put them scars on your legs yourself. Wasn't you scared you was gonna bleed to death?

Risa. They didn't bleed that much.

Sterling. I be scared to do something like that. We had one boy down at the Toner Institute . . . name of Eddie Langston . . . I never will forget that. He cut his wrists and bled to death. We was about thirteen. I tried to wake him up in the morning and the whole bed was filled with blood. That stopped me from doing something like that. You wanna go to this rally with me? They having this rally for Malcolm X. You ought to come and go with me. It right down there at the Savoy Ballroom. They might have some dancing. You like to dance?

Risa. If it be with the right person.

Sterling. I can't dance. I ain't never danced. I guess I could slow-dance. Seem like anybody can do that. That ain't but so much grinding. I can't fast-dance though. It seems kinda stupid to be moving around like that. Like you should know better than to make yourself look silly.

Risa. It ain't silly. You can't dance for real?

Sterling. I asked this girl one time and she said no. I ain't never asked nobody else. I started to one time. Something told me not to. It was down at the workmen's club. I went in there and seen this woman. She was dancing with some other guys. She was laughing and having her a good time. I started to ask her to dance and changed my mind. Then I just forgot about dancing for good.

Risa. You just didn't ask the right person.

Sterling. You ought to hang that announcement up there. Somebody might wanna go. It say, "Come one, come all." You ought to come and go with me.

Risa. I don't want to go down there with all them people. I stay away from all that kind of stuff. You never see me hanging around a bunch of people.

Sterling. People don't pay you half as much mind as you think they do. That just be in your head. Most people so busy trying to live their own lives they ain't got time to pay attention to nobody else. I found that out. I used to think everybody cared what I did. I robbed that bank and thought people would be mad at me. Half of them didn't even know I was gone. Five years and ain't nobody missed me. They didn't even think about me till they saw me again. You can go down there with me and won't nobody even notice.

Risa. I don't care if they notice or not. I don't want to go down there with them niggers. There might be a riot or something.

Sterling. If a fight break out, you just get behind me. I won't let nobody hurt you. Not when you with me. I don't care if he was King Kong or Mighty Joe Young. He got to come through me first. Mrs. Johnson taught me that. Told me not to let nobody hurt my sister. Say she'd rather see me hurt than her hurt. That made me kinda important. Made me feel strong. Like when I robbed the bank. That made me feel strong too. Like I had everything under control. I did until they arrested me.

Risa. I still ain't going down there.

Sterling.   I can't find no job, I got to keep trying to hit the numbers. You play numbers?

Risa.   I don't throw my money away like that.

Sterling.   I know a lot of people play numbers. If you lucky you can do alright. I been trying to hit since I got out. I dreamt about dogs and looked it up in the dream book. That didn't work. I found a quarter on the fourth step of my house and played four twenty-five. That didn't work. Now I'm counting cars. I count all the Buicks I see and play that with all the Cadillacs and Fords I see. If I had a telephone number I'd play that.

Risa.   I don't know why people throw their money away. That twenty-five cents you found is twenty-five cents you could have had. You could have played the jukebox or something.

Sterling.   I'm trying to get twenty-five hundred dollars. I wouldn't mind taking a chance on that if I had me a good number.

Risa.   Play seven eighty-one.

Sterling.   How you come up with that?

Risa.   I got seven scars on one leg and eight on the other.

Sterling.   Where you get the one from?

Risa.   That's my business.

Sterling.   One what?

Risa.   Go on, Sterling, I ain't playing with you.

Sterling.   What? I just say, "Where you get the one from?" You getting all embarrassed. What you getting embarrassed about? I ought to play seven eighty-two. We can put one and one together.

Risa.   Go on, Sterling. You asked me for a number and I give you one now. If you want to play it go on and play it.

Sterling.   I'm gonna put five dollars on that number seven eighty-one. Wait— let me see how much money I got.

(He looks in his pocket.)

I ain't got nothing right now, but as soon as I get me some money I'm gonna play that seven eighty-one. If it come out we gonna get married.

(Holloway enters.)

Hey, Holloway.

Holloway.   Hey, Sterling. How you doing, Risa?

Sterling.   Hey, Holloway, you talking about that fence that run in back of Lutz's Meat Market where he put his garbage, back of that alley there, across from that billboard above Eddie's Restaurant? Is that the fence Hambone painted?

Holloway.   Yeah, that's it.

Sterling.   That fence run all up the side and all the way around the back there. He ought to have give him two hams. I wouldn't paint that fence for no ham.

He'd have to give me a case of chickens or one of them half-cows he got hanging over there. He'd have to give me something like that. That fence run all the way back around there.

Holloway. Used to have another part closer to the front, but Lutz tore that down.

Sterling. I looked at it. He did a good job. Some of the paint done chipped off but you can tell he did a good job. I started to go over there and get his ham for him. But then he wouldn't have nothing to do in the morning. I didn't want to take that away from him. He have more cause to get up out of the bed in the morning than I do. I consider him lucky. I get up cause I wake up and can't think of nothing else to do. Get up and see what's out here. Only it be the same thing as yesterday. I guess it be that for him, too. Only Lutz just might shock him to death one day and say, "Here, take your ham!" Best thing that might happen to me is I get a woman and an extra twenty dollars from somewhere. The jukebox still broke?

Risa. Yeah. They supposed to fix it. It ain't gonna do nothing but break again if they do fix it.

Sterling. I don't know why I want to play it. That's just like paying a quarter to hear yourself sing. You ought to get a radio or something. That's free.

Holloway. Let me get some sugar, Risa.

Sterling. How come you don't give nobody no sugar? You make them ask for it.

Risa. I give it to them. All they got to do is ask. West ask for sugar and then half the time don't use it. You watch him. First thing he do is ask for sugar and then it look like he change his mind.

Sterling. West got a sweet tooth. I'm surprised he don't use it. As much pie as he eat.

(Wolf enters.)

Wolf. How's everybody in here? Risa, here go some stockings. And put this cologne back over there for Memphis. He like that English Leather cologne.

Risa. What size is they?

Wolf. They your size. I wouldn't be giving them to you otherwise.

Risa. How much I owe you?

Wolf. You don't owe me nothing. If I come up with one of them fur coats we can sit down and talk. We can do some real nice negotiating.

Risa. I don't want no fur coat.

Wolf. You don't want none till you see it. After you put one of them on and see what it feel like . . . then you want one.

Sterling. Hey, Wolf . . . loan me two dollars. I wanna play a number. Me and Risa got something going. Luck might be trying to get in my door today. I need me some money to buy Risa a present.

Wolf. I ain't got it, Sterling.

Sterling. I'm gonna hit the numbers and buy Risa a present, then I'm gonna get me one of them Buick Electra deuce and a quarter.

Holloway. You need to be trying to find you a job.

Sterling. I been trying to get one. Ain't nobody got none. I wish I could get one of them white folks' job making eight or nine thousand dollars a year.

Holloway. You ain't got none of them white folks' education . . . how you gonna get one of their jobs?

Sterling. Hey, I can do anything. I told the judge I could do his job. I got enough sense to sit up there and tell right from wrong. I can tell when somebody getting rail-roaded . . . when the lawyer is talking too much. I got sense enough to know when it's lunch time and how to say "recess." I can do anything the white man can do. If the truth be told . . . most things I can do better.

Holloway. I see where you gonna end up back down there.

Sterling. Not in this life. All I do is try to live in the world, but the world done gone crazy. I'm sorry I was ever born into it. This woman told me one time, "Sterling, I wanna have your baby." I told her if we have a baby he might live to be seventy-five years old. Just think how much hell he gonna catch. I wouldn't do that to nobody. She told me I was crazy. Hell, maybe she was right. But nobody will ever come to me and say, "You responsible for this. You brought me into this crazy world."

Wolf. That's why I don't have no kids. I said the same thing.

Sterling. Hey, Wolf . . . tell him . . . what kind of world is this?

Holloway. You sit around talking about you want this . . . you want the other . . . you want a job . . . you want a car. What you don't know is everybody that want one got one. You talking about you want one and ain't doing nothing to get none. The people that have them is the people that wanted them. You don't do nothing but sit around and talk about what you ain't got. The more you sit around and talk about what you ain't got the more you have to talk about. Wait two or three years and see what you have to talk about then.

Sterling. I know what I'm doing. I'm gonna get me two or three Cadillacs and everything that go with them. If I can't find no job I might have to find me a gun. Hey, Wolf, you know anybody got a gun they want to sell?

Wolf. What you looking for?

Sterling. Something that shoot straight. I don't care what it is. I don't want no .22. A .38 too big and heavy. Everybody can see it's bulging out under your coat. I'll take me a snub-nosed .32 if I can get one. I don't want no silver gun that shine in the dark. I'll take a black one. Other than that I don't care what it is.

Wolf. Tony Jackson got an Army .45 he trying to sell.

Sterling. I don't want no .45. He probably got the same one I had. You liable to end up shooting yourself with that. I was shooting at some birds one time and couldn't even hit the tree.

Wolf. I'll ask around. Let me get some sugar, Risa.

Holloway. I see where you want to go back down the penitentiary. I thought you was trying to stay out.

Sterling. You subject to end up there anyway. You don't have to do nothing to go to jail.

Wolf. You right about that. I know. You can walk down there . . . just walk down the street and ask people . . . every nigger you see done been to jail one time or another. The white man don't feel right unless he got a record on these niggers. Walk on down there . . . I'll give you a dollar for every nigger you find that ain't been to jail. Ain't that right, Sterling. I been to jail. Stayed down there three months. Tried to make bond and couldn't do it. They kept me down there in the county jail for three months. Ain't done nothing but walk down the street. I was walking down Centre Avenue . . . police was chasing somebody and wasn't looking where he was going, and I wasn't looking where I was going either . . . he ran into me so hard it knocked us both down. I started to get up and there was two, three policemen with their guns pointed at my head. Told me not to move. They arrested me for obstructing justice. Kept me down there for three months before the judge had a chance to throw it out. But I learned a lot from that. I learned to watch where I was going at all times. Cause you always under attack.

Sterling. That's why I said if I was going I was going for something.

(Hambone enters.)

Hey, my man. How you doing, Hambone?

Hambone. He gonna give me my ham. He gonna give me my ham.

Sterling. Risa, give him something to eat.

Risa. You hungry, Hambone? You want a bowl of beans?

Hambone. He gonna give me my ham. He gonna give me my ham.

Wolf. Hey, Holloway, you know Bubba Boy, don't you? Him and his woman?

Holloway. Yeah . . . be together all the time. When you see him you see her.

Wolf. I just found out she died. She overdosed last night. West just went down to pick up her body. She dead and he in jail. He went down to Surrey's to get a dress to be buried in. You know them dresses down there cost two, three hundred dollars. He went down there like a fool and was walking out the door with the dress . . . they arrested him. He can't even go to her funeral. The people taking up a collection to see if they can get him out on bond. You wanna give anything?

Holloway. Here go a dollar.

Sterling. Holloway . . . loan me two dollars.

Holloway. I ain't got no two dollars. If you had a job you'd have two dollars.

Risa. Holloway ain't got no money. . . . Here.

(Risa hands Sterling two dollars. Sterling hands them to Wolf.)

Sterling. That's for me and Hambone.

Holloway. How much is his bail?

Wolf. They got him on a two-thousand-dollar bond. I got to get two hundred dollars.

Sterling. Go ask West. He got all that money.

Wolf. West ain't gonna give a dime.

Sterling. Whoever hit the numbers ought to put in ten or twenty.

Wolf. That's what I say, but it don't always work like that. Thanks, I'll see you all later.

Holloway. Let me get a dime on that nine sixty-eight before you go. I dreamt about snakes.

(Wolf writes the slip.)

Wolf. I don't know what Bubba Boy's gonna do now. I ain't never seen him without her. You see him you see her. It's been like that for fifteen years. I used to look at them and say that's how deep love get. I don't know what he gonna do now.

Wolf. I don't know either. But we gonna try and get him out of jail.

(Wolf exits. Sterling moves over to the stool next to Hambone. Risa gives Hambone a bowl of beans.)

Sterling. Hey, Hambone. How you doing?

Hambone. He gonna give me my ham.

Sterling. You want your ham?

Risa. Sterling, don't be playing with him like that.

Sterling. I ain't playing with him. Me and Hambone got us a thing going. Ain't we, Hambone?

Hambone. He gonna give me my ham.

Sterling. I'm trying to build up his confidence in me. Ain't that right, Hambone? You don't know nothing about this. We talking man to man. Okay, Hambone, check this out. Now . . . you ready? First I say it . . . and then you say it. You ready?

(Sterling lines up in front of Hambone.)

Now listen. Take your time. Don't worry about getting it wrong. Okay.

(He pronounces each word carefully.)

Black—is—beautiful. See? Come on now. Black . . .

Hambone. Black . . .

Sterling. Is . . .

Hambone. Is . . .

Sterling. Beautiful.

Hambone. Beautiful.

Sterling. Yeah, see—you got it. Black is beautiful.

Hambone. Black is beautiful.

(Hambone grins at his accomplishment.)

Sterling.   I want you to remember that now . . . for the next time I see you. Then I'll teach you something else. Okay?

Hambone.   He gonna give me my ham. He gonna give me my ham.

(Memphis enters.)

Memphis.   These white folks crazy. Tell me my deed say they can give me anything they want for my building. Say it got a clause. I told them I don't care nothing about no clause. What kind of sense that make if they can give me what they want?

Holloway.   How much they offer you?

Memphis.   Fifteen thousand dollars! I raised all kind of hell. The judge looked at me like I was crazy. I told them I got a clause too. They ain't the only one got a clause. My clause say they got to give me what I want for it. It's my building. If they wanna buy it they got to meet my price. That's just common sense. I raised so much hell the judge postponed it . . . told me talk to my lawyer. The lawyer looked at the deed and told me that they was right. I told him, "I don't need you no more." Fired him on the spot. He supposed to be on my side. They left it like that till I could get me another lawyer.

Holloway.   Who was your lawyer?

Memphis.   Chauncey Ward. Supposed to be a big nigger down there. Chauncey Ward III. His daddy was a judge. You remember Chauncey Ward. The first black judge they had down there. He was death on niggers. Give one fellow five hundred years.

Holloway.   I know Chauncey Ward.

Memphis.   This his son. Ain't even looked at the paper good . . . talking about they right. I don't care what the paper say, he supposed to fix it so they meet my price. I left out of there and called me one of them white lawyers, which is what I should have done in the first place. Fellow named Joseph Bartoromo.

Sterling.   You got insurance? If you got insurance you could burn it down.

Memphis.   Nigger, is you crazy! Insurance cost five times what the building is worth. That's why I keep me some good tenants upstairs. I don't put none of them fools up there that's liable to get drunk and burn down the place. When Mr. Collins died I let it set empty three months till I got somebody up there that was responsible. Look back in the kitchen . . . ask Risa . . . I got four or five fire extinguishers back there . . . and you talking about burning down the place. That's the one thing I am scared of. If it burn down I don't get nothing. I don't even get the fifteen thousand. See, they don't know. The half ain't never been told. I'm ready to walk through fire. I don't bother nobody. The last person I bothered is dead. My mama died in '54. I said then I wasn't going for no more draws. They don't know I feel just like I did when my mama died. She got old and gray and sat by the window till she died. She must have done that cause she ain't had nothing else to do. I was gone. My brother was gone. Sister gone. Everybody gone. My daddy was gone. She sat there till she died. I was staying down on Logan Street. Got the letter one day and telegram the next. They usually fall on top of one another . . . but not that close. I got the letter say, "If you wanna see your mother you better come home." Before I could get out the door the telegram came saying, "It's too late . . . your mother gone." I was trying to borrow some money. Called the train station and found out the schedule and I'm trying to borrow some money. I can't go down there broke. I don't know how long I got to be there. I ain't even got the train fare. I got twelve dollars and sixty-three cents. I got the telegram and sat down and cried like a baby. I could beat any newborn baby in the world crying. I cried till the tears all run down in my ears. Got up and went out the door and everything looked different. Everything had changed. I felt like I had been cut loose. All them years something had a hold of me and I didn't know it. I didn't find out till it cut me loose. I walked out the door and everything had different colors to it. I felt great. I didn't owe nobody nothing. The last person I owed anything to was gone. I borrowed fifty dollars from West and went on down to her funeral. I come back and said, "Everybody better get out my way." You couldn't hold me down. It look like then I had somewhere to go fast. I didn't know where, but I damn sure was going there. That's the way I feel now. They don't know I got a clause of my own.

I'll get up off the canvas if I have to. They can carry me out feet first . . . but my clause say . . . they got to meet my price!

(*The lights go down on the scene.*)

Act II

Scene 1

(*The lights come up on the restaurant. Risa sits on one of the stools. The flyer about the rally is taped to the wall behind the counter. Sterling enters with a handful of flowers and a five-gallon gas can. He is dressed in different clothes. He wears a cap instead of a hat.*)

Sterling. Hey, Risa. Here.
Risa. What's that?
Sterling. What they look like? Them some flowers. I got them for you.
Risa. Sterling, where you get these flowers from?
Sterling. What you worried about where I got them from? God made them. You don't ask him where he got them from. I got them, that's all that counts.

Risa. Sterling, where you get these flowers from?

Sterling. I got them from across the street. I wasn't gonna buy them. I think that's silly to buy flowers. White folks do that. If I want to buy you something I buy you earrings or something. But I got them. And I got them for you. I saw them and I said, "I'm gonna take these to Risa. She a woman. Woman supposed to like nice things. Flowers and lace and all that kind of stuff." You better look at those flowers and see where they got your name on them. That's all you got to know.

Risa. I don't want no flowers you stole from a dead man.

Sterling. He don't mind. The man got so many flowers West don't know where to put them. West had to postpone his funeral and the flowers sitting over there dying. If I was gonna steal the man's flowers I'd pull a truck up there at night and go on and take the whole load. I picked them four or five cause I was thinking of you and I looked and seen where they had your name on it. Now you talking about you don't want them. Hell, a flower's a flower. They gonna be dead in a minute if you don't put them in some water. They gonna be dead in two or three days even if you do. Go on and put them in a glass and enjoy them. Prophet Samuel can't smell them. He don't even know they there. People throwing all that money away buying flowers.

(Risa puts the flowers in a glass.)

Risa. West gonna come over here and see these flowers. I'm gonna tell him where I got them from.

Sterling. I'll tell him myself. West don't care. He ain't gonna do nothing but take them out there and throw them in the ground.

(Holloway enters.)

Hey, Holloway, you think Aunt Ester be well yet?

Holloway. You can go back up there. Eighteen thirty-nine Wylie. In the back. Knock on the red door.

Sterling. I got something I wanna ask her about Risa.

Risa. You ain't got nothing to ask her about me.

Sterling. I wanna find out something. I asked God to send me an angel. He said he couldn't do that but he'd send me a teasing brown. I wanna find out if you her. If you is, then . . . look out, woman! We gonna make all kinds of babies.

(Risa sees the gas can.)

Risa. Sterling, what's that? Where you get that from?

Sterling. I found it in back of the alley down there off of Centre. In back of that drugstore. It was just sitting there . . . wasn't nobody around . . . so I picked it up. It got five gallon of gas in it.

Risa. You done went and stole somebody's gas.

Sterling. I told you I found it, woman.

Holloway.   You ought to put them flowers in a bigger glass. Put a little salt in the glass. They last longer then. That's what my grandmother used to do.

(Hambone enters.)

Sterling.   There he is! Hey, Hambone. Black is beautiful!

(Hambone looks at him for a moment, confused.)

Hambone.   I want my ham.
Sterling.   You stick with me . . . you gonna get your ham. Okay? Me and you. Brothers.

(He clasps his hands together.)

See? Like that. Black is beautiful. Remember? Now, I'm gonna teach you something else. United . . . come on now. Come on—first I say it . . . then you say it. United we stand . . .
Hambone.   United we stand . . .
Sterling.   Divided we fall.
Hambone.   Divided we fall.
Sterling.   Yeah, that's right. See? You can do it! United we stand . . . divided we fall. I learned that in the penitentiary. You ever been in the penitentiary?

(Hambone looks at him. Sterling suddenly shouts.)

I want my ham!
Hambone.   I want my ham!
Sterling.   I want my ham!
Hambone.   I want my ham!
Sterling.   I want my ham!
Hambone.   I want my ham!
Sterling.   Malcolm lives!
Hambone.   I want my ham!
Sterling.   Malcolm lives!
Hambone.   I want my ham!
Sterling.   Malcolm lives!
Hambone.   I want my ham!

(Memphis enters.)

Sterling.   Malcolm lives!
Hambone.   I want my ham!
Sterling.   Malcolm lives!
Hambone.   I want my ham!
Memphis.   Stop all the hollering in here! This a business. Risa . . .

Hambone.   I want my ham!

Memphis.   Stop all that hollering! Risa!

Risa.   What?

Memphis.   What's all this hollering in here? You supposed to be running a business. This ain't no schoolyard!

(To Sterling.)

Go on outside if you wanna holler. Take that out on the street and holler all you want.

Sterling.   We was just having some fun. Say, Memphis, you wanna buy some gas? I got five gallon of gas I found in the alley down there off of Centre. Let you have it for two dollars.

Memphis.   I got gas.

Sterling.   That gas you got ain't gonna last forever. I'll carry it out there and put it in your car if you want. It ain't gonna cost but two dollars. You know how much gas cost? Bean charge seventy-two cents a gallon. He charge three cent more than the white man.

(Memphis gives him two dollars.)

Memphis.   Here. Bring the can back.

Sterling.   I ain't said I was selling the can. That's two dollars if you wanna buy that. This a regulation United States Army gas can. Made with good metal and everything. Bullet probably bounce right off it.

Memphis.   I don't want to buy the can. I just say bring it back empty.

Sterling.   Give me the key and let me drive it around the block a couple of times.

Memphis.   Nigger . . . give me back my two dollars!

Sterling.   I was just playing around. I wouldn't even look right driving a Cadillac.

(Sterling exits.)

Memphis.   That boy ain't got good sense. I don't want all that hollering in here. Hambone paid you for these beans?

Risa.   Naw.

Memphis.   That's sixty-five cent. You got sixty-five cent?

(Hambone gives him three quarters. He goes to the register and rings it up. He takes Hambone's change and slaps it down on the table in front of him.)

Go on and finish your beans and get on where you going. Give him another muffin, Risa.

(To Hambone.)

You eat that and get on with your business.

(The phone rings. Memphis answers it.)

Hello? . . . Wolf don't work here.

(He slams down the phone.)

Risa, Wolf been taking numbers out of here?
Risa. I don't know.
Memphis.   I told him about that. This ain't no number station. First thing you know they be raiding the place. Have my picture in the paper for racketeering. If there's one thing I can say, I ain't never had my picture in the paper.

(Sterling enters with the gas can.)

Sterling.   Hey, Risa . . . hold this for me.
Memphis.   You carry that right on back out there where you got it from—I don't want no part of it.

(Wolf enters.)

Wolf.   How's everybody in here? I can smell them short ribs. Fix me up a plate, Risa.
Risa.   They ain't done yet.
Wolf.   Give me a bowl of beans. I'll be back for the short ribs. Hey, Sterling . . . look here.

(Wolf takes out a brown paper bag.)

You got twenty dollars?
Sterling.   What for?

(Wolf hands him the bag. He looks inside.)

Wolf.   That's the best I can do. Tony Jackson say he want twenty dollars for it.
Sterling.   I ain't got but two dollars and it ain't worth but fifteen.
Wolf.   He say twenty. I'll loan it to you if you ain't got it.
Sterling.   I can't pay you back till next week.
Wolf.   That's alright. Pay me next week.

(Sterling takes the bag and shoves it in his pants.)

What you got there, Risa? That look like some of Prophet Samuel's flowers.
Risa.   They ain't his no more.

Sterling.   Let me spend my last two dollars. Give me two dollars on seven eighty-one straight. Seven eighty-one . . . right, Risa? If that come out me and Risa getting married.

(He picks up his gas can and starts to exit.)

Risa, fix me up a plate of them short ribs. I'll be right back.

(Sterling exits.)

Memphis.   I give that boy three weeks. You hear me, Holloway? Three weeks. And he gonna be laying over there across the street or back down there in the penitentiary. You watch. Three weeks.

(Risa sets Wolf's beans in front of him. The phone rings and Wolf goes to answer it. Memphis beats him to it.)

Hello? . . . Wolf don't work here!
Wolf.   What you do that for, Memphis? That's my livelihood.
Memphis.   This my restaurant. I told you about taking numbers out of here. This is a legitimate business. This ain't no number station. Go on down to Seefus . . . give people the number down there. Risa . . . get these dishes cleaned up.
Wolf.   Here you go, Risa . . . let me get out of here before I get in trouble.

(He drops the money for his dinner on the counter.)

Memphis.   You gonna do more than get in trouble if you messing with me.
Wolf.   See . . . I ain't said nothing to you now, Memphis. You starting something?
Memphis.   This my place, nigger! This my place. How you gonna have people call you at my place?
Wolf.   I ain't told nobody to call me. People know I be here and they trying to catch me. I get messages everywhere I go. Nobody else don't say nothing about it.
Memphis.   Well, go on and get them, cause you ain't getting no more here.

(Wolf exits. Memphis smells something.)

What's that burning? Risa?

(Memphis crosses behind the counter.)

Risa, watch you don't burn these short ribs. You got the fire way up high. What you doing back there?

Risa. I'm getting the food ready.

Memphis. That don't take all day. Them short ribs need some more water. Put some water in there.

(Risa goes to put some water in the short ribs.)

Turn the fire down and get on down to the store and get some corn meal. Where's the corn meal? How you gonna make muffins without corn meal?

(West enters.)

Hey, West.

West. Somebody done busted out my window. A great big old six-foot piece of glass! People ain't got sense enough to walk through the door. Over there pushing and carrying on. Let me get some coffee, Risa. I don't care how many people be lined up there to see Prophet Samuel . . . he leaving my place tomorrow. I'm talking about a big piece of glass! Ain't no telling how much it cost to replace that.

Risa. You ought to put a board up there.

West. I ain't gonna put up no board. They better get out here with that piece of glass. I spent twelve years putting up board. I worked hard not to put up board. Let them cut a piece of glass and bring it out and bill me. There was a time when they wouldn't do that. When I was down there on Centre I couldn't get the windows fixed. The toilet break down it be two weeks before somebody come and fix it. When I built that over there I said that wasn't gonna happen. Something go wrong I call the man who built it and he come right out and take care of it. No, sweetheart, West ain't gonna put up no board.

Memphis. I hear tell somebody tried to break in there.

West. Tried to come in through the basement window. Let me get a little sugar here, Risa. I hired Mason to sit over there tonight. I want to see them come in with him there.

Holloway. They be a fool to tangle with Mason and that twelve-gauge shotgun. The police sorry they had to retire him, as many niggers as he done shot.

West. Say, Memphis, I told you what was gonna happen when you went down there. But you don't listen to nobody. They got it all stacked up against you before you walk through the door.

Memphis. That's alright. I know how to deal with white folks. Ask Holloway. Down from where we come from you learn how to deal with white folks quick. It won't be the first time I bucked heads with white folks about my property.

West. I tell you what I do . . . you wanna be stubborn . . . I'll go ahead and give you twenty thousand for it.

Memphis. You gonna give me twenty thousand?

West. We can go right on down to the bank now. I'll give you fifteen now and five thousand after I sell it to the city.

Memphis.   I knew there was a catch to it.

West.   I can't give it all to you now. You know I gotta leverage it with my other property. It's liable to be two or three years before I get my money. I'm fighting with the insurance company now about my two places that burned down. I got to wait and see how all that turns out. I'll give you the fifteen now and five later.

Memphis.   That's alright. I see what you doing. You gonna use me to leverage your property and string me out for five thousand while you collect the interest and settle up on your insurance till you get big money and then after you get it in your pocket in two or three years then you kick me out my little five thousand dollars. That ain't right. That ain't the way to do business.

West.   That's the only way to do business. I'm trying to help you and quite naturally I got to look for every little advantage that I can get. You ought to be able to understand that.

Memphis.   I understand it. That's why I'm going downtown to the city and get my twenty-five thousand dollars. Just like I'm going back to Jackson and get my land one of these days. I still got the deed. They ran me out of there but I'm going back. I got me a piece of farm down there. Everybody said I was crazy to buy it cause it didn't have no water on it. They didn't know my grandaddy knew how to find water. If there was water anywhere under the ground he'd find it. He told me where to dig and I dug a well. Dug sixty feet down. You ain't got no idea how far that is. Took me six months hauling dirt out this little hole. Found me some water and made me a nice little crop.

   Jim Stovall, who I bought the land from, told me my deed say if I found any water the sale was null and void. Went down to the court to straighten it out and come to find out he had a bunch of these fellows get together to pick on me. He try to act like he ain't had nothing to do with it. They took and cut my mule's belly out while it standing there. Just took a knife and sliced it open. I stood there and watched them. They was laughing about it. I look and see where they got me covered. There's too many of them to fool around with. I didn't want to die. But I loved that old mule. Me and him had been through a lot together. He was a good old mule. Remind me of myself. He only do so much amount of work and that was it. He didn't mind working. He liked to get out there and exercise. Do anything you asked him. He didn't like you to half-work him. If you gonna work him . . . he want you to work him. Or else let him lay. He didn't like no stop-and-start work. That wasn't to his suiting. Don't tell him you gonna do one thing and then do something else. He'd lay down and tell you, "God damn it, make up your mind!" I used to take him down there and let him mate with Jimmy Hollis's mule. I figure I get mine, let him get his. A man like him a woman after a hard day's work. I stood there and watched them cut his belly open. He kinda reared back, took a few steps, and fell over. One of them reached down, grabbed hold of his dick, and cut that off. I stood there looking at them. I say, "Okay. I know the rules now. If you do that to something that ain't never done nothing to you . . . then I know what you would do to me. So I tell you what. You go on and get your laugh now. Cause if I get out of this alive I know how to play as good as anyone." Once I know the rules, whatever they are, I can play by them.

Went in there, saw the judge, and he say the deed was null and void. Now I got to walk home. I was looking for them to try something. But I didn't see nobody. Got home and they had set fire to my crop. To get to my house I'd have to walk through fire. I wasn't ready to do that. I turned around and walked up the hill to Natchez. Called it a draw. Said I was going back. Got up there and got tied up with one of them Mississippi gals and one year led to two led to five. Then I come on up here in '36. But I'm going back one of these days.

(Sterling enters.)

Sterling. Say, Mr. West, I was thinking, you know, I ain't never driven me no Cadillac. I figure everybody supposed to drive a Cadillac at least once before they die. A man got seven Cadillacs need somebody to drive them, right? You should see me drive. Can't nobody beat me driving. I drove a getaway car once. We got away, too. So, do you need any drivers?

West. No, I got everybody I need.

Sterling. If you ever need anybody just let me know. Okay? I done been in the penitentiary. I'll tell you that up front. I don't want to go back. I figure everybody should work at what they like to do. So I asked myself, "Sterling, what you like to do?" The closest I could come up with was I like to drive a Cadillac. So if you ever need anybody you think of me. Do you have to wash the cars if you drive them? I don't want to wash them without driving them. But if I could wash them seven at a time every day for about five dollars apiece I might do that. How long you reckon it take to do that? I don't reckon it take more than three hours. If you do a good job. I could do that for you.

West. Naw, I got somebody to wash my cars.

Sterling. I know. Every time I see them they be clean. Except for the grille. I could clean the grille better than that. You ought to tell them to get a little brush to scrub in them little spots with. It won't hurt the chrome none. Mr. Lewis taught me how to do that.

West. If I ever need anybody I'll let you know.

Holloway. Did you go back up there to see Aunt Ester?

Sterling. I went back up there they told me she was asleep.

Holloway. You give her a chance to get her rest, then you go on back up there. I'm going up and see her myself. West been up there. He don't like to tell nobody, but he been up there.

West. I don't care who know. Yeah, I been up there.

Memphis. You been up there, West?

West. Yeah, I went up there and saw her. I didn't take her to be no more than a hundred or so.

Holloway. Tell him when that was. Tell him how long that's been.

West. It's been twenty-two years. That don't mean she still alive. I ain't seen her in twenty-two years and she look like she was half-dead then. I can't imagine what she look like now.

Holloway. She look like she looked then. She wasn't but three hundred years old then. I don't reckon them twenty-two years make that much difference to her.

West. The oldest person I buried was Miss Sarah Degree and she was a hundred and twelve. I don't think nobody can live too much longer than that.

Holloway. You can go on back up and see her. She still there.

Memphis. What you go up there for, West?

West. I went up there to see if my wife was in heaven. I done buried a whole lot of people, but she the first one I ever wondered about. See, people don't understand about death, but if you ever hear one of them coffin sounds you'd know. There ain't nothing like it. That coffin get to talking and you know that this here . . . this what we call life ain't nothing. You can blow it away with a blink of an eye. But death . . . you can't blow away death. It lasts forever. I didn't understand about it till my wife died. Before that it was just a job. Then when she died I come to understand it. You can live to be a hundred and fifty and you'll never have a greater moment than when you breathe your last breath. Ain't nothing you can do in life compared to it. See, right then you done something. You became a part of everything that come before. And that's a great thing. Ain't nothing you can do in life compared to that. So I heard about Aunt Ester and went to see if my wife was in heaven. I figure if anybody know she would.

Memphis. What she tell you?

West. She told me to take and throw twenty dollars in the river and come back and see her. I thought she was crazy, to tell you the truth. I didn't pay her no mind. I knew she was old, but I figure she had gotten too old.

Holloway. That's what your problem is. You don't want to do nothing for yourself. You want somebody else to do it for you. Aunt Ester don't work that way. She say you got to pull your part of the load. But you didn't want to do that. That's why you don't know. And it didn't cost you but twenty dollars.

West. I wasn't gonna throw my money in the river, nigger.

Holloway. That's why you don't know. You don't know what might have happened if you did that. If you had gone on back up there she might have told you.

West. I offered to give her the twenty dollars just for her time . . . but she wouldn't take it. Told me to throw it in the river. I'd rather see her with it than to see it at the bottom of the river. I just wasn't gonna do that with my money.

Holloway. That's why you don't know.

West. If it take throwing my money in the river to find out then I ain't never gonna know.

Memphis. What you go up to see her about, Holloway? What happened when you threw your twenty dollars in?

Holloway. I went up there to see her cause I wanted to kill my grandfather. I went up there and got that feeling off me. I had to throw twenty dollars every week for a month. But I got it off me. He died from natural causes. Ask West . . . he buried him. He died in his sleep. That's why I knew it worked. Cause he died of natural death.

Memphis.   What you wanna kill your grandfather for?

Holloway.   Now you getting in my business. Ask West if he ain't died a natural death. That's all you need to know.

Memphis.   I don't care nothing about your business. You the one brought it up. I ain't even know you had a grandfather.

Holloway.   Had two of them. One on my mother's side and one on my father's side. One of them I never knew. The other one wasn't no good for nobody. That was the worse Negro I ever known. He think if it wasn't for white people there wouldn't be no daylight. If you let him tell it, God was a white man who had a big plantation in the sky and sat around drinking mint juleps and smoking Havana cigars. He couldn't wait to die to get up in heaven to pick cotton. If he overheard you might wanna go down and get you some extra meat out the white man's smokehouse . . . he'd run and tell him. He see you put a rabbit in your sack to weigh up with the cotton, he'd run and tell. The white man would give him a couple pounds of bacon. He'd bring that home and my grandmother would throw it out with the garbage. That's the kind of woman she was. I don't know how she got tied up with him. She used to curse the day she laid down with him. That rubbed off on me. I got a little older to where I could see what kind of man he was . . . I figure if he want to go to heaven to pick cotton, I'd help him. I got real serious about it. It stayed on me so didn't nobody want to be around me cause of the bad energy I was carrying. Couldn't keep me a woman. Seemed like nothing wouldn't work out for me. I went up to see Aunt Ester and got that bad energy off me. And it worked too. Ask West. He died in his sleep. Caught pneumonia and laid down and died. They wouldn't let him in the hospital cause he didn't have any insurance. He crawled up in the bed in my grandmother's house and laid there till he died. March 5, 1952. So can't nobody tell me nothing about Aunt Ester. I know what she can do for you.

West.   Let me get on. Say, Memphis, if you change your mind about the building, let me know.

(West exits.)

Sterling.   I'm going back up there soon as I get some money. I'll throw twenty dollars in the river if it help me get a job.

Holloway.   You go on back up there.

Sterling.   Say, Memphis . . . you know how many people be down at the steel mill hanging around there at lunch time? You ever seen that? Must be five or six hundred. I figure we could make some money selling chicken sandwiches. All you need is a little truck . . . have Risa fry up the chicken and I go over there and sell them. You ever thought about that? We could go in business together.

Memphis. I'm in business already. You go on and get your truck and go on over there. Risa . . . get these dishes cleaned up.

Sterling (*starting toward the door*). That alright . . . if that seven eighty-one come out I'll have me enough money I won't need to go in no business. If that seven eighty-one come out me and Risa gonna get married. Ain't that right, Risa?

(*Risa doesn't say anything.*)

She shy. She don't want to let everybody know. Hey, Memphis, if I find some more gas I'll bring it on around. Okay?

(*Sterling exits.*)

Memphis. I changed that, Holloway. I give him two weeks.

(*The lights go down on the scene.*)

Scene 2

(*The lights come up on the restaurant. Risa sits on a stool, reading a magazine. Holloway enters.*)

Holloway. Risa, you seen Hambone today?

Risa. Naw, he ain't been in here.

Holloway. You know he wasn't over there this morning. Lutz asked me about him.

Risa. He ain't been in here. Anybody know where he stay at?

Holloway. He was staying up there on Arcena Street. He stayed up there for the longest time. He ain't up there no more. Nobody know where he stay at.

Risa. Maybe he just quit coming. He might have moved to Homewood or East Liberty. Got tired of waiting on Lutz to give him his ham.

Holloway. I ain't known him to miss a day in nine and a half years. He come and stand there even on Sunday just in case Lutz show up. That don't sound like nobody got tired of waiting.

(*Wolf enters.*)

Wolf. Hey . . . Holloway. Did you see that out there this morning? West was having a fit trying to bury Prophet Samuel.

Holloway. Yeah, I was out there. They say the hearse was at the cemetery and some of the cars hadn't even left from in front of the funeral home.

Wolf. They had the boulevard backed up two miles. People's cars overheating. They tried to block off the street and let the cars go in two lanes, but the people was arguing with the police and wouldn't let them do it. They had helicopters flying all over the place.

Risa.   Look like they had more people watching than was in the funeral. They was lined up on both sides of the street. Half of them was in here.

Wolf.   I know. I couldn't get near the door. That was the biggest funeral West ever had.

Holloway.   It wasn't as big as Patchneck Red's funeral. This wasn't nothing but Pittsburgh niggers. For Patchneck Red's funeral they came from Detroit, Cleveland, and all parts of Ohio and New Jersey. Youngstown . . . Newark . . . Jersey City. Come from West Virginia. They had eleven Cadillacs full of women come all the way from Vegas. People didn't leave the cemetery till the next morning. They was out there pouring whiskey on the grave . . . had two five-gallon buckets full of dice and fifty-eleven decks of cards they dumped in the grave with him. Prophet Samuel wasn't nothing like that. You find out anything about Hambone?

Wolf.   I been asking around. Ain't anybody seen him. Last time anybody seen him was yesterday.

Holloway.   Lutz say he ain't seen him either.

Wolf.   How you doing, Risa? You lucky to see me today. If that six fifty-seven had come out I'd be in Atlanta right now.

Holloway.   Who you know in Atlanta, Wolf?

Wolf.   I got me a woman down there. Got two. Got one up on Jackson Hill and the other one stay on Lombard Street. One of them got four or five other men, but that's alright with me. All I got to do is call. All she got to do is hear my voice and she drop them other niggers. All she got to do is hear my voice and she come running. Any time of day or night.

Holloway.   Well, why ain't you down there, then? You walking around here without a woman talking about you got two in Atlanta. Why ain't you there?

Wolf.   I can't go down there unless I got some money. One of them think I'm a rich man. Last time she seen me I had six or seven hundred dollars in my pocket. Spent two hundred of it on her. She think I got that kind of money all the time. If that six fifty-seven had come out I'd been right there sitting on her doorstep. I had ten dollars straight on it. That's Harvey's number. He hit on that two or three times a year. I figured today might have been his lucky day.

Holloway.   I see you and Memphis got in a little hassle yesterday.

Wolf.   We alright. Memphis gets beside himself sometimes. See, he don't know he lucky I understand him. Without that understanding it be a different thing.

(Memphis enters.)

Holloway.   Hey, Memphis. You know Hambone didn't come today? You ain't seen him, have you?

Memphis.   Naw, I ain't seen him.

Holloway.   That ain't like him not to show up.

Memphis.   Risa, get these dishes cleaned off the counter.

(He and Wolf glare at each other.)

Holloway.   Hey, Wolf, give me a dime on nine sixty-eight. I'm gonna keep playing it till it come out.

Wolf.   I got to ask Memphis. Memphis, is it okay if I take Holloway's number? I mean, since this is a legitimate business and all.

Memphis.   I said I didn't want you using my phone, Wolf. You can twist it all out of shape if you want. I can't have them running in here raiding my place. I don't take no numbers out of here. Seem like you be able to understand that.

Wolf.   I understand it. What you want, Holloway?

Holloway.   Give me a dime on nine sixty-eight. Box it for a nickel.

(Wolf writes down his number.)

Memphis.   Give me a dollar on four seventy-eight.

Wolf.   You know, Sterling hit for two dollars yesterday on that seven eighty-one? He ain't gonna like it none, but they cut the number. They cut it in half. They ain't paying but half of it. I don't know what it was . . . seem like every nigger in Pittsburgh played seven eighty-one. Ain't nobody gonna like it, but he ain't gonna like it especially. I started to carry my pistol today, but I say, "Naw . . . I might kill somebody." Most people understand when they cut the numbers . . . but I don't know about Sterling. He got his own way of looking at things. Holloway, if you see him would you try and explain it to him that it ain't my fault cause I will go to the pawnshop and get my pistol. So if you could explain that to him before I see him I'd appreciate it. That way you be helping us both out.

Holloway.   If I know him like I think I do, he gonna wanna know why everybody play his number instead of their own. Then he gonna come to understand that he don't care how many people played it . . . the Alberts still owe him all his money. And since you work for the Alberts, if you don't get him his money, then you all in cahoots, and the Alberts is splitting it with you, and you gonna buy a Cadillac next week with his money . . . therefore you gonna need your pistol. And if it go that way . . . West is gonna get a chance to bury one of you. If he go up there and mess with the Alberts, then West gonna have to bury him in a closed casket. Now . . . I'm sixty-five years old and I got that way by staying out of people's business, so no . . . I ain't gonna tell him nothing. If he come in here right now I'd walk out. Come back tomorrow and Risa will have to tell me what happened.

Wolf.   Well, I ain't gonna pay him out my pocket. The hell with it. You right. I got to go to the pawnshop and get my pistol. Hey, Risa, I'll be back. If Sterling comes, tell him I was looking to see him.

(Wolf exits.)

Holloway.   I don't know why I play the numbers. The Alberts want all the advantages. They got six hundred-to-one odds, but that ain't enough for them. If thirty or forty niggers get lucky enough to hit the numbers the same day, they don't even want them to enjoy their luck. They want to take that away from them. They don't say nothing about cutting the numbers when six thousand niggers guess wrong.

Memphis.   They been cutting numbers for the past hundred years. That's part of the game. You supposed to understand that when you play your money. If I was—

(He spies the flyer on the wall.)

What the hell this doing up here?

(He tears it down and crumples it up.)

I don't want this up in my place. I ain't putting no sanction on nothing like that. That's what the problem is now. All them niggers wanna do is have a rally. Soon as they finish with one rally they start planning for the next. They forget about what goes in between. You rally to spur you into action. When it comes time for action these niggers sit down and scratch their heads. They had that boy Begaboo. The police walked up and shot him in the head and them same niggers went down there to see the mayor. Raised all kind of hell. Trying to get the cop charged with murder. They raised hell for three weeks. After that it was business as usual. The only thing anybody remember is the funeral. That's the Sterling boy bringing that stuff in here. Something wrong with that boy. That boy ain't right.

(To Risa.)

If I was you I'd stay away from him. He ain't gonna do nothing but end up right back down there in the penitentiary.

Holloway.   You might be right. Now he done got him a gun. What he gonna do with it? A nigger with a gun is bad news. You can't even use the word "nigger" and "gun" in the same sentence. You say the word "gun" in the same sentence with the word "nigger" and you in trouble. The white man panic. Unless you say, "The policeman shot the nigger with his gun" . . . then that be alright. Other than that he panic. He ain't had nothing but guns for the last five hundred years . . . got the atomic bomb and everything. But you say the word "nigger" and "gun" in the same sentence and they'll try and arrest you. Accuse you of sabotage, disturbing the peace, inciting a riot, plotting to overthrow the government and anything else they can think of. You think I'm lying? You go down there and stand in front of the number two police station and say, "The niggers is tired of this mistreatment—they gonna get some guns," and see if they don't arrest you.

Memphis.   As young and as crazy as that boy is, he need to carry one.

(Sterling enters.)

Sterling.   How you doing, Memphis? Risa . . . Wolf been in here?

Risa.   He just left. He say he be back.

Sterling.   I was out there watching them bury Prophet Samuel. Harvey gave me a ride to the cemetery. Was you over there, Risa? I was looking for you.

Risa.   Everybody running over there to see him cause he dead. They didn't go see him when he was alive. He was right up there on Herron Avenue. They wasn't lining up there then.

Sterling.   It be like that with everything. People don't care nothing about you till you dead. Then they walk around and tell everybody how well they knew you and that make them special for a day or two. You always have more followers when you dead than when you living.

Risa.   That's what I'm saying. Prophet Samuel used to preach about hypocrites and that's what half them people is. If you be a hypocrite it don't count with God. He want you all the time. That's what Prophet Samuel say. God can look into your heart and tell. But see . . . I knew Prophet Samuel when he was living.

(She hands Sterling a card. He takes it and reads.)

Sterling *(reading).*   "This certifies that Risa Thomas is a member in good standing of the First African Congregational Kingdom, having duly paid all tithing. . . . Signed, Prophet Samuel."

(He hands her back the card.)

I remember Prophet Samuel, but I ain't paid preachers or nothing like that no mind.

Risa.   Prophet Samuel wasn't no preacher. He was a prophet like they have in the Bible. God sent him to help the colored people get justice.

Memphis.   The people ain't thinking about no justice when they lined up there. They thinking about money like Prophet Samuel. That's all he thought about. Justice come second. When God send you he pay your way. God ain't paid Prophet Samuel's way. The people paid Prophet Samuel's way hoping they get a financial blessing. You running up there giving him your little bit of change—what it get you? I wish I had three, four hundred people bringing me money every week. That be all the financial blessing I need.

Risa.   That's cause you don't believe in nothing. Whatever Prophet Samuel prophesied, it come true.

Sterling.   Did he say anything about these being the last days? That's what I believe. I believe the world coming to an end.

Risa.   He said God was gonna send a sign. That's all he said about that. Said you would see it, but only the wise men would know what it meant.

Sterling.   I be looking at the moon. Seem like it's getting closer and closer. You ever notice that? You look up and see if it ain't getting closer. Maybe that's what he meant by a sign. You look next time when the moon be full and see if it ain't getting closer. You look and then go right back in your house. I don't go outside when it's a full moon. There be at least three or four people killed that night. I believe the world coming to an end.

(Risa exits into the back.)

Memphis.   If it do be the end of the world, what you gonna do? You can't do nothing but go down with it. It's foolish to worry about something like that. Something you ain't got no control over. If these niggers spent half the time they spend worrying about stuff like that and more time trying to figure out how to get out of the situation they in . . . they wouldn't have all the problems they got now.

Sterling.   Soon as I find Wolf I ain't gonna have no more problems. Hey, Risa . . . if you see Wolf . . . tell him I'm looking for him. He knows what it's about.

(Sterling exits.)

Memphis *(calling).*   Risa!

Risa.   What?

Memphis.   Come here, woman. *(Pause.)* If you want your pay you better get out here.

(Risa enters.)

I owe you forty-six dollars with the ten you took.

Risa.   I don't owe you but seven.

Memphis.   You ain't counting the three dollars you got the other day to buy some hair grease. You ain't counting that.

Risa.   I told you I put the three dollars back cause they ain't had the kind I wanted.

Memphis.   Well, write a note saying you put it back. How in the hell I'm supposed to know you put it back? Here . . . take this forty-nine dollars. I got some business to take care of . . . don't forget to put the bread in the refrigerator when you lock up. Put the bread in the refrigerator and make sure you pull the shade down on the door. I got to go down to the courthouse in the morning . . . make sure you got enough eggs before you leave out of here.

Well, Holloway . . . I was talking to my lawyer . . . Joseph Bartoromo . . . I was talking to him on the phone. He said let him handle it. I ain't gonna let him handle it but so far. I told him like I tell you . . . I ain't going for no more draws . . . and I ain't taking a penny less than twenty-five thousand dollars.

(He starts to exit and stops at the door.)

What's that address?
Holloway.　Eighteen thirty-nine Wylie. In the back. Knock on the red door.

(The lights go down on the scene.)

Scene 3

(The lights come up on Risa and Holloway. Wolf sits at the table doing his bookkeeping. Risa is sweeping. It is later the same day.)

Holloway.　He was staying up there on Herron Avenue. They found him up there today. His landlady found him. He just laid down across the bed with his clothes on and died. Say he died real peaceful. West went down to the morgue to get him . . . he got some kind of contract with the welfare and they called him up. Hambone ain't had no people. Most anybody know about him is he come from Alabama. Don't nobody even know his right name.

Risa.　That's a shame. Lutz gonna rot in hell.

Wolf.　Lutz ain't thinking about no hell. All he thinking about is his ham.

Holloway.　I went up there and told him about it cause he asked me to let him know what I found out. He didn't say nothing. He just looked at me.

(Risa accidentally sweeps Wolf's feet.)

Wolf.　Don't sweep me with that broom, girl. Ain't your mama never taught you nothing?

Risa.　Well, move your feet out the way then.

Wolf.　You sweep me with that broom and I'll end up in jail.

Holloway.　That's what's wrong with half these niggers now. They don't know what causes their trouble. They around here breaking mirrors, opening umbrellas in the house, and everything else.

Wolf.　Come on, Risa!

Risa.　Move your feet then, Wolf! You be gone to jail twice you don't move your feet.

(She sweeps him again.)

Wolf.　Hey, Risa. Come on, now!

(He gets up and gathers his papers.)

A man can't get no peace around here. If you see Sterling, tell him I'm look-ing for him. Tell him to wait here, I'll be back.

(Wolf exits.)

Holloway.   A man was driving a truck . . . hauling a whole truck full of mirrors . . . lost the brakes and ran into a telephone pole. He wasn't hurt or nothing. He looked back there and saw all them mirrors broke . . . he was staring at two hundred years of bad luck. They had to carry him away in a straitjacket.

(West enters.)

Hey, West . . . I see you finally got Prophet Samuel buried.
West.   Yeah . . . I got him in the ground and turned around and went down there and got Hambone. It don't never stop. Time you bury one nigger you got to go get another. Man had so many scars on his body . . . I ain't never seen nothing like that. All on his back, his chest . . . his legs. I'm gonna lay him out tomorrow and bury him on Saturday.
Risa.   You ought to lay him out in a nice casket. I hate to see people laid out in them welfare caskets.
West.   That's a poor man's casket. What you call a pauper's casket. He wouldn't look right laying in a bronze or silver casket.
Risa.   I hate to see him in a welfare casket. Like his life ain't meant nothing. How much one of them other caskets cost?
West.   You talking about a seven-hundred-dollar difference. The welfare don't pay but three hundred and fifty dollars. That don't even cover laying him out. I'm laying him out for free. I'm gonna lay him out for two hours tomorrow and take him on out there and bury him. You talking about a bronze casket you talking about seven hundred dollars. At least.
Risa.   Ain't you got some other caskets over there?
West.   I don't get them for free, woman. I call the company and order the cas-ket, they send me the bill. We talking about a seven-hundred-dollar differ-ence.
Risa.   I wish I had seven hundred dollars to give you. I'd lay him out in a gold casket.
West.   Now you talking about a seventeen-hundred-dollar difference. People don't understand. I got overhead. I got seven cars I got to keep up. Got sup-plies I got to order. How much you think that embalming fluid cost? I got all kinds of bills. People owe me money and won't pay me. It ain't all like every-body think with Mr. West.
Risa.   I ain't said nothing about that.

West.   You talking about why don't I lay him out in a different casket. That three hundred and fifty dollars barely cover my expenses. You can't put nobody in the ground for three hundred and fifty dollars no more. I bury him in a different casket I'm out seven hundred dollars. I try to tell these niggers to keep up their insurance.

(Sterling enters.)

Risa.   Sterling, Wolf was looking for you.

Sterling.   Naw, he ain't. I'm looking for him. Nigger owe me twelve hundred dollars. Come on, let's go to Vegas. I got me a grubstake, I might get lucky. These niggers ain't got no money around here. Come on . . . take off that apron. How you doing, Mr. West?

West.   Fine.

Sterling.   Say, Mr. West . . . you ever been to Vegas? You ought to let me take you to Vegas and teach you how to gamble. We can make us some money.

West.   I was gambling before you was born. Give me some sugar, Risa. I ran two or three crap games. Sold bootleg liquor and ran numbers too. The only thing you get out of that is an early grave. I know. I seen it happening. I looked up one day and so many people was dying from that fast life I figured I could make me some money burying them and live a long life too. I figured I could make a living from it. I didn't know I was gonna get rich. I found out life's hard but it ain't impossible.

Sterling.   That's what I figure. I get my money from Wolf . . . get in one of them white folks' crap games it be impossible to stop me. I'm gonna get me two or three Cadillacs like you. Get Risa to be my woman and I'll be alright. That's all a man need is a pocketful of money, a Cadillac, and a good woman. That's all he need on the surface. I ain't gonna talk about that other part of satisfaction. But I got sense enough to know it's there. I know if you get the surface it don't mean nothing unless you got the other. I know that, Mr. West. Sometimes I think I'll just take the woman part. And then sometimes that don't seem like it's enough.

West.   That's cause you walking around here with a ten-gallon bucket. Somebody put a little cupful in and you get mad cause it's empty. You can't go through life carrying a ten-gallon bucket. Get you a little cup. That's all you need. Get you a little cup and somebody put a little bit in and it's half full. That ten-gallon bucket ain't never gonna be full. Carry you a little cup through life and you'll never be disappointed. I'll tell you what my daddy told me. I was a young man just finding my way through life. I told him I wanted to find me a woman and go away and get me a ranch and raise horses like my grandaddy. I was still waiting around to find the woman. He told me to get the ranch first and the woman would come. And he was right. I never did get me the ranch, but he was right.

Sterling.   That's what I'm gonna do, Mr. West. You hear that, Risa? Soon as I get my money we going to Vegas and I'm gonna get me enough money to buy us a ranch. You like horses? I ain't never seen a real horse. I wouldn't know how to act around one. But if that's what it takes to get a woman like you I'm willing to do that. What's the matter? Don't you wanna go to Vegas with me?

Risa. Go on, Sterling, I don't feel like playing.

(To West.)

Ain't you got no other kind of metal casket over there? What about one of them copper caskets?

West. The government don't pay but three hundred and fifty dollars, woman! I'm doing him a favor laying him out. How you expect me to meet my expenses? If I laid everybody out in a bronze casket at my expense I'd be out of business.

Risa. I ain't talking about everybody. I'm talking about Hambone.

West. Insurance don't cost but two dollars a month. I try to tell people that.

Sterling. Hambone dead? Risa . . . Hambone dead?

Risa. They found him this morning laying across his bed.

(Sterling is thrown for a moment, but recovers quickly.)

Sterling. That don't surprise me. Don't nothing surprise me no more.

(Wolf enters.)

Hey, Wolf . . . just the man I want to see. I need my money. Me and Risa getting married and Reverend Flowers want fifty dollars . . . the cake man want fifty dollars . . . the jewelry man want two hundred dollars. Hey, Risa . . . you want to invite Wolf? She say yeah. We ain't set the date yet . . . but we let you know. Where's my money, nigger? You got my money?

Wolf. Look, Sterling . . . it ain't my fault . . . but they cut the number. They cut it in half. They ain't paying but six hundred dollars.

Sterling. I'm like Joe Louis.[5] They cut the odds on Joe Louis all the time. That seven eighty-one was like a knockout punch. I knew it was gonna hit. I'm going up and tell the Alberts that seven eighty-one don't hit like a .45. Mr. West, you don't bury white people, do you? That's alright. I ain't gonna kill nobody. I'll just put them in a wheelchair.

(To Wolf.)

And I'm gonna start with you if you don't give me my twelve hundred dollars.

Wolf. I'm gonna tell you one more time, Sterling. I ain't had nothing to do with it. I know you mad. Everybody mad. They mad out in East Liberty.

---

[5] Joe Louis (1914–1981), African American champion heavyweight boxer from 1937 to 1949, was often called the "Brown Bomber."

People in Beltzhoover . . . everybody all up and down the avenue mad. I ain't had nothing to do with it. If it was up to me I'd pay everybody what they due. This is a job to me. That little bit they pay me ain't worth all that. They call me, say, "Wolf, the numbers cut in half." I say, "Okay." That's the way that go. The best I can say is you lucky they didn't cut it seven ways.

Sterling.   Naw . . . naw, what you telling me is me and Risa got to postpone our getting married.

Risa.   I ain't said nothing about getting married. Don't be telling everybody that. Wolf, don't pay him no mind about that.

Sterling.   See what I mean? Risa done changed her mind. I'm going up and see the Alberts, see if they change theirs. Give me my six hundred dollars, nigger.

(Wolf pays him the money.)

I'm going up there and give it back to them. See Old Man Albert himself. Let him know an airplane can fall on his head.

(Sterling starts to exit.)

Wolf.   Don't do that, Sterling. Them people don't play.

Sterling.   If I don't play . . . that mean there can't be no game. I'm going up there and carry me a big sign say "Game Canceled." See? Cause I don't play either.

(Sterling exits.)

Risa *(calling after him).*   Sterling!

(The lights go down on the scene.)

Scene 4

(The lights come up on the restaurant. Risa is sweeping the floor. Sterling enters.)

Sterling.   I come by to see if you wanna go to the rally.

(He doesn't get a response.)

It done started already but I figure we won't be too late.

Risa.   You left out of here talking about you was gonna see the Alberts. . . . We didn't know if we was gonna see you again.

Sterling.   I didn't know it mattered to nobody. I heard you calling me. What you calling after me for?

Risa.   I just didn't want to see you get killed.

Sterling. I went up there to see Old Man Albert. He sitting up there with four or five bodyguards. They let me in to see him and I told him to give me back my two dollars. Said I was calling off the bet. He gave me the two dollars and asked me for his six hundred back. I told him no. Told him I was gonna keep that. That way I have something that belong to him for a change. He just looked at me funny and told me to leave the same way I had come in. Told one of his bodyguards to show me the door. I left out of there and was walking by Aunt Ester's. I saw the light on and I figure she might be up, so I stopped to see her. They led me into the hallway and then through some curtains into this room . . . and she was just sitting there. I talked to her a long while. Told her my whole life story. She real nice. Ain't nobody ever talk to me like that. "I cannot swim does not walk by the lakeside." It took me a while to figure out what she meant. Told me, "Make better what you have and you have best." Then she wrote down something on a piece of paper, put it in a little envelope, told me to put it in my shoe and walk around on it for three days. I asked her how much I owed her. She told me to take twenty dollars and throw it in the river. Say she get it. She had this look about her real calm and sweet like. I asked her how old she was. She say she was three hundred and forty-nine years old. Holloway had it wrong. I figured anybody that old know what she talking about. I took twenty dollars and carried it down there. Didn't even think about it. I just took and threw it in the river. I'm gonna wait them three days and see what happen. You ought to go up there and see her. She a real nice old lady. She say yeah, you the one God sent when he told me he couldn't send no angel.

Risa. Sterling, you crazy.

Sterling. I figure me and you get us a nice little old place. . . . Ain't you tired of sleeping by yourself? I am.

Risa. Naw, I'm just fine taking care of me.

Sterling. You ain't got to take care of you . . . let me do that. I'll take care of you real good.

(He sings.)

Wake up, Pretty Mama
See what I got for you
I got everything
Set your poor heart at ease
I got everything for you, woman.
I got a list of things
long as my right arm.

Risa. Naw, that's alright.

Sterling. Woman, you everything a man need. Know how to cook . . . pay nice attention to yourself . . . except for those legs. You ought not to have done that. What you do that for anyway?

Risa. You wouldn't understand, Sterling.

Sterling. You be surprised . . . I got good understanding. That's what Aunt Ester told me. She looked at me and say, "I like to work with people like you cause you got good understanding." She say that before I could say anything to her. She just looked at me and said that. Now why can't you do that?

Risa. What you looking at my legs for anyway?

Sterling. That's part of life, woman. You don't think I'm not gonna look at them? Even if you tried to make them ugly. So you wanted to have ugly legs . . . you got them. Now what? I done looked at your legs, your hips, your titties, and everything else. Now what? I don't care if you got scars on your legs.

Risa. That's why I did it. To make them ugly.

Sterling. You did a good job. You and God both. He made them pretty and you made them ugly. You both got what you wanted. Now why can't I get what I want?

Risa. That's what the problem is.

Sterling. I know that's a problem. I'm trying to solve it.

Risa. You just want what everybody else want.

Sterling. Risa . . . you in the world, baby. You a woman in the world. You here like everybody else. You got to make the best of it. Quite naturally when men see you with that big ass and them pretty legs they gonna try and talk you into a bed somewhere. That's common sense. They be less than a man if they didn't. Ain't no sense in you getting upset about that. You ought to take it as a compliment. All you got to do is say no and keep on stepping.

Risa. That just what I done.

Sterling. I know that. Been telling me no since I met you. By rights I should be talking to somebody else. I tried that. But I was talking to her and thinking of you. So I come on back.

Risa. You ain't got no job. You going back to the penitentiary. I don't want to be tied up with nobody I got to be worrying is they gonna rob another bank or something.

Sterling. When I was living with Mrs. Johnson before she died I used to watch her husband. He get up every morning at six o'clock. Sunday too. Six-thirty he out the door. Now . . . he ain't coming back till ten o'clock at night. He going down to J&L and lift hundred-pound slabs of steel till three o'clock. Then he going over after they close the fish market and clean up over there. Now what he got? He got six kids of his own, not to mention me. He got a raggedy house with some beat-up furniture. Can't buy no house cause he can't get a loan. Now that sound like a hard-working man. Good. Clean. Honest. Upright. He work thirty years at the mill and ain't even got a union card. You got to work six months straight. They lay him off for two weeks every five and a half months. He got to call the police after he clean up the fish market so they can let him out of the building. Make sure he don't steal anything. What they got? Two pound of catfish? There got to be something else. I ain't sure I want to do all that.

Risa. You got to do something.

Sterling.   Okay. Okay. If you don't want to get married and have babies and all that . . . then can we be cousins? Can we be kissing cousins? How's that?

(He has cornered her. Risa pushes him away.)

Risa.   Go on, Sterling . . . leave me alone now.
Sterling.   Risa, baby . . .
Risa.   What?
Sterling.   I ain't never met no woman like you.
Risa.   I ain't met no man like you either. But that don't mean I'm gonna get tied up with you. You'll never have me sitting and worrying what you gonna do next.
Sterling.   Well, come on and go to the rally with me.
Risa.   I ain't going to no rally. You can just go on by yourself.

(Risa goes over to the jukebox and puts in a quarter. "Take a Look" by Aretha Franklin begins to play.)

Sterling.   When did that get fixed?
Risa.   Today.
Sterling *(hesitant).*   You wanna dance?
Risa.   Yeah.

(They begin to dance. Sterling kisses her lightly.)

Sterling.   How's that? You wanna be kissing cousins?

(He kisses her passionately.)

   Goddamn, baby!
Risa.   Sterling.
Sterling.   I didn't know it was gonna be like this. You can be my first cousin.
Risa *(between kisses).*   I wanna be your only cousin.
Sterling.   That too.

(Sterling kisses her as the lights go down.)

Scene 5

(The lights come up on the restaurant. The menu board reads, "Funeral for Hambone Saturday One O'Clock." Holloway sits in a booth. Risa is cooking. Sterling stands looking out the window.)

Holloway.   That's all you got. You got love and you got death. Death will find you . . . it's up to you to find love. That's where most people fall down at.

Death got room for everybody. Love pick and choose. Now, most people won't admit that. They tell you they love this one and that one. Most don't even love their mother. You can see that by the way they treat her. But they'll tell you anything. But they got to know in their heart. I believe West loved his wife. And Bubba Boy loved his woman. Them's the only two people I can say found love. The rest of us play at it. That's cause love cost. Love got a price to it. Everybody don't want to pay. They put it on credit. Time it come due they got it on credit somewhere else. That's the way I see the world. That's what I done learned all these years.

(Wolf enters.)

Wolf. It look like Hong Kong out there. I didn't know there was that many niggers in Pittsburgh. If you drive by you'd swear didn't nobody have no home. They all out there on the street.

Holloway. The people out there looking for opportunity. Whatever's out there in the way of opportunity, sooner or later it's got to pass through. You can't find out what's out there sitting at home.

(To Wolf.)

Why ain't you home? Talking about the people. You just come in from out there.

Wolf. I got business to take care of. I can't take care of it sitting at home.

Holloway. That's what I'm trying to tell you. You can't separate yourself from everybody else. The people out there trying to figure out how they gonna eat. It's day off on the plantation. They waiting for the white man to call them back to work.

Wolf. I went over there to see Hambone. West got him laid out real nice. He look like he sleeping. You been over, Sterling?

Sterling. I just left from over there.

Wolf. Don't he look real nice and peaceful? Look like he sleeping.

Sterling. He look like he dead to me. I sat there awhile. I signed the book. Ain't but three or four people signed it.

Wolf. I signed it. I see Holloway signed it. Risa, you going over?

Risa. No . . . I don't want to see him like that.

Wolf. I saw you all down at the rally last night. Wasn't that something? Everybody was down there. Even the niggers that swear up and down on two stacks of Bibles that they ain't black . . . they was down there. Ain't had but five hundred chairs and three thousand people. Wasn't no fight or nothing. It was real nice.

Sterling. The police was down there taking people's pictures.

Wolf. I seen that. Wasn't that something? They don't go out there where the white folks at and take their pictures.

Sterling. I smiled when they took mine.

Wolf. I was standing down there watching that drugstore. It's still smoking from the fire last night. They ain't put it out yet. They must have had every fire truck in the world down there. Did you all see that? It wasn't nothing but a little old drugstore. Had ten, eleven fire trucks and near about a hundred police. Say it started in the back by the alley. A couple of people seen some of them black power niggers around there.

Holloway. That ain't nothing but talk. Everybody know the man burned down his own store so he could get the insurance. That's the only way he get anything out of it. If he pack up and leave he don't get nothing. This way he get paid for everything . . . all his stock . . . his building . . . everything. That's the best way to sell a business don't nobody want to buy. Sell it to the insurance company. All them niggers standing down there watching the fire . . . they don't know . . . but somebody's going to jail. The police got to snatch one of them. That way the insurance company pay quicker. Meyer's gonna walk away with two hundred thousand dollars and somebody going to jail for three years. See if I ain't right. You watch over the next two or three days and see if they don't arrest somebody as he walking by there. Meyer's gonna be down there in Florida playing golf and laying on the beach . . . and the fire inspector's gonna be right there with him. That's the way it works in America.

Wolf. You right about that. It's hard to live in America. Did you all hear where Petey Brown killed his old lady last night? Caught her in the Ellis Hotel with his best friend. Killed him too. That's why I don't have no one woman. When I die every woman in Pittsburgh gonna cry. They ain't gonna know what to do with themselves. My woman come and told me she had another man. I told her say, "Alright, baby, but he can't hear and he can't see. He can't see like I do. You got to be able to pull a whole lot of boxcars to keep up with me." I'm like Prophet Samuel . . . if a man can get him seven women . . . if he can find seven women want to be with him . . . let him have them seven and one or two more. Seven women wanna lay down with him must see something they like. Hell, it's hard to get one, let alone seven. It's hard to get one you can trust that far. See, when you lay down with her, you trusting her with your life. You lay down you got to close your eyes. It wouldn't be nothing for somebody to walk up and slit your throat. That's why you lock the door at night. You lock the door and it be just you and her. That's a whole lot of trust there. If I had that I wouldn't give it up for nothing. Other than that when I die every woman in Pittsburgh gonna cry.

(West enters.)

Holloway. Hey, West.

Wolf. Mr. West himself!

West. How you doing, Holloway? Hey, Risa, give me a cup of coffee. Memphis ain't come back yet?

Holloway. I hope he didn't go down there and act a fool to where they had to lock him up. The courthouse been closed.

Sterling. Say, Mr. West . . . I just wanna tell you . . . you did a good job on Hambone. I just wanna tell you that.

West. I got him laid out there for two hours tonight . . . just in case anybody wanna see him . . . then I'm gonna take him on out there and bury him tomorrow. Lutz come by to see him after he closed his store.

Risa. Lutz gonna rot in hell.

Wolf. Lutz gonna go to hell with a ham under each arm.

Risa. You want some coffee, Sterling?

Sterling. Yeah, give me a cup.

West. Let me get some sugar, Risa.

Holloway. Things done quieted down over there now with Prophet Samuel gone.

West. It took seven hours to bury him.

Holloway. Hey, West, tell him . . . that wasn't nothing like Patchneck Red.

West. I ain't never seen nothing like that. The way them people carried on . . . it was sinful. I buried that boy Begaboo but it wasn't nothing like that. There was just as many people, but they was respectful. Them niggers come to bury Patchneck Red act like it was a party.

Sterling. Here's your twenty dollars, Wolf. Hey, Risa . . . hold this for me.

Risa. What's that?

Sterling. That's my money. All five hundred and sixty-two dollars of it. Hold it for me . . . I'll be right back.

(Sterling exits.)

Wolf. Risa, what's going on with you and Sterling? Something going on. Don't get me wrong now, I ain't said nothing wrong with it. You know me. I live and let live. I think it's nice.

Risa. Wolf, ain't nobody paying you no mind.

Wolf. Naw, Sterling's alright with me. He act kind of crazy sometime. But he alright with me. I think it's nice.

(Memphis enters, singing. He has been drinking.)

Memphis.

We don't care what Mama don't allow
We gonna barrelhouse anyhow

Hey . . . Hey . . . Holloway. You know the Brass Rail down there by the courthouse? Man . . . they got a barmaid down there you can stand up right next to Risa. She gonna wait on me till I come back. She down there now. I told her I'll be back. She get off at seven o'clock. I left the courthouse, stopped down there and got me a few drinks. Hey . . . hey . . . Risa, fix me something to eat. Holloway . . . I took that twenty dollars and threw it in the river . . . right down there in the Monongahela River. . . . I went and stood on the Brady Street Bridge . . . I didn't just let it drop. I took and tied a rock around it and threw it . . . just like Aunt Ester say. She told me if I do that everything be alright. And she was right too. She told me, "If you can't fight the fire, don't mess with it." Only I'm ready to fight it now. Hey, West . . . look here . . . I went down there to the courthouse ready to fight for that twenty-five thousand dollars I want for my property. I wasn't taking no fifteen. I wasn't taking no twenty. I want twenty-five thousand. They told me, "Well, Mr. Lee . . . we got a clause, and the city is prepared to put into motion"—that's the part I like, "prepared to put into motion"—"the securing of your property at sixteen twenty-one Wylie Avenue"—they had the address right and everything—"for the sum of thirty-five thousand dollars." I liked to fell over. The lawyer standing there, he know I'm mad and he ready to fight it. I told him, "Don't you say a word. Don't you open your mouth." Thirty-five thousand dollars! I started to go up and tell my wife. She up there. She up there at the house. She come back to get her things and ended up staying. I moved out. She moved back in and I moved out. Told her I had something to do and if she be there when I get back—if I get back—then we can sit down and talk. You know what I'm gonna do? Aunt Ester clued me on this one. I went up there and told her my whole life story. She say, "If you drop the ball, you got to go back and pick it up. Ain't no need in keeping running, cause if you get to the end zone it ain't gonna be a touchdown." She didn't say it in them words but that's what she meant. Told me . . . "You got to go back and pick up the ball." That's what I'm gonna do. I'm going back to Jackson and see Stovall. If he ain't there, then I'm gonna see his son. He enjoying his daddy's benefits he got to carry his daddy's weight. I'm going on back up to Jackson and pick up the ball.

(He notices the sign on the menu board.)

"Funeral for Hambone Saturday One O'Clock." Hambone dead? He dead?
Risa. He died in his sleep.
Memphis. Lutz never did give him his ham, did he? I always figured one day Lutz would break down and give it to him. Either that or he'd take it.

(He mimics Hambone:)

He gonna give me my ham. He gonna give me my ham. I want my ham.

(He is in pain, wounded by all the cruel and cold ironies of life. He reaches into his pocket.)

Risa . . . take this fifty dollars and get some flowers.

(He gives her some money.)

Get him a big bunch. Put on there where it say who it's from . . . say it's from everybody . . . everybody who ever dropped the ball and went back to pick it up. Risa, where's my plate? I got to eat something. I'm going on back down there to the Brass Rail. Me and . . . me and . . . I forget her name . . . we gonna celebrate. You believe that, Holloway? Hey, West . . . thirty-five thousand dollars. When I get back . . . if I get back from seeing Stovall . . . I'm gonna open me up a big restaurant right down there on Centre Avenue. I'm gonna need two or three cooks and seven or eight waitresses. I'm gonna fix it up real nice. Gonna put me a jukebox . . . fix it so the lights go up and down and everything.

(The sound of glass breaking and a burglar alarm is heard.)

Hell, I might even put a carpet on the floor. Put little chandeliers . . . get me a neon sign. I'm talking about a big neon. You be able to see it from Herron Avenue. I'm gonna put everything on the menu. Short ribs. Bar-B-Que . . . I might have me a little takeout on the side . . . put in a separate entrance. . . .

(Sterling enters, carrying a large ham. He is bleeding from his face and his hands. He grins and lays the ham on the counter.)

Sterling.   Say, Mr. West . . . that's for Hambone's casket.

(The lights go down to black.)

For Analysis
1. Identify the various story lines in the play. How are they related to one another? Does the play achieve unity despite the fact that there is not much **plot** in the conventional sense? **2.** Which character seems most fully developed? Least fully developed? Explain. **3.** Which character seems to come closest to embodying the themes of the play? **4.** What does Aunt Ester represent? **5.** What does West represent? **6.** How would you characterize the play's treatment of racism? Which character strikes you as having the most perceptive views on the subject? **7.** In what sense might this play be described as a celebration of African American life and culture?

On Style
There are no white characters in the cast although the presence of the white world permeates the play. Examine the ways in which that presence is created. What does the white world represent?

Making Connections
What similarities do you find in the depiction of black life in this play and Toni Cade Bambara's "The Lesson" (p. 115)?

Writing Topics
1. In a program note for the play, Wilson explained the meaning of the title: "There are always and only two trains running. There is life and there is death. Each of us

rides them both." A reviewer of the play had this to say about the title: "Two Trains subtly embodies the entire black political dialectic from [the late 1960s to today]— isolation vs. assimilation, hostility toward vs. cooperation with whites, clinging to bitter memory vs. moving on into a better world." Use these two comments as the basis for an analysis of the play. **2.** Write an essay arguing for or against the proposition that the play embodies a generally upbeat and positive view.

Essays

Jonathan Swift   [1667–1745]

A Modest Proposal   1729

It is a melancholy object to those who walk through this great town[1] or travel in the country, when they see the streets, the roads, and cabin doors, crowded with beggars of the female sex, followed by three, four, or six children, all in rags and importuning every passenger for an alms. These mothers, instead of being able to work for their honest livelihood, are forced to employ all their time in strolling to beg sustenance for their helpless infants, who, as they grow up, either turn thieves for want of work, or leave their dear native country to fight for the Pretender in Spain, or sell themselves to the Barbados.[2]

I think it is agreed by all parties that this prodigious number of children in the arms, or on the backs, or at the heels of their mothers, and frequently of their fathers, is in the present deplorable state of the kingdom a very great additional grievance; and therefore whoever could find out a fair, cheap, and easy method of making these children sound, useful members of the commonwealth would deserve so well of the public as to have his statue set up for a preserver of the nation.

But my intention is very far from being confined to provide only for the children of professed beggars; it is of a much greater extent, and shall take in the whole number of infants at a certain age who are born of parents in effect as little able to support them as those who demand our charity in the streets.

As to my own part, having turned my thoughts for many years upon this important subject, and maturely weighed the several schemes of other projectors,[3] I have always found them grossly mistaken in their computation. It is true, a

---

[1] Dublin.

[2] Many Irish men joined the army of the exiled James Stuart (1688–1766), who laid claim to the British throne. Others exchanged their labor for passage to the British colony of Barbados, in the Caribbean.

[3] People with projects.

628

child just dropped from its dam may be supported by her milk for a solar year, with little other nourishment; at most not above the value of two shillings,[4] which the mother may certainly get, or the value in scraps, by her lawful occupation of begging; and it is exactly at one year that I propose to provide for them in such a manner as instead of being a charge upon their parents or the parish, or wanting food and raiment for the rest of their lives, they shall on the contrary contribute to the feeding, and partly to the clothing, of many thousands.

There is likewise another great advantage in my scheme, that it will prevent   5 those voluntary abortions, and that horrid practice of women murdering their bastard children, alas, too frequent among us, sacrificing the poor innocent babes, I doubt, more to avoid the expense than the shame, which would move tears and pity in the most savage and inhuman breast.

The number of souls in this kingdom being usually reckoned one million and a half, of these I calculate there may be about two hundred thousand couples whose wives are breeders; from which number I subtract thirty thousand couples who are able to maintain their own children, although I apprehend there cannot be so many under the present distress of the kingdom; but this being granted, there will remain an hundred and seventy thousand breeders. I again subtract fifty thousand for those women who miscarry, or whose children die by accident or disease within the year. There only remain an hundred and twenty thousand children of poor parents annually born. The question therefore is, how this number shall be reared and provided for, which, as I have already said, under the present situation of affairs, is utterly impossible by all the methods hitherto proposed. For we can neither employ them in handicraft or agriculture; we neither build houses (I mean in the country) nor cultivate land. They can very seldom pick up a livelihood by stealing till they arrive at six years old except where they are of towardly parts;[5] although I confess they learn the rudiments much earlier, during which time they can however be looked upon only as probationers, as I have been informed by a principal gentleman in the country of Cavan, who protested to me that he never knew above one or two instances under the age of six, even in a part of the kingdom so renowned for the quickest proficiency in that art.

I am assured by our merchants that a boy or a girl before twelve years old is no salable commodity; and even when they come to this age they will not yield above three pounds, or three pounds and half a crown at most on the Exchange;[6] which cannot turn to account either to the parents or the kingdom, the charge of nutriment and rags having been at least four times that value.

I shall now therefore humbly propose my own thoughts, which I hope will not be liable to the least objection.

I have been assured by a very knowing American of my acquaintance in London, that a young healthy child well nursed is at a year old a most delicious,

---

[4] A shilling was worth about twenty-five cents.
[5] Able and eager to learn.
[6] A pound was twenty shillings; a crown, five shillings.

nourishing, and wholesome food, whether stewed, roasted, baked, or boiled; and I make no doubt that it will equally serve in a fricassee or a ragout.

I do therefore humbly offer it to public consideration that of the hundred and 10 twenty thousand children, already computed, twenty thousand may be reserved for breed, whereof only one fourth part to be males, which is more than we allow to sheep, black cattle, or swine; and my reason is that these children are seldom the fruits of marriage, a circumstance not much regarded by our savages, therefore one male will be sufficient to serve four females. That the remaining hundred thousand may at a year old be offered in sale to the persons of quality and fortune through the kingdom, always advising the mother to let them suck plentifully in the last month, so as to render them plump and fat for a good table. A child will make two dishes at an entertainment for friends; and when the family dines alone, the fore or hind quarter will make a reasonable dish, and seasoned with a little pepper or salt will be very good boiled on the fourth day, especially in winter.

I have reckoned upon a medium that a child just born will weigh twelve pounds, and in a solar year if tolerably nursed increaseth to twenty-eight pounds.

I grant this food will be somewhat dear, and therefore very proper for landlords, who, as they have already devoured most of the parents, seem to have the best title to the children.

Infant's flesh will be in season throughout the year, but more plentiful in March, and a little before and after. For we are told by a grave author, an eminent French physician,[7] that fish being a prolific diet, there are more children born in Roman Catholic countries about nine months after Lent than at any other season; therefore, reckoning a year after Lent, the markets will be more glutted than usual, because the number of popish infants is at least three to one in this kingdom; and therefore it will have one other collateral advantage, by lessening the number of Papists among us.

I have already computed the charge of nursing a beggar's child (in which list I reckon all cottagers, laborers, and four-fifths of the farmers) to be about two shillings per annum, rags included; and I believe no gentleman would repine to give ten shillings for the carcass of a good fat child, which, as I have said, will make four dishes of excellent nutritive meat, when he hath only some particular friend or his own family to dine with him. Thus the squire will learn to be a good landlord, and grow popular among the tenants; the mother will have eight shillings net profit, and be fit for work till she produces another child.

Those who are more thrifty (as I must confess the times require) may flay the 15 carcass; the skin of which artificially[8] dressed will make admirable gloves for ladies, and summer boots for fine gentlemen.

As to our city of Dublin, shambles[9] may be appointed for this purpose in the

---

[7] François Rabelais, sixteenth-century French comic writer.
[8] Skillfully.
[9] Slaughterhouses.

most convenient parts of it, and butchers we may be assured will not be wanting; although I rather recommend buying the children alive, and dressing them
hot from the knife as we do roasting pigs.

A very worthy person, a true lover of his country, and whose virtues I highly
esteem, was lately pleased in discoursing on this matter to offer a refinement
upon my scheme. He said that many gentlemen of his kingdom, having of late
destroyed their deer, he conceived that the want of venison might be well supplied by the bodies of young lads and maidens, not exceeding fourteen years of
age nor under twelve, so great a number of both sexes in every country being
now ready to starve for want of work or service; and these to be disposed of by
their parents, if alive, or otherwise by their nearest relations. But with due deference to so excellent a friend and so deserving a patriot, I cannot be altogether
in his sentiments; for as to the males, my American acquaintance assured me
from frequent experience that their flesh was generally tough and lean, like that
of our schoolboys, by continual exercise, and their taste disagreeable; and to fat-
ten them would not answer the charge. Then as to the females; it would, I think
with humble submission, be a loss to the public, because they soon would become breeders themselves; and besides, it is not improbable that some scrupulous people might be apt to censure such a practice (although indeed very
unjustly) as a little bordering upon cruelty; which, I confess, hath always been
with me the strongest objection against any project, how well soever intended.

But in order to justify my friend, he confessed that this expedient was put into
his head by the famous Psalmanazar,[10] a native of the island Formosa, who came
from thence to London above twenty years ago, and in conversation told my
friend that in his country when any young person happened to be put to death,
the executioner sold the carcass to persons of quality as a prime dainty; and that
in his time the body of a plump girl of fifteen, who was crucified for an attempt
to poison the emperor, was sold to his Imperial Majesty's prime minister of
state, and other great mandarins of the court, in joints from the gibbet, at four
hundred crowns. Neither indeed can I deny that if the same use were made of
several plump young girls in this town, who without one single groat[11] to their
fortunes cannot stir abroad without a chair,[12] and appear at the playhouse and
assemblies in foreign fineries which they never will pay for, the kingdom would
not be the worse.

Some persons of a desponding spirit are in great concern about the vast number of poor people who are aged, diseased, or maimed, and I have been desired
to employ my thoughts what course may be taken to ease the nation of so grievous an encumberance. But I am not in the least pain upon the matter, because
it is very well known that they are every day dying and rotting by cold and
famine, and filth and vermin, as fast as can be reasonably expected. And as to

---

[10] George Psalmanazar was a Frenchman who passed himself off as a native of Formosa (the former name for Taiwan).

[11] A coin worth about four cents.

[12] A sedan chair, an enclosed chair carried by poles on the front and back.

the younger laborers, they are now in almost as hopeful a condition. They cannot get work, and consequently pine away for want of nourishment to a degree that if any time they are accidently hired to common labor, they have not the strength to perform it; and thus the country and themselves are happily delivered from the evils to come.

I have too long digressed, and therefore I shall return to my subject. I think   20
the advantages by the proposal which I have made are obvious and many, as well as of the highest importance.

For first, I have already observed, it would greatly lessen the number of Papists, with whom we are yearly overrun, being the principal breeders of the nation as well as our most dangerous enemies; and who stay at home on purpose to deliver the kingdom to the Pretender, hoping to take their advantage by the absence of so many good Protestants, who have chose rather to leave their country than to stay at home and pay tithes against their conscience to an Episcopal curate.

Secondly, the poorer tenants will have something valuable of their own, which by law may be made liable to distress,[13] and help to pay their landlord's rent, their corn and cattle being already seized and money a thing unknown.

Thirdly, whereas the maintenance of a hundred thousand children, from two years old and upwards, cannot be computed at less than ten shillings a piece per annum, the nation's stock will be thereby increased fifty thousand pounds per annum, besides the profit of a new dish introduced to the tables of all gentlemen of fortune in the kingdom who have any refinement in taste. And all the money will circulate among ourselves, the goods being entirely of our own growth and manufacture.

Fourthly, the constant breeders, besides the gain of eight shillings sterling per annum by the sale of their children, will be rid of the charge of maintaining them after the first year.

Fifthly, this food would likewise bring great custom to taverns, where the   25
vintners will certainly be so prudent as to procure the best receipts[14] for dressing it to perfection, and consequently have their houses frequented by all the fine gentlemen, who justly value themselves upon their knowledge in good eating; and a skillful cook, who understands how to oblige his guests, will contrive to make it as expensive as they please.

Sixthly, this would be a great inducement to marriage, which all wise nations have either encouraged by rewards or enforced by laws and penalties. It would increase the care and tenderness of mothers towards their children, when they were sure of a settlement for life to the poor babes, provided in some sort by the public, to their annual profit instead of expense. We should see an honest emulation among the married women, which of them could bring the fattest child to the market. Men would become as fond of their wives during the time of their pregnancy as they are now of their mares in foal, their cows in calf, or sows

[13] Seizure for payment of debts.
[14] Recipes.

when they are ready to farrow; nor offer to beat or kick them (as is too frequent a practice) for fear of a miscarriage.

Many other advantages might be enumerated. For instance, the addition of some thousand carcasses in our exportation of barreled beef, the propagation of swine's flesh, and improvements in the art of making good bacon, so much wanted among us by the great destruction of pigs, too frequent at our tables, which are no way comparable in taste or magnificence to a well-grown, fat, yearling child, which roasted whole will make a considerable figure at a lord mayor's feast or any other public entertainment. But this and many others I omit, being studious of brevity.

Supposing that one thousand families in this city would be constant customers for infants' flesh, besides others who might have it at merry meetings, particularly weddings and christenings, I compute that Dublin would take off annually about twenty thousand carcasses, and the rest of the kingdom (where probably they will be sold somewhat cheaper) the remaining eighty thousand.

I can think of no one objection that will possibly be raised against this proposal unless it should be urged that the number of people will be thereby much lessened in the kingdom. This I freely own, and it was indeed one principal design in offering it to the world. I desire the reader will observe, that I calculate my remedy for this one individual kingdom of Ireland and for no other that ever was, is, or I think ever can be upon earth. Therefore let no man talk to me of other expedients: of taxing our absentees at five shillings a pound: of using neither clothes nor household furniture except what is of our own growth and manufacture: of utterly rejecting the materials and instruments that promote foreign luxury: of curing the expensiveness of pride, vanity, idleness, and gaming in our women: of introducing a vein of parsimony, prudence, and temperance: of learning to love our country, in the want of which we differ even from Laplanders and the inhabitants of Topinamboo:[15] of quitting our animosities and factions, nor acting any longer like the Jews, who were murdering one another at the very moment their city was taken:[16] of being a little cautious not to sell our country and conscience for nothing: of teaching landlords to have at least one degree of mercy toward their tenants: lastly, of putting a spirit of honesty, industry, and skill into our shopkeepers; who, if a resolution could now be taken to buy only our native goods, would immediately unite to cheat and exact upon us in the price, the measure, and the goodness, nor could ever yet be brought to make one fair proposal of just dealing, though often and earnestly invited to it.

Therefore, I repeat, let no man talk to me of these and the like expedients, till   30
he hath at least some glimpse of hope that there will be some hearty and sincere attempt to put them in practice.

But as to myself, having been wearied out for many years of offering vain,

---

[15] A district in Brazil, inhabited in Swift's day by primitive tribes.
[16] While the Roman emperor Titus laid siege to Jerusalem in 70 A.D., bloody fighting erupted among factions within the city.

idle, visionary thoughts, and at length utterly despairing of success, I fortunately fell upon this proposal, which, as it is wholly new, so it hath something solid and real, of no expense and little trouble, full in our own power, and whereby we can incur no danger in disobliging England. For this kind of commodity will not bear exportation, the flesh being of too tender a consistence to admit a long continuance in salt, although perhaps I could name a country[17] which would be glad to eat up our whole nation without it.

After all, I am not so violently bent upon my own opinion as to reject any offer proposed by wise men, which shall be found equally innocent, cheap, easy, and effectual. But before something of that kind shall be advanced in contradiction to my scheme, and offering a better, I desire the author or authors will be pleased maturely to consider two points. First, as things now stand, how they will be able to find food and raiment for an hundred thousand useless mouths and backs. And secondly, there being a round million of creatures in human figure throughout this kingdom, whose sole subsistence put into a common stock would leave them in debt two millions of pounds sterling, adding those who are beggars by profession to the bulk of farmers, cottagers, and laborers, with their wives and children who are beggars in effect; I desire those politicians who dislike my overture, and may perhaps be so bold to attempt to answer, that they will first ask the parents of these mortals whether they would not at this day think it a great happiness to have been sold for food at a year old in this manner I prescribe, and thereby have avoided such a perpetual scene of misfortunes as they have since gone through by the oppression of landlords, the impossibility of paying rent without money or trade, the want of common sustenance, with neither house nor clothes to cover them from the inclemencies of the weather, and the most inevitable prospect of entailing the like or greater miseries upon their breed forever.

I profess, in the sincerity of my heart, that I have not the least personal interest in endeavoring to promote this necessary work, having no other motive than the public good of my country, by advancing our trade, providing for infants, relieving the poor, and giving some pleasure to the rich. I have no children by which I can propose to get a single penny; the youngest being nine years old, and my wife past childbearing.

For Analysis
1. What kind of person is the speaker? What does his tone of voice reveal about who he is? Is his voice direct and transparent, or does it seem deliberately created to achieve a specific effect? **2.** In what sense is the proposal "modest"? **3.** Where are the major divisions of the essay? What function does each serve? **4.** What function does paragraph 29 serve? **5.** Explain what Swift means when he says in paragraph 20, "I have too long digressed. . . ." **6.** Whom is Swift addressing in this essay?

On Style
Characterize the **tone** of the essay, paying particular attention to the speaker's diction. How does the tone contribute to the effectiveness of the piece?

---

[17] England.

Making Connections

Some other works in this anthology that use **satire** include: Robert Frost, "Departmental" (p. 715); E. E. Cummings, "the Cambridge ladies who live in furnished souls" (p. 724); W. H. Auden, "The Unknown Citizen" (p. 448); Edwin Arlington Robinson, "Miniver Cheevy" (p. 440); Harlan Ellison, " 'Repent, Harlequin!' Said the Ticktockman" (p. 395); and Woody Allen, "Death Knocks" (p. 1305). Compare and contrast the use of satire in one of these works with Swift's use of satire.

Writing Topics

1. Some background information on Swift's life and other works would make it clear that in this essay he is being satiric. Without that background, that is, on the basis of this essay alone, how would you demonstrate that Swift is writing satire? **2.** In a single, brief paragraph, paraphrase the major arguments Swift uses to support his plan.

Emma Goldman   [1869–1940]

Defense[1]   1916

Your Honor: My presence before you this afternoon proves conclusively that there is no free speech in the city or county of New York. I hope that there is free speech in your court.

I have delivered the lecture which caused my arrest in at least fifty cities throughout the country, always in the presence of detectives. I have never been arrested. I delivered the same address in New York City seven times, prior to my arrest, always in the presence of detectives, because in my case, Your Honor, "the police never cease out of the land." Yet for some reason unknown to me I have never been molested until February 11th, nor would I have been then, if free speech were a living factor, and not a dead letter to be celebrated only on the 4th of July.

Your Honor, I am charged with the crime of having given information to men and women as to how to prevent conception. For the last three weeks, every night before packed houses, a stirring social indictment is being played at the Candler Theatre. I refer to "Justice" by John Galsworthy.[2] The council for the Defense in summing up the charge against the defendant says among other things: "Your Honor: back of the commission of every crime, is life, palpitating life."

Now what is the palpitating life back of my crime? I will tell you, Your Honor. According to the bulletin of the Department of Health, 30,000,000 people in America are underfed. They are always in a state of semi-starvation. Not only because their average income is too small to sustain them properly—the bulletin states that eight hundred dollars a year is the minimum income necessary for every family—but because there are too many members in each family to be sustained on a meagre income. Hence 30,000,000 people in this land go through life underfed and overworked.

Your Honor: what kind of children do you suppose these parents can bring into the world? I will tell you: children so poor and anemic that they take their leave from this, our kind world, before their first year of life. In that way, 300,000 babies, according to the baby welfare association, are sacrificed in the   5

---

[1] Emma Goldman was arrested while lecturing in New York on February 11, 1916. She was charged with violating Section 1142 of the New York Penal Code, which made it a misdemeanor to "sell, lend, or give away" or to advertise, loan, or distribute "any recipe, drug, or medicine for the prevention of conception." Tried and convicted on April 20, she was offered the choice between a hundred-dollar fine or fifteen days in jail. As a matter of principle, she chose jail.

[2] John Galsworthy (1867–1933), English novelist and playwright, whose play *Justice* (1909) deals with crime and disproportionate punishment.

United States each year. This, Your Honor, is the palpitating life which has confronted me for many years, and which is back of the commission of my crime. I have been part of the great social struggle of this country for twenty-six years, as nurse, as lecturer, as publisher. During this time I have gone up and down the land in the large industrial centres, in the mining region, in the slums of our large cities. I have seen conditions appalling and heart-rending, which no creative genius could adequately describe. I do not intend to take up the time of the court to go into many of these cases, but I must mention a few.

A woman, married to a consumptive husband has eight children, six are in the tuberculosis hospital. She is on the way with the ninth child.

A woman whose husband earns $12 per week has six children, on the way with the seventh child.

A woman with twelve children living in three squalid rooms, dies in confinement with the 13th child, the oldest, now the mainstay of the 12 orphans, is 14 years of age.

These are but very few of the victims of our economic grinding mill, which sets a premium upon poverty, and our puritanic law which maintains a conspiracy of silence.

Your Honor: if giving one's life for the purpose of awakening race consciousness in the masses, a consciousness which will impel them to bring quality and not quantity into society, if that be a crime, I am glad to be such a criminal. But I assure you I am in good company. I have as my illustrious colleagues the greatest men and women of our time; scientists, political economists, artists, men of letters in Europe and America. And what is even more important, I have the working class, and women in every walk of life, to back me. No isolated individuals here and there, but thousands of them.

After all, the question of birth control is largely a workingman's question, above all a workingwoman's question. She it is who risks her health, her youth, her very life in giving out of herself the units of the race. She it is who ought to have the means and the knowledge to say how many children she shall give, and to what purpose she shall give them, and under what conditions she shall bring forth life.

Statesmen, politicians, men of the cloth, men, who own the wealth of the world, need a large race, no matter how poor in quality. Who else would do their work, and fight their wars? But the people who toil and drudge and create, and receive a mere pittance in return, what reason have they to bring hapless children into the world? They are beginning to realize their debt to the children already in existence, and in order to make good their obligations, they absolutely refuse to go on like cattle breeding more and more.

That which constitutes my crime, Your Honor, is therefore, enabling the mass of humanity to give to the world fewer and better children—birth control, which in the last two years has grown to such gigantic dimensions that no amount of laws can possibly stop the ever-increasing tide.

And this is true, not only because of what I may or may not say, or of how many propagandists may or may not be sent to jail; there is a much profounder

10

reason for the tremendous growth and importance of birth control. That reason is conditioned in the great modern social conflict, or rather social war, I should say. A war not for military conquest or material supremacy, a war of the oppressed and disinherited of the earth against their enemies, capitalism and the state, a war for a seat at the table of life, a war for well-being, for beauty, for liberty. Above all, this war is for a free motherhood and a joyous playful, glorious childhood.

Birth control, Your Honor, is only one of the ways which leads to the victory   15
in that war, and I am glad and proud to be able to indicate that way.

For Analysis
1. What are the strengths and weaknesses of Goldman's argument? Reflect on your own feelings about birth control. How persuasive is she? **2.** Do you think Goldman is right to characterize birth control as "largely a workingman's question, above all a workingwoman's question" (par. 11)? **3.** Are Goldman's arguments equally relevant to the issue of abortion? Explain.

On Style
Goldman invokes many cases and examples to support her argument. How do these examples strengthen her argument?

Making Connections
What similarities do you find between Martin Luther King Jr.'s arguments to support civil disobedience (p. 643) and those Emma Goldman makes in her "Defense"? Which essay do you find more persuasive?

Writing Topic
In criminal trials that concern larger political and social issues, defendants will sometimes forgo a narrow legal defense and attempt instead to use the trial as a forum for expounding their views to the public. Analyze Goldman's defense in terms of the audiences she is trying to reach.

Willard Gaylin   [b. 1925]

What's So Special about Being Human?   1990

We are in urgent need of reacquainting ourselves with our nature. Our self-respect as a species is alarmingly low. The late twentieth century has seen a confluence of events destined to diminish self-confidence and self-esteem. Along with the great wars, the Depression, the Holocaust, and the ecological disasters—enough to drive any introspective creature to self-doubts—have come a series of seemingly unrelated intellectual movements that have independently and unwittingly diminished our stature in our own eyes.

The "dignity of man" is attacked indirectly by those who, drawing from modern biology and using the principles of sociobiology, have consciously attempted to lessen the distinction between us and our fellow creatures. Anthropologists in particular—Lorenz, Tiger, Fox, Morris, and others—have tended to emphasize the hostile, aggressive, and territorial aspects of human nature while ignoring the caring and nurturing aspects. They have envisioned man at best as a naked ape, and at worst as a marauding beast.

Fortunately, some of our most literate, respected, and brilliant biologists, while marveling at, and honoring the lower animals, have had no doubts about the special quality of being human. Such great humanistic twentieth-century biologists as Dobzhansky, Tax, and Portmann have been elegant spokesmen within their disciplines for the special nature of human beings. They have not, however, gone beyond their disciplines to indicate the moral implications of our biological uniqueness.

The reputation of our species is also under attack, in a way that is half direct and half indirect, through what has come to be known as the animal-rights movement. The purpose of the people in this movement is not to diminish *Homo sapiens* but to protect the beast. They do so by elevating animals, often endowing them anthropomorphically with features the animals do not possess. Their purpose is noble—to protect helpless creatures from unnecessary suffering—but one untoward consequence of this decent enterprise is a reduction of the distance between the nature of people and that of animals. Animal rights advocates constantly emphasize the similarity between the human and the subhuman in a worthy attempt to mitigate our abuses of the subhuman. But in so doing they seriously undermine the special nature of being human.

Peter Singer,[1] perhaps the most eloquent spokesman for animal rights, acknowledges a quantitative difference between the worth of lower animals and   5

---

[1] Peter Singer (b. 1946), author of *Animal Liberation* (1975) and *In Defense of Animals* (1985).

human beings. (Some of his colleagues do not.) He rejects, however, any suggestion that there is a qualitative difference, which would preclude *any* measurement of the worth of a human life against that of an animal life, seeing such a construction as immoral in itself. On the contrary, he insists, the failure to consider such a calculus constitutes a breach of ethics.

This leads him into the dangerous readiness to measure humans and animals on the same scale. Although he certainly would not equate the life of a rat with the life of a human being, he has inevitably been forced to take a position whereby thousands of rats would be judged more worthy of life than one child, since he is prepared to see differences only in degree.

I am not clear where on his social scale the cockroach would need to be in relation to the rat, so that we might extrapolate the number of cockroaches necessary to balance the life of a child.

I see a danger in the animal-rights movement that is more than theoretical. It is beginning to impinge on the lifesaving research necessary to solve such human miseries as AIDS, cancer, and degenerative diseases of the nervous system. I acknowledge my bias. In my world, trees may have standing but animals have no "rights." In the world of morality—as in the world of politics—the animate (and inanimate) exist—valued, considered, dealt with, or destroyed, all in the service of the purposes and interests of humankind.

This position has been attacked in the past as being unfairly anthropocentric. Anthropocentric it certainly is. But what else can a human being be? Beyond man are only the claims of nature or the hand of God. Though not a religious person myself, I have profound respect for religion, and I would point out to critics that the position I hold was most firmly established, not out of the anthropocentricism of science and psychology, but in the religious tradition of the Old Testament and as confirmed, in that same tradition, by such modern philosophers as Kant.[2]

Kant was capable of a great tenderness toward animals, as Mary Midgeley observed in her excellent book *Beast and Man,* citing the following statement by Kant: "Liebnitz used a tiny worm for purposes of observation and then carefully replaced it with its leaf on the tree so that it should not come to harm through any act of his. He would have been sorry—a natural feeling for a humane man—to destroy such a creature for no reason."   10

Yet the very same Kant, with the inherent self-confidence of his Lutheran morality, said: "The first time he [man] ever said to the sheep, 'Nature has given you the skin you wear for my use, not for yours' . . . he became aware of the way in which his nature privileged and raised him above all animals."

I oppose the attribution of rights to animals not out of any religious conviction or invocation of divine authority, and not because I have no affection for animals, but because I fear animal-rights arguments diminish the special status of *Homo sapiens.* Respect for human beings requires that dignity be granted our species beyond any qualitative comparison with others. In insisting on that dig-

---

[2] Immanuel Kant (1724–1804), German philosopher.

nity, I do not shirk our responsibility toward other creatures. A position of such privilege and power imposes a special moral obligation on our species. That is why only we human beings are capable of, willing to, and even obliged to agonize about other species.

It is directly within the purposes of humankind to treat animals with compassion, even empathy; to have reverence for those common qualities we share with the higher primates; and to be aware that, given the mutability of our nature, the way we honor and revere other creatures and other things will define the degree to which we have been true to our humanity. If human nature is so perverted as to be indifferent to suffering and blind to beauty, what is left is no longer "human" and therefore not worthy of its special role in the moral universe.

All animals are not created equal, however. Some animals have less value even than inanimate structures; some have negative value. I do not grieve for the destruction of *Treponema pallidum,* that beautiful and delicate spiral organism that is the cause of human syphilis. To destroy this entire species would be a blessing; whereas blowing up the Grand Tetons or willfully destroying Michelangelo's *David* would constitute a greater moral crime, these are inanimate "things."

Recently I was confronted with a difficult case of the ethical permissibility of using chimpanzee hearts in experimentation to facilitate human organ transplants. Chimpanzees have enormous charm, sensitivity, great intelligence, and a strong kinship to humanity. Should they be sacrificed for human ends? If so, what are the limits? 15

It seems to me that the implicit issue evolved into the following dilemmas. Assuming a promising and prudent research procedure, would you sacrifice a chimpanzee for a trivial human need? I suspect most of us would not. Would you sacrifice a chimpanzee for a child's life? I know most of us would. Would you sacrifice the entire species of chimpanzees for the entire species of *Homo sapiens?* I hope most of us would. Finally, the hard question: would you risk sacrificing the entire species of chimpanzees, a real and not just a theoretical possibility, to relieve the pain and suffering and premature death of many children? I emphatically would. Others would not. It is here that my bias for the specialness, for the extraordinary specialness, of the human being emerges.

Our current understanding of anthropology is replete with the suggestion of humanoid species—*higher* than the chimpanzee—that have become extinct for unknown reasons of climate or competition. Such is the moral indifference of nature. It is only with the introduction of human sensibility, human empathy, and human capacity for identification that we—alone among creatures—even consider the "rights" of other species.

The nobility of the human being is expressed in this readiness of some of our misguided members to sacrifice human children for the preservation of a kindred living creature. To these spokesmen the overvaluation of the human child is a form of "anthropocentrism," a prejudice like racism or sexism. I am pleased about the presence of such advocates—their unselfishness does honor to our species—even while I reject their sentimentalities. But with my coarser sensibilities, my willingness to sacrifice the chimpanzee, I am still within the limits of decency that define that glorious creature whom I defend, *Homo sapiens.*

For Analysis

1. Some proponents of animal rights make an important distinction between animals that experience pain and those that (apparently) don't and argue that humans have a moral obligation not to inflict pain on any creature for whatever reason. How do you think Gaylin would respond to such a distinction? **2.** Do you agree with Gaylin's assertion that emphasis on the similarity between humans and animals and attributing rights to animals "seriously undermine[s] the special nature of being human" (par. 4)? Explain. **3.** Do you see any practical problems with acceptance of Gaylin's view? For example, how would Gaylin deal with the dissection of animals in biology classes or with experimentation on animals in the development of new cosmetics? **4.** Gaylin says that he is not religious, but he appeals to religion to support his contention that "animal-rights arguments diminish the special status of *Homo sapiens*" (par. 12). Is his appeal to religion persuasive?

On Style

What is the audience Gaylin is appealing to? What in this essay reveals his attitude toward this audience?

Making Connections

1. Compare the ways in which Gaylin and Bill McKibben in "A Path of More Resistance (p. 657) appeal to religion or religious sentiment to support their arguments. **2.** Which essay, Gaylin's or Bill McKibben's "A Path of More Resistance" (p. 657) do you find written in an easier or more interesting style? Does the better written essay also make the most persuasive arguments? Explain.

Writing Topics

1. Write a brief reaction from the point of view of a defender of animal rights to Gaylin's arguments. You might generate ideas either by reading or by interviewing an activist. **2.** Write a paper debating animal rights in the form of a dialogue with three characters: a moderator (who introduces the subject), Willard Gaylin, and Bill McKibben.

Martin Luther King Jr. [1929–1968]

Letter from Birmingham Jail[1] 1963

M Y DEAR FELLOW CLERGYMEN:
  While confined here in the Birmingham city jail, I came across your recent statement calling my present activities "unwise and untimely." Seldom do I pause to answer criticism of my work and ideas. If I sought to answer all the criticisms that cross my desk, my secretaries would have little time for anything other than such correspondence in the course of the day, and I would have no time for constructive work. But since I feel that you are men of genuine good will and that your criticisms are sincerely set forth, I want to try to answer your statement in what I hope will be patient and reasonable terms.

I think I should indicate why I am here in Birmingham, since you have been influenced by the view which argues against "outsiders coming in." I have the honor of serving as president of the Southern Christian Leadership Conference, an organization operating in every southern state, with headquarters in Atlanta, Georgia. We have some eighty-five affiliated organizations across the South, and one of them is the Alabama Christian Movement for Human Rights. Frequently we share staff, educational, and financial resources with our affiliates. Several months ago the affiliate here in Birmingham asked us to be on call to engage in a nonviolent direct-action program if such were deemed necessary. We readily consented, and when the hour came we lived up to our promise. So I, along with several members of my staff, am here because I was invited here. I am here because I have organizational ties here.

But more basically, I am in Birmingham because injustice is here. Just as the prophets of the eighth century B.C. left their villages and carried their "thus saith the Lord" far beyond the boundaries of their home towns, and just as the Apostle Paul left his village of Tarsus[2] and carried the gospel of Jesus Christ to

---

[1] This response to a published statement by eight fellow clergymen from Alabama (Bishop C. C. J. Carpenter, Bishop Joseph A. Durick, Rabbi Hilton L. Grafman, Bishop Paul Hardin, Bishop Holan B. Harmon, the Reverend George M. Murray, the Reverend Edward V. Ramage and the Reverend Earl Stallings) was composed under somewhat constricting circumstances. Begun on the margins of the newspaper in which the statement appeared while I was in jail, the letter was continued on scraps of writing paper supplied by a friendly Negro trusty, and concluded on a pad my attorneys were eventually permitted to leave me. Although the text remains in substance unaltered, I have indulged in the author's prerogative of polishing it for publication [King's note].

[2] Birthplace of St. Paul, in present-day Turkey.

the far corners of the Greco-Roman world, so am I compelled to carry the gospel of freedom beyond my own home town. Like Paul, I must constantly respond to the Macedonian call for aid.[3]

Moreover, I am cognizant of the interrelatedness of all communities and states. I cannot sit idly by in Atlanta and not be concerned about what happens in Birmingham. Injustice anywhere is a threat to justice everywhere. We are caught in an inescapable network of mutuality, tied in a single garment of destiny. Whatever affects one directly, affects all indirectly. Never again can we afford to live with the narrow, provincial "outside agitator" idea. Anyone who lives inside the United States can never be considered an outsider anywhere within its bounds.

You deplore the demonstrations taking place in Birmingham. But your state-   5
ment, I am sorry to say, fails to express a similar concern for the conditions that brought about the demonstrations. I am sure that none of you would want to rest content with the superficial kind of social analysis that deals merely with effects and does not grapple with the underlying causes. It is unfortunate that demonstrations are taking place in Birmingham, but it is even more unfortunate that the city's white power structure left the Negro community with no alternative.

In any nonviolent campaign there are four basic steps: collection of the facts to determine whether injustices exist; negotiation; self-purification; and direct action. We have gone through all these steps in Birmingham. There can be no gainsaying the fact that racial injustice engulfs this community. Birmingham is probably the most thoroughly segregated city in the United States. Its ugly record of brutality is widely known. Negroes have experienced grossly unjust treatment in the courts. There have been more unsolved bombings of Negro homes and churches in Birmingham than in any other city in the nation. These are the hard, brutal facts of the case. On the basis of these conditions, Negro leaders sought to negotiate with the city fathers. But the latter consistently refused to engage in good-faith negotiation.

Then, last September, came the opportunity to talk with leaders of Birmingham's economic community. In the course of the negotiations, certain promises were made by the merchants—for example, to remove the stores' humiliating racial signs. On the basis of these promises, the Reverend Fred Shuttlesworth and the leaders of the Alabama Christian Movement for Human Rights agreed to a moratorium on all demonstrations. As the weeks and months went by, we realized that we were the victims of a broken promise. A few signs, briefly removed, returned; the others remained.

As in so many past experiences, our hopes had been blasted, and the shadow of deep disappointment settled upon us. We had no alternative except to prepare for direct action, whereby we would present our very bodies as a means of laying our case before the conscience of the local and the national community. Mindful of the difficulties involved, we decided to undertake a process of self-

---

[3] St. Paul was frequently called upon to aid the Christian community in Macedonia.

purification. We began a series of workshops on nonviolence, and we repeatedly asked ourselves: "Are you able to accept blows without retaliating?" "Are you able to endure the ordeal of jail?" We decided to schedule our direct-action program for the Easter season, realizing that except for Christmas, this is the main shopping period of the year. Knowing that a strong economic-withdrawal program would be the by-product of direct action, we felt that this would be the best time to bring pressure to bear on the merchants for the needed change.

Then it occurred to us that Birmingham's mayoral election was coming up in March, and we speedily decided to postpone action until after election-day. When we discovered that the Commissioner of Public Safety, Eugene "Bull" Connor, had piled up enough votes to be in the run-off, we decided again to postpone action until the day after the run-off so that the demonstrations could not be used to cloud the issues. Like many others, we waited to see Mr. Connor defeated, and to this end we endured postponement after postponement. Having aided in this community need, we felt that our direct-action program could be delayed no longer.

You may well ask, "Why direct action? Why sit-ins, marches, and so forth? Isn't negotiation a better path?" You are quite right in calling for negotiation. Indeed, this is the very purpose of direct action. Nonviolent direct action seeks to create such a crisis and foster such a tension that a community which has constantly refused to negotiate is forced to confront the issue. It seeks so to dramatize the issue that it can no longer be ignored. My citing the creation of tension as part of the work of the nonviolent-resister may sound rather shocking. But I must confess that I am not afraid of the word "tension." I have earnestly opposed violent tension, but there is a type of constructive, nonviolent tension which is necessary for growth. Just as Socrates[4] felt that it was necessary to create a tension in the mind so that individuals could rise from the bondage of myths and half-truths to the unfettered realm of creative analysis and objective appraisal, so must we see the need for nonviolent gadflies to create the kind of tension in society that will help men rise from the dark depths of prejudice and racism to the majestic heights of understanding and brotherhood.

The purpose of our direct-action program is to create a situation so crisis-packed that it will inevitably open the door to negotiation. I therefore concur with you in your call for negotiation. Too long has our beloved Southland been bogged down in a tragic effort to live in monologue rather than dialogue.

One of the basic points in your statement is that the action that I and my associates have taken in Birmingham is untimely. Some have asked: "Why didn't you give the new city administration time to act?" The only answer that I can give to this query is that the new Birmingham administration must be prodded about as much as the outgoing one, before it will act. We are sadly mistaken if we feel that the election of Albert Boutwell as mayor will bring the millennium to Birmingham. While Mr. Boutwell is a much more gentle person than

10

---

[4] Socrates (469–399 B.C.), a Greek philosopher who often pretended ignorance in arguments in order to expose the errors in his opponent's reasoning.

Mr. Connor, they are both segregationists, dedicated to maintenance of the status quo. I have hoped that Mr. Boutwell will be reasonable enough to see the futility of massive resistance to desegregation. But he will not see this without pressure from devotees of civil rights. My friends, I must say to you that we have not made a single gain in civil rights without determined legal and nonviolent pressure. Lamentably, it is an historical fact that privileged groups seldom give up their privileges voluntarily. Individuals may see the moral light and voluntarily give up their unjust posture; but, as Reinhold Niebuhr[5] has reminded us, groups tend to be more immoral than individuals.

We know through painful experience that freedom is never voluntarily given by the oppressor; it must be demanded by the oppressed. Frankly, I have yet to engage in a direct-action campaign that was "well timed" in the view of those who have not suffered unduly from the disease of segregation. For years now I have heard the word "Wait!" It rings in the ear of every Negro with piercing familiarity. This "Wait" has almost always meant "Never." We must come to see, with one of our distinguished jurists, that "justice too long delayed is justice denied."

We have waited for more than 340 years for our constitutional and God-given rights. The nations of Asia and Africa are moving with jetlike speed toward gaining political independence, but we still creep at horse-and-buggy pace toward gaining a cup of coffee at a lunch counter. Perhaps it is easy for those who have never felt the stinging darts of segregation to say, "Wait." But when you have seen vicious mobs lynch your mothers and fathers at will and drown your sisters and brothers at whim; when you have seen hate-filled policemen curse, kick, and even kill your black brothers and sisters; when you see the vast majority of your twenty million Negro brothers smothering in an airtight cage of poverty in the midst of an affluent society; when you suddenly find your tongue twisted and your speech stammering as you seek to explain to your six-year-old daughter why she can't go to the public amusement park that has just been advertised on television, and see tears welling up in her eyes when she is told that Funtown is closed to colored children, and see ominous clouds of inferiority beginning to form in her little mental sky, and see her beginning to distort her personality by developing an unconscious bitterness toward white people; when you have to concoct an answer for a five-year-old son who is asking, "Daddy, why do white people treat colored people so mean?"; when you take a cross-country drive and find it necessary to sleep night after night in the uncomfortable corners of your automobile because no motel will accept you; when you are humiliated day in and day out by nagging signs reading "white" and "colored"; when your first name becomes "nigger," your middle name becomes "boy" (however old you are) and your last name becomes "John," and your wife and mother are never given the respected title "Mrs."; when you are harried by day and haunted by night by the fact that you are a Negro, living constantly at tiptoe stance, never quite knowing what to expect next, and are

---

[5] Reinhold Niebuhr (1892–1971), American philosopher and theologian.

plagued with inner fears and outer resentments; when you are forever fighting a degenerating sense of "nobodiness"—then you will understand why we find it difficult to wait. There comes a time when the cup of endurance runs over, and men are no longer willing to be plunged into the abyss of despair. I hope, sirs, you can understand our legitimate and unavoidable impatience.

You express a great deal of anxiety over our willingness to break laws. This is certainly a legitimate concern. Since we so diligently urge people to obey the Supreme Court's decision of 1954 outlawing segregation in the public schools, at first glance it may seem rather paradoxical for us consciously to break laws. One may well ask: "How can you advocate breaking some laws and obeying others?" The answer lies in the fact that there are two types of laws: just and unjust. I would be the first to advocate obeying just laws. One has not only a legal but a moral responsibility to obey just laws. Conversely, one has a moral responsibility to disobey unjust laws. I would agree with St. Augustine that "an unjust law is no law at all."

Now, what is the difference between the two? How does one determine whether a law is just or unjust? A just law is a man-made code that squares with the moral law or the law of God. An unjust law is a code that is out of harmony with the moral law. To put it in the terms of St. Thomas Aquinas: An unjust law is a human law that is not rooted in eternal law and natural law. Any law that uplifts human personality is just. Any law that degrades human personality is unjust. All segregation statutes are unjust because segregation distorts the soul and damages the personality. It gives the segregator a false sense of superiority and the segregated a false sense of inferiority. Segregation, to use the terminology of the Jewish philosopher Martin Buber, substitutes an "I-it" relationship for an "I-thou" relationship and ends up relegating persons to the status of things. Hence segregation is not only politically, economically, and sociologically unsound, it is morally wrong and sinful. Paul Tillich has said that sin is separation. Is not segregation an existential expression of man's tragic separation, his awful estrangement, his terrible sinfulness? Thus it is that I can urge men to obey the 1954 decision of the Supreme Court, for it is morally right; and I can urge them to disobey segregation ordinances, for they are morally wrong.

Let us consider a more concrete example of just and unjust laws. An unjust law is a code that a numerical or power majority group compels a minority group to obey but does not make binding on itself. This is *difference* made legal. By the same token, a just law is a code that a majority compels a minority to follow and that it is willing to follow itself. This is *sameness* made legal.

Let me give another explanation. A law is unjust if it is inflicted on a minority that, as a result of being denied the right to vote, had no part in enacting or devising the law. Who can say that the legislature of Alabama which set up that state's segregation laws was democratically elected? Throughout Alabama all sorts of devious methods are used to prevent Negroes from becoming registered voters, and there are some counties in which, even though Negroes constitute a majority of the population, not a single Negro is registered. Can any law enacted under such circumstances be considered democratically structured?

Sometimes a law is just on its face and unjust in its application. For instance, I have been arrested on a charge of parading without a permit. Now, there is nothing wrong in having an ordinance which requires a permit for a parade. But such an ordinance becomes unjust when it is used to maintain segregation and to deny citizens the First-Amendment privilege of peaceful assembly and protest.

I hope you are able to see the distinction I am trying to point out. In no sense   20
do I advocate evading or defying the law, as would the rabid segregationist. That would lead to anarchy. One who breaks an unjust law must do so openly, lovingly, and with a willingness to accept the penalty. I submit that an individual who breaks a law that conscience tells him is unjust, and who willingly accepts the penalty of imprisonment in order to arouse the conscience of the community over its injustice, is in reality expressing the highest respect for law.

Of course, there is nothing new about this kind of civil disobedience. It was evidenced sublimely in the refusal of Shadrach, Meshach, and Abednego to obey the laws of Nebuchadnezzar, on the ground that a higher moral law was at stake.[6] It was practiced superbly by the early Christians, who were willing to face hungry lions and the excruciating pain of chopping blocks rather than submit to certain unjust laws of the Roman Empire. To a degree, academic freedom is a reality today because Socrates practiced civil disobedience. In our own nation, the Boston Tea Party represented a massive act of civil disobedience.

We should never forget that everything Adolf Hitler did in Germany was "legal" and everything the Hungarian freedom fighters did in Hungary was "illegal." It was "illegal" to aid and comfort a Jew in Hitler's Germany. Even so, I am sure that, had I lived in Germany at the time, I would have aided and comforted my Jewish brothers. If today I lived in a Communist country where certain principles dear to the Christian faith are suppressed, I would openly advocate disobeying that country's anti-religious laws.

I must make two honest confessions to you, my Christian and Jewish brothers. First, I must confess that over the past few years I have been gravely disappointed with the white moderate. I have almost reached the regrettable conclusion that the Negro's great stumbling block in his stride toward freedom is not the white Citizen's Counciler[7] or the Ku Klux Klanner, but the white moderate, who is more devoted to "order" than to justice; who prefers a negative peace which is the absence of tension to a positive peace which is the presence of justice; who constantly says, "I agree with you in the goal you seek, but I cannot agree with your methods of direct action"; who paternalistically believes he can set the timetable for another man's freedom; who lives by a mythical concept of time and who constantly advises the Negro to wait for a "more convenient season." Shallow understanding from people of good will is more

[6] See Daniel 1:7–3:30.
[7] White Citizen's Councils sprang up in the South after 1954 (the year the Supreme Court declared segregated education unconstitutional) to fight against desegregation.

frustrating than absolute misunderstanding from people of ill will. Lukewarm acceptance is much more bewildering than outright rejection.

I had hoped that the white moderate would understand that law and order exist for the purpose of establishing justice and that when they fail in this purpose they become the dangerously structured dams that block the flow of social progress. I had hoped that the white moderate would understand that the present tension in the South is a necessary phase of the transition from an obnoxious negative peace, in which the Negro passively accepted his unjust plight, to a substantive and positive peace, in which all men will respect the dignity and worth of human personality. Actually, we who engage in nonviolent direct action are not the creators of tension. We merely bring to the surface the hidden tension that is already alive. We bring it out in the open, where it can be seen and dealt with. Like a boil that can never be cured so long as it is covered up but must be opened with all its ugliness to the natural medicines of air and light, injustice must be exposed, with all the tension its exposure creates, to the light of human conscience and the air of national opinion, before it can be cured.

In your statement you assert that our actions, even though peaceful, must be condemned because they precipitate violence. But is this a logical assertion? Isn't this like condemning a robbed man because his possession of money precipitated the evil act of robbery? Isn't this like condemning Socrates because his unswerving commitment to truth and his philosophical inquiries precipitated the act by the misguided populace in which they made him drink hemlock? Isn't this like condemning Jesus because his unique God-consciousness and never-ceasing devotion to God's will precipitated the evil act of crucifixion? We must come to see that, as the federal courts have consistently affirmed, it is wrong to urge an individual to cease his efforts to gain his basic constitutional rights because the quest may precipitate violence. Society must protect the robbed and punish the robber. 25

I had also hoped that the white moderate would reject the myth concerning time in relation to the struggle for freedom. I have just received a letter from a white brother in Texas. He writes: "All Christians know that the colored people will receive greater equal rights eventually, but it is possible that you are in too great a religious hurry. It has taken Christianity almost two thousand years to accomplish what it has. The teachings of Christ take time to come to earth." Such an attitude stems from a tragic misconception of time, from the strangely irrational notion that there is something in the very flow of time that will inevitably cure all ills. Actually, time itself is neutral; it can be used either destructively or constructively. More and more I feel that the people of ill will have used time much more effectively than have the people of good will. We will have to repent in this generation not merely for the hateful words and actions of the bad people, but for the appalling silence of the good people. Human progress never rolls in on wheels of inevitability; it comes through the tireless efforts of men willing to be co-workers with God, and without this hard work, time itself becomes an ally of the forces of social stagnation. We must use time creatively, in the knowledge that the time is always ripe to do right. Now is the time to make real the promise of democracy and transform our pending national elegy into a creative psalm of brotherhood. Now is the time to lift our national policy from the quicksand of racial injustice to the solid rock of human dignity.

You speak of our activity in Birmingham as extreme. At first I was rather disappointed that fellow clergymen would see my nonviolent efforts as those of an extremist. I began thinking about the fact that I stand in the middle of two opposing forces in the Negro community. One is a force of complacency, made up in part of Negroes, who, as a result of long years of oppression, are so drained of self-respect and a sense of "somebodiness" that they have adjusted to segregation; and in part of a few middle-class Negroes who, because of a degree of academic and economic security and because in some ways they profit by segregation, have become insensitive to the problems of the masses. The other force is one of bitterness and hatred, and it comes perilously close to advocating violence. It is expressed in the various black nationalist groups that are springing up across the nation, the largest and best-known being Elijah Muhammad's Muslim movement.[8] Nourished by the Negro's frustration over the continued existence of racial discrimination, this movement is made up of people who have lost faith in America, who have absolutely repudiated Christianity, and who have concluded that the white man is an incorrigible "devil."

I have tried to stand between these two forces, saying that we need emulate neither the "do-nothingism" of the complacent nor the hatred and despair of the black nationalist. For there is the more excellent way of love and nonviolent protest. I am grateful to God that, through the influence of the Negro church, the way of nonviolence became an integral part of our struggle.

If this philosophy had not emerged, by now many streets of the South would, I am convinced, be flowing with blood. And I am further convinced that if our white brothers dismiss as "rabble-rousers" and "outside agitators" those of us who employ nonviolent direct action, and if they refuse to support our nonviolent efforts, millions of Negroes will, out of frustration and despair, seek solace and security in black-nationalist ideologies—a development that would inevitably lead to a frightening racial nightmare.

Oppressed people cannot remain oppressed forever. The yearning for freedom eventually manifests itself, and that is what has happened to the American Negro. Something within has reminded him of his birthright of freedom, and something without has reminded him that it can be gained. Consciously or unconsciously, he has been caught up by the *Zeitgeist*,[9] and with his black brothers of Africa and his brown and yellow brothers of Asia, South America, and the Caribbean, the United States Negro is moving with a sense of great urgency toward the promised land of racial justice. If one recognizes this vital urge that has engulfed the Negro community, one should readily understand why public

30

[8] Elijah Muhammad (1897–1975), leader of the Nation of Islam, a black Muslim religious group that rejected integration and called upon blacks to fight to establish their own nation.
[9] The spirit of the time.

demonstrations are taking place. The Negro has many pent-up resentments and latent frustrations, and he must release them. So let him march; let him make prayer pilgrimages to the city hall; let him go on freedom rides[10]—and try to understand why he must do so. If his repressed emotions are not released in nonviolent ways, they will seek expression through violence; this is not a threat but a fact of history. So I have not said to my people, "Get rid of your discontent." Rather, I have tried to say that this normal and healthy discontent can be channeled into the creative outlet of nonviolent direct action. And now this approach is being termed extremist.

But though I was initially disappointed at being categorized as an extremist, as I continued to think about the matter I gradually gained a measure of satisfaction from the label. Was not Jesus an extremist for love: "Love your enemies, bless them that curse you, do good to them that hate you, and pray for them that despitefully use you, and persecute you." Was not Amos an extremist for justice: "Let justice roll down like waters and righteousness like an ever-flowing stream." Was not Paul an extremist for the Christian gospel: "I bear in my body the marks of the Lord Jesus." Was not Martin Luther an extremist: "Here I stand; I cannot do otherwise, so help me God." And John Bunyan: "I will stay in jail to the end of my days before I make a butchery of my conscience." And Abraham Lincoln: "This nation cannot survive half slave and half free." And Thomas Jefferson: "We hold these truths to be self-evident, that all men are created equal. . . . " So the question is not whether we will be extremists, but what kind of extremists we will be. Will we be extremists for the preservation of injustice or for the extension of justice? In that dramatic scene on Calvary's hill three men were crucified. We must never forget that all three were crucified for the same crime—the crime of extremism. Two were extremists for immorality, and thus fell below their environment. The other, Jesus Christ, was an extremist for love, truth, and goodness, and thereby rose above his environment. Perhaps the South, the nation, and the world are in dire need of creative extremists.

I had hoped that the white moderate would see this need. Perhaps I was too optimistic; perhaps I expected too much. I suppose I should have realized that few members of the oppressor race can understand the deep groans and passionate yearnings of the oppressed race, and still fewer have the vision to see that injustice must be rooted out by strong, persistent, and determined action. I am thankful, however, that some of our white brothers in the South have grasped the meaning of this social revolution and committed themselves to it. They are still all too few in quantity, but they are big in quality. Some—such as Ralph McGill, Lillian Smith, Harry Golden, James McBride Dabbs, Ann Braden, and Sarah Patton Boyle—have written about our struggle in eloquent and prophetic terms. Others have marched with us down nameless streets of the South. They have languished in filthy, roach-infested jails, suffering the

---

[10] In 1961, hundreds of blacks and whites, under the direction of the Congress of Racial Equality (CORE), deliberately violated laws in southern states that required segregation in buses and bus terminals.

abuse and brutality of policemen who view them as "dirty nigger-lovers." Unlike so many of their moderate brothers and sisters, they have recognized the urgency of the moment and sensed the need for powerful "action" antidotes to combat the disease of segregation.

Let me take note of my other major disappointment. I have been so greatly disappointed with the white church and its leadership. Of course, there are some notable exceptions. I am not unmindful of the fact that each of you has taken some significant stands on this issue. I commend you, Reverend Stallings, for your Christian stand on this past Sunday, in welcoming Negroes to your worship service on a nonsegregated basis. I commend the Catholic leaders of this state for integrating Spring Hill College several years ago.

But despite these notable exceptions, I must honestly reiterate that I have been disappointed with the church. I do not say this as one of those negative critics who can always find something wrong with the church. I say this as a minister of the gospel, who loves the church; who was nurtured in its bosom; who has been sustained by its spiritual blessings and who will remain true to it as long as the cord of life shall lengthen.

When I was suddenly catapulted into the leadership of the bus protest in Montgomery, Alabama, a few years ago, I felt we would be supported by the white church. I felt that the white ministers, priests, and rabbis of the South would be among our strongest allies. Instead, some have been outright opponents, refusing to understand the freedom movement and misrepresenting its leaders; all too many others have been more cautious than courageous and have remained silent behind the anesthetizing security of stained-glass windows. 35

In spite of my shattered dreams, I came to Birmingham with the hope that the white religious leadership of this community would see the justice of our cause and, with deep moral concern, would serve as the channel through which our just grievances could reach the power structure. I had hoped that each of you would understand. But again I have been disappointed.

I have heard numerous southern religious leaders admonish their worshipers to comply with a desegregation decision because it is the law, but I have longed to hear white ministers declare: "Follow this decree because integration is morally right and because the Negro is your brother." In the midst of blatant injustices inflicted upon the Negro, I have watched white churchmen stand on the sideline and mouth pious irrelevancies and sanctimonious trivialities. In the midst of a mighty struggle to rid our nation of racial and economic injustice, I have heard many ministers say: "Those are social issues, with which the gospel has no real concern." And I have watched many churches commit themselves to a completely otherworldly religion which makes a strange, unBiblical distinction between body and soul, between the sacred and the secular.

I have traveled the length and breadth of Alabama, Mississippi, and all the other southern states. On sweltering summer days and crisp autumn mornings I have looked at the South's beautiful churches with their lofty spires pointing heavenward. I have beheld the impressive outlines of her massive religious-education buildings. Over and over I have found myself asking: "What kind of people worship here? Who is their God? Where were their voices when the lips of Governor Barnett dripped with words of interposition and nullification? Where were they when Governor Wallace gave a clarion call for defiance and hatred? Where were their voices of support when bruised and weary Negro men and women decided to rise from the dark dungeons of complacency to the bright hills of creative protest?"

Yes, these questions are still in mind. In deep disappointment I have wept over the laxity of the church. But be assured that my tears have been tears of love. There can be no deep disappointment where there is not deep love. Yes, I love the church. How could I do otherwise? I am in the rather unique position of being the son, the grandson, and the great-grandson of preachers. Yes, I see the church as the body of Christ. But, oh! How we have blemished and scarred the body through social neglect and through fear of being nonconformists.

There was a time when the church was very powerful—in the time when the early Christians rejoiced at being deemed worthy to suffer for what they believed. In those days the church was not merely a thermometer that transformed the mores of society. Whenever the early Christians entered a town, the people in power became disturbed and immediately sought to convict the Christians for being "disturbers of the peace" and "outside agitators." But the Christians pressed on, in the conviction that they were "a colony of heaven," called to obey God rather than man. Small in number, they were big in commitment. They were too God-intoxicated to be "astronomically intimidated." By their effort and example they brought an end to such ancient evils as infanticide and gladiatorial contests. 40

Things are different now. So often the contemporary church is a weak, ineffectual voice with an uncertain sound. So often it is an archdefender of the status quo. Far from being disturbed by the presence of the church, the power structure of the average community is consoled by the church's silent—and often even vocal—sanction of things as they are.

But the judgment of God is upon the church as never before. If today's church does not recapture the sacrificial spirit of the early church, it will lose its authenticity, forfeit the loyalty of millions, and be dismissed as an irrelevant social club with no meaning for the twentieth century. Every day I meet young people whose disappointment with the church has turned into outright disgust.

Perhaps I have once again been too optimistic. Is organized religion too inextricably bound to the status quo to save our nation and the world? Perhaps I must turn my faith to the inner spiritual church, the church within the church, as the true *ekklesia*[11] and the hope of the world. But again I am thankful to God that some noble souls from the ranks of organized religion have broken loose from the paralyzing chains of conformity and joined us as active partners in the struggle for freedom. They have left their secure congregations and walked the streets of Albany, Georgia, with us. They have gone down the highways of the South on tortuous rides for freedom. Yes, they have gone to jail with us.

[11] The Greek *New Testament* word for the early Christian church.

Some have been dismissed from their churches, have lost the support of their bishops and fellow ministers. But they have acted in the faith that right defeated is stronger than evil triumphant. Their witness has been the spiritual salt that has preserved the true meaning of the gospel in these troubled times. They have carved a tunnel of hope through the dark mountain of disappointment.

I hope that the church as a whole will meet the challenge of this decisive hour. But even if the church does not come to the aid of justice, I have no despair about the future. I have no fear about the outcome of our struggle in Birmingham, even if our motives are at present misunderstood. We will reach the goal of freedom in Birmingham and all over the nation, because the goal of America is freedom. Abused and scorned though we may be, our destiny is tied up with America's destiny. Before the pilgrims landed at Plymouth, we were here. Before the pen of Jefferson etched the majestic words of the Declaration of Independence across the pages of history, we were here. For more than two centuries our forebears labored in this country without wages; they made cotton king; they built the homes of their masters while suffering gross injustice and shameful humiliation—and yet out of a bottomless vitality they continued to thrive and develop. If the inexpressible cruelties of slavery could not stop us, the opposition we now face will surely fail. We will win our freedom because the sacred heritage of our nation and the eternal will of God are embodied in our echoing demands.

Before closing I feel impelled to mention one other point in your statement   45
that has troubled me profoundly. You warmly commended the Birmingham police force for keeping "order" and "preventing violence." I doubt that you would have so warmly commended the police force if you had seen its dogs sinking their teeth into unarmed, nonviolent Negroes. I doubt that you would so quickly commend the policemen if you were to observe their ugly and inhumane treatment of Negroes here in the city jail; if you were to watch them push and curse old Negro women and young Negro girls; if you were to see them slap and kick old Negro men and young boys; if you were to observe them, as they did on two occasions, refuse to give us food because we wanted to sing our grace together. I cannot join you in your praise of the Birmingham police department.

It is true that the police have exercised a degree of discipline in handling the demonstrators. In this sense they have conducted themselves rather "nonviolently" in public. But for what purpose? To preserve the evil system of segregation. Over the past few years I have consistently preached that nonviolence demands that the means we use must be as pure as the ends we seek. I have tried to make clear that it is wrong to use immoral means to attain moral ends. But now I must affirm that it is just as wrong, or perhaps even more so, to use moral means to preserve immoral ends. Perhaps Mr. Connor and his policemen have been rather nonviolent in public, as was Chief Pritchett in Albany, Georgia, but they have used the moral means of nonviolence to maintain the immoral end of racial injustice. As T. S. Eliot[12] has said, "The last temptation is the greatest treason: To do the right deed for the wrong reason."

---

[12] Thomas Stearns Eliot (1888–1965), American-born poet.

I wish you had commended the Negro sit-inners and demonstrators of Birmingham for their sublime courage, their willingness to suffer, and their amazing discipline in the midst of great provocation. One day the South will recognize its real heroes. They will be the James Merediths,[13] with the noble sense of purpose that enables them to face jeering and hostile mobs, and with the agonizing loneliness that characterizes the life of the pioneer. They will be old, oppressed, battered Negro women, symbolized in a seventy-two-year-old woman in Montgomery, Alabama, who rose up with a sense of dignity and with her people decided not to ride segregated buses, and who responded with ungrammatical profundity to one who inquired about her weariness: "My feets is tired, but my soul is at rest." They will be the young high school and college students, the young ministers of the gospel and a host of their elders, courageously and nonviolently sitting in at lunch counters and willingly going to jail for conscience' sake. One day the South will know that when these disinherited children of God sat down at lunch counters, they were in reality standing up for what is best in the American dream and for the most sacred values in our Judaeo-Christian heritage, thereby bringing our nation back to those great wells of democracy which were dug deep by the founding fathers in their formulation of the Constitution and the Declaration of Independence.

Never before have I written so long a letter. I'm afraid it is much too long to take your precious time. I can assure you that it would have been much shorter if I had been writing from a comfortable desk, but what else can one do when he is alone in a narrow jail cell, other than write long letters, think long thoughts, and pray long prayers?

If I have said anything in this letter that overstates the truth and indicates an unreasonable impatience, I beg you to forgive me. If I have said anything that understates the truth and indicates my having a patience that allows me to settle for anything less than brotherhood, I beg God to forgive me.

I hope this letter finds you strong in the faith. I hope that circumstances will   50 soon make it possible for me to meet each of you, not as an integrationist or a civil-rights leader but as a fellow clergyman and a Christian brother. Let us all hope that the dark clouds of a racial prejudice will soon pass away and the deep fog of misunderstanding will be lifted from our fear-drenched communities, and in some not too distant tomorrow the radiant stars of love and brotherhood will shine over our great nation with all their scintillating beauty.

Yours for the cause of Peace and Brotherhood,
MARTIN LUTHER KING JR.

For Analysis

1. What is King's definition of civil disobedience? **2.** Summarize and explain the argument King makes in paragraph 46 about "means" and "ends." **3.** Those opposed to civil disobedience frequently argue that in a democratic society, change should be pursued through legislation and the courts because if people are allowed to disobey laws with which they disagree, there will be chaos and violence. How does King

[13] James Meredith was the first black to be admitted as a student at the University of Mississippi.

seek to allay those fears? **4.** How does King deal with the charge that he is an outsider meddling in the affairs of others? **5.** What are the "four basic steps" (par. 6) in a non-violent campaign, according to King? **6.** What is King's answer to his critics who urge negotiation instead of direct action?

On Style
1. Readers have often found King's **tone** and **style** strongly influenced by pulpit oratory in its eloquence, elevated **diction,** biblical allusions, and didacticism. Select one or two paragraphs from the essay, and show how it reflects these qualities. **2.** Rewrite some of King's sentences by eliminating the **metaphors** and comment on the effects of the change (see, for example, the metaphors in par. 14, 26, 43, and 50). **3.** Characterize King's tone. Throughout the essay, does the tone change to any significant degree? Explain.

Making Connections
1. Does your own experience bear out King's distinction (par. 10) between "violent" and "nonviolent" tension? **2.** Have you ever been in a situation in which you were required to obey what you considered an unjust law? If so, describe the law, why you felt it was unjust, and the course of action you chose. **3.** What similarities do you find between King's arguments to support civil disobedience and those Emma Goldman makes in her "Defense" (p. 636)? **4.** King argues that civil disobedience contributes to the avoidance of violence by giving people an opportunity to release their frustration and anger (par. 30). Does James Baldwin's essay "Rage" (p. 937) give indirect support to that argument?

Writing Topics
1. King offers a philosophical justification for civil disobedience (par. 15–22), at the heart of which is his distinction between a just and an unjust law. Defend or take issue with that distinction. **2.** In your opinion, has the history of race relations in America since King's assassination in 1968 strengthened or weakened his arguments on the necessity and value of civil disobedience?

Bill McKibben   [b. 1960]

A Path of More Resistance   1989

Several years ago, Jim Stolz shouldered a pack at the Mexican border and hiked eight or nine hundred miles north to the Idaho mountains for a meeting of a small environmental group.

This, he told me as we sat by a stream three months later, was not all that unusual for him. Some years earlier, he had walked the Appalachian Trail, Georgia to Maine. "I spent the next two years going coast to coast. I took the northern route—I spent a couple of months on snowshoes through Wisconsin and Minnesota." He'd never seen the Pacific till he got there on his own two feet. After that, he walked the Continental Divide trail. And then he began to lay out a new trek—the Grand West Trail, he calls it. It runs north and south between the Pacific Crest and the Continental Divide trails, traversing the Grand Canyon and the lava plains, climbing over the Sawtooths. All it lacks is people. "I spent one nine-and-a-half-day stretch this trip when I didn't see anyone," Stolz said. "I see someone else maybe every fourth day."

In the course of his long walks he had twelve times come across grizzly bears, the continent's grandest mammals, now nearly gone from the lower forty-eight. "The last one, he stood on his hind legs, clicked his jaws, woofed three times. I was too close to him, and he was just letting me know. Another one circled me about forty feet away and wouldn't look me in the eye. When you get that close, you realize you're part of the food chain. When we go into grizzly country, we're going into *their* home. We're the intruders. We're used to being top dog. But in griz country we're part of the food chain."

That seemed a quietly radical idea to me—the idea that we don't necessarily belong at the top in every way. It seemed to me, thinking about it later, that it might be a good way to describe a philosophy that is the opposite of the defiant, consumptive course we've traditionally followed. What would it mean to our ways of life, our demographics, our economics, our output of carbon dioxide and methane if we began to truly and viscerally think of ourselves as just one species among many?

The logic of our present thinking—that we should increase in numbers and, especially, in material wealth and ease—leads inexorably in the direction of the managed world. It is, as a few rebels have maintained, a rut, a system of beliefs in which we are trapped. When Thoreau declared that the masses of men lead lives of quiet desperation,[1] it was to this rut that he referred. He went to live at

---

[1] Henry David Thoreau (1817–1862) made this declaration in *Walden, or Life in the Woods* (1854).

Walden Pond to prove how little man needed to survive—$61.99¾ for eight months, including the cost of his house.

But most of us have lived in that rut without rebelling. A few, often under Thoreau's influence, may have chucked their sophomore year to live in a tent by some wild lake, but even most of them returned to normal society. Thoreau's explanation—that we think there's no choice—may help explain this fact. But the terrible truth is that most of us rather like the rut. We like acquiring more things; the aphorists notwithstanding, they make us happy. We like the easy life. I was skimming through an old copy of the *New Yorker* not long ago and came across an advertisement, from what in 1949 was still the Esso Company, that summed up our century to this point. "The better you live," it shouted, "the more oil you use." And we live well. The world, as most of us in the West experience it in the late twentieth century, is a reasonably sweet place. That is why there aren't more hippies camped by the lake. We like to camp, but for the weekend.

The only trouble is that this system of beliefs, this pleasant rut, seems not to be making *the planet* happy. The atmosphere and the forests are less satisfied than we are. In fact, they are changing, dying. And those changes affect us, body and soul. The end of nature sours all my material pleasures. The prospect of living in a genetically engineered world sickens me. And yet it is toward such a world that our belief in endless material advancement hurries us.

As long as that desire drives us, there is no way to set limits. We won't develop genetic engineering to eradicate disease and not use it to manufacture perfectly efficient chickens; there is nothing in the logic of our ingrained beliefs that would lead us to draw those lines. Direct our beliefs into a new stream, and that stream would soon be a torrent just like the present one: if we use fusion energy instead of coal, we will still plow ahead at our basic business, accumulation, with all its implications for the natural world. If there is one notion that virtually every successful politician on earth—socialist or fascist or capitalist—agrees on, it is that "economic growth" is good, necessary, the proper end of organized human activity. But where does economic growth end? It ends—or, at least, it runs straight through—the genetically engineered dead world that the optimists envision. That is, provided we can surmount our present environmental troubles.

Those troubles, though, just might give us the chance to change the way we think. What if they gave us a practical—as opposed to a moral or an aesthetic—reason to climb out of our rut and find a new one that leads in some different direction? A reason based on atmospheric chemistry, not Eastern spirituality. That is why Stolz's phrase caught my ear, his notion that we might be no more important than anything else. If a new idea—a *humble* idea, in contrast to the conventional defiant attitude—is going to rise out of the wreckage we have made of the world, this is the gut feeling, the impulse, it will come from.

The idea that the rest of creation might count for as much as we do is spectacularly foreign, even to most environmentalists. The ecological movement has always had its greatest success in convincing people that we are threatened by

10

some looming problem—or, if we are not threatened directly, then some creature that we find appealing, such as the seal or the whale or the songbird. The tropical rain forests must be saved because they contain millions of species of plants that may have medical uses—that was the single most common argument against tropical deforestation until it was replaced by the greenhouse effect. Even the American wilderness movement, in some ways a radical crusade, has argued for wilderness largely as places for man—places big enough for backpackers to lose themselves in and for stressed city dwellers to find themselves.

But what if we began to believe in the rain forest *for its own sake?* This attitude has very slowly begun to spread in recent years, both in America and abroad, as the effects of man's domination have become clearer. Some few people have begun to talk of two views of the world—the traditional, man-centered—anthropocentric—view and the biocentric vision of people as a part of the world, just like bears.

Many of those who take the biocentric view are, of course, oddballs, the sort who would walk two thousand miles instead of flying. (Prophets, false or true, are inevitably oddballs. There's not much need for prophets who are in synch with their society.) And theirs is, admittedly, a radical idea, almost an unrealistic idea. It strikes at the root of our identities. But we live at a radical, unrealistic moment. We live at the end of nature, the moment when the essential character of the world we've known since we stopped swinging from our tails is suddenly changing. I'm not intrinsically attracted to radical ideas anymore. I have a house, and a bank account, and I'd like my life, all other things being equal, to continue in its current course. But all other things are not equal—we live at an odd moment in human history when the most basic elements of our lives are changing. I love the trees outside my window; they are a part of my life. I don't want to see them shrivel in the heat, nor sprout in perfect cloned rows. The damage we have done to the planet, and the damage we seem set to do in a genetically engineered business-as-usual future, make me wonder if there isn't some other way. If there isn't a humbler alternative—one that would let us hew closer to what remains of nature, and give it room to recover, if it can. An alternative that would involve changing not only the way we act but also the way we think.

Such ideas are not brand-new. Almost as far back as people have gathered in societies, there are records of ascetics and hermits. Thoreau diluted the religion in this strain of thinking and injected it into the modern bloodstream, but, as we have seen, he went to the woods to redeem man, not nature. (It is curious, in fact, just how little description of nature *Walden* contains.) His is an intensely anthropocentric account—man's desecration of nature worried him less than man's desecration of himself. Nature mattered, but as a wonderful text. "Let us spend one day as deliberately as Nature," he pleads, "and not be thrown off the track by every nutshell and mosquito wing that falls on the rails. Let us rise early and fast, or break fast, gently and without perturbation." Nature was a lesson.

The crucial next step in the development of this humble philosophy—the idea that the rest of creation mattered for its own sake, and that man didn't matter all that much—awaited other writers. It is implicit throughout the works of John Muir,[2] and sometimes it is explicit. In the journal of his thousand-mile hike to the Gulf of Mexico, for instance, there is a passage that stands in perfect contrast to Professor Baxter's argument that men matter entirely and penguins not at all.[3] Muir is writing about alligators, animals as revolting by our standards as any on the continent. He acknowledges that alligators "cannot be called the friends of man" (though he had heard of "one big fellow that was caught young and partially civilized and made to work in harness"). But that, he declares, is not the point. "Many good people believe the alligators were created by the Devil, thus accounting for their all-consuming appetite and ugliness. But doubtless these creatures are happy and fill the place assigned for them by the great Creator of us all. Fierce and cruel they appear to us, but beautiful in the eyes of God." This is more than an ecological, Darwinian vision; it is a moral one: "How narrow we selfish, conceited creatures are in our sympathies! How blind to the rights of all the rest of creation! . . . Though alligators, snakes etc. naturally repel us, they are not mysterious evils. They dwell happily in these flowery wilds, are part of God's family, unfallen, undepraved, and cared for with the same species of tenderness as is bestowed on angels in heaven or saints on earth." Muir ends his swampy sermonette with a benediction that stands as a good epigram for this humbler approach: "Honorable representatives of the great saurians of older creation, may you long enjoy your lilies and rushes, and be blessed now and then with a mouthful of terror-stricken man by way of dainty!"

Of the many heirs to this philosophical tradition, the most striking was Edward Abbey. A funny, moving novelist and an able critic, Abbey was, more than anything else, an apostle of a place—the desert Southwest, where he lived for many years. Abbey, who died in the spring of 1989, spent long stretches working for the government in various fire towers and ranger shacks—long stretches utterly alone. And alone in the part of nature—the desert—that seems least hospitable, most alienating. Though he loved the desert's beauty, he also recognized its overwhelming alienness. In one of the essays in his first collection he wrote: "The desert says nothing. Completely passive, acted upon but never acting, the desert lies there like the bare skeleton of Being, spare, sparse, austere, utterly worthless, inviting not love but contemplation. In its simplicity and order it suggests the classical, except that *the desert is a realm beyond the human* and in the classicist view only the human is regarded as significant or even recognized as real." 15

The idea of "a realm beyond the human" but still on this earth is at odds with our deepest notions, our sense of all creation as our private domain. It is no accident that Abbey wrote from the desert. If you lived in the Garden of Eden, or even in, say, Fort Lauderdale, it might be possible to think that the earth had

---

[2] John Muir (1838–1914), American naturalist and writer.
[3] William F. Baxter, *People or Penguins: The Case for Optimal Pollution* (1974).

been made for you and your pleasure. But not if you lived in the desert of the Southwest. If the desert was made for you, why is there so little water? It's infinitely more plausible that the desert was made for buzzards.

No wonder, then, that in all the world the desert of the Southwest was one of the last places left more or less untouched. Prospectors had come and gone, and their traces could still be seen in the preserving sand, but when Abbey arrived most of the area lay in its natural state. As a result, he got to watch the developers, miners, and promoters lay their defiant siege to the land. Abbey wrote a novel, *The Monkey Wrench Gang*, out of his anger at the uranium mines and the copper smelters fouling the clean air, and at the endless road building and river damming. Though it is an "action novel," a wild account of a campaign of sabotage against bulldozers and dams, it crystallizes in a single scene the difference between our conventional, defiant view of the world and the biocentric vision.

Early in the book, Hayduke, the hero, decides to disrupt the construction of a road that is being laid out through the Arizona desert. As he follows the planned route, pulling up the surveyor's orange flags, he comes to the stony rim of a small canyon. On the opposite wall, four hundred feet away, he could see the line of stakes, with their Day-Glo ribbons, marching on. "This canyon, then, was going to be bridged. It was only a small and little known canyon, to be sure, with a tiny stream coursing down its bed, meandering in lazy bights over the sand, lolling in pools under the acid-green leafery of the cottonwoods, falling over lip of stone into basin below, barely enough water even in spring to sustain a resident population of spotted toads, red-winged dragonflies, a snake or two, a few canyon wrens, nothing special. And yet Hayduke demurred; he didn't want a bridge here, ever; he liked this little canyon, which he had never seen before, the name of which he didn't even know, quite well enough as it was. Hayduke knelt and wrote a message in the sand to all highway construction contractors: 'Go home.'" This canyon is not Yosemite, or even Hetch Hetchy— there is no way to rally a crowd to its defense by virtue of its splendor or its opportunities for recreation. It has no human use. If the road isn't built, no one will ever come here. This canyon can only be paved over or be left alone to no constructive end. Abbey's radicalism was that he chose the latter.

For Analysis
1. Are you persuaded by McKibben's arguments? What evidence does he offer that seems persuasive? **2.** What does McKibben mean by "a path of more resistance"? **3.** What does McKibben mean when he asserts that the destructive changes inflicted on the planet "affect us, body and soul" (par. 7)? **4.** What does it mean "to believe in the rain forest *for its own sake*" (par. 11)?

On Style
Consider the way McKibben presents himself in the context of earlier writers and thinkers. What is McKibben's relationship to these writers? How effective is his use of these examples?

Making Connections

Compare the style of "A Path of More Resistance" to Willard Gaylin's "What's So Special about Being Human?" (p. 639). Which author's book would you choose to read in its entirety? Why?

Writing Topic

Write an analysis of McKibben's essay, evaluating his claims and supporting evidence.

Conformity and Rebellion

Questions and Writing Topics

1. What support do the works in this section offer for Emily Dickinson's assertion that "Much Madness is divinest Sense"? **Writing Topic:** The central characters in Melville's "Bartleby the Scrivener" and Ellison's " 'Repent, Harlequin!' Said the Ticktockman" are viewed by society as mad. How might it be argued that they exhibit "divinest sense"?

2. In a number of these works, a single individual rebels against society and suffers defeat or death. Are these works therefore pessimistic and despairing? If not, then what is the purpose of the rebellions, and why do the authors choose to bring their characters to such ends? **Writing Topic:** Compare two works from this section that offer support for the idea that a single individual can have a decisive effect on society.

3. Examine some of the representatives of established order—the lawyer in "Bartleby the Scrivener," Creon in *Antigonê,* the Ticktockman—and discuss what attitudes they share and how effectively they function as spokespeople for law and order. **Writing Topic:** Compare and evaluate the kinds of order that each represents.

4. Lawrence Ferlinghetti's "In Goya's Greatest Scenes" and Bertolt Brecht's "War Has Been Given a Bad Name" are, in different ways, antiwar poems. In which of these poems do you find the most articulate and convincing antiwar statement? **Writing Topic:** Discuss the argument that, while condemning war, neither of these poems examines the specific reasons that a nation may be obliged to fight—self-defense and national self-interest, for example—and that consequently they are irresponsible.

5. Most of us live out our lives in the ordinary and humdrum world that is rejected in poems such as Wordsworth's "The World Is Too Much with Us" and Auden's "The Unknown Citizen." Can it be said that these poems are counsels to social irresponsibility? **Writing Topic:** Consider whether "we" in Wordsworth's poem and the unknown citizen are simply objects of scorn or whether they deserve sympathy and perhaps even respect.

6. Characters in several works in this section—the Harlequin in " 'Repent, Harlequin!' Said the Ticktockman," Bartleby in "Bartleby the Scrivener," Jack Smurch in "The Greatest Man in the World," and Antigonê in *Antigonê*—are rebels. What similarities do you find among these rebels? **Writing Topic:** Explain how the attitudes and actions of these characters constitute an attack on the status quo.

7. Many works in this section deal explicitly with the relationship between the individual and the state. What similarities of outlook do you find among them? **Writing Topic:** Compare and contrast the way that relationship is perceived in Ellison's " 'Repent, Harlequin!' Said the Ticktockman" and King's "Letter from Birmingham Jail."

Culture and Identity

At Connie's Inn, 1974 by Romare Bearden.

Historically, a group of people bound together by kinship and geography will form a society that exhibits a *culture*—common language, behavioral rules, traditions, skills, mores, religion, and art that define the civilization of that group. Literary works, including folklore and myth, are inseparable from the particular human society from which they emerge.

Until relatively recently with the invention of trains, automobiles, and airplanes, travel over long distances was difficult. Instant communication—the telephone, the computer network—is an innovation of this century. Originally, information about societies could be heard only as far away as a human could shout. Letters helped transmit ideas and cultural values over time and distance, but no more quickly than a horse could gallop. For thousands of years cultures lived in relative isolation from each other and, hence, tended to develop distinctive traits and values. Within China, for instance, we discover numerous well-defined cultures: the Uighurs of the northwest, the coastal Chinese of Shanghai, the Tibetan mountain people, the Szechwanese of the southwest. They eat different foods, they practice different religions, they speak different dialects.

Though technological advances have made the world seem smaller and, generally, ended the geographical isolation of various cultures, those advances have not diminished the powerful cultural distinctions that mark societies all over the world. In fact, modern communication and transport sometimes have served to bring cultures into conflict. The works in this section, varied as they are, share a preoccupation with the connection between culture and identity. Some of them, such as Louise Erdrich's "The Red Convertible," Athol Fugard's *"Master Harold" . . . and the Boys,* and George Orwell's "Shooting an Elephant," examine the devastating consequences of cultural imperialism. Others, such as David Henry Hwang's *M. Butterfly* and James Baldwin's "Rage," focus on the way dominant cultural stereotypes distort and undermine the sense of self of those who are different. Chinua Achebe's "Marriage Is a Private Affair" examines the assault of cultural assimilation on tradition.

The works in this section reveal how culture powerfully shapes identity. They reveal the tension and offer insight into the conflict generated by interacting cultures. But these works also provide an opportunity for us to step outside the bounds and bonds of our own culture and to experience just how complex, diverse, and interesting, the human condition can be.

FOR THINKING AND WRITING

As you read the selections in this section, consider the following questions. You may want to write out your thoughts informally, in a journal if you are keeping one, as a way of preparing to respond to the selections. Or you may wish to make one of these questions the basis for a formal essay.

1. What cultural tradition(s) do you come from? Describe that tradition as fully as you can. Do you feel that you live in or out of the cultural mainstream? Explain.

2. Except for Native Americans, the people of the United States descended from or arrived as citizens of foreign cultures. Is there, nonetheless, an American culture? Explain. America was once called a cultural "melting pot." Now it is sometimes called a cultural "salad." Which metaphor strikes you as more apt? Explain.

3. Do economic considerations affect culture? Are the rich (aside from their wealth) different from the poor? Explain. Does education strengthen or weaken traditional culture? Explain.

4. What are some of the positive and negative associations you have with the values in the cultural traditions you come from? Is the preservation of these traditional cultural values a good thing or a bad thing? Explain.

Fiction

William Faulkner   [1897–1962]

A Rose for Emily   1931

I

When Miss Emily Grierson died, our whole town went to her funeral: the men through a sort of respectful affection for a fallen monument, the women mostly out of curiosity to see the inside of her house, which no one save an old manservant—a combined gardener and cook—had seen in at least ten years.

It was a big, squarish frame house that had once been white, decorated with cupolas and spires and scrolled balconies in the heavily lightsome style of the seventies, set on what had once been our most select street. But garages and cotton gins had encroached and obliterated even the august names of that neighborhood; only Miss Emily's house was left, lifting its stubborn and coquettish decay above the cotton wagons and the gasoline pumps—an eyesore among eyesores. And now Miss Emily had gone to join the representatives of those august names where they lay in the cedar-bemused cemetery among the ranked and anonymous graves of Union and Confederate soldiers who fell at the battle of Jefferson.

Alive, Miss Emily had been a tradition, a duty, and a care; a sort of hereditary obligation upon the town, dating from that day in 1894 when Colonel Sartoris, the mayor—he who fathered the edict that no Negro woman should appear on the streets without an apron—remitted her taxes, the dispensation dating from the death of her father on into perpetuity. Not that Miss Emily would have accepted charity. Colonel Sartoris invented an involved tale to the effect that Miss Emily's father had loaned money to the town, which the town, as a matter of business, preferred this way of repaying. Only a man of Colonel Sartoris' generation and thought could have invented it, and only a woman could have believed it.

When the next generation, with its more modern ideas, became mayors and aldermen, this arrangement created some little dissatisfaction. On the first of the year they mailed her a tax notice. February came, and there was no reply. They wrote her a formal letter, asking her to call at the sheriff's office at her convenience. A week later the mayor wrote her himself, offering to call or to send his car for her, and received in reply a note on paper of an archaic shape, in a thin, flowing calligraphy in faded ink, to the effect that she no longer went out at all. The tax notice was also enclosed, without comment.

They called a special meeting of the Board of Aldermen. A deputation waited 5 upon her, knocked at the door through which no visitor had passed since she ceased giving china-painting lessons eight or ten years earlier. They were admitted by the old Negro into a dim hall from which a stairway mounted into still more shadow. It smelled of dust and disuse—a close, dank smell. The Negro led them into the parlor. It was furnished in heavy, leather-covered furniture. When the Negro opened the blinds of one window, they could see that the leather was cracked; and when they sat down, a faint dust rose sluggishly about their thighs, spinning with slow motions in the single sun-ray. On a tarnished gilt easel before the fireplace stood a crayon portrait of Miss Emily's father.

They rose when she entered—a small, fat woman in black, with a thin gold chain descending to her waist and vanishing into her belt, leaning on an ebony cane with a tarnished gold head. Her skeleton was small and spare; perhaps that was why what would have been merely plumpness in another was obesity in her. She looked bloated, like a body long submerged in motionless water, and of that pallid hue. Her eyes, lost in the fatty ridges of her face, looked like two small pieces of coal pressed into a lump of dough as they moved from one face to another while the visitors stated their errand.

She did not ask them to sit. She just stood in the door and listened quietly until the spokesman came to a stumbling halt. Then they could hear the invisible watch ticking at the end of the gold chain.

Her voice was dry and cold. "I have no taxes in Jefferson. Colonel Sartoris explained it to me. Perhaps one of you can gain access to the city records and satisfy yourselves."

"But we have. We are the city authorities, Miss Emily. Didn't you get a notice from the sheriff, signed by him?"

"I received a paper, yes," Miss Emily said. "Perhaps he considers himself the 10 sheriff . . . I have no taxes in Jefferson."

"But there is nothing on the books to show that, you see. We must go by the—"

"See Colonel Sartoris." (Colonel Sartoris had been dead almost ten years.) "I have no taxes in Jefferson. Tobe!" The Negro appeared. "Show these gentlemen out."

II

So she vanquished them, horse and foot, just as she had vanquished their fathers thirty years before about the smell. That was two years after her father's death and a short time after her sweetheart—the one we believed would marry her—had deserted her. After her father's death she went out very little; after her sweetheart went away, people hardly saw her at all. A few of the ladies had the temerity to call, but were not received, and the only sign of life about the place was the Negro man—a young man then—going in and out with a market basket.

"Just as if a man—any man—could keep a kitchen properly," the ladies said; so they were not surprised when the smell developed. It was another link between the gross, teeming world and the high and mighty Griersons.

A neighbor, a woman, complained to the mayor, Judge Stevens, eighty years   15
old.

"But what will you have me do about it, madam?" he said.

"Why, send her word to stop it," the woman said. "Isn't there a law?"

"I'm sure that won't be necessary," Judge Stevens said. "It's probably just a snake or a rat that nigger of hers killed in the yard. I'll speak to him about it."

The next day he received two more complaints, one from a man who came in diffident deprecation. "We really must do something about it, Judge. I'd be the last one in the world to bother Miss Emily, but we've got to do something." That night the Board of Aldermen met—three graybeards and one younger man, a member of the rising generation.

"It's simple enough," he said. "Send her word to have her place cleaned up.   20
Give her a certain time to do it in, and if she don't . . ."

"Dammit, sir," Judge Stevens said, "will you accuse a lady to her face of smelling bad?"

So the next night, after midnight, four men crossed Miss Emily's lawn and slunk about the house like burglars, sniffing along the base of the brickwork and at the cellar openings while one of them performed a regular sowing motion with his hand out of a sack slung from his shoulder. They broke open the cellar door and sprinkled lime there, and in all the outbuildings. As they recrossed the lawn, a window that had been dark was lighted and Miss Emily sat in it, the light behind her, and her upright torso motionless as that of an idol. They crept quietly across the lawn and into the shadow of the locusts that lined the street. After a week or two the smell went away.

That was when people had begun to feel really sorry for her. People in our town, remembering how old lady Wyatt, her great-aunt, had gone completely crazy at last, believed that the Griersons held themselves a little too high for what they really were. None of the young men were quite good enough for Miss Emily and such. We had long thought of them as a tableau, Miss Emily a slender figure in white in the background, her father a spraddled silhouette in the foreground, his back to her and clutching a horsewhip, the two of them framed by the back-flung front door. So when she got to be thirty and was still single, we were not pleased exactly, but vindicated; even with insanity in the family she wouldn't have turned down all of her chances if they had really materialized.

When her father died, it got about that the house was all that was left to her; and in a way, people were glad. At last they could pity Miss Emily. Being left alone, and a pauper, she had become humanized. Now she too would know the old thrill and the old despair of a penny more or less.

The day after his death all the ladies prepared to call at the house and offer   25 condolence and aid, as is our custom. Miss Emily met them at the door, dressed as usual and with no trace of grief on her face. She told them that her father was not dead. She did that for three days, with the ministers calling on her, and the doctors, trying to persuade her to let them dispose of the body. Just as they were about to resort to law and force, she broke down, and they buried her father quickly.

We did not say she was crazy then. We believed she had to do that. We remembered all the young men her father had driven away, and we knew that with nothing left, she would have to cling to that which had robbed her, as people will.

III

She was sick for a long time. When we saw her again, her hair was cut short, making her look like a girl, with a vague resemblance to those angels in colored church windows—sort of tragic and serene.

The town had just let the contracts for paving the sidewalks, and in the summer after her father's death they began the work. The construction company came with niggers and mules and machinery, and a foreman named Homer Barron, a Yankee—a big, dark, ready man, with a big voice and eyes lighter than his face. The little boys would follow in groups to hear him cuss the niggers, and the niggers singing in time to the rise and fall of picks. Pretty soon he knew everybody in town. Whenever you heard a lot of laughing anywhere about the square, Homer Barron would be in the center of the group. Presently we began to see him and Miss Emily on Sunday afternoons driving in the yellow-wheeled buggy and the matched team of bays from the livery stable.

At first we were glad that Miss Emily would have an interest, because the ladies all said, "Of course a Grierson would not think seriously of a Northerner, a day laborer." But there were still others, older people, who said that even grief could not cause a real lady to forget *noblesse oblige*—without calling it *noblesse oblige*. They just said, "Poor Emily. Her kinsfolk should come to her." She had some kin in Alabama; but years ago her father had fallen out with them over the estate of old lady Wyatt, the crazy woman, and there was no communication between the two families. They had not even been represented at the funeral.

And as soon as the old people said, "Poor Emily," the whispering began. "Do you suppose it's really so?" they said to one another. "Of course it is. What else could . . ." This behind their hands; rustling of craned silk and satin behind jalousies closed upon the sun of Sunday afternoon as the thin, swift clop-clop-clop of the matched team passed: "Poor Emily."

She carried her head high enough—even when we believed that she was fallen. It was as if she demanded more than ever the recognition of her dignity as the last Grierson; as if it had wanted that touch of earthiness to reaffirm her imperviousness. Like when she bought the rat poison, the arsenic. That was over a year after they had begun to say "Poor Emily," and while the two female cousins were visiting her.

30

"I want some poison," she said to the druggist. She was over thirty then, still a slight woman, though thinner than usual, with cold, haughty black eyes in a face the flesh of which was strained across the temples and about the eye-sockets as you imagine a lighthouse-keeper's face ought to look. "I want some poison," she said.

"Yes, Miss Emily. What kind? For rats and such? I'd recom—"

"I want the best you have. I don't care what kind."

The druggist named several. "They'll kill anything up to an elephant. But   35
what you want is—"

"Arsenic," Miss Emily said. "Is that a good one?"

"Is . . . arsenic? Yes, ma'am. But what you want—"

"I want arsenic."

The druggist looked down at her. She looked back at him, erect, her face like a strained flag. "Why, of course," the druggist said. "If that's what you want. But the law requires you to tell what you are going to use it for."

Miss Emily just stared at him, her head tilted back in order to look him eye   40
for eye, until he looked away and went and got the arsenic and wrapped it up. The Negro delivery boy brought her package; the druggist didn't come back. When she opened the package at home there was written on the box, under the skull and bones: "For rats."

IV

So the next day we all said, "She will kill herself"; and we said it would be the best thing. When she had first begun to be seen with Homer Barron, we had said, "She will marry him." Then we said, "She will persuade him yet," because Homer himself had remarked—he liked men, and it was known that he drank with the younger men in the Elks' Club—that he was not a marrying man. Later we said, "Poor Emily" behind the jalousies as they passed on Sunday afternoon in the glittering buggy, Miss Emily with her head high and Homer Barron with his hat cocked and a cigar in his teeth, reins and whip in a yellow glove.

Then some of the ladies began to say that it was a disgrace to the town and a bad example to the young people. The men did not want to interfere, but at last the ladies forced the Baptist minister—Miss Emily's people were Episcopal—to call upon her. He would never divulge what happened during that interview, but he refused to go back again. The next Sunday they again drove about the streets, and the following day the minister's wife wrote to Miss Emily's relations in Alabama.

So she had blood-kin under her roof again and we sat back to watch develop-ments. At first nothing happened. Then we were sure that they were to be mar-ried. We learned that Miss Emily had been to the jeweler's and ordered a man's toilet set in silver, with the letters H.B. on each piece. Two days later we learned that she had bought a complete outfit of men's clothing, including a nightshirt, and we said, "They are married." We were really glad. We were glad because the two female cousins were even more Grierson than Miss Emily had ever been.

So we were not surprised when Homer Barron—the streets had been finished some time since—was gone. We were a little disappointed that there was not a public blowing-off, but we believed that he had gone on to prepare for Miss Emily's coming, or to give her a chance to get rid of the cousins. (By that time it was a cabal, and we were all Miss Emily's allies to help circumvent the cousins.) Sure enough, after another week they departed. And, as we had expected all along, within three days Homer Barron was back in town. A neighbor saw the Negro man admit him at the kitchen door at dusk one evening.

And that was the last we saw of Homer Barron. And of Miss Emily for some 45 time. The Negro man went in and out with the market basket, but the front door remained closed. Now and then we would see her at the window for a moment, as the men did that night when they sprinkled the lime, but for almost six months she did not appear on the streets. Then we knew that this was to be expected too; as if that quality of her father which had thwarted her woman's life so many times had been too virulent and too furious to die.

When we next saw Miss Emily, she had grown fat and her hair was turning gray. During the next few years it grew grayer and grayer until it attained an even pepper-and-salt iron-gray, when it ceased turning. Up to the day of her death at seventy-four it was still that vigorous iron-gray, like the hair of an active man.

From that time on her front door remained closed, save during a period of six or seven years, when she was about forty, during which she gave lessons in china-painting. She fitted up a studio in one of the downstairs rooms, where the daughters and granddaughters of Colonel Sartoris' contemporaries were sent to her with the same regularity and in the same spirit that they were sent to church on Sundays with a twenty-five-cent piece for the collection plate. Meanwhile her taxes had been remitted.

Then the newer generation became the backbone and the spirit of the town, and the painting pupils grew up and fell away and did not send their children to her with boxes of color and tedious brushes and pictures cut from the ladies' magazines. The front door closed upon the last one and remained closed for good. When the town got free postal delivery, Miss Emily alone refused to let them fasten the metal numbers above her door and attach a mailbox to it. She would not listen to them.

Daily, monthly, yearly we watched the Negro grow grayer and more stooped, going in and out with the market basket. Each December we sent her a tax notice, which would be returned by the post office a week later, unclaimed. Now and then we would see her in one of the downstairs windows—she had evidently shut up the top floor of the house—like the carven torso of an idol in a niche, looking or not looking at us, we could never tell which. Thus she passed from generation to generation—dear, inescapable, impervious, tranquil, and perverse.

And so she died. Fell ill in the house filled with dust and shadows, with only 50 a doddering Negro man to wait on her. We did not even know she was sick; we had long since given up trying to get any information from the Negro. He talked to no one, probably not even to her, for his voice had grown harsh and rusty, as if from disuse.

She died in one of the downstairs rooms, in a heavy walnut bed with a curtain, her gray head propped on a pillow yellow and moldy with age and lack of sunlight.

V

The Negro met the first of the ladies at the front door and let them in, with their hushed, sibilant voices and their quick, curious glances, and then he disappeared. He walked right through the house and out the back and was not seen again.

The two female cousins came at once. They held the funeral on the second day, with the town coming to look at Miss Emily beneath a mass of bought flowers, with the crayon face of her father musing profoundly above the bier and the ladies sibilant and macabre; and the very old men—some in their brushed Confederate uniforms—on the porch and the lawn, talking of Miss Emily as if she had been a contemporary of theirs, believing they had danced with her and courted her perhaps, confusing time with its mathematical progression, as the old do, to whom all the past is not a diminishing road but, instead, a huge meadow which no winter ever quite touches, divided from them now by the narrow bottle-neck of the most recent decade of years.

Already we knew that there was one room in that region above stairs which no one had seen in forty years, and which would have to be forced. They waited until Miss Emily was decently in the ground before they opened it.

The violence of breaking down the door seemed to fill this room with pervading dust. A thin, acrid pall as of the tomb seemed to lie everywhere upon this room decked and furnished as for a bridal: upon the valance curtains of faded rose color, upon the rose-shaded lights, upon the dressing table, upon the delicate array of crystal and the man's toilet things backed with tarnished silver, silver so tarnished that the monogram was obscured. Among them lay a collar and tie, as if they had just been removed, which, lifted, left upon the surface a pale crescent in the dust. Upon a chair hung the suit, carefully folded; beneath it the two mute shoes and the discarded socks.

The man himself lay in the bed.

For a long while we just stood there, looking down at the profound and fleshless grin. The body had apparently once lain in the attitude of an embrace, but now the long sleep that outlasts love, that conquers even the grimace of love, had cuckolded him. What was left of him, rotted beneath what was left of the nightshirt, had become inextricable from the bed in which he lay; and upon him and upon the pillow beside him lay that even coating of the patient and biding dust.

Then we noticed that in the second pillow was the indentation of a head. One of us lifted something from it, and leaning forward, that faint and invisible dust dry and acrid in the nostrils, we saw a long strand of iron-gray hair.

For Analysis

1. Why does Faulkner title the narrative "A Rose for Emily"? **2.** At the end of section two, the narrator says "we remembered all the young men her father had driven away." What is the significance of this statement? How would you characterize Emily's relationship with her father? Her father's relationship with the town? **3.** In section three, we learn that "the ladies all said, 'Of course a Grierson would not think seriously of a Northerner, a day laborer.' " Why not? What are Emily's alternatives? **4.** What is the effect of the final paragraph?

On Style

1. Why do you suppose the narrator uses the pronoun "we"? The narrator often speaks of "the town." What does "the town" signify? **2.** Reread the description of Emily's house in the second paragraph. What does that description suggest to you? **3.** What does the author accomplish by not presenting the story in chronological order?

Making Connections

1. Consider your own relationship with your parents. Does it parallel or contrast with Emily's relationship with her father? Explain. **2.** In this story the town sometimes is treated like one of the **protagonists**—the narrator refers to himself as "we," and "the town" has significant opinions and reactions. Have you ever lived in a social setting that dictated your behavior? Explain.

Writing Topic

Write a brief essay discussing the role of time in this story. How does the town's response to the Griersons in general, and Emily in particular, change as time passes?

Chinua Achebe [b. 1930]

Marriage Is a Private Affair 1972

"Have you written to your dad yet?" asked Nene one afternoon as she sat with Nnaemeka in her room at 16 Kasanga Street, Lagos.[1]

"No. I've been thinking about it. I think it's better to tell him when I get home on leave!"

"But why? Your leave is such a long way off yet—six whole weeks. He should be let into our happiness now."

Nnaemeka was silent for a while, and then began very slowly as if he groped for his words: "I wish I were sure it would be happiness to him."

"Of course it must," replied Nene, a little surprised. "Why shouldn't it?"   5

"You have lived in Lagos all your life, and you know very little about people in remote parts of the country."

"That's what you always say. But I don't believe anybody will be so unlike other people that they will be unhappy when their sons are engaged to marry."

"Yes. They are most unhappy if the engagement is not arranged by them. In our case it's worse—you are not even an Ibo."

This was said so seriously and so bluntly that Nene could not find speech immediately. In the cosmopolitan atmosphere of the city it had always seemed to her something of a joke that a person's tribe could determine whom he married.

At last she said, "You don't really mean that he will object to your marrying   10
me simply on that account? I had always thought you Ibos were kindly disposed to other people."

"So we are. But when it comes to marriage, well, it's not quite so simple. And this," he added, "is not peculiar to the Ibos. If your father were alive and lived in the heart of Ibibio-land he would be exactly like my father."

"I don't know. But anyway, as your father is so fond of you, I'm sure he will forgive you soon enough. Come on then, be a good boy and send him a nice lovely letter . . ."

"It would not be wise to break the news to him by writing. A letter will bring it upon him with a shock. I'm quite sure about that."

"All right, honey, suit yourself. You know your father."

As Nnaemeka walked home that evening he turned over in his mind the dif-   15
ferent ways of overcoming his father's opposition, especially now that he had gone and found a girl for him. He had thought of showing his letter to Nene but decided on second thoughts not to, at least for the moment. He read it again when he got home and couldn't help smiling to himself. He remembered Ugoye

---

[1] The former capital of Nigeria, Lagos is the largest city in sub-Saharan Africa.

quite well, an Amazon of a girl who used to beat up all the boys, himself included, on the way to the stream, a complete dunce at school.

> I have found a girl who will suit you admirably—Ugoye Nweke, the eldest daughter of our neighbour, Jacob Nweke. She has a proper Christian upbringing. When she stopped schooling some years ago her father (a man of sound judgment) sent her to live in the house of a pastor where she has received all the training a wife could need. Her Sunday School teacher has told me that she reads her Bible very fluently. I hope we shall begin negotiations when you come home in December.

On the second evening of his return from Lagos Nnaemeka sat with his father under a cassia tree. This was the old man's retreat where he went to read his Bible when the parching December sun had set and a fresh, reviving wind blew on the leaves.[2]

"Father," began Nnaemeka suddenly, "I have come to ask forgiveness."

"Forgiveness? For what, my son?" he asked in amazement.

"It's about this marriage question."

"Which marriage question?"

"I can't—we must—I mean it is impossible for me to marry Nweke's daugh-   20
ter."

"Impossible? Why?" asked his father.

"I don't love her."

"Nobody said you did. Why should you?" he asked.

"Marriage today is different . . ."

"Look here, my son," interrupted his father, "nothing is different. What one   25
looks for in a wife are a good character and a Christian background."

Nnaemeka saw there was no hope along the present line of argument.

"Moreover," he said, "I am engaged to marry another girl who has all of Ugoye's good qualities, and who . . ."

His father did not believe his ears. "What did you say?" he asked slowly and disconcertingly.

"She is a good Christian," his son went on, "and a teacher in a Girls' School in Lagos."

"Teacher, did you say? If you consider that a qualification for a good wife I   30
should like to point out to you, Emeka, that no Christian woman should teach. St. Paul in his letter to the Corinthians says that women should keep silence." He rose slowly from his seat and paced forwards and backwards. This was his pet subject, and he condemned vehemently those church leaders who encouraged women to teach in their schools. After he had spent his emotion on a long homily he at last came back to his son's engagement, in a seemingly milder tone.

"Whose daughter is she, anyway?"

"She is Nene Atang."

---

[2] Although traditional Ibo religion centers on ancestor and nature worship, many Ibos became Christians under British colonial and missionary influence.

"What!" All the mildness was gone again. "Did you say Neneataga, what does that mean?"

"Nene Atang from Calabar. She is the only girl I can marry." This was a very rash reply and Nnaemeka expected the storm to burst. But it did not. His father merely walked away into his room. This was most unexpected and perplexed Nnaemeka. His father's silence was infinitely more menacing than a flood of threatening speech. That night the old man did not eat.

When he sent for Nnaemeka a day later he applied all possible ways of dissuasion. But the young man's heart was hardened, and his father eventually gave him up as lost. 35

"I owe it to you, my son, as a duty to show you what is right and what is wrong. Whoever put this idea into your head might as well have cut your throat. It is Satan's work." He waved his son away.

"You will change your mind, Father, when you know Nene."

"I shall never see her," was the reply. From that night the father scarcely spoke to his son. He did not, however, cease hoping that he would realize how serious was the danger he was heading for. Day and night he put him in his prayers.

Nnaemeka, for his own part, was very deeply affected by his father's grief. But he kept hoping that it would pass away. If it had occurred to him that never in the history of his people had a man married a woman who spoke a different tongue, he might have been less optimistic. "It has never been heard," was the verdict of an old man speaking a few weeks later. In that short sentence he spoke for all of his people. This man had come with others to commiserate with Okeke when news went round about his son's behaviour. By that time the son had gone back to Lagos.

"It has never been heard," said the old man again with a sad shake of his head. 40

"What did Our Lord say?" asked another gentleman. "Sons shall rise against their Fathers; it is there in the Holy Book."

"It is the beginning of the end," said another.

The discussion thus tending to become theological, Madubogwu, a highly practical man, brought it down once more to the ordinary level.

"Have you thought of consulting a native doctor about your son?" he asked Nnaemeka's father.

"He isn't sick," was the reply. 45

"What is he then? The boy's mind is diseased and only a good herbalist can bring him back to his right senses. The medicine he requires is *Amalile*, the same that women apply with success to recapture their husbands' straying affection."

"Madubogwu is right," said another gentleman. "This thing calls for medicine."

"I shall not call in a native doctor." Nnaemeka's father was known to be obstinately ahead of his more superstitious neighbours in these matters. "I will not be another Mrs. Ochuba. If my son wants to kill himself let him do it with his own hands. It is not for me to help him."

"But it was her fault," said Madubogwu. "She ought to have gone to an honest herbalist. She was a clever woman, nevertheless."

"She was a wicked murderess," said Jonathan who rarely argued with his ⁵⁰ neighbours because, he often said, they were incapable of reasoning. "The medicine was prepared for her husband, it was his name they called in its preparation and I am sure it would have been perfectly beneficial to him. It was wicked to put it into the herbalist's food, and say you were only trying it out."

Six months later, Nnaemeka was showing his young wife a short letter from his father:

> It amazes me that you could be so unfeeling as to send me your wedding picture. I would have sent it back. But on further thought I decided just to cut off your wife and send it back to you because I have nothing to do with her. How I wish that I had nothing to do with you either.

When Nene read through this letter and looked at the mutilated picture her eyes filled with tears, and she began to sob.

"Don't cry, my darling," said her husband. "He is essentially good-natured and will one day look more kindly on our marriage." But years passed and that one day did not come.

For eight years, Okeke would have nothing to do with his son, Nnaemeka. Only three times (when Nnaemeka asked to come home and spend his leave) did he write to him.

"I can't have you in my house," he replied on one occasion. "It can be of no ⁵⁵ interest to me where or how you spend your leave—or your life, for that matter."

The prejudice against Nnaemeka's marriage was not confined to his little village. In Lagos, especially among his people who worked there, it showed itself in a different way. Their women, when they met at their village meeting were not hostile to Nene. Rather, they paid her such excessive deference as to make her feel she was not one of them. But as time went on, Nene gradually broke through some of this prejudice and even began to make friends among them. Slowly and grudgingly they began to admit that she kept her home much better than most of them.

The story eventually got to the little village in the heart of the Ibo country that Nnaemeka and his young wife were a most happy couple. But his father was one of the few people who knew nothing about this. He always displayed so much temper whenever his son's name was mentioned that everyone avoided it in his presence. By a tremendous effort of will he had succeeded in pushing his son to the back of his mind. The strain had nearly killed him but he had persevered, and won.

Then one day he received a letter from Nene, and in spite of himself he began to glance through it perfunctorily until all of a sudden the expression on his face changed and he began to read more carefully.

> . . . Our two sons, from the day they learnt that they have a grandfather, have insisted on being taken to him. I find it impossible to tell them that you will not see them. I

implore you to allow Nnaemeka to bring them home for a short time during his leave next month. I shall remain here in Lagos . . .

The old man at once felt the resolution he had built up over so many years falling in. He was telling himself that he must not give in. He tried to steel his heart against all emotional appeals. It was a reenactment of that other struggle. He leaned against a window and looked out. The sky was overcast with heavy black clouds and a high wind began to blow filling the air with dust and dry leaves. It was one of those rare occasions when even Nature takes a hand in a human fight. Very soon it began to rain, the first rain in the year. It came down in large sharp drops and was accompanied by the lightning and thunder which mark a change of season. Okeke was trying hard not to think of his two grandsons. But he knew he was now fighting a losing battle. He tried to hum a favourite hymn but the pattering of large rain drops on the roof broke up the tune. His mind immediately returned to the children. How could he shut his door against them? By a curious mental process he imagined them standing, sad and forsaken, under the harsh angry weather—shut out from his house.

That night he hardly slept, from remorse—and a vague fear that he might die without making it up to them. 60

For Analysis
1. What are the various forms the conflict between modernism and tradition takes in this story? **2.** Nnaemeka's father, Okeke, rejects a neighbor's suggestion that he call a doctor to treat his son's "sickness" because, we are told, he is "ahead of his more superstitious neighbours" (par. 48). Does the story provide evidence that Okeke is more enlightened than the others in his village? Explain.

On Style
What is the narrator's attitude toward the story he is telling? How does his attitude affect your reading of it?

Making Connections
Like this story, Faulkner's "A Rose for Emily" (p. 667) and Mukherjee's "Orbiting" (p. 680) focus on courtship and marriage to dramatize the theme of cultural conflict. In what ways are the conflicts similar? In what ways different?

Writing Topic
Have you or someone you know experienced family resistance or criticism for forming a relationship with someone from a different cultural background? Write a page explaining how you dealt with the problem.

Bharati Mukherjee   [b. 1940]

Orbiting   1988

On Thanksgiving morning I'm still in my nightgown thinking of Vic when Dad raps on my apartment door. Who's he rolling joints for, who's he initiating now into the wonders of his inner space? What got me on Vic is remembering last Thanksgiving and his famous cranberry sauce with Grand Marnier, which Dad had interpreted as a sign of permanence in my life. A man who cooks like Vic is ready for other commitments. Dad cannot imagine cooking as self-expression. You cook *for* someone. Vic's sauce was a sign of his permanent isolation, if you really want to know.

Dad's come to drop off the turkey. It's a seventeen-pounder. Mr. Vitelli knows to reserve a biggish one for us every Thanksgiving and Christmas. But this November what with Danny in the Marines, Uncle Carmine having to be very careful after the bypass, and Vic taking off for outer space as well, we might as well have made do with one of those turkey rolls you pick out of the freezer. And in other years, Mr. Vitelli would not have given us a frozen bird. We were proud of that, our birds were fresh killed. I don't bring this up to Dad.

"Your mama took care of the thawing," Dad says. "She said you wouldn't have room in your Frigidaire."

"You mean Mom said Rindy shouldn't be living in a dump, right?" Mom has the simple, immigrant faith that children should do better than their parents, and her definition of better is comfortingly rigid. Fair enough—I believed it, too. But the fact is all I can afford is this third-floor studio with an art deco shower. The fridge fits under the kitchenette counter. The room has potential. I'm content with that. And I *like* my job even though it's selling, not designing, jewelry made out of seashells and semiprecious stones out of a boutique in Bellevue Plaza.

Dad shrugs. "You're an adult, Renata." He doesn't try to lower himself into   5
one of my two deck chairs. He was a minor league catcher for a while and his knees went. The fake zebra-skin cushions piled as seats on the rug are out of the question for him. My futon bed folds up into a sofa, but the satin sheets are still lasciviously tangled. My father stands in a slat of sunlight, trying not to look embarrassed.

"Dad, I'd have come to the house and picked it up. You didn't have to make the extra trip out from Verona." A sixty-five-year-old man in wingtips and a Borsalino[1] hugging a wet, heavy bird is so poignant I have to laugh.

---

[1] A stylish brim hat.

"You wouldn't have gotten out of bed until noon, Renata." But Dad smiles. I know what he's saying. He's saying *he's* retired and *he* should be able to stay in bed till noon if he wants to, but he can't and he'd rather drive twenty miles with a soggy bird than read the *Ledger* one more time.

Grumbling and scolding are how we deMarcos express love. It's the North Italian way, Dad used to tell Cindi, Danny, and me when we were kids. Sicilians and Calabrians are emotional; we're contained. Actually, *he's* contained, the way Vic was contained for the most part. Mom's a Calabrian and she was born and raised there. Dad's very American, so Italy's a safe source of pride for him. I once figured it out: *his* father, Arturo deMarco, was a fifteen-week-old fetus when his mother planted her feet on Ellis Island. Dad, a proud son of North Italy, had one big adventure in his life, besides fighting in the Pacific, and that was marrying a Calabrian peasant. He made it sound as though Mom was a Korean or something, and their marriage was a kind of taming of the West, and that everything about her could be explained as a cultural deficiency. Actually, Vic could talk beautifully about his feelings. He'd brew espresso, pour it into tiny blue pottery cups and analyze our relationship. I should have listened. I mean really listened. I thought he was talking about us, but I know now he was only talking incessantly about himself. I put too much faith in mail-order nightgowns and bras.

"Your mama wanted me out of the house," Dad goes on. "She didn't used to be like this, Renata."

Renata and Carla are what we were christened. We changed to Rindy and   10
Cindi in junior high. Danny didn't have to make such leaps, unless you count dropping out of Montclair State and joining the Marines. He was always Danny, or Junior.

I lug the turkey to the kitchen sink where it can drip away at a crazy angle until I have time to deal with it.

"Your mama must have told you girls I've been acting funny since I retired."

"No, Dad, she hasn't said anything about you acting funny." What she *has* said is do we think she ought to call Doc Brunetti and have a chat about Dad? Dad wouldn't have to know. He and Doc Brunetti are, or were, on the same church league bowling team. So is, or was, Vic's dad, Vinny Riccio.

"Your mama thinks a man should have an office to drive to every day. I sat at a desk for thirty-eight years and what did I get? Ask Doc, I'm too embarrassed to say." Dad told me once Doc—his real name was Frankie, though no one ever called him that—had been called Doc since he was six years old and growing up with Dad in Little Italy. There was never a time in his life when Doc wasn't Doc, which made his professional decision very easy. Dad used to say, no one ever called me Adjuster when I was a kid. Why didn't they call me something like Sarge or Teach? Then I would have known better.

I wish I had something breakfasty in my kitchen cupboard to offer him. He   15
wants to stay and talk about Mom, which is the way old married people have. Let's talk about me means: What do you think of Mom? I'll take the turkey over means: When will Rindy settle down? I wish this morning I had bought the

Goodwill sofa for ten dollars instead of letting Vic haul off the fancy deck chairs from Fortunoff's. Vic had flash. He'd left Jersey a long time before he actually took off.

"I can make you tea."

"None of that herbal stuff."

We don't talk about Mom, but I know what he's going through. She's just started to find herself. He's not burned out, he's merely stuck. I remember when Mom refused to learn to drive, wouldn't leave the house even to mail a letter. Her litany those days was: when you've spent the first fifteen years of your life in a mountain village, when you remember candles and gaslight and carrying water from a well, not to mention holding in your water at night because of wolves and the unlit outdoor privy, you *like* being housebound. She used those wolves for all they were worth, as though imaginary wolves still nipped her heels in the Clifton Mall.

Before Mom began to find herself and signed up for a class at Paterson, she used to nag Cindi and me about finding the right men. "Men," she said; she wasn't coy, never. Unembarrassed, she'd tell me about her wedding night, about her first sighting of Dad's "thing" ("Land Ho!" Cindi giggled. "Thar she blows!" I chipped in.) and she'd giggle at our word for it, the common word, and she'd use it around us, never around Dad. Mom's peasant, she's earthy but never coarse. If I could get that across to Dad, how I admire it in men or in women, I would feel somehow redeemed of all my little mistakes with them, with men, with myself. Cindi and Brent were married on a cruise ship by the ship's captain. Tony, Vic's older brother, made a play for me my senior year. Tony's solid now. He manages a funeral home but he's invested in crayfish ponds on the side.

"You don't even own a dining table." Dad sounds petulant. He uses "even" a 20 lot around me. Not just a judgment, but a comparative judgment. Other people have dining tables. *Lots* of dining tables. He softens it a bit, not wanting to hurt me, wanting more for me to judge him a failure. "We've always had a sit-down dinner, hon."

Okay, so traditions change. This year dinner's potluck. So I don't have real furniture. I eat off stack-up plastic tables as I watch the evening news. I drink red wine and heat a pita bread on the gas burner and wrap it around alfalfa sprouts or green linguine. The Swedish knockdown dresser keeps popping its sides because Vic didn't glue it properly. Swedish engineering, he said, doesn't need glue. Think of Volvos, he said, and Ingmar Bergman. He isn't good with directions that come in four languages. At least he wasn't.

"Trust me, Dad." This isn't the time to spring new lovers on him. "A friend made me a table. It's in the basement."

"How about chairs?" Ah, my good father. He could have said, friend? What friend?

Marge, my landlady, has all kinds of junky stuff in the basement. "Jorge and I'll bring up what we need. You'd strain your back, Dad." Shot knees, bad back: daily pain but nothing fatal. Not like Carmine.

"Jorge? Is that the new boyfriend?" 25

Shocking him makes me feel good. It would serve him right if Jorge were my new boyfriend. But Jorge is Marge's other roomer. He gives Marge Spanish lessons, and does the heavy cleaning and the yard work. Jorge has family in El Salvador he's hoping to bring up. I haven't met Marge's husband yet. He works on an offshore oil rig in some emirate with a funny name.

"No, Dad." I explain about Jorge.

"El Salvador!" he repeats. "That means 'the Savior.' " He passes on the information with a kind of awe. It makes Jorge's homeland, which he's shown me pretty pictures of, seem messy and exotic, at the very rim of human comprehension.

After Dad leaves, I call Cindi, who lives fifteen minutes away on Upper Mountainside Road. She's eleven months younger and almost a natural blond, but we're close. Brent wasn't easy for me to take, not at first. He owns a discount camera and electronics store on Fifty-fourth in Manhattan. Cindi met him through Club Med. They sat on a gorgeous Caribbean beach and talked of hogs. His father is an Amish farmer in Kalona, Iowa. Brent, in spite of the obvious hairpiece and the gold chain, is a rebel. He was born Schwartzendruber, but changed his name to Schwartz. Now no one believes the Brent, either. They call him Bernie on the street and it makes everyone more comfortable. His father's never taken their buggy out of the county.

The first time Vic asked me out, he talked of feminism and holism and macrobiotics. Then he opened up on cinema and literature, and I was very impressed, as who wouldn't be? Ro, my current lover, is very different. He picked me up in an uptown singles bar that I and sometimes Cindi go to. He bought me a Cinzano and touched my breast in the dark. He was direct, and at the same time weirdly courtly. I took him home though usually I don't, at first. I learned in bed that night that the tall brown drink with the lemon twist he'd been drinking was Tab.

I went back on the singles circuit even though the break with Vic should have made me cautious. Cindi thinks Vic's a romantic. I've told her how it ended. One Sunday morning in March he kissed me awake as usual. He'd brought in the *Times* from the porch and was reading it. I made us some cinnamon rose tea. We had a ritual, starting with the real estate pages, passing remarks on the latest tacky towers. Not for us, we'd say, the view is terrible! No room for the servants, things like that. And our imaginary children's imaginary nanny. "Hi, gorgeous," I said. He is gorgeous, not strong, but showy. He said, "I'm leaving, babe. New Jersey doesn't do it for me anymore." I said, "Okay, so where're we going?" I had an awful job at the time, taking orders for MCI. Vic said, "I didn't say we, babe." So I asked, "You mean it's over? Just like that?" And he said, "Isn't that the best way? No fuss, no hang-ups." Then I got a little whiny. "But *why?*" I wanted to know. But he was macrobiotic in lots of things, including relationships. Yin and yang, hot and sour, green and yellow. "You know, Rindy, there are *places*. You don't fall off the earth when you leave Jersey, you know. Places you see pictures of and read about. Different weathers, different trees, different everything. Places that get the Cubs on cable instead of the Mets." He

30

was into that. For all the sophisticated things he liked to talk about, he was a very local boy. "Vic," I pleaded, "you're crazy. You need help." "I need help because I want to get out of Jersey? You gotta be kidding!" He stood up and for a moment I thought he would do something crazy, like destroy something, or hurt me. "Don't ever call me crazy, got that? And give me the keys to the van."

He took the van. Danny had sold it to me when the Marines sent him overseas. I'd have given it to him anyway, even if he hadn't asked.

"Cindi, I need a turkey roaster," I tell my sister on the phone.

"I'll be right over," she says. "The brat's driving me crazy."

"Isn't Franny's visit working out?"   35

"I could kill her. I think up ways. How does that sound?"

"Why not send her home?" I'm joking. Franny is Brent's twelve-year-old and he's shelled out a lot of dough to lawyers in New Jersey and Florida to work out visitation rights.

"Poor Brent. He feels so *divided,*" Cindi says. "He shouldn't have to take sides."

I want her to ask who my date is for this afternoon, but she doesn't. It's important to me that she like Ro, that Mom and Dad more than tolerate him.

All over the country, I tell myself, women are towing new lovers home to   40
meet their families. Vic is simmering cranberries in somebody's kitchen and explaining yin and yang. I check out the stuffing recipe. The gravy calls for cream and freshly grated nutmeg. Ro brought me six whole nutmegs in a Ziplock bag from his friend, a Pakistani, who runs a spice store in SoHo.[2] The nuts look hard and ugly. I take one out of the bag and sniff it. The aroma's so exotic my head swims. On an impulse I call Ro.

The phone rings and rings. He doesn't have his own place yet. He has to crash with friends. He's been in the States three months, maybe less. I let it ring fifteen, sixteen, seventeen times.

Finally someone answers. "Yes?" The voice is guarded, the accent obviously foreign even though all I'm hearing is a one-syllable word. Ro has fled here from Kabul. He wants to take classes at NJIT and become an electrical engineer. He says he's lucky his father got him out. A friend of Ro's father, a man called Mumtaz, runs a fried chicken restaurant in Brooklyn in a neighborhood Ro calls "Little Kabul," though probably no one else has ever noticed. Mr. Mumtaz puts the legal immigrants to work as waiters out front. The illegals hide in a backroom as pluckers and gutters.

"Ro? I miss you. We're eating at three, remember?"

"Who is speaking, please?"

So I fell for the accent, but it isn't a malicious error. I *can* tell one Afghan tribe   45
from another now, even by looking at them or by their names. I can make out

---

[2] A neighborhood south of Houston Street in Manhattan.

some Pashto words. "Tell Ro it's Rindy. Please? I'm a friend. He wanted me to call this number."

"Not knowing any Ro."

"Hey, wait. Tell him it's Rindy deMarco."

The guy hangs up on me.

I'm crumbling cornbread into a bowl for the stuffing when Cindi honks half of "King Cotton" from the parking apron in the back. Brent bought her the BMW on the gray market and saved a bundle—once discount, always discount—then spent three hundred dollars to put in a horn that beeps a Sousa march. I wave a potato masher at her from the back window. She doesn't get out of the car. Instead she points to the pan in the back seat. I come down, wiping my hands on a dish towel.

"I should stay and help." Cindi sounds ready to cry. But I don't want her with 50 me when Ro calls back.

"You're doing too much already, kiddo." My voice at least sounds comforting. "You promised one veg and the salad."

"I ought to come up and help. That or get drunk." She shifts the stick. When Brent bought her the car, the dealer threw in driving gloves to match the upholstery.

"Get Franny to shred the greens," I call as Cindi backs up the car. "Get her involved."

The phone is ringing in my apartment. I can hear it ring from the second-floor landing.

"Ro?" 55

"You're taking a chance, my treasure. It could have been any other admirer, then where would you be?"

"I don't have any other admirers." Ro is not a conventionally jealous man, not like the types I have known. He's totally unlike any man I have ever known. He wants men to come on to me. Lately when we go to a bar he makes me sit far enough from him so some poor lonely guy thinks I'm looking for action. Ro likes to swagger out of a dark booth as soon as someone buys me a drink. I go along. He comes from a macho culture.

"How else will I know you are as beautiful as I think you are? I would not want an unprized woman," he says. He is asking me for time, I know. In a few more months he'll know I'm something of a catch in my culture, or at least I've never had trouble finding boys. Even Brent Schwartzendruber has begged me to see him alone.

"I'm going to be a little late," Ro says. "I told you about my cousin, Abdul, no?"

Ro has three or four cousins that I know of in Manhattan. They're all named 60 Abdul something. When I think of Abdul, I think of a giant black man with goggles on, running down a court. Abdul is the teenage cousin whom immigration officials nabbed as he was gutting chickens in Mumtaz's backroom. Abdul doesn't have the right papers to live and work in this country, and now he's been locked up in a detention center on Varick Street. Ro's afraid Abdul will be deported back to Afghanistan. If that happens, he'll be tortured.

"I have to visit him before I take the DeCamp bus. He's talking nonsense. He's talking of starting a hunger fast."

"A hunger strike! God!" When I'm with Ro I feel I am looking at America through the wrong end of a telescope. He makes it sound like a police state, with sudden raids, papers, detention centers, deportations, and torture and death waiting in the wings. I'm not a political person. Last fall I wore the Ferraro button because she's a woman and Italian.

"Rindy, all night I've been up and awake. All night I think of your splendid breasts. Like clusters of grapes, I think. I am stroking and fondling your grapes this very minute. My talk gets you excited?"

I tell him to test me, please get here before three. I remind him he can't buy his ticket on the bus.

"We got here too early, didn't we?" Dad stands just outside the door to my apartment, looking embarrassed. He's in his best dark suit, the one he wears every Thanksgiving and Christmas. This year he can't do up the top button of his jacket. 65

"Don't be so formal, Dad." I give him a showy hug and pull him indoors so Mom can come in.

"As if your papa ever listens to me!" Mom laughs. But she sits primly on the sofa bed in her velvet cloak, with her tote bag and evening purse on her lap. Before Dad started courting her, she worked as a seamstress. Dad rescued her from a sweatshop. He married down, she married well. That's the family story.

"She told me to rush."

Mom isn't in a mood to squabble. I think she's reached the point of knowing she won't have him forever. There was Carmine, at death's door just a month ago. Anything could happen to Dad. She says, "Renata, look what I made! Crostolis." She lifts a cake tin out of her tote bag. The pan still feels warm. And for dessert, I know, there'll be a jar of super-thick, super-rich Death by Chocolate.

The story about Grandma deMarco, Dad's mama, is that every Thanksgiving she served two full dinners, one American with the roast turkey, candied yams, pumpkin pie, the works, and another with Grandpa's favorite pastas. 70

Dad relaxes. He appoints himself bartender. "Don't you have more ice cubes, sweetheart?"

I tell him it's good Glenlivet. He shouldn't ruin it with ice, just a touch of water if he must. Dad pours sherry in Vic's pottery espresso cups for his women. Vic made them himself, and I used to think they were perfect blue jewels. Now I see they're lumpy, uneven in color.

"Go change into something pretty before Carla and Brent come." Mom believes in dressing up. Beaded dresses lift her spirits. She's wearing a beaded green dress today.

I take the sherry and vanish behind a four-panel screen, the kind long-legged showgirls change behind in black and white movies while their mous-tached lovers keep talking. My head barely shows above the screen's top, since I'm no long-legged showgirl. My best points, as Ro has said, are my clusters of grapes. Vic found the screen at a country auction in the Adirondacks. It had filled the van. Now I use the panels as a bulletin board and I'm worried Dad'll spot the notice for the next meeting of Amnesty International, which will bother him. He will think the two words stand for draft dodger and commu-nist. I was going to drop my membership, a legacy of Vic, when Ro saw it and approved. Dad goes to the Sons of Italy Anti-Defamation dinners. He met Frank Sinatra at one. He voted for Reagan last time because the Democrats ran an Italian woman.

Instead of a thirties lover, it's my moustached papa talking to me from the   75
other side of the screen. "So where's this dining table?"

"Ro's got the parts in the basement. He'll bring it up, Dad."

I hear them whispering. "Bo? Now she's messing with a Southerner?" and "Shh, it's her business."

I'm just smoothing on my pantyhose when Mom screams for the cops. Dad shouts too, at Mom for her to shut up. It's my fault, I should have warned Ro not to use his key this afternoon.

I peek over the screen's top and see my lover the way my parents see him. He's a slight, pretty man with hazel eyes and a tufty moustache, so whom can he intimidate? I've seen Jews and Greeks, not to mention Sons of Italy, darker-skinned than Ro. Poor Ro resorts to his Kabuli prep-school man-ners.

"How do you do, Madam! Sir! My name is Roashan."   80

Dad moves closer to Ro but doesn't hold out his hand. I can almost read his mind: *he speaks.* "Come again?" he says, baffled.

I cringe as he spells his name. My parents are so parochial. With each letter he does a graceful dip and bow. "Try it syllable by syllable, sir. Then it is not so hard."

Mom stares past him at me. The screen doesn't hide me because I've strayed too far in to watch the farce. "Renata, you're wearing only your camisole."

I pull my crew neck over my head, then kiss him. I make the kiss really sexy so they'll know I've slept with this man. Many times. And if he asks me, I will marry him. I had not known that till now. I think my mother guesses.

He's brought flowers: four long-stemmed, stylish purple blossoms in a florist's   85
paper cone. "For you, madam." He glides over the dirty broadloom to Mom who fills up more than half the sofa bed. "This is my first Thanksgiving dinner, for which I have much to give thanks, no?"

"He was born in Afghanistan," I explain. But Dad gets continents wrong. He says, "We saw your famine camps on TV. Well, you won't starve this afternoon."

"They smell good," Mom says. "Thank you very much but you shouldn't spend a fortune."

"No, no, madam. What you smell good is my cologne. Flowers in New York have no fragrance."

"His father had a garden estate outside Kabul." I don't want Mom to think he's putting down American flowers, though in fact he is. Along with American fruits, meats, and vegetables. "The Russians bulldozed it," I add.

Dad doesn't want to talk politics. He senses, looking at Ro, this is not the face   90
of Ethiopian starvation. "Well, what'll it be, Roy? Scotch and soda?" I wince. It's not going well.

"Thank you but no. I do not imbibe alcoholic spirits, though I have no objection for you, sir." My lover goes to the fridge and reaches down. He knows just where to find his Tab. My father is quietly livid, staring down at his drink.

In my father's world, grown men bowl in leagues and drink the best whiskey they can afford. Dad whistles "My Way." He must be under stress. That's his usual self-therapy: how would Francis Albert handle this?

"Muslims have taboos, Dad." Cindi didn't marry a Catholic, so he has no right to be upset about Ro, about us.

"Jews," Dad mutters. "So do Jews." He knows because catty-corner from Vitelli's is a kosher butcher. This isn't the time to parade new words before him, like *halal*, the Muslim kosher. An Italian-American man should be able to live sixty-five years never having heard the word, I can go along with that. Ro, fortunately, is cosmopolitan. Outside of pork and booze, he eats anything else I fix.

Brent and Cindi take forever to come. But finally we hear his MG squeal in   95
the driveway. Ro glides to the front window; he seems to blend with the ficus tree and hanging ferns. Dad and I wait by the door.

"Party time!" Brent shouts as he maneuvers Cindi and Franny ahead of him up three flights of stairs. He looks very much the head of the family, a rich man steeply in debt to keep up appearances, to compete, to head off middle age. He's at that age—and Cindi's nowhere near that age—when people notice the difference and quietly judge it. I know these things from Cindi—I'd never guess it from looking at Brent. If he feels divided, as Cindi says he does, it doesn't show. Misery, anxiety, whatever, show on Cindi though; they bring her cheekbones out. When I'm depressed, my hair looks rough, my skin breaks out. Right now, I'm lustrous.

Brent does a lot of whooping and hugging at the door. He even hugs Dad who looks grave and funereal like an old-world Italian gentleman because of his outdated, pinched dark suit. Cindi makes straight for the fridge with her casserole of squash and browned marshmallow. Franny just stands in the middle of the room holding two biggish Baggies of salad greens and vinaigrette in an old Dijon mustard jar. Brent actually bought the mustard in Dijon, a story that Ro is bound to hear and not appreciate. Vic was mean enough last year to tell him that he could have gotten it for more or less the same price at the Italian specialty foods store down on Watchung Plaza. Franny doesn't seem to have her own winter clothes. She's wearing Cindi's car coat over a Dolphins sweatshirt. Her mother moved down to Florida the very day the divorce became final. She's got a Walkman tucked into the pocket of her cords.

"You could have trusted me to make the salad dressing at least," I scold my sister.

Franny gives up the Baggies and the jar of dressing to me. She scrutinizes us—Mom, Dad, me and Ro, especially Ro, as though she can detect something strange about him—but doesn't take off her earphones. A smirk starts twitching her tanned, feral features. I see what she is seeing. Asian men carry their bodies differently, even these famed warriors from the Khyber Pass. Ro doesn't stand like Brent or Dad. His hands hang kind of stiffly from the shoulder joints, and when he moves, his palms are tucked tight against his thighs, his stomach sticks out like a slightly pregnant woman's. Each culture establishes its own manly posture, different ways of claiming space. Ro, hiding among my plants, holds himself in a way that seems both too effeminate and too macho. I hate Franny for what she's doing to me. I am twenty-seven years old, I should be more mature. But I see now how wrong Ro's clothes are. He shows too much white collar and cuff. His shirt and his wool-blend flare-leg pants were made to measure in Kabul. The jacket comes from a discount store on Canal Street, part of a discontinued line of two-trousered suits. I ought to know, I took him there. I want to shake Franny or smash the earphones.

Cindi catches my exasperated look. "Don't pay any attention to her. She's   100
unsociable this weekend. We can't compete with the Depeche Mode."

I intend to compete.

Franny, her eyes very green and very hostile, turns on Brent. "How come she never gets it right, Dad?"

Brent hi-fives his daughter, which embarrasses her more than anyone else in the room. "It's a Howard Jones, hon," Brent tells Cindi.

Franny, close to tears, runs to the front window where Ro's been hanging back. She has an ungainly walk for a child whose support payments specify weekly ballet lessons. She bores in on Ro's hidey hole like Russian artillery. Ro moves back to the perimeter of family intimacy. I have no way of helping yet. I have to set out the dips and Tostitos. Brent and Dad are talking sports, Mom and Cindi are watching the turkey. Dad's going on about the Knicks. He's in despair, so early in the season. He's on his second Scotch. I see Brent try. "What do you think, Roy?" He's doing his best to get my lover involved. "Maybe we'll get lucky, huh? We can always hope for a top draft pick. End up with Patrick Ewing!" Dad brightens. "That guy'll change the game. Just wait and see. He'll fill the lane better than Russell." Brent gets angry, since for some strange Amish reason he's a Celtics fan. So was Vic. "Bird'll make a monkey out of him." He looks to Ro for support.

Ro nods. Even his headshake is foreign. "You are undoubtedly correct,   105
Brent," he says. "I am deferring to your judgment because currently I have not familiarized myself with these practices."

Ro loves squash, but none of my relatives have ever picked up a racket. I want to tell Brent that Ro's skied in St. Moritz, lost a thousand dollars in a casino in Beirut, knows where to buy Havana cigars without getting hijacked. He's sophisticated, he could make monkeys out of us all, but they think he's a retard.

Brent drinks three Scotches to Dad's two; then all three men go down to the basement. Ro and Brent do the carrying, negotiating sharp turns in the stairwell. Dad supervises. There are two trestles and a wide, splintery plywood top. "Try not to take the wall down!" Dad yells.

When they make it back in, the men take off their jackets to assemble the table. Brent's wearing a red lamb's wool turtleneck under his camel hair blazer. Ro unfastens his cuff links—they are 24-karat gold and his father's told him to sell them if funds run low—and pushes up his very white shirt sleeves. There are scars on both arms, scars that bubble against his dark skin, scars like lightning flashes under his thick black hair. Scar tissue on Ro is the color of freshwater pearls. I want to kiss it.

Cindi checks the turkey one more time. "You guys better hurry. We'll be ready to eat in fifteen minutes."

Ro, the future engineer, adjusts the trestles. He's at his best now. He's become quite chatty. From under the plywood top, he's holding forth on the Soviet menace in Kabul. Brent may actually have an idea where Afghanistan is, in a general way, but Dad is lost. He's talking of being arrested for handing out pro-American pamphlets on his campus. Dad stiffens at "arrest" and blanks out the rest. He talks of this "so-called leader," this "criminal" named Babrak Karmal and I hear other buzz-words like Kandahār and Pamir, words that might have been Polish to me a month ago, and I can see even Brent is slightly embarrassed. It's his first exposure to Third World passion. He thought only Americans had informed political opinion—other people staged coups out of spite and misery. It's an unwelcome revelation to him that a reasonably educated and rational man like Ro would die for things that he, Brent, has never heard of and would rather laugh about. Ro was tortured in jail. Franny has taken off her earphones. Electrodes, canes, freezing tanks. He leaves nothing out. Something's gotten into Ro.

Dad looks sick. The meaning of Thanksgiving should not be so explicit. But Ro's in a daze. He goes on about how—*inshallah*[3]—his father, once a rich landlord, had stashed away enough to bribe a guard, sneak him out of this cell and hide him for four months in a tunnel dug under a servant's adobe hut until a forged American visa could be bought. Franny's eyes are wide, Dad joins Mom on the sofa bed, shaking his head. Jail, bribes, forged, what is this? I can read his mind. "For six days I must orbit one international airport to another," Ro is saying. "The main trick is having a valid ticket, that way the airline has to carry you, even if the country won't take you in. Colombo, Seoul, Bombay, Geneva, Frankfurt, I know too too well the transit lounges of many airports. We travel the world with our gym bags and prayer rugs, unrolling them in the transit lounges. The better airports have special rooms."

[3] "God willing." Here, it is apparently used to mean "Thank God."

Brent tries to ease Dad's pain. "Say, buddy," he jokes, "you wouldn't be ripping us off, would you?"

Ro snakes his slender body from under the makeshift table. He hasn't been watching the effect of his monologue. "I am a working man," he says stiffly. I have seen his special permit. He's one of the lucky ones, though it might not last. He's saving for NJIT. Meantime he's gutting chickens to pay for room and board in Little Kabul. He describes the gutting process. His face is transformed as he sticks his fist into imaginary roasters and grabs for gizzards, pulls out the squishy stuff. He takes an Afghan dagger out of the pocket of his pants. You'd never guess, he looks like such a victim. "This," he says, eyes glinting. "This is all I need."

"Cool," Franny says.

"Time to eat," Mom shouts. "I made the gravy with the nutmeg as you said, 115 Renata."

I lead Dad to the head of the table. "Everyone else sit where you want to."

Franny picks out the chair next to Ro before I can put Cindi there. I want Cindi to know him, I want her as an ally.

Dad tests the blade of the carving knife. Mom put the knife where Dad always sits when she set the table. He takes his thumb off the blade and pushes the switch. "That noise makes me feel good."

But I carry in the platter with the turkey and place it in front of Ro. "I want you to carve," I say.

He brings out his dagger all over again. Franny is practically licking his fin- 120 gers. "You mean this is a professional job?"

We stare fascinated as my lover slashes and slices, swiftly, confidently, at the huge, browned, juicy beast. The dagger scoops out flesh.

Now I am the one in a daze. I am seeing Ro's naked body as though for the first time, his nicked, scarred, burned body. In his body, the blemishes seem embedded, more beautiful, like wood. I am seeing character made manifest. I am seeing Brent and Dad for the first time, too. They have their little scars, things they're proud of, football injuries and bowling elbows they brag about. Our scars are so innocent; they are invisible and come to us from rough-housing gone too far. Ro hates to talk about his scars. If I trace the puckered tissue on his left thigh and ask "How, Ro?" he becomes shy, dismissive: a pack of dogs attacked him when he was a boy. The skin on his back is speckled and lumpy from burns, but when I ask he laughs. A crazy villager whacked him with a burning stick for cheekiness, he explains. He's ashamed that he comes from a culture of pain.

The turkey is reduced to a drying, whitened skeleton. On our plates, the slices are symmetrical, elegant. I realize all in a rush how much I love this man with his blemished, tortured body. I will give him citizenship if he asks. Vic was beautiful, but Vic was self-sufficient. Ro's my chance to heal the world.

I shall teach him how to walk like an American, how to dress like Brent but better, how to fill up a room as Dad does instead of melting and blending but sticking out in the Afghan way. In spite of the funny way he holds himself and the funny way he moves his head from side to side when he wants to say yes, Ro is Clint Eastwood, scarred hero and survivor. Dad and Brent are children. I realize Ro's the only circumcised man I've slept with.

Mom asks, "Why are you grinning like that, Renata?"   125

For Analysis
1. During the conversation with her father, early in the story, Renata thinks: "This isn't the time to spring new lovers on him" (par. 22). What is she referring to? **2.** Characterize Renata's previous lover, Vic. What relevance do her comments about him have to the theme of the story? **3.** What do Brent and Renata's father talk about before dinner? What does Ro talk about? What do you make of the differences in their interests? **4.** How do the various members of Renata's family feel about Ro? How does the family express its disapproval of Renata's choice of a boyfriend? How does Renata react to her family's disapproval? **5.** What does the title mean? **6.** Are Renata's expectations, described in paragraph 124, realistic? Explain.

On Style
Analyze the ways in which the **first-person narration** shapes the **theme** of this story.

Making Connections
1. What similarities and differences do you find between this story and Chinua Achebe's "Marriage Is a Private Affair" (p. 675)? **2.** Have you ever experienced or known an example of the kind of cultural conflict dealt with in this story? Have you ever found yourself the outsider? Describe the experience.

Writing Topic
Write an essay analyzing how this story dramatizes the ways in which cultural barriers prevent Renata's family from seeing who Ro really is.

Alice Walker [b. 1944]

Everyday Use 1973
For Your Grandmama

I will wait for her in the yard that Maggie and I made so clean and wavy yesterday afternoon. A yard like this is more comfortable than most people know. It is not just a yard. It is like an extended living room. When the hard clay is swept clean as a floor and the fine sand around the edges lined with tiny, irregular grooves anyone can come and sit and look up into the elm tree and wait for the breezes that never come inside the house.

Maggie will be nervous until after her sister goes: she will stand hopelessly in corners homely and ashamed of the burn scars down her arms and legs, eyeing her sister with a mixture of envy and awe. She thinks her sister has held life always in the palm of one hand, that "no" is a word the world never learned to say to her.

You've no doubt seen those TV shows where the child who has "made it" is confronted, as a surprise, by her own mother and father, tottering in weakly from backstage. (A pleasant surprise, of course: What would they do if parent and child came on the show only to curse out and insult each other?) On TV mother and child embrace and smile into each other's faces. Sometimes the mother and father weep, the child wraps them in her arms and leans across the table to tell how she would not have made it without their help. I have seen these programs.

Sometimes I dream a dream in which Dee and I are suddenly brought together on a TV program of this sort. Out of a dark and soft-seated limousine I am ushered into a bright room filled with many people. There I meet a smiling, gray, sporty man like Johnny Carson who shakes my hand and tells me what a fine girl I have. Then we are on the stage and Dee is embracing me with tears in her eyes. She pins on my dress a large orchid, even though she has told me once that she thinks orchids are tacky flowers.

In real life I am a large, big-boned woman with rough, man-working hands.   5
In the winter I wear flannel nightgowns to bed and overalls during the day. I can kill and clean a hog as mercilessly as a man. My fat keeps me hot in zero weather. I can work outside all day, breaking ice to get water for washing. I can eat pork liver cooked over the open fire minutes after it comes steaming from the hog. One winter I knocked a bull calf straight in the brain between the eyes with a sledge hammer and had the meat hung up to chill before nightfall. But of course all this does not show on television. I am the way my daughter would

693

want me to be: a hundred pounds lighter, my skin like an uncooked barley pan-cake. My hair glistens in the hot bright lights. Johnny Carson has much to do to keep up with my quick and witty tongue.

But that is a mistake. I know even before I wake up. Who ever knew a Johnson with a quick tongue? Who can even imagine me looking a strange white man in the eye? It seems to me I have talked to them always with one foot raised in flight, with my head turned in whichever way is farthest from them. Dee, though. She would always look anyone in the eye. Hesitation was no part of her nature.

"How do I look, Mama?" Maggie says, showing just enough of her thin body enveloped in pink skirt and red blouse for me to know she's there, almost hid-den by the door.

"Come out into the yard," I say.

Have you ever seen a lame animal, perhaps a dog run over by some careless person rich enough to own a car, sidle up to someone who is ignorant enough to be kind to him? That is the way my Maggie walks. She has been like this, chin on chest, eyes on ground, feet in shuffle, ever since the fire that burned the other house to the ground.

Dee is lighter than Maggie, with nicer hair and a fuller figure. She's a woman now, though sometimes I forget. How long ago was it that the other house burned? Ten, twelve years? Sometimes I can still hear the flames and feel Mag-gie's arms sticking to me, her hair smoking and her dress falling off her in little black papery flakes. Her eyes seemed stretched open, blazed open by the flames reflected in them. And Dee. I see her standing off under the sweet gum tree she used to dig gum out of; a look of concentration on her face as she watched the last dingy gray board of the house fall in toward the red-hot brick chimney. Why don't you do a dance around the ashes? I'd wanted to ask her. She had hated the house that much.

I used to think she hated Maggie, too. But that was before we raised the money, the church and me, to send her to Augusta to school. She used to read to us without pity; forcing words, lies, other folks' habits, whole lives upon us two, sitting trapped and ignorant underneath her voice. She washed us in a river of make-believe, burned us with a lot of knowledge we didn't necessarily need to know. Pressed us to her with the serious way she read, to shove us away at just the moment, like dimwits, we seemed about to understand.

Dee wanted nice things. A yellow organdy dress to wear to her graduation from high school; black pumps to match a green suit she'd made from an old suit somebody gave me. She was determined to stare down any disaster in her efforts. Her eyelids would not flicker for minutes at a time. Often I fought off the temptation to shake her. At sixteen she had a style of her own: and knew what style was.

I never had an education myself. After second grade the school was closed down. Don't ask me why: in 1927 colored asked fewer questions than they do now. Sometimes Maggie reads to me. She stumbles along good-naturedly but can't see well. She knows she is not bright. Like good looks and money, quickness passed her by. She will marry John Thomas (who has mossy teeth in an earnest face) and then I'll be free to sit here and I guess just sing church songs to myself. Although I never was a good singer. Never could carry a tune. I was always better at a man's job. I used to love to milk till I was hoofed in the side in '49. Cows are soothing and slow and don't bother you, unless you try to milk them the wrong way.

I have deliberately turned my back on the house. It is three rooms, just like the one that burned, except the roof is tin; they don't make shingle roofs any more. There are no real windows, just some holes cut in the sides, like the portholes in a ship, but not round and not square, with rawhide holding the shutters up on the outside. This house is in a pasture, too, like the other one. No doubt when Dee sees it she will want to tear it down. She wrote me once that no matter where we "choose" to live, she will manage to come see us. But she will never bring her friends. Maggie and I thought about this and Maggie asked me, "Mama, when did Dee ever *have* any friends?"

She had a few. Furtive boys in pink shirts hanging about on washday after   15
school. Nervous girls who never laughed. Impressed with her they worshiped the well-turned phrase, the cute shape, the scalding humor that erupted like bubbles in lye. She read to them.

When she was courting Jimmy T she didn't have much time to pay to us, but turned all her faultfinding power on him. He *flew* to marry a cheap gal from a family of ignorant flashy people. She hardly had time to recompose herself.

When she comes I will meet—but there they are!

Maggie attempts to make a dash for the house, in her shuffling way, but I stay her with my hand. "Come back here," I say. And she stops and tries to dig a well in the sand with her toe.

It is hard to see them clearly through the strong sun. But even the first glimpse of leg out of the car tells me it is Dee. Her feet were always neat-looking, as if God himself had shaped them with a certain style. From the other side of the car comes a short, stocky man. Hair is all over his head a foot long and hanging from his chin like a kinky mule tail. I hear Maggie suck in her breath. "Uhnnnh," is what it sounds like. Like when you see the wriggling end of a snake just in front of your foot on the road. "Uhnnnh."

Dee next. A dress down to the ground, in this hot weather. A dress so loud it   20
hurts my eyes. There are yellows and oranges enough to throw back the light of the sun. I feel my whole face warming from the heat waves it throws out. Earrings, too, gold and hanging down to her shoulders. Bracelets dangling and making noises when she moves her arm up to shake the folds of the dress out of her armpits. The dress is loose and flows, and as she walks closer, I like it. I hear Maggie go "Uhnnnh" again. It is her sister's hair. It stands straight up like the wool on a sheep. It is black as night and around the edges are two long pigtails that rope about like small lizards disappearing behind her ears.

"Wa-su-zo-Tean-o!" she says, coming on in that gliding way the dress makes her move. The short stocky fellow with the hair to his navel is all grinning and he follows up with "Asalamalakim, my mother and sister!" He moves to hug Maggie but she falls back, right up against the back of my chair. I feel her trembling there and when I look up I see the perspiration falling off her chin.

"Don't get up," says Dee. Since I am stout it takes something of a push. You can see me trying to move a second or two before I make it. She turns, showing white heels through her sandals, and goes back to the car. Out she peeks next with a Polaroid. She stoops down quickly and lines up picture after picture of me sitting there in front of the house with Maggie cowering behind me. She never takes a shot without making sure the house is included. When a cow comes nibbling around the edge of the yard she snaps it and me and Maggie *and* the house. Then she puts the Polaroid in the back seat of the car, and comes up and kisses me on the forehead.

Meanwhile Asalamalakim is going through motions with Maggie's hand. Maggie's hand is as limp as a fish, and probably as cold, despite the sweat, and she keeps trying to pull it back. It looks like Asalamalakim wants to shake hands but wants to do it fancy. Or maybe he don't know how people shake hands. Anyhow, he soon gives up on Maggie.

"Well," I say. "Dee."

"No, Mama," she says. "Not 'Dee,' Wangero Leewanika Kemanjo!"   25

"What happened to 'Dee'?" I wanted to know.

"She's dead," Wangero said. "I couldn't bear it any longer being named after the people who oppress me."

"You know as well as me you was named after your aunt Dicie," I said. Dicie is my sister. She named Dee. We called her "Big Dee" after Dee was born.

"But who was *she* named after?" asked Wangero.

"I guess after Grandma Dee," I said.   30

"And who was she named after?" asked Wangero.

"Her mother," I said, and saw Wangero was getting tired. "That's about as far back as I can trace it," I said. Though, in fact, I probably could have carried it back beyond the Civil War through the branches.

"Well," said Asalamalakim, "there you are."

"Uhnnnh," I heard Maggie say.

"There I was not," I said, "before 'Dicie' cropped up in our family, so why   35 should I try to trace it that far back?"

He just stood there grinning, looking down on me like somebody inspecting a Model A car. Every once in a while he and Wangero sent eye signals over my head.

"How do you pronounce this name?" I asked.

"You don't have to call me by it if you don't want to," said Wangero.

"Why shouldn't I?" I asked. "If that's what you want us to call you, we'll call you."

"I know it might sound awkward at first," said Wangero.   40

"I'll get used to it," I said. "Ream it out again."

Well, soon we got the name out of the way. Asalamalakim had a name twice as long and three times as hard. After I tripped over it two or three times he told me to just call him Hakim-a-barber. I wanted to ask him was he a barber, but I didn't really think he was, so I didn't ask.

"You must belong to those beef-cattle peoples down the road," I said. They said "Asalamalakim" when they met you, too, but they didn't shake hands. Always too busy: feeding the cattle, fixing the fences, putting up salt-lick shelters, throwing down hay. When the white folks poisoned some of the herd the men stayed up all night with rifles in their hands. I walked a mile and a half just to see the sight.

Hakim-a-barber said, "I accept some of their doctrines, but farming and raising cattle is not my style." (They didn't tell me, and I didn't ask, whether Wangero [Dee] had really gone and married him.)

We sat down to eat and right away he said he didn't eat collards and pork was   45
unclean. Wangero, though, went on through the chitlins and corn bread, the greens and everything else. She talked a blue streak over the sweet potatoes. Everything delighted her. Even the fact that we still used the benches her daddy made for the table when we couldn't afford to buy chairs.

"Oh, Mama!" she cried. Then turned to Hakim-a-barber. "I never knew how lovely these benches are. You can feel the rump prints," she said, running her hands underneath her and along the bench. Then she gave a sigh and her hand closed over Grandma Dee's butter dish. "That's it!" she said. "I knew there was something I wanted to ask you if I could have." She jumped up from the table and went over in the corner where the churn stood, the milk in its clabber by now. She looked at the churn and looked at it.

"This churn top is what I need," she said. "Didn't Uncle Buddy whittle it out of a tree you all used to have?"

"Yes," I said.

"Uh huh," she said happily. "And I want the dasher, too."

"Uncle Buddy whittle that, too?" asked the barber.   50

Dee (Wangero) looked up at me.

"Aunt Dee's first husband whittled the dash," said Maggie so low you almost couldn't hear her. "His name was Henry, but they called him Stash."

"Maggie's brain is like an elephant's," Wangero said, laughing. "I can use the churn top as a centerpiece for the alcove table," she said, sliding a plate over the churn, "and I'll think of something artistic to do with the dasher."

When she finished wrapping the dasher the handle stuck out. I took it for a moment in my hands. You didn't even have to look close to see where hands pushing the dasher up and down to make butter had left a kind of sink in the wood. In fact, there were a lot of small sinks; you could see where thumbs and fingers had sunk into the wood. It was beautiful light yellow wood, from a tree that grew in the yard where Big Dee and Stash had lived.

After dinner Dee (Wangero) went to the trunk at the foot of my bed and   55
started rifling through it. Maggie hung back in the kitchen over the dishpan. Out came Wangero with two quilts. They had been pieced by Grandma Dee and then Big Dee and me had hung them on the quilt frames on the front porch and quilted them. One was in the Lone Star pattern. The other was Walk Around the Mountain. In both of them were scraps of dresses Grandma Dee had worn fifty and more years ago. Bits and pieces of Grandpa Jarrell's Paisley shirts. And one teeny faded blue piece, about the size of a penny matchbox, that was from Great Grandpa Ezra's uniform that he wore in the Civil War.

"Mama," Wangero said sweet as a bird. "Can I have these old quilts?"

I heard something fall in the kitchen, and a minute later the kitchen door slammed.

"Why don't you take one or two of the others?" I asked. "These old things was just done by me and Big Dee from some tops your grandma pieced before she died."

"No," said Wangero. "I don't want those. They are stitched around the borders by machine."

"That'll make them last better," I said.   60

"That's not the point," said Wangero. "These are all pieces of dresses Grandma used to wear. She did all this stitching by hand. Imagine!" She held the quilts securely in her arms, stroking them.

"Some of the pieces, like those lavender ones, come from old clothes her mother handed down to her," I said, moving up to touch the quilts. Dee (Wangero) moved back just enough so that I couldn't reach the quilts. They already belonged to her.

"Imagine!" she breathed again, clutching them closely to her bosom.

"The truth is," I said, "I promised to give them quilts to Maggie, for when she marries John Thomas."

She gasped like a bee had stung her.   65

"Maggie can't appreciate these quilts!" she said. "She'd probably be backward enough to put them to everyday use."

"I reckon she would," I said. "God knows I been saving 'em for long enough with nobody using 'em. I hope she will!" I didn't want to bring up how I had offered Dee (Wangero) a quilt when she went away to college. Then she had told me they were old-fashioned, out of style.

"But they're *priceless!*" she was saying now, furiously; for she has a temper. "Maggie would put them on the bed and in five years they'd be in rags. Less than that!"

"She can always make some more," I said. "Maggie knows how to quilt."

Dee (Wangero) looked at me with hatred. "You just will not understand. The   70
point is these quilts, *these* quilts!"

"Well," I said, stumped. "What would *you* do with them?"

"Hang them," she said. As if that was the only thing you *could* do with quilts.

Maggie by now was standing in the door. I could almost hear the sound her feet made as they scraped over each other.

"She can have them, Mama," she said, like somebody used to never winning anything, or having anything reserved for her. "I can 'member Grandma Dee without the quilts."

I looked at her hard. She had filled her bottom lip with checkerberry snuff   75
and it gave her face a kind of dopey, hangdog look. It was Grandma Dee and Big Dee who taught her how to quilt herself. She stood there with her scarred hands hidden in the folds of her skirt. She looked at her sister with something like fear but she wasn't mad at her. This was Maggie's portion. This was the way she knew God to work.

When I looked at her like that something hit me in the top of my head and ran down to the soles of my feet. Just like when I'm in church and the spirit of God touches me and I get happy and shout. I did something I never had done before: hugged Maggie to me, then dragged her on into the room, snatched the quilts out of Miss Wangero's hands and dumped them into Maggie's lap. Maggie just sat there on my bed with her mouth open.

"Take one or two of the others," I said to Dee.

But she turned without a word and went out to Hakim-a-barber.

"You just don't understand," she said, as Maggie and I came out to the car.

"What don't I understand?" I wanted to know.   80

"Your heritage," she said. And then she turned to Maggie, kissed her, and said, "You ought to try to make something of yourself, too, Maggie. It's really a new day for us. But from the way you and Mama still live you'd never know it."

She put on some sunglasses that hid everything above the tip of her nose and her chin.

Maggie smiled; maybe at the sunglasses. But a real smile, not scared. After we watched the car dust settle I asked Maggie to bring me a dip of snuff. And then the two of us sat there just enjoying, until it was time to go in the house and go to bed.

For Analysis

1. What are the narrator's outstanding traits, her weaknesses and her strengths? **2.** How would you characterize the narrator's feelings about her daughter Dee? About her daughter Maggie? **3.** How would you characterize the narrator's descriptions of herself? Are her actions consistent with the kind of person she says she is? Explain. **4.** Why does the narrator recall the burning of the house? How does this event from the past help the reader understand the present action? **5.** What are the sources of the story's humor? **6.** What does Dee's boyfriend Asalamalakim represent? **7.** Why does the narrator give the quilt to Maggie? **8.** Explain the title. What is the meaning of the subtitle, "For Your Grandmama"?

On Style

1. Examine the function of the quilt as a **symbol**. **2.** Analyze the way in which Walker creates the sense of a narrator speaking spontaneously while in fact the story is carefully structured.

Making Connections

Compare Dee in this story, Hulga in Flannery O'Connor's "Good Country People" (p. 99), and Mrs. Moore in Bambara's "The Lesson" (p. 115) as characters whose intellectual and educational superiority enables them to unsettle the tranquillity of those around them.

Writing Topics

1. Analyze the opening two paragraphs of the story, showing how they set the **tone** and establish the tension of the story. **2.** Write an essay analyzing the **conflict** in this story and the way it is resolved. Is the resolution satisfying?

Barry Holstun Lopez [b. 1945]

Winter Count 1973: Geese, They Flew Over in a Storm 1981

He followed the bellboy off the elevator, through a foyer with forlorn leather couches, noting how low the ceiling was, with its white plaster flowers in bas-relief—and that there were no windows. He followed him down a long corridor dank with an air of fugitives, past dark, impenetrable doors. At the distant end of the next corridor he saw gray thunderheads and the black ironwork of a fire escape. The boy slowed down and reached out to slide a thick key into the lock and he heard the sudden alignment of steel tumblers and their ratchet click. The door swung open and the boy entered, with the suitcase bouncing against the crook at the back of his knee.

He tipped the boy, having no idea what amount was now thought proper. The boy departed, leaving the room sealed off as if in a vacuum. The key with the ornate brass fob lay on a glass table. The man stood by the bed with his hands folded at his lips as though in prayer. Slowly he cleared away the drapes, the curtains and the blinds and stared out at the bare sky. Wind whipped rain in streaks across the glass. He had never been to New Orleans. It was a vague streamer blowing in his memory, like a boyhood acquaintance with Lafcadio Hearn. Natchez Trace. Did Choctaw live here? he wondered. Or Chitamacha? Before them, worshippers of the sun.

He knew the plains better. Best. The high plains north of the Platte River.

He took off his shoes and lay on the bed. He was glad for the feel of the candlewick bedspread. Or was it chenille? He had had this kind of spread on his bed when he was a child. He removed his glasses and pinched the bridge of his nose. In all these years he had delivered so few papers, had come to enjoy much more listening to them, to the stories unfolding in them. It did not matter to him that the arguments were so abstruse they were all but impregnable, that the thought in them would turn to vapor, an arrested breath. He came to hear a story unfold, to regard its shape and effect. He thought one unpacked history, that it came like pemmican in a parfleche and was to be consumed in a hard winter.

The wind sucked at the windows and released them suddenly to rattle in their metal frames. It made him think of home, of the Sand Hills. He lay motionless on the bed and thought of the wind. Crow men racing naked in an April rain, 5 with their hair, five-foot-long black banners, spiraling behind, splashing on the muscled rumps of white horses with brown ears.

1847 One man alone defended the Hat in a fight with the Crow

1847 White buffalo, Dusk killed it

1847 Daughter of Turtle Head, her clothes caught fire and she was burned up

1847 Three men who were women came

He got up and went to his bag. He took out three stout willow sticks and bound them as a tripod. From its apex he hung a beaded bag of white elk hide with long fringe. The fringe was wrinkled from having been folded against itself in his suit pocket.

1891 Medicine bundles, police tore them open

What did they want from him? A teacher. He taught, he did not write papers. He told the story of people coming up from the Tigris-Euphrates, starting there. Other years he would start in a different place—Olduvai, Afar Valley. Or in Tierra del Fuego with the Onas. He could as easily start in the First World of the Navajo. The point, he told his students, was not this. There was no point. It was a slab of meat. It was a rhythm to dance to. It was a cloak that cut the wind when it blew hard enough to crack your soul.

1859 Ravens froze, fell over

1804 Heavy spring snow. Even the dogs went snow-blind

He slept. In his rumpled suit. In the flat, reflected storm light his face appeared ironed smooth. The wind fell away from the building and he dreamed.

For a moment he was lost. Starlight Room. Tarpon Room. Oak Room. He was due—he thought suddenly of aging, of illness: *when our children, they had strangulations of the throat,* of the cure for *any* illness as he scanned the long program—in the Creole Room. He was due in the Creole Room. Roger Callahan, Nebraska State College: "Winter Counts from the Dakota, the Crow and the Blackfeet: Personal Histories." Jesus, he thought, why had he come? He had been asked. They had asked.

"Aha, Roger."

"I'm on time? I got—"

"You come right this way. I want you in front here. Everyone is very excited, very excited, you know. We're very glad you came. And how is Margaret?"

"Yes—. Margaret died. She died two years ago."

10

1837 Straight Calf took six horses from the Crow and gave them to Blue Cloud Woman's father and took her

1875 White Hair, he was killed in a river by an Omaha man

1943 John Badger Heart killed in an automobile crash

He did not hear the man. He sat. The histories began to cover him over like willows, thick as creek willows, and he reached out to steady himself in the pool of time.

He listened patiently to the other papers. Edward Rice Phillips, Purdue: 15 "The Okipa Ceremony and Mandan Sexual Habits." The Mandan, he thought, they were all dead. Who would defend them? Renata Morrison, University of Texas: "The Role of Women in Northern Plains Religious Ceremonials."

1818 Sparrow Woman promised the Sun Dance in winter if the Cree didn't find us

1872 Comes Out of the Water, she ran off the Assiniboine horses

1904 Moving Gently, his sister hung herself

He tried to listen, but the words fell away like tumbled leaves. Cottonwoods. Winters so bad they would have to cut down cottonwood trees for the horses to eat. *So cold we got water from beaver holes only.* And years when they had to eat the horses. *We killed our ponies and ate them. No buffalo.*

Inside the windowless room (he could not remember which floor the elevator had opened on) everyone was seated in long rows. From the first row he could not see anyone. He shifted in his seat and his leather bag fell with a slap against the linoleum floor. How long had he been carrying papers from one place to another like this? He remembered a friend's poem about a snowy owl dead behind glass in a museum, no more to soar, to hunch and spread his wings and tail and fall silent as moonlight.

1809 Blue feathers found on the ground from unknown birds

1811 Weasel Sits Down came into camp with blue feathers tied in his hair

There was distant applause, like dry brush rattling in the wind.

Years before, defense of theory had concerned him. Not now. "I've thrown away everything that is no good," he told a colleague one summer afternoon on his porch, as though shouting over the roar of a storm. "I can no longer think of anything worse than proving you are right." He took what was left and he went on from there.

1851 No meat in camp. A man went to look for buffalo and was killed by two Arapaho

1854 The year they dragged the Arapaho's head through camp

"... and my purpose in aligning these four examples is to clearly demonstrate   20
an irrefutable, or what I consider an irrefutable, relationship: the Arikara
never ..."

When he was a boy his father had taken him one April morning to watch
whooping cranes on estuaries of the Platte, headed for Alberta. The morning
was crucial in the unfolding of his own life.

> 1916 My father drives east for hours in silence. We walk out into a field covered all
> over with river fog. The cranes, just their legs are visible

His own count would be personal, more personal, as though he were the only
one.

> 1918 Father, shot dead. Argonne forest

The other years came around him now like soft velvet noses of horses touching his arms in the dark.

"... while the Cheyenne, contrary to what Greenwold has had to say on this
point but reinforcing what has been stated previously by Gregg and Houston,
were more inclined ..."

He wished for something to hold, something to touch, to strip leaves bare-   25
handed from a chokecherry branch or to hear rain falling on the surface of a
lake. In this windowless room he ached.

> 1833 Stars blowing around like snow. Some fall to the earth

> 1856 Reaches into the Enemy's Tipi has a dream and can't speak

> 1869 Fire Wagon, it comes

Applause.

He stood up and walked in quiet shoes to the stage. (Once in the middle of
class he had stopped to explain his feeling about walking everywhere in silence.)
He set his notes on the podium and covered them with his hands. In a clear
voice, without apology for his informality or a look at his papers, he unfolded the
winter counts of the Sioux warrior Blue Thunder, of the Blackfeet Bad Head,
and of the Crow Extends His Paw. He stated that these were personal views of
history, sometimes metaphorical, bearing on a larger, tribal history. He spoke of
the confusion caused by translators who had tried to force agreement among
several winter counts or who mistook mythic time for some other kind of real
time. He concluded by urging less contention. "As professional historians, we
have too often subordinated one system to another and forgotten all together
the individual view, the poetic view, which is as close to the truth as the consensus. Or it can be as distant."

He felt the necklace of hawk talons pressing against his clavicles under the
weight of his shirt.

The applause was respectful, thin, distracted. As he stepped away from the podium he realized it was perhaps foolish to have accepted the invitation. He could no longer make a final point. He had long ago lost touch with the definitive, the awful distance of reason. He wanted to go back to the podium. You can only tell the story as it was given to you, he wanted to say. Do not lie. Do not make it up.

He hesitated for a moment at the edge of the stage. He wished he were back   30
in Nebraska with his students, to warn them: it is too dangerous for everyone to have the same story. The same things do not happen to everyone.

He passed through the murmuring crowd, through a steel fire door, down a hallway, up a flight of stairs, another, and emerged into palms in the lobby.

> 1823 A man, he was called Fifteen Horses, who was heyoka, a contrary, sacred clown, ran at the Crow backwards, shooting arrows at his own people. The Crow shot him in midair like a quail. He couldn't fool them

He felt the edge of self-pity, standing before a plate-glass window as wide as the spread of his arms and as tall as his house. He watched the storm that still raged, which he could not hear, which he had not been able to hear, bend trees to breaking, slash the surface of Lake Pontchartrain and raise air boiling over the gulf beyond. "Everything is held together with stories," he thought. "That is all that is holding us together, stories and compassion."

He turned quickly from the cold glass and went up in the silent elevator and ordered dinner. When it came, he threw back the drapes and curtains and opened the windows. The storm howled through his room and roared through his head. He breathed the wet air deep into his lungs. In the deepest distance, once, he heard the barking-dog sounds of geese, running like horses before a prairie thunderstorm.

For Analysis

1. Examine the diction of the opening paragraph, the objects that are described, and the adjectives that are used to characterize them. What kind of tone do they establish? **2.** Why does Roger Callahan prefer listening to papers rather than delivering them? **3.** Why do you suppose Roger Callahan carries a "medicine bag" and wears a hawk talon necklace? **4.** Who do you imagine Margaret was (par. 12)? What is the relevance of the brief dialogue about her? **5.** How does Callahan's own "count" about his father fit into the pattern of the narrative? How does it help explain the power Callahan feels counts have? **6.** Is there any relationship between Callahan and the last winter count anecdote about the "contrary" who ran backwards (par. 31)? Explain.

On Style

1. What is the effect of the various "counts" that punctuate the narrative? What connections are there among them and the narrative? **2.** The story is comprised of various levels of narrative: (1) the narrative voice telling the story, (2) the various "counts," (3) flashbacks, and (4) Roger Callahan's reading of his paper. Examine the way Lopez weaves these different narrative levels into a coherent story.

Making Connections
Compare this story and Louise Erdrich's "The Red Convertible" (p. 706) as celebrations of Native American culture within the context of the dominant American culture. Do these very different stories embody, in a broad sense, similar views about Native American culture? In what sense do these stories criticize the dominant culture?

Writing Topics
1. In an essay, expand on Callahan's statement to his colleague: " 'I can no longer think of anything worse than proving you are right' " (par. 19). **2.** Keeping in mind the contrast between Native American historical observations and the scholarly papers being read at the academic meeting, discuss Callahan's concluding remark: "As professional historians, we have too often subordinated one system to another and forgotten all together the individual view, the poetic view, which is as close to the truth as the consensus. Or it can be as distant" (par. 27).

Louise Erdrich [b. 1954]

The Red Convertible 1984
Lyman Lamartine

I was the first one to drive a convertible on my reservation. And of course it was red, a red Olds. I owned that car along with my brother Henry Junior. We owned it together until his boots filled with water on a windy night and he bought out my share. Now Henry owns the whole car, and his youngest brother Lyman (that's myself), Lyman walks everywhere he goes.

How did I earn enough money to buy my share in the first place? My own talent was I could always make money. I had a touch for it, unusual in a Chippewa. From the first I was different that way, and everyone recognized it. I was the only kid they let in the American Legion Hall to shine shoes, for example, and one Christmas I sold spiritual bouquets for the mission door to door. The nuns let me keep a percentage. Once I started, it seemed the more money I made the easier the money came. Everyone encouraged it. When I was fifteen I got a job washing dishes at the Joliet Café, and that was where my first big break happened.

It wasn't long before I was promoted to bussing tables, and then the short-order cook quit and I was hired to take her place. No sooner than you know it I was managing the Joliet. The rest is history. I went on managing. I soon became part owner, and of course there was no stopping me then. It wasn't long before the whole thing was mine.

After I'd owned the Joliet for one year, it blew over in the worst tornado ever seen around here. The whole operation was smashed to bits. A total loss. The fryalator was up in a tree, the grill torn in half like it was paper. I was only sixteen. I had it all in my mother's name, and I lost it quick, but before I lost it I had every one of my relatives, and their relatives, to dinner, and I also bought that red Olds I mentioned, along with Henry.

The first time we saw it! I'll tell you when we first saw it. We had gotten a ride up to Winnipeg, and both of us had money. Don't ask me why, because we never mentioned a car or anything, we just had all our money. Mine was cash, a big bankroll from the Joliet's insurance. Henry had two checks—a week's extra pay for being laid off, and his regular check from the Jewel Bearing Plant.

We were walking down Portage anyway, seeing the sights, when we saw it. There it was, parked, large as life. Really as *if* it was alive. I thought of the word *repose*, because the car wasn't simply stopped, parked, or whatever. That car reposed, calm and gleaming, a FOR SALE sign in its left front window. Then, before we had thought it over at all, the car belonged to us and our pockets were empty. We had just enough money for gas back home.

We went places in that car, me and Henry. We took off driving all one whole summer. We started off toward the Little Knife River and Mandaree in Fort Berthold and then we found ourselves down in Wakpala somehow, and then suddenly we were over in Montana on the Rocky Boys, and yet the summer was not even half over. Some people hang on to details when they travel, but we didn't let them bother us and just lived our everyday lives here to there.

I do remember this one place with willows. I remember I laid under those trees and it was comfortable. So comfortable. The branches bent down all around me like a tent or a stable. And quiet, it was quiet, even though there was a powwow close enough so I could see it going on. The air was not too still, not too windy either. When the dust rises up and hangs in the air around the dancers like that, I feel good. Henry was asleep with his arms thrown wide. Later on, he woke up and we started driving again. We were somewhere in Montana, or maybe on the Blood Reserve—it could have been anywhere. Anyway it was where we met the girl.

All her hair was in buns around her ears, that's the first thing I noticed about her. She was posed alongside the road with her arm out, so we stopped. That girl was short, so short her lumber shirt looked comical on her, like a nightgown. She had jeans on and fancy moccasins and she carried a little suitcase.

"Hop on in," says Henry. So she climbs in between us.   10

"We'll take you home," I says. "Where do you live?"

"Chicken," she says.

"Where the hell's that?" I ask her.

"Alaska."

"Okay," says Henry, and we drive.   15

We got up there and never wanted to leave. The sun doesn't truly set there in summer, and the night is more a soft dusk. You might doze off, sometimes, but before you know it you're up again, like an animal in nature. You never feel like you have to sleep hard or put away the world. And things would grow up there. One day just dirt or moss, the next day flowers and long grass. The girl's name was Susy. Her family really took to us. They fed us and put us up. We had our own tent to live in by their house, and the kids would be in and out of there all day and night. They couldn't get over me and Henry being brothers, we looked so different. We told them we knew we had the same mother, anyway.

One night Susy came in to visit us. We sat around in the tent talking of this thing and that. The season was changing. It was getting darker by that time, and the cold was even getting just a little mean. I told her it was time for us to go. She stood up on a chair.

"You never seen my hair," Susy said.

That was true. She was standing on a chair, but still, when she unclipped her buns the hair reached all the way to the ground. Our eyes opened. You couldn't tell how much hair she had when it was rolled up so neatly. Then my brother Henry did something funny. He went up to the chair and said, "Jump on my shoulders." So she did that, and her hair reached down past his waist, and he started twirling, this way and that, so her hair was flung out from side to side.

"I always wondered what it was like to have long pretty hair," Henry says. 20
Well we laughed. It was a funny sight, the way he did it. The next morning we got up and took leave of those people.

On to greener pastures, as they say. It was down through Spokane and across Idaho then Montana and very soon we were racing the weather right along under the Canadian border through Columbus, Des Lacs, and then we were in Bottineau County and soon home. We'd made most of the trip, that summer, without putting up the car hood at all. We got home just in time, it turned out, for the army to remember Henry had signed up to join it.

I don't wonder that the army was so glad to get my brother that they turned him into a Marine. He was built like a brick outhouse anyway. We liked to tease him that they really wanted him for his Indian nose. He had a nose big and sharp as a hatchet, like the nose on Red Tomahawk, the Indian who killed Sitting Bull, whose profile is on signs all along the North Dakota highways. Henry went off to training camp, came home once during Christmas, then the next thing you know we got an overseas letter from him. It was 1970, and he said he was stationed up in the northern hill country. Whereabouts I did not know. He wasn't such a hot letter writer, and only got off two before the enemy caught him. I could never keep it straight, which direction those good Vietnam soldiers were from.

I wrote him back several times, even though I didn't know if those letters would get through. I kept him informed all about the car. Most of the time I had it up on blocks in the yard or half taken apart, because that long trip did a hard job on it under the hood.

I always had good luck with numbers, and never worried about the draft myself. I never even had to think about what my number was. But Henry was never lucky in the same way as me. It was at least three years before Henry came home. By then I guess the whole war was solved in the government's mind, but for him it would keep on going. In those years I'd put his car into almost perfect shape. I always thought of it as his car while he was gone, even though when he left he said, "Now it's yours," and threw me his key.

"Thanks for the extra key," I'd say. "I'll put it up in your drawer just in case I 25
need it." He laughed.

When he came home, though, Henry was very different, and I'll say this: the change was no good. You could hardly expect him to change for the better, I know. But he was quiet, so quiet, and never comfortable sitting still anywhere but always up and moving around. I thought back to times we'd sat still for whole afternoons, never moving a muscle, just shifting our weight along the ground, talking to whoever sat with us, watching things. He'd always had a joke, then, too, and now you couldn't get him to laugh, or when he did it was more the sound of a man choking, a sound that stopped up the throats of other people around him. They got to leaving him alone most of the time, and I didn't blame them. It was a fact: Henry was jumpy and mean.

I'd bought a color TV set for my mom and the rest of us while Henry was away. Money still came very easy. I was sorry I'd ever bought it though, because of Henry. I was also sorry I'd bought color, because with black-and-white the pictures seem older and farther away. But what are you going to do? He sat in front of it, watching it, and that was the only time he was completely still. But it was the kind of stillness that you see in a rabbit when it freezes and before it will bolt. He was not easy. He sat in his chair gripping the armrests with all his might, as if the chair itself was moving at a high speed and if he let go at all he would rocket forward and maybe crash right through the set.

Once I was in the room watching TV with Henry and I heard his teeth click at something. I looked over, and he'd bitten through his lip. Blood was going down his chin. I tell you right then I wanted to smash that tube to pieces. I went over to it but Henry must have known what I was up to. He rushed from his chair and shoved me out of the way, against the wall. I told myself he didn't know what he was doing.

My mom came in, turned the set off real quiet, and told us she had made something for supper. So we went and sat down. There was still blood going down Henry's chin, but he didn't notice it and no one said anything, even though every time he took a bit of his bread his blood fell onto it until he was eating his own blood mixed in with the food.

While Henry was not around we talked about what was going to happen to   30
him. There were no Indian doctors on the reservation, and my mom was afraid of trusting Old Man Pillager because he courted her long ago and was jealous of her husbands. He might take revenge through her son. We were afraid that if we brought Henry to a regular hospital they would keep him.

"They don't fix them in those places," Mom said; "they just give them drugs."

"We wouldn't get him there in the first place," I agreed, "so let's just forget about it."

Then I thought about the car.

Henry had not even looked at the car since he'd gotten home, though like I said, it was in tip-top condition and ready to drive. I thought the car might bring the old Henry back somehow. So I bided my time and waited for my chance to interest him in the vehicle.

One night Henry was off somewhere. I took myself a hammer. I went out to   35
that car and I did a number on its underside. Whacked it up. Bent the tail pipe double. Ripped the muffler loose. By the time I was done with the car it looked worse than any typical Indian car that has been driven all its life on reservation roads, which they always say are like government promises—full of holes. It just

about hurt me, I'll tell you that! I threw dirt in the carburetor and I ripped all the electric tape off the seats. I made it look just as beat up as I could. Then I sat back and waited for Henry to find it.

Still, it took him over a month. That was all right, because it was just getting warm enough, not melting, but warm enough to work outside.

"Lyman," he says, walking in one day, "that red car looks like shit."

"Well it's old," I says. "You got to expect that."

"No way!" says Henry. "That car's a classic! But you went and ran the piss right out of it, Lyman, and you know it don't deserve that. I kept that car in A-one shape. You don't remember. You're too young. But when I left, that car was running like a watch. Now I don't even know if I can get it to start again, let alone get it anywhere near its old condition."

"Well you try," I said, like I was getting mad, "but I say it's a piece of junk."   40

Then I walked out before he could realize I knew he'd strung together more than six words at once.

After that I thought he'd freeze himself to death working on that car. He was out there all day, and at night he rigged up a little lamp, ran a cord out the window, and had himself some light to see by while he worked. He was better than he had been before, but that's still not saying much. It was easier for him to do the things the rest of us did. He ate more slowly and didn't jump up and down during the meal to get this or that or look out the window. I put my hand in the back of the TV set, I admit, and fiddled around with it good, so that it was almost impossible now to get a clear picture. He didn't look at it very often anyway. He was always out with that car or going off to get parts for it. By the time it was really melting outside, he had it fixed.

I had been feeling down in the dumps about Henry around this time. We had always been together before. Henry and Lyman. But he was such a loner now that I didn't know how to take it. So I jumped at the chance one day when Henry seemed friendly. It's not that he smiled or anything. He just said, "Let's take that old shitbox for a spin." Just the way he said it made me think he could be coming around.

We went out to the car. It was spring. The sun was shining very bright. My only sister, Bonita, who was just eleven years old, came out and made us stand together for a picture. Henry leaned his elbow on the red car's windshield, and he took his other arm and put it over my shoulder, very carefully, as though it was heavy for him to lift and he didn't want to bring the weight down all at once.

"Smile," Bonita said, and he did.   45

That picture, I never look at it anymore. A few months ago, I don't know why, I got his picture out and tacked it on the wall. I felt good about Henry at the time, close to him. I felt good having his picture on the wall, until one night when I was looking at television. I was a little drunk and stoned. I looked up at the wall and Henry was staring at me. I don't know what it was, but his smile had changed, or maybe it was gone. All I know is I couldn't stay in the same room with that picture. I was shaking. I got up, closed the door, and went into the kitchen. A little later my friend Ray came over and we both went back into that room. We put the picture in a brown bag, folded the bag over and over tightly, then put it way back in a closet.

I still see that picture now, as if it tugs at me, whenever I pass that closet door. The picture is very clear in my mind. It was so sunny that day Henry had to squint against the glare. Or maybe the camera Bonita held flashed like a mirror, blinding him, before she snapped the picture. My face is right out in the sun, big and round. But he might have drawn back, because the shadows on his face are deep as holes. There are two shadows curved like little hooks around the ends of his smile, as if to frame it and try to keep it there—that one, first smile that looked like it might have hurt his face. He has his field jacket on and the worn-in clothes he'd come back in and kept wearing ever since. After Bonita took the picture, she went into the house and we got into the car. There was a full cooler in the trunk. We started off, east, toward Pembina and the Red River because Henry said he wanted to see the high water.

The trip over there was beautiful. When everything starts changing, drying up, clearing off, you feel like your whole life is starting. Henry felt it, too. The top was down and the car hummed like a top. He'd really put it back in shape, even the tape on the seats was very carefully put down and glued back in layers. It's not that he smiled again or even joked, but his face looked to me as if it was clear, more peaceful. It looked as though he wasn't thinking of anything in particular except the bare fields and windbreaks and houses we were passing.

The river was high and full of winter trash when we got there. The sun was still out, but it was colder by the river. There were still little clumps of dirty snow here and there on the banks. The water hadn't gone over the banks yet, but it would, you could tell. It was just at its limit, hard swollen glossy like an old gray scar. We made ourselves a fire, and we sat down and watched the current go. As I watched it I felt something squeezing inside me and tightening and trying to let go all at the same time. I knew I was not just feeling it myself; I knew I was feeling what Henry was going through at that moment. Except that I couldn't stand it, the closing and opening. I jumped to my feet. I took Henry by the shoulders and I started shaking him. "Wake up," I says, "wake up, wake up, wake up!" I didn't know what had come over me. I sat down beside him again.

His face was totally white and hard. Then it broke, like stones break all of a 50
sudden when water boils up inside them.

"I know it," he says. "I know it. I can't help it. It's no use."

We start talking. He said he knew what I'd done with the car. It was obvious it had been whacked out of shape and not just neglected. He said he wanted to give the car to me for good now, it was no use. He said he'd fixed it just to give it back and I should take it.

"No way," I says, "I don't want it."

"That's okay," he says, "you take it."

"I don't want it, though," I says back to him, and then to emphasize, just to 55
emphasize, you understand, I touch his shoulder. He slaps my hand off.

"Take that car," he says.

"No," I say, "make me," I say, and then he grabs my jacket and rips the arm loose. That jacket is a class act, suede with tags and zippers. I push Henry backwards, off the log. He jumps up and bowls me over. We go down in a clinch and come up swinging hard, for all we're worth, with our fists. He socks my jaw so hard I feel like it swings loose. Then I'm at his ribcage and land a good one under his chin so his head snaps back. He's dazzled. He looks at me and I look at him and then his eyes are full of tears and blood and at first I think he's crying. But no, he's laughing. "Ha! Ha!" he says. "Ha! Ha! Take good care of it."

"Okay," I says, "okay, no problem. Ha! Ha!"

I can't help it, and I start laughing, too. My face feels fat and strange, and after a while I get a beer from the cooler in the trunk, and when I hand it to Henry he takes his shirt and wipes my germs off. "Hoof-and-mouth disease," he says. For some reason this cracks me up, and so we're really laughing for a while, and then we drink all the rest of the beers one by one and throw them in the river and see how far, how fast, the current takes them before they fill up and sink.

"You want to go on back?" I ask after a while. "Maybe we could snag a couple 60 nice Kashpaw girls."

He says nothing. But I can tell his mood is turning again.

"They're all crazy, the girls up here, every damn one of them."

"You're crazy too," I say, to jolly him up. "Crazy Lamartine boys!"

He looks as though he will take this wrong at first. His face twists, then clears, and he jumps up on his feet. "That's right!" he says. "Crazier 'n hell. Crazy Indians!"

I think it's the old Henry again. He throws off his jacket and starts swinging 65 his legs out from the knees like a fancy dancer. He's down doing something between a grouse dance and a bunny hop, no kind of dance I ever saw before, but neither has anyone else on all this green growing earth. He's wild. He wants to pitch whoopee! He's up and at me and all over. All this time I'm laughing so hard, so hard my belly is getting tied up in a knot.

"Got to cool me off!" he shouts all of a sudden. Then he runs over to the river and jumps in.

There's boards and other things in the current. It's so high. No sound comes from the river after the splash he makes, so I run right over. I look around. It's getting dark. I see he's halfway across the water already, and I know he didn't swim there but the current took him. It's far. I hear his voice, though, very clearly across it.

"My boots are filling," he says.

He says this in a normal voice, like he just noticed and he doesn't know what to think of it. Then he's gone. A branch comes by. Another branch. And I go in.

By the time I get out of the river, off the snag I pulled myself onto, the sun is 70 down. I walk back to the car, turn on the high beams, and drive it up the bank. I put it in first gear and then I take my foot off the clutch. I get out, close the door, and watch it plow softly into the water. The headlights reach in as they go down, searching, still lighted even after the water swirls over the back end. I wait. The wires short out. It is all finally dark. And then there is only the water, the sound of it going and running and going and running and running.

For Analysis

1. What sort of person is Lyman? **2.** Why does Lyman feel that *repose* is the precise word to describe the red convertible? **3.** Characterize Susy's family. Is there any thematic significance to the generosity this Alaskan family extends to the brothers? Explain. **4.** How does the episode about Susy's hair relate to the **theme** of the story? **5.** What function does the fifth section (par. 30–41) serve? **6.** Does it make a difference that it is the Vietnam War (rather than, say, the Second World War) that Henry never recovers from? Explain. **7.** What is the significance of the fight over the car in the seventh section (par. 48–69)? **8.** Why does Lyman let the red convertible roll down the bank and into the river? **9.** Is the fact that Lyman and Henry are Native Americans incidental or central to the meaning of this story? Explain.

On Style

1. What is the **theme** that unifies the eight sections of this story? **2.** Why does Lyman adopt the third-person **point of view** in referring to himself in the opening paragraph? **3.** The only exception to the straightforward chronological narrative occurs in the sixth section of the story (par. 46), when Lyman moves forward in time to describe the photograph taken by his sister and his feelings about it. What purpose does this interruption serve?

Making Connections

1. How might Tim O'Brien's story "On the Rainy River" (p. 420) help explain Henry's character? **2.** Compare the reasons for Henry's withdrawal from life with Brown's in Nathaniel Hawthorne's "Young Goodman Brown" (p. 61), Bartleby's in Herman Melville's "Bartleby the Scrivener" (p. 313), and Fred Daniels's in Richard Wright's "The Man Who Lived Underground" (p. 351).

Writing Topics

1. Write an essay showing how section four, dealing with Henry and the Vietnam War, is pivotal in stating the theme of the story and in shifting to a **tone** more appropriate to the impending tragedy. **2.** In what ways is it significant that Lyman and Henry are Native Americans?

Poetry

Emily Dickinson [1830–1886]

What Soft— Cherubic Creatures— ca. 1862

What Soft—Cherubic Creatures—
These Gentlewomen are—
One would as soon assault a Plush—
Or violate a Star—

Such Dimity Convictions—
A Horror so refined
Of freckled Human Nature—
Of Deity—ashamed—

It's such a common-Glory—
A Fisherman's—Degree—   10
Redemption—Brittle Lady—
Be so—ashamed of Thee—

Paul Laurence Dunbar [1872–1906]

We Wear the Mask 1896

We wear the mask that grins and lies,
It hides our cheeks and shades our eyes—
This debt we pay to human guile;
With torn and bleeding hearts we smile,
And mouth with myriad subtleties.

714

Why should the world be over-wise,
In counting all our tears and sighs?
Nay, let them only see us, while
   We wear the mask.

We smile, but, O great Christ, our cries   10
To thee from tortured souls arise.
We sing, but oh the clay is vile
Beneath our feet, and long the mile;
But let the world dream otherwise,
   We wear the mask!

Robert Frost   [1874–1963]

Departmental   1936

An ant on the table cloth
Ran into a dormant moth
Of many times his size.
He showed not the least surprise.
His business wasn't with such.
He gave it scarcely a touch,
And was off on his duty run.
Yet if he encountered one
Of the hive's enquiry squad
Whose work is to find out God   10
And the nature of time and space,
He would put him onto the case.
Ants are a curious race;
One crossing with hurried tread
The body of one of their dead
Isn't given a moment's arrest—
Seems not even impressed.
But he no doubt reports to any
With whom he crosses antennae,
And they no doubt report   20
To the higher up at court.
Then word goes forth in Formic:
"Death's come to Jerry McCormic,
Our selfless forager Jerry.
Will the special Janizary

Whose office it is to bury
The dead of the commissary
Go bring him home to his people.
Lay him in state on a sepal.
Wrap him for shroud in a petal.   30
Embalm him with ichor of nettle.
This is the word of your Queen."
And presently on the scene
Appears a solemn mortician;
And taking formal position
With feelers calmly atwiddle,
Seizes the dead by the middle,
And heaving him high in air,
Carries him out of there.
No one stands round to stare.   40
It is nobody else's affair.
It couldn't be called ungentle.
But how thoroughly departmental.

For Analysis

1. What comment does this poem make on human society? Is ant society a good metaphor for human society? Explain. **2.** How do the **diction** and **rhyme** help establish the **tone**?

Writing Topic

How does the diction in this poem convey the speaker's attitude toward the social order he describes?

Amy Lowell   [1874–1925]

Patterns   1916

I walk down the garden-paths,
And all the daffodils
Are blowing, and the bright blue squills.
I walk down the patterned garden-paths
In my stiff, brocaded gown.
With my powdered hair and jeweled fan,
I too am a rare
Pattern. As I wander down
The garden-paths.

My dress is richly figured,   10
And the train
Makes a pink and silver stain
On the gravel, and the thrift
Of the borders.
Just a plate of current fashion,
Tripping by in high-heeled, ribboned shoes.
Not a softness anywhere about me,
Only whalebone and brocade.
And I sink on a seat in the shade
Of a lime tree. For my passion   20
Wars against the stiff brocade.
The daffodils and squills
Flutter in the breeze
As they please.
And I weep;
For the lime-tree is in blossom
And one small flower has dropped upon my bosom.

And the plashing of waterdrops
In the marble fountain
Comes down the garden-paths.   30
The dripping never stops.
Underneath my stiffened gown
Is the softness of a woman bathing in a marble basin,
A basin in the midst of hedges grown
So thick, she cannot see her lover hiding,
But she guesses he is near,
And the sliding of the water
Seems the stroking of a dear
Hand upon her.
What is Summer in a fine brocaded gown!   40
I should like to see it lying in a heap upon the ground.
All the pink and silver crumpled up on the ground.

I would be the pink and silver as I ran along the paths,
And he would stumble after,
Bewildered by my laughter.
I should see the sun flashing from his sword-hilt and the buckles on his shoes.
I would choose
To lead him in a maze along the patterned paths,
A bright and laughing maze for my heavy-booted lover.
Till he caught me in the shade,   50
And the buttons of his waistcoat bruised my body as he clasped me,

Aching, melting, unafraid.
With the shadows of the leaves and the sundrops,
And the plopping of the waterdrops,
All about us in the open afternoon—
I am very like to swoon
With the weight of this brocade,
For the sun sifts through the shade.

Underneath the fallen blossom
In my bosom   60
Is a letter I have hid.
It was brought to me this morning by a rider from the Duke.
"Madam, we regret to inform you that Lord Hartwell
Died in action Thursday se'nnight."[1]
As I read it in the white, morning sunlight,
The letters squirmed like snakes.
"Any answer, Madam," said my footman.
"No," I told him.
"See that the messenger takes some refreshment.
No, no answer."   70
And I walked into the garden,
Up and down the patterned paths,
In my stiff, correct brocade.
The blue and yellow flowers stood up proudly in the sun,
Each one.
I stood upright too,
Held rigid to the pattern
By the stiffness of my gown;
Up and down I walked,
Up and down.   80

In a month he would have been my husband.
In a month, here, underneath this lime,
We would have broke the pattern;
He for me, and I for him,
He as Colonel, I as Lady,
On this shady seat.
He had a whim
That sunlight carried blessing.
And I answered, "It shall be as you have said."
Now he is dead.   90

---

[1] Seven nights (i.e., a week) ago.

In Summer and in Winter I shall walk
Up and down
The patterned garden-paths
In my stiff, brocaded gown.
The squills and daffodils
Will give place to pillared roses, and to asters, and to snow.
I shall go
Up and down
In my gown.
Gorgeously arrayed,   100
Boned and stayed.
And the softness of my body will be guarded from embrace
By each button, hook, and lace.
For the man who should loose me is dead,
Fighting with the Duke in Flanders,[2]
In a pattern called a war.
Christ! What are patterns for?

For Analysis

1. What period of time does the poem seem to be set in? Explain. **2.** Identify the various kinds of patterns in the poem. **3.** In line 83, the speaker refers to the pattern "We would have broke." What is that pattern? How might it have been broken? **4.** Does the poem provide an answer to the question the speaker asks in the final line? Explain.

Writing Topics

1. Describe a pattern in your family that has limited your life. **2.** Describe a societal pattern that has limited your life. **3.** Write an essay in which you argue that patterns, while perhaps limiting, are necessary.

T. S. Eliot   [1888–1965]

The Love Song of J. Alfred Prufrock   1917

S'io credessi che mia risposta fosse
a persona che mai tornasse al mondo,
questa fiamma staria senza più scosse.

Patterns
  [2] A region of Belgium where battles were fought during wars in the eighteenth, nineteenth, and twentieth centuries.

Ma per ciò che giammai di questo fondo
non tornò vivo alcun, s'i'odo il vero,
senza tema d'infamia ti rispondo.[1]

Let us go then, you and I,
When the evening is spread out against the sky
Like a patient etherized upon a table;
Let us go, through certain half-deserted streets,
The muttering retreats
Of restless nights in one-night cheap hotels
And sawdust restaurants with oyster shells:
Streets that follow like a tedious argument
Of insidious intent
To lead you to an overwhelming question . . .   10
Oh, do not ask, "What is it?"
Let us go and make our visit.

In the room the women come and go
Talking of Michelangelo.

The yellow fog that rubs its back upon the windowpanes,
The yellow smoke that rubs its muzzle on the windowpanes
Licked its tongue into the corners of the evening,
Lingered upon the pools that stand in drains,
Let fall upon its back the soot that falls from chimneys,
Slipped by the terrace, made a sudden leap,   20
And seeing that it was a soft October night,
Curled once about the house, and fell asleep.

And indeed there will be time
For the yellow smoke that slides along the street,
Rubbing its back upon the windowpanes;
There will be time, there will be time
To prepare a face to meet the faces that you meet;
There will be time to murder and create,
And time for all the works and days of hands
That lift and drop a question on your plate;   30
Time for you and time for me,

---

[1] From Dante, *Inferno*, XXVII, 61–66. The speaker is Guido da Montefeltro, who is imprisoned in a flame in the level of Hell reserved for false counselors. He tells Dante and Virgil, "If I thought my answer were given to one who might return to the world, this flame would stay without further movement. But since from this depth none has ever returned alive, if what I hear is true, I answer you without fear of infamy."

And time yet for a hundred indecisions,
And for a hundred visions and revisions,
Before the taking of a toast and tea.

In the room the women come and go
Talking of Michelangelo.

And indeed there will be time
To wonder, "Do I dare?" and, "Do I dare?"
Time to turn back and descend the stair,
With a bald spot in the middle of my hair—   40
(They will say: "How his hair is growing thin!")
My morning coat, my collar mounting firmly to the chin,
My necktie rich and modest, but asserted by a simple pin—
(They will say: "But how his arms and legs are thin!")
Do I dare
Disturb the universe?
In a minute there is time
For decisions and revisions which a minute will reverse.

For I have known them all already, known them all—
Have known the evenings, mornings, afternoons,   50
I have measured out my life with coffee spoons;
I know the voices dying with a dying fall
Beneath the music from a farther room.
    So how should I presume?

And I have known the eyes already, known them all—
The eyes that fix you in a formulated phrase,
And when I am formulated, sprawling on a pin,
When I am pinned and wriggling on the wall,
Then how should I begin
To spit out all the butt-ends of my days and ways?   60
    And how should I presume?

And I have known the arms already, known them all—
Arms that are braceleted and white and bare
(But in the lamplight, downed with light brown hair!)
Is it perfume from a dress
That makes me so digress?
Arms that lie along a table, or wrap about a shawl.
    And should I then presume?
    And how should I begin?

                    .   .   .   .

Shall I say, I have gone at dusk through narrow streets   70
And watched the smoke that rises from the pipes
Of lonely men in shirt-sleeves, leaning out of windows? . . .

I should have been a pair of ragged claws
Scuttling across the floors of silent seas.

. . . .

And the afternoon, the evening, sleeps so peacefully!
Smoothed by long fingers,
Asleep . . . tired . . . or it malingers,
Stretched on the floor, here beside you and me.
Should I, after tea and cakes and ices,
Have the strength to force the moment to its crisis?   80
But though I have wept and fasted, wept and prayed,
Though I have seen my head (grown slightly bald) brought in upon a platter,[2]
I am no prophet—and here's no great matter;
I have seen the moment of my greatness flicker,
And I have seen the eternal Footman hold my coat, and snicker,
And in short, I was afraid.

And would it have been worth it, after all,
After the cups, the marmalade, the tea,
Among the porcelain, among some talk of you and me,
Would it have been worth while,   90
To have bitten off the matter with a smile,
To have squeezed the universe into a ball
To roll it toward some overwhelming question,
To say: "I am Lazarus,[3] come from the dead,
Come back to tell you all, I shall tell you all"—
If one, settling a pillow by her head,
  Should say: "That is not what I meant at all.
  That is not it, at all."

And would it have been worth it, after all,
Would it have been worth while,   100
After the sunsets and the dooryards and the sprinkled streets,
After the novels, after the teacups, after the skirts that trail along the floor—
And this, and so much more?—
It is impossible to say just what I mean!
But as if a magic lantern threw the nerves in patterns on a screen:
Would it have been worth while
If one, settling a pillow or throwing off a shawl,

---

[2] Like the head of John the Baptist. See Matthew 14:3–12.
[3] See John 11:1–14 and Luke 16:19–26.

And turning toward the window, should say:
  "That is not it at all,
  That is not what I meant, at all."   110

.   .   .   .

No! I am not Prince Hamlet, nor was meant to be;
Am an attendant lord, one that will do
To swell a progress,° start a scene or two,   _state journey_
Advise the prince; no doubt, an easy tool,
Deferential, glad to be of use,
Politic, cautious, and meticulous;
Full of high sentence,° but a bit obtuse;   _sententiousness_
At times, indeed, almost ridiculous—
Almost, at times, the Fool.

I grow old . . . I grow old . . .   120
I shall wear the bottoms of my trousers rolled.°   _cuffed_

Shall I part my hair behind? Do I dare to eat a peach?
I shall wear white flannel trousers, and walk upon the beach.
I have heard the mermaids singing, each to each.

I do not think that they will sing to me.

I have seen them riding seaward on the waves
Combing the white hair of the waves blown back
When the wind blows the water white and black.

We have lingered in the chambers of the sea
By sea-girls wreathed with seaweed red and brown   130
Till human voices wake us, and we drown.

For Analysis

1. This poem may be understood as a stream of consciousness passing through the mind of Prufrock. The "you and I" of line 1 may be different aspects of his personality. Or perhaps the "you and I" is parallel to Guido who speaks the epigraph and Dante to whom he tells the story that resulted in his damnation—hence, "you" is the reader and "I" is Prufrock. The poem is disjointed because it proceeds by psychological rather than logical stages. To what social class does Prufrock belong? How does Prufrock respond to the attitudes and values of his class? Does he change in the course of the poem? **2.** Line 92 provides a good example of literary allusion (see the last stanza of Marvel's "To His Coy Mistress," p. 1002). How does an awareness of the allusion contribute to the reader's response to the stanza here? **3.** What might the song of the mermaids (l. 124) signify, and why does Prufrock think they will not sing to him (l. 125)? **4.** T. S. Eliot once said that some poetry "can communicate without being understood." Is this such a poem?

Writing Topic

What sort of man is J. Alfred Prufrock? How does the poet establish his characteristics?

E. E. Cummings   [1894–1962]

the Cambridge ladies
who live in furnished souls   1923

the Cambridge ladies who live in furnished souls
are unbeautiful and have comfortable minds
(also, with the church's protestant blessings
daughters, unscented shapeless spirited)
they believe in Christ and Longfellow, both dead,
are invariably interested in so many things—
at the present writing one still finds
delighted fingers knitting for the is it Poles?
perhaps. While permanent faces coyly bandy
scandal of Mrs. N. and Professor D   10
. . . . the Cambridge ladies do not care, above
Cambridge if sometimes in its box of
sky lavender and cornerless, the
moon rattles like a fragment of angry candy

For Analysis
1. What **images** does the poet use to describe "the Cambridge ladies"? What do the images suggest? **2.** What is the effect of the interruption "is it" in line 8? **3.** In the final lines, the moon seems to protest against the superficiality of these women. What is the effect of comparing the moon to a fragment of candy?

Writing Topic
Compare this poem with Emily Dickinson's "What Soft—Cherubic Creatures—" on p. 714.

W. H. Auden   [1907–1973]

from
Five Songs   1937

That night when joy began
Our narrowest veins to flush,
We waited for the flash
Of morning's levelled gun.

But morning let us pass,
And day by day relief
Outgrew his nervous laugh,
Grows credulous of peace.

As mile by mile is seen
No trespasser's reproach,   10
And love's best glasses reach
No fields but are his own.

For Analysis
1. Describe the sound relationships among the last words in the lines of each stanza.
2. What is the controlling **metaphor** in the poem? Is it appropriate for a love poem?
3. If it were suggested that the poem describes a homosexual relationship, would your response to the poem's **figurative language** change?

<u>Richard Wright</u> [1908–1960]

Between the World and Me   1935

And one morning while in the woods I stumbled suddenly upon the thing,
Stumbled upon it in a grassy clearing guarded by scaly oaks and elms.
And the sooty details of the scene rose, thrusting themselves between the
    world and me. . . .
There was a design of white bones slumbering forgottenly upon a cushion
    of ashes.
There was a charred stump of a sapling pointing a blunt finger accusingly
    at the sky.
There were torn tree limbs, tiny veins of burnt leaves, and a scorched
    coil of greasy hemp;
A vacant shoe, an empty tie, a ripped shirt, a lonely hat, and a pair of
    trousers stiff with black blood.
And upon the trampled grass were buttons, dead matches, butt-ends of
    cigars and cigarettes, peanut shells, a drained gin-flask, and a whore's
    lipstick;
Scattered traces of tar, restless arrays of feathers, and the lingering smell
    of gasoline.
And through the morning air the sun poured yellow surprise into the eye
    sockets of a stony skull. . . .   10
And while I stood my mind was frozen with a cold pity for the life that
    was gone.

The ground gripped my feet and my heart was circled by icy walls of fear—
The sun died in the sky; a night wind muttered in the grass and fumbled the
    leaves in the trees; the woods poured forth the hungry yelping of hounds;
    the darkness screamed with thirsty voices; and the witnesses rose and
    lived: The dry bones stirred, rattled, lifted, melting themselves into my
    bones.
The grey ashes formed flesh firm and black, entering into my flesh.
The gin-flask passed from mouth to mouth; cigars and cigarettes glowed,
    the whore smeared the lipstick red upon her lips,
And a thousand faces swirled around me, clamoring that my life be
    burned. . . .
And then they had me, stripped me, battering my teeth into my throat till
    I swallowed my own blood.
My voice was drowned in the roar of their voices, and my black wet body
    slipped and rolled in their hands as they bound me to the sapling.
And my skin clung to the bubbling hot tar, falling from me in limp patches.
And the down and quills of the white feathers sank into my raw flesh, and
    I moaned in my agony.   20
Then my blood was cooled mercifully, cooled by a baptism of gasoline.
And in a blaze of red I leaped to the sky as pain rose like water, boiling my
    limbs.
Panting, begging I clutched childlike, clutched to the hot sides of death.
Now I am dry bones and my face a stony skull staring in my yellow
    surprise at the sun. . . .

Henry Reed   [1914–1986]

Naming of Parts   1946

Today we have naming of parts. Yesterday,
We had daily cleaning. And tomorrow morning
We shall have what to do after firing. But today,
Today we have naming of parts. Japonica
Glistens like coral in all of the neighboring gardens,
    And today we have naming of parts.

This is the lower sling swivel. And this
Is the upper sling swivel, whose use you will see,
When you are given your slings. And this is the piling swivel,
Which in your case you have not got. The branches   10
Hold in the gardens their silent, eloquent gestures,
    Which in our case we have not got.

This is the safety-catch, which is always released
With an easy flick of the thumb. And please do not let me
See anyone using his finger. You can do it quite easy
If you have any strength in your thumb. The blossoms
Are fragile and motionless, never letting anyone see
    Any of them using their finger.

And this you can see is the bolt. The purpose of this
Is to open the breech, as you see. We can slide it   20
Rapidly backwards and forwards: we call this
Easing the spring. And rapidly backwards and forwards
The early bees are assaulting and fumbling the flowers:
    They call it easing the Spring.

They call it easing the Spring: it is perfectly easy
If you have any strength in your thumb: like the bolt,
And the breech, and the cocking-piece, and the point of balance,
Which in our case we have not got; and the almond-blossom
Silent in all of the gardens and the bees going backwards and forwards,
    For today we have naming of parts.   30

For Analysis

1. The poem has two speakers. Identify their voices, and characterize the speakers.
2. The last line of each stanza repeats a phrase from within the stanza. What is the effect of the repetition?

Writing Topic

This poem incorporates a subtle underlying sexuality. Trace the language that generates it. What function does that sexuality serve in the poem?

M. Carl Holman   [1919–1988]

Mr. Z   1967

Taught early that his mother's skin was the sign of error,
He dressed and spoke the perfect part of honor;
Won scholarships, attended the best schools,
Disclaimed kinship with jazz and spirituals;
Chose prudent, raceless views for each situation,
Or when he could not cleanly skirt dissension,
Faced up to the dilemma, firmly seized
Whatever ground was Anglo-Saxonized.

In diet, too, his practice was exemplary:
Of pork in its profane forms he was wary;   10
Expert in vintage wines, sauces and salads,
His palate shrank from cornbread, yams and collards.

He was as careful whom he chose to kiss:
His bride had somewhere lost her Jewishness,
But kept her blue eyes; an Episcopalian
Prelate proclaimed them matched chameleon.
Choosing the right addresses, here, abroad,
They shunned those places where they might be barred;
Even less anxious to be asked to dine
Where hosts catered to kosher accent or exotic skin.   20

And so he climbed, unclogged by ethnic weights,
An airborne plant, flourishing without roots.
Not one false note was struck—until he died:
His subtly grieving widow could have flayed
The obit writers, ringing crude changes on a clumsy phrase:
"One of the most distinguished members of his race."

For Analysis
1. Explain the title of this poem. What might "Z" stand for? **2.** What is the significance of the description of Mr. Z's wife? **3.** In what sense is the comment of the final line the only "false note" in an otherwise successful and exemplary life?

On Style
Describe the use of **irony** in this poem.

Writing Topics
1. Describe an experience you have had in which you successfully conformed to a set of expectations in order to achieve a goal only to discover that you were denied that goal. **2.** If you have lived as a minority (ethnic, religious, racial, or other) in a community, describe the pressures you felt to conform and the costs (social, economic, or emotional) of your attempts or your refusal to conform.

Anne Sexton   [1928–1974]

Cinderella   1971

You always read about it:
the plumber with twelve children
who wins the Irish Sweepstakes.

From toilets to riches.
That story.

Or the nursemaid,
some luscious sweet from Denmark
who captures the oldest son's heart.
From diapers to Dior.
That story.   10

Or a milkman who serves the wealthy,
eggs, cream, butter, yogurt, milk,
the white truck like an ambulance
who goes into real estate
and makes a pile.
From homogenized to martinis at lunch.

Or the charwoman
who is on the bus when it cracks up
and collects enough from the insurance.
From mops to Bonwit Teller.   20
That story.

Once
the wife of a rich man was on her deathbed
and she said to her daughter Cinderella:
Be devout. Be good. Then I will smile
down from heaven in the seam of a cloud.
The man took another wife who had
two daughters, pretty enough
but with hearts like blackjacks.
Cinderella was their maid.   30
She slept on the sooty hearth each night
and walked around looking like Al Jolson.
Her father brought presents home from town,
jewels and gowns for the other women
but the twig of a tree for Cinderella.
She planted that twig on her mother's grave
and it grew to a tree where a white dove sat.
Whenever she wished for anything the dove
would drop it like an egg upon the ground.
The bird is important, my dears, so heed him.   40

Next came the ball, as you all know.
It was a marriage market.
The prince was looking for a wife.

All but Cinderella were preparing
and gussying up for the big event.
Cinderella begged to go too.
Her stepmother threw a dish of lentils
into the cinders and said: Pick them
up in an hour and you shall go.
The white dove brought all his friends;   50
all the warm wings of the fatherland came,
and picked up the lentils in a jiffy.
No, Cinderella, said the stepmother,
you have no clothes and cannot dance.
That's the way with stepmothers.

Cinderella went to the tree at the grave
and cried forth like a gospel singer:
Mama! Mama! My turtledove,
send me to the prince's ball!
The bird dropped down a golden dress   60
and delicate little gold slippers.
Rather a large package for a simple bird.
So she went. Which is no surprise.
Her stepmother and sisters didn't
recognize her without her cinder face
and the prince took her hand on the spot
and danced with no other the whole day.

As nightfall came she thought she'd better
get home. The prince walked her home
and she disappeared into the pigeon house   70
and although the prince took an axe and broke
it open she was gone. Back to her cinders.
These events repeated themselves for three days.
However on the third day the prince
covered the palace steps with cobbler's wax
and Cinderella's gold shoe stuck upon it.

Now he would find whom the shoe fit
and find his strange dancing girl for keeps.
He went to their house and the two sisters
were delighted because they had lovely feet.   80
The eldest went into a room to try the slipper on
but her big toe got in the way so she simply
sliced it off and put on the slipper.
The prince rode away with her until the white dove
told him to look at the blood pouring forth.

That is the way with amputations.
They don't just heal up like a wish.
The other sister cut off her heel
but the blood told as blood will.
The prince was getting tired.   90
He began to feel like a shoe salesman
but he gave it one last try.
This time Cinderella fit into the shoe
like a love letter into its envelope.

At the wedding ceremony
the two sisters came to curry favor
and the white dove pecked their eyes out.
Two hollow spots were left
like soup spoons.

Cinderella and the prince   100
lived, they say, happily ever after,
like two dolls in a museum case
never bothered by diapers or dust,
never arguing over the timing of an egg,
never telling the same story twice,
never getting a middle-aged spread,
their darling smiles pasted on for eternity.
Regular Bobbsey Twins.[1]
That story.

For Analysis

1. Where does one usually find the first four "stories" mentioned in the poem? Why do such stories interest readers? **2.** Do you remember your feelings as a child in response to the story of Cinderella and at the success of Cinderella? How are those feelings modified by the last stanza?

Writing Topic

The language and formal structure of this poem resemble prose. Describe, by examining the image patterns and individual lines, the qualities that make the piece a poem.

[1] The ever-cheerful central figures in a series of children's books.

Etheridge Knight [1933–1991]

Hard Rock Returns to Prison from the Hospital for the Criminal Insane 1968

Hard Rock was "known not to take no shit
From nobody," and he had the scars to prove it:
Split purple lips, lumped ears, welts above
His yellow eyes, and one long scar that cut
Across his temple and plowed through a thick
Canopy of kinky hair.

The WORD was that Hard Rock wasn't a mean nigger
Anymore, that the doctors had bored a hole in his head,
Cut out part of his brain, and shot electricity
Through the rest. When they brought Hard Rock back,   10
Handcuffed and chained, he was turned loose,
Like a freshly gelded stallion, to try his new status.
And we all waited and watched, like Indians at a corral,
To see if the WORD was true.

As we waited we wrapped ourselves in the cloak
Of his exploits: "Man, the last time, it took eight
Screws to put him in the Hole." "Yeah, remember when he
Smacked the captain with his dinner tray?" "He set
The record for time in the Hole—67 straight days!"
"Ol Hard Rock! man, that's one crazy nigger."   20
And then the jewel of a myth that Hard Rock had once bit
A screw on the thumb and poisoned him with syphilitic spit.

The testing came, to see if Hard Rock was really tame.
A hillbilly called him a black son of a bitch
And didn't lose his teeth, a screw who knew Hard Rock
From before shook him down and barked in his face.
And Hard Rock did *nothing*. Just grinned and looked silly,
His eyes empty like knot holes in a fence.

And even after we discovered that it took Hard Rock
Exactly 3 minutes to tell you his first name,   30
We told ourselves that he had just wised up,
Was being cool; but we could not fool ourselves for long,
And we turned away, our eyes on the ground. Crushed.

He had been our Destroyer, the doer of things
We dreamed of doing but could not bring ourselves to do,
The fears of years, like a biting whip,
Had cut grooves too deeply across our backs.

Felix Mnthali   [b. 1933]

The Stranglehold of English Lit.   1961
(For Molara Ogundipe-Leslie)

Those questions, sister,
those questions
           stand
           stab
           jab
           and gore
too close to the centre!

For if we had asked
why Jane Austen's people[1]
carouse all day   10
and do no work

would Europe in Africa
have stood
the test of time?
and would she still maul
the flower of our youth
in the south?
Would she?

Your elegance of deceit,
Jane Austen,   20
lulled the sons and daughters
of the dispossessed
into a calf-love
with irony and satire
around imaginary people.

The Stranglehold
  [1] Characters in the novels of Jane Austen (1775–1817), a standard author in English literature courses. Her ironic domestic comedies are peopled with English country gentlefolk who, apparently, do not have to work for a living.

While history went on mocking
the victims of branding irons
and sugar-plantations
that made Jane Austen's people
wealthy beyond compare!   30

Eng. Lit., my sister,
was more than a cruel joke—
it was the heart
of alien conquest.

How could questions be asked
at Makerere and Ibadan,
Dakar and Ford Hare[2]—
with Jane Austen
at the centre?
How could they be answered?   40

For Analysis
1. Some would argue that studying Jane Austen is appropriate because her work embodies "universal" values. Does the poet agree? Explain. **2.** In the fifth stanza, the
poet moves from derision to an attack; discuss the issues he raises. **3.** Do you agree
with the assertion of the sixth stanza? Explain.

Writing Topic
Discuss the political and cultural implications of the poem's title.

Yevgeny Yevtushenko   [b. 1933]

I Would Like   trans. 1962

I would like
            to be born
                        in every country,
have a passport
            for them all,
to throw
        all foreign offices
                    into panic,

The Stranglehold
    [2] The sites of major African Universities whose students, among others, participated in Africa's
struggle to free itself from European domination.

be every fish
          in every ocean   10
and every dog
            along the path.
I don't want to bow down
                  before any idols
or play at being
            an Orthodox church hippy,
but I would like to plunge
                 deep into Lake Baikal[1]
and surface snorting
               somewhere,   20
                      why not in the Mississippi?
In my beloved universe
               I would like
to be a lonely weed,
             but not a delicate Narcissus[2]
kissing his own mug
            in the mirror.
I would like to be
            any of God's creatures
right down to the last mangy hyena—   30
but never a tyrant
            or even the cat of a tyrant.
I would like to be
            reincarnated as a man
                  in any circumstance:
a victim of Paraguayan prison tortures,
a homeless child in the slums of Hong Kong,
a living skeleton in Bangladesh,
a holy beggar in Tibet,
a black in Cape Town,   40
but never
            in the image of Rambo
The only people whom I hate
                  are the hypocrites—
pickled hyenas
            in heavy syrup.
I would like to lie
            under the knives of all the surgeons in the world,

[1] A large lake in Siberia, just north of Mongolia.
[2] In Greek myth, a beautiful youth who pined away for love of his own reflection and was changed into a flower.

be hunchbacked, blind,
     suffer all kinds of diseases,   50
            wounds and scars,
be a victim of war,
     or a sweeper of cigarette butts,
just so a filthy microbe of superiority
        doesn't creep inside.
I would not like to be in the elite,
nor of course,
    in the cowardly herd,
nor be a guard-dog of that herd,
nor a shepherd,   60
     sheltered by that herd.
And I would like happiness,
      but not at the expense of the unhappy,
and I would like freedom,
      but not at the expense of the unfree.
I would like to love
     all the women in the world,
and I would like to be a woman, too—
       just once. . . .
Men have been diminished   70
     by Mother Nature.
Suppose she'd given motherhood
      to men?
If an innocent child
    stirred
     below his heart,
man would probably
     not be so cruel.
I would like to be man's daily bread—
say,   80
  a cup of rice
    for a Vietnamese woman in mourning,
cheap wine
    in a Neapolitan workers' trattoria,[3]
or a tiny tube of cheese
     in orbit round the moon:
let them eat me,
    let them drink me,
only let my death
    be of some use.   90

[3] A small inexpensive restaurant in Italy.

I would like to belong to all times,
                          shock all history so much
that it would be amazed
                    what a smart aleck I was.
I would like to bring Nefertiti
                      to Pushkin in a troika.[4]
I would like to increase
                  the space of a moment
                            a hundredfold,
so that in the same moment   100
                I could drink vodka with fishermen in Siberia
and sit together with Homer,
                      Dante,
                          Shakespeare,
                              and Tolstoy,
drinking anything,
                except of course,
                      Coca-Cola,
—dance to the tom-toms in the Congo,
—strike at Renault,   110
—chase a ball with Brazilian boys
                  at Copacabana Beach.
I would like
          to know every language,
                    the secret waters under the earth,
and do all kinds of work at once.
                  I would make sure
that one Yevtushenko was merely a poet,
                the second—an underground fighter,
                        somewhere,   120
I couldn't say where
                for security reasons,
the third—a student at Berkeley,
                  the fourth—a jolly Georgian[5] drinker,
and the fifth—
              maybe a teacher of Eskimo children in Alaska,
the sixth—
          a young president,
                  somewhere, say even in Sierra Leone,

---

[4] Nefertiti was a famously beautiful fourteenth-century B.C. queen of Egypt. Aleksandr Sergeyevich Pushkin (1799–1837) was, perhaps, the greatest Russian writer and poet of his time. A troika is a Russian vehicle drawn by a team of three horses.
   [5] Georgia is one of the republics that made up the former Soviet Union. It lies along the east coast of the Black Sea.

the seventh— 130
        would still be shaking a rattle in his stroller,
and the tenth . . .
          the hundredth . . .
                the millionth . . .
For me it's not enough to be myself,
          let me be everyone!
Every creature
        usually has a double,
but God was stingy
          with the carbon paper, 140
and in his Paradise Publishing Company
            made a unique copy of me.
But I shall muddle up
        all God's cards—
            I shall confound God!
I shall be in a thousand copies
          to the end of my days,
so that the earth buzzes with me,
          and computers go berserk
in the world census of me. 150
I would like to fight on all your barricades,
          humanity,
dying each night
        an exhausted moon,
and being resurrected each morning
          like a newborn sun,
with an immortal soft spot
        on my skull.
And when I die,
        a smart-aleck Siberian François Villon,[6] 160
do not lay me in the earth
        of France
        or Italy,
but in our Russian, Siberian earth,
        on a still green hill,
where I first felt
      that I was
        everyone.

For Analysis

1. The poet declares that he would like to be a certain kind of person. What kind of person? What specific **images** lead you to your judgment? **2.** What kind of person does he *not* wish to be? What images support your conclusion? **3.** Discuss the images

---

[6] A French balladeer, born in 1431, who was often in trouble with the law.

that address chronological time. Discuss those that address geographical distance. Discuss those that address a sort of chain of being among creatures, moving from "low" to "high." How does Yevtushenko use these images to define his social and political views?

Writing Topic
In an essay, characterize the poet's notion of an ideal person, and speculate on how that person would get along in the real world. Do you accept, or would you modify, Yevtushenko's ideal? Explain.

Mary Oliver [b. 1935]

The Black Walnut Tree 1992

My mother and I debate:
we could sell
the black walnut tree
to the lumberman,
and pay off the mortgage.
Likely some storm anyway
will churn down its dark boughs,
smashing the house. We talk
slowly, two women trying
in a difficult time to be wise.   10
Roots in the cellar drains,
I say, and she replies
that the leaves are getting heavier
every year, and the fruit
harder to gather away.
But something brighter than money
moves in our blood—an edge
sharp and quick as a trowel
that wants us to dig and sow.
So we talk, but we don't do   20
anything. That night I dream
of my fathers out of Bohemia
filling the blue fields
of fresh and generous Ohio
with leaves and vines and orchards.
What my mother and I both know
is that we'd crawl with shame
in the emptiness we'd made
in our own and our fathers' backyard.

So the black walnut tree   30
swings through another year
of sun and leaping winds,
of leaves and bounding fruit,
and, month after month, the whip-
crack of the mortgage.

For Analysis
1. What arguments support selling the black walnut tree? **2.** Why do the mother and daughter not sell it?

Writing Topics
1. In an essay, describe the benefits to the mother and daughter of not selling the tree, despite all the trouble it causes. Consider what "fathers" (ll. 22 and 29) have to do with the issue. **2.** Write about a time when "something brighter than money" moved in your blood (ll. 16–17).

Wendy Cope   [b. 1945]

Lonely Hearts   1986

Can someone make my simple wish come true?
Male biker seeks female for touring fun.
Do you live in North London? Is it you?

Gay vegetarian whose friends are few,
I'm into music, Shakespeare and the sun,
Can someone make my simple wish come true?

Executive in search of something new—
Perhaps bisexual woman, arty, young.
Do you live in North London? Is it you?

Successful, straight and solvent? I am too—   10
Attractive Jewish lady with a son.
Can someone make my simple wish come true?

I'm Libran, inexperienced and blue—
Need slim non-smoker, under twenty-one.
Do you live in North London? Is it you?

Please write (with photo) to Box 152.
Who knows where it may lead once we've begun?

Can someone make my simple wish come true?
Do you live in North London? Is it you?

Ira Sadoff   [b. 1945]

Nazis   1989

Thank God they're all gone
except for one or two in Clinton Maine
who come home from work
at Scott Paper or Diamond Match
to make a few crank calls
to the only Jew in New England
they can find

These make-shift students of history
whose catalogue of facts include
every Jew who gave a dollar   10
to elect the current governor
every Jew who'd sell this country out
to the insatiable Israeli state

I know exactly how they feel
when they say they want to smash my face

Someone's cheated them
they want to know who it is
they want to know who makes them beg
It's true Let's Be Fair
it's tough for almost everyone   20
I exaggerate the facts
to make a point

Just when I thought I could walk to the market
just when Jean the check-out girl
asks me how many cords of wood I chopped
and wishes me a Happy Easter
as if I've lived here all my life

Just when I can walk into the bank
and nod at the tellers who know my name
where I work who lived in my house in 1832   30

who know to the penny the amount
of my tiny Jewish bank account

Just when I'm sure we can all live together
and I can dine in their saltbox dining rooms
with the melancholy painting of Christ
on the wall their only consolation
just when I can borrow my neighbor's ladder
to repair one of the holes in my roof

I pick up the phone
and listen to my instructions   40

I see the town now from the right perspective
the gunner in the glass bubble
of his fighter plane shadowing the tiny man
with the shopping bag and pointy nose
his overcoat two sizes too large for him
skulking from one doorway to the next
trying to make his own way home

I can see he's not one of us

For Analysis
1. The stanza beginning at line 16 suggests the origins of the anti-Semitism described in the poem. Who, do you suppose, has cheated whom out of what? **2.** Explain lines 39–40: "I pick up the phone / and listen to my instructions." **3.** At line 41, the **point of view** seems to change. Who is the "gunner" (l. 42) and who is the "tiny man" (l. 43)?

Writing Topic
In a reflective essay, describe the effect of some stereotypical view (based on nationality, religion, ethnicity, gender, or sexual orientation) held by you or someone you know.

Linda Hogan   [b. 1947]

First Light   1991

In early morning
I forget I'm in this world
with crooked chiefs
who make federal deals.

In the first light
I remember who rewards me for living,
not bosses
but singing birds and blue sky.

I know I can bathe and stretch,
make jewelry and love   10
the witch and wise woman
living inside, needing to be silenced
and put at rest for work's long day.

In the first light
I offer cornmeal
and tobacco.
I say hello to those who came before me,
and to birds
under the eaves,
and budding plants.   20

I know the old ones are here.
And every morning I remember the song
about how buffalo left through a hole in the sky
and how the grandmothers look out from those holes
watching over us
from there and from there.

For Robin

For Analysis

1. Explain what "this world" of line 2 is. **2.** Who are the "crooked chiefs"? What is a "federal" deal? Is the speaker part of the world of chiefs and federal deals? **3.** Why does the speaker offer cornmeal and tobacco? **4.** Explain the title.

Writing Topic

Write an essay in which you speculate on who the poet is and what might have led her to write this poem.

Catherine Anderson   [b. 1954]

Womanhood   1987

She slides over
the hot upholstery
of her mother's car,
this schoolgirl of fifteen
who loves humming & swaying
with the radio.
Her entry into womanhood
will be like all the other girls'—
a cigarette and a joke,
as she strides up with the rest   10
to a brick factory
where she'll sew rag rugs
from textile strips of kelly green,
bright red, aqua.

When she enters,
and the millgate closes,
final as a slap,
there'll be silence.
She'll see fifteen high windows
cemented over to cut out light.   20
Inside, a constant, deafening noise
and warm air smelling of oil,
the shifts continuing on . . .
All day she'll guide cloth along a line
of whirring needles, her arms & shoulders
rocking back & forth
with the machines—
200 porch size rugs behind her
before she can stop
to reach up, like her mother,   30
and pick the lint
out of her hair.

For Analysis
1. Who are the "other girls" of line 8? **2.** Explain line 9. What is the effect of the contrast between the "silence" (l. 18) and the "deafening noise" (l. 21)? **3.** Explain the final four lines.

Taslima Nasrin   [b. 1962]

Things Cheaply Had[1]   1991

In the market nothing can be had as cheap as women.
If they get a small bottle of *alta*[2] for their feet
       they spend three nights sleepless for sheer joy.
If they get a few bars of soap to scrub their skin
       and some scented oil for their hair
they become so submissive that they scoop out
       chunks of their flesh
to be sold in the flea market twice a week.
If they get a jewel for their nose
       they lick feet for seventy days or so,   10
a full three and a half months
       if it's a single striped sari.[3]

Even the mangy cur of the house barks now and then,
and over the mouths of women cheaply had
       there's a lock
a golden lock.

---

[1] Translated by Carolyne Wright with Mohammad Nurul Huda.

[2] *Alta,* or lac-dye, is a red liquid with which South Asian women decorate the borders of their feet on ceremonial occasions, such as weddings and dance performances. *Alta* is more in vogue among Hindus, but Bangladeshi women also use it, and it can be seen on the feet of Muslim heroines and harem women in Moghul miniature paintings. [Translator's note.]

[3] An outer garment worn chiefly by women of India and Pakistan, consisting of a length of cloth wrapped around the waist at one end and draped over the shoulder or head at the other.

Culture and Identity

Drama

Arthur Miller   [b. 1915]

Death of a Salesman   1949

**CERTAIN PRIVATE CONVERSATIONS IN TWO ACTS AND
A REQUIEM**

CAST

Willy Loman	**Uncle Ben**
Linda	**Howard Wagner**
Biff	**Jenny**
Happy	**Stanley**
Bernard	**Miss Forsythe**
The Woman	**Letta**
Charley	

scene: *The action takes place in Willy Loman's house and yard and in various places he visits in the New York and Boston of today.*

Throughout the play, in the stage directions, left and right mean stage left and stage right.

Act I

A melody is heard, played upon a flute. It is small and fine, telling of grass and trees and the horizon. The curtain rises.

Before us is the Salesman's house. We are aware of towering, angular shapes behind it, surrounding it on all sides. Only the blue light of the sky falls upon the house and forestage; the surrounding area shows an angry glow of orange. As more light appears, we see a solid vault of apartment houses around the small, fragile-seeming home. An air of the dream clings to the place, a dream rising out of reality. The kitchen at center seems actual enough, for there is a kitchen table with three chairs, and a refrigerator. But no other fixtures are seen. At the back of the kitchen there is a draped entrance, which leads to the living-room. To the right of the kitchen, on a level raised two feet, is a bedroom furnished only with a brass bedstead and a straight chair. On a shelf over the bed a silver athletic trophy stands. A window opens onto the apartment house at the side.

Behind the kitchen, on a level raised six and a half feet, is the boys' bedroom, at present barely visible. Two beds are dimly seen, and at the back of the room a dormer window. (This bedroom is above the unseen living-room.) At the left a stairway curves up to it from the kitchen.

The entire setting is wholly or, in some places, partially transparent. The roof-line of the house is one-dimensional; under and over it we see the apartment buildings. Before the house lies an apron, curving beyond the forestage into the orchestra. This forward area serves as the back yard as well as the locale of all Willy's imaginings and of his city scenes. Whenever the action is in the present the actors observe the imaginary wall-lines, entering the house only through its door at the left. But in the scenes of the past these boundaries are broken, and characters enter or leave a room by stepping "through" a wall onto the forestage.

From the right, Willy Loman, the Salesman, enters, carrying two large sample cases. The flute plays on. He hears but is not aware of it. He is past sixty years of age, dressed quietly. Even as he crosses the stage to the doorway of the house, his exhaustion is apparent. He unlocks the door, comes into the kitchen, and thankfully lets his burden down, feeling the soreness of his palms. A word-sigh escapes his lips—it might be "Oh, boy, oh, boy." He closes the door, then carries his cases out into the living-room, through the draped kitchen doorway.

Linda, his wife, has stirred in her bed at the right. She gets out and puts on a robe, listening. Most often jovial, she has developed an iron repression of her exceptions to Willy's behavior—she more than loves him, she admires him, as though his mercurial nature, his temper, his massive dreams and little cruelties, served her only as sharp reminders of the turbulent longings within him, longings which she shares but lacks the temperament to utter and follow to their end.

Linda *(hearing Willy outside the bedroom, calls with some trepidation).* Willy!

Willy.   It's all right. I came back.

Linda.   Why? What happened? *(Slight pause.)* Did something happen, Willy?

Willy.   No, nothing happened.

Linda.   You didn't smash the car, did you?

Willy *(with casual irritation).* I said nothing happened. Didn't you hear me?

Linda.   Don't you feel well?

Willy.   I'm tired to the death. *(The flute has faded away. He sits on the bed beside her, a little numb.)* I couldn't make it. I just couldn't make it, Linda.

Linda *(very carefully, delicately).*   Where were you all day? You look terrible.

Willy.   I got as far as a little above Yonkers. I stopped for a cup of coffee. Maybe it was the coffee.

Linda.   What?

Willy *(after a pause).*   I suddenly couldn't drive any more. The car kept going off onto the shoulder, y'know?

Linda *(helpfully).*   Oh. Maybe it was the steering again. I don't think Angelo knows the Studebaker.

Willy.   No, it's me, it's me. Suddenly I realize I'm goin' sixty miles an hour and I don't remember the last five minutes. I'm—I can't seem to—keep my mind to it.

Linda.   Maybe it's your glasses. You never went for your new glasses.

Willy.   No, I see everything. I came back ten miles an hour. It took me nearly four hours from Yonkers.

Linda *(resigned).*   Well, you'll just have to take a rest, Willy, you can't continue this way.

Willy.   I just got back from Florida.

Linda.   But you didn't rest your mind. Your mind is overactive, and the mind is what counts, dear.

Willy.   I'll start out in the morning. Maybe I'll feel better in the morning. *(She is taking off his shoes.)* These goddam arch supports are killing me.

Linda.   Take an aspirin. Should I get you an aspirin? It'll soothe you.

Willy *(with wonder).*   I was driving along, you understand? And I was fine. I was even observing the scenery. You can imagine, me looking at scenery, on the road every week of my life. But it's so beautiful up there, Linda, the trees are so thick, and the sun is warm. I opened the windshield and just let the warm air bathe over me. And then all of a sudden I'm goin' off the road! I'm tellin' ya, I absolutely forgot I was driving. If I'd've gone the other way over the white line I might've killed somebody. So I went on again—and five minutes later I'm dreamin' again, and I nearly—*(He presses two fingers against his eyes.)* I have such thoughts, I have such strange thoughts.

Linda.   Willy, dear. Talk to them again. There's no reason why you can't work in New York.

Willy.   They don't need me in New York. I'm the New England man. I'm vital in New England.

Linda.   But you're sixty years old. They can't expect you to keep traveling every week.

Willy.   I'll have to send a wire to Portland. I'm supposed to see Brown and Morrison tomorrow morning at ten o'clock to show the line. Goddammit, I could sell them! *(He starts putting on his jacket.)*

Linda *(taking the jacket from him).*   Why don't you go down to the place tomorrow and tell Howard you've simply got to work in New York? You're too accommodating, dear.

Willy.   If old man Wagner was alive I'd a been in charge of New York now! That man was a prince, he was a masterful man. But that boy of his, that

Howard, he don't appreciate. When I went north the first time, the Wagner Company didn't know where New England was!

Linda.   Why don't you tell those things to Howard, dear?

Willy *(encouraged).*   I will, I definitely will. Is there any cheese?

Linda.   I'll make you a sandwich.

Willy.   No, go to sleep. I'll take some milk. I'll be up right away. The boys in?

Linda.   They're sleeping. Happy took Biff on a date tonight.

Willy *(interested).*   That so?

Linda.   It was so nice to see them shaving together, one behind the other, in the bathroom. And going out together. You notice? The whole house smells of shaving lotion.

Willy.   Figure it out. Work a lifetime to pay off a house. You finally own it, and there's nobody to live in it.

Linda.   Well, dear, life is a casting off. It's always that way.

Willy.   No, no, some people—some people accomplish something. Did Biff say anything after I went this morning?

Linda.   You shouldn't have criticized him, Willy, especially after he just got off the train. You mustn't lose your temper with him.

Willy.   When the hell did I lose my temper? I simply asked him if he was making any money. Is that a criticism?

Linda.   But, dear, how could he make any money?

Willy *(worried and angered).*   There's such an undercurrent in him. He became a moody man. Did he apologize when I left this morning?

Linda.   He was crestfallen, Willy. You know how he admires you. I think if he finds himself, then you'll both be happier and not fight any more.

Willy.   How can he find himself on a farm? Is that a life? A farmhand? In the beginning, when he was young, I thought, well, a young man, it's good for him to tramp around, take a lot of different jobs. But it's more than ten years now and he has yet to make thirty-five dollars a week!

Linda.   He's finding himself, Willy.

Willy.   Not finding yourself at the age of thirty-four is a disgrace!

Linda.   Shh!

Willy.   The trouble is he's lazy, goddammit!

Linda.   Willy, please!

Willy.   Biff is a lazy bum!

Linda.   They're sleeping. Get something to eat. Go on down.

Willy.   Why did he come home? I would like to know what brought him home.

Linda.   I don't know. I think he's still lost, Willy. I think he's very lost.

Willy.   Biff Loman is lost. In the greatest country in the world a young man with such—personal attractiveness, gets lost. And such a hard worker. There's one thing about Biff—he's not lazy.

Linda.   Never.

Willy *(with pity and resolve).*   I'll see him in the morning; I'll have a nice talk with him. I'll get him a job selling. He could be big in no time. My God! Remember how they used to follow him around in high school? When he smiled at one of them their faces lit up. When he walked down the street . . . *(He loses himself in reminiscences.)*

Linda *(trying to bring him out of it).* Willy, dear, I got a new kind of American-type cheese today. It's whipped.

Willy. Why do you get American when I like Swiss?

Linda. I just thought you'd like a change—

Willy. I don't want a change! I want Swiss cheese. Why am I always being contradicted?

Linda *(with a covering laugh).* I thought it would be a surprise.

Willy. Why don't you open a window in here, for God's sake?

Linda *(with infinite patience).* They're all open, dear.

Willy. The way they boxed us in here. Bricks and windows, windows and bricks.

Linda. We should've bought the land next door.

Willy. The street is lined with cars. There's not a breath of fresh air in the neighborhood. The grass don't grow any more, you can't raise a carrot in the back yard. They should've had a law against apartment houses. Remember those two beautiful elm trees out there? When I and Biff hung the swing between them?

Linda. Yeah, like being a million miles from the city.

Willy. They should've arrested the builder for cutting those down. They massacred the neighborhood. *(Lost.)* More and more I think of those days, Linda. This time of year it was lilac and wisteria. And then the peonies would come out, and the daffodils. What fragrance in this room!

Linda. Well, after all, people had to move somewhere.

Willy. No, there's more people now.

Linda. I don't think there's more people. I think—

Willy. There's more people! That's what's ruining this country! Population is getting out of control. The competition is maddening! Smell the stink from that apartment house! And another one on the other side . . . How can they whip cheese?

On Willy's last line, Biff and Happy raise themselves up in their beds, listening.

Linda. Go down, try it. And be quiet.

Willy *(turning to Linda, guiltily).* You're not worried about me, are you, sweetheart?

Biff. What's the matter?

Happy. Listen!

Linda. You've got too much on the ball to worry about.

Willy. You're my foundation and my support, Linda.

Linda. Just try to relax, dear. You make mountains out of molehills.

Willy. I won't fight with him any more. If he wants to go back to Texas, let him go.

Linda. He'll find his way.

Willy. Sure. Certain men just don't get started till later in life. Like Thomas Edison, I think. Or B. F. Goodrich. One of them was deaf. *(He starts for the bedroom doorway.)* I'll put my money on Biff.

Linda. And Willy—if it's warm Sunday we'll drive in the country. And we'll open the windshield, and take lunch.

Willy. No, the windshields don't open on the new cars.

Linda. But you opened it today.

Willy. Me? I didn't. *(He stops.)* Now isn't that peculiar! Isn't that a remarkable—*(He breaks off in amazement and fright as the flute is heard distantly.)*

Linda. What, darling?

Willy. That is the most remarkable thing.

Linda. What, dear?

Willy. I was thinking of the Chevy. *(Slight pause.)* Nineteen twenty-eight . . . when I had that red Chevy—*(Breaks off.)* That funny? I coulda sworn I was driving that Chevy today.

Linda. Well, that's nothing. Something must've reminded you.

Willy. Remarkable. Ts. Remember those days? The way Biff used to simonize that car? The dealer refused to believe there was eighty thousand miles on it. *(He shakes his head.)* Heh! *(To Linda.)* Close your eyes, I'll be right up. *(He walks out of the bedroom.)*

Happy *(to Biff).* Jesus, maybe he smashed up the car again!

Linda *(calling after Willy).* Be careful on the stairs, dear! The cheese is on the middle shelf! *(She turns, goes over to the bed, takes his jacket, and goes out of the bedroom.)*

Light has risen on the boys' room. Unseen, Willy is heard talking to himself, "Eighty thousand miles," and a little laugh. Biff gets out of bed, comes downstage a bit, and stands attentively. Biff is two years older than his brother Happy, well built, but in these days bears a worn air and seems less self-assured. He has succeeded less, and his dreams are stronger and less acceptable than Happy's. Happy is tall, powerfully made. Sexuality is like a visible color on him, or a scent that many women have discovered. He, like his brother, is lost, but in a different way, for he has never allowed himself to turn his face toward defeat and is thus more confused and hard-skinned, although seemingly more content.

Happy *(getting out of bed).* He's going to get his license taken away if he keeps that up. I'm getting nervous about him, y'know, Biff?

Biff. His eyes are going.

Happy. No, I've driven with him. He sees all right. He just doesn't keep his mind on it. I drove into the city with him last week. He stops at a green light and then it turns red and he goes. *(He laughs.)*

Biff. Maybe he's color-blind.

Happy. Pop? Why he's got the finest eye for color in the business. You know that.

Biff *(sitting down on his bed).* I'm going to sleep.

Happy.   You're not still sour on Dad, are you, Biff?

Biff.   He's all right, I guess.

Willy (*underneath them, in the living-room*).   Yes, sir, eighty thousand miles—eighty-two thousand!

Biff.   You smoking?

Happy (*holding out a pack of cigarettes*).   Want one?

Biff (*taking a cigarette*).   I can never sleep when I smell it.

Willy.   What a simonizing job, heh!

Happy (*with deep sentiment*).   Funny, Biff, y'know? Us sleeping in here again? The old beds. (*He pats his bed affectionately.*) All the talk that went across those two beds, huh? Our whole lives.

Biff.   Yeah. Lotta dreams and plans.

Happy (*with a deep and masculine laugh*).   About five hundred women would like to know what was said in this room.

They share a soft laugh.

Biff.   Remember that big Betsy something—what the hell was her name—over on Bushwick Avenue?

Happy (*combing his hair*).   With the collie dog!

Biff.   That's the one. I got you in there, remember?

Happy.   Yeah, that was my first time—I think. Boy, there was a pig! (*They laugh, almost crudely.*) You taught me everything I know about women. Don't forget that.

Biff.   I bet you forgot how bashful you used to be. Especially with girls.

Happy.   Oh, I still am, Biff.

Biff.   Oh, go on.

Happy.   I just control it, that's all. I think I got less bashful and you got more so. What happened, Biff? Where's the old humor, the old confidence? (*He shakes Biff's knee. Biff gets up and moves restlessly about the room.*) What's the matter?

Biff.   Why does Dad mock me all the time?

Happy.   He's not mocking you, he—

Biff.   Everything I say there's a twist of mockery on his face. I can't get near him.

Happy.   He just wants you to make good, that's all. I wanted to talk to you about Dad for a long time, Biff. Something's—happening to him. He—talks to himself.

Biff.   I noticed that this morning. But he always mumbled.

Happy.   But not so noticeable. It got so embarrassing I sent him to Florida. And you know something? Most of the time he's talking to you.

Biff.   What's he say about me?

Happy.   I can't make it out.

Biff.   What's he say about me?

Happy. I think the fact that you're not settled, that you're still kind of up in the air . . .

Biff. There's one or two other things depressing him, Happy.

Happy. What do you mean?

Biff. Never mind. Just don't lay it all to me.

Happy. But I think if you just got started—I mean—is there any future for you out there?

Biff. I tell ya, Hap, I don't know what the future is. I don't know—what I'm supposed to want.

Happy. What do you mean?

Biff. Well, I spent six or seven years after high school trying to work myself up. Shipping clerk, salesman, business of one kind or another. And it's a measly manner of existence. To get on that subway on the hot mornings in summer. To devote your whole life to keeping stock, or making phone calls, or selling or buying. To suffer fifty weeks of the year for the sake of a two-week vacation, when all you really desire is to be outdoors, with your shirt off. And always to have to get ahead of the next fella. And still—that's how you build a future.

Happy. Well, you really enjoy it on a farm? Are you content out there?

Biff (*with rising agitation*). Hap, I've had twenty or thirty different kinds of jobs since I left home before the war, and it always turns out the same. I just realized it lately. In Nebraska when I herded cattle, and the Dakotas, and Arizona, and now in Texas. It's why I came home now, I guess, because I realized it. This farm I work on, it's spring there now, see? And they've got about fifteen new colts. There's nothing more inspiring or—beautiful than the sight of a mare and a new colt. And it's cool there now, see? Texas is cool now, and it's spring. And whenever spring comes to where I am, I suddenly get the feeling, my God, I'm not gettin' anywhere! What the hell am I doing, playing around with horses, twenty-eight dollars a week! I'm thirty-four years old, I oughta be makin' my future. That's when I come running home. And now, I get here, and I don't know what to do with myself. (*After a pause.*) I've always made a point of not wasting my life, and everytime I come back here I know that all I've done is to waste my life.

Happy. You're a poet, you know that, Biff? You're a—you're an idealist!

Biff. No, I'm mixed up very bad. Maybe I oughta get married. Maybe I oughta get stuck into something. Maybe that's my trouble. I'm like a boy. I'm not married. I'm not in business, I just—I'm like a boy. Are you content, Hap? You're a success, aren't you? Are you content?

Happy. Hell, no!

Biff. Why? You're making money, aren't you?

Happy (*moving about with energy, expressiveness*). All I can do now is wait for the merchandise manager to die. And suppose I get to be merchandise manager? He's a good friend of mine, and he just built a terrific estate on Long Island. And he lived there about two months and sold it, and now he's building another one. He can't enjoy it once it's finished. And I know that's just what I would do. I don't know what the hell I'm workin' for. Sometimes I sit in my apartment—all alone. And I think of the rent I'm paying. And it's crazy. But then, it's what I always wanted. My own apartment, a car, and plenty of women. And still, goddammit, I'm lonely.

Biff *(with enthusiasm).*   Listen, why don't you come out West with me?

Happy.   You and I, heh?

Biff.   Sure, maybe we could buy a ranch. Raise cattle, use our muscles. Men built like we are should be working out in the open.

Happy *(avidly).*   The Loman Brothers, heh?

Biff *(with vast affection).*   Sure, we'd be known all over the counties!

Happy *(enthralled).*   That's what I dream about, Biff. Sometimes I want to just rip my clothes off in the middle of the store and outbox that goddam merchandise manager. I mean I can outbox, outrun, and outlift anybody in that store, and I have to take orders from those common, petty sons-of-bitches till I can't stand it any more.

Biff.   I'm tellin' you, kid, if you were with me I'd be happy out there.

Happy *(enthused).*   See, Biff, everybody around me is so false that I'm constantly lowering my ideals . . .

Biff.   Baby, together we'd stand up for one another, we'd have someone to trust.

Happy.   If I were around you—

Biff.   Hap, the trouble is we weren't brought up to grub for money. I don't know how to do it.

Happy.   Neither can I!

Biff.   Then let's go!

Happy.   The only thing is—what can you make out there?

Biff.   But look at your friend. Builds an estate and then hasn't the peace of mind to live in it.

Happy.   Yeah, but when he walks into the store the waves part in front of him. That's fifty-two thousand dollars a year coming through the revolving door, and I got more in my pinky finger than he's got in his head.

Biff.   Yeah, but you just said—

Happy.   I gotta show some of those pompous, self-important executives over there that Hap Loman can make the grade. I want to walk into the store the way he walks in. Then I'll go with you, Biff. We'll be together yet, I swear. But take those two we had tonight. Now weren't they gorgeous creatures?

Biff.   Yeah, yeah, most gorgeous I've had in years.

Happy.   I get that any time I want, Biff. Whenever I feel disgusted. The trouble is, it gets like bowling or something. I just keep knockin' them over and it doesn't mean anything. You still run around a lot?

Biff.   Naa. I'd like to find a girl—steady, somebody with substance.

Happy.   That's what I long for.

Biff.   Go on! You'd never come home.

Happy. I would! Somebody with character, with resistance! Like Mom, y'know? You're gonna call me a bastard when I tell you this. That girl Charlotte I was with tonight is engaged to be married in five weeks. *(He tries on his new hat.)*

Biff. No kiddin'!

Happy. Sure, the guy's in line for the vice-presidency of the store. I don't know what gets into me, maybe I just have an overdeveloped sense of competition or something, but I went and ruined her, and furthermore I can't get rid of her. And he's the third executive I've done that to. Isn't that a crummy characteristic? And to top it all, I go to their weddings! *(Indignantly, but laughing.)* Like I'm not supposed to take bribes. Manufacturers offer me a hundred-dollar bill now and then to throw an order their way. You know how honest I am, but it's like this girl, see. I hate myself for it. Because I don't want the girl, and, still, I take it and—I love it!

Biff. Let's go to sleep.

Happy. I guess we didn't settle anything, heh?

Biff. I just got one idea that I think I'm going to try.

Happy. What's that?

Biff. Remember Bill Oliver?

Happy. Sure, Oliver is very big now. You want to work for him again?

Biff. No, but when I quit he said something to me. He put his arm on my shoulder, and he said, "Biff, if you ever need anything, come to me."

Happy. I remember that. That sounds good.

Biff. I think I'll go to see him. If I could get ten thousand or even seven or eight thousand dollars I could buy a beautiful ranch.

Happy. I bet he'd back you. 'Cause he thought highly of you, Biff. I mean, they all do. You're well liked, Biff. That's why I say to come back here, and we both have the apartment. And I'm tellin' you, Biff, any babe you want . . .

Biff. No, with a ranch I could do the work I like and still be something. I just wonder though. I wonder if Oliver still thinks I stole that carton of basketballs.

Happy. Oh, he probably forgot that long ago. It's almost ten years. You're too sensitive. Anyway, he didn't really fire you.

Biff. Well, I think he was going to. I think that's why I quit. I was never sure whether he knew or not. I know he thought the world of me, though. I was the only one he'd let lock up the place.

Willy *(below).* You gonna wash the engine, Biff?

Happy. Shh!

Biff looks at Happy, who is gazing down, listening. Willy is mumbling in the parlor.

Happy. You hear that?

They listen. Willy laughs warmly.

Biff *(growing angry)*. Doesn't he know Mom can hear that?
Willy. Don't get your sweater dirty, Biff!

A look of pain crosses Biff's face.

Happy. Isn't that terrible? Don't leave again, will you? You'll find a job here. You gotta stick around. I don't know what to do about him, it's getting embarrassing.
Willy. What a simonizing job!
Biff. Mom's hearing that!
Willy. No kiddin', Biff, you got a date? Wonderful!
Happy. Go on to sleep. But talk to him in the morning, will you?
Biff *(reluctantly getting into bed)*. With her in the house. Brother!
Happy *(getting into bed)*. I wish you'd have a good talk with him.

The light on their room begins to fade.

Biff *(to himself in bed)*. That selfish, stupid . . .
Happy. Sh . . . Sleep, Biff.

Their light is out. Well before they have finished speaking, Willy's form is dimly seen below in the darkened kitchen. He opens the refrigerator, searches in there, and takes out a bottle of milk. The apartment houses are fading out, and the entire house and surroundings become covered with leaves. Music insinuates itself as the leaves appear.

Willy. Just wanna be careful with those girls, Biff, that's all. Don't make any promises. No promises of any kind. Because a girl, y'know, they always believe what you tell 'em, and you're very young, Biff, you're too young to be talking seriously to girls.

Light rises on the kitchen. Willy, talking, shuts the refrigerator door and comes downstage to the kitchen table. He pours milk into a glass. He is totally immersed in himself, smiling faintly.

Willy. Too young entirely, Biff. You want to watch your schooling first. Then when you're all set, there'll be plenty of girls for a boy like you. *(He smiles broadly at a kitchen chair.)* That so? The girls pay for you? *(He laughs.)* Boy, you must really be makin' a hit.

Willy is gradually addressing—physically—a point offstage, speaking through the wall of the kitchen, and his voice has been rising in volume to that of a normal conversation.

Willy. I been wondering why you polish the car so careful. Ha! Don't leave the hubcaps, boys. Get the chamois to the hubcaps. Happy, use newspaper on the windows, it's the easiest thing. Show him how to do it, Biff! You see, Happy? Pad it up, use it like a pad. That's it, that's it, good work. You're doin' all right, Hap. (*He pauses, then nods in approbation for a few seconds, then looks upward.*) Biff, first thing we gotta do when we get time is clip that big branch over the house. Afraid it's gonna fall in a storm and hit the roof. Tell you what. We get a rope and sling her around, and then we climb up there with a couple of saws and take her down. Soon as you finish the car, boys, I wanna see ya. I got a surprise for you, boys.

Biff (*offstage*). Whatta ya got, Dad?

Willy. No, you finish first. Never leave a job till you're finished—remember that. (*Looking toward the "big trees."*) Biff, up in Albany I saw a beautiful hammock. I think I'll buy it next trip, and we'll hang it right between those two elms. Wouldn't that be something? Just swingin' there under those branches. Boy, that would be . . .

Young Biff and Young Happy appear from the direction Willy was addressing. Happy carries rags and a pail of water. Biff, wearing a sweater with a block "S," carries a football.

Biff (*pointing in the direction of the car offstage*). How's that, Pop, professional?

Willy. Terrific. Terrific job, boys. Good work, Biff.

Happy. Where's the surprise, Pop?

Willy. In the back seat of the car.

Happy. Boy! (*He runs off.*)

Biff. What is it, Dad? Tell me, what'd you buy?

Willy (*laughing, cuffs him*). Never mind, something I want you to have.

Biff (*turns and starts off*). What is it, Hap?

Happy (*offstage*). It's a punching bag!

Biff. Oh, Pop!

Willy. It's got Gene Tunney's signature on it!

Happy runs onstage with a punching bag.

Biff. Gee, how'd you know we wanted a punching bag?

Willy. Well, it's the finest thing for the timing.

Happy (*lies down on his back and pedals with his feet*). I'm losing weight, you notice, Pop?

Willy (*to Happy*). Jumping rope is good too.

Biff. Did you see the new football I got?

Willy (*examining the ball*). Where'd you get a new ball?

Biff. The coach told me to practice my passing.

Willy. That so? And he gave you the ball, heh?

Biff.   Well, I borrowed it from the locker room. (*He laughs confidentially.*)

Willy (*laughing with him at the theft*).   I want you to return that.

Happy.   I told you he wouldn't like it!

Biff (*angrily*).   Well, I'm bringing it back!

Willy (*stopping the incipient argument, to Happy*).   Sure, he's gotta practice with a regulation ball, doesn't he? (*To Biff.*) Coach'll probably congratulate you on your initiative!

Biff.   Oh, he keeps congratulating my initiative all the time, Pop.

Willy.   That's because he likes you. If somebody else took that ball there'd be an uproar. So what's the report, boys, what's the report?

Biff.   Where'd you go this time, Dad? Gee we were lonesome for you.

Willy (*pleased, puts an arm around each boy and they come down to the apron*).   Lonesome, heh?

Biff.   Missed you every minute.

Willy.   Don't say? Tell you a secret, boys. Don't breathe it to a soul. Someday I'll have my own business, and I'll never have to leave home any more.

Happy.   Like Uncle Charley, heh?

Willy.   Bigger than Uncle Charley! Because Charley is not—liked. He's liked, but he's not—well liked.

Biff.   Where'd you go this time, Dad?

Willy.   Well, I got on the road, and I went north to Providence. Met the Mayor.

Biff.   The Mayor of Providence!

Willy.   He was sitting in the hotel lobby.

Biff.   What'd he say?

Willy.   He said, "Morning!" And I said, "You got a fine city here, Mayor." And then he had coffee with me. And then I went to Waterbury. Waterbury is a fine city. Big clock city, the famous Waterbury clock. Sold a nice bill there. And then Boston—Boston is the cradle of the Revolution. A fine city. And a couple of other towns in Mass., and on to Portland and Bangor and straight home!

Biff.   Gee, I'd love to go with you sometime, Dad.

Willy.   Soon as summer comes.

Happy.   Promise?

Willy.   You and Hap and I, and I'll show you all the towns. America is full of beautiful towns and fine, upstanding people. And they know me, boys, they know me up and down New England. The finest people. And when I bring you fellas up, there'll be open sesame for all of us, 'cause one thing, boys: I have friends. I can park my car in any street in New England, and the cops protect it like their own. This summer, heh?

Biff and Happy (*together*).   Yeah! You bet!

Willy.   We'll take our bathing suits.

Happy.   We'll carry your bags, Pop!

Willy.   Oh, won't that be something! Me comin' into the Boston stores with you boys carryin' my bags. What a sensation!

Biff is prancing around, practicing passing the ball.

Willy. You nervous, Biff, about the game?
Biff. Not if you're gonna be there.
Willy. What do they say about you in school, now that they made you captain?
Happy. There's a crowd of girls behind him everytime the classes change.
Biff *(taking Willy's hand).* This Saturday, Pop, this Saturday—just for you, I'm going to break through for a touchdown.
Happy. You're supposed to pass.
Biff. I'm takin' one play for Pop. You watch me, Pop, and when I take off my helmet, that means I'm breakin' out. Then you watch me crash through that line!
Willy *(kisses Biff).* Oh, wait'll I tell this in Boston!

Bernard enters in knickers. He is younger than Biff, earnest and loyal, a worried boy.

Bernard. Biff, where are you? You're supposed to study with me today.
Willy. Hey, looka Bernard. What're you lookin' so anemic about, Bernard?
Bernard. He's gotta study, Uncle Willy. He's got Regents next week.
Happy *(tauntingly, spinning Bernard around).* Let's box, Bernard!
Bernard. Biff! *(He gets away from Happy.)* Listen, Biff, I heard Mr. Birnbaum say that if you don't start studyin' math, he's gonna flunk you, and you won't graduate. I heard him!
Willy. You better study with him, Biff. Go ahead now.
Bernard. I heard him!
Biff. Oh, Pop, you didn't see my sneakers! *(He holds up a foot for Willy to look at.)*
Willy. Hey, that's a beautiful job of printing!
Bernard *(wiping his glasses).* Just because he printed University of Virginia on his sneakers doesn't mean they've got to graduate him, Uncle Willy!
Willy *(angrily).* What're you talking about? With scholarships to three universities they're gonna flunk him?
Bernard. But I heard Mr. Birnbaum say—
Willy. Don't be a pest, Bernard! *(To his boys.)* What an anemic!
Bernard. Okay, I'm waiting for you in my house, Biff.

Bernard goes off. The Lomans laugh.

Willy. Bernard is not well liked, is he?
Biff. He's liked, but he's not well liked.
Happy. That's right, Pop.
Willy. That's just what I mean. Bernard can get the best marks in school, y'understand, but when he gets out in the business world, y'understand, you are going to be five times ahead of him. That's why I thank Almighty God

you're both built like Adonises.[1] Because the man who makes an appearance in the business world, the man who creates personal interest, is the man who gets ahead. Be liked and you will never want. You take me, for instance. I never have to wait in line to see a buyer. "Willy Loman is here!" That's all they have to know, and I go right through.

Biff. Did you knock them dead, Pop?

Willy. Knocked 'em cold in Providence, slaughtered 'em in Boston.

Happy (*on his back, pedaling again*). I'm losing weight, you notice, Pop?

Linda enters, as of old, a ribbon in her hair, carrying a basket of washing.

Linda (*with youthful energy*). Hello, dear!

Willy. Sweetheart!

Linda. How'd the Chevy run?

Willy. Chevrolet, Linda, is the greatest car ever built. (*To the boys.*) Since when do you let your mother carry wash up the stairs?

Biff. Grab hold there, boy!

Happy. Where to, Mom?

Linda. Hang them up on the line. And you better go down to your friends, Biff. The cellar is full of boys. They don't know what to do with themselves.

Biff. Ah, when Pop comes home they can wait!

Willy (*laughs appreciatively*). You better go down and tell them what to do, Biff.

Biff. I think I'll have them sweep out the furnace room.

Willy. Good work, Biff.

Biff (*goes through wall-line of kitchen to doorway at back and calls down*). Fellas! Everybody sweep out the furnace room! I'll be right down!

Voices. All right! Okay, Biff.

Biff. George and Sam and Frank, come out back! We're hangin' up the wash! Come on, Hap, on the double! (*He and Happy carry out the basket.*)

Linda. The way they obey him!

Willy. Well, that's training, the training. I'm tellin' you, I was sellin' thousands and thousands, but I had to come home.

Linda. Oh, the whole block'll be at that game. Did you sell anything?

Willy. I did five hundred gross in Providence and seven hundred gross in Boston.

Linda. No! Wait a minute, I've got a pencil. (*She pulls pencil and paper out of her apron pocket.*) That makes your commission . . . Two hundred—my God! Two hundred and twelve dollars!

Willy. Well, I didn't figure it yet, but . . .

Linda. How much did you do?

Willy. Well, I—I did—about a hundred and eighty gross in Providence. Well, no—it came to—roughly two hundred gross on the whole trip.

---

[1] In Greek mythology, Adonis was a young man known for his good looks and favored by Aphrodite, goddess of love and beauty.

Linda (*without hesitation*).   Two hundred gross. That's . . . (*She figures.*)

Willy.   The trouble was that three of the stores were half closed for inventory in Boston. Otherwise I woulda broke records.

Linda.   Well, it makes seventy dollars and some pennies. That's very good.

Willy.   What do we owe?

Linda.   Well, on the first there's sixteen dollars on the refrigerator—

Willy.   Why sixteen?

Linda.   Well, the fan belt broke, so it was a dollar eighty.

Willy.   But it's brand new.

Linda.   Well, the man said that's the way it is. Till they work themselves in, y'know.

They move through the wall-line into the kitchen.

Willy.   I hope we didn't get stuck on that machine.

Linda.   They got the biggest ads of any of them!

Willy.   I know, it's a fine machine. What else?

Linda.   Well, there's nine-sixty for the washing machine. And for the vacuum cleaner there's three and a half due on the fifteenth. Then the roof, you got twenty-one dollars remaining.

Willy.   It don't leak, does it?

Linda.   No, they did a wonderful job. Then you owe Frank for the carburetor.

Willy.   I'm not going to pay that man! That goddam Chevrolet, they ought to prohibit the manufacture of that car!

Linda.   Well, you owe him three and a half. And odds and ends, comes to around a hundred and twenty dollars by the fifteenth.

Willy.   A hundred and twenty dollars! My God, if business don't pick up I don't know what I'm gonna do!

Linda.   Well, next week you'll do better.

Willy.   Oh, I'll knock 'em dead next week. I'll go to Hartford. I'm very well liked in Hartford. You know, the trouble is, Linda, people don't seem to take to me.

They move onto the forestage.

Linda.   Oh, don't be foolish.

Willy.   I know it when I walk in. They seem to laugh at me.

Linda.   Why? Why would they laugh at you? Don't talk that way, Willy.

Willy moves to the edge of the stage. Linda goes into the kitchen and starts to darn stockings.

Willy.   I don't know the reason for it, but they just pass me by. I'm not noticed.

Linda.   But you're doing wonderful, dear. You're making seventy to a hundred dollars a week.

Willy.   But I gotta be at it ten, twelve hours a day. Other men—I don't know—
   they do it easier. I don't know why—I can't stop myself—I talk too much. A
   man oughta come in with a few words. One thing about Charley. He's a man
   of few words, and they respect him.

Linda.   You don't talk too much, you're just lively.

Willy *(smiling).*   Well, I figure, what the hell, life is short, a couple of jokes. *(To
   himself.)* I joke too much! *(The smile goes.)*

Linda.   Why? You're—

Willy.   I'm fat. I'm very—foolish to look at, Linda. I didn't tell you, but Christmas time I happened to be calling on F. H. Stewarts, and a salesman I know,
   as I was going in to see the buyer I heard him say something about—walrus.
   And I—I cracked him right across the face. I won't take that. I simply will not
   take that. But they do laugh at me. I know that.

Linda.   Darling . . .

Willy.   I gotta overcome it. I know I gotta overcome it. I'm not dressing to advantage, maybe.

Linda.   Willy, darling, you're the handsomest man in the world—

Willy.   Oh, no, Linda.

Linda.   To me you are. *(Slight pause.)* The handsomest.

*From the darkness is heard the laughter of a woman. Willy doesn't turn to it, but
it continues through Linda's lines.*

Linda.   And the boys, Willy. Few men are idolized by their children the way
   you are.

*Music is heard as behind a scrim, to the left of the house, The Woman, dimly
seen, is dressing.*

Willy *(with great feeling).*   You're the best there is, Linda, you're a pal, you
   know that? On the road—on the road I want to grab you sometimes and just
   kiss the life outa you.

*The laughter is loud now, and he moves into a brightening area at the left, where
The Woman has come from behind the scrim and is standing, putting on her hat,
looking into a "mirror" and laughing.*

Willy.   'Cause I get so lonely—especially when business is bad and there's nobody to talk to. I get the feeling that I'll never sell anything again, that I won't
   make a living for you, or a business, a business for the boys. *(He talks through
   The Woman's subsiding laughter; The Woman primps at the "mirror.")*
   There's so much I want to make for—

The Woman.   Me? You didn't make me, Willy. I picked you.

Willy *(pleased).*   You picked me?

The Woman *(who is quite proper-looking, Willy's age).*   I did. I've been sitting at that desk watching all the salesmen go by, day in, day out. But you've

got such a sense of humor, and we do have such a good time together, don't we?

Willy. Sure, sure. *(He takes her in his arms.)* Why do you have to go now?

The Woman. It's two o'clock . . .

Willy. No, come on in! *(He pulls her.)*

The Woman. . . . my sisters'll be scandalized. When'll you be back?

Willy. Oh, two weeks about. Will you come up again?

The Woman. Sure thing. You do make me laugh. It's good for me. *(She squeezes his arm, kisses him.)* And I think you're a wonderful man.

Willy. You picked me, heh?

The Woman. Sure. Because you're so sweet. And such a kidder.

Willy. Well, I'll see you next time I'm in Boston.

The Woman. I'll put you right through to the buyers.

Willy *(slapping her bottom).* Right. Well, bottoms up!

The Woman *(slaps him gently and laughs).* You just kill me, Willy. *(He suddenly grabs her and kisses her roughly.)* You kill me. And thanks for the stockings. I love a lot of stockings. Well, good night.

Willy. Good night. And keep your pores open!

The Woman. Oh, Willy!

The Woman bursts out laughing, and Linda's laughter blends in. The Woman disappears into the dark. Now the area at the kitchen table brightens. Linda is sitting where she was at the kitchen table, but now is mending a pair of her silk stockings.

Linda. You are, Willy. The handsomest man. You've got no reason to feel that—

Willy *(coming out of The Woman's dimming area and going over to Linda).* I'll make it all up to you, Linda, I'll—

Linda. There's nothing to make up, dear. You're doing fine, better than—

Willy *(noticing her mending).* What's that?

Linda. Just mending my stockings. They're so expensive—

Willy *(angrily, taking them from her).* I won't have you mending stockings in this house! Now throw them out!

Linda puts the stockings in her pocket.

Bernard *(entering on the run).* Where is he? If he doesn't study!

Willy *(moving to the forestage, with great agitation).* You'll give him the answers!

Bernard. I do, but I can't on a Regents! That's a state exam! They're liable to arrest me!

Willy. Where is he? I'll whip him, I'll whip him!

Linda. And he'd better give back that football, Willy, it's not nice.

Willy. Biff! Where is he? Why is he taking everything?

Linda. He's too rough with the girls, Willy. All the mothers are afraid of him!

Willy.   I'll whip him!
Bernard.   He's driving the car without a license!

The Woman's laugh is heard.

Willy.   Shut up!
Linda.   All the mothers—
Willy.   Shut up!
Bernard (*backing quietly away and out*).   Mr. Birnbaum says he's stuck up.
Willy.   Get outa here!
Bernard.   If he doesn't buckle down he'll flunk math! (*He goes off.*)
Linda.   He's right, Willy, you've gotta—
Willy (*exploding at her*).   There's nothing the matter with him! You want him
   to be a worm like Bernard? He's got spirit, personality . . .

*As he speaks, Linda, almost in tears, exits into the living-room. Willy is alone in
the kitchen, wilting and staring. The leaves are gone. It is night again, and the
apartment houses look down from behind.*

Willy.   Loaded with it. Loaded! What is he stealing? He's giving it back, isn't
   he? Why is he stealing? What did I tell him? I never in my life told him anything but decent things.

*Happy in pajamas has come down the stairs; Willy suddenly becomes aware of
Happy's presence.*

Happy.   Let's go now, come on.
Willy (*sitting down at the kitchen table*).   Huh! Why did she have to wax the
   floors herself? Everytime she waxes the floors she keels over. She knows that!
Happy.   Shh! Take it easy. What brought you back tonight?
Willy.   I got an awful scare. Nearly hit a kid in Yonkers. God! Why didn't I go
   to Alaska with my brother Ben that time! Ben! That man was a genius, that
   man was success incarnate! What a mistake! He begged me to go.
Happy.   Well, there's no use in—
Willy.   You guys! There was a man started with the clothes on his back and
   ended up with diamond mines!
Happy.   Boy, someday I'd like to know how he did it.
Willy.   What's the mystery? The man knew what he wanted and went out and
   got it! Walked into a jungle, and comes out, the age of twenty-one, and he's
   rich! The world is an oyster, but you don't crack it open on a mattress!
Happy.   Pop, I told you I'm gonna retire you for life.
Willy.   You'll retire me for life on seventy goddam dollars a week? And your
   women and your car and your apartment, and you'll retire me for life! Christ's
   sake, I couldn't get past Yonkers today! Where are you guys, where are you?
   The woods are burning! I can't drive a car!

Charley has appeared in the doorway. He is a large man, slow of speech, laconic, immovable. In all he says, despite what he says, there is pity, and, now, trepidation. He has a robe over pajamas, slippers on his feet. He enters the kitchen.

Charley. Everything all right?

Happy. Yeah, Charley, everything's . . .

Willy. What's the matter?

Charley. I heard some noise. I thought something happened. Can't we do something about the walls? You sneeze in here, and in my house hats blow off.

Happy. Let's go to bed, Dad. Come on.

Charley signals to Happy to go.

Willy. You go ahead, I'm not tired at the moment.

Happy *(to Willy).* Take it easy, huh? *(He exits.)*

Willy. What're you doin' up?

Charley *(sitting down at the kitchen table opposite Willy).* Couldn't sleep good. I had a heartburn.

Willy. Well, you don't know how to eat.

Charley. I eat with my mouth.

Willy. No, you're ignorant. You gotta know about vitamins and things like that.

Charley. Come on, let's shoot. Tire you out a little.

Willy *(hesitantly).* All right. You got cards?

Charley *(taking a deck from his pocket).* Yeah, I got them. Someplace. What is it with those vitamins?

Willy *(dealing).* They build up your bones. Chemistry.

Charley. Yeah, but there's no bones in a heartburn.

Willy. What are you talkin' about? Do you know the first thing about it?

Charley. Don't get insulted.

Willy. Don't talk about something you don't know anything about.

They are playing. Pause.

Charley. What're you doin' home?

Willy. A little trouble with the car.

Charley. Oh. *(Pause.)* I'd like to take a trip to California.

Willy. Don't say.

Charley. You want a job?

Willy. I got a job, I told you that. *(After a slight pause.)* What the hell are you offering me a job for?

Charley. Don't get insulted.

Willy. Don't insult me.

Charley. I don't see no sense in it. You don't have to go on this way.

Willy.   I got a good job. (*Slight pause.*) What do you keep comin' in here for?

Charley.   You want me to go?

Willy (*after a pause, withering*).   I can't understand it. He's going back to Texas again. What the hell is that?

Charley.   Let him go.

Willy.   I got nothin' to give him, Charley, I'm clean, I'm clean.

Charley.   He won't starve. None a them starve. Forget about him.

Willy.   Then what have I got to remember?

Charley.   You take it too hard. To hell with it. When a deposit bottle is broken you don't get your nickel back.

Willy.   That's easy enough for you to say.

Charley.   That ain't easy for me to say.

Willy.   Did you see the ceiling I put up in the living-room?

Charley.   Yeah, that's a piece of work. To put up a ceiling is a mystery to me. How do you do it?

Willy.   What's the difference?

Charley.   Well, talk about it.

Willy.   You gonna put up a ceiling?

Charley.   How could I put up a ceiling?

Willy.   Then what the hell are you bothering me for?

Charley.   You're insulted again.

Willy.   A man who can't handle tools is not a man. You're disgusting.

Charley.   Don't call me disgusting, Willy.

Uncle Ben, carrying a valise and an umbrella, enters the forestage from around the right corner of the house. He is a stolid man, in his sixties, with a mustache and an authoritative air. He is utterly certain of his destiny, and there is an aura of far places about him. He enters exactly as Willy speaks.

Willy.   I'm getting awfully tired, Ben.

Ben's music is heard. Ben looks around at everything.

Charley.   Good, keep playing; you'll sleep better. Did you call me Ben?

Ben looks at his watch.

Willy.   That's funny. For a second there you reminded me of my brother Ben.

Ben.   I only have a few minutes. (*He strolls, inspecting the place. Willy and Charley continue playing.*)

Charley.   You never heard from him again, heh? Since that time?

Willy.   Didn't Linda tell you? Couple of weeks ago we got a letter from his wife in Africa. He died.

Charley.   That so.

Ben (*chuckling*).   So this is Brooklyn, eh?

Charley.   Maybe you're in for some of his money.

Willy.   Naa, he had seven sons. There's just one opportunity I had with that man . . .

Ben.   I must make a train, William. There are several properties I'm looking at in Alaska.

Willy.   Sure, sure! If I'd gone with him to Alaska that time, everything would've been totally different.

Charley.   Go on, you'd froze to death up there.

Willy.   What're you talking about?

Ben.   Opportunity is tremendous in Alaska, William. Surprised you're not up there.

Willy.   Sure, tremendous.

Charley.   Heh?

Willy.   There was the only man I ever met who knew the answers.

Charley.   Who?

Ben.   How are you all?

Willy (*taking a pot, smiling*).   Fine, fine.

Charley.   Pretty sharp tonight.

Ben.   Is mother living with you?

Willy.   No, she died a long time ago.

Charley.   Who?

Ben.   That's too bad. Fine specimen of a lady, Mother.

Willy (*to Charley*).   Heh?

Ben.   I'd hoped to see the old girl.

Charley.   Who died?

Ben.   Heard anything from Father, have you?

Willy (*unnerved*).   What do you mean, who died?

Charley (*taking a pot*).   What're you talkin' about?

Ben (*looking at his watch*).   William, it's half-past eight!

Willy (*as though to dispel his confusion he angrily stops Charley's hand*). That's my build!

Charley.   I put the ace—

Willy.   If you don't know how to play the game I'm not gonna throw my money away on you!

Charley (*rising*).   It was my ace, for God's sake!

Willy.   I'm through, I'm through!

Ben.   When did Mother die?

Willy.   Long ago. Since the beginning you never knew how to play cards.

Charley (*picks up the cards and goes to the door*).   All right! Next time I'll bring a deck with five aces.

Willy.   I don't play that kind of game!

Charley (*turning to him*).   You ought to be ashamed of yourself!

Willy.   Yeah?

Charley.   Yeah! (*He goes out.*)

Willy (*slamming the door after him*).   Ignoramus!

Ben (*as Willy comes toward him through the wall-line of the kitchen*). So you're William.

Willy (*shaking Ben's hand*). Ben! I've been waiting for you so long! What's the answer? How did you do it?

Ben. Oh, there's a story in that.

Linda enters the forestage, as of old, carrying the wash basket.

Linda. Is this Ben?

Ben (*gallantly*). How do you do, my dear.

Linda. Where've you been all these years? Willy's always wondered why you—

Willy (*pulling Ben away from her impatiently*). Where is Dad? Didn't you follow him? How did you get started?

Ben. Well, I don't know how much you remember.

Willy. Well, I was just a baby, of course, only three or four years old—

Ben. Three years and eleven months.

Willy. What a memory, Ben!

Ben. I have many enterprises, William, and I have never kept books.

Willy. I remember I was sitting under the wagon in—was it Nebraska?

Ben. It was South Dakota, and I gave you a bunch of wild flowers.

Willy. I remember you walking away down some open road.

Ben (*laughing*). I was going to find Father in Alaska.

Willy. Where is he?

Ben. At that age I had a very faulty view of geography, William. I discovered after a few days that I was heading due south, so instead of Alaska, I ended up in Africa.

Linda. Africa!

Willy. The Gold Coast!

Ben. Principally diamond mines.

Linda. Diamond mines!

Ben. Yes, my dear. But I've only a few minutes—

Willy. No! Boys! Boys! (*Young Biff and Happy appear.*) Listen to this. This is your Uncle Ben, a great man! Tell my boys, Ben!

Ben. Why, boys, when I was seventeen I walked into the jungle, and when I was twenty-one I walked out. (*He laughs.*) And by God I was rich.

Willy (*to the boys*). You see what I been talking about? The greatest things can happen!

Ben (*glancing at his watch*). I have an appointment in Ketchikan Tuesday week.

Willy. No, Ben! Please tell about Dad. I want my boys to hear. I want them to know the kind of stock they spring from. All I remember is a man with a big beard, and I was in Mamma's lap, sitting around a fire, and some kind of high music.

Ben.   His flute. He played the flute.

Willy.   Sure, the flute, that's right!

New music is heard, a high, rollicking tune.

Ben.   Father was a very great and a very wild-hearted man. We would start in Boston, and he'd toss the whole family into the wagon, and then he'd drive the team right across the country; through Ohio, and Indiana, Michigan, Illinois, and all the Western states. And we'd stop in the towns and sell the flutes that he'd made on the way. Great inventor, Father. With one gadget he made more in a week than a man like you could make in a lifetime.

Willy.   That's just the way I'm bringing them up, Ben—rugged, well liked, all-around.

Ben.   Yeah? *(To Biff.)* Hit that, boy—hard as you can. *(He pounds his stomach.)*

Biff.   Oh, no, sir!

Ben *(taking boxing stance).*   Come on, get to me. *(He laughs.)*

Willy.   Go to it, Biff! Go ahead, show him!

Biff.   Okay! *(He cocks his fists and starts in.)*

Linda *(to Willy).*   Why must he fight, dear?

Ben *(sparring with Biff).*   Good boy! Good boy!

Willy.   How's that, Ben, heh?

Happy.   Give him the left, Biff!

Linda.   Why are you fighting?

Ben.   Good boy! *(Suddenly comes in, trips Biff, and stands over him, the point of his umbrella poised over Biff's eye.)*

Linda.   Look out, Biff!

Biff.   Gee!

Ben *(patting Biff's knee).*   Never fight fair with a stranger, boy. You'll never get out of the jungle that way. *(Taking Linda's hand and bowing):* It was an honor and a pleasure to meet you, Linda.

Linda *(withdrawing her hand coldly, frightened).*   Have a nice—trip.

Ben *(to Willy).*   And good luck with your—what do you do?

Willy.   Selling.

Ben.   Yes. Well . . . *(He raises his hand in farewell to all.)*

Willy.   No, Ben, I don't want you to think . . . *(He takes Ben's arm to show him.)* It's Brooklyn, I know, but we hunt too.

Ben.   Really, now.

Willy.   Oh, sure, there's snakes and rabbits and—that's why I moved out here. Why, Biff can fell any one of these trees in no time! Boys! Go right over to where they're building the apartment house and get some sand. We're gonna rebuild the entire front stoop now! Watch this, Ben!

Biff.   Yes, sir! On the double, Hap!

Happy *(as he and Biff run off).*   I lost weight, Pop, you notice?

Charley enters in knickers, even before the boys are gone.

Charley.   Listen, if they steal any more from that building the watchman'll put the cops on them!

Linda (*to Willy*).   Don't let Biff . . .

Ben laughs lustily.

Willy.   You shoulda seen the lumber they brought home last week. At least a dozen six-by-tens worth all kinds a money.

Charley.   Listen, if that watchman—

Willy.   I gave them hell, understand. But I got a couple of fearless characters there.

Charley.   Willy, the jails are full of fearless characters.

Ben (*clapping Willy on the back, with a laugh at Charley*).   And the stock exchange, friend!

Willy (*joining in Ben's laughter*).   Where are the rest of your pants?

Charley.   My wife bought them.

Willy.   Now all you need is a golf club and you can go upstairs and go to sleep. (*To Ben.*) Great athlete! Between him and his son Bernard they can't hammer a nail!

Bernard (*rushing in*).   The watchman's chasing Biff!

Willy (*angrily*).   Shut up! He's not stealing anything!

Linda (*alarmed, hurrying off left*).   Where is he? Biff, dear! (*She exits.*)

Willy (*moving toward the left, away from Ben*).   There's nothing wrong. What's the matter with you?

Ben.   Nervy boy. Good!

Willy (*laughing*).   Oh, nerves of iron, that Biff!

Charley.   Don't know what it is. My New England man comes back and he's bleedin', they murdered him up there.

Willy.   It's contacts, Charley, I got important contacts!

Charley (*sarcastically*).   Glad to hear it, Willy. Come in later, we'll shoot a little casino. I'll take some of your Portland money. (*He laughs at Willy and exits.*)

Willy (*turning to Ben*).   Business is bad, it's murderous. But not for me, of course.

Ben.   I'll stop by on my way back to Africa.

Willy (*longingly*).   Can't you stay a few days? You're just what I need, Ben, because I—I have a fine position here, but I—well, Dad left when I was such a baby and I never had a chance to talk to him and I still feel—kind of temporary about myself.

Ben.   I'll be late for my train.

They are at opposite ends of the stage.

Willy. Ben, my boys—can't we talk? They'd go into the jaws of hell for me, see, but I—

Ben. William, you're being first-rate with your boys. Outstanding, manly chaps!

Willy (*hanging on to his words*). Oh, Ben, that's good to hear! Because sometimes I'm afraid that I'm not teaching them the right kind of—Ben, how should I teach them?

Ben (*giving great weight to each word, and with a certain vicious audacity*). William, when I walked into the jungle, I was seventeen. When I walked out I was twenty-one. And, by God, I was rich! (*He goes off into darkness around the right corner of the house.*)

Willy. . . . was rich! That's just the spirit I want to imbue them with! To walk into a jungle! I was right! I was right! I was right!

Ben is gone, but Willy is still speaking to him as Linda, in nightgown and robe, enters the kitchen, glances around for Willy, then goes to the door of the house, looks out, and sees him. Comes down to his left. He looks at her.

Linda. Willy, dear? Willy?

Willy. I was right!

Linda. Did you have some cheese? (*He can't answer.*) It's very late, darling. Come to bed, heh?

Willy (*looking straight up*). Gotta break your neck to see a star in this yard.

Linda. You coming in?

Willy. Whatever happened to that diamond watch fob? Remember? When Ben came from Africa that time? Didn't he give me a watch fob with a diamond in it?

Linda. You pawned it, dear. Twelve, thirteen years ago. For Biff's radio correspondence course.

Willy. Gee, that was a beautiful thing. I'll take a walk.

Linda. But you're in your slippers.

Willy (*starting to go around the house at the left*). I was right! I was! (*Half to Linda, as he goes, shaking his head.*) What a man! There was a man worth talking to. I was right!

Linda (*calling after Willy*). But in your slippers, Willy!

Willy is almost gone when Biff, in his pajamas, comes down the stairs and enters the kitchen.

Biff. What is he doing out there?

Linda. Sh!

Biff. God Almighty, Mom, how long has he been doing this?

Linda. Don't, he'll hear you.

Biff. What the hell is the matter with him?

Linda. It'll pass by morning.

Biff. Shouldn't we do anything?

Linda. Oh, my dear, you should do a lot of things, but there's nothing to do, so go to sleep.

Happy comes down the stairs and sits on the steps.

Happy. I never heard him so loud, Mom.

Linda. Well, come around more often; you'll hear him. (*She sits down at the table and mends the lining of Willy's jacket.*)

Biff. Why didn't you ever write me about this, Mom?

Linda. How would I write to you? For over three months you had no address.

Biff. I was on the move. But you know I thought of you all the time. You know that, don't you, pal?

Linda. I know, dear, I know. But he likes to have a letter. Just to know that there's still a possibility for better things.

Biff. He's not like this all the time, is he?

Linda. It's when you come home he's always the worst.

Biff. When I come home?

Linda. When you write you're coming, he's all smiles, and talks about the future, and—he's just wonderful. And then the closer you seem to come, the more shaky he gets, and then, by the time you get here, he's arguing, and he seems angry at you. I think it's just that maybe he can't bring himself to—to open up to you. Why are you so hateful to each other? Why is that?

Biff (*evasively*). I'm not hateful, Mom.

Linda. But you no sooner come in the door than you're fighting!

Biff. I don't know why. I mean to change. I'm tryin', Mom, you understand?

Linda. Are you home to stay now?

Biff. I don't know. I want to look around, see what's doin'.

Linda. Biff, you can't look around all your life, can you?

Biff. I just can't take hold, Mom. I can't take hold of some kind of a life.

Linda. Biff, a man is not a bird, to come and go with the springtime.

Biff. Your hair . . . (*He touches her hair.*) Your hair got so gray.

Linda. Oh, it's been gray since you were in high school. I just stopped dyeing it, that's all.

Biff. Dye it again, will ya? I don't want my pal looking old. (*He smiles.*)

Linda. You're such a boy! You think you can go away for a year and . . . You've got to get it into your head now that one day you'll knock on this door and there'll be strange people here—

Biff. What are you talking about? You're not even sixty, Mom.

Linda. But what about your father?

Biff (*lamely*). Well, I meant him too.

Happy. He admires Pop.

Linda. Biff, dear, if you don't have any feeling for him, then you can't have any feeling for me.

Biff. Sure I can, Mom.

Linda. No. You can't just come to see me, because I love him. (*With a threat, but only a threat, of tears.*) He's the dearest man in the world to me, and I won't have anyone making him feel unwanted and low and blue. You've got to make up your mind now, darling, there's no leeway any more. Either he's your father and you pay him that respect, or else you're not to come here. I know he's not easy to get along with—nobody knows that better than me—but . . .

Willy (*from the left, with a laugh*). Hey, hey, Biffo!

Biff (*starting to go out after Willy*). What the hell is the matter with him? (*Happy stops him.*)

Linda. Don't—don't go near him!

Biff. Stop making excuses for him! He always, always wiped the floor with you. Never had an ounce of respect for you.

Happy. He's always had respect for—

Biff. What the hell do you know about it?

Happy (*surlily*). Just don't call him crazy!

Biff. He's got no character—Charley wouldn't do this. Not in his own house—spewing out that vomit from his mind.

Happy. Charley never had to cope with what he's got to.

Biff. People are worse off than Willy Loman. Believe me, I've seen them!

Linda. Then make Charley your father, Biff. You can't do that, can you? I don't say he's a great man. Willy Loman never made a lot of money. His name was never in the paper. He's not the finest character that ever lived. But he's a human being, and a terrible thing is happening to him. So attention must be paid. He's not to be allowed to fall into his grave like an old dog. Attention, attention must be finally paid to such a person. You called him crazy—

Biff. I didn't mean—

Linda. No, a lot of people think he's lost his—balance. But you don't have to be very smart to know what his trouble is. The man is exhausted.

Happy. Sure!

Linda. A small man can be just as exhausted as a great man. He works for a company thirty-six years this March, opens up unheard-of territories to their trademark, and now in his old age they take his salary away.

Happy (*indignantly*). I didn't know that, Mom.

Linda. You never asked, my dear! Now that you get your spending money someplace else you don't trouble your mind with him.

Happy. But I gave you money last—

Linda. Christmas time, fifty dollars! To fix the hot water it cost ninety-seven fifty! For five weeks he's been on straight commission, like a beginner, an unknown!

Biff. Those ungrateful bastards!

Linda. Are they any worse than his sons? When he brought them business, when he was young, they were glad to see him. But now his old friends, the old buyers that loved him so and always found some order to hand him in a pinch—they're all dead, retired. He used to be able to make six, seven calls a day in Boston. Now he takes his valises out of the car and puts them back and takes them out again and he's exhausted. Instead of walking he talks now. He drives seven hundred miles, and when he gets there no one knows him any more, no one welcomes him. And what goes through a man's mind, driving seven hundred miles home without having earned a cent? Why shouldn't he talk to himself? Why? When he has to go to Charley and borrow fifty dollars a week and pretend to me that it's his pay? How long can that go on? How long? You see what I'm sitting here and waiting for? And you tell me he has no character? The man who never worked a day but for your benefit? When does he get the medal for that? Is this his reward—to turn around at the age of sixty-three and find his sons, who he loved better than his life, one a philandering bum—

Happy. Mom!

Linda. That's all you are, my baby! *(To Biff.)* And you! What happened to the love you had for him? You were such pals! How you used to talk to him on the phone every night! How lonely he was till he could come home to you!

Biff. All right, Mom. I'll live here in my room, and I'll get a job. I'll keep away from him, that's all.

Linda. No, Biff. You can't stay here and fight all the time.

Biff. He threw me out of this house, remember that.

Linda. Why did he do that? I never knew why.

Biff. Because I know he's a fake and he doesn't like anybody around who knows!

Linda. Why a fake? In what way? What do you mean?

Biff. Just don't lay it all at my feet. It's between me and him—that's all I have to say. I'll chip in from now on. He'll settle for half my pay check. He'll be all right. I'm going to bed. *(He starts for the stairs.)*

Linda. He won't be all right.

Biff *(turning on the stairs, furiously)*. I hate this city and I'll stay here. Now what do you want?

Linda. He's dying, Biff.

Happy turns quickly to her, shocked.

Biff *(after a pause)*. Why is he dying?

Linda. He's been trying to kill himself.

Biff *(with great horror)*. How?

Linda. I live from day to day.

Biff. What're you talking about?

Linda. Remember I wrote you that he smashed up the car again? In February?

Biff. Well?

Linda. The insurance inspector came. He said that they have evidence. That all these accidents in the last year—weren't—weren't—accidents.

Happy. How can they tell that? That's a lie.

Linda. It seems there's a woman . . . *(She takes a breath as):*
  { **Biff** *(sharply but contained).* What woman?
  { **Linda** *(simultaneously).* . . . and this woman . . .
Linda. What?
Biff. Nothing. Go ahead.
Linda. What did you say?
Biff. Nothing. I just said what woman?
Happy. What about her?
Linda. Well, it seems she was walking down the road and saw his car. She says that he wasn't driving fast at all, and that he didn't skid. She says he came to that little bridge, and then deliberately smashed into the railing, and it was only the shallowness of the water that saved him.
Biff. Oh, no, he probably just fell asleep again.
Linda. I don't think he fell asleep.
Biff. Why not?
Linda. Last month . . . *(With great difficulty.)* Oh, boys, it's so hard to say a thing like this! He's just a big stupid man to you, but I tell you there's more good in him than in many other people. *(She chokes, wipes her eyes.)* I was looking for a fuse. The lights blew out, and I went down the cellar. And behind the fuse box—it happened to fall out—was a length of rubber pipe—just short.
Happy. No kidding?
Linda. There's a little attachment on the end of it. I knew right away. And sure enough, on the bottom of the water heater there's a new little nipple on the gas pipe.
Happy *(angrily).* That—jerk.
Biff. Did you have it taken off?
Linda. I'm—I'm ashamed to. How can I mention it to him? Every day I go down and take away that little rubber pipe. But, when he comes home, I put it back where it was. How can I insult him that way? I don't know what to do. I live from day to day, boys. I tell you, I know every thought in his mind. It sounds so old-fashioned and silly, but I tell you he put his whole life into you and you've turned your backs on him. *(She is bent over in chair, weeping, her face in her hands.)* Biff, I swear to God! Biff, his life is in your hands!
Happy *(to Biff).* How do you like that damned fool!
Biff *(kissing her).* All right, pal, all right. It's all settled now. I've been remiss. I know that, Mom. But now I'll stay, and I swear to you, I'll apply myself. *(Kneeling in front of her, in a fever of self-reproach.)* It's just—you see, Mom, I don't fit in business. Not that I won't try. I'll try, and I'll make good.
Happy. Sure you will. The trouble with you in business was you never tried to please people.
Biff. I know, I—
Happy. Like when you worked for Harrison's. Bob Harrison said you were tops, and then you go and do some damn fool thing like whistling whole songs in the elevator like a comedian.

Biff *(against Happy).*   So what? I like to whistle sometimes.

Happy.   You don't raise a guy to a responsible job who whistles in the elevator!

Linda.   Well, don't argue about it now.

Happy.   Like when you'd go off and swim in the middle of the day instead of taking the line around.

Biff *(his resentment rising).*   Well, don't you run off? You take off sometimes, don't you? On a nice summer day?

Happy.   Yeah, but I cover myself!

Linda.   Boys!

Happy.   If I'm going to take a fade the boss can call any number where I'm supposed to be and they'll swear to him that I just left. I'll tell you something that I hate to say, Biff, but in the business world some of them think you're crazy.

Biff *(angered).*   Screw the business world!

Happy.   All right, screw it! Great, but cover yourself!

Linda.   Hap, Hap!

Biff.   I don't care what they think! They've laughed at Dad for years, and you know why? Because we don't belong in this nuthouse of a city! We should be mixing cement on some open plain, or—or carpenters. A carpenter is allowed to whistle!

Willy walks in from the entrance of the house, at left.

Willy.   Even your grandfather was better than a carpenter. *(Pause. They watch him.)* You never grew up. Bernard does not whistle in the elevator, I assure you.

Biff *(as though to laugh Willy out of it).*   Yeah, but you do, Pop.

Willy.   I never in my life whistled in an elevator! And who in the business world thinks I'm crazy?

Biff.   I didn't mean it like that, Pop. Now don't make a whole thing out of it, will ya?

Willy.   Go back to the West! Be a carpenter, a cowboy, enjoy yourself!

Linda.   Willy, he was just saying—

Willy.   I heard what he said!

Happy *(trying to quiet Willy).*   Hey, Pop, come on now . . .

Willy *(continuing over Happy's line).*   They laugh at me, heh? Go to Filene's, go to the Hub, go to Slattery's, Boston. Call out the name Willy Loman and see what happens! Big shot!

Biff.   All right, Pop.

Willy.   Big!

Biff.   All right!

Willy.   Why do you always insult me?

Biff.   I didn't say a word. *(To Linda.)* Did I say a word?

Linda.   He didn't say anything, Willy.

Willy *(going to the doorway of the living-room).*   All right, good night, good night.

Linda.   Willy, dear, he just decided . . .

Willy *(to Biff)*.   If you get tired hanging around tomorrow, paint the ceiling I put up in the living-room.

Biff.   I'm leaving early tomorrow.

Happy.   He's going to see Bill Oliver, Pop.

Willy *(interestedly)*.   Oliver? For what?

Biff *(with reserve, but trying, trying)*.   He always said he'd stake me. I'd like to go into business, so maybe I can take him up on it.

Linda.   Isn't that wonderful?

Willy.   Don't interrupt. What's wonderful about it? There's fifty men in the City of New York who'd stake him. *(To Biff.)* Sporting goods?

Biff.   I guess so. I know something about it and—

Willy.   He knows something about it! You know sporting goods better than Spalding, for God's sake! How much is he giving you?

Biff.   I don't know, I didn't even see him yet, but—

Willy.   Then what're you talkin' about?

Biff *(getting angry)*.   Well, all I said was I'm gonna see him, that's all!

Willy *(turning away)*.   Ah, you're counting your chickens again.

Biff *(starting left for the stairs)*.   Oh, Jesus, I'm going to sleep!

Willy *(calling after him)*.   Don't curse in this house!

Biff *(turning)*.   Since when did you get so clean?

Happy *(trying to stop them)*.   Wait a . . .

Willy.   Don't use that language to me! I won't have it!

Happy *(grabbing Biff, shouts)*.   Wait a minute! I got an idea. I got a feasible idea. Come here, Biff, let's talk this over now, let's talk some sense here. When I was down in Florida last time, I thought of a great idea to sell sporting goods. It just came back to me. You and I, Biff—we have a line, the Loman Line. We train a couple of weeks, and put on a couple of exhibitions, see?

Willy.   That's an idea!

Happy.   Wait! We form two basketball teams, see? Two water-polo teams. We play each other. It's a million dollars' worth of publicity. Two brothers, see? The Loman Brothers. Displays in the Royal Palms—all the hotels. And banners over the ring and the basketball court: "Loman Brothers." Baby, we could sell sporting goods!

Willy.   That is a one-million-dollar idea!

Linda.   Marvelous!

Biff.   I'm in great shape as far as that's concerned.

Happy.   And the beauty of it is, Biff, it wouldn't be like a business. We'd be out playin' ball again . . .

Biff *(enthused)*.   Yeah, that's . . .

Willy.   Million-dollar . . .

Happy.   And you wouldn't get fed up with it, Biff. It'd be the family again. There'd be the old honor, and comradeship, and if you wanted to go off for a swim or somethin'—well, you'd do it! Without some smart cooky gettin' up ahead of you!

Willy. Lick the world! You guys together could absolutely lick the civilized world.

Biff. I'll see Oliver tomorrow. Hap, if we could work that out . . .

Linda. Maybe things are beginning to—

Willy *(wildly enthused, to Linda).* Stop interrupting! *(To Biff.)* But don't wear sport jacket and slacks when you see Oliver.

Biff. No, I'll—

Willy. A business suit, and talk as little as possible, and don't crack any jokes.

Biff. He did like me. Always liked me.

Linda. He loved you!

Willy *(to Linda).* Will you stop! *(To Biff.)* Walk in very serious. You are not applying for a boy's job. Money is to pass. Be quiet, fine, and serious. Everybody likes a kidder, but nobody lends him money.

Happy. I'll try to get some myself, Biff. I'm sure I can.

Willy. I see great things for you kids, I think your troubles are over. But remember, start big and you'll end big. Ask for fifteen. How much you gonna ask for?

Biff. Gee, I don't know—

Willy. And don't say "Gee." "Gee" is a boy's word. A man walking in for fifteen thousand dollars does not say "Gee!"

Biff. Ten, I think, would be top though.

Willy. Don't be so modest. You always started too low. Walk in with a big laugh. Don't look worried. Start off with a couple of your good stories to lighten things up. It's not what you say, it's how you say it—because personality always wins the day.

Linda. Oliver always thought the highest of him—

Willy. Will you let me talk?

Biff. Don't yell at her, Pop, will ya?

Willy *(angrily).* I was talking, wasn't I?

Biff. I don't like you yelling at her all the time, and I'm tellin' you, that's all.

Willy. What're you, takin' over this house?

Linda. Willy—

Willy *(turning on her).* Don't take his side all the time, goddammit!

Biff *(furiously).* Stop yelling at her!

Willy *(suddenly pulling on his cheek, beaten down, guilt ridden).* Give my best to Bill Oliver—he may remember me. *(He exits through the living-room doorway.)*

Linda *(her voice subdued).* What'd you have to start that for? *(Biff turns away.)* You see how sweet he was as soon as you talked hopefully? *(She goes over to Biff.)* Come up and say good night to him. Don't let him go to bed that way.

Happy. Come on, Biff, let's buck him up.

Linda. Please, dear. Just say good night. It takes so little to make him happy. Come. *(She goes through the living-room doorway, calling upstairs from within the living-room.)* Your pajamas are hanging in the bathroom, Willy!

Happy (*looking toward where Linda went out*).   What a woman! They broke the mold when they made her. You know that, Biff?

Biff.   He's off salary. My God, working on commission!

Happy.   Well, let's face it: he's no hot-shot selling man. Except that sometimes, you have to admit, he's a sweet personality.

Biff (*deciding*).   Lend me ten bucks, will ya? I want to buy some new ties.

Happy.   I'll take you to a place I know. Beautiful stuff. Wear one of my striped shirts tomorrow.

Biff.   She got gray. Mom got awful old. Gee, I'm gonna go in to Oliver tomorrow and knock him for a—

Happy.   Come on up. Tell that to Dad. Let's give him a whirl. Come on.

Biff (*steamed up*).   You know, with ten thousand bucks, boy!

Happy (*as they go into the living-room*).   That's the talk, Biff, that's the first time I've heard the old confidence out of you! (*From within the living-room, fading off.*) You're gonna live with me, kid, and any babe you want just say the word . . . (*The last lines are hardly heard. They are mounting the stairs to their parents' bedroom.*)

Linda (*entering her bedroom and addressing Willy, who is in the bathroom. She is straightening the bed for him*).   Can you do anything about the shower? It drips.

Willy (*from the bathroom*).   All of a sudden everything falls to pieces! Goddam plumbing, oughta be sued, those people. I hardly finished putting it in and the thing . . . (*His words rumble off.*)

Linda.   I'm just wondering if Oliver will remember him. You think he might?

Willy (*coming out of the bathroom in his pajamas*).   Remember him? What's the matter with you, you crazy? If he'd've stayed with Oliver he'd be on top by now! Wait'll Oliver gets a look at him. You don't know the average caliber any more. The average young man today—(*he is getting into bed*)—is got a caliber of zero. Greatest thing in the world for him was to bum around.

Biff and Happy enter the bedroom. Slight pause.

Willy (*stops short, looking at Biff*).   Glad to hear it, boy.

Happy.   He wanted to say good night to you, sport.

Willy (*to Biff*).   Yeah. Knock him dead, boy. What'd you want to tell me?

Biff.   Just take it easy, Pop. Good night. (*He turns to go.*)

Willy (*unable to resist*).   And if anything falls off the desk while you're talking to him—like a package or something—don't you pick it up. They have office boys for that.

Linda.   I'll make a big breakfast—

Willy.   Will you let me finish? (*To Biff.*) Tell him you were in the business in the West. Not farm work.

Biff.   All right, Dad.

Linda.   I think everything—

Willy *(going right through her speech).*   And don't undersell yourself. No less than fifteen thousand dollars.

Biff *(unable to bear him).*   Okay. Good night, Mom. *(He starts moving.)*

Willy.   Because you got a greatness in you, Biff, remember that. You got all kinds a greatness . . . *(He lies back, exhausted. Biff walks out.)*

Linda *(calling after Biff).*   Sleep well, darling!

Happy.   I'm gonna get married, Mom. I wanted to tell you.

Linda.   Go to sleep, dear.

Happy *(going).*   I just wanted to tell you.

Willy.   Keep up the good work. *(Happy exits.)* God . . . remember that Ebbets Field game? The championship of the city?

Linda.   Just rest. Should I sing to you?

Willy.   Yeah. Sing to me. *(Linda hums a soft lullaby.)* When that team came out—he was the tallest, remember?

Linda.   Oh, yes. And in gold.

Biff enters the darkened kitchen, takes a cigarette, and leaves the house. He comes downstage into a golden pool of light. He smokes, staring at the night.

Willy.   Like a young god. Hercules—something like that. And the sun, the sun all around him. Remember how he waved to me? Right up from the field, with the representatives of three colleges standing by? And the buyers I brought, and the cheers when he came out—Loman, Loman, Loman! God Almighty, he'll be great yet. A star like that, magnificent, can never really fade away!

The light on Willy is fading. The gas heater begins to glow through the kitchen wall, near the stairs, a blue flame beneath red coils.

Linda *(timidly).*   Willy dear, what has he got against you?

Willy.   I'm so tired. Don't talk any more.

Biff slowly returns to the kitchen. He stops, stares toward the heater.

Linda.   Will you ask Howard to let you work in New York?

Willy.   First thing in the morning. Everything'll be all right.

Biff reaches behind the heater and draws out a length of rubber tubing. He is horrified and turns his head toward Willy's room, still dimly lit, from which the strains of Linda's desperate but monotonous humming rise.

Willy *(staring through the window into the moonlight).*   Gee, look at the moon moving between the buildings!

Biff wraps the tubing around his hand and quickly goes up the stairs.

Curtain

Act II

Music is heard, gay and bright. The curtain rises as the music fades away. Willy, in shirt sleeves, is sitting at the kitchen table, sipping coffee, his hat in his lap. Linda is filling his cup when she can.

Willy. Wonderful coffee. Meal in itself.

Linda. Can I make you some eggs?

Willy. No. Take a breath.

Linda. You look so rested, dear.

Willy. I slept like a dead one. First time in months. Imagine, sleeping till ten on a Tuesday morning. Boys left nice and early, heh?

Linda. They were out of here by eight o'clock.

Willy. Good work!

Linda. It was so thrilling to see them leaving together. I can't get over the shaving lotion in this house!

Willy *(smiling).* Mmm—

Linda. Biff was very changed this morning. His whole attitude seemed to be hopeful. He couldn't wait to get downtown to see Oliver.

Willy. He's heading for a change. There's no question, there simply are certain men that take longer to get—solidified. How did he dress?

Linda. His blue suit. He's so handsome in that suit. He could be a—anything in that suit!

Willy gets up from the table. Linda holds his jacket for him.

Willy. There's no question, no question at all. Gee, on the way home tonight I'd like to buy some seeds.

Linda *(laughing).* That'd be wonderful. But not enough sun gets back there. Nothing'll grow any more.

Willy. You wait, kid, before it's all over we're gonna get a little place out in the country, and I'll raise some vegetables, a couple of chickens . . .

Linda. You'll do it yet, dear.

Willy walks out of his jacket. Linda follows him.

Willy. And they'll get married, and come for a weekend. I'd build a little guest house. 'Cause I got so many fine tools, all I'd need would be a little lumber and some peace of mind.

Linda (*joyfully*). I sewed the lining . . .

Willy. I could build two guest houses, so they'd both come. Did he decide how much he's going to ask Oliver for?

Linda (*getting him into the jacket*). He didn't mention it, but I imagine ten or fifteen thousand. You going to talk to Howard today?

Willy. Yeah. I'll put it to him straight and simple. He'll just have to take me off the road.

Linda. And Willy, don't forget to ask for a little advance, because we've got the insurance premium. It's the grace period now.

Willy. That's a hundred . . . ?

Linda. A hundred and eight, sixty-eight. Because we're a little short again.

Willy. Why are we short?

Linda. Well, you had the motor job on the car . . .

Willy. That goddam Studebaker!

Linda. And you got one more payment on the refrigerator . . .

Willy. But it just broke again!

Linda. Well, it's old, dear.

Willy. I told you we should've bought a well-advertised machine. Charley bought a General Electric and it's twenty years old and it's still good, that son-of-a-bitch.

Linda. But, Willy—

Willy. Whoever heard of a Hastings refrigerator? Once in my life I would like to own something outright before it's broken! I'm always in a race with the junkyard! I just finished paying for the car and it's on its last legs. The refrigerator consumes belts like a goddam maniac. They time those things. They time them so when you finally paid for them, they're used up.

Linda (*buttoning up his jacket as he unbuttons it*). All told, about two hundred dollars would carry us, dear. But that includes the last payment on the mortgage. After this payment, Willy, the house belongs to us.

Willy. It's twenty-five years!

Linda. Biff was nine years old when we bought it.

Willy. Well, that's a great thing. To weather a twenty-five year mortgage is—

Linda. It's an accomplishment.

Willy. All the cement, the lumber, the reconstruction I put in this house! There ain't a crack to be found in it any more.

Linda. Well, it served its purpose.

Willy. What purpose? Some stranger'll come along, move in, and that's that. If only Biff would take this house, and raise a family . . . (*He starts to go.*) Good-by, I'm late.

Linda (*suddenly remembering*). Oh, I forgot! You're supposed to meet them for dinner.

Willy. Me?

Linda.   At Frank's Chop House on Forty-eighth near Sixth Avenue.

Willy.   Is that so! How about you?

Linda.   No, just the three of you. They're gonna blow you to a big meal!

Willy.   Don't say! Who thought of that?

Linda.   Biff came to me this morning, Willy, and he said, "Tell Dad, we want to blow him to a big meal." Be there six o'clock. You and your two boys are going to have dinner.

Willy.   Gee whiz! That's really somethin'. I'm gonna knock Howard for a loop, kid. I'll get an advance, and I'll come home with a New York job. Goddammit, now I'm gonna do it!

Linda.   Oh, that's the spirit, Willy!

Willy.   I will never get behind a wheel the rest of my life!

Linda.   It's changing, Willy, I can feel it changing!

Willy.   Beyond a question. G'by, I'm late. (*He starts to go again.*)

Linda (*calling after him as she runs to the kitchen table for a handkerchief*). You got your glasses?

Willy (*feels for them, then comes back in*).   Yeah, yeah, got my glasses.

Linda (*giving him the handkerchief*).   And a handkerchief.

Willy.   Yeah, handkerchief.

Linda.   And your saccharine?

Willy.   Yeah, my saccharine.

Linda.   Be careful on the subway stairs.

She kisses him, and a silk stocking is seen hanging from her hand. Willy notices it.

Willy.   Will you stop mending stockings? At least while I'm in the house. It gets me nervous. I can't tell you. Please.

Linda hides the stocking in her hand as she follows Willy across the forestage in front of the house.

Linda.   Remember, Frank's Chop House.

Willy (*passing the apron*).   Maybe beets would grow out there.

Linda (*laughing*).   But you tried so many times.

Willy.   Yeah. Well, don't work hard today. (*He disappears around the right corner of the house.*)

Linda.   Be careful!

As Willy vanishes, Linda waves to him. Suddenly the phone rings. She runs across the stage and into the kitchen and lifts it.

Linda.   Hello? Oh, Biff! I'm so glad you called, I just . . . Yes, sure, I just told him. Yes, he'll be there for dinner at six o'clock, I didn't forget. Listen, I was just dying to tell you. You know that little rubber pipe I told you about? That he connected to the gas heater? I finally decided to go down the cellar this morning and take it away and destroy it. But it's gone! Imagine? He took it away himself, it isn't there! *(She listens.)* When? Oh, then you took it. Oh—nothing, it's just that I'd hoped he'd taken it away himself. Oh, I'm not worried, darling, because this morning he left in such high spirits, it was like the old days! I'm not afraid any more. Did Mr. Oliver see you? . . . Well, you wait there then. And make a nice impression on him, darling. Just don't perspire too much before you see him. And have a nice time with Dad. He may have big news too! . . . That's right, a New York job. And be sweet to him tonight, dear. Be loving to him. Because he's only a little boat looking for a harbor. *(She is trembling with sorrow and joy.)* Oh, that's wonderful, Biff, you'll save his life. Thanks, darling. Just put your arm around him when he comes into the restaurant. Give him a smile. That's the boy . . . Good-by, dear. . . . You got your comb? . . . That's fine. Good-by, Biff dear.

In the middle of her speech, Howard Wagner, thirty-six, wheels in a small typewriter table on which is a wire-recording machine and proceeds to plug it in. This is on the left forestage. Light slowly fades on Linda as it rises on Howard. Howard is intent on threading the machine and only glances over his shoulder as Willy appears.

Willy.   Pst! Pst!
Howard.   Hello, Willy, come in.
Willy.   Like to have a little talk with you, Howard.
Howard.   Sorry to keep you waiting. I'll be with you in a minute.
Willy.   What's that, Howard?
Howard.   Didn't you ever see one of these? Wire recorder.
Willy.   Oh. Can we talk a minute?
Howard.   Records things. Just got delivery yesterday. Been driving me crazy, the most terrific machine I ever saw in my life. I was up all night with it.
Willy.   What do you do with it?
Howard.   I bought it for dictation, but you can do anything with it. Listen to this. I had it home last night. Listen to what I picked up. The first one is my daughter. Get this. *(He flicks the switch and "Roll Out the Barrel" is heard being whistled.)* Listen to that kid whistle.
Willy.   That is lifelike, isn't it?
Howard.   Seven years old. Get that tone.
Willy.   Ts, ts. Like to ask a little favor if you . . .

The whistling breaks off, and the voice of Howard's daughter is heard.

His Daughter.   "Now you, Daddy."
Howard.   She's crazy for me! *(Again the same song is whistled.)* That's me! Ha! *(He winks.)*

Willy. You're very good!

The whistling breaks off again. The machine runs silent for a moment.

Howard. Sh! Get this now, this is my son.
His Son. "The capital of Alabama is Montgomery; the capital of Arizona is Phoenix; the capital of Arkansas is Little Rock; the capital of California is Sacramento . . ." *(and on, and on).*
Howard *(holding up five fingers).* Five years old, Willy!
Willy. He'll make an announcer some day!
His Son *(continuing).* "The capital . . ."
Howard. Get that—alphabetical order! *(The machine breaks off suddenly.)* Wait a minute. The maid kicked the plug out.
Willy. It certainly is a—
Howard. Sh, for God's sake!
His Son. "It's nine o'clock, Bulova watch time. So I have to go to sleep."
Willy. That really is—
Howard. Wait a minute! The next is my wife.

They wait.

Howard's Voice. "Go on, say something." *(Pause.)* "Well, you gonna talk?"
His Wife. "I can't think of anything."
Howard's Voice. "Well, talk—it's turning."
His Wife *(shyly, beaten).* "Hello." *(Silence.)* "Oh, Howard, I can't talk into this . . ."
Howard *(snapping the machine off).* That was my wife.
Willy. That is a wonderful machine. Can we—
Howard. I tell you, Willy, I'm gonna take my camera, and my bandsaw, and all my hobbies, and out they go. This is the most fascinating relaxation I ever found.
Willy. I think I'll get one myself.
Howard. Sure, they're only a hundred and a half. You can't do without it. Supposing you wanna hear Jack Benny, see? But you can't be at home at that hour. So you tell the maid to turn the radio on when Jack Benny comes on, and this automatically goes on with the radio . . .
Willy. And when you come home you . . .
Howard. You can come home twelve o'clock, one o'clock, any time you like, and you get yourself a Coke and sit yourself down, throw the switch, and there's Jack Benny's program in the middle of the night!
Willy. I'm definitely going to get one. Because lots of time I'm on the road, and I think to myself, what I must be missing on the radio!
Howard. Don't you have a radio in the car?
Willy. Well, yeah, but who ever thinks of turning it on?

Howard. Say, aren't you supposed to be in Boston?

Willy. That's what I want to talk to you about, Howard. You got a minute? *(He draws a chair in from the wing.)*

Howard. What happened? What're you doing here?

Willy. Well . . .

Howard. You didn't crack up again, did you?

Willy. Oh, no. No . . .

Howard. Geez, you had me worried there for a minute. What's the trouble?

Willy. Well, tell you the truth, Howard. I've come to the decision that I'd rather not travel any more.

Howard. Not travel! Well, what'll you do?

Willy. Remember, Christmas time, when you had the party here? You said you'd try to think of some spot for me here in town.

Howard. With us?

Willy. Well, sure.

Howard. Oh, yeah, yeah. I remember. Well, I couldn't think of anything for you, Willy.

Willy. I tell ya, Howard. The kids are all grown up, y'know. I don't need much any more. If I could take home—well, sixty-five dollars a week, I could swing it.

Howard. Yeah, but Willy, see I—

Willy. I tell ya why, Howard. Speaking frankly and between the two of us, y'know—I'm just a little tired.

Howard. Oh, I could understand that, Willy. But you're a road man, Willy, and we do a road business. We've only got a half-dozen salesmen on the floor here.

Willy. God knows, Howard, I never asked a favor of any man. But I was with the firm when your father used to carry you in here in his arms.

Howard. I know that, Willy, but—

Willy. Your father came to me the day you were born and asked me what I thought of the name of Howard, may he rest in peace.

Howard. I appreciate that, Willy, but there just is no spot here for you. If I had a spot I'd slam you right in, but I just don't have a single solitary spot.

He looks for his lighter. Willy has picked it up and gives it to him. Pause.

Willy *(with increasing anger).* Howard, all I need to set my table is fifty dollars a week.

Howard. But where am I going to put you, kid?

Willy. Look, it isn't a question of whether I can sell merchandise, is it?

Howard. No, but it's a business, kid, and everybody's gotta pull his own weight.

Willy *(desperately).* Just let me tell you a story, Howard—

Howard. 'Cause you gotta admit, business is business.

Willy *(angrily).* Business is definitely business, but just listen for a minute.

You don't understand this. When I was a boy—eighteen, nineteen—I was already on the road. And there was a question in my mind as to whether selling had a future for me. Because in those days I had a yearning to go to Alaska. See, there were three gold strikes in one month in Alaska, and I felt like going out. Just for the ride, you might say.

Howard (*barely interested*).   Don't say.

Willy.   Oh, yeah, my father lived many years in Alaska. He was an adventurous man. We've got quite a little streak of self-reliance in our family. I thought I'd go out with my older brother and try to locate him, and maybe settle in the North with the old man. And I was almost decided to go, when I met a salesman in the Parker House. His name was Dave Singleman. And he was eighty-four years old, and he'd drummed merchandise in thirty-one states. And old Dave, he'd go up to his room, y'understand, put on his green velvet slippers—I'll never forget—and pick up his phone and call the buyers, and without ever leaving his room, at the age of eighty-four, he made his living. And when I saw that, I realized that selling was the greatest career a man could want. 'Cause what could be more satisfying than to be able to go, at the age of eighty-four, into twenty or thirty different cities, and pick up a phone, and be remembered and loved and helped by so many different people? Do you know? when he died—and by the way he died the death of a salesman, in his green velvet slippers in the smoker of the New York, New Haven, and Hartford, going into Boston—when he died, hundreds of salesmen and buyers were at his funeral. Things were sad on a lotta trains for months after that. (*He stands up. Howard has not looked at him.*) In those days there was personality in it, Howard. There was respect, and comradeship, and gratitude in it. Today, it's all cut and dried, and there's no chance for bringing friendship to bear—or personality. You see what I mean? They don't know me any more.

Howard (*moving away, to the right*).   That's just the thing, Willy.

Willy.   If I had forty dollars a week—that's all I'd need. Forty dollars, Howard.

Howard.   Kid, I can't take blood from a stone, I—

Willy (*desperation is on him now*).   Howard, the year Al Smith[2] was nominated, your father came to me and—

Howard (*starting to go off*).   I've got to see some people, kid.

Willy (*stopping him*).   I'm talking about your father! There were promises made across this desk! You mustn't tell me you've got people to see—I put thirty-four years into this firm, Howard, and now I can't pay my insurance! You can't eat the orange and throw the peel away—a man is not a piece of fruit! (*After a pause.*) Now pay attention. Your father—in 1928 I had a big year. I averaged a hundred and seventy dollars a week in commissions.

Howard (*impatiently*).   Now, Willy, you never averaged—

Willy (*banging his hand on the desk*).   I averaged a hundred and seventy dollars a week in the year of 1928! And your father came to me—or rather, I was

---

[2] The Democratic candidate for president in 1928; he lost to Herbert Hoover.

in the office here—it was right over this desk—and he put his hand on my shoulder—

Howard (*getting up*).   You'll have to excuse me, Willy, I gotta see some people. Pull yourself together. (*Going out.*) I'll be back in a little while.

On Howard's exit, the light on his chair grows very bright and strange.

Willy.   Pull myself together! What the hell did I say to him? My God, I was yelling at him! How could I! (*Willy breaks off, staring at the light, which occupies the chair, animating it. He approaches this chair, standing across the desk from it.*) Frank, Frank, don't you remember what you told me that time? How you put your hand on my shoulder, and Frank . . . (*He leans on the desk and as he speaks the dead man's name he accidentally switches on the recorder, and instantly*):

Howard's Son.   ". . . of New York is Albany. The capital of Ohio is Cincinnati, the capital of Rhode Island is . . . " (*The recitation continues.*)

Willy (*leaping away with fright, shouting*).   Ha! Howard! Howard! Howard!

Howard (*rushing in*).   What happened?

Willy (*pointing at the machine, which continues nasally, childishly, with the capital cities*).   Shut it off! Shut it off!

Howard (*pulling the plug out*).   Look, Willy . . .

Willy (*pressing his hands to his eyes*).   I gotta get myself some coffee. I'll get some coffee . . .

Willy starts to walk out. Howard stops him.

Howard (*rolling up the cord*).   Willy, look . . .

Willy.   I'll go to Boston.

Howard.   Willy, you can't go to Boston for us.

Willy.   Why can't I go?

Howard.   I don't want you to represent us. I've been meaning to tell you for a long time now.

Willy.   Howard, are you firing me?

Howard.   I think you need a good long rest, Willy.

Willy.   Howard—

Howard.   And when you feel better, come back, and we'll see if we can work something out.

Willy.   But I gotta earn money, Howard. I'm in no position to—

Howard.   Where are your sons? Why don't your sons give you a hand?

Willy.   They're working on a very big deal.

Howard.   This is no time for false pride, Willy. You go to your sons and you tell them that you're tired. You've got two great boys, haven't you?

Willy.   Oh, no question, no question, but in the meantime . . .

Howard.   Then that's that, heh?

Willy. All right, I'll go to Boston tomorrow.

Howard. No, no.

Willy. I can't throw myself on my sons. I'm not a cripple!

Howard. Look, kid, I'm busy this morning.

Willy (*grasping Howard's arm*). Howard, you've got to let me go to Boston!

Howard (*hard, keeping himself under control*). I've got a line of people to see this morning. Sit down, take five minutes, and pull yourself together, and then go home, will ya? I need the office, Willy. (*He starts to go, turns, remembering the recorder, starts to push off the table holding the recorder.*) Oh, yeah. Whenever you can this week, stop by and drop off the samples. You'll feel better, Willy, and then come back and we'll talk. Pull yourself together, kid, there's people outside.

Howard exits, pushing the table off left. Willy stares into space, exhausted. Now the music is heard—Ben's music—first distantly, then closer, closer. As Willy speaks, Ben enters from the right. He carries valise and umbrella.

Willy. Oh, Ben, how did you do it? What is the answer? Did you wind up the Alaska deal already?

Ben. Doesn't take much time if you know what you're doing. Just a short business trip. Boarding ship in an hour. Wanted to say good-by.

Willy. Ben, I've got to talk to you.

Ben (*glancing at his watch*). Haven't the time, William.

Willy (*crossing the apron to Ben*). Ben, nothing's working out. I don't know what to do.

Ben. Now, look here, William. I've bought timberland in Alaska and I need a man to look after things for me.

Willy. God, timberland! Me and my boys in those grand outdoors!

Ben. You've a new continent at your doorstep, William. Get out of these cities, they're full of talk and time payments and courts of law. Screw on your fists and you can fight for a fortune up there.

Willy. Yes, yes! Linda, Linda!

Linda enters as of old, with the wash.

Linda. Oh, you're back?

Ben. I haven't much time.

Willy. No, wait! Linda, he's got a proposition for me in Alaska.

Linda. But you've got—(*To Ben.*) He's got a beautiful job here.

Willy. But in Alaska, kid, I could—

Linda. You're doing well enough, Willy!

Ben (*to Linda*). Enough for what, my dear?

Linda (*frightened of Ben and angry at him*). Don't say those things to him! Enough to be happy right here, right now. (*To Willy, while Ben laughs.*) Why must everybody conquer the world? You're well liked, and the boys love you, and someday—*(to Ben)*—why, old man Wagner told him just the other day that if he keeps it up he'll be a member of the firm, didn't he, Willy?

Willy. Sure, sure. I am building something with this firm, Ben, and if a man is building something he must be on the right track, mustn't he?

Ben. What are you building? Lay your hand on it. Where is it?

Willy *(hesitantly).* That's true, Linda, there's nothing.

Linda. Why? *(To Ben.)* There's a man eighty-four years old—

Willy. That's right, Ben, that's right. When I look at that man I say, what is there to worry about?

Ben. Bah!

Willy. It's true, Ben. All he has to do is go into any city, pick up the phone, and he's making his living and you know why?

Ben *(picking up his valise).* I've got to go.

Willy *(holding Ben back).* Look at this boy!

Biff, in his high school sweater, enters carrying suitcase. Happy carries Biff's shoulder guards, gold helmet, and football pants.

Willy. Without a penny to his name, three great universities are begging for him, and from there the sky's the limit, because it's not what you do, Ben. It's who you know and the smile on your face! It's contacts, Ben, contacts! The whole wealth of Alaska passes over the lunch table at the Commodore Hotel, and that's the wonder, the wonder of this country, that a man can end with diamonds here on the basis of being liked! *(He turns to Biff.)* And that's why when you get out on that field today it's important. Because thousands of people will be rooting for you and loving you. *(To Ben, who has again begun to leave.)* And Ben! when he walks into a business office his name will sound out like a bell and all the doors will open to him! I've seen it, Ben, I've seen it a thousand times! You can't feel it with your hand like timber, but it's there!

Ben. Good-by, William.

Willy. Ben, am I right? Don't you think I'm right? I value your advice.

Ben. There's a new continent at your doorstep, William. You could walk out rich. Rich! *(He is gone.)*

Willy. We'll do it here, Ben! You hear me? We're gonna do it here!

Young Bernard rushes in. The gay music of the Boys is heard.

Bernard. Oh, gee, I was afraid you left already!

Willy. Why? What time is it?

Bernard. It's half-past one!

Willy. Well, come on, everybody! Ebbets Field next stop! Where's the pennants? *(He rushes through the wall-line of the kitchen and out into the living-room.)*

Linda (*to Biff*).   Did you pack fresh underwear?

Biff (*who has been limbering up*).   I want to go!

Bernard.   Biff, I'm carrying your helmet, ain't I?

Happy.   I'm carrying the helmet.

Bernard.   How am I going to get in the locker room?

Linda.   Let him carry the shoulder guards. (*She puts her coat and hat on in the kitchen.*)

Bernard.   Can I, Biff? 'Cause I told everybody I'm going to be in the locker room.

Happy.   In Ebbets Field it's the clubhouse.

Bernard.   I meant the clubhouse. Biff!

Happy.   Biff!

Biff (*grandly, after a slight pause*).   Let him carry the shoulder guards.

Happy (*as he gives Bernard the shoulder guards*).   Stay close to us now.

Willy rushes in with the pennants.

Willy (*handing them out*).   Everybody wave when Biff comes out on the field. (*Happy and Bernard run off.*) You set now, boy?

The music has died away.

Biff.   Ready to go, Pop. Every muscle is ready.

Willy (*at the edge of the apron*).   You realize what this means?

Biff.   That's right, Pop.

Willy (*feeling Biff's muscles*).   You're comin' home this afternoon captain of the All-Scholastic Championship Team of the City of New York.

Biff.   I got it, Pop. And remember, pal, when I take off my helmet, that touchdown is for you.

Willy.   Let's go! (*He is starting out, with his arm around Biff, when Charley enters, as of old, in knickers.*) I got no room for you, Charley.

Charley.   Room? For what?

Willy.   In the car.

Charley.   You goin' for a ride? I wanted to shoot some casino.

Willy (*furiously*).   Casino! (*Incredulously.*) Don't you realize what today is?

Linda.   Oh, he knows, Willy. He's just kidding you.

Willy.   That's nothing to kid about!

Charley.   No, Linda, what's goin' on?

Linda.   He's playing in Ebbets Field.

Charley.   Baseball in this weather?

Willy.   Don't talk to him. Come on, come on! (*He is pushing them out.*)

Charley.   Wait a minute, didn't you hear the news?

Willy.   What?

Charley.   Don't you listen to the radio? Ebbets Field just blew up.

Willy. You go to hell! *(Charley laughs. Pushing them out.)* Come on, come on! We're late.

Charley *(as they go).* Knock a homer, Biff, knock a homer!

Willy *(the last to leave, turning to Charley).* I don't think that was funny, Charley. This is the greatest day of his life.

Charley. Willy, when are you going to grow up?

Willy. Yeah, heh? When this game is over, Charley, you'll be laughing out of the other side of your face. They'll be calling him another Red Grange. Twenty-five thousand a year.

Charley *(kidding).* Is that so?

Willy. Yeah, that's so.

Charley. Well, then, I'm sorry, Willy. But tell me something.

Willy. What?

Charley. Who is Red Grange?

Willy. Put up your hands. Goddam you, put up your hands!

Charley, chuckling, shakes his head and walks away, around the left corner of the stage. Willy follows him. The music rises to a mocking frenzy.

Willy. Who the hell do you think you are, better than everybody else? You don't know everything, you big, ignorant, stupid . . . Put up your hands!

Light rises, on the right side of the forestage, on a small table in the reception room of Charley's office. Traffic sounds are heard. Bernard, now mature, sits whistling to himself. A pair of tennis rackets and an overnight bag are on the floor beside him.

Willy *(offstage).* What are you walking away for? Don't walk away! If you're going to say something say it to my face! I know you laugh at me behind my back. You'll laugh out of the other side of your goddam face after this game. Touchdown! Touchdown! Eighty thousand people! Touchdown! Right between the goal posts.

Bernard is a quiet, earnest, but self-assured young man. Willy's voice is coming from right upstage now. Bernard lowers his feet off the table and listens. Jenny, his father's secretary, enters.

Jenny *(distressed).* Say, Bernard, will you go out in the hall?

Bernard. What is that noise? Who is it?

Jenny. Mr. Loman. He just got off the elevator.

Bernard *(getting up).* Who's he arguing with?

Jenny. Nobody. There's nobody with him. I can't deal with him any more, and your father gets all upset everytime he comes. I've got a lot of typing to do, and your father's waiting to sign it. Will you see him?

Willy (*entering*).   Touchdown! Touch—(*He sees Jenny.*) Jenny, Jenny, good to see you. How're ya? Workin'? Or still honest?

Jenny.   Fine. How've you been feeling?

Willy.   Not much any more, Jenny. Ha, ha! (*He is surprised to see the rackets.*)

Bernard.   Hello, Uncle Willy.

Willy (*almost shocked*).   Bernard! Well, look who's here! (*He comes quickly, guiltily, to Bernard and warmly shakes his hand.*)

Bernard.   How are you? Good to see you.

Willy.   What are you doing here?

Bernard.   Oh, just stopped by to see Pop. Get off my feet till my train leaves. I'm going to Washington in a few minutes.

Willy.   Is he in?

Bernard.   Yes, he's in his office with the accountant. Sit down.

Willy (*sitting down*).   What're you going to do in Washington?

Bernard.   Oh, just a case I've got there, Willy.

Willy.   That so? (*Indicating the rackets.*) You going to play tennis there?

Bernard.   I'm staying with a friend who's got a court.

Willy.   Don't say. His own tennis court. Must be fine people, I bet.

Bernard.   They are, very nice. Dad tells me Biff's in town.

Willy (*with a big smile*).   Yeah, Biff's in. Working on a very big deal, Bernard.

Bernard.   What's Biff doing?

Willy.   Well, he's been doing very big things in the West. But he decided to establish himself here. Very big. We're having dinner. Did I hear your wife had a boy?

Bernard.   That's right. Our second.

Willy.   Two boys! What do you know!

Bernard.   What kind of a deal has Biff got?

Willy.   Well, Bill Oliver—very big sporting-goods man—he wants Biff very badly. Called him in from the West. Long distance, carte blanche, special deliveries. Your friends have their own private tennis court?

Bernard.   You still with the old firm, Willy?

Willy (*after a pause*).   I'm—I'm overjoyed to see how you made the grade, Bernard, overjoyed. It's an encouraging thing to see a young man really—really—Looks very good for Biff—very—(*He breaks off, then.*) Bernard—(*He is so full of emotion, he breaks off again.*)

Bernard.   What is it, Willy?

Willy (*small and alone*).   What—what's the secret?

Bernard.   What secret?

Willy.   How—how did you? Why didn't he ever catch on?

Bernard.   I wouldn't know that, Willy.

Willy (*confidentially, desperately*).   You were his friend, his boyhood friend. There's something I don't understand about it. His life ended after that Ebbets Field game. From the age of seventeen nothing good ever happened to him.

Bernard.   He never trained himself for anything.

Willy.   But he did, he did. After high school he took so many correspondence courses. Radio mechanics; television; God knows what, and never made the slightest mark.

Bernard (*taking off his glasses*).   Willy, do you want to talk candidly?

Willy (*rising, faces Bernard*).   I regard you as a very brilliant man, Bernard. I value your advice.

Bernard.   Oh, the hell with the advice, Willy. I couldn't advise you. There's just one thing I've always wanted to ask you. When he was supposed to graduate, and the math teacher flunked him—

Willy.   Oh, that son-of-a-bitch ruined his life.

Bernard.   Yeah, but, Willy, all he had to do was go to summer school and make up that subject.

Willy.   That's right, that's right.

Bernard.   Did you tell him not to go to summer school?

Willy.   Me? I begged him to go. I ordered him to go!

Bernard.   Then why wouldn't he go?

Willy.   Why? Why! Bernard, that question has been trailing me like a ghost for the last fifteen years. He flunked the subject, and laid down and died like a hammer hit him!

Bernard.   Take it easy, kid.

Willy.   Let me talk to you—I got nobody to talk to. Bernard, Bernard, was it my fault? Y'see? It keeps going around in my mind, maybe I did something to him. I got nothing to give him.

Bernard.   Don't take it so hard.

Willy.   Why did he lay down? What is the story there? You were his friend!

Bernard.   Willy, I remember, it was June, and our grades came out. And he'd flunked math.

Willy.   That son-of-a-bitch!

Bernard.   No, it wasn't right then. Biff just got very angry, I remember, and he was ready to enroll in summer school.

Willy (*surprised*).   He was?

Bernard.   He wasn't beaten by it at all. But then, Willy, he disappeared from the block for almost a month. And I got the idea that he'd gone up to New England to see you. Did he have a talk with you then?

Willy stares in silence.

Bernard.   Willy?

Willy (*with a strong edge of resentment in his voice*).   Yeah, he came to Boston. What about it?

Bernard.   Well, just that when he came back—I'll never forget this, it always mystifies me. Because I'd thought so well of Biff, even though he'd always taken advantage of me. I loved him, Willy, y'know? And he came back after that month and took his sneakers—remember those sneakers with "University of Virginia" printed on them? He was so proud of those, wore them every day. And he took them down in the cellar, and burned them up in the furnace. We had a fist fight. It lasted at least half an hour. Just the two of us, punching each other down the cellar, and crying right through it. I've often thought of how strange it was that I knew he'd given up his life. What happened in Boston, Willy?

Willy looks at him as at an intruder.

Bernard.   I just bring it up because you asked me.
Willy (*angrily*).   Nothing. What do you mean, "What happened?" What's that got to do with anything?
Bernard.   Well, don't get sore.
Willy.   What are you trying to do, blame it on me? If a boy lays down is that my fault?
Bernard.   Now, Willy, don't get—
Willy.   Well, don't—don't talk to me that way! What does that mean, "What happened?"

Charley enters. He is in his vest, and he carries a bottle of bourbon.

Charley.   Hey, you're going to miss that train. (*He waves the bottle.*)
Bernard.   Yeah, I'm going. (*He takes the bottle.*) Thanks, Pop. (*He picks up his rackets and bag.*) Good-by, Willy, and don't worry about it. You know. "If at first you don't succeed . . ."
Willy.   Yes, I believe in that.
Bernard.   But sometimes, Willy, it's better for a man just to walk away.
Willy.   Walk away?
Bernard.   That's right.
Willy.   But if you can't walk away?
Bernard (*after a slight pause*).   I guess that's when it's tough. (*Extending his hand.*) Good-by, Willy.
Willy (*shaking Bernard's hand*).   Good-by, boy.
Charley (*an arm on Bernard's shoulder*).   How do you like this kid? Gonna argue a case in front of the Supreme Court.
Bernard (*protesting*).   Pop!
Willy (*genuinely shocked, pained, and happy*).   No! The Supreme Court!
Bernard.   I gotta run. 'By, Dad!
Charley.   Knock 'em dead, Bernard!

Bernard goes off.

Willy (*as Charley takes out his wallet*).   The Supreme Court! And he didn't even mention it!
Charley (*counting out money on the desk*).   He don't have to—he's gonna do it.

Willy. And you never told him what to do, did you? You never took any interest in him.

Charley. My salvation is that I never took any interest in any thing. There's some money—fifty dollars. I got an accountant inside.

Willy. Charley, look . . . *(With difficulty.)* I got my insurance to pay. If you can manage it—I need a hundred and ten dollars.

Charley doesn't reply for a moment; merely stops moving.

Willy. I'd draw it from my bank but Linda would know, and I . . .

Charley. Sit down, Willy.

Willy *(moving toward the chair).* I'm keeping an account of everything, remember. I'll pay every penny back. *(He sits.)*

Charley. Now listen to me, Willy.

Willy. I want you to know I appreciate . . .

Charley *(sitting down on the table).* Willy, what're you doin'? What the hell is goin' on in your head?

Willy. Why? I'm simply . . .

Charley. I offered you a job. You can make fifty dollars a week. And I won't send you on the road.

Willy. I've got a job.

Charley. Without pay? What kind of a job is a job without pay? *(He rises.)* Now, look, kid, enough is enough. I'm no genius but I know when I'm being insulted.

Willy. Insulted!

Charley. Why don't you want to work for me?

Willy. What's the matter with you? I've got a job.

Charley. Then what're you walkin' in here every week for?

Willy *(getting up).* Well, if you don't want me to walk in here—

Charley. I am offering you a job.

Willy. I don't want your goddam job!

Charley. When the hell are you going to grow up?

Willy *(furiously).* You big ignoramus, if you say that to me again I'll rap you one! I don't care how big you are! *(He's ready to fight.)*

Pause.

Charley *(kindly, going to him).* How much do you need, Willy?

Willy. Charley, I'm strapped. I'm strapped. I don't know what to do. I was just fired.

Charley. Howard fired you?

Willy. That snotnose. Imagine that? I named him. I named him Howard.

Charley. Willy, when're you gonna realize that them things don't mean anything? You named him Howard, but you can't sell that. The only thing you got in this world is what you can sell. And the funny thing is that you're a salesman, and you don't know that.

Willy. I've always tried to think otherwise, I guess. I always felt that if a man was impressive, and well liked, that nothing—

Charley. Why must everybody like you? Who liked J. P. Morgan? Was he impressive? In a Turkish bath he'd look like a butcher. But with his pockets on he was very well liked. Now listen, Willy, I know you don't like me, and nobody can say I'm in love with you, but I'll give you a job because—just for the hell of it, put it that way. Now what do you say?

Willy. I—I just can't work for you, Charley.

Charley. What're you, jealous of me?

Willy. I can't work for you, that's all, don't ask me why.

Charley (*angered, takes out more bills*). You been jealous of me all your life, you damned fool! Here, pay your insurance. (*He puts the money in Willy's hand.*)

Willy. I'm keeping strict accounts.

Charley. I've got some work to do. Take care of yourself. And pay your insurance.

Willy (*moving to the right*). Funny, y'know? After all the highways, and the trains, and the appointments, and the years, you end up worth more dead than alive.

Charley. Willy, nobody's worth nothin' dead. (*After a slight pause.*) Did you hear what I said?

Willy stands still, dreaming.

Charley. Willy!

Willy. Apologize to Bernard for me when you see him. I didn't mean to argue with him. He's a fine boy. They're all fine boys, and they'll end up big—all of them. Someday they'll all play tennis together. Wish me luck, Charley. He saw Bill Oliver today.

Charley. Good luck.

Willy (*on the verge of tears*). Charley, you're the only friend I got. Isn't that a remarkable thing? (*He goes out.*)

Charley. Jesus!

Charley stares after him a moment and follows. All light blacks out. Suddenly raucous music is heard, and a red glow rises behind the screen at right. Stanley, a young waiter, appears, carrying a table, followed by Happy, who is carrying two chairs.

Stanley (*putting the table down*). That's all right, Mr. Loman, I can handle it myself. (*He turns and takes the chairs from Happy and places them at the table.*)

Happy (*glancing around*).   Oh, this is better.

Stanley.   Sure, in the front there you're in the middle of all kinds a noise. Whenever you got a party, Mr. Loman, you just tell me and I'll put you back here. Y'know, there's a lotta people they don't like it private, because when they go out they like to see a lotta action around them because they're sick and tired to stay in the house by theirself. But I know you, you ain't from Hackensack. You know what I mean?

Happy (*sitting down*).   So how's it coming, Stanley?

Stanley.   Ah, it's a dog's life. I only wish during the war they'd a took me in the Army. I coulda been dead by now.

Happy.   My brother's back, Stanley.

Stanley.   Oh, he come back, heh? From the Far West.

Happy.   Yeah, big cattle man, my brother, so treat him right. And my father's coming too.

Stanley.   Oh, your father too!

Happy.   You got a couple of nice lobsters?

Stanley.   Hundred per cent, big.

Happy.   I want them with the claws.

Stanley.   Don't worry, I don't give you no mice. (*Happy laughs.*) How about some wine? It'll put a head on the meal.

Happy.   No. You remember, Stanley, that recipe I brought you from overseas? With the champagne in it?

Stanley.   Oh, yeah, sure. I still got it tacked up yet in the kitchen. But that'll have to cost a buck apiece anyways.

Happy.   That's all right.

Stanley.   What'd you, hit a number or somethin'?

Happy.   No, it's a little celebration. My brother is—I think he pulled off a big deal today. I think we're going into business together.

Stanley.   Great! That's the best for you. Because a family business, you know what I mean?—that's the best.

Happy.   That's what I think.

Stanley.   'Cause what's the difference? Somebody steals? It's in the family. Know what I mean? (*Sotto voce.*[3]) Like this bartender here. The boss is goin' crazy what kinda leak he's got in the cash register. You put it in but it don't come out.

Happy (*raising his head*).   Sh!

Stanley.   What?

Happy.   You notice I wasn't lookin' right or left, was I?

Stanley.   No.

Happy.   And my eyes are closed.

Stanley.   So what's the—?

Happy.   Strudel's comin'.

Stanley (*catching on, looks around*).   Ah, no, there's no—

---

[3] "Softly" in Italian.

He breaks off as a furred, lavishly dressed girl enters and sits at the next table. Both follow her with their eyes.

Stanley. Geez, how'd ya know?
Happy. I got radar or something. (*Staring directly at her profile.*) Oooooooo . . . Stanley.
Stanley. I think that's for you, Mr. Loman.
Happy. Look at that mouth. Oh, God. And the binoculars.
Stanley. Geez, you got a life, Mr. Loman.
Happy. Wait on her.
Stanley (*going to the girl's table*). Would you like a menu, ma'am?
Girl. I'm expecting someone, but I'd like a—
Happy. Why don't you bring her—excuse me, miss, do you mind? I sell champagne, and I'd like you to try my brand. Bring her a champagne, Stanley.
Girl. That's awfully nice of you.
Happy. Don't mention it. It's all company money. (*He laughs.*)
Girl. That's a charming product to be selling, isn't it?
Happy. Oh, gets to be like everything else. Selling is selling, y'know.
Girl. I suppose.
Happy. You don't happen to sell, do you?
Girl. No, I don't sell.
Happy. Would you object to a compliment from a stranger? You ought to be on a magazine cover.
Girl (*looking at him a little archly*). I have been.

Stanley comes in with a glass of champagne.

Happy. What'd I say before, Stanley? You see? She's a cover girl.
Stanley. Oh, I could see, I could see.
Happy (*to the Girl*). What magazine?
Girl. Oh, a lot of them. (*She takes the drink.*) Thank you.
Happy. You know what they say in France, don't you? "Champagne is the drink of the complexion"—Hya, Biff!

Biff has entered and sits with Happy.

Biff. Hello, kid. Sorry I'm late.
Happy. I just got here. Uh, Miss—?
Girl. Forsythe.
Happy. Miss Forsythe, this is my brother.
Biff. Is Dad here?
Happy. His name is Biff. You might've heard of him. Great football player.
Girl. Really? What team?
Happy. Are you familiar with football?

Girl.   No, I'm afraid I'm not.

Happy.   Biff is quarterback with the New York Giants.

Girl.   Well, that is nice, isn't it? *(She drinks.)*

Happy.   Good health.

Girl.   I'm happy to meet you.

Happy.   That's my name. Hap. It's really Harold, but at West Point they called me Happy.

Girl *(now really impressed).*   Oh, I see. How do you do? *(She turns her profile.)*

Biff.   Isn't Dad coming?

Happy.   You want her?

Biff.   Oh, I could never make that.

Happy.   I remember the time that idea would never come into your head. Where's the old confidence, Biff?

Biff.   I just saw Oliver—

Happy.   Wait a minute. I've got to see that old confidence again. Do you want her? She's on call.

Biff.   Oh, no. *(He turns to look at the Girl.)*

Happy.   I'm telling you. Watch this. *(Turning to the Girl.)* Honey? *(She turns to him.)* Are you busy?

Girl.   Well, I am . . . but I could make a phone call.

Happy.   Do that, will you, honey? And see if you can get a friend. We'll be here for a while. Biff is one of the greatest football players in the country.

Girl *(standing up).*   Well, I'm certainly happy to meet you.

Happy.   Come back soon.

Girl.   I'll try.

Happy.   Don't try, honey, try hard.

The Girl exits. Stanley follows, shaking his head in bewildered admiration.

Happy.   Isn't that a shame now? A beautiful girl like that? That's why I can't get married. There's not a good woman in a thousand. New York is loaded with them, kid!

Biff.   Hap, look—

Happy.   I told you she was on call!

Biff *(strangely unnerved).*   Cut it out, will ya? I want to say something to you.

Happy.   Did you see Oliver?

Biff.   I saw him all right. Now look, I want to tell Dad a couple of things and I want you to help me.

Happy.   What? Is he going to back you?

Biff.   Are you crazy? You're out of your goddam head, you know that?

Happy.   Why? What happened?

Biff *(breathlessly).*   I did a terrible thing today, Hap. It's been the strangest day I ever went through. I'm all numb, I swear.

Happy.   You mean he wouldn't see you?

Biff.   Well, I waited six hours for him, see? All day. Kept sending my name in. Even tried to date his secretary so she'd get me to him, but no soap.

Happy.   Because you're not showin' the old confidence, Biff. He remembered you, didn't he?

Biff *(stopping Happy with a gesture).*   Finally, about five o'clock, he comes out. Didn't remember who I was or anything. I felt like such an idiot, Hap.

Happy.   Did you tell him my Florida idea?

Biff.   He walked away. I saw him for one minute. I got so mad I could've torn the walls down! How the hell did I ever get the idea I was a salesman there? I even believed myself that I'd been a salesman for him! And then he gave me one look and—I realized what a ridiculous lie my whole life has been! We've been talking in a dream for fifteen years. I was a shipping clerk.

Happy.   What'd you do?

Biff *(with great tension and wonder).*   Well, he left, see. And the secretary went out. I was all alone in the waiting-room. I don't know what came over me, Hap. The next thing I know I'm in his office—paneled walls, everything. I can't explain it. I—Hap, I took his fountain pen.

Happy.   Geez, did he catch you?

Biff.   I ran out. I ran down all eleven flights. I ran and ran and ran.

Happy.   That was an awful dumb—what'd you do that for?

Biff *(agonized).*   I don't know, I just—wanted to take something, I don't know. You gotta help me, Hap, I'm gonna tell Pop.

Happy.   You crazy? What for?

Biff.   Hap, he's got to understand that I'm not the man somebody lends that kind of money to. He thinks I've been spiting him all these years and it's eating him up.

Happy.   That's just it. You tell him something nice.

Biff.   I can't.

Happy.   Say you got a lunch date with Oliver tomorrow.

Biff.   So what do I do tomorrow?

Happy.   You leave the house tomorrow and come back at night and say Oliver is thinking it over. And he thinks it over for a couple of weeks, and gradually it fades away and nobody's the worse.

Biff.   But it'll go on forever!

Happy.   Dad is never so happy as when he's looking forward to something!

Willy enters.

Happy.   Hello, scout!

Willy.   Gee, I haven't been here in years!

Stanley has followed Willy in and sets a chair for him. Stanley starts off but Happy stops him.

Happy.   Stanley!

Stanley stands by, waiting for an order.

Biff *(going to Willy with guilt, as to an invalid).*   Sit down, Pop. You want a
drink?

Willy.   Sure, I don't mind.

Biff.   Let's get a load on.

Willy.   You look worried.

Biff.   N-no. *(To Stanley.)* Scotch all around. Make it doubles.

Stanley.   Doubles, right. *(He goes.)*

Willy.   You had a couple already, didn't you?

Biff.   Just a couple, yeah.

Willy.   Well, what happened, boy? *(Nodding affirmatively, with a smile.)*
Everything go all right?

Biff *(takes a breath, then reaches out and grasps Willy's hand.)* Pal . . . *(He is
smiling bravely, and Willy is smiling too.)* I had an experience today.

Happy.   Terrific, Pop.

Willy.   That so? What happened?

Biff *(high, slightly alcoholic, above the earth).*   I'm going to tell you everything
from first to last. It's been a strange day. *(Silence. He looks around, composes
himself as best he can, but his breath keeps breaking the rhythm of his voice.)*
I had to wait quite a while for him, and—

Willy.   Oliver.

Biff.   Yeah, Oliver. All day, as a matter of cold fact. And a lot of—instances—
facts, Pop, facts about my life came back to me. Who was it, Pop? Who ever
said I was a salesman with Oliver?

Willy.   Well, you were.

Biff.   No, Dad, I was a shipping clerk.

Willy.   But you were practically—

Biff *(with determination).*   Dad, I don't know who said it first, but I was never
a salesman for Bill Oliver.

Willy.   What're you talking about?

Biff.   Let's hold on to the facts tonight, Pop. We're not going to get anywhere
bullin' around. I was a shipping clerk.

Willy *(angrily).*   All right, now listen to me—

Biff.   Why don't you let me finish?

Willy.   I'm not interested in stories about the past or any crap of that kind because the woods are burning, boys, you understand? There's a big blaze going
on all around. I was fired today.

Biff *(shocked).*   How could you be?

Willy.   I was fired, and I'm looking for a little good news to tell your mother,
because the woman has waited and the woman has suffered. The gist of it is
that I haven't got a story left in my head, Biff. So don't give me a lecture about
facts and aspects. I am not interested. Now what've you got to say to me?

Stanley enters with three drinks. They wait until he leaves.

Willy.   Did you see Oliver?

Biff. Jesus, Dad!

Willy. You mean you didn't go up there?

Happy. Sure he went up there.

Biff. I did. I—saw him. How could they fire you?

Willy (*on the edge of his chair*). What kind of a welcome did he give you?

Biff. He won't even let you work on commission?

Willy. I'm out! (*Driving.*) So tell me, he gave you a warm welcome?

Happy. Sure, Pop, sure!

Biff (*driven*). Well, it was kind of—

Willy. I was wondering if he'd remember you. (*To Happy.*) Imagine, man doesn't see him for ten, twelve years and gives him that kind of a welcome!

Happy. Damn right!

Biff (*trying to return to the offensive*). Pop, look—

Willy. You know why he remembered you, don't you? Because you impressed him in those days.

Biff. Let's talk quietly and get this down to the facts, huh?

Willy (*as though Biff had been interrupting*). Well, what happened? It's great news, Biff. Did he take you into his office or'd you talk in the waiting-room?

Biff. Well, he came in, see, and—

Willy (*with a big smile*). What'd he say? Betcha he threw his arm around you.

Biff. Well, he kinda—

Willy. He's a fine man. (*To Happy.*) Very hard man to see, y'know.

Happy (*agreeing*). Oh, I know.

Willy (*to Biff*). Is that where you had the drinks?

Biff. Yeah, he gave me a couple of—no, no!

Happy (*cutting in*). He told him my Florida idea.

Willy. Don't interrupt. (*To Biff.*) How'd he react to the Florida idea?

Biff. Dad, will you give me a minute to explain?

Willy. I've been waiting for you to explain since I sat down here! What happened? He took you into his office and what?

Biff. Well—I talked. And—and he listened, see.

Willy. Famous for the way he listens, y'know. What was his answer?

Biff. His answer was—(*He breaks off, suddenly angry.*) Dad, you're not letting me tell you what I want to tell you!

Willy (*accusing, angered*). You didn't see him, did you?

Biff. I did see him!

Willy. What'd you insult him or something? You insulted him, didn't you?

Biff. Listen, will you let me out of it, will you just let me out of it!

Happy. What the hell!

Willy. Tell me what happened!

Biff (*to Happy*). I can't talk to him!

A single trumpet note jars the ear. The light of green leaves stains the house, which holds the air of night and a dream. Young Bernard enters and knocks on the door of the house.

Young Bernard (*frantically*).   Mrs. Loman, Mrs. Loman!
Happy.   Tell him what happened!
Biff (*to Happy*).   Shut up and leave me alone!
Willy.   No, no! You had to go and flunk math!
Biff.   What math? What're you talking about?
Young Bernard.   Mrs. Loman, Mrs. Loman!

Linda appears in the house, as of old.

Willy (*wildly*).   Math, math, math!
Biff.   Take it easy, Pop!
Young Bernard.   Mrs. Loman!
Willy (*furiously*).   If you hadn't flunked you'd've been set by now!
Biff.   Now, look, I'm gonna tell you what happened, and you're going to listen to me.
Young Bernard.   Mrs. Loman!
Biff.   I waited six hours—
Happy.   What the hell are you saying?
Biff.   I kept sending in my name but he wouldn't see me. So finally he . . . (*He continues unheard as light fades low on the restaurant.*)
Young Bernard.   Biff flunked math!
Linda.   No!
Young Bernard.   Birnbaum flunked him! They won't graduate him!
Linda.   But they have to. He's gotta go to the university. Where is he? Biff! Biff!
Young Bernard.   No, he left. He went to Grand Central.
Linda.   Grand—You mean he went to Boston!
Young Bernard.   Is Uncle Willy in Boston?
Linda.   Oh, maybe Willy can talk to the teacher. Oh, the poor, poor boy!

Light on house area snaps out.

Biff (*at the table, now audible, holding up a gold fountain pen*).   . . . so I'm washed up with Oliver, you understand? Are you listening to me?
Willy (*at a loss*).   Yeah, sure. If you hadn't flunked—
Biff.   Flunked what? What're you talking about?
Willy.   Don't blame everything on me! I didn't flunk math—you did! What pen?
Happy.   That was awful dumb, Biff, a pen like that is worth—
Willy (*seeing the pen for the first time*).   You took Oliver's pen?
Biff (*weakening*).   Dad, I just explained it to you.
Willy.   You stole Bill Oliver's fountain pen!
Biff.   I didn't exactly steal it! That's just what I've been explaining to you!
Happy.   He had it in his hand and just then Oliver walked in, so he got nervous and stuck it in his pocket!

Willy. My God, Biff!

Biff. I never intended to do it, Dad!

Operator's Voice. Standish Arms, good evening!

Willy *(shouting).* I'm not in my room!

Biff *(frightened).* Dad, what's the matter? *(He and Happy stand up.)*

Operator. Ringing Mr. Loman for you!

Willy. I'm not there, stop it!

Biff *(horrified, gets down on one knee before Willy).* Dad, I'll make good, I'll make good. *(Willy tries to get to his feet. Biff holds him down.)* Sit down now.

Willy. No, you're no good, you're no good for anything.

Biff. I am, Dad, I'll find something else, you understand? Now don't worry about anything. *(He holds up Willy's face.)* Talk to me, Dad.

Operator. Mr. Loman does not answer. Shall I page him?

Willy *(attempting to stand, as though to rush and silence the Operator).* No, no, no!

Happy. He'll strike something, Pop.

Willy. No, no . . .

Biff *(desperately, standing over Willy).* Pop, listen! Listen to me! I'm telling you something good. Oliver talked to his partner about the Florida idea. You listening? He—he talked to his partner, and he came to me . . . I'm going to be all right, you hear? Dad, listen to me, he said it was just a question of the amount!

Willy. Then you . . . got it?

Happy. He's gonna be terrific, Pop!

Willy *(trying to stand).* Then you got it, haven't you? You got it! You got it!

Biff *(agonized, holds Willy down).* No, no. Look, Pop. I'm supposed to have lunch with them tomorrow. I'm just telling you this so you'll know that I can still make an impression, Pop. And I'll make good somewhere, but I can't go tomorrow, see?

Willy. Why not? You simply—

Biff. But the pen, Pop!

Willy. You give it to him and tell him it was an oversight!

Happy. Sure, have lunch tomorrow!

Biff. I can't say that—

Willy. You were doing a crossword puzzle and accidentally used his pen!

Biff. Listen, kid, I took those balls years ago, now I walk in with his fountain pen? That clinches it, don't you see? I can't face him like that! I'll try elsewhere.

Page's Voice. Paging Mr. Loman!

Willy. Don't you want to be anything?

Biff. Pop, how can I go back?

Willy. You don't want to be anything, is that what's behind it?

Biff *(now angry at Willy for not crediting his sympathy).* Don't take it that way! You think it was easy walking into that office after what I'd done to him? A team of horses couldn't have dragged me back to Bill Oliver!

Willy. Then why'd you go?

Biff. Why did I go? Why did I go! Look at you! Look at what's become of you!

Off left, The Woman laughs.

Willy. Biff, you're going to lunch tomorrow, or—

Biff. I can't go. I've got no appointment!

Happy. Biff, for . . . !

Willy. Are you spiting me?

Biff. Don't take it that way! Goddammit!

Willy (*strikes Biff and falters away from the table*). You rotten little louse! Are you spiting me?

The Woman. Someone's at the door, Willy!

Biff. I'm no good, can't you see what I am?

Happy (*separating them*). Hey, you're in a restaurant! Now cut it out, both of you! (*The girls enter.*) Hello, girls, sit down.

The Woman laughs, off left.

Miss Forsythe. I guess we might as well. This is Letta.

The Woman. Willy, are you going to wake up?

Biff (*ignoring Willy*). How're ya, miss, sit down. What do you drink?

Miss Forsythe. Letta might not be able to stay long.

Letta. I gotta get up very early tomorrow. I got jury duty. I'm so excited! Were you fellows ever on a jury?

Biff. No, but I been in front of them! (*The girls laugh.*) This is my father.

Letta. Isn't he cute? Sit down with us, Pop.

Happy. Sit him down, Biff!

Biff (*going to him*). Come on, slugger, drink us under the table. To hell with it! Come on, sit down, pal.

On Biff's last insistence, Willy is about to sit.

The Woman (*now urgently*). Willy, are you going to answer the door!

The Woman's call pulls Willy back. He starts right, befuddled.

Biff. Hey, where are you going?

Willy. Open the door.

Biff. The door?

Willy. The washroom . . . the door . . . where's the door?

Biff (*leading Willy to the left*). Just go straight down.

Willy moves left.

The Woman. Willy, Willy, are you going to get up, get up, get up, get up?

Willy exits left.

Letta. I think it's sweet you bring your daddy along.

Miss Forsythe. Oh, he isn't really your father!

Biff (*at left, turning to her resentfully*). Miss Forsythe, you've just seen a prince walk by. A fine, troubled prince. A hard-working, unappreciated prince. A pal, you understand? A good companion. Always for his boys.

Letta. That's so sweet.

Happy. Well, girls, what's the program? We're wasting time. Come on, Biff. Gather round. Where would you like to go?

Biff. Why don't you do something for him?

Happy. Me!

Biff. Don't you give a damn for him, Hap?

Happy. What're you talking about? I'm the one who—

Biff. I sense it, you don't give a good goddamn about him. (*He takes the rolled-up hose from his pocket and puts it on the table in front of Happy.*) Look what I found in the cellar, for Christ's sake. How can you bear to let it go on?

Happy. Me? Who goes away? Who runs off and—

Biff. Yeah, but he doesn't mean anything to you. You could help him—I can't! Don't you understand what I'm talking about? He's going to kill himself, don't you know that?

Happy. Don't I know it! Me!

Biff. Hap, help him! Jesus . . . help him . . . Help me, help me, I can't bear to look at his face! (*Ready to weep, he hurries out, up right.*)

Happy (*starting after him*). Where are you going?

Miss Forsythe. What's he so mad about?

Happy. Come on, girls, we'll catch up with him.

Miss Forsythe (*as Happy pushes her out*). Say, I don't like that temper of his!

Happy. He's just a little overstrung, he'll be all right!

Willy (*off left, as The Woman laughs*). Don't answer! Don't answer!

Letta. Don't you want to tell your father—

Happy. No, that's not my father. He's just a guy. Come on, we'll catch Biff, and, honey, we're going to paint this town! Stanley, where's the check! Hey, Stanley!

They exit. Stanley looks toward left.

Stanley (*calling to Happy indignantly*). Mr. Loman! Mr. Loman!

Stanley picks up a chair and follows them off. Knocking is heard off left. The Woman enters, laughing. Willy follows her. She is in a black slip; he is buttoning his shirt. Raw, sensuous music accompanies their speech.

Willy. Will you stop laughing? Will you stop?

The Woman. Aren't you going to answer the door? He'll wake the whole hotel.

Willy. I'm not expecting anybody.

The Woman. Whyn't you have another drink, honey, and stop being so damn self-centered?

Willy. I'm so lonely.

The Woman. You know you ruined me, Willy? From now on, whenever you come to the office, I'll see that you go right through to the buyers. No waiting at my desk any more, Willy. You ruined me.

Willy. That's nice of you to say that.

The Woman. Gee, you are self-centered! Why so sad? You are the saddest, self-centeredest soul I ever did see-saw. (*She laughs. He kisses her.*) Come on inside, drummer boy. It's silly to be dressing in the middle of the night. (*As knocking is heard.*) Aren't you going to answer the door?

Willy. They're knocking on the wrong door.

The Woman. But I felt the knocking. And he heard us talking in here. Maybe the hotel's on fire!

Willy (*his terror rising*). It's a mistake.

The Woman. Then tell him to go away!

Willy. There's nobody there.

The Woman. It's getting on my nerves, Willy. There's somebody standing out there and it's getting on my nerves!

Willy (*pushing her away from him*). All right, stay in the bathroom here, and don't come out. I think there's a law in Massachusetts about it, so don't come out. It may be that new room clerk. He looked very mean. So don't come out. It's a mistake, there's no fire.

The knocking is heard again. He takes a few steps away from her, and she vanishes into the wing. The light follows him, and now he is facing Young Biff, who carries a suitcase. Biff steps toward him. The music is gone.

Biff. Why didn't you answer?

Willy. Biff! What are you doing in Boston?

Biff. Why didn't you answer? I've been knocking for five minutes, I called you on the phone—

Willy. I just heard you. I was in the bathroom and had the door shut. Did anything happen home?

Biff. Dad—I let you down.

Willy. What do you mean?

Biff. Dad . . .

Willy. Biffo, what's this about? (*Putting his arm around Biff.*) Come on, let's go downstairs and get you a malted.

Biff. Dad, I flunked math.

Willy. Not for the term?

Biff. The term. I haven't got enough credits to graduate.

Willy.   You mean to say Bernard wouldn't give you the answers?

Biff.   He did, he tried, but I only got a sixty-one.

Willy.   And they wouldn't give you four points?

Biff.   Birnbaum refused absolutely. I begged him, Pop, but he won't give me those points. You gotta talk to him before they close the school. Because if he saw the kind of man you are, and you just talked to him in your way, I'm sure he'd come through for me. The class came right before practice, see, and I didn't go enough. Would you talk to him? He'd like you, Pop. You know the way you could talk.

Willy.   You're on. We'll drive right back.

Biff.   Oh, Dad, good work! I'm sure he'll change it for you!

Willy.   Go downstairs and tell the clerk I'm checkin' out. Go right down.

Biff.   Yes, sir! See, the reason he hates me, Pop—one day he was late for class so I got up at the blackboard and imitated him. I crossed my eyes and talked with a lithp.

Willy *(laughing).*   You did? The kids like it?

Biff.   They nearly died laughing!

Willy.   Yeah? What'd you do?

Biff.   The thquare root of thixthy twee is . . . *(Willy bursts out laughing; Biff joins him.)* And in the middle of it he walked in!

Willy laughs and The Woman joins in offstage.

Willy *(without hesitation).*   Hurry downstairs and—

Biff.   Somebody in there?

Willy.   No, that was next door.

The Woman laughs offstage.

Biff.   Somebody got in your bathroom!

Willy.   No, it's the next room, there's a party—

The Woman *(enters, laughing. She lisps this):*   Can I come in? There's something in the bathtub, Willy, and it's moving!

Willy looks at Biff, who is staring open-mouthed and horrified at The Woman.

Willy.   Ah—you better go back to your room. They must be finished painting by now. They're painting her room so I let her take a shower here. Go back, go back . . . *(He pushes her.)*

The Woman *(resisting).*   But I've got to get dressed, Willy, I can't—

Willy.   Get out of here! Go back, go back . . . *(Suddenly striving for the ordinary):* This is Miss Francis, Biff, she's a buyer. They're painting her room. Go back, Miss Francis, go back . . .

The Woman.   But my clothes, I can't go out naked in the hall!

Willy *(pushing her offstage).*   Get outa here! Go back, go back!

Biff slowly sits down on his suitcase as the argument continues offstage.

The Woman.   Where's my stockings? You promised me stockings, Willy!

Willy.   I have no stockings here!

The Woman.   You had two boxes of size nine sheers for me, and I want them!

Willy.   Here, for God's sake, will you get outa here!

The Woman *(enters holding a box of stockings).*   I just hope there's nobody in the hall. That's all I hope. *(To Biff.)* Are you football or baseball?

Biff.   Football.

The Woman *(angry, humiliated).*   That's me too. G'night. *(She snatches her clothes from Willy, and walks out.)*

Willy *(after a pause).*   Well, better get going. I want to get to the school first thing in the morning. Get my suits out of the closet. I'll get my valise. *(Biff doesn't move.)* What's the matter? *(Biff remains motionless, tears falling.)* She's a buyer. Buys for J. H. Simmons. She lives down the hall—they're painting. You don't imagine—*(He breaks off. After a pause.)* Now listen, pal, she's just a buyer. She sees merchandise in her room and they have to keep it looking just so . . . *(Pause. Assuming command.)* All right, get my suits. *(Biff doesn't move.)* Now stop crying and do as I say. I gave you an order. Biff, I gave you an order! Is that what you do when I give you an order? How dare you cry! *(Putting his arm around Biff.)* Now look, Biff, when you grow up you'll understand about these things. You mustn't—you mustn't overemphasize a thing like this. I'll see Birnbaum first thing in the morning.

Biff.   Never mind.

Willy *(getting down beside Biff).*   Never mind! He's going to give you those points. I'll see to it.

Biff.   He wouldn't listen to you.

Willy.   He certainly will listen to me. You need those points for the U. of Virginia.

Biff.   I'm not going there.

Willy.   Heh? If I can't get him to change that mark you'll make it up in summer school. You've got all summer to—

Biff *(his weeping breaking from him).*   Dad . . .

Willy *(infected by it).*   Oh, my boy . . .

Biff.   Dad . . .

Willy.   She's nothing to me, Biff. I was lonely, I was terribly lonely.

Biff.   You—you gave her Mama's stockings! *(His tears break through and he rises to go.)*

Willy *(grabbing for Biff).*   I gave you an order!

Biff.   Don't touch me, you—liar!

Willy.   Apologize for that!

Biff.   You fake! You phony little fake! You fake! *(Overcome, he turns quickly and weeping fully goes out with his suitcase. Willy is left on the floor on his knees.)*

Willy.   I gave you an order! Biff, come back here or I'll beat you! Come back here! I'll whip you!

Stanley comes quickly in from the right and stands in front of Willy.

Willy (*shouts at Stanley*).   I gave you an order . . .
Stanley.   Hey, let's pick it up, pick it up, Mr. Loman. (*He helps Willy to his feet.*) Your boys left with the chippies. They said they'll see you home.

A second waiter watches some distance away.

Willy.   But we were supposed to have dinner together.

Music is heard, Willy's theme.

Stanley.   Can you make it?
Willy.   I'll—sure, I can make it. (*Suddenly concerned about his clothes.*) Do I—I look all right?
Stanley.   Sure, you look all right. (*He flicks a speck off Willy's lapel.*)
Willy.   Here—here's a dollar.
Stanley.   Oh, your son paid me. It's all right.
Willy (*putting it in Stanley's hand*).   No, take it. You're a good boy.
Stanley.   Oh, no, you don't have to . . .
Willy.   Here—here's some more, I don't need it any more. (*After a slight pause.*) Tell me—is there a seed store in the neighborhood?
Stanley.   Seeds? You mean like to plant?

As Willy turns, Stanley slips the money back into his jacket pocket.

Willy.   Yes. Carrots, peas . . .
Stanley.   Well, there's hardware stores on Sixth Avenue, but it may be too late now.
Willy (*anxiously*).   Oh, I'd better hurry. I've got to get some seeds. (*He starts off to the right.*) I've got to get some seeds, right away. Nothing's planted. I don't have a thing in the ground.

Willy hurries out as the light goes down. Stanley moves over to the right after him, watches him off. The other waiter has been staring at Willy.

Stanley (*to the waiter*).   Well, whatta you looking at?

The waiter picks up the chairs and moves off right. Stanley takes the table and follows him. The light fades on this area. There is a long pause, the sound of the flute coming over. The light gradually rises on the kitchen, which is empty. Happy appears at the door of the house, followed by Biff. Happy is carrying a large bunch of long-stemmed roses. He enters the kitchen, looks around for Linda. Not seeing her, he turns to Biff, who is just outside the house door, and makes a gesture with his hands, indicating "Not here, I guess." He looks into the living-room and freezes. Inside, Linda, unseen, is seated, Willy's coat on her lap. She rises ominously and quietly and moves toward Happy, who backs up into the kitchen, afraid.

Happy.   Hey, what're you doing up? (*Linda says nothing but moves toward him implacably.*) Where's Pop? (*He keeps backing to the right, and now Linda is in full view in the doorway to the living-room.*) Is he sleeping?

Linda.   Where were you?

Happy (*trying to laugh it off*).   We met two girls, Mom, very fine types. Here, we brought you some flowers. (*Offering them to her.*) Put them in your room, Ma.

She knocks them to the floor at Biff's feet. He has now come inside and closed the door behind him. She stares at Biff, silent.

Happy.   Now what'd you do that for? Mom, I want you to have some flowers—

Linda (*cutting Happy off, violently to Biff*).   Don't you care whether he lives or dies?

Happy (*going to the stairs*).   Come upstairs, Biff.

Biff (*with a flare of disgust, to Happy*).   Go away from me! (*To Linda.*) What do you mean, lives or dies? Nobody's dying around here, pal.

Linda.   Get out of my sight! Get out of here!

Biff.   I wanna see the boss.

Linda.   You're not going near him!

Biff.   Where is he? (*He moves into the living-room and Linda follows.*)

Linda (*shouting after Biff*).   You invite him for dinner. He looks forward to it all day—(*Biff appears in his parents' bedroom, looks around, and exits.*)—and then you desert him there. There's no stranger you'd do that to!

Happy.   Why? He had a swell time with us. Listen, when I—(*Linda comes back into the kitchen*)—desert him I hope I don't outlive the day!

Linda.   Get out of here!

Happy.   Now look, Mom . . .

Linda.   Did you have to go to women tonight? You and your lousy rotten whores!

Biff re-enters the kitchen.

Happy.   Mom, all we did was follow Biff around trying to cheer him up! (*To Biff.*) Boy, what a night you gave me!

Linda.   Get out of here, both of you, and don't come back! I don't want you tormenting him any more. Go on now, get your things together! (*To Biff.*) You can sleep in his apartment. (*She starts to pick up the flowers and stops herself.*) Pick up this stuff, I'm not your maid any more. Pick it up, you bum, you!

Happy turns his back to her in refusal. Biff slowly moves over and gets down on his knees, picking up the flowers.

Linda. You're a pair of animals! Not one, not another living soul would have had the cruelty to walk out on that man in a restaurant!

Biff *(not looking at her).* Is that what he said?

Linda. He didn't have to say anything. He was so humiliated he nearly limped when he came in.

Happy. But, Mom, he had a great time with us—

Biff *(cutting him off violently).* Shut up!

Without another word, Happy goes upstairs.

Linda. You! You didn't even go in to see if he was all right!

Biff *(still on the floor in front of Linda, the flowers in his hand; with self-loathing).* No. Didn't. Didn't do a damned thing. How do you like that, heh? Left him babbling in a toilet.

Linda. You louse. You . . .

Biff. Now you hit it on the nose! *(He gets up, throws the flowers in the waste-basket.)* The scum of the earth, and you're looking at him!

Linda. Get out of here!

Biff. I gotta talk to the boss, Mom. Where is he?

Linda. You're not going near him. Get out of this house!

Biff *(with absolute assurance, determination).* No. We're gonna have an abrupt conversation, him and me.

Linda. You're not talking to him!

Hammering is heard from outside the house, off right. Biff turns toward the noise.

Linda *(suddenly pleading).* Will you please leave him alone?

Biff. What's he doing out there?

Linda. He's planting the garden!

Biff *(quietly).* Now? Oh, my God!

Biff moves outside, Linda following. The light dies down on them and comes up on the center of the apron as Willy walks into it. He is carrying a flashlight, a hoe, and handful of seed packets. He raps the top of the hoe sharply to fix it firmly, and then moves to the left, measuring off the distance with his foot. He holds the flashlight to look at the seed packets, reading off the instructions. He is in the blue of night.

Willy. Carrots . . . quarter-inch apart. Rows . . . one-foot rows. *(He measures it off.)* One foot. *(He puts down a package and measures off.)* Beets. *(He puts down another package and measures again.)* Lettuce. *(He reads the package, puts it down.)* One foot—*(He breaks off as Ben appears at the right and moves slowly down to him.)* What a proposition, ts, ts. Terrific, terrific. 'Cause she's suffered, Ben, the woman has suffered. You understand me? A man can't go out the way he came in, Ben, a man has got to add up to something. You can't, you can't—(*Ben moves toward him as though to interrupt.*) You gotta consider, now. Don't answer so quick. Remember, it's a guaranteed twenty-thousand-dollar proposition. Now look, Ben, I want you to go through the ins and outs of this thing with me. I've got nobody to talk to, Ben, and the woman has suffered, you hear me?

Ben (*standing still, considering*).   What's the proposition?

Willy.   It's twenty thousand dollars on the barrelhead. Guaranteed, gilt-edged, you understand?

Ben.   You don't want to make a fool of yourself. They might not honor the policy.

Willy.   How can they dare refuse? Didn't I work like a coolie to meet every premium on the nose? And now they don't pay off? Impossible!

Ben.   It's called a cowardly thing, William.

Willy.   Why? Does it take more guts to stand here the rest of my life ringing up a zero?

Ben (*yielding*).   That's a point, William. (*He moves, thinking, turns.*) And twenty thousand—that *is* something one can feel with the hand, it is there.

Willy (*now assured, with rising power*).   Oh, Ben, that's the whole beauty of it! I see it like a diamond, shining in the dark, hard and rough, that I can pick up and touch in my hand. Not like—like an appointment! This would not be another damned-fool appointment, Ben, and it changes all the aspects. Because he thinks I'm nothing, see, and so he spites me. But the funeral—(*Straightening up.*) Ben, that funeral will be massive! They'll come from Maine, Massachusetts, Vermont, New Hampshire! All the old-timers with the strange license plates—that boy will be thunder-struck, Ben, because he never realized—I am known! Rhode Island, New York, New Jersey—I am known, Ben, and he'll see it with his eyes once and for all. He'll see what I am, Ben! He's in for a shock, that boy!

Ben (*coming to the edge of the garden*).   He'll call you a coward.

Willy (*suddenly fearful*).   No, that would be terrible.

Ben.   Yes. And a damned fool.

Willy.   No, no, he mustn't, I won't have that! (*He is broken and desperate.*)

Ben.   He'll hate you William.

The gay music of the Boys is heard.

Willy.   Oh, Ben, how do we get back to all the great times? Used to be so full of light, and comradeship, the sleigh-riding in winter, and the ruddiness on his cheeks. And always some kind of good news coming up, always something nice coming up ahead. And never even let me carry the valises in the house, and simonizing, simonizing that little red car! Why, why can't I give him something and not have him hate me?

Ben.   Let me think about it. (*He glances at his watch.*) I still have a little time. Remarkable proposition, but you've got to be sure you're not making a fool of yourself.

Ben drifts off upstage and goes out of sight. Biff comes down from the left.

Willy (*suddenly conscious of Biff, turns and looks up at him, then begins picking up the packages of seeds in confusion*).   Where the hell is that seed? (*Indignantly.*) You can't see nothing out here! They boxed in the whole goddamn neighborhood!

Biff.   There are people all around here. Don't you realize that?

Willy.   I'm busy. Don't bother me.

Biff (*taking the hoe from Willy*).   I'm saying good-by to you, Pop. (*Willy looks at him, silent, unable to move.*) I'm not coming back any more.

Willy.   You're not going to see Oliver tomorrow?

Biff.   I've got no appointment, Dad.

Willy.   He put his arm around you, and you've got no appointment?

Biff.   Pop, get this now, will you? Everytime I've left it's been a fight that sent me out of here. Today I realized something about myself and I tried to explain it to you and I—I think I'm just not smart enough to make any sense out of it for you. To hell with whose fault it is or anything like that. (*He takes Willy's arm.*) Let's just wrap it up, heh? Come on in, we'll tell Mom. (*He gently tries to pull Willy to left.*)

Willy (*frozen, immobile, with guilt in his voice*).   No, I don't want to see her.

Biff.   Come on! (*He pulls again, and Willy tries to pull away.*)

Willy (*highly nervous*).   No, no, I don't want to see her.

Biff (*tries to look into Willy's face, as if to find the answer there*).   Why don't you want to see her?

Willy (*more harshly now*).   Don't bother me, will you?

Biff.   What do you mean, you don't want to see her? You don't want them calling you yellow, do you? This isn't your fault; it's me, I'm a bum. Now come inside! (*Willy strains to get away.*) Did you hear what I said to you?

Willy pulls away and quickly goes by himself into the house. Biff follows.

Linda (*to Willy*).   Did you plant, dear?

Biff (*at the door, to Linda*).   All right, we had it out. I'm going and I'm not writing any more.

Linda (*going to Willy in the kitchen*).   I think that's the best way, dear. 'Cause there's no use drawing it out, you'll just never get along.

Willy doesn't respond.

Biff.   People ask where I am and what I'm doing, you don't know, and you don't care. That way it'll be off your mind and you can start brightening up again. All right? That clears it, doesn't it? (*Willy is silent, and Biff goes to him.*) You gonna wish me luck, scout? (*He extends his hand.*) What do you say?

Linda.   Shake his hand, Willy.

Willy (*turning to her, seething with hurt*).   There's no necessity to mention the pen at all, y'know.

Biff (*gently*).   I've got no appointment, Dad.

Willy (*erupting fiercely*).   He put his arm around . . . ?

Biff.   Dad, you're never going to see what I am, so what's the use of arguing? If I strike oil I'll send you a check. Meantime forget I'm alive.

Willy (*to Linda*).   Spite, see?

Biff.   Shake hands, Dad.

Willy.   Not my hand.

Biff.   I was hoping not to go this way.

Willy.   Well, this is the way you're going. Good-by.

Biff looks at him a moment, then turns sharply and goes to the stairs.

Willy (*stops him with*).   May you rot in hell if you leave this house!

Biff (*turning*).   Exactly what is it that you want from me?

Willy.   I want you to know, on the train, in the mountains, in the valleys, wherever you go, that you cut down your life for spite!

Biff.   No, no.

Willy.   Spite, spite, is the word of your undoing! And when you're down and out, remember what did it. When you're rotting somewhere beside the railroad tracks, remember, and don't you dare blame it on me!

Biff.   I'm not blaming it on you!

Willy.   I won't take the rap for this, you hear?

Happy comes down the stairs and stands on the bottom step, watching.

Biff.   That's just what I'm telling you!

Willy (*sinking into a chair at the table, with full accusation*).   You're trying to put a knife in me—don't think I don't know what you're doing!

Biff.   All right, phony! Then let's lay it on the line. (*He whips the rubber tube out of his pocket and puts it on the table.*)

Happy.   You crazy—

Linda.   Biff! (*She moves to grab the hose, but Biff holds it down with his hand.*)

Biff.   Leave it there! Don't move it!

Willy (*not looking at it*).   What is that?

Biff.   You know goddam well what that is.

Willy (*caged, wanting to escape*).   I never saw that.

Biff.   You saw it. The mice didn't bring it into the cellar! What is this supposed to do, make a hero out of you? This supposed to make me sorry for you?

Willy.   Never heard of it.

Biff.   There'll be no pity for you, you hear it? No pity!

Willy (*to Linda.*)   You hear the spite!

Biff.   No, you're going to hear the truth—what you are and what I am!

Linda.   Stop it!

Willy.   Spite!

Happy (*coming down toward Biff*).   You cut it now!

Biff *(to Happy).*   The man don't know who we are! The man is gonna know! *(To Willy.)* We never told the truth for ten minutes in this house!

Happy.   We always told the truth!

Biff *(turning on him).*   You big blow, are you the assistant buyer? You're one of the two assistants to the assistant, aren't you?

Happy.   Well, I'm practically—

Biff.   You're practically full of it! We all are! And I'm through with it. *(To Willy.)* Now hear this, Willy, this is me.

Willy.   I know you!

Biff.   You know why I had no address for three months? I stole a suit in Kansas City and I was in jail. *(To Linda, who is sobbing.)* Stop crying. I'm through with it.

Linda turns away from them, her hands covering her face.

Willy.   I suppose that's my fault!

Biff.   I stole myself out of every good job since high school!

Willy.   And whose fault is that?

Biff.   And I never got anywhere because you blew me so full of hot air I could never stand taking orders from anybody! That's whose fault it is!

Willy.   I hear that!

Linda.   Don't, Biff!

Biff.   It's goddam time you heard that! I had to be boss big shot in two weeks, and I'm through with it!

Willy.   Then hang yourself! For spite, hang yourself!

Biff.   No! Nobody's hanging himself, Willy! I ran down eleven flights with a pen in my hand today. And suddenly I stopped, you hear me? And in the middle of that office building, do you hear this? I stopped in the middle of that building and I saw—the sky. I saw the things that I love in this world. The work and the food and time to sit and smoke. And I looked at the pen and said to myself, what the hell am I grabbing this for? Why am I trying to become what I don't want to be? What am I doing in an office, making a contemptuous, begging fool of myself, when all I want is out there, waiting for me the minute I say I know who I am! Why can't I say that, Willy? *(He tries to make Willy face him, but Willy pulls away and moves to the left.)*

Willy *(with hatred, threateningly).*   The door of your life is wide open!

Biff.   Pop! I'm a dime a dozen, and so are you!

Willy *(turning on him now in an uncontrolled outburst).*   I am not a dime a dozen! I am Willy Loman, and you are Biff Loman!

Biff starts for Willy, but is blocked by Happy. In his fury, Biff seems on the verge of attacking his father.

Biff.   I am not a leader of men, Willy, and neither are you. You were never anything but a hard-working drummer who landed in the ash can like all the rest of them! I'm one dollar an hour, Willy! I tried seven states and couldn't raise it. A buck an hour! Do you gather my meaning? I'm not bringing home any prizes any more, and you're going to stop waiting for me to bring them home!

Willy (*directly to Biff*).   You vengeful, spiteful mutt!

Biff breaks from Happy. Willy, in fright, starts up the stairs. Biff grabs him.

Biff (*at the peak of his fury*).   Pop, I'm nothing! I'm nothing, Pop. Can't you understand that? There's no spite in it any more. I'm just what I am, that's all.

Biff's fury has spent itself, and he breaks down, sobbing, holding on to Willy, who dumbly fumbles for Biff's face.

Willy (*astonished*).   What're you doing? What're you doing? (*To Linda.*) Why is he crying?

Biff (*crying, broken*).   Will you let me go, for Christ's sake? Will you take that phony dream and burn it before something happens? (*Struggling to contain himself, he pulls away and moves to the stairs.*) I'll go in the morning. Put him—put him to bed. (*Exhausted, Biff moves up the stairs to his room.*)

Willy (*after a long pause, astonished, elevated*).   Isn't that—isn't that remarkable? Biff—he likes me!

Linda.   He loves you, Willy!

Happy (*deeply moved*).   Always did, Pop.

Willy.   Oh, Biff! (*Staring wildly.*) He cried! Cried to me. (*He is choking with his love, and now cries out his promise.*) That boy—that boy is going to be magnificent!

Ben appears in the light just outside the kitchen.

Ben.   Yes, outstanding, with twenty thousand behind him.

Linda (*sensing the racing of his mind, fearfully, carefully*).   Now come to bed, Willy. It's all settled now.

Willy (*finding it difficult not to rush out of the house*).   Yes, we'll sleep. Come on. Go to sleep, Hap.

Ben.   And it does take a great kind of a man to crack the jungle.

In accents of dread, Ben's idyllic music starts up.

Happy (*his arm around Linda*).   I'm getting married, Pop, don't forget it. I'm changing everything. I'm gonna run that department before the year is up. You'll see, Mom. (*He kisses her.*)

Ben.   The jungle is dark but full of diamonds, Willy.

Willy turns, moves, listening to Ben.

Linda.   Be good. You're both good boys, just act that way, that's all.

Happy.   'Night, Pop. (*He goes upstairs.*)

Linda *(to Willy).*   Come, dear.

Ben *(with greater force).*   One must go in to fetch a diamond out.

Willy *(to Linda, as he moves slowly along the edge of the kitchen, toward the door).*   I just want to get settled down, Linda. Let me sit alone for a little.

Linda *(almost uttering her fear).*   I want you upstairs.

Willy *(taking her in his arms).*   In a few minutes, Linda. I couldn't sleep right now. Go on, you look awful tired. *(He kisses her.)*

Ben.   Not like an appointment at all. A diamond is rough and hard to the touch.

Willy.   Go on now. I'll be right up.

Linda.   I think this is the only way, Willy.

Willy.   Sure, it's the best thing.

Ben.   Best thing!

Willy.   The only way. Everything is gonna be—go on, kid, get to bed. You look so tired.

Linda.   Come right up.

Willy.   Two minutes.

Linda goes into the living-room, then reappears in her bedroom. Willy moves just outside the kitchen door.

Willy.   Loves me. *(Wonderingly.)* Always loved me. Isn't that a remarkable thing? Ben, he'll worship me for it!

Ben *(with promise).*   It's dark there, but full of diamonds.

Willy.   Can you imagine that magnificence with twenty thousand dollars in his pocket?

Linda *(calling from her room).*   Willy! Come up!

Willy *(calling into the kitchen).*   Yes! Yes. Coming! It's very smart, you realize that, don't you, sweetheart? Even Ben sees it. I gotta go, baby. 'By! 'By! *(Going over to Ben, almost dancing.)* Imagine? When the mail comes he'll be ahead of Bernard again!

Ben.   A perfect proposition all around.

Willy.   Did you see how he cried to me? Oh, if I could kiss him, Ben!

Ben.   Time, William, time!

Willy.   Oh, Ben, I always knew one way or another we were gonna make it, Biff and I!

Ben *(looking at his watch).*   The boat. We'll be late. *(He moves slowly off into the darkness.)*

Willy *(elegiacally, turning to the house).*   Now when you kick off, boy, I want a seventy-yard boot, and get right down the field under the ball, and when you hit, hit low and hit hard, because it's important, boy. *(He swings around and faces the audience.)* There's all kinds of important people in the stands, and the first thing you know . . . *(Suddenly realizing he is alone.)* Ben! Ben, where do I . . . ? *(He makes a sudden movement of search.)* Ben, how do I . . . ?

Linda *(calling).*   Willy, you coming up?

Willy (*uttering a gasp of fear, whirling about as if to quiet her*).   Sh! (*He turns around as if to find his way; sounds, faces, voices, seem to be swarming in upon him and he flicks at them, crying.*) Sh! Sh! (*Suddenly music, faint and high, stops him. It rises in intensity, almost to an unbearable scream. He goes up and down on his toes, and rushes off around the house.*) Shhh!

Linda.   Willy?

There is no answer. Linda waits. Biff gets up off his bed. He is still in his clothes. Happy sits up. Biff stands listening.

Linda (*with real fear*).   Willy, answer me! Willy!

There is the sound of a car starting and moving away at full speed.

Linda.   No!
Biff (*rushing down the stairs*).   Pop!

As the car speeds off, the music crashes down in a frenzy of sound, which becomes the soft pulsation of a single cello string. Biff slowly returns to his bedroom. He and Happy gravely don their jackets. Linda slowly walks out of her room. The music has developed into a dead march. The leaves of day are appearing over everything. Charley and Bernard, somberly dressed, appear and knock on the kitchen door. Biff and Happy slowly descend the stairs to the kitchen as Charley and Bernard enter. All stop a moment when Linda, in clothes of mourning, bearing a little bunch of roses, comes through the draped doorway into the kitchen. She goes to Charley and takes his arm. Now all move toward the audience, through the wall-line of the kitchen. At the limit of the apron, Linda lays down the flowers, kneels, and sits back on her heels. All stare down at the grave.

Requiem

Charley.   It's getting dark, Linda.

Linda doesn't react. She stares at the grave.

Biff.   How about it, Mom? Better get some rest, heh? They'll be closing the gate soon.

Linda makes no move. Pause.

Happy (*deeply angered*).   He had no right to do that. There was no necessity for it. We would've helped him.
Charley (*grunting*).   Hmmm.
Biff.   Come along, Mom.

Linda. Why didn't anybody come?

Charley. It was a very nice funeral.

Linda. But where are all the people he knew? Maybe they blame him.

Charley. Naa. It's a rough world, Linda. They wouldn't blame him.

Linda. I can't understand it. At this time especially. First time in thirty-five years we were just about free and clear. He only needed a little salary. He was even finished with the dentist.

Charley. No man only needs a little salary.

Linda. I can't understand it.

Biff. There were a lot of nice days. When he'd come home from a trip; or on Sundays, making the stoop; finishing the cellar; putting on the new porch; when he built the extra bathroom; and put up the garage. You know something, Charley, there's more of him in that front stoop than in all the sales he ever made.

Charley. Yeah. He was a happy man with a batch of cement.

Linda. He was so wonderful with his hands.

Biff. He had the wrong dreams. All, all, wrong.

Happy (*almost ready to fight Biff*). Don't say that!

Biff. He never knew who he was.

Charley (*stopping Happy's movement and reply. To Biff*). Nobody dast blame this man. You don't understand: Willy was a salesman. And for a salesman, there is no rock bottom to the life. He don't put a bolt to a nut, he don't tell you the law or give you medicine. He's a man way out there in the blue, riding on a smile and a shoeshine. And when they start not smiling back—that's an earthquake. And then you get yourself a couple of spots on your hat, and you're finished. Nobody dast blame this man. A salesman is got to dream, boy. It comes with the territory.

Biff. Charley, the man didn't know who he was.

Happy (*infuriated*). Don't say that!

Biff. Why don't you come with me, Happy?

Happy. I'm not licked that easily. I'm staying right in this city, and I'm gonna beat this racket! (*He looks at Biff, his chin set.*) The Loman Brothers!

Biff. I know who I am, kid.

Happy. All right, boy. I'm gonna show you and everybody else that Willy Loman did not die in vain. He had a good dream. It's the only dream you can have—to come out number-one man. He fought it out here, and this is where I'm gonna win it for him.

Biff (*with a hopeless glance at Happy, bends toward his mother*). Let's go, Mom.

Linda. I'll be with you in a minute. Go on, Charley. (*He hesitates.*) I want to, just for a minute. I never had a chance to say good-by.

Charley moves away, followed by Happy. Biff remains a slight distance up and left of Linda. She sits there, summoning herself. The flute begins, not far away, playing behind her speech.

Linda.   Forgive me, dear. I can't cry. I don't know what it is, but I can't cry. I don't understand it. Why did you ever do that? Help me. Willy, I can't cry. It seems to me that you're just on another trip. I keep expecting you. Willy, dear, I can't cry. Why did you do it? I search and search and I search, and I can't understand it, Willy. I made the last payment on the house today. Today, dear. And there'll be nobody home. (*A sob rises in her throat.*) We're free and clear. (*Sobbing more fully, released.*) We're free. (*Biff comes slowly toward her.*) We're free . . . We're free . . .

Biff lifts her to her feet and moves out up right with her in his arms. Linda sobs quietly. Bernard and Charley come together and follow them, followed by Happy. Only the music of the flute is left on the darkening stage as over the house the hard towers of the apartment buildings rise into sharp focus, and

The Curtain Falls

For Analysis

1. What is Linda's role in the tragedy of Willy? Do you admire her? **2.** In what ways are Biff and Happy similar? In what ways different? Is Biff, as Willy asserts, a failure? Explain. **3.** Which of the brothers is most likely to become another Willy Loman? Explain. **4.** What does Uncle Ben represent to Willy? Are we meant to see Uncle Ben as Willy sees him? Explain. **5.** The play contains many references to the outdoors, the West, working with one's hands. What purpose do these references serve?

On Style

1. Consider the first long stage direction in which Miller describes a **setting** that can move from the present to the past on stage before the audience. The film version of the play simply alternated between the two time periods. Some critics have argued that the ability of the film to realistically recreate the different times damaged the play by diminishing the significant presence of the past in the Loman household. Discuss the difference between the methods, and defend your choice of the better method. **2.** The last paragraph of the first stage direction describes Linda. Comment on the parts of the stage direction that cannot be translated into dramatic action. Why do you suppose Miller wrote of Linda as he did?

Making Connections

1. What advantages do Arthur Miller and David Henry Hwang in *M. Butterfly* (p. 860) gain by interrupting the chronological narrative with flashbacks? **2.** Compare the depiction of the family in this play and Tennessee Williams's *The Glass Menagerie* (p. 209). **3.** Use the following comment by Arthur Miller as the basis for a comparison of this play with Sophocles' *Oedipus Rex* (p. 166) and *Antigonê* (p. 460): ". . . I think the tragic feeling is evoked in us when we are in the presence of a character who is ready to lay down his life, if need be, to secure one thing—his sense of personal dignity."

Writing Topics

1. In an essay, either support or refute the assertion that Willy is a victim of the American Dream. **2.** Argue for or against the view that Biff's treatment of Willy is justified.

Athol Fugard   [b. 1932]

"MASTER HAROLD"...and the Boys   1982

CHARACTERS

Hally
Sam
Willie

The St. George's Park Tea Room on a wet and windy Port Elizabeth afternoon.

Tables and chairs have been cleared and are stacked on one side except for one which stands apart with a single chair. On this table a knife, fork, spoon and side plate in anticipation of a simple meal, together with a pile of comic books.

Other elements: a serving counter with a few stale cakes under glass and a not very impressive display of sweets, cigarettes and cool drinks, etc.; a few cardboard advertising handouts—Cadbury's Chocolate, Coca-Cola—and a blackboard on which an untrained hand has chalked up the prices of Tea, Coffee, Scones, Milkshakes—all flavors—and Cool Drinks; a few sad ferns in pots; a telephone; an old-style jukebox.

There is an entrance on one side and an exit into a kitchen on the other.

Leaning on the solitary table, his head cupped in one hand as he pages through one of the comic books, is Sam. A black man in his mid-forties. He wears the white coat of a waiter. Behind him on his knees, mopping down the floor with a bucket of water and a rag, is Willie. Also black and about the same age as Sam. He has his sleeves and trousers rolled up.

The Year: 1950

Willie *(Singing as he works).*   "She was scandalizin' my name,
   She took my money
   She called me honey
   But she was scandalizin' my name.
   Called it love but was playin' a game . . ."

(He gets up and moves the bucket. Stands thinking for a moment, then, raising his arms to hold an imaginary partner, he launches into an intricate ballroom

dance step. Although a mildly comic figure, he reveals a reasonable degree of accomplishment)

Hey, Sam.

(Sam, absorbed in the comic book, does not respond)

Hey, Boet[1] Sam!

(Sam looks up)

I'm getting it. The quickstep. Look now and tell me. *(He repeats the step)* Well?

Sam *(Encouragingly).*   Show me again.

Willie.   Okay, count for me.

Sam.   Ready?

Willie.   Ready.

Sam.   Five, six, seven, eight . . . *(Willie starts to dance)* A-n-d one two three four . . . and one two three four. . . . *(Ad libbing as Willie dances)* Your shoulders, Willie . . . your shoulders! Don't look down! Look happy, Willie! Relax, Willie!

Willie *(Desperate but still dancing).*   I am relax.

Sam.   No, you're not.

Willie *(He falters).*   Ag no man, Sam! Mustn't talk. You make me make mistakes.

Sam.   But you're too stiff.

Willie.   Yesterday I'm not straight . . . today I'm too stiff!

Sam.   Well, you are. You asked me and I'm telling you.

Willie.   Where?

Sam.   Everywhere. Try to glide through it.

Willie.   Glide?

Sam.   Ja, make it smooth. And give it more style. It must look like you're enjoying yourself.

Willie *(Emphatically).*   I wasn't.

Sam.   Exactly.

Willie.   How can I enjoy myself? No straight, too stiff and now it's also glide, give it more style, make it smooth. . . . Haai! Is hard to remember all those things, Boet Sam.

Sam.   That's your trouble. You're trying too hard.

Willie.   I try hard because it *is* hard.

Sam.   But don't let me see it. The secret is to make it look easy. Ballroom must look happy, Willie, not like hard work. It must . . . Ja! . . . it must look like romance.

---

[1] Afrikaans, meaning "brother."

Willie. Now another one! What's romance?

Sam. Love story with happy ending. A handsome man in tails, and in his arms, smiling at him, a beautiful lady in evening dress!

Willie. Fred Astaire, Ginger Rogers.

Sam. You got it. Tapdance or ballroom, it's the same. Romance. In two weeks' time when the judges look at you and Hilda, they must see a man and a woman who are dancing their way to a happy ending. What I saw was you holding her like you were frightened she was going to run away.

Willie. Ja! Because that is what she wants to do! I got no romance left for Hilda anymore, Boet Sam.

Sam. Then pretend. When you put your arms around Hilda, imagine she is Ginger Rogers.

Willie. With no teeth? You try.

Sam. Well, just remember, there's only two weeks left.

Willie. I know, I know! (*To the jukebox*) I do it better with music. You got sixpence for Sarah Vaughan?

Sam. That's a slow foxtrot. You're practicing the quickstep.

Willie. I'll practice slow foxtrot.

Sam (*Shaking his head*). It's your turn to put money in the jukebox.

Willie. I only got bus fare to go home. (*He returns disconsolately to his work*) Love story and happy ending! She's doing it all right, Boet Sam, but is not me she's giving happy endings. Fuckin' whore! Three nights now she doesn't come practice. I wind up gramophone, I get record ready and I sit and wait. What happens? Nothing. Ten o'clock I start dancing with my pillow. You try and practice romance by yourself, Boet Sam. Struesgod,[2] she doesn't come tonight I take back my dress and ballroom shoes and I find me new partner. Size twenty-six. Shoes size seven. And now she's also making trouble for me with the baby again. Reports me to Child Wellfed, that I'm not giving her money. She lies! Every week I am giving her money for milk. And how do I know is my baby? Only his hair looks like me. She's fucking around all the time I turn my back. Hilda Samuels is a bitch! (*Pause*) Hey, Sam!

Sam. Ja.

Willie. You listening?

Sam. Ja.

Willie. So what you say?

Sam. About Hilda?

Willie. Ja.

Sam. When did you last give her a hiding?

Willie (*Reluctantly*). Sunday night.

Sam. And today is Thursday.

Willie (*He knows what's coming*). Okay.

---

[2] Regional slang, meaning "As true as God." A mild oath.

Sam.   Hiding on Sunday night, then Monday, Tuesday and Wednesday she doesn't come to practice . . . and you are asking me why?

Willie.   I said okay, Boet Sam!

Sam.   You hit her too much. One day she's going to leave you for good.

Willie.   So? She makes me the hell-in too much.

Sam (*Emphasizing his point*).   *Too* much and *too* hard. You had the same trouble with Eunice.

Willie.   Because she also make the hell-in, Boet Sam. She never got the steps right. Even the waltz.

Sam.   Beating her up every time she makes a mistake in the waltz? (*Shaking his head*) No, Willie! That takes the pleasure out of ballroom dancing.

Willie.   Hilda is not too bad with the waltz, Boet Sam. Is the quickstep where the trouble starts.

Sam (*Teasing him gently*).   How's your pillow with the quickstep?

Willie (*Ignoring the tease*).   Good! And why? Because it got no legs. That's her trouble. She can't move them quick enough, Boet Sam. I start the record and before halfway Count Basie is already winning. Only time we catch up with him is when gramophone runs down.

(*Sam laughs*)

Haaikona,[3] Boet Sam, is not funny.

Sam (*Snapping his fingers*).   I got it! Give her a handicap.

Willie.   What's that?

Sam.   Give her a ten-second start and then let Count Basie go. Then I put my money on her. Hot favorite in the Ballroom Stakes: Hilda Samuels ridden by Willie Malopo.

Willie (*Turning away*).   I'm not talking to you no more.

Sam (*Relenting*).   Sorry, Willie . . .

Willie.   It's finish between us.

Sam.   Okay, okay . . . I'll stop.

Willie.   You can also fuck off.

Sam.   Willie, listen! I want to help you!

Willie.   No more jokes?

Sam.   I promise.

Willie.   Okay. Help me.

Sam (*His turn to hold an imaginary partner*).   Look and learn. Feet together. Back straight. Body relaxed. Right hand placed gently in the small of her back and wait for the music. Don't start worrying about making mistakes or the judges or the other competitors. It's just you, Hilda and the music, and you're going to have a good time. What Count Basie do you play?

Willie.   "You the cream in my coffee, you the salt in my stew."

---

[3] Zulu word meaning, "Don't"; here meaning, "Don't laugh."

Sam.   Right. Give it to me in strict tempo.
Willie.   Ready?
Sam.   Ready.
Willie.   A-n-d . . . (*Singing*)
  "You the cream in my coffee.
  You the salt in my stew.
  You will always be my necessity.
  I'd be lost without you. . . ." (*etc.*)

(*Sam launches into the quickstep. He is obviously a much more accomplished dancer than Willie. Hally enters. A seventeen-year-old white boy. Wet raincoat and school case. He stops and watches Sam. The demonstration comes to an end with a flourish. Applause from Hally and Willie*)

Hally.   Bravo! No question about it. First place goes to Mr. Sam Semela.
Willie (*In total agreement*).   You was gliding with style, Boet Sam.
Hally (*Cheerfully*).   How's it, chaps?
Sam.   Okay, Hally.
Willie (*Springing to attention like a soldier and saluting*).   At your service, Master Harold!
Hally.   Not long to the big event, hey!
Sam.   Two weeks.
Hally.   You nervous?
Sam.   No.
Hally.   Think you stand a chance?
Sam.   Let's just say I'm ready to go out there and dance.
Hally.   It looked like it. What about you, Willie?

(*Willie groans*)

  What's the matter?
Sam.   He's got leg trouble.
Hally (*Innocently*).   Oh, sorry to hear that, Willie.
Willie.   Boet Sam! You promised. (*Willie returns to his work*)

(*Hally deposits his school case and takes off his raincoat. His clothes are a little neglected and untidy: black blazer with school badge, gray flannel trousers in need of an ironing, khaki shirt and tie, black shoes. Sam has fetched a towel for Hally to dry his hair*)

Hally.   God, what a lousy bloody day. It's coming down cats and dogs out there. Bad for business, chaps . . . (*Conspiratorial whisper*) . . . but it also means we're in for a nice quiet afternoon.
Sam.   You can speak loud. Your Mom's not here.

Hally. Out shopping?

Sam. No. The hospital.

Hally. But it's Thursday. There's no visiting on Thursday afternoons. Is my Dad okay?

Sam. Sounds like it. In fact, I think he's going home.

Hally (*Stopped short by Sam's remark*). What do you mean?

Sam. The hospital phoned.

Hally. To say what?

Sam. I don't know. I just heard your Mom talking.

Hally. So what makes you say he's going home?

Sam. It sounded as if they were telling her to come and fetch him.

(*Hally thinks about what Sam has said for a few seconds*)

Hally. When did she leave?

Sam. About an hour ago. She said she would phone you. Want to eat?

(*Hally doesn't respond*)

Hally, want your lunch?

Hally. I suppose so. (*His mood has changed*) What's on the menu? . . . as if I don't know.

Sam. Soup, followed by meat pie and gravy.

Hally. Today's?

Sam. No.

Hally. And the soup?

Sam. Nourishing pea soup.

Hally. Just the soup. (*The pile of comic books on the table*) And these?

Sam. For your Dad. Mr. Kempston brought them.

Hally. You haven't been reading them, have you?

Sam. Just looking.

Hally (*Examining the comics*). *Jungle Jim* . . . *Batman and Robin* . . . *Tarzan* . . . God, what rubbish! Mental pollution. Take them away.

(*Sam exits waltzing into the kitchen. Hally turns to Willie*)

Hally. Did you hear my Mom talking on the telephone, Willie?

Willie. No, Master Hally. I was at the back.

Hally. And she didn't say anything to you before she left?

Willie. She said I must clean the floors.

Hally. I mean about my Dad.

Willie. She didn't say anything to me about him, Master Hally.

Hally (*With conviction*). No! It can't be. They said he needed at least another three weeks of treatment. Sam's definitely made a mistake. (*Rummages* *through his school case, finds a book and settles down at the table to read)* So, Willie!

Willie. Yes, Master Hally! Schooling okay today?

Hally. Yes, okay. . . . *(He thinks about it)* . . . No, not really. Ag, what's the difference? I don't care. And Sam says you've got problems.

Willie. Big problems.

Hally. Which leg is sore?

(Willie groans)

Both legs.

Willie. There is nothing wrong with my legs. Sam is just making jokes.

Hally. So then you *will* be in the competition.

Willie. Only if I can find me a partner.

Hally. But what about Hilda?

Sam *(Returning with a bowl of soup).* She's the one who's got trouble with her legs.

Hally. What sort of trouble, Willie?

Sam. From the way he describes it, I think the lady has gone a bit lame.

Hally. Good God! Have you taken her to see a doctor?

Sam. I think a vet would be better.

Hally. What do you mean?

Sam. What do you call it again when a racehorse goes very fast?

Hally. Gallop?

Sam. That's it!

Willie. Boet Sam!

Hally. "A gallop down the homestretch to the winning post." But what's that got to do with Hilda?

Sam. Count Basie always gets there first.

(Willie lets fly with his slop rag. It misses Sam and hits Hally)

Hally *(Furious).* For Christ's sake, Willie! What the hell do you think you're doing!

Willie. Sorry, Master Hally, but it's him. . . .

Hally. Act your bloody age! *(Hurls the rag back at Willie)* Cut out the nonsense now and get on with your work. And you too, Sam. Stop fooling around.

(Sam moves away)

No. Hang on. I haven't finished! Tell me exactly what my Mom said.

Sam. I have. "When Hally comes, tell him I've gone to the hospital and I'll phone him."

Hally. She didn't say anything about taking my Dad home?

Sam. No. It's just that when she was talking on the phone . . .

Hally *(Interrupting him).* No, Sam. They can't be discharging him. She would have said so if they were. In any case, we saw him last night and he wasn't in good shape at all. Staff nurse even said there was talk about taking more X-rays. And now suddenly today he's better? If anything, it sounds more like a bad turn to me . . . which I sincerely hope it isn't. Hang on . . . how long ago did you say she left?

Sam. Just before two . . . *(His wrist watch)* . . . hour and a half.

Hally. I know how to settle it. *(Behind the counter to the telephone. Talking as he dials)* Let's give her ten minutes to get to the hospital, ten minutes to load him up, another ten, at the most, to get home and another ten to get him inside. Forty minutes. They should have been home for at least half an hour already. *(Pause—he waits with the receiver to his ear)* No reply, chaps. And you know why? Because she's at his bedside in hospital helping him pull through a bad turn. You definitely heard wrong.

Sam. Okay.

(As far as Hally is concerned, the matter is settled. He returns to his table, sits down and divides his attention between the book and his soup. Sam is at his school case and picks up a textbook)

Modern Graded Mathematics for Standards Nine and Ten. *(Opens it at random and laughs at something he sees)* Who is this supposed to be?

Hally. Old fart-face Prentice.

Sam. Teacher?

Hally. Thinks he is. And believe me, that is not a bad likeness.

Sam. Has he seen it?

Hally. Yes.

Sam. What did he say?

Hally. Tried to be clever, as usual. Said I was no Leonardo da Vinci and that bad art had to be punished. So, six of the best, and his are bloody good.

Sam. On your bum?

Hally. Where else? The days when I got them on my hands are gone forever, Sam.

Sam. With your trousers down!

Hally. No. He's not quite that barbaric.

Sam. That's the way they do it in jail.

Hally *(Flicker of morbid interest).* Really?

Sam. Ja. When the magistrate sentences you to "strokes with a light cane."

Hally. Go on.

Sam. They make you lie down on a bench. One policeman pulls down your trousers and holds your ankles, another one pulls your shirt over your head and holds your arms . . .

Hally. Thank you! That's enough.

Sam. . . . and the one that gives you the strokes talks to you gently and for a long time between each one. (*He laughs*)

Hally. I've heard enough, Sam! Jesus! It's a bloody awful world when you come to think of it. People can be real bastards.

Sam. That's the way it is, Hally.

Hally. It doesn't *have* to be that way. There is something called progress, you know. We don't exactly burn people at the stake anymore.

Sam. Like Joan of Arc.

Hally. Correct. If she was captured today, she'd be given a fair trial.

Sam. And then the death sentence.

Hally (*A world-weary-sigh*). I know, I know! I oscillate between hope and despair for this world as well, Sam. But things will change, you wait and see. One day somebody is going to get up and give history a kick up the backside and get it going again.

Sam. Like who?

Hally (*After thought*). They're called social reformers. Every age, Sam, has got its social reformer. My history book is full of them.

Sam. So where's ours?

Hally. Good question. And I hate to say it, but the answer is: I don't know. Maybe he hasn't even been born yet. Or is still only a babe in arms at his mother's breast. God, what a thought.

Sam. So we just go on waiting.

Hally. Ja, looks like it. (*Back to his soup and the book*)

Sam (*Reading from the textbook*). "Introduction: In some mathematical problems only the magnitude . . ." (*He mispronounces the word "magnitude"*)

Hally (*Correcting him without looking up*). Magnitude.

Sam. What's it mean?

Hally. How big it is. The size of the thing.

Sam (*Reading*). ". . . magnitude of the quantities is of importance. In other problems we need to know whether these quantities are negative or positive. For example, where there is a debit or credit bank balance . . ."

Hally. Whether you're broke or not.

Sam. ". . . whether the temperature is above or below Zero . . ."

Hally. Naught degrees. Cheerful state of affairs! No cash and you're freezing to death. Mathematics won't get you out of that one.

Sam. "All these quantities are called . . ." (*Spelling the word*) . . . s-c-a-l . . .

Hally. Scalars.

Sam. Scalars! (*Shaking his head with a laugh*) You understand all that?

Hally (*Turning a page*). No. And I don't intend to try.

Sam. So what happens when the exams come?

Hally. Failing a maths exam isn't the end of the world, Sam. How many times have I told you that examination results don't measure intelligence?

Sam. I would say about as many times as you've failed one of them.

Hally (*Mirthlessly*). Ha, ha, ha.

Sam *(Simultaneously)*.   Ha, ha, ha.

Hally.   Just remember Winston Churchill didn't do particularly well at school.

Sam.   You've also told me that one many times.

Hally.   Well, it just so happens to be the truth.

Sam *(Enjoying the word)*.   Magnitude! Magnitude! Show me how to use it.

Hally *(After thought)*.   An intrepid social reformer will not be daunted by the magnitude of the task he has undertaken.

Sam *(Impressed)*.   Couple of jaw-breakers in there!

Hally.   I gave you three for the price of one. Intrepid, daunted and magnitude. I did that once in an exam. Put five of the words I had to explain in one sentence. It was half a page long.

Sam.   Well, I'll put my money on you in the English exam.

Hally.   Piece of cake. Eighty percent without even trying.

Sam *(Another textbook from Hally's case)*.   And history?

Hally.   So-so. I'll scrape through. In the fifties if I'm lucky.

Sam.   You didn't do too badly last year.

Hally.   Because we had World War One. That at least had some action. You try to find that in the South African Parliamentary system.

Sam *(Reading from the history textbook)*.   "Napoleon and the principle of equality." Hey! This sounds interesting. "After concluding peace with Britain in 1802, Napoleon used a brief period of calm to in-sti-tute . . ."

Hally.   Introduce.

Sam.   ". . . many reforms. Napoleon regarded all people as equal before the law and wanted them to have equal opportunities for advancement. All vesti-ges of the feu-dal system with its oppression of the poor were abolished." Vestiges, feudal system and abolished. I'm all right on oppression.

Hally.   I'm thinking. He swept away . . . abolished . . . the last remains . . . vestiges . . . of the bad old days . . . feudal system.

Sam.   Ha! There's the social reformer we're waiting for. He sounds like a man of some magnitude.

Hally.   I'm not so sure about that. It's a damn good title for a book, though. A man of magnitude!

Sam.   He sounds pretty big to me, Hally.

Hally.   Don't confuse historical significance with greatness. But maybe I'm being a bit prejudiced. Have a look in there and you'll see he's two chapters long. And hell! . . . has he only got dates, Sam, all of which you've got to remember! This campaign and that campaign, and then, because of all the fighting, the next thing is we get Peace Treaties all over the place. And what's the end of the story? Battle of Waterloo, which he loses. Wasn't worth it. No, I don't know about him as a man of magnitude.

Sam.   Then who would you say was?

Hally.   To answer that, we need a definition of greatness, and I suppose that would be somebody who . . . somebody who benefited all mankind.

Sam.   Right. But like who?

Hally (*He speaks with total conviction*).   Charles Darwin. Remember him? That big book from the library. *The Origin of the Species.*

Sam.   Him?

Hally.   Yes. For his Theory of Evolution.

Sam.   You didn't finish it.

Hally.   I ran out of time. I didn't finish it because my two weeks was up. But I'm going to take it out again after I've digested what I read. It's safe. I've hidden it away in the Theology section. Nobody ever goes in there. And anyway who are you to talk? You hardly even looked at it.

Sam.   I tried. I looked at the chapters in the beginning and I saw one called "The Struggle for an Existence." Ah ha, I thought. At last! But what did I get? Something called the mistiltoe which needs the apple tree and there's too many seeds and all are going to die except one . . . ! No, Hally.

Hally (*Intellectually outraged*).   What do you mean, No! The poor man had to start somewhere. For God's sake, Sam, he revolutionized science. Now we know.

Sam.   What?

Hally.   Where we come from and what it all means.

Sam.   And that's a benefit to mankind? Anyway, I still don't believe it.

Hally.   God, you're impossible. I showed it to you in black and white.

Sam.   Doesn't mean I got to believe it.

Hally.   It's the likes of you that kept the Inquisition in business. It's called bigotry. Anyway, that's my man of magnitude. Charles Darwin! Who's yours?

Sam (*Without hesitation*).   Abraham Lincoln.

Hally.   I might have guessed as much. Don't get sentimental, Sam. You've never been a slave, you know. And anyway we freed your ancestors here in South Africa long before the Americans. But if you want to thank somebody on their behalf, do it to Mr. William Wilberforce.[4] Come on. Try again. I want a real genius.

(*Now enjoying himself, and so is Sam. Hally goes behind the counter and helps himself to a chocolate*)

Sam.   William Shakespeare.

Hally (*No enthusiasm*).   Oh. So you're also one of them, are you? You're basing that opinion on only one play, you know. You've only read my *Julius Caesar* and even I don't understand half of what they're talking about. They should do what they did with the old Bible: bring the language up to date.

Sam.   That's all you've got. It's also the only one *you've* read.

Hally.   I know. I admit it. That's why I suggest we reserve our judgment until we've checked up on a few others. I've got a feeling, though, that by the end

---

[4] William Wilberforce (1759–1833), an English statesman whose vigorous opposition to slavery led to the Emancipation Act of 1833 that ended slavery in the British Empire.

of this year one is going to be enough for me, and I can give you the names of twenty-nine other chaps in the Standard Nine class of the Port Elizabeth Technical College who feel the same. But if you want him, you can have him. My turn now. *(Pacing)* This is a damned good exercise, you know! It started off looking like a simple question and here it's got us really probing into the intellectual heritage of our civilization.

Sam. So who is it going to be?

Hally. My next man . . . and he gets the title on two scores: social reform and literary genius . . . is Leo Nikolaevich Tolstoy.

Sam. That Russian.

Hally. Correct. Remember the picture of him I showed you?

Sam. With the long beard.

Hally *(Trying to look like Tolstoy)*. And those burning, visionary eyes. My God, the face of a social prophet if ever I saw one! And remember my words when I showed it to you? Here's a *man*, Sam!

Sam. Those were words, Hally.

Hally. Not many intellectuals are prepared to shovel manure with the peasants and then go home and write a "little book" called *War and Peace*. Incidentally, Sam, he was somebody else who, to quote, ". . . did not distinguish himself scholastically."

Sam. Meaning?

Hally. He was also no good at school.

Sam. Like you and Winston Churchill.

Hally *(Mirthlessly)*. Ha, ha, ha.

Sam *(Simultaneously)*. Ha, ha, ha.

Hally. Don't get clever, Sam. That man freed his serfs of his own free will.

Sam. No argument. He was a somebody, all right. I accept him.

Hally. I'm sure Count Tolstoy will be very pleased to hear that. Your turn. Shoot. *(Another chocolate from behind the counter)* I'm waiting, Sam.

Sam. I've got him.

Hally. Good. Submit your candidate for examination.

Sam. Jesus.

Hally *(Stopped him dead in his tracks)*. Who?

Sam. Jesus Christ.

Hally. Oh, come on, Sam!

Sam. The Messiah.

Hally. Ja, but still . . . No, Sam. Don't let's get started on religion. We'll just spend the whole afternoon arguing again. Suppose I turn around and say Mohammed?

Sam. All right.

Hally. You can't have them both on the same list!

Sam. Why not? You like Mohammed, I like Jesus.

Hally. I *don't* like Mohammed. I never have. I was merely being hypothetical.

As far as I'm concerned, the Koran is as bad as the Bible. No. Religion is out! I'm not going to waste my time again arguing with you about the existence of God. You know perfectly well I'm an atheist . . . and I've got homework to do.

Sam. Okay, I take him back.

Hally. You've got time for one more name.

Sam *(After thought).* I've got one I know we'll agree on. A simple straightforward great Man of Magnitude . . . and no arguments. And *he* really *did* benefit all mankind.

Hally. I wonder. After your last contribution I'm beginning to doubt whether anything in the way of an intellectual agreement is possible between the two of us. Who is he?

Sam. Guess.

Hally. Socrates? Alexandre Dumas? Karl Marx? Dostoevsky? Nietzsche?

(Sam shakes his head after each name)

Give me a clue.

Sam. The letter P is important . . .

Hally. Plato!

Sam. . . . and his name begins with an F.

Hally. I've got it. Freud and Psychology.

Sam. No. I didn't understand him.

Hally. That makes two of us.

Sam. Think of mouldy apricot jam.

Hally *(After a delighted laugh).* Penicillin and Sir Alexander Fleming! And the title of the book: *The Microbe Hunters. (Delighted)* Splendid, Sam! Splendid. For once we are in total agreement. The major breakthrough in medical science in the Twentieth Century. If it wasn't for him, we might have lost the Second World War. It's deeply gratifying, Sam, to know that I haven't been wasting my time in talking to you. *(Strutting around proudly)* Tolstoy may have educated his peasants, but I've educated you.

Sam. Standard Four to Standard Nine.

Hally. Have we been at it as long as that?

Sam. Yep. And my first lesson was geography.

Hally *(Intrigued).* Really? I don't remember.

Sam. My room there at the back of the old Jubilee Boarding House. I had just started working for your Mom. Little boy in short trousers walks in one afternoon and asks me seriously: "Sam, do you want to see South Africa?" Hey man! Sure I wanted to see South Africa!

Hally. Was that me?

Sam. . . . So the next thing I'm looking at a map you had just done for homework. It was your first one and you were very proud of yourself.

Hally. Go on.

Sam. Then came my first lesson. "Repeat after me, Sam: Gold in the Transvaal, mealies in the Free State, sugar in Natal and grapes in the Cape." I still know it!

Hally. Well, I'll be buggered. So that's how it all started.

Sam. And your next map was one with all the rivers and the mountains they came from. The Orange, the Vaal, the Limpopo, the Zambezi . . .

Hally. You've got a phenomenal memory!

Sam. You should be grateful. That is why you started passing your exams. You tried to be better than me.

(They laugh together. Willie is attracted by the laughter and joins them)

Hally. The old Jubilee Boarding House. Sixteen rooms with board and lodging, rent in advance and one week's notice. I haven't thought about it for donkey's years . . . and I don't think that's an accident. God, was I glad when we sold it and moved out. Those years are not remembered as the happiest ones of an unhappy childhood.

Willie *(Knocking on the table to imitate a woman's voice).* "Hally, are you there?"

Hally. Who's that supposed to be?

Willie. "What you doing in there, Hally? Come out at once!"

Hally *(To Sam).* What's he talking about?

Sam. Don't you remember?

Willie. "Sam, Willie . . . is he in there with you boys?"

Sam. Hiding away in our room when your mother was looking for you.

Hally *(Another good laugh).* Of course! I used to crawl and hide under your bed! But finish the story, Willie. Then what used to happen? You chaps would give the game away by telling her I was in there with you. So much for friendship.

Sam. We couldn't lie to her. She knew.

Hally. Which meant I got another rowing for hanging around the "servants' quarters." I think I spent more time in there with you chaps than anywhere else in that dump. And do you blame me? Nothing but bloody misery wherever you went. Somebody was always complaining about the food, or my mother was having a fight with Micky Nash because she'd caught her with a petty officer in her room. Maud Meiring was another one. Remember those two? They were prostitutes, you know. Soldiers and sailors from the troopships. Bottom fell out of the business when the war ended. God, the flotsam and jetsam that life washed up on our shores! No joking, if it wasn't for your room, I would have been the first certified ten-year-old in medical history. Ja, the memories are coming back now. Walking home from school and thinking: "What can I do this afternoon?" Try out a few ideas, but sooner or later I'd end up in there with you fellows. I bet you I could still find my way to your room with my eyes closed. *(He does exactly that)* Down the corridor . . . telephone on the right, which my Mom keeps locked because somebody is using it on the sly and not paying . . . past the kitchen and unappetizing cooking smells . . . around the corner into the backyard, hold my breath again because there are more smells coming when I pass your lavatory, then into that little passageway, first door on the right and into your room. How's that?

Sam. Good. But, as usual, you forgot to knock.

Hally. Like that time I barged in and caught you and Cynthia . . . at it. Remember? God, was I embarrassed! I didn't know what was going on at first.

Sam. Ja, that taught you a lesson.

Hally. And about a lot more than knocking on doors, I'll have you know, and I don't mean geography either. Hell, Sam, couldn't you have waited until it was dark?

Sam. No.

Hally. Was it that urgent?

Sam. Yes, and if you don't believe me, wait until your time comes.

Hally. No, thank you. I am not interested in girls. *(Back to his memories . . . Using a few chairs he recreates the room as he lists the items)* A gray little wall . . . and I now know why the mattress sags so much! . . . Willie's bed . . . it's propped up on bricks because one leg is broken . . . that wobbly little table with the washbasin and jug of water . . . Yes! . . . stuck to the wall above it are some pin-up pictures from magazines. Joe Louis . . .

Willie. Brown Bomber. World Title. *(Boxing pose)* Three rounds and knockout.

Hally. Against who?

Sam. Max Schmeling.

Hally. Correct. I can also remember Fred Astaire and Ginger Rogers, and Rita Hayworth in a bathing costume which always made me hot and bothered when I looked at it. Under Willie's bed is an old suitcase with all his clothes in a mess, which is why I never hide there. Your things are neat and tidy in a trunk next to your bed, and on it there is a picture of you and Cynthia in your ballroom clothes, your first silver cup for third place in a competition and an old radio which doesn't work anymore. Have I left out anything?

Sam. No.

Hally. Right, so much for the stage directions. Now the characters. *(Sam and Willie move to their appropriate positions in the bedroom)* Willie is in bed, under his blankets with his clothes on, complaining non-stop about something, but we can't make out a word of what he's saying because he's got his head under the blankets as well. You're on your bed trimming your toenails with a knife—not a very edifying sight—and as for me . . . What am I doing?

Sam. You're sitting on the floor giving Willie a lecture about being a good loser while you get the checker board and pieces ready for a game. Then you go to Willie's bed, pull off the blankets and make him play with you first because you know you're going to win, and that gives you the second game with me.

Hally. And you certainly were a bad loser, Willie!

Willie. Haai!

Hally. Wasn't he, Sam? And so slow! A game with you almost took the whole afternoon. Thank God I gave up trying to teach you how to play chess.

Willie. You and Sam cheated.

Hally. I never saw Sam cheat, and mine were mostly the mistakes of youth.

Willie. Then how is it you two was always winning?

Hally. Have you ever considered the possibility, Willie, that it was because we were better than you?

Willie. Every time better?

Hally. Not every time. There were occasions when we deliberately let you win a game so that you would stop sulking and go on playing with us. Sam used to wink at me when you weren't looking to show me it was time to let you win.

Willie. So then you two didn't play fair.

Hally. It was for your benefit, Mr. Malopo, which is more than being fair. It was an act of self-sacrifice. *(To Sam)* But you know what my best memory is, don't you?

Sam. No.

Hally. Come on, guess. If your memory is so good, you must remember it as well.

Sam. We got up to a lot of tricks in there, Hally.

Hally. This one was special, Sam.

Sam. I'm listening.

Hally. It started off looking like another of those useless nothing-to-do afternoons. I'd already been down to Main Street looking for adventure, but nothing had happened. I didn't feel like climbing trees in the Donkin Park or pretending I was a private eye and following a stranger . . . so as usual: See what's cooking in Sam's room. This time it was you on the floor. You had two thin pieces of wood and you were smoothing them down with a knife. It didn't look particularly interesting, but when I asked you what you were doing, you just said, "Wait and see, Hally. Wait . . . and see" . . . in that secret sort of way of yours, so I knew there was a surprise coming. You teased me, you bugger, by being deliberately slow and not answering my questions!

(Sam laughs)

And whistling while you worked away! God, it was infuriating! I could have brained you! It was only when you tied them together in a cross and put that down on the brown paper that I realized what you were doing. "Sam is making a kite?" And when I asked you and you said "Yes" . . . ! *(Shaking his head with disbelief)* The sheer audacity of it took my breath away. I mean, seriously, what the hell does a black man know about flying a kite? I'll be honest with you, Sam, I had no hopes for it. If you think I was excited and happy, you got another guess coming. In fact, I was shit-scared that we were going to make fools of ourselves. When we left the boarding house to go up onto the hill, I was praying quietly that there wouldn't be any other kids around to laugh at us.

Sam (*Enjoying the memory as much as Hally*).   Ja, I could see that.

Hally.   I made it obvious, did I?

Sam.   Ja. You refused to carry it.

Hally.   Do you blame me? Can you remember what the poor thing looked like? Tomato-box wood and brown paper! Flour and water for glue! Two of my mother's old stockings for a tail, and then all those bits and pieces of string you made me tie together so that we could fly it! Hell, no, that was now only asking for a miracle to happen.

Sam.   Then the big argument when I told you to hold the string and run with it when I let go.

Hally.   I was prepared to run, all right, but straight back to the boarding house.

Sam (*Knowing what's coming*).   So what happened?

Hally.   Come on, Sam, you remember as well as I do.

Sam.   I want to hear it from you.

(*Hally pauses. He wants to be as accurate as possible*)

Hally.   You went a little distance from me down the hill, you held it up ready to let it go. . . . "This is it," I thought. "Like everything else in my life, here comes another fiasco." Then you shouted, "Go, Hally!" and I started to run. (*Another pause*) I don't know how to describe it, Sam. Ja! The miracle happened! I was running, waiting for it to crash to the ground, but instead suddenly there was something alive behind me at the end of the string, tugging at it as if it wanted to be free. I looked back . . . (*Shakes his head*) . . . I still can't believe my eyes. It was flying! Looping around and trying to climb even higher into the sky. You shouted to me to let it have more string. I did, until there was none left and I was just holding that piece of wood we had tied it to. You came up and joined me. You were laughing.

Sam.   So were you. And shouting, "It works, Sam! We've done it!"

Hally.   And we had! I was so proud of us! It was the most splendid thing I had ever seen. I wished there were hundreds of kids around to watch us. The part that scared me, though, was when you showed me how to make it dive down to the ground and then just when it was on the point of crashing, swoop up again!

Sam.   You didn't want to try yourself.

Hally.   Of course not! I would have been suicidal if anything had happened to it. Watching you do it made me nervous enough. I was quite happy just to see it up there with its tail fluttering behind it. You left me after that, didn't you? You explained how to get it down, we tied it to the bench so that I could sit and watch it, and you went away. I wanted you to stay, you know. I was a little scared of having to look after it by myself.

Sam (*Quietly*).   I had work to do, Hally.

Hally.   It was sort of sad bringing it down, Sam. And it looked sad again when it was lying there on the ground. Like something that had lost its soul. Just tomato-box wood, brown paper and two of my mother's old stockings! But, hell, I'll never forget that first moment when I saw it up there. I had a stiff neck the next day from looking up so much.

(*Sam laughs. Hally turns to him with a question he never thought of asking before*)

Why did you make that kite, Sam?

Sam (*Evenly*).   I can't remember.

Hally.   Truly?

Sam.   Too long ago, Hally.

Hally.   Ja, I suppose it was. It's time for another one, you know.

Sam.   Why do you say that?

Hally.   Because it feels like that. Wouldn't be a good day to fly it, though.

Sam.   No. You can't fly kites on rainy days.

Hally (*He studies Sam. Their memories have made him conscious of the man's presence in his life*).   How old are you, Sam?

Sam.   Two score and five.

Hally.   Strange, isn't it?

Sam.   What?

Hally.   Me and you.

Sam.   What's strange about it?

Hally.   Little white boy in short trousers and a black man old enough to be his father flying a kite. It's not every day you see that.

Sam.   But why strange? Because the one is white and the other black?

Hally.   I don't know. Would have been just as strange, I suppose, if it had been me and my Dad . . . cripple man and a little boy! Nope! There's no chance of me flying a kite without it being strange. (*Simple statement of fact—no self-pity*) There's a nice little short story there. "The Kite-Flyers." But we'd have to find a twist in the ending.

Sam.   Twist?

Hally.   Yes. Something unexpected. The way it ended with us was too straightforward . . . me on the bench and you going back to work. There's no drama in that.

Willie.   And me?

Hally.   You?

Willie.   Yes me.

Hally.   You want to get into the story as well, do you? I got it! Change the title: "Afternoons in Sam's Room" . . . expand it and tell all the stories. It's on its way to being a novel. Our days in the old Jubilee. Sad in a way that they're over. I almost wish we were still in that little room.

Sam.   We're still together.

Hally.   That's true. It's just that life felt the right size in there . . . not too big and not too small. Wasn't so hard to work up a bit of courage. It's got so bloody complicated since then.

(*The telephone rings. Sam answers it*)

Sam.   St. George's Park Tea Room . . . Hello, Madam . . . Yes, Madam, he's here . . . Hally, it's your mother.

Hally.   Where is she phoning from?

Sam.   Sounds like the hospital. It's a public telephone.

Hally (*Relieved*).   You see! I told you. (*The telephone*) Hello, Mom . . . Yes . . . Yes no fine. Everything's under control here. How's things with poor old Dad? . . . Has he had a bad turn? . . . What? . . . Oh, God! . . . Yes, Sam told me, but I was sure he'd made a mistake. But what's this all about, Mom? He didn't look at all good last night. How can he get better so quickly? . . . Then very obviously you must say no. Be firm with him. You're the boss. . . . You know what it's going to be like if he comes home. . . . Well then, don't blame me when I fail my exams at the end of the year. . . . Yes! How am I expected to be fresh for school when I spend half the night massaging his gammy leg? . . . So am I! . . . So tell him a white lie. Say Dr. Colley wants more X-rays of his stump. Or bribe him. We'll sneak in double tots of brandy in future. . . . What? . . . Order him to get back into bed at once! If he's going to behave like a child, treat him like one. . . . All right, Mom! I was just trying to . . . I'm sorry. . . . I said I'm sorry. . . . Quick, give me your number. I'll phone you back. (*He hangs up and waits a few seconds*) Here we go again! (*He dials*) I'm sorry, Mom. . . . Okay . . . But now listen to me carefully. All it needs is for you to put your foot down. Don't take no for an answer. . . . Did you hear me? And whatever you do, don't discuss it with him. . . . Because I'm frightened you'll give in to him. . . . Yes, Sam gave me lunch. . . . I ate all of it! . . . No, Mom, not a soul. It's still raining here. . . . Right, I'll tell them. I'll just do some homework and then lock up. . . . But remember now, Mom. Don't listen to anything he says. And phone me back and let me know what happens. . . . Okay. Bye, Mom. (*He hangs up. The men are staring at him*) My Mom says that when you're finished with the floors you must do the windows. (*Pause*) Don't misunderstand me, chaps. All I want is for him to get better. And if he was, I'd be the first person to say: "Bring him home." But he's not, and we can't give him the medical care and attention he needs at home. That's what hospitals are there for. (*Brusquely*) So don't just stand there! Get on with it!

(*Sam clears Hally's table*)

You heard right. My Dad wants to go home.

Sam.   Is he better?

Hally (*Sharply*).   No! How the hell can he be better when last night he was groaning with pain? This is not an age of miracles!

Sam.   Then he should stay in hospital.

Hally (*Seething with irritation and frustration*).   Tell me something I don't know, Sam. What the hell do you think I was saying to my Mom? All I can say is fuck-it-all.

Sam.   I'm sure he'll listen to your Mom.

Hally.   You don't know what she's up against. He's already packed his shaving kit and pajamas and is sitting on his bed with his crutches, dressed and ready to go. I know him when he gets in that mood. If she tries to reason with him, we've had it. She's no match for him when it comes to a battle of words. He'll tie her up in knots. (*Trying to hide his true feelings*)

Sam.   I suppose it gets lonely for him in there.

Hally.   With all the patients and nurses around? Regular visits from the Salvation Army? Balls! It's ten times worse for him at home. I'm at school and my mother is here in the business all day.

Sam.   He's at least got you at night.

Hally (*Before he can stop himself*).   And we've got him! Please! I don't want to talk about it anymore. (*Unpacks his school case, slamming down books on the table*) Life is just a plain bloody mess, that's all. And people are fools.

Sam.   Come on, Hally.

Hally.   Yes, they are! They bloody well deserve what they get.

Sam.   Then don't complain.

Hally.   Don't try to be clever, Sam. It doesn't suit you. Anybody who thinks there's nothing wrong with this world needs to have his head examined. Just when things are going along all right, without fail someone or something will come along and spoil everything. Somebody should write that down as a fundamental law of the Universe. The principle of perpetual disappointment. If there is a God who created this world, he should scrap it and try again.

Sam.   All right, Hally, all right. What you got for homework?

Hally.   Bullshit, as usual. (*Opens an exercise book and reads*) "Write five hundred words describing an annual event of cultural or historical significance."

Sam.   That should be easy enough for you.

Hally.   And also plain bloody boring. You know what he wants, don't you? One of their useless old ceremonies. The commemoration of the 1820 Settlers, or if it's going to be culture, Carols by Candlelight every Christmas.

Sam.   It's an impressive sight. Make a good description, Hally. All those candles glowing in the dark and the people singing hymns.

Hally.   And it's called religious hysteria. (*Intense irritation*) Please, Sam! Just leave me alone and let me get on with it. I'm not in the mood for games this afternoon. And remember my Mom's orders . . . you're to help Willie with the windows. Come on now, I don't want any more nonsense in here.

Sam.   Okay, Hally, okay.

(Hally settles down to his homework; determined preparations . . . pen, ruler, exercise book, dictionary, another cake . . . all of which will lead to nothing.)

(Sam waltzes over to Willie and starts to replace tables and chairs. He practices a ballroom step while doing so. Willie watches. When Sam is finished, Willie tries) Good! But just a little bit quicker on the turn and only move in to her after she's crossed over. What about this one?

(Another step. When Sam is finished, Willie again has a go)

Much better. See what happens when you just relax and enjoy yourself? Remember that in two weeks' time and you'll be all right.

Willie.   But I haven't got partner, Boet Sam.

Sam.   Maybe Hilda will turn up tonight.

Willie.   No, Boet Sam. *(Reluctantly)* I gave her a good hiding.

Sam.   You mean a bad one.

Willie.   Good bad one.

Sam.   Then you mustn't complain either. Now you pay the price for losing your temper.

Willie.   I also pay two pounds ten shilling entrance fee.

Sam.   They'll refund you if you withdraw now.

Willie *(Appalled).*   You mean, don't dance?

Sam.   Yes.

Willie.   No! I wait too long and I practice too hard. If I find me new partner, you think I can be ready in two weeks? I ask Madam for my leave now and we practice every day.

Sam.   Quickstep non-stop for two weeks. World record, Willie, but you'll be mad at the end.

Willie.   No jokes, Boet Sam.

Sam.   I'm not joking.

Willie.   So then what?

Sam.   Find Hilda. Say you're sorry and promise you won't beat her again.

Willie.   No.

Sam.   Then withdraw. Try again next year.

Willie.   No.

Sam.   Then I give up.

Willie.   Haaikona, Boet Sam, you can't.

Sam.   What do you mean, I can't? I'm telling you: I give up.

Willie *(Adamant).*   No! *(Accusingly)* It was you who start me ballroom dancing.

Sam.   So?

Willie.   Before that I use to be happy. And is you and Miriam who bring me to Hilda and say here's partner for you.

Sam.   What are you saying, Willie?

Willie. You!

Sam. But me what? To blame?

Willie. Yes.

Sam. Willie . . . ? (*Bursts into laughter*)

Willie. And now all you do is make jokes at me. You wait. When Miriam leaves you is my turn to laugh. Ha! Ha! Ha!

Sam (*He can't take Willie seriously any longer*). She can leave me tonight! I know what to do. (*Bowing before an imaginary partner*) May I have the pleasure? (*He dances and sings*)

"Just a fellow with his pillow . . .

Dancin' like a willow . . .

In an autumn breeze . . ."

Willie. There you go again!

(*Sam goes on dancing and singing*)

Boet Sam!

Sam. There's the answer to your problem! Judges' announcement in two weeks' time: "Ladies and gentlemen, the winner in the open section . . . Mr. Willie Malopo and his pillow!"

(*This is too much for a now really angry Willie. He goes for Sam, but the latter is too quick for him and puts Hally's table between the two of them*)

Hally (*Exploding*). For Christ's sake, you two!

Willie (*Still trying to get at Sam*). I donner you, Sam! Struesgod!

Sam (*Still laughing*). Sorry, Willie . . . Sorry . . .

Hally. Sam! Willie! (*Grabs his ruler and gives Willie a vicious whack on the bum*) How the hell am I supposed to concentrate with the two of you behaving like bloody children!

Willie. Hit him too!

Hally. Shut up, Willie.

Willie. He started jokes again.

Hally. Get back to your work. You too, Sam. (*His ruler*) Do you want another one, Willie?

(*Sam and Willie return to their work. Hally uses the opportunity to escape from his unsuccessful attempt at homework. He struts around like a little despot, ruler in hand, giving vent to his anger and frustration*)

Suppose a customer had walked in then? Or the Park Superintendent. And seen the two of you behaving like a pair of hooligans. That would have been the end of my mother's license, you know. And your jobs! Well, this is the end of it. From now on there will be no more of your ballroom nonsense in here. This is a business establishment, not a bloody New Brighton dancing school.

I've been far too lenient with the two of you. (*Behind the counter for a green cool drink and a dollop of ice cream. He keeps up his tirade as he prepares it*) But what really makes me bitter is that I allow you chaps a little freedom in here when business is bad and what do you do with it? The foxtrot! Specially you, Sam. There's more to life than trotting around a dance floor and I thought at least you knew it.

Sam. It's a harmless pleasure, Hally. It doesn't hurt anybody.

Hally. It's also a rather simple one, you know.

Sam. You reckon so? Have you ever tried?

Hally. Of course not.

Sam. Why don't you? Now.

Hally. What do you mean? Me dance?

Sam. Yes. I'll show you a simple step—the waltz—then you try it.

Hally. What will that prove?

Sam. That it might not be as easy as you think.

Hally. I didn't say it was easy. I said it was simple—like in simple-minded, meaning mentally retarded. You can't exactly say it challenges the intellect.

Sam. It does other things.

Hally. Such as?

Sam. Make people happy.

Hally (*The glass in his hand*). So do American cream sodas with ice cream. For God's sake, Sam, you're not asking me to take ballroom dancing serious, are you?

Sam. Yes.

Hally (*Sigh of defeat*). Oh well, so much for trying to give you a decent education. I've obviously achieved nothing.

Sam. You still haven't told me what's wrong with admiring something that's beautiful and then trying to do it yourself.

Hally. Nothing. But we happen to be talking about a foxtrot, not a thing of beauty.

Sam. But that is just what I'm saying. If you were to see two champions doing, two masters of the art . . . !

Hally. Oh, God, I give up. So now it's also art!

Sam. Ja.

Hally. There's a limit, Sam. Don't confuse art and entertainment.

Sam. So then what is art?

Hally. You want a definition?

Sam. Ja.

Hally (*He realizes he has got to be careful. He gives the matter a lot of thought before answering*). Philosophers have been trying to do that for centuries. What is Art? What is Life? But basically I suppose it's . . . the giving of meaning to matter.

Sam. Nothing to do with beautiful?

Hally. It goes beyond that. It's the giving of form to the formless.

Sam. Ja, well, maybe it's not art, then. But I still say it's beautiful.

Hally.   I'm sure the word you mean to use is entertaining.

Sam *(Adamant).*   No. Beautiful. And if you want proof, come along to the Centenary Hall in New Brighton in two weeks' time.

(The mention of the Centenary Hall draws Willie over to them)

Hally.   What for? I've seen the two of you prancing around in here often enough.

Sam *(He laughs).*   This isn't the real thing, Hally. We're just playing around in here.

Hally.   So? I can use my imagination.

Sam.   And what do you get?

Hally.   A lot of people dancing around and having a so-called good time.

Sam.   That all?

Hally.   Well, basically it is that, surely.

Sam.   No, it isn't. Your imagination hasn't helped you at all. There's a lot more to it than that. We're getting ready for the championships, Hally, not just another dance. There's going to be a lot of people, all right, and they're going to have a good time, but they'll only be spectators, sitting around and watching. It's just the competitors out there on the dance floor. Party decorations and fancy lights all around the walls! The ladies in beautiful evening dresses!

Hally.   My mother's got one of those, Sam, and quite frankly, it's an embarrassment every time she wears it.

Sam *(Undeterred).*   Your imagination left out the excitement.

(Hally scoffs)

Oh, yes. The finalists are not going to be out there just to have a good time. One of those couples will be the 1950 Eastern Province Champions. And your imagination left out the music.

Willie.   Mr. Elijah Gladman Guzana and his Orchestral Jazzonions.

Sam.   The sound of the big band, Hally. Trombone, trumpet, tenor and alto sax. And then, finally, your imagination also left out the climax of the evening when the dancing is finished, the judges have stopped whispering among themselves and the Master of Ceremonies collects their scorecards and goes up onto the stage to announce the winners.

Hally.   All right. So you make it sound like a bit of a do. It's an occasion. Satisfied?

Sam *(Victory).*   So you admit that!

Hally.   Emotionally yes, intellectually no.

Sam.   Well, I don't know what you mean by that, all I'm telling you is that it is going to be *the* event of the year in New Brighton. It's been sold out for two weeks already. There's only standing room left. We've got competitors coming from Kingwilliamstown, East London, Port Alfred.

(Hally starts pacing thoughtfully)

Hally.   Tell me a bit more.

Sam.   I thought you weren't interested . . . intellectually.

Hally (*Mysteriously*).   I've got my reasons.

Sam.   What do you want to know?

Hally.   It takes place every year?

Sam.   Yes. But only every third year in New Brighton. It's East London's turn to have the championships next year.

Hally.   Which, I suppose, makes it an even more significant event.

Sam.   Ah ha! We're getting somewhere. Our "occasion" is now a "significant event."

Hally.   I wonder.

Sam.   What?

Hally.   I wonder if I would get away with it.

Sam.   But what?

Hally (*To the table and his exercise book*).   "Write five hundred words describing an annual event of cultural or historical significance." Would I be stretching poetic license a little too far if I called your ballroom championships a cultural event?

Sam.   You mean . . . ?

Hally.   You think we could get five hundred words out of it, Sam?

Sam.   Victor Sylvester has written a whole book on ballroom dancing.

Willie.   You going to write about it, Master Hally?

Hally.   Yes, gentlemen, that is precisely what I am considering doing. Old Doc Bromely—he's my English teacher—is going to argue with me, of course. He doesn't like natives. But I'll point out to him that in strict anthropological terms the culture of a primitive black society includes its dancing and singing. To put my thesis in a nutshell: The war-dance has been replaced by the waltz. But it still amounts to the same thing: the release of primitive emotions through movement. Shall we give it a go?

Sam.   I'm ready.

Willie.   Me also.

Hally.   Ha! This will teach the old bugger a lesson. (*Decision taken*) Right. Let's get ourselves organized. (*This means another cake on the table. He sits*) I think you've given me enough general atmosphere, Sam, but to build the tension and suspense I need facts. (*Pencil poised*)

Willie.   Give him facts, Boet Sam.

Hally.   What you call the climax . . . how many finalists?

Sam.   Six couples.

Hally (*Making notes*).   Go on. Give me the picture.

Sam.   Spectators seated right around the hall. (*Willie becomes a spectator*)

Hally.   . . . and it's a full house.

Sam.   At one end, on the stage, Gladman and his Orchestral Jazzonions. At the other end is a long table with the three judges. The six finalists go onto the dance floor and take up their positions. When they are ready and the spectators have settled down, the Master of Ceremonies goes to the microphone. To start with, he makes some jokes to get the people laughing . . .

Hally.   Good touch! (*As he writes*) "... creating a relaxed atmosphere which will change to one of tension and drama as the climax is approached."

Sam (*Onto a chair to act out the M.C.*).   "Ladies and gentlemen, we come now to the great moment you have all been waiting for this evening. ... The finals of the 1950 Eastern Province Open Ballroom Dancing Championships. But first let me introduce the finalists! Mr. and Mrs. Welcome Tchabalala from Kingwilliamstown ..."

Willie (*He applauds after every name*).   Is when the people clap their hands and whistle and make a lot of noise, Master Hally.

Sam.   "Mr. Mulligan Njikelane and Miss Nomhle Nkonyeni of Grahamstown; Mr. and Mrs. Norman Nchinga from Port Alfred; Mr. Fats Bokolane and Miss Dina Plaatjies from East London; Mr. Sipho Dugu and Mrs. Mable Magada from Peddie; and from New Brighton our very own Mr. Willie Malopo and Miss Hilda Samuels."

(*Willie can't believe his ears. He abandons his role as spectator and scrambles in position as a finalist*)

Willie.   Relaxed and ready to romance!

Sam.   The applause dies down. When everybody is silent, Gladman lifts up his sax, nods at the Orchestral Jazzonions ...

Willie.   Play the jukebox please, Boet Sam!

Sam.   I also only got bus fare, Willie.

Hally.   Hold it, everybody. (*Heads for the cash register behind the counter*) How much is in the till, Sam?

Sam.   Three shillings. Hally ... your Mom counted it before she left.

(*Hally hesitates*)

Hally.   Sorry, Willie. You know how she carried on the last time I did it. We'll just have to pool our combined imaginations and hope for the best. (*Returns to the table*) Back to work. How are the points scored, Sam?

Sam.   Maximum of ten points each for individual style, deportment, rhythm and general appearance.

Willie.   Must I start?

Hally.   Hold it for a second, Willie. And penalties?

Sam.   For what?

Hally.   For doing something wrong. Say you stumble or bump into somebody ... do they take off any points?

Sam (*Aghast*).   Hally ...!

Hally.   When you're dancing. If you and your partner collide into another couple.

(*Hally can get no further. Sam has collapsed with laughter. He explains to Willie*)

Sam.   If me and Miriam bump into you and Hilda . . .

(*Willie joins him in another good laugh*)

Hally, Hally . . . !
Hally (*Perplexed*).   Why? What did I say?
Sam.   There's no collisions out there, Hally. Nobody trips or stumbles or bumps into anybody else. That's what that moment is all about. To be one of those finalists on that dance floor is like . . . like being in a dream about a world in which accidents don't happen.
Hally (*Genuinely moved by Sam's image*).   Jesus, Sam! That's beautiful!
Willie (*Can endure waiting no longer*).   I'm starting! (*Willie dances while Sam talks*)
Sam.   Of course it is. That's what I've been trying to say to you all afternoon. And it's beautiful because that is what we want life to be like. But instead, like you said, Hally, we're bumping into each other all the time. Look at the three of us this afternoon: I've bumped into Willie, the two of us have bumped into you, you've bumped into your mother, she bumping into your Dad. . . . None of us knows the steps and there's no music playing. And it doesn't stop with us. The whole world is doing it all the time. Open a newspaper and what do you read? America has bumped into Russia, England is bumping into India, rich man bumps into poor man. Those are big collisions, Hally. They make for a lot of bruises. People get hurt in all that bumping, and we're sick and tired of it now. It's been going on for too long. Are we never going to get it right! . . . Learn to dance life like champions instead of always being just a bunch of beginners at it?
Hally (*Deep and sincere admiration of the man*).   You've got a vision, Sam!
Sam.   Not just me. What I'm saying to you is that everybody's got it. That's why there's only standing room left for the Centenary Hall in two weeks' time. For as long as the music lasts, we are going to see six couples get it right, the way we want life to be.
Hally.   But is that the best we can do, Sam . . . watch six finalists dreaming about the way it should be?
Sam.   I don't know. But it starts with that. Without the dream we won't know what we're going for. And anyway I reckon there are a few people who have got past just dreaming about it and are trying for something real. Remember that thing we read once in the paper about the Mahatma Gandhi? Going without food to stop those riots in India?
Hally.   You're right. He certainly was trying to teach people to get the steps right.
Sam.   And the Pope.
Hally.   Yes, he's another one. Our old General Smuts as well, you know. He's also out there dancing. You know, Sam, when you come to think of it, that's what the United Nations boils down to . . . a dancing school for politicians!
Sam.   And let's hope they learn.

Hally (*A little surge of hope*).   You're right. We mustn't despair. Maybe there's some hope for mankind after all. Keep it up, Willie. (*Back to his table with determination*) This is a lot bigger than I thought. So what have we got? Yes, our title: "A World Without Collisions."

Sam.   That sounds good! "A World Without Collisions."

Hally.   Subtitle: "Global Politics on the Dance Floor." No. A bit too heavy, hey? What about "Ballroom Dancing as a Political Vision"?

(*The telephone rings. Sam answers it*)

Sam.   St. George's Park Tea Room . . . Yes, Madam . . . Hally, it's your Mom.

Hally (*Back to reality*).   Oh, God, yes! I'd forgotten all about that. Shit! Remember my words, Sam? Just when you're enjoying yourself, someone or something will come along and wreck everything.

Sam.   You haven't heard what she's got to say yet.

Hally.   Public telephone?

Sam.   No.

Hally.   Does she sound happy or unhappy?

Sam.   I couldn't tell. (*Pause*) She's waiting, Hally.

Hally (*To the telephone*).   Hello, Mom . . . No, everything is okay here. Just doing my homework. . . . What's your news? . . . You've what? . . . (*Pause. He takes the receiver away from his ear for a few seconds. In the course of Hally's telephone conversation, Sam and Willie discreetly position the stacked tables and chairs. Hally places the receiver back to his ear*) Yes, I'm still here. Oh, well, I give up now. Why did you do it, Mom? . . . Well, I just hope you know what you've let us in for. . . . (*Loudly*) I said I hope you know what you've let us in for! It's the end of the peace and quiet we've been having. (*Softly*) Where is he? (*Normal voice*) He can't hear us from in there. But for God's sake, Mom, what happened? I told you to be firm with him. . . . Then you and the nurses should have held him down, taken his crutches away. . . . I know only too well he's my father! . . . I'm not being disrespectful, but I'm sick and tired of emptying stinking chamberpots full of phlegm and piss. . . . Yes, I do! When you're not there, he asks *me* to do it. . . . If you really want to know the truth, that's why I've got no appetite for my food. . . . Yes! There's a lot of things you don't know about. For your information, I still haven't got that science textbook I need. And you know why? He borrowed the money you gave me for it. . . . Because I didn't want to start another fight between you two. . . . He says that every time. . . . All right, Mom! (*Viciously*) Then just remember to start hiding your bag away again, because he'll be at your purse before long for money for booze. And when he's well enough to come down here, you better keep an eye on the till as well, because that is going to develop a leak. . . . Then don't complain to me when he starts his old tricks. . . . Yes, you do. I get it from you on one side and from him on the other, and it makes life hell for me. I'm not going to be the peacemaker anymore. I'm warning you now: when the two of you start fighting again, I'm leaving home. . . . Mom, if you start crying, I'm going to put down the receiver. . . .

Okay . . . (*Lowering his voice to a vicious whisper*) Okay, Mom. I heard you. (*Desperate*) No. . . . Because I don't want to. I'll see him when I get home! Mom! . . . (*Pause. When he speaks again, his tone changes completely. It is not simply pretense. We sense a genuine emotional conflict*) Welcome home, chum! . . . What's that? . . . Don't be silly, Dad. You being home is just about the best news in the world. . . . I bet you are. Bloody depressing there with everybody going on about their ailments, hey! . . . How you feeling? . . . Good . . . Here as well, pal. Coming down cats and dogs. . . . That's right. Just the day for a kip and a toss in your old Uncle Ned. . . . Everything's just hunkydory on my side, Dad. . . . Well, to start with, there's a nice pile of comics for you on the counter. . . . Yes, old Kemple brought them in. *Batman and Robin, Submariner* . . . just your cup of tea . . . I will. . . . Yes, we'll spin a few yarns tonight. . . . Okay, chum, see you in a little while. . . . No, I promise. I'll come straight home. . . . (*Pause—his mother comes back on the phone*) Mom? Okay. I'll lock up now. . . . What? . . . Oh, the brandy . . . Yes, I'll remember! . . . I'll put it in my suitcase now, for God's sake. I know well enough what will happen if he doesn't get it. . . . (*Places a bottle of brandy on the counter*) I *was* kind to him, Mom. I didn't say anything nasty! . . . All right. Bye. (*End of telephone conversation. A desolate Hally doesn't move. A strained silence*)

Sam (*Quietly*).   That sounded like a bad bump, Hally.

Hally (*Having a hard time controlling his emotions. He speaks carefully*). Mind your own business, Sam.

Sam.   Sorry. I wasn't trying to interfere. Shall we carry on? Hally? (*He indicates the exercise book. No response from Hally*)

Willie (*Also trying*).   Tell him about when they give out the cups, Boet Sam.

Sam.   Ja! That's another big moment. The presentation of the cups after the winners have been announced. You've got to put that in.

(*Still no response from Hally*)

Willie.   A big silver one, Master Hally, called floating trophy for the champions.

Sam.   We always invite some big-shot personality to hand them over. Guest of honor this year is going to be His Holiness Bishop Jabulani of the All African Free Zionist Church.

(*Hally gets up abruptly, goes to his table and tears up the page he was writing on*)

Hally.   So much for a bloody world without collisions.

Sam.   Too bad. It was on its way to being a good composition.

Hally.   Let's stop bullshitting ourselves, Sam.

Sam.   Have we been doing that?

Hally.   Yes! That's what all our talk about a decent world has been . . . just so much bullshit.

Sam.   We did say it was still only a dream.

Hally. And a bloody useless one at that. Life's a fuck-up and it's never going to change.

Sam. Ja, maybe that's true.

Hally. There's no maybe about it. It's a blunt and brutal fact. All we've done this afternoon is waste our time.

Sam. Not if we'd got your homework done.

Hally. I don't give a shit about my homework, so, for Christ's sake, just shut up about it. *(Slamming books viciously into his school case)* Hurry up now and finish your work. I want to lock up and get out of here. *(Pause)* And then go where? Home-sweet-fucking-home. Jesus, I hate that word.

(Hally goes to the counter to put the brandy bottle and comics in his school case. After a moment's hesitation, he smashes the bottle of brandy. He abandons all further attempts to hide his feelings. Sam and Willie work away as unobtrusively as possible)

Do you want to know what is really wrong with your lovely little dream, Sam? It's not just that we are all bad dancers. That does happen to be perfectly true, but there's much more to it than just that. You left out the cripples.

Sam. Hally!

Hally *(Now totally reckless).* Ja! Can't leave them out, Sam. That's why we always end up on our backsides on the dance floor. They're also out there dancing . . . like a bunch of broken spiders trying to do the quickstep! *(An ugly attempt at laughter)* When you come to think of it, it's a bloody comical sight. I mean, it's bad enough on two legs . . . but one and a pair of crutches! Hell, no, Sam. That's guaranteed to turn that dance floor into a shambles. Why you shaking your head? Picture it, man. For once this afternoon let's use our imaginations sensibly.

Sam. Be careful, Hally.

Hally. Of what? The truth? I seem to be the only one around here who is prepared to face it. We've had the pretty dream, it's time now to wake up and have a good long look at the way things really are. Nobody knows the steps, there's no music, the cripples are also out there tripping up everybody and trying to get into the act, and it's all called the All-Comers-How-to-Make-a-Fuckup-of-Life Championships. *(Another ugly laugh)* Hang on, Sam! The best bit is still coming. Do you know what the winner's trophy is? A beautiful big chamber-pot with roses on the side, and it's full to the brim with piss. And guess who I think is going to be this year's winner.

Sam *(Almost shouting).* Stop now!

Hally *(Suddenly appalled by how far he has gone).* Why?

Sam. Hally? It's your father you're talking about.

Hally. So?

Sam. Do you know what you've been saying?

(Hally can't answer. He is rigid with shame. Sam speaks to him sternly)

No, Hally, you mustn't do it. Take back those words and ask for forgiveness! It's a terrible sin for a son to mock his father with jokes like that. You'll be punished if you carry on. Your father is your father, even if he is a . . . cripple man.

Willie. Yes, Master Hally. Is true what Sam say.

Sam. I understand how you are feeling, Hally, but even so . . .

Hally. No, you don't!

Sam. I think I do.

Hally. And I'm telling you you don't. Nobody does. (*Speaking carefully as his shame turns to rage at Sam*) It's your turn to be careful, Sam. Very careful! You're treading on dangerous ground. Leave me and my father alone.

Sam. I'm not the one who's been saying things about him.

Hally. What goes on between me and my Dad is none of your business!

Sam. Then don't tell me about it. If that's all you've got to say about him, I don't want to hear.

(*For a moment Hally is at a loss for a response*)

Hally. Just get on with your bloody work and shut up.

Sam. Swearing at me won't help you.

Hally. Yes, it does! Mind your own fucking business and shut up!

Sam. Okay. If that's the way you want it, I'll stop trying.

(*He turns away. This infuriates Hally even more*)

Hally. Good. Because what you've been trying to do is meddle in something you know nothing about. All that concerns you in here, Sam, is to try and do what you get paid for—keep the place clean and serve the customers. In plain words, just get on with your job. My mother is right. She's always warning me about allowing you to get too familiar. Well this time you've gone too far. It's going to stop right now.

(*No response from Sam*)

You're only a servant in here, and don't forget it.

(*Still no response. Hally is trying hard to get one*)

And as far as my father is concerned, all you need to remember is that he is your boss.

Sam (*Needled at last*). No, he isn't. I get paid by your mother.

Hally. Don't argue with me, Sam!

Sam. Then don't say he's my boss.

Hally. He's a white man and that's good enough for you.

Sam. I'll try to forget you said that.

Hally.   Don't! Because you won't be doing me a favor if you do. I'm telling you to remember it.

(*A pause. Sam pulls himself together and makes one last effort*)

Sam.   Hally, Hally . . . ! Come on now. Let's stop before it's too late. You're right. We *are* on dangerous ground. If we're not careful, somebody is going to get hurt.

Hally.   It won't be me.

Sam.   Don't be so sure.

Hally.   I don't know what you're talking about, Sam.

Sam.   Yes, you do.

Hally (*Furious*).   Jesus, I wish you would stop trying to tell me what I do and what I don't know.

(*Sam gives up. He turns to Willie*)

Sam.   Let's finish up.

Hally.   Don't turn your back on me! I haven't finished talking.

(*He grabs Sam by the arm and tries to make him turn around. Sam reacts with a flash of anger*)

Sam.   Don't do that, Hally! (*Facing the boy*) All right, I'm listening. Well? What do you want to say to me?

Hally (*Pause as Hally looks for something to say*).   To begin with, why don't you also start calling me Master Harold, like Willie.

Sam.   Do you mean that?

Hally.   Why the hell do you think I said it?

Sam.   And if I don't?

Hally.   You might just lose your job.

Sam (*Quietly and very carefully*).   If you make me say it once, I'll never call you anything else again.

Hally.   So? (*The boy confronts the man*) Is that meant to be a threat?

Sam.   Just telling you what will happen if you make me do that. You must decide what it means to you.

Hally.   Well, I have. It's good news. Because that is exactly what Master Harold wants from now on. Think of it as a little lesson in respect, Sam, that's long overdue, and I hope you remember it as well as you do your geography. I can tell you now that somebody who will be glad to hear I've finally given it to you will be my Dad. Yes! He agrees with my Mom. He's always going on about it as well. "You must teach the boys to show you more respect, my son."

Sam.   So now you can stop complaining about going home. Everybody is going to be happy tonight.

Hally.   That's perfectly correct. You see, you mustn't get the wrong idea about me and my Dad, Sam. We also have our good times together. Some bloody good laughs. He's got a marvelous sense of humor. Want to know what our favorite joke is? He gives out a big groan, you see, and says: "It's not fair, is it, Hally?" Then I have to ask: "What, chum?" And then he says: "A nigger's arse" . . . and we both have a good laugh.

(*The men stare at him with disbelief*)

What's the matter, Willie? Don't you catch the joke? You always were a bit slow on the uptake. It's what is called a pun. You see, fair means both light in color and to be just and decent. (*He turns to Sam*) I thought *you* would catch it, Sam.

Sam.   Oh ja, I catch it all right.

Hally.   But it doesn't appeal to your sense of humor.

Sam.   Do you really laugh?

Hally.   Of course.

Sam.   To please him? Make him feel good?

Hally.   No, for heaven's sake! I laugh because I think it's a bloody good joke.

Sam.   You're really trying hard to be ugly, aren't you? And why drag poor old Willie into it? He's done nothing to you except show you the respect you want so badly. That's also not being fair, you know . . . and *I* mean just or decent.

Willie.   It's all right, Sam. Leave it now.

Sam.   It's me you're after. You should just have said "Sam's arse" . . . because that's the one you're trying to kick. Anyway, how do you know it's not fair? You've never seen it. Do you want to? (*He drops his trousers and underpants and presents his backside for Hally's inspection*) Have a good look. A real Basuto arse . . . which is about as nigger as they can come. Satisfied? (*Trousers up*) Now you can make your Dad even happier when you go home tonight. Tell him I showed you my arse and he is quite right. It's not fair. And if it will give him an even better laugh next time, I'll also let *him* have a look. Come, Willie, let's finish up and go.

(*Sam and Willie start to tidy up the tea room. Hally doesn't move. He waits for a moment when Sam passes him*)

Hally (*Quietly*).   Sam . . .

(*Sam stops and looks expectantly at the boy. Hally spits in his face. A long and heartfelt groan from Willie. For a few seconds Sam doesn't move*)

Sam (*Taking out a handkerchief and wiping his face*).   It's all right, Willie.

(*To Hally*)

Ja, well, you've done it . . . Master Harold. Yes, I'll start calling you that from now on. It won't be difficult anymore. You've hurt yourself, Master Harold. I saw it coming. I warned you, but you wouldn't listen. You've just hurt yourself *bad.* And you're a coward, Master Harold. The face you should be spitting in is your father's . . . but you used mine, because you think you're safe inside your fair skin . . . and this time I don't mean just or decent. *(Pause, then moving violently towards Hally)* Should I hit him, Willie?

Willie *(Stopping Sam).*   No, Boet Sam.

Sam *(Violently).*   Why not?

Willie.   It won't help, Boet Sam.

Sam.   I don't want to help! I want to hurt him.

Willie.   You also hurt yourself.

Sam.   And if he had done it to you, Willie?

Willie.   Me? Spit at me like I was a dog? *(A thought that had not occurred to him before. He looks at Hally)* Ja. Then I want to hit him. I want to hit him hard!

(A dangerous few seconds as the men stand staring at the boy. Willie turns away shaking his head)

But maybe all I do is go cry at the back. He's little boy, Boet Sam. Little *white* boy. Long trousers now, but he's still little boy.

Sam *(His violence ebbing away into defeat as quickly as it flooded).*   You're right. So go on, then: groan again, Willie. You do it better than me. *(To Hally)* You don't know all of what you've just done . . . Master Harold. It's not just that you've made me feel dirtier than I've ever been in my life . . . I mean, how do I wash off yours and your father's filth? . . . I've also failed. A long time ago I promised myself I was going to try and do something, but you've just shown me . . . Master Harold . . . that I've failed. *(Pause)* I've also got a memory of a little white boy when he was still wearing short trousers and a black man, but they're not flying a kite. It was the old Jubilee days, after dinner one night. I was in my room. You came in and just stood against the wall, looking down at the ground, and only after I'd asked you what you wanted, what was wrong, I don't know how many times, did you speak and even then so softly I almost didn't hear you. "Sam, please help me to go and fetch my Dad." Remember? He was dead drunk on the floor of the Central Hotel Bar. They'd phoned for your Mom, but you were the only one at home. And do you remember how we did it? You went in first by yourself to ask permission for me to go into the bar. Then I loaded him onto my back like a baby and carried him back to the boarding house with you following behind carrying his crutches. *(Shaking his head as he remembers)* A crowded Main Street with all the people watching a little white boy following his drunk father on a nigger's back! I felt for that little boy . . . Master Harold. I felt for him. After that we still had to clean him up, remember? He'd messed in his trousers, so we had to clean him up and get him into bed.

Hally *(Great pain).*   I love him, Sam.

Sam.   I know you do. That's why I tried to stop you from saying these things about him. It would have been so simple if you could have just despised him for being a weak man. But he's your father. You love him and you're ashamed of him. You're ashamed of so much! . . . And now that's going to include yourself. That was the promise I made to myself: to try and stop that happening. *(Pause)* After we got him to bed you came back with me to my room and sat in a corner and carried on just looking down at the ground. And for days after that! You hadn't done anything wrong, but you went around as if you owed the world an apology for being alive. I didn't like seeing that! That's not the way a boy grows up to be a man! . . . But the one person who should have been teaching you what that means was the cause of your shame. If you really want to know, that's why I made you that kite. I wanted you to look up, be proud of something, of yourself . . . *(Bitter smile at the memory)* . . . and you certainly were that when I left you with it up there on the hill. Oh, ja . . . something else! . . . If you ever do write it as a short story, there *was* a twist in our ending. I couldn't sit down there and stay with you. It was a "Whites Only" bench. You were too young, too excited to notice then. But not anymore. If you're not careful . . . Master Harold . . . you're going to be sitting up there by yourself for a long time to come, and there won't be a kite in the sky. *(Sam has got nothing more to say. He exits into the kitchen, taking off his waiter's jacket)*

Willie.   Is bad. Is all all bad in here now.

Hally *(Books into his school case, raincoat on)*.   Willie . . . *(It is difficult to speak)* Will you lock up for me and look after the keys?

Willie.   Okay.

(Sam returns. Hally goes behind the counter and collects the few coins in the cash register. As he starts to leave . . .)

Sam.   Don't forget the comic books.

(Hally returns to the counter and puts them in his case. He starts to leave again)

Sam *(To the retreating back of the boy)*.   Stop . . . Hally . . .

(Hally stops, but doesn't turn to face him)

Hally . . . I've got no right to tell you what being a man means if I don't behave like one myself, and I'm not doing so well at that this afternoon. Should we try again, Hally?

Hally.   Try what?

Sam.   Fly another kite, I suppose. It worked once, and this time I need it as much as you do.

Hally.   It's still raining, Sam. You can't fly kites on rainy days, remember.

Sam.   So what do we do? Hope for better weather tomorrow?

Hally *(Helpless gesture)*.   I don't know. I don't know anything anymore.

Sam.   You sure of that, Hally? Because it would be pretty hopeless if that was true. It would mean nothing has been learnt in here this afternoon, and there was a hell of a lot of teaching going . . . one way or the other. But anyway, I don't believe you. I reckon there's one thing you know. You don't *have* to sit up there by yourself. You know what that bench means now, and you can leave it any time you choose. All you've got to do is stand up and walk away from it.

(*Hally leaves. Willie goes up quietly to Sam*)

Willie. Is okay, Boet Sam. You see. Is . . . (*He can't find any better words*) . . . *is* going to be okay tomorrow. (*Changing his tone*) Hey, Boet Sam! (*He is trying hard*) You right. I think about it and you right. Tonight I find Hilda and say sorry. And make promise I won't beat her no more. You hear me, Boet Sam?

Sam. I hear you, Willie.

Willie. And when we practice I relax and romance with her from beginning to end. Non-stop! You watch! Two weeks' time: "First prize for promising newcomers: Mr. Willie Malopo and Miss Hilda Samuels." (*Sudden impulse*) To hell with it! I walk home. (*He goes to the jukebox, puts in a coin and selects a record. The machine comes to life in the gray twilight, blushing its way through a spectrum of soft, romantic colors*) How did you say it, Boet Sam? Let's dream. (*Willie sways with the music and gestures for Sam to dance*)

(*Sarah Vaughan sings*)

"Little man you're crying,
I know why you're blue,
Someone took your kiddy car away;
Better go to sleep now,
Little man you've had a busy day." (*etc. etc.*)

You lead. I follow.

(*The men dance together*)

"Johnny won your marbles,
Tell you what we'll do;
Dad will get you new ones right away;
Better go to sleep now,
Little man you've had a busy day."

For Analysis
1. Does Hally's brutal attack on Sam at the end of the play come as a surprise? Explain. **2.** What is the relevance of the stories about whippings that Hally and Sam exchange? **3.** Why does the kite figure so powerfully in Hally's memory? **4.** What bearing does Hally's feelings about his father have on his relationship with Sam? **5.** Is the ending of the play optimistic or pessimistic?

On Style

1. Although this play addresses the political oppression embodied in the recently ended apartheid system in the Union of South Africa, it also examines the qualities of fatherhood. How does the playwright reveal Hally's attitude toward his biological father? Who is Hally's spiritual father, and how is the audience made aware of that relationship?

Making Connections

What circumstances might cause you to look to a friend rather than your father or mother as a confidante and protector?

Writing Topics

1. Analyze the opening dialogue between Sam and Willie (up to the appearance of Hally) and show how it establishes the mood and major themes of the play. **2.** Write an essay discussing Hally's attitude toward his father and toward Sam.

David Henry Hwang [b. 1957]

M. Butterfly 1988

CHARACTERS

Rene Gallimard
Song Liling
Marc / Man No. 2 / Consul
  Sharpless
Renee / Woman at Party /
  Pinup Girl

Comrade Chin / Suzuki /
  Shu-Fang
Helga
Toulon / Man No. 1 / Judge
Dancers

Playwright's Notes

This play was suggested by international newspaper accounts of a recent espionage trial. For purposes of dramatization, names have been changed, characters created, and incidents devised or altered, and this play does not purport to be a factual record of real events or real people.

A former French diplomat and a Chinese opera singer have been sentenced to six years in jail for spying for China after a two-day trial that traced a story of clandestine love and mistaken sexual identity. . . .
  Mr. Bouriscot was accused of passing information to China after he fell in love with Mr. Shi, whom he believed for twenty years to be a woman.
  —*The New York Times*, May 11, 1986

I could escape this feeling
With my China girl . . .
  —David Bowie & Iggy Pop

Time and Place

The action of the play takes place in a Paris prison in the present, and, in recall, during the decade 1960–1970 in Beijing, and from 1966 to the present in Paris.

Act I

Scene 1. M. Gallimard's prison cell. Paris. 1988.

Lights fade up to reveal Rene Gallimard, sixty-five, in a prison cell. He wears a comfortable bathrobe, and looks old and tired. The sparsely furnished cell contains a wooden crate, upon which sits a hot plate with a kettle, and a portable tape recorder. Gallimard sits on the crate staring at the recorder, a sad smile on his face.

Upstage Song, who appears as a beautiful woman in traditional Chinese garb, dances a traditional piece from the Peking Opera, surrounded by the percussive clatter of Chinese music.

Then, slowly, lights and sound cross-fade; the Chinese opera music dissolves into a Western opera, the "Love Duet" from Puccini's Madame Butterfly. *Song continues dancing, now to the Western accompaniment. Though her movements are the same, the difference in music now gives them a balletic quality.*

Gallimard rises, and turns upstage towards the figure of Song, who dances without acknowledging him.

Gallimard.   Butterfly, Butterfly . . .

He forces himself to turn away, as the image of Song fades out, and talks to us.

Gallimard.   The limits of my cell are as such: four-and-a-half meters by five. There's one window against the far wall; a door, very strong, to protect me from autograph hounds. I'm responsible for the tape recorder, the hot plate, and this charming coffee table.

When I want to eat, I'm marched off to the dining room—hot, steaming slop appears on my plate. When I want to sleep, the light bulb turns itself off—the work of fairies. It's an enchanted space I occupy. The French—we know how to run a prison.

But, to be honest, I'm not treated like an ordinary prisoner. Why? Because I'm a celebrity. You see, I make people laugh.

I never dreamed this day would arrive. I've never been considered witty or clever. In fact, as a young boy, in an informal poll among my grammar school classmates, I was voted "least likely to be invited to a party." It's a title I managed to hold on to for many years. Despite some stiff competition.

But now, how the tables turn! Look at me: the life of every social function in Paris. Paris? Why be modest: My fame has spread to Amsterdam, London, New York. Listen to them! In the world's smartest parlors, I'm the one who lifts their spirits!

With a flourish, Gallimard directs our attention to another part of the stage.

Scene 2.   A party. 1988.

Lights go up on a chic-looking parlor, where a well-dressed trio, two men and one woman, make conversation. Gallimard also remains lit; he observes them from his cell.

Woman.   And what of Gallimard?
Man 1.   Gallimard?

Man 2. Gallimard!

Gallimard *(to us).* You see? They're all determined to say my name, as if it were some new dance.

Woman. He still claims not to believe the truth.

Man 1. What? Still? Even since the trial?

Woman. Yes. Isn't it mad?

Man 2 *(laughing).* He says . . . it was dark . . . and she was very modest!

The trio break into laughter.

Man 1. So—what? He never touched her with his hands?

Man 2. Perhaps he did, and simply misidentified the equipment. A compelling case for sex education in the schools.

Woman. To protect the National Security—the Church can't argue with that.

Man 1. That's impossible! How could he not know?

Man 2. Simple ignorance.

Man 1. For twenty years?

Man 2. Time flies when you're being stupid.

Woman. Well, I thought the French were ladies' men.

Man 2. It seems Monsieur Gallimard was overly anxious to live up to his national reputation.

Woman. Well, he's not very good-looking.

Man 1. No, he's not.

Man 2. Certainly not.

Woman. Actually, I feel sorry for him.

Man 2. A toast! To Monsieur Gallimard!

Woman. Yes! To Gallimard!

Man 1. To Gallimard!

Man 2. *Vive la différence!*

They toast, laughing. Lights down on them.

Scene 3. M. Gallimard's cell.

Gallimard *(smiling).* You see? They toast me. I've become a patron saint of the socially inept. Can they really be so foolish? Men like that—they should be scratching at my door, begging to learn my secrets! For I, Rene Gallimard, you see, I have known, and been loved by . . . the Perfect Woman.

   Alone in this cell, I sit night after night, watching our story play through my head, always searching for a new ending, one which redeems my honor, where she returns at last to my arms. And I imagine you—my ideal audience—who come to understand and even, perhaps just a little, to envy me.

He turns on his tape recorder. Over the house speakers, we hear the opening phrases of Madame Butterfly.

Gallimard.   In order for you to understand what I did and why, I must introduce you to my favorite opera: *Madame Butterfly.* By Giacomo Puccini. First produced at La Scala, Milan, in 1904, it is now beloved throughout the Western world.

As Gallimard describes the opera, the tape segues in and out to sections he may be describing.

Gallimard.   And why not? Its heroine, Cio-Cio-San, also known as Butterfly, is a feminine ideal, beautiful and brave. And its hero, the man for whom she gives up everything, is—(*He pulls out a naval officer's cap from under his crate, pops it on his head, and struts about*)—not very good-looking, not too bright, and pretty much a wimp: Benjamin Franklin Pinkerton of the U.S. Navy. As the curtain rises, he's just closed on two great bargains: one on a house, the other on a woman—call it a package deal.

Pinkerton purchased the rights to Butterfly for one hundred yen—in modern currency, equivalent to about . . . sixty-six cents. So, he's feeling pretty pleased with himself as Sharpless, the American consul, arrives to witness the marriage.

Marc, wearing an official cap to designate Sharpless, enters and plays the character.

Sharpless/Marc.   Pinkerton!
Pinkerton/Gallimard.   Sharpless! How's it hangin'? It's a great day, just great. Between my house, my wife, and the rickshaw ride in from town, I've saved nineteen cents just this morning.
Sharpless.   Wonderful. I can see the inscription on your tombstone already: "I saved a dollar, here I lie." (*He looks around.*) Nice house.
Pinkerton.   It's artistic. Artistic, don't you think? Like the way the shoji screens slide open to reveal the wet bar and disco mirror ball? Classy, huh? Great for impressing the chicks.
Sharpless.   "Chicks"? Pinkerton, you're going to be a married man!
Pinkerton.   Well, sort of.
Sharpless.   What do you mean?
Pinkerton.   This country—Sharpless, it is okay. You got all these geisha girls running around—
Sharpless.   I know! I live here!
Pinkerton.   Then, you know the marriage laws, right? I split for one month, it's annulled!
Sharpless.   Leave it to you to read the fine print. Who's the lucky girl?
Pinkerton.   Cio-Cio-San. Her friends call her Butterfly. Sharpless, she eats out of my hand!
Sharpless.   She's probably very hungry.

Pinkerton.   Not like American girls. It's true what they say about Oriental girls. They want to be treated bad!

Sharpless.   Oh, please!

Pinkerton.   It's true!

Sharpless.   Are you serious about this girl?

Pinkerton.   I'm marrying her, aren't I?

Sharpless.   Yes—with generous trade-in terms.

Pinkerton.   When I leave, she'll know what it's like to have loved a real man. And I'll even buy her a few nylons.

Sharpless.   You aren't planning to take her with you?

Pinkerton.   Huh? Where?

Sharpless.   Home!

Pinkerton.   You mean, America? Are you crazy? Can you see her trying to buy rice in St. Louis?

Sharpless.   So, you're not serious.

Pause

Pinkerton/Gallimard (*as Pinkerton*).   Consul, I am a sailor in port. (*As Gallimard.*) They then proceed to sing the famous duet, "The Whole World Over."

The duet plays on the speakers. Gallimard, as Pinkerton, lip-syncs his lines from the opera.

Gallimard.   To give a rough translation: "The whole world over, the Yankee travels, casting his anchor wherever he wants. Life's not worth living unless he can win the hearts of the fairest maidens, then hotfoot it off the premises ASAP." (*He turns towards Marc.*) In the preceding scene, I played Pinkerton, the womanizing cad, and my friend Marc from school . . . (*Marc bows grandly for our benefit.*) played Sharpless, the sensitive soul of reason. In life, however, our positions were usually—no, always—reversed.

Scene 4.   École Nationale.[1] Aix-en-Provence. 1947.

Gallimard.   No, Marc, I think I'd rather stay home.

Marc.   Are you crazy?! We are going to Dad's condo in Marseilles! You know what happened last time?

Gallimard.   Of course I do.

Marc.   Of course you don't! You never know. . . . They stripped, Rene!

Gallimard.   Who stripped?

---

[1] National School.

Marc. The girls!

Gallimard. Girls? Who said anything about girls?

Marc. Rene, we're a buncha university guys goin' up to the woods. What are we gonna do—talk philosophy?

Gallimard. What girls? Where do you get them?

Marc. Who cares? The point is, they come. On trucks. Packed in like sardines. The back flips open, babes hop out, we're ready to roll.

Gallimard. You mean, they just—?

Marc. Before you know it, every last one of them—they're stripped and splashing around my pool. There's no moon out, they can't see what's going on, their boobs are flapping, right? You close your eyes, reach out—it's grab bag, get it? Doesn't matter whose ass is between whose legs, whose teeth are sinking into who. You're just in there, going at it, eyes closed, on and on for as long as you can stand. *(Pause.)* Some fun, huh?

Gallimard. What happens in the morning?

Marc. In the morning, you're ready to talk some philosophy. *(Beat.)* So how 'bout it?

Gallimard. Marc, I can't . . . I'm afraid they'll say no—the girls. So I never ask.

Marc. You don't have to ask! That's the beauty—don't you see? They don't have to say yes. It's perfect for a guy like you, really.

Gallimard. You go ahead . . . I may come later.

Marc. Hey, Rene—it doesn't matter that you're clumsy and got zits—they're not looking!

Gallimard. Thank you very much.

Marc. Wimp.

Marc walks over to the other side of the stage, and starts waving and smiling at women in the audience.

Gallimard *(to us).* We now return to my version of *Madame Butterfly* and the events leading to my recent conviction for treason.

Gallimard notices Marc making lewd gestures.

Gallimard. Marc, what are you doing?

Marc. Huh? *(Sotto voce.)* Rene, there're a lotta great babes out there. They're probably lookin' at me and thinking, "What a dangerous guy."

Gallimard. Yes—how could they help but be impressed by your cool sophistication?

Gallimard pops the Sharpless cap on Marc's head, and points him offstage. Marc exits, leering.

Scene 5. M. Gallimard's cell.

Gallimard. Next, Butterfly makes her entrance. We learn her age—fifteen . . . but very mature for her years.

Lights come up on the area where we saw Song dancing at the top of the play. She appears there again, now dressed as Madame Butterfly, moving to the "Love Duet." Gallimard turns upstage slightly to watch, transfixed.

Gallimard. But as she glides past him, beautiful, laughing softly behind her fan, don't we who are men sigh with hope? We, who are not handsome, nor brave, nor powerful, yet somehow believe, like Pinkerton, that we deserve a Butterfly. She arrives with all her possessions in the folds of her sleeves, lays them all out, for her man to do with as he pleases. Even her life itself—she bows her head as she whispers that she's not even worth the hundred yen he paid for her. He's already given too much, when we know he's really had to give nothing at all.

Music and lights on Song out. Gallimard sits at his crate.

Gallimard. In real life, women who put their total worth at less than sixty-six cents are quite hard to find. The closest we come is in the pages of these magazines. (*He reaches into his crate, pulls out a stack of girlie magazines, and begins flipping through them.*) Quite a necessity in prison. For three or four dollars, you get seven or eight women.

I first discovered these magazines at my uncle's house. One day, as a boy of twelve. The first time I saw them in his closet . . . all lined up—my body shook. Not with lust—no, with power. Here were women—a shelf-full—who would do exactly as I wanted.

The "Love Duet" creeps in over the speakers. Special comes up, revealing, not Song this time, but a pinup girl in a sexy negligee, her back to us. Gallimard turns upstage and looks at her.

Girl. I know you're watching me.
Gallimard. My throat . . . it's dry.
Girl. I leave my blinds open every night before I go to bed.
Gallimard. I can't move.
Girl. I leave my blinds open and the lights on.
Gallimard. I'm shaking. My skin is hot, but my penis is soft. Why?
Girl. I stand in front of the window.
Gallimard. What is she going to do?
Girl. I toss my hair, and I let my lips part . . . barely.
Gallimard. I shouldn't be seeing this. It's so dirty. I'm so bad.
Girl. Then, slowly, I lift off my nightdress.

Gallimard. Oh, god. I can't believe it. I can't—

Girl. I toss it to the ground.

Gallimard. Now, she's going to walk away. She's going to—

Girl. I stand there, in the light, displaying myself.

Gallimard. No. She's—why is she naked?

Girl. To you.

Gallimard. In front of a window? This is wrong. No—

Girl. Without shame.

Gallimard. No, she must . . . like it.

Girl. I like it.

Gallimard. She . . . she wants me to see.

Girl. I want you to see.

Gallimard. I can't believe it! She's getting excited!

Girl. I can't see you. You can do whatever you want.

Gallimard. I can't do a thing. Why?

Girl. What would you like me to do . . . next?

Lights go down on her. Music off. Silence, as Gallimard puts away his maga-
zines. Then he resumes talking to us.

Gallimard. Act Two begins with Butterfly staring at the ocean. Pinkerton's
been called back to the U.S., and he's given his wife a detailed schedule of his
plans. In the column marked "return date," he's written "when the robins
nest." This failed to ignite her suspicions. Now, three years have passed without a peep from him. Which brings a response from her faithful servant,
Suzuki.

Comrade Chin enters, playing Suzuki.

Suzuki. Girl, he's a loser. What'd he ever give you? Nineteen cents and those
ugly Day-Glo stockings? Look, it's finished! Kaput! Done! And you should be
glad! I mean, the guy was a woofer! He tried before, you know—before he
met you, he went down to geisha central and plunked down his spare change
in front of the usual candidates—everyone else gagged! These are hungry
prostitutes, and they were not interested, get the picture? Now, stop slather-
ing when an American ship sails in, and let's make some bucks—I mean, yen!
We are broke!

Now, what about Yamadori? Hey, hey—don't look away—the man is a
prince—figuratively, and, what's even better, literally. He's rich, he's handsome, he says he'll die if you don't marry him—and he's even willing to overlook the little fact that you've been deflowered all over the place by a foreign
devil. What do you mean, "But he's Japanese"? What do you think you are?
You think you've been touched by the whitey god? He was a sailor with dirty
hands!

Suzuki stalks offstage.

Gallimard.   She's also visited by Consul Sharpless, sent by Pinkerton on a minor errand.

Marc enters, as Sharpless.

Sharpless.   I hate this job.

Gallimard.   This Pinkerton—he doesn't show up personally to tell his wife he's abandoning her. No, he sends a government diplomat . . . at taxpayers' expense.

Sharpless.   Butterfly? Butterfly? I have some bad—I'm going to be ill. Butterfly, I came to tell you—

Gallimard.   Butterfly says she knows he'll return and if he doesn't she'll kill herself rather than go back to her own people. *(Beat.)* This causes a lull in the conversation.

Sharpless.   Let's put it this way . . .

Gallimard.   Butterfly runs into the next room, and returns holding—

Sound cue: a baby crying. Sharpless, "seeing" this, backs away.

Sharpless.   Well, good. Happy to see things going so well. I suppose I'll be going now. Ta ta. Ciao. *(He turns away. Sound cue out.)* I hate this job. *(He exits.)*

Gallimard.   At that moment, Butterfly spots in the harbor an American ship—the *Abramo Lincoln!*

Music cue: "The Flower Duet." Song, still dressed as Butterfly, changes into a wedding kimono, moving to the music.

Gallimard.   This is the moment that redeems her years of waiting. With Suzuki's help, they cover the room with flowers—

Chin, as Suzuki, trudges onstage and drops a lone flower without much enthusiasm.

Gallimard.   —and she changes into her wedding dress to prepare for Pinkerton's arrival.

Suzuki helps Butterfly change. Helga enters, and helps Gallimard change into a tuxedo.

Gallimard.   I married a woman older than myself—Helga.

Helga.   My father was ambassador to Australia. I grew up among criminals and kangaroos.

Gallimard.   Hearing that brought me to the altar—

Helga exits.

Gallimard.   —where I took a vow renouncing love. No fantasy woman would ever want me, so, yes, I would settle for a quick leap up the career ladder. Passion, I banish, and in its place—practicality!
   But my vows had long since lost their charm by the time we arrived in China. The sad truth is that all men want a beautiful woman, and the uglier the man, the greater the want.

Suzuki makes final adjustments of Butterfly's costume, as does Gallimard of his tuxedo.

Gallimard.   I married late, at age thirty-one. I was faithful to my marriage for eight years. Until the day when, as a junior-level diplomat in puritanical Peking, in a parlor at the German ambassador's house, during the "Reign of a Hundred Flowers,"[2] I first saw her . . . singing the death scene from *Madame Butterfly.*

Suzuki runs offstage.

Scene 6.   German ambassador's house. Beijing. 1960.

The upstage special area now becomes a stage. Several chairs face upstage, representing seating for some twenty guests in the parlor. A few "diplomats"—Renee, Marc, Toulon—in formal dress enter and take seats.
   Gallimard also sits down, but turns towards us and continues to talk. Orchestral accompaniment on the tape is now replaced by a simple piano. Song picks up the death scene from the point where Butterfly uncovers the hara-kiri knife.

Gallimard.   The ending is pitiful. Pinkerton, in an act of great courage, stays home and sends his American wife to pick up Butterfly's child. The truth, long deferred, has come up to her door.

Song, playing Butterfly, sings the lines from the opera in her own voice—which, though not classical, should be decent.

Song.   *"Con onor muore / chi non puo serbar / vita con onore."*
Gallimard *(simultaneously).*   "Death with honor / Is better than life / Life with dishonor."

---

[2] The name given to a short-lived encouragement of free expression in China in 1957.

The stage is illuminated; we are now completely within an elegant diplomat's residence. Song proceeds to play out an abbreviated death scene. Everyone in the room applauds. Song, shyly, takes her bows. Others in the room rush to congratulate her. Gallimard remains with us.

Gallimard.   They say in opera the voice is everything. That's probably why I'd never before enjoyed opera. Here . . . here was a Butterfly with little or no voice—but she had the grace, the delicacy . . . I believed this girl. I believed her suffering. I wanted to take her in my arms—so delicate, even I could protect her, take her home, pamper her until she smiled.

Over the course of the preceding speech, Song has broken from the upstage crowd and moved directly upstage of Gallimard.

Song.   Excuse me. Monsieur . . . ?

Gallimard turns upstage, shocked.

Gallimard.   Oh! Gallimard. Mademoiselle . . . ? A beautiful . . .
Song.   Song Liling.
Gallimard.   A beautiful performance.
Song.   Oh, please.
Gallimard.   I usually—
Song.   You make me blush. I'm no opera singer at all.
Gallimard.   I usually don't like *Butterfly*.
Song.   I can't blame you in the least.
Gallimard.   I mean, the story—
Song.   Ridiculous.
Gallimard.   I like the story, but . . . what?
Song.   Oh, you like it?
Gallimard.   I . . . what I mean is, I've always seen it played by huge women in so much bad makeup.
Song.   Bad makeup is not unique to the West.
Gallimard.   But, who can believe them?
Song.   And you believe me?
Gallimard.   Absolutely. You were utterly convincing. It's the first time—
Song.   Convincing? As a Japanese woman? The Japanese used hundreds of our people for medical experiments during the war, you know. But I gather such an irony is lost on you.
Gallimard.   No! I was about to say, it's the first time I've seen the beauty of the story.
Song.   Really?
Gallimard.   Of her death. It's a . . . a pure sacrifice. He's unworthy, but what can she do? She loves him . . . so much. It's a very beautiful story.
Song.   Well, yes, to a Westerner.

Gallimard.   Excuse me?

Song.   It's one of your favorite fantasies, isn't it? The submissive Oriental woman and the cruel white man.

Gallimard.   Well, I didn't quite mean . . .

Song.   Consider it this way: what would you say if a blonde homecoming queen fell in love with a short Japanese businessman? He treats her cruelly, then goes home for three years, during which time she prays to his picture and turns down marriage from a young Kennedy. Then, when she learns he has remarried, she kills herself. Now, I believe you would consider this girl to be a deranged idiot, correct? But because it's an Oriental who kills herself for a Westerner—ah!—you find it beautiful.

Silence.

Gallimard.   Yes . . . well . . . I see your point . . .

Song.   I will never do Butterfly again, Monsieur Gallimard. If you wish to see some real theater, come to the Peking Opera sometime. Expand your mind.

Song walks offstage. Other guests exit with her.

Gallimard *(to us).*   So much for protecting her in my big Western arms.

Scene 7.   M. Gallimard's apartment. Beijing. 1960.

Gallimard changes from his tux into a casual suit. Helga enters.

Gallimard.   The Chinese are an incredibly arrogant people.

Helga.   They warned us about that in Paris, remember?

Gallimard.   Even Parisians consider them arrogant. That's a switch.

Helga.   What is it that Madame Su says? "We are a very old civilization." I never know if she's talking about her country or herself.

Gallimard.   I walk around here, all I hear every day, everywhere is how *old* this culture is. The fact that "old" may be synonymous with "senile" doesn't occur to them.

Helga.   You're not going to change them. "East is east, west is west, and . . ." whatever that guy said.

Gallimard.   It's just that—silly. I met . . . at Ambassador Koening's tonight— you should've been there.

Helga.   Koening? Oh god, no. Did he enchant you all again with the history of Bavaria?

Gallimard.   No. I met, I suppose, the Chinese equivalent of a diva. She's a singer in the Chinese opera.

Helga.   They have an opera, too? Do they sing in Chinese? Or maybe—in Italian?

Gallimard.　Tonight, she did sing in Italian.

Helga.　How'd she manage that?

Gallimard.　She must've been educated in the West before the Revolution. Her French is very good also. Anyway, she sang the death scene from *Madame Butterfly.*

Helga.　*Madame Butterfly!* Then I should have come. (*She begins humming, floating around the room as if dragging long kimono sleeves.*) Did she have a nice costume? I think it's a classic piece of music.

Gallimard.　That's what *I* thought, too. Don't let her hear you say that.

Helga.　What's wrong?

Gallimard.　Evidently the Chinese hate it.

Helga.　She hated it, but she performed it anyway? Is she perverse?

Gallimard.　They hate it because the white man gets the girl. Sour grapes if you ask me.

Helga.　Politics again? Why can't they just hear it as a piece of beautiful music? So, what's in their opera?

Gallimard.　I don't know. But, whatever it is, I'm sure it must be *old.*

Helga exits.

Scene 8.　Chinese opera house and the streets of Beijing. 1960.

The sound of gongs clanging fills the stage.

Gallimard.　My wife's innocent question kept ringing in my ears. I asked around, but no one knew anything about the Chinese opera. It took four weeks, but my curiosity overcame my cowardice. This Chinese diva—this unwilling Butterfly—what did she do to make her so proud?

　　The room was hot, and full of smoke. Wrinkled faces, old women, teeth missing—a man with a growth on his neck, like a human toad. All smiling, pipes falling from their mouths, cracking nuts between their teeth, a live chicken pecking at my foot—all looking, screaming, gawking . . . at her.

The upstage area is suddenly hit with a harsh white light. It has become the stage for the Chinese opera performance. Two dancers enter, along with Song. Gallimard stands apart, watching. Song glides gracefully amidst the two dancers. Drums suddenly slam to a halt. Song strikes a pose, looking straight at Gallimard. Dancers exit. Light change. Pause, then Song walks right off the stage and straight up to Gallimard.

Song.　Yes. You. White man. I'm looking straight at you.

Gallimard.　Me?

Song.　You see any other white men? It was too easy to spot you. How often does a man in my audience come in a tie?

Song starts to remove her costume. Underneath, she wears simple baggy clothes. They are now backstage. The show is over.

Song. So, you are an adventurous imperialist?

Gallimard. I . . . thought it would further my education.

Song. It took you four weeks. Why?

Gallimard. I've been busy.

Song. Well, education has always been undervalued in the West, hasn't it?

Gallimard *(laughing).* I don't think that's true.

Song. No, you wouldn't. You're a Westerner. How can you objectively judge your own values?

Gallimard. I think it's possible to achieve some distance.

Song. Do you? *(Pause.)* It stinks in here. Let's go.

Gallimard. These are the smells of your loyal fans.

Song. I love them for being my fans, I hate the smell they leave behind. I too can distance myself from my people. *(She looks around, then whispers in his ear.)* "Art for the masses" is a shitty excuse to keep artists poor. *(She pops a cigarette in her mouth.)* Be a gentleman, will you? And light my cigarette.

Gallimard fumbles for a match.

Gallimard. I don't . . . smoke.

Song *(lighting her own).* Your loss. Had you lit my cigarette, I might have blown a puff of smoke right between your eyes. Come.

They start to walk about the stage. It is a summer night on the Beijing streets. Sounds of the city play on the house speakers.

Song. How I wish there were even a tiny café to sit in. With cappuccinos, and men in tuxedos and bad expatriate jazz.

Gallimard. If my history serves me correctly, you weren't even allowed into the clubs in Shanghai before the Revolution.

Song. Your history serves you poorly, Monsieur Gallimard. True, there were signs reading "No dogs and Chinamen." But a woman, especially a delicate Oriental woman—we always go where we please. Could you imagine it otherwise? Clubs in China filled with pasty, big-thighed white women, while thousands of slender lotus blossoms wait just outside the door? Never. The clubs would be empty. *(Beat.)* We have always held a certain fascination for you Caucasian men, have we not?

Gallimard. But . . . that fascination is imperialist, or so you tell me.

Song. Do you believe everything I tell you? Yes. It is always imperialist. But sometimes . . . sometimes, it is also mutual. Oh—this is my flat.

Gallimard. I didn't even—

Song. Thank you. Come another time and we will further expand your mind.

Song exits. Gallimard continues roaming the streets as he speaks to us.

Gallimard.   What was that? What did she mean, "Sometimes . . . it is mutual"? Women do not flirt with me. And I normally can't talk to them. But tonight, I held up my end of the conversation.

Scene 9.   Gallimard's bedroom. Beijing. 1960.

Helga enters.

Helga.   You didn't tell me you'd be home late.
Gallimard.   I didn't intend to. Something came up.
Helga.   Oh? Like what?
Gallimard.   I went to the . . . to the Dutch ambassador's home.
Helga.   Again?
Gallimard.   There was a reception for a visiting scholar. He's writing a six-volume treatise on the Chinese revolution. We all gathered that meant he'd have to live here long enough to actually write six volumes, and we all expressed our deepest sympathies.
Helga.   Well, I had a good night too. I went with the ladies to a martial arts demonstration. Some of those men—when they break those thick boards— *(she mimes fanning herself.)* whoo-whoo!

Helga exits. Lights dim.

Gallimard.   I lied to my wife. Why? I've never had any reason to lie before. But what reason did I have tonight? I didn't do anything wrong. That night, I had a dream. Other people, I've been told, have dreams when angels appear. Or dragons, or Sophia Loren in a towel. In my dream, Marc from school appeared.

Marc enters, in a nightshirt and cap.

Marc.   Rene! You met a girl!

Gallimard and Marc stumble down the Beijing streets. Night sounds over the speakers.

Gallimard.   It's not that amazing, thank you.
Marc.   No! It's so monumental, I heard about it halfway around the world in my sleep!
Gallimard.   I've met girls before, you know.
Marc.   Name one. I've come across time and space to congratulate you. *(He hands Gallimard a bottle of wine.)*
Gallimard.   Marc, this is expensive.

Marc.   On those rare occasions when you become a formless spirit, why not steal the best?

Marc pops open the bottle, begins to share it with Gallimard.

Gallimard.   You embarrass me. She . . . there's no reason to think she likes me.

Marc.   "Sometimes, it is mutual"?

Gallimard.   Oh.

Marc.   "Mutual"? "Mutual"? What does that mean?

Gallimard.   You heard?

Marc.   It means the money is in the bank, you only have to write the check!

Gallimard.   I am a married man!

Marc.   And an excellent one too. I cheated after . . . six months. Then again and again, until now—three hundred girls in twelve years.

Gallimard.   I don't think we should hold that up as a model.

Marc.   Of course not! My life—it is disgusting! Phooey! Phooey! But, you—you are the model husband.

Gallimard.   Anyway, it's impossible. I'm a foreigner.

Marc.   Ah, yes. She cannot love you, it is taboo, but something deep inside her heart . . . she cannot help herself . . . she must surrender to you. It is her destiny.

Gallimard.   How do you imagine all this?

Marc.   The same way you do. It's an old story. It's in our blood. They fear us, Rene. Their women fear us. And their men—their men hate us. And, you know something? They are all correct.

They spot a light in a window.

Marc.   There! There, Rene!

Gallimard.   It's her window.

Marc.   Late at night—it burns. The light—it burns for you.

Gallimard.   I won't look. It's not respectful.

Marc.   We don't have to be respectful. We're foreign devils.

Enter Song, in a sheer robe, her face completely swathed in black cloth. The "One Fine Day" aria creeps in over the speakers. With her back to us, Song mimes attending to her toilette. Her robe comes loose, revealing her white shoulders.

Marc.   All your life you've waited for a beautiful girl who would lay down for you. All your life you've smiled like a saint when it's happened to every other man you know. And you see them in magazines and you see them in movies. And you wonder, what's wrong with me? Will anyone beautiful ever want me? As the years pass, your hair thins and you struggle to hold on to even your hopes. Stop struggling, Rene. The wait is over. *(He exits.)*

Gallimard. Marc? Marc?

At that moment, Song, her back still towards us, drops her robe. A second of her naked back, then a sound cue: a phone ringing, very loud. Blackout, followed in the next beat by a special up on the bedroom area, where a phone now sits. Gallimard stumbles across the stage and picks up the phone. Sound cue out. Over the course of his conversation, area lights fill in the vicinity of his bed. It is the following morning.

Gallimard. Yes? Hello?
Song *(offstage).* Is it very early?
Gallimard. Why, yes.
Song *(offstage).* How early?
Gallimard. It's . . . it's 5:30. Why are you—?
Song *(offstage).* But it's light outside. Already.
Gallimard. It is. The sun must be in confusion today.

Over the course of Song's next speech, her upstage special comes up again. She sits in a chair, legs crossed, in a robe, telephone to her ear.

Song. I waited until I saw the sun. That was as much discipline as I could manage for one night. Do you forgive me?
Gallimard. Of course . . . for what?
Song. Then I'll ask you quickly. Are you really interested in the opera?
Gallimard. Why, yes. Yes I am.
Song. Then come again next Thursday. I am playing *The Drunken Beauty.* May I count on you?
Gallimard. Yes. You may.
Song. Perfect. Well, I must be getting to bed. I'm exhausted. It's been a very long night for me.

Song hangs up; special on her goes off. Gallimard begins to dress for work.

Scene 10. Song Liling's apartment. Beijing. 1960.

Gallimard. I returned to the opera that next week, and the week after that . . . she keeps our meetings so short—perhaps fifteen, twenty minutes at most. So I am left each week with a thirst which is intensified. In this way, fifteen weeks have gone by. I am starting to doubt the words of my friend Marc. But no, not really. In my heart, I know she has . . . an interest in me. I suspect this is her way. She is outwardly bold and outspoken, yet her heart is shy and afraid. It is the Oriental in her at war with her Western education.
Song *(offstage).* I will be out in an instant. Ask the servant for anything you want.
Gallimard. Tonight, I have finally been invited to enter her apartment. Though the idea is almost beyond belief, I believe she is afraid of me.

Gallimard looks around the room. He picks up a picture in a frame, studies it. Without his noticing, Song enters, dressed elegantly in a black gown from the twenties. She stands in the doorway looking like Anna May Wong.[3]

Song. That is my father.
Gallimard *(surprised).* Mademoiselle Song . . .

She glides up to him, snatches away the picture.

Song. It is very good that he did not live to see the Revolution. They would, no doubt, have made him kneel on broken glass. Not that he didn't deserve such a punishment. But he is my father. I would've hated to see it happen.
Gallimard. I'm very honored that you've allowed me to visit your home.

Song curtseys.

Song. Thank you. Oh! Haven't you been poured any tea?
Gallimard. I'm really not—
Song *(to her offstage servant).* Shu-Fang! Cha! Kwai-lah! *(To Gallimard.)* I'm sorry. You want everything to be perfect—
Gallimard. Please.
Song. —and before the evening even begins—
Gallimard. I'm really not thirsty.
Song. —it's ruined.
Gallimard *(sharply).* Mademoiselle Song!

Song sits down.

Song. I'm sorry.
Gallimard. What are you apologizing for now?

Pause; Song starts to giggle.

Song. I don't know!

Gallimard laughs.

Gallimard. Exactly my point.
Song. Oh, I am silly. Light-headed. I promise not to apologize for anything else tonight, do you hear me?
Gallimard. That's a good girl.

Shu-Fang, a servant girl, comes out with a tea tray and starts to pour.

---

[3] (1905–1961), a beautiful Chinese-American actress, was the first Asian woman to become a movie star in the United States.

Song *(to Shu-Fang).*   No! I'll pour myself for the gentleman!

Shu-Fang, staring at Gallimard, exits.

Gallimard.   You have a beautiful home.
Song.   No, I . . . I don't even know why I invited you up.
Gallimard.   Well, I'm glad you did.

Song looks around the room.

Song.   There is an element of danger to your presence.
Gallimard.   Oh?
Song.   You must know.
Gallimard.   It doesn't concern me. We both know why I'm here.
Song.   It doesn't concern me either. No . . . well perhaps . . .
Gallimard.   What?
Song.   Perhaps I am slightly afraid of scandal.
Gallimard.   What are we doing?
Song.   I'm entertaining you. In my parlor.
Gallimard.   In France, that would hardly—
Song.   France. France is a country living in the modern era. Perhaps even ahead of it. China is a nation whose soul is firmly rooted two thousand years in the past. What I do, even pouring the tea for you now . . . it has . . . implications. The walls and windows say so. Even my own heart, strapped inside this Western dress . . . even it says things—things I don't care to hear.

Song hands Gallimard a cup of tea. Gallimard puts his hand over both the teacup and Song's hand.

Gallimard.   This is a beautiful dress.
Song.   Don't.
Gallimard.   What?
Song.   I don't even know if it looks right on me.
Gallimard.   Believe me—
Song.   You are from France. You see so many beautiful women.
Gallimard.   France? Since when are the European women—?
Song.   Oh! What am I trying to do, anyway?!

Song runs to the door, composes herself, then turns towards Gallimard.

Song.   Monsieur Gallimard, perhaps you should go.
Gallimard.   But . . . why?
Song.   There's something wrong about this.
Gallimard.   I don't see what.
Song.   I feel . . . I am not myself.

Gallimard.   No. You're nervous.

Song.   Please. Hard as I try to be modern, to speak like a man, to hold a Western woman's strong face up to my own . . . in the end, I fail. A small, frightened heart beats too quickly and gives me away. Monsieur Gallimard, I'm a Chinese girl. I've never . . . never invited a man up to my flat before. The forwardness of my actions makes my skin burn.

Gallimard.   What are you afraid of? Certainly not me, I hope.

Song.   I'm a modest girl.

Gallimard.   I know. And very beautiful. *(He touches her hair.)*

Song.   Please—go now. The next time you see me, I shall again be myself.

Gallimard.   I like you the way you are right now.

Song.   You are a cad.

Gallimard.   What do you expect? I'm a foreign devil.

Gallimard walks downstage. Song exits.

Gallimard *(to us).*   Did you hear the way she talked about Western women? Much differently than the first night. She does—she feels inferior to them— and to me.

Scene 11.   The French embassy. Beijing. 1960.

Gallimard moves towards a desk.

Gallimard.   I determined to try an experiment. In *Madame Butterfly*, Cio-Cio-San fears that the Western man who catches a butterfly will pierce its heart with a needle, then leave it to perish. I began to wonder: had I, too, caught a butterfly who would writhe on a needle?

Marc enters, dressed as a bureaucrat, holding a stack of papers. As Gallimard speaks, Marc hands papers to him. He peruses, then signs, stamps, or rejects them.

Gallimard.   Over the next five weeks, I worked like a dynamo. I stopped going to the opera, I didn't phone or write her. I knew this little flower was waiting for me to call, and, as I wickedly refused to do so, I felt for the first time that rush of power—the absolute power of a man.

Marc continues acting as the bureaucrat, but he now speaks as himself.

Marc.   Rene! It's me.

Gallimard.   Marc—I hear your voice everywhere now. Even in the midst of work.

Marc. That's because I'm watching you—all the time.

Gallimard. You were always the most popular guy in school.

Marc. Well, there's no guarantee of failure in life like happiness in high school. Somehow I knew I'd end up in the suburbs working for Renault and you'd be in the Orient picking exotic women off the trees. And they say there's no justice.

Gallimard. That's why you were my friend?

Marc. I gave you a little of my life, so that now you can give me some of yours. *(Pause.)* Remember Isabelle?

Gallimard. Of course I remember! She was my first experience.

Marc. We all wanted to ball her. But she only wanted me.

Gallimard. I had her.

Marc. Right. You balled her.

Gallimard. You were the only one who ever believed me.

Marc. Well, there's a good reason for that. *(Beat.)* C'mon. You must've guessed.

Gallimard. You told me to wait in the bushes by the cafeteria that night. The next thing I knew, she was on me. Dress up in the air.

Marc. She never wore underwear.

Gallimard. My arms were pinned to the dirt.

Marc. She loved the superior position. A girl ahead of her time.

Gallimard. I looked up, and there was this woman . . . bouncing up and down on my loins.

Marc. Screaming, right?

Gallimard. Screaming, and breaking off the branches all around me, and pounding my butt up and down into the dirt.

Marc. Huffing and puffing like a locomotive.

Gallimard. And in the middle of all this, the leaves were getting into my mouth, my legs were losing circulation, I thought, "God. So this is *it?*"

Marc. You thought that?

Gallimard. Well, I was worried about my legs falling off.

Marc. You didn't have a good time?

Gallimard. No, that's not what I—I had a great time!

Marc. You're sure?

Gallimard. Yeah. Really.

Marc. 'Cuz I wanted you to have a good time.

Gallimard. I did.

Pause.

Marc. Shit. *(Pause.)* When all is said and done, she was kind of a lousy lay, wasn't she? I mean, there was a lot of energy there, but you never knew what she was doing with it. Like when she yelled "I'm coming!"—hell, it was so loud, you wanted to go, "Look, it's not that big a deal."

Gallimard.   I got scared. I thought she meant someone was actually coming. *(Pause.)* But, Marc?

Marc.   What?

Gallimard.   Thanks.

Marc.   Oh, don't mention it.

Gallimard.   It was my first experience.

Marc.   Yeah. You got her.

Gallimard.   I got her.

Marc.   Wait! Look at that letter again!

Gallimard picks up one of the papers he's been stamping, and rereads it.

Gallimard *(to us).*   After six weeks, they began to arrive. The letters.

Upstage special on Song, as Madame Butterfly. The scene is underscored by the "Love Duet."

Song.   Did we fight? I do not know. Is the opera no longer of interest to you? Please come—my audiences miss the white devil in their midst.

Gallimard looks up from the letter, towards us.

Gallimard *(to us).*   A concession, but much too dignified. *(Beat; he discards the letter.)* I skipped the opera again that week to complete a position paper on trade.

The bureaucrat hands him another letter.

Song.   Six weeks have passed since last we met. Is this your practice—to leave friends in the lurch? Sometimes I hate you, sometimes I hate myself, but always I miss you.

Gallimard *(to us).*   Better, but I don't like the way she calls me "friend." When a woman calls a man her "friend," she's calling him a eunuch or a homosexual. *(Beat; he discards the letter.)* I was absent from the opera for the seventh week, feeling a sudden urge to clean out my files.

Bureaucrat hands him another letter.

Song.   Your rudeness is beyond belief. I don't deserve this cruelty. Don't bother to call. I'll have you turned away at the door.

Gallimard *(to us).*   I didn't. *(He discards the letter; bureaucrat hands him another.)* And then finally, the letter that concluded my experiment.

Song.   I am out of words. I can hide behind dignity no longer. What do you want? I have already given you my shame.

Gallimard gives the letter back to Marc, slowly. Special on Song fades out.

Gallimard *(to us).*   Reading it, I became suddenly ashamed. Yes, my experiment had been a success. She was turning on my needle. But the victory seemed hollow.

Marc.   Hollow?! Are you crazy?

Gallimard.   Nothing, Marc. Please go away.

Marc *(exiting, with papers).*   Haven't I taught you anything?

Gallimard.   "I have already given you my shame." I had to attend a reception that evening. On the way, I felt sick. If there is a God, surely he would punish me now. I had finally gained power over a beautiful woman, only to abuse it cruelly. There must be justice in the world. I had the strange feeling that the ax would fall this very evening.

Scene 12.   Ambassador Toulon's residence. Beijing. 1960.

Sound cue: party noises. Light change. We are now in a spacious residence. Toulon, the French ambassador, enters and taps Gallimard on the shoulder.

Toulon.   Gallimard? Can I have a word? Over here.

Gallimard *(to us).*   Manuel Toulon. French ambassador to China. He likes to think of us all as his children. Rather like God.

Toulon.   Look, Gallimard, there's not much to say. I've liked you. From the day you walked in. You were no leader, but you were tidy and efficient.

Gallimard.   Thank you, sir.

Toulon.   Don't jump the gun. Okay, our needs in China are changing. It's embarrassing that we lost Indochina. Someone just wasn't on the ball there. I don't mean you personally, of course.

Gallimard.   Thank you, sir.

Toulon.   We're going to be doing a lot more information-gathering in the future. The nature of our work here is changing. Some people are just going to have to go. It's nothing personal.

Gallimard.   Oh.

Toulon.   Want to know a secret? Vice-Consul LeBon is being transferred.

Gallimard *(to us).*   My immediate superior!

Toulon.   And most of his department.

Gallimard *(to us).*   Just as I feared! God has seen my evil heart—

Toulon.   But not you.

Gallimard *(to us).*   —and he's taking her away just as . . . *(To Toulon.)* Excuse me, sir?

Toulon.   Scare you? I think I did. Cheer up, Gallimard. I want you to replace LeBon as vice-consul.

Gallimard.   You—? Yes, well, thank you, sir.

Toulon.   Anytime.

Gallimard.   I . . . accept with great humility.

Toulon.   Humility won't be part of the job. You're going to coordinate the re-vamped intelligence division. Want to know a secret? A year ago, you would've been out. But the past few months, I don't know how it happened, you've become this new aggressive confident . . . thing. And they also tell me you get along with the Chinese. So I think you're a lucky man, Gallimard. Congratulations.

They shake hands. Toulon exits. Party noises out. Gallimard stumbles across a darkened stage.

Gallimard.   Vice-consul? Impossible! As I stumbled out of the party, I saw it written across the sky: There is no God. Or, no—say that there is a God. But that God . . . understands. Of course! God who creates Eve to serve Adam, who blesses Solomon with his harem but ties Jezebel to a burning bed[4]—that God is a man. And he understands! At age thirty-nine, I was suddenly initiated into the way of the world.

Scene 13.   Song Liling's apartment. Beijing. 1960.

Song enters, in a sheer dressing gown.

Song.   Are you crazy?
Gallimard.   Mademoiselle Song—
Song.   To come here—at this hour? After . . . after eight weeks?
Gallimard.   It's the most amazing—
Song.   You bang on my door? Scare my servants, scandalize the neighbors?
Gallimard.   I've been promoted. To vice-consul.

Pause.

Song.   And what is that supposed to mean to me?
Gallimard.   Are you my Butterfly?
Song.   What are you saying?
Gallimard.   I've come tonight for an answer: are you my Butterfly?
Song.   Don't you know already?
Gallimard.   I want you to say it.
Song.   I don't want to say it.
Gallimard.   So, that is your answer?
Song.   You know how I feel about—
Gallimard.   I do remember one thing.
Song.   What?
Gallimard.   In the letter I received today.

---

[4] Biblical allusions. See Genesis 2:18–25, I Kings 11:1–8, and II Kings 9:30–37.

Song.   Don't.

Gallimard.   "I have already given you my shame."

Song.   It's enough that I even wrote it.

Gallimard.   Well, then—

Song.   I shouldn't have it splashed across my face.

Gallimard.   —if that's all true—

Song.   Stop!

Gallimard.   Then what is one more short answer?

Song.   I don't want to!

Gallimard.   Are you my Butterfly? *(Silence; he crosses the room and begins to touch her hair.)* I want from you honesty. There should be nothing false between us. No false pride.

Pause.

Song.   Yes, I am. I am your Butterfly.

Gallimard.   Then let me be honest with you. It is because of you that I was promoted tonight. You have changed my life forever. My little Butterfly, there should be no more secrets: I love you.

He starts to kiss her roughly. She resists slightly.

Song.   No . . . no . . . gently . . . please, I've never . . .

Gallimard.   No?

Song.   I've tried to appear experienced, but . . . the truth is . . . no.

Gallimard.   Are you cold?

Song.   Yes. Cold.

Gallimard.   Then we will go very, very slowly.

He starts to caress her; her gown begins to open.

Song.   No . . . let me . . . keep my clothes . . .

Gallimard.   But . . .

Song.   Please . . . it all frightens me. I'm a modest Chinese girl.

Gallimard.   My poor little treasure.

Song.   I am your treasure. Though inexperienced, I am not . . . ignorant. They teach us things, our mothers, about pleasing a man.

Gallimard.   Yes?

Song.   I'll do my best to make you happy. Turn off the lights.

Gallimard gets up and heads for a lamp. Song, propped up on one elbow, tosses her hair back and smiles.

Song.   Monsieur Gallimard?

Gallimard.   Yes, Butterfly?

Song. *"Vieni, vieni!"*
Gallimard. "Come, darling."
Song. *"Ah! Dolce notte!"*
Gallimard. "Beautiful night."
Song. *"Tutto estatico d'amor ride il ciel!"*
Gallimard. "All ecstatic with love, the heavens are filled with laughter."

He turns off the lamp. Blackout.

Act II

Scene 1. M. Gallimard's cell. Paris. 1988.

Lights up on Gallimard. He sits in his cell, reading from a leaflet.

Gallimard. This, from a contemporary critic's commentary on *Madame Butterfly:* "Pinkerton suffers from . . . being an obnoxious bounder whom every man in the audience itches to kick." Bully for us men in the audience! Then, in the same note: "Butterfly is the most irresistibly appealing of Puccini's 'Little Women.' Watching the succession of her humiliations is like watching a child under torture." *(He tosses the pamphlet over his shoulder.)* I suggest that, while we men may all want to kick Pinkerton, very few of us would pass up the opportunity to *be* Pinkerton.

Gallimard moves out of his cell.

Scene 2. Gallimard and Butterfly's flat. Beijing. 1960.

We are in a simple but well-decorated parlor. Gallimard moves to sit on a sofa, while Song, dressed in a chong sam,[5] enters and curls up at his feet.

Gallimard *(to us).* We secured a flat on the outskirts of Peking. Butterfly, as I was calling her now, decorated our "home" with Western furniture and Chinese antiques. And there, on a few stolen afternoons or evenings each week, Butterfly commenced her education.
Song. The Chinese men—they keep us down.
Gallimard. Even in the "New Society"?

---

[5] A tight-fitting dress with side slits in the skirt.

Song.   In the "New Society," we are all kept ignorant equally. That's one of the exciting things about loving a Western man. I know you are not threatened by a woman's education.

Gallimard.   I'm no saint, Butterfly.

Song.   But you come from a progressive society.

Gallimard.   We're not always reminding each other how "old" we are, if that's what you mean.

Song.   Exactly. We Chinese—once, I suppose, it is true, we ruled the world. But so what? How much more exciting to be part of the society ruling the world today. Tell me—what's happening in Vietnam?

Gallimard.   Oh, Butterfly—you want me to bring my work home?

Song.   I want to know what you know. To be impressed by my man. It's not the particulars so much as the fact that you're making decisions which change the shape of the world.

Gallimard.   Not the world. At best, a small corner.

Toulon enters, and sits at a desk upstage.

Scene 3.   French embassy. Beijing. 1961.

Gallimard moves downstage, to Toulon's desk. Song remains upstage, watching.

Toulon.   And a more troublesome corner is hard to imagine.

Gallimard.   So, the Americans plan to begin bombing?

Toulon.   This is very secret, Gallimard: yes. The Americans don't have an embassy here. They're asking us to be their eyes and ears. Say Jack Kennedy signed an order to bomb North Vietnam, Laos. How would the Chinese react?

Gallimard.   I think the Chinese will squawk—

Toulon.   Uh-huh.

Gallimard.   —but, in their hearts, they don't even like Ho Chi Minh.[6]

Pause.

Toulon.   What a bunch of jerks. Vietnam was *our* colony. Not only didn't the Americans help us fight to keep them, but now, seven years later, they've come back to grab the territory for themselves. It's very irritating.

Gallimard.   With all due respect, sir, why should the Americans have won our war for us back in 'fifty-four if we didn't have the will to win it ourselves?

Toulon.   You're kidding, aren't you?

Pause.

---

[6] Revolutionary leader and president of North Vietnam, 1954–1969.

Gallimard. The Orientals simply want to be associated with whoever shows the most strength and power. You live with the Chinese, sir. Do you think they like Communism?

Toulon. I live in China. Not with the Chinese.

Gallimard. Well, I—

Toulon. *You* live with the Chinese.

Gallimard. Excuse me?

Toulon. I can't keep a secret.

Gallimard. What are you saying?

Toulon. Only that I'm not immune to gossip. So, you're keeping a native mistress? Don't answer. It's none of my business. *(Pause.)* I'm sure she must be gorgeous.

Gallimard. Well . . .

Toulon. I'm impressed. You had the stamina to go out into the streets and hunt one down. Some of us have to be content with the wives of the expatriate community.

Gallimard. I do feel . . . fortunate.

Toulon. So, Gallimard, you've got the inside knowledge—what *do* the Chinese think?

Gallimard. Deep down, they miss the old days. You know, cappuccinos, men in tuxedos—

Toulon. So what do we tell the Americans about Vietnam?

Gallimard. Tell them there's a natural affinity between the West and the Orient.

Toulon. And that you speak from experience?

Gallimard. The Orientals are people too. They want the good things we can give them. If the Americans demonstrate the will to win, the Vietnamese will welcome them into a mutually beneficial union.

Toulon. I don't see how the Vietnamese can stand up to American firepower.

Gallimard. Orientals will always submit to a greater force.

Toulon. I'll note your opinions in my report. The Americans always love to hear how "welcome" they'll be. *(He starts to exit.)*

Gallimard. Sir?

Toulon. Mmmm?

Gallimard. This . . . rumor you've heard.

Toulon. Uh-huh?

Gallimard. How . . . widespread do you think it is?

Toulon. It's only widespread within this embassy. Where nobody talks because everybody is guilty. We were worried about you, Gallimard. We thought you were the only one here without a secret. Now you go and find a lotus blossom . . . and top us all. *(He exits.)*

Gallimard *(to us).* Toulon knows! And he approves! I was learning the benefits of being a man. We form our own clubs, sit behind thick doors, smoke—and celebrate the fact that we're still boys. *(He starts to move downstage, towards Song.)* So, over the—

Suddenly Comrade Chin enters. Gallimard backs away.

Gallimard *(to Song).*   No! Why does she have to come in?
Song.   Rene, be sensible. How can they understand the story without her? Now, don't embarrass yourself.

Gallimard moves down center.

Gallimard *(to us).*   Now, you will see why my story is so amusing to so many people. Why they snicker at parties in disbelief. Please—try to understand it from my point of view. We are all prisoners of our time and place. *(He exits.)*

Scene 4.   Gallimard and Butterfly's flat. Beijing. 1961.

Song *(to us).*   1961. The flat Monsieur Gallimard rented for us. An evening after he has gone.
Chin.   Okay, see if you can find out when the Americans plan to start bombing Vietnam. If you can find out what cities, even better.
Song.   I'll do my best, but I don't want to arouse his suspicions.
Chin.   Yeah, sure, of course. So, what else?
Song.   The Americans will increase troops in Vietnam to 170,000 soldiers with 120,000 militia and 11,000 American advisors.
Chin *(writing).*   Wait, wait, 120,000 militia and—
Song.   —11,000 American—
Chin.   —American advisors. *(Beat.)* How do you remember so much?
Song.   I'm an actor.
Chin.   Yeah. *(Beat.)* Is that how come you dress like that?
Song.   Like what, Miss Chin?
Chin.   Like that dress! You're wearing a dress. And every time I come here, you're wearing a dress. Is that because you're an actor? Or what?
Song.   It's a . . . disguise, Miss Chin.
Chin.   Actors, I think they're all weirdos. My mother tells me actors are like gamblers or prostitutes or—
Song.   It helps me in my assignment.

Pause.

Chin.   You're not gathering information in any way that violates Communist Party principles, are you?
Song.   Why would I do that?
Chin.   Just checking. Remember: when working for the Great Proletarian State, you represent our Chairman Mao in every position you take.
Song.   I'll try to imagine the Chairman taking my positions.
Chin.   We all think of him this way. Good-bye, comrade. *(She starts to exit.)* Comrade?

Song. Yes?
Chin. Don't forget: there is no homosexuality in China!
Song. Yes, I've heard.
Chin. Just checking. *(She exits.)*
Song *(to us).* What passes for a woman in modern China.

Gallimard sticks his head out from the wings.

Gallimard. Is she gone?
Song. Yes, Rene. Please continue in your own fashion.

Scene 5. Beijing. 1961–1963.

Gallimard moves to the couch where Song still sits. He lies down in her lap, and she strokes his forehead.

Gallimard *(to us).* And so, over the years 1961, '62, '63, we settled into our routine, Butterfly and I. She would always have prepared a light snack and then, ever so delicately, and only if I agreed, she would start to pleasure me. With her hands, her mouth . . . too many ways to explain, and too sad, given my present situation. But mostly we would talk. About my life. Perhaps there is nothing more rare than to find a woman who passionately listens.

Song remains upstage, listening, as Helga enters and plays a scene downstage with Gallimard.

Helga. Rene, I visited Dr. Bolleart this morning.
Gallimard. Why? Are you ill?
Helga. No, no. You see, I wanted to ask him . . . that question we've been discussing.
Gallimard. And I told you, it's only a matter of time. Why did you bring a doctor into this? We just have to keep trying—like a crapshoot, actually.
Helga. I went, I'm sorry. But listen: he says there's nothing wrong with me.
Gallimard. You see? Now, will you stop—?
Helga. Rene, he says he'd like you to go in and take some tests.
Gallimard. Why? So he can find there's nothing wrong with both of us?
Helga. Rene, I don't ask for much. One trip! One visit! And then, whatever you want to do about it—you decide.
Gallimard. You're assuming he'll find something defective!
Helga. No! Of course not! Whatever he finds—if he finds nothing, we decide what to do about nothing! But go!
Gallimard. If he finds nothing, we keep trying. Just like we do now.
Helga. But at least we'll know! *(Pause.)* I'm sorry. *(She starts to exit.)*
Gallimard. Do you really want me to see Dr. Bolleart?

Helga. Only if you want a child, Rene. We have to face the fact that time is running out. Only if you want a child. *(She exits.)*

Gallimard *(to Song).* I'm a modern man, Butterfly. And yet, I don't want to go. It's the same old voodoo. I feel like God himself is laughing at me if I can't produce a child.

Song. You men of the West—you're obsessed by your odd desire for equality. Your wife can't give you a child, and *you're* going to the doctor?

Gallimard. Well, you see, she's already gone.

Song. And because this incompetent can't find the defect, you now have to subject yourself to him? It's unnatural.

Gallimard. Well, what is the "natural" solution?

Song. In Imperial China, when a man found that one wife was inadequate, he turned to another—to give him his son.

Gallimard. What do you—? I can't . . . marry you, yet.

Song. Please. I'm not asking you to be my husband. But I am already your wife.

Gallimard. Do you want to . . . have my child?

Song. I thought you'd never ask.

Gallimard. But, your career . . . your—

Song. Phooey on my career! That's your Western mind, twisting itself into strange shapes again. Of course I love my career. But what would I love most of all? To feel something inside me—day and night—something I know is yours. *(Pause.)* Promise me . . . you won't go to this doctor. Who is this Western quack to set himself as judge over the man I love? I know who is a man, and who is not. *(She exits.)*

Gallimard *(to us).* Dr. Bolleart? Of course I didn't go. What man would?

Scene 6. Beijing. 1963.

Party noises over the house speakers. Renee enters, wearing a revealing gown.

Gallimard. 1963. A party at the Austrian embassy. None of us could remember the Austrian ambassador's name, which seemed somehow appropriate. *(To Renee.)* So, I tell the Americans, Diem[7] must go. The U.S. wants to be respected by the Vietnamese, and yet they're propping up this nobody seminarian as her president. A man whose claim to fame is his sister-in-law imposing fanatic "moral order" campaigns? Oriental women—when they're good, they're very good, but when they're bad, they're Christians.

Renee. Yeah.

Gallimard. And what do you do?

Renee. I'm a student. My father exports a lot of useless stuff to the Third World.

Gallimard. How useless?

Renee. You know. Squirt guns, confectioner's sugar, Hula Hoops . . .

---

[7] Ngo Dinh Diem (1901–1963), president of South Vietnam, 1955–1963. He was assassinated in a U.S.-supported coup d'etat.

Gallimard.   I'm sure they appreciate the sugar.

Renee.   I'm here for two years to study Chinese.

Gallimard.   Two years!

Renee.   That's what everybody says.

Gallimard.   When did you arrive?

Renee.   Three weeks ago.

Gallimard.   And?

Renee.   I like it. It's primitive, but . . . well, this is the place to learn Chinese, so here I am.

Gallimard.   Why Chinese?

Renee.   I think it'll be important someday.

Gallimard.   You do?

Renee.   Don't ask me when, but . . . that's what I think.

Gallimard.   Well, I agree with you. One hundred percent. That's very far-sighted.

Renee.   Yeah. Well of course, my father thinks I'm a complete weirdo.

Gallimard.   He'll thank you someday.

Renee.   Like when the Chinese start buying Hula Hoops?

Gallimard.   There're a billion bellies out there.

Renee.   And if they end up taking over the world—well, then I'll be lucky to know Chinese too, right?

Pause.

Gallimard.   At this point, I don't see how the Chinese can possibly take—

Renee.   You know what I *don't* like about China?

Gallimard.   Excuse me? No—what?

Renee.   Nothing to do at night.

Gallimard.   You come to parties at embassies like everyone else.

Renee.   Yeah, but they get out at ten. And then what?

Gallimard.   I'm afraid the Chinese idea of a dance hall is a dirt floor and a man with a flute.

Renee.   Are you married?

Gallimard.   Yes. Why?

Renee.   You wanna . . . fool around?

Pause.

Gallimard.   Sure.

Renee.   I'll wait for you outside. What's your name?

Gallimard.   Gallimard. Rene.

Renee.   Weird. I'm Renee too. (*She exits.*)

Gallimard (*to us*).   And so, I embarked on my first extra-extramarital affair. Renee was picture perfect. With a body like those girls in the magazines. If I put a tissue paper over my eyes, I wouldn't have been able to tell the difference. And it was exciting to be with someone who wasn't afraid to be seen completely naked. But is it possible for a woman to be *too* uninhibited, *too* willing, so as to seem almost too . . . masculine?

Chuck Berry blares from the house speakers, then comes down in volume as Renee enters, toweling her hair.

Renee. You have a nice weenie.
Gallimard. What?
Renee. Penis. You have a nice penis.
Gallimard. Oh. Well, thank you. That's very . . .
Renee. What—can't take a compliment?
Gallimard. No, it's very . . . reassuring.
Renee. But most girls don't come out and say it, huh?
Gallimard. And also . . . what did you call it?
Renee. Oh. Most girls don't call it a "weenie," huh?
Gallimard. It sounds very—
Renee. Small, I know.
Gallimard. I was going to say, "young."
Renee. Yeah. Young, small, same thing. Most guys are pretty, uh, sensitive about that. Like, you know, I had a boyfriend back home in Denmark. I got mad at him once and called him a little weeniehead. He got so mad! He said at least I should call him a great big weeniehead.
Gallimard. I suppose I just say "penis."
Renee. Yeah. That's pretty clinical. There's "cock," but that sounds like a chicken. And "prick" is painful, and "dick" is like you're talking about someone who's not in the room.
Gallimard. Yes. It's a . . . bigger problem than I imagined.
Renee. I—I think maybe it's because I really don't know what to do with them—that's why I call them "weenies."
Gallimard. Well, you did quite well with . . . mine.
Renee. Thanks, but I mean, really *do* with them. Like, okay, have you ever looked at one? I mean, really?
Gallimard. No, I suppose when it's part of you, you sort of take it for granted.
Renee. I guess. But, like, it just hangs there. This little . . . flap of flesh. And there's so much fuss that we make about it. Like, I think the reason we fight wars is because we wear clothes. Because no one knows—between the men, I mean—who has the biggest . . . weenie. So, if I'm a guy with a small one, I'm going to build a really big building or take over a really big piece of land or write a really long book so the other men don't know, right? But, see, it never really works, that's the problem. I mean, you conquer the country, or whatever, but you're still wearing clothes, so there's no way to prove absolutely whose is bigger or smaller. And that's what we call a civilized society. The whole world run by a bunch of men with pricks the size of pins. *(She exits.)*
Gallimard *(to us).* This was simply not acceptable.

A high-pitched chime rings through the air. Song, dressed as Butterfly, appears in the upstage special. She is obviously distressed. Her body swoons as she attempts to clip the stems of flowers she's arranging in a vase.

Gallimard. But I kept up our affair, wildly, for several months. Why? I believe because of Butterfly. She knew the secret I was trying to hide. But, unlike a Western woman, she didn't confront me, threaten, even pout. I remembered the words of Puccini's *Butterfly:*

Song. *"Noi siamo gente avvezza / alle piccole cose / umili e silenziose."*

Gallimard. "I come from a people / Who are accustomed to little / Humble and silent." I saw Pinkerton and Butterfly, and what she would say if he were unfaithful . . . nothing. She would cry, alone, into those wildly soft sleeves, once full of possessions, now empty to collect her tears. It was her tears and her silence that excited me, every time I visited Renee.

Toulon (*offstage*). Gallimard!

Toulon enters. Gallimard turns towards him. During the next section, Song, up center, begins to dance with the flowers. It is a drunken, reckless dance, where she breaks small pieces off the stems.

Toulon. They're killing him.

Gallimard. Who? I'm sorry? What?

Toulon. Bother you to come over at this late hour?

Gallimard. No . . . of course not.

Toulon. Not after you hear my secret. Champagne?

Gallimard. Um . . . thank you.

Toulon. You're surprised. There's something that you've wanted, Gallimard. No, not a promotion. Next time. Something in the world. You're not aware of this, but there's an informal gossip circle among intelligence agents. And some of ours heard from some of the Americans—

Gallimard. Yes?

Toulon. That the U.S. will allow the Vietnamese generals to stage a coup . . . and assassinate President Diem.

The chime rings again. Toulon freezes. Gallimard turns upstage and looks at Butterfly, who slowly and deliberately clips a flower off its stem. Gallimard turns back towards Toulon.

Gallimard. I think . . . that's a very wise move!

Toulon unfreezes.

Toulon. It's what you've been advocating. A toast?

Gallimard. Sure. I consider this a vindication.

Toulon. Not exactly. "To the test. Let's hope you pass."

They drink. The chime rings again. Toulon freezes. Gallimard turns upstage, and Song clips another flower.

Gallimard *(to Toulon).*   The test?

Toulon *(unfreezing).*   It's a test of everything you've been saying. I personally think the generals probably will stop the Communists. And you'll be a hero. But if anything goes wrong, then your opinions won't be worth a pig's ear. I'm sure that won't happen. But sometimes it's easier when they don't listen to you.

Gallimard.   They're your opinions too, aren't they?

Toulon.   Personally, yes.

Gallimard.   So we agree.

Toulon.   But my opinions aren't on that report. Yours are. Cheers.

Toulon turns away from Gallimard and raises his glass. At that instant Song picks up the vase and hurls it to the ground. It shatters. Song sinks down amidst the shards of the vase, in a calm, childlike trance. She sings softly, as if reciting a child's nursery rhyme.

Song *(repeat as necessary).*   "The whole world over, the white man travels, setting anchor, wherever he likes. Life's not worth living, unless he finds, the finest maidens, of every land . . ."

Gallimard turns downstage towards us. Song continues singing.

Gallimard.   I shook as I left his house. That coward! That worm! To put the burden for his decisions on my shoulders!

   I started for Renee's. But no, that was all I needed. A schoolgirl who would question the role of the penis in modern society. What I wanted was revenge. A vessel to contain my humiliation. Though I hadn't seen her in several weeks, I headed for Butterfly's.

Gallimard enters Song's apartment.

Song.   Oh! Rene . . . I was dreaming!

Gallimard.   You've been drinking?

Song.   If I can't sleep, then yes, I drink. But then, it gives me these dreams which—Rene, it's been almost three weeks since you visited me last.

Gallimard.   I know. There's been a lot going on in the world.

Song.   Fortunately I am drunk. So I can speak freely. It's not the world, it's you and me. And an old problem. Even the softest skin becomes like leather to a man who's touched it too often. I confess I don't know how to stop it. I don't know how to become another woman.

Gallimard.   I have a request.

Song.   Is this a solution? Or are you ready to give up the flat?

Gallimard.   It may be a solution. But I'm sure you won't like it.

Song. Oh well, that's very important. "Like it?" Do you think I "like" lying here alone, waiting, always waiting for your return? Please—don't worry about what I may not "like."

Gallimard. I want to see you . . . naked.

Silence.

Song. I thought you understood my modesty. So you want me to—what— strip? Like a big cowboy girl? Shiny pasties on my breasts? Shall I fling my kimono over my head and yell "ya-hoo" in the process? I thought you respected my shame!

Gallimard. I believe you gave me your shame many years ago.

Song. Yes—and it is just like a white devil to use it against me. I can't believe it. I thought myself so repulsed by the passive Oriental and the cruel white man. Now I see—we are always most revolted by the things hidden within us.

Gallimard. I just mean—

Song. Yes?

Gallimard. —that it will remove the only barrier left between us.

Song. No, Rene. Don't couch your request in sweet words. Be yourself—a cad—and know that my love is enough, that I submit—submit to the worst you can give me. *(Pause.)* Well, come. Strip me. Whatever happens, know that you have willed it. Our love, in your hands. I'm helpless before my man.

Gallimard starts to cross the room.

Gallimard. Did I not undress her because I knew, somewhere deep down, what I would find? Perhaps. Happiness is so rare that our mind can turn somersaults to protect it.

At the time, I only knew that I was seeing Pinkerton stalking towards his Butterfly, ready to reward her love with his lecherous hands. The image sickened me, pulled me to my knees, so I was crawling towards her like a worm. By the time I reached her, Pinkerton . . . had vanished from my heart. To be replaced by something new, something unnatural, that flew in the face of all I'd learned in the world—something very close to love.

He grabs her around the waist; she strokes his hair.

Gallimard. Butterfly, forgive me.

Song. Rene . . .

Gallimard. For everything. From the start.

Song. I'm . . .

Gallimard. I want to—

Song. I'm pregnant. *(Beat.)* I'm pregnant. *(Beat.)* I'm pregnant.

Beat.

Gallimard. I want to marry you!

Scene 7.   Gallimard and Butterfly's flat. Beijing. 1963.

Downstage, Song paces as Comrade Chin reads from her notepad. Upstage, Gallimard is still kneeling. He remains on his knees throughout the scene, watching it.

Song.   I need a baby.
Chin *(from pad)*.   He's been spotted going to a dorm.
Song.   I need a baby.
Chin.   At the Foreign Language Institute.
Song.   I need a baby.
Chin.   The room of a Danish girl. . . . What do you mean, you need a baby?!
Song.   Tell Comrade Kang—last night, the entire mission, it could've ended.
Chin.   What do you mean?
Song.   Tell Kang—he told me to strip.
Chin.   Strip?!
Song.   Write!
Chin.   I tell you, I don't understand nothing about this case anymore. Nothing.
Song.   He told me to strip, and I took a chance. Oh, we Chinese, we know how to gamble.
Chin *(writing)*.   ". . . told him to strip."
Song.   My palms were wet, I had to make a split-second decision.
Chin.   Hey! Can you slow down?!

Pause.

Song.   You write faster, I'm the artist here. Suddenly, it hit me—"All he wants is for her to submit. Once a woman submits, a man is always ready to become 'generous.'"
Chin.   You're just gonna end up with rough notes.
Song.   And it worked! He gave in! Now, if I can just present him with a baby. A Chinese baby with blond hair—he'll be mine for life!
Chin.   Kang will never agree! The trading of babies has to be a counterrevolutionary act!
Song.   Sometimes, a counterrevolutionary act is necessary to counter a counterrevolutionary act.

Pause.

Chin.   Wait.
Song.   I need one . . . in seven months. Make sure it's a boy.
Chin.   This doesn't sound like something the Chairman would do. Maybe you'd better talk to Comrade Kang yourself.
Song.   Good. I will.

Chin gets up to leave.

Song.   Miss Chin? Why, in the Peking Opera, are women's roles played by men?

Chin.   I don't know. Maybe, a reactionary remnant of male—

Song.   No. *(Beat.)* Because only a man knows how a woman is supposed to act.

Chin exits. Song turns upstage, towards Gallimard.

Gallimard *(calling after Chin).*   Good riddance! *(To Song.)* I could forget all that betrayal in an instant, you know. If you'd just come back and become Butterfly again.

Song.   Fat chance. You're here in prison, rotting in a cell. And I'm on a plane, winging my way back to China. Your President pardoned me of our treason, you know.

Gallimard.   Yes, I read about that.

Song.   Must make you feel . . . lower than shit.

Gallimard.   But don't you, even a little bit, wish you were here with me?

Song.   I'm an artist, Rene. You were my greatest . . . acting challenge. *(She laughs.)* It doesn't matter how rotten I answer, does it? You still adore me. That's why I love you, Rene. *(She points to us.)* So—you were telling your audience about the night I announced I was pregnant.

Gallimard puts his arms around Song's waist. He and Song are in the positions they were in at the end of Scene 6.

Scene 8.   Same.

Gallimard.   I'll divorce my wife. We'll live together here, and then later in France.

Song.   I feel so . . . ashamed.

Gallimard.   Why?

Song.   I had begun to lose faith. And now, you shame me with your generosity.

Gallimard.   Generosity? No, I'm proposing for very selfish reasons.

Song.   Your apologies only make me feel more ashamed. My outburst a moment ago!

Gallimard.   Your outburst? What about my request?!

Song.   You've been very patient dealing with my . . . eccentricities. A Western man, used to women freer with their bodies—

Gallimard.   It was sick! Don't make excuses for me.

Song.   I have to. You don't seem willing to make them for yourself.

Pause.

Gallimard. You're crazy.

Song. I'm happy. Which often looks like crazy.

Gallimard. Then make me crazy. Marry me.

Pause.

Song. No.

Gallimard. What?

Song. Do I sound silly, a slave, if I say I'm not worthy?

Gallimard. Yes. In fact you do. No one has loved me like you.

Song. Thank you. And no one ever will. I'll see to that.

Gallimard. So what is the problem?

Song. Rene, we Chinese are realists. We understand rice, gold, and guns. You are a diplomat. Your career is skyrocketing. Now, what would happen if you divorced your wife to marry a Communist Chinese actress?

Gallimard. That's not being realistic. That's defeating yourself before you begin.

Song. We conserve our strength for the battles we can win.

Gallimard. That sounds like a fortune cookie!

Song. Where do you think fortune cookies come from!

Gallimard. I don't care.

Song. You do. So do I. And we should. That is why I say I'm not worthy. I'm worthy to love and even to be loved by you. But I am not worthy to end the career of one of the West's most promising diplomats.

Gallimard. It's not that great a career! I made it sound like more than it is!

Song. Modesty will get you nowhere. Flatter yourself, and you flatter me. I'm flattered to decline your offer. *(She exits.)*

Gallimard *(to us).* Butterfly and I argued all night. And, in the end, I left, knowing I would never be her husband. She went away for several months—to the countryside, like a small animal. Until the night I received her call.

A baby's cry from offstage. Song enters, carrying a child.

Song. He looks like you.

Gallimard. Oh! *(Beat; he approaches the baby.)* Well, babies are never very attractive at birth.

Song. Stop!

Gallimard. I'm sure he'll grow more beautiful with age. More like his mother.

Song. *"Chi vide mai / a bimbo del Giappon . . ."*

Gallimard. "What baby, I wonder, was ever born in Japan"—or China, for that matter—

Song. *". . . occhi azzurrini?"*

Gallimard. "With azure eyes"—they're actually sort of brown, wouldn't you say?

Song. *"E il labbro."*

Gallimard. "And such lips!" *(He kisses Song.)* And such lips.

Song. *"E i ricciolini d'oro schietto?"*

Gallimard. "And such a head of golden"—if slightly patchy—"curls?"

Song. I'm going to call him "Peepee."

Gallimard. Darling, could you repeat that because I'm sure a rickshaw just flew by overhead.

Song. You heard me.

Gallimard. "Song Peepee"? May I suggest Michael, or Stephan, or Adolph?

Song. You may, but I won't listen.

Gallimard. You can't be serious. Can you imagine the time this child will have in school?

Song. In the West, yes.

Gallimard. It's worse than naming him Ping Pong or Long Dong or—

Song. But he's never going to live in the West, is he?

Pause.

Gallimard. That wasn't my choice.

Song. It is mine. And this is my promise to you: I will raise him, he will be our child, but he will never burden you outside of China.

Gallimard. Why do you make these promises? I want to be burdened! I want a scandal to cover the papers!

Song *(to us).* Prophetic.

Gallimard. I'm serious.

Song. So am I. His name is as I registered it. And he will never live in the West.

Song exits with the child.

Gallimard *(to us).* It is possible that her stubbornness only made me want her more. That drawing back at the moment of my capitulation was the most brilliant strategy she could have chosen. It is possible. But it is also possible that by this point she could have said, could have done . . . anything, and I would have adored her still.

Scene 9. Beijing. 1966.

A driving rhythm of Chinese percussion fills the stage.

Gallimard. And then, China began to change. Mao became very old, and his cult became very strong. And, like many old men, he entered his second childhood. So he handed over the reins of state to those with minds like his own. And children ruled the Middle Kingdom[8] with complete caprice. The doctrine of the Cultural Revolution[9] implied continuous anarchy. Contact between Chinese and foreigners became impossible. Our flat was confiscated. Her fame and my money now counted against us.

Two dancers in Mao suits and red-starred caps enter, and begin crudely mimicking revolutionary violence, in an agitprop fashion.

Gallimard.   And somehow the American war went wrong too. Four hundred thousand dollars were being spent for every Viet Cong[10] killed; so General Westmoreland's[11] remark that the Oriental does not value life the way Americans do was oddly accurate. Why weren't the Vietnamese people giving in? Why were they content instead to die and die and die again?

Toulon enters. Percussion and dancers continue upstage.

Toulon.   Congratulations, Gallimard.
Gallimard.   Excuse me, sir?
Toulon.   Not a promotion. That was last time. You're going home.
Gallimard.   What?
Toulon.   Don't say I didn't warn you.
Gallimard.   I'm being transferred . . . because I was wrong about the American war?
Toulon.   Of course not. We don't care about the Americans. We care about your mind. The quality of your analysis. In general, everything you've predicted here in the Orient . . . just hasn't happened.
Gallimard.   I think that's premature.
Toulon.   Don't force me to be blunt. Okay, you said China was ready to open to Western trade. The only thing they're trading out there are Western heads. And, yes, you said the Americans would succeed in Indochina. You were kidding, right?
Gallimard.   I think the end is in sight.
Toulon.   Don't be pathetic. And don't take this personally. You were wrong. It's not your fault.
Gallimard.   But I'm going home.
Toulon.   Right. Could I have the number of your mistress? *(Beat.)* Joke! Joke! Eat a croissant for me.

[8] From early in its history, the Chinese have called their country the Middle (or Central) Kingdom.   [9] The name given to the period from 1965 to 1967 during which any opposition to the ideological ideas of Chinese leader Mao Tse-tung were fiercely suppressed.   [10] Those in the Vietnamese Communist movement rebelling against the South Vietnam government. U.S. military forces were sent to suppress the Viet Cong.   [11] William Westmoreland commanded American military forces in Vietnam from 1964 to 1968.

Toulon exits. Song, wearing a Mao suit, is dragged in from the wings as part of the upstage dance. They "beat" her, then lampoon the acrobatics of the Chinese opera, as she is made to kneel onstage.

Gallimard *(simultaneously).* I don't care to recall how Butterfly and I said our hurried farewell. Perhaps it was better to end our affair before it killed her.

Gallimard exits. Percussion rises in volume. The lampooning becomes faster, more frenetic. At its height, Comrade Chin walks across the stage with a banner reading: "The Actor Renounces His Decadent Profession!" She reaches the kneeling Song. At the moment Chin touches Song's chin, percussion stops with a thud. Dancers strike poses.

Chin. Actor-oppressor, for years you have lived above the common people and looked down on their labor. While the farmer ate millet—
Song. I ate pastries from France and sweetmeats from silver trays.
Chin. And how did you come to live in such an exalted position?
Song. I was a plaything for the imperialists!
Chin. What did you do?
Song. I shamed China by allowing myself to be corrupted by a foreigner . . .
Chin. What does this mean? The People demand a full confession!
Song. I engaged in the lowest perversions with China's enemies!
Chin. What perversions? Be more clear!
Song. I let him put it up my ass!

Dancers look over, disgusted.

Chin. Aaaa-ya! How can you use such sickening language?!
Song. My language . . . is only as foul as the crimes I committed . . .
Chin. Yeah. That's better. So—what do you want to do . . . now?
Song. I want to serve the people.

Percussion starts up, with Chinese strings.

Chin. What?
Song. I want to serve the people!

Dancers regain their revolutionary smiles, and begin a dance of victory.

Chin. What?!
Song. I want to serve the people!!

Dancers unveil a banner: "The Actor Is Re-Habilitated!" Song remains kneeling before Chin, as the dancers bounce around them, then exit. Music out.

Scene 10.   A commune. Hunan Province. 1970.

Chin.   How you planning to do that?
Song.   I've already worked four years in the fields of Hunan, Comrade Chin.
Chin.   So? Farmers work all their lives. Let me see your hands.

Song holds them out for her inspection.

Chin.   Goddamn! Still so smooth! How long does it take to turn you actors into good anythings? Hunh. You've just spent too many years in luxury to be any good to the Revolution.
Song.   I served the Revolution.
Chin.   Served the Revolution? Bullshit! You wore dresses! Don't tell me—I was there. I saw you! You and your white vice-consul! Stuck up there in your flat, living off the People's Treasury! Yeah, I knew what was going on! You two . . . homos! Homos! Homos! *(Pause; she composes herself.)* Ah! Well . . . you will serve the people, all right. But not with the Revolution's money. This time, you use your own money.
Song.   I have no money.
Chin.   Shut up! And you won't stink up China anymore with your pervert stuff. You'll pollute the place where pollution begins—the West.
Song.   What do you mean?
Chin.   Shut up! You're going to France. Without a cent in your pocket. You find your consul's house, you make him pay your expenses—
Song.   No.
Chin.   And you give us weekly reports! Useful information!
Song.   That's crazy. It's been four years.
Chin.   Either that, or back to the rehabilitation center!
Song.   Comrade Chin, he's not going to support me! Not in France! He's a white man! I was just his plaything—
Chin.   Oh yuck! Again with the sickening language? Where's my stick?
Song.   You don't understand the mind of a man.

Pause.

Chin.   Oh no? No I don't? Then how come I'm married, huh? How come I got a man? Five, six years ago, you always tell me those kind of things, I felt very bad. But not now! Because what does the Chairman say? He tells us *I'm* now the smart one, you're now the nincompoop! *You're* the blockhead, the hare-brain, the nitwit! You think you're so smart? You understand "The Mind of a Man"? Good! Then *you* go to France and be a pervert for Chairman Mao!

Chin and Song exit in opposite directions.

Scene 11.   Paris. 1968–1970.

Gallimard enters.

Gallimard.   And what was waiting for me back in Paris? Well, better Chinese food than I'd eaten in China. Friends and relatives. A little accounting, regular schedule, keeping track of traffic violations in the suburbs. . . . And the indignity of students shouting the slogans of Chairman Mao at me—in French.

Helga.   Rene? Rene? *(She enters, soaking wet.)* I've had a . . . problem. *(She sneezes.)*

Gallimard.   You're wet.

Helga.   Yes, I . . . coming back from the grocer's. A group of students, waving red flags, they—

Gallimard fetches a towel.

Helga.   —they ran by, I was caught up along with them. Before I knew what was happening—

Gallimard gives her the towel.

Helga.   Thank you. The police started firing water cannons at us. I tried to shout, to tell them I was the wife of a diplomat, but—you know how it is . . . *(Pause.)* Needless to say, I lost the groceries. Rene, what's happening to France?

Gallimard.   What's—? Well, nothing, really.

Helga.   Nothing?! The storefronts are in flames, there's glass in the streets, buildings are toppling—and I'm wet!

Gallimard.   Nothing! . . . that I care to think about.

Helga.   And is that why you stay in this room?

Gallimard.   Yes, in fact.

Helga.   With the incense burning? You know something? I hate incense. It smells so sickly sweet.

Gallimard.   Well, I hate the French. Who just smell—period!

Helga.   And the Chinese were better?

Gallimard.   Please—don't start.

Helga.   When we left, this exact same thing, the riots—

Gallimard.   No, no . . .

Helga.   Students screaming slogans, smashing down doors—

Gallimard.   Helga—

Helga.   It was all going on in China, too. Don't you remember?!

Gallimard.   Helga! Please! *(Pause.)* You have never understood China, have you? You walk in here with these ridiculous ideas, that the West is falling apart, that China was spitting in our faces. You come in, dripping of the streets, and you leave water all over my floor. *(He grabs Helga's towel, begins mopping up the floor.)*

Helga.   But it's the truth!

Gallimard.   Helga, I want a divorce.

Pause; Gallimard continues mopping the floor.

Helga.   I take it back. China is . . . beautiful. Incense, I like incense.

Gallimard.   I've had a mistress.

Helga.   So?

Gallimard.   For eight years.

Helga.   I knew you would. I knew you would the day I married you. And now what? You want to marry her?

Gallimard.   I can't. She's in China.

Helga.   I see. You know that no one else is ever going to marry me, right?

Gallimard.   I'm sorry.

Helga.   And you want to leave. For someone who's not here, is that right?

Gallimard.   That's right.

Helga.   You can't live with her, but still you don't want to live with me.

Gallimard.   That's right.

Pause.

Helga.   Shit. How terrible that I can figure that out. *(Pause.)* I never thought I'd say it. But, in China, I was happy. I knew, in my own way, I knew that you were not everything you pretended to be. But the pretense—going on your arm to the embassy ball, visiting your office and the guards saying, "Good morning, good morning, Madame Gallimard"—the pretense . . . was very good indeed. *(Pause.)* I hope everyone is mean to you for the rest of your life. *(She exits.)*

Gallimard *(to us).*   Prophetic.

Marc enters with two drinks.

Gallimard *(to Marc).*   In China, I was different from all other men.

Marc.   Sure. You were white. Here's your drink.

Gallimard.   I felt . . . touched.

Marc.   In the head? Rene, I don't want to hear about the Oriental love goddess. Okay? One night—can we just drink and throw up without a lot of conversation?

Gallimard.   You still don't believe me, do you?

Marc.   Sure I do. She was the most beautiful, et cetera, et cetera, blasé, blasé.

Pause.

Gallimard.   My life in the West has been such a disappointment.

Marc.   Life in the West is like that. You'll get used to it. Look, you're driving me away. I'm leaving. Happy, now? *(He exits, then returns.)* Look, I have a date tomorrow night. You wanna come? I can fix you up with—

Gallimard.   Of course. I would love to come.

Pause.

Marc.   Uh—on second thought, no. You'd better get ahold of yourself first.

He exits; Gallimard nurses his drink.

Gallimard *(to us).*   This is the ultimate cruelty, isn't it? That I can talk and talk and to anyone listening, it's only air—too rich a diet to be swallowed by a mundane world. Why can't anyone understand? That in China, I once loved, and was loved by, very simply, the Perfect Woman.

Song enters, dressed as Butterfly in wedding dress.

Gallimard *(to Song).*   Not again. My imagination is hell. Am I asleep this time? Or did I drink too much?

Song.   Rene!

Gallimard.   God, it's too painful! That you speak?

Song.   What are you talking about? Rene—touch me.

Gallimard.   Why?

Song.   I'm real. Take my hand.

Gallimard.   Why? So you can disappear again and leave me clutching at the air? For the entertainment of my neighbors who—?

Song touches Gallimard.

Song.   Rene?

Gallimard takes Song's hand. Silence.

Gallimard.   Butterfly? I never doubted you'd return.

Song.   You hadn't . . . forgotten—?

Gallimard.   Yes, actually, I've forgotten everything. My mind, you see—there wasn't enough room in this hard head—not for the world *and* for you. No, there was only room for one. *(Beat.)* Come, look. See? Your bed has been waiting, with the Klimt[12] poster you like, and—see? The *xiang lu*[13] you gave me?

---

[12] Gustav Klimt (1862–1918), an Austrian painter.   [13] Incense burner.

Song. I . . . I don't know what to say.

Gallimard. There's nothing to say. Not at the end of a long trip. Can I make you some tea?

Song. But where's your wife?

Gallimard. She's by my side. She's by my side at last.

Gallimard reaches to embrace Song. Song sidesteps, dodging him.

Gallimard. Why?!

Song *(to us).* So I did return to Rene in Paris. Where I found—

Gallimard. Why do you run away? Can't we show them how we embraced that evening?

Song. Please. I'm talking.

Gallimard. You have to do what I say! I'm conjuring you up in *my* mind!

Song. Rene, I've never done what you've said. Why should it be any different in your mind? Now split—the story moves on, and I must change.

Gallimard. I welcomed you into my home! I didn't have to, you know! I could've left you penniless on the streets of Paris! But I took you in!

Song. Thank you.

Gallimard. So . . . please . . . don't change.

Song. You know I have to. You know I will. And anyway, what difference does it make? No matter what your eyes tell you, you can't ignore the truth. You already know too much.

Gallimard exits. Song turns to us.

Song. The change I'm going to make requires about five minutes. So I thought you might want to take this opportunity to stretch your legs, enjoy a drink, or listen to the musicians. I'll be here, when you return, right where you left me.

Song goes to a mirror in front of which is a washbasin of water. She starts to remove her makeup as stagelights go to half and houselights come up.

Act III

Scene 1. A courthouse in Paris. 1986.

As he promised, Song has completed the bulk of his transformation onstage by the time the houselights go down and the stagelights come up full. As he speaks to us, he removes his wig and kimono, leaving them on the floor. Underneath, he wears a well-cut suit.

Song. So I'd done my job better than I had a right to expect. Well, give him some credit, too. He's right—I was in a fix when I arrived in Paris. I walked from the airport into town, then I located, by blind groping, the Chinatown district. Let me make one thing clear: whatever else may be said about the Chinese, they are stingy! I slept in doorways three days until I could find a tailor who would make me this kimono on credit. As it turns out, maybe I didn't even need it. Maybe he would've been happy to see me in a simple shift and mascara. But . . . better safe than sorry.

That was 1970, when I arrived in Paris. For the next fifteen years, yes, I lived a very comfy life. Some relief, believe me, after four years on a fucking commune in Nowheresville, China. Rene supported the boy and me, and I did some demonstrations around the country as part of my "cultural exchange" cover. And then there was the spying.

Song moves upstage, to a chair. Toulon enters as a judge, wearing the appropriate wig and robes. He sits near Song. It's 1986, and Song is testifying in a courtroom.

Song. Not much at first. Rene had lost all his high-level contacts. Comrade Chin wasn't very interested in parking-ticket statistics. But finally, at my urging, Rene got a job as a courier, handling sensitive documents. He'd photograph them for me, and I'd pass them on to the Chinese embassy.
Judge. Did he understand the extent of his activity?
Song. He didn't ask. He knew that I needed those documents, and that was enough.
Judge. But he must've known he was passing classified information.
Song. I can't say.
Judge. He never asked what you were going to do with them?
Song. Nope.

Pause.

Judge. There is one thing that the court—indeed, that all of France—would like to know.
Song. Fire away.
Judge. Did Monsieur Gallimard know you were a man?
Song. Well, he never saw me completely naked. Ever.
Judge. But surely, he must've . . . how can I put this?
Song. Put it however you like. I'm not shy. He must've felt around?
Judge. Mmmmm.
Song. Not really. I did all the work. He just laid back. Of course we did enjoy more . . . complete union, and I suppose he *might* have wondered why I was always on my stomach, but. . . . But what you're thinking is, "Of course a wrist must've brushed . . . a hand hit . . . over twenty years!" Yeah. Well, Your

Honor, it was my job to make him think I was a woman. And chew on this: it wasn't all that hard. See, my mother was a prostitute along the Bundt before the Revolution. And, uh, I think it's fair to say she learned a few things about Western men. So I borrowed her knowledge. In service to my country.

Judge.   Would you care to enlighten the court with this secret knowledge? I'm sure we're all very curious.

Song.   I'm sure you are. *(Pause.)* Okay, Rule One is: Men always believe what they want to hear. So a girl can tell the most obnoxious lies and the guys will believe them every time—"This is my first time"—"That's the biggest I've ever seen"—or *both*, which, if you really think about it, is not possible in a single lifetime. You've maybe heard those phrases a few times in your own life, yes, Your Honor?

Judge.   It's not my life, Monsieur Song, which is on trial today.

Song.   Okay, okay, just trying to lighten up the proceedings. Tough room.

Judge.   Go on.

Song.   Rule Two: As soon as a Western man comes into contact with the East—he's already confused. The West has sort of an international rape mentality towards the East. Do you know rape mentality?

Judge.   Give us your definition, please.

Song.   Basically, "Her mouth says no, but her eyes say yes."

The West thinks of itself as masculine—big guns, big industry, big money—so the East is feminine—weak, delicate, poor . . . but good at art, and full of inscrutable wisdom—the feminine mystique.

Her mouth says no, but her eyes say yes. The West believes the East, deep down, *wants* to be dominated—because a woman can't think for herself.

Judge.   What does this have to do with my question?

Song.   You expect Oriental countries to submit to your guns, and you expect Oriental women to be submissive to your men. That's why you say they make the best wives.

Judge.   But why would that make it possible for you to fool Monsieur Gallimard? Please—get to the point.

Song.   One, because when he finally met his fantasy woman, he wanted more than anything to believe that she was, in fact, a woman. And second, I am an Oriental. And being an Oriental, I could never be completely a man.

Pause.

Judge.   Your armchair political theory is tenuous, Monsieur Song.

Song.   You think so? That's why you'll lose in all your dealings with the East.

Judge.   Just answer my question: did he know you were a man?

Pause.

Song.   You know, Your Honor, I never asked.

Scene 2.   Same.

Music from the "Death Scene" from Butterfly *blares over the house speakers. It is the loudest thing we've heard in this play.*
      Gallimard enters, crawling towards Song's wig and kimono.

Gallimard.   Butterfly? Butterfly?

Song remains a man, in the witness box, delivering a testimony we do not hear.

Gallimard *(to us)*.   In my moment of greatest shame, here, in this court-room—with that . . . person up there, telling the world. . . . What strikes me especially is how shallow he is, how glib and obsequious . . . completely . . . without substance! The type that prowls around discos with a gold medallion stinking of garlic. So little like my Butterfly.
      Yet even in this moment my mind remains agile, flip-flopping like a man on a trampoline. Even now, my picture dissolves, and I see that . . . witness . . . talking to me.

Song suddenly stands straight up in his witness box, and looks at Gallimard.

Song.   Yes. You. White man.

Song steps out of the witness box, and moves downstage towards Gallimard. Light change.

Gallimard *(to Song)*.   Who? Me?
Song.   Do you see any other white men?
Gallimard.   Yes. There're white men all around. This is a French courtroom.
Song.   So you are an adventurous imperialist. Tell me, why did it take you so long? To come back to this place?
Gallimard.   What place?
Song.   This theater in China. Where we met many years ago.
Gallimard *(to us)*.   And once again, against my will, I am transported.

Chinese opera music comes up on the speakers. Song begins to do opera moves, as he did the night they met.

Song.   Do you remember? The night you gave your heart?
Gallimard.   It was a long time ago.
Song.   Not long enough. A night that turned your world upside down.
Gallimard.   Perhaps.
Song.   Oh, be honest with me. What's another bit of flattery when you've al-

ready given me twenty years' worth? It's a wonder my head hasn't swollen to the size of China.

Gallimard. Who's to say it hasn't?

Song. Who's to say? And what's the shame? In pride? You think I could've pulled this off if I wasn't already full of pride when we met? No, not just pride. Arrogance. It takes arrogance, really—to believe you can will, with your eyes and your lips, the destiny of another. *(He dances.)* C'mon. Admit it. You still want me. Even in slacks and a button-down collar.

Gallimard. I don't see what the point of—

Song. You don't? Well maybe, Rene, just maybe—I want you.

Gallimard. You do?

Song. Then again, maybe I'm just playing with you. How can you tell? *(Reprising his feminine character, he sidles up to Gallimard.)* "How I wish there were even a small café to sit in. With men in tuxedos, and cappuccinos, and bad expatriate jazz." Now you want to kiss me, don't you?

Gallimard *(pulling away).* What makes you—?

Song. —so sure? See? I take the words from your mouth. Then I wait for you to come and retrieve them. *(He reclines on the floor.)*

Gallimard. Why?! Why do you treat me so cruelly?

Song. Perhaps I *was* treating you cruelly. But now—I'm being nice. Come here, my little one.

Gallimard. I'm not your little one!

Song. My mistake. It's I who am *your* little one, right?

Gallimard. Yes, I—

Song. So come get your little one. If you like, I may even let you strip me.

Gallimard. I mean, you were! Before . . . but not like this!

Song. I was? Then perhaps I still am. If you look hard enough. *(He starts to remove his clothes.)*

Gallimard. What—what are you doing?

Song. Helping you to see through my act.

Gallimard. Stop that! I don't want to! I don't—

Song. Oh, but you asked me to strip, remember?

Gallimard. What? That was years ago! And I took it back!

Song. No. You postponed it. Postponed the inevitable. Today, the inevitable has come calling.

From the speakers, cacophony: Butterfly mixed in with Chinese gongs.

Gallimard. No! Stop! I don't want to see!

Song. Then look away.

Gallimard. You're only in my mind! All this is in my mind! I order you! To stop!

Song. To what? To strip? That's just what I'm—

Gallimard. No! Stop! I want you—!

Song. You want me?

Gallimard.   To stop!

Song.   You know something, Rene? Your mouth says no, but your eyes say yes. Turn them away. I dare you.

Gallimard.   I don't have to! Every night, you say you're going to strip, but then I beg you and you stop!

Song.   I guess tonight is different.

Gallimard.   Why? Why should that be?

Song.   Maybe I've become frustrated. Maybe I'm saying "Look at me, you fool!" Or maybe I'm just feeling . . . sexy. *(He is down to his briefs.)*

Gallimard.   Please. This is unnecessary. I know what you are.

Song.   You do? What am I?

Gallimard.   A—a man.

Song.   You don't really believe that.

Gallimard.   Yes I do! I knew all the time somewhere that my happiness was temporary, my love a deception. But my mind kept the knowledge at bay. To make the wait bearable.

Song.   Monsieur Gallimard—the wait is over.

Song drops his briefs. He is naked. Sound cue out. Slowly, we and Song come to the realization that what we had thought to be Gallimard's sobbing is actually his laughter.

Gallimard.   Oh god! What an idiot! Of course!

Song.   Rene—what?

Gallimard.   Look at you! You're a man! *(He bursts into laughter again.)*

Song.   I fail to see what's so funny!

Gallimard.   "You fail to see—!" I mean, you never did have much of a sense of humor, did you? I just think it's ridiculously funny that I've wasted so much time on just a man!

Song.   Wait. I'm not "just a man."

Gallimard.   No? Isn't that what you've been trying to convince me of?

Song.   Yes, but what I mean—

Gallimard.   And now, I finally believe you, and you tell me it's not true? I think you must have some kind of identity problem.

Song.   Will you listen to me?

Gallimard.   Why?! I've been listening to you for twenty years. Don't I deserve a vacation?

Song.   I'm not just any man!

Gallimard.   Then, what exactly are you?

Song.   Rene, how can you ask—? Okay, what about this?

He picks up Butterfly's robes, starts to dance around. No music.

Gallimard.   Yes, that's very nice. I have to admit.

Song holds out his arm to Gallimard.

Song.   It's the same skin you've worshipped for years. Touch it.
Gallimard.   Yes, it does feel the same.
Song.   Now—close your eyes.

Song covers Gallimard's eyes with one hand. With the other, Song draws Galli-mard's hand up to his face. Gallimard, like a blind man, lets his hands run over Song's face.

Gallimard.   This skin, I remember. The curve of her face, the softness of her cheek, her hair against the back of my hand . . .
Song.   I'm your Butterfly. Under the robes, beneath everything, it was always me. Now, open your eyes and admit it—you adore me. *(He removes his hand from Gallimard's eyes.)*
Gallimard.   You, who knew every inch of my desires—how could you, of all people, have made such a mistake?
Song.   What?
Gallimard.   You showed me your true self. When all I loved was the lie. A perfect lie, which you let fall to the ground—and now, it's old and soiled.
Song.   So—you never really loved me? Only when I was playing a part?
Gallimard.   I'm a man who loved a woman created by a man. Everything else—simply falls short.

Pause.

Song.   What am I supposed to do now?
Gallimard.   You were a fine spy, Monsieur Song, with an even finer accomplice. But now I believe you should go. Get out of my life!
Song.   Go where? Rene, you can't live without me. Not after twenty years.
Gallimard.   I certainly can't live with you—not after twenty years of betrayal.
Song.   Don't be stubborn! Where will you go?
Gallimard.   I have a date . . . with my Butterfly.
Song.   So, throw away your pride. And come . . .
Gallimard.   Get away from me! Tonight, I've finally learned to tell fantasy from reality. And, knowing the difference, I choose fantasy.
Song.   *I'm* your fantasy!
Gallimard.   You? You're as real as hamburger. Now get out! I have a date with my Butterfly and I don't want your body polluting the room! *(He tosses Song's suit at him.)* Look at these—you dress like a pimp.
Song.   Hey! These are Armani slacks and—! *(He puts on his briefs and slacks.)* Let's just say . . . I'm disappointed in you, Rene. In the crush of your adoration, I thought you'd become something more. More like . . . a woman.

But no. Men. You're like the rest of them. It's all in the way we dress, and make up our faces, and bat our eyelashes. You really have so little imagination!

Gallimard. You, Monsieur Song? Accuse me of too little imagination? You, if anyone, should know—I am pure imagination. And in imagination I will remain. Now get out!

Gallimard bodily removes Song from the stage, taking his kimono.

Song. Rene! I'll never put on those robes again! You'll be sorry!

Gallimard *(to Song).* I'm already sorry! *(Looking at the kimono in his hands.)* Exactly as sorry . . . as a Butterfly.

Scene 3. M. Gallimard's prison cell. Paris. 1988.

Gallimard. I've played out the events of my life night after night, always searching for a new ending to my story, one where I leave this cell and return forever to my Butterfly's arms.

Tonight I realize my search is over. That I've looked all along in the wrong place. And now, to you, I will prove that my love was not in vain—by returning to the world of fantasy where I first met her.

He picks up the kimono; dancers enter.

Gallimard. There is a vision of the Orient that I have. Of slender women in chong sams and kimonos who die for the love of unworthy foreign devils. Who are born and raised to be the perfect women. Who take whatever punishment we give them, and bounce back, strengthened by love, unconditionally. It is a vision that has become my life.

Dancers bring the washbasin to him and help him make up his face.

Gallimard. In public, I have continued to deny that Song Liling is a man. This brings me headlines, and is a source of great embarrassment to my French colleagues, who can now be sent into a coughing fit by the mere mention of Chinese food. But alone, in my cell, I have long since faced the truth.

And the truth demands a sacrifice. For mistakes made over the course of a lifetime. My mistakes were simple and absolute—the man I loved was a cad, a bounder. He deserved nothing but a kick in the behind, and instead I gave him . . . all my love.

Yes—love. Why not admit it all? That was my undoing, wasn't it? Love warped my judgment, blinded my eyes, rearranged the very lines on my face . . . until I could look in the mirror and see nothing but . . . a woman.

Dancers help him put on the Butterfly wig.

Gallimard.   I have a vision. Of the Orient. That, deep within its almond eyes, there are still women. Women willing to sacrifice themselves for the love of a man. Even a man whose love is completely without worth.

Dancers assist Gallimard in donning the kimono. They hand him a knife.

Gallimard.   Death with honor is better than life . . . life with dishonor. *(He sets himself center stage, in a seppuku position.)* The love of a Butterfly can withstand many things—unfaithfulness, loss, even abandonment. But how can it face the one sin that implies all others? The devastating knowledge that, underneath it all, the object of her love was nothing more, nothing less than . . . a man. *(He sets the tip of the knife against his body.)* It is 1988. And I have found her at last. In a prison on the outskirts of Paris. My name is Rene Gallimard—also known as Madame Butterfly.

Gallimard turns upstage and plunges the knife into his body, as music from the "Love Duet" blares over the speakers. He collapses into the arms of the dancers, who lay him reverently on the floor. The image holds for several beats. Then a tight special up on Song, who stands as a man, staring at the dead Gallimard. He smokes a cigarette; the smoke filters up through the lights. Two words leave his lips.

Song.   Butterfly? Butterfly?

Smoke rises as lights fade slowly to black.

For Analysis
1. Explain the title of the play. Who was Madame Butterfly? Why does Hwang use the abbreviation *M*? **2.** Describe the Western stereotypes of Chinese and Japanese women that figure in the play. How do they contribute to the play's impact? **3.** Are we meant to admire Gallimard? Explain. **4.** What function is served by the minor characters such as Marc and Helga? **5.** Is this play about international spying? Odd and obsessive sexuality? Political systems? Or something else? Explain. **6.** The story of this play was inspired by an actual case of mistaken sexual identity between a French diplomatic officer, stationed in Communist China, and an opera singer he thought was a woman. How does that affect your reaction to the story, if at all?

On Style
How does the play's complex structure (its movements back and forth in time, in and out of the story of Madame Butterfly and the Chinese opera) serve to develop the play's central **themes**?

Making Connections

1. Compare the way in which cultural stereotypes blind people to truth in this play and in Susan Glaspell's *Trifles* (p. 551). **2.** In this play, in Flannery O'Connor's "Good Country People" (p. 99), and in Henrik Ibsen's *A Doll's House* (p. 492), the **protagonists** are driven by a powerful illusion that is finally shattered. Compare the nature of those illusions and the needs that create them as well as the degree of success each of the characters has in coping with the trauma of discovering the truth.

Writing Topics

1. Analyze the implications of the play's ending. Who does Gallimard emulate? How has he changed? **2.** Write an essay exploring whether or not the events in the play are believable.

Essays

Virginia Woolf   [1882–1941]

What if Shakespeare Had Had a Sister?[1]   1928

It was disappointing not to have brought back in the evening some important statement, some authentic fact. Women are poorer than men because—this or that. Perhaps now it would be better to give up seeking for the truth, and receiving on one's head an avalanche of opinion hot as lava, discoloured as dishwater. It would be better to draw the curtains; to shut out distractions; to light the lamp; to narrow the enquiry and to ask the historian, who records not opinions but facts, to describe under what conditions women lived, not throughout the ages, but in England, say in the time of Elizabeth.

For it is a perennial puzzle why no woman wrote a word of that extraordinary literature when every other man, it seemed, was capable of song or sonnet. What were the conditions in which women lived, I asked myself; for fiction, imaginative work that is, is not dropped like a pebble upon the ground, as science may be; fiction is like a spider's web, attached ever so lightly perhaps, but still attached to life at all four corners. Often the attachment is scarcely perceptible; Shakespeare's plays, for instance, seem to hang there complete by themselves. But when the web is pulled askew, hooked up at the edge, torn in the middle, one remembers that these webs are not spun in midair by incorporeal creatures, but are the work of suffering human beings, and are attached to grossly material things, like health and money and the houses we live in.

I went, therefore, to the shelf where the histories stand and took down one of the latest, Professor Trevelyan's *History of England*. Once more I looked up

---

[1] A *Room of One's Own,* from which this essay is taken, is based on two lectures Woolf delivered on women and literature at Newnham College and Girton College, Cambridge University. In the opening chapter, Woolf declares that without "money and a room of her own" a woman cannot write fiction. In the following chapter, she recounts her unsuccessful attempt to turn up information at the British Library on the lives of women. This essay is from Chapter 3, from which a few passages are omitted. It ends with the concluding paragraph of the book.

Women, found "position of," and turned to the pages indicated. "Wife-beating," I read, "was a recognized right of man, and was practiced without shame by high as well as low. . . . Similarly," the historian goes on, "the daughter who refused to marry the gentleman of her parents' choice was liable to be locked up, beaten and flung about the room, without any shock being inflicted on public opinion. Marriage was not an affair of personal affection, but of family avarice, particularly in the 'chivalrous' upper classes. . . . Betrothal often took place while one or both of the parties was in the cradle, and marriage when they were scarcely out of the nurses' charge." That was about 1470, soon after Chaucer's time. The next reference to the position of women is some two hundred years later, in the time of the Stuarts. "It was still the exception for women of the upper and middle class to choose their own husbands, and when the husband had been assigned, he was lord and master, so far at least as law and custom could make him. Yet even so," Professor Trevelyan concludes, "neither Shakespeare's women nor those of authentic seventeenth-century memoirs, like the Verneys and the Hutchinsons, seem wanting in personality and character." Certainly, if we consider it, Cleopatra must have had a way with her; Lady Macbeth, one would suppose, had a will of her own; Rosalind, one might conclude, was an attractive girl. Professor Trevelyan is speaking no more than the truth when he remarks that Shakespeare's women do not seem wanting in personality and character. Not being a historian, one might go even further and say that women have burnt like beacons in all the works of all the poets from the beginning of time—Clytemnestra, Antigone, Cleopatra, Lady Macbeth, Phèdre, Cressida, Rosalind, Desdemona, the Duchess of Malfi, among the dramatists; then among the prose writers: Millamant, Clarissa, Becky Sharp, Anna Karenina, Emma Bovary, Madame de Guermantes[2]—the names flock to mind, nor do they recall women "lacking in personality and character." Indeed, if woman had no existence save in the fiction written by men, one would imagine her a person of the utmost importance; very various; heroic and mean; splendid and sordid; infinitely beautiful and hideous in the extreme; as great as a man, some think even greater. But this is woman in fiction. In fact, as Professor Trevelyan points out, she was locked up, beaten and flung about the room.

A very queer, composite being thus emerges. Imaginatively she is of the highest importance; practically she is completely insignificant. She pervades poetry from cover to cover; she is all but absent from history. She dominates the lives of kings and conquerors in fiction; in fact she was the slave of any boy whose parents forced a ring upon her finger. Some of the most inspired words, some of the most profound thoughts in literature fell from her lips; in real life she could hardly read, could scarcely spell, and was the property of her husband.

It was certainly an odd monster that one made up by reading the historians   5
first and the poets afterwards—a worm winged like an eagle; the spirit of life and beauty in a kitchen chopping up suet. But these monsters, however amusing to the imagination, have no existence in fact. What one must do to bring her

[2] Female characters from great works of literature.

to life was to think poetically and prosaically at one and the same moment, thus keeping in touch with fact—that she is Mrs. Martin, aged thirty-six, dressed in blue, wearing a black hat and brown shoes; but not losing sight of fiction either—that she is a vessel in which all sorts of spirits and forces are coursing and flashing perpetually. The moment, however, that one tries this method with the Elizabethan woman, one branch of illumination fails; one is held up by the scarcity of facts. One knows nothing detailed, nothing perfectly true and substantial about her. History scarcely mentions her. And I turned to Professor Trevelyan again to see what history meant to him. I found by looking at his chapter headings that it meant—

"The Manor Court and the Methods of Open-field Agriculture . . . The Cistercians and Sheep-farming . . . The Crusades . . . The University . . . The House of Commons . . . The Hundred Years' War . . . The Wars of the Roses . . . The Renaissance Scholars . . . The Dissolution of the Monasteries . . . Agrarian and Religious Strife . . . The Origin of English Seapower . . . The Armada . . ." and so on. Occasionally an individual woman is mentioned, an Elizabeth, or a Mary; a queen or a great lady. But by no possible means could middle-class women with nothing but brains and character at their command have taken part in any one of the great movements which, brought together, constitute the historian's view of the past. Nor shall we find her in any collection of anecdotes. Aubrey hardly mentions her.[3] She never writes her own life and scarcely keeps a diary; there are only a handful of her letters in existence. She left no plays or poems by which we can judge her. . . . Here am I asking why women did not write poetry in the Elizabethan age, and I am not sure how they were educated; whether they were taught to write; whether they had sitting-rooms to themselves; how many women had children before they were twenty-one; what, in short, they did from eight in the morning till eight at night. They had no money evidently; according to Professor Trevelyan they were married whether they liked it or not before they were out of the nursery, at fifteen or sixteen very likely. It would have been extremely odd, even upon this showing, had one of them suddenly written the plays of Shakespeare, I concluded, and I thought of that old gentleman, who is dead now, but was a bishop, I think, who declared that it was impossible for any woman, past, present, or to come, to have the genius of Shakespeare. He wrote to the papers about it. He also told a lady who applied to him for information that cats do not as a matter of fact go to heaven, though they have, he added, souls of a sort. How much thinking those old gentlemen used to save one! How the borders of ignorance shrank back at their approach! Cats do not go to heaven. Women cannot write the plays of Shakespeare.

Be that as it may, I could not help thinking, as I looked at the works of Shakespeare on the shelf, that the bishop was right at least in this; it would have been impossible, completely and entirely, for any woman to have written the plays of Shakespeare in the age of Shakespeare. Let me imagine, since facts are so hard to come by, what would have happened had Shakespeare had a wonderfully

---

[3] John Aubrey (1626–1697), author of *Brief Lives,* a biographical work.

gifted sister, called Judith, let us say. Shakespeare himself went, very probably—
his mother was an heiress—to the grammar school, where he may have learnt
Latin—Ovid, Virgil and Horace—and the elements of grammar and logic. He
was, it is well known, a wild boy who poached rabbits, perhaps shot a deer, and
had, rather sooner than he should have done, to marry a woman in the neigh-
bourhood, who bore him a child rather quicker than was right. That escapade
sent him to seek his fortune in London. He had, it seemed, a taste for the theatre; he began by holding horses at the stage door. Very soon he got work in the
theatre, became a successful actor, and lived in the hub of the universe, meeting everybody, knowing everybody, practising his art on the boards, exercising
his wits in the streets, and even getting access to the palace of the queen. Meanwhile his extraordinarily gifted sister, let us suppose, remained at home. She was
as adventurous, as imaginative, as agog to see the world as he was. But she was
not sent to school. She had no chance of learning grammar and logic, let alone
of reading Horace and Virgil. She picked up a book now and then, one of her
brother's perhaps, and read a few pages. But then her parents came in and told
her to mend the stockings or mind the stew and not moon about with books and
papers. They would have spoken sharply but kindly, for they were substantial
people who knew the conditions of life for a woman and loved their daughter—
indeed, more likely than not she was the apple of her father's eye. Perhaps she
scribbled some pages up in an apple loft on the sly, but was careful to hide them
or set fire to them. Soon, however, before she was out of her teens, she was to
be betrothed to the son of a neighbouring wool-stapler. She cried out that marriage was hateful to her, and for that she was severely beaten by her father. Then
he ceased to scold her. He begged her instead not to hurt him, not to shame him
in this matter of her marriage. He would give her a chain of beads or a fine petticoat, he said; and there were tears in his eyes. How could she disobey him?
How could she break his heart? The force of her own gift alone drove her to it.
She made up a small parcel of her belongings, let herself down by a rope one
summer's night and took the road to London. She was not seventeen. The birds
that sang in the hedge were not more musical than she was. She had the quickest fancy, a gift like her brother's, for the tune of words. Like him, she had a taste
for the theatre. She stood at the stage door; she wanted to act, she said. Men
laughed in her face. The manager—a fat, loose-lipped man—guffawed. He bellowed something about poodles dancing and women acting—no woman, he
said, could possibly be an actress.[4] He hinted—you can imagine what. She could
get no training in her craft. Could she even seek her dinner in a tavern or roam
the streets at midnight? Yet her genius was for fiction and lusted to feed abun-
dantly upon the lives of men and women and the study of their ways. At last—
for she was very young, oddly like Shakespeare the poet in her face, with the
same grey eyes and rounded brows—at last Nick Greene the actor-manager
took pity on her; she found herself with child by that gentleman and so—who
shall measure the heat and violence of the poet's heart when caught and tangled

---

[4] In Shakespeare's day, women's roles were played by boys.

in a woman's body?—killed herself one winter's night and lies buried at some cross-roads where the omnibuses now stop outside the Elephant and Castle.[5]

That, more or less, is how the story would run, I think, if a woman in Shakespeare's day had had Shakespeare's genius. But for my part, I agree with the deceased bishop, if such he was—it is unthinkable that any woman in Shakespeare's day should have had Shakespeare's genius. For genius like Shakespeare's is not born among labouring, uneducated, servile people. It was not born in England among the Saxons and the Britons. It is not born today among the working classes. How, then, could it have been born among women whose work began, according to Professor Trevelyan, almost before they were out of the nursery, who were forced to it by their parents and held to it by all the power of law and custom? Yet genius of a sort must have existed among women as it must have existed among the working classes. Now and again an Emily Brontë or a Robert Burns blazes out and proves its presence.[6] But certainly it never got itself on to paper. When, however, one reads of a witch being ducked, of a woman possessed by devils, of a wise woman selling herbs, or even of a very remarkable man who had a mother, then I think we are on the track of a lost novelist, a suppressed poet, of some mute and inglorious[7] Jane Austen, some Emily Brontë who dashed her brains out on the moor or mopped and mowed about the highways crazed with the torture that her gift had put her to. Indeed, I would venture to guess that Anon, who wrote so many poems without signing them, was often a woman. It was a woman Edward Fitzgerald,[8] I think, suggested who made the ballads and the folk-songs, crooning them to her children, beguiling her spinning with them, or the length of the winter's night.

This may be true or it may be false—who can say?—but what is true in it, so it seemed to me, reviewing the story of Shakespeare's sister as I had made it, is that any woman born with a great gift in the sixteenth century would certainly have gone crazed, shot herself, or ended her days in some lonely cottage outside the village, half witch, half wizard, feared and mocked at. For it needs little skill in psychology to be sure that a highly gifted girl who had tried to use her gift for poetry would have been so thwarted and hindered by other people, so tortured and pulled asunder by her own contrary instincts, that she must have lost her health and sanity to a certainty. No girl could have walked to London and stood at a stage door and forced her way into the presence of actor-managers without doing herself a violence and suffering an anguish which may have been irrational—for chastity may be a fetish invented by certain societies for unknown reasons—but were none the less inevitable. Chastity had then, it has even now, a religious importance in a woman's life, and has so wrapped itself round with nerves and instincts that to cut it free and bring it to the light of day demands courage of the rarest. To have lived a free life in London in the sixteenth cen-

---

[5] A London neighborhood.

[6] Emily Brontë (1818–1848), English novelist, and Robert Burns (1759–1796), Scottish poet.

[7] Thomas Gray's description in "Elegy Written in a Country Churchyard" of a peasant whose underdeveloped poetic genius might be as powerful as the great John Milton's.

[8] Edward Fitzgerald (1809–1883), translator and poet.

tury would have meant for a woman who was poet and playwright a nervous stress and dilemma which might well have killed her. Had she survived, whatever she had written would have been twisted and deformed, issuing from a strained and morbid imagination. And undoubtedly, I thought, looking at the shelf where there are no plays by women, her work would have gone unsigned. That refuge she would have sought certainly. It was the relic of the sense of chastity that dictated anonymity to women even so late as the nineteenth century. Currer Bell, George Eliot, George Sand,[9] all the victims of inner strife as their writings prove, sought ineffectively to veil themselves by using the name of a man. Thus they did homage to the convention, which if not implanted by the other sex was liberally encouraged by them (the chief glory of a woman is not to be talked of, said Pericles,[10] himself a much-talked-of man), that publicity in women is detestable. . . .

That woman, then, who was born with a gift of poetry in the sixteenth century, was an unhappy woman, a woman at strife against herself. All the conditions of her life, all her own instincts, were hostile to the state of mind which is needed to set free whatever is in the brain. But what is the state of mind that is most propitious to the act of creation, I asked? Can one come by any notion of the state that furthers and makes possible that strange activity? Here I opened the volume containing the Tragedies of Shakespeare. What was Shakespeare's state of mind, for instance, when he wrote *Lear* and *Antony and Cleopatra?* It was certainly the state of mind most favourable to poetry that there has ever existed. But Shakespeare himself said nothing about it. We only know casually and by chance that he "never blotted a line."[11] Nothing indeed was ever said by the artist himself about his state of mind until the eighteenth century perhaps. Rousseau[12] perhaps began it. At any rate, by the nineteenth century self-consciousness had developed so far that it was the habit for men of letters to describe their minds in confessions and autobiographies. Their lives also were written, and their letters were printed after their deaths. Thus, though we do not know what Shakespeare went through when he wrote *Lear,* we do know what Carlyle went through when he wrote the *French Revolution;* what Flaubert went through when he wrote *Madame Bovary;* what Keats was going through when he tried to write poetry against the coming of death and the indifference of the world.

And one gathers from this enormous modern literature of confession and self-analysis that to write a work of genius is almost always a feat of prodigious difficulty. Everything is against the likelihood that it will come from the writer's mind whole and entire. Generally material circumstances are against it. Dogs will bark; people will interrupt; money must be made; health will break down.

10

---

[9] The pseudonyms of Charlotte Brontë (1816–1855) and Mary Ann Evans (1819–1880), English novelists, and Amandine Aurore Lucie Dupin (1804–1876), French novelist.

[10] Pericles (d. 429 B.C.), Athenian statesman and general.

[11] According to Ben Jonson, Shakespeare's contemporary.

[12] Jean-Jacques Rousseau (1712–1778), French philosopher, author of *The Confessions of Jean-Jacques Rousseau.*

Further, accentuating all these difficulties and making them harder to bear is the world's notorious indifference. It does not ask people to write poems and novels and histories; it does not need them. It does not care whether Flaubert finds the right word or whether Carlyle scrupulously verifies this or that fact. Naturally, it will not pay for what it does not want. And so the writer, Keats, Flaubert, Carlyle, suffers, especially in the creative years of youth, every form of distraction and discouragement. A curse, a cry of agony, rises from those books of analysis and confession. "Mighty poets in their misery dead"[13]—that is the burden of their song. If anything comes through in spite of this, it is a miracle, and probably no book is born entire and uncrippled as it was conceived.

But for women, I thought, looking at the empty shelves, these difficulties were infinitely more formidable. In the first place, to have a room of her own, let alone a quiet room or a sound-proof room, was out of the question, unless her parents were exceptionally rich or very noble, even up to the beginning of the nineteenth century. Since her pin money, which depended on the good will of her father, was only enough to keep her clothed, she was debarred from such alleviations as came even to Keats or Tennyson or Carlyle, all poor men, from a walking tour, a little journey to France, from the separate lodging which, even if it were miserable enough, sheltered them from the claims and tyrannies of their families. Such material difficulties were formidable; but much worse were the immaterial. The indifference of the world which Keats and Flaubert and other men of genius have found so hard to bear was in her case not indifference but hostility. The world did not say to her as it said to them, Write if you choose; it makes no difference to me. The world said with a guffaw, Write? What's the good of your writing? . . .

I told you in the course of this paper that Shakespeare had a sister; but do not look for her in Sir Sidney Lee's life of the poet. She died young—alas, she never wrote a word. She lies buried where the omnibuses now stop, opposite the Elephant and Castle. Now my belief is that this poet who never wrote a word and was buried at the cross-roads still lives. She lives in you and me, and in many other women who are not here tonight, for they are washing up the dishes and putting the children to bed. But she lives; for great poets do not die; they are continuing presences; they need only the opportunity to walk among us in the flesh. This opportunity, as I think, it is now coming within your power to give her. For my belief is that if we live another century or so—I am talking of the common life which is the real life and not of the little separate lives which we live as individuals—and have five hundred a year each of us and rooms of our own; if we have the habit of freedom and the courage to write exactly what we think; if we escape a little from the common sitting-room and see human beings not always in their relation to each other but in relation to reality; and the sky, too, and the trees or whatever it may be in themselves; if we look past Milton's bogey, for no human being should shut out the view; if we face the fact, for it is a fact, that there is no arm to cling to, but that we go alone and that our relation

---

[13] From William Wordsworth's poem "Resolution and Independence."

is to the world of reality and not only to the world of men and women, then the opportunity will come and the dead poet who was Shakespeare's sister will put on the body which she has so often laid down. Drawing her life from the lives of the unknown who were her forerunners, as her brother did before her, she will be born. As for her coming without that preparation, without that effort on our part, without that determination that when she is born again she shall find it possible to live and write her poetry, that we cannot expect, for that would be impossible. But I maintain that she would come if we worked for her, and that so to work, even in poverty and obscurity, is worth while.

For Analysis

1. How does Woolf explain the contrast between the women of fact and women as they have been portrayed in fiction? **2.** What answers do historians provide to the "perennial puzzle" Woolf mentions in the first sentence of the second paragraph? What generalizations might we make about the meaning of "history" on the basis of Woolf's research into the position of women? **3.** Analyze the effect of Woolf's concluding remarks about the bishop (par. 6): "Cats do not go to heaven. Women cannot write the plays of Shakespeare." Then consider her later comment (par. 8), "I agree with the deceased bishop, if such he was—it is unthinkable that any woman in Shakespeare's day should have had Shakespeare's genius." Does this contradict what she has been saying? **4.** Explain the link Woolf makes (par. 9) between chastity and the problem of the gifted woman writer.

On Style

1. How would you describe Woolf's general **tone** throughout the essay? Where and for what purpose does she adopt an **ironic** tone? **2.** In what ways does the first part of Woolf's essay prepare the reader to accept her imagined life of Shakespeare's sister?

Making Connections

1. Among the women who "have burnt like beacons" (par. 3) in the works of great male writers, Woolf cites Antigonê in Sophocles' *Antigonê* (p. 460) and Desdemona in Shakespeare's *Othello* (p. 1041). Do you agree with her assessment of these two women? Might Woolf have included Nora in Henrik Ibsen's *A Doll's House* (p. 492) and Risa in August Wilson's *Two Trains Running* (p. 565)? Explain. **2.** What do you suppose Woolf would think of Mrs. Peters and Mrs. Hale in Susan Glaspell's *Trifles* (p. 551), Cynthia in Alice Childress's *Wine in the Wilderness* (p. 262), and Calixta in Kate Chopin's "The Storm" (p. 947)?

Writing Topics

1. Do you believe that our culture has changed so significantly in its attitudes toward women that Woolf's arguments have lost their relevance? Write an essay explaining why or why not. **2.** Speculate on why it was the case that, while economically women were as dependent on men as servants throughout much of Western history, they were sometimes portrayed in fiction "as great as a man, some think even greater" (par. 3).

George Orwell   [1903–1950]

Shooting an Elephant   1936

In Moulmein, in lower Burma, I was hated by large numbers of people—the only time in my life that I have been important enough for this to happen to me. I was sub-divisional police officer of the town, and in an aimless, petty kind of way anti-European feeling was very bitter. No one had the guts to raise a riot, but if a European woman went through the bazaars alone somebody would probably spit betel juice over her dress. As a police officer I was an obvious target and was baited whenever it seemed safe to do so. When a nimble Burman tripped me up on the football field and the referee (another Burman) looked the other way, the crowd yelled with hideous laughter. This happened more than once. In the end the sneering yellow faces of young men that met me everywhere, the insults hooted after me when I was at a safe distance, got badly on my nerves. The young Buddhist priests were the worst of all. There were several thousands of them in the town and none of them seemed to have anything to do except stand on street corners and jeer at Europeans.

All this was perplexing and upsetting. For at that time I had already made up my mind that imperialism was an evil thing and the sooner I chucked up my job and got out of it the better. Theoretically—and secretly, of course—I was all for the Burmese and all against their oppressors, the British. As for the job I was doing, I hated it more bitterly than I can perhaps make clear. In a job like that you see the dirty work of Empire at close quarters. The wretched prisoners huddling in the stinking cages of the lock-ups, the grey, cowed faces of the long-term convicts, the scarred buttocks of the men who had been flogged with bamboos—all these oppressed me with an intolerable sense of guilt. But I could get nothing into perspective. I was young and ill-educated and I had had to think out my problems in the utter silence that is imposed on every Englishman in the East. I did not even know that the British Empire is dying, still less did I know that it is a great deal better than the younger empires that are going to supplant it. All I knew was that I was stuck between my hatred of the empire I served and my rage against the evil-spirited little beasts who tried to make my job impossible. With one part of my mind I thought of the British[1] as an unbreakable tyranny, as something clamped down, *in saecula saeculorum,*[2] upon the will of prostrate peoples; with another part I thought that the greatest joy in the world would be to drive a bayonet into a Buddhist priest's guts. Feelings like these are

[1] The imperial British government of India and Burma.
[2] For eternity.

the normal by-products of imperialism; ask any Anglo-Indian official, if you can catch him off duty.

One day something happened which in a roundabout way was enlightening. It was a tiny incident in itself, but it gave me a better glimpse than I had had before of the real nature of imperialism—the real motive for which despotic governments act. Early one morning the sub-inspector at a police station the other end of the town rang me up on the 'phone and said that an elephant was ravaging the bazaar. Would I please come and do something about it? I did not know what I could do, but I wanted to see what was happening and I got on to a pony and started out. I took my rifle, an old .44 Winchester and much too small to kill an elephant, but I thought the noise might be useful *in terrorem.* Various Burmans stopped me on the way and told me about the elephant's doings. It was not, of course, a wild elephant, but a tame one which had gone "must." It had been chained up, as tame elephants always are when their attack of "must" is due, but on the previous night it had broken its chain and escaped. Its mahout,[3] the only person who could manage it when it was in that state, had set out in pursuit, but had taken the wrong direction and was now twelve hours' journey away, and in the morning the elephant had suddenly reappeared in the town. The Burmese population had no weapons and were quite helpless against it. It had already destroyed somebody's bamboo hut, killed a cow and raided some fruit-stalls and devoured the stock; also it had met the municipal rubbish van and, when the driver jumped out and took to his heels, had turned the van over and inflicted violences upon it.

The Burmese sub-inspector and some Indian constables were waiting for me in the quarter where the elephant had been seen. It was a very poor quarter, a labyrinth of squalid bamboo huts, thatched with palm-leaf, winding all over a steep hillside. I remember that it was a cloudy, stuffy morning at the beginning of the rains. We began questioning the people as to where the elephant had gone and, as usual, failed to get any definite information. That is invariably the case in the East; a story always sounds clear enough at a distance, but the nearer you get to the scene of events the vaguer it becomes. Some of the people said that the elephant had gone in one direction, some said that he had gone in another, some professed not even to have heard of any elephant. I had almost made up my mind that the whole story was a pack of lies, when we heard yells a little distance away. There was a loud, scandalized cry of "Go away, child! Go away this instant!" and an old woman with a switch in her hand came round the corner of a hut, violently shooing away a crowd of naked children. Some more women followed, clicking their tongues and exclaiming; evidently there was something that the children ought not to have seen. I rounded the hut and saw a man's dead body sprawling in the mud. He was an Indian, a black Dravidian coolie, almost naked, and he could not have been dead many minutes. The people said that the elephant had come suddenly upon him round the corner of the hut, caught him with its trunk, put its foot on his back and ground him into

---

[3] The keeper and driver of an elephant.

the earth. This was the rainy season and the ground was soft, and his face had scored a trench a foot deep and a couple of yards long. He was lying on his belly with arms crucified and head sharply twisted to one side. His face was coated with mud, the eyes wide open, the teeth bared and grinning with an expression of unendurable agony. (Never tell me, by the way, that the dead look peaceful. Most of the corpses I have seen look devilish.) The friction of the great beast's foot had stripped the skin from his back as neatly as one skins a rabbit. As soon as I saw the dead man I sent an orderly to a friend's house nearby to borrow an elephant rifle. I had already sent back the pony, not wanting it to go mad with fright and throw me if it smelt the elephant.

The orderly came back in a few minutes with a rifle and five cartridges, and 5
meanwhile some Burmans had arrived and told us that the elephant was in the paddy fields below, only a few hundred yards away. As I started forward practically the whole population of the quarter flocked out of the houses and followed me. They had seen the rifle and were all shouting excitedly that I was going to shoot the elephant. They had not shown much interest in the elephant when he was merely ravaging their homes, but it was different now that he was going to be shot. It was a bit of fun to them, as it would be to an English crowd; besides they wanted the meat. It made me vaguely uneasy. I had no intention of shooting the elephant—I had merely sent for the rifle to defend myself if necessary—and it is always unnerving to have a crowd following you. I marched down the hill, looking and feeling a fool, with the rifle over my shoulders and an ever-growing army of people jostling at my heels. At the bottom, when you got away from the huts, there was a metalled road and beyond that a miry waste of paddy fields a thousand yards across, not yet ploughed but soggy from the first rains and dotted with coarse grass. The elephant was standing eight yards from the road, his left side towards us. He took not the slightest notice of the crowd's approach. He was tearing up branches of grass, beating them against his knees to clean them and stuffing them into his mouth.

I had halted on the road. As soon as I saw the elephant I knew with perfect certainty that I ought not to shoot him. It is a serious matter to shoot a working elephant—it is comparable to destroying a huge and costly piece of machinery—and obviously one ought not to do it if it can possibly be avoided. And at that distance, peacefully eating, the elephant looked no more dangerous than a cow. I thought then and I think now that his attack of "must" was already passing off; in which case he would merely wander harmlessly about until the mahout came back and caught him. Moreover, I did not in the least want to shoot him. I decided that I would watch him for a little while to make sure that he did not turn savage again, and then go home.

But at that moment I glanced round at the crowd that had followed me. It was an immense crowd, two thousand at the least and growing every minute. It blocked the road for a long distance on either side. I looked at the sea of yellow faces above the garish clothes—faces all happy and excited over this bit of fun, all certain that the elephant was going to be shot. They were watching me as they would watch a conjurer about to perform a trick. They did not like me, but with the magical rifle in my hands I was momentarily worth watching. And suddenly I realized that I should have to shoot the elephant after all. The people expected it of me and I had got to do it; I could feel their two thousand wills pressing me forward, irresistibly. And it was at this moment, as I stood there with the rifle in my hands, that I first grasped the hollowness, the futility of the white man's dominion in the East. Here was I, the white man with his gun, standing in front of the unarmed native crowd—seemingly the leading actor of the piece; but in reality I was only an absurd puppet pushed to and fro by the will of those yellow faces behind. I perceived in this moment that when the white man turns tyrant it is his own freedoms that he destroys. He becomes a sort of hollow, posing dummy, the conventionalized figure of a sahib. For it is the condition of his rule that he shall spend his life in trying to impress the "natives," and so in every crisis he has got to do what the "natives" expect of him. He wears a mask, and his face grows to fit it. I had got to shoot the elephant. I had committed myself to doing it when I sent for the rifle. A sahib has got to act like a sahib; he has got to appear resolute, to know his own mind and do definite things. To come all that way, rifle in hand, with two thousand people marching at my heels, and then to trail feebly away, having done nothing—no, that was impossible. The crowd would laugh at me. And my whole life, every white man's life in the East, was one long struggle not to be laughed at.

But I did not want to shoot the elephant. I watched him beating his bunch of grass against his knees, with that preoccupied grandmotherly air that elephants have. It seemed to me that it would be murder to shoot him. At that age I was not squeamish about killing animals, but I had never shot an elephant and never wanted to. (Somehow it always seems worse to kill a *large* animal.) Besides, there was the beast's owner to be considered. Alive, the elephant was worth at least a hundred pounds; dead, he would only be worth the value of his tusks, five pounds, possibly. But I had to act quickly. I turned to some experienced-looking Burmans who had been there when we arrived, and asked them how the elephant had been behaving. They all said the same thing: he took no notice of you if you left him alone, but he might charge if you went too close to him.

It was perfectly clear to me what I ought to do. I ought to walk up to within, say, twenty-five yards of the elephant and test his behavior. If he charged, I could shoot; if he took no notice of me, it would be safe to leave him until the mahout came back. But also I knew that I was going to do no such thing. I was a poor shot with a rifle and the ground was soft mud into which one would sink at every step. If the elephant charged and I missed him, I should have about as much chance as a toad under a steam-roller. But even then I was not thinking particularly of my own skin, only of the watchful yellow faces behind. For at that moment, with the crowd watching me, I was not afraid in the ordinary sense, as I would have been if I had been alone. A white man mustn't be frightened in front of "natives"; and so, in general, he isn't frightened. The sole thought in my mind was that if anything went wrong those two thousand Burmans would see me pursued, caught, trampled on and reduced to a grinning corpse like that Indian up the hill. And if that happened it was quite probable that some of them would laugh. That would never do. There was only one alternative. I shoved the cartridges into the magazine and lay down on the road to get a better aim.

The crowd grew very still, and a deep, low, happy sigh, as of people who see the theatre curtain go up at last, breathed from innumerable throats. They were going to have their bit of fun after all. The rifle was a beautiful German thing with cross-hair sights. I did not then know that in shooting an elephant one would shoot to cut an imaginary bar running from ear-hole to ear-hole. I ought, therefore, as the elephant was sideways on, to have aimed straight at his ear-hole; actually I aimed several inches in front of this, thinking the brain would be further forward. 10

When I pulled the trigger I did not hear the bang or feel the kick—one never does when a shot goes home—but I heard the devilish roar of glee that went up from the crowd. In that instant, in too short a time, one would have thought, even for the bullet to get there, a mysterious, terrible change had come over the elephant. He neither stirred nor fell, but every line of his body had altered. He looked suddenly stricken, shrunken, immensely old, as though the frightful impact of the bullet had paralysed him without knocking him down. At last, after what seemed a long time—it might have been five seconds, I dare say—he sagged flabbily to his knees. His mouth slobbered. An enormous senility seemed to have settled upon him. One could have imagined him thousands of years old. I fired again into the same spot. At the second shot he did not collapse but climbed with desperate slowness to his feet and stood weakly upright, with legs sagging and head drooping. I fired a third time. That was the shot that did for him. You could see the agony of it jolt his whole body and knock the last remnant of strength from his legs. But in falling he seemed for a moment to rise, for as his hind legs collapsed beneath him he seemed to tower upward like a huge rock toppling, his trunk reaching skywards like a tree. He trumpeted, for the first and only time. And then down he came, his belly towards me, with a crash that seemed to shake the ground even where I lay.

I got up. The Burmans were already racing past me across the mud. It was obvious that the elephant would never rise again, but he was not dead. He was breathing very rhythmically with long rattling gasps, his great mound of a side painfully rising and falling. His mouth was wide open—I could see far down into caverns of pale pink throat. I waited a long time for him to die, but his breathing did not weaken. Finally I fired my two remaining shots into the spot where I thought his heart must be. The thick blood welled out of him like red velvet, but still he did not die. His body did not even jerk when the shots hit him, the tortured breathing continued without a pause. He was dying, very slowly and in great agony, but in some world remote from me where not even a bullet could damage him further. I felt that I had got to put an end to that dreadful noise. It seemed dreadful to see the great beast lying there, powerless to move and yet powerless to die, and not even to be able to finish him. I sent back for my small rifle and poured shot after shot into his heart and down his throat. They seemed to make no impression. The tortured gasps continued as steadily as the ticking of a clock.

In the end I could not stand it any longer and went away. I heard later that it took him half an hour to die. Burmans were bringing dahs[4] and baskets even before I left, and I was told they had stripped his body almost to the bones by the afternoon.

Afterwards, of course, there were endless discussions about the shooting of the elephant. The owner was furious, but he was only an Indian and could do nothing. Besides, legally I had done the right thing, for a mad elephant has to be killed, like a mad dog, if its owner fails to control it. Among the Europeans opinion was divided. The older men said I was right, the younger men said it was a damn shame to shoot an elephant for killing a coolie, because an elephant was worth more than any damn Coringhee coolie. And afterwards I was very glad that the coolie had been killed; it put me legally in the right and it gave me a sufficient pretext for shooting the elephant. I often wondered whether any of the others grasped that I had done it solely to avoid looking a fool.

For Analysis

1. Examine carefully paragraphs 11 and 12, in which Orwell describes the death of the elephant. Is the reader meant to take the passage only literally, or can a case be made that the elephant's death is imbued with symbolic meaning? Explain. **2.** Orwell tells us repeatedly that his sympathies are with the Burmese. Yet he describes them as "evil-spirited little beasts" (par. 2). How might this ambivalence be explained? **3.** What does the experience described in paragraph 7 teach Orwell? **4.** Do you agree with Orwell's rationalization that under the circumstances he had no choice but "to shoot the elephant" (par. 7)? **5.** What is your reaction to Orwell's final comment, "I was very glad that the coolie had been killed; it put me legally in the right and it gave me a sufficient pretext for shooting the elephant. I often wondered whether any of the others grasped that I had done it solely to avoid looking a fool"?

On Style

Midway through the essay (par. 7), Orwell discloses the significance the event had for him. Why does he disclose it then rather than save it for the conclusion?

Making Connections

1. Compare this essay with Jonathan Swift's "A Modest Proposal" (p. 628) in the techniques and arguments used to attack imperialism. **2.** While they are dissimilar in subject matter, this story and Toni Cade Bambara's "The Lesson" (p. 115) culminate in climactic events that change the **protagonists**. Compare those events and their effect on the two protagonists.

Writing Topics

1. In a brief paragraph, summarize the lesson Orwell learned from his experience. **2.** What does Orwell conclude regarding the position of foreign authorities in a hostile country? **3.** Describe a situation in which you were required to behave in an official capacity that contradicted your personal beliefs.

---

[4] Knives.

Lewis Thomas   [1913–1993]

The Iks   1974

The small tribe of Iks, formerly nomadic hunters and gatherers in the mountain valley of northern Uganda, have become celebrities, literary symbols of the ultimate fate of disheartened, heartless mankind at large. Two disastrously conclusive things happened to them: the government decided to have a national park, so they were compelled by law to give up hunting in the valleys and become farmers on poor hillside soil, and then they were visited for two years by an anthropologist who detested them and wrote a book about them.

The message of the book is that the Iks have transformed themselves into an irreversibly disagreeable collection of unattached, brutish creatures, totally selfish and loveless, in response to the dismantling of their traditional culture. Moreover, this is what the rest of us are like in our inner selves, and we will all turn into Iks when the structure of our society comes all unhinged.

The argument rests, of course, on certain assumptions about the core of human beings, and is necessarily speculative. You have to agree in advance that man is fundamentally a bad lot, out for himself alone, displaying such graces as affection and compassion only as learned habits. If you take this view, the story of the Iks can be used to confirm it. These people seem to be living together, clustered in small, dense villages, but they are really solitary, unrelated individuals with no evident use for each other. They talk, but only to make ill-tempered demands and cold refusals. They share nothing. They never sing. They turn the children out to forage as soon as they can walk, and desert the elders to starve whenever they can, and the foraging children snatch food from the mouths of the helpless elders. It is a mean society.

They breed without love or even casual regard. They defecate on each other's doorsteps. They watch their neighbors for signs of misfortune, and only then do they laugh. In the book they do a lot of laughing, having so much bad luck. Several times they even laughed at the anthropologist, who found this especially repellent (one senses, between the lines, that the scholar is not himself the world's luckiest man). Worse, they took him into the family, snatched his food, defecated on his doorstep, and hooted dislike at him. They gave him two bad years.

It is a depressing book. If, as he suggests, there is only Ikness at the center of each of us, our sole hope for hanging onto the name of humanity will be in endlessly mending the structure of our society, and it is changing so quickly and completely that we may never find the threads in time. Meanwhile, left to ourselves alone, solitary, we will become the same joyless, zestless, untouching lone animals.

930

But this may be too narrow a view. For one thing, the Iks are extraordinary. They are absolutely astonishing, in fact. The anthropologist has never seen people like them anywhere, nor have I. You'd think, if they were simply examples of the common essence of mankind, they'd seem more recognizable. Instead, they are bizarre, anomalous. I have known my share of peculiar, difficult, nervous, grabby people, but I've never encountered any genuinely, consistently detestable human beings in all my life. The Iks sound more like abnormalities, maladies.

I cannot accept it. I do not believe that the Iks are representative of isolated, revealed man, unobscured by social habits. I believe their behavior is something extra, something laid on. This unremitting, compulsive repellence is a kind of complicated ritual. They must have learned to act this way; they copied it, somehow.

I have a theory, then. The Iks have gone crazy.

The solitary Ik, isolated in the ruins of an exploded culture, has built a new defense for himself. If you live in an unworkable society you can make up one of your own, and this is what the Iks have done. Each Ik has become a group, a one-man tribe on its own, a constituency.

Now everything falls into place. This is why they do seem, after all, vaguely   10 familiar to all of us. We've seen them before. This is precisely the way groups of one size or another, ranging from communities to nations, behave. It is, of course, this aspect of humanity that has lagged behind the rest of evolution, and this is why the Ik seems so primitive. In his absolute selfishness, his incapacity to give anything away, no matter what, he is a successful committee. When he stands at the door of his hut, shouting insults at his neighbors in a loud harangue, he is a city addressing another city.

Cities have all the Ik characteristics. They defecate on doorsteps, in rivers and lakes, their own or anyone else's. They leave rubbish. They detest all neighboring cities, give nothing away. They even build institutions for deserting elders out of sight.

Nations are the most Iklike of all. No wonder the Iks seem familiar. For total greed, rapacity, heartlessness, and irresponsibility there is nothing to match a nation. Nations, by law, are solitary, self-centered, withdrawn into themselves. There is no such thing as affection between nations, and certainly no nation ever loved another. They bawl insults from their doorsteps, defecate into whole oceans, snatch all the food, survive by detestation, take joy in the bad luck of others, celebrate the death of others, live for the death of others.

That's it, and I shall stop worrying about the book. It does not signify that man is a sparse, inhuman thing at his center. He's all right. It only says what we've always known and never had enough time to worry about, that we haven't yet learned how to stay human when assembled in masses. The Ik, in his despair, is acting out this failure, and perhaps we should pay closer attention. Nations have themselves become too frightening to think about, but we might learn some things by watching these people.

For Analysis

1. To what, in the "civilized" world, do the Iks correspond? **2.** Is this essay about the Iks or about us? Explain. **3.** What is Thomas's view of human nature in this essay? How does it differ from the anthropologist's?

On Style

Examine the sentence structure of the next to the last paragraph. The paragraph defines *nation* with sentences of varied length and forcefulness. Describe the relationship between the paragraph's structure (including sentence length, rhythm, balance, sequence of assertions) and the message it conveys.

Making Connections

Explain how your own experience supports or refutes Thomas's assertion that Iks behave "precisely the way groups of one size or another, ranging from communities to nations, behave" (par. 10).

Writing Topic

Write an essay arguing for or against the assertion that "For total greed, rapacity, heartlessness, and irresponsibility there is nothing to match a nation" (par. 12).

Jessica Mitford   [1917–1996]

The American Way of Death   1963

O Death, where is thy sting? O grave, where is thy victory?[1] Where, indeed. Many a badly stung survivor, faced with the aftermath of some relative's funeral, has ruefully concluded that the victory has been won hands down by a funeral establishment—in disastrously unequal battle.

Much has been written of late about the affluent society in which we live, and much fun poked at some of the irrational "status symbols" set out like golden snares to trap the unwary consumer at every turn. Until recently, little has been said about the most irrational and weirdest of the lot, lying in ambush for all of us at the end of the road—the modern American funeral.

If the Dismal Traders (as an eighteenth-century English writer calls them) have traditionally been cast in a comic role in literature, a universally recognized symbol of humor from Shakespeare to Dickens to Evelyn Waugh, they have successfully turned the tables in recent years to perpetrate a huge, macabre and expensive practical joke on the American public. It is not consciously conceived as a joke, of course; on the contrary, it is hedged with admirably contrived rationalizations.

Gradually, almost imperceptibly, over the years the funeral men have constructed their own grotesque cloud-cuckooland where the trappings of Gracious Living are transformed, as in a nightmare, into the trappings of Gracious Dying. The same familiar Madison Avenue language, with its peculiar adjectival range designed to anesthetize sales resistance to all sorts of products, has seeped into the funeral industry in a new and bizarre guise. The emphasis is on the same desirable qualities that we have all been schooled to look for in our daily search for excellence: comfort, durability, beauty, craftsmanship. The attuned ear will recognize too the convincing quasi-scientific language, so reassuring even if unintelligible.

So that this too, too solid flesh might not melt, we are offered "solid copper—   5
a quality casket which offers superb value to the client seeking long-lasting protection," or "the Colonial Classic Beauty—18 gauge lead coated steel, seamless top, lap-jointed welded body construction." Some are equipped with foam rubber, some with innerspring mattresses. Elgin offers "the revolutionary 'Perfect-Posture' bed." Not every casket need have a silver lining, for one may choose between "more than 60 color matched shades, magnificent and unique masterpieces" by the Cheney casket-lining people. Shrouds no longer exist. Instead,

---

[1] See 1 Corinthians 15:55.

you may patronize a grave-wear couturière who promises "handmade original fashions—styles from the best in life for the last memory—dresses, men's suits, negligees, accessories." For the final, perfect grooming: "Nature-Glo—the ultimate in cosmetic embalming." And, where have we heard the phrase "peace of mind protection" before? No matter. In funeral advertising, it is applied to the Wilbert Burial Vault, with its ⅜-inch precast asphalt inner liner plus extra-thick, reinforced concrete—all this "guaranteed by Good Housekeeping." Here again the Cadillac, status symbol par excellence, appears in all its gleaming glory, this time transformed into a pastel-colored funeral hearse.

You, the potential customer for all this luxury, are unlikely to read the lyrical descriptions quoted above, for they are culled from *Mortuary Management* and *Casket and Sunnyside,* two of the industry's eleven trade magazines. For you there are ads in your daily newspaper, generally found on the obituary page, stressing dignity, refinement, high-caliber professional service and that intangible quality, *sincerity.* The trade advertisements are, however, instructive, because they furnish an important clue to the frame of mind into which the funeral industry has hypnotized itself.

A new mythology, essential to the twentieth-century American funeral rite, has grown up—or rather has been built up step by step—to justify the peculiar customs surrounding the disposal of our dead. And, just as the witch doctor must be convinced of his own infallibility in order to maintain a hold over his clientele, so the funeral industry has had to "sell itself" on its articles of faith in the course of passing them along to the public.

The first of these is the tenet that today's funeral procedures are founded in "American tradition." The story comes to mind of a sign on the freshly sown lawn of a brand-new Midwest college: "There is a tradition on this campus that students never walk on this strip of grass. This tradition goes into effect next Tuesday." The most cursory look at American funerals of past times will establish this parallel. Simplicity to the point of starkness, the plain pine box, the laying out of the dead by friends and family who also bore the coffin to the grave—these were the hallmarks of the traditional funeral until the end of the nineteenth century.

Secondly, there is a myth that the American public is only being given what it wants—an opportunity to keep up with the Joneses to the end. "In keeping with our high standard of living, there should be an equally high standard of dying," says the past president of the Funeral Directors of San Francisco. "The cost of a funeral varies according to individual taste and the niceties of living the family has been accustomed to." Actually, choice doesn't enter the picture for the average individual, faced, generally for the first time, with the necessity of buying a product of which he is totally ignorant, at a moment when he is least in a position to quibble. In point of fact the cost of a funeral almost always varies, not "according to individual taste" but according to what the traffic will bear.

Thirdly, there is an assortment of myths based on half-digested psychiatric theories. The importance of the "memory picture" is stressed—meaning the last glimpse of the deceased in open casket, done up with the latest in embalming techniques and finished off with a dusting of makeup. A newer one, impres-

10

sively authentic-sounding, is the need for "grief therapy," which is beginning to go over big in mortuary circles. A historian of American funeral directing hints at the grief-therapist idea when speaking of the new role of the undertaker— "the dramaturgic role, in which the undertaker becomes a stage manager to create an appropriate atmosphere and to move the funeral party through a drama in which social relationships are stressed and an emotional catharsis or release is provided through ceremony."

Lastly, a whole new terminology, as ornately shoddy as the satin rayon casket liner, has been invented by the funeral industry to replace the direct and serviceable vocabulary of former times. Undertaker has been supplanted by "funeral director" or "mortician." (Even the classified section of the telephone directory gives recognition to this; in its pages you will find "Undertakers—see Funeral Directors.") Coffins are "caskets"; hearses are "coaches," or "professional cars"; flowers are "floral tributes"; corpses generally are "loved ones," but mortuary etiquette dictates that a specific corpse be referred to by name only— as, "Mr. Jones"; cremated ashes are "cremains." Euphemisms such as "slumber room," "reposing room," and "calcination—the *kindlier* heat" abound in the funeral business.

If the undertaker is the stage manager of the fabulous production that is the modern American funeral, the stellar role is reserved for the occupant of the open casket. The decor, the stagehands, the supporting cast are all arranged for the most advantageous display of the deceased, without which the rest of the paraphernalia would lose its point—*Hamlet* without the Prince of Denmark. It is to this end that a fantastic array of costly merchandise and services is pyramided to dazzle the mourners and facilitate the plunder of the next of kin.

Grief therapy, anyone? But it's going to come high. According to the funeral industry's own figures, the *average* undertaker's bill in 1961 was $708 for casket and "services," to which must be added the cost of a burial vault, flowers, clothing, clergy and musician's honorarium, and cemetery charges. When these costs are added to the undertaker's bill, the total average cost for an adult's funeral is, as we shall see, close to $1,450.

The question naturally arises, *is* this what most people want for themselves and their families? For several reasons, this has been a hard one to answer until recently. It is a subject seldom discussed. Those who have never had to arrange for a funeral frequently shy away from its implications, preferring to take comfort in the thought that sufficient unto the day is the evil thereof. Those who have acquired personal and painful knowledge of the subject would often rather forget about it. Pioneering "Funeral Societies" or "Memorial Associations," dedicated to the principle of dignified funerals at reasonable cost, have existed in a number of communities throughout the country, but their membership has been limited for the most part to the more sophisticated element in the population—university people, liberal intellectuals—and those who, like doctors and lawyers, come up against problems in arranging funerals for their clients.

Some indication of the pent-up resentment felt by vast numbers of people against the funeral interests was furnished by the astonishing response to an article by Roul Tunley, titled "Can You Afford to Die?" in *The Saturday Evening* 15

Post of June 17, 1961. As though a dike had burst, letters poured in from every part of the country to the *Post*, to the funeral societies, to local newspapers. They came from clergymen, professional people, old-age pensioners, trade unionists. Three months after the article appeared, an estimated six thousand had taken pen in hand to comment on some phase of the high cost of dying. Many recounted their own bitter experiences at the hands of funeral directors; hundreds asked for advice on how to establish a consumer organization in communities where none exists; others sought information about pre-need plans. The membership of funeral societies skyrocketed. The funeral industry, finding itself in the glare of public spotlight, has begun to engage in serious debate about its own future course—as well it might.

Is the funeral inflation bubble ripe for bursting? A few years ago, the United States public suddenly rebelled against the trend in the auto industry towards ever more showy cars, with their ostentatious and nonfunctional fins, and a demand was created for compact cars patterned after European models. The all-powerful auto industry, accustomed to *telling* the customer what sort of car he wanted, was suddenly forced to *listen* for a change. Overnight, the little cars became for millions a new kind of status symbol. Could it be that the same cycle is working itself out in the attitude towards the final return of dust to dust, that the American public is becoming sickened by ever more ornate and costly funerals, and that a status symbol of the future may indeed be the simplest kind of "funeral without fins"?

For Analysis

1. What four "articles of faith" does Mitford attribute to the funeral industry? **2.** In the final three paragraphs, Mitford speculates about what most people want. Make a list of the assumptions she puts forward. Do you agree with her? Explain.

On Style

Consider the opening sentences of the first and fifth paragraphs. Identify the **allusions,** and comment on how Mitford's allusiveness contributes to her argument.

Making Connections

What other "costly and ornate" cultural customs would you consider open to ridicule?

Writing Topic

Imitating Mitford's approach and style, write an essay critical of the American Way of _____. Possible subjects might include high school proms, weddings, football half-time shows, debutante balls, bar mitzvahs or confirmations, or New Year's Eve celebrations.

James Baldwin [1924–1987]

Rage 1955

. . . The year which preceded my father's death had made a great change in my life. I had been living in New Jersey, working in defense plants, working and living among southerners, white and black. I knew about the south, of course, and about how southerners treated Negroes and how they expected them to behave, but it had never entered my mind that anyone would look at me and expect *me* to behave that way. I learned in New Jersey that to be a Negro meant, precisely, that one was never looked at but was simply at the mercy of the reflexes the color of one's skin caused in other people. I acted in New Jersey as I had always acted, that is as though I thought a great deal of myself—I had to *act* that way— with results that were, simply, unbelievable. I had scarcely arrived before I had earned the enmity, which was extraordinarily ingenious, of all my superiors and nearly all my co-workers. In the beginning, to make matters worse, I simply did not know what was happening. I did not know what I had done, and I shortly began to wonder what *anyone* could possibly do, to bring about such unanimous, active, and unbearably vocal hostility. I knew about jim-crow but I had never experienced it. I went to the same self-service restaurant three times and stood with all the Princeton boys before the counter, waiting for a hamburger and coffee; it was always an extraordinarily long time before anything was set before me, but it was not until the fourth visit that I learned that, in fact, nothing had ever been set before me: I had simply picked something up. Negroes were not served there, I was told, and they had been waiting for me to realize that I was always the only Negro present. Once I was told this, I determined to go there all the time. But now they were ready for me and, though some dreadful scenes were subsequently enacted in that restaurant, I never ate there again.

It was the same story all over New Jersey, in bars, bowling alleys, diners, places to live. I was always being forced to leave, silently, or with mutual imprecations. I very shortly became notorious and children giggled behind me when I passed and their elders whispered or shouted—they really believed that I was mad. And it did begin to work on my mind, of course; I began to be afraid to go anywhere and to compensate for this I went places to which I really should not have gone and where, God knows, I had no desire to be. My reputation in town naturally enhanced my reputation at work and my working day became one long series of acrobatics designed to keep me out of trouble. I cannot say that these acrobatics succeeded. It began to seem that the machinery of the organization I worked for was turning over, day and night, with but one aim: to eject me. I was fired once, and contrived, with the aid of a friend from New York, to get back on the payroll; was fired again, and bounced back again. It took a while to fire me for a third time, but the third time took. There were no loopholes anywhere. There was not even any way of getting back inside the gates.

That year in New Jersey lives in my mind as though it were the year during which, having unsuspected predilection for it, I first contracted some dread, chronic disease, the unfailing symptom of which is a kind of blind fever, a pounding in the skull and fire in the bowels. Once this disease is contracted, one can never be really carefree again, for the fever, without an instant's warning, can recur at any moment. It can wreck more important things than race relations. There is not a Negro alive who does not have this rage in his blood—one has the choice, merely, of living with it consciously or surrendering to it. As for me, this fever has recurred in me, and does, and will until the day I die.

My last night in New Jersey, a white friend from New York took me to the nearest big town, Trenton, to go to the movies and have a few drinks. As it turned out, he also saved me from, at the very least, a violent whipping. Almost every detail of that night stands out very clearly in my memory. I even remember the name of the movie we saw because its title impressed me as being so patly ironical. It was a movie about the German occupation of France, starring Maureen O'Hara and Charles Laughton and called *This Land is Mine*. I remember the name of the diner we walked into when the movie ended: it was the "American Diner." When we walked in the counterman asked what we wanted and I remember answering with the casual sharpness which had become my habit: "We want a hamburger and a cup of coffee, what do you think we want?" I do not know why, after a year of such rebuffs, I so completely failed to anticipate his answer, which was, of course, "We don't serve Negroes here." This reply failed to discompose me, at least for the moment. I made some sardonic comment about the name of the diner and we walked out into the streets.

This was the time of what was called the "brown-out," when the lights in all   5
American cities were very dim. When we re-entered the streets something happened to me which had the force of an optical illusion, or a nightmare. The streets were very crowded and I was facing north. People were moving in every direction but it seemed to me, in that instant, that all of the people I could see, and many more than that, were moving toward me, against me, and that everyone was white. I remember how their faces gleamed. And I felt, like a physical sensation, a *click* at the nape of my neck as though some interior string connecting my head to my body had been cut. I began to walk. I heard my friend call after me, but I ignored him. Heaven only knows what was going on in his mind, but he had the good sense not to touch me—I don't know what would have happened if he had—and to keep me in sight. I don't know what was going on in my mind, either; I certainly had no conscious plan. I wanted to do something to crush these white faces, which were crushing me. I walked for perhaps a block or two until I came to an enormous, glittering, and fashionable restaurant in which I knew not even the intercession of the Virgin would cause me to be served. I pushed through the doors and took the first vacant seat I saw, at a table for two, and waited.

I do not know how long I waited and I rather wonder, until today, what I could possibly have looked like. Whatever I looked like, I frightened the waitress who shortly appeared, and the moment she appeared all of my fury flowed towards her. I hated her for her white face, and for her great, astounded, frightened eyes. I felt that if she found a black man so frightening I would make her fright worthwhile.

She did not ask me what I wanted, but repeated, as though she had learned it somewhere, "We don't serve Negroes here." She did not say it with the blunt, derisive hostility to which I had grown so accustomed, but, rather, with a note of apology in her voice, and fear. This made me colder and more murderous than ever. I felt I had to do something with my hands. I wanted her to come close enough for me to get her neck between my hands.

So I pretended not to have understood her, hoping to draw her closer. And she did step a very short step closer, with her pencil poised incongruously over her pad, and repeated the formula: ". . . don't serve Negroes here."

Somehow, with the repetition of that phrase, which was already ringing in my head like a thousand bells of a nightmare, I realized that she would never come any closer and that I would have to strike from a distance. There was nothing on the table but an ordinary watermug half full of water, and I picked this up and hurled it with all my strength at her. She ducked and it missed her and shattered against the mirror behind the bar. And, with that sound, my frozen blood abruptly thawed, I returned from wherever I had been, I *saw*, for the first time, the restaurant, the people with their mouths open, already, as it seemed to me, rising as one man, and I realized what I had done, and where I was, and I was frightened. I rose and began running for the door. A round, potbellied man grabbed me by the nape of the neck just as I reached the doors and began to beat me about the face. I kicked him and got loose and ran into the streets. My friend whispered, "*Run!*" and I ran.

My friend stayed outside the restaurant long enough to misdirect my pur-   10
suers and the police, who arrived, he told me, at once. I do not know what I said to him when he came to my room that night. I could not have said much. I felt, in the oddest, most awful way, that I had somehow betrayed him. I lived it over and over and over again, the way one relives an automobile accident after it has happened and one finds oneself alone and safe. I could not get over two facts, both equally difficult for the imagination to grasp, and one was that I could have been murdered. But the other was that I had been ready to commit murder. I saw nothing very clearly but I did see this: that my life, my *real* life, was in danger, and not from anything other people might do but from the hatred I carried in my own heart.

For Analysis

1. What does Baldwin mean in the opening paragraph when he says, "I acted . . . as though I thought a great deal of myself—I had to *act* that way"? **2.** What are the various stages Baldwin passes through in his response to racism? **3.** Does Baldwin's powerful description of the rage he felt support his generalization at the end of paragraph 3: "There is not a Negro alive who does not have this rage in his blood . . ."? **4.** What does Baldwin mean by the final sentence of the essay?

On Style
Discuss the **imagery** of the third paragraph. Do you find the characterization of racism's effect as a chronic disease convincing?

Making Connections
Compare the sources of hatred described in Thomas's "The Iks" (p. 930) and in Baldwin's essay.

Writing Topic
In an essay, describe how hatred in you or someone you know became self-destructive.

Culture and Identity

Questions and Writing Topics

1. Bharati Mukherjee's "Orbiting" is told from the daughter's **point of view** while Alice Walker's "Everyday Use" is told from the mother's point of view. How might the stories differ if the viewpoints were reversed? How would the parents see their daughter's situation in "Orbiting," and how would the educated daughter see her mother's situation in "Everyday Use"? **Writing Topic:** In each of these stories, the daughter has broken away from the parents' culture. Describe the nature of each break; have the daughters acted constructively or destructively? Explain.

2. Felix Mnthali's "The Stranglehold of English Lit." examines one culture's imposition of values on another. Consider the excerpt from W. H. Auden's "Five Songs," M. Carl Holman's "Mr. Z," and Amy Lowell's "Patterns" in the light of Mnthali's observations. How do these poems demonstrate the effect of cultural imperialism? **Writing Topic:** Examine a literary work chosen from this book and explore how that work fails to embody (or violates) the cultural values of your own tradition.

3. Explain how Virginia Woolf's observations in "What If Shakespeare Had Had a Sister?" illuminate Emily's situation in William Faulkner's "A Rose for Emily." **Writing Topic:** In an essay, argue for or against the proposition that women have achieved absolute equality in the United States.

4. Explain the cultural sources of the downfall of Gallimard in David Henry Hwang's *M. Butterfly* and of Willy Loman in Arthur Miller's *Death of a Salesman*. In what respects are Gallimard's and Loman's culturally determined attitudes similar and different? **Writing Topic:** Compare and contrast Willy Loman and Gallimard as "tragic heroes."

5. Anne Sexton's "Cinderella," Amy Lowell's "Patterns," E. E. Cummings's "the Cambridge ladies who live in furnished souls," and Emily Dickinson's "What Soft—Cherubic Creatures—" all address certain culturally determined behavior patterns among women. Describe the behavior depicted in these poems. How do the authors feel about the behavior? What devices reveal the authors' attitudes? **Writing Topic:** Define the social tradition that produced the women in these poems. Either defend that tradition as crucial to the social order or offer a cultural variation that would give women a different social role.

6. The speakers in Yevgeny Yevtushenko's "I Would Like" and T. S. Eliot's "The Love Song of J. Alfred Prufrock" exhibit quite different attitudes about their identities. Describe each speaker's attitude toward his identity and identify which aspects of the poems define those attitudes. In what sense are the speakers' identities culturally determined? **Writing Topic:** In an imaginative essay, describe each speaker's early life, and suggest what cultural forces shaped them.

7. In both George Orwell's "Shooting an Elephant" and Athol Fugard's *"Master Harold" . . . and the Boys,* characters do things they don't want to do. Why do they behave as they do? **Writing Topic:** Describe a situation in which you acted as other people expected rather than as you wished. Explain why you did so and what the results were.

8. Many of the works in this section deal with the tension and conflict that result when a minority culture is threatened or overpowered by another, dominant culture. **Writing Topic:** Examine the nature of that conflict in Louise Erdrich's "The Red Convertible," Barry Holstun Lopez's "Winter Count 1973," Bharati Mukherjee's "Orbiting," and David Henry Hwang's *M. Butterfly.*

9. Some of the works in this section focus on intergenerational tensions within a culture. **Writing Topic:** Compare such tensions in William Faulkner's "A Rose for Emily," Chinua Achebe's "Marriage Is a Private Affair," and Alice Walker's "Everyday Use."

10. The struggle of women to achieve equality is the subject of many works in this section. **Writing Topic:** Examine some of the feminist works in this section. What, if any, common threads do you find running through them, either in content or in the use of literary devices?

11. Homer in William Faulkner's "A Rose for Emily," Prufrock in T. S. Eliot's "The Love Song of J. Alfred Prufrock," Ro in Bharati Mukherjee's "Orbiting," and Callahan in Barry Holstun Lopez's "Winter Count 1973," are all, in some sense, cultural outsiders. **Writing Topic:** Compare their positions in the dominant culture, the resulting conflicts or tensions, and the strategies they employ in dealing with their status.

Love and Hate

Room in New York, 1932 by Edward Hopper.

Love and death, it is often noted, are the two great themes of literature. Many of the literary works we have placed in the sections "Innocence and Experience," "Conformity and Rebellion," and "Culture and Identity" speak of love and death as well. But in those works, other thematic interests dominate. In this section, we gather a number of works in which love and hate are thematically central.

The rosy conception of love presented in many popular and sentimental stories does not prepare us for the complicated reality we face. We know that the course of true love never runs smooth, but in those popular stories the obstacles that hinder the lovers are simple and external. If the young lover can land the high-paying job or convince the beloved's parents that he or she is worthy despite social differences, all will be well. But love in life is rarely that simple. The external obstacles may be insuperable, or the obstacles may lie deep within the personality. The major obstacle may well be an individual's difficult and painful effort to understand that he or she has been deceived by an immature or sentimental conception of love.

In this age of psychological awareness, the claims of the flesh are well recognized. But psychology teaches us, as well, to recognize the aggressive aspect of the human condition. The omnipresent selfishness that civilization attempts to check may be aggressively violent as well as lustful. Thus we have the simple eroticism of Kate Chopin's "The Storm." And Matthew Arnold in "Dover Beach" finds love the only refuge from a chaotic world in which "ignorant armies clash by night."

The cliché has it that love and hate are closely related, and much evidence supports this proposition. But why should love and hate, seeming opposites, lie so close together in the emotional lives of men and women? We are all egos, separate from each other. And as separate individuals, we develop elaborate behavior mechanisms that defend us from each other. But the erotic love relationship differs from other relationships in that it may be defined as a rejection of separateness. The common metaphor speaks of two lovers as joining, as merging into one. That surrender of the "me" to join in an "us" leaves lovers uniquely vulnerable to psychic injury. In short, the defenses are down, and the self-esteem of each of the lovers depends importantly on the behavior of the other. If the lover is betrayed by the beloved, the emotional consequences are uniquely disastrous—hence the peculiarly close relationship between passionate hatred and erotic love.

Words like *love* and *hate* are so general that poets rarely use them except as one term in a metaphor designed to project sharply some aspect of emotional life. The simple sexuality in poems such as Andrew Marvell's "To His Coy Mistress," Christopher Marlowe's "The Passionate Shepherd to His Love," and Thomas Campion's "I Care Not for These Ladies" may be juxtaposed with the hatred and violence generated in *Othello* by sexual jealousy or with the quick reprisal of the slighted Barbara Allan. And Shakespeare's description of lust in "Th' expense of spirit in a waste of shame" notes an aspect of love quite overlooked by Edmund Waller in his song, "Go, Lovely Rose!"

Perhaps more than anything, the works in this section celebrate the elemental impulses of men and women that run counter to those rational formulations by which we govern our lives. We pursue Othello's love for Desdemona and Iago's hate for Othello and arrive at an irreducible mystery, for neither Othello's love nor Iago's hate yields satisfactorily to rational explanation. Reason does not tell us why Othello and Desdemona love one another or why Iago hates rather than honors Othello.

Love is an act of faith springing from our deep-seated need to join with another human being not only in physical nakedness but in emotional and spiritual nakedness as well. While hate is a denial of that faith and, therefore, a retreat into spiritual isolation, love is an attempt to break out of the isolation.

FOR THINKING AND WRITING

As you read the selections in this section, consider the following questions. You may want to write out your thoughts informally in a journal or notebook as a way of preparing to respond to the selections, or you may wish to make one of these questions the basis for a formal essay.

1. What is love? What is the source of your definition (literature, personal observation, discussions with those you trust)? Have you ever been in love? How did you know? Do you know someone who is in love? How do you know?

2. Have you ever truly hated someone or something? Describe the circumstances, and characterize your hatred.

3. Do you believe that love and hate are closely related? Have you experienced a change from love to hatred, or do you know someone who has? Explain.

4. There are different kinds of love—love of family, of humankind, of a cause. Characterize several different kinds of love, and examine your own motives and behavior in different love relationships. Is it possible that certain kinds of love necessarily generate certain hatreds? Explain.

Fiction

Kate Chopin [1851–1904]

The Storm 1898

I

The leaves were so still that even Bibi thought it was going to rain. Bobinôt, who was accustomed to converse on terms of perfect equality with his little son, called the child's attention to certain sombre clouds that were rolling with sinister intention from the west, accompanied by a sullen, threatening roar. They were at Friedheimer's store and decided to remain there till the storm had passed. They sat within the door on two empty kegs. Bibi was four years old and looked very wise.

"Mama'll be 'fraid, yes," he suggested with blinking eyes.

"She'll shut the house. Maybe she got Sylvie helpin' her this evenin'," Bobinôt responded reassuringly.

"No; she ent got Sylvie. Sylvie was helpin' her yistiday," piped Bibi.

Bobinôt arose and going across to the counter purchased a can of shrimps, of   5 which Calixta was very fond. Then he returned to his perch on the keg and sat stolidly holding the can of shrimps while the storm burst. It shook the wooden store and seemed to be ripping great furrows in the distant field. Bibi laid his little hand on his father's knee and was not afraid.

II

Calixta, at home, felt no uneasiness for their safety. She sat at a side window sewing furiously on a sewing machine. She was greatly occupied and did not notice the approaching storm. But she felt very warm and often stopped to mop her face on which the perspiration gathered in beads. She unfastened her white sacque at the throat. It began to grow dark, and suddenly realizing the situation she got up hurriedly and went about closing windows and doors.

Out on the small front gallery she had hung Bobinôt's Sunday clothes to air and she hastened out to gather them before the rain fell. As she stepped outside, Alcée Laballière rode in at the gate. She had not seen him very often since her marriage, and never alone. She stood there with Bobinôt's coat in her hands, and the big rain drops began to fall. Alcée rode his horse under the shelter of a side projection where the chickens had huddled and there were plows and a harrow piled up in the corner.

"May I come and wait on your gallery till the storm is over, Calixta?" he asked.

"Come 'long in, M'sieur Alcée."

His voice and her own startled her as if from a trance, and she seized Bobinôt's vest. Alcée, mounting to the porch, grabbed the trousers and snatched Bibi's braided jacket that was about to be carried away by a sudden gust of wind. He expressed an intention to remain outside, but it was soon apparent that he might as well have been out in the open: the water beat in upon the boards in driving sheets, and he went inside, closing the door after him. It was even necessary to put something beneath the door to keep the water out.

"My! what a rain! It's good two years sence it rain' like that," exclaimed Calixta as she rolled up a piece of bagging and Alcée helped her to thrust it beneath the crack.

She was a little fuller of figure than five years before when she married; but she had lost nothing of her vivacity. Her blue eyes still retained their melting quality; and her yellow hair, dishevelled by the wind and rain, kinked more stubbornly than ever about her ears and temples.

The rain beat upon the low, shingled roof with a force and clatter that threatened to break an entrance and deluge them there. They were in the dining room—the sitting room—the general utility room. Adjoining was her bed room, with Bibi's couch along side her own. The door stood open, and the room with its white, monumental bed, its closed shutters, looked dim and mysterious.

Alcée flung himself into a rocker and Calixta nervously began to gather up from the floor the lengths of a cotton sheet which she had been sewing.

"If this keeps up, *Dieu sait*[1] if the levees goin' to stan' it!" she exclaimed.

"What have you got to do with the levees?"

"I got enough to do! An' there's Bobinôt with Bibi out in that storm—if he only didn' left Friedheimer's!"

"Let us hope, Calixta, that Bobinôt's got sense enough to come in out of a cyclone."

She went and stood at the window with a greatly disturbed look on her face. She wiped the frame that was clouded with moisture. It was stiflingly hot. Alcée got up and joined her at the window, looking over her shoulder. The rain was coming down in sheets obscuring the view of far-off cabins and enveloping the distant wood in a gray mist. The playing of the lightning was incessant. A bolt struck a tall chinaberry tree at the edge of the field. It filled all visible space with a blinding glare and the crash seemed to invade the very boards they stood upon.

Calixta put her hands to her eyes, and with a cry, staggered backward. Alcée's arm encircled her, and for an instant he drew her close and spasmodically to him.

---

[1] God knows.

"*Bonté!*"[2] she cried, releasing herself from his encircling arm and retreating from the window, "the house'll go next! If I only knew w'ere Bibi was!" She would not compose herself; she would not be seated. Alcée clasped her shoulders and looked into her face. The contact of her warm, palpitating body when he had unthinkingly drawn her into his arms, had aroused all the old-time infatuation and desire for her flesh.

"Calixta," he said, "don't be frightened. Nothing can happen. The house is too low to be struck, with so many tall trees standing about. There! aren't you going to be quiet? say, aren't you?" He pushed her hair back from her face that was warm and steaming. Her lips were as red and moist as pomegranate seed. Her white neck and a glimpse of her full, firm bosom disturbed him powerfully. As she glanced up at him the fear in her liquid blue eyes had given place to a drowsy gleam that unconsciously betrayed a sensuous desire. He looked down into her eyes and there was nothing for him to do but to gather her lips in a kiss. It reminded him of Assumption.[3]

"Do you remember—in Assumption, Calixta?" he asked in a low voice broken by passion. Oh! she remembered; for in Assumption he had kissed her and kissed and kissed her; until his senses would well nigh fail, and to save her he would resort to a desperate flight. If she was not an immaculate dove in those days, she was still inviolate; a passionate creature whose very defenselessness had made her defense, against which his honor forbade him to prevail. Now—well, now—her lips seemed in a manner free to be tasted, as well as her round, white throat and her whiter breasts.

They did not heed the crashing torrents, and the roar of the elements made her laugh as she lay in his arms. She was a revelation in that dim, mysterious chamber; as white as the couch she lay upon. Her firm, elastic flesh that was knowing for the first time its birthright, was like a creamy lily that the sun invites to contribute its breath and perfume to the undying life of the world.

The generous abundance of her passion, without guile or trickery, was like a white flame which penetrated and found response in depths of his own sensuous nature that had never yet been reached.   25

When he touched her breasts they gave themselves up in quivering ecstasy, inviting his lips. Her mouth was a fountain of delight. And when he possessed her, they seemed to swoon together at the very borderland of life's mystery.

He stayed cushioned upon her, breathless, dazed, enervated, with his heart beating like a hammer upon her. With one hand she clasped his head, her lips lightly touching his forehead. The other hand stroked with a soothing rhythm his muscular shoulders.

The growl of the thunder was distant and passing away. The rain beat softly

[2] An exclamation: Goodness!
[3] A holiday commemorating the ascent of the Virgin Mary to heaven. Assumption is also the name of a Louisiana parish (county) where Calixta and Alcée had had a rendezvous in an earlier story.

upon the shingles, inviting them to drowsiness and sleep. But they dared not yield.

The rain was over; and the sun was turning the glistening green world into a palace of gems. Calixta, on the gallery, watched Alcée ride away. He turned and smiled at her with a beaming face; and she lifted her pretty chin in the air and laughed aloud.

III

Bobinôt and Bibi, trudging home, stopped without at the cistern to make them-   30
selves presentable.

"My! Bibi, w'at will yo' mama say! You ought to be ashame'. You oughtn' put on those good pants. Look at 'em! An' that mud on yo' collar! How you got that mud on yo' collar, Bibi? I never saw such a boy!" Bibi was the picture of pathetic resignation. Bobinôt was the embodiment of serious solicitude as he strove to remove from his own person and his son's the signs of their tramp over heavy roads and through wet fields. He scraped the mud off Bibi's bare legs and feet with a stick and carefully removed all traces from his heavy brogans. Then, prepared for the worst—the meeting with an over-scrupulous housewife, they entered cautiously at the back door.

Calixta was preparing supper. She had set the table and was dripping coffee at the hearth. She sprang up as they came in.

"Oh, Bobinôt! You back! My! but I was uneasy. W'ere you been during the rain? An' Bibi? he ain't wet? he ain't hurt?" She had clasped Bibi and was kissing him effusively. Bobinôt's explanations and apologies which he had been composing all along the way, died on his lips as Calixta felt him to see if he were dry, and seemed to express nothing but satisfaction at their safe return.

"I brought you some shrimps, Calixta," offered Bobinôt, hauling the can from his ample side pocket and laying it on the table.

"Shrimps! Oh, Bobinôt! you too good fo' anything!" and she gave him a   35
smacking kiss on the cheek that resounded. "*J'vous réponds,*[4] we'll have a feas' to night! umph-umph!"

Bobinôt and Bibi began to relax and enjoy themselves, and when the three seated themselves at table they laughed much and so loud that anyone might have heard them as far away as Laballière's.

IV

Alcée Laballière wrote to his wife, Clarisse, that night. It was a loving letter, full of tender solicitude. He told her not to hurry back, but if she and the babies liked it at Biloxi, to stay a month longer. He was getting on nicely; and though he missed them, he was willing to bear the separation a while longer—realizing that their health and pleasure were the first things to be considered.

---

[4] I'm telling you.

V

As for Clarisse, she was charmed upon receiving her husband's letter. She and the babies were doing well. The society was agreeable; many of her old friends and acquaintances were at the bay. And the first free breath since her marriage seemed to restore the pleasant liberty of her maiden days. Devoted as she was to her husband, their intimate conjugal life was something which she was more than willing to forego for a while.

So the storm passed and everyone was happy.

For Analysis
1. Aside from the child Bibi, there are four characters in this story—two married couples. How did you respond to each of those characters? What are the sources for your reactions? **2.** How do the characters in the story feel about themselves? About each other? Upon what evidence in the story do you base your response? **3.** Discuss the title of the story.

On Style
1. During the second half of the nineteenth century, certain American writers, including Kate Chopin, evoked a sense of region in their work. What region of the country provides the **setting** for this story? How do you know? **2.** What aspects of this story's **style** contribute to its realism? **3.** Discuss the first part of the story, analyzing the stylistic differences between the first paragraph and the exchange between Bobinôt and Bibi that follows it.

Making Connections
1. Contrast this story with Irwin Shaw's "The Girls in Their Summer Dresses" (p. 952). Which strikes you as more "realistic"? **2.** How might your response to this story differ if it had been written by a man? Explain.

Writing Topic
Write an essay on modern marriage, using this story to support your analysis.

Irwin Shaw   [1913–1984]

The Girls in Their Summer Dresses   1939

Fifth Avenue was shining in the sun when they left the Brevoort.[1] The sun was
warm, even though it was February, and everything looked like Sunday
morning—the buses and the well-dressed people walking slowly in couples and
the quiet buildings with the windows closed.

Michael held Frances' arm tightly as they walked toward Washington Square[2]
in the sunlight. They walked lightly, almost smiling, because they had slept late
and had a good breakfast and it was Sunday. Michael unbuttoned his coat and
let it flap around him in the mild wind.

"Look out," Frances said as they crossed Eighth Street. "You'll break your
neck." Michael laughed and Frances laughed with him.

"She's not so pretty," Frances said. "Anyway, not pretty enough to take a
chance of breaking your neck."

Michael laughed again. "How did you know I was looking at her?"   5

Frances cocked her head to one side and smiled at her husband under the
brim of her hat. "Mike, darling," she said.

"O.K.," he said. "Excuse me."

Frances patted his arm lightly and pulled him along a little faster toward
Washington Square. "Let's not see anybody all day," she said. "Let's just hang
around with each other. You and me. We're always up to our neck in people,
drinking their Scotch or drinking our Scotch; we only see each other in bed. I
want to go out with my husband all day long. I want him to talk only to me and
listen only to me."

"What's to stop us?" Michael asked.

"The Stevensons. They want us to drop by around one o'clock and they'll   10
drive us into the country."

"The cunning Stevensons," Mike said. "Transparent. They can whistle. They
can go driving in the country by themselves."

"Is it a date?"

"It's a date."

Frances leaned over and kissed him on the tip of the ear.

"Darling," Michael said, "this is Fifth Avenue."   15

---

[1] The Brevoort was a New York hotel on lower Fifth Avenue. At the time that this story was written, the Brevoort's bar was famous as a gathering place for literary people.

[2] A park at the south end of Fifth Avenue.

"Let me arrange a program," Frances said. "A planned Sunday in New York for a young couple with money to throw away."

"Go easy."

"First let's go to the Metropolitan Museum of Art," Frances suggested, because Michael had said during the week he wanted to go. "I haven't been there in three years and there're at least ten pictures I want to see again. Then we can take the bus down to Radio City and watch them skate. And later we'll go down to Cavanagh's and get a steak as big as a blacksmith's apron, with a bottle of wine, and after that there's a French picture at the Filmarte that everybody says—say, are you listening to me?"

"Sure," he said. He took his eyes off the hatless girl with the dark hair, cut dancer-style like a helmet, who was walking past him.

"That's the program for the day," Frances said flatly. "Or maybe you'd just   20
rather walk up and down Fifth Avenue."

"No," Michael said. "Not at all."

"You always look at other women," Frances said. "Everywhere. Every damned place we go."

"No, darling," Michael said, "I look at everything. God gave me eyes and I look at women and men in subway excavations and moving pictures and the little flowers of the field. I casually inspect the universe."

"You ought to see the look in your eye," Frances said, "as you casually inspect the universe on Fifth Avenue."

"I'm a happily married man." Michael pressed her elbow tenderly. "Example   25
for the whole twentieth century—Mr. and Mrs. Mike Loomis. Hey, let's have a drink," he said, stopping.

"We just had breakfast."

"Now listen, darling," Mike said, choosing his words with care, "it's a nice day and we both felt good and there's no reason why we have to break it up. Let's have a nice Sunday."

"All right. I don't know why I started this. Let's drop it. Let's have a good time."

They joined hands consciously and walked without talking among the baby carriages and the old Italian men in their Sunday clothes and the young women with Scotties in Washington Square Park.

"At least once a year everyone should go to the Metropolitan Museum of   30
Art," Frances said after a while, her tone a good imitation of the tone she had used at breakfast and at the beginning of their walk. "And it's nice on Sunday. There're a lot of people looking at the pictures and you get the feeling maybe Art isn't on the decline in New York City, after all—"

"I want to tell you something," Michael said very seriously. "I have not touched another woman. Not once. In all the five years."

"All right," Frances said.

"You believe that, don't you?"

"All right."

They walked between the crowded benches, under the scrubby city-park trees.   35

"I try not to notice it," Frances said, "but I feel rotten inside, in my stomach, when we pass a woman and you look at her and I see that look in your eye and that's the way you looked at me the first time. In Alice Maxwell's house. Standing there in the living room, next to the radio, with a green hat on and all those people."

"I remember the hat," Michael said.

"The same look," Frances said. "And it makes me feel bad. It makes me feel terrible."

"Sh-h-h, please, darling, sh-h-h."

"I think I would like a drink now," Frances said.   40

They walked over to a bar on Eighth Street, not saying anything, Michael automatically helping her over curbstones and guiding her past automobiles. They sat near a window in the bar and the sun streamed in and there was a small, cheerful fire in the fireplace. A little Japanese waiter came over and put down some pretzels and smiled happily at them.

"What do you order after breakfast?" Michael asked.

"Brandy, I suppose," Frances said.

"Courvoisier," Michael told the waiter. "Two Courvoisiers."

The waiter came with the glasses and they sat drinking the brandy in the sun-   45
light. Michael finished half his and drank a little water.

"I look at women," he said. "Correct. I don't say it's wrong or right. I look at them. If I pass them on the street and I don't look at them, I'm fooling you, I'm fooling myself."

"You look at them as though you want them," Frances said, playing with her brandy glass. "Every one of them."

"In a way," Michael said, speaking softly and not to his wife, "in a way that's true. I don't do anything about it, but it's true."

"I know it. That's why I feel bad."

"Another brandy," Michael called. "Waiter, two more brandies."   50

He sighed and closed his eyes and rubbed them gently with his fingers. "I love the way women look. One of the things I like best about New York is the battalions of women. When I first came to New York from Ohio that was the first thing I noticed, the million wonderful women, all over the city. I walked around with my heart in my throat."

"A kid," Frances said. "That's a kid's feeling."

"Guess again," Michael said. "Guess again. I'm older now. I'm a man getting near middle age, putting on a little fat, and I still love to walk along Fifth Avenue at three o'clock on the east side of the street between Fiftieth and Fifty-seventh Streets. They're all out then, shopping, in their furs and their crazy hats, everything all concentrated from all over the world into seven blocks—the best furs, the best clothes, the handsomest women, out to spend money and feeling good about it."

The Japanese waiter put the two drinks down, smiling with great happiness.

"Everything is all right?" he asked.   55

"Everything is wonderful," Michael said.

"If it's just a couple of fur coats," Frances said, "and forty-five dollar hats—"

"It's not the fur coats. Or the hats. That's just the scenery for that particular kind of woman. Understand," he said, "you don't have to listen to this."

"I want to listen."

"I like the girls in the offices. Neat with their eyeglasses, smart, chipper, knowing what everything is about. I like the girls on Forty-fourth Street at lunchtime, the actresses, all dressed up on nothing a week. I like the salesgirls in the stores, paying attention to you first because you're a man, leaving the lady customers waiting. I got all this stuff accumulated in me because I've been thinking about it for ten years and now you've asked for it and here it is."

"Go ahead," Frances said.

"When I think of New York City, I think of all the girls on parade in the city. I don't know whether it's something special with me or whether every man in the city walks around with the same feeling inside him, but I feel as though I'm at a picnic in this city. I like to sit near the women in the theatres, the famous beauties who've taken six hours to get ready and look it. And the young girls at the football games, with the red cheeks, and when the warm weather comes, the girls in their summer dresses." He finished his drink. "That's the story."

Frances finished her drink and swallowed two or three times extra. "You say you love me?"

"I love you."

"I'm pretty, too," Frances said. "As pretty as any of them."

"You're beautiful," Michael said.

"I'm good for you," Frances said, pleading. "I've made a good wife, a good housekeeper, a good friend. I'd do any damn thing for you."

"I know," Michael said. He put his hand out and grasped hers.

"You'd like to be free to—" Frances said.

"Sh-h-h."

"Tell the truth." She took her hand away from under his.

Michael flicked the edge of his glass with his finger. "O.K.," he said gently. "Sometimes I feel I would like to be free."

"Well," Frances said, "any time you say."

"Don't be foolish." Michael swung his chair around to her side of the table and patted her thigh.

She began to cry silently into her handkerchief, bent over just enough so that nobody else in the bar would notice. "Someday," she said, crying, "you're going to make a move."

Michael didn't say anything. He sat watching the bartender slowly peel a lemon.

"Aren't you?" Frances asked harshly. "Come on, tell me. Talk. Aren't you?"

"Maybe," Michael said. He moved his chair back again. "How the hell do I know?"

"You know," Frances persisted. "Don't you know?"

"Yes," Michael said after a while, "I know."

Frances stopped crying then. Two or three snuffles into the handkerchief and she put it away and her face didn't tell anything to anybody. "At least do me one favor," she said.

"Sure."

"Stop talking about how pretty this woman is or that one. Nice eyes, nice breasts, a pretty figure, good voice." She mimicked his voice. "Keep it to yourself. I'm not interested."

Michael waved to the waiter. "I'll keep it to myself," he said.

Frances flicked the corners of her eyes. "Another brandy," she told the waiter.   85

"Two," Michael said.

"Yes, ma'am, yes, sir," said the waiter, backing away.

Frances regarded Michael coolly across the table. "Do you want me to call the Stevensons?" she asked. "It'll be nice in the country."

"Sure," Michael said. "Call them."

She got up from the table and walked across the room toward the telephone.   90
Michael watched her walk, thinking what a pretty girl, what nice legs.

For Analysis
1. How does Frances react to Michael's roving eyes? **2.** When Michael admits, "Sometimes I feel I would like to be free" (par. 72), what is Frances's response? Do you feel her response is justified? **3.** Why do you suppose Michael suggests they have a drink? Why does Frances agree? What causes Frances to order a third drink? **4.** What is the significance of their decision to spend the afternoon with the Stevensons? **5.** What effect does the final sentence of the story create?

On Style
1. How does the author's description of Fifth Avenue and the weather affect your initial response to the narrative? **2.** When Frances and Michael order their third brandies, the waiter responds while "backing away." What does that movement suggest?

Making Connections
Have you ever experienced the sort of sexual jealousy that animates this story? Upon reflection, was your response appropriate?

Writing Topic
Kate Chopin's "The Storm" deals with sexual infidelity in marriage. Contrast the relationship between spouses in that story and this.

Edna O'Brien   [b. 1936]

Sin   1994

They were in. In. Mother, father, and daughter. She waited to hear them come in, stayed awake. She would be awake anyhow, because sleep was paying her less and less court as the years went on. Occasionally, she took a tablet, but dreaded being at the mercy of any drug and had a secondary dread of one day not being able to get it, or not being able to afford it. In those wide-awake vigils she prayed or tried to, but prayer, like sleep, was on the wane now, at the very time when she should be pressing her maker for favors. The prayers came only from her lips, not from deep within—she had lost that heartfelt rapport she once had with God. When the prayers became meaningless, she went around her house in her mind and thought of improvements she would make this year or next—new wallpaper in the big room, where the pink was soiled around the window frames, brown smears from all the damp. And then in the vacant room, where apples were stored, the wallpaper had been hung upside-down and had survived the years without anyone knowing that the acorns and the branches were the wrong way around. She might have that replaced, too, just to get the better of those fools who hung it incorrectly. She was a woman who liked to be always in the right. Funny that on the day the paper was hung she had consulted some seer in the city about a certain matter and had been told that she would go home and find these fruits and bobbins the wrong way up, and she did. In other quarters of her house, she was more spartan with her improvements; she thought of maybe a new strip of linoleum inside the hall door, to save the tiles from trampling boots. Scrubbing was hard for her now, hard on her lower back. Then there were little things, like new towels and tea towels and dishcloths— dishcloths smelled of milk no matter how she soaked or boiled them. They had that sour, gone-off smell. Smell was her strongest sense, and when these paying guests arrived that morning she smelled the woman's perfume and the daughter's—identical, and yet nothing else about them seemed alike. The daughter, Samantha, blond and cocksure, screwed up her eyes as if she were thinking something mathematical, when all she was thinking was Look at me, admire me. She touted for their attention. Her hair was her chief weapon—long hair, which she swept along the table as she looked carefully at the wallpaper or at her parents or at a picture over the whatnot, of pussycats who were trying to move the hands of a clock on to feeding time. She kept insisting that her parents have a bite of her toast, or a taste of her porridge, because it was yummy. Her skirt was nothing short of nude—a bib, really, to draw attention to her thighs, like pillars of solid nougat inside her cream lace stockings. The mother was dark and plump and made a habit of touching the daughter whenever she jumped up in one of her fits of simulated exuberance. The father smoked a pipe. He was a handsome man, tall and distant.

They ate breakfast, then had to have a basket packed with hard-boiled eggs and sandwiches for their boating expedition. She explained that they must make their own arrangements for dinner. When they came back, she heard them say "Sh-h-h-, sh-h-h" repeatedly as they climbed the stairs. They used the bathroom in turn. She could tell by their footsteps, and had to concede that they were doing their best to be quiet—that is, until something went crash-crash and the mother went to the rescue of the daughter. She reckoned it was the china tooth mug. She loved that tooth mug, cream with green fluting and little garlands of shamrock, and she wanted to get up and tackle them, but something stopped her. Also, she did not have a dressing gown. Would they be in their dressing gowns? The woman possibly yes, and the man in his shirtsleeves. She would miss the tooth mug, she would mourn it. Her things had become her beloveds, all else gone, or scattered in distant places. She knew—oh yes, she knew—that the love of children gets fainter and fainter, like a garment that's washed and re-washed until it is only a shadow of its original color, its crimson or royal blue. Their daughter, like Samantha, would be like that soon, would skedaddle once she had other interests, men and so forth.

The parents had the blue room, which had been her and her husband's bridal room, the one where her children were born and where as the years went on she slept as little as possible and went only when she was compelled to, when he roared for her. She went to keep him quiet, to keep him off the batter—went in disgust and stayed in disgust and afterward rinsed and washed herself of it all. Five children were enough for any woman. Four scattered children and one dead, and a daughter-in-law who had made her son, her only son, the essence of graspingness. Still, she must not be too hard on them. The girls remembered when they remembered, they sent gifts, especially the one overseas, and next time when asked what she wanted she would say a dressing gown, and then she could confront her lodgers.

She only kept people in summer, partly because they only came then but also because to heat the house in winter would be impossible, as it swallowed up tankers of oil. Moreover, she never kept people for more than two nights, believing they might get forward and start to think the house was theirs, opening wardrobes and doors, making free. Her other reason was more of a secret. She was afraid that she might grow attached to them and ask them to stay. With the takings, she made improvements to the house but never indulged in a luxury herself except for the jams and tins of biscuits for her sweet tooth.

Yes, they were in her marriage bed, a wide bed with an oak headboard that rattled and a rose quilt that she had made during her betrothal, stitching all her dreamings into it. She imagined them, man and wife, lying side by side, the square pouches of the quilt rising and sinking with their breath, and she remembered the clutching of it and the plucking of some of the feathers as her husband made wrathful and unloving love to her. How might it have been with

5

another man, a gentler, more considerate man? The girl was probably not asleep, but shaping her eyebrows or brushing the long spill of hair, brushing it slowly and maybe even examining herself in the mirror, admiring her plump, firm little figure inside her short nightgown. After they went out to dinner, she had peered into their rooms. She did not open their suitcases, as a point of honor, but she studied some of their possessions, the woman's string of pearls, her cosmetics, and her dark-brown hair net, which lay stealthily next to his pipes, pipes of different-colored wood, and a folded swag of mulchy tobacco. Their money, English money, was piled into two little banks—his money and her money, she felt. On the girl's dressing table there was only the hairbrush, cotton buds, and baby oil. The diaphanous nightie was laid out on the pillow and looked lifelike, as if there were a doll inside it.

Sleep would not come. She got up, intending to go look at the broken tooth mug, but as soon as she reached the door something prevented her. She was ashamed of being heard by them. It was as if the house had become theirs and she, the lodger, beholden to them. Something about their being a family and all over each other, and blowing about what a brilliant time they were having galled her. She paced. Pacing was one of the things she did at night, but now she felt that it, too, was wrong—revealing—and so she crept back into her bed and waited for the blessing of sleep. Sleep often came unbeknownst to her. It was not preceded by yawning or drowsiness. There she would be, totting up what guests owed her, taking it and putting it in the big orange bowl where the spoils of the summer were kept, and all of a sudden it would be morning, the sun giving a rich, red-wine glow to the velvet curtains, or the rain pouring down and her little dog, Gigi, on his hind legs, looking up at her window, waiting for her to get up and come down and open the back door and serve him a saucer of tea with milk. Over the years, he had grown more like a human and was undoubtedly her most faithful friend.

With some visitors she found it more difficult to get to sleep. They unnerved her or she began thinking about them, speculating about their lives, their earnings, their happiness, and so forth, and so it was with these three. It was as if she had to be awake, to keep a watch.

Exactly half an hour after they had retired, it happened. She heard a creak, the girl's door opening slowly, and she thought it was bathroom need, but, no, she heard her go toward their room on tiptoe and then she heard a tap, a series of taps, light and playful—not the tapping of a sick or overwrought child, not the tapping of someone disturbed by a mouse or a bumblebee—and in that second she knew it. Her whole body went into spasm. She heard the girl go into their room, and then everything became so silent, the atmosphere so tense, that her hand, jerking her own doorknob, made her jump. She opened her door very softly and moved in their direction, not certain what exactly she would do. The whole house seemed to wait. They were not talking, yet what reached her ears could not be called silence. Something terrible was being enacted in there, a rite of whispering and tittering and lewd laughter. She could not see, yet her eyes seemed to penetrate through the panelled door as if it were sheer glass and she could picture them—hands, mouths, limbs, all searching for one another. They had not dared to put on a light. The girl was probably naked, or else wore her scarf like a sarong, moving with them in their macabre dance, yielding, allowing them to fondle her, the man fondling her in one place, the woman fondling her elsewhere—an orgy of caresses and whispers and sighs that rent the air. Those sighs and whispers magnified.

She would break the door down. It was not enough simply to open it. She would catch them out, the man, lord of his harem, straddled over a girl who was in no way his daughter, and the woman ministering, because that was the only way she could hold on to him. Vile. Vile. There was a poker in there, in the coal scuttle, left since her last confinement, thirty years ago, and she was already picking it up. She would break it on their bare romping bodies. What detained her she could not say. Everything determined that she go in, and yet she waited in some wanton hesitation, as if she were waiting for their smell.

Their exclamations were what sent her scurrying back to her own room, the   10
three pitches of sound so different—the woman's loud and gusty, the girl's helpless, almost as if she were crying, and, sometime later, his, like a jackass down in the woods with his lady love. She sat on the edge of her bed in a simmer. They would have to go in the morning. She would let them know why. She would convey it to them, insinuate that the girl was not their daughter, but she would never know for sure, and that, plus the vile pageant in the dark, would torment her and be a plague on her house until the day she died.

For Analysis

1. How sympathetically is the woman who owns the house presented? **2.** What is the connection between the woman's loss of religious faith noted in the opening paragraph and her opinions about the guests? **3.** In what ways does the woman's past help to explain her reaction to the guests? **4.** Explain the meaning of the final sentence of the story. **5.** How do you interpret the title of the story?

On Style

1. The story is not a first-person narrative; its viewpoint is limited to a **central intelligence**—referred to as "she." Suggest how the story would have been altered had the author used a first-person **narrator**. **2.** Do you think the story would be improved had the narrative been presented chronologically? Explain.

Making Connections

Do you find either Kate Chopin's "The Storm" or O'Brien's story morally offensive? Explain why or why not.

Writing Topics

1. Argue for or against the proposition that the woman who owns the house is justified in her opinions about who the guests are and what they are doing in their room. **2.** Study the **imagery** of the story—perhaps compile a list of images—and comment on how the images manipulate the reader's response. For example, note that in the first paragraph the landlady sees the daughter's thighs as "pillars of solid nougat inside her cream lace stockings."

Raymond Carver   [1938–1988]

What We Talk about When We Talk about Love   1981

M y friend Mel McGinnis was talking. Mel McGinnis is a cardiologist, and sometimes that gives him the right.

The four of us were sitting around his kitchen table drinking gin. Sunlight filled the kitchen from the big window behind the sink. There were Mel and me and his second wife, Teresa—Terri, we called her—and my wife, Laura. We lived in Albuquerque then. But we were all from somewhere else.

There was an ice bucket on the table. The gin and the tonic water kept going around, and we somehow got on the subject of love. Mel thought real love was nothing less than spiritual love. He said he'd spent five years in a seminary before quitting to go to medical school. He said he still looked back on those years in the seminary as the most important years in his life.

Terri said the man she lived with before she lived with Mel loved her so much he tried to kill her. Then Terri said, "He beat me up one night. He dragged me around the living room by my ankles. He kept saying, 'I love you, I love you, you bitch.' He went on dragging me around the living room. My head kept knocking on things." Terri looked around the table. "What do you do with love like that?"

She was a bone-thin woman with a pretty face, dark eyes, and brown hair that   5 hung down her back. She liked necklaces made of turquoise, and long pendant earrings.

"My God, don't be silly. That's not love, and you know it," Mel said. "I don't know what you'd call it, but I sure know you wouldn't call it love."

"Say what you want to, but I know it was," Terri said. "It may sound crazy to you, but it's true just the same. People are different, Mel. Sure, sometimes he may have acted crazy. Okay. But he loved me. In his own way maybe, but he loved me. There was love there, Mel. Don't say there wasn't."

Mel let out his breath. He held his glass and turned to Laura and me. "The man threatened to kill me," Mel said. He finished his drink and reached for the gin bottle. "Terri's a romantic. Terri's of the kick-me-so-I'll-know-you-love-me school. Terri, hon, don't look that way." Mel reached across the table and touched Terri's cheek with his fingers. He grinned at her.

"Now he wants to make up," Terri said.

"Make up what?" Mel said. "What is there to make up? I know what I know.   10 That's all."

"How'd we get started on this subject, anyway?" Terri said. She raised her

961

glass and drank from it. "Mel always has love on his mind," she said. "Don't you, honey?" She smiled, and I thought that was the last of it.

"I just wouldn't call Ed's behavior love. That's all I'm saying, honey," Mel said. "What about you guys?" Mel said to Laura and me. "Does that sound like love to you?"

"I'm the wrong person to ask," I said. "I didn't even know the man. I've only heard his name mentioned in passing. I wouldn't know. You'd have to know the particulars. But I think what you're saying is that love is an absolute."

Mel said, "The kind of love I'm talking about is. The kind of love I'm talking about, you don't try to kill people."

Laura said, "I don't know anything about Ed, or anything about the situation. But who can judge anyone else's situation?"

I touched the back of Laura's hand. She gave me a quick smile. I picked up Laura's hand. It was warm, the nails polished, perfectly manicured. I encircled the broad wrist with my fingers, and I held her.

"When I left, he drank rat poison," Terri said. She clasped her arms with her hands. "They took him to the hospital in Sante Fe. That's where we lived then, about ten miles out. They saved his life. But his gums went crazy from it. I mean they pulled away from his teeth. After that, his teeth stood out like fangs. My God," Terri said. She waited a minute, then let go of her arms and picked up her glass.

"What people won't do!" Laura said.

"He's out of the action now," Mel said. "He's dead."

Mel handed me the saucer of limes. I took a section, squeezed it over my drink, and stirred the ice cubes with my finger.

"It gets worse," Terri said. "He shot himself in the mouth. But he bungled that too. Poor Ed," she said. Terri shook her head.

"Poor Ed nothing," Mel said. "He was dangerous."

Mel was forty-five years old. He was tall and rangy with curly soft hair. His face and arms were brown from the tennis he played. When he was sober, his gestures, all his movements, were precise, very careful.

"He did love me though, Mel. Grant me that," Terri said. "That's all I'm asking. He didn't love me the way you love me. I'm not saying that. But he loved me. You can grant me that, can't you?"

"What do you mean, he bungled it?" I said.

Laura leaned forward with her glass. She put her elbows on the table and held her glass in both hands. She glanced from Mel to Terri and waited with a look of bewilderment on her open face, as if amazed that such things happened to people you were friendly with.

"How'd he bungle it when he killed himself?" I said.

"I'll tell you what happened," Mel said. "He took this twenty-two pistol he'd bought to threaten Terri and me with. Oh, I'm serious, the man was always threatening. You should have seen the way we lived in those days. Like fugitives. I even bought a gun myself. Can you believe it? A guy like me? But I did. I bought one for self-defense and carried it in the glove compartment. Sometimes I'd have to leave the apartment in the middle of the night. To go to the hospital, you know? Terri and I weren't married then, and my first wife had the house and kids, the dog, everything, and Terri and I were living in this apartment here. Sometimes, as I say, I'd get a call in the middle of the night and have to go in to the hospital at two or three in the morning. It'd be dark out there in the parking lot, and I'd break into a sweat before I could even get to my car. I never knew if he was going to come up out of the shrubbery or from behind a car and start shooting. I mean, the man was crazy. He was capable of wiring a bomb, anything. He used to call my service at all hours and say he needed to talk to the doctor, and when I'd return the call, he'd say, 'Son of a bitch, your days are numbered.' Little things like that. It was scary, I'm telling you."

"I still feel sorry for him," Terri said.

"It sounds like a nightmare," Laura said. "But what exactly happened after he   30 shot himself?"

Laura is a legal secretary. We'd met in a professional capacity. Before we knew it, it was a courtship. She's thirty-five, three years younger than I am. In addition to being in love, we like each other and enjoy one another's company. She's easy to be with.

"What happened?" Laura said.

Mel said, "He shot himself in the mouth in his room. Someone heard the shot and told the manager. They came in with a passkey, saw what had happened, and called an ambulance. I happened to be there when they brought him in, alive but past recall. The man lived for three days. His head swelled up to twice the size of a normal head. I'd never seen anything like it, and I hope I never do again. Terri wanted to go in and sit with him when she found out about it. We had a fight over it. I didn't think she should see him like that. I didn't think she should see him, and I still don't."

"Who won the fight?" Laura said.

"I was in the room with him when he died," Terri said. "He never came up   35 out of it. But I sat with him. He didn't have anyone else."

"He was dangerous," Mel said. "If you call that love, you can have it."

"It was love," Terri said. "Sure, it's abnormal in most people's eyes. But he was willing to die for it. He did die for it."

"I sure as hell wouldn't call it love," Mel said. "I mean, no one knows what he did it for. I've seen a lot of suicides, and I couldn't say anyone ever knew what they did it for."

Mel put his hands behind his neck and tilted his chair back. "I'm not interested in that kind of love," he said. "If that's love, you can have it."

Terri said, "We were afraid. Mel even made a will out and wrote to his brother   40 in California who used to be a Green Beret. Mel told him who to look for if something happened to him."

Terri drank from her glass. She said, "But Mel's right—we lived like fugitives. We were afraid. Mel was, weren't you, honey? I even called the police at one

point, but they were no help. They said they couldn't do anything until Ed actually did something. Isn't that a laugh?" Terri said.

She poured the last of the gin into her glass and waggled the bottle. Mel got
up from the table and went to the cupboard. He took down another bottle.

"Well, Nick and I know what love is," Laura said. "For us, I mean," Laura
said. She bumped my knee with her knee. "You're supposed to say something
now," Laura said, and turned her smile on me.

For an answer, I took Laura's hand and raised it to my lips. I made a big production out of kissing her hand. Everyone was amused.

"We're lucky," I said.   45

"You guys," Terri said. "Stop that now. You're making me sick. You're still on
the honeymoon, for God's sake. You're still gaga, for crying out loud. Just wait.
How long have you been together now? How long has it been? A year? Longer
than a year?"

"Going on a year and a half," Laura said, flushed and smiling.

"Oh, now," Terri said. "Wait a while."

She held her drink and gazed at Laura.

"I'm only kidding," Terri said.   50

Mel opened the gin and went around the table with the bottle.

"Here, you guys," he said. "Let's have a toast. I want to propose a toast. A toast
to love. To true love," Mel said.

We touched glasses.

"To love," we said.

Outside in the backyard, one of the dogs began to bark. The leaves of the as-   55
pen that leaned past the window ticked against the glass. The afternoon sun was
like a presence in this room, the spacious light of ease and generosity. We could
have been anywhere, somewhere enchanted. We raised our glasses again and
grinned at each other like children who had agreed on something forbidden.

"I'll tell you what real love is," Mel said. "I mean, I'll give you a good example.
And then you can draw your own conclusions." He poured more gin into his
glass. He added an ice cube and a sliver of lime. We waited and sipped our
drinks. Laura and I touched knees again. I put a hand on her warm thigh and
left it there.

"What do any of us really know about love?" Mel said. "It seems to me we're
just beginners at love. We say we love each other and we do, I don't doubt it. I
love Terri and Terri loves me, and you guys love each other too. You know the
kind of love I'm talking about now. Physical love, that impulse that drives you to
someone special, as well as love of the other person's being, his or her essence,
as it were. Carnal love and, well, call it sentimental love, the day-to-day caring
about the other person. But sometimes I have a hard time accounting for the
fact that I must have loved my first wife too. But I did, I know I did. So I suppose I am like Terri in that regard. Terri and Ed." He thought about it and then
he went on. "There was a time when I thought I loved my first wife more than

life itself. But now I hate her guts. I do. How do you explain that? What happened to that love? What happened to it, is what I'd like to know. I wish someone could tell me. Then there's Ed. Okay, we're back to Ed. He loves Terri so much he tries to kill her and he winds up killing himself." Mel stopped talking and swallowed from his glass. "You guys have been together eighteen months and you love each other. It shows all over you. You glow with it. But you both loved other people before you met each other. You've both been married before, just like us. And you probably loved other people before that too, even. Terri and I have been together five years, been married for four. And the terrible thing, the terrible thing is, but the good thing too, the saving grace, you might say, is that if something happened to one of us—excuse me for saying this—but if something happened to one of us tomorrow I think the other one, the other person, would grieve for a while, you know, but then the surviving party would go out and love again, have someone else soon enough. All this, all of this love we're talking about, it would just be a memory. Maybe not even a memory. Am I wrong? Am I way off base? Because I want you to set me straight if you think I'm wrong. I want to know. I mean, I don't know anything, and I'm the first one to admit it."

"Mel, for God's sake," Terri said. She reached out and took hold of his wrist. "Are you getting drunk? Honey? Are you drunk?"

"Honey, I'm just talking," Mel said. "All right? I don't have to be drunk to say what I think. I mean, we're all just talking, right?" Mel said. He fixed his eyes on her.

"Sweetie, I'm not criticizing," Terri said.   60

She picked up her glass.

"I'm not on call today," Mel said. "Let me remind you of that. I am not on call," he said.

"Mel, we love you," Laura said.

Mel looked at Laura. He looked at her as if he could not place her, as if she was not the woman she was.

"Love you too, Laura," Mel said. "And you, Nick, love you too. You know   65
something?" Mel said. "You guys are our pals," Mel said.

He picked up his glass.

Mel said, "I was going to tell you about something. I mean, I was going to prove a point. You see, this happened a few months ago, but it's still going on right now, and it ought to make us feel ashamed when we talk like we know what we're talking about when we talk above love."

"Come on now," Terri said. "Don't talk like you're drunk if you're not drunk."

"Just shut up for once in your life," Mel said very quietly. "Will you do me a favor and do that for a minute? So as I was saying, there's this old couple who had this car wreck out on the interstate. A kid hit them and they were all torn to shit and nobody was giving them much chance to pull through."

Terri looked at us and then back at Mel. She seemed anxious, or maybe that's   70
too strong a word.

Mel was handing the bottle around the table.

"I was on call that night," Mel said. "It was May or maybe it was June. Terri and I had just sat down to dinner when the hospital called. There'd been this thing out on the interstate. Drunk kid, teenager, plowed his dad's pickup into this camper with this old couple in it. They were up in their mid-seventies, that couple. The kid—eighteen, nineteen, something—he was DOA. Taken the steering wheel through his sternum. The old couple, they were alive, you understand. I mean, just barely. But they had everything. Multiple fractures, internal injuries, hemorrhaging, contusions, lacerations, the works, and they each of them had themselves concussions. They were in a bad way, believe me. And, of course, their age was two strikes against them. I'd say she was worse off than he was. Ruptured spleen along with everything else. Both kneecaps broken. But they'd been wearing their seatbelts and, God knows, that's what saved them for the time being."

"Folks, this is an advertisement for the National Safety Council," Terri said. "This is your spokesman, Dr. Melvin R. McGinnis, talking." Terri laughed. "Mel," she said, "sometimes you're just too much. But I love you, hon," she said.

"Honey, I love you," Mel said.

He leaned across the table. Terri met him halfway. They kissed.   75

"Terri's right," Mel said as he settled himself again. "Get those seatbelts on. But seriously, they were in some shape, those oldsters. By the time I got down there, the kid was dead, as I said. He was off in a corner, laid out on a gurney. I took one look at the old couple and told the ER nurse to get me a neurologist and an orthopedic man and a couple of surgeons down there right away."

He drank from his glass. "I'll try to keep this short," he said. "So we took the two of them up to the OR and worked like fuck on them most of the night. They had these incredible reserves, those two. You see that once in a while. So we did everything that could be done, and toward morning we're giving them a fifty-fifty chance, maybe less than that for her. So here they are, still alive the next morning. So, okay, we move them into the ICU, which is where they both kept plugging away at it for two weeks, hitting it better and better on all the scopes. So we transfer them out to their own room."

Mel stopped talking. "Here," he said, "let's drink this cheapo gin the hell up. Then we're going to dinner, right? Terri and I know a new place. That's where we'll go, to this new place we know about. But we're not going until we finish up this cut-rate, lousy gin."

Terri said, "We haven't actually eaten there yet. But it looks good. From the outside, you know."

"I like food," Mel said. "If I had it to do all over again, I'd be a chef, you   80
know? Right, Terri?" Mel said.

He laughed. He fingered the ice in his glass.

"Terri knows," he said. "Terri can tell you. But let me say this. If I could come back again in a different life, a different time and all, you know what? I'd like to come back as a knight. You were pretty safe wearing all that armor. It was all right being a knight until gunpowder and muskets and pistols came along."

"Mel would like to ride a horse and carry a lance," Terri said.

"Carry a woman's scarf with you everywhere," Laura said.

"Or just a woman," Mel said.   85

"Shame on you," Laura said.

Terri said, "Suppose you came back as a serf. The serfs didn't have it so good in those days," Terri said.

"The serfs never had it good," Mel said. "But I guess even the knights were vessels to someone. Isn't that the way it worked? But then everyone is always a vessel to someone. Isn't that right? Terri? But what I liked about knights, besides their ladies, was that they had that suit of armor, you know, and they couldn't get hurt very easy. No cars in those days, you know? No drunk teenagers to tear into your ass."

"Vassals," Terri said.

"What?" Mel said.   90

"Vassals," Terri said. "They were called vassals, not vessels."

"Vassals, vessels," Mel said, "what the fuck's the difference? You knew what I meant anyway. All right," Mel said. "So I'm not educated. I learned my stuff. I'm a heart surgeon, sure, but I'm just a mechanic. I go in and I fuck around and I fix things. Shit," Mel said.

"Modesty doesn't become you," Terri said.

"He's just a humble sawbones," I said. "But sometimes they suffocated in all that armor, Mel. They'd even have heart attacks if it got too hot and they were too tired and worn out. I read somewhere that they'd fall off their horses and not be able to get up because they were too tired to stand with all that armor on them. They got trampled by their own horses sometimes."

"That's terrible," Mel said. "That's a terrible thing, Nicky. I guess they'd just   95
lay there and wait until somebody came along and made a shish kebab out of them."

"Some other vessel," Terri said.

"That's right," Mel said. "Some vassal would come along and spear the bastard in the name of love. Or whatever the fuck it was they fought over in those days."

"Same things we fight over these days," Terri said.

Laura said, "Nothing's changed."

The color was still high in Laura's cheeks. Her eyes were bright. She brought   100
her glass to her lips.

Mel poured himself another drink. He looked at the label closely as if studying a long row of numbers. Then he slowly put the bottle down on the table and slowly reached for the tonic water.

"What about the old couple?" Laura said. "You didn't finish that story you started."

Laura was having a hard time lighting her cigarette. Her matches kept going out.

The sunshine inside the room was different now, changing, getting thinner. But the leaves outside the window were still shimmering, and I stared at the pattern they made on the panes and on the Formica counter. They weren't the same patterns, of course.

"What about the old couple?" I said. 105

"Older but wiser," Terri said.

Mel stared at her.

Terri said, "Go on with your story, hon. I was only kidding. Then what happened?"

"Terri, sometimes," Mel said.

"Please, Mel," Terri said. "Don't always be so serious, sweetie. Can't you take 110 a joke?"

"Where's the joke?" Mel said.

He held his glass and gazed steadily at his wife.

"What happened?" Laura said.

Mel fastened his eyes on Laura. He said, "Laura, if I didn't have Terri and if I didn't love her so much, and if Nick wasn't my best friend, I'd fall in love with you, I'd carry you off, honey," he said.

"Tell your story," Terri said. "Then we'll go to that new place, okay?" 115

"Okay," Mel said. "Where was I?" he said. He stared at the table and then he began again.

"I dropped in to see each of them every day, sometimes twice a day if I was up doing other calls anyway. Casts and bandages, head to foot, the both of them. You know, you've seen it in the movies. That's just the way they looked, just like in the movies. Little eye-holes and nose-holes and mouth-holes. And she had to have her legs slung up on top of it. Well, the husband was very depressed for the longest while. Even after he found out that his wife was going to pull through, he was still very depressed. Not about the accident, though. I mean, the accident was one thing, but it wasn't everything. I'd get up to his mouth-hole, you know, and he'd say no, it wasn't the accident exactly but it was because he couldn't see her through his eye-holes. He said that was what was making him feel so bad. Can you imagine? I'm telling you, the man's heart was breaking because he couldn't turn his goddamn head and *see* his goddamn wife."

Mel looked around the table and shook his head at what he was going to say.

"I mean, it was killing the old fart just because he couldn't *look* at the fucking woman."

We all looked at Mel. 120

"Do you see what I'm saying?" he said.

Maybe we were a little drunk by then. I know it was hard keeping things in focus. The light was draining out of the room, going back through the window where it had come from. Yet nobody made a move to get up from the table to turn on the overhead light.

"Listen," Mel said. "Let's finish this fucking gin. There's about enough left here for one shooter all around. Then let's go eat. Let's go to the new place."

"He's depressed," Terri said. "Mel, why don't you take a pill?"

Mel shook his head. "I've taken everything there is."   125

"We all need a pill now and then," I said.

"Some people are born needing them," Terri said.

She was using her finger to rub at something on the table. Then she stopped rubbing.

"I think I want to call my kids," Mel said. "Is that all right with everybody? I'll call my kids," he said.

Terri said, "What if Marjorie answers the phone? You guys, you've heard us   130
on the subject of Marjorie? Honey, you know you don't want to talk to Marjorie. It'll make you feel even worse."

"I don't want to talk to Marjorie," Mel said. "But I want to talk to my kids."

"There isn't a day goes by that Mel doesn't say he wishes she'd get married again. Or else die," Terri said. "For one thing," Terri said, "she's bankrupting us. Mel says it's just to spite him that she won't get married again. She has a boyfriend who lives with her and the kids, so Mel is supporting the boyfriend too."

"She's allergic to bees," Mel said. "If I'm not praying she'll get married again, I'm praying she'll get herself stung to death by a swarm of fucking bees."

"Shame on you," Laura said.

"Bzzzzzzz," Mel said, turning his fingers into bees and buzzing them at Terri's   135
throat. Then he let his hands drop all the way to his sides.

"She's vicious," Mel said. "Sometimes I think I'll go up there dressed like a beekeeper. You know, that hat that's like a helmet with the plate that comes down over your face, the big gloves, and the padded coat? I'll knock on the door and let loose a hive of bees in the house. But first I'd make sure the kids were out, of course."

He crossed one leg over the other. It seemed to take him a lot of time to do it. Then he put both feet on the floor and leaned forward, elbows on the table, his chin cupped in his hands.

"Maybe I won't call the kids, after all. Maybe it isn't such a hot idea. Maybe we'll just go eat. How does that sound?"

"Sounds fine to me," I said. "Eat or not eat. Or keep drinking. I could head right on out into the sunset."

"What does that mean, honey?" Laura said.   140

"It just means what I said," I said. "It means I could just keep going. That's all it means."

"I could eat something myself," Laura said. "I don't think I've ever been so hungry in my life. Is there something to nibble on?"

"I'll put out some cheese and crackers," Terri said.

But Terri just sat there. She did not get up to get anything.

Mel turned his glass over. He spilled it out on the table.   145

"Gin's gone," Mel said.

Terri said, "Now what?"

I could hear my heart beating. I could hear everyone's heart. I could hear the human noise we sat there making, not one of us moving, not even when the room went dark.

For Analysis

1. How would you characterize the relationship between Mel and Terri? Between Nick and Laura? **2.** What is your reaction to Mel? Is he likable? What does his profession—a scientist and a cardiologist—represent? **3.** Do you agree with Mel or Terri about Ed? Explain. **4.** What is the significance of Mel's account of the old couple injured in an accident? **5.** Do Mel's feelings about his ex-wife parallel Ed's feelings about Terri? Explain.

On Style

1. The story begins in the sunlight of midday and ends in darkness. How does this transition affect our understanding of what the story says about love and marriage? **2.** Identify the elements in Carver's style that suggest Mel's increasing drunkenness. **3.** Are the assertions in the last paragraph literal or **figurative**? Explain.

Making Connections

1. Have you ever come to hate someone you had once loved, or wanted to injure someone you once cherished? Given the circumstances, can you justify your feelings? **2.** Compare the relationships between Mel and Marjorie, Terri and Ed, with that of Harvey and Susu in Stephanie Vaughn's "Other Women" (p. 979). What attitudes about marriage and divorce do these ex-spouses reveal?

Writing Topic

In an essay, examine the various relationships in the story: Nick and Laura, Mel and Terri, Terri and Ed, Mel and his ex-wife Marjorie, and the injured old couple. Conclude with a comment on "what we talk about when we talk about love."

Barbara Neely   [b. 1941]

Spilled Salt   1990

"I'm home, Ma."

Myrna pressed down hard on the doorknob and stared blankly up into Kenny's large brown eyes and freckled face so much like her own he was nearly her twin. But he was taller than she remembered. Denser.

He'd written to say he was getting out. She hadn't answered his letter, hoping her lack of response would keep him away.

"You're here." She stepped back from the door, pretending not to see him reach out and try to touch her.

But a part of her had leaped to life at the sight of him. No matter what, she   5 was glad he hadn't been maimed or murdered in prison. He at least looked whole and healthy of body. She hoped it was a sign that he was all right inside, too.

She tried to think of something to say as they stood staring at each other in the middle of the living room. A fly buzzed against the window screen in a desperate attempt to get out.

"Well, Ma, how've you—"

"I'll fix you something to eat," Myrna interrupted. "I know you must be starved for decent cooking." She rushed from the room as though a meal were already in the process of burning.

For a moment she was lost in her own kitchen. The table, with its dented metal legs, the green-and-white cotton curtains, and the badly battered coffeepot were all familiar-looking strangers. She took a deep breath and leaned against the back of a chair.

In the beginning she'd flinched from the very word. She couldn't even think   10 it, let alone say it. Assault, attack, molest, anything but rape. Anyone but her son, her bright and funny boy, her high school graduate.

At the time, she'd been sure it was a frame-up on the part of the police. They did things like that. It was in the newspapers every day. Or the girl was trying to get revenge because he hadn't shown any interest in her. Kenny's confession put paid to all those speculations.

She'd have liked to believe that remorse had made him confess. But she knew better. He'd simply told the wrong lie. If he'd said he'd been with the girl but it hadn't been rape, he might have built a case that someone would have believed—although she didn't know how he could have explained away the wound on her neck where he'd held his knife against her throat to keep her docile. Instead, he'd claimed not to have offered her a ride home from the bar where she worked, never to have had her in his car. He'd convinced Myrna. So thoroughly convinced her that she'd fainted dead away when confronted with the semen, fiber, and hair evidence the police quickly collected from his car, and the word of the woman who reluctantly came forth to say she'd seen Kenny ushering Crystal Roberts into his car on the night Crystal was raped.

Only then had Kenny confessed. He'd said he'd been doing the girl a favor by offering her a ride home. In return, she'd teased and then refused him, he'd said. "I lost my head," he'd said.

"I can't sleep. I'm afraid to sleep." The girl had spoken in barely a whisper. The whole courtroom had seemed to tilt as everyone leaned toward her. "Every night he's there in my mind, making me go through it all over again, and again, and again."

Was she free now that Kenny had done his time? Or was she flinching from   15
hands with short, square fingers, and crying when the first of September came near? Myrna moved around the kitchen like an old, old woman with bad feet.

After Kenny had confessed, Myrna spent days that ran into weeks rifling through memories of the past she shared with him, searching for some incident, some trait or series of events that would explain why he'd done such a thing. She'd tried to rationalize his actions with circumstances: Kenny had seen his father beat her. They'd been poorer than dirt. And when Kenny had just turned six, she'd finally found the courage to leave Buddy to raise their son alone. What had she really known about raising a child? What harm might she have done out of ignorance, out of impatience and concentration on warding off the pains of her own life?

Still, she kept stumbling over the knowledge of other boys, from far worse circumstances, with mothers too tired and worried to do more than strike out at them. Yet those boys had managed to grow up and not do the kind of harm Kenny had done. The phrases "I lost my head," and "doing the girl a favor," reverberated through her brain, mocking her, making her groan out loud and startle people around her.

Myrna dragged herself around the room, turning eggs, bacon, milk, and margarine into a meal. In the beginning the why of Kenny's crime was like a tapeworm in her belly, consuming all her strength and sustenance, all her attention. In the first few months of his imprisonment she'd religiously paid a neighbor to drive her the long distance to the prison each visiting day. The visits were as much for her benefit as for his.

"But why?" she'd kept asking him, just as she'd asked him practically every day since he'd confessed.

He would only say that he knew he'd done wrong. As the weeks passed, si-   20
lence became his only response—a silence that had remained intact despite questions like: "Would you have left that girl alone if I'd bought a shotgun and blown your daddy's brains out after the first time he hit me in front of you?" and, "Is there a special thrill you feel when you make a woman ashamed of her sex?" and, "Was this the first time? The second? The last?"

Perhaps silence was best, now, after so long. Anything could happen if she let those five-year-old questions come rolling out of her mouth. Kenny might begin to question her, might ask her what there was about her mothering that made him want to treat a woman like a piece of toilet paper. And what would she say to that?

It was illness that had finally put an end to her visits with him. She'd written the first letter—a note really—to say she was laid up with the flu. A hacking cough had lingered. She hadn't gotten her strength back for nearly two months. By that time their correspondence was established. Letters full of: How are you? I'm fine. . . . The weather is . . . The print shop is . . . The dress I made for Mrs. Rothstein was . . . were so much more manageable than those silence-laden visits. And she didn't have to worry about making eye contact with Kenny in a letter.

Now Myrna stood staring out the kitchen window while Kenny ate his bacon and eggs. The crisp everydayness of clothes flapping on the line surprised her. A leaf floated into her small cemented yard and landed on a potted pansy. Outside, nothing had changed; the world was still in spring.

"I can't go through this again," she mouthed soundlessly to the breeze.

"Come talk to me, Ma," her son called softly around a mouthful of food. 25

Myrna turned to look at him. He smiled an egg-flecked smile she couldn't return. She wanted to ask him what he would do now, whether he had a job lined up, whether he planned to stay long. But she was afraid of his answers, afraid of how she might respond if he said he had no job, no plans, no place to stay except with her and that he hadn't changed in any important way.

"I'm always gonna live with you, Mommy," he'd told her when he was a child. "Always." At the time, she'd wished it was true, that they could always be together, she and her sweet, chubby boy. Now the thought frightened her.

"Be right back," she mumbled, and scurried down the hall to the bathroom. She eased the lock over so that it made barely a sound.

"He's my son!" she hissed at the drawn woman in the mirror. Perspiration dotted her upper lip and glistened around her hair line.

"My son!" she repeated pleadingly. But the words were not as powerful as the 30 memory of Crystal Roberts sitting in the courtroom, her shoulders hunched and her head hung down, as though she were the one who ought to be ashamed. Myrna wished him never born, before she flushed the toilet and unlocked the door.

In the kitchen Kenny had moved to take her place by the window. His dishes littered the table. He'd spilled the salt, and there were crumbs on the floor.

"It sure is good to look out the window and see something besides guard towers and cons." Kenny stretched, rubbed his belly, and turned to face her.

"It's good to see you, Ma." His eyes were soft and shiny.

Oh, Lord! Myrna moaned to herself. She turned her back to him and began carrying his dirty dishes to the sink: first the plate, then the cup, the knife, fork, and spoon, drawing out the chore.

"This place ain't got as much room as the old place," she told him while she   35
made dishwater in the sink.

"It's fine, Ma, just fine."

Oh, Lord, Myrna prayed.

Kenny came to lean against the stove to her right. She dropped a knife and
made the dishwater too cold.

"Seen Dad?"

"Where and why would I see *him?*" She tried to put ice in her voice. It   40
trembled.

"Just thought you might know where he is." Kenny moved back to the window.

Myrna remembered the crippling shock of Buddy's fist in her groin and
scoured Kenny's plate and cup with a piece of steel wool before rinsing them in
scalding water.

"Maybe I'll hop a bus over to the old neighborhood. See some of the guys,
how things have changed."

He paced the floor behind her. Myrna sensed his uneasiness and was startled
by a wave of pleasure at his discomfort.

After he'd gone, she fixed herself a large gin and orange juice and carried it   45
into the living room. She flicked on the TV and sat down to stare at it. After two
minutes of frenetic, over-bright commercials, she got up and turned it off again.
Outside, children screamed each other to the finish line of a footrace. She remembered that Kenny had always liked to run. So had she. But he'd had more
childhood than she'd had. She'd been hired out as a mother's helper by the time
she was twelve, and pregnant and married at sixteen. She didn't begrudge him
his childhood fun. It just seemed so wasted now.

Tears slid down her face and salted her drink. Tears for the young Myrna who
hadn't understood that she was raising a boy who needed special handling to
keep him from becoming a man she didn't care to know. Tears for Kenny who
was so twisted around inside that he could rape a woman. Myrna drained her
gin, left Kenny a note reminding him to leave her door key on the kitchen table,
and went to bed.

Of course, she was still awake when he came in. He bumped into the coffee
table, ran water in the bathroom sink for a long time, then quiet. Myrna lay
awake in the dark blue-gray night listening to the groan of the refrigerator, the
hiss of the hot-water heater, and the rumble of large trucks on a distant street.
He made no sound where he lay on the opened-out sofa, surrounded by her
sewing machine, dress dummy, marking tape, and pins.

When sleep finally came, it brought dreams of walking down brilliantly lit
streets, hand in hand with a boy about twelve who looked, acted, and talked like
Kenny but who she knew with certainty was not her son, at the same time she
also knew he could be no one else.

She woke to a cacophony of church bells. It was late. Too late to make it to
church service. She turned her head to look at the crucifix hanging by her bed
and tried to pray, to summon up that feeling of near weightlessness that came
over her in those moments when she was able to free her mind of all else and

give herself over to prayer. Now nothing came but a dull ache in the back of her throat.

She had begun attending church regularly after she stopped visiting Kenny. His refusal to respond to her questions made it clear she'd have to seek answers elsewhere. She'd decided to talk to Father Giles. He'd been at St. Mark's, in their old neighborhood, before she and Kenny had moved there. He'd seen Kenny growing up. Perhaps he'd noticed something, understood something about the boy, about her, that would explain what she could not understand.

"It's God's will, my child—put it in His hands," he'd urged, awkwardly patting her arm and averting his eyes.

Myrna took his advice wholeheartedly. She became quite adept at quieting the questions boiling in her belly with, "His will," or "My cross to bear." Many nights she'd "Our Fathered" herself to sleep. Acceptance of Kenny's inexplicable act became a test God had given her. One she passed by visiting the sick, along with other women from the church; working on the neighborhood cleanup committee; avoiding all social contact with men. With sex. She put "widowed" on job applications and never mentioned a son to new people she met. Once she'd moved away from the silent accusation of their old apartment, prayer and good works became a protective shield separating her from the past.

Kenny's tap on her door startled her back to the present. She cleared her throat and straightened the covers before calling to him to come in.

A rich, aromatic steam rose from the coffee he'd brought her. The toast was just the right shade of brown, and she was sure that when she cracked the poached egg it would be cooked exactly to her liking. Not only was everything perfectly prepared, it was the first time she'd had breakfast in bed since he'd been arrested. Myrna couldn't hold back the tears or the flood of memories of many mornings, just so: him bending over her with a breakfast tray.

"You wait on people in the restaurant all day and sit up all night making other people's clothes. You need some waiting on, too."

Had he actually said that, this man as a boy? Could this man have been such a boy? Myrna nearly tilted the tray in her confusion.

"I need to brush my teeth." She averted her face and reached for her bathrobe.

But she couldn't avoid her eyes in the medicine cabinet mirror, eyes that reminded her that despite what Kenny had done, she hadn't stopped loving him. But her love didn't need his company. It thrived only on memories of him that were more than four years old. It was as much a love remembered as a living thing. But it was love, nonetheless. Myrna pressed her clenched fist against her lips and wondered if love was enough. She stayed in the bathroom until she heard him leave her bedroom and turn on the TV in the living room.

When he came back for the tray, she told him she had a sick headache and had decided to stay in bed. He was immediately sympathetic, fetching aspirin and a cool compress for her forehead, offering to massage her neck and temples, to lower the blinds and block out the bright morning sun. Myrna told him she wanted only to rest.

All afternoon she lay on her unmade bed, her eyes on the ceiling or idly roam-   60
ing the room, her mind moving across the surface of her life, poking at old
wounds, so amazingly raw after all these years. First there'd been Buddy. He'd
laughed at her country ways and punched her around until he'd driven her and
their child into the streets. But at least she was rid of him. Then there was his
son. Her baby. He'd tricked a young woman into getting into his car where he
proceeded to ruin a great portion of her life. Now he'd come back to spill salt in
her kitchen.

I'm home, Ma, homema, homema. His words echoed in her inner ear and
made her heart flutter. Her neighbors would want to know where he'd been all
this time and why. Fear and disgust would creep into their faces and voices. Her
nights would be full of listening. Waiting.

And she would have to live with the unblanketed reality that whatever anger
and meanness her son held toward the world, he had chosen a woman to take it
out on.

A woman.

Someone like me, she thought, like Great Aunt Faye, or Valerie, her eight-
year-old niece; like Lucille, her oldest friend, or Dr. Ramsey, her dentist. A
woman like all the women who'd helped feed, clothe, and care for Kenny;
who'd tried their damnedest to protect him from as much of the ugly and awful
in life as they could; who'd taught him to ride a bike and cross the street. All
women. From the day she'd left Buddy, not one man had done a damned thing
for Kenny. Not one.

And he might do it again, she thought. The idea sent Myrna rolling back and   65
forth across the bed as though she could actually escape her thoughts. She'd allowed herself to believe she was done with such thoughts. Once she accepted
Kenny's crime as the will of God, she immediately saw that it wouldn't have
made any difference how she'd raised him if this was God's unfathomable plan
for him. It was a comforting idea, one that answered her question of why and
how her much-loved son could be a rapist. One that answered the question of
the degree of her responsibility for Kenny's crime by clearing her of all possible
blame. One that allowed her to forgive him. Or so she'd thought.

Now she realized all her prayers, all her studied efforts to accept and forgive
were like blankets thrown on a forest fire. All it took was the small breeze created by her opening the door to her only child to burn those blankets to cinders
and release her rage—as wild and fierce as the day he'd confessed.

She closed her eyes and saw her outraged self dash wildly into the living room
to scream imprecations in his face until her voice failed. Specks of froth gathered at the corners of her mouth. Her flying spit peppered his face. He cringed
before her, his eyes full of shame as he tore at his own face and chest in self-
loathing.

Yet, even as she fantasized, she knew Kenny could no more be screamed into
contrition than Crystal or any woman could be bullied into willing sex. And
what, in fact, was there for him to say or do that would satisfy her? The response

she really wanted from him was not available: there was no way he could become the boy he'd been before that night four years ago.

No more than I can treat him as if he were that boy, she thought.

And the thought stilled her. She lay motionless, considering.   70

When she rose from her bed, she dragged her old green Samsonite suitcase out from the back of the closet. She moved with the easy, effortless grace of someone who knows what she is doing and feels good about it. Without even wiping off the dust, she plopped the suitcase on the bed. When she lifted the lid, the smell of leaving and good-bye flooded the room and quickened her pulse. For the first time in two days, her mouth moved in the direction of a smile.

She hurried from dresser drawer to closet, choosing her favorites: the black two-piece silk knit dress she'd bought on sale, her comfortable gray shoes, the lavender sweater she'd knitted as a birthday present to herself but had never worn, both her blue and her black slacks, the red crepe blouse she'd made to go with them, and the best of her underwear. She packed in a rush, as though her bus or train were even now pulling out of the station.

When she'd packed her clothes, Myrna looked around the room for other necessary items. She gathered up her comb and brush and the picture of her mother from the top of her bureau, then walked to the wall on the left side of her bed and lifted down the shiny metal and wooden crucifix that hung there. She ran her finger down the slim, muscular body. The Aryan plaster-of-Paris Christ seemed to writhe in bittersweet agony. Myrna stared at the crucifix for a few moments, then gently hung it back on the wall.

When she'd finished dressing, she sat down in the hard, straight-backed chair near the window to think through her plan. Kenny tapped at her door a number of times until she was able to convince him that she was best left alone and would be fine in the morning. When dark came, she waited for the silence of sleep, then quietly left her room. She set her suitcase by the front door, tiptoed by Kenny, where he slept on the sofa, and went into the kitchen. By the glow from the back alley streetlight, she wrote him a note and propped it against the sugar bowl:

> Dear Kenny,
>   I'm sorry. I just can't be your mother right now. I will be back in one week. Please be gone. Much love, Myrna.

Kenny flinched and frowned in his sleep as the front door clicked shut.

For Analysis

1. If Kenny had been convicted of some other crime—say, burglary—would his mother have responded differently to his return? Explain. **2.** What effect does Kenny's serving his mother breakfast in bed and ministering to her "headache" have on your assessment of his character? **3.** What do you think is the significance of the spilled salt? **4.** Do you believe that Myrna's parenting was somehow responsible for Kenny's crime? Explain.

On Style
1. Though this story begins with Kenny's homecoming from prison, it includes a great deal of information about the family's past. How does the author get that information into the story? **2.** Consider the **point of view** from which the story is told. How might the story be different if other viewpoints were used?

Making Connections
Not all destructive behavior is criminal. Have you been the victim or the source of any kind of destructive behavior? Were you able to reestablish some viable connection with your tormentor or your victim? Explain.

Writing Topics
1. Explain the relevance of Buddy's abusive behavior to Kenny's crime. **2.** Though Myrna has become religious, she cannot forgive Kenny. Discuss the relationship between her religiousness and her understanding of her son's behavior.

Stephanie Vaughn   [b. 1943]

Other Women   1990

Suddenly the world is composed of infinitely divisible parts, and things, it seems, grow bigger as they grow smaller. An atom, once a tiny creature, is now a giant compared to a quark. And inside the quark, who knows? Maybe a whole universe of colliding specks, some of them red-haired, some blond, some sleek and dusky skinned, some of them with silicone implants, and some of the plainer ones, like me, still going to the shopping center in thrift-shop shoes.

Harvey has a former wife named Susu, and who am I? A single woman and not getting any younger: I can settle for a compromise.

Harvey's former wife has given us both lice, serially, of course, first to Harvey, who passed them right along to me. For the two years since the divorce she's been living in Italy, where she uses the money from the sale of their house to finance the reinvention of her face and figure—a thinner nose and bigger breasts. Also thicker eyelashes—three hundred dollars per transplant from an unspecified part of her body. For two weeks now, she has been sleeping on Harvey's sofa, but, you know, as my friend Lila likes to say, people who did it once can do it again, and anyway with husbands and wives there's always the long good-bye. "Smile," Lila says. "Keep your sense of humor. Everything will be all right."

"She was my wife," Harvey says, as we drive around the shopping center looking for a space near the self-serve drugstore. "I was married to her," he says, enunciating the word *married* as if it were part of a foreign language I have not yet mastered.

"It's certainly a comfort to know these are just postconnubial crabs," I say, and   5
Harvey laughs.

He stops the car in a loading zone and hunches over the wheel like a getaway driver. When I push through the plate-glass door I look back and see him glancing over his shoulder for signs of people who will recognize us and, with their extrasensory perception, discern immediately that we are on a shady errand. At the rear of the store I find what I am looking for, a selection of colorful boxes advertising a cure for certain skin conditions and, in smaller print, for three different kinds of lice infestation. These boxes are prominently displayed next to an arrangement of condoms and spermicidal jellies, and free pamphlets describing sexually transmitted diseases. Next to them is a line of eight people, most of them well-groomed older women waiting for their prescriptions. I decide to linger near cough remedies and hemorrhoid preparations, but now here come two more people to the prescription line.

979

"Take me to the Women's Health Collective," I tell Harvey back in the car. "We need the privacy of a prescription."

"You know you can get these things off of toilets now," he says. "You can even get them off of sofas and chairs in even very clean houses."

"We know where we got these, Harvey."

"Okay, you take the wheel, and I'll go in."   10

Now it's my turn to drive around the shopping center, through the clots of Saturday morning traffic and fearful pedestrians. This is the very place where Harvey and I met just nine months ago only moments after I hit his parked car, and now here we are raising a family of tiny creatures.

"I was daydreaming," I said. "I didn't think to look before I made my cut."

"It's my fault," he said. "I parked too close." It was his voice that attracted me to him first, rich and golden like oak turned to sound, a big, solid voice a person could lean against. Then there was his height, six feet four inches of him; even now I think there must be enough of Harvey to go around, while there is so little of me that when I offer affection to someone, I feel as if I am handing over some of my very cells. Harvey loves everyone, and I love only Harvey.

"I don't know much about small cars," I told him. I was driving the enormous old Ford I had had since college. "Is yours a Datsun or a Toyota?"

"It's an Audi," he said, and then he added, before I had the time to become   15
depressed by the prospect of increased insurance premiums, "Don't worry. I'm very handy. I think I can knock out that dent with a hammer."

Now he stands by the curb in front of the drugstore, a huge man with a very small sack in his hand. "I hope you got enough for three," I say. "Well," he says, "I ran into someone from the office. I had to buy this instead." Inside the sack is a bottle of dandruff shampoo.

"Why can't we get Susu to do this?" I say as we enter the freeway traffic on our way to the Women's Health Collective, which is twelve miles from here and suitably anonymous. I love to say the name "Susu." I say it so that the name sounds ridiculous, and it helps me to think of Susu as a ridiculous person instead of a lovesick woman just like me. Every morning for two weeks Susu has been going into the bathroom with ordinary, sleep-flattened hair and emerging an hour later with a rococo tangle of back-combed frizzes and knotted tendrils. "Her hair looks like a place where small animals go to browse in the night," I say to Harvey. "But what am I saying? Her hair *is* a place where small animals go to browse in the night."

"She's always on the verge of a nervous collapse," Harvey says.

This much I know about the marriage. Susu took many weight-reducing pills and cried a great deal, while Harvey was complimentary and apologetic. When Susu was angry, she threw plates. When Harvey was angry, he went to his office and spent the night designing small houses that will never be built—modular units for the common people, each unit embellished with a medieval detail. "But who wants lancet windows when they can have a second bathroom instead?" Harvey likes to say, making the houses sound like a fool's invention. But the houses—and there are dozens of them now—are his secret hopes, the places where he can curl up in his mind's eye when times get bad.

"Look," Harvey says. "It's not like this is AIDS or anything. It's not even her- 20 pes. It's not even a urinary tract infection."

My friend Lila is an engineer who would like to be an antiques dealer or maybe the curator of a small museum. "I think I missed my century," she likes to say. "I think I would have been very happy doing needlepoint pictures in 1750."

Instead Lila has worked for ten years in the semiconductor industry develop-ing new ways to make a computer smaller than your hand. "In 1750 you would have been a washerwoman," I tell her. "Or maybe a slave." Lila is an adopted child. She has dark skin and light gray eyes. She could be anybody, a Scandina-vian Indian or an Irish black woman. She grew up in a series of mobile-home parks and now lives in an apartment full of authentic Chippendale and Hepple-white, baroque silver, and antique beaded purses.

"Be sure and ask for Dr. L'Heureux," she tells me now as I stand at a pay phone across the street from the Women's Health Collective. "Dr. L'Heureux is the one who will be lighthearted and make you feel that the situation is very funny."

As it turns out, Dr. L'Heureux is on vacation in Hawaii, and the young recep-tionist at the desk does not think that anyone is available right now. You would think that a place called the Women's Health Collective would be staffed with sympathetic, generous-hearted people. But except for the absence of men, this place is like any other large clinic, with people on the front desk who make you feel that dealing with your medical problem is an inconvenience.

"This is a gynecological problem?" the receptionist says very loudly. "Yes," I 25 say in a low voice meant to be a cue.

"And you can't come back and see us on Monday?"

"No," I say, trying to give the word just the right degree of quiet urgency.

She consults once again the form I have just filled out. "You have an infec-tion?"

"No, that word is infestation."

"You have a yeast infection?" 30

"No, I don't." I am thirty-one years old and have never had a yeast infection or cystitis. I also never have had gonorrhea, syphilis, or an abortion. I have a checkup once a year and am a healthy specimen. I bend close to the small curve of the woman's ear and say, "I have"—and here my voice drops away altogether as I feel the loathsome word scraping along the back of my throat—"I have the crubs."

"CRUBS? You have CRUBS?" She is perplexed, then amused. She smiles, unsure whether I have intentionally made a joke or am one of those patients the medical people like to laugh about on their coffee breaks—uneducated women who cannot name their parts and say "bajiva" instead of "vagina," or rich women who say they got the clap from the cleaning woman who brought germs to the bathroom. "I have the crubs," I say again, this time as loudly as the receptionist, because now everyone in the waiting room has already heard it anyway, and the doctors will be told, and the nurse practitioners, and the med techs and the janitors. Suddenly I can imagine the lice down there building a new life for themselves in the wilderness of my pubic hair, clearing the forests, planting farms, and sending east for a spinster schoolteacher. "I have the crubs," I say. "And I need help now."

"Well, at least you know nobody's going to have any sex for the next few days," Lila says. We are resting at the edge of the apartment pool between our laps. I admire Lila's slender, muscular legs and think that Susu would pay ten thousand dollars for those legs if the surgeons in Italy could figure out a way to make them. It is early evening, the water is cool, the oleanders are still in bloom, there is a fragrance of invisible eucalyptus trees in the air, and behind the apartment building, the red sunlight billows like sheet silk. This is not a bad life.

"My first husband's ex-wife was just like her," Lila says. "She had lots of affairs but always went back to him in between to be told that she was still a desirable woman."

"You think this could go on indefinitely?" I have a vision of Harvey and me   35
seated at a candlelit table twenty years from now in one of his small Gothic houses, and in from the kitchen comes Susu with her large Italian breasts and a nose that is beginning to slide out of place like an old boxer's.

"Maybe she'll marry a plastic surgeon," Lila says.

We look up toward Harvey's lighted kitchen window, where Susu is preparing supper. Harvey is bent over the dining table like a willow tree, while Susu stands by the counter like a box hedge. "I think the time has come for me to have a little talk with the happy couple," I say.

Susu's meal for the three of us consists of a packaged spaghetti dinner and, on the side, some slices of canned pineapple decorating small bowls of cottage cheese. "Look what Susu did," Harvey says, giving me a cautious glance.

"How nice, Susu. Did you learn this in Italy?"

Susu laughs as we sit down at the table. That is one good thing about her: she   40
can usually take a joke.

"Susu was always a rotten cook, wasn't I, sweetie?" Susu says to Harvey. Why does she have that coy way of referring to herself in the third person, as if she's a character even in her own life?

"Really, this is great," Harvey says. I see that he has decided to discuss this meal at length in order to avoid more delicate topics. "Would you believe that she did all this in only twenty minutes?"

Already he is halfway through his meal, and I realize once again that this is a Harvey I have not seen much of in the nine months since I dented the side of his car. This is a Harvey who is attracted to food largely because it is fuel, and whose heart is gladdened as much by the sight of the kind that comes pulpy from a can as by my own aromatic sauce, simmered for hours with fresh herbs. In the last two weeks I have discovered that Harvey really cannot tell the difference between scrambled eggs and a soufflé or between Campbell's chicken noodle soup and the kind I make from scratch.

"No wonder you're so thin," Susu says to me. "You're not eating anything."

"Maybe I need some silicone implants," I say, and I am just mean and small enough to feel a thrill of pleasure when Susu looks back at her plate without smiling. Harvey gives me a warning look. Susu, I must remember, is not playing with a full deck this week. Apparently, this is her best culinary effort, and it has been offered as a peace token—Susu, the repentant crab-carrier trying to make amends with the other woman. 45

"I was never pretty," she says. "I always had these big hips and no breasts to go with them. Not like you, Angelina. You have a nice compact little figure."

"Yes, you do," Harvey says to me. "And you have one, too. Both of your figures have always been very nice."

"You always lie," Susu says. "You lie to make everybody feel good about you."

That is not true. In fact, Harvey never lies. He is simply one of those people who rarely perceive an inadequacy in another person. Right now I can see the old guilt resurrecting itself as I watch Harvey watching Susu over a shaker of Kraft cheese and a plate of soft white bread. He is about to take the blame once again for the failure of the marriage. I can see the tenderness in his eyes, the pity that will cause him to offer Susu a place to stay for weeks and weeks if that's how long it takes her to find a job. She begins to cry, and Harvey reaches out to touch her hand.

"Now come on," he says in his beautiful voice. 50

"Excuse me," I say, although no one is listening. I leave the apartment and go back over to Lila's.

"He was always a sucker for the basket cases," she says. "After her he went out with a sculptress who had had shock treatment and who used to send him obscene, jealous postcards at the office. Then he took up with a woman who ate only fruit and nuts and liked to throw drinks on other women at parties."

"Don't you ever want to get married again?" I say. "Don't you want to move into a little house with daffodils pushing up along the front walk in the spring?"

"Listen, I have thousands of dollars' worth of antiques and a good job. Things could be worse. I could be in love with a man like Harvey."

Every Sunday night Harvey and I watch the science program on the PBS channel. Tonight we are watching it on Harvey's bed with the door closed and the volume turned up high, so that we cannot be overheard by Susu, who is pretending to read foreign-language fashion magazines in the next room. 55

"She's actually a sweet person," he says. "She's having a hard time thinking about her future."

"How can she think with a hairdo like that? Her brain never gets any light or air."

"Please," he says. "Please, please, please."

Last week's topic on the PBS program was atoms and quarks. This week the program is about the miracles of microphotography. Harvey and I watch with genuine fascination as a lens focuses on a human eyelid and magnifies it fifty thousand times to reveal that there are tiny, fish-shaped mites living between the hairs. The announcer says that these mites live on everyone.

"See," says Harvey. "We already had things living on our bodies."   60

In the next scene, the amazing lens focuses on a piece of ordinary bedroom carpet to reveal that in between the fibers there are thousands of living dust mites, each much smaller than the head of a pin. These dust mites, the announcer explains, are in all our homes. They subsist entirely on the cells of sloughed-off human skin. Harvey gets down on the floor and crawls around the bed on his hands and knees. He rests his chin on the sheets by my foot. "Skin," he murmurs and kisses my little toe.

"We can't do anything before Monday or Tuesday," I say, really just as a test of how much he wants me. "We all have to give our bodies another chemical shampoo before we're safe."

He moves his head along my leg and kisses the inside of my thigh. "We can fool around," he says.

"Hello, hello," a voice says from the other side of the door. "Anybody alive in there? *Les personae morte?*"

"What language is it speaking?" I say.   65

Harvey crawls to the door and opens it a crack. "I can't find the detergent," Susu says to me. "What's the matter with him?"

"Harvey is a dust mite."

"He was always like this, you know. So neat you could never find even the most common thing."

"Back in a second," Harvey says as he stands up and steps into the hall. I notice that he shrewdly leaves the door open so that I can monitor the search for the soap. But Susu drops the subject of detergent as soon as they reach the kitchen and begins to tell another one of her third-person stories about life in Italy. In this one Susu goes riding on the beach on the Riviera although she has never been on a horse before. "So there goes Susu in her bikini and there goes Greggie galloping ahead of me." I wonder whether Greggie is the one with the insect problem. On television the dust mites stand like tiny armadillos among colossal strands of shag carpet. In the kitchen Susu's horse kneels toward the beach because he wants to take a sand bath. " 'Mi scuzi,' I say to the Italians. I think the horse is dying. 'Help, help!' " In this anecdote, Susu is the silly, helpless person who needs to be protected. I hear Harvey's deep laugh, and I close the door and turn off the television. I get in bed as I hear Susu say, "Yes, I did, I did." I put the pillow over my head. "I did. It was unbelievable."

I stretch over Harvey's part of the bed and think of the dust mites alive all   70
over the room. There must be whole families of them, generations and generations, living off the great god Harvey as his cells float through the air like manna. Probably after these last nine months a few colonies of Angelinites have sprung

up, too. I wonder whether different species have grown dependent on different tastes—cells flavored by spaghetti sauce, or spilled alcohol, or chocolate syrup, perfumed cells from breasts and inner thighs—Chanel No. 5, L'Air du Temps, Heaven Scent—creamed cells from hands and faces, cells lathered thick with lipstick (these would be Susu's cells), and maybe right now a whole race of dust mites is dividing itself into small communities and setting out in covered wagons for more fertile shag, and the community that has been subsisting on Pond's Dry Skin Cream begins to die out when I switch, arbitrarily, to another brand. I can imagine the dust-mite priests down there pleading for cells saturated with lanolin, cornstarch, rosewater, building little fires, chanting beads, trying to make do with Oil of Olay cells, to which they are allergic.

"*Andiamo,*" says Susu as I gallop toward sleep.

It is 7 A.M. on Monday morning, and Susu's underwear blooms around the bathroom like California poppies. There are scarlet-orange bras hanging from the towel racks, each bra cup stitched in concentric circles meant to suggest a target. There are scarlet-orange panties—some with cut-out crotches—dripping their color along the plastic of the shower curtain. And in the tub and sink there is more underwear seeping mauve into the sudsy water.

"Where are the whips, Harvey?" I say when he comes to stand behind me in the doorway. "Where are the chains?"

He laughs. "I thought she was doing this stuff last night."

"This does not look to me like the underwear of Emily Dickinson," I say. 75

"Shh," he says, still laughing. "She'll hear you."

"For God's sake, it's seven o'clock in the morning," I say loudly. "Please tell Miss Frederick's of Hollywood we would like to take a shower."

"Here is Miss Frederick's in person," Susu says, stepping between us into the bathroom. "Please excuse Miss Frederick's if she has to wash the lice out of her clothes before she goes to her job interview."

"Everybody's been excusing you for two weeks," I say. "When are you leaving?"

"Maybe we could all go into the kitchen and have some coffee," Harvey says. 80

"I gave you the only three thin years I ever had in my life," Susu says to Harvey. "And what did you give me in return? You gave me lice."

I look at Harvey. "You had lice when you were married?" Harvey looks away.

"He gave me lice last week," Susu says and sits on the edge of the tub.

"He couldn't have given you lice," I say. "He gave them to me." But somewhere in the back of my head a camera lens is panning the landscape of my life, and a tree is no longer a tree but a place where other lives and whole worlds will be revealed if the eye looks closely enough at what's under the bark.

Susu begins to cry. "I had to put up with this for years," she says. "You think 85 you're so special? You think you're the only signorina on the block?"

"I suppose now we're going to have to hear a story about the virgin birth of the crabs," I say. I feel that all my good qualities—restraint, perceptiveness, and the ability to handle bad luck—are being stripped away in a violent wind, and I am trying to hold everything together with a joke. I look toward Harvey, but he has slipped into another room. I sit on the edge of the tub and lean against the wet shower curtain. "It was my pal Lila," I say. "Wasn't it?"

Here is what I do at work: I make small houses, office buildings, even airports. I also make streets, trees, shrubs, flower beds, ponds, streams, and miniature people. I work for a large group of architects, creating three-dimensional mock-ups of their designs. Harvey still talks about leaving the firm and going into business for himself. Lila is thinking about going back to graduate school in art history. Susu sells real estate but would rather have a job in broadcasting. I am the only person I know happy at work, except for a writer I met the other night at a party. He has pale green eyes and hair so thick it makes me think his brain must be a very fertile place. His name is Anthony, which is the name of the patron of lost things. An irony, since he owns so few of the things the rest of us seem to regard as necessities. He lives in a one-room apartment furnished in someone else's taste.

"I think he lives in his head," I tell Lila. "I think in his head he owns stereo sets and three-piece suits and takes trips to Mexico in the winter." Lila and I are sitting on one of her Persian carpets near a cherry cabinet full of beaded antique purses. It's been two months since I stopped seeing Harvey, and now Lila and I are having drinks to demonstrate that we are still friends, as indeed we are. If I could choose to be someone else I might actually choose to be Lila, who is smart and beautiful, and whom everybody likes, but who seems to have found a way to close the door of this museum of an apartment and ignore the mucky terrain over which the rest of us must walk. For me the closed door is my work, where I create a stationary world, ageless and colorful, a shopping center or school no bigger than the top of a desk, and completely manageable.

"Once a week he comes over here to tell me how much he misses you," Lila says. She is talking about Harvey. I truly am not interested, so I turn and open the cabinet to look at the purses. Each purse is covered with glass beads and, I see, each bead is faceted so that it gives off many pinpoints of light. "He thinks that you're perfect," Lila says. "He thinks you're a nice cross between Susu, who is crazy, and me. I'm much too independent for just about everybody." We have already established that in Harvey's life Lila occurred briefly between the sculptress and the fruit-and-nut woman, and that she reentered it briefly during the Susu-and-me period. I truly do not care, I told her. I now look back on those months as a phase of temporary insanity that began with an accident in a parking lot.

"You can tell Harvey that I do not wish to be attractive to someone because of my characteristics as a hybrid."

"You're crazy, too," Lila says. "You're a dreamer, you don't have any courage."

"I'm not unhappy," I say. "I'm fine." All week long I have been working on the Janet Freeman Elementary School project, which may be the last elementary school built in California for a generation, now that the taxpayers have voted

90

once again against education. This school will slide on Teflon joints during the earthquakes and will save all the children and the teachers. "Besides, I've just met this writer. He only owns seven shirts and doesn't have any other girl-friends. He leads a simple life." Already I can imagine the two of us moving to the country. Lila leaves the room to refill the drinks, and I turn back to the purses, where there are beads giving off light of every color, amethyst light and rose light, gold and platinum light, the silver light of oat fields in early summer, the coppery light of rivers stirring with mud after a spring thaw. Each bead twinkles like an eye, and it seems to me that if you could get close enough to one it would be like looking into a pupil to see your own reflection, and in the back-ground there would be trees and hills and bridges, each bead different, here a mountainscape in the Himalayas, tiny goats grazing below the snow line, there a tropical shore in Rarotonga, pink orchids strewn across the sand, and always in the foreground, the oval face of Angelina.

For Analysis

1. What sort of man is Harvey? Do you like him? **2.** Why do you suppose Angelina ends her relationship with Harvey rather than Lila? **3.** What function does Susu's din-ner serve in the story? **4.** Angelina asserts that she is happy at work. How does her job provide insight into her character? **5.** Describe the men that Angelina seems to find attractive. What do her preferences contribute to her characterization? **6.** What does each of the four characters in this story want?

On Style

1. What evidence in the story suggests that Angelina is an **unreliable narrator**? How does that unreliability affect your response? **2.** What function does the first paragraph of this story serve?

Making Connections

1. Compare Angelina to the narrator of Pam Houston's "How to Talk to a Hunter" (p. 988). Next, compare Harvey to the hunter. How are the characters similar? How do they differ? **2.** Compare and contrast this story with Kate Chopin's "The Storm" (p. 947). Note that Chopin's story ends, "So the storm passed and everyone was happy." Why isn't everyone happy at the end of "Other Women"?

Writing Topic

Imagine yourself in Angelina's position: she discovers that her lover has slept with her best friend. Write for no more than a page, describing how you would handle such a situation.

Pam Houston   [b. 1962]

How to Talk to a Hunter   1990

When he says "Skins or blankets?" it will take you a moment to realize that he's asking which you want to sleep under. And in your hesitation he'll decide that he wants to see your skin wrapped in the big black moosehide. He carried it, he'll say, soaking wet and heavier than a dead man, across the tundra for two—was it hours or days or weeks? But the payoff, now, will be to see it fall across one of your white breasts. It's December, and your skin is never really warm, so you will pull the bulk of it around you and pose for him, pose for his camera, without having to narrate this moose's death.

You will spend every night in this man's bed without asking yourself why he listens to top-forty country. Why he donated money to the Republican party. Why he won't play back his messages while you are in the room. You are there so often the messages pile up. Once, you noticed the bright green counter reading as high as fifteen.

He will have lured you here out of a careful independence that you spent months cultivating; though it will finally be winter, the dwindling daylight and the threat of Christmas, that makes you give in. Spending nights with this man means suffering the long face of your sheep dog, who likes to sleep on your bed, who worries when you don't come home. But the hunter's house is so much warmer than yours, and he'll give you a key, and just like a woman, you'll think that means something. It will snow hard for thirteen straight days. Then it will really get cold. When it is sixty below there will be no wind and no clouds, just still air and cold sunshine. The sun on the windows will lure you out of bed, but he'll pull you back under. The next two hours he'll devote to your body. With his hands, with his tongue, he'll express what will seem to you like the most eternal of loves. Like the house key, this is just another kind of lie. Even in bed; especially in bed, you and he cannot speak the same language. The machine will answer the incoming calls. From under an ocean of passion and hide and hair you'll hear a woman's muffled voice between the beeps.

Your best female friend will say, "So what did you think? That a man who sleeps under a dead moose is capable of commitment?"

This is what you learned in college: A man desires the satisfaction of his desire; a woman desires the condition of desiring.   5

The hunter will talk about spring in Hawaii, summer in Alaska. The man who says he was always better at math will form the sentences so carefully it will be

988

impossible to tell if you are included in these plans. When he asks you if you would like to open a small guest ranch way out in the country, understand that this is a rhetorical question. Label these conversations future perfect, but don't expect the present to catch up with them. Spring is an inconceivable distance from the December days that just keep getting shorter and gray.

He'll ask you if you've ever shot anything, if you'd like to, if you ever thought about teaching your dog to retrieve. Your dog will like him too much, will drop the stick at his feet every time, will roll over and let the hunter scratch his belly.

One day he'll leave you sleeping to go split wood or get the mail and his phone will ring again. You'll sit very still while a woman who calls herself something like Patty Coyote leaves a message on his machine: she's leaving work, she'll say, and the last thing she wanted to hear was the sound of his beautiful voice. Maybe she'll talk only in rhyme. Maybe the counter will change to sixteen. You'll look a question at the mule deer on the wall, and the dark spots on either side of his mouth will tell you he shares more with this hunter than you ever will. One night, drunk, the hunter told you he was sorry for taking that deer, that every now and then there's an animal that isn't meant to be taken, and he should have known that deer was one.

Your best male friend will say, "No one who needs to call herself Patty Coyote can hold a candle to you, but why not let him sleep alone a few nights, just to make sure?"

10

The hunter will fill your freezer with elk burger, venison sausage, organic potatoes, fresh pecans. He'll tell you to wear your seat belt, to dress warmly, to drive safely. He'll say you are always on his mind, that you're the best thing that's ever happened to him, that you make him glad that he's a man.

Tell him it don't come easy, tell him freedom's just another word for nothing left to lose.

These are the things you'll know without asking: The coyote woman wears her hair in braids. She uses words like "howdy." She's man enough to shoot a deer.

A week before Christmas you'll rent *It's a Wonderful Life* and watch it together, curled on your couch, faces touching. Then you'll bring up the word "monogamy." He'll tell you how badly he was hurt by your predecessor. He'll tell you he couldn't be happier spending every night with you. He'll say there's just a few questions he doesn't have the answers for. He'll say he's just scared and confused. Of course this isn't exactly what he means. Tell him you understand. Tell him you are scared too. Tell him to take all the time he needs. Know that you could never shoot an animal, and be glad of it.

Your best female friend will say, "You didn't tell him you loved him, did you?" Don't even tell her the truth. If you do, you'll have to tell her that he said this: "I feel exactly the same way."

Your best male friend will say, "Didn't you know what would happen when   15
you said the word 'commitment'?"
But that isn't the word that you said.
He'll say, "Commitment, monogamy, it all means just one thing."

The coyote woman will come from Montana with the heavier snows. The hunter will call you on the day of the solstice to say he has a friend in town and can't see you. He'll leave you hanging your Christmas lights; he'll give new meaning to the phrase "longest night of the year." The man who has said he's not so good with words will manage to say eight things about his friend without using a gender-determining pronoun. Get out of the house quickly. Call the most understanding person you know that will let you sleep in his bed.

Your best female friend will say, "So what did you think? That he was capable of living outside his gender?"

When you get home in the morning there's a candy tin on your pillow. Santa,   20
obese and grotesque, fondles two small children on the lid. The card will say something like, From your not-so-secret admirer. Open it. Examine each carefully made truffle. Feed them, one at a time, to the dog. Call the hunter's machine. Tell him you don't speak chocolate.

Your best female friend will say, "At this point, what is it about him that you could possibly find appealing?"

Your best male friend will say, "Can't you understand that this is a good sign? Can't you understand that this proves how deep he's in with you?" Hug your best male friend. Give him the truffles the dog wouldn't eat.

Of course the weather will cooperate with the coyote woman. The highways will close, she will stay another night. He'll tell her he's going to work so he can come and see you. He'll even leave her your number and write "Me at Work" on the yellow pad of paper by his phone. Although you shouldn't, you'll have to be there. It will be you and your nauseous dog and your half-trimmed tree all waiting for him like a series of questions.

This is what you learned in graduate school: In every assumption is contained the possibility of its opposite.

In your kitchen he'll hug you like you might both die there. Sniff him for coy-   25
ote. Don't hug him back.

He will say whatever he needs to win. He'll say it's just an old friend. He'll say the visit was all the friend's idea. He'll say the night away from you has given him time to think about how much you mean to him. Realize that nothing short of sleeping alone will ever make him realize how much you mean to him. He'll say that if you can just be a little patient, some good will come out of this for the two of you after all. He still won't use a gender-specific pronoun.

Put your head in your hands. Think about what it means to be patient. Think about the beautiful, smart, strong, clever woman you thought he saw when he looked at you. Pull on your hair. Rock your body back and forth. Don't cry.

He'll say that after holding you it doesn't feel right holding anyone else. For "holding," substitute "fucking." Then take it as a compliment.

He will get frustrated and rise to leave. He may or may not be bluffing. Stall for time. Ask a question he can't immediately answer. Tell him you want to make love on the floor. When he tells you your body is beautiful, say, "I feel exactly the same way." Don't, under any circumstances, stand in front of the door.

Your best female friend will say, "They lie to us, they cheat on us, and we love them more for it." She'll say, "It's our fault. We raise them to be like that." 30

Tell her it can't be your fault. You've never raised anything but dogs.

The hunter will say it's late and he has to go home to sleep. He'll emphasize the last word in the sentence. Give him one kiss that he'll remember while he's fucking the coyote woman. Give him one kiss that ought to make him cry if he's capable of it, but don't notice when he does. Tell him to have a good night.

Your best male friend will say, "We all do it. We can't help it. We're self-destructive. It's the old bad-boy routine. You have a male dog, don't you?"

The next day the sun will be out and the coyote woman will leave. Think about how easy it must be for the coyote woman and a man who listens to top-forty country. The coyote woman would never use a word like "monogamy"; the coyote woman will stay gentle on his mind.

If you can, let him sleep alone for at least one night. If you can't, invite him over to finish trimming your Christmas tree. When he asks how you are, tell him you think it's a good idea to keep your sense of humor during the holidays. 35

Plan to be breezy and aloof and full of interesting anecdotes about all the other men you've ever known. Plan to be hotter than ever before in bed, and a little cold out of it. Remember that necessity is the mother of invention. Be flexible.

First, he will find the faulty bulb that's been keeping all the others from lighting. He will explain in great detail the most elementary electrical principles. You will take turns placing the ornaments you and other men, he and other women, have spent years carefully choosing. Under the circumstances, try to let this be a comforting thought.

He will thin the clusters of tinsel you put on the tree. He'll say something ambiguous like, Next year you should string popcorn and cranberries. Finally, his arm will stretch just high enough to place the angel on the top of the tree.

Your best female friend will say, "Why can't you ever fall in love with a man who will be your friend?"

Your best male friend will say, "You ought to know this by now: Men always cheat on the best women." 40

This is what you learned in the pop psychology book: Love means letting go of fear.

Play Willie Nelson's "Pretty Paper." He'll ask you to dance, and before you can answer he'll be spinning you around your wood stove, he'll be humming in your ear. Before the song ends he'll be taking off your clothes, setting you lightly under the tree, hovering above you with tinsel in his hair. Through the spread of the branches the all-white lights you insisted on will shudder and blur, outlining the ornaments he brought: a pheasant, a snow goose, a deer.

The record will end. Above the crackle of the wood stove and the rasp of the hunter's breathing you'll hear one long low howl break the quiet of the frozen night: your dog, chained and lonely and cold. You'll wonder if he knows enough to stay in his dog house. You'll wonder if he knows that the nights are getting shorter now.

For Analysis

1. What is the difference between the advice offered by the male and the female friend? Which advice is more accurate and useful? Explain. **2.** The second paragraph, with three unasked questions, characterizes both the hunter and the narrator. What do the questions reveal about each of them? What is the significance of the order of the questions? **3.** Describe the difference between the narrator and the "coyote woman." What does the narrator think of the "coyote woman"? What specific advice does the narrator give about talking to a hunter? **4.** What is the significance of the narrator lying to her best female friend? **5.** Why does the story end with the narrator's thoughts about the dog?

On Style

The story is written as if it were a series of notes or journal entries. How does that **style** and the **tone** of these notes affect your response to the story?

Making Connections

Does the relationship in this story remind you of any of your own courtship experiences? Explain.

Writing Topic

In an essay, and, perhaps, drawing on your own experiences, analyze Houston's assertions about the differences between what men and women expect from a relationship.

Poetry

Sappho [ca. 610–ca. 580 B.C.]

With His Venom[1]

With his venom

Irresistible
and bittersweet

that loosener
of limbs, Love

reptile-like
strikes me down

Anonymous

Bonny Barbara Allan

It was in and about the Martinmas[1] time,
　　When the green leaves were a falling,
That Sir John Graeme, in the West Country,
　　Fell in love with Barbara Allan.

With His Venom
　[1] Translated by Mary Barnard.
Bonny Barbara Allan
　[1] November 11.

He sent his man down through the town,
   To the place where she was dwelling:
"O haste and come to my master dear,
   Gin° ye be Barbara Allan."   *if*

O hooly,° hooly rose she up,   *slowly*
   To the place where he was lying,   10
And when she drew the curtain by:
   "Young man, I think you're dying."

"O it's I'm sick, and very, very sick,
   And 'tis a' for Barbara Allan."
"O the better for me ye s'° never be,   *ye shall*
   Tho your heart's blood were a-spilling.

"O dinna° ye mind,° young man," said she,   *don't/remember*
   "When ye was in the tavern a drinking,
That ye made the healths gae° round and round,   *go*
   And slighted Barbara Allan?"   20

He turned his face unto the wall,
   And death was with him dealing:
"Adieu, adieu, my dear friends all,
   And be kind to Barbara Allan."

And slowly, slowly raise she up,
   And slowly, slowly left him,
And sighing said she could not stay,
   Since death of life had reft him.

She had not gane a mile but twa,
   When she heard the dead-bell ringing,   30
And every jow° that the dead-bell geid,°   *stroke/gave*
   It cried, "Woe to Barbara Allan!"

"O mother, mother, make my bed!
   O make it saft and narrow!
Since my love died for me to-day,
   I'll die for him to-morrow."

Christopher Marlowe   [1564–1593]

The Passionate Shepherd to His Love[1]   1600

Come live with me and be my love,
And we will all the pleasures prove
That valleys, groves, hills, and fields,
Woods, or steepy mountain yields.

And we will sit upon the rocks,
Seeing the shepherds feed their flocks,
By shallow rivers to whose falls
Melodious birds sing madrigals.

And I will make thee beds of roses
And a thousand fragrant posies,   10
A cap of flowers, and a kirtle°   skirt
Embroidered all with leaves of myrtle;

A gown made of the finest wool
Which from our pretty lambs we pull;
Fair lined slippers for the cold,
With buckles of the purest gold;

A belt of straw and ivy buds,
With coral clasps and amber studs:
And if these pleasures may thee move,
Come live with me, and be my love.   20

The shepherds' swains shall dance and sing
For thy delight each May morning:
If these delights thy mind may move,
Then live with me and be my love.

---

[1] This poem has elicited many responses over the centuries. Sir Walter Ralegh's early answer follows. C. Day Lewis's twentieth-century response appears on p. 1014.

Sir Walter Ralegh   [1552?–1618][1]

The Nymph's Reply
to the Shepherd   1600

If all the world and love were young,
And truth in every shepherd's tongue,
These pretty pleasures might me move
To live with thee and be thy love.

Time drives the flocks from field to fold,
When rivers rage and rocks grow cold,
And Philomel° becometh dumb;   the nightingale
The rest complains of cares to come.

The flowers do fade, and wanton fields
To wayward winter reckoning yields;   10
A honey tongue, a heart of gall,
Is fancy's spring, but sorrow's fall.

Thy gowns, thy shoes, thy beds of roses,
Thy cap, thy kirtle, and thy posies
Soon break, soon wither, soon forgotten—
In folly ripe, in reason rotten.

Thy belt of straw and ivy buds,
Thy coral clasps and amber studs,
All these in me no means can move
To come to thee and be thy love.   20

But could youth last and love still breed,
Had joys no date° nor age no need,   end
Then these delights my mind might move
To live with thee and be thy love.

[1] *Editor's Note:* Chronology has been dispensed with in this instance to facilitate comparison with Marlowe's "Passionate Shepherd."

William Shakespeare   [1564–1616]

Sonnets   1609

18

Shall I compare thee to a summer's day?
Thou art more lovely and more temperate:
Rough winds do shake the darling buds of May,
And summer's lease hath all too short a date:
Sometime too hot the eye of heaven shines,
And often is his gold complexion dimmed;
And every fair from fair sometimes declines,
By chance or nature's changing course untrimmed;
But thy eternal summer shall not fade,
Nor lose possession of that fair thou ow'st,°   owns
Nor shall death brag thou wander'st in his shade,   11
When in eternal lines to time thou grow'st:
    So long as men can breathe, or eyes can see,
    So long lives this, and this gives life to thee.

For Analysis
1. Why does the poet argue that "a summer's day" is an inappropriate **metaphor** for his beloved? **2.** What is "this" in line 14?

29

When, in disgrace with fortune and men's eyes,
I all alone beweep my outcast state
And trouble deaf heaven with my bootless cries
And look upon myself and curse my fate,
Wishing me like to one more rich in hope,
Featured like him, like him with friends possessed,
Desiring this man's art and that man's scope,
With what I most enjoy contented least;
Yet in these thoughts myself almost despising,
Haply I think on thee, and then my state,   10
Like to the lark at break of day arising
From sullen earth, sings hymns at heaven's gate;
    For thy sweet love remembered such wealth brings
    That then I scorn to change my state with kings.

129

Th' expense of spirit in a waste of shame
Is lust in action; and till action, lust
Is perjured, murderous, bloody, full of blame,
Savage, extreme, rude, cruel, not to trust;
Enjoyed no sooner but despiséd straight;
Past reason hunted; and no sooner had,
Past reason hated, as a swallowed bait,
On purpose laid to make the taker mad:
Mad in pursuit, and in possession so;
Had, having, and in quest to have, extreme;   10
A bliss in proof,° and proved, a very woe;   experience
Before, a joy proposed; behind, a dream.
    All this the world well knows; yet none knows well
    To shun the heaven that leads men to this hell.

For Analysis
1. Paraphrase "Th' expense of spirit in a waste of shame / Is lust in action." **2.** Describe the sound patterns and metrical variations in lines 3 and 4. What do they contribute to the "sense" of the lines?

Writing Topic
How do the sound patterns, the variations in **meter**, and the **paradox** in the final **couplet** contribute to the sense of this sonnet?

130

My mistress' eyes are nothing like the sun;
Coral is far more red than her lips' red;
If snow be white, why then her breasts are dun;
If hairs be wires, black wires grow on her head.
I have seen roses damasked,° red and white,   variegated
But no such roses see I in her cheeks;
And in some perfumes is there more delight
Than in the breath that from my mistress reeks.
I love to hear her speak, yet well I know
That music hath a far more pleasing sound;   10
I grant I never saw a goddess go;
My mistress, when she walks, treads on the ground.
    And yet, by heaven, I think my love as rare
    As any she belied with false compare.[1]

Sonnet 130
  [1] I.e., as any woman misrepresented with false comparisons.

Thomas Campion [1567–1620]

I Care Not for These Ladies   1601

I care not for these ladies,
That must be wooed and prayed:
Give me kind Amaryllis,[1]
The wanton country maid.
Nature art disdaineth,
Her beauty is her own.
    Who, when we court and kiss,
    She cries, "Forsooth, let go!"
    But when we come where comfort is,
    She never will say no.   10

If I love Amaryllis,
She gives me fruit and flowers:
But if we love these ladies,
We must give golden showers.
Give them gold, that sell love,
Give me the nut-brown lass,
    Who, when we court and kiss,
    She cries, "Forsooth, let go!"
    But when we come where comfort is,
    She never will say no.   20

These ladies must have pillows,
And beds by strangers wrought;
Give me a bower of willows,
Of moss and leaves unbought,
And fresh Amaryllis,
With milk and honey fed;
    Who, when we court and kiss,
    She cries, "Forsooth, let go!"
    But when we come where comfort is,
    She never will say no.   30

---

[1] A conventional name for a country girl in pastoral poetry.

John Donne   [1572–1631]

A Valediction: Forbidding Mourning   1633

As virtuous men pass mildly away,
   And whisper to their souls to go,
Whilst some of their sad friends do say
   The breath goes now, and some say, No;

So let us melt, and make no noise,
   No tear-floods, nor sigh-tempests move,
'Twere profanation of our joys
   To tell the laity our love.

Moving of th' earth° brings harms and fears,   earthquake
   Men reckon what it did and meant;   10
But trepidation of the spheres,
   Though greater far, is innocent.[1]

Dull sublunary° lovers' love   under the moon
   (Whose soul is sense) cannot admit
Absence, because it doth remove
   Those things which elemented it.

But we by a love so much refined
   That our selves know not what it is,
Inter-assuréd of the mind,
   Care less, eyes, lips, and hands to miss.   20

Our two souls therefore, which are one,
   Though I must go, endure not yet
A breach, but an expansion,
   Like gold to airy thinness beat.

If they be two, they are two so
   As stiff twin compasses are two;
Thy soul, the fixed foot, makes no show
   To move, but doth, if th' other do.

---

[1] The movement of the heavenly spheres is harmless.

And though it in the center sit,
    Yet when the other far doth roam,   30
It leans and harkens after it,
    And grows erect, as that comes home.

Such wilt thou be to me, who must
    Like th' other foot, obliquely run;
Thy firmness makes my circle just,
    And makes me end where I begun.

For Analysis

1. Two kinds of love are described in this poem—spiritual and physical. How does the **simile** drawn in the first two stanzas help define the differences between them? **2.** How does the contrast between earthquakes and the movement of the spheres in stanza three further develop the contrast between the two types of lovers? **3.** Explain the comparison between a drawing compass and the lovers in the last three stanzas.

<u>Ben</u> <u>Jonson</u>   [1572–1637]

Doing, a filthy pleasure is, and short[1] 1585

Doing, a filthy pleasure is, and short;
And done, we straight repent us of the sport:
Let us not then rush blindly on unto it,
Like lustful beasts, that only know to do it:
For lust will languish, and that heat decay,
But thus, thus, keeping endless Holy-day,
Let us together closely lie, and kiss,
There is no labour, nor no shame in this;
This hath pleased, doth please, and long will please; never
Can this decay, but is beginning ever.   10

Doing, . . .
   [1] Translated from the Latin poem by Petronius Arbiter (d. ca. A.D. 66).

Edmund Waller [1606–1687]

Go, Lovely Rose! 1645

    Go, lovely rose!
Tell her that wastes her time and me
    That now she knows,
When I resemble° her to thee,   compare
How sweet and fair she seems to be.

    Tell her that's young,
And shuns to have her graces spied,
    That hadst thou sprung
In deserts, where no men abide,
Thou must have uncommended died.   10

    Small is the worth
Of beauty from the light retired;
    Bid her come forth,
Suffer herself to be desired,
And not blush so to be admired.

    Then die! that she
The common fate of all things rare
    May read in thee;
How small a part of time they share
That are so wondrous sweet and fair!   20

Andrew Marvell [1621–1678]

To His Coy Mistress 1681

    Had we but world enough, and time,
This coyness, lady, were no crime.
We would sit down, and think which way
To walk, and pass our long love's day.
Thou by the Indian Ganges' side
Shouldst rubies find; I by the tide
Of Humber would complain. I would
Love you ten years before the flood,
And you should, if you please, refuse

Til the conversion of the Jews.   10
My vegetable love should grow
Vaster than empires and more slow;
An hundred years should go to praise
Thine eyes, and on thy forehead gaze;
Two hundred to adore each breast,
But thirty thousand to the rest;
An age at least to every part,
And the last age should show your heart.
For, lady, you deserve this state,
Nor would I love at lower rate.   20
    But at my back I always hear
Time's wingéd chariot hurrying near;
And yonder all before us lie
Deserts of vast eternity.
Thy beauty shall no more be found,
Nor, in thy marble vault, shall sound
My echoing song; then worms shall try
That long-preserved virginity,
And your quaint honor turn to dust,
And into ashes all my lust: 30
The grave's a fine and private place,
But none, I think, do there embrace.
    Now therefore, while the youthful hue
Sits on thy skin like morning dew,
And while thy willing soul transpires
At every pore with instant fires,
Now let us sport us while we may,
And now, like amorous birds of prey,
Rather at once our time devour   39
Than languish in his slow-chapped° power.   slow-jawed
Let us roll our strength and all
Our sweetness up into one ball,
And tear our pleasures with rough strife
Thorough° the iron gates of life: through
Thus, though we cannot make our sun
Stand still, yet we will make him run.

For Analysis

1. State the argument of the poem (see ll. 1–2, 21–22, 33–34). **2.** Compare the figures of speech in the first verse paragraph with those in the last. How do they differ? **3.** Characterize the attitude toward life recommended by the poet.

Writing Topic

In what ways does the conception of love in this poem differ from that in John Donne's "A Valediction: Forbidding Mourning" (p. 1000)? In your discussion consider the **imagery** in both poems.

William Blake [1757–1827]

A Poison Tree 1794

I was angry with my friend:
I told my wrath, my wrath did end.
I was angry with my foe:
I told it not, my wrath did grow.

And I watered it in fears,
Night & morning with my tears;
And I sunnéd it with smiles,
And with soft deceitful wiles.

And it grew both day and night,
Till it bore an apple bright.   10
And my foe beheld it shine,
And he knew that it was mine,

And into my garden stole,
When the night had veil'd the pole;
In the morning glad I see
My foe outstretched beneath the tree.

For Analysis
1. Is anything gained from the parallel readers might draw between this tree and the tree in the Garden of Eden? Explain. **2.** Can you articulate what the "poison" is? **3.** Does your own experience verify the first stanza of the poem?

Robert Burns [1759–1796]

A Red, Red Rose 1796

O My Luve's like a red, red rose,
    That's newly sprung in June;
O My Luve's like a melodie
    That's sweetly played in tune.

1004

As fair art thou, my bonnie lass,
    So deep in luve am I;
And I will luve thee still, my dear,
    Til a' the seas gang dry.

Till a' the seas gang dry, my dear,
    And the rocks melt wi' the sun: 10
O I will love thee still, my dear,
    While the sands o' life shall run.

And fare thee weel, my only luve,
    And fare thee weel awhile!
And I will come again, my luve,
    Though it were ten thousand mile.

Walt Whitman   [1819–1892]

from
Song of Myself 1855

11

Twenty-eight young men bathe by the shore,
Twenty-eight young men and all so friendly;
Twenty-eight years of womanly life and all so lonesome.

She owns the fine house by the rise of the bank,
She hides handsome and richly drest aft the blinds of the window.

Which of the young men does she like the best?
Ah the homeliest of them is beautiful to her.

Where are you off to, lady? for I see you,
You splash in the water there, yet stay stock still in your room.

Dancing and laughing along the beach came the twenty-ninth bather,   10
The rest did not see her, but she saw them and loved them.

The beards of the young men glisten'd with wet, it ran from their long
    hair,
Little streams pass'd all over their bodies.

An unseen hand also pass'd over their bodies,
It descended tremblingly from their temples and ribs.

The young men float on their backs, their white bellies bulge to the sun,
    they do not ask who seizes fast to them,
They do not know who puffs and declines with pendant and bending
    arch,
They do not think whom they souse with spray.

Matthew Arnold   [1822–1888]

Dover Beach   1867

The sea is calm tonight.
The tide is full, the moon lies fair
Upon the straits; on the French coast the light
Gleams and is gone; the cliffs of England stand,
Glimmering and vast, out in the tranquil bay.
Come to the window, sweet is the night-air!
Only, from the long line of spray
Where the sea meets the moon-blanched land,
Listen! you hear the grating roar
Of pebbles which the waves draw back, and fling,   10
At their return, up the high strand,
Begin, and cease, and then again begin,
With tremulous cadence slow, and bring
The eternal note of sadness in.

Sophocles long ago
Heard it on the Aegean, and it brought
Into his mind the turbid ebb and flow
Of human misery; we
Find also in the sound a thought,
Hearing it by this distant northern sea.   20

The Sea of Faith
Was once, too, at the full, and round earth's shore
Lay like the folds of a bright girdle furled.
But now I only hear

Its melancholy, long, withdrawing roar,
Retreating, to the breath
Of the night-wind, down the vast edges drear
And naked shingles° of the world.   pebble beaches

Ah, love, let us be true
To one another! for the world, which seems   30
To lie before us like a land of dreams,
So various, so beautiful, so new,
Hath really neither joy, nor love, nor light,
Nor certitude, nor peace, nor help for pain;
And we are here as on a darkling plain
Swept with confused alarms of struggle and flight,
Where ignorant armies clash by night.

Emily Dickinson [1830–1886]

Mine Enemy is growing old ca. 1881

Mine Enemy is growing old—
I have at last Revenge—
The Palate of the Hate departs—
If any would avenge

Let him be quick—the Viand flits—
It is a faded Meat—
Anger as soon as fed is dead—
'Tis starving makes it fat—

For Analysis
Explain the **paradox** contained in the last two lines.

Writing Topic
Compare this poem with William Blake's "A Poison Tree," (p. 1004).

Gerard Manley Hopkins [1844–1889]

Pied Beauty   1877

Glory be to God for dappled things—
    For skies of couple-colour as a brinded° cow;   brindled
        For rose-moles all in stipple upon trout that swim;
Fresh-firecoal chestnut-falls;[1] finches' wings;
    Landscape plotted and pieced[2]—fold, fallow, and plough;
        And all trades, their gear and tackle, and trim.°   equipment
All things counter,° original, spare, strange;   contrasted
    Whatever is fickle, freckled (who knows how?)
      With swift, slow; sweet, sour; adazzle, dim;
He fathers-forth whose beauty is past change: 10
             Praise him.

Robert Frost   [1874–1963]

Fire and Ice   1923

Some say the world will end in fire,
Some say in ice,
From what I've tasted of desire
I hold with those who favor fire.
But if it had to perish twice,
I think I know enough of hate
To say that for destruction ice
Is also great
And would suffice.

The Silken Tent   1942

She is as in a field a silken tent
At midday when a sunny summer breeze
Has dried the dew and all its ropes relent,
So that in guys it gently sways at ease,

Pied Beauty
  [1] Fallen chestnuts, with the outer husks removed, colored like fresh fire coal.
  [2] Reference to the variegated pattern of land put to different uses.

1008

And its supporting central cedar pole,
That is its pinnacle to heavenward
And signifies the sureness of the soul,
Seems to owe naught to any single cord,
But strictly held by none, is loosely bound
By countless silken ties of love and thought
To everything on earth the compass round,
And only by one's going slightly taut
In the capriciousness of summer air
Is of the slightest bondage made aware.

10

Edna St. Vincent Millay   [1892–1950]

Love Is Not All   1931

Love is not all: it is not meat nor drink
Nor slumber nor a roof against the rain;
Nor yet a floating spar to men that sink
And rise and sink and rise and sink again;
Love can not fill the thickened lung with breath,
Nor clean the blood, nor set the fractured bone;
Yet many a man is making friends with death
Even as I speak, for lack of love alone.
It well may be that in a difficult hour,
Pinned down by pain and moaning for release,
Or nagged by want past resolution's power,
I might be driven to sell your love for peace,
Or trade the memory of this night for food.
It well may be. I do not think I would.

10

Dorothy Parker   [1893–1967]

One Perfect Rose   1926

A single flow'r he sent me, since we met.
   All tenderly his messenger he chose;
Deep-hearted, pure, with scented dew still wet—
   One perfect rose.

I knew the language of the floweret;
 "My fragile leaves," it said, "his heart enclose."
Love long has taken for his amulet
 One perfect rose.

Why is it no one ever sent me yet
 One perfect limousine, do you suppose?   10
Ah no, it's always just my luck to get
 One perfect rose.

E. E. Cummings   [1894–1962]

if everything happens
that can't be done   1944

if everything happens that can't be done
(and anything's righter
than books
could plan)
the stupidest teacher will almost guess
(with a run
skip
around we go yes)
there's nothing as something as one

one hasn't a why or because or although   10
(and buds know better
than books
don't grow)
one's anything old being everything new
(with a what
which
around we come who)
one's everyanything so

so world is a leaf so tree is a bough
(and birds sing sweeter   20
than books
tell how)
so here is away and so your is a my
(with a down

up
around again fly)
forever was never till now

now i love you and you love me
(and books are shuter
than books   30
can be)
and deep in the high that does nothing but fall
(with a shout
each
around we go all)
there's somebody calling who's we

we're anything brighter than even the sun
(we're everything greater
than books
might mean)   40
we're everyanything more than believe
(with a spin
leap
alive we're alive)
we're wonderful one times one

For Analysis
1. What fundamental contrast is stated by the poem? **2.** Lines 2–4 and 6–8 of each
stanza could be printed as single lines. Why do you think Cummings decided to print
them as he does? **3.** What common attitude toward lovers is expressed by the last
lines of the stanzas? **4.** Is the poem **free verse** or formal verse?

Writing Topic
What relation do the parenthetical lines in each stanza bear to the poem as a whole?

when serpents bargain
for the right to squirm   1923

when serpents bargain for the right to squirm
and the sun strikes to gain a living wage—
when thorns regard their roses with alarm
and rainbows are insured against old age

when every thrush may sing no new moon in
if all screech-owls have not okayed his voice
—and any wave signs on the dotted line
or else an ocean is compelled to close

when the oak begs permission of the birch
to make an acorn—valleys accuse their   10
mountains of having altitude—and march
denounces april as a saboteur

then we'll believe in that incredible
unanimal mankind (and not until)

Stevie Smith   [1902–1971]

The Frog Prince   1966

I am a frog
I live under a spell
I live at the bottom
Of a green well

And here I must wait
Until a maiden places me
On her royal pillow
And kisses me
In her father's palace.

The story is familiar   10
Everybody knows it well
But do other enchanted people feel as nervous
As I do? The stories do not tell,

Ask if they will be happier
When the changes come
As already they are fairly happy
In a frog's doom?

I have been a frog now
For a hundred years
And in all this time   20
I have not shed many tears,

I am happy, I like the life,
Can swim for many a mile
(When I have hopped to the river)
And am for ever agile.

And the quietness,
Yes, I like to be quiet
I am habituated
To a quiet life,

But always when I think these thoughts   30
As I sit in my well
Another thought comes to me and says:
It is part of the spell

To be happy
To work up contentment
To make much of being a frog
To fear disenchantment

Says, It will be *heavenly*
To be set free,
Cries, *Heavenly* the girl who disenchants   40
And the royal times, *heavenly*,
And I think it will be.

Come then, royal girl and royal times,
Come quickly,
I can be happy until you come
But I cannot be heavenly,
Only disenchanted people
Can be heavenly.

For Analysis
1. Discuss the possibilities suggested by the words *disenchantment* and *heavenly*.
2. What are the advantages of remaining a frog? The disadvantages?

Writing Topic
In an essay, defend or rebut the assertion at the end of the poem that "Only disenchanted people / Can be heavenly."

C. Day Lewis   [1904–1972]

Song[1]   1935

Come, live with me and be my love,
And we will all the pleasures prove
Of peace and plenty, bed and board,
That chance employment may afford.

I'll handle dainties on the docks
And thou shalt read of summer frocks:
At evening by the sour canals
We'll hope to hear some madrigals.

Care on thy maiden brow shall put
A wreath of wrinkles, and thy foot   10
Be shod with pain: not silken dress
But toil shall tire thy loveliness.

Hunger shall make thy modest zone
And cheat fond death of all but bone—
If these delights thy mind may move,
Then live with me and be my love.

Theodore Roethke   [1908–1963]

My Papa's Waltz   1948

The whiskey on your breath
Could make a small boy dizzy;
But I hung on like death:
Such waltzing was not easy.

We romped until the pans
Slid from the kitchen shelf;
My mother's countenance
Could not unfrown itself.

Song
[1] See Christopher Marlowe's "The Passionate Shepherd to His Love," p. 995.

The hand that held my wrist
Was battered on one knuckle;   10
At every step you missed
My right ear scraped a buckle.

You beat time on my head
With a palm caked hard by dirt,
Then waltzed me off to bed
Still clinging to your shirt.

For Analysis

1. Why is iambic trimeter an appropriate **meter** for this poem? **2.** Identify the details that reveal the kind of person the father is. **3.** How would you characterize the boy's feelings about his father? The father's about the boy?

Writing Topic

Robert Hayden's "Those Winter Sundays" (p. 1017), and Sylvia Plath's "Daddy" (p. 1027) also deal with a child's feelings about a parent. Compare one of them with this poem.

Elizabeth Bishop   [1911–1979]

One Art   1976

The art of losing isn't hard to master;
so many things seem filled with the intent
to be lost that their loss is no disaster.

Lose something every day. Accept the fluster
of lost door keys, the hour badly spent.
The art of losing isn't hard to master.

Then practice losing farther, losing faster:
places, and names, and where it was you meant
to travel. None of these will bring disaster.

I lost my mother's watch. And look! my last, or   10
next-to-last, of three loved houses went.
The art of losing isn't hard to master.

I lost two cities, lovely ones. And, vaster,
some realms I owned, two rivers, a continent.
I miss them, but it wasn't a disaster.

—Even losing you (the joking voice, a gesture
I love) I shan't have lied. It's evident
the art of losing's not too hard to master
though it may look like (*Write* it!) like disaster.

May Sarton [1912–1995]

AIDS 1988

We are stretched to meet a new dimension
Of love, a more demanding range
Where despair and hope must intertwine.
How grow to meet it? Intention
Here can neither move nor change
The raw truth. Death is on the line.
It comes to separate and estrange
Lover from lover in some reckless design.
Where do we go from here?

Fear.   Fear.   Fear.   Fear.   10

Our world has never been more stark
Or more in peril.
It is very lonely now in the dark.
Lonely and sterile.

And yet in the simple turn of a head
Mercy lives. I heard it when someone said
"I must go now to a dying friend.
Every night at nine I tuck him into bed,
And give him a shot of morphine,"
And added, "I go where I have never been."   20
I saw he meant into a new discipline
He had not imagined before, and a new grace.

Every day now we meet it face to face.
Every day now devotion is the test.
Through the long hours, the hard, caring nights
We are forging a new union. We are blest.

As closed hands open to each other
Closed lives open to strange tenderness.
We are learning the hard way how to mother.
Who says it is easy? But we have the power.   30
I watch the faces deepen all around me.
It is the time of change, the saving hour.
The word is not fear, the word we live,
But an old word suddenly made new,
As we learn it again, as we bring it alive:

Love.   Love.   Love.   Love.

For Analysis
1. Paraphrase the first three lines. **2.** Explain the difference between "separate" and "estrange" (l. 7). **3.** What is the meaning of "reckless design" (l. 8)? **4.** What does the speaker mean by "new discipline" (l. 21) and "new grace" (l. 22)? **5.** Who are the "We" of line 26, and why are they "blest"?

Writing Topic
Argue either for or against the assertion that the specter of AIDS has brought about a "time of change" and that fear is giving way to love.

Robert Hayden   [1913–1980]

Those Winter Sundays   1975

Sundays too my father got up early
and put his clothes on in the blueblack cold,
then with cracked hands that ached
from labor in the weekday weather made
banked fires blaze. No one ever thanked him.

I'd wake and hear the cold splintering, breaking.
When the rooms were warm, he'd call,
and slowly I would rise and dress,
fearing the chronic angers of that house,

Speaking indifferently to him,   10
who had driven out the cold
and polished my good shoes as well.
What did I know, what did I know
of love's austere and lonely offices?

Duane Locke   [b. 1921]

Out in a Pasture   1991

Out in a pasture, pouring wine into glasses,
comparing the ruby reflection on grasses,
with the ruby coloring of sundews' globes,
we commented on the beauty of the sound *carnivorous*,
and how, remembering Alexander Pope,[1]
the sound did not fit the sense.
We speculated on what sounds make sense of a bird:
pájaro, Vogel, oiseaux, uccèllo.[2]
We settled on the Italian for warblers,
the German for eagles, the French for swallows,   10
and dismissed the Spanish.
We turned to the sounds for butterflies,
as a butterfly was flying over,
darkening our hands with fluttering shadows;
mariposa, Schmetterling, papillon, farfalla.
All sounds seemed appropriate, even the German.
We repeated the sounds for love:
amor, Liebe, amour, amore.
None seemed to fit, not even English.

For Analysis
1. What arguments would you use to defend the poet's assertion, in lines 9–11, that certain foreign words suggest particular birds, while the Spanish word seems utterly unbirdlike? What about the English word? **2.** Extend your arguments to the words for butterfly. Does English work?

Writing Topic
Make up some words that would sound like different kinds of love—young love, affection, brotherly love, passion, spiritual love. As best you can, explain why the sounds you select suggest certain emotions.

---

[1] English poet (1688–1744) who argued in his poem "An Essay on Criticism" that the sounds within a poem should seem an echo to the sense.
[2] The foreign word sequence is, in each case, Spanish, German, French, Italian.

Richard Wilbur [b. 1921]

A Late Aubade   1968

You could be sitting now in a carrel
Turning some liver-spotted page,
Or rising in an elevator-cage
Toward Ladies' Apparel.

You could be planting a raucous bed
Of salvia, in rubber gloves,
Or lunching through a screed of someone's loves
With pitying head,

Or making some unhappy setter
Heel, or listening to a bleak   10
Lecture on Schoenberg's serial technique.[1]
Isn't this better?

Think of all the time you are not
Wasting, and would not care to waste,
Such things, thank God, not being to your taste.
Think what a lot

Of time, by woman's reckoning,
You've saved, and so may spend on this,
You who had rather lie in bed and kiss
Than anything.   20

It's almost noon, you say? If so,
Time flies, and I need not rehearse
The rosebuds-theme of centuries of verse.[2]
If you *must* go,

Wait for a while, then slip downstairs
And bring us up some chilled white wine,
And some blue cheese, and crackers, and some fine
Ruddy-skinned pears.

---

[1] Arnold Schoenberg (1874–1951), Austrian-born composer.
[2] Refers to the *Carpe Diem* theme (see Glossary of Literary Terms).

For Analysis
1. Look up *aubade* in a dictionary and explain the poem's title. **2.** Is the speaker sexist? Why or why not? **3.** Explain lines 16–18.

Anthony Hecht [b. 1923]

The Dover Bitch 1968
A Criticism Of Life

So there stood Matthew Arnold and this girl
With the cliffs of England crumbling away behind them,
And he said to her, "Try to be true to me,
And I'll do the same for you, for things are bad
All over, etc., etc."
Well now, I knew this girl. It's true she had read
Sophocles in a fairly good translation
And caught that bitter allusion to the sea,
But all the time he was talking she had in mind
The notion of what his whiskers would feel like   10
On the back of her neck. She told me later on
That after a while she got to looking out
At the lights across the channel, and really felt sad,
Thinking of all the wine and enormous beds
And blandishments in French and the perfumes.
And then she got really angry. To have been brought
All the way down from London, and then be addressed
As a sort of mournful cosmic last resort
Is really tough on a girl, and she was pretty.
Anyway, she watched him pace the room   20
And finger his watch-chain and seem to sweat a bit,
And then she said one or two unprintable things.
But you mustn't judge her by that. What I mean to say is,
She's really all right. I still see her once in a while
And she always treats me right. We have a drink
And I give her a good time, and perhaps it's a year
Before I see her again, but there she is,
Running to fat, but dependable as they come,
And sometimes I bring her a bottle of *Nuit d'Amour.*

For Analysis
1. This poem is a response to Matthew Arnold's "Dover Beach," which appears on p. 1006 in this section. Arnold's poem is often read as a pained response to the break-

down of religious tradition and social and political order in the mid-nineteenth century. Is this poem, in contrast, optimistic? Is the relationship between the speaker and the girl at the end of the poem admirable? Explain. **2.** Do you suppose Hecht was moved to write this poem out of admiration for "Dover Beach"? Explain.

Writing Topic
What is the fundamental difference between the speaker's conception of love in Arnold's poem and the "girl's" conception of love as reported in this poem?

Denise Levertov   [b. 1923]

The Mutes   1967

Those groans men use
passing a woman on the street
or on the steps of the subway

to tell her she is a female
and their flesh knows it,

are they a sort of tune,
an ugly enough song, sung
by a bird with a slit tongue

but meant for music?

Or are they the muffled roaring   10
of deafmutes trapped in a building that is
slowly filling with smoke?

Perhaps both.

Such men most often
look as if groan were all they could do,
yet a woman, in spite of herself,

knows it's a tribute:
if she were lacking all grace
they'd pass her in silence:

so it's not only to say she's   20
a warm hole. It's a word

in grief-language, nothing to do with
primitive, not an ur-language;[1]
language stricken, sickened, cast down

in decrepitude. She wants to
throw the tribute away, disgusted, and can't,

it goes on buzzing in her ear,
it changes the pace of her walk,
the torn posters in echoing corridors   30

spell it out, it
quakes and gnashes as the train comes in.
Her pulse sullenly

had picked up speed,
but the cars slow down and
jar to a stop while her understanding

keeps on translating:
'Life after life after life goes by

without poetry,
without seemliness,   40
without love.'

For Analysis
1. Explain the title. **2.** Why does the tribute go on "buzzing in her ear" (l. 28)? **3.** Is
this poem an attack on men? Explain.

Carolyn Kizer   [b. 1925]

Bitch   1984

Now, when he and I meet, after all these years,
I say to the bitch inside me, don't start growling.
He isn't a trespasser anymore,
Just an old acquaintance tipping his hat.

The Mutes
  [1] Primordial language.

My voice says, "Nice to see you,"
As the bitch starts to bark hysterically.
He isn't an enemy now,
Where are your manners, I say, as I say,
"How are the children? They must be growing up."
At a kind word from him, a look like the old days,   10
The bitch changes her tone: she begins to whimper.
She wants to snuggle up to him, to cringe.
Down, girl! Keep your distance
Or I'll give you a taste of the choke-chain.
"Fine, I'm just fine," I tell him.
She slobbers and grovels.
After all, I am her mistress. She is basically loyal.
It's just that she remembers how she came running
Each evening, when she heard his step;
How she lay at his feet and looked up adoringly   20
Though he was absorbed in his paper;
Or, bored with her devotion, ordered her to the kitchen
Until he was ready to play.
But the small careless kindnesses
When he'd had a good day, or a couple of drinks,
Come back to her now, seem more important
Than the casual cruelties, the ultimate dismissal.
"It's nice to know you are doing so well," I say.
He couldn't have taken you with him;
You were too demonstrative, too clumsy,   30
Not like the well-groomed pets of his new friends.
"Give my regards to your wife," I say. You gag
As I drag you off by the scruff,
Saying, "Goodbye! Goodbye! Nice to have seen you again."

For Analysis

1. Who is being addressed in lines 13 and 14? **2.** In what ways does the title suit the poem? Consider the **tone** of "Bitch," as well as the many connotations of the word, in answering this question. **3.** What is "the ultimate dismissal" referred to in line 27? **4.** How would you describe the speaker's present feelings about her former relationship?

Carol Bergé [b. 1928]

Position 1964

i stand before you
to represent all of the women
you have ever hated

your mother who
whipped the spirit out of you
your aunt who
kibitzed the life out of your life
the girl who didnt
or wouldnt or couldnt   but didnt
etc   etc   etc   10

what chance have i got
unless you consider
that you stand before me too

Elaine Magarrell [b. 1928]

The Joy of Cooking 1988

I have prepared my sister's tongue,
scrubbed and skinned it,
trimmed the roots, small bones, and gristle.
Carved through the hump it slices thin and neat.
Best with horseradish
and economical—it probably will grow back.
Next time perhaps a creole sauce
or mold of aspic?
I will have my brother's heart,
which is firm and rather dry,   10
slow cooked. It resembles muscle
more than organ meat
and needs an apple-onion stuffing
to make it interesting at all.
Although beef heart serves six
my brother's heart barely feeds two.
I could also have it braised
and served in sour sauce.

For Analysis

1. Can you suggest some other meaty parts of the poet's brother and sister that might be added to the menu? How might they (in view of the poet's expressed feelings) be cooked? **2.** *Tongue* and *heart* are figures of speech called **synecdoches**. What human behaviors do they represent?

Writing Topic

Select one person you love or admire and one you despise. Choose a part to cook that most reveals each person's nature, and write a recipe that would most tellingly reveal the lovable and hateful quality of each person.

Anne Sexton   [1928–1974]

The Farmer's Wife   1960

From the hodge porridge
of their country lust,
their local life in Illinois,
where all their acres look
like a sprouting broom factory,
they name just ten years now
that she has been his habit;
as again tonight he'll say
honey bunch let's go
and she will not say how there   10
must be more to living
than this brief bright bridge
of the raucous bed or even
the slow braille touch of him
like a heavy god grown light,
that old pantomime of love
that she wants although
it leaves her still alone,
built back again at last,
minds apart from him, living   20
her own self in her own words
and hating the sweat of the house
they keep when they finally lie
each in separate dreams
and then how she watches him,
still strong in the blowzy bag
of his usual sleep while
her young years bungle past

their same marriage bed
and she wishes him cripple, or poet,   30
or even lonely, or sometimes,
better, my lover, dead.

Thom Gunn   [b. 1929]

Memory Unsettled   1992

Your pain still hangs in air,
Sharp motes of it suspended;
The voice of your despair—
That also is not ended:

When near your death a friend
Asked you what he could do,
'Remember me,' you said.
We will remember you.

Once when you went to see
Another with a fever   10
In a like hospital bed,
With terrible hothouse cough
And terrible hothouse shiver
That soaked him and then dried him,
And you perceived that he
Had to be comforted,

You climbed in there beside him
And hugged him plain in view,
Though you were sick enough,
And had your own fears too.   20

Adrienne Rich   [b. 1929]

Living in Sin   1955

She had thought the studio would keep itself;
no dust upon the furniture of love.
Half heresy, to wish the taps less vocal,
the panes relieved of grime. A plate of pears,
a piano with a Persian shawl, a cat
stalking the picturesque amusing mouse
had risen at his urging.
Not that at five each separate stair would writhe
under the milkman's tramp; that morning light
so coldly would delineate the scraps   10
of last night's cheese and three sepulchral bottles;
that on the kitchen shelf among the saucers
a pair of beetle-eyes would fix her own—
Envoy from some village in the moldings . . .
Meanwhile, he, with a yawn,
sounded a dozen notes upon the keyboard,
declared it out of tune, shrugged at the mirror,
rubbed at his beard, went out for cigarettes;
while she, jeered by the minor demons,
pulled back the sheets and made the bed and found   20
a towel to dust the table-top,
and let the coffee-pot boil over on the stove.
By evening she was back in love again,
though not so wholly but throughout the night
she woke sometimes to feel the daylight coming
like a relentless milkman up the stairs.

Sylvia Plath   [1932–1963]

Daddy   1965

You do not do, you do not do
Any more, black shoe
In which I have lived like a foot
For thirty years, poor and white,
Barely daring to breathe or Achoo.

Daddy, I have had to kill you,
You died before I had time—
Marble-heavy, a bag full of God,
Ghastly statue with one gray toe
Big as a Frisco seal   10

And a head in the freakish Atlantic
Where it pours bean green over blue
In the waters off beautiful Nauset.
I used to pray to recover you.
Ach, du.¹

In the German tongue, in the Polish town
Scraped flat by the roller
Of wars, wars, wars.
But the name of the town is common.
My Polack friend   20

Says there are a dozen or two.
So I never could tell where you
Put your foot, your root,
I never could talk to you.
The tongue stuck in my jaw.

It stuck in a barb wire snare.
Ich, ich, ich, ich,²
I could hardly speak.
I thought every German was you.
And the language obscene   30

An engine, an engine
Chuffing me off like a Jew.
A Jew to Dachau, Auschwitz, Belsen.
I began to talk like a Jew.
I think I may well be a Jew.

The snows of the Tyrol, the clear beer of Vienna
Are not very pure or true.
With my gypsy ancestress and my weird luck
And my Taroc pack and my Taroc pack
I may be a bit of a Jew.   40

¹ German for "Oh, you."
² German for "I, I, I, I."

I have always been scared of *you*,
With your Luftwaffe,[3] your gobbledygoo.
And your neat mustache
And your Aryan eye, bright blue.
Panzer-man,[4] panzer-man, O You—

Not God but a swastika
So black no sky could squeak through.
Every woman adores a Fascist,
The boot in the face, the brute
Brute heart of a brute like you.   50

You stand at the blackboard, daddy,
In the picture I have of you,
A cleft in your chin instead of your foot
But no less a devil for that, no not
Any less the black man who

Bit my pretty red heart in two.
I was ten when they buried you.
At twenty I tried to die
And get back, back, back to you.
I thought even the bones would do   60

But they pulled me out of the sack,
And they stuck me together with glue.
And then I knew what to do.
I made a model of you,
A man in black with a Meinkampf[5] look

And a love of the rack and the screw.
And I said I do, I do.
So daddy, I'm finally through.
The black telephone's off at the root,
The voices just can't worm through.   70

If I've killed one man, I've killed two—
The vampire who said he was you
And drank my blood for a year,
Seven years, if you want to know.
Daddy, you can lie back now.

---

[3] Name of the German air force during World War II.
[4] Panzer refers to German armored divisions during World War II.
[5] *My Battle*, the title of Adolf Hitler's political autobiography.

There's a stake in your fat black heart
And the villagers never liked you.
They are dancing and stamping on you.
They always *knew* it was you.
Daddy, daddy, you bastard, I'm through.   80

For Analysis

1. How do the allusions to Nazism function in the poem? **2.** Does the poem exhibit the speaker's love for her father or her hatred for him? Explain. **3.** What sort of man does the speaker marry (see stanzas 13 and 14)? **4.** How does the speaker characterize her husband and her father in the last two stanzas? Might the "Daddy" of the last line of the poem refer to something more than the speaker's father? Explain.

Writing Topics

1. What is the effect of the peculiar structure, idiosyncratic **rhyme**, unusual words (such as *achoo, gobbledygoo*), and repetitions in the poem? **2.** What emotional associations does the title "Daddy" possess? Are those associations reinforced or contradicted by the poem?

Audre Lorde [1934–1992]

Power[1] 1978

The difference between poetry and rhetoric
is being
ready to kill
yourself
instead of your children.

I am trapped on a desert of raw gunshot wounds
and a dead child dragging his shattered black
face off the edge of my sleep
blood from his punctured cheeks and shoulders

Power

[1] " 'Power' . . . is a poem written about Clifford Glover, the ten-year-old Black child shot by a cop who was acquitted by a jury on which a Black woman sat. In fact, the day I heard on the radio that O'Shea had been acquitted, I was going across town on Eighty-eighth Street and I had to pull over. A kind of fury rose up in me; the sky turned red. I felt so sick. I felt as if I would drive this car into a wall, into the next person I saw. So I pulled over. I took out my journal just to air some of my fury, to get it out of my fingertips. Those expressed feelings are that poem" (Audre Lorde, "My Words Will Be There," in *Black Women Writers* (1950–1980), ed. Mari Evans, New York, 1983, p. 266).

is the only liquid for miles and my stomach   10
churns at the imagined taste while
my mouth splits into dry lips
without loyalty or reason
thirsting for the wetness of his blood
as it sinks into the whiteness
of the desert where I am lost
without imagery or magic
trying to make power out of hatred and destruction
trying to heal my dying son with kisses
only the sun will bleach his bones quicker.   20

The policeman who shot down a 10-year-old in Queens[2]
stood over the boy with his cop shoes in childish blood
and a voice said "Die you little motherfucker" and
there are tapes to prove that. At his trial
this policeman said in his own defense
"I didn't notice the size or nothing else
only the color." and
there are tapes to prove that, too.

Today that 37-year-old white man with 13 years of police forcing
has been set free   30
by 11 white men who said they were satisfied
justice had been done
and one black woman who said
"They convinced me" meaning
they had dragged her 4′ 10″ black woman's frame
over the hot coals of four centuries of white male approval
until she let go the first real power she ever had
and lined her own womb with cement
to make a graveyard for our children.

I have not been able to touch the destruction within me.   40
But unless I learn to use
the difference between poetry and rhetoric
my power too will run corrupt as poisonous mold
or lie limp and useless as an unconnected wire
and one day I will take my teenaged plug
and connect it to the nearest socket
raping an 85-year-old white woman
who is somebody's mother
and as I beat her senseless and set a torch to her bed

[2] A borough of New York City.

a greek chorus will be singing in ¾ time[3]   50
"Poor thing. She never hurt a soul. What beasts they are."

Lucille Clifton   [b. 1936]

There Is a Girl Inside   1977

there is a girl inside.
she is randy as a wolf.
she will not walk away
and leave these bones
to an old woman.

she is a green tree
in a forest of kindling.
she is a green girl
in a used poet.

she has waited   10
patient as a nun
for the second coming,
when she can break through gray hairs
into blossom

and her lovers will harvest
honey and thyme
and the woods will be wild
with the damn wonder of it.

For Analysis
1. Who is the "girl" of this poem? What is she "inside" of? **2.** What are the "bones" of the first stanza? What does the speaker's statement that she will not defer to old women tell us about her? **3.** Describe the prevailing **metaphor** of the poem.

Writing Topic
Compare this poem with Helen Sorrells's "From a Correct Address in a Suburb of a Major City" (p. 449) What do the two speakers share? In what ways are they different?

Power
   [3] In classical Greek tragedy, a chorus chanted in response to the action in the play. Three-quarter time is waltz rhythm.

Seamus Heaney   [b. 1939]

Valediction   1966

Lady with the frilled blouse
And simple tartan skirt,
Since you have left the house
Its emptiness has hurt
All thought. In your presence
Time rode easy, anchored
On a smile; but absence
Rocked love's balance, unmoored
The days. They buck and bound
Across the calendar   10
Pitched from the quiet sound
Of your flower-tender
Voice. Need breaks on my strand;
You've gone, I am at sea.
Until you resume command
Self is in mutiny.

For Analysis
1. What is the central figure of speech (beginning in the middle of line 5) that animates this poem? **2.** How are *time, love's balance,* and *the days* affected by the lady's
behavior? **3.** What sort of voice would a "flower-tender / Voice" (ll. 12–13) be?

Writing Topic
Write an essay or a poem, serious or humorous, in which you use an extended
metaphor to describe a fundamental emotion or experience. For example, how
falling in love is like racing a car, or how the anguish of separation is like a visit to a
dentist, or how attending classes is like a twenty-mile hike through a desert.

Sharon Olds   [b. 1942]

Sex without Love   1984

How do they do it, the ones who make love
without love? Beautiful as dancers,
gliding over each other like ice skaters
over the ice, fingers hooked
inside each other's bodies, faces

red as steak, wine, wet as the
children at birth whose mothers are going to
give them away. How do they come to the
come to the   come to the   God   come to the
still waters, and not love   10
the one who came there with them, light
rising slowly as steam off their joined
skin? These are the true religious,
the purists, the pros, the ones who will not
accept a false Messiah, love the
priest instead of the God. They do not
mistake the lover for their own pleasure,
they are like great runners: they know they are alone
with the road surface, the cold, the wind,
the fit of their shoes, their over-all cardio-   20
vascular health—just factors, like the partner
in the bed, and not the truth, which is the
single body alone in the universe
against its own best time.

For Analysis
1. Characterize the speaker's attitude toward "the ones who make love without love."
2. Who are the "These" of line 13? **3.** What is the effect of the repetitions in lines 8
and 9? **4.** What does "factors" of line 21 refer to? **5.** Put into your own words the
"truth" referred to in the final three lines. Is the speaker using the word straightfor-
wardly or ironically? Explain.

The Victims   1984

When Mother divorced you, we were glad. She took it and
took it, in silence, all those years and then
kicked you out, suddenly, and her
kids loved it. Then you were fired, and we
grinned inside, the way people grinned when
Nixon's helicopter lifted off the South
Lawn for the last time. We were tickled
to think of your office taken away,
your secretaries taken away,
your lunches with three double bourbons,   10
your pencils, your reams of paper. Would they take your
suits back, too, those dark
carcasses hung in your closet, and the black
noses of your shoes with their large pores?
She had taught us to take it, to hate you and take it
until we pricked with her for your

annihilation, Father. Now I
pass the bums in doorways, the white
slugs of their bodies gleaming through slits in their
suits of compressed silt, the stained   20
flippers of their hands, the underwater
fire of their eyes, ships gone down with the
lanterns lit, and I wonder who took it and
took it from them in silence until they had
given it all away and had nothing
left but this.

For Analysis

1. Characterize the **tone** of this poem. Who are the victims? **2.** Identify and analyze
the effects of the **metaphors** the speaker uses in the final lines to describe the "bums."
3. How does the speaker's description of the "bums" clarify her feelings about her
father?

Molly Peacock   [b. 1947]

Say You Love Me   1989

What happened earlier I'm not sure of.
Of course he was drunk, but often he was.
His face looked like a ham on a hook above

me—I was pinned to the chair because
he'd hunkered over me with arms like jaws
pried open by the chair arms. "Do you love

me?" he began to sob. "Say you love me!"
I held out. I was probably fifteen.
What had happened? Had my mother—had she

said or done something? Or had he just been   10
drinking too long after work? "He'll get *mean*,"
my sister hissed, "just *tell* him." I brought my knee

up to kick him, but was too scared. Nothing
could have got the words out of me then. Rage
shut me up, yet "DO YOU?" was beginning

to peel, as of live layers of skin, age
from age from age from him until he gazed
through hysteria as a wet baby thing

repeating, "Do you love me? Say you do,"
in baby chokes, only loud, for they came   20
from a man. There wouldn't be a rescue

from my mother, still at work. The same
choking sobs said, "Love me, love me," and my game
was breaking down because I couldn't do

anything, not escape into my own
refusal, *I won't, I won't,* not fantasize
a kind, rich father, not fill the narrowed zone,

empty except for confusion until the size
of my fear ballooned as I saw his eyes,
blurred, taurean—my sister screamed—unknown,   30

unknown to me, a voice rose and leveled
off, "I love you," I said. *"Say 'I love you,*
Dad!' " "I love you, Dad," I whispered, leveled

by defeat into a cardboard image, untrue,
unbending. I was surprised I could move
as I did to get up, but he stayed, burled

onto the chair—my monstrous fear—she screamed,
my sister, "Dad, the phone! Go answer it!"
The phone wasn't ringing, yet he seemed

to move toward it, and I ran. He had a fit—   40
"It's not ringing!"—but I was at the edge of it
as he collapsed into the chair and blamed

both of us at a distance. No, the phone
was not ringing. There was no world out there,
so there we remained, completely alone.

For Analysis

1. Is the speaker a child or an adult? Explain. **2.** How do the **images** of the sixth stanza capture the speaker's feelings? **3.** When the speaker finally capitulates to her father's demand, she describes herself in lines 33–35 as "leveled / by defeat into a cardboard image, untrue, / unbending." What does she mean? **4.** Explain what the speaker means by "my game" (l. 23).

Writing Topic

What would motivate a parent, even a drunken one, to make the kind of demand the father makes on his daughter?

Susan Musgrave   [b. 1951]

Right through the Heart   1982

and out the other side,
pumping like a bitch in heat,
beast with two backs, the
left and right ventricles.

It has to be love
when it goes straight through;
no bone can stop it,
no barb impede its journey.

When it happens you have to bleed,
you want to kiss and hold on   10

despite all the messy blood
you want to embrace it.

You want it to last forever,
you want to own it.
You want to take love's tiny life
in your hands

and crush it to death before it dies.

For Analysis

1. What goes "Right through the Heart?" **2.** How are the "left and right ventricles" characterized? **3.** Explain the **paradox** of the last three lines.

Writing Topic

Analyze the last three lines of this poem in an essay on the dangers of unbounded passion.

Gary Soto   [b. 1952]

Oranges   1987

The first time I walked
With a girl, I was twelve,
Cold, and weighted down
With two oranges in my jacket.
December. Frost cracking
Beneath my steps, my breath
Before me, then gone,
As I walked toward
Her house, the one whose
Porch light burned yellow   10
Night and day, in any weather.
A dog barked at me, until
She came out pulling
At her gloves, face bright
With rouge. I smiled,
Touched her shoulder, and led
Her down the street, across
A used car lot and a line
Of newly planted trees,
Until we were breathing   20
Before a drugstore. We
Entered, the tiny bell
Bringing a saleslady
Down a narrow aisle of goods.
I turned to the candies
Tiered like bleachers,
And asked what she wanted—
Light in her eyes, a smile
Starting at the corners
Of her mouth. I fingered   30
A nickel in my pocket,
And when she lifted a chocolate
That cost a dime,
I didn't say anything.
I took the nickel from
My pocket, then an orange,
And set them quietly on
The counter. When I looked up,

The lady's eyes met mine,
And held them, knowing   40
Very well what it was all
About.

      Outside,
A few cars hissing past,
Fog hanging like old
Coats between the trees.
I took my girl's hand
In mine for two blocks,
Then released it to let
Her unwrap the chocolate.
I peeled my orange   50
That was so bright against
The gray of December
That, from some distance,
Someone might have thought
I was making a fire in my hands.

Liu Kexiang   [b. 1957]

Descendants of Myths   1992

they invented myths
myths transformed them

mammals with dignity
strictly territorial hunters

advanced in their social organization
not at all hirsute, on a mixed diet
with a strong sexual drive
they once lived in jungles
polite, they know how to smile
but resent strangers   10

they can kill each other from a distance
from a longer and longer distance

For Analysis

1. Who are "they" in the opening line? **2.** In what sense might "they" be transformed by the myths they invent? **3.** What is the significance of the final two lines?

Writing Topic

Write an essay on this poem's implicit observations on historical changes and developments.

Drama

William Shakespeare [1564–1616]

Othello ca. 1604

CHARACTERS

Duke of Venice
Brabantio, a Senator
Senators
Gratiano, Brother to Brabantio
Lodovico, Kinsman to Brabantio
Othello, a noble Moor; in the service of the Venetian State
Cassio, his Lieutenant
Iago, his Ancient
Roderigo, a Venetian Gentleman

Montano, Othello's predecessor in the Government of Cyprus
Clown, Servant to Othello
Desdemona, Daughter to Brabantio, and Wife to Othello
Emilia, Wife to Iago
Bianca, Mistress to Cassio
Sailor, Officers, Gentlemen, Messengers, Musicians, Heralds, Attendants

Scene

For the first Act, in Venice; during the rest of the Play, at a Sea-port in Cyprus

Act I

Scene 1. Venice. A Street.

(Enter Roderigo and Iago.)

Roderigo. Tush! Never tell me; I take it much unkindly
That thou, Iago, who has had my purse
As if the strings were thine, shouldst know of this.[1]

---

[1] I.e., Othello's successful courtship of Desdemona.

1041

Iago. 'Sblood,[2] but you will not hear me:
    If ever I did dream of such a matter,
    Abhor me.
Roderigo. Thou told'st me thou didst hold him[3] in thy hate.
Iago. Despise me if I do not. Three great ones of the city,
    In personal suit to make me his lieutenant,
    Off-capp'd[4] to him; and, by the faith of man,   10
    I know my price, I am worth no worse a place;
    But he, as loving his own pride and purposes,
    Evades them, with a bombast circumstance[5]
    Horribly stuff'd with epithets of war;
    And, in conclusion,
    Nonsuits[6] my mediators;[7] for, 'Certes,'[8] says he,
    'I have already chosen my officer.'
    And what was he?
    Forsooth, a great arithmetician,
    One Michael Cassio, a Florentine,   20
    A fellow almost damn'd in a fair wife;[9]
    That never set a squadron in the field,
    Nor the division of a battle knows
    More than a spinster; unless[10] the bookish theoric,[11]
    Wherein the toged consuls can propose
    As masterly as he: mere prattle, without practice,
    Is all his soldiership. But he, sir, had the election;
    And I—of whom his eyes had seen the proof
    At Rhodes, at Cyprus, and on other grounds
    Christian and heathen—must be be-lee'd[12] and calm'd   30
    By debitor and creditor; this counter-caster,[13]
    He, in good time, must his lieutenant be,
    And I—God bless the mark!—his Moorship's ancient.[14]
Roderigo. By heaven, I rather would have been his hangman.
Iago. Why, there's no remedy: 'tis the curse of service,
    Preferment goes by letter and affection,
    Not by the old gradation,[15] where each second
    Stood heir to the first. Now, sir, be judge yourself,
    Whe'r[16] I in any just term am affin'd[17]
    To love the Moor.

---

[2] By God's blood.   [3] I.e., Othello.   [4] Took off their caps.   [5] Pompous wordiness, circumlocution.   [6] Turns down.   [7] Spokesmen.   [8] In truth.   [9] A much debated phrase. In the Italian source the Captain (i.e., Cassio) was married, and it may be that Shakespeare originally intended Bianca to be Cassio's wife but later changed his mind and failed to alter the phrase here accordingly. Or perhaps Iago simply sneers at Cassio as a notorious ladies' man.   [10] Except.   [11] Theory.   [12] Left without wind for my sails.   [13] Bookkeeper (cf. "arithmetician" above).   [14] Ensign (but Iago's position in the play seems to be that of Othello's aide-de-camp).   [15] Seniority.   [16] Whether.   [17] Obliged.

Roderigo.   I would not follow him then.   40
Iago.   O! sir, content you;
  I follow him to serve my turn upon him;
  We cannot all be masters, nor all masters
  Cannot be truly follow'd. You shall mark
  Many a duteous and knee-crooking knave,
  That, doting on his own obsequious bondage,
  Wears out his time, much like his master's ass,
  For nought but provender, and when he's old, cashier'd;
  Whip me such honest knaves. Others there are
  Who, trimm'd in forms and visages of duty,   50
  Keep yet their hearts attending on themselves,
  And, throwing but shows of service on their lords,
  Do well thrive by them, and when they have lin'd their coats
  Do themselves homage: these fellows have some soul;
  And such a one do I profess myself. For, sir,
  It is as sure as you are Roderigo,
  Were I the Moor, I would not be Iago:
  In following him, I follow but myself;
  Heaven is my judge, not I for love and duty,
  But seeming so, for my peculiar end: 60
  For when my outward action doth demonstrate
  The native act and figure of my heart
  In compliment extern,[18] 'tis not long after
  But I will wear my heart upon my sleeve
  For daws to peck at: I am not what I am.
Roderigo.   What a full fortune does the thick-lips owe,[19]
  If he can carry 't thus!
Iago.   Call up her father;
  Rouse him, make after him, poison his delight,
  Proclaim him in the streets, incense her kinsmen,
  And, though he in a fertile climate dwell,[20]   70
  Plague him with flies; though that his joy be joy,
  Yet throw such changes of vexation on 't
  As it may lose some colour.
Roderigo.   Here is her father's house; I'll call aloud.
Iago.   Do; with like timorous[21] accent and dire yell
  As when, by night and negligence, the fire
  Is spied in populous cities.
Roderigo.   What, ho! Brabantio: Signior Brabantio, ho!
Iago.   Awake! what, ho! Brabantio! thieves! thieves! thieves!
  Look to your house, your daughter, and your bags!   80
  Thieves! thieves!

---

[18] External show.   [19] Own.   [20] I.e., is fortunate.   [21] Frightening.

(*Enter Brabantio, above, at a window.*)

Brabantio.   What is the reason of this terrible summons?
  What is the matter there?
Roderigo.   Signior, is all your family within?
Iago.   Are your doors lock'd?
Brabantio.   Why? wherefore ask you this?
Iago.   'Zounds!²² sir, you're robb'd; for shame, put on your gown;
  Your heart is burst, you have lost half your soul;
  Even now, now, very now, an old black ram
  Is tupping²³ your white ewe. Arise, arise!
  Awake the snorting²⁴ citizens with the bell,   90
  Or else the devil will make a grandsire of you.
  Arise, I say.
Brabantio.   What! have you lost your wits?
Roderigo.   Most reverend signior, do you know my voice?
Brabantio.   Not I, what are you?
Roderigo.   My name is Roderigo.
Brabantio.   The worser welcome:
  I have charg'd thee not to haunt about my doors:
  In honest plainness thou hast heard me say
  My daughter is not for thee; and now, in madness,
  Being full of supper and distempering draughts,
  Upon malicious knavery dost thou come   100
  To start my quiet.
Roderigo.   Sir, sir, sir!
Brabantio.   But thou must needs be sure
  My spirit and my place²⁵ have in them power
  To make this bitter to thee.
Roderigo.   Patience, good sir.
Brabantio.   What tell'st thou me of robbing? this is Venice;
  My house is not a grange.²⁶
Roderigo.   Most grave Brabantio,
  In simple and pure soul I come to you.
Iago.   'Zounds! sir, you are one of those that will not serve God if the devil bid
  you. Because we come to do you service and you think we are ruffians, you'll
  have your daughter covered with a Barbary horse; you'll have your nephews
  neigh to you; you'll have coursers for cousins and gennets²⁷ for germans.²⁸
Brabantio.   What profane wretch art thou?
Iago.   I am one, sir, that comes to tell you, your daughter and the Moor are
  now making the beast with two backs.
Brabantio.   Thou art a villain.

---

²² By God's wounds.   ²³ Copulating.   ²⁴ Snoring.   ²⁵ Position.   ²⁶ Isolated farmhouse.
²⁷ Spanish horses.   ²⁸ Blood relations.

Iago.   You are—a senator.

Brabantio.   This thou shalt answer; I know thee, Roderigo.

Roderigo.   Sir, I will answer any thing. But, I beseech you,   120
If 't be your pleasure and most wise consent,—
As partly, I find, it is,—that your fair daughter,
At this odd-even[29] and dull watch o' the night,
Transported with no worse nor better guard
But with a knave of common hire, a gondolier,
To the gross clasps of a lascivious Moor,—
If this be known to you, and your allowance,[30]
We then have done you bold and saucy wrongs;
But if you know not this, my manners tell me
We have your wrong rebuke. Do not believe   130
That, from[31] the sense of all civility,
I thus would play and trifle with your reverence:
Your daughter, if you have not given her leave,
I say again, hath made a gross revolt;
Tying her duty, beauty, wit and fortunes
In[32] an extravagant[33] and wheeling stranger
Of here and every where. Straight satisfy yourself:
If she be in her chamber or your house,
Let loose on me the justice of the state
For thus deluding you.

Brabantio.   Strike on the tinder, ho!   140
Give me a taper! call up all my people!
This accident[34] is not unlike my dream;
Belief of it oppresses me already.
Light, I say! light!   *(Exit, from above.)*

Iago.   Farewell, for I must leave you:
It seems not meet nor wholesome to my place
To be produc'd,[35] as, if I stay, I shall,
Against the Moor; for I do know the state,
However this may gall him with some check,[36]
Cannot with safety cast him; for he's embark'd
With such loud reason to the Cyprus wars,—   150
Which even now stand in act,—that, for their souls,
Another of his fathom[37] they have none,
To lead their business; in which regard,
Though I do hate him as I do hell-pains,
Yet, for necessity of present life,
I must show out a flag and sign of love,

---

[29] Between night and morning.   [30] By your approval.   [31] Away from.   [32] To.   [33] Expatriate.   [34] Happening.   [35] I.e., as a witness.   [36] Restraining adversity.   [37] Caliber, ability.

Which is indeed but sign. That you shall surely find him,
Lead to the Sagittary[38] the raised search;
And there will I be with him. So, farewell.   (*Exit.*)

(*Enter below, Brabantio, and servants with torches.*)

Brabantio.   It is too true an evil: gone she is,   160
   And what's to come of my despised time
   Is nought but bitterness. Now, Roderigo,
   Where didst thou see her? O, unhappy girl!
   With the Moor, sayst thou? Who would be a father!
   How didst thou know 'twas she? O, she deceives me
   Past thought. What said she to you? Get more tapers!
   Raise all my kindred! Are they married, think you?
Roderigo.   Truly, I think they are.
Brabantio.   O heaven! How got she out? O treason of the blood:
   Fathers, from hence trust not your daughters' minds   170
   By what you see them act. Are there not charms
   By which the property of youth and maidhood
   May be abus'd? Have you not read, Roderigo,
   Of some such thing?
Roderigo.   Yes, sir, I have indeed.
Brabantio.   Call up my brother. O! that you had had her.
   Some one way, some another! Do you know
   Where we may apprehend her and the Moor?
Roderigo.   I think I can discover him, if you please
   To get good guard and go along with me.   180
Brabantio.   Pray you, lead on. At every house I'll call;
   I may command at most. Get weapons, ho!
   And raise some special officers of night.
   On, good Roderigo; I'll deserve[39] your pains.   (*Exeunt.*)

Scene 2.   Another street.

(*Enter Othello, Iago, and Attendants, with torches.*)

Iago.   Though in the trade of war I have slain men,
   Yet do I hold it very stuff o' the conscience
   To do no contriv'd murder: I lack iniquity
   Sometimes to do me service. Nine or ten times
   I had thought to have yerk'd[40] him here under the ribs.
Othello.   'Tis better as it is.

---

[38] The name of an inn (?).   [39] I.e., reward.   [40] Stabbed.

Iago.   Nay, but he prated,
And spoke such scurvy and provoking terms
Against your honour
That, with the little godliness I have,
I did full hard forbear him. But, I pray, sir,   10
Are you fast married? Be assur'd of this,
That the magnifico[41] is much belov'd,
And hath in his effect a voice potential
As double[42] as the duke's; he will divorce you,
Or put upon you what restraint and grievance
The law—with all his might to enforce it on—
Will give him cable.[43]
Othello.   Let him do his spite:
My services which I have done the signiory[44]
Shall out-tongue his complaints. 'Tis yet to know,[45]
Which when I know that boasting is an honour   20
I shall promulgate, I fetch my life and being
From men of royal siege, and my demerits[46]
May speak unbonneted[47] to as proud a fortune
As this[48] that I have reach'd; for know, Iago,
But that I love the gentle Desdemona,
I would not my unhoused[49] free condition
Put into circumscription and confine
For the sea's worth. But, look! what lights come yond?
Iago.   Those are the raised[50] father and his friends:
You were best[51] go in.
Othello.   Not I; I must be found: 30
My parts, my title, and my perfect[52] soul
Shall manifest me rightly. Is it they?
Iago.   By Janus,[53] I think no.

(*Enter Cassio and certain Officers, with torches.*)

Othello.   The servants of the duke, and my lieutenant.
The goodness of the night upon you, friends!
What is the news?
Cassio.   The duke does greet you, general,
And he requires your haste-post-haste appearance,
Even on the instant.

---

[41] One of the grandees, or rulers, of Venice; here, Brabantio.   [42] Iago means that Brabantio's influence equals that of the Doge's with his double vote.   [43] I.e., scope.   [44] The Venetian government.   [45] I.e., the signiory does not as yet know.   [46] Merits.   [47] I.e., as equals.   [48] I.e., that of Desdemona's family.   [49] Unconfined.   [50] Aroused.   [51] Had better.   [52] Untroubled by a bad conscience.   [53] The two-faced Roman god of portals and doors and (hence) of beginnings and ends.

Othello.   What is the matter, think you?
Cassio.   Something from Cyprus, as I may divine.
   It is a business of some heat;[54] the galleys   40
   Have sent a dozen sequent[55] messengers
   This very night at one another's heels,
   And many of the consuls,[56] rais'd and met,
   Are at the duke's already. You have been hotly call'd for;
   When, being not at your lodging to be found,
   The senate hath sent about three several[57] quests
   To search you out.
Othello.   'Tis well I am found by you.
   I will but spend a word here in the house,
   And go with you.   (*Exit.*)
Cassio.   Ancient, what makes he here?
Iago.   Faith, he to-night hath boarded a land carrack;[58]   50
   If it prove lawful prize, he's made for ever.
Cassio.   I do not understand.
Iago.   He's married.
Cassio.   To who?

(*Re-enter Othello.*)

Iago.   Marry,[59] to—Come, captain, will you go?
Othello.   Have with you.
Cassio.   Here comes another troop to seek for you.
Iago.   It is Brabantio. General, be advis'd;
   He comes to bad intent.

(*Enter Brabantio, Roderigo, and Officers, with torches and weapons.*)

Othello.   Holla! stand there!
Roderigo.   Signior, it is the Moor.
Brabantio.   Down with him, thief!

(*They draw on both sides.*)

Iago.   You, Roderigo! Come, sir, I am for you.[60]
Othello.   Keep up your bright swords, for the dew will rust them.
   Good signior, you shall more command with years   60
   Than with your weapons.
Brabantio.   O thou foul thief! where hast thou stow'd my daughter?
   Damn'd as thou art, thou hast enchanted her;

---

[54] Urgency.   [55] Following one another.   [56] I.e., senators.   [57] Separate.   [58] Treasure ship.
[59] By the Virgin Mary.   [60] Let you and me fight.

For I'll refer me to all things of sense,
If she in chains of magic were not bound,
Whether a maid so tender, fair, and happy,
So opposite to marriage that she shunn'd
The wealthy curled darlings of our nation,
Would ever have, to incur a general mock,
Run from her guardage to the sooty bosom   70
Of such a thing as thou; to fear, not to delight.
Judge me the world, if 'tis not gross in sense[61]
That thou hast practis'd on her with foul charms,
Abus'd her delicate youth with drugs or minerals
That weaken motion:[62] I'll have 't disputed on;
'Tis probable, and palpable to thinking.
I therefore apprehend and do attach[63] thee
For an abuser of the world, a practiser
Of arts inhibited and out of warrant.[64]
Lay hold upon him: if he do resist,   80
Subdue him at his peril.
Othello.   Hold your hands,
Both you of my inclining,[65] and the rest:
Were it my cue to fight, I should have known it
Without a prompter. Where will you that I go
To answer this your charge?
Brabantio.   To prison; till fit time
Of law and course of direct session[66]
Call thee to answer.
Othello.   What if I do obey?
How may the duke be therewith satisfied,
Whose messengers are here about my side,
Upon some present[67] business of the state   90
To bring me to him?
Officer.   'Tis true, most worthy signior;
The duke's in council, and your noble self,
I am sure, is sent for.
Brabantio.   How! the duke in council!
In this time of the night! Bring him away.
Mine's not an idle cause: the duke himself,
Or any of my brothers of the state,[68]
Cannot but feel this wrong as 'twere their own;
For if such actions may have passage free,
Bond-slaves and pagans shall our statesmen be.   *(Exeunt.)*

---

[61] Obvious.   [62] Normal reactions.   [63] Arrest.   [64] Prohibited and illegal.   [65] Party.
[66] Normal process of law.   [67] Immediate, pressing.   [68] Fellow senators.

Scene 3.   A Council Chamber.

(*The Duke and Senators sitting at a table. Officers attending.*)

Duke.   There is no composition[69] in these news
   That gives them credit.
First Senator.   Indeed, they are disproportion'd;
   My letters say a hundred and seven galleys.
Duke.   And mine, a hundred and forty.
Second Senator.   And mine, two hundred:
   But though they jump[70] not on a just[71] account,—
   As in these cases, where the aim[72] reports,
   'Tis oft with difference,—yet do they all confirm
   A Turkish fleet, and bearing up to Cyprus.
Duke.   Nay, it is possible enough to judgment:
   I do not so secure me in[73] the error,   10
   But the main article[74] I do approve[75]
   In fearful sense.
Sailor (*within*).   What, ho! what, ho! what, ho!
Officer.   A messenger from the galleys.

(*Enter a Sailor.*)

Duke.   Now, what's the business?
Sailor.   The Turkish preparation makes for Rhodes;
   So was I bid report here to the state
   By Signior Angelo.
Duke.   How say you by this change?
First Senator.   This cannot be
   By no[76] assay[77] of reason; 'tis a pageant[78]
   To keep us in false gaze.[79] When we consider
   The importancy of Cyprus to the Turk,   20
   And let ourselves again but understand,
   That as it more concerns the Turk than Rhodes,
   So may he with more facile question bear[80] it,
   For that it stands not in such warlike brace,[81]
   But altogether lacks the abilities
   That Rhodes is dress'd in: if we make thought of this,
   We must not think the Turk is so unskilful
   To leave that latest which concerns him first,
   Neglecting an attempt of ease and gain,
   To wake and wage a danger profitless.   30

---

[69] Consistency, agreement.   [70] Coincide.   [71] Exact.   [72] Conjecture.   [73] Draw comfort from.   [74] Substance.   [75] Believe.   [76] Any.   [77] Test.   [78] (Deceptive) show.   [79] Looking in the wrong direction.   [80] More easily capture.   [81] State of defense.

Duke. Nay, in all confidence, he's not for Rhodes.
Officer. Here is more news.

(*Enter a Messenger.*)

Messenger. The Ottomites,[82] reverend and gracious,
    Steering with due course toward the isle of Rhodes,
    Have there injointed[83] them with an after fleet.[84]
First Senator. Ay, so I thought. How many, as you guess?
Messenger. Of thirty sail; and now they do re-stem[85]
    Their backward course, bearing with frank appearance
    Their purposes toward Cyprus. Signior Montano,
    Your trusty and most valiant servitor,   40
    With his free duty[86] recommends[87] you thus,
    And prays you to believe him.
Duke. 'Tis certain then, for Cyprus.
    Marcus Luccicos, is not he in town?
First Senator. He's now in Florence.
Duke. Write from us to him; post-post-haste dispatch.
First Senator. Here comes Brabantio and the valiant Moor.

(*Enter Brabantio, Othello, Iago, Roderigo, and Officers.*)

Duke. Valiant Othello, we must straight employ you
    Against the general enemy Ottoman.
    (*To Brabantio*) I did not see you; welcome, gentle signior;   50
    We lack'd your counsel and your help to-night.
Brabantio. So did I yours. Good your Grace, pardon me;
    Neither my place nor aught I heard of business
    Hath rais'd me from my bed, nor doth the general care
    Take hold of me, for my particular grief
    Is of so flood-gate[88] and o'erbearing nature
    That it engluts and swallows other sorrows
    And it is still itself.
Duke. Why, what's the matter?
Brabantio. My daughter! O! my daughter.
Duke.
Senators. } Dead?
Brabantio. Ay, to me;   60
    She is abus'd, stol'n from me, and corrupted
    By spells and medicines bought of mountebanks;
    For nature so preposterously to err,

---

[82] Turks.   [83] Joined.   [84] Fleet that followed after.   [85] Steer again.   [86] Unqualified expressions of respect.   [87] Informs.   [88] Torrential.

Being not deficient, blind, or lame of sense,
Sans[89] witchcraft could not.
Duke. Whoe'er he be that in this foul proceeding
Hath thus beguil'd your daughter of herself
And you of her, the bloody book of law
You shall yourself read in the bitter letter
After your own sense; yea, though our proper[90] son
Stood[91] in your action.[92]
Brabantio. Humbly I thank your Grace. 70
Here is the man, this Moor; whom now, it seems,
Your special mandate for the state affairs
Hath hither brought.
Duke.
Senators. } We are very sorry for it.
Duke (*to Othello*). What, in your own part, can you say to this?
Brabantio. Nothing, but this is so.
Othello. Most potent, grave, and reverend signiors,
My very noble and approv'd[93] good masters,
That I have ta'en away this old man's daughter,
It is most true; true, I have married her:
The very head and front of my offending 80
Hath this extent, no more. Rude am I in my speech,
And little bless'd with the soft phrase of peace;
For since these arms of mine had seven years' pith,[94]
Till now some nine moons wasted,[95] they have us'd
Their dearest action in the tented field;
And little of this great world can I speak,
More than pertains to feats of broil and battle;
And therefore little shall I grace my cause
In speaking for myself. Yet, by your gracious patience,
I will a round[96] unvarnish'd tale deliver 90
Of my whole course of love; what drugs, what charms,
What conjuration, and what mighty magic,
For such proceeding I am charg'd withal,
I won his daughter.
Brabantio. A maiden never bold;
Of spirit so still and quiet, that her motion
Blush'd at herself;[97] and she, in spite of nature,
Of years, of country, credit, every thing,
To fall in love with what she fear'd to look on!
It is a judgment maim'd and most imperfect

---

[89] Without. [90] Own. [91] Were accused. [92] Suit. [93] Tested (by past experience).
[94] Strength. [95] Past. [96] Blunt. [97] I.e., (her modesty was such that) she blushed at her own emotions; or: could not move without blushing.

That will confess[98] perfection so could err   100
Against all rules of nature, and must be driven
To find out practices of cunning hell,
Why this should be. I therefore vouch again
That with some mixtures powerful o'er the blood,
Or with some dram conjur'd to this effect,
He wrought upon her.

Duke.   To vouch this, is no proof,
Without more certain and more overt test
Than these thin habits[99] and poor likelihoods
Of modern[100] seeming do prefer against him.

First Senator.   But, Othello, speak: 110
Did you by indirect and forced courses
Subdue and poison this young maid's affections;
Or came it by request and such fair question[101]
As soul to soul affordeth?

Othello.   I do beseech you;
Send for the lady to the Sagittary,
And let her speak of me before her father:
If you do find me foul in her report,
The trust, the office I do hold of you,
Not only take away, but let your sentence
Even fall upon my life.

Duke.   Fetch Desdemona hither.   120

Othello.   Ancient, conduct them; you best know the place.

(*Exeunt Iago and Attendants.*)

And, till she come, as truly as to heaven
I do confess the vices of my blood,
So justly to your grave ears I'll present
How I did thrive in this fair lady's love,
And she in mine.

Duke.   Say it, Othello.

Othello.   Her father lov'd me; oft invited me;
Still[102] question'd me the story of my life
From year to year, the battles, sieges, fortunes   130
That I have pass'd.
I ran it through, even from my boyish days
To the very moment that he bade me tell it;
Wherein I spake of most disastrous chances,
Of moving accidents by flood and field,

[98] Assert.   [99] Weak appearances.   [100] Commonplace.   [101] Conversation.   [102] Always, regularly.

Of hair-breadth 'scapes i' the imminent deadly breach,
Of being taken by the insolent foe
And sold to slavery, of my redemption thence
And portance[103] in my travel's history;
Wherein of antres[104] vast and deserts idle,[105]   140
Rough quarries, rocks, and hills whose heads touch heaven,
It was my hint[106] to speak, such was the process;
And of the Cannibals that each other eat,
The Anthropophagi,[107] and men whose heads
Do grow beneath their shoulders. This to hear
Would Desdemona seriously incline;
But still the house-affairs would draw her thence;
Which ever as she could with haste dispatch,
She'd come again, and with a greedy ear
Devour up my discourse. Which I observing,   150
Took once a pliant[108] hour, and found good means
To draw from her a prayer of earnest heart
That I would all my pilgrimage dilate,[109]
Whereof by parcels[110] she had something heard,
But not intentively:[111] I did consent;
And often did beguile her of her tears,
When I did speak of some distressful stroke
That my youth suffer'd. My story being done,
She gave me for my pains a world of sighs:
She swore, in faith, 'twas strange, 'twas passing[112] strange;   160
'Twas pitiful, 'twas wondrous pitiful:
She wish'd she had not heard it, yet she wish'd
That heaven had made her[113] such a man; she thank'd me,
And bade me, if I had a friend that lov'd her,
I should but teach him how to tell my story,
And that would woo her. Upon this hint I spake.
She lov'd me for the dangers I had pass'd,
And I lov'd her that she did pity them.
This only is the witchcraft I have us'd:
Here comes the lady; let her witness it.   170

(*Enter Desdemona, Iago, and Attendants.*)

Duke. I think this tale would win my daughter too.
Good Brabantio,
Take up this mangled matter at the best;

---

[103] Behavior.   [104] Caves.   [105] Empty, sterile.   [106] Opportunity.   [107] Man-eaters.
[108] Suitable.   [109] Relate in full.   [110] Piecemeal.   [111] In sequence.   [112] Surpassing.   [113] Direct object; not "for her."

Men do their broken weapons rather use
Than their bare hands.

Brabantio.   I pray you, hear her speak:
If she confess that she was half the wooer,
Destruction on my head, if my bad blame
Light on the man! Come hither, gentle mistress:
Do you perceive in all this noble company
Where most you owe obedience?

Desdemona.   My noble father,   180
I do perceive here a divided duty:
To you I am bound for life and education;
My life and education both do learn[114] me
How to respect you; you are the lord of duty,
I am hitherto your daughter: but here's my husband;
And so much duty as my mother show'd
To you, preferring you before her father,
So much I challenge[115] that I may profess
Due to the Moor my lord.

Brabantio.   God be with you! I have done.
Please it your Grace, on to the state affairs;   190
I had rather to adopt a child than get it.
Come hither, Moor:
I here do give thee that with all my heart
Which, but thou hast[116] already, with all my heart
I would keep from thee. For your sake,[117] jewel,
I am glad at soul I have no other child;
For thy escape would teach me tyranny,
To hang clogs on them. I have done, my lord.

Duke.   Let me speak like yourself and lay a sentence,[118]
Which as a grize[119] or step, may help these lovers   200
Into your favour.
When remedies are past, the griefs are ended
By seeing the worst, which[120] late on hopes depended.
To mourn a mischief that is past and gone
Is the next way to draw new mischief on.
What cannot be preserv'd when Fortune takes,
Patience her injury a mockery makes.[121]
The robb'd that smiles steals something from the thief;
He robs himself that spends a bootless grief.

Brabantio.   So let the Turk of Cyprus us beguile;   210
We lose it not so long as we can smile.

---

[114] Teach.   [115] Claim as right.   [116] Didn't you have it.   [117] Because of you.   [118] Provide a maxim.   [119] Step.   [120] The antecedent is "griefs."   [121] To suffer an irreparable loss patiently is to make light of injury (i.e., to triumph over adversity).

He bears the sentence[122] well that nothing bears
But the free comfort which from thence he hears;
But he bears both the sentence and the sorrow
That, to pay grief, must of poor patience borrow.
These sentences, to sugar, or to gall,
Being strong on both sides, are equivocal:[123]
But words are words: I never yet did hear
That the bruis'd heart was pierced[124] through the ear.
I humbly beseech you, proceed to the affairs of state.   220

Duke.   The Turk with a most mighty preparation makes for Cyprus. Othello,
the fortitude[125] of the place is best known to you; and though we have there a
substitute of most allowed sufficiency,[126] yet opinion, a sovereign mistress of
effects, throws a more safer voice on you:[127] you must therefore be content to
slubber[128] the gloss of your new fortunes with this more stubborn[129] and boisterous expedition.

Othello.   The tyrant custom, most grave senators,
Hath made the flinty and steel couch of war
My thrice-driven[130] bed of down: I do agnize[131]
A natural and prompt alacrity   230
I find in hardness, and do undertake
These present wars against the Ottomites.
Most humbly therefore bending to your state,[132]
I crave fit disposition[133] for my wife,
Due reference of place and exhibition,[134]
With such accommodation and besort[135]
As levels with[136] her breeding.

Duke.   If you please,
Be 't at her father's.

Brabantio.   I'll not have it so.

Othello.   Nor I.

Desdemona.   Nor I; I would not there reside,
To put my father in impatient thoughts   240
By being in his eye. Most gracious duke,
To my unfolding[137] lend your gracious ear;
And let me find a charter[138] in your voice
To assist my simpleness.

Duke.   What would you, Desdemona?

Desdemona.   That I did love the Moor to live with him,
My downright violence and storm of fortunes

---

[122] (1) Verdict, (2) Maxim.   [123] Sententious comfort (like the Duke's trite maxims) can hurt
as well as soothe.   [124] (1) Lanced (i.e., cured), (2) Wounded.   [125] Strength.   [126] Admitted
competence.   [127] General opinion, which mainly determines action, thinks Cyprus safer with
you in command.   [128] Besmear.   [129] Rough.   [130] Made as soft as possible.   [131] Recognize.
[132] Submitting to your authority.   [133] Disposal.   [134] Provision.   [135] Fitness.   [136] Is proper to.
[137] Explanation.   [138] Permission.

May trumpet to the world; my heart's subdu'd
Even to the very quality of my lord;[139]
I saw Othello's visage in his mind,   250
And to his honours and his valiant parts
Did I my soul and fortunes consecrate.
So that, dear lords, if I be left behind,
A moth of peace, and he go to the war,
The rites[140] for which I love him are bereft me,
And I a heavy interim shall support[141]
By his dear[142] absence. Let me go with him.

Othello.   Let her have your voices.
Vouch with me, heaven, I therefore beg it not
To please the palate of my appetite,   260
Nor to comply with heat,—the young affects[143]
In me defunct,—and proper satisfaction,
But to be free and bounteous to her mind;
And heaven defend[144] your good souls that you think
I will your serious and great business scant
For[145] she is with me. No, when light-wing'd toys
Of feather'd Cupid seel[146] with wanton dulness
My speculative and offic'd instruments,[147]
That[148] my disports corrupt and taint my business,
Let housewives make a skillet of my helm,   270
And all indign[149] and base adversities
Make head against my estimation![150]

Duke.   Be it as you shall privately determine,
Either for her stay or going. The affair cries haste,
And speed must answer it.

First Senator.   You must away to-night.

Othello.   With all my heart.

Duke.   At nine i' the morning here we'll meet again.
Othello, leave some officer behind,
And he shall our commission bring to you;
With such things else of quality and respect   280
As doth import you.[151]

Othello.   So please your Grace, my ancient;
A man he is of honesty and trust:
To his conveyance I assign my wife,
With what else needful your good grace shall think
To be sent after me.

---

[139] I.e., I have become a soldier, like Othello.   [140] I.e., of marriage, or of war, or of both.
[141] Endure.   [142] Closely concerning (i.e., Desdemona).   [143] The passions of youth (hence, here,
immoderate sexual passion).   [144] Forbid.   [145] Because.   [146] Blind (v.) by sewing up the eyelids
(a term from falconry).   [147] Reflective and executive faculties and organs.   [148] So that.
[149] Shameful.   [150] Reputation.   [151] Concern.

Duke.   Let it be so.
  Good-night to every one. (*To Brabantio*) And, noble signior,
  If virtue no delighted[152] beauty lack,
  Your son-in-law is far more fair than black.
First Senator.   Adieu, brave Moor! use Desdemona well.
Brabantio.   Look to her, Moor, if thou hast eyes to see: 290
  She has deceiv'd her father, and may thee.

                    (*Exeunt Duke, Senators, Officers, &c.*)

Othello.   My life upon her faith! Honest Iago,
  My Desdemona must I leave to thee:
  I prithee, let thy wife attend on her;
  And bring them after in the best advantage.[153]
  Come, Desdemona; I have but an hour
  Of love, of worldly matters and direction,
  To spend with thee: we must obey the time.

                    (*Exeunt Othello and Desdemona.*)

Roderigo.   Iago!
Iago.   What sayst thou, noble heart?   300
Roderigo.   What will I do, think'st thou?
Iago.   Why, go to bed, and sleep.
Roderigo.   I will incontinently[154] drown myself.
Iago.   Well, if thou dost, I shall never love thee after.
  Why, thou silly gentleman!
Roderigo.   It is silliness to live when to live is torment; and then have we a
  prescription to die when death is our physician.
Iago.   O! villainous; I have looked upon the world for four times seven years,
  and since I could distinguish betwixt a benefit and an injury, I never found
  man that knew how to love himself. Ere I would say, I would drown myself
  for the love of a guinea-hen, I would change my humanity with a baboon.
Roderigo.   What should I do? I confess it is my shame to be so fond;[155] but it
  is not in my virtue[156] to amend it.
Iago.   Virtue! a fig! 'tis in ourselves that we are thus, or thus. Our bodies are
  our gardens, to the which our wills are gardeners; so that if we will plant
  nettles or sow lettuce, set hyssop and weed up thyme, supply it with one gender[157] of herbs or distract it with many, either to have it sterile with idleness
  or manured with industry, why, the power and corrigible[158] authority of this
  lies in our wills. If the balance of our lives had not one scale of reason to poise

---

[152] Delightful.   [153] Opportunity.   [154] Forthwith.   [155] Infatuated.   [156] Strength.   [157] Kind.
[158] Corrective.

another of sensuality, the blood and baseness of our natures would conduct us to most preposterous conclusions; but we have reason to cool our raging motions, our carnal stings, our unbitted[159] lusts, whereof I take this that you call love to be a sect or scion.[160]

Roderigo. It cannot be.

Iago. It is merely a lust of the blood and a permission of the will. Come, be a man. Drown thyself! drown cats and blind puppies. I have professed me thy friend, and I confess me knit to thy deserving with cables of perdurable toughness; I could never better stead thee than now. Put money in thy purse; follow these wars; defeat thy favour[161] with a usurped[162] beard; I say, put money in thy purse. It cannot be that Desdemona should long continue her love to the Moor,—put money in thy purse,—nor he his to her. It was a violent commencement in her, and thou shalt see an answerable sequestration;[163] put but money in thy purse. These Moors are changeable in their wills;—fill thy purse with money:—the food that to him now is as luscious as locusts,[164] shall be to him shortly as bitter as coloquintida.[165] She must change for youth: when she is sated with his body, she will find the error of her choice. She must have change, she must: therefore put money in thy purse. If thou wilt needs damn thyself, do it a more delicate way than drowning. Make all the money thou canst. If sanctimony and a frail vow betwixt an erring[166] barbarian and a supersubtle[167] Venetian be not too hard for my wits and all the tribe of hell, thou shalt enjoy her; therefore make money. A pox of drowning thyself! it is clean out of the way: seek thou rather to be hanged in compassing thy joy than to be drowned and go without her.

Roderigo. Wilt thou be fast to my hopes, if I depend on the issue?[168]

Iago. Thou art sure of me: go, make money. I have told thee often, and I retell thee again and again, I hate the Moor; my cause is hearted; thine hath no less reason. Let us be conjunctive[169] in our revenge against him; if thou canst cuckold him, thou dost thyself a pleasure, me a sport. There are many events in the womb of time which will be delivered. Traverse;[170] go: provide thy money. We will have more of this to-morrow. Adieu.

Roderigo. Where shall we meet i' the morning?

Iago. At my lodging.

Roderigo. I'll be with thee betimes.

Iago. Go to: farewell. Do you hear, Roderigo?

Roderigo. What say you?

Iago. No more of drowning, do you hear?

Roderigo. I am changed. I'll sell all my land.

Iago. Go to; farewell! put money enough in your purse. (*Exit Roderigo.*)
　Thus do I ever make my fool my purse;
　For I mine own gain'd knowledge should profane,　　　　360

---

[159] I.e., uncontrolled.　[160] Offshoot.　[161] Change thy appearance (for the worse?).　[162] Assumed.　[163] Estrangement.　[164] Sweet-tasting fruits (perhaps the carob, the edible seedpod of an evergreen tree in the Mediterranean area).　[165] Purgative derived from a bitter apple. [166] Vagabond.　[167] Exceedingly refined.　[168] Rely on the outcome.　[169] Allied.　[170] March.

If I would time expend with such a snipe[171]
But for my sport and profit. I hate the Moor,
And it is thought abroad[172] that 'twixt my sheets
He has done my office: I know not if 't be true,
But I, for mere suspicion in that kind,
Will do as if for surety.[173] He holds me well;[174]
The better shall my purpose work on him.
Cassio's a proper[175] man; let me see now:
To get his place; and to plume up[176] my will
In double knavery; how, how? Let's see: 370
After some time to abuse Othello's ear
That he[177] is too familiar with his wife:
He hath a person and a smooth dispose[178]
To be suspected; framed[179] to make women false,
The Moor is of a free and open nature,
That thinks men honest that but seem to be so,
And will as tenderly be led by the nose
As asses are.
I have 't; it is engender'd: hell and night
Must bring this monstrous birth to the world's light.   (*Exit.*)

Act II

Scene 1.   A Sea-port Town in Cyprus. An open place near the Quay.

(*Enter Montano and two Gentlemen.*)

Montano.   What from the cape can you discern at sea?
First Gentleman.   Nothing at all: it is a high-wrought flood;
  I cannot 'twixt the heaven and the main[180]
  Descry a sail.
Montano.   Methinks the wind hath spoke aloud at land;
  A fuller blast ne'er shook our battlements;
  If it hath ruffian'd so upon the sea,
  What ribs of oak, when mountains melt on them,
  Can hold the mortise?[181] What shall we hear of this?
Second Gentleman.   A segregation[182] of the Turkish fleet;   10
  For do but stand upon the foaming shore,
  The chidden billow seems to pelt the clouds;

---

[171] Dupe.   [172] People think.   [173] As if it were certain.   [174] In high regard.   [175] Handsome.   [176] Make ready.   [177] I.e., Cassio.   [178] Bearing.   [179] Designed, apt.   [180] Ocean.
[181] Hold the joints together.   [182] Scattering.

The wind-shak'd surge, with high and monstrous mane,
Seems to cast water on the burning bear[183]
And quench the guards of the ever-fixed pole:[184]
I never did like[185] molestation view
On the enchafed[186] flood.
Montano.   If that[187] the Turkish fleet
Be not enshelter'd and embay'd, they are drown'd;
It is impossible they bear it out.

(*Enter a Third Gentleman.*)

Third Gentleman.   News, lad! our wars are done.   20
The desperate tempest hath so bang'd the Turks
That their designment halts;[188] a noble ship of Venice
Hath seen a grievous wrack and suffrance[189]
On most part of their fleet.
Montano.   How! is this true?
Third Gentleman.   The ship is here put in,
A Veronesa;[190] Michael Cassio,
Lieutenant to the warlike Moor Othello,
Is come on shore: the Moor himself's at sea,
And is in full commission here for Cyprus.
Montano.   I am glad on 't; 'tis a worthy governor.   30
Third Gentleman.   But this same Cassio, though he speak of comfort
Touching the Turkish loss, yet he looks sadly
And prays the Moor be safe; for they were parted
With foul and violent tempest.
Montano.   Pray heaven he be;
For I have serv'd him, and the man commands
Like a full soldier. Let's to the sea-side, ho!
As well to see the vessel that's come in
As to throw out our eyes for brave Othello,
Even till we make the main and the aerial blue
An indistinct regard.[191]
Third Gentleman.   Come, let's do so;   40
For every minute is expectancy
Of more arrivance.

(*Enter Cassio.*)

---

[183] Ursa Minor (the Little Dipper).   [184] Polaris, the North Star, almost directly above the Earth's axis, is part of the constellation of the Little Bear, or Dipper.   [185] Similar.   [186] Agitated. [187] If.   [188] Plan is stopped.   [189] Damage.   [190] Probably a *type* of ship, rather than a ship from Verona—not only because Verona is an inland city but also because of "a noble ship of Venice" above.   [191] Till our (straining) eyes can no longer distinguish sea and sky.

Cassio.   Thanks, you the valiant of this warlike isle,
That so approve the Moor. O! let the heavens
Give him defence against the elements,
For I have lost him on a dangerous sea.
Montano.   Is he well shipp'd?
Cassio.   His bark is stoutly timber'd, and his pilot
Of very expert and approv'd allowance;[192]
Therefore my hopes, not surfeited to death,[193]   50
Stand in bold cure.[194]

(*Within,* 'A sail!—a sail!—a sail!' *Enter a Messenger.*)

Cassio.   What noise?
Messenger.   The town is empty; on the brow o' the sea
Stand ranks of people, and they cry 'A sail!'
Cassio.   My hopes do shape him for the governor.

(*Guns heard.*)

Second Gentleman.   They do discharge their shot of courtesy;
Our friends at least.
Cassio.   I pray you, sir, go forth.
And give us truth who 'tis that is arriv'd.
Second Gentleman.   I shall.   (*Exit.*)
Montano.   But, good lieutenant, is your general wiv'd?   60
Cassio.   Most fortunately: he hath achiev'd a maid
That paragons[195] description and wild fame;
One that excels the quirks[196] of blazoning pens,
And in th' essential vesture of creation [197]
Does tire the ingener.[198]

(*Re-enter Second Gentleman.*)

How now! who has put in?
Second Gentleman.   'Tis one Iago, ancient to the general.
Cassio.   He has had most favourable and happy speed:
Tempests themselves, high seas, and howling winds,
The gutter'd[199] rocks, and congregated sands,
Traitors ensteep'd[200] to clog the guiltless keel,   70
As having sense of beauty, do omit

---

[192] Admitted and proven to be expert.   [193] Overindulged.   [194] With good chance of being fulfilled.   [195] Exceeds, surpasses.   [196] Ingenuities.   [197] I.e., just as God made her; or: (even in) the (mere) essence of human nature.   [198] Inventor (i.e., of her praises?).   [199] Jagged; or: submerged.   [200] Submerged.

Their mortal[201] natures, letting go safely by
The divine Desdemona.

Montano.   What is she?

Cassio.   She that I spake of, our great captain's captain,
Left in the conduct of the bold Iago,
Whose footing[202] here anticipates our thoughts
A se'nnight's[203] speed. Great Jove, Othello guard,
And swell his sail with thine own powerful breath,
That he may bless this bay with his tall[204] ship,
Make love's quick pants in Desdemona's arms,   80
Give renew'd fire to our extincted spirits,
And bring all Cyprus comfort!

(*Enter Desdemona, Emilia, Iago, Roderigo, and Attendants.*)

                        O! behold,
The riches of the ship is come on shore.
Ye men of Cyprus, let her have your knees.
Hail to thee, lady! and the grace of heaven,
Before, behind thee, and on every hand,
Enwheel thee round!

Desdemona.   I thank you, valiant Cassio.
What tidings can you tell me of my lord?

Cassio.   He is not yet arriv'd; nor know I aught
But that he's well, and will be shortly here.   90

Desdemona.   O! but I fear—How lost you company?

Cassio.   The great contention of the sea and skies
Parted our fellowship. But hark! a sail.

(*Cry within,* 'A sail—a sail!' *Guns heard.*)

Second Gentleman.   They give their greeting to the citadel:
This likewise is a friend.

Cassio.   See for the news!   (*Exit Gentleman.*)
Good ancient, you are welcome:—(*To Emilia*) welcome, mistress.
Let it not gall your patience, good Iago,
That I extend my manners; 'tis my breeding
That gives me this bold show of courtesy.   (*Kissing her.*)

Iago.   Sir, would she give you so much of her lips   100
As of her tongue she oft bestows on me,
You'd have enough.

Desdemona.   Alas! she has no speech.

---

[201] Deadly.   [202] Landing.   [203] Week's.   [204] Brave.

Iago.   In faith, too much;
  I find it still when I have list[205] to sleep:
  Marry, before your ladyship, I grant,
  She puts her tongue a little in her heart,
  And chides with thinking.[206]
Emilia.   You have little cause to say so.
Iago.   Come on, come on; you are pictures[207] out of doors,
  Bells[208] in your parlours, wild cats in your kitchens,   110
  Saints in your injuries, devils being offended,
  Players[209] in your housewifery,[210] and housewives[211] in your beds.
Desdemona.   O! fie upon thee, slanderer.
Iago.   Nay, it is true, or else I am a Turk:
  You rise to play and go to bed to work.
Emilia.   You shall not write my praise.
Iago.   No, let me not.
Desdemona.   What wouldst thou write of me, if thou shouldst praise me?
Iago.   O gentle lady, do not put me to 't,
  For I am nothing if not critical.
Desdemona.   Come on; assay. There's one gone to the harbour?   120
Iago.   Ay, madam.
Desdemona (*aside*).   I am not merry, but I do beguile
  The thing I am by seeming otherwise.
  (*To Iago.*) Come, how wouldst thou praise me?
Iago.   I am about it; but indeed my invention
  Comes from my pate[212] as birdlime does from frize;[213]
  It plucks out brains and all: but my muse labours
  And thus she is deliver'd.
  If she be fair and wise, fairness and wit,
  The one's for use, the other useth it.   130
Desdemona.   Well prais'd! How if she be black and witty?
Iago.   If she be black,[214] and thereto have a wit,
  She'll find a white that shall her blackness fit.
Desdemona.   Worse and worse.
Emilia.   How if fair and foolish?
Iago.   She never yet was foolish that was fair,
  For even her folly[215] help'd to an heir.
Desdemona.   These are old fond[216] paradoxes to make fools laugh i' the ale-
  house. What miserable praise has thou for her that's foul and foolish?
Iago.   There's none so foul and foolish thereunto,   140
  But does foul pranks which fair and wise ones do.

---

[205] Wish.   [206] I.e., without words.   [207] I.e., made up, "painted."   [208] I.e., jangly.   [209] Tri-
flers, wastrels.   [210] Housekeeping.   [211] (1) Hussies, (2) (unduly) frugal with their sexual favors,
(3) businesslike, serious.   [212] Head.   [213] Coarse cloth.   [214] Brunette, dark haired.   [215] Here
also, wantonness.   [216] Foolish.

Desdemona. O heavy ignorance! thou praisest the worst best. But what praise couldst thou bestow on a deserving woman indeed, one that, in the authority of her merit, did justly put on the vouch[217] of very malice itself?

Iago. She that was ever fair and never proud,
Had tongue at will and yet was never loud,
Never lack'd gold and yet went never gay,
Fled from her wish and yet said 'Now I may,'
She that being anger'd, her revenge being nigh,
Bade her wrong stay and her displeasure fly, 150
She that in wisdom never was so frail
To change the cod's head for the salmon's tail,[218]
She that could think and ne'er disclose her mind,
See suitors following and not look behind,
She was a wight, if ever such wight were,—

Desdemona. To do what?

Iago. To suckle fools and chronicle small beer.[219]

Desdemona. O most lame and impotent conclusion! Do not learn of him, Emilia, though he be thy husband. How say you, Cassio? Is he not a most profane and liberal[220] counsellor? 160

Cassio. He speaks home,[221] madam; you may relish him more in the soldier than in[222] the scholar.

Iago (*aside*). He takes her by the palm: ay, well said, whisper; with as little a web as this will I ensnare as great a fly as Cassio. Ay, smile upon her, do; I will gyve[223] thee in thine own courtship. You say true, 'tis so, indeed. If such tricks as these strip you out of your lieutenantry, it had been better you had not kissed your three fingers so oft, which now again you are most apt to play the sir[224] in. Very good; well kissed! an excellent courtesy! 'tis so, indeed. Yet again your fingers to your lips? would they were clyster-pipes[225] for your sake! (*A trumpet heard.*) The Moor! I know his trumpet.[226] 170

Cassio. 'Tis truly so.

Desdemona. Let's meet him and receive him.

Cassio. Lo! where he comes.

(*Enter Othello and Attendants.*)

Othello. O my fair warrior!

Desdemona. My dear Othello!

Othello. It gives me wonder great as my content
To see you here before me. O my soul's joy!
If after every tempest come such calms,

---

[217] Compel the approval. [218] To make a foolish exchange (a bawdy secondary meaning is probable). [219] I.e., keep petty household accounts. [220] Free-spoken, licentious. [221] To the mark, aptly. [222] As . . . as. [223] Entangle. [224] Gentleman. [225] Syringes, enema pipes. [226] I.e., Othello's distinctive trumpet call.

May the winds blow till they have waken'd death!
And let the labouring bark climb hills of seas   180
Olympus-high, and duck again as low
As hell's from heaven! If it were now to die,
'Twere now to be most happy, for I fear
My soul hath her content so absolute
That not another comfort like to this
Succeeds in unknown fate.
Desdemona.   The heavens forbid
But that our loves and comforts should increase
Even as our days do grow!
Othello.   Amen to that, sweet powers!
I cannot speak enough of this content;
It stops me here; it is too much of joy:
And this, and this, the greatest discords be   (*Kissing her.*)
That e'er our hearts shall make!
Iago (*aside*).   O! you are well tun'd now,   190
But I'll set down[227] the pegs that make this music,
As honest as I am.
Othello.   Come, let us to the castle.
News, friends; our wars are done, the Turks are drown'd.
How does my old acquaintance of this isle?
Honey, you shall be well desir'd[228] in Cyprus;
I have found great love amongst them. O my sweet,
I prattle out of fashion, and I dote
In mine own comforts. I prithee, good Iago,
Go to the bay and disembark my coffers.
Bring thou the master to the citadel;   200
He is a good one, and his worthiness
Does challenge much respect. Come, Desdemona,
Once more well met at Cyprus.

           (*Exeunt all except Iago and Roderigo.*)

Iago.   Do thou meet me presently at the harbour. Come hither. If thou be'st valiant, as they say base men being in love have then a nobility in their natures more than is native to them, list[229] me. The lieutenant to-night watches on the court of guard:[230] first, I must tell thee this, Desdemona is directly in love with him.

Roderigo.   With him! Why, 'tis not possible.

Iago.   Lay thy finger thus, and let thy soul be instructed. Mark me with what violence she first loved the Moor but for bragging and telling her fantastical lies; and will she love him still for prating? let not thy discreet heart think it.

---

[227] Loosen.   [228] Welcomed.   [229] Listen to.   [230] Guardhouse.

Her eye must be fed; and what delight shall she have to look on the devil? When the blood is made dull with the act of sport, there should be, again to inflame it, and to give satiety a fresh appetite, loveliness in favour, sympathy in years, manners, and beauties; all which the Moor is defective in. Now, for want of these required conveniences, her delicate tenderness will find itself abused, begin to heave the gorge,[231] disrelish and abhor the Moor; very nature will instruct her in it, and compel her to some second choice. Now, sir, this granted, as it is a most pregnant[232] and unforced position, who stands so eminently in the degree of this fortune as Cassio does? a knave very voluble, no further conscionable[233] than in putting on the mere form of civil and humane seeming, for the better compassing of his salt[234] and most hidden loose affection? why, none; why, none: a slipper[235] and subtle knave, a finder-out of occasions, that has an eye can stamp and counterfeit advantages, though true advantage never present itself; a devilish knave! Besides, the knave is handsome, young, and hath all those requisites in him that folly and green minds look after; a pestilent complete knave! and the woman hath found him already.

Roderigo. I cannot believe that in her; she is full of most blessed condition.

Iago. Blessed fig's end! the wine she drinks is made of grapes;[236] if she had been blessed she would never have loved the Moor; blessed pudding! Didst thou not see her paddle with the palm of his hand? didst not mark that?

Roderigo. Yes, that I did; but that was but courtesy.

Iago. Lechery, by this hand! an index[237] and obscure prologue to the history of lust and foul thoughts. They met so near with their lips, that their breaths embraced together. Villainous thoughts, Roderigo! when these mutualities so marshal the way, hard at hand comes the master and main exercise, the incorporate[238] conclusion. Pish![239] But, sir, be you ruled by me: I have brought you from Venice. Watch you to-night; for the command, I'll lay 't upon you: Cassio knows you not. I'll not be far from you: do you find some occasion to anger Cassio, either by speaking too loud, or tainting[240] his discipline; or from what other course you please, which the time shall more favourably minister.

Roderigo. Well.

Iago. Sir, he is rash and very sudden in choler, and haply may strike at you: provoke him, that he may; for even out of that will I cause these of Cyprus to mutiny, whose qualification[241] shall come into no true taste again but by the displanting of Cassio. So shall you have a shorter journey to your desires by the means I shall then have to prefer[242] them; and the impediment most profitably removed, without the which there were no expectation of our prosperity.

Roderigo. I will do this, if I can bring it to any opportunity.

Iago. I warrant thee. Meet me by and by at the citadel: I must fetch his necessaries ashore. Farewell.

---

[231] Vomit. [232] Obvious. [233] Conscientious. [234] Lecherous. [235] Slippery. [236] I.e., she is only flesh and blood. [237] Pointer. [238] Carnal. [239] Exclamation of disgust. [240] Disparaging. [241] Appeasement. [242] Advance.

Roderigo.   Adieu.   (*Exit.*)
Iago.   That Cassio loves her, I do well believe it;
That she loves him, 'tis apt,[243] and of great credit:[244]
The Moor, howbeit that I endure him not,
Is of a constant, loving, noble nature;
And I dare think he'll prove to Desdemona   260
A most dear[245] husband. Now, I do love her too;
Not out of absolute lust,—though peradventure[246]
I stand accountant[247] for as great a sin,—
But partly led to diet my revenge,
For that I do suspect the lusty Moor
Hath leap'd into my seat; the thought whereof
Doth like a poisonous mineral gnaw my inwards;
And nothing can or shall content my soul
Till I am even'd with him, wife for wife;
Or failing so, yet that I put the Moor   270
At least into a jealousy so strong
That judgment cannot cure. Which thing to do,
If this poor trash[248] of Venice, whom I trash[249]
For his quick hunting, stand the putting-on,[250]
I'll have our Michael Cassio on the hip;
Abuse him to the Moor in the rank garb,[251]
For I fear Cassio with my night-cap too,
Make the Moor thank me, love me, and reward me
For making him egregiously an ass
And practising upon his peace and quiet   280
Even to madness. 'Tis here, but yet confus'd:
Knavery's plain face is never seen till us'd.   (*Exit.*)

Scene 2.   A Street.

(*Enter a Herald with a proclamation; people following.*)

Herald.   It is Othello's pleasure, our noble and valiant general, that, upon certain tidings now arrived, importing the mere[252] perdition of the Turkish fleet,
every man put himself into triumph; some to dance, some to make bonfires,
each man to what sport and revels his addiction leads him; for, besides these
beneficial news, it is the celebration of his nuptial. So much was his pleasure
should be proclaimed. All offices[253] are open, and there is full liberty of feast-
ing from this present hour of five till the bell have told eleven. Heaven bless
the isle of Cyprus and our noble general Othello!   (*Exeunt.*)

---

[243] Natural, probable.   [244] Easily believable.   [245] A pun on the word in the sense of expensive.
[246] Perchance, perhaps.   [247] Accountable.   [248] I.e., Roderigo.   [249] Check, control.   [250] Inciting.   [251] Gross manner.   [252] Utter.   [253] Kitchens and storehouses.

Scene 3.   A Hall in the Castle.

(*Enter Othello, Desdemona, Cassio, and Attendants.*)

Othello.   Good Michael, look you to the guard to-night:
   Let's teach ourselves that honourable stop,²⁵⁴
   Not to outsport discretion.
Cassio.   Iago hath direction what to do:
   But, notwithstanding, with my personal²⁵⁵ eye
   Will I look to 't.
Othello.   Iago is most honest.
   Michael, good-night; to-morrow with your earliest
   Let me have speech with you. (*To Desdemona.*) Come, my dear love,
   The purchase made, the fruits are to ensue;
   That profit's yet to come 'twixt me and you.   10
   Good-night.

               (*Exeunt Othello, Desdemona, and Attendants.*)

(*Enter Iago.*)

Cassio.   Welcome, Iago; we must to the watch.
Iago.   Not this hour, lieutenant; 'tis not yet ten o' the clock. Our general casts
   us thus early for the love of his Desdemona, who let us not therefore blame;
   he hath not yet made wanton the night with her, and she is sport for Jove.
Cassio.   She's a most exquisite lady.
Iago.   And, I'll warrant her, full of game.
Cassio.   Indeed, she is a most fresh and delicate creature.
Iago.   What an eye she has! methinks it sounds a parley²⁵⁶ of provocation.
Cassio.   An inviting eye: and yet methinks right modest.   20
Iago.   And when she speaks, is it not an alarum²⁵⁷ to love?
Cassio.   She is indeed perfection.
Iago.   Well, happiness to their sheets! Come, lieutenant, I have a stoup of
   wine, and here without are a brace²⁵⁸ of Cyprus gallants that would fain have
   a measure to the health of black Othello.
Cassio.   Not to-night, good Iago: I have very poor and unhappy brains for
   drinking: I could well wish courtesy would invent some other custom of en-
   tertainment.
Iago.   O! they are our friends; but one cup: I'll drink for you.
Cassio.   I have drunk but one cup to-night, and that was craftily qualified²⁵⁹

---

²⁵⁴ Discipline.   ²⁵⁵ Own.   ²⁵⁶ Conference.   ²⁵⁷ Call-to-arms.   ²⁵⁸ Pair.   ²⁵⁹ Diluted.

too, and, behold, what innovation[260] it makes here: I am unfortunate in the infirmity, and dare not task my weakness with any more.

Iago.   What, man! 'tis a night of revels; the gallants desire it.

Cassio.   Where are they?

Iago.   Here at the door; I pray you, call them in.

Cassio.   I'll do 't; but it dislikes me.   (*Exit.*)

Iago.   If I can fasten but one cup upon him,
With that which he hath drunk to-night already,
He'll be as full of quarrel and offence
As my young mistress' dog. Now, my sick fool Roderigo,   40
Whom love has turn'd almost the wrong side out,
To Desdemona hath to-night carous'd
Potations pottle-deep;[261] and he's to watch.
Three lads of Cyprus, noble swelling spirits,
That hold their honours in a wary distance,[262]
The very elements[263] of this warlike isle,
Have I to-night fluster'd with flowing cups,
And they watch too. Now, 'mongst this flock of drunkards,
Am I to put our Cassio in some action
That may offend the isle. But here they come.   50
If consequence[264] do but approve my dream,
My boat sails freely, both with wind and stream.

(*Re-enter Cassio, with him Montano, and Gentlemen. Servant following with wine.*)

Cassio.   'Fore God, they have given me a rouse[265] already.

Montano.   Good faith, a little one; not past a pint, as I am a soldier.

Iago.   Some wine, ho!
(*Sings.*) And let me the canakin[266] clink, clink;
          And let me the canakin clink:
          A soldier's a man;
          A life's but a span;
          Why then let a soldier drink.   60
Some wine, boys!

Cassio.   'Fore God, an excellent song.

Iago.   I learned it in England, where indeed they are most potent in potting; your Dane, your German, and your swag-bellied[267] Hollander,—drink ho!—are nothing to your English.

Cassio.   Is your Englishman so expert in his drinking?

Iago.   Why, he drinks you[268] with facility your Dane dead drunk; he sweats not

---

[260] Change, revolution.   [261] Bottoms-up.   [262] Take offense easily.   [263] Types.   [264] Succeeding events.   [265] Drink.   [266] Small cup.   [267] With a pendulous belly.   [268] The "ethical" dative, i.e., you'll see that he drinks.

to overthrow your Almain;[269] he gives your Hollander a vomit ere the next pottle can be filled.

Cassio. To the health of our general! 70

Montano. I am for it, lieutenant; and I'll do you justice.

Iago. O sweet England!

(*Sings.*) King Stephen was a worthy peer,
    His breeches cost him but a crown;
    He held them sixpence all too dear,
       With that he call'd the tailor lown.[270]
    He was a wight of high renown,
       And thou art but of low degree:
    'Tis pride that pulls the country down,
       Then take thine auld cloak about thee. 80

Some wine, ho!

Cassio. Why, this is a more exquisite song than the other.

Iago. Will you hear 't again?

Cassio. No; for I hold him to be unworthy of his place that does those things. Well, God's above all; and there be souls must be saved, and there be souls must not be saved.

Iago. It's true, good lieutenant.

Cassio. For mine own part,—no offence to the general, nor any man of quality,—I hope to be saved.

Iago. And so do I too, lieutenant. 90

Cassio. Ay; but, by your leave, not before me; the lieutenant is to be saved before the ancient. Let's have no more of this; let's to our affairs. God forgive us our sins! Gentlemen, let's look to our business. Do not think, gentlemen, I am drunk: this is my ancient; this is my right hand, and this is my left hand. I am not drunk now; I can stand well enough, and speak well enough.

All. Excellent well.

Cassio. Why, very well, then; you must not think then that I am drunk.

(*Exit.*)

Montano. To the platform, masters; come, let's set the watch.

Iago. You see this fellow that is gone before;
He is a soldier fit to stand by Caesar 100
And give direction; and do but see his vice;
'Tis to his virtue a just equinox,[271]
The one as long as the other; 'tis pity of him.
I fear the trust Othello puts him in,
On some odd time of his infirmity,
Will shake this island.

Montano.   But is he often thus?

Iago. 'Tis evermore the prologue to his sleep;

---

[269] German. [270] Lout, rascal. [271] Equivalent.

He'll watch the horologe a double set,[272]
If drink rock not his cradle.
Montano.   It were well   110
The general were put in mind of it.
Perhaps he sees it not; or his good nature
Prizes the virtue that appears in Cassio,
And looks not on his evils. Is not this true?

(*Enter Roderigo.*)

Iago (*aside to him*).   How now, Roderigo!
I pray you, after the lieutenant; go.   (*Exit Roderigo.*)
Montano.   And 'tis great pity that the noble Moor
Should hazard such a place as his own second
With one of an ingraft[273] infirmity;
It were an honest action to say   120
So to the Moor.
Iago.   Not I, for this fair island:
I do love Cassio well, and would do much
To cure him of this evil. But hark! what noise?

(*Cry within,* 'Help! Help!' *Re-enter Cassio, driving in Roderigo.*)

Cassio.   You rogue! you rascal!
Montano.   What's the matter, lieutenant?
Cassio.   A knave teach me my duty!
I'll beat the knave into a twiggen[274] bottle.
Roderigo.   Beat me!
Cassio.   Dost thou prate, rogue?

(*Striking Roderigo.*)

Montano (*staying him*).   Nay, good lieutenant;
I pray you, sir, hold your hand.
Cassio.   Let me go, sir,
Or I'll knock you o'er the mazzard.[275]
Montano.   Come, come; you're drunk.   130
Cassio.   Drunk!

(*They fight.*)

Iago (*aside to Roderigo*).   Away, I say! go out, and cry a mutiny.
                                                    (*Exit Roderigo.*)

---

[272] Stand watch twice twelve hours.   [273] Ingrained.   [274] Wicker.   [275] Head.

Nay, good lieutenant! God's will, gentlemen!
Help, ho! Lieutenant! sir! Montano! sir!
Help, masters! Here's a goodly watch indeed!

(*Bell rings.*)

Who's that that rings the bell? Diablo, ho!
The town will rise: God's will! lieutenant, hold!
You will be sham'd for ever.

(*Re-enter Othello and Attendants.*)

Othello.   What is the matter here?
Montano.   'Zounds! I bleed still; I am hurt to the death.

(*He faints.*)

Othello.   Hold, for your lives!
Iago.   Hold, ho, lieutenant! Sir! Montano! gentlemen!   140
    Have you forgot all sense of place and duty?
    Hold! the general speaks to you; hold for shame!
Othello.   Why, how now, ho! from whence ariseth this?
    Are we turn'd Turks, and to ourselves do that
    Which heaven hath forbid the Ottomites?
    For Christian shame put by this barbarous brawl;
    He that stirs next to carve for his own rage
    Holds his soul light; he dies upon his motion.
    Silence that dreadful bell! it frights the isle
    From her propriety. What is the matter, masters?   150
    Honest Iago, that look'st dead with grieving,
    Speak, who began this? On thy love, I charge thee.
Iago.   I do not know; friends all but now, even now,
    In quarter[276] and in terms like bride and groom
    Devesting[277] them for bed; and then, but now,—
    As if some planet had unwitted men,—
    Swords out, and tilting one at other's breast,
    In opposition bloody. I cannot speak
    Any beginning to this peevish odds,[278]
    And would in action glorious I had lost   160
    Those legs that brought me to a part of it!
Othello.   How comes it, Michael, you are thus forgot?
Cassio.   I pray you, pardon me; I cannot speak.
Othello.   Worthy Montano, you were wont be civil;

[276] On duty.   [277] Undressing.   [278] Silly quarrel.

The gravity and stillness of your youth
The world hath noted, and your name is great
In mouths of wisest censure:[279] what's the matter,
That you unlace[280] your reputation thus
And spend your rich opinion[281] for the name
Of a night-brawler? give me answer to it.   170

Montano.   Worthy Othello, I am hurt to danger;
Your officer, Iago, can inform you,
While I spare speech, which something now offends[282] me,
Of all that I do know; nor know I aught
By me that's said or done amiss this night,
Unless self-charity be sometimes a vice,
And to defend ourselves it be a sin
When violence assails us.

Othello.   Now, by heaven,
My blood begins my safer guides to rule,
And passion, having my best judgment collied,[283]   180
Assays to lead the way. If I once stir,
Or do but lift this arm, the best of you
Shall sink in my rebuke. Give me to know
How this foul rout began, who set it on;
And he that is approv'd[284] in this offence,
Though he had twinn'd with me—both at a birth—
Shall lose me. What! in a town of war,
Yet wild, the people's hearts brimful of fear,
To manage private and domestic quarrel,
In night, and on the court and guard of safety!   190
'Tis monstrous. Iago, who began 't?

Montano.   If partially affin'd,[285] or leagu'd in office,
Thou dost deliver more or less than truth,
Thou art not soldier.

Iago.   Touch me not so near;
I had rather[286] have this tongue cut from my mouth
Than it should do offence to Michael Cassio;
Yet, I persuade myself, to speak the truth
Shall nothing wrong him. Thus it is, general.
Montano and myself being in speech,
There comes a fellow crying out for help,   200
And Cassio following with determin'd sword
To execute upon him. Sir, this gentleman

---

[279] Judgment.   [280] Undo.   [281] High reputation.   [282] Pains, harms.   [283] Clouded.
[284] Proved (i.e., guilty).   [285] Favorably biased (by ties of friendship, or as Cassio's fellow officer).
[286] More quickly.

Steps in to Cassio, and entreats his pause;
Myself the crying fellow did pursue,
Lest by his clamour, as it so fell out,
The town might fall in fright; he, swift of foot,
Outran my purpose, and I return'd the rather
For that I heard the clink and fall of swords,
And Cassio high in oath, which till to-night
I ne'er might say before. When I came back,— 210
For this was brief,—I found them close together,
At blow and thrust, even as again they were
When you yourself did part them.
More of this matter can I not report:
But men are men; the best sometimes forget:
Though Cassio did some little wrong to him,
As men in rage strike those that wish them best,
Yet, surely Cassio, I believe, receiv'd
From him that fled some strange indignity,
Which patience could not pass.

Othello.   I know, Iago. 220
Thy honesty and love doth mince[287] this matter,
Making it light to Cassio. Cassio, I love thee;
But never more be officer of mine.

(*Enter Desdemona, attended.*)

Look! if my gentle love be not rais'd up;
(*To Cassio.*) I'll make thee an example.
Desdemona.   What's the matter?
Othello.   All's well now, sweeting; come away to bed.
Sir, for your hurts, myself will be your surgeon.
Lead him off.   (*Montano is led off.*)
Iago, look with care about the town,
And silence those whom this vile brawl distracted. 230
Come, Desdemona; 'tis the soldier's life,
To have their balmy slumbers wak'd with strife.

(*Exeunt all but Iago and Cassio.*)

Iago.   What! are you hurt, lieutenant?
Cassio.   Ay; past all surgery.
Iago.   Marry, heaven forbid!

---

[287] Tone down.

Cassio. Reputation, reputation, reputation! O! I have lost my reputation. I have lost the immortal part of myself, and what remains is bestial. My reputation, Iago, my reputation!

Iago. As I am an honest man, I thought you had received some bodily wound; there is more offence in that than in reputation. Reputation is an idle and most false imposition;[288] oft got without merit, and lost without deserving: you have lost no reputation at all, unless you repute yourself such a loser. What! man; there are ways to recover the general again; you are but now cast in his mood,[289] a punishment more in policy[290] than in malice; even so as one would beat his offenceless dog to affright an imperious lion. Sue to him again, and he is yours.

Cassio. I will rather sue to be despised than to deceive so good a commander with so slight, so drunken and so indiscreet an officer. Drunk! and speak parrot![291] and squabble, swagger, swear, and discourse fustian[292] with one's own shadow! O thou invisible spirit of wine! if thou hast no name to be known by, let us call thee devil!

Iago. What was he that you followed with your sword? What hath he done to you?

Cassio. I know not.

Iago. Is 't possible?

Cassio. I remember a mass of things, but nothing distinctly; a quarrel, but nothing wherefore. O God! that men should put an enemy in their mouths to steal away their brains; that we should, with joy, pleasance,[293] revel, and applause, transform ourselves into beasts.

Iago. Why, but you are now well enough; how came you thus recovered?

Cassio. It hath pleased the devil drunkenness to give place to the devil wrath; one unperfectness shows me another, to make me frankly despise myself.

Iago. Come, you are too severe a moraler. As the time, the place, and the condition of this country stands, I could heartily wish this had not befallen, but since it is as it is, mend it for your own good.

Cassio. I will ask him for my place again; he shall tell me I am a drunkard! Had I as many mouths as Hydra,[294] such an answer would stop them all. To be now a sensible man, by and by a fool, and presently a beast! O strange! Every inordinate cup is unblessed and the ingredient[295] is a devil.

Iago. Come, come; good wine is a good familiar creature if it be well used; exclaim no more against it. And, good lieutenant, I think you think I love you.

Cassio. I have well approved it, sir. I drunk!

Iago. You or any man living may be drunk at some time, man. I'll tell you what you shall do. Our general's wife is now the general; I may say so in this respect, for that he hath devoted and given up himself to the contemplation, mark, and denotement of her parts and graces: confess yourself freely to her;

---

[288] Something external.   [289] Dismissed because he is angry.   [290] I.e., more for the sake of the example, or to show his fairness.   [291] I.e., without thinking.   [292] I.e., nonsense.   [293] Pleasure.   [294] Many-headed snake in Greek mythology.   [295] Contents.

importune her; she'll help to put you in your place again. She is of so free, so kind, so apt, so blessed a disposition, that she holds it a vice in her goodness not to do more than she is requested. This broken joint between you and her husband entreat her to splinter;[296] and, my fortunes against any lay[297] worth naming, this crack of your love shall grow stronger than it was before.

Cassio.   You advise me well.

Iago.   I protest, in the sincerity of love and honest kindness.

Cassio.   I think it freely; and betimes in the morning I will beseech the virtuous Desdemona to undertake for me. I am desperate of my fortunes if they check me here.

Iago.   You are in the right. Good-night, lieutenant; I must to the watch.

Cassio.   Good-night, honest Iago!   (*Exit.*)

Iago.   And what's he then that says I play the villain?   290
When this advice is free I give and honest,
Probal[298] to thinking and indeed the course
To win the Moor again? For 'tis most easy
The inclining Desdemona to subdue
In any honest suit; she's fram'd as fruitful[299]
As the free elements. And then for her
To win the Moor, were 't to renounce his baptism,
All seals and symbols of redeemed sin,
His soul is so enfetter'd to her love,
That she may make, unmake, do what she list,   300
Even as her appetite shall play the god
With his weak function.[300] How am I then a villain
To counsel Cassio to this parallel[301] course,
Directly to his good? Divinity of hell!
When devils will the blackest sins put on,
They do suggest at first with heavenly shows,
As I do now; for while this honest fool
Plies Desdemona to repair his fortunes,
And she for him pleads strongly to the Moor,
I'll pour this pestilence into his ear   310
That she repeals[302] him for her body's lust;
And, by how much she strives to do him good,
She shall undo her credit with the Moor.
So will I turn her virtue into pitch,
And out of her own goodness make the net
That shall enmesh them all.

(*Re-enter Roderigo.*)

---

[296] Bind up with splints.   [297] Wager.   [298] Provable.   [299] Generous.   [300] Faculties.
[301] Purposeful.   [302] I.e., seeks to recall.

Iago.   How now, Roderigo!

Roderigo.   I do follow here in the chase, not like a hound that hunts, but one
that fills up the cry.[303] My money is almost spent; I have been to-night exceedingly well cudgelled; and I think the issue will be, I shall have so much
experience for my pains; and so, with no money at all and a little more wit, return again to Venice.

Iago.   How poor are they that have not patience!
What wound did ever heal but by degrees?
Thou know'st we work by wit and not by witchcraft,
And wit depends on dilatory time.
Does 't not go well? Cassio hath beaten thee,
And thou by that small hurt hast cashiered Cassio.
Though other things grow fair against the sun,
Yet fruits that blossom first will first be ripe:
Content thyself awhile. By the mass, 'tis morning;   330
Pleasure and action make the hours seem short.
Retire thee; go where thou art billeted:
Away, I say; thou shalt know more hereafter:
Nay, get thee gone. (*Exit Roderigo.*) Two things are to be done,
My wife must move for Cassio to her mistress;
I'll set her on;
Myself the while to draw the Moor apart,
And bring him jump[304] when he may Cassio find
Soliciting his wife: ay, that's the way:
Dull not device by coldness and delay.   (*Exit.*)

Act III

Scene 1.   Cyprus. Before the Castle.

(*Enter Cassio, and some Musicians.*)

Cassio.   Masters, play here, I will content your pains;[305]
Something that's brief; and bid 'Good-morrow, general.'   (*Music.*)

(*Enter Clown.*)

Clown.   Why, masters, have your instruments been in Naples, that they speak
i' the nose[306] thus?

---

[303] Pack (hunting term).   [304] At the exact moment.   [305] Reward your efforts.   [306] Naples
was notorious for venereal disease, and syphilis was believed to affect the nose.

First Musician.   How, sir, how?

Clown.   Are these, I pray you, wind-instruments?

First Musician.   Ay, marry, are they, sir.

Clown.   O! thereby hangs a tale.

First Musician.   Whereby hangs a tale, sir?

Clown.   Marry, sir, by many a wind-instrument that I know. But, masters, here's money for you; and the general so likes your music, that he desires you, for love's sake, to make no more noise with it.

First Musician.   Well, sir, we will not.

Clown.   If you have any music that may not be heard, to 't again; but, as they say, to hear music the general does not greatly care.

First Musician.   We have none such, sir.

Clown.   Then put up your pipes in your bag, for I'll away.
Go; vanish into air; away!   (*Exeunt Musicians.*)

Cassio.   Dost thou hear, mine honest friend?

Clown.   No, I hear not your honest friend; I hear you.   20

Cassio.   Prithee, keep up thy quillets.[307] There's a poor piece of gold for thee. If the gentlewoman that attends the general's wife be stirring, tell her there's one Cassio entreats her a little favour of speech: wilt thou do this?

Clown.   She is stirring, sir: if she will stir hither, I shall seem to notify unto her.

Cassio.   Do, good my friend.   (*Exit Clown.*)

(*Enter Iago.*)

In happy time, Iago.

Iago.   You have not been a-bed, then?

Cassio.   Why, no; the day had broke
Before we parted. I have made bold, Iago,
To send in to your wife; my suit to her
Is, that she will to virtuous Desdemona   30
Procure me some access.

Iago.   I'll send her to you presently;
And I'll devise a mean to draw the Moor
Out of the way, that your converse and business
May be more free.

Cassio.   I humbly thank you for 't.   (*Exit Iago.*)
                              I never knew
A Florentine more kind and honest.[308]

(*Enter Emilia.*)

---

[307] Quibbles.   [308] Cassio means that not even a fellow Florentine could behave to him in a friendlier fashion than does Iago.

Emilia.   Good-morrow, good lieutenant: I am sorry
  For your displeasure,[309] but all will soon be well.
  The general and his wife are talking of it,
  And she speaks for you stoutly: the Moor replies   40
  That he you hurt is of great fame in Cyprus
  And great affinity,[310] and that in wholesome wisdom
  He might not but refuse you; but he protests he loves you,
  And needs no other suitor but his likings
  To take the safest occasion by the front[311]
  To bring you in again.[312]
Cassio.   Yet, I beseech you,
  If you think fit, or that it may be done,
  Give me advantage of some brief discourse
  With Desdemona alone.
Emilia.   Pray you, come in:
  I will bestow you where you shall have time   50
  To speak your bosom[313] freely.
Cassio.   I am much bound to you.   *(Exeunt.)*

Scene 2.   A Room in the Castle.

(Enter Othello, Iago, and Gentlemen.)

Othello.   These letters give, Iago, to the pilot,
  And by him do my duties to the senate;
  That done, I will be walking on the works;
  Repair there to me.
Iago.   Well, my good lord, I'll do 't.
Othello.   This fortification, gentlemen, shall we see 't?
Gentlemen.   We'll wait upon your lordship.   *(Exeunt.)*

Scene 3.   Before the Castle.

(Enter Desdemona, Cassio, and Emilia.)

Desdemona.   Be thou assur'd, good Cassio, I will do
  All my abilities in thy behalf.
Emilia.   Good madam, do: I warrant it grieves my husband,
  As if the case were his.
Desdemona.   O! that's an honest fellow. Do not doubt, Cassio,
  But I will have my lord and you again
  As friendly as you were.

[309] Disgrace.   [310] Family connection.   [311] Forelock.   [312] Restore you (to Othello's favor).
[313] Heart, inmost thoughts.

Cassio.   Bounteous madam,
  Whatever shall become of Michael Cassio,
  He's never any thing but your true servant.
Desdemona. I know 't; I thank you. You do love my lord;   10
  You have known him long; and be you well assur'd
  He shall in strangeness[314] stand no further off
  Than in a politic[315] distance.
Cassio.   Ay, but, lady,
  That policy may either last so long,
  Or feed upon such nice[316] and waterish diet,
  Or breed itself so out of circumstance,
  That, I being absent and my place supplied,
  My general will forget my love and service.
Desdemona. Do not doubt[317] that; before Emilia here
  I give thee warrant of thy place. Assure thee,   20
  If I do vow a friendship, I'll perform it
  To the last article; my lord shall never rest;
  I'll watch him tame,[318] and talk him out of patience;
  His bed shall seem a school, his board a shrift;[319]
  I'll intermingle every thing he does
  With Cassio's suit. Therefore be merry, Cassio;
  For thy solicitor shall rather die
  Than give thy cause away.[320]

(Enter Othello, and Iago at a distance.)

Emilia. Madam, here comes my lord.
Cassio. Madam, I'll take my leave.   30
Desdemona. Why, stay, and hear me speak.
Cassio. Madam, not now; I am very ill at ease,
  Unfit for mine own purposes.
Desdemona. Well, do your discretion.   *(Exit Cassio.)*
Iago. Ha! I like not that.
Othello.   What dost thou say?
Iago. Nothing, my lord: or if—I know not what.
Othello. Was not that Cassio parted from my wife?
Iago. Cassio, my lord? No, sure, I cannot think it,
  That he would steal away so guilty-like,
  Seeing you coming.
Othello.   I do believe 'twas he.   40
Desdemona. How now, my lord!

---

[314] Aloofness.   [315] I.e., dictated by policy.   [316] Slight, trivial.   [317] Fear.   [318] Outwatch him (i.e., keep him awake) till he submits.   [319] Confessional.   [320] Abandon your cause.

I have been talking with a suitor here,
A man that languishes in your displeasure.
Othello.   Who is 't you mean?
Desdemona.   Why, your lieutenant, Cassio. Good my lord,
If I have any grace or power to move you,
His present[321] reconciliation take;
For if he be not one that truly loves you,
That errs in ignorance and not in cunning,
I have no judgment in an honest face.   50
I prithee[322] call him back.
Othello.   Went he hence now?
Desdemona.   Ay, sooth; so humbled,
That he hath left part of his grief with me,
To suffer with him. Good love, call him back.
Othello.   Not now, sweet Desdemona; some other time.
Desdemona.   But shall 't be shortly?
Othello.   The sooner, sweet, for you.
Desdemona.   Shall 't be to-night at supper?
Othello.   No, not to-night.
Desdemona.   To-morrow dinner, then?
Othello.   I shall not dine at home;
I meet the captains at the citadel.
Desdemona.   Why, then, to-morrow night; or Tuesday morn;   60
Or Tuesday noon, or night; or Wednesday morn:
I prithee name the time, but let it not
Exceed three days: in faith, he's penitent;
And yet his trespass, in our common reason,—
Save that they say, the wars must make examples
Out of their best,—is not almost[323] a fault
To incur a private check.[324] When shall he come?
Tell me, Othello: I wonder in my soul,
What you could ask me, that I should deny,
Or stand so mammering[325] on. What! Michael Cassio,   70
That came a wooing with you, and so many a time,
When I have spoke of you dispraisingly,
Hath ta'en your part; to have so much to do
To bring him in! Trust me, I could do much,—
Othello.   Prithee, no more; let him come when he will;
I deny thee nothing.
Desdemona.   Why, this is not a boon;
'Tis as I should entreat you wear your gloves,
Or feed on nourishing dishes, or keep you warm,

---

[321] Immediate.   [322] Pray thee.   [323] Hardly.   [324] (Even) a private reprimand.   [325] Shilly-
shallying.

Or sue to you to do a peculiar profit
To your own person: nay, when I have a suit   80
Wherein I mean to touch your love indeed,
It shall be full of poise[326] and difficult weight,
And fearful to be granted.
Othello.   I will deny thee nothing:
Whereon, I do beseech thee, grant me this,
To leave me but a little to myself.
Desdemona.   Shall I deny you? no: farewell, my lord.
Othello.   Farewell, my Desdemona: I'll come to thee straight.
Desdemona.   Emilia, come. Be as your fancies teach you;
Whate'er you be, I am obedient.   (*Exit, with Emilia.*)
Othello.   Excellent wretch![327] Perdition catch my soul,   90
But I do love thee! and when I love thee not,
Chaos is[328] come again.
Iago.   My noble lord,—
Othello.   What dost thou say, Iago?
Iago.   Did Michael Cassio, when you woo'd my lady,
Know of your love?
Othello.   He did, from first to last: why dost thou ask?
Iago.   But for a satisfaction of my thought;
No further harm.
Othello.   Why of thy thought, Iago?
Iago.   I did not think he had been acquainted with her.
Othello.   O! yes; and went between us very oft.   100
Iago.   Indeed!
Othello.   Indeed! ay, indeed; discern'st thou aught in that?
Is he not honest?
Iago.   Honest, my lord?
Othello.   Honest! ay, honest.
Iago.   My lord, for aught I know.
Othello.   What dost thou think?
Iago.   Think, my lord!
Othello.   Think, my lord!
By heaven, he echoes me,
As if there were some monster in his thought
Too hideous to be shown. Thou dost mean something:
I heard thee say but now, thou lik'dst not that,
When Cassio left my wife; what didst not like?   110
And when I told thee he was of my counsel
In my whole course of wooing, thou criedst, 'Indeed!'
And didst contract and purse thy brow together,
As if thou then hadst shut up in thy brain

---

[326] Weight.   [327] Here, a term of endearment.   [328] Will have.

Some horrible conceit.[329] If thou dost love me,
Show me thy thought.
Iago.   My lord, you know I love you.
Othello.   I think thou dost;
And, for[330] I know thou art full of love and honesty,
And weigh'st thy words before thou givest them breath,
Therefore these stops[331] of thine fright me the more;   120
For such things in a false disloyal knave
Are tricks of custom, but in a man that's just
They are close dilations,[332] working from the heart
That passion cannot rule.
Iago.   For Michael Cassio,
I dare be sworn I think that he is honest.
Othello.   I think so too.
Iago.   Men should be what they seem;
Or those that be not, would they might seem none!
Othello.   Certain men should be what they seem.
Iago.   Why then, I think Cassio's an honest man.
Othello.   Nay, yet there's more in this.   130
I pray thee, speak to me as to thy thinkings,
As thou dost ruminate, and give thy worst of thoughts
The worst of words.
Iago.   Good my lord, pardon me;
Though I am bound to every act of duty,
I am not bound to[333] that all slaves are free to.
Utter my thoughts? Why, say they are vile and false;
As where's that palace whereinto foul things
Sometimes intrude not? who has a breast so pure
But some uncleanly apprehensions[334]
Keep leets and law-days,[335] and in session sit   140
With meditations lawful?
Othello.   Thou dost conspire against thy friend, Iago,
If thou but think'st him wrong'd, and mak'st his ear
A stranger to thy thoughts.
Iago.   I do beseech you,
Though I perchance am vicious in my guess,—
As, I confess, it is my nature's plague
To spy into abuses, and oft my jealousy[336]
Shapes faults that are not,—that your wisdom yet,
From one that so imperfectly conceits,
Would take no notice, nor build yourself a trouble   150

---

[329] Fancy.   [330] Because.   [331] Interruptions, hesitations.   [332] Secret (i.e., involuntary, unconscious) revelations.   [333] Bound with regard to.   [334] Conceptions.   [335] Sittings of the local courts.   [336] Suspicion.

Out of his scattering and unsure observance.
It were not for your quiet nor your good,
Nor for my manhood, honesty, or wisdom,
To let you know my thoughts.

Othello.   What dost thou mean?

Iago.   Good name in man and woman, dear my lord,
Is the immediate jewel of[337] their souls:
Who steals my purse steals trash; 'tis something, nothing;
'Twas mine, 'tis his, and has been slave to thousands;
But he that filches from me my good name
Robs me of that which not enriches him,   160
And makes me poor indeed.

Othello.   By heaven, I'll know thy thoughts.

Iago.   You cannot, if my heart were in your hand;
Nor shall not, whilst 'tis in my custody.

Othello.   Ha!

Iago.   O! beware, my lord, of jealousy;
It is the green-ey'd monster which doth mock
The meat it feeds on: that cuckold[338] lives in bliss
Who, certain of his fate, loves not his wronger;
But, O! what damned minutes tells[339] he o'er
Who dotes, yet doubts; suspects, yet soundly loves!   170

Othello.   O misery!

Iago.   Poor and content is rich, and rich enough,
But riches fineless[340] is as poor as winter
To him that ever fears he shall be poor.
Good heaven, the souls of all my tribe defend
From jealousy!

Othello.   Why, why is this?
Think'st thou I'd make a life of jealousy,
To follow still the changes of the moon
With fresh suspicions? No; to be once in doubt
Is once to be resolved. Exchange me for a goat   180
When I shall turn the business of my soul
To such exsufflicate[341] and blown[342] surmises,
Matching thy inference. 'Tis not to make me jealous
To say my wife is fair, feeds well, loves company,
Is free of speech, sings, plays, and dances well;
Where virtue is, these are more virtuous:
Nor from mine own weak merits will I draw
The smallest fear, or doubt of her revolt;
For she had eyes, and chose me. No, Iago;

---

[337] Jewel closest to.   [338] Husband of an adulterous woman.   [339] Counts.   [340] Boundless.
[341] Spat out (?).   [342] Fly-blown.

I'll see before I doubt; when I doubt, prove; 190
And, on the proof, there is no more but this,
Away at once with love or jealousy!

Iago. I am glad of it; for now I shall have reason
To show the love and duty that I bear you
With franker spirit; therefore, as I am bound,
Receive it from me; I speak not yet of proof.
Look to your wife; observe her well with Cassio;
Wear your eye thus, not jealous nor secure:
I would not have your free and noble nature
Out of self-bounty[343] be abus'd; look to 't: 200
I know our country disposition[344] well;
In Venice they do let heaven see the pranks
They dare not show their husbands; their best conscience
Is not to leave 't undone, but keep 't unknown.

Othello. Dost thou say so?

Iago. She did deceive her father, marrying you;
And when she seem'd to shake and fear your looks,
She lov'd them most.

Othello. And so she did.

Iago. Why, go to,[345] then;
She that so young could give out such a seeming,
To seel her father's eyes up close as oak, 210
He thought 'twas witchcraft; but I am much to blame;
I humbly do beseech you of your pardon
For too much loving you.

Othello. I am bound to thee for ever.

Iago. I see, this hath a little dash'd your spirits.

Othello. Not a jot, not a jot.

Iago. I' faith, I fear it has.
I hope you will consider what is spoke
Comes from my love. But I do see you're mov'd;
I am to pray you not to strain my speech
To grosser issues nor to larger reach
Than to suspicion. 220

Othello. I will not.

Iago. Should you do so, my lord,
My speech should fall into such vile success
As my thoughts aim not at. Cassio's my worthy friend—
My lord, I see you're mov'd.

Othello. No, not much mov'd:
I do not think but Desdemona's honest.[346]

---

[343] Innate generosity. [344] I.e., that of Venice. [345] Colloquialism; here, something like "all right." [346] Chaste.

Iago.   Long live she so! and long live you to think so!

Othello.   And yet, how nature erring from itself,—

Iago.   Ay, there's the point: as, to be bold with you,
Not to affect many proposed matches
Of her own clime,[347] complexion, and degree,[348]   230
Whereto, we see, in all things nature tends;
Foh! one may smell in such, a will most rank,
Foul disproportion, thoughts unnatural.
But pardon me; I do not in position[349]
Distinctly[350] speak of her, though I may fear
Her will, recoiling[351] to her better judgment,
May fall to match you with her country forms
And happily[352] repent.

Othello.   Farewell, farewell:
If more thou dost perceive, let me know more;
Set on thy wife to observe. Leave me, Iago.   240

Iago.   My lord, I take my leave.   (*Going.*)

Othello.   Why did I marry? This honest creature, doubtless,
Sees and knows more, much more, than he unfolds.

Iago (*returning*).   My lord, I would I might entreat your honour
To scan this thing no further; leave it to time.
Although 'tis fit that Cassio have his place,
For, sure he fills it up with great ability,
Yet, if you please to hold him off awhile,
You shall by that perceive him and his means:
Note if your lady strain his entertainment[353]   250
With any strong or vehement importunity;
Much will be seen in that. In the mean time,
Let me be thought too busy[354] in my fears,
As worthy cause I have to fear I am,
And hold her free, I do beseech your honour.

Othello.   Fear not my government.

Iago.   I once more take my leave.   (*Exit.*)

Othello.   This fellow's of exceeding honesty,
And knows all qualities, with a learned spirit,
Of human dealings; if I do prove her haggard,[355]   260
Though that her jesses[356] were my dear heart-strings,
I'd whistle her off and let her down the wind,[357]
To prey at fortune. Haply, for I am black,
And have not those soft parts of conversation

---

[347] Country.   [348] Social rank.   [349] In definite assertion.   [350] Specifically.   [351] Reverting.
[352] Perhaps.   [353] Urge his re-welcome (i.e., to Othello's trust and favor).   [354] Meddlesome.
[355] Wild hawk.   [356] Leather thongs by which the hawk's legs were strapped to the trainer's wrist.
[357] I'd let her go and take care of herself.

That chamberers[358] have, or, for I am declin'd
Into the vale of years—yet that's not much—
She's gone, I am abus'd;[359] and my relief
Must be to loathe her. O curse of marriage!
That we can call these delicate creatures ours,
And not their appetites. I had rather be a toad,   270
And live upon the vapour of a dungeon,
Than keep a corner in the thing I love
For others' uses. Yet, 'tis the plague of great ones;
Prerogativ'd[360] are they less than the base;
'Tis destiny unshunnable, like death:
Even then this forked plague[361] is fated to us
When we do quicken.[362]
                Look! where she comes.
If she be false, O! then heaven mocks itself.
I'll not believe it.

(*Re-enter Desdemona and Emilia.*)

Desdemona.   How now, my dear Othello!
Your dinner and the generous[363] islanders   280
By you invited, do attend your presence.
Othello.   I am to blame.
Desdemona.   Why do you speak so faintly?
Are you not well?
Othello.   I have a pain upon my forehead here.[364]
Desdemona.   Faith, that's with watching; 'twill away again:
Let me but bind it hard, within this hour
It will be well.
Othello.   Your napkin[365] is too little:

(*She drops her handkerchief.*)

Let it alone. Come, I'll go in with you.
Desdemona.   I am very sorry that you are not well.

(*Exeunt Othello and Desdemona.*)

Emilia.   I am glad I have found this napkin;   290
This was her first remembrance from the Moor;
My wayward husband hath a hundred times

---

[358] Courtiers; or (more specifically): gallants, frequenters of bed chambers.   [359] Deceived. [360] Privileged.   [361] I.e., the cuckold's proverbial horns.   [362] Are conceived, come alive. [363] Noble.   [364] Othello again refers to his cuckoldom.   [365] Handkerchief.

Woo'd me to steal it, but she so loves the token,
For he conjur'd her she should ever keep it,
That she reserves it evermore about her
To kiss and talk to. I'll have the work ta'en out,[366]
And giv 't Iago:
What he will do with it heaven knows, not I;
I nothing but[367] to please his fantasy.[368]

(*Enter Iago.*)

Iago.   How now! what do you here alone?   300
Emilia.   Do not you chide; I have a thing for you.
Iago.   A thing for me? It is a common thing—
Emilia.   Ha!
Iago.   To have a foolish wife.
Emilia.   O! is that all? What will you give me now
     For that same handkerchief?
Iago.   What handkerchief?
Emilia.   What handkerchief!
     Why, that the Moor first gave to Desdemona:
     That which so often you did bid me steal.
Iago.   Hath stol'n it from her?   310
Emilia.   No, faith; she let it drop by negligence,
     And, to the advantage, I, being there, took 't up.
     Look, here it is.
Iago.   A good wench; give it me.
Emilia.   What will you do with 't, that you have been so earnest
     To have me filch it?
Iago.   Why, what's that to you?   (*Snatches it.*)
Emilia.   If it be not for some purpose of import
     Give 't me again; poor lady! she'll run mad
     When she shall lack it.
Iago.   Be not acknown on 't;[369] I have use for it.
     Go, leave me.   (*Exit Emilia.*)
     I will in Cassio's lodging lose this napkin,   321
     And let him find it; trifles light as air
     Are to the jealous confirmations strong
     As proofs of holy writ; this may do something.
     The Moor already changes with my poison:
     Dangerous conceits are in their natures poisons,
     Which at the first are scarce found to distaste,[370]

---

[366] Pattern copied.   [367] I.e., only want.   [368] Whim.   [369] You know nothing about it.
[370] Scarce can be tasted.

But with a little act upon the blood,
Burn like the mines of sulphur. I did say so:
Look! where he comes!

(*Enter Othello.*)

Not poppy,[371] nor mandragora,[372]   330
Nor all the drowsy syrups[373] of the world,
Shall ever medicine thee to that sweet sleep
Which thou ow'dst yesterday.
Othello.   Ha! ha! false to me?
Iago.   Why, how now, general! no more of that.
Othello.   Avaunt! be gone! thou hast set me on the rack;
I swear 'tis better to be much abus'd
Than but to know 't a little.
Iago.   How now, my lord!
Othello.   What sense had I of her stol'n hours of lust?
I saw 't not, thought it not, it harm'd not me;
I slept the next night well, was free and merry;   340
I found not Cassio's kisses on her lips;
He that is robb'd, not wanting what is stol'n,
Let him not know 't, and he's not robb'd at all.
Iago.   I am sorry to hear this.
Othello.   I had been happy, if the general camp,[374]
Pioners[375] and all, had tasted her sweet body,
So[376] I had nothing known. O! now, for ever
Farewell the tranquil mind; farewell content!
Farewell the plumed troop and the big wars
That make ambition virtue! O, farewell!   350
Farewell the neighing steed, and the shrill trump,
The spirit-stirring drum, the ear-piercing fife,
The royal banner, and all quality,
Pride, pomp, and circumstance[377] of glorious war!
And, O you mortal engines,[378] whose rude throats
The immortal Jove's dread clamours counterfeit,
Farewell! Othello's occupation's gone!
Iago.   Is it possible, my lord?
Othello.   Villain, be sure thou prove my love a whore,
Be sure of it; give me the ocular proof;   360
Or, by the worth of mine eternal soul,
Thou hadst been better have been born a dog
Than answer my wak'd wrath.

---

[371] Opium.   [372] A soporific.   [373] I.e., soporifics.   [374] Whole army.   [375] Lowest rank of manual laborers in the army.   [376] As long as.   [377] Pageantry.   [378] Deadly artillery.

Iago.   Is 't come to this?

Othello.   Make me to see 't; or, at the least, so prove it,
    That the probation[379] bear no hinge nor loop
    To hang a doubt on; or woe upon thy life!

Iago.   My noble lord—

Othello.   If thou dost slander her and torture me,
    Never pray more; abandon all remorse;
    On horror's head horrors accumulate;   370
    Do deeds to make heaven weep, all earth amaz'd;
    For nothing canst thou to damnation add
    Greater than that.

Iago.   O grace! O heaven forgive me!
    Are you a man! have you a soul or sense?
    God be wi' you; take mine office. O wretched fool!
    That liv'st to make thine honesty a vice.
    O monstrous world! Take note, take note, O world!
    To be direct and honest is not safe.
    I thank you for this profit,[380] and, from hence
    I'll love no friend, sith[381] love breeds such offence.   380

Othello.   Nay, stay; thou shouldst be honest.

Iago.   I should be wise; for honesty's a fool,
    And loses that it works for.

Othello.   By the world,
    I think my wife be honest and think she is not;
    I think that thou art just and think thou art not.
    I'll have some proof. Her name, that was as fresh
    As Dian's[382] visage, is now begrim'd and black
    As mine own face. If there be cords or knives,
    Poison or fire or suffocating streams,
    I'll not endure it. Would I were satisfied!   390

Iago.   I see, sir, you are eaten up with passion.
    I do repent me that I put it to you.
    You would be satisfied?

Othello.   Would! nay, I will.

Iago.   And may; but how? how satisfied, my lord?
    Would you, the supervisor,[383] grossly gape on;
    Behold her tupp'd?

Othello.   Death and damnation! O!

Iago.   It were a tedious[384] difficulty, I think,
    To bring them to that prospect; damn them then,
    If ever mortal eyes do see them bolster[385]

---

[379] Proof.   [380] Lesson.   [381] Since.   [382] Diana's, the goddess of the moon.   [383] Observer.
[384] Laborious.   [385] Lie together.

More[386] than their own! What then? how then?   400
What shall I say? Where's satisfaction?
It is impossible you should see this,
Were they as prime[387] as goats, as hot as monkeys,
As salt as wolves in pride,[388] and fools as gross
As ignorance made drunk; but yet, I say,
If imputation, and strong circumstances,
Which lead directly to the door of truth,
Will give you satisfaction, you may have it.

Othello.   Give me a living reason she's disloyal.

Iago.   I do not like the office;   410
But, sith I am enter'd in this cause so far,
Prick'd to 't by foolish honesty and love,
I will go on. I lay with Cassio lately;
And, being troubled with a raging tooth,
I could not sleep.
There are a kind of men so loose of soul
That in their sleeps will mutter their affairs;
One of this kind is Cassio.
In sleep I heard him say, 'Sweet Desdemona,
Let us be wary, let us hide our loves!'   420
And then, sir, would he gripe[389] and wring my hand,
Cry, 'O, sweet creature!' and then kiss me hard,
As if he pluck'd up kisses by the roots,
That grew upon my lips; then laid his leg
Over my thigh, and sigh'd, and kiss'd; and then
Cried, 'Cursed fate, that gave thee to the Moor!'

Othello.   O monstrous! monstrous!

Iago.   Nay, this was but his dream.

Othello.   But this denoted a foregone conclusion:[390]
'Tis a shrewd doubt,[391] though it be but a dream.

Iago.   And this may help to thicken other proofs   430
That do demonstrate thinly.

Othello.   I'll tear her all to pieces.

Iago.   Nay, but be wise; yet we see nothing done;
She may be honest yet. Tell me but this:
Have you not sometimes seen a handkerchief
Spotted with strawberries in your wife's hand?

Othello.   I gave her such a one; 'twas my first gift.

Iago.   I know not that; but such a handkerchief—
I am sure it was your wife's—did I to-day
See Cassio wipe his beard with.

---

[386] Other.   [387] Lustful.   [388] Heat.   [389] Seize.   [390] Previous consummation.   [391] (1) Cursed, (2) Acute, suspicion.

Othello.   If it be that,—
Iago.   If it be that, or any that was hers,   440
  It speaks against her with the other proofs.
Othello.   O! that the slave had forty thousand lives;
  One is too poor, too weak for my revenge.
  Now do I see 'tis true. Look here, Iago;
  All my fond love thus do I blow to heaven:
  'Tis gone.
  Arise, black vengeance, from the hollow hell!
  Yield up, O love! thy crown and hearted throne
  To tyrannous hate. Swell, bosom, with thy fraught,[392]
  For 'tis of aspics'[393] tongues!
Iago.   Yet be content.[394]   450
Othello.   O! blood, blood, blood!
Iago.   Patience, I say; your mind, perhaps, may change.
Othello.   Never, Iago. Like to the Pontic sea,[395]
  Whose icy current and compulsive course
  Ne'er feels retiring ebb, but keeps due on
  To the Propontic and the Hellespont,[396]
  Even so my bloody thoughts, with violent pace,
  Shall ne'er look back, ne'er ebb to humble love,
  Till that a capable[397] and wide revenge
  Swallow them up.   (*Kneels.*)
                    Now, by yond marble heaven,   460
  In the due reverence of a sacred vow
  I here engage my words.
Iago.   Do not rise yet.   (*Kneels.*)
  Witness, you ever-burning lights above!
  You elements that clip[398] us round about!
  Witness, that here Iago doth give up
  The execution of his wit, hands, heart,
  To wrong'd Othello's service! Let him command,
  And to obey shall be in me remorse,[399]
  What bloody business ever.[400]   (*They rise.*)
Othello.   I greet thy love,
  Not with vain thanks, but with acceptance bounteous,   470
  And will upon the instant put thee to 't:
  Within these three days let me hear thee say
  That Cassio 's not alive.
Iago.   My friend is dead; 'tis done at your request:
  But let her live.

---

[392] Burden.   [393] Poisonous snakes.   [394] Patient.   [395] The Black Sea.   [396] The Sea of Marmara, the Dardanelles.   [397] Comprehensive.   [398] Encompass.   [399] Probably a corrupt line; the meaning appears to be: "to obey shall be my solemn obligation."   [400] Soever.

Othello.   Damn her, lewd minx! O, damn her!
  Come, go with me apart; I will withdraw.
  To furnish me with some swift means of death
  For the fair devil. Now art thou my lieutenant.
Iago.   I am your own for ever.   (*Exeunt.*)

Scene 4.   Before the Castle.

(*Enter Desdemona, Emilia, and Clown.*)

Desdemona.   Do you know, sirrah,[401] where Lieutenant Cassio lies?[402]
Clown.   I dare not say he lies any where.
Desdemona.   Why, man?
Clown.   He is a soldier; and for one to say a soldier lies, is stabbing.[403]
Desdemona.   Go to;[404] where lodges he?
Clown.   To tell you where he lodges is to tell you where I lie.
Desdemona.   Can anything be made of this?
Clown.   I know not where he lodges, and for me to devise[405] a lodging, and say
  he lies here or he lies there, were to lie in mine own throat.
Desdemona.   Can you inquire him out, and be edified by report?
Clown.   I will catechize the world for him; that is, make questions, and by
  them answer.
Desdemona.   Seek him, bid him come hither; tell him I have moved my lord
  in his behalf, and hope all will be well.
Clown.   To do this is within the compass of man's wit, and therefore I will at-
  tempt the doing it.   (*Exit.*)
Desdemona.   Where should I lose that handkerchief, Emilia?
Emilia.   I know not, madam.
Desdemona.   Believe me, I had rather have lost my purse
  Full of cruzadoes;[406] and, but my noble Moor   20
  Is true of mind, and made of no such baseness
  As jealous creatures are, it were enough
  To put him to ill thinking.
Emilia.   Is he not jealous?
Desdemona.   Who! he? I think the sun where he was born
  Drew all such humours from him.
Emilia.   Look! where he comes.
Desdemona.   I will not leave him now till Cassio
  Be call'd to him.

(*Enter Othello.*)

---

[401] Common form of address to inferiors.   [402] Lives.   [403] I.e., is cause for stabbing.
[404] Here apparently: "Come on!"   [405] Invent.   [406] Portuguese gold coins.

Desdemona.   How is 't with you, my lord?

Othello.   Well, my good lady. (*Aside.*) O! hardness to dissemble.
   How do you, Desdemona?

Desdemona.   Well, my good lord.

Othello.   Give me your hand. This hand is moist,[407] my lady.   30

Desdemona.   It yet has felt no age nor known no sorrow.

Othello.   This argues fruitfulness and liberal[408] heart;
   Hot, hot, and moist; this hand of yours requires
   A sequester[409] from liberty, fasting and prayer,
   Much castigation, exercise devout;
   For here 's a young and sweating devil here,
   That commonly rebels. 'Tis a good hand,
   A frank one.

Desdemona.   You may, indeed, say so;
   For 'twas that hand that gave away my heart.

Othello.   A liberal hand; the hearts of old gave hands,   40
   But our new heraldry[410] is hands not hearts.

Desdemona.   I cannot speak of this. Come now, your promise.

Othello.   What promise, chuck?[411]

Desdemona.   I have sent to bid Cassio come speak with you.

Othello.   I have a salt and sorry rheum offends me.
   Lend me thy handkerchief.

Desdemona.   Here, my lord.

Othello.   That which I gave you.

Desdemona.   I have it not about me.

Othello.   Not?

Desdemona.   No, indeed, my lord.

Othello.   That is a fault.
   That handkerchief
   Did an Egyptian[412] to my mother give;   50
   She was a charmer,[413] and could almost read
   The thoughts of people; she told her, while she kept it,
   'Twould make her amiable[414] and subdue my father
   Entirely to her love, but if she lost it
   Or made a gift of it, my father's eye
   Should hold her loathed, and his spirits should hunt
   After new fancies.[415] She dying gave it me;
   And bid me, when my fate would have me wive,
   To give it her. I did so; and take heed on 't;
   Make it a darling like your precious eye;   60

---

[407] A supposed symptom of a lustful nature.   [408] With overtones of: too free, loose.   [409] Separation.   [410] I.e., new heraldic symbolism (Othello means that the new way is not to give the heart together with the hand).   [411] Common term of endearment.   [412] Gypsy.   [413] Sorceress.   [414] Lovable, desirable.   [415] Loves.

To lose 't or give 't away, were such perdition
As nothing else could match.
Desdemona.   Is 't possible?
Othello.   'Tis true; there 's magic in the web of it;
A sibyl,[416] that had number'd in the world
The sun to course two hundred compasses,
In her prophetic fury sew'd the work;
The worms were hallow'd that did breed the silk,
And it was dy'd in mummy[417] which the skilful
Conserv'd of maidens' hearts.
Desdemona.   Indeed! is 't true?
Othello.   Most veritable; therefore look to 't well.   70
Desdemona.   Then would to heaven that I had never seen it!
Othello.   Ha! wherefore?
Desdemona.   Why do you speak so startingly and rash?
Othello.   Is 't lost? is 't gone? speak, is it out o' the way?
Desdemona.   Heaven bless us!
Othello.   Say you?
Desdemona.   It is not lost; but what an if[418] it were?
Othello.   How!
Desdemona.   I say, it is not lost.
Othello.   Fetch 't, let me see 't!
Desdemona.   Why, so I can, sir, but I will not now.
This is a trick to put me from my suit: 80
Pray you let Cassio be receiv'd again.
Othello.   Fetch me the handkerchief; my mind misgives.
Desdemona.   Come, come;
You'll never meet a more sufficient[419] man.
Othello.   The handkerchief!
Desdemona.   I pray, talk[420] me of Cassio.
Othello.   The handkerchief!
Desdemona.   A man that all his time
Hath founded his good fortunes on your love,
Shar'd dangers with you,—
Othello.   The handkerchief!
Desdemona.   In sooth, you are to blame.   90
Othello.   Away!   (*Exit.*)
Emilia.   Is not this man jealous?
Desdemona.   I ne'er saw this before.
Sure, there's some wonder in this handkerchief;
I am most unhappy in the loss of it.

---

[416] Prophetess.   [417] Drug (medicinal or magic) derived from embalmed bodies.   [418] If.
[419] Adequate.   [420] Talk to.

Emilia.   'Tis not a year or two shows us a man;
They are all but[421] stomachs, and we all but[421] food;
They eat us hungerly, and when they are full
They belch us. Look you! Cassio and my husband.

(*Enter Iago and Cassio.*)

Iago.   There is no other way; 'tis she must do 't:
And, lo! the happiness;[422] go and importune her.   100
Desdemona.   How now, good Cassio! what 's the news with you?
Cassio.   Madam, my former suit: I do beseech you
That by your virtuous means I may again
Exist, and be a member of his love
Whom I with all the office[423] of my heart
Entirely honour; I would not be delay'd.
If my offence be of such mortal kind
That nor my service past, nor present sorrows,
Nor purpos'd merit in futurity,
Can ransom me into his love again,   110
But to know so must be my benefit;
So shall I clothe me in a forc'd content,
And shut myself up in some other course
To fortune's alms.
Desdemona.   Alas! thrice-gentle Cassio!
My advocation is not now in tune;
My lord is not my lord, nor should I know him,
Were he in favour[424] as in humour alter'd.
So help me every spirit sanctified,
As I have spoken for you all my best
And stood within the blank of[425] his displeasure   120
For my free speech. You must awhile be patient;
What I can do I will, and more I will
Than for myself I dare: let that suffice you.
Iago.   Is my lord angry?
Emilia.   He went hence but now,
And certainly in strange unquietness.
Iago.   Can he be angry? I have seen the cannon,
When it hath blown his ranks[426] into the air,
And, like the devil, from his very arm
Puff'd his own brother; and can he be angry?
Something of moment[427] then; I will go meet him;   130
There's matter in 't indeed, if he be angry.

---

[421] Only . . . only.   [422] "What luck!"   [423] Duty.   [424] Appearance.   [425] As the target for.
[426] I.e., his soldiers.   [427] Important.

Desdemona.   I prithee, do so. (*Exit Iago.*) Something, sure, of state,[428]
Either from Venice, or some unhatch'd[429] practice
Made demonstrable here in Cyprus to him,
Hath puddled[430] his clear spirit; and, in such cases
Men's natures wrangle with inferior things,
Though great ones are their object. 'Tis even so;
For let our finger ache, and it indues[431]
Our other healthful members even to that sense
Of pain. Nay, we must think men are not gods,   140
Nor of them look for such observancy[432]
As fits the bridal.[433] Beshrew me much, Emilia,
I was—unhandsome warrior as I am—
Arraigning his unkindness with[434] my soul;
But now I find I had suborn'd the witness,[435]
And he 's indicted falsely.
Emilia.   Pray heaven it be state matters, as you think,
And no conception,[436] nor no jealous toy[437]
Concerning you.
Desdemona.   Alas the day! I never gave him cause.   150
Emilia.   But jealous souls will not be answer'd so;
They are not ever jealous for the cause,
But jealous for they are jealous; 'tis a monster
Begot upon itself, born on itself.
Desdemona.   Heaven keep that monster from Othello's mind!
Emilia.   Lady, amen.
Desdemona.   I will go seek him. Cassio, walk hereabout;
If I do find him fit, I'll move your suit
And seek to effect it to my uttermost.
Cassio.   I humbly thank your ladyship.   160

(*Exeunt Desdemona and Emilia.*)

(*Enter Bianca.*)

Bianca.   Save you, friend Cassio!
Cassio.   What make you from home?
How is it with you, my most fair Bianca?
I' faith, sweet love, I was coming to your house.

---

[428] Public affairs.   [429] Abortive or budding plot.   [430] Muddied.   [431] Brings, leads.   [432] Attention.   [433] Wedding.   [434] To.   [435] I.e., caused my soul to bring in wrong charges.   [436] Fancy, supposition.   [437] Fancy.

Bianca.   And I was going to your lodging, Cassio.
  What! keep a week away? seven days and nights?
  Eight score eight hours? and lovers' absent hours,
  More tedious than the dial eight score times?
  O weary reckoning!
Cassio.   Pardon me, Bianca,
  I have this while with leaden thoughts been press'd;
  But I shall, in a more continuate[438] time,   170
  Strike off[439] this score of absence. Sweet Bianca,

(Giving her Desdemona's handkerchief.)

  Take me this work out.
Bianca.   O Cassio! whence came this?
  This is some token from a newer friend;
  To the felt absence now I feel a cause;
  Is 't come to this? Well, well.
Cassio.   Go to, woman!
  Throw your vile guesses in the devil's teeth,
  From whence you have them. You are jealous now
  That this is from some mistress, some remembrance:
  No, in good troth, Bianca.
Bianca.   Why, whose is it?   180
Cassio.   I know not, sweet; I found it in my chamber.
  I like the work well; ere it be demanded,—[440]
  As like enough it will,—I'd have it copied;
  Take it and do 't; and leave me for this time.
Bianca.   Leave you! wherefore?
Cassio.   I do attend here on[441] the general,
  And think it no addition,[442] nor my wish,
  To have him see me woman'd.
Bianca.   Why, I pray you?
Cassio.   Not that I love you not.
Bianca.   But that you do not love me.
  I pray you, bring me on the way a little   190
  And say if I shall see you soon at night.
Cassio.   'Tis but a little way that I can bring you,
  For I attend here; but I'll see you soon.
Bianca.   'Tis very good; I must be circumstanc'd.[443]   *(Exeunt.)*

---

[438] Uninterrupted.   [439] Cancel (i.e., make up for).   [440] Asked for.   [441] Wait for.   [442] Advantage, credit.   [443] Governed by circumstances.

Act IV

Scene 1.   Cyprus. Before the Castle.

(*Enter Othello and Iago.*)

Iago.   Will you think so?
Othello.   Think so, Iago!
Iago.   What!
    To kiss in private?
Othello.   An unauthoriz'd kiss.
Iago.   Or to be naked with her friend a-bed
    An hour or more, not meaning any harm?
Othello.   Naked a-bed, Iago, and not mean harm?
    It is hypocrisy against the devil:[444]
    They that mean virtuously, and yet do so,
    The devil their virtue tempts, and they tempt heaven.
Iago.   If they do nothing, 'tis a venial slip;
    But if I give my wife a handkerchief,—   10
Othello.   What then?
Iago.   Why, then, 'tis hers, my lord; and, being hers,
    She may, I think, bestow 't on any man.
Othello.   She is protectress of her honour too;
    May she give that?
Iago.   Her honour is an essence that 's not seen;
    They have it very oft that have it not:[445]
    But for the handkerchief,—
Othello.   By heaven, I would most gladly have forgot it:—
    Thou said'st,—O! it comes o'er my memory,   20
    As doth the raven[446] o'er the infected house,
    Boding to all,—he had my handkerchief.
Iago.   Ay, what of that?
Othello.   That's not so good now.
Iago.   What,
    If I had said I had seen him do you wrong?
    Or heard him say, as knaves be such abroad,[447]
    Who having, by their own importunate suit,
    Or voluntary dotage[448] of some mistress,
    Convinced or supplied them,[449] cannot choose
    But they must blab.

---

[444] I.e., by not committing the sin which the situation invites.   [445] I.e., some unchaste women are thought chaste.   [446] (1) A bad omen, (2) A carrier of the plague.   [447] As there are some such in the world.   [448] Foolish affection.   [449] Overcome (their reluctance) or satisfied (their desires).

Othello.　　　　　Hath he said any thing?

Iago.　He hath, my lord; but be you well assur'd,　　　　　　　　30
No more than he'll unswear.

Othello.　　　　　What hath he said?

Iago.　Faith, that he did— I know not what he did.

Othello.　What? what?

Iago.　Lie—

Othello.　With her?

Iago.　　　　　With her, on her; what you will.

Othello.　Lie with her; lie on her! We say, lie on her, when they belie her. Lie with her! that's fulsome. Handkerchief,—confessions,—handkerchief! To confess, and be hanged for his labour. First, to be hanged, and then to confess: I tremble at it. Nature would not invest herself in such shadowing passion without some instruction.[450] It is not words that shake me thus. Pish! Noses, ears, and lips. Is it possible?—Confess!—Handkerchief!—O devil!

(*Falls in a trance.*)

Iago.　Work on,
My medicine, work! Thus credulous fools are caught;
And many worthy and chaste dames even thus,
All guiltless, meet reproach. What, ho! my lord!
My lord, I say! Othello!

(*Enter Cassio.*)

　　　　　How now, Cassio!

Cassio.　What's the matter?

Iago.　My lord is fallen into an epilepsy;[451]
This is his second fit; he had one yesterday.

Cassio.　Rub him about the temples.

Iago.　　　　　No, forbear;
The lethargy[452] must have his quiet course,　　　　　　　　50
If not, he foams at mouth, and by and by
Breaks out to savage madness. Look! he stirs;
Do you withdraw yourself a little while,
He will recover straight; when he is gone,
I would on great occasion[453] speak with you.　　　　(*Exit Cassio.*)
How is it, general? have you not hurt your head?

Othello.　Dost thou mock me?[454]

Iago.　　　　　I mock you! no, by heaven.
Would you would bear your fortune like a man!

---

[450] I would not fall into such passion unless there were some real grounds for it.　[451] Seizure, fit.
[452] Coma.　[453] Important matter.　[454] Another allusion to the cuckold's horns.

Othello.   A horned man's a monster and a beast.

Iago.   There's many a beast then, in a populous city,   60
And many a civil[455] monster.

Othello.   Did he confess it?

Iago.   Good sir, be a man;
Think every bearded fellow that's but yok'd
May draw[456] with you; there's millions now alive
That nightly lie in those unproper[457] beds
Which they dare swear peculiar;[458] your case is better.
O! 'tis the spite of hell, the fiend's arch-mock,
To lip[459] a wanton in a secure[460] couch,
And to suppose her chaste. No, let me know;
And knowing what I am, I know what she shall be.   70

Othello.   O! thou art wise; 'tis certain.

Iago.   Stand you awhile apart;
Confine yourself but in a patient list.[461]
Whilst you were here o'erwhelmed with your grief,—
A passion most unsuiting such a man,—
Cassio came hither; I shifted him away,
And laid good 'scuse upon your ecstasy;[462]
Bade him anon return and here speak with me;
The which he promis'd. Do but encave yourself,
And mark the fleers, the gibes, and notable scorns,
That dwell in every region of his face;   80
For I will make him tell the tale anew,
Where, how, how oft, how long ago, and when
He hath, and is again to cope[463] your wife:
I say, but mark his gesture. Marry, patience;
Or I shall say you are all in all in spleen,[464]
And nothing of a man.

Othello.   Dost thou hear, Iago?
I will be found most cunning in my patience;
But—dost thou hear?—most bloody.

Iago.   That's not amiss:
But yet keep time[465] in all. Will you withdraw?   *(Othello goes apart.)*
Now will I question Cassio of Bianca,   90
A housewife[466] that by selling her desires
Buys herself bread and clothes; it is a creature
That dotes on Cassio; as 'tis the strumpet's plague
To beguile many and be beguil'd by one.

---

[455] Citizen.   [456] I.e., pull the burden of cuckoldom.   [457] Not exclusively their own.   [458] Exclusively their own.   [459] Kiss.   [460] I.e., without suspicion of having a rival.   [461] Bounds of patience.   [462] Derangement, trance.   [463] Close with.   [464] Completely overcome by passion.   [465] Maintain control.   [466] Hussy.

He, when he hears of her, cannot refrain
From the excess of laughter. Here he comes:

(*Re-enter Cassio.*)

As he shall smile, Othello shall go mad;
And his unbookish[467] jealousy must construe
Poor Cassio's smiles, gestures, and light behaviour
Quite in the wrong. How do you now, lieutenant?   100
Cassio.   The worser that you give me the addition[468]
Whose want[469] even kills me.
Iago.   Ply Desdemona well, and you are sure on 't.
(*Speaking lower.*) Now, if this suit lay in Bianca's power,
How quickly should you speed!
Cassio.   Alas! poor caitiff![470]
Othello.   Look! how he laughs already!
Iago.   I never knew woman love man so.
Cassio.   Alas! poor rogue, I think i' faith, she loves me.
Othello.   Now he denies it faintly, and laughs it out.
Iago.   Do you hear, Cassio?
Othello.   Now he importunes him   110
To tell it o'er: go to; well said, well said.
Iago.   She gives it out that you shall marry her;
Do you intend it?
Cassio.   Ha, ha, ha!
Othello.   Do you triumph, Roman?[471] do you triumph?
Cassio.   I marry her! what? a customer?[472] I prithee, bear some charity to my
wit;[473] do not think it so unwholesome. Ha, ha, ha!
Othello.   So, so, so, so. They laugh that win.[474]
Iago.   Faith, the cry goes that you shall marry her.
Cassio.   Prithee, say true.   120
Iago.   I am a very villain else.
Othello.   Have you scored me?[475] Well.
Cassio.   This is the monkey's own giving out: she is persuaded I will marry her,
out of her own love and flattery, not out of my promise.
Othello.   Iago beckons me;[476] now he begins the story.
Cassio.   She was here even now; she haunts me in every place. I was the other
day talking on the sea-bank with certain Venetians, and thither comes this
bauble,[477] and, by this hand, she falls me thus about my neck;—
Othello.   Crying, 'O dear Cassio!' as it were; his gesture imports it.

---

[467] Unpracticed, naive.   [468] Title.   [469] The want of which.   [470] Wretch.   [471] I.e., one who
triumphs (?).   [472] Courtesan, prostitute.   [473] Give me credit for some sense.   [474] "He who
laughs last laughs longest" (?).   [475] Wounded, defaced (?); or: settled my account (?).   [476] Signals.   [477] Plaything.

Cassio.   So hangs and lolls and weeps upon me; so hales[478] and pulls me; ha, ha, ha!

Othello.   Now he tells how she plucked him to my chamber. O! I see that nose of yours, but not the dog I shall throw it to.

Cassio.   Well, I must leave her company.

Iago.   Before me![479] look, where she comes.

Cassio.   'Tis such another fitchew![480] marry, a perfumed one.

(Enter Bianca.)

What do you mean by this haunting of me?

Bianca.   Let the devil and his dam haunt you! What did you mean by that same handkerchief you gave me even now? I was a fine fool to take it. I must take out the work! A likely piece of work, that you should find it in your chamber, and not know who left it there! This is some minx's token, and I must take out the work! There, give it your hobby-horse;[481] wheresoever you had it I'll take out no work on 't.

Cassio.   How now, my sweet Bianca! how now, how now!

Othello.   By heaven, that should be[482] my handkerchief!

Bianca.   An you'll come to supper to-night, you may; an you will not, come when you are next prepared[483] for.   *(Exit.)*

Iago.   After her, after her.

Cassio.   Faith, I must; she'll rail in the street else.

Iago.   Will you sup there?   150

Cassio.   Faith, I intend so.

Iago.   Well, I may chance to see you, for I would very fain[484] speak with you.

Cassio.   Prithee come; will you?

Iago.   Go to; say no more.   *(Exit Cassio.)*

Othello (*advancing*).   How shall I murder him, Iago?

Iago.   Did you perceive how he laughed at his vice?

Othello.   O! Iago!

Iago.   And did you see the handkerchief?

Othello.   Was that mine?

Iago.   Yours, by this hand; and to see how he prizes the foolish woman your wife! she gave it him, and he hath given it his whore.

Othello.   I would have him nine years a-killing. A fine woman! a fair woman! a sweet woman!

Iago.   Nay, you must forget that.

Othello.   Ay, let her rot, and perish, and be damned to-night; for she shall not live. No, my heart is turned to stone; I strike it, and it hurts my hand. O! the

---

[478] Hauls.   [479] An exclamation of surprise.   [480] Polecat, noted both for its strong smell and for its lechery.   [481] Harlot.   [482] I.e., I think that is.   [483] Expected (Bianca means that if he does not come that night, she will never want to see him again).   [484] Gladly.

world hath not a sweeter creature; she might lie by an emperor's side and command him tasks.

Iago.   Nay, that's not your way.[485]

Othello.   Hang her! I do but say what she is. So delicate with her needle! An admirable musician! O, she will sing the savageness out of a bear. Of so high and plenteous wit and invention!

Iago.   She's the worse for all this.

Othello.   O! a thousand, a thousand times. And then, of so gentle a condition![486]

Iago.   Ay, too gentle.[487]

Othello.   Nay, that's certain;—but yet the pity of it, Iago!
O! Iago, the pity of it, Iago!

Iago.   If you are so fond over her iniquity, give her patent to offend; for, if it touch not you, it comes near nobody.

Othello.   I will chop her into messes.[488] Cuckold me!

Iago.   O! 'tis foul in her.

Othello.   With mine officer!

Iago.   That's fouler.

Othello.   Get me some poison, Iago; this night: I'll not expostulate with her, lest her body and beauty unprovide my mind again.[489] This night, Iago.

Iago.   Do it not with poison, strangle her in her bed, even the bed she hath contaminated.

Othello.   Good, good; the justice of it pleases; very good.

Iago.   And for Cassio, let me be his undertaker;[490] you shall hear more by midnight.

Othello.   Excellent good. (*A trumpet within.*) What trumpet is that same?

Iago.   Something from Venice, sure. 'Tis Lodovico,
Come from the duke; and see, your wife is with him.

(*Enter Lodovico, Desdemona, and Attendants.*)

Lodovico.   God save you, worthy general!

Othello.   With all my heart, sir.

Lodovico.   The duke and senators of Venice greet you.

(*Gives him a packet.*)

Othello.   I kiss the instrument of their pleasures.

(*Opens the packet, and reads.*)

---

[485] Proper course.   [486] So much the high-born lady.   [487] I.e., yielding.   [488] Bits.   [489] Unsettle my intention.   [490] Dispatcher.

Desdemona.   And what's the news, good cousin Lodovico?

Iago.   I am very glad to see you, signior;
   Welcome to Cyprus.

Lodovico.   I thank you. How does Lieutenant Cassio?

Iago.   Lives, sir.   200

Desdemona.   Cousin, there's fall'n between him and my lord
   An unkind⁴⁹¹ breach; but you shall make all well.

Othello.   Are you sure of that?

Desdemona.   My lord?

Othello (*reads*).   'This fail you not to do, as you will'—

Lodovico.   He did not call; he's busy in the paper.
   Is there division⁴⁹² twixt my lord and Cassio?

Desdemona.   A most unhappy one; I would do much
   To atone⁴⁹³ them, for the love I bear to Cassio.

Othello.   Fire and brimstone!

Desdemona.   My lord?

Othello.   Are you wise?   210

Desdemona.   What! is he angry?

Lodovico.   May be the letter mov'd him;
   For, as I think, they do command him home,
   Deputing Cassio in his government.

Desdemona.   Trust me, I am glad on 't.

Othello.   Indeed!

Desdemona.   My lord?

Othello.   I am glad to see you mad.

Desdemona.   Why, sweet Othello?

Othello.   Devil!   (*Strikes her.*)

Desdemona.   I have not deserved this.

Lodovico.   My lord, this would not be believ'd in Venice,
   Though I should swear I saw 't; 'tis very much;
   Make her amends, she weeps.

Othello.   O devil, devil!
   If that the earth could teem with woman's tears,   220
   Each drop she falls⁴⁹⁴ would prove a crocodile.⁴⁹⁵
   Out of my sight!

Desdemona.   I will not stay to offend you.   (*Going.*)

Lodovico.   Truly, an obedient lady;
   I do beseech your lordship, call her back.

Othello.   Mistress!

Desdemona.   My lord?

Othello.   What would you with her, sir?

Lodovico.   Why, I, my lord?

---

⁴⁹¹ Unnatural.   ⁴⁹² Estrangement.   ⁴⁹³ Reconcile.   ⁴⁹⁴ Lets fall.   ⁴⁹⁵ The crocodile's tears
were supposed to be hypocritical.

Othello. Ay; you did wish that I would make her turn:
    Sir, she can turn, and turn, and yet go on,
    And turn again; and she can weep, sir, weep;
    And she's obedient, as you say, obedient,   230
    Very obedient. Proceed you in your tears.
    Concerning this, sir—O well-painted passion!—
    I am commanded home. Get you away;
    I'll send for you anon. Sir, I obey the mandate,
    And will return to Venice. Hence! avaunt![496]   *(Exit Desdemona.)*
    Cassio shall have my place. And, sir, to-night,
    I do entreat that we may sup together;
    You are welcome, sir, to Cyprus. Goats and monkeys!   *(Exit.)*
Lodovico. Is this the noble Moor whom our full senate
    Call all-in-all sufficient? is this the noble nature   240
    Whom passion could not shake? whose solid virtue
    The shot of accident nor dart of chance
    Could neither graze nor pierce?
Iago.   He is much chang'd.
Lodovico. Are his wits safe? is he not light of brain?
Iago. He's that he is; I may not breathe my censure.
    What he might be, if, what he might, he is not,
    I would to heaven he were![497]
Lodovico.   What! strike his wife!
Iago. Faith, that was not so well; yet would I knew
    That stroke would prove the worst!
Lodovico.   Is it his use?
    Or did the letters work upon his blood,   250
    And new-create this fault?
Iago.   Alas, alas!
    It is not honesty in me to speak
    What I have seen and known. You shall observe him,
    And his own courses[498] will denote him so
    That I may save my speech. Do but go after
    And mark how he continues.
Lodovico. I am sorry that I am deceiv'd in him.   *(Exeunt.)*

Scene 2. A Room in the Castle.

(Enter Othello and Emilia.)

Othello. You have seen nothing, then?
Emilia. Nor ever heard, nor ever did suspect.

---

[496] Begone!   [497] Another of Iago's gnomic speeches; perhaps approximately: "If now he is not himself, I wish he would be what he could be!"   [498] Actions.

Othello.   Yes, you have seen Cassio and her together.
Emilia.   But then I saw no harm, and then I heard
　Each syllable that breath made up between them.
Othello.   What! did they never whisper?
Emilia.   Never, my lord.
Othello.   Nor send you out o' the way?
Emilia.   Never.
Othello.   To fetch her fan, her gloves, her mask, nor nothing?[499]
Emilia.   Never, my lord.   10
Othello.   That's strange.
Emilia.   I durst, my lord, to wager she is honest,
　Lay down my soul at stake: if you think other,
　Remove your thought; it doth abuse your bosom.
　If any wretch have put this in your head,
　Let heaven requite it with the serpent's curse!
　For, if she be not honest, chaste, and true,
　There's no man happy; the purest of their wives
　Is foul as slander.
Othello.   Bid her come hither; go.   (*Exit Emilia.*)
　She says enough; yet she 's a simple[500] bawd
　That cannot say as much. This is a subtle whore,   20
　A closet lock and key of villainous secrets;
　And yet she 'll kneel and pray; I have seen her do 't.

(*Re-enter Emilia with Desdemona.*)

Desdemona.   My lord, what is your will?
Othello.   Pray, chuck, come hither.
Desdemona.   What is your pleasure?
Othello.   Let me see your eyes;
　Look in my face.
Desdemona.   What horrible fancy 's this?
Othello (*to Emilia*).   Some of your function,[501] mistress;
　Leave procreants alone and shut the door;
　Cough or cry 'hem' if any body come;
　Your mystery,[502] your mystery; nay, dispatch.   (*Exit Emilia.*)
Desdemona.   Upon my knees, what doth your speech import?
　I understand a fury in your words.
　But not the words.
Othello.   Why, what art thou?
Desdemona.   Your wife, my lord; your true
　And loyal wife.

---

[499] Anything.   [500] Simpleminded.   [501] To your duty, business.   [502] Trade.

Othello.   Come, swear it, damn thyself;
 Lest, being like one of heaven, the devils themselves
 Should fear to seize thee; therefore be double-damn'd;
 Swear thou art honest.
Desdemona.   Heaven doth truly know it.
Othello. Heaven truly knows that thou art false as hell.
Desdemona. To whom, my lord? with whom? how am I false?   40
Othello. Ah! Desdemona; away, away, away!
Desdemona. Alas, the heavy day!—Why do you weep?
 Am I the motive of these tears, my lord?
 If haply you my father do suspect
 An instrument of this your calling back,
 Lay not your blame on me; if you have lost him,
 Why, I have lost him too.
Othello.   Had it pleas'd heaven
 To try me with affliction, had he rain'd
 All kinds of sores and shames on my bare head,
 Steep'd me in poverty to the very lips,   50
 Given to captivity me and my utmost hopes,
 I should have found in some part of my soul
 A drop of patience; but, alas! to make me
 The fixed figure for the time of scorn[503]
 To point his slow and moving finger at;
 Yet could I bear that too; well, very well:
 But there, where I have garner'd[504] up my heart,
 Where either I must live or bear no life,
 The fountain from the which my current runs
 Or else dries up; to be discarded thence!   60
 Or keep it as a cistern for foul toads
 To knot and gender in![505] Turn thy complexion there,[506]
 Patience, thou young and rose-lipp'd cherubin;
 Ay, there, look grim as hell!
Desdemona. I hope my noble lord esteems me honest.
Othello. O! ay; as summer flies are in the shambles,[507]
 That quicken even with blowing. O thou weed!
 Who art so lovely fair and smell'st so sweet
 That the sense aches at thee, would thou hadst ne'er been born.
Desdemona. Alas! what ignorant sin have I committed?   70
Othello. Was this fair paper, this most goodly book,
 Made to write 'whore' upon? What committed!
 Committed! O thou public commoner![508]
 I should make very forges of my cheeks,

---

[503] I.e., the scornful world. [504] Stored. [505] Bunch up and procreate. [506] I.e., change your color to suit the "cistern for foul toads." [507] Slaughterhouse. [508] Harlot.

That would to cinders burn up modesty,
Did I but speak thy deeds. What committed!
Heaven stops the nose at it and the moon winks,[509]
The bawdy wind that kisses all it meets
Is hush'd within the hollow mine of earth,
And will not hear it. What committed!   80
Impudent strumpet!
Desdemona.   By heaven, you do me wrong.
Othello.   Are not you a strumpet?
Desdemona.   No, as I am a Christian.
   If to preserve this vessel for my lord
   From any other foul unlawful touch
   Be not to be a strumpet, I am none.
Othello.   What! not a whore?
Desdemona.   No, as I shall be sav'd.
Othello.   Is it possible?
Desdemona.   O! heaven forgive us.
Othello.   I cry you mercy,[510] then;
   I took you for that cunning whore of Venice
   That married with Othello. You, mistress,   90
   That have the office opposite to Saint Peter,
   And keep the gate of hell!

(Re-enter Emilia.)

                        You, you, ay, you!
   We have done our course; there's money for your pains.
   I pray you, turn the key and keep our counsel.   *(Exit.)*
Emilia.   Alas! what does this gentleman conceive?[511]
   How do you, madam? how do you, my good lady?
Desdemona.   Faith, half asleep.
Emilia.   Good madam, what 's the matter with my lord?
Desdemona.   With who?
Emilia.   Why, with my lord, madam.   100
Desdemona.   Who is thy lord?
Emilia.   He that is yours, sweet lady.
Desdemona.   I have none; do not talk to me, Emilia;
   I cannot weep, nor answer have I none,
   But what should go by water.[512] Prithee, to-night
   Lay on my bed my wedding sheets: remember:
   And call thy husband hither.
Emilia.   Here is a change indeed!   *(Exit.)*

---

[509] Closes her eyes.   [510] Beg your pardon.   [511] Imagine.   [512] Be conveyed by means of tears.

Desdemona. 'Tis meet I should be us'd so, very meet.
How have I been behav'd, that he might stick
The small'st opinion on my least misuse?[513]

(*Re-enter Emilia, with Iago.*)

Iago. What is your pleasure, madam? How is it with you?   110
Desdemona. I cannot tell. Those that do teach young babes
Do it with gentle means and easy tasks;
He might have chid me so; for, in good faith,
I am a child to chiding.
Iago.   What 's the matter, lady?
Emilia. Alas, Iago, my lord hath so bewhor'd her,
Thrown such despite[514] and heavy terms upon her,
As true hearts cannot bear.
Desdemona. Am I that name, Iago?
Iago.   What name, fair lady?
Desdemona. Such as she says my lord did say I was.
Emilia. He call'd her whore; a beggar in his drink   120
Could not have laid such terms upon his callat.[515]
Iago. Why did he so?
Desdemona. I do not know; I am sure I am none such.
Iago. Do not weep, do not weep. Alas the day!
Emilia. Has she forsook so many noble matches,
Her father and her country and her friends,
To be call'd whore? would it not make one weep?
Desdemona. It is my wretched fortune.
Iago.   Beshrew[516] him for it!
How comes this trick upon him?
Desdemona.   Nay, heaven doth know.
Emilia. I will be hang'd, if some eternal villain,   130
Some busy and insinuating rogue,
Some cogging[517] cozening slave, to get some office,
Have not devis'd this slander; I'll be hang'd else.
Iago. Fie! there is no such man; it is impossible.
Desdemona. If any such there be, heaven pardon him!
Emilia. A halter pardon him, and hell gnaw his bones!
Why should he call her whore? who keeps her company?
What place? what time? what form? what likelihood?
The Moor 's abus'd by some most villainous knave,
Some base notorious knave, some scurvy fellow.   140
O heaven! that such companions[518] thou'dst unfold,

---

[513] The least suspicion on my slightest misconduct.   [514] Abuse.   [515] Slut.   [516] Curse.
[517] Cheating.   [518] Fellows (derogatory).

And put in every honest hand a whip
To lash the rascals naked through the world,
Even from the east to west!

Iago.   Speak within door.

Emilia.   O! fie upon them. Some such squire he was
That turn'd your wit the seamy side without,[519]
And made you to suspect me with the Moor.

Iago.   You are a fool; go to.

Desdemona.   O good Iago,
What shall I do to win my lord again?
Good friend, go to him; for, by this light of heaven,   150
I know not how I lost him. Here I kneel:
If e'er my will did trespass 'gainst his love,
Either in discourse of thought or actual deed,
Or that mine eyes, mine ears, or any sense,
Delighted them[520] in any other form;
Or that I do not yet,[521] and ever did,
And ever will, though he do shake me off
To beggarly divorcement, love him dearly,
Comfort forswear me! Unkindness may do much;
And his unkindness may defeat[522] my life,   160
But never taint my love. I cannot say 'whore':
It does abhor me now I speak the word;
To do the act that might the addition earn
Not the world's mass of vanity could make me.

Iago.   I pray you be content, 'tis but his humour;
The business of the state does him offence,
And he does chide with you.

Desdemona.   If 'twere no other,—

Iago.   'Tis but so, I warrant.   *(Trumpets.)*
Hark! how these instruments summon to supper;
The messengers of Venice stay the meat: 170
Go in, and weep not; all things shall be well.

(Exeunt Desdemona and Emilia.)

(Enter Roderigo.)

How now, Roderigo!

Roderigo.   I do not find that thou dealest justly with me.

Iago.   What in the contrary?[523]

Roderigo.   Every day thou daffest me[524] with some device, Iago; and rather,
as it seems to me now, keepest from me all conveniency,[525] than suppliest me

---

[519] Outward.   [520] Found delight.   [521] Still.   [522] Destroy.   [523] I.e., what reason do you have
for saying that.   [524] You put me off.   [525] Favorable circumstances.

with the least advantage of hope. I will indeed no longer endure it, nor am I yet persuaded to put up[526] in peace what already I have foolishly suffered.

Iago. Will you hear me, Roderigo?

Roderigo. Faith, I have heard too much, for your words and performances are no kin together.

Iago. You charge me most unjustly.

Roderigo. With nought but truth. I have wasted myself out of my means. The jewels you have had from me to deliver to Desdemona would half have corrupted a votarist;[527] you have told me she has received them, and returned me expectations and comforts of sudden respect[528] and acquaintance, but I find none.

Iago. Well; go to; very well.

Roderigo. Very well! go to! I cannot go to, man; nor 'tis not very well: by this hand, I say, it is very scurvy, and begin to find myself fobbed[529] in it.

Iago. Very well.

Roderigo. I tell you 'tis not very well. I will make myself known to Desdemona; if she will return me my jewels, I will give over my suit and repent my unlawful solicitation; if not, assure yourself I will seek satisfaction of you.

Iago. You have said now.[530]

Roderigo. Ay, and said nothing, but what I protest intendment of doing.

Iago. Why, now I see there's mettle in thee, and even from this instant do build on thee a better opinion than ever before. Give me thy hand, Roderigo; thou hast taken against me a most just exception; but yet, I protest, I have dealt most directly in thy affair.

Roderigo. It hath not appeared.

Iago. I grant indeed it hath not appeared, and your suspicion is not without wit and judgment. But, Roderigo, if thou hast that in thee indeed, which I have greater reason to believe now than ever, I mean purpose, courage, and valour, this night show it: if thou the next night following enjoy not Desdemona, take me from this world with treachery and devise engines for[531] my life.

Roderigo. Well, what is it? is it within reason and compass?

Iago. Sir, there is especial commission come from Venice to depute Cassio in Othello's place.

Roderigo. Is that true? why, then Othello and Desdemona return again to Venice.

Iago. O, no! he goes into Mauritania, and takes away with him the fair Desdemona, unless his abode be lingered here by some accident; wherein none can be so determinate[532] as the removing of Cassio.

Roderigo. How do you mean, removing of him?

Iago. Why, by making him uncapable of Othello's place; knocking out his brains.

---

[526] Put up with.   [527] Nun.   [528] Immediate consideration.   [529] Cheated.   [530] I.e., "I suppose you're through?" (?); or: "Now you're talking" (?).   [531] Devices against.   [532] Effective.

Roderigo.   And that you would have me do?

Iago.   Ay; if you dare do yourself a profit and a right. He sups to-night with a harlotry,[533] and thither will I go to him; he knows not yet of his honourable fortune. If you will watch his going thence,—which I will fashion to fall out between twelve and one,—you may take him at your pleasure; I will be near to second your attempt, and he shall fall between us. Come, stand not amazed at it, but go along with me; I will show you such a necessity in his death that you shall think yourself bound to put it on him. It is now high supper-time, and the night grows to waste; about it.

Roderigo.   I will hear further reason for this.

Iago.   And you shall be satisfied.   (*Exeunt.*)

Scene 3.   Another Room in the Castle.

(*Enter Othello, Lodovico, Desdemona, Emilia, and Attendants.*)

Lodovico.   I do beseech you, sir, trouble yourself no further.

Othello.   O! pardon me; 'twill do me good to walk.

Lodovico.   Madam, good-night; I humbly thank your ladyship.

Desdemona.   Your honour is most welcome.

Othello.   Will you walk, sir?
  O! Desdemona,—

Desdemona.   My lord?

Othello.   Get you to bed on the instant; I will be returned forthwith; dismiss your attendant there; look it be done.

Desdemona.   I will, my lord.   (*Exeunt Othello, Lodovico, and Attendants.*)

Emilia.   How goes it now? He looks gentler than he did.   10

Desdemona.   He says he will return incontinent;[534]
  He hath commanded me to go to bed,
  And bade me to dismiss you.

Emilia.   Dismiss me!

Desdemona.   It was his bidding; therefore, good Emilia,
  Give me my nightly wearing, and adieu:
  We must not now displease him.

Emilia.   I would you had never seen him.

Desdemona.   So would not I; my love doth so approve him,
  That even his stubbornness,[535] his checks[536] and frowns,—
  Prithee, unpin me,—have grace and favour in them.   20

Emilia.   I have laid those sheets you bade me on the bed.

Desdemona.   All's one.[537] Good faith! how foolish are our minds!
  If I do die before thee, prithee, shroud me
  In one of those same sheets.

---

[533] Harlot.   [534] At once.   [535] Roughness.   [536] Rebukes.   [537] I.e., it doesn't matter.

Emilia.   Come, come, you talk.
Desdemona.   My mother had a maid call'd Barbara;
   She was in love, and he she lov'd prov'd mad[538]
   And did forsake her; she had a song of 'willow';
   An old thing 'twas, but it express'd her fortune,
   And she died singing it; that song to-night
   Will not go from my mind; I have much to do   30
   But to go hang my head all at one side,
   And sing it like poor Barbara. Prithee, dispatch.
Emilia.   Shall I go fetch your night-gown?
Desdemona.   No, unpin me here.
   This Lodovico is a proper man.
Emilia.   A very handsome man.
Desdemona.   He speaks well.
Emilia.   I know a lady in Venice would have walked barefoot to Palestine for
a touch of his nether lip.
Desdemona (*sings*).
   The poor soul sat sighing by a sycamore tree,
     Sing all a green willow;   40
   Her hand on her bosom, her head on her knee,
     Sing willow, willow, willow:
   The fresh streams ran by her, and murmur'd her moans;
     Sing willow, willow, willow:
   Her salt tears fell from her and soften'd the stones;—

   Lay by these:—
     Sing willow, willow, willow:

   Prithee, hie thee;[539] he 'll come anon.—

     Sing all a green willow must be my garland.
      Let nobody blame him, his scorn I approve,—   50
   Nay, that's not next. Hark! who is it that knocks?
Emilia.   It is the wind.
Desdemona.
   I call'd my love false love; but what said he then?
     Sing willow, willow, willow:
   If I court moe[540] women, you 'll couch with moe men.

   So, get thee gone; good-night. Mine eyes do itch;
   Doth that bode weeping?
Emilia.   'Tis neither here nor there.
Desdemona.   I have heard it said so. O! these men, these men!

---

[538] Wild.   [539] Hurry.   [540] More.

Dost thou in conscience think, tell me, Emilia,
That there be women do abuse their husbands   60
In such gross kind?

Emilia.   There be some such, no question.

Desdemona.   Wouldst thou do such a deed for all the world?

Emilia.   Why, would not you?

Desdemona.   No, by this heavenly light!

Emilia.   Nor I neither by this heavenly light;
I might do 't as well i' the dark.

Desdemona.   Wouldst thou do such a deed for all the world?

Emilia.   The world is a huge thing; 'tis a great price
For a small vice.

Desdemona.   In troth, I think thou wouldst not.

Emilia.   In troth, I think I should, and undo 't when I had done. Marry, I
would not do such a thing for a joint-ring,[541] nor measures of lawn,[542] nor for
gowns, petticoats, nor caps, nor any petty exhibition;[543] but for the whole
world, who would not make her husband a cuckold to make him a monarch?
I should venture purgatory for 't.

Desdemona.   Beshrew me, if I would do such a wrong
For the whole world.

Emilia.   Why, the wrong is but a wrong i' the world; and having the world for
your labour, 'tis a wrong in your own world, and you might quickly make it
right.

Desdemona.   I do not think there is any such woman.

Emilia.   Yes, a dozen; and as many to the vantage,[544] as   80
Would store[545] the world they played for.
But I do think it is their husbands' faults
If wives do fall. Say that they slack their duties,
And pour our treasures into foreign laps,
Or else break out in peevish jealousies,
Throwing restraint upon us; or say they strike us,
Or scant[546] our former having[547] in despite;
Why, we have galls;[548] and though we have some grace,
Yet have we some revenge. Let husbands know
Their wives have sense like them; they see and smell,   90
And have their palates both for sweet and sour,
As husbands have. What is it that they do
When they change us for others? Is it sport?[549]
I think it is; and doth affection breed it?
I think it doth; is 't frailty that thus errs?
It is so too; and have not we affections,
Desires for sport, and frailty, as men have?

---

[541] Ring made in separable halves.   [542] Fine linen.   [543] Offer, gift.   [544] Over and above.
[545] Populate.   [546] Reduce.   [547] Allowance.   [548] Spirits, temper.   [549] Lust, sexual enjoyment.

Then, let them use us well; else let them know,
The ills we do, their ills instruct us so.

Desdemona.   Good-night, good night; heaven me such usage[550] send,   100
Not to pick bad from bad, but by bad mend!   (*Exeunt.*)

Act V

Scene 1.   Cyprus. A Street.

(*Enter Iago and Roderigo.*)

Iago.   Here, stand behind this bulk,[551] straight will he come:
Wear thy good rapier bare, and put it home.
Quick, quick; fear nothing; I 'll be at thy elbow.
It makes us, or it mars us; think on that,
And fix most firm thy resolution.

Roderigo.   Be near at hand; I may miscarry in 't.

Iago.   Here, at thy hand: be bold, and take thy stand.   (*Retires.*)

Roderigo.   I have no great devotion to the deed;
And yet he has given me satisfying reasons:
'Tis but a man gone: forth, my sword; he dies.   10

Iago.   I have rubb'd this young quat[552] almost to the sense,[553]
And he grows angry. Now, whether he kill Cassio,
Or Cassio him, or each do kill the other,
Every way makes my gain: live Roderigo,
He calls me to a restitution large
Of gold and jewels that I bobb'd[554] from him,
As gifts to Desdemona;
It must not be: if Cassio do remain,
He hath a daily beauty in his life
That makes me ugly: and, besides, the Moor   20
May unfold me to him; there stand I in much peril.
No, he must die. But so;[555] I hear him coming.

(*Enter Cassio.*)

Roderigo.   I know his gait; 'tis he. Villain, thou diest!

(*Makes a pass at Cassio.*)

---

[550] Habits (?), treatment (?).   [551] Jutting part of a wall.   [552] Pimple.   [553] To the quick.
[554] Swindled.   [555] I.e., that's the only way.

Cassio.   That thrust had been mine enemy indeed
  But that my coat is better than thou know'st;
  I will make proof of thine.

(*Draws, and wounds Roderigo.*)

Roderigo.   O! I am slain.

(*Iago from behind wounds Cassio in the leg, and exit.*)

Cassio.   I am maim'd for ever. Help, ho! murder! murder!   (*Falls.*)

(*Enter Othello, at a distance.*)

Othello.   The voice of Cassio: Iago keeps his word.
Roderigo.   O! villain that I am!
Othello.   It is e'en so.
Cassio.   O, help, ho! light! a surgeon!   30
Othello.   'Tis he: O brave Iago, honest and just!
  That hast such noble sense of thy friend's wrong;
  Thou teachest me. Minion,[556] your dear lies dead,
  And your unblest fate hies; strumpet, I come!
  Forth of my heart those charms, thine eyes, are blotted;
  Thy bed lust-stain'd shall with lust's blood be spotted.   (*Exit.*)

(*Enter Lodovico and Gratiano, at a distance.*)

Cassio.   What ho! no watch? no passage?[557] murder! murder!
Gratiano.   'Tis some mischance; the cry is very direful.
Cassio.   O, help!
Lodovico.   Hark!   40
Roderigo.   O wretched villain!
Lodovico.   Two or three groans: it is a heavy[558] night;
  These may be counterfeits; let 's think 't unsafe
  To come in to the cry[559] without more help.
Roderigo.   Nobody come? then shall I bleed to death.
Lodovico.   Hark!

(*Re-enter Iago, with a light.*)

Gratiano.   Here 's one comes in his shirt, with light and weapons.
Iago.   Who 's there? whose noise is this that cries on murder?

---

[556] (Cassio's) darling, i.e., Desdemona.   [557] Passer-by.   [558] Dark.   [559] Where the cry comes from.

Lodovico.   We do not know.
Iago.   Did not you hear a cry?
Cassio.   Here, here! for heaven's sake, help me.
Iago.   What's the matter?   50
Gratiano.   This is Othello's ancient, as I take it.
Lodovico.   The same indeed; a very valiant fellow.
Iago.   What are you here that cry so grievously?
Cassio.   Iago? O! I am spoil'd, undone by villains!
   Give me some help.
Iago.   O me, lieutenant! what villains have done this?
Cassio.   I think that one of them is hereabout,
   And cannot make away.
Iago.   O treacherous villains!
   (*To Lodovico and Gratiano.*) What are you there? come in, and
   give some help.
Roderigo.   O! help me here.   60
Cassio.   That's one of them.
Iago.   O murderous slave! O villain!

(*Stabs Roderigo.*)

Roderigo.   O damn'd Iago! O inhuman dog!
Iago.   Kill men i' the dark! Where be these bloody thieves?
   How silent is this town! Ho! murder! murder!
   What may you be? are you of good or evil?
Lodovico.   As you shall prove us, praise us.
Iago.   Signior Lodovico?
Lodovico.   He, sir.
Iago.   I cry you mercy. Here 's Cassio hurt by villains.
Gratiano.   Cassio!   70
Iago.   How is it, brother?
Cassio.   My leg is cut in two.
Iago.   Marry, heaven forbid.
   Light, gentlemen; I 'll bind it with my shirt.

(*Enter Bianca.*)

Bianca.   What is the matter, ho? who is 't that cried?
Iago.   Who is 't that cried!
Bianca.   O my dear Cassio! my sweet Cassio!
   O Cassio, Cassio, Cassio!
Iago.   O notable strumpet! Cassio, may you suspect
   Who they should be that have thus mangled you?
Cassio.   No.   80
Gratiano.   I am sorry to find you thus; I have been to seek you.

Iago.   Lend me a garter. So. O! for a chair,
  To bear him easily hence!
Bianca.   Alas; he faints! O Cassio, Cassio, Cassio!
Iago.   Gentlemen all, I do suspect this trash[560]
  To be a party in this injury.
  Patience awhile, good Cassio. Come, come.
  Lend me a light. Know we this face, or no?
  Alas! my friend and my dear countryman,
  Roderigo? no: yes, sure, O heaven! Roderigo.   90
Gratiano.   What! of Venice?
Iago.   Even he, sir, did you know him?
Gratiano.   Know him! ay.
Iago.   Signior Gratiano? I cry you gentle pardon;
  These bloody accidents must excuse my manners,
  That so neglected you.
Gratiano.   I am glad to see you.
Iago.   How do you, Cassio? O! a chair, a chair!
Gratiano.   Roderigo!

(*A chair brought in.*)

Iago.   He, he, 'tis he,—O! that 's well said; the chair:
  Some good men bear him carefully from hence;
  I 'll fetch the general's surgeon. (*To Bianca.*) For you, mistress,   100
  Save you your labour. He that lies slain here, Cassio,
  Was my dear friend. What malice was between you?
Cassio.   None in the world; nor do I know that man.
Iago (*to Bianca*).   What! look you pale? O! bear him out o' the air—

(*Cassio and Roderigo are borne off.*)

  Stay you, good gentlemen. Look you pale, mistress?—
  Do you perceive the gastness[561] of her eye?
  Nay, if you stare, we shall hear more anon.
  Behold her well; I pray you, look upon her.
  Do you see, gentlemen? nay, guiltiness will speak
  Though tongues were out of use.   110

(*Enter Emilia.*)

Emilia.   'Las! what 's the matter? what 's the matter, husband?
Iago.   Cassio hath here been set on in the dark

---

[560] I.e., Bianca.   [561] Terror.

By Roderigo and fellows that are 'scaped:
He 's almost slain, and Roderigo dead.

Emilia.   Alas! good gentleman; alas! good Cassio!

Iago.   This is the fruit of whoring. Prithee, Emilia,
Go know of Cassio where he supp'd to-night.
(*To Bianca.*) What! do you shake at that?

Bianca.   He supp'd at my house; but I therefore shake not.

Iago.   O! did he so? I charge you, go with me.   120

Emilia.   Fie, fie, upon thee, strumpet!

Bianca.   I am no strumpet, but of life as honest
As you that thus abuse me.

Emilia.   As I! foh! fie upon thee!

Iago.   Kind gentlemen, let 's go see poor Cassio dress'd.[562]
Come, mistress, you must tell 's another tale.
Emilia, run you to the citadel,
And tell my lord and lady what hath happ'd.
Will you go on afore? (*Aside.*) This is the night
That either makes me or fordoes[563] me quite.   (*Exeunt.*)

Scene 2.   A Bedchamber in the Castle. Desdemona in bed asleep. A light
burning.

(*Enter Othello.*)

Othello.   It is the cause,[564] it is the cause, my soul;
Let me not name it to you, you chaste stars!
It is the cause. Yet I 'll not shed her blood,
Nor scar that whiter skin of hers than snow,
And smooth as monumental alabaster.
Yet she must die, else she 'll betray more men.
Put out the light, and then put out the light:
If I quench thee, thou flaming minister,[565]
I can again thy former light restore,
Should I repent me; but once put out thy light,   10
Thou cunning'st[566] pattern of excelling nature,
I know not where is that Promethean[567] heat
That can thy light relume.[568] When I have pluck'd the rose,
I cannot give it vital growth again,
It needs must wither: I 'll smell it on the tree. (*Kisses her.*)
O balmy breath, that dost almost persuade

---

[562] Bandaged.   [563] Ruins.   [564] I.e., Desdemona's unchastity (Othello means that the severity
of the punishment is required by the nature of her sin).   [565] I.e., the candle.   [566] Most intricately
wrought.   [567] In Greek mythology the demigod Prometheus stole fire from the gods and gave it to
man.   [568] Relight.

Justice to break her sword! One more, one more.
Be thus when thou art dead, and I will kill thee,
And love thee after. One more, and this the last:
So sweet was ne'er so fatal. I must weep,   20
But they are cruel tears; this sorrow 's heavenly,
It strikes where it doth love. She wakes.
Desdemona.   Who 's there? Othello?
Othello.   Ay, Desdemona.
Desdemona.   Will you come to bed, my lord?
Othello.   Have you pray'd to-night, Desdemona?
Desdemona.   Ay, my lord.
Othello.   If you bethink yourself of any crime
Unreconcil'd as yet to heaven and grace,
Solicit for it straight.
Desdemona.   Alas! my lord, what may you mean by that?
Othello.   Well, do it, and be brief; I will walk by:[569]   30
I would not kill thy unprepared spirit;
No; heaven forfend![570] I would not kill thy soul.
Desdemona.   Talk you of killing?
Othello.   Ay, I do.
Desdemona.   Then heaven
Have mercy on me!
Othello.   Amen! with all my heart.
Desdemona.   If you say so, I hope you will not kill me.
Othello.   Hum!
Desdemona.   And yet I fear you; for you are fatal then
When your eyes roll so. Why I should fear I know not,
Since guiltiness I know not; but yet I feel I fear.
Othello.   Think on thy sins.
Desdemona.   They are loves I bear to you.   40
Othello.   Ay, and for that thou diest.
Desdemona.   That death's unnatural that kills for loving.
Alas! why gnaw you so your nether lip?
Some bloody passion shakes your very frame;
These are portents,[571] but yet, I hope, I hope
They do not point on me.
Othello.   Peace, and be still!
Desdemona.   I will so. What 's the matter?
Othello.   That handkerchief which I so lov'd and gave thee
Thou gav'st to Cassio.
Desdemona.   No, by my life and soul!
Send for the man and ask him.

---

[569] Nearby.   [570] Forbid.   [571] Omens.

Othello.   Sweet soul, take heed,   50
Take heed of perjury; thou 'rt on thy death-bed.
Desdemona.   Ay, but not yet to die.
Othello.   Yes, presently;[572]
Therefore confess thee freely of thy sin;
For to deny each article with oath
Cannot remove nor choke the strong conception[573]
That I do groan withal. Thou art to die.
Desdemona.   Then Lord have mercy on me!
Othello.   I say, amen.
Desdemona.   And have you mercy too! I never did
Offend you in my life; never lov'd Cassio
But with such general warranty[574] of heaven   60
As I might love; I never gave him token.
Othello.   By heaven, I saw my handkerchief in 's hand.
O perjur'd woman! thou dost stone[575] my heart,
And mak'st me call what I intend to do
A murder, which I thought a sacrifice:
I saw the handkerchief.
Desdemona.   He found it then;
I never gave it him. Send for him hither;
Let him confess a truth.
Othello.   He had confessed.
Desdemona.   What, my lord?
Othello.   That he hath us'd thee.
Desdemona.   How? Unlawfully?
Othello.   Ay.   70
Desdemona.   He will not say so.
Othello.   No; his mouth is stopp'd:
Honest Iago hath ta'en order for 't.[576]
Desdemona.   O! my fear interprets. What! is he dead?
Othello.   Had all his hairs been lives, my great revenge
Had stomach[577] for them all.
Desdemona.   Alas! he is betray'd and I undone.
Othello.   Out, strumpet! Weep'st thou for him to my face?
Desdemona.   O! banish me, my lord, but kill me not!
Othello.   Down, strumpet!
Desdemona.   Kill me to-morrow; let me live to-night!   80
Othello.   Nay, if you strive,—
Desdemona.   But half an hour!
Othello.   Being done, there is no pause.
Desdemona.   But while I say one prayer!

---

[572] At once.   [573] Belief.   [574] Permission.   [575] Turn to stone.   [576] Taken steps.   [577] Appetite.

Othello.   It is too late.   (*He smothers her.*)

Emilia (*within*).   My lord, my lord! what, ho! my lord, my lord!

Othello.   What noise is this? Not dead? Not yet quite dead?
  I that am cruel am yet merciful;
  I would not have thee linger in thy pain.
  So, so.

Emilia (*within*).   What, ho! my lord, my lord!

Othello.   Who's there?

Emilia (*within*).   O! good my lord, I would speak a word with you!   90

Othello.   Yes; 'tis Emilia: by and by.[578] She's dead.
  'Tis like[579] she comes to speak of Cassio's death;
  The noise was high. Ha! no more moving?
  Still as the grave. Shall she come in? were 't good?[580]
  I think she stirs again: no. What 's best to do?
  If she come in she'll sure speak to my wife:
  My wife! my wife! what wife? I have no wife;
  O, insupportable! O heavy hour!
  Methinks it should be now a huge eclipse
  Of sun and moon, and that the affrighted globe   100
  Should yawn[581] at alteration.

Emilia (*within*).   I do beseech you
  That I may speak with you, O! good my lord.

Othello.   I had forgot thee: O! come in, Emilia:
  Soft, by and by: let me the curtains draw.
  Where art thou?   (*Unlocks the door.*)

(*Enter Emilia.*)

                    What 's the matter with thee now?

Emilia.   O! my good lord, yonder 's foul murder done.

Othello.   What! now?

Emilia.   But now, my lord.

Othello.   It is the very error[582] of the moon;
  She comes more near the earth than she was wont,   110
  And makes men mad.

Emilia.   Cassio, my lord, has kill'd a young Venetian
  Call'd Roderigo.

Othello.   Roderigo kill'd!
  And Cassio kill'd?

Emilia.   No, Cassio is not kill'd.

Othello.   Not Cassio kill'd! then murder 's out of tune,
  And sweet revenge grows harsh.

---

[578] I.e., "just a moment."   [579] Likely.   [580] Would that be wise.   [581] Open up (as in an earthquake).   [582] Straying.

Desdemona.   O! falsely, falsely murder'd.

Emilia.   Alas! what cry is that?

Othello.   That! what?

Emilia.   Out, and alas! that was my lady's voice:

    Help! Help, ho! help! O lady, speak again!   120

    Sweet Desdemona! O! sweet mistress, speak.

Desdemona.   A guiltless death I die.

Emilia.   O! who hath done this deed?

Desdemona.   Nobody; I myself; farewell:

    Commend me to my kind lord. O! farewell!   (*Dies.*)

Othello.   Why, how should she be murder'd?

Emilia.   Alas! who knows?

Othello.   You heard her say herself it was not I.

Emilia.   She said so; I must needs report the truth.

Othello.   She 's like a liar gone to burning hell;

    'Twas I that kill'd her.

Emilia.   O! the more angel she,   130

    And you the blacker devil.

Othello.   She turn'd to folly, and she was a whore.

Emilia.   Thou dost belie her, and thou art a devil.

Othello.   She was false as water.

Emilia.   Thou art rash as fire to say

    That she was false! O! she was heavenly true.

Othello.   Cassio did tup her; ask thy husband else.

    O! I were damn'd beneath all depth in hell

    But that I did proceed[583] upon just grounds

    To this extremity. Thy husband knew it all.

Emilia.   My husband!   140

Othello.   Thy husband.

Emilia.   That she was false to wedlock?

Othello.   Ay, with Cassio. Nay, had she been true,

    If heaven would make me such another world

    Of one entire and perfect chrysolite,[584]

    I'd not have sold her for it.

Emilia.   My husband!

Othello.   Ay, 'twas he that told me first:

    An honest man he is, and hates the slime

    That sticks on filthy deeds.

Emilia.   My husband!

Othello.   What needs this iterance,[585] woman? I say thy husband.   150

Emilia.   O mistress! villany hath made mocks with love.

    My husband say that she was false!

---

[583] Had I not proceeded.   [584] Topaz.   [585] Repetition.

Othello.   He, woman;
  I say, thy husband: dost understand the word?
  My friend, thy husband, honest, honest Iago.
Emilia.   If he say so, may his pernicious soul
  Rot half a grain a day! he lies to the heart:
  She was too fond of her most filthy bargain.[586]
Othello.   Ha!
Emilia.   Do thy worst:
  This deed of thine is no more worthy heaven   160
  Than thou wast worthy her.
Othello.   Peace! you were best.[587]
Emilia.   Thou hast not half the power to do me harm
  As I have to be hurt. O gull! O dolt!
  As ignorant as dirt! thou hast done a deed,—
  I care not for thy sword; I'll make thee known,
  Though I lost twenty lives. Help! help, ho! help!
  The Moor has kill'd my mistress! murder! murder!

(Enter Montano, Gratiano, Iago, and others.)

Montano.   What is the matter? How now, general!
Emilia.   O! are you come, Iago? you have done well,
  That men must lay their murders on your neck.   170
Gratiano.   What is the matter?
Emilia.   Disprove this villain if thou be'st a man:
  He says thou told'st him that his wife was false.
  I know thou didst not, thou 'rt not such a villain.
  Speak, for my heart is full.
Iago.   I told him what I thought, and told no more
  Than what he found himself was apt and true.
Emilia.   But did you ever tell him she was false?
Iago.   I did.
Emilia.   You told a lie, an odious damned lie;   180
  Upon my soul, a lie, a wicked lie;
  She false with Cassio! Did you say with Cassio?
Iago.   With Cassio, mistress. Go to, charm[588] your tongue.
Emilia.   I will not charm my tongue; I am bound to speak.
  My mistress here lies murder'd in her bed.
All.   O heavens forfend!
Emilia.   And your reports have set the murder on.
Othello.   Nay, stare not, masters; it is true, indeed.
Gratiano.   'Tis a strange truth.
Montano.   O monstrous act!

---

[586] I.e., Othello.   [587] You'd better be quiet.   [588] I.e., into silence.

Emilia.   Villany! villany! villany!   190
  I think upon 't, I think, I smell 't; O villany!
  I thought so then;[589] I'll kill myself for grief.
  O! villany, villany!
Iago.   What! are you mad? I charge you, get you home.
Emilia.   Good gentlemen, let me have leave to speak:
  'Tis proper I obey him, but not now.
  Perchance, Iago, I will ne'er go home.
Othello.   O! O! O!   *(Falls on the bed.)*
Emilia.   Nay, lay thee down and roar,
  For thou hast kill'd the sweetest innocent
  That e'er did lift up eye.
Othello.   O! she was foul.   *(Rises.)*
  I scarce did know you, uncle. There lies your niece,   201
  Whose breath, indeed, these hands have newly stopp'd:
  I know this act shows terrible and grim.
Gratiano.   Poor Desdemona! I am glad thy father 's dead.
  Thy match was mortal to him, and pure grief
  Shore[590] his old thread in twain: did he live now,
  This sight would make him do a desperate turn,
  Yea, curse his better angel from his side,
  And fall to reprobation.[591]
Othello.   'Tis pitiful; but yet Iago knows   210
  That she with Cassio hath the act of shame
  A thousand times committed; Cassio confess'd it:
  And she did gratify[592] his amorous works
  With that recognizance and pledge of love
  Which I first gave her. I saw it in his hand:
  It was a handkerchief, an antique token
  My father gave my mother.
Emilia.   O heaven! O heavenly powers!
Iago.   Come, hold your peace.
Emilia.   'Twill out, 'twill out; I hold my peace, sir? no;
  No, I will speak as liberal as the north;[593]   220
  Let heaven and men and devils, let them all,
  All, all, cry shame against me, yet I'll speak.
Iago.   Be wise, and get you home.
Emilia.   I will not.

(Iago threatens to stab Emilia.)

---

[589] *Cf.* "I will be hang'd, if some eternal villain, / Some busy and insinuating rogue, / Some cogging cozening slave, to get some office, / Have not devis'd this slander; . . ." (IV, 2, 130 ff.). Emilia means, not that she guessed Iago's guilt, but that she rightly guessed the slanderer's motive. [590] Cut.   [591] Damnation.   [592] Reward.   [593] I.e., the north wind (?), the supposedly free-spoken people of north England (?).

Gratiano.   Fie!
   Your sword upon a woman!
Emilia.   O thou dull Moor! that handkerchief thou speak'st of
   I found by fortune and did give my husband;
   For often, with a solemn earnestness,
   More than, indeed, belong'd to such a trifle,
   He begg'd of me to steal it.
Iago.   Villainous whore!
Emilia.   She give it Cassio! no, alas! I found it,   230
   And I did give 't my husband.
Iago.   Filth, thou liest!
Emilia.   By heaven, I do not, I do not, gentlemen.
   O murderous coxcomb![594] what should such a fool
   Do with so good a wife?
Othello.   Are there no stones[595] in heaven
   But what serve for the thunder? Precious villain!

(He runs at Iago. Iago stabs Emilia.)

Gratiano.   The woman falls; sure, he has kill'd his wife.   *(Exit Iago.)*
Emilia.   Ay, ay; O! lay me by my mistress' side.
Gratiano.   He 's gone; but his wife 's kill'd.
Montano.   'Tis a notorious[596] villain. Take you this weapon,
   Which I have here recover'd from the Moor.   240
   Come, guard the door without; let him not pass,
   But kill him rather. I'll after that same villain,
   For 'tis a damned slave.   *(Exeunt Montano and Gratiano.)*
Othello.   I am not valiant neither,
   But every puny whipster[597] gets my sword.
   But why should honour outlive honesty?
   Let it go all.
Emilia.   What did thy song bode, lady?
   Hark, canst thou hear me? I will play the swan,
   And die in music:—
   (Sings.)   Willow, willow, willow.
   Moor, she was chaste; she lov'd thee, cruel Moor;
   So come my soul to bliss as I speak true;   250
   So speaking as I think, I die, I die.   *(Dies.)*
Othello.   I have another weapon in this chamber;
   It is a sword of Spain, the ice-brook's temper.[598]
   O! here it is. Uncle, I must come forth.

---

[594] Idiot.   [595] I.e., thunderbolts (to strike Iago down).   [596] Notable.   [597] I.e., a small boy whipping a top.   [598] Tempered in icy water (or the reference may be to Innsbruck, famed for the quality of its steel, but this hardly fits "a sword of Spain").

Gratiano (*within*).   If thou attempt it, it will cost thee dear:
  Thou hast no weapon, and perforce must suffer.
Othello.   Look in upon me then, and speak with me,
  Or, naked[599] as I am, I will assault thee.

(*Re-enter Gratiano.*)

Gratiano.   What is the matter?
Othello.   Behold! I have a weapon;
  A better never did itself sustain   260
  Upon a soldier's thigh: I have seen the day,
  That with this little arm, and this good sword,
  I have made my way through more impediments
  Than twenty times your stop: but, O vain boast!
  Who can control his fate? 'tis not so now.
  Be not afraid, though you do see me weapon'd;
  Here is my journey's end, here is my butt,[600]
  And very sea-mark of my utmost sail.[601]
  Do you go back dismay'd? 'tis a lost fear;
  Man but a rush[602] against Othello's breast,   270
  And he retires. Where should Othello go?
  Now how dost thou look now? O ill-starr'd wench!
  Pale as thy smock! when we shall meet at compt,[603]
  This look of thine will hurl my soul from heaven,
  And fiends will snatch at it. Cold, cold, my girl!
  Even like thy chastity.
  O! cursed, cursed slave. Whip me, ye devils,
  From the possession of this heavenly sight!
  Blow me about in winds! roast me in sulphur!
  Wash me in steep-down gulfs of liquid fire!   280
  O Desdemona! Desdemona! dead!
  Oh! Oh! Oh!

(*Enter Lodovico, Montano, Cassio carried in a chair, and Officers with Iago, prisoner.*)

Lodovico.   Where is this rash and most unfortunate man?
Othello.   That's he that was Othello; here I am.
Lodovico.   Where is that viper? bring the villain forth.
Othello.   I look down towards his feet;[604] but that's a fable.
  If that thou be'st a devil, I cannot kill thee.   (*Wounds Iago.*)
Lodovico.   Wrench his sword from him.   (*Othello is disarmed.*)

---

[599] Unarmed.   [600] Goal, end, limit.   [601] Destination of my farthest journey.   [602] Wield but a reed.   [603] On the day of judgment.   [604] I.e., for the Devil's cloven hoof.

Iago. I bleed, sir; but not kill'd.

Othello. I am not sorry neither; I'd have thee live;
For, in my sense,[605] 'tis happiness to die.   290

Lodovico. O thou Othello! that wert once so good,
Fall'n in the practice[606] of a damned slave,[607]
What shall be said to thee?

Othello. Why, any thing:
An honourable murderer, if you will;
For nought did I in hate, but all in honour.

Lodovico. This wretch hath part confess'd his villany:
Did you and he consent in Cassio's death?

Othello. Ay.

Cassio. Dear general, I never gave you cause.

Othello. I do believe it, and I ask your pardon.   300
Will you, I pray, demand that demi-devil
Why he hath thus ensnar'd my soul and body?

Iago. Demand me nothing: what you know, you know:
From this time forth I never will speak word.

Lodovico. What! not to pray?

Gratiano. Torments will ope[608] your lips.

Othello. Well, thou dost best.

Lodovico. Sir, you shall understand what hath befall'n,
Which, as I think, you know not. Here is a letter
Found in the pocket of the slain Roderigo,
And here another; the one of them imports   310
The death of Cassio to be undertook
By Roderigo.

Othello. O villain!

Cassio. Most heathenish and most gross!

Lodovico. Now here's another discontented paper,
Found in his pocket too; and this, it seems,
Roderigo meant to have sent this damned villain,
But that, belike,[609] Iago in the interim[610]
Came in and satisfied him.

Othello. O the pernicious caitiff!
How came you, Cassio, by that handkerchief
That was my wife's?

Cassio. I found it in my chamber;   320
And he himself confess'd but even now
That there he dropp'd it for a special purpose
Which wrought to his desire.

Othello. O fool! fool! fool!

---

[605] The way I feel.   [606] Plot, machination.   [607] I.e., Iago.   [608] Open.   [609] Most likely.
[610] In the meantime.

Cassio.   There is besides in Roderigo's letter
How he upbraids Iago that he made him
Brave me upon the watch; whereon it came
That I was cast:[611] and even but now he spake,
After long seeming dead, Iago hurt him,
Iago set him on.

Lodovico.   You must forsake this room and go with us;   330
Your power and your command is taken off,
And Cassio rules in Cyprus. For this slave,
If there be any cunning cruelty
That can torment him much and hold him long,
It shall be his. You shall close prisoner rest,
Till that the nature of your fault be known
To the Venetian state. Come, bring him away.

Othello.   Soft you; a word or two before you go.
I have done the state some service, and they know 't;
No more of that. I pray you, in your letters,   340
When you shall these unlucky deeds relate,
Speak of me as I am; nothing extenuate,
Nor set down aught[612] in malice: then, must you speak
Of one that lov'd not wisely but too well;
Of one not easily jealous, but, being wrought,
Perplex'd[613] in the extreme; of one whose hand
Like the base Indian,[614] threw a pearl away
Richer than all his tribe; of one whose subdu'd[615] eyes
Albeit unused to the melting mood,
Drop tears as fast as the Arabian trees   350
Their med'cinable gum. Set you down this;
And say besides, that in Aleppo once,
Where a malignant and a turban'd Turk
Beat a Venetian and traduc'd the state,
I took by the throat the circumcised dog,
And smote him, thus.   (*Stabs himself.*)

Lodovico.   O bloody period![616]

Gratiano.   All that's spoke is marr'd.

Othello.   I kiss'd thee ere I killed thee; no way but this.
                                    (*Falling upon Desdemona.*)
Killing myself to die upon a kiss.   (*Dies.*)

Cassio.   This did I fear, but thought he had no weapon;
For he was great of heart.

Lodovico (*to Iago*).   O Spartan dog!
More fell[617] than anguish, hunger, or the sea.

---

[611] Dismissed.   [612] Anything.   [613] Distracted.   [614] The Folio reads "Iudean." Both readings denote the foolish infidel who fails to appreciate the treasure he possesses.   [615] Overcome (by grief).   [616] Ending.   [617] Grim, cruel.

Look on the tragic loading of this bed;
This is thy work; the object poisons sight;
Let it be hid. Gratiano, keep the house,
And seize upon the fortunes of the Moor,
For they succeed on you. To you, lord governor,
Remains the censure of this hellish villain,
The time, the place, the torture; O! enforce it.
Myself will straight aboard, and to the state   370
This heavy act with heavy heart relate.   (*Exeunt.*)

For Analysis

1. In what sense might it be said that Othello is responsible for his own downfall?
2. Do you find the reasons that Iago gives for his actions consistent and convincing?
3. Discuss the functions of the minor characters, such as Roderigo, Bianca, and
Emilia. **4.** Is the rapidity of Othello's emotional collapse (Act III, Scene 3) plausible?
Does his race contribute to his emotional turmoil? Explain. **5.** The first part of Act IV,
Scene 2 (until Othello exits), is sometimes called the "brothel" scene. What features
of Othello's language and behavior justify that designation? **6.** Why does Iago kill
Roderigo? **7.** What are the benefits of moving the main characters to Cyprus rather
than setting the drama in Venice?

On Style

1. Compare the speeches of Cassio and Iago in Act II, Scene 1. What do the differences in language and **style** reveal about their characters? **2.** Review the play to carefully determine how much time elapses between the arrival in Cyprus and the end of
the action. Can you find narrated events that could not possibly have occurred within
that time? What effect do the chronological inconsistencies have on you? Explain.

Making Connections

1. Place yourself in Othello's position. How would you respond to Iago's machinations? If you were in Desdemona's position, how would you deal with Othello's (apparently) bizarre behavior? **2.** Compare Desdemona's hope that her virtue will win
out to the hope (or cynicism) of the wives in Irwin Shaw's "The Girls in Their Summer
Dresses" (p. 952) and Raymond Carver's "What We Talk about When We Talk about
Love" (p. 961). Why do you think Desdemona remains submissive?

Writing Topics

1. Write an analysis of the **figurative language** in Iago's soliloquies at the end of Act
I and at the end of Act II, Scene 1. **2.** Choose a minor character, such as Roderigo,
Emilia, or Bianca, and in a carefully reasoned essay, explain how the character contributes to the design of the play. **3.** Discuss the relationship between love and hate
in this tragedy.

Paul   [d. ca. A.D. 64]

1 Corinthians 13   ca. 56

If I speak in the tongues of men° and of angels, but have not love, I am a noisy gong or a clanging cymbal. ² And if I have prophetic powers, and understand all mysteries and all knowledge, and if I have all faith, so as to remove mountains, but have not love, I am nothing. ³ If I give away all I have, and if I deliver my body to be burned, but have not love, I gain nothing.

⁴ Love is patient and kind; love is not jealous or boastful; ⁵ it is not arrogant or rude. Love does not insist on its own way; it is not irritable or resentful; ⁶ it does not rejoice at wrong, but rejoices in the right. ⁷ Love bears all things, believes all things, hopes all things, endures all things.

⁸ Love never ends; as for prophesies, they will pass away; as for tongues, they will cease; as for knowledge, it will pass away. ⁹ For our knowledge is imperfect and our prophecy is imperfect; ¹⁰ but when the perfect comes, the imperfect will pass away. ¹¹ When I was a child, I spoke like a child, I thought like a child, I reasoned like a child; when I became a man, I gave up childish ways. ¹² For now we see in a mirror dimly, but then face to face. Now I know in part; then I shall understand fully, even as I have been fully understood. ¹³ So faith, hope, love abide, these three; but the greatest of these is love.

For Analysis

1. How does Paul emphasize the significance of love in verses 1–3? **2.** What does Paul mean by "now" and "then" in verse 12? **3.** In verse 13, Paul mentions "faith, hope, love" as abiding conditions. What do you understand by "faith" and "hope"? What do you think "love" means to Paul?

° Glossolalia, the ecstatic uttering of unintelligible sounds that some interpret as a deeply religious experience.

On Style

Examine Paul's method of argument. Note that his definition of love embodies assertions of what love is and, equally important, what it is not. How effective do you find this definition by exclusion? Explain.

Making Connections

How do you think the characters in Raymond Carver's "What We Talk about When We Talk about Love" (p. 961) would respond to Paul's definitions of "love" or the absence of "love"?

Writing Topics

1. Read Paul's First Epistle to the Corinthians (preferably in a well-annotated study Bible), and analyze the relationship of Chapter 13 to the rest of the epistle. **2.** This text, translated from the original Greek, is taken from the Revised Standard Version of the Bible. Read the same passage in two or three other versions (for example, the King James Version, the Douay Version, the New American Bible), and compare the translations in terms of style and effectiveness.

Jill Tweedie   [1936–1993]

The Experience   1979

"Some day my prince will come . . . "

I have no particular qualifications to write about love but then, who has? There are no courses of higher learning offered in the subject except at the University of Life, as they say, and there I have put in a fair amount of work. So I offer my own thoughts, experiences and researches into love in the only spirit possible to such an enterprise—a combination of absolute humility and utter arrogance that will cause the reader either to deride my wrongheadedness or, with luck, to recognize some of the same lessons.

I am a white, Anglo-Saxon, heterosexual, happily married, middle-income female whose experience of what is called love spans forty years of the mid-twentieth century in one of the most fortunate parts of the globe. I mention this because I am profoundly aware of the limits these facts give to my vision; also because, in spite of such advantages, my experience of love has hardly been uplifting and yet, because of them too, I have at least been vouchsafed a glimpse of what love might be, some day.

I took my first steps in what I was told was love when the idea of high romance and living happily ever after still held sway. They said that whatever poisoned apple I might bite would surely be dislodged by a Prince's kiss and I would then rise from all the murderous banalities of living and, enfolded in a strong man's arms, gallop away on a white charger to the better land called love. The way it turned out, this dream of love did not do much to irradiate my life. The ride was nice enough but 'twas better to travel than to arrive and—oh, shame—there was more than one Prince. Of two previous marriages and a variety of other lovings, very little remains and that mostly ugly. However sweet love's initial presence, when it goes it leaves horrid scars. Unlike friendship and other forms of love, the tide of male/female sex love does not ebb imperceptibly, leaving the stones it reveals gleaming and covetable. No. It only shows that what was taken to be precious is simply a bare, dull pebble like any other.

Loving, lovers fill each other's lives, Siamese twins joined at the heart, bees that suck honey from each other's blossoms. When love ebbs, nothing remains. Ex-lovers rarely meet again or write or offer each other even those small kindnesses and comforts that strangers would not withhold. Birthdays, high days and holidays pass unmarked where once they were entered in New Year diaries and planned for months ahead. Photographs of the beloved are discarded or curl up, yellowing, in some dusty drawer. What was once the world becomes a no-man's land, fenced with barbed wire, where trespassers are prosecuted and even the civilities given a passing acquaintance are forbidden. What was the most intimate—private thoughts, dreams, nightmares and childhood panics soothed in warm arms—are now merely coinage for a pub joke, a hostess flippancy, worth a line or two in the local paper or the old school magazine. Divorced. Separated. Split.

For the first man I thought I loved, and therefore married, I bear, at most, a 5 distant anger for injuries received. For the second I carefully suppress the good times, burying them with the bad. All those hours, weeks, months, years passed in the same bed have vanished, leaving only the traces of an old wound, an ache where a growth was removed.

Was either a part of love, ever? Of a kind. The best we could manage at the time, a deformed seedling planted in fertile ground. The three of us, each of them and me, carried loads on our backs when we met, all the clobber of past generations. This I must do, that you must be, this is good, that is bad, you must, I must, we must. By the time we met, we were already proficient puppeteers, hands stuck up our stage dolls, our real selves well concealed behind the striped canvas. You Punch, me Judy. Me Jane, you Tarzan.

I had a conventional 1940s and 1950s childhood, cut to the pattern of time. I adored and admired my father and my father did not adore or admire me. My mother was there like the curtains and the carpets were there, taken for loving granted in early childhood and then ruthlessly discarded, the living symbol of everything my world did not regard and that I, therefore, did not wish to become. Rejecting her caused a very slight wreckage inside, nothing you'd notice, though transfusions would later be necessary. Powerful unloving father, powerless loving mother. Cliché.

So I did what I could to make my way and married an older man. Love and marriage go together like a horse and carriage. This act imposed certain conditions. First of all, you cannot grow up if you marry a father figure because this is no part of the contract, and besides, growing up is a disagreeable occupation. Then, of course, a continuing virginity of mind, if not of body, is essential because Daddy's girl has never known other men and any evidence of sexual curiosity or, worse, a touch of ribaldry might cause him to withdraw his protection. Indeed, a daughter must not know much of anything at all because Daddy must teach and daughter learn, for ever. Competence, independence, selfsufficiency, talent in anything but the most girlish endeavours, toughness of any kind, is against the rules. Light-heartedness, giggling, little tantrums and a soupçon of mischief are permitted because Daddy is a Daddy, after all, and likes to be amused after a long day or even smack a naughty bum, in his wisdom. My first marriage was a romper room and each day I laid plans to negotiate the next, with my thumb stuck endearingly in my mouth.

To begin with, we both enjoyed the game we didn't know we were playing. He was a proper husband in the eyes of the outside world, protective and admonitory, and I was a proper wife, that is to say, a child; charming and irresponsible. But quite soon these playful rituals began to harden into concrete, so that we could no longer move, even if we wished, as long as we were together. For a few years I was satisfied enough, the drama of my life absorbed me, it was a stage and I was the star. First a house to play with and later, in case the audience began to cough and fidget, a pregnancy to hold them riveted. Later, like Alice in Wonderland, I came across the cake labelled 'eat me' and whenever my husband was away at work, I ate and I grew. My legs stuck out of the windows, my arms snaked round the doors, my head above an endless neck loomed through the chimney and my heartbeat rocked the room. Each day, just before 5 P.M., I nibbled the other side of Alice's cake and, in the nick of time, shrank to being a little woman again. Hullo, darling, how was your day? Me? Oh, nothing happened. Terrified, I knew that one day I wouldn't make it down again and my husband, returning from work, would fall back in horror at the monster who had taken over his home and push me out into the big wide world.[1]

Writing this now perhaps suggests that I was aware of a pretence and set up my false self knowingly, for reward. Not so. The boundaries given me in girlhood were strictly defined, allowing only minimum growth and that mainly physical. To sprout the titivating secondary sexual characteristics was expected, but woe betide the *enfant terrible* who tried to burst that tight cocoon and emerge as a full-grown adult in mind as well as body. The penalty was ill-defined but all-pervasive, like those sci-fi novels of a postnuclear generation bred to fear the radioactive world above their subterranean tunnels that threatens isolation, mutilation and death. The reward for my self-restraint (in the most literal sense) was a negative one—be good and tractable and you will be looked after—but it was none the less powerful for that. So my real self, or hints of it, was as frightening to me as I feared it would be to my husband, a dark shadow given to emerging at less and less acceptable times. I was Mr. Rochester[2] secure in his mansion but I was also his mad wife in the attic. I had to conceal her existence to preserve my way of life but all the time she was setting matches to the bedding, starting a flame at the hem of the curtains, hoping to burn the mansion down.

Things became more and more schizoid. The demure façade of a prim girl hid a raucous fishwife who folded her massive arms against her chest and cursed. She horrified me, so much so—threatening, as she did, my exile from society—that in spite of increasing marital quarrels and even spurts of pure hatred, never once did I let that fishwife out to hurl the oaths she could have hurled or yelled the truths she knew. How could I, without revealing what I really was, to him and to myself?

The inner split opened wider. When my husband said he loved me, I knew he meant he loved the doll I had created and I accepted his love smugly enough, on her behalf. She was worth it. She wore the right clothes, she said the right

[1] The allusion to *Alice in Wonderland* refers to a number of affairs Tweedie had during her first marriage.
[2] The hero of Charlotte Brontë's novel *Jane Eyre* (1847), who keeps his insane wife secluded.

things, the span of her waist would bring tears to your eyes and the tiny staccato of her heels across a floor would melt the sternest heart. She turned her head upon its graceful stem just so and her camellia hands, laced on her lap, could make a stone bleed. She smiled just enough to give a man the wildest expectations and frowned just enough to make him feel safe. This doll is a good doll. This doll is a marriageable doll. This doll is a real doll.

I knew, of course, that my doll self was only a front but it was the one I had deliberately created in response to popular demand. My real self knew all the things the doll did not wish to know. She was human and therefore hopelessly unfeminine, she had no pretty ways. Her voice was harsh, pumped from the guts instead of issuing sweetly from the throat, and every now and then she howled and the doll was forced to look at her face, bare as a picked bone. No wonder the poor dolly gathered up her ruffled skirts and ran shrieking down corridors to find reassurance in a man's eyes. See my soft red lips, my white skin, feel how smooth the shaven legs, smell the scented underarms, tell me you love me, dolly me.

There were, of course, other ways to accommodate the spectre within and other ways became more necessary as the spectre grew stronger and rattled the bars of the cage. My husband was a man of uncertain temper. I was quite aware of this before we married. He came from a country ravaged by war, his home had been destroyed, his brother killed, his family made refugees and he, corralled off the streets of his town, had spent two years starving in the polar wastes of a Russian prison camp. Understandably, he was outside the conventional pale. I was afraid of him.

The fear was seductive. The dolly shook with it at times, was martyred by it. 15 Hit, punched, she fell to the floor and lay, a poor pale victim, her lashes fanned against an appealingly white cheek stained, briefly, dull red. Later, kindly, she accepted the remorse of her attacker, grovelling before her. Yes, I forgive you, she said. And well she might forgive, because down in the dungeon beneath, her other self was quiet for the time being, gorged to quiescence on the thick hot adrenaline provided by the man. A small price to pay.

I do not know how many people stand at the altar repeating the marriage vows and knowing, however unclearly, that what they say is false and what they do calamitous. My doll stood stiffly in her stiff dress, the groom beside her, and there was not a hope for them. Upbringing had set us against each other from the start and each was busily preparing to hammer the other into an appropriate frame. After the service well-wishers launched our raft with champagne; lashed together, not far out, we sank.

Next time, I chose more carefully. The doll, anyway, was aware that her days were numbered. Winning ways must be adjusted if they are to go on being useful and a good actress acknowledges that she has aged out of *ingénue* roles before the casting director says don't call us. Besides, I was no longer enamoured of my puppet and did not want to extend her life much further. She had become more obstacle than defence, the way a wall, originally built to keep enemies out, can come to be a prison keeping you in.

So I let my real self out on probation, to be called in only now and then for discipline. And now I needed a male with all the right worldly appurtenances, whom I could use as a hermit crab uses a shell, to reach full growth without exposing vulnerable flesh. Using him, I could flex my own muscles in safety until they were strong enough to risk exposure.

So I fell in love with my second husband. This time, the emotion was much more powerful because I knew he had seen something of my real self before he took me on. I thought him beautiful, a golden man, flamboyant and seductively hollow, like a rocket into which I could squeeze myself and guide the flight, using his engines. He was so large he filled a room, his laugh set it shaking, his shining head topped everyone, he drew all eyes. In the turmoil of his wake I found breathing space, I could advance or retreat as I chose. He had another desirable asset and that was his lack of self-restraint. He never talked if he could shout, he never saved if he could spend, he was full of tall stories and the drinks were always on him. All of which combined to make him a natural force and natural forces can be harnessed for other ends. By his noisy, infuriating, unpredictable, ebullient and blustering existence he made me look, in comparison, a good, calm, reasonable and deeply feminine woman and thus I was able, over the years with him, to allow my real self out for airings in the sure knowledge that though I might not be as adorable as the doll, I was bound to appear more acceptable than I actually was.

There were drawbacks, of course. Originally, the space within our relation-   20
ship was almost entirely taken up with the volume of his ego and I made do in a little left-over corner. He breathed deeply, his lungs fully expanded, and I breathed lightly, in short thin gasps, and there was air enough for both of us. But then things changed. I learned a trade, began to work, worked hard and earned money. Hey, he said, getting a little stuffy in here, isn't it? Sorry, darling, I said. I breathed more deeply and new ideas rushed in. The voices of American women reached me, ideas on women's rights that linked me to the clamour of the outside world. For the first time I saw myself face to face, recognized myself, realised that I was not my own creation, uniquely formed in special circumstances, but much of a muchness with other women, a fairly standard female product made by a conveyor-belt society. Inner battles, to be fought for myself alone, became outer battles, to be fought alongside the whole female sex. Release, euphoria. Look, said my husband, I haven't enough room. Neither have I, I said. I would not placate, I would not apologise, I would not give ground any more because I was connected now to a larger army that waged a bigger war, and rescue was at hand. The slaves had revolted and even the most abject gained strength for their individual skirmishes from the growing awareness that they were not personally slavish but merely enslaved. My poor man had his problems, too, but I felt no pity, then. The walls of our relationship were closing in, we fought each other as the oxygen gave out and finally I made it into the cold, invigorating fresh air. The dolly died of double pneumonia but I was still alive.

That is a brief sketch of two marriages, founded on something we all called love because we lived in the romantic West and what other reason is allowed for marriage, if not love? On the surface, of course, the upheavals were not so apparent, being thought of as private quarrels, and I have anyway condensed them greatly—they were actually spread over seven years each, the seven years they say it takes a human to replace every cell of body skin. In the lulls between there were good times, when we laughed together and shared quite a deal of tenderness and celebrated the birth of children, and just ordinary times when we went about the business of marriage, the paying of bills, the buying of goods, the cooking and the cleaning and the entertainment of friends, as every couple does. I make very little of them because the world made so much, crowding around the happy wife, the successful husband, and abruptly turning away, turning a blind and embarrassed eye to the sobbing wife and the angry, frustrated husband. Besides, the violence was endemic and perhaps because of that, ignored as much as possible. Each of us thought we were building new houses, especially designed for us, but we didn't know about the quicksand beneath or the death-watch beetles munching the timbers. An all-pervading dishonesty hung over our enterprise. I was not what I pretended and neither were they. I sold my soul for a mess of sacrificial femininity, sugar and spice and all things nice. They built a prison with their own masculinity, so constricting it made them red in the face, choleric. And the impulse to act on our roles, the sheer effort it took, left little time or energy to investigate small sounds of protest within. What reward, anyway, would there be for such investigation? In fact, only penalties would be paid. Loss of social approval, isolation from friends and family, accusations of bizarre behaviour and, for the woman, selfishness, that sin forbidden to any female unless she be extraordinarily rich, beautiful or old. To let the human being show behind the mask of gender was to risk even madness. They might come and take us away to the funny farm, make arrangements for derangement.

Much safer to be what they wanted, what was considered respectable. Much better to lean heavily upon each other for support and set up a quarrel, some drama, whenever the inner voices grew querulous and needed to be drowned. *Men,* said my mother, wiping my tears away. *Women,* said my father, soothing a husband. They sounded calm and quite pleased. Well, it was all very natural, wasn't it?

Long before all this, in my very first close encounter with the opposite sex, the pattern was laid down. I was ten at the time and jaunted daily back and forth to school on a bus. Every morning a boy was also waiting at the stop, he with his mates and I with mine. I liked the way he looked, I laughed a little louder when he was about. One afternoon, on the way home, it happened. I was sitting right at the front of the bus and he was two rows behind. There came a rustle, sounds of suppressed mirth, a hand stuck itself over my shoulder and thrust a small piece of paper at me. I unfolded it. There upon the graph-lined page were fat letters in pencil. "Dear Girl," said the letters, "I love you."

I read the message and stared out of the window and watched the grass that lined the road grow as green as emeralds, as if a light had been lit under every leaf. An ache started at my chest and spread through every vein until I was heavy, drugged with glucose, banjaxed by that most potent of love-surrogates— thick undiluted narcissism. A boy, a stranger, a member of the male sex, encased in his own unknown life, lying on his unknown bed, had thought of me and, by doing so, given me surreality. Until that moment "I" was who I thought I was. From then on for a very long time, "I" was whoever a man thought I was. That pencilled note signalled the end of an autonomy I was not to experience again for many years. As I turned towards that boy, tilting my chin, narrowing my eyes, pulling down my underlip to show my pearly teeth, giving him my first consciously manufactured, all synthetic skin-deep smile, I entered into my flawed inheritance.

Looking back on all this and other episodes of lust and affection, encounters that lasted a week or a year, the picture seems at first glance chaotic and a gloomy sort of chaos at that. Love and failure. By the standards of my time, success in love is measured in bronze and gold and diamonds, anniversaries of the day when love was firstly publicly seen to be there, at the altar. Thus I am found wanting, like any other whose marriage and relationships have ended in separation, and to be found wanting is meant to induce a sense of failure because those who do not conform must be rendered impotent.

In fact, people of my generation, like all the generations before, have had little chance of success in love of any kind. Many of those who offer the longevity of their marriage as proof of enduring love are often only revealing their own endurance in the face of ravaging compromises and a resulting anaesthesia that has left them half-way dead. In the name of that love they have jettisoned every grace considered admirable in any other part or act of life: honesty, dignity, self-respect, courtesy, kindness, integrity, steadfastness of principle. They have said those things to each other that are unsayable and done those things that are undoable and there is no health in them. They have not been true to themselves and therefore they are false to everyone else, including their children. The man has become and been allowed to become an autocrat, a tinpot dictator in love's police state. The woman has lowered herself upon the floor to lick his jackboots. Or, sometimes, vice versa. What would never have been permitted strangers is given a free licence under love—abuse, insults, petty denigration, physical attack, intrusions on personal privacy, destruction of personal beliefs, destruction of any other friendships, destruction of sex itself. In order to enter the kingdom of love they have shrunk themselves to the space of less than one and, atrophied in every part, they claim love's crown. Two individuals who could have reached some stature have settled for being pygmies whose life's work, now, is the similar distortion of their offspring.

If love takes any other form than this tight, monogamous, heterosexual, lifelong reproductive unit, blessed by the law, the State, the priests and sanctified by gods, it is dismissed as an aberration, hounded as a perversion, insulted as a failure and refused the label "love." The incredible shrinking couple is presented to the world as the central aim and reward of life, a holy grail for which it is never too early to begin searching. Worst of all, we are given to believe that these dwarfish twosomes form the rock upon which all the rest of life is built, from the mental health of children to whole political systems and to remain outside it is to opt out of a cosmic responsibility and threaten the very roots of the human community. Love is all, they say. Love makes the world go round, they say. And you know it's true love, they say, when two people remain together from youth to death.

But you don't and it doesn't and you can't. The truth is that we have not yet created upon this earth the conditions in which true love can exist. Most of us are quite aware that most of mankind's other developments, emotional or technological, have been dependent upon certain prerequisites. Fire had to be discovered before we could develop a taste for cooked food and a pot to cook it in. Mass literacy was only possible after the invention of printing and printing itself depended on the much earlier Chinese discovery of paper-making. The geodesic dome was an absolute impossibility before the computer age. The emotions are based on something of the same rules. Men's lives were not overshadowed by the certainty of death (and this is still so in some primitive tribes) until life itself was safer and death could be seen inevitably to arrive without sudden injury or accident. Unlike his fellow Greeks, Xenophanes[3] was a monotheist, largely because he guessed that the physical characteristics of the earth changed with time and belief in one universal god is dependent upon belief in universal rules. And man can only be said to have become truly self-conscious after Freud's delineation of the unconscious. Just so has love its necessary prerequisites, its birth-time in history, its most favourable climatic conditions.

So for all that we lay claim to an eternal heritage of love, man's bosom companion since the dawn of time, we have got it wrong. We have called other emotions love and they do not smell as sweet. Love itself has been very nearly impossible for most of us most of our history and is only just becoming possible today. I failed in love, like many others, because given the tools I had to hand the work could not be done. More hopelessly still, the very blueprint was flawed, rough sketch of the eventual edifice without a single practical instruction, without a brick or a nail, without a vital part or principle. Dreams are not enough.

For Analysis
1. What function does the opening **epigraph** serve? What tone does the epigraph evoke? **2.** How do Tweedie's first and second husbands differ? Suggest a "cause" for the divorce in each case. **3.** In paragraph 28, the author asserts that "we have not yet created upon this earth the conditions in which true love can exist." What do you suppose she means by "true love"? Do you agree or disagree with her assertion?

On Style
1. Focus on the figures of speech Tweedie uses to describe herself as she moves through her marriages. How does the **figurative language** contribute to her argu-

---

[3] Greek philosopher (b. ca. 570 B.C.).

ment? **2.** Discuss the appropriateness of the extended **metaphor** embodied in the last three sentences of the essay.

Making Connections

1. In paragraph 27, Tweedie rather bitterly describes the prevailing social attitudes toward love and marriage. Explain how your own experience supports or refutes her assertions. **2.** How does Tweedie's attempt to define love compare with the narrator's view of love and commitment in Pam Houston's "How to Talk to a Hunter" (p. 988)? Do you think Houston's narrator would agree with Tweedie? Explain.

Writing Topics

1. Describe the circumstances of a divorce you know about. Was one of the parties clearly at fault? Could (or should) the divorce have been prevented? **2.** Write about a successful marriage you know of, focusing on what makes it successful.

Robert C. Solomon [b. 1942]

Love Stories 1988

Tell me *who*—
Who wrote the book of love?
—THE MONOTONES, 1957

At the root of "romantic" love is the romance—a story. Love is not just a momentary passion but an emotional development, a structured *narrative* that is so familiar and seemingly "natural" to us that we rarely think of it as a story, a scenario that we are taught to follow, with all of its predictable progressions and conflicts and resolutions. When we hear the folk tales of other cultures, it is often easy to find them quaint or peculiar, but it is essential that we recognize our own romantic heritage as itself an anthropological oddity, a conflict-ridden and sometimes destructive set of scenarios. For example, our romantic love stories often center on the very young, though the fact is that love is just as inspiring and important to those of us who have made it past the watershed age of thirty. Our romantic protagonists are often rich, spoiled and exotic, though love since the last century or so has become thoroughly domesticated, middle-class and democratic. Indeed, our favorite protagonists are typically ill suited for long-term love, and it is not unusual for them to be killed off while still in their prime. The paradigm of romance is often forbidden or impossible love, from Lancelot's illicit love for Guinevere to the consumptive love of *La Bohème*.[1] Or else the story is cut off with a happy ending, with an embrace and a suspicious "happily ever after." But whether the story is a tragedy or a "happily ever after," it excludes the rich development of love over time.

I once asked a group of graduate literature students what made *Romeo and Juliet*—supposedly our paradigmatic love story—romantic. They listed, in order of elicitation, the fact that the two lovers:

die
don't get to know each other
face serious opposition to their love
face danger
live in an exotic setting
have to meet secretly
confide in each other
are young and beautiful

[1] Lancelot, a knight at King Arthur's Court, has an adulterous relationship with Arthur's Queen Guinevere. Puccini's opera *La Bohème* ends with the tragic death of the consumptive Mimi.

1144

make speeches proclaiming their love
are impatient, full of longing and passion
have confidence in themselves
are obstinate
have no concern for pragmatics or practicability
can't think of anyone else
have a strong sexual urge for each other

One doesn't have to be a romantic scholar to be struck by this list, which quite innocently dismisses couples over twenty, not beautiful, living in Lake Wobegon, Minnesota,[2] who enjoy the approval of parents and friends, date in the open and don't have to die at the end of the fifth act. The fact is that our favorite love story gives a very misleading impression of the nature of love and its narrative, and yet it and stories like it have defined the genre of romance since at least the twelfth century, with the first popular stories of Lancelot and Guinevere, whose love was adulterous and destroyed a kingdom.

But even without the illicitness, secrecy and fatality, it is not hard to pinpoint our paradigm love story: "Boy meets girl. Boy loses girl. Boy gets girl." (Why not vice versa?) They live "happily ever after." Our first question should be why we use "girl" and "boy" when love is or ought to be the main concern of adulthood, not just adolescence. It is also worth noting how unthinkingly we assume that two lovers have to *meet* one another. That is, they didn't grow up together. They encounter each other essentially *as* lovers, and all other attributes are pretty much beside the point. Presumably they are strangers, meeting most likely by chance. And what is worse is the ending. We cut off the real story line before it even begins with the disingenuous phrase "happily ever after." Marriage signifies the culmination of love rather than its vehicle. (Of course, weddings aren't often included. They're not usually dramatic events.)

Of course the heart of the love story, what makes it romantic, is the "problem," the conflict, the suspense. This is where romance writers get to ply their skill, rend our hearts, purple our language. Love is a challenge, an enormous and often pathologically stubborn effort to overcome misunderstandings, tragedies and apparent betrayals. "Why doesn't she just get herself another fellow?" is not one of the options. Love is perseverance and agony, even to the point of personal destruction. Of necessity the love story ends when the "problem" is solved and done away with. "Boy gets girl"—or vice versa. That is when we get the quasi-literary cop-out ("and they lived happily ever after") or the death of one or preferably both of the lovers (*Love Story, Romeo and Juliet, Tristan and Isolde, Sophie's Choice*). Occasionally the love abruptly ends (*Gone with the Wind*) or suffers a heroic parting (*Casablanca*), but all of these options are, on reflection, utterly remarkable: our paradigm story of love leaves out the heart of love. It includes the initial melodrama but excludes the countless con-

5

---

[2] A fictional town, created and populated by humor writer Garrison Keillor, used here to represent the antithesis of exoticism.

tinuing details of real-life love. The story of love, in other words, leaves out love. It does not deny that love demands a protracted and possibly lifelong time together ("happily ever after" and premature death both point to that), but it totally ignores this. How, then, are we supposed to live our lives according to it? Surely we should not emulate those brief periods in history, for example the time of the publication of Goethe's unhappy romantic novel *The Sorrows of Young Werther* in 1774, when literary fashion dictated a rash of suicides among the young and lovelorn.

But here is another love story, one that, you can be sure, would not make it into a Harlequin romance.[3] That elderly couple walk into breakfast at a Wisconsin Holiday Inn. They are sharing the morning paper and he offers dutifully to see to the acquisition of coffee and Danish. Their story is one of lifelong companionship. One can dimly imagine a brief but clumsy courtship, but this possibly forgettable or even (in their own minds) laughable experience is of little importance to this love story. They may remember some little misunderstanding, some early rival for affection, but probably not. They may remember the wedding, but most likely they were both too dazed and confused at the time. There may have been passion. There may have been some doubts at the beginning, but those were on page twenty of a 1,600-page novel. It is not hard to imagine that there have been days, weeks or even years of anger, resentment, contempt, even violence, but these passions, too, disperse into the mist of the years together. One can be sure that they rarely talk of love, perhaps an occasional "I love you" (on anniversaries), but certainly no philosophical discussions of love, no metaphysical skepticism about whether or not it's "the real thing," no agonizing personal reflections about "Is this what I really want?" and whether love is actually narcissism or an unjustifiable need for dependency. No question about its going on (the word "forever" would be superfluous). Their love just *is*. It is as real and as solid a foundation as the Midwestern granite they walk on. It does not even need a name.

It is tragic and absurd that our idealized storybook romance should be so different and so detached from the real story of love and our conception of love should, consequently, be so divided into two wholly separate parts, one romantic and exciting but unrealistic and the other a dull tale of domesticity and endurance, devoid of the excitement that many of us now insist upon to make life worthwhile. The two parts of this unfortunate conception of love complement each other in a thoroughly disappointing way. The romantic story is all about the thrill of newfound love, but it is so filled with suspense and excitement or pathos that it cannot bear the weight of the future. "Forever" is thus an evasion of time rather than a celebration of it. The infinitely less romantic part of the story is about the formation and working out of a partnership, legally defined as such by marriage. It is a topic fit for accountants, advisers and counselors, in which the market virtues of honesty and fair exchange and the business skills of negotiation and compromise are of great value. Or, for the less affluent, there is a lifetime of

---

[3] A publisher's imprint noted for overheated love stories.

"seeing it through," raising children, waiting for grandchildren, earning the mortgage, coping with life. In other words, first there is the thrill, then there is the coping. In the beginning there are two independent people engaged in a melodrama; then they have to "work it out." One reason why love fades, it is not unreasonable to hypothesize, is because we define it in such a hopelessly schizoid and ultimately dreary way. By definition the suspense and excitement of romance cannot continue, the partners become compatible and confident in their love for each other, and, besides, there are simply too many other things to do.

The flaws in the two-part story of love are as conducive to unhappiness as they are unliterary. A good novel doesn't climax in the second chapter, five hundred pages from the end. Romantic love is not just the story of the initial melodrama, nor is what follows anything so dreary as a mere partnership. Love is not initial conquest followed by a relationship, much less by "happily ever after." It is the continuing story of self-definition, in which plots, themes, characters, beginnings, middles and ends are very much up to the authorship of the indeterminate selves engaged in love. Indeed, another problem with our love stories is that they sound as if they give us a complete outline and a detailed recipe for love, when in fact every romance just gives us one possible version of it. Even at the beginning, every story is different, and once one gets to the reality hidden beneath the "happily ever after" cop-out, it is every couple for themselves. We get disappointed when we don't have a storybook romance, but the truth is that all of us have to create our own story, our own romance.

Not all love stories get told; some of them we are forced to live, and at least some of the love stories with which we are most familiar are not all romantic. Emotions are learned in standard behavioral situations, in what philosopher Ronald De Sousa calls paradigm scenarios. Anger, for example, is learned in a situation where one is frustrated and learns to blame other people. And so we should ask "What is the paradigm scenario of love?" It is embarrassing to say that, for most of us, it was the *dating* situation. How should we describe this? It is an extremely artificially contrived circumstance in which two people are wrenched away from familiar contexts and the support of friends and forced to seek a complete stranger's approval, admiration and more. In other words, the story of love begins for most of us, not with a blank page, but with a character who has been imposed upon us, no background or history to appeal to and no real sense of who or what we are supposed to be or do. No wonder we need the comfort of the more sentimental love stories to soothe us through such an ordeal. And no wonder our current conception of love is so much at odds with our more general notions of comfort and sociability, so private and exclusive and so walled off from all other sources of support and appeal. We learn love in these conditions of total isolation, and we learn it as a cruel game of acceptance and rejection. And so of course finding love strikes us as both a necessity and a great relief. As one recent book puts it, an overwhelming reason for falling in love and living with someone is that one doesn't have to date anymore.

Life is notoriously sloppy, from a literary point of view. It begins before we know how to narrate and we never know how it will end. Philosophers such as

10

Nietzsche[4] may insist that we should "live life as a work of art," but the truth is that no work of art could be so complex, could fill up such a vast amount of time or deal with such a bewildering array of details. But in love, more than anywhere else, we recognize our urge for living life as a simple story, following a narrative with a beginning, a plot, a development and a climax. Of course it is not always clear where the climax is to be found (first kiss, making love, saying "I love you," marriage, first child, death?), but *closure* is what every story must have. It is its resolution. A novel might end just after the climax, but our story must go on. We try to live our lives as narrative, but we always find ourselves in the middle. And so when we try to find closure in any particular culmination of love—whether first kiss or marriage—we are haunted by the literary phrase "happily ever after." For us there is no phrase, just more life to live, more to work out. And so we try to start the story again, keeping conflict and frustrating plot twists to a minimum, or we invent sequels, which, as in the movies, too often seem imitative and inferior to the originals. We want to close it off and seal it with a definitive word or phrase—like all of those familiar romances. But we go on. And, paradoxically though not surprisingly, we periodically try to create closure, by provoking a crisis, by walking out, for "no" creates a closure where "yes" only means that the story must go on. And there is nothing worse than a boring story, even if—especially if—it is one's own.

For Analysis
1. What dangers await lovers whose notions of love and marriage are formed by fiction? Can you suggest a solution to this problem? **2.** How, ideally should young people learn what "love" is? **3.** In some detail, explain the meaning of "happily ever after." In what sense does this typical conclusion begin, rather than end, an interesting story?

On Style
Solomon uses many examples of dramas, films, and novels to support his argument about storybook romance. How effective are the examples he's chosen? Can you think of any stories that he might have used that are similar to the story of the elderly couple?

Making Connections
Which stories in this section support or undermine Solomon's ideas about love?

Writing Topics
1. In an essay, first analyze Solomon's warnings about the pernicious effects of both tragic and happy love stories on the young, and, second, suggest some solutions to the problem these stories create. **2.** Write a definition of love. **3.** Write an account of an experience you had that either validates or contradicts Solomon's argument.

---

[4] Friedrich Wilhelm Nietzsche (1844–1900), a German philosopher.

Love and Hate

Questions and Writing Topics

1. Almost every story in this section incorporates some sexual element. Distinguish among the functions served by the sexual themes and issues of the stories. **Writing Topic:** Contrast the function of sexuality in Edna O'Brien's "Sin" and Stephanie Vaughn's "Other Women."

2. Examine the works in this section in terms of the support they provide for the contention that love and hate are closely related emotions. **Writing Topic:** Discuss the relationship between love and hate in Carver's "What We Talk about When We Talk about Love" and Shakespeare's *Othello*.

3. What images are characteristically associated with love in the prose and poetry of this section? What images are associated with hate? **Writing Topic:** Compare the image patterns in Shakespeare's sonnets 18 and 130 or the image patterns in John Donne's "A Valediction: Forbidding Mourning" and Christopher Marlowe's "The Passionate Shepherd to His Love."

4. The Greeks have three words that can be translated by the English word *love: eros, agape,* and *philia.* Describe the differences among these three types of love. **Writing Topic:** Find a story or poem that you think is representative of each type of love. In analyzing each work, discuss the extent to which the primary notion of love being addressed or celebrated is tempered by the other two types.

5. William Blake's "A Poison Tree," Emily Dickinson's "Mine Enemy is growing old," Elaine Magarrell's "The Joy of Cooking," and Sylvia Plath's "Daddy" all seem to describe aspects of hate. Distinguish the different varieties of hatred expressed in each poem. **Writing Topic:** Compare and contrast the source of the speaker's hatred in two of these poems.

6. Kate Chopin's "The Storm" and Stephanie Vaughn's "Other Women" deal with infidelity. Distinguish between the attitudes toward infidelity developed by these stories. **Writing Topic:** Describe the effects of marital infidelity on the lives of the major characters in each story.

7. Raymond Carver's "What We Talk about When We Talk about Love" and Irwin Shaw's "The Girls in Their Summer Dresses" deal with jealousy. Contrast the sources of the jealousy and the resolution of the problems caused by the jealousy in both stories. **Writing Topic:** Who, in your opinion, has the better reason for being jealous, Mel in Carver's story or the wife in "The Girls in Their Summer Dresses"? Explain.

8. Which works in this section treat love or hate in a way that corresponds most closely with your own experience or conception of those emotional states? Which contradict your experience? **Writing Topic:** Isolate, in each case, the elements in the work that provoke your response and discuss them in terms of their "truth" or "falsity."

The Presence of Death

The Dead Mother, 1899–1900 by Edvard Munch.

The inevitability of death is not implied in the Biblical story of creation; an act of disobedience causes an angry God to pass a sentence of hard labor and mortality on humankind: "In the sweat of your face you shall eat bread till you return to the ground, for out of it you were taken; you are dust and to dust you shall return." These words, written down some 2,800 years ago, preserve one ancient explanation for a persistently enigmatic condition of life. Though we cannot know what death is like, from earliest times men and women have attempted to characterize death, to cultivate beliefs about it. The mystery and certainty of death, in every age, make it an important theme for literary art.

Beliefs about the nature of death vary widely. The ancient Jews of the Pentateuch reveal no conception of immortality. Ancient Buddhist writings describe death as a mere translation from one painful life to another in an ongoing process of atonement that only the purest can avoid. The Christians came to conceive of a soul, separate from the body, which at the body's death is freed for a better (or worse) disembodied eternal life. More recently, the attitudes about death reflect the great intellectual revolutions that affected all thought. For example, the Darwinian revolution replaced humans, the greatest glory of God's creation, with upright primates whose days are likely to be numbered by the flux between the fire and ice of geological history; and the Freudian revolution robbed men and women of their proudest certainty, the conviction that they possessed a dependable and controlling rational mind. In the context of Western tradition, these ideas serve to diminish us, to mock our self-importance. And, inevitably, these shifts lead us to alter our conception of death.

But despite the impact of intellectual history, death remains invested with a special awe—perhaps because it infallibly mediates between all human differences. For many, death, like birth and marriage, is the occasion for a solemn, reaffirming ritual. Although for Christians death holds promise of a better life hereafter, the belief in immortality does not eliminate sadness and regret. For those for whom there is no immortality, death is nonetheless a ceremonial affair, full of awe, for nothing human is so purely defined, so utterly important, as a life ended. Furthermore, both the religious and the secular see death in moral terms. For both, the killer is hateful. For both, there are some deaths that are deserved, some deaths that human weakness makes inevitable, some deaths that are outrageously unfair. For both, there are courageous deaths, which exalt the community, and embarrassing deaths that go unrecognized.

The speaker in Robert Frost's "Stopping by Woods on a Snowy Evening" gazes into the dark woods filling up with snow, momentarily drawn toward the peace it represents. But Frost's is a secular poem and the speaker turns back to life. In much religious poetry—John Donne's sonnet "Death, Be Not Proud" is an outstanding example—death is celebrated as a release from a burdensome existence into the eternal happiness of the afterlife.

The view that establishes death as the great leveler, bringing citizens and

1151

emperors to the selfsame dust, is apparent in such poems as Nashe's "A Litany in Time of Plague" and Shakespeare's "Fear No More the Heat o' the Sun." This leveling view of death leads easily to the tradition wherein life itself is made absurd by the fact of death. You may remember that Macbeth finally declares that life is "a tale / Told by an idiot, full of sound and fury, / Signifying nothing." And the contemplation of suicide, which the pain and absurdity of life would seem to commend, provokes responses such as Edwin Arlington Robinson's ironic "Richard Cory." Some rage against death—Dylan Thomas in "Do Not Go Gentle into That Good Night;" others caution a quiet resignation—Frost in "After Apple-Picking" and Catherine Davis in "After a Time," her answer to Thomas. Much fine poetry on death is elegiac—it speaks the melancholy response of the living to the fact of death in poems such as A. E. Housman's "To an Athlete Dying Young" and Theodore Roethke's "Elegy for Jane."

In short, literary treatments of death display immense diversity. In Leo Tolstoy's "The Death of Iván Ilých," dying leads to a redemptive awareness. In Bernard Malamud's tragicomic "Idiots First," the protagonist insists upon and wins fair treatment from death, and in E. E. Cummings's "nobody loses all the time" and in Woody Allen's *Death Knocks,* the comic lightens the weight of death. The inevitability of death and the way one confronts it paradoxically lend to life its meaning and its value.

FOR THINKING AND WRITING

As you read the selections in this section, consider the following questions. You may want to write out your thoughts informally in a journal, if you are keeping one, as a way of preparing to respond to the selections, or you may wish to make one of these questions the basis for a formal essay.

1. Have you had a close relative or friend who died? Was the person young or old, vigorous or feeble? How did you feel? How might the circumstances of death alter one's feelings toward death, or toward the person who died?

2. Do you believe that some essential part of you will survive the death of your body? On what do you base the belief? How does it alter your feelings about the death of people close to you? How does it alter your own behavior?

3. Are there any circumstances that justify suicide? Explain. If you feel that some suicides are justifiable, would it also be justifiable to help someone end his or her life? Explain.

4. Are there any circumstances that justify killing someone? Explain.

5. Imagine as best you can the circumstances of your own death. Describe them.

Fiction

Edgar Allan Poe   [1809–1849]

Ligeia   1838

And the will therein lieth, which dieth not. Who knoweth the mysteries of the will,
with its vigor? For God is but a great will pervading all things by nature of its intentness. Man doth not yield himself to the angels, nor unto death utterly, save only
through the weakness of his feeble will.

—Joseph Glanvill

I cannot, for my soul, remember how, when, or even precisely where, I first became acquainted with the lady Ligeia. Long years have since elapsed, and my
memory is feeble through much suffering. Or, perhaps, I cannot *now* bring
these points to mind, because, in truth, the character of my beloved, her rare
learning, her singular yet placid cast of beauty, and the thrilling and enthralling
eloquence of her low musical language, made their way into my heart by paces
so steadily and stealthily progressive that they have been unnoticed and unknown. Yet I believe that I met her first and most frequently in some large, old,
decaying city near the Rhine. Of her family—I have surely heard her speak.
That it is of a remotely ancient date cannot be doubted. Ligeia! Ligeia! Buried
in studies of a nature more than all else adapted to deaden impressions of the
outward world, it is by that sweet word alone—by Ligeia—that I bring before
mine eyes in fancy the image of her who is no more. And now, while I write, a
recollection flashes upon me that I have *never known* the paternal name of her
who was my friend and my betrothed, and who became the partner of my studies, and finally the wife of my bosom. Was it a playful charge on the part of my
Ligeia? or was it a test of my strength of affection, that I should institute no inquiries upon this point? or was it rather a caprice of my own—a wildly romantic
offering on the shrine of the most passionate devotion? I but indistinctly recall
the fact itself—what wonder that I have utterly forgotten the circumstances
which originated or attended it? And, indeed, if ever that spirit which is entitled

Romance—if ever she, the wan and the misty-winged *Ashtophet*[1] of idolatrous Egypt, presided, as they tell, over marriages ill-omened, then most surely she presided over mine.

There is one dear topic, however, on which my memory fails me not. It is the *person* of Ligeia. In stature she was tall, somewhat slender, and, in her latter days, even emaciated. I would in vain attempt to portray the majesty, the quiet ease of her demeanor, or the incomprehensible lightness and elasticity of her footfall. She came and departed as a shadow. I was never made aware of her entrance into my closed study save by the dear music of her low sweet voice, as she placed her marble hand upon my shoulder. In beauty of face no maiden ever equalled her. It was the radiance of an opium-dream—an airy and spirit-lifting vision more wildly divine than the phantasies which hovered about the slumbering souls of the daughters of Delos.[2] Yet her features were not of that regular mould which we have been falsely taught to worship in the classical labors of the heathen. "There is no exquisite beauty," says Bacon, Lord Verulam, speaking truly of all the forms and *genera* of beauty, "without some *strangeness* in the proportion." Yet, although I saw that the features of Ligeia were not of a classic regularity—although I perceived that her loveliness was indeed "exquisite," and felt that there was much of "strangeness" pervading it, yet I have tried in vain to detect the irregularity and to trace home my own perception of "the strange." I examined the contour of the lofty and pale forehead—it was faultless—how cold indeed that word when applied to a majesty so divine!—the skin rivalling the purest ivory, the commanding extent and repose, the gentle prominence of the regions above the temples; and then the raven-black, the glossy, the luxuriant and naturally-curling tresses, setting forth the full force of the Homeric epithet, "hyacinthine!" I looked at the delicate outlines of the nose—and nowhere but in the graceful medallions of the Hebrews had I beheld a similar perfection. There were the same luxurious smoothness of surface, the same scarcely perceptible tendency to the aquiline, the same harmoniously curved nostrils speaking the free spirit. I regarded the sweet mouth. Here was indeed the triumph of all things heavenly—the magnificent turn of the short upper lip—the soft, voluptuous slumber of the under—the dimples which sported, and the color which spoke—the teeth glancing back, with a brilliancy almost startling, every ray of the holy light which fell upon them in her serene and placid yet most exultingly radiant of all smiles. I scrutinized the formation of the chin—and, here too, I found the gentleness of breadth, the softness and the majesty, the fullness and the spirituality, of the Greek—the contour which the god Apollo revealed but in a dream, to Cleomenes,[3] the son of the Athenian. And then I peered into the large eyes of Ligeia.

---

[1] A Phoenician fertility goddess.
[2] According to Greek mythology, the twins Apollo and Artemis were born on Delos, an island of the Cyclades. The reference here may be to the maidens, sworn to chastity, who attended Artemis.
[3] An Athenian sculptor to whom the *Venus de'Medici* has been attributed.

For eyes we have no models in the remotely antique. It might have been, too, that in these eyes of my beloved lay the secret to which Lord Verulam alludes. They were, I must believe, far larger than the ordinary eyes of our own race. They were even fuller than the fullest of the gazelle eyes of the tribe of the valley of Nourjahad.[4] Yet it was only at intervals—in moments of intense excitement—that this peculiarity became more than slightly noticeable in Ligeia. And at such moments was her beauty—in my heated fancy thus it appeared perhaps—the beauty of beings either above or apart from the earth—the beauty of the fabulous Houri[5] of the Turk. The hue of the orbs was the most brilliant of black, and, far over them, hung jetty lashes of great length. The brows, slightly irregular in outline, had the same tint. The "strangeness," however, which I found in the eyes, was of a nature distinct from the formation, or the color, or the brilliancy of the features, and must, after all, be referred to the *expression*. Ah, word of no meaning! behind whose vast latitude of mere sound we intrench our ignorance of so much of the spiritual. The expression of the eyes of Ligeia! How for long hours have I pondered upon it! How have I, through the whole of a midsummer night, struggled to fathom it! What was it—that something more profound than the well of Democritus[6]—which lay far within the pupils of my beloved? What was it? I was possessed with a passion to discover. Those eyes! those large, those shining, those divine orbs! they became to me twin stars of Leda,[7] and I to them devoutest of astrologers.

There is no point, among the many incomprehensible anomalies of the science of mind, more thrillingly exciting than the fact—never, I believe, noticed in the schools—that in our endeavors to recall to memory something long forgotten, we often find ourselves *upon the very verge* of remembrance, without being able, in the end, to remember. And thus how frequently, in my intense scrutiny of Ligeia's eyes, have I felt approaching the full knowledge of their expression—felt it approaching—yet not quite be mine—and so at length entirely depart! And (strange, oh strangest mystery of all!) I found, in the commonest objects of the universe, a circle of analogies to that expression. I mean to say that, subsequently to the period when Ligeia's beauty passed into my spirit, there dwelling as in a shrine, I derived, from many existences in the material world, a sentiment such as I felt always aroused, within me, by her large and luminous orbs. Yet not the more could I define that sentiment, or analyze, or even steadily view it. I recognized it, let me repeat, sometimes in the survey of a rapidly growing vine—in the contemplation of a moth, a butterfly, a chrysalis, a stream of running water. I have felt it in the ocean; in the falling of a meteor. I

---

[4] *The History of Nourjahad* (1767) by Frances Sheridan was an oriental romance familiar in Poe's day.

[5] One of the beautiful virgins, according to Moslem belief, given to those who attain Paradise.

[6] Greek philosopher of the fifth century B.C. credited with the proverb, "Truth lies at the bottom of a well."

[7] Castor and Pollux, named after the twin sons of Leda, are stars in the constellation Gemini.

have felt it in the glances of unusually aged people. And there are one or two stars in heaven—(one especially, a star of the sixth magnitude, double and changeable, to be found near the large star in Lyra)[8] in a telescopic scrutiny of which I have been made aware of the feeling. I have been filled with it by certain sounds from stringed instruments, and not unfrequently by passages from books. Among innumerable other instances, I well remember something in a volume of Joseph Glanvill, which (perhaps from its quaintness—who shall say?) never failed to inspire me with the sentiment;—"And the will therein lieth, which dieth not. Who knoweth the mysteries of the will, with its vigor? For God is but a great will pervading all things by nature of its intentness. Man doth not yield him to the angels, nor unto death utterly, save only through the weakness of his feeble will."

Length of years and subsequent reflection, have enabled me to trace, indeed, some remote connection between this passage in the English moralist and a portion of the character of Ligeia. An *intensity* in thought, action, or speech, was possibly, in her, a result, or at least an index, of that gigantic volition which, during our long intercourse, failed to give other and more immediate evidence of its existence. Of all the women whom I have ever known, she, the outwardly calm, the ever-placid Ligeia, was the most violently a prey to the tumultuous vultures of stern passion. And of such passion I could form no estimate, save by the miraculous expansion of those eyes which at once so delighted and appalled me—by the almost magical melody, modulation, distinctness, and placidity of her very low voice—and by the fierce energy (rendered doubly effective by contrast with her manner of utterance) of the wild words which she habitually uttered.

I have spoken of the learning of Ligeia; it was immense—such as I have never known in woman. In the classical tongues was she deeply proficient, and as far as my own acquaintance extended in regard to the modern dialects of Europe, I have never known her at fault. Indeed upon any theme of the most admired, because simply the most abstruse of the boasted erudition of the academy, have I *ever* found Ligeia at fault? How singularly—how thrillingly, this one point in the nature of my wife has forced itself, at this late period only, upon my attention! I said her knowledge was such as I have never known in woman—but where breathes the man who has traversed, and successfully, *all* the wide areas of moral, physical, and mathematical science? I saw not then what I now clearly perceive, that the acquisitions of Ligeia were gigantic, were astounding; yet I was sufficiently aware of her infinite supremacy to resign myself, with a child-like confidence, to her guidance through the chaotic world of metaphysical investigation at which I was most busily occupied during the earlier years of our marriage. With how vast a triumph—with how vivid a delight—with how much of all that is ethereal in hope—did I *feel*, as she bent over me in studies but little

5

---

[8] The "large star" in the constellation Lyra is Vega, one of the brightest in the heavens. Near it but of lesser magnitude is Epsilon Lyrae, requiring a telescope to be seen.

sought—but less known—that delicious vista by slow degrees expanding before me, down whose long, gorgeous, and all untrodden path, I might at length pass onward to the goal of a wisdom too divinely precious not to be forbidden!

How poignant, then, must have been the grief with which, after some years, I beheld my well-grounded expectations take wings to themselves and fly away! Without Ligeia I was but as a child groping benighted. Her presence, her readings alone, rendered vividly luminous the many mysteries of the transcendentalism in which we were immersed. Wanting the radiant lustre of her eyes, letters, lambent and golden, grew duller than Saturnian lead.[9] And now those eyes shone less and less frequently upon the pages over which I pored. Ligeia grew ill. The wild eyes blazed with a too—too glorious effulgence; the pale fingers became of the transparent waxen hue of the grave; and the blue veins upon the lofty forehead swelled and sank impetuously with the tides of the most gentle emotion. I saw that she must die—and I struggled desperately in spirit with the grim Azrael.[10] And the struggles of the passionate wife were, to my astonishment, even more energetic than my own. There had been much in her stern nature to impress me with the belief that, to her, death would have come without its terrors; but not so. Words are impotent to convey any just idea of the fierceness of resistance with which she wrestled with the Shadow. I groaned in anguish at the pitiable spectacle. I would have soothed—I would have reasoned; but, in the intensity of her wild desire for life,—for life—*but* for life—solace and reason were alike the uttermost folly. Yet not until the last instance, amid the most convulsive writhings of her fierce spirit, was shaken the external placidity of her demeanor. Her voice grew more gentle—grew more low—yet I would not wish to dwell upon the wild meaning of the quietly uttered words. My brain reeled as I hearkened entranced, to a melody more than mortal—to assumptions and aspirations which mortality had never before known.

That she loved me I should not have doubted; and I might have been easily aware that, in a bosom such as hers, love would have reigned no ordinary passion. But in death only was I fully impressed with the strength of her affection. For long hours, detaining my hand, would she pour out before me the overflowing of a heart whose more than passionate devotion amounted to idolatry. How had I deserved to be so blessed by such confessions?—how had I deserved to be so cursed with the removal of my beloved in the hour of her making them? But upon this subject I cannot bear to dilate. Let me say only, that in Ligeia's more than womanly abandonment to a love, alas! all unmerited, all unworthily bestowed, I at length recognized the principle of her longing with so wildly earnest a desire for the life which was now fleeing so rapidly away. It is this wild longing—it is this eager vehemence of desire for life—*but* for life—that I have no power to portray—no utterance capable of expressing.

At high noon of the night in which she departed, beckoning me, perempto-

---

[9] In ancient alchemy, Saturn is the technical term for lead.
[10] The angel of death in Mohammedan and Hebrew mythology.

rily, to her side, she bade me repeat certain verses composed by herself not many days before. I obeyed her.—They were these:

> Lo! 'tis a gala night
> Within the lonesome latter years!
> An angel throng, bewinged, bedight
> In veils, and drowned in tears,
> Sit in a theatre, to see
> A play of hopes and fears,
> While the orchestra breathes fitfully
> The music of the spheres.
>
> Mimes, in the form of God on high,
> Mutter and mumble low,
> And hither and thither fly—
> Mere puppets they, who come and go
> At bidding of vast formless things
> That shift the scenery to and fro,
> Flapping from out their Condor wings
> Invisible Woe!
>
> That motley drama!—oh, be sure
> It shall not be forgot!
> With its Phantom chased forever more,
> By a crowd that seize it not,
> Through a circle that ever returneth in
> To the self-same spot,
> And much of Madness and more of Sin
> And Horror the soul of the plot.
>
> But see, amid the mimic rout,
> A crawling shape intrude!
> A blood-red thing that writhes from out
> The scenic solitude!
> It writhes!—it writhes!—with mortal pangs
> The mimes become its food,
> And the seraphs sob at vermin fangs
> In human gore imbued.
>
> Out—out are the lights—out all!
> And over each quivering form,
> The curtain, a funeral pall,
> Comes down with the rush of a storm,
> And the angels, all pallid and wan,
> Uprising, unveiling, affirm
> That the play is the tragedy, "Man,"
> And its hero the Conqueror Worm.

"O God!" half shrieked Ligeia, leaping to her feet and extending her arms 10
aloft with a spasmodic movement, as I made an end of these lines—"O God! O
Divine Father!—shall these things be undeviatingly so?—shall this Conqueror

be not once conquered? Are we not part and parcel in Thee? Who—who knoweth the mysteries of the will with its vigor? Man doth not yield him to the angels, *nor unto death utterly,* save only through the weakness of his feeble will."

And now, as if exhausted with emotion, she suffered her white arms to fall, and returned solemnly to her bed of death. And as she breathed her last sighs, there came mingled with them a low murmur from her lips. I bent to them my ear, and distinguished, again, the concluding words of the passage in Glanvill— *"Man doth not yield him to the angels, nor unto death utterly, save only through the weakness of his feeble will."*

She died;—and I, crushed into the very dust with sorrow, could no longer endure the lonely desolation of my dwelling in the dim and decaying city by the Rhine. I had no lack of what the world calls wealth. Ligeia had brought me far more, very far more than ordinarily falls to the lot of mortals. After a few months, therefore, of weary and aimless wandering, I purchased, and put in some repair, an abbey, which I shall not name, in one of the wildest and least frequented portions of fair England. The gloomy and dreary grandeur of the building, the almost savage aspect of the domain, the many melancholy and time-honored memories connected with both, had much in unison with the feelings of utter abandonment which had driven me into that remote and unsocial region of the country. Yet although the external abbey, with its verdant decay hanging about it, suffered but little alteration, I gave way, with a child-like perversity, and perchance with a faint hope of alleviating my sorrows, to a display of more than regal magnificence within.—For such follies, even in childhood, I had imbibed a taste, and now they came back to me as if in the dotage of grief. Alas, I feel how much even of incipient madness might have been discovered in the gorgeous and fantastic draperies, in the solemn carvings of Egypt, in the wild cornices and furniture, in the Bedlam patterns of the carpets of tufted gold! I had become a bounden slave in the trammels of opium, and my labors and orders had taken a coloring from my dreams. But these absurdities I must not pause to detail. Let me speak only of that one chamber, ever accursed, whither, in a moment of mental alienation, I led from the altar as my bride—as the successor of the unforgotten Ligeia—the fair-haired and blue-eyed Lady Rowena Trevanion, of Tremaine.

There is no individual portion of the architecture and decoration of that bridal chamber which is not now visible before me. Where were the souls of the haughty family of the bride, when, through thirst of gold, they permitted to pass the threshold of an apartment so bedecked, a maiden and a daughter so beloved? I have said that I minutely remember the details of the chamber—yet I am sadly forgetful on topics of deep moment—and here there was no system, no keeping, in the fantastic display, to take hold upon the memory. The room lay in a high turret of the castellated abbey, was pentagonal in shape, and of capacious size. Occupying the whole southern face of the pentagon was the sole window—an immense sheet of broken glass from Venice—a single pane, and tinted of a leaden hue, so that the rays of either the sun or moon, passing through it, fell with a ghastly lustre on the objects within. Over the upper portion of this huge window, extended the trellis-work of an aged vine, which clambered up the massy walls of the turret. The ceiling, of gloomy-looking oak, was excessively lofty, vaulted, and elaborately fretted with the wildest and most grotesque specimens of a semi-Gothic, semi-Druidical device. From out the most central recess of this melancholy vaulting, depended, by a single chain of gold with long links, a huge censer of the same metal, Saracenic in pattern, and with many perforations so contrived that there writhed in and out of them, as if endued with a serpent vitality, a continual succession of parti-colored fires.

Some few ottomans and golden candelabra, of Eastern figure, were in various stations about—and there was the couch, too—the bridal couch—of an Indian model, and low, and sculptured of solid ebony, with a pall-like canopy above. In each of the angles of the chamber stood on end a gigantic sarcophagus of black granite, from the tombs of the kings over against Luxor,[11] with their aged lids full of immemorial sculpture. But in the draping of the apartment lay, alas! the chief phantasy of all. The lofty walls, gigantic in height—even unproportionably so—were hung from summit to foot, in vast folds, with a heavy and massive-looking tapestry—tapestry of a material which was found alike as a carpet on the floor, as a covering for the ottomans and the ebony bed, as a canopy for the bed and as the gorgeous volutes of the curtains which partially shaded the window. The material was the richest cloth of gold. It was spotted all over, at irregular intervals, with arabesque figures, about a foot in diameter, and wrought upon the cloth in patterns of the most jetty black. But these figures partook of the true character of the arabesque only when regarded from a single point of view. By a contrivance now common, and indeed traceable to a very remote period of antiquity, they were made changeable in aspect. To one entering the room, they bore the appearance of simple monstrosities; but upon a farther advance, this appearance gradually departed; and step by step, as the visitor moved his station in the chamber, he saw himself surrounded by an endless succession of the ghastly forms which belong to the superstition of the Norman, or arise in the guilty slumbers of the monk. The phantasmagoric effect was vastly heightened by the artificial introduction of a strong continual current of wind behind the draperies—giving a hideous and uneasy animation to the whole.

In halls such as these—in a bridal chamber such as this—I passed, with the Lady of Tremaine, the unhallowed hours of the first month of our marriage—passed them with but little disquietude. That my wife dreaded the fierce moodiness of my temper—that she shunned me and loved me but little—I could not help perceiving; but it gave me rather pleasure than otherwise. I loathed her with a hatred belonging more to demon than to man. My memory flew back, (oh, with what intensity of regret!) to Ligeia, the beloved, the august, the beautiful, the entombed. I revelled in recollections of her purity, of her wisdom, of her lofty, her ethereal nature, of her passionate, her idolatrous love. Now, then, did my spirit fully and freely burn with more than all the fires of her own. In the excitement of my opium dreams (for I was habitually fettered in the shackles of

15

---

[11] The ancient site of Thebes, on the Nile in central Egypt.

the drug) I would call aloud upon her name, during the silence of the night, or among the sheltered recesses of the glens by day, as if, through the wild eagerness, the solemn passion, the consuming ardor of my longing for the departed, I could restore her to the pathways she had abandoned—ah, *could* it be forever?—upon the earth.

About the commencement of the second month of the marriage, the Lady Rowena was attacked with sudden illness, from which her recovery was slow. The fever which consumed her rendered her nights uneasy; and in her perturbed state of half-slumber, she spoke of sounds, and of motions, in and above the chamber of the turret, which I concluded had no origin save in the distemper of her fancy, or perhaps in the phantasmagoric influences of the chamber itself. She became at length convalescent—finally well. Yet but a brief period elapsed, ere a second more violent disorder again threw her upon a bed of suffering; and from this attack her frame, at all times feeble, never altogether recovered. Her illnesses were, after this epoch, of alarming character, and of more alarming recurrence, defying alike the knowledge and the great exertions of her physicians. With the increase of the chronic disease which had thus, apparently, taken too sure hold upon her constitution to be eradicated by human means, I could not fail to observe a similar increase in the nervous irritation of her temperament, and in her excitability by trivial causes of fear. She spoke again, and now more frequently and pertinaciously, of the sounds—of the slight sounds—and of the unusual motions among the tapestries, to which she had formerly alluded.

One night, near the closing in of September, she pressed this distressing subject with more than usual emphasis upon my attention. She had just awakened from an unquiet slumber, and I had been watching, with feelings half of anxiety, half of vague terror, the workings of her emaciated countenance. I sat by the side of her ebony bed, upon one of the ottomans of India. She partly arose, and spoke, in an earnest low whisper, of sounds which she *then* heard, but which I could not hear—of motions which she *then* saw, but which I could not perceive. The wind was rushing hurriedly behind the tapestries, and I wished to show her (what, let me confess it, I could not *all* believe) that those almost inarticulate breathings, and those very gentle variations of the figures upon the wall, were but the natural effects of that customary rushing of the wind. But a deadly pallor, overspreading her face, had proved to me that my exertions to reassure her would be fruitless. She appeared to be fainting, and no attendants were within call. I remembered where was deposited a decanter of light wine which had been ordered by her physicians, and hastened across the chamber to procure it. But, as I stepped beneath the light of the censer, two circumstances of a startling nature attracted my attention. I had felt that some palpable although invisible object had passed lightly by my person; and I saw that there lay upon the golden carpet, in the very middle of the rich lustre thrown from the censer, a shadow—a faint, indefinite shadow of angelic aspect—such as might be fancied for the shadow of a shade. But I was wild with the excitement of an immoderate dose of opium, and heeded these things but little, nor spoke of them to Rowena. Having found the wine, I recrossed the chamber, and poured out a gobletful, which I held to the lips of the fainting lady. She had now partially recovered, however, and took the vessel herself, while I sank upon an ottoman near me, with my eyes fastened upon her person. It was then that I became distinctly aware of a gentle foot-fall upon the carpet, and near the couch; and in a second thereafter, as Rowena was in the act of raising the wine to her lips, I saw, or may have dreamed that I saw, fall within the goblet, as if from some invisible spring in the atmosphere of the room, three or four large drops of a brilliant and ruby colored fluid. If this I saw—not so Rowena. She swallowed the wine unhesitatingly, and I forbore to speak to her of a circumstance which must, after all, I considered, have been but the suggestion of a vivid imagination, rendered morbidly active by the terror of the lady, by the opium, and by the hour.

Yet I cannot conceal it from my own perception that, immediately subsequent to the fall of the ruby-drops, a rapid change for the worse took place in the disorder of my wife; so that, on the third subsequent night, the hands of her menials prepared her for the tomb, and on the fourth, I sat alone, with her shrouded body, in that fantastic chamber which had received her as my bride.— Wild visions, opium-engendered, flitted, shadowlike, before me. I gazed with unquiet eye upon the sarcophagi in the angles of the room, upon the varying figures of the drapery, and upon the writhing of the particolored fires in the censer overhead. My eyes then fell, as I called to mind the circumstances of a former night, to the spot beneath the glare of the censer where I had seen the faint traces of the shadow. It was there, however, no longer; and breathing with greater freedom, I turned my glances to the pallid and rigid figure upon the bed. Then rushed upon me a thousand memories of Ligeia—and then came back upon my heart, with the turbulent violence of a flood, the whole of that unutterable woe with which I had regarded *her* thus enshrouded. The night waned; and still, with a bosom full of bitter thoughts of the one only and supremely beloved, I remained gazing upon the body of Rowena.

It might have been midnight, or perhaps earlier, or later, for I had taken no note of time, when a sob, low, gentle, but very distinct, startled me from my revery.—I *felt* that it came from the bed of ebony—the bed of death. I listened in an agony of superstitious terror—but there was no repetition of the sound. I strained my vision to detect any motion in the corpse—but there was not the slightest perceptible. Yet I could not have been deceived. I *had* heard the noise, however faint, and my soul was awakened within me. I resolutely and perseveringly kept my attention riveted upon the body. Many minutes elapsed before any circumstance occurred tending to throw light upon the mystery. At length it became evident that a slight, a very feeble, and barely noticeable tinge of color had flushed up within the cheeks, and along the sunken small veins of the eyelids. Through a species of unutterable horror and awe, for which the language of mortality has no sufficiently energetic expression, I felt my heart cease to beat, my limbs grow rigid where I sat. Yet a sense of duty finally operated to restore my self-possession. I could no longer doubt that we had been precipitate in our preparations—that Rowena still lived. It was necessary that some immediate exertion be made; yet the turret was altogether apart from the portion of the abbey tenanted by the servants—there were none within call—I had no means of summoning them to my aid without leaving the room for many min-utes—and this I could not venture to do. I therefore struggled alone in my en-deavors to call back the spirit still hovering. In a short period it was certain, however, that a relapse had taken place; the color disappeared from both eyelid and cheek, leaving a wanness even more than that of marble; the lips became doubly shrivelled and pinched up in the ghastly expression of death; a repulsive clamminess and coldness overspread rapidly the surface of the body; and all the usual rigorous stiffness immediately supervened. I fell back with a shudder upon the couch from which I had been so startlingly aroused, and again gave myself up to passionate waking visions of Ligeia.

An hour thus elapsed when (could it be possible?) I was a second time aware   20
of some vague sound issuing from the region of the bed. I listened—in extrem-ity of horror. The sound came again—it was a sigh. Rushing to the corpse, I saw—distinctly saw—a tremor upon the lips. In a minute afterward they re-laxed, disclosing a bright line of the pearly teeth. Amazement now struggled in my bosom with the profound awe which had hitherto reigned there alone. I felt that my vision grew dim, that my reason wandered; and it was only by a violent effort that I at length succeeded in nerving myself to the task which duty thus once more had pointed out. There was now a partial glow upon the forehead and upon the cheek and throat; a perceptible warmth pervaded the whole frame; there was even a slight pulsation at the heart. The lady *lived;* and with re-doubled ardor I betook myself to the task of restoration. I chafed and bathed the temples and the hands, and used every exertion which experience, and no little medical reading, could suggest. But in vain. Suddenly, the color fled, the pulsation ceased, the lips resumed the expression of the dead, and, in an instant afterward, the whole body took upon itself the icy chilliness, the livid hue, the intense rigidity, the sunken outline, and all the loathsome peculiarities of that which has been, for many days, a tenant of the tomb.

And again I sunk into visions of Ligeia—and again, (what marvel that I shud-der while I write?) *again* there reached my ears a low sob from the region of the ebony bed. But why shall I minutely detail the unspeakable horrors of that night? Why shall I pause to relate how, time after time, until near the period of the gray dawn, this hideous drama of revivification was repeated; how each ter-rific relapse was only into a sterner and apparently more irredeemable death; how each agony wore the aspect of a struggle with some invisible foe; and how each struggle was succeeded by I know not what of wild change in the personal appearance of the corpse? Let me hurry to a conclusion.

The greater part of the fearful night had worn away, and she who had been dead once again stirred—and now more vigorously than hitherto, although arousing from a dissolution more appalling in its utter hopelessness than any. I had long ceased to struggle or to move, and remained sitting rigidly upon the ot-toman, a helpless prey to a whirl of violent emotions, of which extreme awe was perhaps the least terrible, the least consuming. The corpse, I repeat, stirred, and now more vigorously than before. The hues of life flushed up with un-wonted energy into the countenance—the limbs relaxed—and, save that the eyelids were yet pressed heavily together, and that the bandages and draperies of the grave still imparted their charnel character to the figure, I might have dreamed that Rowena had indeed shaken off, utterly, the fetters of Death. But if this idea was not, even then, altogether adopted, I could at least doubt no longer, when, arising from the bed, tottering, with feeble steps, with closed eyes, and with the manner of one bewildered in a dream, the thing that was enshrouded advanced boldly and palpably into the middle of the apartment.

I trembled not—I stirred not—for a crowd of unutterable fancies connected with the air, the stature, the demeanor of the figure, rushing hurriedly through my brain, had paralyzed—had chilled me into stone. I stirred not—but gazed upon the apparition. There was a mad disorder in my thoughts—a tumult unappeasable. Could it, indeed, be the *living* Rowena who confronted me? Could it, indeed, be Rowena *at all*—the fair-haired, the blue-eyed Lady Rowena Trevanion of Tremaine? Why, *why* should I doubt it? The bandage lay heavily about the mouth—but then might it not be the mouth of the breathing Lady of Tremaine? And the cheeks—there were the roses as in her noon of life—yes, these might indeed be the fair cheeks of the living Lady of Tremaine. And the chin, with its dimples, as in health, might it not be hers?—but *had she then grown taller since her malady?* What inexpressible madness seized me with that thought? One bound, and I had reached her feet! Shrinking from my touch, she let fall from her head, unloosened, the ghastly cerements which had confined it, and there streamed forth into the rushing atmosphere of the chamber huge masses of long and dishevelled hair; *it was blacker than the raven wings of midnight!* And now slowly opened *the eyes* of the figure which stood before me. "Here then, at least," I shrieked aloud, "can I never—can I never be mistaken—these are the full, and the black, and the wild eyes—of my lost love—of the Lady—of the Lady Ligeia."

For Analysis
1. Is this a story of serious moral and psychological meaning or merely a thriller? What evidence can you find in the text to support your answer? **2.** Contrast the attitude toward life expressed in the passage from Joseph Glanvill that opens the story with that in Ligeia's poem.

On Style
1. What do the patterns of color **imagery** contribute to the effect of the story? **2.** How does the decor of the English abbey contribute to the story's atmosphere?

Making Connections
Have you (or has someone you know) ever overcome seemingly insurmountable obstacles by a powerful effort generated by will? Explain.

Writing Topic
Some critics read "Ligeia" as a study in obsessional psychology told by an **unreliable narrator** who, in fact, murdered his second wife. In an essay based on close reading of the text, either support or refute this view.

Leo Tolstoy   [1828–1910]

The Death of Iván Ilých[1]   1886

CHAPTER I

During an interval in the Melvínski trial in the large building of the Law Courts the members and public prosecutor met in Iván Egórovich Shébek's private room, where the conversation turned on the celebrated Krasóvski case. Fëdor Vasílievich warmly maintained that it was not subject to their jurisdiction, Iván Egórovich maintained the contrary, while Peter Ivánovich, not having entered into the discussion at the start, took no part in it but looked through the *Gazette* which had just been handed in.

"Gentlemen," he said, "Iván Ilých has died!"

"You don't say so!"

"Here, read it yourself," replied Peter Ivánovich, handing Fëdor Vasílievich the paper still damp from the press. Surrounded by a black border were the words: "Praskóvya Fëdorovna Gol* viná, with profound sorrow, informs relatives and friends of the demise of her beloved husband Iván Ilých Golovín, Member of the Court of Justice, which occurred on February the 4th of this year 1882. The funeral will take place on Friday at one o'clock in the afternoon."

Iván Ilých had been a colleague of the gentlemen present and was liked by them all. He had been ill for some weeks with an illness said to be incurable. His post had been kept open for him, but there had been conjectures that in case of his death Alexéev might receive his appointment, and that either Vínnikov or Shtábel would succeed Alexéev. So on receiving the news of Iván Ilých's death the first thought of each of the gentlemen in that private room was of the changes and promotions it might occasion among themselves or their acquaintances. 5

"I shall be sure to get Shtábel's place or Vínnikov's," thought Fëdor Vasílievich. "I was promised that long ago, and the promotion means an extra eight hundred rubles a year for me besides the allowance."

"Now I must apply for my brother-in-law's transfer from Kalúga," thought Peter Ivánovich. "My wife will be very glad, and then she won't be able to say that I never do anything for her relations."

"I thought he would never leave his bed again," said Peter Ivánovich aloud. "It's very sad."

"But what really was the matter with him?"

"The doctors couldn't say—at least they could, but each of them said something different. When last I saw him I thought he was getting better." 10

"And I haven't been to see him since the holidays. I always meant to go."

[1] Translated by Aylmer Maude.

"Had he any property?"

"I think his wife had a little—but something quite trifling."

"We shall have to go to see her, but they live so terribly far away."

"Far away from you, you mean. Everything's far away from your place." 15

"You see, he never can forgive my living on the other side of the river," said Peter Ivánovich, smiling at Shébek. Then, still talking of the distances between different parts of the city, they returned to the Court.

Besides considerations as to the possible transfers and promotions likely to result from Iván Ilých's death, the mere fact of the death of a near acquaintance aroused, as usual, in all who heard of it the complacent feeling that, "it is he who is dead and not I."

Each one thought or felt, "Well, he's dead but I'm alive!" But the more intimate of Iván Ilých's acquaintances, his so-called friends, could not help thinking also that they would now have to fulfill the very tiresome demands of propriety by attending the funeral service and paying a visit of condolence to the widow.

Fëdor Vasílievich and Peter Ivánovich had been his nearest acquaintances. Peter Ivánovich had studied law with Iván Ilých and had considered himself to be under obligations to him.

Having told his wife at dinner-time of Iván Ilých's death, and of his conjecture 20 that it might be possible to get her brother transferred to their circuit, Peter Ivánovich sacrificed his usual nap, put on his evening clothes, and drove to Iván Ilých's house.

At the entrance stood a carriage and two cabs. Leaning against the wall in the hall downstairs near the cloak-stand was a coffin-lid covered with cloth of gold, ornamented with gold cord and tassels, that had been polished up with metal powder. Two ladies in black were taking off their fur cloaks. Peter Ivánovich recognized one of them as Iván Ilých's sister, but the other was a stranger to him. His colleague Schwartz was just coming downstairs, but on seeing Peter Ivánovich enter he stopped and winked at him, as if to say: "Iván Ilých has made a mess of things—not like you and me."

Schwartz's face with his Piccadilly whiskers, and his slim figure in evening dress, had as usual an air of elegant solemnity which contrasted with the playfulness of his character and had a special piquancy here, or so it seemed to Peter Ivánovich.

Peter Ivánovich allowed the ladies to precede him and slowly followed them upstairs. Schwartz did not come down but remained where he was, and Peter Ivánovich understood that he wanted to arrange where they should play bridge that evening. The ladies went upstairs to the widow's room, and Schwartz with seriously compressed lips but a playful look in his eyes, indicated by a twist of his eyebrows the room to the right where the body lay.

Peter Ivánovich, like everyone else on such occasions, entered feeling uncertain what he would have to do. All he knew was that at such times it is always safe to cross oneself. But he was not quite sure whether one should make obeisances while doing so. He therefore adopted a middle course. On entering the room he began crossing himself and made a slight movement resembling a bow. At the same time, as far as the motion of his head and arm allowed, he surveyed the room. Two young men—apparently nephews, one of whom was a high-school pupil—were leaving the room, crossing themselves as they did so. An old woman was standing motionless, and a lady with strangely arched eyebrows was saying something to her in a whisper. A vigorous, resolute Church Reader, in a frock-coat, was reading something in a loud voice with an expression that precluded any contradiction. The butler's assistant, Gerásim, stepping lightly in front of Peter Ivánovich, was strewing something on the floor. Noticing this, Peter Ivánovich was immediately aware of a faint odour of a decomposing body.

The last time he had called on Iván Ilých, Peter Ivánovich had seen Gerásim   25
in the study. Iván Ilých had been particularly fond of him and he was performing the duty of a sick nurse.

Peter Ivánovich continued to make the sign of the cross slightly inclining his head in an intermediate direction between the coffin, the Reader, and the icons on the table in a corner of the room. Afterwards, when it seemed to him that this movement of his arm in crossing himself had gone on too long, he stopped and began to look at the corpse.

The dead man lay, as dead men always lie, in a specially heavy way, his rigid limbs sunk in the soft cushions of the coffin, with the head forever bowed on the pillow. His yellow waxen brow with bald patches over his sunken temples was thrust up in the way peculiar to the dead, the protruding nose seeming to press on the upper lip. He was much changed and had grown even thinner since Peter Ivánovich had last seen him, but, as is always the case with the dead, his face was handsomer and above all more dignified than when he was alive. The expression on the face said that what was necessary had been accomplished, and accomplished rightly. Besides this there was in that expression a reproach and a warning to the living. This warning seemed to Peter Ivánovich out of place, or at least not applicable to him. He felt a certain discomfort and so he hurriedly crossed himself once more and turned and went out of the door—too hurriedly and too regardless of propriety, as he himself was aware.

Schwartz was waiting for him in the adjoining room with legs spread wide apart and both hands toying with his top-hat behind his back. The mere sight of that playful, well-groomed, and elegant figure refreshed Peter Ivánovich. He felt that Schwartz was above all these happenings and would not surrender to any depressing influences. His very look said that this incident of a church service for Iván Ilých could not be a sufficient reason for infringing the order of the session—in other words, that it would certainly not prevent his unwrapping a new pack of cards and shuffling them that evening while a footman placed four fresh candles on the table: in fact, there was no reason for supposing that this incident would hinder their spending the evening agreeably. Indeed he said this in a whisper as Peter Ivánovich passed him, proposing that they should meet for a game at Fëdor Vasílievich's. But apparently Peter Ivánovich was not destined to play bridge that evening. Praskóvya Fëdorovna (a short, fat woman who despite all efforts to the contrary had continued to broaden steadily from her shoulders downwards and who had the same extraordinarily arched eyebrows as the lady who had been standing by the coffin), dressed all in black, her head covered with lace, came out of her own room with some other ladies, conducted them to the room where the dead body lay, and said: "The service will begin immediately. Please go in."

Schwartz, making an indefinite bow, stood still, evidently neither accepting nor declining this invitation. Praskóvya Fëdorovna recognizing Peter Ivánovich, sighed, went close up to him, took his hand, and said: "I know you were a true friend to Iván Ilých . . ." and looked at him awaiting some suitable response. And Peter Ivánovich knew that, just as it had been the right thing to cross himself in that room, so what he had to do here was to press her hand, sigh, and say, "Believe me . . ." So he did all this and as he did it felt that the desired result had been achieved: that both he and she were touched.

"Come with me. I want to speak to you before it begins," said the widow. 30 "Give me your arm."

Peter Ivánovich gave her his arm and they went to the inner rooms, passing Schwartz who winked at Peter Ivánovich compassionately.

"That does for our bridge! Don't object if we find another player. Perhaps you can cut in when you do escape," said his playful look.

Peter Ivánovich sighed still more deeply and despondently, and Praskóvya Fëdorovna pressed his arm gratefully. When they reached the drawing-room, upholstered in pink cretonne and lighted by a dim lamp, they sat down at the table—she on a sofa and Peter Ivánovich on a low pouffe, the springs of which yielded spasmodically under his weight. Praskóvya Fëdorovna had been on the point of warning him to take another seat, but felt that such a warning was out of keeping with her present condition and so changed her mind. As he sat down on the pouffe Peter Ivánovich recalled how Iván Ilých had arranged this room and had consulted him regarding this pink cretonne with green leaves. The whole room was full of furniture and knick-knacks, and on her way to the sofa the lace of the widow's black shawl caught on the carved edge of the table. Peter Ivánovich rose to detach it, and the springs of the pouffe, relieved of his weight, rose also and gave him a push. The widow began detaching her shawl herself, and Peter Ivánovich again sat down, suppressing the rebellious springs of the pouffe under him. But the widow had not quite freed herself and Peter Ivánovich got up again, and again the pouffe rebelled and even creaked. When this was all over she took out a clean cambric handkerchief and began to weep. The episode with the shawl and the struggle with the pouffe had cooled Peter Ivánovich's emotions and he sat there with a sullen look on his face. This awkward situation was interrupted by Sokolóv, Iván Ilých's butler, who came to report that the plot in the cemetery that Praskóvya Fëdorovna had chosen would cost two hundred rubles. She stopped weeping and, looking at Peter Ivánovich with the air of a victim, remarked in French that it was very hard for her. Peter Ivánovich made a silent gesture signifying his full conviction that it must indeed be so.

"Please smoke," she said in a magnanimous yet crushed voice, and turned to discuss with Sokolóv the price of the plot for the grave.

Peter Ivánovich while lighting his cigarette heard her inquiring very circum- 35 stantially into the price of different plots in the cemetery and finally decide which she would take. When that was done she gave instructions about engaging the choir. Sokolóv then left the room.

"I look after everything myself," she told Peter Ivánovich, shifting the albums that lay on the table; and noticing that the table was endangered by his cigarette-ash, she immediately passed him an ashtray, saying as she did so: "I consider it an affectation to say that my grief prevents my attending to practical affairs. On the contrary, if anything can—I won't say console me, but—distract me, it is seeing to everything concerning him." She again took out her handkerchief as if preparing to cry, but suddenly, as if mastering her feeling, she shook herself and began to speak calmly. "But there is something I want to talk to you about."

Peter Ivánovich bowed, keeping control of the springs of the pouffe, which immediately began quivering under him.

"He suffered terribly the last few days."

"Did he?" said Peter Ivánovich.

"Oh, terribly! He screamed unceasingly, not for minutes but for hours. For the last three days he screamed incessantly. It was unendurable. I cannot understand how I bore it; you could hear him three rooms off. Oh, what I have suffered!"

"Is it possible that he was conscious all that time?" asked Peter Ivánovich.

"Yes," she whispered. "To the last moment. He took leave of us a quarter of an hour before he died, and asked us to take Volódya away."

The thought of the sufferings of this man he had known so intimately, first as a merry little boy, then as a school-mate, and later as a grown-up colleague, suddenly struck Peter Ivánovich with horror, despite an unpleasant consciousness of his own and this woman's dissimulation. He again saw that brow, and that nose pressing down on the lip, and felt afraid for himself.

"Three days of frightful suffering and then death! Why, that might suddenly, at any time, happen to me," he thought, and for a moment felt terrified. But—he did not himself know how—the customary reflection at once occurred to him that this had happened to Iván Ilých and not to him, and that it should not and could not happen to him, and that to think that it could would be yielding to depression which he ought not to do, as Schwartz's expression plainly showed. After which reflection Peter Ivánovich felt reassured, and began to ask with interest about the details of Iván Ilých's death, as though death was an accident natural to Iván Ilých but certainly not to himself.

After many details of the really dreadful physical sufferings Iván Ilých had endured (which details he learnt only from the effect those sufferings had produced on Praskóvya Fëdorovna's nerves) the widow apparently found it necessary to get to business.

"Oh, Peter Ivánovich, how hard it is! How terribly, terribly hard!" and she again began to weep.

Peter Ivánovich sighed and waited for her to finish blowing her nose. When she had done so he said, "Believe me . . ." and she again began talking and brought out what was evidently her chief concern with him—namely, to question him as to how she could obtain a grant of money from the government on the occasion of her husband's death. She made it appear that she was asking Peter Ivánovich's advice about her pension, but he soon saw that she already knew about that to the minutest detail, more even than he did himself. She knew how much could be got out of the government in consequence of her husband's death, but wanted to find out whether she could not possibly extract something more. Peter Ivánovich tried to think of some means of doing so, but after reflecting for a while and, out of propriety, condemning the government for its niggardliness, he said he thought that nothing more could be got. Then she sighed and evidently began to devise means of getting rid of her visitor. Noticing this, he put out his cigarette, rose, pressed her hand, and went out into the anteroom.

In the dining-room where the clock stood that Iván Ilých had liked so much and had bought at an antique shop, Peter Ivánovich met a priest and a few acquaintances who had come to attend the service, and he recognized Iván Ilých's daughter, a handsome young woman. She was in black and her slim figure appeared slimmer than ever. She had a gloomy, determined, almost angry expression, and bowed to Peter Ivánovich as though he were in some way to blame. Behind her, with the same offended look, stood a wealthy young man, an examining magistrate, whom Peter Ivánovich also knew and who was her fiancé, as he had heard. He bowed mournfully to them and was about to pass into the death-chamber, when from under the stairs appeared the figure of Iván Ilých's school-boy son, who was extremely like his father. He seemed a little Iván Ilých, such as Peter Ivánovich remembered when they studied law together. His tear-stained eyes had in them the look that is seen in the eyes of boys of thirteen or fourteen who are not pure-minded. When he saw Peter Ivánovich he scowled morosely and shamefacedly. Peter Ivánovich nodded to him and entered the death-chamber. The service began: candles, groans, incense, tears, and sobs. Peter Ivánovich stood looking gloomily down at his feet. He did not look once at the dead man, did not yield to any depressing influence, and was one of the first to leave the room. There was no one in the anteroom, but Gerásim darted out of the dead man's room, rummaged with his strong hands among the fur coats to find Peter Ivánovich's and helped him on with it.

"Well, friend Gerásim," said Peter Ivánovich, so as to say something. "It's a sad affair, isn't it?"

"It's God's will. We shall all come to it some day," said Gerásim, displaying his   50 teeth—the even, white teeth of a healthy peasant—and, like a man in the thick of urgent work, he briskly opened the front door, called the coachman, helped Peter Ivánovich into the sledge, and sprang back to the porch as if in readiness for what he had to do next.

Peter Ivánovich found the fresh air particularly pleasant after the smell of incense, the dead body, and carbolic acid.

"Where to, sir?" asked the coachman.

"It's not too late even now. . . . I'll call round on Fëdor Vasílievich."

He accordingly drove there and found them just finishing the first rubber, so that it was quite convenient for him to cut in.

CHAPTER II

Iván Ilých's life had been most simple and most ordinary and therefore most ter-   55
rible.

He had been a member of the Court of Justice, and died at the age of forty-
five. His father had been an official who after serving in various ministries and
departments in Petersburg had made the sort of career which brings men to positions from which by reason of their long service they cannot be dismissed,
though they are obviously unfit to hold any responsible position, and for whom
therefore posts are specially created, which though fictitious carry salaries of
from six to ten thousand rubles that are not fictitious, and in receipt of which
they live on to a great age.

Such was the Privy Councillor and superfluous member of various superfluous institutions, Ilyá Epímovich Golovín.

He had three sons, of whom Iván Ilých was the second. The eldest son was
following in his father's footsteps only in another department, and was already
approaching that stage in the service at which a similar sinecure would be
reached. The third son was a failure. He had ruined his prospects in a number
of positions and was now serving in the railway department. His father and
brothers, and still more their wives, not merely disliked meeting him, but
avoided remembering his existence unless compelled to do so. His sister had
married Baron Greff, a Petersburg official of her father's type. Iván Ilých was *le
phénix de la famille*[2] as people said. He was neither as cold and formal as his
elder brother nor as wild as the younger, but was a happy mean between them—
an intelligent, polished, lively and agreeable man. He had studied with his
younger brother at the School of Law, but the latter had failed to complete the
course and was expelled when he was in the fifth class. Iván Ilých finished the
course well. Even when he was at the School of Law he was just what he remained for the rest of his life: a capable, cheerful, good-natured, and sociable
man, though strict in the fulfilment of what he considered to be his duty: and he
considered his duty to be what was so considered by those in authority. Neither
as a boy nor as a man was he a toady, but from early youth was by nature attracted to people of high station as a fly is drawn to the light, assimilating their
ways and views of life and establishing friendly relations with them. All the en-
thusiasms of childhood and youth passed without leaving much trace on him; he
succumbed to sensuality, to vanity, and latterly among the highest classes to liberalism, but always within limits which his instinct unfailingly indicated to him
as correct.

At school he had done things which had formerly seemed to him very horrid
and made him feel disgusted with himself when he did them; but when later on
he saw that such actions were done by people of good position and that they did
not regard them as wrong, he was able not exactly to regard them as right, but
to forget about them entirely or not be at all troubled at remembering them.

[2] The phoenix of the family, here meaning "rare bird" or "prodigy."

Having graduated from the School of Law and qualified for the tenth rank of   60
the civil service, and having received money from his father for his equipment,
Iván Ilých ordered himself clothes at Scharmer's, the fashionable tailor, hung a
medallion inscribed *respice finem*[3] on his watch-chain, took leave of his professor and the prince who was patron of the school, had a farewell dinner with his
comrades at Donon's first-class restaurant, and with his new and fashionable
portmanteau, linen, clothes, shaving and other toilet appliances, and a travelling
rug, all purchased at the best shops, he set off for one of the provinces where,
through his father's influence, he had been attached to the Governor as an official for special service.

In the province Iván Ilých soon arranged as easy and agreeable a position for
himself as he had had at the School of Law. He performed his official tasks,
made his career, and at the same time amused himself pleasantly and decorously. Occasionally he paid official visits to country districts, where he behaved
with dignity both to his superiors and inferiors, and performed the duties en-
trusted to him, which related chiefly to the sectarians,[4] with an exactness and in-
corruptible honesty of which he could not but feel proud.

In official matters, despite his youth and taste for frivolous gaiety, he was exceedingly reserved, punctilious, and even severe; but in society he was often
amusing and witty, and always good-natured, correct in his manner, and *bon enfant*, as the governor and his wife—with whom he was like one of the family—
used to say of him.

In the provinces he had an affair with a lady who made advances to the elegant young lawyer, and there was also a milliner; and there were carousals with
aides-de-camp who visited the district, and after-supper visits to a certain out-
lying street of doubtful reputation; and there was too some obsequiousness to
his chief and even to his chief's wife, but all this was done with such a tone of
good breeding that no hard names could be applied to it. It all came under the
heading of the French saying: "Il faut que jeunesse se passe."[5] It was all done
with clean hands, in clean linen, with French phrases, and above all among
people of the best society and consequently with the approval of people of rank.

So Iván Ilých served for five years and then came a change in his official life.
The new and reformed judicial institutions were introduced, and new men were
needed. Iván Ilých became such a new man. He was offered the post of Examining Magistrate, and he accepted it though the post was in another province
and obliged him to give up the connections he had formed and to make new
ones. His friends met to give him a send-off; they had a group-photograph taken
and presented him with a silver cigarette-case, and he set off to his new post.

As examining magistrate Iván Ilých was just as *comme il faut*[6] and decorous a   65

---

[3] Regard the end.
[4] A large sect, whose members were placed under many legal restrictions, which broke away
from the Orthodox Church in the seventeenth century.
[5] Youth must have its fling.
[6] Proper.

man, inspiring general respect and capable of separating his official duties from his private life, as he had been when acting as an official on special service. His duties now as examining magistrate were far more interesting and attractive than before. In his former position it had been pleasant to wear an undress uniform made by Scharmer, and to pass through the crowd of petitioners and officials who were timorously awaiting an audience with the governor, and who envied him as with free and easy gait he went straight into his chief's private room to have a cup of tea and a cigarette with him. But not many people had then been directly dependent on him—only police officials and the sectarians when he went on special missions—and he liked to treat them politely, almost as comrades, as if he were letting them feel that he who had the power to crush them was treating them in this simple, friendly way. There were then but few such people. But now, as an examining magistrate, Iván Ilých felt that everyone without exception, even the most important and self-satisfied, was in his power, and that he need only write a few words on a sheet of paper with a certain heading, and this or that important, self-satisfied person would be brought before him in the role of an accused person or a witness, and if he did not choose to allow him to sit down, would have to stand before him and answer his questions. Iván Ilých never abused his power; he tried on the contrary to soften its expression, but the consciousness of it and of the possibility of softening its effect, supplied the chief interest and attraction of his office. In his work itself, especially in his examinations, he very soon acquired a method of eliminating all considerations irrelevant to the legal aspect of the case, and reducing even the most complicated case to a form in which it would be presented on paper only in its externals, completely excluding his personal opinion of the matter, while above all observing every prescribed formality. The work was new and Iván Ilých was one of the first men to apply the new Code of 1864.[7]

On taking up the post of examining magistrate in a new town, he made new acquaintances and connections, placed himself on a new footing, and assumed a somewhat different tone. He took up an attitude of rather dignified aloofness towards the provincial authorities, but picked out the best circle of legal gentlemen and wealthy gentry living in the town and assumed a tone of slight dissatisfaction with the government, of moderate liberalism, and of enlightened citizenship. At the same time, without at all altering the elegance of his toilet, he ceased shaving his chin and allowed his beard to grow as it pleased.

Iván Ilých settled down very pleasantly in this new town. The society there, which inclined towards opposition to the Governor, was friendly, his salary was larger, and he began to play *vint*,[8] which he found added not a little to the pleasure of life, for he had a capacity for cards, played good-humouredly, and calculated rapidly and astutely, so that he usually won.

After living there for two years he met his future wife, Praskóvya Fëdorovna

---

[7] Judicial procedures were thoroughly reformed after the emancipation of the serfs in 1861.
[8] A card game similar to bridge.

Míkhel, who was the most attractive, clever, and brilliant girl of the set in which he moved, and among other amusements and relaxations from his labours as examining magistrate, Iván Ilých established light and playful relations with her.

While he had been an official on special service he had been accustomed to dance, but now as an examining magistrate it was exceptional for him to do so. If he danced now, he did it as if to show that though he served under the reformed order of things, and had reached the fifth official rank, yet when it came to dancing he could do it better than most people. So at the end of an evening he sometimes danced with Praskóvya Fëdorovna, and it was chiefly during these dances that he captivated her. She fell in love with him. Iván Ilých had at first no definite intention of marrying, but when the girl fell in love with him he said to himself: "Really, why shouldn't I marry?"

Praskóvya Fëdorovna came of a good family, was not bad looking and had some little property. Iván Ilých might have aspired to a more brilliant match, but even this was good. He had his salary, and she, he hoped, would have an equal income. She was well connected, and was a sweet, pretty, and thoroughly correct young woman. To say that Iván Ilých married because he fell in love with Praskóvya Fëdorovna and found that she sympathized with his views of life would be as incorrect as to say that he married because his social circle approved of the match. He was swayed by both these considerations: the marriage gave him personal satisfaction, and at the same time it was considered the right thing by the most highly placed of his associates.

So Iván Ilých got married.

The preparations for marriage and the beginning of married life, with its conjugal caresses, the new furniture, new crockery, and new linen, were very pleasant until his wife became pregnant—so that Iván Ilých had begun to think that marriage would not impair the easy, agreeable, gay and always decorous character of his life, approved of by society and regarded by himself as natural, but would even improve it. But from the first months of his wife's pregnancy, something new, unpleasant, depressing, and unseemly, and from which there was no way of escape, unexpectedly showed itself.

His wife, without any reason—*de gaieté de coeur* as Iván Ilých expressed it to himself—began to disturb the pleasure and propriety of their life. She began to be jealous without any cause, expected him to devote his whole attention to her, found fault with everything, and made coarse and ill-mannered scenes.

At first Iván Ilých hoped to escape from the unpleasantness of this state of affairs by the same easy and decorous relation to life that had served him heretofore: he tried to ignore his wife's disagreeable moods, continued to live in his usual easy and pleasant way, invited friends to his house for a game of cards, and also tried going out to his club or spending his evenings with friends. But one day his wife began upbraiding him so vigorously, using such coarse words, and continued to abuse him every time he did not fulfil her demands, so resolutely and with such evident determination not to give way till he submitted—that is, till he stayed at home and was bored just as she was—that he became alarmed.

He now realized that matrimony—at any rate with Praskóvya Fëdorovna—was not always conducive to the pleasures and amenities of life but on the contrary often infringed both comfort and propriety, and that he must therefore entrench himself against such infringement. And Iván Ilých began to seek for means of doing so. His official duties were the one thing that imposed upon Praskóvya Fëdorovna, and by means of his official work and the duties attached to it he began struggling with his wife to secure his own independence.

With the birth of their child, the attempts to feed it and the various failures in doing so, and with the real and imaginary illnesses of mother and child, in which Iván Ilých's sympathy was demanded but about which he understood nothing, the need of securing for himself an existence outside his family life became still more imperative. 75

As his wife grew more irritable and exacting and Iván Ilých transferred the centre of gravity of his life more and more to his official work, so did he grow to like his work better and became more ambitious than before.

Very soon, within a year of his wedding, Iván Ilých had realized that marriage, though it may add some comforts to life, is in fact a very intricate and difficult affair towards which in order to perform one's duty, that is, to lead a decorous life approved of by society, one must adopt a definite attitude just as towards one's official duties.

And Iván Ilých evolved such an attitude towards married life. He only required of it those conveniences—dinner at home, housewife, and bed—which it could give him, and above all that propriety of external forms required by public opinion. For the rest he looked for light-hearted pleasure and propriety, and was very thankful when he found them, but if he met with antagonism and querulousness he at once retired into his separate fenced-off world of official duties, where he found satisfaction.

Iván Ilých was esteemed a good official, and after three years was made Assistant Public Prosecutor. His new duties, their importance, the possibility of indicting and imprisoning anyone he chose, the publicity his speeches received, and the success he had in all these things, made his work still more attractive.

More children came. His wife became more and more querulous and ill- 80 tempered, but the attitude Iván Ilých had adopted towards his home life rendered him almost impervious to her grumbling.

After seven years' service in that town he was transferred to another province as Public Prosecutor. They moved, but were short of money and his wife did not like the place they moved to. Though the salary was higher the cost of living was greater, besides which two of their children died and family life became still more unpleasant for him.

Praskóvya Fëdorovna blamed her husband for every inconvenience they encountered in their new home. Most of the conversations between husband and wife, especially as to the children's education, led to topics which recalled former disputes, and those disputes were apt to flare up again at any moment. There remained only those rare periods of amorousness which still came to them at times but did not last long. These were islets at which they anchored for a while and then again set out upon that ocean of veiled hostility which showed itself in their aloofness from one another. This aloofness might have grieved Iván Ilých had he considered that it ought not to exist, but he now regarded the position as normal, and even made it the goal at which he aimed in family life. His aim was to free himself more and more from those unpleasantnesses and to give them a semblance of harmlessness and propriety. He attained this by spending less and less time with his family, and when obliged to be at home he tried to safeguard his position by the presence of outsiders. The chief thing however was that he had his official duties. The whole interest of his life now centered in the official world and that interest absorbed him. The consciousness of his power, being able to ruin anybody he wished to ruin, the importance, even the external dignity of his entry into court, or meetings with his subordinates, his success with superiors and inferiors, and above all his masterly handling of cases, of which he was conscious—all this gave him pleasure and filled his life, together with chats with his colleagues, dinners, and bridge. So that on the whole Iván Ilých's life continued to flow as he considered it should do—pleasantly and properly.

So things continued for another seven years. His eldest daughter was already sixteen, another child had died, and only one son was left, a schoolboy and a subject of dissension. Iván Ilých wanted to put him in the School of Law, but to spite him Praskóvya Fëdorovna entered him at the High School. The daughter had been educated at home and had turned out well: the boy did not learn badly either.

CHAPTER III

So Iván Ilých lived for seventeen years after his marriage. He was already a Public Prosecutor of long standing, and had declined several proposed transfers while awaiting a more desirable post, when an unanticipated and unpleasant occurrence quite upset the peaceful course of his life. He was expecting to be offered the post of presiding judge in a University town, but Happe somehow came to the front and obtained the appointment instead. Iván Ilých became irritable, reproached Happe, and quarreled both with him and with his immediate superiors—who became colder to him and again passed him over when other appointments were made.

This was in 1880, the hardest year of Iván Ilých's life. It was then that it became evident on the one hand that his salary was insufficient for them to live on, and on the other that he had been forgotten, and not only this, but that what was for him the greatest and most cruel injustice appeared to others a quite ordinary occurrence. Even his father did not consider it his duty to help him. Iván Ilých felt himself abandoned by everyone, and that they regarded his position with a salary of 3,500 rubles as quite normal and even fortunate. He alone knew that with the consciousness of the injustices done him, with his wife's incessant nagging, and with the debts he had contracted by living beyond his means, his position was far from normal.

In order to save money that summer he obtained leave of absence and went with his wife to live in the country at her brother's place.

In the country, without his work, he experienced *ennui* for the first time in his life, and not only *ennui* but intolerable depression, and he decided that it was impossible to go on living like that, and that it was necessary to take energetic measures.

Having passed a sleepless night pacing up and down the veranda, he decided to go to Petersburg and bestir himself, in order to punish those who had failed to appreciate him and to get transferred to another ministry.

Next day, despite many protests from his wife and her brother, he started for Petersburg with the sole object of obtaining a post with a salary of five thousand rubles a year. He was no longer bent on any particular department, or tendency, or kind of activity. All he now wanted was an appointment to another post with a salary of five thousand rubles, either in the administration, in the banks, with the railways, in one of the Empress Márya's Institutions,[9] or even in the customs—but it had to carry with it a salary of five thousand rubles and be in a ministry other than that in which they had failed to appreciate him.

And this quest of Iván Ilých's was crowned with remarkable and unexpected success. At Kursk an acquaintance of his, F. I. Ilyín, got into the first-class carriage, sat down beside Iván Ilých, and told him of a telegram just received by the Governor of Kursk announcing that a change was about to take place in the ministry: Peter Ivánovich was to be superseded by Iván Semënovich.   90

The proposed change, apart from its significance for Russia, had a special significance for Iván Ilých, because by bringing forward a new man, Peter Petróvich, and consequently his friend Zachár Ivánovich, it was highly favourable for Iván Ilých, since Zachár Ivánovich was a friend and colleague of his.

In Moscow this news was confirmed, and on reaching Petersburg Iván Ilých found Zachár Ivánovich and received a definite promise of an appointment in his former Department of Justice.

A week later he telegraphed to his wife: "Zachár in Miller's place. I shall receive appointment on presentation of report."

Thanks to this change of personnel, Iván Ilých had unexpectedly obtained an appointment in his former ministry which placed him two stages above his former colleagues besides giving him five thousand rubles salary and three thousand five hundred rubles for expenses connected with his removal. All his ill humour towards his former enemies and the whole department vanished, and Iván Ilých was completely happy.

He returned to the country more cheerful and contented than he had been for a long time. Praskóvya Fëdorovna also cheered up and a truce was arranged between them. Iván Ilých told of how he had been fêted by everybody in Petersburg, how all those who had been his enemies were put to shame and now fawned on him, how envious they were of his appointment, and how much everybody in Petersburg had liked him.   95

[9] A charitable organization founded in the late eighteenth century by the Empress Márya.

Praskóvya Fëdorovna listened to all this and appeared to believe it. She did not contradict anything, but only made plans for their life in the town to which they were going. Iván Ilých saw with delight that these plans were his plans, that he and his wife agreed, and that, after a stumble, his life was regaining its due and natural character of pleasant lightheartedness and decorum.

Iván Ilých had come back for a short time only, for he had to take up his new duties on the 10th of September. Moreover, he needed time to settle into the new place, to move all his belongings from the province, and to buy and order many additional things: in a word, to make such arrangements as he had resolved on, which were almost exactly what Praskóvya Fëdorovna too had decided on.

Now that everything had happened so fortunately, and that he and his wife were at one in their aims and moreover saw so little of one another, they got on together better than they had done since the first years of marriage. Iván Ilých had thought of taking his family away with him at once, but the insistence of his wife's brother and her sister-in-law, who had suddenly become particularly amiable and friendly to him and his family, induced him to depart alone.

So he departed, and the cheerful state of mind induced by his success and by the harmony between his wife and himself, the one intensifying the other, did not leave him. He found a delightful house, just the thing both he and his wife had dreamt of. Spacious, lofty reception rooms in the old style, a convenient and dignified study, rooms for his wife and daughter, a study for his son—it might have been specially built for them. Iván Ilých himself superintended the arrangements, chose the wallpapers, supplemented the furniture (preferably with antiques which he considered particularly *comme il faut*), and supervised the upholstering. Everything progressed and progressed and approached the ideal he had set himself: even when things were only half completed they exceeded his expectations. He saw what a refined and elegant character, free from vulgarity, it would all have when it was ready. On falling asleep he pictured to himself how the reception-room would look. Looking at the yet unfinished drawing-room he could see the fireplace, the screen, the what-not, the little chairs dotted here and there, the dishes and plates on the walls, and the bronzes, as they would be when everything was in place. He was pleased by the thought of how his wife and daughter, who shared his taste in this matter, would be impressed by it. They were certainly not expecting as much. He had been particularly successful in finding, and buying cheaply, antiques which gave a particularly aristocratic character to the whole place. But in his letters he intentionally understated everything in order to be able to surprise them. All this so absorbed him that his new duties—though he liked his official work—interested him less than he had expected. Sometimes he even had moments of absent-mindedness during the Court Sessions, and would consider whether he should have straight or curved cornices for his curtains. He was so interested in it all that he often did things himself, rearranging the furniture, or rehanging the curtains. Once when mounting a step-ladder to show the upholsterer, who did not understand, how he wanted the hangings draped, he made a false step and slipped, but being a strong and agile man he clung on and only knocked his side against the knob of the window frame. The bruised place was painful but the pain soon passed, and he felt particularly bright and well just then. He wrote: "I feel fifteen years younger." He thought he would have everything ready by September, but it dragged on till mid-October. But the result was charming not only in his eyes but to everyone who saw it.

In reality it was just what is usually seen in the houses of people of moderate means who want to appear rich, and therefore succeed only in resembling others like themselves: there were damasks, dark wood, plants, rugs, and dull and polished bronzes—all the things people of a certain class have in order to resemble other people of that class. His house was so like the others that it would never have been noticed, but to him it all seemed to be quite exceptional. He was very happy when he met his family at the station and brought them to the newly furnished house all lit up, where a footman in a white tie opened the door into the hall decorated with plants, and when they went on into the drawing room and the study uttering exclamations of delight. He conducted them everywhere, drank in their praises eagerly, and beamed with pleasure. At tea that evening, when Praskóvya Fëdorovna among other things asked him about his fall, he laughed and showed them how he had gone flying and had frightened the upholsterer.

"It's a good thing I'm a bit of an athlete. Another man might have been killed, but I merely knocked myself, just here; it hurts when it's touched, but it's passing off already—it's only a bruise."

So they began living in their new home—in which, as always happens, when they got thoroughly settled in they found they were just one room short—and with the increased income, which as always was just a little (some five hundred rubles) too little, but it was all very nice.

Things went particularly well at first, before everything was finally arranged and while something had still to be done: this thing bought, that thing ordered, another thing moved, and something else adjusted. Though there were some disputes between husband and wife, they were both so well satisfied and had so much to do that it all passed off without any serious quarrels. When nothing was left to arrange it became rather dull and something seemed to be lacking, but they were then making acquaintances, forming habits, and life was growing fuller.

Iván Ilých spent his mornings at the law court and came home to dinner, and at first he was generally in a good humour, though he occasionally became irritable just on account of his house. (Every spot on the tablecloth or the upholstery, and every broken window-blind string, irritated him. He had devoted so much trouble to arranging it all that every disturbance of it distressed him.) But on the whole his life ran its course as he believed life should do: easily, pleasantly, and decorously.

He got up at nine, drank his coffee, read the paper, and then put on his undress uniform and went to the law courts. There the harness in which he worked had already been stretched to fit him and he donned it without a hitch: petitioners, inquiries at the chancery, the chancery itself, and the sittings public and administrative. In all this the thing was to exclude everything fresh and vital, which always disturbs the regular course of official business, and to admit only official relations with people, and then only on official grounds. A man would come, for instance, wanting some information. Iván Ilých, as one in whose sphere the matter did not lie, would have nothing to do with him: but if the man had some business with him in his official capacity, something that could be expressed on officially stamped paper, he would do everything, positively everything he could within the limits of such relations, and in doing so would maintain the semblance of friendly human relations, that is, would observe the courtesies of life. As soon as the official relations ended, so did everything else. Iván Ilých possessed this capacity to separate his real life from the official side of affairs and not mix the two, in the highest degree, and by long practice and natural aptitude had brought it to such a pitch that sometimes, in the manner of a virtuoso, he would even allow himself to let the human and official relations mingle. He let himself do this just because he felt that he could at any time he chose resume the strictly official attitude again and drop the human relation. And he did it all easily, pleasantly, correctly, and even artistically. In the intervals between the sessions he smoked, drank tea, chatted a little about politics, a little about general topics, a little about cards, but most of all about official appointments. Tired, but with the feelings of a virtuoso—one of the first violins who has played his part in an orchestra with precision—he would return home to find that his wife and daughter had been out paying calls, or had a visitor, and that his son had been to school, had done his homework with his tutor, and was duly learning what is taught at High Schools. Everything was as it should be. After dinner, if they had no visitors, Iván Ilých sometimes read a book that was being much discussed at the time, and in the evening settled down to work, that is, read official papers, compared the depositions of witnesses, and noted paragraphs of the Code applying to them. This was neither dull nor amusing. It was dull when he might have been playing bridge, but if no bridge was available it was at any rate better than doing nothing or sitting with his wife. Iván Ilých's chief pleasure was giving little dinners to which he invited men and women of good social position, and just as his drawing-room resembled all other drawing-rooms so did his enjoyable little parties resemble all other such parties.

Once they even gave a dance. Iván Ilých enjoyed it and everything went off well, except that it led to a violent quarrel with his wife about the cakes and sweets. Praskóvya Fëdorovna had made her own plans, but Iván Ilých insisted on getting everything from an expensive confectioner and ordered too many cakes, and the quarrel occurred because some of those cakes were left over and the confectioner's bill came to forty-five rubles. It was a great and disagreeable quarrel. Praskóvya Fëdorovna called him "a fool and an imbecile," and he clutched at his head and made angry allusions to divorce.

But the dance itself had been enjoyable. The best people were there, and Iván Ilých had danced with Princess Trúfonova, a sister of the distinguished founder of the Society "Bear My Burden."

The pleasures connected with his work were pleasures of ambition; his social pleasures were those of vanity; but Iván Ilých's greatest pleasure was playing bridge. He acknowledged that whatever disagreeable incident happened in his life, the pleasure that beamed like a ray of light above everything else was to sit down to bridge with good players, not noisy partners, and of course to four-handed bridge (with five players it was annoying to have to stand out, though one pretended not to mind), to play a clever and serious game (when the cards allowed it) and then to have supper and drink a glass of wine. After a game of bridge, especially if he had won a little (to win a large sum was unpleasant), Iván Ilých went to bed in specially good humour.

So they lived. They formed a circle of acquaintances among the best people and were visited by people of importance and by young folk. In their views as to their acquaintances, husband, wife and daughter were entirely agreed, and tacitly and unanimously kept at arm's length and shook off the various shabby friends and relations who, with much show of affection, gushed into the drawing-room with its Japanese plates on the walls. Soon these shabby friends ceased to obtrude themselves and only the best people remained in the Golovíns' set.

Young men made up to Lisa, and Petríshchev, an examining magistrate and Dmítri Ivanovich Petríshchev's son and sole heir, began to be so attentive to her that Iván Ilých had already spoken to Praskóvya Fëdorovna about it, and considered whether they should not arrange a party for them or get up some private theatricals.

So they lived, and all went well, without change, and life flowed pleasantly.

110

CHAPTER IV

They were all in good health. It could not be called ill health if Iván Ilých sometimes said that he had a queer taste in his mouth and felt some discomfort in his left side.

But this discomfort increased and, though not exactly painful, grew into a sense of pressure in his side accompanied by ill humour. And his irritability became worse and worse and began to mar the agreeable, easy, and correct life that had established itself in the Golovín family. Quarrels between husband and wife became more and more frequent, and soon the ease and amenity disappeared and even the decorum was barely maintained. Scenes again became frequent, and very few of those islets remained on which husband and wife could meet without explosion. Praskóvya Fëdorovna now had good reason to say that her husband's temper was trying. With characteristic exaggeration she said he had always had a dreadful temper, and that it had needed all her good nature to put up with it for twenty years. It was true that now the quarrels were started by him. His bursts of temper always came just before dinner, often just as he began to eat his soup. Sometimes he noticed that a plate or dish was chipped, or the food was not right, or his son put his elbow on the table, or his daughter's hair was not done as he liked it, and for all this he blamed Praskóvya Fëdorovna. At first she retorted and said disagreeable things to him, but once or twice he fell into such a rage at the beginning of dinner that she realized it was due to some physical derangement brought on by taking food, and so she restrained herself and did not answer, but only hurried to get the dinner over. She regarded this self-restraint as highly praiseworthy. Having come to the conclusion that her husband had a dreadful temper and made her life miserable, she began to feel sorry for herself, and the more she pitied herself the more she hated her husband. She began to wish he would die; yet she did not want him to die because then his salary would cease. And this irritated her against him still more. She considered herself dreadfully unhappy just because not even his death could save her, and though she concealed her exasperation, that hidden exasperation of hers increased his irritation also.

After one scene in which Iván Ilých had been particularly unfair and after which he had said in explanation that he certainly was irritable but that it was due to his not being well, she said that if he was ill it should be attended to, and insisted on his going to see a celebrated doctor.

He went. Everything took place as he had expected and as it always does. There was the usual waiting and the important air assumed by the doctor, with which he was so familiar (resembling that which he himself assumed in court), and the sounding and listening, and the questions which called for answers that were foregone conclusions and were evidently unnecessary, and the look of importance which implied that "if only you put yourself in our hands we will arrange everything—we know indubitably how it has to be done, always in the same way for everybody alike." It was all just as it was in the law courts. The doctor put on just the same air towards him as he himself put on towards an accused person.

The doctor said that so-and-so indicated that there was so-and-so inside the patient, but if the investigation of so-and-so did not confirm this, then he must assume that and that. If he assumed that and that, then . . . and so on. To Iván Ilých only one question was important: was his case serious or not? But the doctor ignored that inappropriate question. From his point of view it was not the one under consideration, the real question was to decide between a floating kidney, chronic catarrh, or appendicitis. It was not a question of Iván Ilých's life or death, but one between a floating kidney and appendicitis. And that question the doctor solved brilliantly, as it seemed to Iván Ilých, in favour of the appendix, with the reservation that should an examination of the urine give fresh indications the matter would be reconsidered. All this was just what Iván Ilých had himself brilliantly accomplished a thousand times in dealing with men on trial. The doctor summed up just as brilliantly, looking over his spectacles triumphantly and even gaily at the accused. From the doctor's summing up Iván Ilých concluded that things were bad, but that for the doctor, and perhaps for

115

everybody else, it was a matter of indifference, though for him it was bad. And this conclusion struck him painfully, arousing in him a great feeling of pity for himself and of bitterness towards the doctor's indifference to a matter of such importance.

He said nothing of this, but rose, placed the doctor's fee on the table, and remarked with a sigh: "We sick people probably often put inappropriate questions. But tell me, in general, is this complaint dangerous, or not? . . ."

The doctor looked at him sternly over his spectacles with one eye, as if to say: "Prisoner, if you will not keep to the questions put to you, I shall be obliged to have you removed from the court."

"I have already told you what I consider necessary and proper. The analysis may show something more." And the doctor bowed.

Iván Ilých went out slowly, seated himself disconsolately in his sledge, and drove home. All the way home he was going over what the doctor had said, trying to translate those complicated, obscure, scientific phrases into plain language and find in them an answer to the question: "Is my condition bad? Is it very bad? Or is there as yet nothing much wrong?" And it seemed to him that the meaning of what the doctor had said was that it was very bad. Everything in the streets seemed depressing. The cabmen, the houses, the passers-by, and the shops, were dismal. His ache, this dull gnawing ache that never ceased for a moment, seemed to have acquired a new and more serious significance from the doctor's dubious remarks. Iván Ilých now watched it with a new and oppressive feeling.

He reached home and began to tell his wife about it. She listened, but in the middle of his account his daughter came in with her hat on, ready to go out with her mother. She sat down reluctantly to listen to this tedious story, but could not stand it long, and her mother too did not hear him to the end.

"Well, I am very glad," she said. "Mind now to take your medicine regularly. Give me the prescription and I'll send Gerásim to the chemist's." And she went to get ready to go out.

While she was in the room Iván Ilých had hardly taken time to breathe, but he sighed deeply when she left it.

"Well," he thought, "perhaps it isn't so bad after all."

He began taking his medicine and following the doctor's directions, which had been altered after the examination of the urine. But then it happened that there was a contradiction between the indications drawn from the examination of the urine and the symptoms that showed themselves. It turned out that what was happening differed from what the doctor had told him, and that he had either forgotten, or blundered, or hidden something from him. He could not, however, be blamed for that, and Iván Ilých still obeyed his orders implicitly and at first derived some comfort from doing so.

From the time of his visit to the doctor, Iván Ilých's chief occupation was the exact fulfilment of the doctor's instructions regarding hygiene and the taking of medicine, and the observation of his pain and his excretions. His chief interests came to be people's ailments and people's health. When sickness, deaths, or recoveries were mentioned in his presence, especially when the illness resembled his own, he listened with agitation which he tried to hide, asked questions, and applied what he heard to his own case.

The pain did not grow less, but Iván Ilých made efforts to force himself to think that he was better. And he could do this so long as nothing agitated him. But as soon as he had any unpleasantness with his wife, any lack of success in his official work, or held bad cards at bridge, he was at once acutely sensible of his disease. He had formerly borne such mischances, hoping soon to adjust what was wrong, to master it and attain success, or make a grand slam. But now every mischance upset him and plunged him into despair. He would say to himself: "There now, just as I was beginning to get better and the medicine had begun to take effect, comes this accursed misfortune, or unpleasantness. . . ." And he was furious with the mishap, or with the people who were causing the unpleasantness and killing him, for he felt that this fury was killing him but could not restrain it. One would have thought that it should have been clear to him that this exasperation with circumstances and people aggravated his illness, and that he ought therefore to ignore unpleasant occurrences. But he drew the very opposite conclusion: he said that he needed peace, and he watched for everything that might disturb it and became irritable at the slightest infringement of it. His condition was rendered worse by the fact that he read medical books and consulted doctors. The progress of his disease was so gradual that he could deceive himself when comparing one day with another—the difference was so slight. But when he consulted the doctors it seemed to him that he was getting worse, and even very rapidly. Yet despite this he was continually consulting them.

That month he went to see another celebrity, who told him almost the same as the first had done but put his questions rather differently, and the interview with this celebrity only increased Iván Ilých's doubts and fears. A friend of a friend of his, a very good doctor, diagnosed his illness again quite differently from the others, and though he predicted recovery, his questions and suppositions bewildered Iván Ilých still more and increased his doubts. A homeopathist diagnosed the disease in yet another way, and prescribed medicine which Iván Ilých took secretly for a week. But after a week, not feeling any improvement and having lost confidence both in the former doctor's treatment and in this one's, he became still more despondent. One day a lady acquaintance mentioned a cure effected by a wonder-working icon. Iván Ilých caught himself listening attentively and beginning to believe that it had occurred. This incident alarmed him. "Has my mind really weakened to such an extent?" he asked himself. "Nonsense! It's all rubbish. I mustn't give way to nervous fears but having chosen a doctor must keep strictly to his treatment. That is what I will do. Now it's all settled. I won't think about it, but will follow the treatment seriously till summer, and then we shall see. From now there must be no more of this wavering!" This was easy to say but impossible to carry out. The pain in his side oppressed him and seemed to grow worse and more incessant, while the taste in his mouth grew stranger and stranger. It seemed to him that his breath had a disgusting smell, and he was conscious of a loss of appetite and strength. There was no deceiving himself: something terrible, new, and more important than anything before in his life, was taking place within him of which he alone was aware. Those about him did not understand or would not understand it, but thought everything in the world was going on as usual. That tormented Iván Ilých more than anything. He saw that his household, especially his wife and daughter who were in a perfect whirl of visiting, did not understand anything of it and were annoyed that he was so depressed and so exacting, as if he were to blame for it. Though they tried to disguise it he saw that he was an obstacle in their path, and that his wife had adopted a definite line in regard to his illness and kept to it regardless of anything he said or did. Her attitude was this: "You know," she would say to her friends, "Iván Ilých can't do as other people do, and keep to the treatment prescribed for him. One day he'll take his drops and keep strictly to his diet and go to bed in good time, but the next day unless I watch him he'll suddenly forget his medicine, eat sturgeon—which is forbidden—and sit up playing cards till one o'clock in the morning."

"Oh, come, when was that?" Iván Ilých would ask in vexation. "Only once at Peter Ivánovich's."

"And yesterday with Shébek."   130

"Well, even if I hadn't stayed up, this pain would have kept me awake."

"Be that as it may you'll never get well like that, but will always make us wretched."

Praskóvya Fëdorovna's attitude to Iván Ilých's illness, as she expressed it both to others and to him, was that it was his own fault and was another of the annoyances he caused her. Iván Ilých felt that this opinion escaped her involuntarily—but that did not make it easier for him.

At the law courts too, Iván Ilých noticed, or thought he noticed, a strange attitude towards himself. It sometimes seemed to him that people were watching him inquisitively as a man whose place might soon be vacant. Then again, his friends would suddenly begin to chaff him in a friendly way about his low spirits, as if the awful, horrible, and unheard-of thing that was going on within him, incessantly gnawing at him and irresistibly drawing him away, was a very agreeable subject for jests. Schwartz in particular irritated him by his jocularity, vivacity, and *savoir-faire*, which reminded him of what he himself had been ten years ago.

Friends came to make up a set and they sat down to cards. They dealt, bend-   135 ing the new cards to soften them, and he sorted the diamonds in his hand and found he had seven. His partner said "No trumps" and supported him with two diamonds. What more could be wished for? It ought to be jolly and lively. They would make a grand slam. But suddenly Iván Ilých was conscious of that gnawing pain, that taste in his mouth, and it seemed ridiculous that in such circumstances he should be pleased to make a grand slam.

He looked at his partner Mikháil Mikháylovich, who rapped the table with his strong hand and instead of snatching up the tricks pushed the cards courteously and indulgently towards Iván Ilých that he might have the pleasure of gathering them up without the trouble of stretching out his hand for them. "Does he think

I am too weak to stretch out my arm?" thought Iván Ilých, and forgetting what he was doing he over-trumped his partner, missing the grand slam by three tricks. And what was most awful of all was that he saw how upset Mikháil Mikháylovich was about it but did not himself care. And it was dreadful to realize why he did not care.

They all saw that he was suffering and said: "We can stop if you are tired. Take a rest." Lie down? No, he was not at all tired, and he finished the rubber. All were gloomy and silent. Iván Ilých felt that he had diffused this gloom over them and could not dispel it. They had supper and went away, and Iván Ilých was left alone with the consciousness that his life was poisoned and was poisoning the lives of others, and that this poison did not weaken but penetrated more and more deeply into his whole being.

With this consciousness, and with physical pain besides the terror, he must go to bed, often to lie awake the greater part of the night. Next morning he had to get up again, dress, go to the law courts, speak, and write; or if he did not go out, spend at home those twenty-four hours a day each of which was a torture. And he had to live thus all alone on the brink of an abyss, with no one who understood or pitied him.

CHAPTER V

So one month passed and then another. Just before the New Year his brother-in-law came to town and stayed at their house. Iván Ilých was at the law courts and Praskóvya Fëdorovna had gone shopping. When Iván Ilých came home and entered his study he found his brother-in-law there—a healthy, florid man—unpacking his portmanteau himself. He raised his head on hearing Iván Ilých's footsteps and looked up at him for a moment without a word. That stare told Iván Ilých everything. His brother-in-law opened his mouth to utter an exclamation of surprise but checked himself, and that action confirmed it all.

"I have changed, eh?"

"Yes, there is a change."

And after that, try as he would to get his brother-in-law to return to the subject of his looks, the latter would say nothing about it. Praskóvya Fëdorovna came home and her brother went out to her. Iván Ilých locked the door and began to examine himself in the glass, first full face, then in profile. He took up a portrait of himself taken with his wife, and compared it with what he saw in the glass. The change in him was immense. Then he bared his arms to the elbow, looked at them, drew the sleeves down again, sat down on an ottoman, and grew blacker than night.

"No, no, this won't do!" he said to himself, and jumped up, went to the table, took up some law papers and began to read them, but could not continue. He unlocked the door and went into the reception-room. The door leading to the drawing room was shut. He approached it on tiptoe and listened.

"No, you are exaggerating!" Praskóvya Fëdorovna was saying.

140

"Exaggerating! Don't you see it? Why, he's a dead man! Look at his eyes— 145
there's no light in them. But what is it that is wrong with him?"

"No one knows. Nikoláevich (that was another doctor) said something, but I
don't know what. And Leshchetítsky (this was the celebrated specialist) said
quite the contrary . . ."

Iván Ilých walked away, went to his own room, lay down, and began musing:
"The kidney, a floating kidney." He recalled all the doctors had told him of how
it detached itself and swayed about. And by an effort of imagination he tried to
catch that kidney and arrest it and support it. So little was needed for this, it
seemed to him. "No, I'll go to see Peter Ivánovich again." (That was the friend
whose friend was a doctor.) He rang, ordered the carriage, and got ready to go.

"Where are you going, Jean?" asked his wife, with a specially sad and exceptionally kind look.

This exceptionally kind look irritated him. He looked morosely at her.

"I must go to see Peter Ivánovich." 150

He went to see Peter Ivánovich, and together they went to see his friend, the
doctor. He was in, and Iván Ilých had a long talk with him.

Reviewing the anatomical and physiological details of what in the doctor's
opinion was going on inside him, he understood it all.

There was something, a small thing, in the vermiform appendix. It might all
come right. Only stimulate the energy of one organ and check the activity of another, then absorption would take place and everything would come right. He got
home rather late for dinner, ate his dinner, and conversed cheerfully, but could
not for a long time bring himself to go back to work in his room. At last, however,
he went to his study and did what was necessary, but the consciousness that he
had put something aside—an important, intimate matter which he would revert
to when his work was done—never left him. When he had finished his work he
remembered that this intimate matter was the thought of his vermiform appendix. But he did not give himself up to it, and went to the drawing-room for tea.
There were callers there, including the examining magistrate who was a desirable
match for his daughter, and they were conversing, playing the piano and singing.
Iván Ilých, as Praskóvya Fëdorovna remarked, spent that evening more cheerfully than usual, but he never for a moment forgot that he had postponed the important matter of the appendix. At eleven o'clock he said good-night and went to
his bedroom. Since his illness he had slept alone in a small room next to his study.
He undressed and took up a novel by Zola, but instead of reading it he fell into
thought, and in his imagination that desired improvement in the vermiform appendix occurred. There was the absorption and evacuation and the reestablish-
ment of normal activity. "Yes, that's it!" he said to himself. "One need only assist
nature, that's all." He remembered his medicine, rose, took it, and lay down on
his back watching for the beneficent action of the medicine and for it to lessen
the pain. "I need only take it regularly and avoid all injurious influences. I am already feeling better, much better." He began touching his side: it was not painful
to the touch. "There, I really don't feel it. It's much better already." He put out

the light and turned on his side . . . "The appendix is getting better, absorption is occurring." Suddenly he felt the old, familiar, dull, gnawing pain, stubborn and serious. There was the same familiar loathsome taste in his mouth. His heart sank and he felt dazed. "My God! My God!" he muttered. "Again, again! and it will never cease." And suddenly the matter presented itself in a quite different aspect. "Vermiform appendix! Kidney!" he said to himself. "It's not a question of appendix or kidney, but of life and . . . death. Yes, life was there and now it is going, going and I cannot stop it. Yes. Why deceive myself? Isn't it obvious to everyone but me that I'm dying, and that it's only a question of weeks, days . . . it may happen this moment. There was light and now there is darkness. I was here and now I'm going there! Where?" A chill came over him, his breathing ceased, and he felt only the throbbing of his heart.

"When I am not, what will there be? There will be nothing. Then where shall I be when I am no more? Can this be dying? No, I don't want to!" He jumped up and tried to light the candle, felt for it with trembling hands, dropped candle and candlestick on the floor, and fell back on his pillow.

"What's the use? It makes no difference," he said to himself, staring with   155
wide-open eyes into the darkness. "Death. Yes, death. And none of them know or wish to know it, and they have no pity for me. Now they are playing." (He heard through the door the distant sound of a song and its accompaniment.) "It's all the same to them, but they will die too! Fools! I first, and they later, but it will be the same for them. And now they are merry . . . the beasts!"

Anger choked him and he was agonizingly, unbearably miserable. "It is impossible that all men have been doomed to suffer this awful horror!" He raised himself.

"Something must be wrong. I must calm myself—must think it all over from the beginning." And he again began thinking. "Yes, the beginning of my illness: I knocked my side, but I was still quite well that day and the next. It hurt a little, then rather more. I saw the doctors, then followed despondency and anguish, more doctors, and I drew nearer to the abyss. My strength grew less and I kept coming nearer and nearer, and now I have wasted away and there is no light in my eyes. I think of the appendix—but this is death! I think of mending the appendix, and all the while here is death! Can it really be death?" Again terror seized him and he gasped for breath. He leant down and began feeling for the matches, pressing with his elbow on the stand beside the bed. It was in his way and hurt him, he grew furious with it, pressed on it still harder, and upset it. Breathless and in despair he fell on his back, expecting death to come immediately.

Meanwhile the visitors were leaving. Praskóvya Fëdorovna was seeing them off. She heard something fall and came in.

"What has happened?"

"Nothing. I knocked it over accidentally."   160

She went out and returned with a candle. He lay there panting heavily, like a man who has run a thousand yards, and stared upwards at her with a fixed look.

"What is it, Jean?"

"No . . . o . . . thing. I upset it." ("Why speak of it? She won't understand," he thought.)

And in truth she did not understand. She picked up the stand, lit his candle, and hurried away to see another visitor off. When she came back he still lay on his back, looking upwards.

"What is it? Do you feel worse?"   165

"Yes."

She shook her head and sat down.

"Do you know, Jean, I think we must ask Leshchetítsky to come and see you here."

This meant calling in the famous specialist, regardless of expense. He smiled malignantly and said "No." She remained a little longer and then went up to him and kissed his forehead.

While she was kissing him he hated her from the bottom of his soul and with   170
difficulty refrained from pushing her away.

"Good-night. Please God you'll sleep."

"Yes."

CHAPTER VI

Iván Ilých saw that he was dying, and he was in continual despair.

In the depth of his heart he knew he was dying, but not only was he not ac-customed to the thought, he simply did not and could not grasp it.

The syllogism he had learnt from Kiezewetter's Logic:[10] "Caius is a man, men   175
are mortal, therefore Caius is mortal," had always seemed to him correct as ap-plied to Caius, but certainly not as applied to himself. That Caius—man in the abstract—was mortal, was perfectly correct, but he was not Caius, not an ab-stract man, but a creature quite, quite separate from all others. He had been little Ványa, with a mamma and a papa; with Mitya and Volódya, and the toys, a coachman and a nurse, afterwards with Kátenka and with all the joys, griefs, and delights of childhood, boyhood, and youth. What did Caius know of the smell of that striped leather ball Ványa had been so fond of? Had Caius kissed his mother's hand like that, and did the silk of her dress rustle so for Caius? Had he rioted like that at school when the pastry was bad? Had Caius been in love like that? Could Caius preside at a session as he did? "Caius really was mortal, and it was right for him to die; but for me, little Ványa, Iván Ilých, with all my thoughts and emotions, it's altogether a different matter. It cannot be that I ought to die. That would be too terrible."

Such was his feeling.

"If I had to die like Caius I should have known it was so. An inner voice would have told me so, but there was nothing of the sort in me and I and all my friends

---

[10] Karl Kiezewetter (1766–1819), author of an outline of logic widely used in Russian schools at the time.

felt that our case was quite different from that of Caius. And now here it is!" he said to himself. "It can't be. It's impossible! But here it is. How is this? How is one to understand it?"

He could not understand it, and tried to drive this false, incorrect, morbid thought away and to replace it by other proper and healthy thoughts. But that thought, and not the thought only but the reality itself, seemed to come and confront him.

And to replace that thought he called up a succession of others, hoping to find in them some support. He tried to get back into the former current of thoughts that had once screened the thought of death from him. But strange to say, all that had formerly shut off, hidden, and destroyed, his consciousness of death, no longer had that effect. Iván Ilých now spent most of his time in attempting to re-establish that old current. He would say to himself: "I will take up my duties again—after all I used to live by them." And banishing all doubts he would go to the law courts, enter into conversation with his colleagues, and sit carelessly as was his wont, scanning the crowd with a thoughtful look and leaning both his emaciated arms on the arms of his oak chair; bending over as usual to a colleague and drawing his papers nearer he would interchange whispers with him, and then suddenly raising his eyes and sitting erect would pronounce certain words and open the proceedings. But suddenly in the midst of those proceedings the pain in his side, regardless of the stage the proceedings had reached, would begin its own gnawing work. Iván Ilých would turn his attention to it and try to drive the thought of it away, but without success. *It* would come and stand before him and look at him, and he would be petrified and the light would die out of his eyes, and he would again begin asking himself whether *It* alone was true. And his colleagues and subordinates would see with surprise and distress that he, the brilliant and subtle judge, was becoming confused and making mistakes. He would shake himself, try to pull himself together, manage somehow to bring the sitting to a close, and return home with the sorrowful consciousness that his judicial labours could not as formerly hide from him what he wanted them to hide, and could not deliver him from *It*. And what was worst of all was that *It* drew his attention to itself not in order to make him take some action but only that he should look at *It*, look it straight in the face: look at it and without doing anything, suffer inexpressibly.

And to save himself from this condition Iván Ilých looked for consolations— 180 new screens—and new screens were found and for a while seemed to save him, but then they immediately fell to pieces or rather became transparent, as if *It* penetrated them and nothing could veil *It*.

In these latter days he would go into the drawing-room he had arranged—that drawing-room where he had fallen and for the sake of which (how bitterly ridiculous it seemed) he had sacrificed his life—for he knew that his illness originated with that knock. He would enter and see that something had scratched the polished table. He would look for the cause of this and find that it was the bronze ornamentation of an album, that had got bent. He would take up the expensive album which he had lovingly arranged, and feel vexed with his daughter and her friends for their untidiness—for the album was torn here and there and some of the photographs turned upside down. He would put it carefully in order and bend the ornamentation back into position. Then it would occur to him to place all those things in another corner of the room, near the plants. He could call the footman, but his daughter or wife would come to help him. They would not agree, and his wife would contradict him, and he would dispute and grow angry. But that was all right, for then he did not think about *It*. *It* was invisible.

But then, when he was moving something himself, his wife would say: "Let the servants do it. You will hurt yourself again." And suddenly *It* would flash through the screen and he would see it. It was just a flash, and he hoped it would disappear, but he would involuntarily pay attention to his side. "It sits there as before, gnawing just the same!" And he could no longer forget *It*, but could distinctly see it looking at him from behind the flowers. "What is it all for?"

"It really is so! I lost my life over that curtain as I might have done when storming a fort. Is that possible? How terrible and how stupid. It can't be true! It can't, but it is."

He would go to his study, lie down, and again be alone with *It*: face to face with *It*. And nothing could be done with *It* except to look at it and shudder.

CHAPTER VII

How it happened it is impossible to say because it came about step by step, unnoticed, but in the third month of Iván Ilých's illness, his wife, his daughter, his son, his acquaintances, the doctors, the servants, and above all he himself, were aware that the whole interest he had for other people was whether he would soon vacate his place, and at last release the living from the discomfort caused by his presence and be himself released from his sufferings.

He slept less and less. He was given opium and hypodermic injections of morphine, but this did not relieve him. The dull depression he experienced in a somnolent condition at first gave him a little relief, but only as something new, afterwards it became as distressing as the pain itself or even more so.

Special foods were prepared for him by the doctors' orders, but all those foods became increasingly distasteful and disgusting to him.

For his excretions also special arrangements had to be made, and this was a torment to him every time—a torment from the uncleanliness, the unseemliness, and the smell, and from knowing that another person had to take part in it.

But just through this most unpleasant matter Iván Ilých obtained comfort. Gerásim, the butler's young assistant, always came in to carry the things out. Gerásim was a clean, fresh peasant lad, grown stout on town food and always cheerful and bright. At first the sight of him, in his clean Russian peasant costume, engaged on that disgusting task embarrassed Iván Ilých.

185

Once when he got up from the commode too weak to draw up his trousers, 190
he dropped into a soft armchair and looked with horror at his bare, enfeebled
thighs with the muscles so sharply marked on them.

Gerásim with a firm light tread, his heavy boots emitting a pleasant smell of
tar and fresh winter air, came in wearing a clean Hessian apron, the sleeves of
his print shirt tucked up over his strong bare young arms; and refraining from
looking at his sick master out of consideration for his feelings, and restraining
the joy of life that beamed from his face, he went up to the commode.

"Gerásim!" said Iván Ilých in a weak voice.

Gerásim started, evidently afraid he might have committed some blunder,
and with a rapid movement turned his fresh, kind, simple young face which just
showed the first downy signs of a beard.

"Yes, sir?"

"That must be very unpleasant for you. You must forgive me. I am helpless." 195

"Oh, why, sir," and Gerásim's eyes beamed and he showed his glistening white
teeth, "what's a little trouble? It's a case of illness with you, sir."

And his deft strong hands did their accustomed task, and he went out of the
room stepping lightly. Five minutes later he as lightly returned.

Iván Ilých was still sitting in the same position in the armchair.

"Gerásim," he said when the latter had replaced the freshly-washed utensil.
"Please come here and help me." Gerásim went up to him. "Lift me up. It is
hard for me to get up, and I have sent Dmítri away."

Gerásim went up to him, grasped his master with his strong arms deftly but 200
gently, in the same way that he stepped—lifted him, supported him with one
hand, and with the other drew up his trousers and would have set him down
again, but Iván Ilých asked to be led to the sofa. Gerásim, without an effort and
without apparent pressure, led him, almost lifting him, to the sofa and placed
him on it.

"Thank you. How easily and well you do it all!"

Gerásim smiled again and turned to leave the room. But Iván Ilých felt his
presence such a comfort that he did not want to let him go.

"One thing more, please move up that chair. No, the other one—under my
feet. It is easier for me when my feet are raised."

Gerásim brought the chair, set it down gently in place, and raised Iván Ilých's
legs on to it. It seemed to Iván Ilých that he felt better while Gerásim was holding up his legs.

"It's better when my legs are higher," he said. "Place that cushion under 205
them."

Gerásim did so. He again lifted the legs and placed them, and again Iván
Ilých felt better while Gerásim held his legs. When he set them down Iván Ilých
fancied he felt worse.

"Gerásim," he said. "Are you busy now?"

"Not at all, sir," said Gerásim, who had learnt from the townsfolk how to
speak to gentlefolk.

"What have you still to do?"

"What have I to do? I've done everything except chopping the logs for to-   210
morrow."

"Then hold my legs up a bit higher, can you?"

"Of course I can. Why not?" And Gerásim raised his master's legs higher and
Iván Ilých thought that in that position he did not feel any pain at all.

"And how about the logs?"

"Don't trouble about that, sir. There's plenty of time."

Iván Ilých told Gerásim to sit down and hold his legs, and began to talk to   215
him. And strange to say it seemed to him that he felt better while Gerásim held
his legs up.

After that Iván Ilých would sometimes call Gerásim and get him to hold his
legs on his shoulders, and he liked talking to him. Gerásim did it all easily, willingly, simply, and with a good nature that touched Iván Ilých. Health, strength,
and vitality in other people were offensive to him, but Gerásim's strength and vitality did not mortify but soothed him.

What tormented Iván Ilých most was the deception, the lie, which for some
reason they all accepted, that he was not dying but was simply ill, and that he
only need keep quiet and undergo a treatment and then something very good
would result. He however knew that do what they would nothing would come
of it, only still more agonizing suffering and death. This deception tortured
him—their not wishing to admit what they all knew and what he knew, but
wanting to lie to him concerning his terrible condition, and wishing and forcing
him to participate in that lie. Those lies—lies enacted over him on the eve of his
death and destined to degrade this awful, solemn act to the level of their visit-
ings, their curtains, their sturgeon for dinner—were a terrible agony for Iván
Ilých. And strangely enough, many times when they were going through their
antics over him he had been within a hairbreadth of calling out to them: "Stop
lying! You know and I know that I am dying. Then at least stop lying about it!"
But he had never had the spirit to do it. The awful, terrible act of his dying was,
he could see, reduced by those about him to the level of a casual, unpleasant,
and almost indecorous incident (as if someone entered a drawing-room diffus-
ing an unpleasant odour) and this was done by that very decorum which he had
served all his life long. He saw that no one felt for him, because no one even
wished to grasp his position. Only Gerásim recognized it and pitied him. And so
Iván Ilých felt at ease only with him. He felt comforted when Gerásim supported his legs (sometimes all night long) and refused to go to bed, saying,
"Don't you worry, Iván Ilých. I'll get sleep enough later on," or when he suddenly became familiar and exclaimed: "If you weren't sick it would be another
matter, but as it is, why should I grudge a little trouble?" Gerásim alone did not
lie; everything showed that he alone understood the facts of the case and did not
consider it necessary to disguise them, but simply felt sorry for his emaciated
and enfeebled master. Once when Iván Ilých was sending him away he even said
straight out: "We shall all of us die, so why should I grudge a little trouble?"—

expressing the fact that he did not think his work burdensome, because he was doing it for a dying man and hoped someone would do the same for him when his time came.

Apart from this lying, or because of it, what most tormented Iván Ilých was that no one pitied him as he wished to be pitied. At certain moments after prolonged suffering he wished most of all (though he would have been ashamed to confess it) for someone to pity him as a sick child is pitied. He longed to be petted and comforted. He knew he was an important functionary, that he had a beard turning grey, and that therefore what he longed for was impossible, but still he longed for it. And in Gerásim's attitude towards him there was something akin to what he wished for, and so that attitude comforted him. Iván Ilých wanted to weep, wanted to be petted and cried over, and then his colleague Shébek would come, and instead of weeping and being petted, Iván Ilých would assume a serious, severe, and profound air, and by force of habit would express his opinion on a decision of the Court of Cassation and would stubbornly insist on that view. This falsity around him and within him did more than anything else to poison his last days.

CHAPTER VIII

It was morning. He knew it was morning because Gerásim had gone, and Peter the footman had come and put out the candles, drawn back one of the curtains, and begun quietly to tidy up. Whether it was morning or evening, Friday or Sunday, made no difference, it was all just the same: the gnawing, unmitigated, agonizing pain, never ceasing for an instant, the consciousness of life inexorably waning but not yet extinguished, that approach of that ever dreaded and hateful Death which was the only reality, and always the same falsity. What were days, weeks, hours, in such a case?

"Will you have some tea, sir?"   220

"He wants things to be regular, and wishes the gentlefolk to drink tea in the morning," thought Iván Ilých, and only said "No."

"Wouldn't you like to move onto the sofa, sir?"

"He wants to tidy up the room, and I'm in the way. I am uncleanliness and disorder," he thought, and said only:

"No, leave me alone."

The man went on bustling about. Iván Ilých stretched out his hand. Peter   225
came up, ready to help.

"What is it, sir?"

"My watch."

Peter took the watch which was close at hand and gave it to his master.

"Half-past eight. Are they up?"

"No, sir, except Vladímir Ivánich" (the son) "who has gone to school.   230
Praskóvya Fëdorovna ordered me to wake her if you asked for her. Shall I do so?"

"No, there's no need to." "Perhaps I'd better have some tea," he thought, and added aloud: "Yes, bring me some tea."

Peter went to the door but Iván Ilých dreaded being left alone. "How can I keep him here? Oh yes, my medicine." "Peter, give me my medicine." "Why not? Perhaps it may still do me some good." He took a spoonful and swallowed it. "No, it won't help. It's all tomfoolery, all deception," he decided as soon as he became aware of the familiar, sickly, hopeless taste. "No, I can't believe in it any longer. But the pain, why this pain? If it would only cease just for a moment!" And he moaned. Peter turned towards him. "It's all right. Go and fetch me some tea."

Peter went out. Left alone Iván Ilých groaned not so much with pain, terrible though that was, as from mental anguish. Always and for ever the same, always these endless days and nights. If only it would come quicker! If only *what* would come quicker? Death, darkness? . . . No, no! Anything rather than death!

When Peter returned with the tea on a tray, Iván Ilých stared at him for a time in perplexity, not realizing who and what he was. Peter was disconcerted by that look and his embarrassment brought Iván Ilých to himself.

"Oh, tea! All right, put it down. Only help me to wash and put on a clean shirt."

And Iván Ilých began to wash. With pauses for rest, he washed his hands and then his face, cleaned his teeth, brushed his hair, and looked in the glass. He was terrified by what he saw, especially by the limp way in which his hair clung to his pallid forehead.

While his shirt was being changed he knew that he would be still more frightened at the sight of his body, so he avoided looking at it. Finally he was ready. He drew on a dressing-gown, wrapped himself in a plaid, and sat down in the armchair to take his tea. For a moment he felt refreshed, but as soon as he began to drink the tea he was again aware of the same taste, and the pain also returned. He finished it with an effort, and then lay down stretching out his legs, and dismissed Peter.

Always the same. Now a spark of hope flashes up, then a sea of despair rages, and always pain; always pain, always despair, and always the same. When alone he had a dreadful and distressing desire to call someone, but he knew beforehand that with others present it would be still worse. "Another dose of morphine—to lose consciousness. I will tell him, the doctor, that he must think of something else. It's impossible, impossible, to go on like this."

An hour and another pass like that. But now there is a ring at the door bell. Perhaps it's the doctor? It is. He comes in fresh, hearty, plump, and cheerful, with that look on his face that seems to say: "There now, you're in a panic about something, but we'll arrange it all for you directly!" The doctor knows this expression is out of place here, but he has put it on once for all and can't take it off—like a man who has put on a frock-coat in the morning to pay a round of calls.

The doctor rubs his hands vigorously and reassuringly.

"Brr! How cold it is! There's such a sharp frost; just let me warm myself!" he says, as if it were only a matter of waiting till he was warm, and then he would put everything right.

"Well now, how are you?"

Iván Ilých feels that the doctor would like to say: "Well, how are our affairs?" but that even he feels that this would not do, and says instead: "What sort of a night have you had?"

Iván Ilých looks at him as much as to say: "Are you really never ashamed of lying?" But the doctor does not wish to understand this question, and Iván Ilých says: "Just as terrible as ever. The pain never leaves me and never subsides. If only something . . ."

"Yes, you sick people are always like that. . . . There, now I think I am warm   245
enough. Even Praskóvya Fëdorovna, who is so particular, could find no fault with my temperature. Well, now I can say good-morning," and the doctor presses his patient's hand.

Then, dropping his former playfulness, he begins with a most serious face to examine the patient, feeling his pulse and taking his temperature, and then begins the sounding and auscultation.

Iván Ilých knows quite well and definitely that all this is nonsense and pure deception, but when the doctor, getting down on his knee, leans over him, putting his ear first higher then lower, and performs various gymnastic movements over him with a significant expression on his face, Iván Ilých submits to it all as he used to submit to the speeches of the lawyers, though he knew very well that they were all lying and why they were lying.

The doctor, kneeling on the sofa, is still sounding him when Praskóvya Fëdorovna's silk dress rustles at the door and she is heard scolding Peter for not having let her know of the doctor's arrival.

She comes in, kisses her husband, and at once proceeds to prove that she has been up a long time already, and only owing to a misunderstanding failed to be there when the doctor arrived.

Iván Ilých looks at her, scans her all over, sets against her the whiteness and   250
plumpness and cleanness of her hands and neck, the gloss of her hair, and the sparkle of her vivacious eyes. He hates her with his whole soul. And the thrill of hatred he feels for her makes him suffer from her touch.

Her attitude towards him and his disease is still the same. Just as the doctor had adopted a certain relation to his patient which he could not abandon, so had she formed one towards him—that he was not doing something he ought to do and was himself to blame, and that she reproached him lovingly for this—and she could not now change that attitude.

"You see he doesn't listen to me and doesn't take his medicine at the proper time. And above all he lies in a position that is no doubt bad for him—with his legs up."

She described how he made Gerásim hold his legs up.

The doctor smiled with a contemptuous affability that said: "What's to be done? These sick people do have foolish fancies of that kind, but we must forgive them."

When the examination was over the doctor looked at his watch, and then 255 Praskóvya Fëdorovna announced to Iván Ilých that it was of course as he pleased, but she had sent to-day for a celebrated specialist who would examine him and have a consultation with Michael Danílovich (their regular doctor).

"Please don't raise any objections. I am doing this for my own sake," she said ironically, letting it be felt that she was doing it all for his sake and only said this to leave him no right to refuse. He remained silent, knitting his brows. He felt that he was so surrounded and involved in a mesh of falsity that it was hard to unravel anything.

Everything she did for him was entirely for her own sake, and she told him she was doing for herself what she actually was doing for herself, as if that was so incredible that he must understand the opposite.

At half-past eleven the celebrated specialist arrived. Again the sounding began and the significant conversations in his presence and in another room, about the kidneys and the appendix, and the questions and answers, with such an air of importance that again, instead of the real question of life and death which now alone confronted him, the question arose of the kidney and appendix which were not behaving as they ought to and would now be attacked by Michael Danílovich and the specialist and forced to amend their ways.

The celebrated specialist took leave of him with a serious though not hopeless look, and in reply to the timid question Iván Ilých, with eyes glistening with fear and hope, put to him as to whether there was a chance of recovery, said that he could not vouch for it but there was a possibility. The look of hope with which Iván Ilých watched the doctor out was so pathetic that Praskóvya Fëdorovna, seeing it, even wept as she left the room to hand the doctor his fee.

The gleam of hope kindled by the doctor's encouragement did not last long. 260 The same room, the same pictures, curtains, wall-paper, medicine bottles, were all there, and the same aching suffering body, and Iván Ilých began to moan. They gave him a subcutaneous injection and he sank into oblivion.

It was twilight when he came to. They brought him his dinner and he swallowed some beef tea with difficulty, and then everything was the same again and night was coming on.

After dinner, at seven o'clock, Praskóvya Fëdorovna came into the room in evening dress, her full bosom pushed up by her corset, and with traces of powder on her face. She had reminded him in the morning that they were going to the theater. Sarah Bernhardt was visiting the town and they had a box, which he had insisted on their taking. Now he had forgotten about it and her toilet offended him, but he concealed his vexation when he remembered that he had himself insisted on their securing a box and going because it would be an instructive and aesthetic pleasure for the children.

Praskóvya Fëdorovna came in, self-satisfied but yet with a rather guilty air. She sat down and asked how he was, but, as he saw, only for the sake of asking and not in order to learn about it, knowing that there was nothing to learn—and then went on to what she really wanted to say: that she would not on any account have gone but that the box had been taken and Helen and their daughter were going, as well as Petríshchev (the examining magistrate, their daughter's fiancé) and that it was out of the question to let them go alone; but that she would have much preferred to sit with him for a while; and he must be sure to follow the doctor's orders while she was away.

"Oh, and Fëdor Petróvich" (the fiancé) "would like to come in. May he? And Lisa?"

"All right." 265

Their daughter came in in full evening dress, her fresh young flesh exposed (making a show of that very flesh which in his own case caused so much suffering), strong, healthy, evidently in love, and impatient with illness, suffering, and death, because they interfered with her happiness.

Fëdor Petróvich came in too, in evening dress, his hair curled *á la Capoul*, a tight stiff collar round his long sinewy neck, an enormous white shirt-front and narrow black trousers tightly stretched over his strong thighs. He had one white glove tightly drawn on, and was holding his opera hat in his hand.

Following him the schoolboy crept in unnoticed, in a new uniform, poor little fellow, and wearing gloves. Terribly dark shadows showed under his eyes, the meaning of which Iván Ilých knew well.

His son had always seemed pathetic to him, and now it was dreadful to see the boy's frightened look of pity. It seemed to Iván Ilých that Vásya was the only one besides Gerásim who understood and pitied him.

They all sat down and again asked how he was. A silence followed. Lisa asked 270 her mother about the opera-glasses, and there was an altercation between mother and daughter as to who had taken them and where they had been put. This occasioned some unpleasantness.

Fëdor Petróvich inquired of Iván Ilých whether he had ever seen Sarah Bernhardt. Iván Ilých did not at first catch the question, but then replied: "No, have you seen her before?"

"Yes, in *Adrienne Lecouvreur*."[11]

Praskóvya Fëdorovna mentioned some roles in which Sarah Bernhardt was particularly good. Her daughter disagreed. Conversation sprang up as to the elegance and realism of her acting—the sort of conversation that is always repeated and is always the same.

In the midst of the conversation Fëdor Petróvich glanced at Iván Ilých and became silent. The others also looked at him and grew silent. Iván Ilých was staring with glittering eyes straight before him, evidently indignant with them. This had to be rectified, but it was impossible to do so. The silence had to be broken, but for a time no one dared to break it and they all became afraid that the conventional deception would suddenly become obvious and the truth become plain to all. Lisa was the first to pluck up courage and break that silence, but by trying to hide what everybody was feeling, she betrayed it.

"Well, if we are going it's time to start," she said, looking at her watch, a pres- 275

---

[11] A play by the French dramatist Eugène Scribe (1791–1861).

ent from her father, and with a faint and significant smile at Fëdor Petróvich relating to something known only to them. She got up with a rustle of her dress.

They all rose, said good-night, and went away.

When they had gone it seemed to Iván Ilých that he felt better; the falsity had gone with them. But the pain remained—that same pain and that same fear that made everything monotonously alike, nothing harder and nothing easier. Everything was worse.

Again minute followed minute and hour followed hour. Everything remained the same and there was no cessation. And the inevitable end of it all became more and more terrible.

"Yes, send Gerásim here," he replied to a question Peter asked.

CHAPTER IX

His wife returned late at night. She came in on tiptoe, but he heard her, opened   280
his eyes, and made haste to close them again. She wished to send Gerásim away and to sit with him herself, but he opened his eyes and said: "No, go away."

"Are you in great pain?"

"Always the same."

"Take some opium."

He agreed and took some. She went away.

Till about three in the morning he was in a state of stupefied misery. It   285
seemed to him that he and his pain were being thrust into a narrow, deep black sack, but though they were pushed further and further in they could not be pushed to the bottom. And this, terrible enough in itself, was accompanied by suffering. He was frightened yet wanted to fall through the sack, he struggled but yet co-operated. And suddenly he broke through, fell, and regained consciousness. Gerásim was sitting at the foot of the bed dozing quietly and patiently, while he himself lay with his emaciated stockinged legs resting on Gerásim's shoulders; the same shaded candle was there and the same unceasing pain.

"Go away, Gerásim," he whispered.

"It's all right, sir. I'll stay a while."

"No. Go away."

He removed his legs from Gerásim's shoulders, turned sideways onto his arm, and felt sorry for himself. He only waited till Gerásim had gone into the next room and then restrained himself no longer but wept like a child. He wept on account of his helplessness, his terrible loneliness, the cruelty of man, the cruelty of God, and the absence of God.

"Why hast Thou done all this? Why hast Thou brought me here? Why, why   290
dost Thou torment me so terribly?"

He did not expect an answer and yet wept because there was no answer and could be none. The pain again grew more acute, but he did not stir and did not call. He said to himself: "Go on! Strike me! But what is it for? What have I done to Thee? What is it for?"

Then he grew quiet and not only ceased weeping but even held his breath and became all attention. It was as though he were listening not to an audible voice but to the voice of his soul, to the current of thoughts arising within him.

"What is it you want?" was the first clear conception capable of expression in words, that he heard.

"What do you want? What do you want?" he repeated to himself.

"What do I want? To live and not to suffer," he answered.   295

And again he listened with such concentrated attention that even his pain did not distract him.

"To live? How?" asked his inner voice.

"Why, to live as I used to—well and pleasantly."

"As you lived before, well and pleasantly?" the voice repeated.

And in imagination he began to recall the best moments of his pleasant life.   300
But strange to say none of those best moments of his pleasant life now seemed at all what they had then seemed—none of them except the first recollections of childhood. There, in childhood, there had been something really pleasant with which it would be possible to live if it could return. But the child who had ex- perienced that happiness existed no longer, it was like a reminiscence of some- body else.

As soon as the period began which had produced the present Iván Ilých, all that had then seemed joys now melted before his sight and turned into some- thing trivial and often nasty.

And the further he departed from childhood and the nearer he came to the present the more worthless and doubtful were the joys. This began with the School of Law. A little that was really good was still found there—there was light-heartedness, friendship, and hope. But in the upper classes there had al- ready been fewer of such good moments. Then during the first years of his offi- cial career, when he was in the service of the Governor, some pleasant moments again occurred: they were the memories of love for a woman. Then all became confused and there was still less of what was good; later on again there was still less that was good, and the further he went the less there was. His marriage, a mere accident, then the disenchantment that followed it, his wife's bad breath and the sensuality and hypocrisy: then that deadly official life and those preoc- cupations about money, a year of it, and two, and ten, and twenty, and always the same thing. And the longer it lasted the more deadly it became. "It is as if I had been going downhill while I imagined I was going up. And that is really what it was. I was going up in public opinion, but to the same extent life was ebbing away from me. And now it is all done and there is only death."

"Then what does it mean? Why? It can't be that life is so senseless and horrible. But if it really has been so horrible and senseless, why must I die and die in agony? There is something wrong!"

"Maybe I did not live as I ought to have done," it suddenly occurred to him. "But how could that be, when I did everything properly?" he replied, and im- mediately dismissed from his mind this, the sole solution of all the riddles of life and death, as something quite impossible.

"Then what do you want now? To live? Live how? Live as you lived in the law 305
courts when the usher proclaimed 'The judge is coming!' " "The judge is coming, the judge!" he repeated to himself. "Here he is, the judge. But I am not
guilty!" he exclaimed angrily. "What is it for?" And he ceased crying, but turning his face to the wall continued to ponder on the same question: Why, and for
what purpose, is there all this horror? But however much he pondered he found
no answer. And whenever the thought occurred to him, as it often did, that it all
resulted from his not having lived as he ought to have done, he at once recalled
the correctness of his whole life and dismissed so strange an idea.

CHAPTER X

Another fortnight passed. Iván Ilých now no longer left his sofa. He would not
lie in bed but lay on the sofa, facing the wall nearly all the time. He suffered
ever the same unceasing agonies and in his loneliness pondered always on the
same insoluble question: "What is this? Can it be that it is Death?" And the inner voice answered: "Yes, it is Death."

"Why these sufferings?" And the voice answered, "For no reason—they just
are so." Beyond and besides this there was nothing.

From the very beginning of his illness, ever since he had first been to see the
doctor, Iván Ilých's life had been divided between two contrary and alternating
moods: now it was despair and the expectation of this uncomprehended and terrible death, and now hope and an intently interested observation of the functioning of his organs. Now before his eyes there was only a kidney or an
intestine that temporarily evaded its duty, and now only that incomprehensible
and dreadful death from which it was impossible to escape.

These two states of mind had alternated from the very beginning of his illness, but the further it progressed the more doubtful and fantastic became the
conception of the kidney, and the more real the sense of impending death.

He had but to call to mind what he had been three months before and what 310
he was now, to call to mind with what regularity he had been going downhill, for
every possibility of hope to be shattered.

Latterly during that loneliness in which he found himself as he lay facing the
back of the sofa, a loneliness in the midst of a populous town and surrounded by
numerous acquaintances and relations but that yet could not have been more
complete anywhere—either at the bottom of the sea or under the earth—during that terrible loneliness Iván Ilých had lived only in memories of the past.
Pictures of his past rose before him one after another. They always began with
what was nearest in time and then went back to what was most remote—to his
childhood—and rested there. If he thought of the stewed prunes that had been
offered him that day, his mind went back to the raw shrivelled French plums of
his childhood, their peculiar flavor and the flow of saliva when he sucked their
stones, and along with the memory of that taste came a whole series of memories of those days: his nurse, his brother, and their toys. "No, I mustn't think of
that. . . . It is too painful," Iván Ilých said to himself, and brought himself back

to the present—to the button on the back of the sofa and the creases in its morocco. "Morocco is expensive, but it does not wear well: There had been a quarrel about it. It was a different kind of quarrel and a different kind of morocco that time when we tore father's portfolio and were punished, and mamma brought us some tarts. . . ." And again his thoughts dwelt on his childhood, and again it was painful and he tried to banish them and fix his mind on something else.

Then again together with that chain of memories another series passed through his mind—of how his illness had progressed and grown worse. There also the further back he looked the more life there had been. There had been more of what was good in life and more of life itself. The two merged together. "Just as the pain went on getting worse and worse so my life grew worse and worse," he thought. "There is one bright spot there at the back, at the beginning of life, and afterwards all becomes blacker and blacker and proceeds more and more rapidly—in inverse ratio to the square of the distance from death," thought Iván Ilých. And the example of a stone falling downwards with increasing velocity entered his mind. Life, a series of increasing sufferings, flies, further and further towards its end—the most terrible suffering. "I am flying. . . ." He shuddered, shifted himself, and tried to resist, but was already aware that resistance was impossible, and again with eyes weary of gazing but unable to cease seeing what was before them, he stared at the back of the sofa and waited—awaiting that dreadful fall and shock and destruction.

"Resistance is impossible!" he said to himself. "If I could only understand what it is all for! But that too is impossible. An explanation would be possible if it could be said that I have not lived as I ought to. But it is impossible to say that," and he remembered all the legality, correctitude, and propriety of his life. "That at any rate can certainly not be admitted," he thought, and his lips smiled ironically as if someone could see that smile and be taken in by it. "There is no explanation! Agony, death. . . . What for?"

CHAPTER XI

Another two weeks went by in this way and during that fortnight an event occurred that Iván Ilých and his wife had desired. Petríshchev formally proposed. It happened in the evening. The next day Praskóvya Fëdorovna came into her husband's room considering how best to inform him of it, but that very night there had been a fresh change for the worse in his condition. She found him still lying on the sofa but in a different position. He lay on his back, groaning and staring fixedly straight in front of him.

She began to remind him of his medicines, but he turned his eyes towards 315 her with such a look that she did not finish what she was saying; so great an animosity, to her in particular, did that look express.

"For Christ's sake, let me die in peace!" he said.

She would have gone away, but just then their daughter came in and went up to say good morning. He looked at her as he had done at his wife, and in reply to her inquiry about his health said dryly that he would soon free them all of himself. They were both silent and after sitting with him for a while went away.

"Is it our fault?" Lisa said to her mother. "It's as if we were to blame! I am sorry for papa, but why should we be tortured?"

The doctor came at his usual time. Iván Ilých answered "Yes" and "No," never taking his angry eyes from him, and at last said: "You know you can do nothing for me, so leave me alone."

"We can ease your sufferings." 320

"You can't even do that. Let me be."

The doctor went into the drawing-room and told Praskóvya Fëdorovna that the case was very serious and that the only resource left was opium to allay her husband's sufferings, which must be terrible.

It was true, as the doctor said, that Iván Ilých's physical sufferings were terrible, but worse than the physical sufferings were his mental sufferings which were his chief torture.

His mental sufferings were due to the fact that that night, as he looked at Gerásim's sleepy, good-natured face with its prominent cheek-bones, the question suddenly occurred to him: "What if my whole life has really been wrong?"

It occurred to him that what had appeared perfectly impossible before, 325 namely that he had not spent his life as he should have done, might after all be true. It occurred to him that his scarcely perceptible attempts to struggle against what was considered good by the most highly placed people, those scarcely noticeable impulses which he had immediately suppressed, might have been the real thing, and all the rest false. And his professional duties and the whole arrangement of his life and of his family, and all his social and official interests, might all have been false. He tried to defend all those things to himself and suddenly felt the weakness of what he was defending. There was nothing to defend.

"But if that is so," he said to himself, "and I am leaving this life with the consciousness that I have lost all that was given me and it is impossible to rectify it—what then?"

He lay on his back and began to pass his life in review in quite a new way. In the morning when he saw first his footman, then his wife, then his daughter, and then the doctor, their every word and movement confirmed to him the awful truth that had been revealed to him during the night. In them he saw himself—all that for which he had lived—and saw clearly that it was not real at all, but a terrible and huge deception which had hidden both life and death. This consciousness intensified his physical suffering tenfold. He groaned and tossed about, and pulled at his clothing which choked and stifled him. And he hated them on that account.

He was given a large dose of opium and became unconscious, but at noon his sufferings began again. He drove everybody away and tossed from side to side.

His wife came to him and said:

"Jean, my dear, do this for me. It can't do any harm and often helps. Healthy 330 people often do it."

He opened his eyes wide.

"What? Take communion? Why? It's unnecessary! However. . . ."

She began to cry.

"Yes, do, my dear. I'll send for our priest. He is such a nice man."

"All right. Very well," he muttered.   335

When the priest came and heard his confession, Iván Ilých was softened and seemed to feel a relief from his doubts and consequently from his sufferings, and for a moment there came a ray of hope. He again began to think of the vermiform appendix and the possibility of correcting it. He received the sacrament with tears in his eyes.

When they laid him down again afterwards he felt a moment's ease, and the hope that he might live awoke in him again. He began to think of the operation that had been suggested to him. "To live! I want to live!" he said to himself.

His wife came in to congratulate him after his communion, and when uttering the usual conventional words she added:

"You feel better, don't you?"

Without looking at her he said " Yes."   340

Her dress, her figure, the expression of her face, the tone of her voice, all revealed the same thing. "This is wrong, it is not as it should be. All you have lived for and still live for is falsehood and deception, hiding life and death from you." And as soon as he admitted that thought, his hatred and his agonizing physical suffering again sprang up, and with that suffering a consciousness of the unavoidable, approaching end. And to this was added a new sensation of grinding shooting pain and a feeling of suffocation.

The expression of his face when he uttered that "yes" was dreadful. Having uttered it, he looked her straight in the eyes, turned on his face with a rapidity extraordinary in his weak state and shouted:

"Go away! Go away and leave me alone!"

CHAPTER XII

From that moment the screaming began that continued for three days, and was so terrible that one could not hear it through two closed doors without horror. At the moment he answered his wife he realized that he was lost, that there was no return, that the end had come, the very end, and his doubts were still unsolved and remained doubts.

"Oh! Oh! Oh!" he cried in various intonations. He had begun by screaming "I   345
won't!" and continued screaming on the letter "o."

For three whole days, during which time did not exist for him, he struggled in that black sack into which he was being thrust by an invisible, resistless force. He struggled as a man condemned to death struggles in the hands of the executioner, knowing that he cannot save himself. And every moment he felt that despite all his efforts he was drawing nearer and nearer to what terrified him. He felt that his agony was due to his being thrust into that black hole and still more to his not being able to get right into it. He was hindered from getting into it by his conviction that his life had been a good one. That very justification of his life held him fast and prevented his moving forward, and it caused him most torment of all.

Suddenly some force struck him in the chest and side, making it still harder to breathe, and he fell through the hole and there at the bottom was a light. What had happened to him was like the sensation one sometimes experiences in a railway carriage when one thinks one is going backwards while one is really going forwards and suddenly becomes aware of the real direction.

"Yes, it was all not the right thing," he said to himself, "but that's no matter. It can be done. But what *is* the right thing?" he asked himself, and suddenly grew quiet.

This occurred at the end of the third day, two hours before his death. Just then his schoolboy son had crept softly in and gone up to the bedside. The dying man was still screaming desperately and waving his arms. His hand fell on the boy's head, and the boy caught it, pressed it to his lips, and began to cry.

At that very moment Iván Ilých fell through and caught sight of the light, and   350
it was revealed to him that though his life had not been what it should have been, this could still be rectified. He asked himself, "What *is* the right thing?" and grew still, listening. Then he felt that someone was kissing his hand. He opened his eyes, looked at his son, and felt sorry for him. His wife came up to him and he glanced at her. She was gazing at him open-mouthed, with undried tears on her nose and cheek and a despairing look on her face. He felt sorry for her too.

"Yes, I am making them wretched," he thought. "They are sorry, but it will be better for them when I die." He wished to say this but had not the strength to utter it. "Besides, why speak? I must act," he thought. With a look at his wife he indicated his son and said: "Take him away . . . sorry for him . . . sorry for you too. . . ." He tried to add, "forgive me," but said "forego" and waved his hand, knowing that He whose understanding mattered would understand.

And suddenly it grew clear to him that what had been oppressing him and would not leave him was all dropping away at once from two sides, from ten sides, and from all sides. He was sorry for them, he must act so as not to hurt them: release them and free himself from these sufferings. "How good and how simple!" he thought. "And the pain?" he asked himself. "What has become of it? Where are you, pain?"

He turned his attention to it.

"Yes, here it is. Well, what of it? Let the pain be."

"And death . . . where is it?"   355

He sought his former accustomed fear of death and did not find it. "Where is it? What death?" There was no fear because there was no death.

In place of death there was light.

"So that's what it is!" he suddenly exclaimed aloud. "What joy!"

To him all this happened in a single instant, and the meaning of that instant did not change. For those present his agony continued for another two hours. Something rattled in his throat, his emaciated body twitched, then the gasping and rattle became less and less frequent.

"It is finished!" said someone near him.   360

He heard these words and repeated them in his soul.

"Death is finished," he said to himself. "It is no more!"

He drew in a breath, stopped in the midst of a sigh, stretched out, and died.

For Analysis

1. Discuss the evidence that Ilých's death is a moral judgment—that is, a punishment for his life. **2.** Discuss "The Death of Iván Ilých" from the perspective revealed in Paul's 1 Corinthians 13 (p. 1133). What accounts for the change in Ilých's attitude toward his approaching death? **3.** How do you respond to the fact that Gerásim, Ilých's peasant servant, is more sympathetic than Ilých's family?

On Style

Suggest a reason for Tolstoy's decision to begin the story immediately after Ilých's death and then move back to recount the significant episodes of his life.

Making Connections

Compare the significance of death to the characters in this story with the significance of death in one or two of the following works: Edgar Allan Poe's "Ligeia" (p. 1153), Bernard Malamud's "Idiots First" (p. 1123), Robert Olen Butler's "Preparation" (p. 1234), and Amy Hempel's "In the Cemetery Where Al Jolson Is Buried" (p. 1248).

Writing Topics

1. At the conclusion of the story, Ilých achieves peace and understanding, and the questions that have been torturing him are resolved. He realizes that "though his life had not been what it should have been, this could still be rectified." What does this mean? **2.** In an essay, compare and contrast the attitudes of various characters to Ilých's mortal illness. How do his colleagues respond? His wife? His children? His servant Gerásim?

D. H. Lawrence   [1885–1930]

Odour of Chrysanthemums   1911

I

The small locomotive engine, Number 4, came clanking, stumbling down from Selston with seven full wagons. It appeared round the corner with loud threats of speed, but the colt that it startled from among the gorse, which still flickered indistinctly in the raw afternoon, out-distanced it at a canter. A woman, walking up the railway line to Underwood, drew back into the hedge, held her basket aside, and watched the footplate of the engine advancing. The trucks thumped heavily past, one by one, with slow inevitable movement, as she stood insignificantly trapped between the jolting black wagons and the hedge; then they curved away towards the coppice where the withered oak leaves dropped noiselessly, while the birds, pulling at the scarlet hips beside the track, made off into the dusk that had already crept into the spinney. In the open, the smoke from the engine sank and cleaved to the rough grass. The fields were dreary and forsaken, and in the marshy strip that led to the whimsey, a reedy pit-pond, the fowls had already abandoned their run among the alders, to roost in the tarred fowl-house. The pit-bank loomed up beyond the pond, flames like red sores licking its ashy sides, in the afternoon's stagnant light. Just beyond rose the tapering chimneys and the clumsy black headstocks of Brinsley Colliery. The two wheels were spinning fast up against the sky, and the winding engine rapped out its little spasms. The miners were being turned up.

The engine whistled as it came into the wide bay of railway lines beside the colliery, where rows of trucks stood in harbour.

Miners, single, trailing and in groups, passed like shadows diverging home. At the edge of the ribbed level of sidings squat a low cottage, three steps down from the cinder track. A large bony vine clutched at the house, as if to claw down the tiled roof. Round the bricked yard grew a few wintry primroses. Beyond, the long garden sloped down to a bush-covered brook course. There were some twiggy apple trees, winter-crack trees, and ragged cabbages. Beside the path hung dishevelled pink chrysanthemums, like pink cloths hung on bushes. A woman came stooping out of the felt-covered fowl-house, half-way down the garden. She closed and padlocked the door, then drew herself erect, having brushed some bits from her white apron.

She was a tall woman of imperious mien, handsome, with definite black eyebrows. Her smooth black hair was parted exactly. For a few moments she stood steadily watching the miners as they passed along the railway: then she turned towards the brook course. Her face was calm and set, her mouth was closed with disillusionment. After a moment she called:

"John!" There was no answer. She waited, and then said distinctly:

"Where are you?"

"Here!" replied a child's sulky voice from among the bushes. The woman looked piercingly through the dusk.

"Are you at that brook?" she asked sternly.

For answer the child showed himself before the raspberry-canes that rose like whips. He was a small, sturdy boy of five. He stood quite still, defiantly.

"Oh!" said the mother, conciliated. "I thought you were down at that wet brook—and you remember what I told you———"

The boy did not move or answer.

"Come, come on in," she said more gently, "it's getting dark. There's your grandfather's engine coming down the line!"

The lad advanced slowly, with resentful, taciturn movement. He was dressed in trousers and waistcoat of cloth that was too thick and hard for the size of the garments. They were evidently cut down from a man's clothes.

As they went slowly towards the house he tore at the ragged wisps of chrysanthemums and dropped the petals in handfuls along the path.

"Don't do that—it does look nasty," said his mother. He refrained, and she, suddenly pitiful, broke off a twig with three or four wan flowers and held them against her face. When mother and son reached the yard her hand hesitated, and instead of laying the flower aside, she pushed it in her apron-band. The mother and son stood at the foot of the three steps looking across the bay of lines at the passing home of the miners. The trundle of the small train was imminent. Suddenly the engine loomed past the house and came to a stop opposite the gate.

The engine-driver, a short man with round grey beard, leaned out of the cab high above the woman.

"Have you got a cup of tea?" he said in a cheery, hearty fashion.

It was her father. She went in, saying she would mash.[1] Directly, she returned.

"I didn't come to see you on Sunday," began the little grey-bearded man.

"I didn't expect you," said his daughter.

The engine-driver winced; then, reassuming his cheery, airy manner, he said: "Oh, have you heard then? Well, and what do you think———?"

"I think it is soon enough," she replied.

At her brief censure the little man made an impatient gesture, and said coaxingly, yet with dangerous coldness:

"Well, what's a man to do? It's no sort of life for a man of my years, to sit at my own hearth like a stranger. And if I'm going to marry again it may as well be soon as late—what does it matter to anybody?"

The woman did not reply, but turned and went into the house. The man in the engine-cab stood assertive, till she returned with a cup of tea and a piece of bread and butter on a plate. She went up the steps and stood near the footplate of the hissing engine.

---

[1] Make tea.

"You needn't 'a' brought me bread an' butter," said her father. "But a cup of tea"—he sipped appreciatively—"it's very nice." He sipped for a moment or two, then: "I hear as Walter's got another bout on," he said.

"When hasn't he?" said the woman bitterly.

"I heerd tell of him in the 'Lord Nelson' braggin' as he was going to spend that b—— afore he went: half a sovereign[2] that was."

"When?" asked the woman.   30

"A' Sat'day night—I know that's true."

"Very likely," she laughed bitterly. "He gives me twenty-three shillings."

"Aye, it's a nice thing, when a man can do nothing with his money but make a beast of himself!" said the grey-whiskered man. The woman turned her head away. Her father swallowed the last of his tea and handed her the cup.

"Aye," he sighed, wiping his mouth. "It's a settler,[3] it is———"

He put his hand on the lever. The little engine strained and groaned, and the   35
train rumbled towards the crossing. The woman again looked across the metals. Darkness was settling over the spaces of the railway and trucks: the miners, in grey sombre groups, were still passing home. The winding engine pulsed hurriedly, with brief pauses. Elizabeth Bates looked at the dreary flow of men, then she went indoors. Her husband did not come.

The kitchen was small and full of firelight; red coals piled glowing up the chimney mouth. All the life of the room seemed in the white, warm hearth and the steel fender reflecting the red fire. The cloth was laid for tea; cups glinted in the shadows. At the back, where the lowest stairs protruded into the room, the boy sat struggling with a knife and a piece of white wood. He was almost hidden in the shadow. It was half-past four. They had but to await the father's coming to begin tea. As the mother watched her son's sullen little struggle with the wood, she saw herself in his silence and pertinacity; she saw the father in her child's indifference to all but himself. She seemed to be occupied by her husband. He had probably gone past his home, slunk past his own door, to drink before he came in, while his dinner spoiled and wasted in waiting. She glanced at the clock, then took the potatoes to strain them in the yard. The garden and fields beyond the brook were closed in uncertain darkness. When she rose with the saucepan, leaving the drain steaming into the night behind her, she saw the yellow lamps were lit along the high road that went up the hill away beyond the space of the railway lines and the field.

Then again she watched the men trooping home, fewer now and fewer.

Indoors the fire was sinking and the room was dark red. The woman put her saucepan on the hob, and set a batter-pudding near the mouth of the oven. Then she stood unmoving. Directly, gratefully, came quick young steps to the door. Someone hung on the latch a moment, then a little girl entered and began pulling off her outdoor things, dragging a mass of curls, just ripening from gold to brown, over her eyes with her hat.

---

[2] Ten shillings. A relatively large portion of a miner's weekly wage in 1911.
[3] The final blow.

Her mother chid her for coming late from school, and said she would have to keep her at home the dark winter days.

"Why, mother, it's hardly a bit dark yet. The lamp's not lighted, and my fa- 40 ther's not home."

"No, he isn't. But it's a quarter to five! Did you see anything of him?"

The child became serious. She looked at her mother with large, wistful blue eyes.

"No, mother, I've never seen him. Why? Has he come up an' gone past, to Old Brinsley? He hasn't, mother, 'cos I never saw him."

"He'd watch that," said the mother bitterly, "he'd take care as you didn't see him. But you may depend upon it, he's seated in the 'Prince o' Wales.' He wouldn't be this late."

The girl looked at her mother piteously. 45

"Let's have our teas, mother, should we?" said she.

The mother called John to table. She opened the door once more and looked out across the darkness of the lines. All was deserted: she could not hear the winding-engines.

"Perhaps," she said to herself, "he's stopped to get some ripping[4] done."

They sat down to tea. John, at the end of the table near the door, was almost lost in the darkness. Their faces were hidden from each other. The girl crouched against the fender slowly moving a thick piece of bread before the fire. The lad, his face a dusky mark on the shadow, sat watching her who was transfigured in the red glow.

"I do think it's beautiful to look in the fire," said the child. 50

"Do you?" said her mother. "Why?"

"It's so red, and full of little caves—and it feels so nice, and you can fair smell it."

"It'll want mending directly," replied her mother, "and then if your father comes he'll carry on and say there never is a fire when a man comes home sweating from the pit. A public house is always warm enough."

There was silence till the boy said complainingly: "Make haste, our Annie."

"Well, I am doing! I can't make the fire do it no faster, can I?" 55

"She keeps wafflin' it about so's to make 'er slow," grumbled the boy.

"Don't have such an evil imagination, child," replied the mother.

Soon the room was busy in the darkness with the crisp sound of crunching. The mother ate very little. She drank her tea determinedly, and sat thinking. When she rose her anger was evident in the stern unbending of her head. She looked at the pudding in the fender and broke out:

"It is a scandalous thing as a man can't even come home to his dinner! If it's crozzled up to a cinder I don't see why I should care. Past his very door he goes to get to a public-house, and here I sit with his dinner waiting for him———"

She went out. As she dropped piece after piece of coal on the red fire, the 60 shadows fell on the walls, till the room was almost in total darkness.

---

[4] A mining term: cutting away coal or stone.

"I canna see," grumbled the invisible John. In spite of herself, the mother laughed.

"You know the way to your mouth," she said. She set the dustpan outside the door. When she came again like a shadow on the hearth, the lad repeated, complaining sulkily:

"I canna see."

"Good gracious!" cried the mother irritably, "you're as bad as your father if it's a bit dusk!"

Nevertheless, she took a paper spill from a sheaf on the mantelpiece and proceeded to light the lamp that hung from the ceiling in the middle of the room. As she reached up, her figure displayed itself just rounding with maternity.

"Oh, mother———!" exclaimed the girl.

"What?" said the woman, suspended in the act of putting the lamp-glass over the flame. The copper reflector shone handsomely on her, as she stood with uplifted arm, turning to face her daughter.

"You've got a flower in your apron!" said the child, in a little rapture at this unusual event.

"Goodness me!" exclaimed the woman, relieved. "One would think the house was afire." She replaced the glass and waited a moment before turning up the wick. A pale shadow was seen floating vaguely on the floor.

"Let me smell!" said the child, still rapturously, coming forward and putting her face to her mother's waist.

"Go along, silly!" said the mother, turning up the lamp. The light revealed their suspense so that the woman felt it almost unbearable. Annie was still bending at her waist. Irritably, the mother took the flowers out from her apron-band.

"Oh, mother—don't take them out!" Annie cried, catching her hand and trying to replace the sprig.

"Such nonsense!" said the mother, turning away. The child put the pale chrysanthemums to her lips, murmuring:

"Don't they smell beautiful!"

Her mother gave a short laugh.

"No," she said, "not to me. It was chrysanthemums when I married him, and chrysanthemums when you were born, and the first time they ever brought him home drunk, he'd got brown chrysanthemums in his buttonhole."

She looked at the children. Their eyes and their parted lips were wondering. The mother sat rocking in silence for some time. Then she looked at the clock.

"Twenty minutes to six!" In a tone of fine bitter carelessness she continued: "Eh, he'll not come now till they bring him. There he'll stick! But he needn't come rolling in here in his pit-dirt, for *I* won't wash him. He can lie on the floor———Eh, what a fool I've been, what a fool! And this is what I came here for, to this dirty hole, rats and all, for him to slink past his very door. Twice last week—he's begun now———"

She silenced herself, and rose to clear the table.

While for an hour or more the children played, subduedly intent, fertile of imagination, united in fear of the mother's wrath, and in dread of their father's home-coming, Mrs. Bates sat in her rocking-chair making a "singlet" of thick cream-coloured flannel, which gave a dull wounded sound as she tore off the grey edge. She worked at her sewing with energy, listening to the children, and her anger wearied itself, lay down to rest, opening its eyes from time to time and steadily watching, its ears raised to listen. Sometimes even her anger quailed and shrank, and the mother suspended her sewing, tracing the footsteps that thudded along the sleepers outside; she would lift her head sharply to bid the children "hush," but she recovered herself in time, and the footsteps went past the gate, and the children were not flung out of their play-world.

But at last Annie sighed, and gave in. She glanced at her wagon of slippers, and loathed the game. She turned plaintively to her mother.

"Mother!"—but she was inarticulate.

John crept out like a frog from under the sofa. His mother glanced up.

"Yes," she said, "just look at those shirt-sleeves!"

The boy held them out to survey them, saying nothing. Then somebody 85 called in a hoarse voice away down the line, and suspense bristled in the room, till two people had gone by outside, talking.

"It is time for bed," said the mother.

"My father hasn't come," wailed Annie plaintively. But her mother was primed with courage.

"Never mind. They'll bring him when he does come—like a log." She meant there would be no scene. "And he may sleep on the floor till he wakes himself. I know he'll not go to work tomorrow after this!"

The children had their hands and faces wiped with a flannel. They were very quiet. When they had put on their night-dresses, they said their prayers, the boy mumbling. The mother looked down at them, at the brown silken bush of intertwining curls in the nape of the girl's neck, at the little black head of the lad, and her heart burst with anger at their father, who caused all three such distress. The children hid their faces in her skirts for comfort.

When Mrs. Bates came down, the room was strangely empty, with a tension 90 of expectancy. She took up her sewing and stitched for some time without raising her head. Meantime her anger was tinged with fear.

II

The clock struck eight and she rose suddenly, dropping her sewing on her chair. She went to the stair-foot door, opened it, listening. Then she went out, locking the door behind her.

Something scuffled in the yard, and she started, though she knew it was only the rats with which the place was over-run. The night was very dark. In the great bay of railway lines, bulked with trucks, there was no trace of light, only away back she could see a few yellow lamps at the pit-top, and the red smear of the burning pit-bank on the night. She hurried along the edge of the track, then, crossing the converging lines, came to the stile by the white gates, whence she emerged on the road. Then the fear which had led her shrank. People were walking up to New Brinsley; she saw the lights in the houses; twenty yards farther on were the broad windows of the "Prince of Wales," very warm and bright, and the loud voices of men could be heard distinctly. What a fool she had been to imagine that anything had happened to him! He was merely drinking over there at the "Prince of Wales." She faltered. She had never yet been to fetch him, and she never would go. So she continued her walk towards the long straggling line of houses, standing back on the highway. She entered a passage between the dwellings.

"Mr. Rigley?—Yes! Did you want him? No, he's not in at this minute."

The raw-boned woman leaned forward from her dark scullery and peered at the other, upon whom fell a dim light through the blind of the kitchen window.

"Is it Mrs. Bates?" she asked in a tone tinged with respect.   95

"Yes. I wondered if your Master was at home. Mine hasn't come yet."

" 'Asn't 'e! Oh, Jack's been 'ome an' 'ad 'is dinner an' gone out. 'E's just gone for 'alf an hour afore bed-time. Did you call at the 'Prince of Wales'?"

"No———"

"No, you didn't like———! It's not very nice." The other woman was indulgent. There was an awkward pause. "Jack never said nothink about—about your Master," she said.

"No!—I expect he's stuck in there!"   100

Elizabeth Bates said this bitterly, and with recklessness. She knew that the woman across the yard was standing at her door listening, but she did not care. As she turned:

"Stop a minute! I'll just go an' ask Jack if 'e knows anythink," said Mrs. Rigley.

"Oh no—I wouldn't like to put———!"

"Yes, I will, if you'll just step inside an' see as th' childer doesn't come downstairs and set theirselves afire."

Elizabeth Bates, murmuring a remonstrance, stepped inside. The other   105 woman apologised for the state of the room.

The kitchen needed apology. There were little frocks and trousers and childish undergarments on the squab and on the floor, and a litter of playthings everywhere. On the black American cloth[5] of the table were pieces of bread and cake, crusts, slops, and a teapot with cold tea.

"Eh, ours is just as bad," said Elizabeth Bates, looking at the woman, not at the house. Mrs. Rigley put a shawl over her head and hurried out, saying:

"I shanna be a minute."

The other sat, noting with faint disapproval the general untidiness of the room. Then she fell to counting the shoes of various sizes scattered over the floor. There were twelve. She sighed and said to herself: "No wonder!"— glancing at the litter. There came the scratching of two pairs of feet on the yard, and the Rigleys entered. Elizabeth Bates rose. Rigley was a big man, with very

---

[5] Oilcloth.

large bones. His head looked particularly bony. Across his temple was a blue scar, caused by a wound got in the pit, a wound in which the coal-dust remained blue like tattooing.

" 'Asna 'e come whoam yit?" asked the man, without any form of greeting, 110 but with deference and sympathy. "I couldna say wheer he is—'e's non ower theer!"—he jerked his head to signify the "Prince of Wales."

" 'E's 'appen gone up to th' 'Yew,' " said Mrs. Rigley.

There was another pause. Rigley had evidently something to get off his mind:

"Ah left 'im finishin' a stint," he began. "Loose-all[6] 'ad bin gone about ten minutes when we com'n away, an' I shouted: 'Are ter comin', Walt?' an' 'e said: 'Go on, Ah shanna be but a'ef a minnit,' so we com'n ter th' bottom, me an' Bowers, thinkin' as 'e wor just behint, an' 'ud come up i' th' next bantle[7]———"

He stood perplexed, as if answering a charge of deserting his mate. Elizabeth Bates, now again certain of disaster, hastened to reassure him:

"I expect 'e's gone up to th' 'Yew Tree,' as you say. It's not the first time. I've 115 fretted myself into a fever before now. He'll come home when they carry him."

"Ay, isn't it too bad!" deplored the other woman.

"I'll just step up to Dick's an' see if 'e *is* there," offered the man, afraid of appearing alarmed, afraid of taking liberties.

"Oh, I wouldn't think of bothering you that far," said Elizabeth Bates, with emphasis, but he knew she was glad of his offer.

As they stumbled up the entry, Elizabeth Bates heard Rigley's wife run across the yard and open her neighbour's door. At this, suddenly all the blood in her body seemed to switch away from her heart.

"Mind!" warned Rigley. "Ah've said many a time as Ah'd fill up them ruts in 120 this entry, sumb'dy 'll be breakin' their legs yit."

She recovered herself and walked quickly along with the miner.

"I don't like leaving the children in bed, and nobody in the house," she said.

"No, you dunna!" he replied courteously. They were soon at the gate of the cottage.

"Well, I shanna be many minnits. Dunna you be frettin' now, 'e'll be all right," said the butty.[8]

"Thank you very much, Mr. Rigley," she replied. 125

"You're welcome!" he stammered, moving away. "I shanna be many minnits."

The house was quiet. Elizabeth Bates took off her hat and shawl, and rolled back the rug. When she had finished, she sat down. It was a few minutes past nine. She was startled by the rapid chuff of the winding-engine at the pit, and the sharp whirr of the brakes on the rope as it descended. Again she felt the painful sweep of her blood, and she put her hand to her side, saying aloud:

---

[6] Signal to quit work.
[7] Group.
[8] Workmate.

"Good gracious!—it's only the nine o'clock deputy going down," rebuking her-self.

She sat still listening. Half an hour of this, and she was wearied out.

"What am I working myself up like this for?" she said pitiably to herself, "I s'll only be doing myself some damage."

She took out her sewing again.   130

At a quarter to ten there were footsteps. One person! She watched for the door to open. It was an elderly woman, in a black bonnet and a black woollen shawl—his mother. She was about sixty years old, pale, with blue eyes, and her face all wrinkled and lamentable. She shut the door and turned to her daughter-in-law peevishly.

"Eh, Lizzie, whatever shall we do, whatever shall we do!" she cried.

Elizabeth drew back a little, sharply.

"What is it, mother?" she said.

The elder woman seated herself on the sofa.   135

"I don't know, child, I can't tell you!"—she shook her head slowly. Elizabeth sat watching her, anxious and vexed.

"I don't know," replied the grandmother, sighing very deeply. "There's no end to my troubles, there isn't. The things I've gone through, I'm sure it's enough———!" She wept without wiping her eyes, the tears running.

"But, mother," interrupted Elizabeth, "what do you mean? What is it?"

The grandmother slowly wiped her eyes. The fountains of her tears were stopped by Elizabeth's directness. She wiped her eyes slowly.

"Poor child! Eh, you poor thing!" she moaned. "I don't know what we're go-   140
ing to do, I don't—and you as you are—it's a thing, it is indeed!"

Elizabeth waited.

"Is he dead?" she asked, and at the words her heart swung violently, though she felt a slight flush of shame at the ultimate extravagance of the question. Her words sufficiently frightened the old lady, almost brought her to herself.

"Don't say so, Elizabeth! We'll hope it's not as bad as that; no, may the Lord spare us that, Elizabeth. Jack Rigley came just as I was sittin' down to a glass afore going to bed, an' 'e said: ' 'Appen you'll go down th' line, Mrs. Bates. Walt's had an accident. 'Appen you'll go an' sit wi' 'er till we can get him home.' I hadn't time to ask him a word afore he was gone. An' I put my bonnet on an' come straight down, Lizzie. I thought to myself: 'Eh, that poor blessed child, if anybody should come an' tell her of a sudden, there's no knowin' what'll 'appen to 'er.' You mustn't let it upset you, Lizzie—or you know what to expect. How long is it, six months—or is it five, Lizzie? Ay!"—the old woman shook her head—"time slips on, it slips on! Ay!"

Elizabeth's thoughts were busy elsewhere. If he was killed—would she be able to manage on the little pension and what she could earn?—she counted up rapidly. If he was hurt—they wouldn't take him to the hospital—how tiresome he would be to nurse!—but perhaps she'd be able to get him away from the drink and his hateful ways. She would—while he was ill. The tears offered to come to her eyes at the picture. But what sentimental luxury was this she was beginning? She turned to consider the children. At any rate she was absolutely necessary for them. They were her business.

"Ay!" repeated the old woman, "it seems but a week or two since he brought 145 me his first wages. Ay—he was a good lad, Elizabeth, he was, in his way. I don't know why he got to be such a trouble, I don't. He was a happy lad at home, only full of spirits. But there's no mistake he's been a handful of trouble, he has! I hope the Lord'll spare him to mend his ways. I hope so, I hope so. You've had a sight o' trouble with him, Elizabeth, you have indeed. But he was a jolly enough lad wi' me, he was, I can assure you. I don't know how it is . . ."

The old woman continued to muse aloud, a monotonous irritating sound, while Elizabeth thought concentratedly, startled once, when she heard the winding-engine chuff quickly, and the brakes skirr with a shriek. Then she heard the engine more slowly, and the brakes made no sound. The old woman did not notice. Elizabeth waited in suspense. The mother-in-law talked, with lapses into silence.

"But he wasn't your son, Lizzie, an' it makes a difference. Whatever he was, I remember him when he was little, an' I learned to understand him and to make allowances. You've got to make allowances for them————"

It was half-past ten, and the old woman was saying: "But it's trouble from beginning to end; you're never too old for trouble, never too old for that————" when the gate banged back, and there were heavy feet on the steps.

"I'll go, Lizzie, let me go," cried the old woman, rising. But Elizabeth was at the door. It was a man in pit-clothes.

"They're bringin' 'im, Misses," he said. Elizabeth's heart halted a moment. 150 Then it surged on again, almost suffocating her.

"Is he—is it bad?" she asked.

The man turned away, looking at the darkness:

"The doctor says 'e'd been dead hours. 'E saw 'im i' th' lamp-cabin."

The old woman, who stood just behind Elizabeth, dropped into a chair, and folded her hands, crying: "Oh, my boy, my boy!"

"Hush!" said Elizabeth, with a sharp twitch of a frown. "Be still, mother, don't 155 waken th' children: I wouldn't have them down for anything!"

The old woman moaned softly, rocking herself. The man was drawing away. Elizabeth took a step forward.

"How was it?" she asked.

"Well, I couldn't say for sure," the man replied, very ill at ease. " 'E wor finishin' a stint an' th' butties 'ad gone, an' a lot o' stuff come down atop 'n 'im."

"And crushed him?" cried the widow, with a shudder.

"No," said the man, "it fell at th' back of 'im. 'E wor under th' face, an' it niver 160 touched 'im. It shut 'im in. It seems 'e wor smothered."

Elizabeth shrank back. She heard the old woman behind her cry:

"What?—what did 'e say it was?"

The man replied, more loudly: " 'E wor smothered!"

Then the old woman wailed aloud, and this relieved Elizabeth.

"Oh, mother," she said, putting her hand on the old woman, "don't waken th' 165 children, don't waken th' children."

She wept a little, unknowing, while the old mother rocked herself and moaned. Elizabeth remembered that they were bringing him home, and she must be ready. "They'll lay him in the parlour," she said to herself, standing a moment pale and perplexed.

Then she lighted a candle and went into the tiny room. The air was cold and damp, but she could not make a fire, there was no fireplace. She set down the candle and looked round. The candlelight glittered on the lustre-glasses, on the two vases that held some of the pink chrysanthemums, and on the dark mahogany. There was a cold, deathly smell of chrysanthemums in the room. Elizabeth stood looking at the flowers. She turned away, and calculated whether there would be room to lay him on the floor, between the couch and the chiffonier. She pushed the chairs aside. There would be room to lay him down and to step round him. Then she fetched the old red tablecloth, and another old cloth, spreading them down to save her bit of carpet. She shivered on leaving the parlour; so, from the dresser drawer she took a clean shirt and put it at the fire to air. All the time her mother-in-law was rocking herself in the chair and moaning.

"You'll have to move from there, mother," said Elizabeth. "They'll be bringing him in. Come in the rocker."

The old mother rose mechanically, and seated herself by the fire, continuing to lament. Elizabeth went into the pantry for another candle, and there, in the little pent-house under the naked tiles, she heard them coming. She stood still in the pantry doorway, listening. She heard them pass the end of the house, and come awkwardly down the three steps, a jumble of shuffling footsteps and muttering voices. The old woman was silent. The men were in the yard.

Then Elizabeth heard Matthews, the manager of the pit, say: "You go in first, 170 Jim. Mind!"

The door came open, and the two women saw a collier backing into the room, holding one end of a stretcher, on which they could see the nailed pit-boots of the dead man. The two carriers halted, the man at the head stooping to the lintel of the door.

"Wheer will you have him?" asked the manager, a short, white-bearded man.

Elizabeth roused herself and came from the pantry carrying the unlighted candle.

"In the parlour," she said.

"In there, Jim!" pointed the manager, and the carriers backed round into the 175 tiny room. The coat with which they had covered the body fell off as they awkwardly turned through the two doorways, and the women saw their man, naked to the waist, lying stripped for work. The old woman began to moan in a low voice of horror.

"Lay th' stretcher at th' side," snapped the manager, "an' put 'im on th' cloths. Mind now, mind! Look you now————!"

One of the men had knocked off a vase of chrysanthemums. He stared awkwardly, then they set down the stretcher. Elizabeth did not look at her husband. As soon as she could get in the room, she went and picked up the broken vase and the flowers.

"Wait a minute!" she said.

The three men waited in silence while she mopped up the water with a duster.

"Eh, what a job, what a job, to be sure!" the manager was saying, rubbing his brow with trouble and perplexity. "Never knew such a thing in my life, never! He'd no business to ha' been left. I never knew such a thing in my life! Fell over him clean as a whistle, an' shut him in. Not four foot of space, there wasn't—yet it scarce bruised him." 180

He looked down at the dead man, lying prone, half naked, all grimed with coal-dust.

" ''Sphyxiated,' the doctor said. It *is* the most terrible job I've ever known. Seems as if it was done o' purpose. Clean over him, an' shut 'im in, like a mouse-trap"—he made a sharp, descending gesture with his hand.

The colliers standing by jerked aside their heads in hopeless comment.

The horror of the thing bristled upon them all.

Then they heard the girl's voice upstairs calling shrilly: "Mother, mother—who is it? Mother, who is it?" 185

Elizabeth hurried to the foot of the stairs and opened the door:

"Go to sleep!" she commanded sharply. "What are you shouting about? Go to sleep at once—there's nothing————"

Then she began to mount the stairs. They could hear her on the boards, and on the plaster floor of the little bedroom. They could hear her distinctly:

"What's the matter now?—what's the matter with you, silly thing?"—her voice was much agitated, with an unreal gentleness.

"I thought it was some men come," said the plaintive voice of the child. "Has he come?" 190

"Yes, they've brought him. There's nothing to make a fuss about. Go to sleep now, like a good child."

They could hear her voice in the bedroom, they waited whilst she covered the children under the bedclothes.

"Is he drunk?" asked the girl, timidly, faintly.

"No! No—he's not! He—he's asleep."

"Is he asleep downstairs?" 195

"Yes—and don't make a noise."

There was silence for a moment, then the men heard the frightened child again:

"What's that noise?"

"It's nothing, I tell you, what are you bothering for?"

The noise was the grandmother moaning. She was oblivious of everything, sitting on her chair rocking and moaning. The manager put his hand on her arm and bade her "Sh—sh!!" 200

The old woman opened her eyes and looked at him. She was shocked by this interruption, and seemed to wonder.

"What time is it?" the plaintive thin voice of the child, sinking back unhappily into sleep, asked this last question.

"Ten o'clock," answered the mother more softly. Then she must have bent down and kissed the children.

Matthews beckoned to the men to come away. They put on their caps and took up the stretcher. Stepping over the body, they tiptoed out of the house. None of them spoke till they were far from the wakeful children.

When Elizabeth came down she found her mother alone on the parlour floor, 205 leaning over the dead man, the tears dropping on him.

"We must lay him out," the wife said. She put on the kettle, then returning knelt at the feet, and began to unfasten the knotted leather laces. The room was clammy and dim with only one candle, so that she had to bend her face almost to the floor. At last she got off the heavy boots and put them away.

"You must help me now," she whispered to the old woman. Together they stripped the man.

When they arose, saw him lying in the naïve dignity of death, the women stood arrested in fear and respect. For a few moments they remained still, looking down, the old mother whimpering. Elizabeth felt countermanded. She saw him, how utterly inviolable he lay in himself. She had nothing to do with him. She could not accept it. Stooping, she laid her hand on him, in claim. He was still warm, for the mine was hot where he had died. His mother had his face between her hands, and was murmuring incoherently. The old tears fell in succession as drops from wet leaves; the mother was not weeping, merely her tears flowed. Elizabeth embraced the body of her husband, with cheek and lips. She seemed to be listening, inquiring, trying to get some connection. But she could not. She was driven away. He was impregnable.

She rose, went into the kitchen, where she poured warm water into a bowl, brought soap and flannel and a soft towel.

"I must wash him," she said. 210

Then the old mother rose stiffly, and watched Elizabeth as she carefully washed his face, carefully brushing the big blond moustache from his mouth with the flannel. She was afraid with a bottomless fear, so she ministered to him. The old woman, jealous, said:

"Let me wipe him!"—and she kneeled on the other side drying slowly as Elizabeth washed, her big black bonnet sometimes brushing the dark head of her daughter-in-law. They worked thus in silence for a long time. They never forgot it was death, and the touch of the man's dead body gave them strange emotions, different in each of the women; a great dread possessed them both, the mother felt the lie was given to her womb, she was denied; the wife felt the utter isolation of the human soul, the child within her was a weight apart from her.

At last it was finished. He was a man of handsome body, and his face showed no traces of drink. He was blond, full-fleshed, with fine limbs. But he was dead.

"Bless him," whispered his mother, looking always at his face, and speaking out of sheer terror. "Dear lad—bless him!" She spoke in a faint, sibilant ecstasy of fear and mother love.

Elizabeth sank down again to the floor, and put her face against his neck, and   215
trembled and shuddered. But she had to draw away again. He was dead, and her living flesh had no place against his. A great dread and weariness held her: she was so unavailing. Her life was gone like this.

"White as milk he is, clear as a twelve-month baby, bless him, the darling!" the old mother murmured to herself. "Not a mark on him, clear and clean and white, beautiful as ever a child was made," she murmured with pride. Elizabeth kept her face hidden.

"He went peaceful, Lizzie—peaceful as sleep. Isn't he beautiful, the lamb? Ay—he must ha' made his peace, Lizzie. 'Appen he made it all right, Lizzie, shut in there. He'd have time. He wouldn't look like this if he hadn't made his peace. The lamb, the dear lamb. 'Eh, but he had a hearty laugh. I loved to hear it. He had the heartiest laugh, Lizzie, as a lad————"

Elizabeth looked up. The man's mouth was fallen back, slightly open under the cover of the moustache. The eyes, half shut, did not show glazed in the obscurity. Life with its smoky burning gone from him, had left him apart and utterly alien to her. And she knew what a stranger he was to her. In her womb was ice of fear, because of this separate stranger with whom she had been living as one flesh. Was this what it all meant—utter, intact separateness, obscured by heat of living? In dread she turned her face away. The fact was too deadly. There had been nothing between them, and yet they had come together, exchanging their nakedness repeatedly. Each time he had taken her, they had been two isolated beings, far apart as now. He was no more responsible than she. The child was like ice in her womb. For as she looked at the dead man, her mind, cold and detached, said clearly: "Who am I? What have I been doing? I have been fighting a husband who did not exist. *He* existed all the time. What wrong have I done? What was that I have been living with? There lies the reality, this man." And her soul died in her for fear: she knew she had never seen him, he had never seen her, they had met in the dark and had fought in the dark, not knowing whom they met nor whom they fought. And now she saw, and turned silent in seeing. For she had been wrong. She had said he was something he was not; she had felt familiar with him. Whereas he was apart all the while, living as she never lived, feeling as she never felt.

In fear and shame she looked at his naked body, that she had known falsely. And he was the father of her children. Her soul was torn from her body and stood apart. She looked at his naked body and was ashamed, as if she had denied it. After all, it was itself. It seemed awful to her. She looked at his face, and she turned her own face to the wall. For his look was other than hers, his way was not her way. She had denied him what he was—she saw it now. She had refused him as himself. And this had been her life, and his life. She was grateful to death, which restored the truth. And she knew she was not dead.

And all the while her heart was bursting with grief and pity for him. What had   220 he suffered? What stretch of horror for this helpless man! She was rigid with agony. She had not been able to help him. He had been cruelly injured, this naked man, this other being, and she could make no reparation. There were the children—but the children belonged to life. This dead man had nothing to do with them. He and she were only channels through which life had flowed to issue in the children. She was a mother—but how awful she knew it now to have been a wife. And he, dead now, how awful he must have felt it to be a husband. She felt that in the next world he would be a stranger to her. If they met there, in the beyond, they would only be ashamed of what had been before. The children had come, for some mysterious reason, out of both of them. But the children did not unite them. Now he was dead, she knew how eternally he was apart from her, how eternally he had nothing more to do with her. She saw this episode of her life closed. They had denied each other in life. Now he had withdrawn. An anguish came over her. It was finished then: it had become hopeless between them long before he died. Yet he had been her husband. But how little!

"Have you got his shirt, 'Lizabeth?"

Elizabeth turned without answering, though she strove to weep and behave as her mother-in-law expected. But she could not, she was silenced. She went into the kitchen and returned with the garment.

"It is aired," she said, grasping the cotton shirt here and there to try. She was almost ashamed to handle him; what right had she or anyone to lay hands on him; but her touch was humble on his body. It was hard work to clothe him. He was so heavy and inert. A terrible dread gripped her all the while: that he could be so heavy and utterly inert, unresponsive, apart. The horror of the distance between them was almost too much for her—it was so infinite a gap she must look across.

At last it was finished. They covered him with a sheet and left him lying, with his face bound. And she fastened the door of the little parlour, lest the children should see what was lying there. Then, with peace sunk heavy on her heart, she went about making tidy the kitchen. She knew she submitted to life, which was her immediate master. But from death, her ultimate master, she winced with fear and shame.

For Analysis

1. Explain the last sentence of part I: "Meantime her anger was tinged with fear."

2. What does the encounter between Elizabeth Bates and the Rigleys reveal about Elizabeth Bates's character?

On Style

Analyze the meaning of chrysanthemums as **symbols** in the story.

Making Connections

1. You probably have experienced the death of an elderly relative or acquaintance. You may have experienced the accidental or untimely death of a relative or friend. Did your response to the deaths differ? Explain. Have you ever felt relief, even joy, at the report of someone's death? Explain. **2.** Contrast the families' response to death in "The Death of Iván Ilých" (p. 1165) and "The Odour of Chrysanthemums." Which response corresponds to your own experience of the death of a relative or acquaintance?

Writing Topic

Elizabeth "was grateful to death, which restored the truth." What was "the truth" about her marriage? How does her husband's death restore it?

Bernard Malamud   [1914–1986]

Idiots First   1963

The thick ticking of the tin clock stopped. Mendel, dozing in the dark, awoke in fright. The pain returned as he listened. He drew on his cold embittered clothing, and wasted minutes sitting at the edge of the bed.

"Isaac," he ultimately sighed.

In the kitchen, Isaac, his astonished mouth open, held six peanuts in his palm. He placed each on the table. "One . . . two . . . nine."

He gathered each peanut and appeared in the doorway. Mendel, in loose hat and long overcoat, still sat on the bed. Isaac watched with small eyes and ears, thick hair graying the sides of his head.

"Schlaf," he nasally said.   5

"No," muttered Mendel. As if stifling he rose. "Come, Isaac."

He wound his old watch though the sight of the stopped clock nauseated him. Isaac wanted to hold it to his ear.

"No, it's late." Mendel put the watch carefully away. In the drawer he found the little paper bag of crumpled ones and fives and slipped it into his overcoat pocket. He helped Isaac on with his coat.

Isaac looked at one dark window, then at the other. Mendel stared at both   10
blank windows.

They went slowly down the darkly lit stairs, Mendel first, Isaac watching the moving shadows on the wall. To one long shadow he offered a peanut.

"Hungrig."

In the vestibule the old man gazed through the thin glass. The November night was cold and bleak. Opening the door he cautiously thrust his head out. Though he saw nothing he quickly shut the door.

"Ginzburg, that he came to see me yesterday," he whispered in Isaac's ear.
Isaac sucked air.   15

"You know who I mean?"

Isaac combed his chin with his fingers.

"That's the one, with the black whiskers. Don't talk to him or go with him if he asks you."

Isaac moaned.

"Young people he don't bother so much," Mendel said in afterthought.   20

It was suppertime and the street was empty but the store windows dimly lit their way to the corner. They crossed the deserted street and went on. Isaac, with a happy cry, pointed to the three golden balls. Mendel smiled but was exhausted when they got to the pawnshop.

The pawnbroker, a red-bearded man with black horn-rimmed glasses, was

1223

eating a whitefish at the rear of the store. He craned his head, saw them, and settled back to sip his tea.

In five minutes he came forward, patting his shapeless lips with a large white handkerchief.

Mendel, breathing heavily, handed him the worn gold watch. The pawnbroker, raising his glasses, screwed in his eyepiece. He turned the watch over once. "Eight dollars."

The dying man wet his cracked lips. "I must have thirty-five." 25

"So go to Rothschild."

"Cost me myself sixty."

"In 1905." The pawnbroker handed back the watch. It had stopped ticking. Mendel wound it slowly. It ticked hollowly.

"Isaac must go to my uncle that he lives in California."

"It's a free country," said the pawnbroker. 30

Isaac, watching a banjo, snickered.

"What's the matter with him?" the pawnbroker asked.

"So let be eight dollars," muttered Mendel, "but where will I get the rest till tonight?"

"How much for my hat and coat?" he asked.

"No sale." The pawnbroker went behind the cage and wrote out a ticket. He 35 locked the watch in a small drawer but Mendel still heard it ticking.

In the street he slipped the eight dollars into the paper bag, then searched in his pockets for a scrap of writing. Finding it, he strained to read the address by the light of the street lamp.

As they trudged to the subway, Mendel pointed to the sprinkled sky.

"Isaac, look how many stars are tonight."

"Eggs," said Isaac.

"First we will go to Mr. Fishbein, after we will eat." 40

They got off the train in upper Manhattan and had to walk several blocks before they located Fishbein's house.

"A regular palace," Mendel murmured, looking forward to a moment's warmth.

Isaac stared uneasily at the heavy door of the house.

Mendel rang. The servant, a man with long sideburns, came to the door and said Mr. and Mrs. Fishbein were dining and could see no one.

"He should eat in peace but we will wait till he finishes." 45

"Come back tomorrow morning. Tomorrow morning Mr. Fishbein will talk to you. He don't do business or charity at this time of the night."

"Charity I am not interested—"

"Come back tomorrow."

"Tell him it's life or death—"

"Whose life or death?" 50

"So if not his, then mine."

"Don't be such a big smart aleck."

"Look me in my face," said Mendel, "and tell me if I got time till tomorrow morning?"

The servant stared at him, then at Isaac, and reluctantly let them in.

The foyer was a vast high-ceilinged room with many oil paintings on the walls, voluminous silken draperies, a thick flowered rug at foot, and a marbled staircase.

Mr. Fishbein, a paunchy bald-headed man with hairy nostrils and small patent leather feet, ran lightly down the stairs, a large napkin tucked under a tuxedo coat button. He stopped on the fifth step from the bottom and examined his visitors.

"Who comes on Friday night to a man that he has guests, to spoil him his supper?"

"Excuse me that I bother you, Mr. Fishbein," Mendel said. "If I didn't come now I couldn't come tomorrow."

"Without more preliminaries, please state your business. I'm a hungry man."

"Hungrig," wailed Isaac.

Fishbein adjusted his pince-nez. "What's the matter with him?"

"This is my son Isaac. He is like this all his life."

Isaac mewled.

"I am sending him to California."

"Mr. Fishbein don't contribute to personal pleasure trips."

"I am a sick man and he must go tonight on the train to my Uncle Leo."

"I never give to unorganized charity," Fishbein said, "but if you are hungry I will invite you downstairs in my kitchen. We having tonight chicken with stuffed derma."

"All I ask is thirty-five dollars for the train ticket to my uncle in California. I have already the rest."

"Who is your uncle? How old a man?"

"Eighty-one years, a long life to him."

Fishbein burst into laughter. "Eighty-one years and you are sending him this halfwit."

Mendel, flailing both arms, cried, "Please, without names."

Fishbein politely conceded.

"Where is open the door there we go in the house," the sick man said. "If you will kindly give me thirty-five dollars, God will bless you. What is thirty-five dollars to Mr. Fishbein? Nothing. To me, for my boy, is everything."

Fishbein drew himself up to his tallest height.

"Private contributions I don't make—only to institutions. This is my fixed policy."

Mendel sank to his creaking knees on the rug.

"Please, Mr. Fishbein, if not thirty-five, give maybe twenty."

"Levinson!" Fishbein angrily called.

The servant with the long sideburns appeared at the top of the stairs.

"Show this party where is the door—unless he wishes to partake food before leaving the premises."

"For what I got chicken won't cure it," Mendel said.

"This way if you please," said Levinson, descending.

Isaac assisted his father up.

"Take him to an institution," Fishbein advised over the marble balustrade. He 85
ran quickly up the stairs and they were at once outside, buffeted by winds.

The walk to the subway was tedious. The wind blew mournfully. Mendel, breathless, glanced furtively at shadows. Isaac, clutching his peanuts in his frozen fist, clung to his father's side. They entered a small park to rest for a minute on a stone bench under a leafless two-branched tree. The thick right branch was raised, the thin left one hung down. A very pale moon rose slowly. So did a stranger as they approached the bench.

"Gut yuntif" [Happy holiday], he said hoarsely.

Mendel, drained of blood, waved his wasted arms. Isaac yowled sickly. Then a bell chimed and it was only ten. Mendel let out a piercing anguished cry as the bearded stranger disappeared into the bushes. A policeman came running, and though he beat the bushes with his nightstick, could turn up nothing. Mendel and Isaac hurried out of the little park. When Mendel glanced back the dead tree had its thin arm raised, the thick one down. He moaned.

They boarded a trolley, stopping at the home of a former friend, but he had died years ago. On the same block they went into a cafeteria and ordered two fried eggs for Isaac. The tables were crowded except where a heavy-set man sat eating soup with kasha. After one look at him they left in haste, although Isaac wept.

Mendel had another address on a slip of paper but the house was too far away, 90
in Queens, so they stood in a doorway shivering.

What can I do, he frantically thought, in one short hour?

He remembered the furniture in the house. It was junk but might bring a few dollars. "Come, Isaac." They went once more to the pawnbroker's to talk to him, but the shop was dark and an iron gate—rings and gold watches glinting through it—was drawn tight across his place of business.

They huddled behind a telephone pole, both freezing. Isaac whimpered.

"See the big moon, Isaac. The whole sky is white."

He pointed but Isaac wouldn't look. 95

Mendel dreamed for a minute of the sky lit up, long sheets of light in all directions. Under the sky, in California, sat Uncle Leo drinking tea with lemon. Mendel felt warm but woke up cold.

Across the street stood an ancient brick synagogue.

He pounded on the huge door but no one appeared. He waited till he had breath and desperately knocked again. At last there were footsteps within, and the synagogue door creaked open on its massive brass hinges.

A darkly dressed sexton, holding a dripping candle, glared at them.

"Who knocks this time of night with so much noise on the synagogue door?" 100

Mendel told the sexton his troubles. "Please, I would like to speak to the rabbi."

"The rabbi is an old man. He sleeps now. His wife won't let you see him. Go home and come back tomorrow."

"To tomorrow I said goodbye already. I am a dying man."

Though the sexton seemed doubtful he pointed to an old wooden house next door. "In there he lives." He disappeared into the synagogue with his lit candle casting shadows around him.

Mendel, with Isaac clutching his sleeve, went up the wooden steps and rang the bell. After five minutes a big-faced, gray-haired bulky woman came out on the porch with a torn robe thrown over her nightdress. She emphatically said the rabbi was sleeping and could not be waked.

But as she was insisting, the rabbi himself tottered to the door. He listened a minute and said, "Who wants to see me let them come in."

They entered a cluttered room. The rabbi was an old skinny man with bent shoulders and a wisp of white beard. He wore a flannel nightgown and black skullcap; his feet were bare.

"Vey is mir" [Woe is me], his wife muttered. "Put on shoes or tomorrow comes sure pneumonia." She was a woman with a big belly, years younger than her husband. Staring at Isaac, she turned away.

Mendel apologetically related his errand. "All I need more is thirty-five dollars."

"Thirty-five?" said the rabbi's wife. "Why not thirty-five thousand? Who has so much money? My husband is a poor rabbi. The doctors take away every penny."

"Dear friend," said the rabbi, "if I had I would give you."

"I got already seventy," Mendel said, heavy-hearted. "All I need more is thirty-five."

"God will give you," said the rabbi.

"In the grave," said Mendel. "I need tonight. Come, Isaac."

"Wait," called the rabbi.

He hurried inside, came out with a fur-lined caftan, and handed it to Mendel.

"Yascha," shrieked his wife, "not your new coat!"

"I got my old one. Who needs two coats for one body?"

"Yascha, I am screaming—"

"Who can go among poor people, tell me, in a new coat?"

"Yascha," she cried, "what can this man do with your coat? He needs tonight the money. The pawnbrokers are asleep."

"So let him wake them up."

"No." She grabbed the coat from Mendel.

He held on to a sleeve, wrestling her for the coat. Her I know, Mendel thought. "Shylock," he muttered. Her eyes glittered.

The rabbi groaned and tottered dizzily. His wife cried out as Mendel yanked the coat from her hands.

"Run," cried the rabbi.

"Run, Isaac."

They ran out of the house and down the steps.

"Stop, you thief," called the rabbi's wife.

The rabbi pressed both hands to his temples and fell to the floor.

"Help!" his wife wept. "Heart attack! Help!"

105

110

115

120

125

130

But Mendel and Isaac ran through the streets with the rabbi's new fur-lined caftan. After them noiselessly ran Ginzburg.

It was very late when Mendel bought the train ticket in the only booth open.

There was no time to stop for a sandwich so Isaac ate his peanuts and they hurried to the train in the vast deserted station.

"So in the morning," Mendel gasped as they ran, "there comes a man that he sells sandwiches and coffee. Eat but get change. When reaches California the train, will be waiting for you on the station Uncle Leo. If you don't recognize him he will recognize you. Tell him I send best regards."   135

But when they arrived at the gate to the platform it was shut, the light out. Mendel, groaning, beat on the gate with his fists.

"Too late," said the uniformed ticket collector, a bulky, bearded man with hairy nostrils and a fishy smell.

He pointed to the station clock. "Already past twelve."

"But I see standing there still the train," Mendel said, hopping in his grief.   140

"It just left—in one more minute."

"A minute is enough. Just open the gate."

"Too late I told you."

Mendel socked his bony chest with both hands. "With my whole heart I beg you this little favor."

"Favors you had enough already. For you the train is gone. You shoulda been dead already at midnight. I told you that yesterday. This is the best I can do."   145

"Ginzburg!" Mendel shrank from him.

"Who else?" The voice was metallic, eyes glittered, the expression amused.

"For myself," the old man begged, "I don't ask a thing. But what will happen to my boy?"

Ginzburg shrugged slightly. "What will happen happens. This isn't my responsibility. I got enough to think about without worrying about somebody on one cylinder."

"What then is your responsibility?"   150

"To create conditions. To make happen what happens. I ain't in the anthropomorphic business."

"Whatever business you in, where is your pity?"

"This ain't my commodity. The law is the law."

"Which law is this?"

"The cosmic universal law, goddamit, the one I got to follow myself."   155

"What kind of a law is it?" cried Mendel. "For God's sake, don't you understand what I went through in my life with this poor boy? Look at him. For thirty-nine years, since the day he was born, I wait for him to grow up, but he don't. Do you understand what this means in a father's heart? Why don't you let him go to his uncle?" His voice had risen and he was shouting.

Isaac mewled loudly.

"Better calm down or you'll hurt somebody's feelings," Ginzburg said with a wink toward Isaac.

"All my life," Mendel cried, his body trembling, "what did I have? I was poor.

I suffered from my health. When I worked I worked too hard. When I didn't work was worse. My wife died a young woman. But I didn't ask from anybody nothing. Now I ask a small favor. Be so kind, Mr. Ginzburg."

The ticket collector was picking his teeth with a match stick. 160

"You ain't the only one, my friend, some got it worse than you. That's how it goes in this country."

"You dog you." Mendel lunged at Ginzburg's throat and began to choke. "You bastard, don't you understand what it means human?"

They struggled nose to nose, Ginzburg, though his astonished eyes bulged, began to laugh. "You pipsqueak nothing. I'll freeze you to pieces."

His eyes lit in rage and Mendel felt an unbearable cold like an icy dagger invading his body, all of his parts shriveling.

Now I die without helping Isaac. 165

A crowd gathered. Isaac yelped in fright.

Clinging to Ginzburg in his last agony, Mendel saw reflected in the ticket collector's eyes the depth of his terror. But he saw that Ginzburg, staring at himself in Mendel's eyes, saw mirrored in them the extent of his own awful wrath. He beheld a shimmering, starry, blinding light that produced darkness.

Ginzburg looked astounded. "Who me?"

His grip on the squirming old man slowly loosened, and Mendel, his heart barely beating, slumped to the ground.

"Go." Ginzburg muttered, "take him to the train." 170

"Let pass," he commanded a guard.

The crowd parted. Isaac helped his father up and they tottered down the steps to the platform where the train waited, lit and ready to go.

Mendel found Isaac a coach seat and hastily embraced him. "Help Uncle Leo, Isaakil. Also remember your father and mother."

"Be nice to him," he said to the conductor. "Show him where everything is."

He waited on the platform until the train began slowly to move. Isaac sat at 175 the edge of his seat, his face strained in the direction of his journey. When the train was gone, Mendel ascended the stairs to see what had become of Ginzburg.

For Analysis

1. What traits does the rabbi embody? **2.** What does Ginzburg represent? **3.** What is the significance of the fact that Isaac, for whom Mendel is determined to provide before death claims him, is mentally disabled? **4.** Mendel wins the battle with Ginzburg. What does that victory signify?

On Style

Discuss the function of **dialect** in this story. How does Malamud convey that Isaac is an "idiot?"

Making Connections

Consider the desperate appeals that Mendel makes to the pawnbroker, the "philanthropist" Fishbein, the rabbi's wife, and the rabbi. What do the differing responses reveal about the human condition? Imagine yourself in Mendel's situation and discuss the likely responses of various people—friends, clergy, family, counselors—to your desperate appeal for help.

Writing Topic

How do the various episodes in this story establish Mendel's character? How do they prepare the reader for the climactic confrontation between Mendel and Ginzburg?

Bessie Head   [1937–1986]

Looking for a Rain God   1977

It is lonely at the lands where the people go to plough. These lands are vast clearings in the bush, and the wild bush is lonely too. Nearly all the lands are within walking distance from the village. In some parts of the bush where the underground water is very near the surface, people made little rest camps for themselves and dug shallow wells to quench their thirst while on their journey to their own lands. They experienced all kinds of things once they left the village. They could rest at shady watering places full of lush, tangled trees with delicate pale-gold and purple wildflowers springing up between soft green moss and the children could hunt around for wild figs and any berries that might be in season. But from 1958, a seven-year drought fell upon the land and even the watering places began to look as dismal as the dry open thornbush country; the leaves of the trees curled up and withered; the moss became dry and hard and, under the shade of the tangled trees, the ground turned a powdery black and white, because there was no rain. People said rather humorously that if you tried to catch the rain in a cup it would only fill a teaspoon. Toward the beginning of the seventh year of drought, the summer had become an anguish to live through. The air was so dry and moisture-free that it burned the skin. No one knew what to do to escape the heat and tragedy was in the air. At the beginning of that summer, a number of men just went out of their homes and hung themselves to death from trees. The majority of the people had lived off crops, but for two years past they had all returned from the lands with only their rolled-up skin blankets and cooking utensils. Only the charlatans, incanters, and witch doctors made a pile of money during this time because people were always turning to them in desperation for little talismans and herbs to rub on the plough for the crops to grow and the rain to fall.

The rains were late that year. They came in early November, with a promise of good rain. It wasn't the full, steady downpour of the years of good rain but thin, scanty, misty rain. It softened the earth and a rich growth of green things sprang up everywhere for the animals to eat. People were called to the center of the village to hear the proclamation of the beginning of the ploughing season; they stirred themselves and whole families began to move off to the lands to plough.

The family of the old man, Mokgobja, were among those who left early for the lands. They had a donkey cart and piled everything onto it, Mokgobja—who was over seventy years old; two girls, Neo and Boseyong; their mother Tiro and an unmarried sister, Nesta; and the father and supporter of the family, Ramadi, who drove the donkey cart. In the rush of the first hope of rain, the man, Ramadi, and the two women, cleared the land of thornbush and then hedged their vast ploughing area with this same thornbush to protect the future crop from the goats they had brought along for milk. They cleared out and deepened the old well with its pool of muddy water and still in this light, misty rain, Ramadi inspanned two oxen and turned the earth over with a hand plough.

The land was ready and ploughed, waiting for the crops. At night, the earth was alive with insects singing and rustling about in search of food. But suddenly, by mid-November, the rain flew away; the rain clouds fled away and left the sky bare. The sun danced dizzily in the sky, with a strange cruelty. Each day the land was covered in a haze of mist as the sun sucked up the last drop of moisture out of the earth. The family sat down in despair, waiting and waiting. Their hopes had run so high; the goats had started producing milk, which they had eagerly poured on their porridge, now they ate plain porridge with no milk. It was impossible to plant the corn, maize, pumpkin, and watermelon seeds in the dry earth. They sat the whole day in the shadow of the huts and even stopped thinking, for the rain had fled away. Only the children, Neo and Boseyong, were quite happy in their little-girl world. They carried on their game of making house like their mother and chattered to each other in light, soft tones. They made children from sticks around which they tied rags, and scolded them severely in an exact imitation of their own mother. Their voices could be heard scolding the day long: "You stupid thing, when I send you to draw water, why do you spill half of it out of the bucket!" "You stupid thing! Can't you mind the porridge pot without letting the porridge burn!" And then they would beat the rag dolls on their bottoms with severe expressions.

The adults paid no attention to this; they did not even hear the funny chatter; they sat waiting for rain; their nerves were stretched to the breaking-point willing the rain to fall out of the sky. Nothing was important, beyond that. All their animals had been sold during the bad years to purchase food, and of all their herd only two goats were left. It was the women of the family who finally broke down under the strain of waiting for rain. It was really the two women who caused the death of the little girls. Each night they started a weird, high-pitched wailing that began on a low, mournful note and whipped up to a frenzy. Then they would stamp their feet and shout as though they had lost their heads. The men sat quiet and self-controlled; it was important for men to maintain their self control at all times but their nerve was breaking too. They knew the women were haunted by the starvation of the coming year.

Finally, an ancient memory stirred in the old man, Mokgobja. When he was very young and the customs of the ancestors still ruled the land, he had been witness to a rain-making ceremony. And he came alive a little, struggling to recall the details which had been buried by years and years of prayer in a Christian church. As soon as the mists cleared a little, he began consulting in whispers with his youngest son, Ramadi. There was, he said, a certain rain god who accepted only the sacrifice of the bodies of children. Then the rain would fall; then the crops would grow, he said. He explained the ritual and as he talked, his memory became a conviction and he began to talk with unshakable authority. Ramadi's nerves were smashed by the nightly wailing of the women

5

and soon the two men began whispering with the two women. The children continued their game: "You stupid thing! How could you have lost the money on the way to the shop! You must have been playing again!"

After it was all over and the bodies of the two little girls had been spread across the land, the rain did not fall. Instead, there was a deathly silence at night and the devouring heat of the sun by day. A terror, extreme and deep, overwhelmed the whole family. They packed, rolling up their skin blankets and pots, and fled back to the village.

People in the village soon noted the absence of the two little girls. They had died at the lands and were buried there, the family said. But people noted their ashen, terror-stricken faces and a murmur arose. What had killed the children, they wanted to know? And the family replied they had just died. And people said amongst themselves that it was strange that the two deaths had occurred at the same time. And there was a feeling of great unease at the unnatural looks of the family. Soon the police came around. The family told them the same story of death and burial at the lands. They did not know what the children had died of. So the police asked to see the graves. At this, the mother of the children broke down and told everything.

Throughout that terrible summer the story of the children hung like a dark cloud of sorrow over the village, and the sorrow was not assuaged when the old man and Ramadi were sentenced to death for ritual murder. All they had on the statute books was that ritual murder was against the law and must be stamped out with the death penalty. The subtle story of strain and starvation and breakdown was inadmissible evidence at court; but all the people who lived off the crops knew in their hearts that only a hair's breadth had saved them from sharing a fate similar to that of the Mokgobja family. They could have killed something to make the rain fall.

For Analysis
1. Characterize the lives of the people in the story. What do they live on? What are the consequences of the long drought? **2.** How do the two little girls' games affect you as a reader? **3.** Consider the story's final paragraph. Do you feel the men should be executed? Explain.

On Style
Examine the language Head uses to describe the two girls. Why are they the only people in the story quoted directly? What reason might Head have to portray the girls this way?

Making Connections
Write an essay reflecting on a crisis in your own life and discuss the "sacrifices" you offered in exchange for a resolution of your problem.

Writing Topic
Look up the story's references to animal and human sacrifices in the Hebrew Bible. As well, consider Christianity's view of the crucifixion of Jesus. In an essay, discuss the history of blood sacrifices in the Judeo-Christian tradition. Who performed them? Why?

Robert Olen Butler   [b. 1945]

Preparation   1992

Though Thūy's dead body was naked under the sheet, I had not seen it since we were girls together and our families took us to the beaches of Nha Trang. This was so even though she and I were best friends for all our lives and she became the wife of Lê Văn Lý, the man I once loved. Thūy had a beautiful figure and breasts that were so tempting in the tight bodice of our aó dàis[1] that Lý could not resist her. But the last time I saw Thūy's naked body, she had no breasts yet at all, just the little brown nubs that I also had at seven years old, and we ran in the white foam of the breakers and we watched the sampans out beyond the coral reefs.

We were not common girls, the ones who worked the fields and seemed so casual about their bodies. And more than that, we were Catholics, and Mother Mary was very modest, covered from her throat to her ankles, and we made up our toes beautifully, like the statue of Mary in the church, and we were very modest about all the rest. Except Thūy could seem naked when she was clothed. We both ran in the same surf, but somehow her flesh learned something there that mine did not. She could move like the sea, her body filled her clothes like the living sea, fluid and beckoning. Her mother was always worried about her because the boys grew quiet at her approach and noisy at her departure, and no one was worried about me. I was an expert pair of hands, to bring together the herbs for the lemon grass chicken or to serve the tea with the delicacy of a wind chime or to scratch the eucalyptus oil into the back of a sick child.

And this won for me a good husband, though he was not Lê Văn Lý, nor could ever have been. But he was a good man and a surprised man to learn that my hands could also make him very happy even if my breasts did not seem so delightful in the tight bodice of my aó dài. That man died in the war which came to our country, a war we were about to lose, and I took my sons to America and I settled in this place in New Orleans called Versailles that has only Vietnamese. Soon my best friend Thūy also came to this place, with her husband Lê Văn Lý and her children. They left shortly for California, but after three years they returned, and we all lived another decade together and we expected much longer than that, for Thūy and I would have become fifty years old within a week of each other next month.

---

[1] The national dress of Vietnamese women. It consists of an ankle-length dress with a tight bodice, slit to the hip on both sides. It is worn over loose black slacks.

Except that Thũy was dead now and lying before me in this place that Mr. Hoa, the mortician for our community, called the "preparation room," and she was waiting for me to put the makeup on her face and comb her hair for the last time. She died very quickly, but she knew enough to ask for the work of my hands to make her beautiful in the casket. She let on to no one—probably not even herself—when the signs of the cancer growing in her ovaries caused no pain. She was a fearful person over foolish little things, and such a one as that will sometimes ignore the big things until it is too late. But thank God that when the pain did come and the truth was known, the end came quickly afterward.

She clutched my hand in the hospital room, the curtain drawn around us, and   5
my own grip is very strong, but on that morning she hurt me with the power of her hand. This was a great surprise to me. I looked at our locked hands, and her lovely, slender fingers were white with the strength in them and yet the nails were still perfect, each one a meticulously curved echo of the others, each one carefully stroked with the red paint the color of her favorite Winesap apples. This was a very sad moment for me. It made me sadder even than the sounds of her pain, this hand with its sudden fearful strength and yet the signs of her lovely vanity still there.

But I could not see her hands as I stood beside her in the preparation room. They were somewhere under the sheet and I had work to do, so I looked at her face. Her closed eyes showed the mostly Western lids, passed down by more than one Frenchman among her ancestors. This was a very attractive thing about her, I always knew, though Lý never mentioned her eyes, even though they were something he might well have complimented in public. He could have said to people, "My wife has such beautiful eyes," but he did not. And his certain regard for her breasts, of course, was kept very private. Except with his glance.

We three were young, only sixteen, and Thũy and I were at the Cirque Sportif in Saigon. This was where we met Lý for the first time. We were told that if Mother Mary had known the game of tennis, she would have allowed her spiritual children to wear the costume for the game, even if our legs did show. We loved showing our legs. I have very nice legs, really. Not as nice as Thũy's but I was happy to have my legs bare when I met Lê Văn Lý for the first time. He was a ball boy at the tennis court, and when Thũy and I played, he would run before us and pick up the balls and return them to us. I was a more skillful player than Thũy and it wasn't until too late that I realized how much better it was to hit the ball into the net and have Lý dart before me on this side and then pick up my tennis ball and return it to me. Thũy of course, knew this right away and her game was never worse than when we played with Lê Văn Lý poised at the end of the net waiting for us to make a mistake.

And it was even on that first meeting that I saw his eyes move to Thũy's breasts. It was the slightest of glances but full of meaning. I knew this because I was very attuned to his eyes from the start. They were more like mine, with nothing of the West but everything of our ancestors back to the Kindly Dragon, whose hundred children began Vietnam. But I had let myself forget that the

Kindly Dragon married a fairy princess, not a solid homemaker, so my hopes were still real at age sixteen. He glanced at Thūy's breasts, but he smiled at me when I did miss a shot and he said, very low so only I could hear it, "You're a very good player." It sounded to me at sixteen that this was something he would begin to build his love on. I was a foolish girl.

But now she lay before me on a stainless-steel table, her head cranked up on a chrome support, her hair scattered behind her and her face almost plain. The room had a faint smell, a little itch in the nose of something strong, like the smell when my sons killed insects for their science classes in school. But over this was a faint aroma of flowers, though not real flowers, I knew. I did not like this place and I tried to think about what I'd come for. I was standing before Thūy and I had not moved since Mr. Hoa left me. He tied the smock I was wearing at the back and he told me how he had washed Thūy's hair already. He turned up the air conditioner in the window, which had its glass panes painted a chalky white, and he bowed himself out of the room and closed the door tight.

I opened the bag I'd placed on the high metal chair and I took out Thūy's   10
pearl-handled brush and I bent near her. We had combed each other's hair all our lives. She had always worn her hair down, even as she got older. Even to the day of her death, with her hair laid carefully out on her pillow, something she must have done herself, very near the end, for when Lý and their oldest son and I came into the room that evening and found her, she was dead and her hair was beautiful.

So now I reached out to Thūy and I stroked her hair for the first time since her death and her hair resisted the brush and the resistance sent a chill through me. Her hair was still alive. The body was fixed and cold and absolutely passive, but the hair defied the brush, and though Thūy did not cry out at this first brush stroke as she always did, the hair insisted that she was still alive and I felt something very surprising at that. From the quick fisting of my mind at the image of Thūy, I knew I was angry. From the image of her hair worn long even after she was middle aged instead of worn in a bun at the nape of the neck like all the Vietnamese women our age. I was angry and then I realized that I was angry because she was not completely dead, and this immediately filled me with a shame so hot that it seemed as if I would break into a sweat.

The shame did not last very long. I straightened and turned my face to the flow of cool air from the air conditioner and I looked at all the instruments hanging behind the glass doors of the cabinet in the far wall, all the glinting clamps and tubes and scissors and knives. This was not the place of the living. I looked at Thūy's face and her pale lips were tugged down into a faint frown and I lifted the brush and stroked her hair again and once again, and though it felt just the way it always had felt when I combed it, I continued to brush.

And I spoke a few words to Thūy. Perhaps her spirit was in the room and could hear me. "It's all right, Thūy. The things I never blamed you for in life I won't blame you for now." She had been a good friend. She had always appreciated me. When we brushed each other's hair, she would always say how beautiful mine was and she would invite me also to leave it long, even though I am nearly fifty and I am no beauty at all. And she would tell me how wonderful my talents were. She would urge me to date some man or other in Versailles. I would make such and such a man a wonderful wife, she said. These men were successful men that she recommended, very well off. But they were always older men, in their sixties or seventies. One man was eighty-one, and this one she did not suggest to me directly but by saying casually how she had seen him last week and he was such a vigorous man, such a fine and vigorous man.

And her own husband, Lê Văn Lý, was of course more successful than any of them. And he is still the finest-looking man in Versailles. How fine he is. The face of a warrior. I have seen the high cheeks and full lips of Lê Văn Lý in the statues of warriors in the Saigon Museum, the men who threw the Chinese out of our country many centuries ago. And I lifted Thũy's hair and brushed it out in narrow columns and laid the hair carefully on the bright silver surface behind the support, letting the ends dangle off the table. The hair was very soft and it was yielding to my hands now and I could see this hair hanging perfectly against the back of her pale blue aó dài as she and Lý strolled away across the square near the Continental Palace Hotel.

I wish there had been some clear moment, a little scene; I would even have   15
been prepared not to seem so solid and level-headed; I would have been pre-pared to weep and even to speak in a loud voice. But they were very disarming in the way they let me know how things were. We had lemonades on the ve-randa of the Continental Palace Hotel, and I thought it would be like all the other times, the three of us together in the city, strolling along the river or through the flower markets at Nguyễn Huệ or the bookstalls on Lê ọ'i. We had been three friends together for nearly two years, ever since we'd met at the club. There had been no clear choosing, in my mind. Lý was a very traditional boy, a courteous boy, and he never forced the issue of romance, and so I still had some hopes.

Except that I had unconsciously noticed things, so when Thũy spoke to me and then, soon after, the two of them walked away from the hotel together on the eve of Lý's induction into the Army, I realized something with a shock that I actually had come to understand slowly all along. Like suddenly noticing that you are old. The little things gather for a long time, but one morning you look in the mirror and you understand them in a flash. At the flower market on Nguyễn Huệ I would talk with great spirit of how to arrange the flowers, which ones to put together, how a home would be filled with this or that sort of flower on this or that occasion. But Thũy would be bending into the flowers, her hair falling through the petals, and she would breathe very deeply and rise up and she would be inflated with the smell of flowers and of course her breasts would seem to have grown even larger and more beautiful and Lý would look at them and then he would close his eyes softly in appreciation. And at the bookstalls—I would be the one who asked for the bookstalls—I would be lost in what I thought was the miracle of all these little worlds inviting me in, and I was unaware of the little world near my elbow, Thūy looking at the postcards and talking to Lý about trips to faraway places.

I suppose my two friends were as nice to me as possible at the Continental Palace Hotel, considering what they had to do. Thūy asked me to go to the rest room with her and we were laughing together at something Lý had said. We went to the big double mirror and our two faces were side by side, two girls eighteen years old, and yet beside her I looked much older. Already old. I could see that. And she said, "I am so happy."

We were certainly having fun on this day, but I couldn't quite understand her attitude. After all, Lý was going off to fight our long war. But I replied, "I am, too."

Then she leaned near me and put her hand on my shoulder and she said, "I have a wonderful secret for you. I couldn't wait to tell it to my dear friend."

She meant these words without sarcasm. I'm sure of it. And I still did not understand what was coming. 20

She said, "I am in love."

I almost asked who it was that she loved. But this was only the briefest final pulse of naïveté. I knew who she loved. And after laying her head on the point of my shoulder and smiling at me in the mirror with such tenderness for her dear friend, she said, "And Lý loves me, too."

How had this subject not come up before? The answer is that the two of us had always spoken together of what a wonderful boy Lý was. But my own declarations were as vivid and enthusiastic as Thūy's—rather more vivid, in fact. So if I was to assume that she loved Lý from all that she'd said, then my own declaration of love should have been just as clear. But obviously it wasn't, and that was just as I should have expected it. Thūy never for a moment had considered me a rival for Lý. In fact, it was unthinkable to her that I should even love him in vain.

She lifted her head from my shoulder and smiled at me as if she expected me to be happy. When I kept silent, she prompted me. "Isn't it wonderful?"

I had never spoken of my love for Lý and I knew that this was the last chance 25 I would have. But what was there to say? I could look back at all the little signs now and read them clearly. And Thūy was who she was and I was different from that and the feeling between Lý and her was already decided upon. So I said the only reasonable thing that I could. "It is very wonderful."

This made Thūy even happier. She hugged me. And then she asked me to comb her hair. We had been outside for an hour before coming to the hotel and her long, straight hair was slightly ruffled and she handed me the pearl-handled brush that her mother had given her and she turned her back to me. And I began to brush. The first stroke caught a tangle and Thūy cried out in a pretty, piping voice. I paused briefly and almost threw the brush against the wall and walked out of this place. But then I brushed once again and again, and she was turned away from the mirror so she could not see the terrible pinch of my face when I suggested that she and Lý spend their last hours now alone together. She nearly wept in joy and appreciation at this gesture from her dear friend, and I kept on brushing until her hair was perfect.

And her hair was perfect now beneath my hands in the preparation room. And I had a strange thought. She was doing this once more to me. She was having me make her hair beautiful so she could go off to the spirit world and seduce the one man there who could love me. This would be Thũy's final triumph over me. My hands trembled at this thought and it persisted. I saw this clearly: Thũy arriving in heaven and her hair lying long and soft down her back and her breasts are clearly beautiful even in the white robe of the angels, and the spirit of some great warrior who fought at the side of the Tru'ng sisters[2] comes to her, and though he has waited nineteen centuries for me, he sees Thũy and decides to wait no more. It has been only the work of my hands that he has awaited and he lifts Thũy's hair and kisses it.

I drew back from Thũy and I stared at her face. I saw it in the mirror at the Continental Palace Hotel and it was very beautiful, but this face before me now was rubbery in death, the beauty was hidden, waiting for my hands. Thũy waited for me to make her beautiful. I had always made her more beautiful. Just by being near her. I was tempted once more to turn away. But that would only let her have her condescending smile at me. Someone else would do this job if I did not, and Thũy would fly off to heaven with her beautiful face and I would be alone in my own shame.

I turned to the sheet now, and the body I had never looked upon in its womanly nakedness was hiding there and this was what Lý had given his love for. The hair and the face had invited him, but it was this hidden body, her secret flesh, that he had longed for. I had seen him less than half an hour ago. He was in Mr. Hoa's office when I arrived. He got up and shook my hand with both of his, holding my hand for a long moment as he said how glad he was that I was here. His eyes were full of tears and I felt very sorry for Lê Văn Lý. A warrior should never cry, even for the death of a beautiful woman. He handed me the bag with Thũy's brush and makeup and he said, "You always know what to do."

What did he mean by this? Simply that I knew how to brush Thũy's hair and paint her face? Or was this something he had seen about me in all things, just as he had once seen that I was a very good tennis player? Did it mean he understood that he had never been with a woman like that, a woman who would always know what to do for him as a wife? When he stood before me in Mr. Hoa's office, I felt like a foolish teenage girl again, with that rush of hope. But perhaps it wasn't foolish; Thũy's breasts were no longer there for his eyes to slide away to.

Her breasts. What were these things that had always defined my place in the world of women? They were beneath the sheet and my hand went out and grasped it at the edge, but I stopped. I told myself it was of no matter now. She

30

[2] In 43 A.D., the Tru'ng sisters led a revolt against the Chinese masters of the region.

was dead. I let go of the sheet and turned to her face of rubber and I took out her eye shadow and her lipstick and her mascara and I bent near and painted the life back into this dead thing.

And as I painted, I thought of where she would lie, in the cemetery behind the Catholic church, in a stone tomb above the ground. It was often necessary in New Orleans, the placing of the dead above the ground, because the water table was so high. If we laid Thūy in the earth, one day she would float to the surface and I could see that day clearly, her rising from the earth and awaking and finding her way back to the main street of Versailles in the heat of the day, and I would be talking with Lý, he would be bending near me and listening as I said all the things of my heart, and suddenly his eyes would slide away and there she would be, her face made up and her hair brushed and her breasts would be as beautiful as ever. But the thought of her lying above the ground made me anxious, as well. As if she wasn't quite gone. And she never would be. Lý would sense her out there behind the church, suspended in the air, and he would never forget her and would take all the consolation he needed from his children and grandchildren.

My hand trembled now as I touched her eyes with the brush, and when I held the lipstick, I pressed it hard against her mouth and I cast aside the shame at my anger and I watched this mouth in my mind, the quick smile of it that never changed in all the years, that never sensed any mood in me but loyal, subordinate friendship. Then the paint was all in place and I pulled back and I angled my face once more into the flow of cool air and I tried to just listen to the grinding of the air conditioner and forget all of these feelings, these terrible feelings about the dead woman who had always been my friend, who I had never once challenged in life over any of these things. I thought, What a coward I am.

But instead of hearing this righteous charge against me, I looked at Thūy and I took her hair in my hands and I smoothed it all together and wound it into a bun and I pinned it at the nape of her neck. She was a fifty-year-old woman, after all. She was as much a fifty-year-old woman as I was. Surely she was. And at this I looked to the sheet.

It lay lower across the chest than I thought it might. But her breasts were also fifty years old, and they were spread flat as she lay on her back. She had never let her dear friend see them, these two secrets that had enchanted the man I loved. I could bear to look at them now, vulnerable and weary as they were. I stepped down and I grasped the edge of the sheet at her throat, and with the whisper of the cloth I pulled it back.

And one of her breasts was gone. The right breast was lovely even now, even in death, the nipple large and the color of cinnamon, but the left breast was gone and a large crescent scar began there in its place and curved out of sight under her arm. I could not draw a breath at this, as if the scar was in my own chest where my lungs had been yanked out, and I could see that her scar was old, years old, and I thought of her three years in California and how she had never spoken at all about this, how her smile had hidden all that she must have suffered.

I could not move for a long moment, and then at last my hands acted as if on their own. They pulled the sheet up and gently spread it at her throat. I suppose this should have brought back my shame at the anger I'd had at my friend Thūy, but it did not. That seemed a childish feeling now, much too simple. It was not necessary to explain any of this. I simply leaned forward and kissed Thūy on her brow and I undid the bun at the back of her neck, happy to make her beautiful once more, happy to send her off to a whole body in heaven where she would catch the eye of the finest warrior. And I knew she would understand if I did all I could to make Lê Văn Lý happy.

For Analysis
1. What are the defining characteristics of the narrator? Of Thūy? **2.** How does the narrator feel about Thūy's engagement to Lê? **3.** How does the narrator even the score with her dead friend? How does she respond when she discovers that Thūy had suffered a mastectomy? **4.** Do you envision any further relationship between the narrator and Lý?

On Style
Paragraph by paragraph, note the chronology of the story's events. What is gained (or lost) by the author's unchronological narrative?

Making Connections
Compare the behavior of the narrator of this story with the narrator of Amy Hempel's "In the Cemetery Where Al Jolson Is Buried" (p. 1248). Which would you say was a truer friend? Explain.

Writing Topic
In *Billy Budd,* Herman Melville wrote: "Now envy and antipathy, passions irreconcilable in reason, nevertheless in fact may spring conjoined like Chang and Eng [the original Siamese twins] in one birth." In an essay, show how envy and antipathy influence the narrator's thoughts and behavior.

Art Spiegelman   [b. 1948]

Prisoner on the Hell Planet   1986
A Case History

This self-contained story is imbedded in the relentlessly unsentimental *Maus: A Survivor's Tale*. That work describes, in comic book format, Spiegelman's parents' suffering under the Nazi persecution of the Jews during World War II. The Jews in *Maus* are represented as mice; the Nazis are cats. The book deals, as well, with the author's attempt (as a child of Holocaust survivors) to understand and relate to parents whose lives have been warped by the unspeakable horrors they witnessed and endured. In 1968, Anja, Spiegelman's mother, committed suicide. Spiegelman published "Prisoner on the Hell Planet: A Case History" in Short Order Comix, #1 in 1973—and in 1986 included it in *Maus*—the only segment of the book with human rather than animal characters.

   The passages in Aramaic (a language very close to Hebrew) on page 1245 are the opening lines of the Kaddish—the Jewish prayer for the dead: "Extolled and hallowed be the name of God throughout the world which he has created and which he governs according to his righteous will. . . ." —*Eds.*

1242

For Analysis

1. Explain the title. Why is the central figure dressed as a prisoner throughout the piece? **2.** What are some possible reasons for the mother's suicide? Do you think Artie could have prevented it? **3.** Why does Artie accuse his mother of murdering him? **4.** What is the nature of Artie's imprisonment?

On Style

1. How does Spiegelman use graphics to reinforce the emotional impact of the story? **2.** Compare the graphics of the first panel with those of the second panel on p. 1243. How do they differ and what is the effect of the differences? **3.** Closely examine the faces of each character. How do the visual representations convey meaning?

Making Connections

Examine your own relationship with your parents. Can you remember some act of theirs that profoundly affected you? Did some act of yours profoundly affect them? Write an essay on this event, explaining its significance to you now.

Writing Topic

In an essay, describe an act of either a parent or someone with authority over you that emotionally imprisoned you.

Amy Hempel [b. 1951]

In the Cemetery Where Al Jolson Is Buried 1985

"Tell me things I won't mind forgetting," she said. "Make it useless stuff or skip it."

I began. I told her insects fly through rain, missing every drop, never getting wet. I told her no one in America owned a tape recorder before Bing Crosby did. I told her the shape of the moon is like a banana—you see it looking full, you're seeing it end-on.

The camera made me self-conscious and I stopped. It was trained on us from a ceiling mount—the kind of camera banks use to photograph robbers. It played us to the nurses down the hall in Intensive Care.

"Go on, girl," she said. "You get used to it."

I had my audience. I went on. Did she know that Tammy Wynette had   5
changed her tune? Really. That now she sings "Stand by Your *Friends*"? That Paul Anka did it too, I said. Does "You're Having *Our* Baby." That he got sick of all that feminist bitching.

"What else?" she said. "Have you got something else?"

Oh, yes.

For her I would always have something else.

"Did you know that when they taught the first chimp to talk, it lied? That when they asked her who did it on the desk, she signed back the name of the janitor. And that when they pressed her, she said she was sorry, that it was really the project director. But she was a mother, so I guess she had her reasons."

"Oh, that's good," she said. "A parable."   10

"There's more about the chimp," I said. "But it will break your heart."

"No, thanks," she says, and scratches at her mask.

We look like good-guy outlaws. Good or bad, I am not used to the mask yet. I keep touching the warm spot where my breath, thank God, comes out. She is used to hers. She only ties the strings on top. The other ones—a pro by now—she lets hang loose.

We call this place the Marcus Welby Hospital. It's the white one with the palm trees under the opening credits of all those shows. A Hollywood hospital, though in fact it is several miles west. Off camera, there is a beach across the street.

She introduces me to a nurse as the Best Friend. The impersonal article is   15
more intimate. It tells me that *they* are intimate, the nurse and my friend.

1248

"I was telling her we used to drink Canada Dry ginger ale and pretend we were in Canada."

"That's how dumb we were," I say.

"You could be sisters," the nurse says.

So how come, I'll bet they are wondering, it took me so long to get to such a glamorous place? But do they ask?

They do not ask.   20

Two months, and how long is the drive?

The best I can explain it is this—I have a friend who worked one summer in a mortuary. He used to tell me stories. The one that really got to me was not the grisliest, but it's the one that did. A man wrecked his car on 101 going south. He did not lose consciousness. But his arm was taken down to the wet bone—and when he looked at it—it scared him to death.

I mean, he died.

So I hadn't dared to look any closer. But now I'm doing it—and hoping that I will live through it.

She shakes out a summer-weight blanket, showing a leg you did not want to   25
see. Except for that, you look at her and understand the law that requires *two* people to be with the body at all times.

"I thought of something," she says. "I thought of it last night. I think there is a real and present need here. You know," she says, "like for someone to do it for you when you can't do it yourself. You call them up whenever you want—like when push comes to shove."

She grabs the bedside phone and loops the cord around her neck.

"Hey," she says, "the end o' the line."

She keeps on, giddy with something. But I don't know with what.

"I can't remember," she says. "What does Kübler-Ross[1] say comes after De-   30
nial?"

It seems to me Anger must be next. Then Bargaining, Depression, and so on and so forth. But I keep my guesses to myself.

"The only thing is," she says, "is where's Resurrection? God knows, I want to do it by the book. But she left out Resurrection."

She laughs, and I cling to the sound the way someone dangling above a ravine holds fast to the thrown rope.

"Tell me," she says, "about that chimp with the talking hands. What do they do when the thing ends and the chimp says, 'I don't want to go back to the zoo'?"

When I don't say anything, she says, "Okay—then tell me another animal   35
story. I like animal stories. But not a sick one—I don't want to know about all the seeing-eye dogs going blind."

No, I would not tell her a sick one.

---

[1] Elizabeth Kübler-Ross is the author of *On Death and Dying* (1969), a celebrated book on the psychological stages experienced by the dying.

"How about the hearing-ear dogs?" I say. "They're not going deaf, but they are getting very judgmental. For instance, there's this golden retriever in New Jersey, he wakes up the deaf mother and drags her into the daughter's room because the kid has got a flashlight and is reading under the covers."

"Oh, you're killing me," she says. "Yes, you're definitely killing me."

"They say the smart dog obeys, but the smarter dog knows when to disobey."

"Yes," she says, "the smarter anything knows when to disobey. Now, for example."   40

She is flirting with the Good Doctor, who has just appeared. Unlike the Bad Doctor, who checks the IV drip before saying good morning, the Good Doctor says things like "God didn't give epileptics a fair shake." The Good Doctor awards himself points for the cripples he could have hit in the parking lot. Because the Good Doctor is a little in love with her, he says maybe a year. He pulls a chair up to her bed and suggests I might like to spend an hour on the beach.

"Bring me something back," she says. "Anything from the beach. Or the gift shop. Taste is no object."

He draws the curtain around her bed.

"Wait!" she cries.

I look in at her.   45

"Anything," she says, "except a magazine subscription."

The doctor turns away.

I watch her mouth laugh.

What seems dangerous often is not—black snakes, for example, or clear-air turbulence. While things that just lie there, like this beach, are loaded with jeopardy. A yellow dust rising from the ground, the heat that ripens melons overnight—this is earthquake weather. You can sit here braiding the fringe on your towel and the sand will all of a sudden suck down like an hourglass. The air roars. In the cheap apartments on-shore, bathtubs fill themselves and gardens roll up and over like green waves. If nothing happens, the dust will drift and the heat deepen till fear turns to desire. Nerves like that are only bought off by catastrophe.

"It never happens when you're thinking about it," she once observed. "Earthquake, earthquake, earthquake," she said.   50

"Earthquake, earthquake, earthquake," I said.

Like the aviaphobe who keeps the plane aloft with prayer, we kept it up until an aftershock cracked the ceiling.

That was after the big one in seventy-two. We were in college; our dormitory was five miles from the epicenter. When the ride was over and my jabbering pulse began to slow, she served five parts champagne to one part orange juice, and joked about living in Ocean View, Kansas. I offered to drive her to Hawaii on the new world psychics predicted would surface the next time, or the next.

I could not say that now—next.
Whose next? she could ask. 55

Was I the only one who noticed that the experts had stopped saying *if* and now spoke of *when*? Of course not; the fearful ran to thousands. We watched the traffic of Japanese beetles for deviation. Deviation might mean more natural violence.

I wanted her to be afraid with me. But she said, "I don't know. I'm just not."
She was afraid of nothing, not even of flying.
I have this dream before a flight where we buckle in and the plane moves down the runway. It takes off at thirty-five miles an hour, and then we're airborne, skimming the tree tops. Still, we arrive in New York on time.
It is so pleasant. 60
One night I flew to Moscow this way.

She flew with me once. That time she flew with me she ate macadamia nuts while the wings bounced. She knows the wing tips can bend thirty feet up and thirty feet down without coming off. She believes it. She trusts the laws of aerodynamics. My mind stampedes. I can almost accept that a battleship floats when everybody knows steel sinks.

I see fear in her now, and am not going to try to talk her out of it. She is right to be afraid.

After a quake, the six o'clock news airs a film clip of first-graders yelling at the broken playground per their teacher's instructions.
"*Bad* earth!" they shout, because anger is stronger than fear. 65

But the beach is standing still today. Everyone on it is tranquilized, numb, or asleep. Teenaged girls rub coconut oil on each other's hard-to-reach places. They smell like macaroons. They pry open compacts like clamshells; mirrors catch the sun and throw a spray of white rays across glazed shoulders. The girls arrange their wet hair with silk flowers the way they learned in *Seventeen*. They pose.

A formation of low-riders pulls over to watch with a six-pack. They get vocal when the girls check their tan lines. When the beer is gone, so are they—flexing their cars on up the boulevard.

Above this aggressive health are the twin wrought-iron terraces, painted flamingo pink, of the Palm Royale. Someone dies there every time the sheets are changed. There's an ambulance in the driveway, so the remaining residents line the balconies, rocking and not talking, one-upped.

The ocean they stare at is dangerous, and not just the undertow. You can almost see the slapping tails of sand sharks keeping cruising bodies alive.

If she looked, she could see this, some of it, from her window. She would be 70 the first to say how little it takes to make a thing all wrong.

There was a second bed in the room when I got back to it!
For two beats I didn't get it. Then it hit me like an open coffin.

She wants every minute, I thought. She wants my life.

"You missed Gussie," she said.

Gussie is her parents' three-hundred-pound narcoleptic maid. Her attacks often come at the ironing board. The pillowcases in that family are all bordered with scorch. ⁷⁵

"It's a hard trip for her," I said. "How is she?"

"Well, she didn't fall asleep, if that's what you mean. Gussie's great—you know what she said? She said, 'Darlin', stop this worriation. Just keep prayin', down on your knees'—me, who can't even get out of bed."

She shrugged. "What am I missing?"

"It's earthquake weather," I told her.

"The best thing to do about earthquakes," she said, "is not to live in California." ⁸⁰

"That's useful," I said. "You sound like Reverend Ike—'The best thing to do for the poor is not to be one of them.' "

We're crazy about Reverend Ike.

I noticed her face was bloated.

"You know," she said, "I feel like hell. I'm about to stop having fun."

"The ancients have a saying," I said. " 'There are times when the wolves are silent; there are times when the moon howls.' " ⁸⁵

"What's that, Navaho?"

"Palm Royale lobby graffiti," I said. "I bought a paper there. I'll read you something."

"Even though I care about nothing?"

I turned to the page with the trivia column. I said, "Did you know the more shrimp flamingo birds eat, the pinker their feathers get?" I said, "Did you know that Eskimos need refrigerators? Do you know *why* Eskimos need refrigerators? Did you know that Eskimos need refrigerators because how else would they keep their food from freezing?"

I turned to page three, to a UPI filler datelined Mexico City. I read her MAN ROBS BANK WITH CHICKEN, about a man who bought a barbecued chicken at a stand down the block from a bank. Passing the bank, he got the idea. He walked in and approached a teller. He pointed the brown paper bag at her and she handed over the day's receipts. It was the smell of barbecue sauce that eventually led to his capture. ⁹⁰

The story had made her hungry, she said—so I took the elevator down six floors to the cafeteria, and brought back all the ice cream she wanted. We lay side by side, adjustable beds cranked up for optimal TV-viewing, littering the sheets with Good Humor wrappers, picking toasted almonds out of the gauze. We were Lucy and Ethel, Mary and Rhoda in extremis. The blinds were closed to keep light off the screen.

We watched a movie starring men we used to think we wanted to sleep with. Hers was a tough cop out to stop mine, a vicious rapist who went after cocktail waitresses.

"This is a good movie," she said when snipers felled them both.

I missed her already.

A Filipino nurse tiptoed in and gave her an injection. The nurse removed the pile of popsicle sticks from the nightstand—enough to splint a small animal.

The injection made us both sleepy. We slept.

I dreamed she was a decorator, come to furnish my house. She worked in secret, singing to herself. When she finished, she guided me proudly to the door. "How do you like it?" she asked, easing me inside.

Every beam and sill and shelf and knob was draped in gay bunting, with streamers of pastel crepe looped around bright mirrors.

"I have to go home," I said when she woke up.

She thought I meant home to her house in the Canyon, and I had to say No, *home* home. I twisted my hands in the time-honored fashion of people in pain. I was supposed to offer something. The Best Friend. I could not even offer to come back.

I felt weak and small and failed.

Also exhilarated.

I had a convertible in the parking lot. Once out of that room, I would drive it too fast down the Coast highway through the crab-smelling air. A stop in Malibu for sangria. The music in the place would be sexy and loud. They'd serve papaya and shrimp and watermelon ice. After dinner I would shimmer with lust, buzz with heat, vibrate with life, and stay up all night.

Without a word, she yanked off her mask and threw it on the floor. She kicked at the blankets and moved to the door. She must have hated having to pause for breath and balance before slamming out of Isolation, and out of the second room, the one where you scrub and tie on the white masks.

A voice shouted her name in alarm, and people ran down the corridor. The Good Doctor was paged over the intercom. I opened the door and the nurses at the station stared hard, as if this flight had been my idea.

"Where is she?" I asked, and they nodded to the supply closet.

I looked in. Two nurses were kneeling beside her on the floor, talking to her in low voices. One held a mask over her nose and mouth, the other rubbed her back in slow circles. The nurses glanced up to see if I was the doctor—and when I wasn't, they went back to what they were doing.

"There, there, honey," they cooed.

On the morning she was moved to the cemetery, the one where Al Jolson is buried, I enrolled in a "Fear of Flying" class. "What is your worst fear?" the instructor asked, and I answered, "That I will finish this course and still be afraid."

I sleep with a glass of water on the nightstand so I can see by its level if the coastal earth is trembling or if the shaking is still me.

❖   ❖   ❖

What do I remember?

I remember only the useless things I hear—that Bob Dylan's mother invented Wite-Out, that twenty-three people must be in a room before there is a fifty-fifty chance two will have the same birthday. Who cares whether or not it's true? In my head there are bath towels swaddling this stuff. Nothing else seeps through.

I review those things that will figure in the retelling: a kiss through surgical gauze, the pale hand correcting the position of the wig. I noted these gestures as they happened, not in any retrospect—though I don't know why looking back should show us more than looking *at*.

It is just possible I will say I stayed the night.

And who is there that can say that I did not?   115

I think of the chimp, the one with the talking hands.

In the course of the experiment, that chimp had a baby. Imagine how her trainers must have thrilled when the mother, without prompting, began to sign to her newborn.

Baby, drink milk.

Baby, play ball.

And when the baby died, the mother stood over the body, her wrinkled hands moving with animal grace, forming again and again the words: Baby, come hug,   120
Baby, come hug, fluent now in the language of grief.

for Jessica Wolfson

For Analysis

1. What is the significance of the story's title? **2.** How old are the women and what is their relationship? **3.** How would you characterize the women's conversation? What purpose does their conversation serve? **4.** Why does the narrator feel exhilarated when she leaves? **5.** Why does the narrator contemplate lying about having spent the night with her dying friend?

On Style

1. A significant portion of this story consists of trivia. How does the trivia enhance the story's impact? Would you consider the final section of the story another piece of trivia? Explain. **2.** Describe the author's technique for establishing the **setting** and the circumstances in this story.

Making Connections

1. Compare this story with Tolstoy's "The Death of Iván Ilých" (p. 1165) and Selzer's essay "The Discus Thrower" (p. 1340). Describe the differences in the behavior of each character facing death. Be sure to consider the dying woman's attempt to leave her bed. **2.** What duties do you think the living owe, if any, to dying friends and relatives?

Writing Topics

1. Describe the effect of the story's last section—the account of the chimp with talking hands. Why does the narrator credit the chimp with a greater fluency "in the language of grief"? **2.** The dying woman faults Kübler-Ross for not discussing "Resurrection." In an essay comparing this story with Tolstoy's "The Death of Iván Ilých" (p. 1165), examine the impact of a belief in resurrection on the behavior of the dying.

Poetry

Anonymous

Edward

1

"Why does your brand° sae° drap wi' bluid,   sword/so
    Edward, Edward,
Why does your brand sae drap wi' bluid,
    And why sae sad gang° ye, O?"   go
"O I ha'e killed my hawk sae guid,
    Mither, mither,
O I ha'e killed my hawk sae guid,
    And I had nae mair but he, O."

2

"Your hawke's bluid was never sae reid,°   red
    Edward, Edward,   10
Your hawke's bluid was never sae reid,
    My dear son I tell thee, O."
"O I ha'e killed my reid-roan steed,
    Mither, mither,
O I ha'e killed my reid-roan steed,
    That erst was sae fair and free, O."

3

"Your steed was auld, and ye ha'e gat mair,
    Edward, Edward,
Your steed was auld, and ye ha'e gat mair,
    Some other dule° ye drie,° O."   grief/suffer
"O I ha'e killed my fader dear,
    Mither, mither,
O I ha'e killed my fader dear,
    Alas, and wae° is me, O!"   woe

1256

4

"And whatten penance wul ye drie for that,
     Edward, Edward?
And whatten penance wul ye drie for that,
  My dear son, now tell me, O?"
"I'll set my feet in yonder boat,
     Mither, mither,   30
I'll set my feet in yonder boat,
  And I'll fare over the sea, O."

5

"And what wul ye do wi' your towers and your ha',
     Edward, Edward?
And what wul ye do wi' your towers and your ha',
  That were sae fair to see, O?"
"I'll let them stand tul they down fa',
     Mither, mither,
I'll let them stand tul they down fa',
  For here never mair maun° I be, O."   must

6

"And what wul ye leave to your bairns° and your wife,   children
     Edward, Edward?
And what wul ye leave to your bairns and your wife,
  Whan ye gang over the sea, O?"
"The warlde's° room, let them beg thrae° life,   world's/through
     Mither, mither,
The warlde's room, let them beg thrae life,
  For them never mair wul I see, O."

7

"And what wul ye leave to your ain mither dear,
     Edward, Edward?   50
And what wul ye leave to your ain mither dear,
  My dear son, now tell me, O?"
"The curse of hell frae° me sall° ye bear,   from/shall
     Mither, mither,
The curse of hell frae me sall ye bear,
  Sic° counsels ye gave to me, O."   such

For Analysis
1. Why does the mother reject Edward's answers to her first two questions? **2.** Does the poem provide any clues to the murderer's motive? **3.** Edward has murdered his father and then bitterly turns away from his mother, wife, and children. What basis is there in the poem for nevertheless sympathizing with Edward?

Writing Topic
What effects are achieved through the question-and-answer technique and the repetition of lines?

William Shakespeare   [1564–1616]

Sonnet   1609

73

That time of year thou mayst in me behold
When yellow leaves, or none, or few, do hang
Upon those boughs which shake against the cold,
Bare ruined choirs, where late the sweet birds sang.
In me thou see'st the twilight of such day
As after sunset fadeth in the west;
Which by and by black night doth take away,
Death's second self, that seals up all in rest.
In me thou see'st the glowing of such fire,
That on the ashes of his youth doth lie,   10
As the deathbed whereon it must expire,
Consumed with that which it was nourished by.
This thou perceiv'st, which makes thy love more strong,
To love that well which thou must leave ere long.

Fear No More the Heat o' the Sun   1623

Fear no more the heat o' the sun,[1]
   Nor the furious winter's rages;
Thou thy worldly task hast done,
   Home art gone, and ta'en thy wages:
Golden lads and girls all must,
As chimney-sweepers, come to dust.

Fear No More the Heat o' the Sun
   [1] From *Cymbeline*, Act IV, Scene 2.

Fear no more the frown o' the great;
  Thou art past the tyrant's stroke;
Care no more to clothe and eat;
  To thee the reed is as the oak: 10
The scepter, learning, physic,° must[2]   *medicine*
All follow this, and come to dust.

Fear no more the lightning flash,
  Nor the all-dreaded thunder stone;[3]
Fear not slander, censure rash;
  Thou hast finished joy and moan:
All lovers young, all lovers must
Consign to° thee, and come to dust.   *agree with*

No exorciser harm thee!
Nor no witchcraft charm thee!   20
Ghost unlaid forbear thee!
Nothing ill come near thee!
Quiet consummation have;
And renownéd be thy grave!

from

Richard II   1595

And nothing can we call our own but death
And that small model of the barren earth
Which serves as paste and cover to our bones.
For God's sake, let us sit upon the ground
And tell sad stories of the death of kings:
How some have been deposed; some slain in war;
Some haunted by the ghosts they have deposed;
Some poison'd by their wives; some sleeping kill'd;
All murder'd: for within the hollow crown
That rounds the mortal temples of a king   10
Keeps Death his court and there the antic sits
Scoffing his state and grinning at his pomp,
Allowing him a breath, a little scene,
To monarchize, be fear'd and kill with looks,
Infusing him with self and vain conceit,

Fear No More the Heat o' the Sun
    [2] I.e., kings, scholars, and physicians.
    [3] It was believed that thunder was caused by falling meteorites.

As if this flesh which walls about our life
Were brass impregnable, and humour'd thus
Comes at the last and with a little pin
Bores through his castle wall, and farewell king!

from

Macbeth 1606

She should have died hereafter;
There would have been a time for such a word.
To-morrow, and to-morrow, and to-morrow,
Creeps in this petty pace from day to day
To the last syllable of recorded time,
And all our yesterdays have lighted fools
The way to dusty death. Out, out, brief candle!
Life's but a walking shadow, a poor player
That struts and frets his hour upon the stage
And then is heard no more: it is a tale   10
Told by an idiot, full of sound and fury,
Signifying nothing.

For Analysis
1. Examine the **images** in this meditation by Macbeth on the meaning of life (he has
just received word that Lady Macbeth has died). Do they hold together or are they
confusing; for example, how does the image of the candle (l. 7) relate to the images
that precede and follow it?

from

Hamlet 1601

To be, or not to be, that is the question:
Whether 'tis nobler in the mind to suffer
The slings and arrows of outrageous fortune,
Or to take arms against a sea of troubles,
And by opposing end them. To die, to sleep—
No more; and by a sleep to say we end
The heartache, and the thousand natural shocks
That flesh is heir to. 'Tis a consummation
Devoutly to be wished—to die, to sleep—

To sleep, perchance to dream, ay there's the rub;   10
For in that sleep of death what dreams may come
When we have shuffled off this mortal coil°   turmoil
Must give us pause—there's the respect
That makes calamity of so long life.
For who would bear the whips and scorns of time,
Th' oppressor's wrong, the proud man's contumely,
The pangs of despised love, the law's delay,
The insolence of office, and the spurns
That patient merit of th' unworthy takes,
When he himself might his quietus° make   settlement
With a bare bodkin°? Who would fardels° bear,   dagger/burdens
To grunt and sweat under a weary life,
But that the dread of something after death,
The undiscovered country, from whose bourn°   realm
No traveller returns, puzzles the will,
And makes us rather bear those ills we have
Than fly to others that we know not of?
Thus conscience° does make cowards of us all;   thought
And thus the native hue of resolution
Is sicklied o'er with the pale cast of thought,   30
And enterprises of great pitch° and moment   degree
With this regard their currents turn awry
And lose the name of action.

For Analysis

1. What does Hamlet conclude about man's fear of death? Does he view it as cowardly and ignoble? **2.** Explain line 28.

Thomas Nashe   [1567–1601]

A Litany in Time of Plague   1600

Adieu, farewell, earth's bliss;
This world uncertain is;
Fond° are life's lustful joys;   foolish
Death proves them all but toys;
None from his darts can fly;
I am sick, I must die.
    Lord, have mercy on us!

Rich men, trust not in wealth,
Gold cannot buy you health;
Physic himself must fade.   10
All things to end are made,
The plague full swift goes by;
I am sick, I must die.
    Lord, have mercy on us!

Beauty is but a flower
Which wrinkles will devour;
Brightness falls from the air;
Queens have died young and fair;
Dust hath closed Helen's[1] eye.
I am sick, I must die.   20
    Lord, have mercy on us!

Strength stoops unto the grave,
Worms feed on Hector[2] brave;
Swords may not fight with fate,
Earth still holds ope her gate.
"Come, come!" the bells do cry.
I am sick, I must die.
    Lord, have mercy on us.

Wit with his wantonness
Tasteth death's bitterness;   30
Hell's executioner
Hath no ears for to hear
What vain art can reply.
I am sick, I must die.
    Lord, have mercy on us.

Haste, therefore, each degree,
To welcome destiny;
Heaven is our heritage,
Earth but a player's stage;
Mount we unto the sky.   40
I am sick, I must die.
    Lord, have mercy on us.

[1] Helen of Troy, a fabled beauty.
[2] Commander of the Trojan forces in the Trojan War.

John Donne   [1572–1631]

Death, Be Not Proud   1633

Death be not proud, though some have calléd thee
Mighty and dreadful, for thou art not so;
For those whom thou think'st thou dost overthrow
Die not, poor Death, nor yet canst thou kill me.
From rest and sleep, which but thy pictures be,
Much pleasure; then from thee much more must flow,
And soonest our best men with thee do go,
Rest of their bones, and soul's delivery.
Thou art slave to fate, chance, kings, and desperate men,
And dost with poison, war, and sickness dwell,   10
And poppy or charms can make us sleep as well
And better than thy stroke; why swell'st thou then?
One short sleep past, we wake eternally
And death shall be no more; Death, thou shalt die.

George Gordon, Lord Byron   [1788–1824]

Lines Inscribed upon a Cup Formed from a Skull   1814

Start not—nor deem my spirit fled;
    In me behold the only skull,
From which, unlike a living head,
    Whatever flows is never dull.

I lived, I loved, I quaff'd, like thee:
    I died: let earth my bones resign;
Fill up—thou canst not injure me;
    The worm hath fouler lips than thine.

Better to hold the sparkling grape,
    Than nurse the earth-worm's slimy brood;   10

And circle in the goblet's shape
   The drink of gods, than reptile's food.

Where once my wit, perchance, hath shone,
   In aid of others' let me shine;
And when, alas! our brains are gone,
   What nobler substitute than wine?

Quaff while thou canst: another race,
   When thou and thine, like me, are sped,
May rescue thee from earth's embrace,
   And rhyme and revel with the dead.   20

Why not? since through life's little day
   Our heads such sad effects produce;
Redeem'd from worms and wasting clay,
   This chance is theirs, to be of use.

Percy Bysshe Shelley   [1792–1822]

Ozymandias[1]   1818

I met a traveller from an antique land
Who said: Two vast and trunkless legs of stone
Stand in the desert . . . Near them, on the sand,
Half sunk, a shattered visage lies, whose frown,
And wrinkled lip, and sneer of cold command,
Tell that its sculptor well those passions read
Which yet survive, stamped on these lifeless things,
The hand that mocked them, and the heart that fed:
And on the pedestal these words appear:
"My name is Ozymandias, king of kings: 10
Look on my works, ye Mighty, and despair!"
Nothing beside remains. Round the decay
Of that colossal wreck, boundless and bare
The lone and level sands stretch far away.

Ozymandias
   [1] Egyptian monarch of the thirteenth century B.C., said to have erected a huge statue of himself.

John Keats   [1795–1821]

Ode on a Grecian Urn   1820

I

Thou still unravished bride of quietness,
   Thou foster child of silence and slow time,
Sylvan historian, who canst thus express
   A flowery tale more sweetly than our rhyme:
What leaf-fringed legend haunts about thy shape
   Of deities or mortals, or of both,
      In Tempe or the dales of Arcady?[1]
   What men or gods are these? What maidens loath?
What mad pursuit? What struggle to escape?
      What pipes and timbrels? What wild ecstasy?   10

II

Heard melodies are sweet, but those unheard
   Are sweeter; therefore, ye soft pipes, play on;
Not to the sensual ear, but, more endeared,
   Pipe to the spirit ditties of no tone:
Fair youth, beneath the trees, thou canst not leave
   Thy song, nor ever can those trees be bare;
      Bold Lover, never, never canst thou kiss,
Though winning near the goal—yet, do not grieve;
      She cannot fade, though thou hast not thy bliss,
   Forever wilt thou love, and she be fair!   20

III

Ah, happy, happy boughs! that cannot shed
   Your leaves, nor ever bid the Spring adieu;
And, happy melodist, unweariéd,
   Forever piping songs forever new;
More happy love! more happy, happy love!
   Forever warm and still to be enjoyed,
      Forever panting, and forever young;
All breathing human passion far above,[2]

---

[1] Tempe and Arcady are valleys in Greece famous for their beauty. In ancient times, Tempe was regarded as sacred to Apollo.
[2] I.e., far above all breathing human passion.

That leaves a heart high-sorrowful and cloyed,
   A burning forehead, and a parching tongue.   30

IV

Who are these coming to the sacrifice?
   To what green altar, O mysterious priest,
Lead'st thou that heifer lowing at the skies,
   And all her silken flanks with garlands dressed?
What little town by river or sea shore,
   Or mountain-built with peaceful citadel,
      Is emptied of this folk, this pious morn?
And, little town, thy streets forevermore
   Will silent be; and not a soul to tell
      Why thou art desolate, can e'er return.   40

V

O Attic³ shape! Fair attitude! with brede
   Of marble men and maidens overwrought,
With forest branches and the trodden weed;
   Thou, silent form, dost tease us out of thought
As doth eternity: Cold Pastoral!
   When old age shall this generation waste,
      Thou shalt remain, in midst of other woe
Than ours, a friend to man, to whom thou say'st,
"Beauty is truth, truth beauty,—that is all
      Ye know on earth, and all ye need to know."   50

For Analysis

1. Describe the scene the poet sees depicted on the urn. Describe the scene the poet imagines as a consequence of the scene on the urn. **2.** Why are the boughs, the piper, and the lovers happy in stanza 3? **3.** Explain the assertion of stanza II that "Heard melodies are sweet, but those unheard / Are sweeter." **4.** Does the poem support the assertion of the last two lines? What does that assertion mean?

Writing Topic

In what sense might it be argued that this poem is about mortality and immortality? In this connection, consider the meaning of the phrase "Cold Pastoral!" (l. 45).

---

³ Athenian, thus simple and graceful.

Matthew Arnold   [1822–1888]

Growing Old   1867

What is it to grow old?
Is it to lose the glory of the form,
The luster of the eye?
Is it for beauty to forego her wreath?
—Yes, but not this alone.

Is it to feel our strength—
Not our bloom only, but our strength—decay?
Is it to feel each limb
Grow stiffer, every function less exact,
Each nerve more loosely strung?   10

Yes, this, and more; but not
Ah, 'tis not what in youth we dreamed 'twould be!
'Tis not to have our life
Mellowed and softened as with sunset glow,
A golden day's decline.

'Tis not to see the world
As from a height, with rapt prophetic eyes,
And heart profoundly stirred;
And weep, and feel the fullness of the past,
The years that are no more.   20

It is to spend long days
And not once feel that we were ever young;
It is to add, immured
In the hot prison of the present, month
To month with weary pain.

It is to suffer this,
And feel but half, and feebly, what we feel.
Deep in our hidden heart
Festers the dull remembrance of a change,
But no emotion—none.   30

It is—last stage of all—
When we are frozen up within, and quite

The phantom of ourselves,
To hear the world applaud the hollow ghost
Which blamed the living man.

Emily Dickinson [1830–1886]

After great pain, a formal feeling comes ca. 1862

After great pain, a formal feeling comes—
The Nerves sit ceremonious, like Tombs—
The stiff Heart questions was it He, that bore,
And Yesterday, or Centuries before?

The Feet, mechanical, go round—
Of Ground, or Air, or Ought—
A Wooden way
Regardless grown,
A Quartz contentment, like a stone—

This is the Hour of Lead—   10
Remembered, if outlived,
As Freezing persons, recollect the Snow—
First—Chill—then Stupor—then the letting go—

For Analysis
Is this poem about physical or psychic pain? Explain.

Writing Topic
What is the meaning of "stiff Heart" (l. 3) and "Quartz contentment" (l. 9)? What part
do they play in the larger pattern of images?

I heard a Fly buzz— when I died ca. 1862

I heard a Fly buzz—when I died—
The Stillness in the Room
Was like the Stillness in the Air—
Between the Heaves of Storm—

The Eyes around—had wrung them dry—
And Breaths were gathering firm
For that last Onset—when the King
Be witnessed—in the Room—

I willed my Keepsakes—Signed away
What portion of me be   10
Assignable—and then it was
There interposed a Fly—

With Blue—uncertain stumbling Buzz—
Between the light—and me—
And then the Windows failed—and then
I could not see to see—

Apparently with no surprise   ca. 1884

Apparently with no surprise
To any happy Flower,
The Frost beheads it at its play
In accidental power.
The blond Assassin passes on,
The Sun proceeds unmoved
To measure off another Day
For an Approving God.

A. E. Housman   [1859–1936]

To an Athlete Dying Young   1896

The time you won your town the race
We chaired you through the market place;
Man and boy stood cheering by,
And home we brought you shoulder-high.

Today, the road all runners come,
Shoulder-high we bring you home,
And set you at your threshold down,
Townsman of a stiller town.

Smart lad, to slip betimes away
From fields where glory does not stay,   10
And early though the laurel grows
It withers quicker than the rose.

Eyes the shady night has shut
Cannot see the record cut,
And silence sounds no worse than cheers
After earth has stopped the ears:

Now you will not swell the rout
Of lads that wore their honors out,
Runners whom renown outran
And the name died before the man.   20

So set, before its echoes fade,
The fleet foot on the sill of shade,
And hold to the low lintel up
The still-defended challenge cup.

And round that early-laureled head
Will flock to gaze the strengthless dead
And find unwithered on its curls
The garland briefer than a girl's.

William Butler Yeats   [1865–1939]

Sailing to Byzantium[1]   1927

1

That is no country for old men. The young
In one another's arms, birds in the trees
—Those dying generations—at their song,
The salmon-falls, the mackerel-crowded seas,
Fish, flesh, or fowl, commend all summer long
Whatever is begotten, born, and dies.

Sailing to Byzantium
   [1] Capital of the ancient Eastern Roman Empire, Byzantium (modern Istanbul) is celebrated for
its great art, including mosaics (in ll. 17–18, Yeats addresses the figures in one of these mosaics). In
A Vision, Yeats cites Byzantium as possibly the only civilization which had achieved what he called
"Unity of Being," a state where "religious, aesthetic and practical life were one. . . ."

Caught in that sensual music all neglect
Monuments of unaging intellect.

2

An aged man is but a paltry thing,
A tattered coat upon a stick, unless   10
Soul clap its hands and sing, and louder sing
For every tatter in its mortal dress,
Nor is there singing school but studying
Monuments of its own magnificence;
And therefore I have sailed the seas and come
To the holy city of Byzantium.

3

O sages standing in God's holy fire
As in the gold mosaic of a wall,
Come from the holy fire, perne in a gyre,[2]
And be the singing-masters of my soul.   20
Consume my heart away; sick with desire
And fastened to a dying animal
It knows not what it is; and gather me
Into the artifice of eternity.

4

Once out of nature I shall never take
My bodily form from any natural thing,
But such a form as Grecian goldsmiths make
Of hammered gold and gold enameling
To keep a drowsy Emperor awake;[3]
Or set upon a golden bough to sing   30
To lords and ladies of Byzantium
Of what is past, or passing, or to come.

For Analysis
1. This poem incorporates a series of contrasts, among them "That" country and Byzantium, the real birds of the first stanza and the artificial bird of the final stanza. What others do you find? **2.** What are the meanings of "generations" (l. 3)? **3.** For what is the poet "sick with desire" (l. 21)? **4.** In what sense is eternity an "artifice" (l. 24)?

[2] I.e., whirl in a spiral motion. Yeats associated this motion with the cycles of history and the fate of the individual. Here he entreats the sages represented in the mosaic to take him out of the natural world described in the first stanza and into the eternal world of art.
[3] "I have read somewhere," Yeats wrote, "that in the Emperor's palace at Byzantium was a tree made of gold and silver, and artificial birds that sang." The poet wishes to become an artificial bird (a work of art) in contrast to the real birds of the first stanza.

Writing Topic
In what ways are the **images** of bird and song used throughout this poem?

Edwin Arlington Robinson   [1869–1935]

Richard Cory   1897

Whenever Richard Cory went down town,
We people on the pavement looked at him:
He was a gentleman from sole to crown,
Clean favored, and imperially slim.

And he was always quietly arrayed,
And he was always human when he talked;
But still he fluttered pulses when he said,
"Good-morning," and he glittered when he walked.

And he was rich—yes, richer than a king—
And admirably schooled in every grace: 10
In fine, we thought that he was everything
To make us wish that we were in his place.

So on we worked, and waited for the light,
And went without the meat, and cursed the bread;
And Richard Cory, one calm summer night,
Went home and put a bullet through his head.

Robert Frost   [1874–1963]

After Apple-Picking   1914

My long two-pointed ladder's sticking through a tree
Toward heaven still,
And there's a barrel that I didn't fill

Beside it, and there may be two or three
Apples I didn't pick upon some bough.
But I am done with apple-picking now.
Essence of winter sleep is on the night,
The scent of apples: I am drowsing off.
I cannot rub the strangeness from my sight
I got from looking through a pane of glass   10
I skimmed this morning from the drinking trough
And held against the world of hoary grass.
It melted, and I let it fall and break.
But I was well
Upon my way to sleep before it fell,
And I could tell
What form my dreaming was about to take.
Magnified apples appear and disappear,
Stem end and blossom end,
And every fleck of russet showing clear.   20
My instep arch not only keeps the ache,
It keeps the pressure of a ladder-round.
I feel the ladder sway as the boughs bend.
And I keep hearing from the cellar bin
The rumbling sound
Of load on load of apples coming in.
For I have had too much
Of apple-picking: I am overtired
Of the great harvest I myself desired.
There were ten thousand thousand fruit to touch,   30
Cherish in hand, lift down, and not let fall.
For all
That struck the earth,
No matter if not bruised or spiked with stubble,
Went surely to the cider-apple heap
As of no worth.
One can see what will trouble
This sleep of mine, whatever sleep it is.
Were he not gone,
The woodchuck could say whether it's like his   40
Long sleep, as I describe its coming on,
Or just some human sleep.

For Analysis

1. What does apple-picking symbolize? 2. At the end of the poem, why is the speaker uncertain about what kind of sleep is coming on him?

Nothing Gold Can Stay   1923

Nature's first green is gold,
Her hardest hue to hold.
Her early leaf's a flower;
But only so an hour.
Then leaf subsides to leaf.
So Eden sank to grief,
So dawn goes down to day.
Nothing gold can stay.

For Analysis

1. Does this poem protest or accept the transitoriness of things? **2.** Why does Frost use the word "subsides" in line 5 rather than a word like "expands" or "grows"? **3.** How are "Nature's first green" (l. 1), "Eden" (l. 6), and "dawn" (l. 7) linked together?

'Out, Out—'[1]   1916

The buzz-saw snarled and rattled in the yard
And made dust and dropped stove-length sticks of wood,
Sweet-scented stuff when the breeze drew across it.
And from there those that lifted eyes could count
Five mountain ranges one behind the other
Under the sunset far into Vermont.
And the saw snarled and rattled, snarled and rattled,
As it ran light, or had to bear a load.
And nothing happened: day was all but done.
Call it a day, I wish they might have said   10
To please the boy by giving him the half hour
That a boy counts so much when saved from work.
His sister stood beside them in her apron
To tell them 'Supper.' At the word, the saw,
As if to prove saws knew what supper meant,
Leaped out at the boy's hand, or seemed to leap—
He must have given the hand. However it was,
Neither refused the meeting. But the hand!
The boy's first outcry was a rueful laugh,
As he swung toward them holding up the hand   20

'Out, Out—'
[1] The title is taken from the famous speech of Macbeth upon hearing that his wife has died (*Macbeth,* Act V, Scene 5).

Half in appeal, but half as if to keep
The life from spilling. Then the boy saw all—
Since he was old enough to know, big boy
Doing a man's work, though a child at heart—
He saw all spoiled. 'Don't let him cut my hand off—
The doctor, when he comes. Don't let him, sister!'
So. But the hand was gone already.
The doctor put him in the dark of ether.
He lay and puffed his lips out with his breath.
And then—the watcher at his pulse took fright.   30
No one believed. They listened at his heart.
Little—less—nothing!—and that ended it.
No more to build on there. And they, since they
Were not the one dead, turned to their affairs.

Stopping by Woods on a Snowy Evening   1923

Whose woods these are I think I know.
His house is in the village though;
He will not see me stopping here
To watch his woods fill up with snow.

My little horse must think it queer
To stop without a farmhouse near
Between the woods and frozen lake
The darkest evening of the year.

He gives his harness bells a shake
To ask if there is some mistake.   10
The only other sound's the sweep
Of easy wind and downy flake.

The woods are lovely, dark and deep,
But I have promises to keep,
And miles to go before I sleep,
And miles to go before I sleep.

For Analysis
1. What does the description of the horse tell us about the speaker? **2.** What function
does the repetition in the last two lines of the poem serve? **3.** Why does the speaker
refer to the owner of the woods in the opening stanza?

Design   1936

I found a dimpled spider, fat and white,
On a white heal-all, holding up a moth
Like a white piece of rigid satin cloth—
Assorted characters of death and blight
Mixed ready to begin the morning right,
Like the ingredients of a witches' broth—
A snow-drop spider, a flower like a froth,
And dead wings carried like a paper kite.

What had that flower to do with being white,
The wayside blue and innocent heal-all?   10
What brought the kindred spider to that height,
Then steered the white moth thither in the night?
What but design of darkness to appall?—
If design govern in a thing so small.

Writing Topic
Compare this poem with Emily Dickinson's "Apparently with no surprise" (p. 1269).

Padraic Pearse   [1879–1916]

Last Lines—1916[1]   1916
(Written the night before his execution)

The beauty of the world hath made me sad,
This beauty that will pass;
Sometimes my heart hath shaken with great joy
To see a leaping squirrel in a tree,
Or a red lady-bird upon a stalk,
Or little rabbits in a field at evening,
Lit by a slanting sun,
Or some green hill where shadows drifted by,
Some quiet hill where mountainy man hath sown
And soon would reap, near to the gate of Heaven;   10
Or children with bare feet upon the sands
Of some ebbed sea, or playing on the streets

Last Lines—1916
[1] Padraic Pearse was one of the Irish revolutionaries executed for his role in the Easter 1916 up-
rising. See note to W. B. Yeats's "Easter 1916," p. 438.

Of little towns in Connacht,
Things young and happy.
And then my heart hath told me:
These will pass,
Will pass and change, will die and be no more,
Things bright and green, things young and happy;
And I have gone upon my way
Sorrowful.   20

William Carlos Williams   [1883–1963]

Tract   1917

I will teach you my townspeople
how to perform a funeral—
for you have it over a troop
of artists—
unless one should scour the world—
you have the ground sense necessary.
See! the hearse leads.
I begin with a design for a hearse.
For Christ's sake not black—
nor white either—and not polished!   10
Let it be weathered—like a farm wagon—
with gilt wheels (this could be
applied fresh at small expense)
or no wheels at all:
a rough dray to drag over the ground.

Knock the glass out!
My God—glass, my townspeople!
For what purpose? Is it for the dead
to look out or for us to see
how well he is housed or to see   20
the flowers or the lack of them—
or what?
To keep the rain and snow from him?
He will have a heavier rain soon:
pebbles and dirt and what not.
Let there be no glass—
and no upholstery! phew!

and no little brass rollers
and small easy wheels on the bottom—
my townspeople what are you thinking of!   30

A rough plain hearse then
with gilt wheels and no top at all.
On this the coffin lies
by its own weight.
                No wreaths please—
especially no hot-house flowers.
Some common memento is better,
something he prized and is known by:
his old clothes—a few books perhaps—
God knows what! You realize   40
how we are about these things,
my townspeople—
something will be found—anything—
even flowers if he had come to that.
So much for the hearse.

For heaven's sake though see to the driver!
Take off the silk hat! In fact
that's no place at all for him
up there unceremoniously
dragging our friend out of his own dignity!   50
Bring him down—bring him down!
Low and inconspicuous! I'd not have him ride
on the wagon at all—damn him—
the undertaker's understrapper!
Let him hold the reins
and walk at the side
and inconspicuously too!

Then briefly as to yourselves:
Walk behind—as they do in France,
seventh class, or if you ride   60
Hell take curtains! Go with some show
of inconvenience; sit openly—
to the weather as to grief.
Or do you think you can shut grief in?
What—from us? We who have perhaps
nothing to lose? Share with us
share with us—it will be money
in your pockets.
                Go now
I think you are ready.   70

Wilfred Owen   [1893–1918]

Dulce et Decorum Est   1920

Bent double, like old beggars under sacks,
Knock-kneed, coughing like hags, we cursed through sludge,
Till on the haunting flares we turned our backs,
And towards our distant rest began to trudge.
Men marched asleep. Many had lost their boots,
But limped on, blood-shod. All went lame, all blind;
Drunk with fatigue; deaf even to the hoots
Of gas-shells dropping softly behind.

Gas! GAS! Quick, boys!—An ecstasy of fumbling,
Fitting the clumsy helmets just in time,   10
But someone still was yelling out and stumbling
And flound'ring like a man in fire or lime.—
Dim through the misty panes and thick green light,
As under a green sea, I saw him drowning.
In all my dreams before my helpless sight
He plunges at me, guttering, choking, drowning.

If in some smothering dreams, you too could pace
Behind the wagon that we flung him in,
And watch the white eyes writhing in his face,
His hanging face, like a devil's sick of sin,   20
If you could hear, at every jolt, the blood
Come gargling from the froth-corrupted lungs
Bitter as the cud
Of vile, incurable sores on innocent tongues,—
My friend, you would not tell with such high zest
To children ardent for some desperate glory,
The old lie: *Dulce et decorum est
Pro patria mori.*[1]

Dulce et Decorum Est
[1] A quotation from the Latin poet Horace, "It is sweet and fitting to die for one's country."

E. E. Cummings [1894–1962]

nobody loses all the time   1926

nobody loses all the time

i had an uncle named
Sol who was a born failure and
nearly everybody said he should have gone
into vaudeville perhaps because my Uncle Sol could
sing McCann He Was A Diver on Xmas Eve like Hell Itself which
may or may not account for the fact that my Uncle

Sol indulged in that possibly most inexcusable
of all to use a highfalootin phrase
luxuries that is or to   10
wit farming and be
it needlessly
added

my Uncle Sol's farm
failed because the chickens
ate the vegetables so
my Uncle Sol had a
chicken farm till the
skunks ate the chickens when

my Uncle Sol   20
had a skunk farm but
the skunks caught cold and
died and so
my Uncle Sol imitated the
skunks in a subtle manner

or by drowning himself in the watertank
but somebody who'd given my Uncle Sol a Victor
Victrola and records while he lived presented to
him upon the auspicious occasion of his decease a
scrumptious not to mention splendiferous funeral with   30
tall boys in black gloves and flowers and everything and

i remember we all cried like the Missouri
when my Uncle Sol's coffin lurched because
somebody pressed a button

1280

(and down went
my Uncle
Sol

and started a worm farm)

For Analysis
1. Explain the title. 2. What is the speaker's attitude toward Uncle Sol?

O sweet spontaneous   1923

O sweet spontaneous
earth how often have
the
doting

      fingers of
prurient philosophers pinched
and
poked

thee
, has the naughty thumb   10
of science prodded
thy

    beauty   .how
often have religions taken
thee upon their scraggy knees
squeezing and

buffeting thee that thou mightest conceive
gods
      (but
true   20

to the incomparable
couch of death thy
rhythmic
lover

     thou answerest

them only with

         spring)

For Analysis
1. Analyze the erotic **imagery** in this poem. What does it tell us about the speaker's attitude toward philosophy, science, and religion? **2.** What does the speaker mean by calling death earth's "lover" (l. 24)? And why "rhythmic" lover (l. 23)? **3.** In what sense is "spring" (l. 27) an answer?

Pablo Neruda [1904–1973]

The Dead Woman 1972

If suddenly you do not exist,
if suddenly you are not living,
I shall go on living.

I do not dare,
I do not dare to write it,
if you die.

I shall go on living.

Because where a man has no voice,
there, my voice.

Where blacks are beaten,   10
I can not be dead.
When my brothers go to jail
I shall go with them.

When victory,
not my victory
but the great victory
arrives,
even though I am mute I must speak:
I shall see it come even though I am blind.

No, forgive me.   20
If you are not living,
if you, beloved, my love,
if you
have died,
all the leaves will fall on my breast,

it will rain upon my soul night and day,
the snow will burn my heart,
I shall walk with cold and fire and death and snow,
my feet will want to march toward where you sleep,
but   30
I shall go on living,
because you wanted me to be, above all things,
untamable,
and, love, because you know that I am not just one man
but all men.

W. H. Auden   [1907–1973]

Musée des Beaux Arts   1940

About suffering they were never wrong,
The Old Masters: how well they understood
Its human position; how it takes place
While someone else is eating or opening a window or just walking dully along;
How, when the aged are reverently, passionately waiting
For the miraculous birth, there always must be
Children who did not specially want it to happen, skating
On a pond at the edge of the wood:
They never forgot
That even the dreadful martyrdom must run its course   10
Anyhow in a corner, some untidy spot
Where the dogs go on with their doggy life and the torturer's horse
Scratches its innocent behind on a tree.

In Brueghel's *Icarus*,[1] for instance: how everything turns away
Quite leisurely from the disaster; the plowman may
Have heard the splash, the forsaken cry,
But for him it was not an important failure; the sun shone
As it had to on the white legs disappearing into the green
Water; and the expensive delicate ship that must have seen
Something amazing, a boy falling out of the sky,   20
Had somewhere to get to and sailed calmly on.

Musée des Beaux Arts
  [1] This poem describes and comments on Pieter Brueghel's painting *Landscape with the Fall of Icarus* (reproduced on p. 1354). According to myth, Daedalus and his son Icarus made wings, whose feathers they attached with wax, to escape Crete. Icarus flew so near the sun that the wax melted and he fell into the sea.

Theodore Roethke [1908–1963]

Elegy for Jane 1958
My Student, Thrown By A Horse

I remember the neckcurls, limp and damp as tendrils;
And her quick look, a sidelong pickerel smile;
And how, once startled into talk, the light syllables leaped for her,
And she balanced in the delight of her thought,
A wren, happy, tail into the wind,
Her song trembling the twigs and small branches.
The shade sang with her;
The leaves, their whispers turned to kissing;
And the mold sang in the bleached valleys under the rose.

Oh, when she was sad, she cast herself down into such a pure depth,   10
Even a father could not find her:
Scraping her cheek against straw;
Stirring the clearest water.

My sparrow, you are not here,
Waiting like a fern, making a spiny shadow.
The sides of wet stones cannot console me,
Nor the moss, wound with the last light.

If only I could nudge you from this sleep,
My maimed darling, my skittery pigeon.
Over this damp grave I speak the words of my love: 20
I, with no rights in this matter,
Neither father nor lover.

May Sarton [1912–1995]

The Silence Now 1988

These days the silence is immense.
It is there deep down, not to be escaped.
The twittering flight of goldfinches,

1284

The three crows cawing in the distance
Only brush the surface of this silence
Full of mourning, the long drawn-out
Tug and sigh of waters never still—
The ocean out there, and the inner ocean.

Only animals comfort because they live
In the present and cannot drag us down   10
Into those caverns of memory full of loss.
They pay no attention to the thunder
Of distant waves. My dog's eager eyes
Watch me as I sit by the window, thinking.

At the bottom of the silence what lies in wait?
Is it love? Is it death? Too early or too late?
What is it I can have that I still want?

My swift response is to what cannot stay,
The dying daffodils, peonies on the way.
Iris just opening, lilac turning brown   20
In the immense silence where I live alone.

It is the transient that touches me, old,
Those light-shot clouds as the sky clears,
A passing glory can still move to tears,
Moments of pure joy like some fairy gold
Too evanescent to be kept or told.
And the cat's soft footfall on the stair
Keeps me alive, makes Nowhere into Here.
At the bottom of the silence it is she
Who speaks of an eternal Now to me.   30

Dylan Thomas   [1914–1953]

Do Not Go Gentle into That Good Night   1952

Do not go gentle into that good night,
Old age should burn and rave at close of day;
Rage, rage against the dying of the light.

Though wise men at their end know dark is right,
Because their words had forked no lightning they
Do not go gentle into that good night.

Good men, the last wave by, crying how bright
Their frail deeds might have danced in a green bay,
Rage, rage against the dying of the light.

Wild men who caught and sang the sun in flight,　　　　　　　　10
And learn, too late, they grieved it on its way,
Do not go gentle into that good night.

Grave men, near death, who see with blinding sight
Blind eyes could blaze like meteors and be gay,
Rage, rage against the dying of the light.

And you, my father, there on the sad height,
Curse, bless, me now with your fierce tears, I pray.
Do not go gentle into that good night.
Rage, rage against the dying of the light.

For Analysis
1. What do wise, good, wild, and grave men have in common? **2.** Why does the poet
use the adjective "gentle" rather than the adverb "gently"? **3.** What is the "sad height"
(l. 16)?

Philip Larkin　[1922–1985]

Aubade[1]　1977

I work all day, and get half drunk at night.
Waking at four to soundless dark, I stare.
In time the curtain-edges will grow light.
Till then I see what's really always there:
Unresting death, a whole day nearer now;
Making all thought impossible but how
And where and when I shall myself die.
Arid interrogation: yet the dread
Of dying, and being dead,
Flashes afresh to hold and horrify.　　　　　　　　10

Aubade
　[1] An aubade is a morning song.

The mind blanks at the glare. Not in remorse
—The good not done, the love not given, time
Torn off unused—nor wretchedly because
An only life can take so long to climb
Clear of its wrong beginnings, and may never;
But at the total emptiness for ever,
The sure extinction that we travel to
And shall be lost in always. Not to be here,
Not to be anywhere,
And soon; nothing more terrible, nothing more true.   20

This is a special way of being afraid
No trick dispels. Religion used to try,
That vast moth-eaten musical brocade
Created to pretend we never die,
And specious stuff that says *No rational being*
Can fear a thing it will not feel, not seeing
That this is what we fear—no sight, no sound.
No touch or taste to smell, nothing to think with.
Nothing to love or link with,
The anaesthetic from which none come round.   30

And so it stays just on the edge of vision,
A small unfocused blur, a standing chill
That slows each impulse down to indecision.
Most things may never happen: this one will.
And realisation of it rages out
In furnace-fear when we are caught without
People or drink. Courage is no good:
It means not scaring others. Being brave
Lets no one off the grave.
Death is no different whined at than withstood.   40

Slowly light strengthens, and the room takes shape.
It stands plain as a wardrobe, what we know,
Have always known, know that we can't escape,
Yet can't accept. One side will have to go.
Meanwhile telephones crouch, getting ready to ring
In locked-up offices, and all the uncaring
Intricate rented world begins to rouse.
The sky is white as clay, with no sun.
Work has to be done.
Postmen like doctors go from house to house.   50

Catherine Davis [b. 1924]

After a Time   1961?

After a time, all losses are the same.
One more thing lost is one thing less to lose;
And we go stripped at last the way we came.

Though we shall probe, time and again, our shame,
Who lack the wit to keep or to refuse,
After a time, all losses are the same.

No wit, no luck can beat a losing game;
Good fortune is a reassuring ruse:
And we go stripped at last the way we came.

Rage as we will for what we think to claim,   10
Nothing so much as this bare thought subdues:
After a time, all losses are the same.

The sense of treachery—the want, the blame—
Goes in the end, whether or not we choose,
And we go stripped at last the way we came.

So we, who would go raging, will go tame
When what we have we can no longer use:
After a time, all losses are the same;
And we go stripped at last the way we came.

For Analysis
1. What difference in effect would occur if the **refrain** "After a time" were changed to "When life is done"? **2.** What are the various meanings of "stripped" in line 3 and line 19? **3.** Explain the meaning of "The sense of treachery" (l. 13). **4.** Does this poem say that life is meaningless? Explain.

Writing Topic
Compare the form and attitude asserted in this poem with Dylan Thomas's "Do Not Go Gentle into That Good Night" (p. 1285).

Maxine Kumin [b. 1925]

Woodchucks 1972

Gassing the woodchucks didn't turn out right.
The knockout bomb from the Feed and Grain Exchange
was featured as merciful, quick at the bone
and the case we had against them was airtight
both exits shoehorned shut with puddingstone,
but they had a sub-sub-basement out of range.

Next morning they turned up again, no worse
for the cyanide than we for our cigarettes
and state-store Scotch, all of us up to scratch.
They brought down the marigolds as a matter of course   10
and then took over the vegetable patch
nipping the broccoli shoots, beheading the carrots.

The food from our mouths, I said, righteously thrilling
to the feel of the .22, the bullets' neat noses.
I, a lapsed pacifist fallen from grace
puffed with Darwinian pieties for killing,
now drew a bead on the littlest woodchuck's face.
He died down in the everbearing roses.

Ten minutes later I dropped the mother. She
flipflopped in the air and fell, her needle teeth   20
still hooked in a leaf of early Swiss chard.
Another baby next. O one-two-three
the murderer inside me rose up hard,
the hawkeye killer came on stage forthwith.

There's one chuck left. Old wily fellow, he keeps
me cocked and ready day after day after day.
All night I hunt his humped-up form. I dream
I sight along the barrel in my sleep.
If only they'd all consented to die unseen
gassed underground the quiet Nazi way.   30

Allen Ginsberg   [1926–1997]

To Aunt Rose   1961

Aunt Rose—now—might I see you
with your thin face and buck tooth smile and pain
    of rheumatism—and a long black heavy shoe
     for your bony left leg
  limping down the long hall in Newark on the running carpet
     past the black grand piano
      in the day room
       where the parties were
    and I sang Spanish loyalist songs[1]
     in a high squeaky voice   10
       (hysterical) the committee listening
    while you limped around the room
     collected the money—
Aunt Honey, Uncle Sam, a stranger with a cloth arm
     in his pocket
      and huge young bald head
       of Abraham Lincoln Brigade

—your long sad face
    your tears of sexual frustration
      (what smothered sobs and bony hips   20
       under the pillows of Osborne Terrace)
  —the time I stood on the toilet seat naked
    and you powdered my thighs with Calomine
     against the poison ivy—my tender
      and shamed first black curled hairs
what were you thinking in secret heart then
     knowing me a man already—
and I an ignorant girl of family silence on the thin pedestal
    of my legs in the bathroom—Museum of Newark.

[1] Between 1936 and 1939, a civil war occurred in Spain in which rebel forces under General
Francisco Franco defeated the Loyalist forces supporting the politically liberal monarchy. In some
ways a foreshadowing of World War II, the Spanish Civil War attracted the attention of the great
powers, with Russia supporting the Loyalist forces and Germany and Italy supporting the rebel
forces. Many American writers and intellectuals saw the war as a struggle between fascism and
democracy and supported the Loyalist cause energetically; the Abraham Lincoln Brigade (line 17)
was a volunteer unit of Americans that fought on the Loyalist side.

1290

Aunt Rose 30
Hitler is dead, Hitler is in Eternity; Hitler is with
Tamburlane and Emily Brontë[2]

Though I see you walking still, a ghost on Osborne Terrace
down the long dark hall to the front door
limping a little with a pinched smile
in what must have been a silken
flower dress
welcoming my father, the Poet, on his visit to Newark
—see you arriving in the living room
dancing on your crippled leg 40
and clapping hands his book
had been accepted by Liveright[3]

Hitler is dead and Liveright's gone out of business
The Attic of the Past and *Everlasting Minute* are out of print
Uncle Harry sold his last silk stocking
Claire quit interpretive dancing school
Buba sits a wrinkled monument in Old
Ladies Home blinking at new babies

last time I saw you was the hospital
pale skull protruding under ashen skin 50
blue veined unconscious girl
in an oxygen tent
the war in Spain has ended long ago
Aunt Rose

James Merrill   [1926–1995]

Casual Wear   1984

Your average tourist: Fifty. 2.3
Times married. Dressed, this year, in Ferdi Plinthbower
Originals. Odds 1 to 9^{10}
Against her strolling past the Embassy

Aunt Rose
  [2] Tamburlane (1336?–1405), Mongol conqueror; Emily Brontë (1818–1848), English novelist.
  [3] A publishing firm.

Today at noon. Your average terrorist:
Twenty-five. Celibate. No use for trends,
At least in clothing. Mark, though, where it ends.
People have come forth made of colored mist

Unsmiling on one hundred million screens
To tell of his prompt phone call to the station,   10
"Claiming responsibility"—devastation
Signed with a flourish, like the dead wife's jeans.

Edwin Brock   [b. 1927]

Five Ways to Kill a Man   1963

There are many cumbersome ways to kill a man:
you can make him carry a plank of wood
to the top of a hill and nail him to it. To do this
properly you require a crowd of people
wearing sandals, a cock that crows, a cloak
to dissect, a sponge, some vinegar and one
man to hammer the nails home.

Or you can take a length of steel,
shaped and chased° in a traditional way,   ornamented
and attempt to pierce the metal cage he wears.   10
But for this you need white horses,
English trees, men with bows and arrows,
at least two flags, a prince and a
castle to hold your banquet in.

Dispensing with nobility, you may, if the wind
allows, blow gas at him. But then you need
a mile of mud sliced through with ditches,
not to mention black boots, bomb craters,
more mud, a plague of rats, a dozen songs
and some round hats made of steel.   20

In an age of aeroplanes, you may fly
miles above your victim and dispose of him by
pressing one small switch. All you then

require is an ocean to separate you, two
systems of government, a nation's scientists,
several factories, a psychopath and
land that no one needs for several years.

These are, as I began, cumbersome ways
to kill a man. Simpler, direct, and much more neat
is to see that he is living somewhere in the middle   30
of the twentieth century, and leave him there.

Yevgeny Yevtushenko [b. 1933]

People[1] trans. 1962

No people are uninteresting.
Their fate is like the chronicle of planets.

Nothing in them is not particular,
and planet is dissimilar from planet.

And if a man lived in obscurity
making his friends in that obscurity
obscurity is not uninteresting.

To each his world is private,
and in that world one excellent minute.

And in that world one tragic minute.   10
These are private.

In any man who dies there dies with him
his first snow and kiss and fight.
It goes with him.

They are left books and bridges
and painted canvas and machinery.

People
[1] Translated by Robin Milner-Gulland and Peter Levi.

Whose fate is to survive.
But what has gone is also not nothing:

by the rule of the game something has gone.
Not people die but worlds die in them.   20

Whom we knew as faulty, the earth's creatures.
Of whom, essentially, what did we know?

Brother of a brother? Friend of friends?
Lover of lover?

We who knew our fathers
in everything, in nothing.

They perish. They cannot be brought back.
The secret worlds are not regenerated.

And every time again and again
I make my lament against destruction.   30

Mary Oliver   [b. 1935]

When Death Comes   1992

When death comes
like the hungry bear in autumn;
when death comes and takes all the bright coins from his purse

to buy me, and snaps the purse shut;
when death comes
like the measle-pox;

when death comes
like an iceberg between the shoulder blades,

I want to step through the door full of curiosity, wondering:
what is it going to be like, that cottage of darkness?   10

And therefore I look upon everything
as a brotherhood and a sisterhood,
and I look upon time as no more than an idea,
and I consider eternity as another possibility,

and I think of each life as a flower, as common
as a field daisy, and as singular,

and each name a comfortable music in the mouth,
tending, as all music does, toward silence,

and each body a lion of courage, and something
precious to the earth.   20

When it's over, I want to say: all my life
I was a bride married to amazement.
I was the bridegroom, taking the world into my arms.

When it's over, I don't want to wonder
if I have made of my life something particular, and real.
I don't want to find myself sighing and frightened,
or full of argument.

I don't want to end up simply having visited this world.

For Analysis

1. This poem turns on a series of **images**. Characterize each image associated with approaching death, evaluating its effectiveness and appropriateness. **2.** What is the "cottage of darkness" (l. 10)? **3.** What images are associated with life and experience? Do you find them effective? Explain. **4.** What is wrong with "simply having visited this world" (l. 28)?

Writing Topic

Lines 24–27 express the poet's attitude toward life as its end approaches. In an essay, explain how a life that is "particular, and real," leads naturally to a death that does not generate sighing and fear, or argument.

Marge Piercy   [b. 1936]

The long death   1980

For Wendy Teresa Simon
(September 25, 1954–August 7, 1979)

Radiation is like oppression,
the average daily kind of subliminal toothache
you get almost used to, the stench
of chlorine in the water, of smog in the wind.

We comprehend the disasters of the moment,
the nursing home fire, the river in flood
pouring over the sandbag levee, the airplane
crash with fragments of burnt bodies
scattered among the hunks of twisted metal,
the grenade in the marketplace, the sinking ship.   10

But how to grasp a thing that does not
kill you today or tomorrow
but slowly from the inside in twenty years.
How to feel that a corporate or governmental
choice means we bear twisted genes and our
grandchildren will be stillborn if our
children are very lucky.

Slow death can not be photographed for the six
o'clock news. It's all statistical,
the gross national product or the prime   20
lending rate. Yet if our eyes saw
in the right spectrum, how it would shine,
lurid as magenta neon.

If we could smell radiation like seeping
gas, if we could sense it as heat, if we
could hear it as a low ominous roar
of the earth shifting, then we would not sit
and be poisoned while industry spokesmen
talk of acceptable millirems and .02
cancer per population thousand.   30

We acquiesce at murder so long as it is slow,
murder from asbestos dust, from tobacco,

1296

from lead in the water, from sulphur in the air,
and fourteen years later statistics are printed
on the rise in leukemia among children.
We never see their faces. They never stand,
those poisoned children together in a courtyard,
and are gunned down by men in three-piece suits.

The shipyard workers who built nuclear
submarines, the soldiers who were marched   40
into the Nevada desert to be tested by the H-
bomb, the people who work in power plants,
they die quietly years after in hospital
wards and not on the evening news.

The soft spring rain floats down and the air
is perfumed with pine and earth. Seedlings
drink it in, robins sip it in puddles,
you run in it and feel clean and strong,
the spring rain blowing from the irradiated
cloud over the power plant.   50

Radiation is oppression, the daily average
kind, the kind you're almost used to
and live with as the years abrade you,
high blood pressure, ulcers, cramps, migraine,
a hacking cough: you take it inside
and it becomes pain and you say, not
They are killing me, but *I am sick now.*

For Analysis

1. What sort of corporate or governmental choices (ll. 14–15) might result in "twisted genes"? **2.** In what sense is "slow death . . . statistical" (ll. 18–19)? **3.** Who acquiesces "at murder so long as it is slow" (l. 31)? Why? **4.** Do you find the last three lines **ironic**? Explain. **5.** What "prosaic" qualities do you find in this piece? Do they over-balance its "poetic" qualities? Explain.

Writing Topic

In an argumentative essay, either support or refute the assertion that the benefits derived from some avoidable industrial pollution outweigh the relatively modest damage it causes.

Seamus Heaney   [b. 1939]

Mid-term Break   1966

I sat all morning in the college sick bay
Counting bells knelling classes to a close.
At two o'clock our neighbors drove me home.

In the porch I met my father crying—
He had always taken funerals in his stride—
And Big Jim Evans saying it was a hard blow.

The baby cooed and laughed and rocked the pram
When I came in, and I was embarrassed
By old men standing up to shake my hand

And tell me they were "sorry for my trouble,"   10
Whispers informed strangers I was the eldest,
Away at school, as my mother held my hand

In hers and coughed out angry tearless sighs.
At ten o'clock the ambulance arrived
With the corpse, stanched and bandaged by the nurses.

Next morning I went up into the room. Snowdrops
And candles soothed the bedside; I saw him
For the first time in six weeks. Paler now,

Wearing a poppy bruise on his left temple,
He lay in the four foot box as in his cot.   20
No gaudy scars, the bumper knocked him clear.

A four foot box, a foot for every year.

For Analysis
1. Although it contains little rhyme, this poem is remarkably musical. Identify the **assonance** and **alliteration** that permeate the poem. **2.** What event does the poem describe? **3.** How is the poem's title relevant?

Writing Topic
Characterize the family and the society revealed in this short poem.

Kathleen Norris [b. 1947]

The Ignominy
of the Living 1989

The undertaker had placed pink netting
around your face. I removed it
and gave you a small bouquet, encumbering you
into eternity. "Impedimenta," I hear you say,
scornfully, the way you said it at Penn Station
when we struggled to put your bag onto a contraption
of cords and wheels. "Laurel and Hardy[1] got paid for this,"
I said the third time it fell off,
narrowly missing my foot.

You would have laughed   10
at the place we brought you to, the hush of carpet,
violins sliding through "The Way We Were."
"Please turn the music off," I said, civilly,
to the undertaker's assistant.
We had an open grave—no artificial turf—
and your friends lowered you into the ground.

Once you dreamed your mother sweeping
an earthen floor
in a dark, low-ceilinged room.
I see her now: I, too, want to run.   20
And the "ignominy of the living,"
words you nearly spat out
when one of your beloved dead
was ill-remembered; I thought of that
as I removed the netting.

Today I passed St. Mary's
as the Angelus[2] sounded.
You would have liked that, the ancient practice
in the prairie town not a hundred years old,
the world careering disastrously toward the twenty-first century.   30
I stopped and prayed for you.

[1] Stan Laurel (1890–1965) and Oliver Hardy (1892–1957) were a popular movie comedy team.
[2] In the Roman Catholic Church, a bell rung as a call to prayer.

Then a recording of "My Way" came scratching out
on the electronic carillon.
"Oh, hell," I said,
and prayed for Frank Sinatra, too.

For Analysis
1. Explain the title. **2.** Why does the speaker ask the assistant undertaker to turn off the music? In this connection, why does she say, "Oh, hell" at the end when she hears the electronic carillon playing "My Way"? **3.** Explicate lines 17–19.

Writing Topic
If you have ever attended the funeral of someone you knew well, describe your feelings and reactions to the service. Did it seem appropriate and tasteful? Did it leave you satisfied that the tribute was sincere and honest, that the person being eulogized was the person you knew?

James Fenton [b. 1949]

God, A Poem 1984

A nasty surprise in a sandwich,
A drawing-pin caught in your sock,
The limpest of shakes from a hand which
You'd thought would be firm as a rock,

A serious mistake in a nightie,
A grave disappointment all round
Is all that you'll get from th'Almighty,
Is all that you'll get underground.

Oh he *said*: "If you lay off the crumpet
I'll see you alright in the end.   10
Just hang on until the last trumpet.
Have faith in me, chum—I'm your friend."

But if you remind him, he'll tell you:
"I'm sorry, I must have been pissed—
Though your name rings a sort of a bell. You
Should have guessed that I do not exist.

"I didn't exist at Creation,
I didn't exist at the Flood,

And I won't be around for Salvation
To sort out the sheep from the cud—   20

"Or whatever the phrase is. The fact is
In soteriological terms
I'm a crude existential malpractice
And you are a diet of worms.

"You're a nasty surprise in a sandwich.
You're a drawing-pin caught in my sock.
You're the limpest of shakes from a hand which
I'd have thought would be firm as a rock,

"You're a serious mistake in a nightie,
You're a grave disappointment all round—   30
That's all that you are," says th'Almighty,
"And that's all that you'll be underground."

Elizabeth Spires   [b. 1952]

Easter Sunday, 1955   1995

> Why should anything go wrong in our bodies?
> Why should we not be all beautiful? Why should
> there be decay?—why death?—and, oh, why, damnation?
>   —*Anthony Trollope, in a letter.*

What were we? What have we become?
Light fills the picture, the rising sun,
the three of us advancing, dreamlike,
up the steps of my grandparents' house on Oak Street.
My mother and father, still young, swing me
lightly up the steps, as if I weighed nothing.
From the shadows, my brother and sister watch,
wanting their turn, years away from being born.
Now my aunts and uncles and cousins
gather on the shaded porch of generation,   10
big enough for everyone. No one has died yet.
No vows have been broken. No words spoken
that can never be taken back, never forgotten.
I have a basket of eggs my mother and I dyed yesterday.

I ask my grandmother to choose one, just one,
and she takes me up—O hold me close!—
her cancer not yet diagnosed. I bury my face
in soft flesh, the soft folds of her Easter dress,
breathing her in, wanting to stay forever where I am.
Her death will be long and slow, she will beg   20
to be let go, and I will find myself, too quickly,
in the here-and-now moment of my fortieth year.
It's spring again. Easter. Now my daughter steps
into the light, her basket of eggs bright, so bright.
One, choose one, I hear her say, her face upturned
to mine, innocent of outcome. Beautiful child,
how thoughtlessly we enter the world!
How free we are, how bound, put here in love's name
—death's, too—to be happy if we can.

For Analysis

1. The poem begins with a memory and ends with an account of the present. Why?
2. How does the **epigraph** by Trollope contribute to the poem's effect? **3.** The last sentence (ll. 28–29) embodies a **paradox:** "How free we are, how bound, . . ." How can we be both free and bound?

Writing Topic

Lines 12–13 assert that at the time of the poet's reminiscence, "No vows have been broken. No words spoken / that can never be taken back, never forgotten." In an essay, discuss the implications of these lines. Describe the sort of tensions that may exist within your family, or within a family you know of, that reflect the poet's observations.

Marianne Burke   [b. 1957]

Funeral Home   1991

Let us think of you spared, carried gently
in the arms of the ocean that's piped
through speakers, spreading a hush in Parmele's[1]
where we sit, adrift, on the parlor couch
between time, in death's caesura.

Funeral Home
    [1] The name of the funeral home.

The funeral director ticks off a list
of questions. He wants the facts, reduces you
to an abstract—mother with a capital "**M**."
Nowhere will it say how petite you were,
that your wedding ring fits my pinkie finger,   10

or that, tucked into your coffin, you will look
like a doll we will never outgrow.
Downstairs, he shows us his fleet
of caskets, satin-lined, open-lidded—
music boxes whose strains are too fine

for us to hear, like your voice,
utterless, our names dead on your tongue.
Even here the ocean's cold hush.

You are lost at sea.
To think we must choose a vessel,   20
one that will not float but sink.
Mahogany is what we set you in—
our mother of pearl, our buried treasure.

For Analysis

1. Trace the sea and ship **imagery** within the poem. Do you find it appropriate? Explain. **2.** How is the funeral director characterized? How does the speaker respond to his behavior?

Li-Young Lee   [b. 1957]

Between Seasons   1986

Today I bring you cold chrysanthemums,
white as absence, long-stemmed as my grief.
I stand before your grave, a few unfallen
leaves overhead, the sucking mud beneath.

What survives best are chrysanthemums
in a month which arrives austere as grief.
The hearty blossoms persevere, unfallen.
Suffering even snow, they flourish beneath.

You walked in mornings among chrysanthemums,
and bowed to them as if to hear their grief.
Your sleeves grew damp from brushing unfallen
dew. A drop lay by your eye, and one beneath.

Truest to your nature were chrysanthemums,
brilliant while first snows descended like grief.
You watched them from your bed, your heart unfallen,
steadfast through winter, and then you slipped beneath.

What is it they told you, once, the chrysanthemums?
It made you sigh, *Ah, Grief!*
Who savors you more than us, the unfallen,
long after we've forgotten the fallen beneath?

10

20

Drama

<u>Woody Allen</u>   [b. 1935]

Death Knocks   1968

The play takes place in the bedroom of Nat Ackerman's two-story house, some-where in Kew Gardens.[1] The carpeting is wall-to-wall. There is a big double bed and a large vanity. The room is elaborately furnished and curtained, and on the walls there are several paintings and a not really attractive barometer. Soft theme music as the curtain rises. Nat Ackerman, a bald, paunchy fifty-seven-year-old dress manufacturer, is lying on the bed finishing off tomorrow's Daily News.[2] *He wears a bathrobe and slippers, and reads by a bed light clipped to the white headboard of the bed. The time is near midnight. Suddenly we hear a noise, and Nat sits up and looks at the window.*

Nat.   What the hell is that?

(Climbing awkwardly through the window is a sombre, caped figure. The in-truder wears a black hood and skintight black clothes. The hood covers his head but not his face, which is middle-aged and stark white. He is something like Nat in appearance. He huffs audibly and then trips over the windowsill and falls into the room.)

Death *(for it is no one else).*   Jesus Christ. I nearly broke my neck.
Nat *(watching with bewilderment).*   Who are you?
Death.   Death.
Nat.   Who?
Death.   Death. Listen—can I sit down? I nearly broke my neck. I'm shaking like a leaf.
Nat.   Who *are* you?
Death.   *Death.* You got a glass of water?
Nat.   Death? What do you mean, Death?

---

[1] A middle-class neighborhood in the New York City borough of Queens.   [2] The *Daily News* is a tabloid newspaper; the morning edition used to be distributed at about 10 P.M. of the previous night.

Death. What is wrong with you? You see the black costume and the whitened face?

Nat. Yeah.

Death. Is it Halloween?

Nat. No.

Death. Then I'm Death. Now can I get a glass of water—or a Fresca?

Nat. If this is some joke—

Death. What kind of joke? You're fifty-seven? Nat Ackerman? One eighteen Pacific Street? Unless I blew it—where's that call sheet? (*He fumbles through pocket, finally producing a card with an address on it. It seems to check.*)

Nat. What do you want with me?

Death. What do I want? What do you think I want?

Nat. You must be kidding. I'm in perfect health.

Death (*unimpressed*). Uh-huh. (*Looking around*) This is a nice place. You do it yourself?

Nat. We had a decorator, but we worked with her.

Death (*looking at picture on the wall*). I love those kids with the big eyes.

Nat. I don't want to go yet.

Death. *You* don't want to go? Please don't start in. As it is, I'm nauseous from the climb.

Nat. What climb?

Death. I climbed up the drainpipe. I was trying to make a dramatic entrance. I see the big windows and you're awake reading. I figure it's worth a shot. I'll climb up and enter with a little—you know . . . (*Snaps fingers*) Meanwhile, I get my heel caught on some vines, the drainpipe breaks, and I'm hanging by a thread. Then my cape begins to tear. Look, let's just go. It's been a rough night.

Nat. You broke my drainpipe?

Death. Broke. It didn't break. It's a little bent. Didn't you hear anything? I slammed into the ground.

Nat. I was reading.

Death. . You must have really been engrossed. (*Lifting newspaper Nat was reading*) "NAB COEDS IN POT ORGY." Can I borrow this?

Nat. I'm not finished.

Death. Er—I don't know how to put this to you, pal. . . .

Nat. Why didn't you just ring downstairs?

Death. I'm telling you, I could have, but how does it look? This way I get a little drama going. Something. Did you read "Faust"?

Nat. What?

Death. And what if you had company? You're sitting there with important people. I'm Death—I should ring the bell and traipse right in the front? Where's your thinking?

Nat. Listen, Mister, it's very late.

Death. Yeah. Well, you want to go?

Nat.   Go where?

Death.   Death. It. The Thing. The Happy Hunting Grounds. (*Looking at his own knee*) Y'know, that's a pretty bad cut. My first job, I'm liable to get gangrene yet.

Nat.   Now, wait a minute. I need time. I'm not ready to go.

Death.   I'm sorry. I can't help you. I'd like to, but it's the moment.

Nat.   How can it be the moment? I just merged with Modiste Originals.

Death.   What's the difference, a couple of bucks more or less.

Nat.   Sure, what do you care? You guys probably have all your expenses paid.

Death.   You want to come along now?

Nat (*studying him*).   I'm sorry, but I cannot believe you're Death.

Death.   Why? What'd you expect—Rock Hudson?

Nat.   No, it's not that.

Death.   I'm sorry if I disappointed you.

Nat.   Don't get upset. I don't know, I always thought you'd be . . . uh . . . taller.

Death.   I'm five seven. It's average for my weight.

Nat.   You look a little like me.

Death.   Who should I look like? I'm your death.

Nat.   Give me some time. Another day.

Death.   I can't. What do you want me to say?

Nat.   One more day. Twenty-four hours.

Death.   What do you need it for? The radio said rain tomorrow.

Nat.   Can't we work out something?

Death.   Like what?

Nat.   You play chess?

Death.   No, I don't.

Nat.   I once saw a picture of you playing chess.

Death.   Couldn't be me, because I don't play chess. Gin rummy, maybe.

Nat.   You play gin rummy?

Death.   Do I play gin rummy? Is Paris a city?

Nat.   You're good, huh?

Death.   Very good.

Nat.   I'll tell you what I'll do—

Death.   Don't make any deals with me.

Nat.   I'll play you gin rummy. If you win, I'll go immediately. If I win, give me some more time. A little bit—one more day.

Death.   Who's got time to play gin rummy?

Nat.   Come on. If you're so good.

Death.   Although I feel like a game . . .

Nat.   Come on. Be a sport. We'll shoot for a half hour.

Death.   I really shouldn't.

Nat.   I got the cards right here. Don't make a production.

Death.   All right, come on. We'll play a little. It'll relax me.

Nat (*getting cards, pad, and pencil*).   You won't regret this.

Death. Don't give me a sales talk. Get the cards and give me a Fresca and put out something. For God's sake, a stranger drops in, you don't have potato chips or pretzels.

Nat. There's M&M's downstairs in a dish.

Death. M&M's. What if the President came? He'd get M&M's too?

Nat. You're not the President.

Death. Deal.

(*Nat deals, turns up a five.*)

Nat. You want to play a tenth of a cent a point to make it interesting?

Death. It's not interesting enough for you?

Nat. I play better when money's at stake.

Death. Whatever you say, Newt.

Nat. Nat, Nat Ackerman. You don't know my name?

Death. Newt, Nat—I got such a headache.

Nat. You want that five?

Death. No.

Nat. So pick.

Death (*surveying his hand as he picks*). Jesus, I got nothing here.

Nat. What's it like?

Death. What's what like?

(*Throughout the following, they pick and discard.*)

Nat. Death.

Death. What should it be like? You lay there.

Nat. Is there anything after?

Death. Aha, you're saving twos.

Nat. I'm asking. Is there anything after?

Death (*absently*). You'll see.

Nat. Oh, then I will actually see something?

Death. Well, maybe I shouldn't have put it that way. Throw.

Nat. To get an answer from you is a big deal.

Death. I'm playing cards.

Nat. All right, play, play.

Death. Meanwhile, I'm giving you one card after another.

Nat. Don't look through the discards.

Death. I'm not looking. I'm straightening them up. What was the knock card?

Nat. Four. You ready to knock already?

Death. Who said I'm ready to knock. All I asked was what was the knock card.

Nat. And all I asked was is there anything for me to look forward to.

Death. Play.

Nat. Can't you tell me anything? Where do we go?

Death. We? To tell you the truth, *you* fall in a crumpled heap on the floor.

Nat. Oh, I can't wait for that! Is it going to hurt?

Death. Be over in a second.

Nat. Terrific. *(Sighs)* I needed this. A man merges with Modiste Originals . . .

Death. How's four points?

Nat. You're knocking?

Death. Four points is good?

Nat. No, I got two.

Death. You're kidding.

Nat. No, you lose.

Death. Holy Christ, and I thought you were saving sixes.

Nat. No. Your deal. Twenty points and two boxes. Shoot. *(Death deals.)* I must fall on the floor, eh? I can't be standing over the sofa when it happens?

Death. No. Play.

Nat. Why not?

Death. Because you fall on the floor! Leave me alone. I'm trying to concentrate.

Nat. Why must it be on the floor? That's all I'm saying! Why can't the whole thing happen and I'll stand next to the sofa?

Death. I'll try my best. Now can we play?

Nat. That's all I'm saying. You remind me of Moe Lefkowitz. He's also stubborn.

Death. I remind you of Moe Lefkowitz. I'm one of the most terrifying figures you could possibly imagine, and him I remind of Moe Lefkowitz. What is he, a furrier?

Nat. You should be such a furrier. He's good for eighty thousand a year. Passementeries. He's got his own factory. Two points.

Death. What?

Nat. Two points. I'm knocking. What have you got?

Death. My hand is like a basketball score.

Nat. And it's spades.

Death. If you didn't talk so much.

(They redeal and play on.)

Nat. What'd you mean before when you said this was your first job?

Death. What does it sound like?

Nat. What are you telling me—that nobody ever went before?

Death. Sure they went. But I didn't take them.

Nat. So who did?

Death. Others.

Nat. There's others?

Death. Sure. Each one has his own personal way of going.

Nat. I never knew that.

Death. Why should you know? Who are you?

Nat.   What do you mean who am I? Why—I'm nothing?

Death.   Not nothing. You're a dress manufacturer. Where do you come to knowledge of the eternal mysteries?

Nat.   What are you talking about? I make a beautiful dollar. I sent two kids through college. One is in advertising, the other's married. I got my own home. I drive a Chrysler. My wife has whatever she wants. Maids, mink coat, vacations. Right now she's at the Eden Roc. Fifty dollars a day because she wants to be near her sister. I'm supposed to join her next week, so what do you think I am—some guy off the street?

Death.   All right. Don't be so touchy.

Nat.   Who's touchy?

Death.   How would you like it if I got insulted quickly?

Nat.   Did I insult you?

Death.   You didn't say you were disappointed in me?

Nat.   What do you expect? You want me to throw you a block party?

Death.   I'm not talking about that. I mean me personally. I'm too short, I'm this, I'm that.

Nat.   I said you looked like me. It's like a reflection.

Death.   All right, deal, deal.

(*They continue to play as music steals in and the lights dim until all is in total darkness. The lights slowly come up again, and now it is later and their game is over. Nat tallies.*)

Nat.   Sixty-eight . . . one-fifty . . . Well, you lose.

Death (*dejectedly looking through the deck*).   I knew I shouldn't have thrown that nine. Damn it.

Nat.   So I'll see you tomorrow.

Death.   What do you mean you'll see me tomorrow?

Nat.   I won the extra day. Leave me alone.

Death.   You were serious?

Nat.   We made a deal.

Death.   Yeah, but—

Nat.   Don't "but" me. I won twenty-four hours. Come back tomorrow.

Death.   I didn't know we were actually playing for time.

Nat.   That's too bad about you. You should pay attention.

Death.   Where am I going to go for twenty-four hours?

Nat.   What's the difference? The main thing is I won an extra day.

Death.   What do you want me to do—walk the streets?

Nat.   Check into a hotel and go to a movie. Take a *schvitz*.[3] Don't make a federal case.

Death.   Add the score again.

Nat.   Plus you owe me twenty-eight dollars.

Death.   *What?*

---

[3] Steam bath.

Nat. That's right, Buster. Here it is—read it.

Death *(going through pockets).* I have a few singles—not twenty-eight dollars.

Nat. I'll take a check.

Death. From what account?

Nat. Look who I'm dealing with.

Death. Sue me. Where do I keep my checking account?

Nat. All right, gimme what you got and we'll call it square.

Death. Listen, I need that money.

Nat. Why should you need money?

Death. What are you talking about? You're going to the Beyond.

Nat. So?

Death. So—you know how far that is?

Nat. So?

Death. So where's gas? Where's tolls?

Nat. We're going by car!

Death. You'll find out. *(Agitatedly)* Look—I'll be back tomorrow, and you'll give me a chance to win the money back. Otherwise I'm in definite trouble.

Nat. Anything you want. Double or nothing we'll play. I'm liable to win an extra week or a month. The way you play, maybe years.

Death. Meantime I'm stranded.

Nat. See you tomorrow.

Death *(being edged to the doorway).* Where's a good hotel? What am I talking about hotel, I got no money. I'll go sit in Bickford's[4] *(He picks up the News.)*

Nat. Out. Out. That's my paper. *(He takes it back.)*

Death *(exiting).* I couldn't just take him and go. I had to get involved in rummy.

Nat *(calling after him).* And be careful going downstairs. On one of the steps the rug is loose.

(And, on cue, we hear a terrific crash. Nat sighs, then crosses to the bedside table and makes a phone call.)

Nat. Hello, Moe? Me. Listen, I don't know if somebody's playing a joke, or what, but Death was just here. We played a little gin . . . No, *Death*. In person. Or somebody who claims to be Death. But, Moe, he's such a *schlep!*[5]

Curtain

For Analysis

1. Consider the stage direction that opens the play. What sort of household is described? **2.** The stage direction describes Nat Ackerman as a dress manufacturer. If

---

[4] Bickford's was a chain of inexpensive all-night cafeterias in New York City.   [5] Boring jerk.

you were directing the play, how might you convey that information to your audience? Why do you suppose Allen included the information in a stage direction? **3.** Reread the stage directions and identify any others that are literary rather than dramatic tools.

On Style

Characterize the speech patterns of the characters. How do they contribute to the play's effect?

Making Connections

Compare and contrast the **personifications** of death in Allen's play and in Bernard Malamud's story "Idiots First" (p. 1223).

Writing Topic

Either read or rent a video of Ingmar Bergman's *The Seventh Seal*. In an essay, describe the effects of Allen's central allusion in *Death Knocks*.

Harvey Fierstein [b. 1954]

On Tidy Endings 1987

The curtain rises on a deserted, modern Upper West Side apartment. In the bright daylight that pours in through the windows we can see the living room of the apartment. Far Stage Right is the galley kitchen, next to it the multilocked front door with intercom. Stage Left reveals a hallway that leads to the two bedrooms and baths.

Though the room is still fully furnished (couch, coffee table, etc.), there are boxes stacked against the wall and several photographs and paintings are on the floor leaving shadows on the wall where they once hung. Obviously someone is moving out. From the way the boxes are neatly labeled and stacked, we know that this is an organized person.

From the hallway just outside the door we hear the rattling of keys and two arguing voices:

Jim *(offstage).*   I've got to be home by four. I've got practice.
Marion *(offstage).*   I'll get you to practice, don't worry.
Jim *(offstage).*   I don't want to go in there.
Marion *(offstage).*   Jimmy, don't make Mommy crazy, alright? We'll go inside, I'll call Aunt Helen and see if you can go down and play with Robbie.

(The door opens. Marion is a handsome woman of forty. Dressed in a business suit, her hair conservatively combed, she appears to be going to a business meeting. Jim is a boy of eleven. His playclothes are typical, but someone has obviously just combed his hair. Marion recovers the key from the lock.)

Jim.   Why can't I just go down and ring the bell?
Marion.   Because I said so.

(As Marion steps into the room she is struck by some unexpected emotion. She freezes in her path and stares at the empty apartment. Jim lingers by the door.)

Jim.   I'm going downstairs.
Marion.   Jimmy, please.
Jim.   This place gives me the creeps.
Marion.   This was your father's apartment. There's nothing creepy about it.
Jim.   Says you.
Marion.   You want to close the door, please?

(*Jim reluctantly obeys.*)

Marion. Now, why don't you go check your room and make sure you didn't leave anything.
Jim. It's empty.
Marion. Go look.
Jim. I looked last time.
Marion (*trying to be patient*). Honey, we sold the apartment. You're never going to be here again. Go make sure you have everything you want.
Jim. But Uncle Arthur packed everything.
Marion (*less patiently*). Go make sure.
Jim. There's nothing in there.
Marion (*exploding*). I said make sure!

(*Jim jumps, then realizing that she's not kidding, obeys.*)

Marion. Everything's an argument with that one. (*She looks around the room and breathes deeply. There is sadness here. Under her breath:*) I can still smell you. (*Suddenly not wanting to be alone*) Jimmy? Are you okay?
Jim (*returning*). Nothing. Told you so.
Marion. Uncle Arthur must have worked very hard. Make sure you thank him.
Jim. What for? Robbie says, (*Fey mannerisms*) "They love to clean up things!"
Marion. Sometimes you can be a real joy.
Jim. Did you call Aunt Helen?
Marion. Do I get a break here? (*Approaching the boy understandingly*) Wouldn't you like to say good-bye?
Jim. To who?
Marion. To the apartment. You and your daddy spent a lot of time here together. Don't you want to take one last look around?
Jim. Ma, get a real life.
Marion. "Get a real life." (*Going for the phone*) Nice. Very nice.
Jim. Could you call already?
Marion (*dialing*). Jimmy, what does this look like I'm doing?

(*Jim kicks at the floor impatiently. Someone answers the phone at the other end.*)

Marion (*into the phone*). Helen? Hi, we're upstairs. . . . No, we just walked in the door. Jimmy wants to know if he can come down. . . . Oh, thanks.

(*Hearing that, Jim breaks for the door.*)

Marion (*yelling after him*). Don't run in the halls! And don't play with the elevator buttons!

(*The door slams shut behind him.*)

Marion *(back to the phone).* Hi. . . . No, I'm okay. It's a little weird being here. . . . No. Not since the funeral, and then there were so many people. Jimmy told me to get "a real life." I don't think I could handle anything realer. . . . No, please. Stay where you are. I'm fine. The doorman said Arthur would be right back and my lawyer should have been here already. . . . Well, we've got the papers to sign and a few other odds and ends to clean up. Shouldn't take long.

(The intercom buzzer rings.)

Marion. Hang on, that must be her. *(Marion goes to the intercom and speaks)* Yes? . . . Thank you. *(Back to the phone)* Helen? Yeah, it's the lawyer. I'd better go. . . . Well, I could use a stiff drink, but I drove down. Listen, I'll stop by on my way out. Okay? Okay. 'Bye.

(She hangs up the phone, looks around the room. That uncomfortable feeling returns to her quickly. She gets up and goes to the front door, opens it and looks out. No one there yet. She closes the door, shakes her head knowing that she's being silly and starts back into the room. She looks around, can't make it and retreats to the door. She opens it, looks out, closes it, but stays right there, her hand on the doorknob.
The bell rings. She throws open the door.)

Marion. That was quick.

(June Lowell still has her finger on the bell. Her arms are loaded with contracts. Marion's contemporary, June is less formal in appearance and more hyper in her manner.)

June. *That* was quicker. What, were you waiting by the door?
Marion *(embarrassed).* No. I was just passing it. Come on in.
June. Have you got your notary seal?
Marion. I think so.
June. Great. Then you can witness. I left mine at the office and thanks to gentrification I'm double-parked downstairs. *(Looking for a place to dump her load)* Where?
Marion *(definitely pointing to the coffee table).* Anywhere. You mean you're not staying?
June. If you really think you need me I can go down and find a parking lot. I think there's one over on Columbus. So, I can go down, park the car in the lot and take a cab back if you really think you need me.
Marion. Well . . . ?
June. But you shouldn't have any problems. The papers are about as straightforward as papers get. Arthur is giving you power of attorney to sell the apartment and you're giving him a check for half the purchase price. Everything

else is just signing papers that state that you know that you signed the other papers. Anyway, he knows the deal, his lawyers have been over it all with him, it's just a matter of signatures.

Marion *(not fine).*   Oh, fine.

June.   Unless you just don't want to be alone with him . . . ?

Marion.   With Arthur? Don't be silly.

June *(laying out the papers).*   Then you'll handle it solo? My car thanks you, the parking lot thanks you, and the cab driver that wouldn't have gotten a tip thanks you. Come have a quick look-see.

Marion *(joining her on the couch).*   There are a lot of papers here.

June.   Copies. Not to worry. Start here.

(Marion starts to read.)

June.   I ran into Jimmy playing Elevator Operator.

(Marion jumps.)

June.   I got him off at the sixth floor. Read on.

Marion.   This is definitely not my day for dealing with him.

(June gets up and has a look around.)

June.   I don't believe what's happening to this neighborhood. You made quite an investment when you bought this place.

Marion.   Collin was always very good at figuring out those things.

June.   Well, he sure figured this place right. What, have you tripled your money in ten years?

Marion.   More.

June.   It's a shame to let it go.

Marion.   We're not ready to be a two-dwelling family.

June.   So, sublet it again.

Marion.   Arthur needs the money from the sale.

June.   Arthur got plenty already. I'm not crying for Arthur.

Marion.   I don't hear you starting in again, do I?

June.   Your interests and your wishes are my only concern.

Marion.   Fine.

June.   I still say we should contest Collin's will.

Marion.   June! . . .

June.   You've got a child to support.

Marion.   And a great job, and a husband with a great job. Tell me what Arthur's got.

June.   To my thinking, half of everything that should have gone to you. And more. All of Collin's personal effects, his record collection . . .

Marion.   And I suppose their three years together meant nothing.

June.   When you compare them to your sixteen-year marriage? Not nothing, but not half of everything.

Marion *(trying to change the subject).*   June, who gets which copies?

June.   Two of each to Arthur. One you keep. The originals and anything else come back to me. *(Looking around)* I still say you should've sublet the apartment for a year and then sold it. You would've gotten an even better price. Who wants to buy an apartment when they know someone died in it. No one. And certainly no one wants to buy an apartment when they know the person died of AIDS.

Marion *(snapping).*   June. Enough!

June *(catching herself).*   Sorry. That was out of line. Sometimes my mouth does that to me. Hey, that's why I'm a lawyer. If my brain worked as fast as my mouth I would have gotten a real job.

Marion *(holding out a stray paper).*   What's this?

June.   I forgot. Arthur's lawyer sent that over yesterday. He found it in Collin's safety-deposit box. It's an insurance policy that came along with some consulting job he did in Japan. He either forgot about it when he made out his will or else he wanted you to get the full payment. Either way, it's yours.

Marion.   Are you sure we don't split this?

June.   Positive.

Marion.   But everything else . . . ?

June.   Hey, Arthur found it, his lawyer sent it to me. Relax, it's all yours. Minus my commission, of course. Go out and buy yourself something. Anything else before I have to use my cut to pay the towing bill?

Marion.   I guess not.

June *(starting to leave).*   Great. Call me when you get home. *(Stopping at the door and looking back)* Look, I know that I'm attacking this a little coldly. I am aware that someone you loved has just died. But there's a time and place for everything. This is about tidying up loose ends, not holding hands. I hope you'll remember that when Arthur gets here. Call me.

(And she's gone.)

(Marion looks ill at ease to be alone again. She nervously straightens the papers into neat little piles, looks at them and then remembers:)

Marion.   Pens. We're going to need pens.

(At last a chore to be done. She looks in her purse and finds only one. She goes to the kitchen and opens a drawer where she finds two more. She starts back to the table with them but suddenly remembers something else. She returns to the kitchen and begins going through the cabinets until she finds what she's looking for: a blue Art Deco teapot. Excited to find it, she takes it back to the couch.

Guilt strikes. She stops, considers putting it back, wavers, then:)

Marion (*to herself*).   Oh, he won't care. One less thing to pack.

(*She takes the teapot and places it on the couch next to her purse. She is happier. Now she searches the room with her eyes for any other treasures she may have overlooked. Nothing here. She wanders off into the bedroom.*

We hear keys outside the front door. Arthur lets himself into the apartment carrying a load of empty cartons and a large shopping bag.

Arthur is in his mid-thirties, pleasant looking though sloppily dressed in work clothes and slightly overweight.

Arthur enters the apartment just as Marion comes out of the bedroom carrying a framed watercolor painting. They jump at the sight of each other.)

Marion.   Oh, hi, Arthur. I didn't hear the door.

Arthur (*staring at the painting*).   Well hello, Marion.

Marion (*guiltily*).   I was going to ask you if you were thinking of taking this painting because if you're not going to then I'll take it. Unless, of course, you want it.

Arthur.   No. You can have it.

Marion.   I never really liked it, actually. I hate cats. I didn't even like the show. I needed something for my college dorm room. I was never the rock star poster type. I kept it in the back of a closet for years until Collin moved in here and took it. He said he liked it.

Arthur.   I do too.

Marion.   Well, then you keep it.

Arthur.   No. Take it.

Marion.   We've really got no room for it. You keep it.

Arthur.   I don't want it.

Marion.   Well, if you're sure.

Arthur (*seeing the teapot*).   You want the teapot?

Marion.   If you don't mind.

Arthur.   One less thing to pack.

Marion.   Funny, but that's exactly what I thought. One less thing to pack. You know, my mother gave it to Collin and me when we moved in to our first apartment. Silly sentimental piece of junk, but you know.

Arthur.   That's not the one.

Marion.   Sure it is. Hall used to make them for Westinghouse back in the thirties. I see them all the time at antiques shows and I always wanted to buy another, but they ask such a fortune for them.

Arthur.   We broke the one your mother gave you a couple of years ago. That's a reproduction. You can get them almost anywhere in the Village for eighteen bucks.

Marion.   Really? I'll have to pick one up.

Arthur.   Take this one. I'll get another.

Marion.   No, it's yours. You bought it.

Arthur.   One less thing to pack.

Marion.   Don't be silly. I didn't come here to raid the place.

Arthur.   Well, was there anything else of Collin's that you thought you might like to have?

Marion.   Now I feel so stupid, but actually I made a list. Not for me. But I started thinking about different people; friends, relatives, you know, that might want to have something of Collin's to remember him by. I wasn't sure just what you were taking and what you were throwing out. Anyway, I brought the list. *(Gets it from her purse)* Of course these are only suggestions. You probably thought of a few of these people yourself. But I figured it couldn't hurt to write it all down. Like I said, I don't know what you are planning on keeping.

Arthur *(taking the list).*   I was planning on keeping it all.

Marion.   Oh, I know. But most of these things are silly. Like his high school yearbooks. What would you want with them?

Arthur.   Sure. I'm only interested in his Gay period.

Marion.   I didn't mean it that way. Anyway, you look it over. They're only suggestions. Whatever you decide to do is fine with me.

Arthur *(folding the list).*   It would have to be, wouldn't it. I mean, it's all mine now. He did leave this all to me.

(Marion is becoming increasingly nervous, but tries to keep a light approach as she takes a small bundle of papers from her bag.)

Marion.   While we're on the subject of what's yours. I brought a batch of condolence cards that were sent to you care of me. Relatives mostly.

Arthur *(taking them).*   More cards? I'm going to have to have another printing of thank-you notes done.

Marion.   I answered these last week, so you don't have to bother. Unless you want to.

Arthur.   Forge my signature?

Marion.   Of course not. They were addressed to both of us and they're mostly distant relatives or friends we haven't seen in years. No one important.

Arthur.   If they've got my name on them, then I'll answer them myself.

Marion.   I wasn't telling you not to, I was only saying that you don't have to.

Arthur.   I understand.

(Marion picks up the teapot and brings it to the kitchen.)

Marion.   Let me put this back.

Arthur.   I ran into Jimmy in the lobby.

Marion.   Tell me you're joking.

Arthur.   I got him to Helen's.

Marion.   He's really racking up the points today.

Arthur.   You know, he still can't look me in the face.

Marion.   He's reacting to all of this in strange ways. Give him time. He'll come around. He's really very fond of you.

Arthur.   I know. But he's at that awkward age: under thirty. I'm sure in twenty years we'll be the best of friends.

Marion.   It's not what you think.

Arthur.   What do you mean?

Marion.   Well, you know.

Arthur.   No I don't know. Tell me.

Marion.   I thought that you were intimating something about his blaming you for Collin's illness and I was just letting you know that it's not true. (*Foot in mouth, she braves on*) We discussed it a lot and . . . uh . . . he understands that his father was sick before you two ever met.

Arthur.   I don't believe this.

Marion.   I'm just trying to say that he doesn't blame you.

Arthur.   First of all, who asked you? Second of all, that's between him and me. And third and most importantly, of course he blames me. Marion, he's eleven years old. You can discuss all you want, but the fact is that his father died of a "fag" disease and I'm the only fag around to finger.

Marion.   My son doesn't use that kind of language.

Arthur.   Forget the language. I'm talking about what he's been through. Can you imagine the kind of crap he's taken from his friends? That poor kid's been chased and chastised from one end of town to the other. He's got to have someone to blame just to survive. He can't blame you, you're all he's got. He can't blame his father; he's dead. So, Uncle Arthur gets the shaft. Fine, I can handle it.

Marion.   You are so wrong, Arthur. I know my son and that is not the way his mind works.

Arthur.   I don't know what you know. I only know what I know. And all I know is what I hear and see. The snide remarks, the little smirks . . . And it's not just the illness. He's been looking for a scapegoat since the day you and Collin first split up. Finally he has one.

Marion (*getting very angry now*).   Wait. Are you saying that if he's going to blame someone it should be me?

Arthur.   I think you should try to see things from his point of view.

Marion.   Where do you get off thinking you're privy to my son's point of view?

Arthur.   It's not that hard to imagine. Life's rolling right along, he's having a happy little childhood, when suddenly one day his father's moving out. No explanations, no reasons, none of the fights that usually accompany such things. Divorce is hard enough for a kid to understand when he's listened to years of battles, but yours?

Marion.   So what should we have done? Faked a few months' worth of fights before Collin moved out?

Arthur.   You could have told him the truth, plain and simple.

Marion.   He was seven years old at the time. How the hell do you tell a seven-year-old that his father is leaving his mother to go sleep with other men?

Arthur.   Well, not like that.

Marion.   You know, Arthur, I'm going to say this as nicely as I can: Butt out. You're not his mother and you're not his father.

Arthur.   Thank you. I wasn't acutely aware of that fact. I will certainly keep that in mind from now on.

Marion.   There's only so much information a child that age can handle.

Arthur.   So it's best that he reach his capacity on the street.

Marion.   He knew about the two of you. We talked about it.

Arthur.   Believe me, he knew before you talked about it. He's young, not stupid.

Marion.   It's very easy for you to stand here and criticize, but there are aspects that you will just never be able to understand. You weren't there. You have no idea what it was like for me. You're talking to someone who thought that a girl went to college to meet a husband. I went to protest rallies because I liked the music. I bought a guitar because I thought it looked good on the bed! This lifestyle, this knowledge that you take for granted, was all a little out of left field for me.

Arthur.   I can imagine.

Marion.   No. I don't think you can. I met Collin in college, married him right after graduation and settled down for a nice quiet life of Kids and Careers. You think I had any idea about this? Talk about life's little surprises. You live with someone for sixteen years, you share your life, your bed, you have a child together, and then you wake up one day and he tells you that to him it's all been a lie. A lie. Try that on for size. Here you are the happiest couple you know, fulfilling your every life fantasy and he tells you he's living a lie.

Arthur.   I'm sure he never said that.

Marion.   Don't be so sure. There was a lot of new ground being broken back then and plenty of it was muddy.

Arthur.   You know that he loved you.

Marion.   What's that supposed to do, make things easier? It doesn't. I was brought up to believe, among other things, that if you had love that was enough. So what if I wasn't everything he wanted. Maybe he wasn't exactly everything I wanted either. So, you know what? You count your blessings and you settle.

Arthur.   No one has to settle. Not him. Not you.

Marion.   Of course not. You can say, "Up yours!" to everything and everyone who depends and needs you, and go off to make yourself happy.

Arthur.   It's not that simple.

Marion.   No. This is simpler. Death is simpler. (*Yelling out*) Happy now?

(*They stare at each other. Marion calms the rage and catches her breath. Arthur holds his emotions in check.*)

Arthur.   How about a nice hot cup of coffee? Tea with lemon? Hot cocoa with a marshmallow floating in it?

Marion *(laughs).*   I was wrong. You *are* a mother.

(Arthur goes into the kitchen and starts preparing things. Marion loafs by the doorway.)

Marion.   I lied before. He *was* everything I ever wanted.

(Arthur stops, looks at her, and then changes the subject as he goes on with his work.)

Arthur.   When I came into the building and saw Jimmy in the lobby I absolutely freaked for a second. It's amazing how much they look alike. It was like seeing a little miniature Collin standing there.

Marion.   I know. He's like Collin's clone. There's nothing of me in him.

Arthur.   I always kinda hoped that when he grew up he'd take after me. Not much chance, I guess.

Marion.   Don't do anything fancy in there.

Arthur.   Please. Anything we can consume is one less thing to pack.

Marion.   So you've said.

Arthur.   So *we've* said.

Marion.   I want to keep seeing you and I want you to see Jim. You're still part of this family. No one's looking to cut you out.

Arthur.   Ah, who'd want a kid to grow up looking like me anyway. I had enough trouble looking like this. Why pass on the misery?

Marion.   You're adorable.

Arthur.   Is that like saying I have a good personality?

Marion.   I think you are one of the most naturally handsome men I know.

Arthur.   Natural is right, and the bloom is fading.

Marion.   All you need is a few good nights' sleep to kill those rings under your eyes.

Arthur.   Forget the rings under my eyes, *(Grabbing his middle)* . . . how about the rings around my moon?

Marion.   I like you like this.

Arthur.   From the time that Collin started using the wheelchair until he died, about six months, I lost twenty-three pounds. No gym, no diet. In the last seven weeks I've gained close to fifty.

Marion.   You're exaggerating.

Arthur.   I'd prove it on the bathroom scale, but I sold it in working order.

Marion.   You'd never know.

Arthur.   Marion, *you'd* never know, but ask my belt. Ask my pants. Ask my underwear. Even my stretch socks have stretch marks. I called the ambulance at five A.M., he was gone at nine and by nine-thirty, I was on a first-name basis with Sara Lee. I can quote the business hours of every ice-cream parlor, pizzeria and bakery on the island of Manhattan. I know the location of every twenty-four-hour grocery in the greater New York area, and I have memorized the phone numbers of every Mandarin, Szechuan and Hunan restaurant with free delivery.

Marion.   At least you haven't wasted your time on useless hobbies.

Arthur.   Are you kidding? I'm opening my own Overeater's Hotline. We'll have to start small, but expansion is guaranteed.

Marion.   You're the best, you know that? If I couldn't be everything that Collin wanted then I'm grateful that he found someone like you.

Arthur (*turning on her without missing a beat*).   Keep your goddamned gratitude to yourself. I didn't go through any of this for you. So your thanks are out of line. And he didn't find "someone like" me. It was me.

Marion (*frightened*).   I didn't mean . . .

Arthur.   And I wish you'd remember one thing more: He died in my arms, not yours.

(*Marion is totally caught off guard. She stares disbelieving, open-mouthed. Arthur walks past her as he leaves the kitchen with place mats. He puts them on the coffee table. As he arranges the papers and place mats he speaks, never looking at her.*)

Arthur.   Look, I know you were trying to say something supportive. Don't waste your breath. There's nothing you can say that will make any of this easier for me. There's no way for you to help me get through this. And that's your fault. After three years you still have no idea or understanding of who I am. Or maybe you do know but refuse to accept it. I don't know and I don't care. But at least understand, from my point of view, who you are: You are my husband's *ex*-wife. If you like, the mother of *my* stepson. Don't flatter yourself into thinking you're any more than that. And whatever you are, you're certainly not my friend.

(*He stops, looks up at her, then passes her again as he goes back to the kitchen. Marion is shaken, working hard to control herself. She moves toward the couch.*)

Marion.   Why don't we just sign these papers and I'll be out of your way.

Arthur.   Shouldn't you say *I'll* be out of *your* way? After all, I'm not just signing papers, I'm signing away my home.

Marion (*resolved not to fight, she gets her purse*).   I'll leave the papers here. Please have them notarized and returned to my lawyer.

Arthur.   Don't forget my painting.

Marion (*exploding*).   What do you want from me, Arthur?

Arthur (*yelling back*).   I want you the hell out of my apartment! I want you out of my life! And I want you to leave Collin alone!

Marion.   The man's dead. I don't know how much more alone I can leave him.

(Arthur laughs at the irony, but behind the laughter is something much more desperate.)

Arthur.   Lots more, Marion. You've got to let him go.

Marion.   For the life of me, I don't know what I did, or what you think I did, for you to treat me like this. But you're not going to get away with it. You will not take your anger out on me. I will not stand here and be badgered and insulted by you. I know you've been hurt and I know you're hurting but you're not the only one who lost someone here.

Arthur *(topping her)*.   Yes I am! You didn't just lose him. I did! You lost him five years ago when he divorced you. This is not your moment of grief and loss, it's mine! *(Picking up the bundle of cards and throwing it toward her)* These condolences do not belong to you, they're mine. *(Tossing her list back to her)* His things are not yours to give away, they're mine! This death does not belong to you, it's mine! Bought and paid for outright. I suffered for it, I bled for it. I was the one who cooked his meals. I was the one who spoon-fed them. I pushed his wheelchair. I carried and bathed him. I wiped his backside and changed his diapers. I breathed life into and wrestled fear out of his heart. I kept him alive for two years longer than any doctor thought possible and when it was time I was the one who prepared him for death.

I paid in full for my place in his life and I will *not* share it with you. We are not the two widows of Collin Redding. Your life was not here. Your husband didn't just die. You've got a son and a life somewhere else. Your husband's sitting, waiting for you at home, wondering, as I am, what the hell you're doing here and why you can't let go.

(Marion leans back against the couch. She's blown away. Arthur stands staring at her.)

Arthur *(quietly)*.   Let him go, Marion. He's mine. Dead or alive; mine.

(The teakettle whistles. Arthur leaves the room, goes to the kitchen and pours the water as Marion pulls herself together.

Arthur carries the loaded tray back into the living room and sets it down on the coffee table. He sits and pours a cup.)

Arthur.   One marshmallow or two?

(Marion stares, unsure as to whether the attack is really over or not.)

Arthur *(placing them in her cup)*.   Take three, they're small.

(Marion smiles and takes the offered cup.)

Arthur *(campily)*.   Now let me tell you how I *really* feel.

(Marion jumps slightly, then they share a small laugh. Silence as they each gather themselves and sip their refreshments.)

Marion *(calmly).*   Do you think that I sold the apartment just to throw you out?

Arthur.   I don't care about the apartment . . .

Marion   . . . Because I really didn't. Believe me.

Arthur.   I know.

Marion.   I knew the expenses here were too much for you, and I knew you couldn't afford to buy out my half . . . I figured if we sold it, that you'd at least have a nice chunk of money to start over with.

Arthur.   You could've given me a little more time.

Marion.   Maybe. But I thought the sooner you were out of here, the sooner you could go on with your life.

Arthur.   Or the sooner you could go on with yours.

Marion.   Maybe. *(Pause to gather her thoughts)* Anyway, I'm not going to tell you that I have no idea what you're talking about. I'd have to be worse than deaf and blind not to have seen the way you've been treated. Or mistreated. When I read Collin's obituary in the newspaper and saw my name and Jimmy's name and no mention of you . . . *(Shakes her head, not knowing what to say)* You know that his secretary was the one who wrote that up and sent it in. Not me. But I should have done something about it and I didn't. I know.

Arthur.   Wouldn't have made a difference. I wrote my own obituary for him and sent it to the smaller papers. They edited me out.

Marion.   I'm sorry. I remember, at the funeral, I was surrounded by all of Collin's family and business associates while you were left with your friends. I knew it was wrong. I knew I should have said something but it felt good to have them around me and you looked like you were holding up . . . Wrong. But saying that it's all my fault for not letting go? . . . There were other people involved.

Arthur.   Who took their cue from you.

Marion.   Arthur, you don't understand. Most people that we knew as a couple had no idea that Collin was Gay right up to his death. And even those that did know only found out when he got sick and the word leaked out that it was AIDS. I don't think I have to tell you how stupid and ill-informed most people are about homosexuality. And AIDS . . . ? The kinds of insane behavior that word inspires? . . .

Those people at the funeral, how many times did they call to see how he was doing over these years? How many of them ever went to see him in the hospital? Did any of them even come here? So, why would you expect them to act any differently after his death?

So, maybe that helps to explain their behavior, but what about mine, right? Well, maybe there is no explanation. Only excuses. And excuse number one is that you're right, I have never really let go of him. And I am jealous of you.

Hell, I was jealous of anyone that Collin ever talked to, let alone slept with . . . let alone loved.

The first year, after he moved out, we talked all the time about the different men he was seeing. And I always listened and advised. It was kind of fun. It kept us close. It kept me a part of his intimate life. And the bottom line was always that he wasn't happy with the men he was meeting. So, I was always allowed to hang on to the hope that one day he'd give it all up and come home. Then he got sick.

He called me, told me he was in the hospital and asked if I'd come see him. I ran. When I got to his door there was a sign, INSTRUCTIONS FOR VISITORS OF AN AIDS PATIENT. I nearly died.

Arthur. He hadn't told you?

Marion. No. And believe me a sign is not the way to find these things out. I was so angry . . . And he was so sick . . . I was sure that he'd die right then. If not from the illness then from the hospital staff's neglect. No one wanted to go near him and I didn't bother fighting with them because I understood that they were scared. I was scared. That whole month in the hospital I didn't let Jimmy visit him once.

You learn.

Well, as you know, he didn't die. And he asked if he could come stay with me until he was well. And I said yes. Of course, yes. Now, here's something I never thought I'd ever admit to anyone: had he asked to stay with me for a few weeks I would have said no. But he asked to stay with me until he was well and knowing there was no cure I said yes. In my craziness I said yes because to me that meant forever. That he was coming back to me forever. Not that I wanted him to die, but I assumed from everything I'd read . . . And we'd be back together for whatever time he had left. Can you understand that?

(Arthur nods.)

Marion *(gathers her thoughts again).* Two weeks later he left. He moved in here. Into this apartment that we had bought as an investment. Never to live in. Certainly never to live apart in. Next thing I knew, the name Arthur starts appearing in every phone call, every dinner conversation.

"Did you see the doctor?"

"Yes. Arthur made sure I kept the appointment."

"Are you going to your folks for Thanksgiving?"

"No. Arthur and I are having some friends over."

I don't know which one of us was more of a coward, he for not telling or me for not asking about you. But eventually you became a given. Then, of course, we met and became what I had always thought of as friends.

(Arthur winces in guilt.)

Marion. I don't care what you say, how could we not be friends with something so great in common: love for one of the most special human beings there ever was. And don't try and tell me there weren't times when you enjoyed my being around as an ally. I can think of a dozen occasions when we ganged up on him, teasing him with our intimate knowledge of his personal habits.

(*Arthur has to laugh.*)

Marion. Blanket stealing? Snoring? Excess gas, no less? (*Takes a moment to enjoy this truce*) I don't think that my loving him threatened your relationship. Maybe I'm not being truthful with myself. But I don't. I never tried to step between you. Not that I ever had the opportunity. Talk about being joined at the hip! And that's not to say I wasn't jealous. I was. Terribly. Hatefully. But always lovingly. I was happy for Collin because there was no way to deny that he was happy. With everything he was facing, he was happy. Love did that. You did that.

He lit up with you. He came to life. I envied that and all the time you spent together, but more, I watched you care for him (sometimes *overcare* for him), and I was in awe. I could never have done what you did. I never would have survived. I really don't know how you did.
Arthur. Who said I survived?
Marion. Don't tease. You did an absolutely incredible thing. It's not as if you met him before he got sick. You entered a relationship that you knew in all probability would end this way and you never wavered.
Arthur. Of course I did. Don't have me sainted, Marion. But sometimes you have no choice. Believe me, if I could've gotten away from him I would've. But I was a prisoner of love.

(*He makes a campy gesture and pose.*)

Marion. Stop.
Arthur. And there were lots of pluses. I got to quit a job I hated, stay home all day and watch game shows. I met a lot of doctors and learned a lot of big words. (*Arthur jumps up and goes to the pile of boxes where he extracts one and brings it back to the couch*) And then there was all the exciting traveling I got to do. This box has a souvenir from each one of our trips. Wanna see?

(*Marion nods. He opens the box and pulls things out one by one.*)

Arthur (*continuing*) (*Holding up an old bottle*). This is from the house we rented in Reno when we went to clear out his lungs. (*Holding handmade potholders*) This is from the hospital in Reno. Collin made them. They had a great arts and crafts program. (*Copper bracelets*) These are from a faith healer in Philly. They don't do much for a fever, but they look great with a green sweater. *(Glass ashtrays)* These are from our first visit to the clinic in France. Such lovely people. *(A Bible)* This is from our second visit to the clinic in France. *(A bead necklace)* A Voodoo doctor in New Orleans. Next time we'll have to get there earlier in the year. I think he sold all the pretty ones at Mardi Gras. *(A tiny piñata)* Then there was Mexico. Black market drugs and empty wallets. *(Now pulling things out at random)* L.A., San Francisco, Houston, Boston . . . We traveled everywhere they offered hope for sale and came home with souvenirs. *(Arthur quietly pulls a few more things out and then begins to put them all back into the box slowly. Softly as he works:)*

Marion, I would have done anything, traveled anywhere to avoid . . . or delay . . . Not just because I loved him so desperately, but when you've lived the way we did for three years . . . the battle becomes your life. *(He looks at her and then away)*

His last few hours were beyond any scenario I had imagined. He hadn't walked in nearly six months. He was totally incontinent. If he spoke two words in a week I was thankful. Days went by without his eyes ever focusing on me. He just stared out at I don't know what. Not the meals as I fed him. Not the TV I played constantly for company. Just out. Or maybe in.

It was the middle of the night when I heard his breathing become labored. His lungs were filling with fluid again. I knew the sound. I'd heard it a hundred times before. So, I called the ambulance and got him to the hospital. They hooked him up to the machines, the oxygen, shot him with morphine and told me that they would do what they could to keep him alive.

But, Marion, it wasn't the machines that kept him breathing. He did it himself. It was that incredible will and strength inside him. Whether it came from his love of life or fear of death, who knows. But he'd been counted out a hundred times and a hundred times he fought his way back.

I got a magazine to read him, pulled a chair up to the side of his bed and holding his hand, I wondered whether I should call Helen to let the cleaning lady in or if he'd fall asleep and I could sneak home for an hour. I looked up from the page and he was looking at me. Really looking right into my eyes. I patted his cheek and said, "Don't worry, honey, you're going to be fine."

But there was something else in his eyes. He wasn't satisfied with that. And I don't know why, I have no idea where it came from, I just heard the words coming out of my mouth, "Collin, do you want to die?" His eyes filled and closed, he nodded his head.

I can't tell you what I was thinking, I'm not sure I was. I slipped off my shoes, lifted his blanket and climbed into bed next to him. I helped him to put his arms around me, and mine around him, and whispered as gently as I could into his ear, "It's alright to let go now. It's time to go on." And he did.

Marion, you've got your life and his son. All I have is an intangible place in a man's history. Leave me that. Respect that.

Marion.   I understand.

(Arthur suddenly comes to life, running to get the shopping bag that he'd left at the front door.)

Arthur. Jeez! With all the screamin' and sad storytelling I forget something. *(He extracts a bouquet of flowers from the bag)* I brung you flowers and everything.

Marion. You brought *me* flowers?

Arthur. Well, I knew you'd never think to bring me flowers and I felt that on an occasion such as this somebody oughta get flowers from somebody.

Marion. You know, Arthur, you're really making me feel like a worthless piece of garbage.

Arthur. So what else is new? *(He presents the flowers)* Just promise me one thing: Don't press one in a book. Just stick them in a vase and when they fade just toss them out. No more memorabilia.

Marion. Arthur, I want to do something for you and I don't know what. Tell me what you want.

Arthur. I want little things. Not much. I want to be remembered. If you get a Christmas card from Collin's mother, make sure she sent me one too. If his friends call to see how you are, ask if they've called me. Have me to dinner so I can see Jimmy. Let me take him out now and then. Invite me to his wedding.

(They both laugh.)

Marion. You've got it.

Arthur *(clearing the table).* Let me get all this cold cocoa out of the way. We still have the deed to do.

Marion *(checking her watch).* And I've got to get Jimmy home in time for practice.

Arthur. Band practice?

Marion. Baseball. *(Picking her list off the floor)* About this list, you do what you want.

Arthur. Believe me, I will. But I promise to consider your suggestions. Just don't rush me. I'm not ready to give it all away. *(Arthur is off to the kitchen with his tray and the phone rings. He answers it in the kitchen)* Hello? . . . just a minute. *(Calling out)* It's your eager Little Leaguer.

(Marion picks up the living room extension and Arthur hangs his up.)

Marion *(into phone).* Hello, honey . . . I'll be done in five minutes. No. You know what? You come up here and get me. . . . No, I said you should come up here. . . . I said I want you to come up here. . . . Because I said so. . . . Thank you.

(She hangs the receiver.)

Arthur (*rushing to the papers*).   Alright, where do we start on these?

Marion (*getting out her seal*).   I guess you should just start signing everything and I'll stamp along with you. Keep one of everything on the side for yourself.

Arthur.   Now I feel so rushed. What am I signing?

Marion.   You want to do this another time?

Arthur.   No. Let's get it over with. I wouldn't survive another session like this.

(*He starts to sign and she starts her job.*)

Marion.   I keep meaning to ask you; how are you?

Arthur (*at first puzzled and then*).   Oh, you mean my health? Fine. No, I'm fine. I've been tested, and nothing. We were very careful. We took many precautions. Collin used to make jokes about how we should invest in rubber futures.

Marion.   I'll bet.

Arthur (*stops what he's doing*).   It never occurred to me until now. How about you?

Marion (*not stopping*).   Well, we never had sex after he got sick.

Arthur.   But before?

Marion (*stopping but not looking up*).   I have the antibodies in my blood. No signs that it will ever develop into anything else. And it's been five years so my chances are pretty good that I'm just a carrier.

Arthur.   I'm so sorry. Collin never told me.

Marion.   He didn't know. In fact, other than my husband and the doctors, you're the only one I've told.

Arthur.   You and your husband . . . ?

Marion.   Have invested in rubber futures. There'd only be a problem if we wanted to have a child. Which we do. But we'll wait. Miracles happen every day.

Arthur.   I don't know what to say.

Marion.   Tell me you'll be there if I ever need you.

(*Arthur gets up, goes to her and puts his arms around her. They hold each other. He gently pushes her away to make a joke.*)

Arthur.   Sure! Take something else that should have been mine.

Marion.   Don't even joke about things like that.

(*The doorbell rings. They pull themselves together.*)

Arthur.   You know we'll never get these done today.

Marion.   So, tomorrow.

(*Arthur goes to open the door as Marion gathers her things. He opens the door and Jimmy is standing in the hall.*)

Jim.   C'mon, Ma. I'm gonna be late.
Arthur.   Would you like to come inside?
Jim.   We've gotta go.
Marion.   Jimmy, come on.
Jim.   Ma!

(She glares. He comes in. Arthur closes the door:)

Marion *(holding out the flowers).*   Take these for Mommy.
Jim *(taking them).*   Can we go?
Marion *(picking up the painting).*   Say good-bye to your Uncle Arthur.
Jim.   'Bye, Arthur. Come on.
Marion.   Give him a kiss.
Arthur.   Marion, don't.
Marion.   Give your uncle a kiss good-bye.
Jim.   He's not my uncle.
Marion.   No. He's a hell of a lot more than your uncle.
Arthur *(offering his hand).*   A handshake will do.
Marion.   Tell Uncle Arthur what your daddy told you.
Jim.   About what?
Marion.   Stop playing dumb. You know.
Arthur.   Don't embarrass him.
Marion.   Jimmy, please.
Jim *(he regards his mother's softer tone and then speaks).*   He said that after me and Mommy he loved you the most.
Marion *(standing behind him).*   Go on.
Jim.   And that I should love you too. And make sure that you're not lonely or very sad.
Arthur.   Thank you.

(Arthur reaches down to the boy and they hug. Jim gives him a little peck on the cheek and then breaks away.)

Marion *(going to open the door).*   Alright, kid, you done good. Now let's blow this joint before you muck it up.

(Jim rushes out the door. Marion turns to Arthur.)

Marion.   A child's kiss is magic. Why else would they be so stingy with them. I'll call you.

(Arthur nods understanding. Marion pulls the door closed behind her. Arthur stands quietly as the lights fade to black.)

NOTE: If being performed on film, the final image should be of Arthur leaning his back against the closed door on the inside of the apartment and Marion leaning on the outside of the door. A moment of thought and then they both move on.

For Analysis

1. What is Jimmy's attitude toward homosexuals? How is it revealed? **2.** What is June's view on the disposition of Collin's property? On what does she base her opinion? **3.** How does Marion's relationship to Arthur change during the play? What causes the change? **4.** What do you make of the title of the play? **5.** What is the effect of Jimmy's last encounter with Arthur? **6.** What, exactly, does Arthur ask for from Marion and her family?

On Style

Carefully reread the first two stage directions. Imagine yourself the director of the play. How would you realize the stage directions "Obviously someone is moving out. From the way the boxes are neatly labeled and stacked, we know that this is an organized person" and "she appears to be going to a business meeting"?

Making Connections

1. The idea of marriage for gay couples is being hotly debated by governments, the clergy, and the public. What are your feelings on the issue? Are those feelings affected by your response to this play? Explain. **2.** Reflect on Nora's marriage to Helmer in Henrik Ibsen's *A Doll's House* (p. 492) and the relationship between Arthur and Collin in this play. Which "marriage" corresponds most closely with your own view of marriage? Explain.

Writing Topic

The interaction of Arthur and Marion begins with strained politeness, degenerates into anger, and ends with reconciliation. In an essay, describe the sources of each of these emotional interactions.

John Donne [1572–1631]

Meditation XVII, from *Devotions upon Emergent Occasions* 1623

Nunc lento sonitu dicunt morieris.
Now this bell tolling softly for another says to me, Thou must die.

Perchance he for whom this bell tolls may be so ill as that he knows not it tolls for him; and perchance I may think myself so much better than I am, as that they who are about me and see my state may have caused it to toll for me, and I know not that. The church is catholic, universal, so are all her actions; all that she does belongs to all. When she baptizes a child, that action concerns me; for that child is thereby connected to that head which is my head too, and ingrafted into that body whereof I am a member. And when she buries a man, that action concerns me: all mankind is of one author and is one volume; when one man dies, one chapter is not torn out of the book, but translated into a better language; and every chapter must be so translated. God employs several translators; some pieces are translated by age, some by sickness, some by war, some by justice; but God's hand is in every translation, and his hand shall bind up all our scattered leaves again for that library where every book shall lie open to one another. As therefore the bell that rings to a sermon calls not upon the preacher only, but upon the congregation to come, so this bell calls us all; but how much more me, who am brought so near the door by this sickness. There was a contention as far as a suit[1] (in which piety and dignity, religion and estimation, were mingled) which of the religious orders should ring to prayers first in the morning; and it was determined that they should ring first that rose earliest. If we understand aright the dignity of this bell that tolls for our evening prayer, we would be glad to make it ours by rising early, in that application, that it might be

[1] An argument settled by a lawsuit.

ours as well as his whose indeed it is. The bell doth toll for him that thinks it doth, and though it intermit again, yet from that minute that that occasion wrought upon him, he is united to God. Who casts not up his eye to the sun when it rises? but who takes off his eye from a comet when that breaks out? Who bends not his ear to any bell which upon any occasion rings? but who can remove it from that bell which is passing a piece of himself out of this world? No man is an island, entire of itself; every man is a piece of the continent, a part of the main. If a clod be washed away by the sea, Europe is the less, as well as if a promontory were, as well as if a manor of thy friend's or of thine own were. Any man's death diminishes me, because I am involved in mankind; and therefore never send to know for whom the bell tolls; it tolls for thee. Neither can we call this a begging of misery or a borrowing of misery, as though we were not miserable enough of ourselves but must fetch in more from the next house, in taking upon us the misery of our neighbors. Truly it were an excusable covetousness if we did; for affliction is a treasure, and scarce any man hath enough of it. No man hath affliction enough that is not matured and ripened by it, and made fit for God by that affliction. If a man carry treasure in bullion, or in a wedge of gold, and have none coined into current moneys, his treasure will not defray him as he travels. Tribulation is treasure in the nature of it, but it is not current money in the use of it, except we get nearer and nearer our home, heaven, by it. Another man may be sick too, and sick to death, and this affliction may lie in his bowels as gold in a mine and be of no use to him; but this bell that tells me of his affliction digs out and applies that gold to me, if by this consideration of another's danger I take mine own into contemplation and so secure myself by making my recourse to my God, who is our only security.

For Analysis
1. What does Donne mean when he asserts that the death bell "tolls for thee"? **2.** Toward the end of his meditation, Donne states that "tribulation is treasure." What does he mean? What will that treasure purchase?

On Style
Donne is justly admired for his use of **figurative language**. What extended **metaphors** does he use to characterize humankind and death?

Making Connections
Consider Donne's famous assertion "No man is an island, entire of itself." Is the assertion an accurate description of the human condition? Explain.

Mark Twain   [1835–1910]

Lost in the Snow[1]   1872

Plainly the situation was desperate. We were cold and stiff and the horses were tired. We decided to build a sage-brush fire and camp out till morning. This was wise, because if we were wandering from the right road and the snowstorm continued until another day our case would be the next thing to hopeless if we kept on.

All agreed that a camp fire was what would come nearest to saving us, now, and so we set about building it. We could find no matches, and so we tried to make shift with the pistols. Not a man in the party had ever tried to do such a thing before, but not a man in the party doubted that it could be done, and without any trouble—because every man in the party had read about it in books many a time and had naturally come to believe it, with trusting simplicity, just as he had long ago accepted and believed that other common book-fraud about Indians and lost hunters making a fire by rubbing two dry sticks together.

We huddled together on our knees in the deep snow, and the horses put their noses together and bowed their patient heads over us; and while the feathery flakes eddied down and turned us into a group of white statuary, we proceeded with the momentous experiment. We broke twigs from a sage brush and piled them on a little cleared space in the shelter of our bodies. In the course of ten or fifteen minutes all was ready, and then, while conversation ceased and our pulses beat low with anxious suspense, Ollendorff applied his revolver, pulled the trigger and blew the pile clear out of the county! It was the flattest failure that ever was.

This was distressing, but it paled before a greater horror—the horses were gone! I had been appointed to hold the bridles, but in my absorbing anxiety over the pistol experiment I had unconsciously dropped them and the released animals had walked off in the storm. It was useless to try to follow them, for their footfalls could make no sound, and one could pass within two yards of the creatures and never see them. We gave them up without an effort at recovering them, and cursed the lying books that said horses would stay by their masters for protection and companionship in a distressful time like ours.

We were miserable enough, before; we felt still more forlorn, now. Patiently,   5

---

[1] Mark Twain's Roughing It (1872) recounts his experiences in California and Nevada prospecting for silver. In this episode, Twain and his friends are caught in a snowstorm while returning to Carson City, Nevada, from the Humboldt mining district in California.

but with blighted hope, we broke more sticks and piled them, and once more the Prussian shot them into annihilation. Plainly, to light a fire with a pistol was an art requiring practice and experience, and the middle of a desert at midnight in a snow-storm was not a good place or time for the acquiring of the accomplishment. We gave it up and tried the other. Each man took a couple of sticks and fell to chafing them together. At the end of half an hour we were thoroughly chilled, and so were the sticks. We bitterly execrated the Indians, the hunters and the books that had betrayed us with the silly device, and wondered dismally what was next to be done. At this critical moment Mr. Ballou fished out four matches from the rubbish of an overlooked pocket. To have found four gold bars would have seemed poor and cheap good luck compared to this. One cannot think how good a match looks under such circumstances—or how lovable and precious, and sacredly beautiful to the eye. This time we gathered sticks with high hopes; and when Mr. Ballou prepared to light the first match, there was an amount of interest centered upon him that pages of writing could not describe. The match burned hopefully a moment, and then went out. It could not have carried more regret with it if it had been a human life. The next match simply flashed and died. The wind puffed the third one out just as it was on the imminent verge of success. We gathered together closer than ever, and developed a solicitude that was rapt and painful, as Mr. Ballou scratched our last hope on his leg. It lit, burned blue and sickly, and then budded into a robust flame. Shading it with his hands, the old gentleman bent gradually down and every heart went with him—everybody, too, for that matter—and blood and breath stood still. The flame touched the sticks at last, took gradual hold upon them—hesitated—took a stronger hold—hesitated again—held its breath five heartbreaking seconds, then gave a sort of human gasp and went out.

Nobody said a word for several minutes. It was a solemn sort of silence; even the wind put on a stealthy, sinister quiet and made no more noise than the falling flakes of snow. Finally a sad-voiced conversation began, and it was soon apparent that in each of our hearts lay the conviction that this was our last night with the living. I had so hoped that I was the only one who felt so. When the others calmly acknowledged their conviction, it sounded like the summons itself. Ollendorff said:

"Brothers, let us die together. And let us go without one hard feeling towards each other. Let us forget and forgive bygones. I know that you have felt hard towards me for turning over the canoe, and for knowing too much and leading you round and round in the snow—but I meant well; forgive me. I acknowledge freely that I have had hard feelings against Mr. Ballou for abusing me and calling me a logarithm, which is a thing I do not know what, but no doubt a thing considered disgraceful and unbecoming in America, and it has scarcely been out of my mind and has hurt me a great deal—but let it go; I forgive Mr. Ballou with all my heart and—"

Poor Ollendorff broke down and the tears came. He was not alone, for I was crying too, and so was Mr. Ballou. Ollendorff got his voice again and forgave me for things I had done and said. Then he got out his bottle of whiskey and said that whether he lived or died he would never touch another drop. He said he had given up all hope of life, and although ill-prepared, was ready to submit humbly to his fate; that he wished he could be spared a little longer, not for any selfish reason, but to make a thorough reform in his character, and by devoting himself to helping the poor, nursing the sick, and pleading with the people to guard themselves against the evils of intemperance, make his life a beneficent example to the young, and lay it down at last with the precious reflection that it had not been lived in vain. He ended by saying that his reform should begin at this moment, even here in the presence of death, since no longer time was to be vouchsafed wherein to prosecute it to men's help and benefit—and with that he threw away the bottle of whiskey.

Mr. Ballou made remarks of similar purport, and began the reform he could not live to continue, by throwing away the ancient pack of cards that had solaced our captivity during the flood[2] and made it bearable. He said he never gambled, but still was satisfied that the meddling with cards in any way was immoral and injurious, and no man could be wholly pure and blemishless without eschewing them. "And therefore," continued he, "in doing this act I already feel more in sympathy with that spiritual saturnalia necessary to entire and obsolete reform." These rolling syllables touched him as no intelligible eloquence could have done, and the old man sobbed with a mournfulness not unmingled with satisfaction.

My own remarks were of the same tenor as those of my comrades, and I know that the feelings that prompted them were heartfelt and sincere. We were all sincere, and all deeply moved and earnest, for we were in the presence of death and without hope. I threw away my pipe, and in doing it felt that at last I was free of a hated vice and one that had ridden me like a tyrant all my days. While I yet talked, the thought of the good I might have done in the world and the still greater good I might now do, with these new incentives and higher and better aims to guide me if I could only be spared a few years longer, overcame me and the tears came again. We put our arms about each other's necks and awaited the warning drowsiness that precedes death by freezing.

It came stealing over us presently, and then we bade each other a last farewell. A delicious dreaminess wrought its web about my yielding senses, while the snow-flakes wove a winding sheet about my conquered body. Oblivion came. The battle of life was done.

I do not know how long I was in a state of forgetfulness, but it seemed an age. A vague consciousness grew upon me by degrees, and then came a gathering anguish of pain in my limbs and through all my body. I shuddered. The thought flitted through my brain, "this is death—this is the hereafter."

Then came a white upheaval at my side, and a voice said, with bitterness: "Will some gentleman be so good as to kick me behind?"

10

---

[2] Earlier in the narrative, Twain and his friends had been trapped in a cabin during a flash flood.

It was Ballou—at least it was a towzled snow image in a sitting posture, with   15
Ballou's voice.

I rose up, and there in the gray dawn, not fifteen steps from us, were the
frame buildings of a stage station, and under a shed stood our still saddled and
bridled horses!

An arched snow-drift broke up, now, and Ollendorff emerged from it, and the
three of us sat and stared at the houses without speaking a word. We really had
nothing to say. We were like the profane man who could not "do the subject justice," the whole situation was so painfully ridiculous and humiliating that words
were tame and we did not know where to commence anyhow.

The joy in our hearts at our deliverance was poisoned; well-nigh dissipated,
indeed. We presently began to grow pettish by degrees, and sullen; and then,
angry at each other, angry at ourselves, angry at everything in general, we mood-
ily dusted the snow from our clothing and in unsociable single file plowed our
way to the horses, unsaddled them, and sought shelter in the station.

I have scarcely exaggerated a detail of this curious and absurd adventure. It
occurred almost exactly as I have stated it. We actually went into camp in a
snowdrift in a desert, at midnight in a storm, forlorn and hopeless, within fifteen
steps of a comfortable inn.

For two hours we sat apart in the station and ruminated in disgust. The mys-   20
tery was gone, now, and it was plain enough why the horses had deserted us.
Without a doubt they were under that shed a quarter of a minute after they had
left us, and they must have overheard and enjoyed all our confessions and
lamentations.

After breakfast we felt better, and the zest of life soon came back. The world
looked bright again, and existence was as dear to us as ever. Presently an uneasiness came over me—grew upon me—assailed me without ceasing. Alas, my
regeneration was not complete—I wanted to smoke! I resisted with all my
strength, but the flesh was weak. I wandered away alone and wrestled with
myself for an hour. I recalled my promises of reform and preached to myself
persuasively, upbraidingly, exhaustively. But it was all vain, I shortly found
myself sneaking among the snow-drifts hunting for my pipe. I discovered it after
a considerable search, and crept away to hide myself and enjoy it. I remained
behind the barn a good while, asking myself how I would feel if my braver,
stronger, truer comrades should catch me in my degradation. At last I lit the
pipe, and no human being can feel meaner and baser than I did then. I was
ashamed of being in my own pitiful company. Still dreading discovery, I felt that
perhaps the further side of the barn would be somewhat safer, and so I turned
the corner. As I turned the one corner, smoking, Ollendorff turned the other
with his bottle to his lips, and between us sat unconscious Ballou deep in a game
of "solitaire" with the old greasy cards!

Absurdity could go no further. We shook hands and agreed to say no more
about "reform" and "examples to the rising generation."

For Analysis

1. At the conclusion of this piece, Twain and his friends are disgusted with themselves for backsliding, the author even going so far as to say, "I was ashamed of being in my own pitiful company." Is this a serious judgment the reader is expected to share? Explain. **2.** In paragraph 19, Twain states, "I have scarcely exaggerated a detail of this curious and absurd adventure." Do you believe him? Why or why not?

On Style

Reread the essay, annotating it for any passages that strike you as humorous. What is the first indication that Twain's piece is humorous?

Making Connections

Can you identify a prayer-provoking moment (say, before a test, or at the top of a dangerous ski slope) during which you made a rash promise? Did you keep the promise? Explain.

Writing Topic

By examining both the situations he creates and the language he uses, describe how Twain achieves humor.

Richard Selzer   [b. 1928]

The Discus Thrower   1977

I spy on my patients. Ought not a doctor to observe his patients by any means and from any stance, that he might the more fully assemble evidence? So I stand in the doorways of hospital rooms and gaze. Oh, it is not all that furtive an act. Those in bed need only look up to discover me. But they never do.

From the doorway of Room 542 the man in the bed seems deeply tanned. Blue eyes and close-cropped white hair give him the appearance of vigor and good health. But I know that his skin is not brown from the sun. It is rusted, rather, in the last stage of containing the vile repose within. And the blue eyes are frosted, looking inward like the windows of a snowbound cottage. This man is blind. This man is also legless—the right leg missing from midthigh down, the left from just below the knee. It gives him the look of a bonsai, roots and branches pruned into the dwarfed facsimile of a great tree.

Propped on pillows, he cups his right thigh in both hands. Now and then he shakes his head as though acknowledging the intensity of his suffering. In all of this he makes no sound. Is he mute as well as blind?

The room in which he dwells is empty of all possessions—no get-well cards, small, private caches of food, day-old flowers, slippers, all the usual kickshaws of the sickroom. There is only the bed, a chair, a nightstand, and a tray on wheels that can be swung across his lap for meals.

"What time is it?" he asks.   5

"Three o'clock."

"Morning or afternoon?"

"Afternoon."

He is silent. There is nothing else he wants to know.

"How are you?" I say.   10

"Who is it?" he asks.

"It's the doctor. How do you feel?"

He does not answer right away.

"Feel?" he says.

"I hope you feel better," I say.   15

I press the button at the side of the bed.

"Down you go," I say.

"Yes, down," he says.

He falls back upon the bed awkwardly. His stumps, unweighted by legs and feet, rise in the air, presenting themselves. I unwrap the bandages from the stumps, and begin to cut away the black scabs and the dead, glazed fat with scissors and forceps. A shard of white bone comes loose. I pick it away. I wash the wounds with disinfectant and redress the stumps. All this while, he does not speak. What is he thinking behind those lids that do not blink? Is he remembering a time when he was whole? Does he dream of feet? Of when his body was not a rotting log?

He lies solid and inert. In spite of everything, he remains impressive, as 20 though he were a sailor standing athwart a slanting deck.

"Anything more I can do for you?" I ask.

For a long moment he is silent.

"Yes," he says at last and without the least irony. "You can bring me a pair of shoes."

In the corridor, the head nurse is waiting for me.

"We have to do something about him," she says. "Every morning he orders 25 scrambled eggs for breakfast, and, instead of eating them, he picks up the plate and throws it against the wall."

"Throws his plate?"

"Nasty. That's what he is. No wonder his family doesn't come to visit. They probably can't stand him any more than we can."

She is waiting for me to do something.

"Well?"

"We'll see," I say. 30

The next morning I am waiting in the corridor when the kitchen delivers his breakfast. I watch the aide place the tray on the stand and swing it across his lap. She presses the button to raise the head of the bed. Then she leaves.

In time the man reaches to find the rim of the tray, then on to find the dome of the covered dish. He lifts off the corner and places it on the stand. He fingers across the plate until he probes the eggs. He lifts the plate in both hands, sets it on the palm of his right hand, centers it, balances it. He hefts it up and down slightly, getting the feel of it. Abruptly, he draws back his right arm as far as he can.

There is the crack of the plate breaking against the wall at the foot of his bed and the small wet sound of the scrambled eggs dropping to the floor.

And then he laughs. It is a sound you have never heard. It is something new under the sun. It could cure cancer.

Out in the corridor, the eyes of the head nurse narrow. 35

"Laughed, did he?"

She writes something down on her clipboard.

A second aide arrives, brings a second breakfast tray, puts it on the nightstand, out of his reach. She looks over at me shaking her head and making her mouth go. I see that we are to be accomplices.

"I've got to feed you," she says to the man.

"Oh, no you don't," the man says. 40

"Oh, yes I do," the aide says, "after the way you just did. Nurse says so."

"Get me my shoes," the man says.

"Here's oatmeal," the aide says. "Open." And she touches the spoon to his lower lip.

"I ordered scrambled eggs," says the man.

"That's right," the aide says.   45

I step forward.

"Is there anything I can do?" I say.

"Who are you?" the man asks.

In the evening I go once more to that ward to make my rounds. The head nurse reports to me that Room 542 is deceased. She has discovered this quite by accident, she says. No, there had been no sound. Nothing. It's a blessing, she says.

I go into his room, a spy looking for secrets. He is still there in his bed. His   50
face is relaxed, grave, dignified. After a while, I turn to leave. My gaze sweeps the wall at the foot of the bed, and I see the place where it has been repeatedly washed, where the wall looks very clean and very white.

For Analysis
1. Why does the patient in Room 542 hurl his scrambled eggs against the wall?
2. What unstated assumptions govern the nurse's attitude toward the dying man?

On Style
Analyze the style of the essay, with special attention to sentence structure, **imagery,** and **understatement**. How does Selzer's use of language contribute to his account of the patient's death? How does Selzer's description differ from a dispassionate medical description?

Making Connections
1. Have you known someone in a condition the same or similar to that of the patient in this essay? Did that person behave differently? Explain. **2.** Compare the characterization of this dying man with the characterization of Iván Ilých in Tolstoy's story, "The Death of Ivan Ilých."

Melvin I. Urofsky [b.1939]

Two Scenes from a Hospital 1993

Two things a person does alone, the ancient maxim held, are come into the world and leave it. It is true that for most of human existence, people died by themselves, the victims of predators, war, disease, or aging. As civilization tamed humanity, people died at home, in their own beds, surrounded by loving family who might ease the final pains but could do nothing to delay the death. Only in the recent past have people gone to hospitals to die, and only within the last decade or so has medicine developed drugs, procedures, and technology to hold off death.

These developments raise a host of questions, but in the end they all come down to what does the individual want, and if the individual is incapable of deciding, what does the family want. But there are others who now demand a voice in the decision—doctors, nurses, hospital administrators, insurance companies, and, very often, agents of the state. In most instances, the person dies without interference, since there is still little that medicine can do when age or disease have taken their ultimate toll. But in other situations, instead of death coming peacefully and with dignity, there is conflict and suffering, rage and public controversy.

In these cases, the key issue is who will decide whether or not care should be provided or withheld, whether enormous energy and resources should be expended to delay death, or whether nothing should be done, so that death may have its way. Who decides, and what role, if any, should the law play in this process? These are not easy questions, as can be seen in the following stories.

Rocco Musolino was a big man, one who enjoyed good food and drink and people, a gregarious man who had run a liquor store in College Park, Maryland, until his retirement. He also hated hospitals, and never wanted to end his days in one.[1]

To avoid that possibility, Musolino wrote a living will in 1989 in which he specifically declared that if he were terminally ill, he did not want to be kept alive by machine. Aware that if he were really sick he might not be able to make decisions on his own, he also signed a durable power of attorney giving his wife of fifty years, Edith, the authority to make decisions about his care. Repeatedly he told his family he did not want to be hooked up to any "damn machine" or "kept alive as a vegetable."

[1] Rocco Musolino's story is based on an extensive feature by Susan Okie in the Washington Post, June 16, 1991. [This, and subsequent notes, are Urofsky's.]

Rocco Musolino had drawn up his living will shortly after he had suffered a major heart attack in 1988. While he was in the hospital at that time doctors had performed a catheterization procedure that revealed that he had severe blockages in the coronary arteries and that one-fourth of his heart muscle was already dead. The damage was so extensive that doctors ruled out coronary bypass surgery.

Musolino had no illusions as to the prognosis of the disease, nor the fact that his diabetes seriously compounded the problem. In the two years following his heart attack, his condition deteriorated to the point that he had difficulty moving around his house. "If he made it to the bathroom, that was a big deal," his daughter Edith Scott said. "He couldn't shave. He would get all out of breath."

On October 24, 1990, following a night of chest pains and difficulty breathing, he told his wife he couldn't stand the pain anymore. She called an ambulance to take him to Georgetown University Medical Center. There his regular cardiologist, Dr. Richard Rubin, examined Musolino, and then called in a surgeon, Dr. Nevin Katz, who told the family that Rocco's only hope lay in bypass surgery, the same procedure that had been ruled out two years earlier.

"He'll die without an operation," Katz told Edith Musolino. "He's got a 50-50 chance with it." The family agreed reluctantly, since it appeared that potential kidney failure would also require dialysis, the type of machine treatment that Musolino had always feared. Musolino stayed in the hospital to undergo tests and build up his strength, and the medical staff scheduled him for bypass surgery on November 12. The night before the operation, Dr. Rubin went in to visit his patient, and later said that Rocco expressed a strong desire to live, even if it meant he might have to go onto dialysis for the rest of his life.

Later that night, Musolino suffered two cardiac arrests but survived, and   10
Rubin and Katz decided to go ahead with the surgery. Rubin called to get Edith Musolino's consent and then wrote in the patient's record: "He is awake and wishes to proceed. He is aware of the risk. I have reviewed the high risk of death (40 percent), high risk of renal failure (long term about 50 percent) with wife and daughter." His daughter later said she could not recall any such discussion.

The operation appeared successful, at least in relieving strain on the heart, but Musolino's kidneys failed, and he required dialysis several times a week. Since he could not breathe without a respirator, his wife reluctantly agreed to a tracheotomy, in which doctors inserted a breathing tube into his neck. In addition to causing constant pain, the breathing tube left Rocco unable to talk.

Musolino remained conscious and aware of what was happening, but his family claims he was never fully alert, and his medical records seem to bear this out. Doctors' notes show that he slept a lot, and often responded to questions only with a grimace. A neurologist who examined him noted that his fluctuating state of consciousness resulted from severe medical problems; if he overcame them, he would probably regain full mental clarity.

But Rocco Musolino did not improve, and as the weeks went on his family concluded that he would never recover. In late November they asked the doctors to put a "Do Not Resuscitate" order on his chart, so that he would not be treated if he suffered another cardiac arrest. Dr. Katz refused. When the family requested that he stop some of the medication, he angrily told them: "I stay awake at night trying to keep your father alive, and you want me to kill him. What is wrong with you people?" Only after his patient's condition deteriorated further did Katz agree to a "DNR" order.

Edith Musolino watched her husband's condition worsen. "Everything that could be wrong with him was wrong with him. I knew he was dying. I knew his body couldn't take any more." She made up her mind in December to ask the hospital to stop the dialysis sessions and to let her husband die in peace.

On December 21, 1990, the hospital's ethics committee met to consider the request, and recommended a psychiatric examination to determine whether Musolino was mentally competent. Under District of Columbia law, if he were declared incompetent, then the durable power of attorney would become operative, and his wife would have the authority to make the medical decisions.

The hospital named Dr. Steven A. Epstein to do the evaluation, and he visited Musolino twice at times when the patient seemed to rally a bit. Epstein's initial report, dated December 27, was inconclusive, and the family pushed for a second evaluation. This time the doctor reported the patient "lethargic and barely responding to voice. Today he clearly cannot make health care decisions on his own." Musolino, he told the family, was not mentally competent.

On New Year's Day 1991, Edith Musolino filed a note in her husband's medical records withdrawing her consent for dialysis. According to her, doctors, hospital administrators, and the hospital's lawyers agreed that she had the authority; they ordered dialysis stopped and removed the tube used to connect Musolino to the machine. Advised that without the treatment he would probably die within a few days, she and her children went to a funeral home and made the necessary arrangements.

They returned to the hospital to learn that Katz had changed his mind, and wanted to restart dialysis. He wrote on January 2, "I cannot in good conscience carry out their request," and he asked the hospital's lawyers and the chairman of the ethics committee to reopen the case.

The family now tried to find another physician or to have Musolino transferred to another hospital that would honor their requests. Katz agreed to turn over the case if the family could find a heart specialist with intensive-care experience. As Scott Musolino reported: "I called so many doctors. No one was willing to touch my father."

The next day Georgetown Hospital's lawyers wrote to the family's attorney informing them that the hospital would seek "emergency temporary guardianship" unless the family agreed to resume dialysis. Edith Musolino felt she had no choice but to agree.

Ten days later, her husband's condition deteriorating, her frustration and anger at the indignities that had been heaped upon him in spite of his express wishes finally erupted in a confrontation with Katz at Rocco's bedside. With her husband's legs and arms twitching, his face grimacing, she demanded of Katz: "What are you trying to prove here? You have made him suffer so much."

Katz asked her what she wanted. She said she wanted another doctor, Taveira Da Silva, the head of the hospital's intensive-care unit, who had earlier agreed to

15

20

take the case on condition that dialysis be continued. Katz agreed, and the next morning nurses wheeled Rocco to the ICU, where the staff gradually began treating him as a dying patient. While Da Silva described Musolino as "terminal," he nonetheless continued dialysis, even though by this point the patient had become totally disoriented and his arms had to be tied down during the procedure.

His family had reached the end of their patience as well and had agreed that the only way to save Rocco from further indignity was to take him home. At a meeting on January 24, Dr. Da Silva agreed to stop the dialysis if they wanted to do that. A few days later, however, Da Silva finally came to the conclusion the family had reached much earlier—Rocco Musolino had "virtually a fatal, irreversible disease," that no medical care could help, and that the living will, which the hospital and doctors had ignored for three months, should be enforced. He told Edith that he would stop the dialysis and let her husband die in the hospital.

Instead of relief that her husband's long ordeal would soon be over, Edith Musolino felt only anger. "You know, Doctor," she said, "I was beginning not to know who to pray to anymore. Do I pray to you, or do I pray to God?"

On February 2, 1991, Rocco Musolino died, after a stay of 102 days in Georgetown University Medical Center, a place he had never wanted to be and where he and his family had lost all power to decide his fate. 25

While Rocco Musolino's wife fought to get hospital authorities to stop treating him, halfway across the continent hospital officials were trying to get a patient's family to consent to a cessation of treatment.

On December 14, 1989, Helga Wanglie, an eighty-six-year-old retired schoolteacher, tripped on a scatter rug in her home in Minneapolis and fractured her hip. After surgery in a small private hospital, she developed breathing problems and was transferred to Hennepin County Medical Center. There, although on a respirator, she remained fully conscious and alert, writing notes to her husband, since the breathing tube prevented her from talking.

After five months, the hospital weaned her from the respirator in May 1990, and she entered Bethesda Lutheran Hospital across the river in St. Paul, a facility specializing in the care of respiratory ailments. A few days later, her heart stopped suddenly, and by the time doctors and nurses could resuscitate her, she had suffered severe brain damage. An ambulance brought her back to Hennepin Medical in a comatose state, her breathing sustained by a ventilator. When it became clear that doctors could do nothing for Mrs. Wanglie, they spoke with her husband of fifty-three years, Oliver, a retired attorney, about turning off the ventilator.

Although her husband and sons recognized that Helga had no cognition and might never regain consciousness, they would not hear of turning off the machine. His wife had strong religious convictions, Oliver told reporters, and they had talked about the possibility that if anything happened to her, she wanted "everything" done to keep her alive. "She told me, 'Only He who gave me life has the right to take life.' . . . It seems to me [the hospital officials] are trying to play God. Who are they to determine who's to die and who's to live? I take the position that as long as her heart is beating there's life there."

Eight months after readmitting Helga Wanglie and trying to convince her   30
family to stop treatment, Hennepin Medical Center officials announced they
would go to court seeking the appointment of a guardian to determine Helga
Wanglie's medical treatment. The hospital did not request that the court autho-
rize discontinuing treatment. To the best of my knowledge, no hospital has ever
made such a request, nor has there been any case law on it. Rather, the hospital
sought the appointment of a "stranger" conservator, that is, one independent of
both family and hospital, to make decisions based on the best interests of the
patient. The hospital believed that a neutral party would agree with its position.

While in most right-to-die cases it is the patient or the family that wants the
hospital to stop treatment, the Wanglie case is the rarely seen other side of the
coin. Dr. Michael B. Belzer, the hospital's medical director, said he sympathized
with the Wanglie family, but a heartbeat no longer signified life, since machines
could artificially do the heart's work. The real question, he believed, was whether
the hospital had an obligation to provide "inappropriate medical treatment."

Mrs. Wanglie's medical bills were paid in full by her insurance company, so
money was not an issue in the hospital's decision. "This is a pure ethics case,"
said Dr. Arthur Caplan, director of the Center for Biomedical Ethics at the University of Minnesota. For years, he explained, we've used the "smokescreen of
'Can we afford to do this?' There's been a harder question buried under that
layer of blather about money, namely: 'What's the point of medical care?' "

Dr. Belzer noted that Hennepin had the facilities and "the technology to keep
fifty Helga Wanglies alive for an indefinite period of time. That would be the
easy thing to do. The harder thing is to say just because we can do it, do we have
to do it?"

Hennepin Medical Center is a public hospital, one of the best in the upper
midwest, and before it could petition a court to appoint a conservator or
guardian for Mrs. Wanglie (in order to have consent for turning off the life support), it needed the approval of the county's Board of Commissioners. The
board members gave the hospital permission by a 4–3 vote, with the tiebreaker
cast by a member who had known the Wanglie family for more than thirty years.
It took him a month to make up his mind.

The commissioner, Randy Jackson, said that he finally voted to let the hospi-   35
tal go to the courts because "I don't think this is a decision to be made by a
board of elected commissioners who happen to be trustees of the hospital.
These are issues that we're going to be confronted with more and more often as
medical machinery becomes more and more able to keep people alive."[2]

Hospital attorneys presented their case to county judge Patricia Belois on
May 28, 1991, asking her to appoint a conservator to decide Mrs. Wanglie's fate.
They did not question her husband's sincerity, but argued instead that her condition was hopeless, and respirators had never been intended to prolong life in
such cases.

On July 1, Judge Belois ruled against the hospital and left power to decide decisions on Helga's medical treatment in her husband's hands. "He is in the best

[2] New York Times, January 10, 1991; Time, January 21, 1991, 67.

position to investigate and act upon Helga Wanglie's conscientious, religious, and moral beliefs." After the decision Oliver Wanglie said "I think she'd be proud of me. She knew where I stood. I have a high regard for the sanctity of human life."[3]

A little while after this decision, Helga Wanglie died.

The key issue is that of who decides what is best for a terminally ill person and what role the law and the courts have in that process. In an ideal world, perhaps, the interests of patients, families, doctors, hospitals, and courts would all coincide. But aside from the fact that this is an imperfect world, the interests of these groups are not necessarily congruent.

For centuries doctors have sworn to uphold life, and now for the first time they 40 are being asked, openly and at times defiantly, what gives them the right to decide other people's fate? Hospitals, caught in a crunch between escalating expenses and new technology, must weigh costs that never before mattered. Moreover, in a society as litigious as ours, doctors and hospitals walk in constant fear that a "wrong" judgment will lead to a ruinous lawsuit. While elective bodies are responsible for broad policy decisions, it is difficult if not impossible to frame legislation in such a way as to cover all contingencies, and so courts must step in to interpret not only what the laws say and mean, but also what the limits of self-autonomy are under both the common law and constitutional protection.

Two things a person does alone, the ancient maxim held: come into the world and leave it. But at the end of the twentieth century, before one can leave this world, he or she may find it necessary to traverse a bewildering legal, moral, and medical maze.

For Analysis
1. Do you think Rocco Musolino's physician was justified in putting a "Do Not Resuscitate" order on his patient's chart? Why or why not? **2.** Do you think Helga Wanglie's husband and sons were justified in refusing to give permission to end the treatments that were keeping her alive?

On Style
Compare and contrast the writing style of this essay with the style of Richard Selzer's "The Discus Thrower" on p. 1340. Discuss the relationship between style and purpose in these two works.

Making Connections
Examine the relationships between public officials, the courts, doctors, and the family in the case of Helga Wanglie. Then define your own position on how patients in "right-to-die" cases should be treated.

Writing Topic
In an essay, describe a scene from your own experience of the death of someone close to you.

---

[3] In re the Conservatorship of Wanglie, No. PX-91-283, Minnesota Dist. Ct., Probate Div. [July 1991].

Gary Soto [b. 1952]

The Rhino 1990

I got up quickly on my knees in the back seat of our Chevy and stared at a charging rhino painted on the side of a tire company. His legs were pleated with lines, his horn broken, and his eyes yellow and furious. I stared at the rhino until my father's car pulled around the corner, its sluggish shadows following closely behind, and we flew onto the freeway.

I looked at Father. His shirt was brilliant white in the late sun. He was working something from his teeth with a matchbook cover, and Mother was penciling words into a black book. I wanted to ask about the rhino but I knew that they would shush me.

It scared me to think that tires were being made from rhinoceros hides. So many things were possible. We were eating cows, I knew, and drinking goats milk in cans. Pigs feet came stuffed into cloudy jars. Cheese came in blocks from an animal that ate something very orange or very yellow. The Molinas stirred bony pigeons in pots of boiling water, and a pig's happy grin showed up on the bacon wrapper. Hop-Along Cassidy was a face that appeared on milk cartons, his hand on his pistol, and what I noticed was that his horse didn't have any feet. I imagined that someone had cut off his hooves and the horse had to lay down for the rest of his life.

I knew some of our clothes were cut from hides. Father's belt had an alligator look, his lathering brush was the whiskers of a docile pony, and his shoes, whose tips were mirror-bright, were cowhide. My own shoes were also leather and small as toy trucks. Mother's sweater was wool. Her pillow was a restrained cloud of chicken feathers. Her key chain was a rabbit's foot with a claw that drew blood when raked against the skin.

Our neighbor had a bear skin rug spread on his living room floor. Uncle Junior had a shrunken head that swayed from a car mirror. The mouth was stitched closed with black thread and the left eye was half-open. My aunt wore a fox with claws clipped together in friendship. The fox's eyes were smoke-brown marbles, but his teeth, jagged as my aunt's, were real. And my cousin Isaac, two years older with kindergarten already behind him, showed me a bloody finger in a gift box. He wiggled the finger and I jumped back, terrified.

I sat back down. I watched mostly the sky, billboards, and telephone poles. A sonic boom scared Mother and had me back on my knees looking around. The sky was pink as a scar in the west where the sun struggled to go down. Birds huddled on a chain link fence, and because I could count to ten I used all my fingers to tell Mother there were eight. Mother looked up from her book, turned on her knees, and ran a comb through my hair.

Father pulled off the freeway, and after two sharp turns, he pulled into my nina's yard, scattering chickens and a large black dog. The dog sniffed us as we got out, and I was so scared that he might bite, Father pulled me into his arms and put me on a low peach tree while he went inside the house. I thought of eating one of the peaches but knew that the fuzz would make my face itchy. I pressed a finger into a brown sap, counted the number of peaches, and peeled bark from the limb. The dog trotted away and the chickens returned to peck at the dust.

That evening we watched boxing. Father drank beer and I sat near him with two links of Tinkertoy. The first television was on, and he and my godfather were watching two boxers hurt each other very badly. They sat on the edge of their chairs, their fists opening and closing. Father had taken off his shirt. Godfather's watch lay on an end table, glowing in the semi-dark of the living room. Both shouted and crushed beer cans when their fighter stumbled into the ropes. I let the Tinkertoys fight each other and grunt like boxers. I said, "Mine is winning."

Back home I asked Father if our car tires were made from rhinos, and he laughed. Mother laughed and wiped her hands into a chicken-print apron. Uncle with his panther tattoo, claws tipped with blood, pulled on my cheek and said I was crazy. He assured me tires didn't come from rhino hides but from rubber that dripped from trees into buckets. He turned on the porchlight, a feast of orange light for the moth, and led me down the brick steps to the Chevy that ticked from a cooling engine. He pounded a front tire with his fist. I tried to wiggle free, but his grip held me there. He made me pound the tire and pet it like an animal. Black rhino dust came off, dust and fear that I washed with a white bar of soap when we returned inside.

I was four and already at night thinking of the past. The cat with a sliver in his 10 eye came and went. The blimp came and went, and the black smudge of tire. The rose could hold its fiery petals only so long, and the three sick pups shivered and blinked twilight in their eyes. We wet their noses with water. We pulled muck from the corners of their eyes. Mother fed them a spoonful of crushed aspirin, but the next day they rolled over into their leaf-padded graves.

Now the rhino was dying. We were rolling on his hide and turning corners so sharply that the shadows mingled with the dust. His horn was gone, his hooves and whale eyes. He was a tire pumped with evil air on a road of splattered dogs and cats and broken pigeons in the grills of long, long cars.

For Analysis

1. How does watching boxing (par. 8) relate to the rest of the essay? How does the speaker define the boxing match? What is the child's response to the boxing match? **2.** Why does the speaker call attention to his uncle's tattoo (par. 9)? **3.** What is this essay about, and why do you suppose the editors included it in the section devoted to death?

On Style

Who is the speaker in this essay? What effect does Soto achieve by adopting this **point of view**?

Making Connections

1. Recollect some early childhood misunderstanding of your own, and describe the feelings that the misunderstanding created. **2.** Gary Soto's remembrance of childhood and William Saroyan's in "Five Ripe Pears" (p. 290) both capture the keen observations of young children. How do both writers use a youthful voice to convey a message?

Writing Topic

Examine the animal **images** in this piece—you might include descriptive passages about humans as well. In an essay, analyze the animal images and describe the feelings they generate.

The Presence of Death _____

Questions and Writing Topics

1. Although A. E. Housman's "To an Athlete Dying Young," Pablo Neruda's "The Dead Woman," and Theodore Roethke's "Elegy for Jane" employ different poetic forms, they all embody a poetic mode called *elegy*. Define *elegy* in terms of the characteristic tone of these poems. Compare the elegiac tone of these poems. **Writing Topic:** Compare the elegiac tone of one of these poems with the tone of Wilfred Owen's "Dulce et Decorum Est" or Dylan Thomas's "Do Not Go Gentle into That Good Night."

2. What figurative language in the prose and poetry of this section is commonly associated with death itself? With dying? Contrast the characteristic imagery of this section with the characteristic imagery of love poetry. **Writing Topic:** Compare the imagery in Shakespeare's sonnet 18 with the imagery in sonnet 73.

3. In Leo Tolstoy's "The Death of Iván Ilých" and John Donne's sonnet "Death, Be Not Proud," death and dying are considered from a religious viewpoint. **Writing Topic:** Discuss whether these works develop a similar attitude toward death, or whether the attitudes they develop differ crucially.

4. State the argument against resignation to death made in Dylan Thomas's "Do Not Go Gentle into That Good Night." State the argument of Catherine Davis's reply, "After a Time." **Writing Topic:** Using these positions as the basis of your discussion, select for analysis two works that support Thomas's argument and two works that support Davis's.

5. Contrast the attitude toward death revealed in John Donne's "Meditation XVII" and Richard Selzer's "The Discus Thrower." **Writing Topic:** Analyze the figurative language in each essay. How does style contribute to the contrasting attitudes toward death expressed in these essays?

6. Bernard Malamud's "Idiots First" and James Fenton's "God, A Poem" both present a grim picture of the human condition, yet they are often funny. What function does humor serve in each work? **Writing Topic:** Which work embodies a more hopeful vision of the human condition? Explain.

7. Which works in this section treat death and dying in a way that corresponds most closely with your own attitudes toward mortality? Which contradict your attitudes? **Writing Topic:** Choose two works, each of which affects you differently, and isolate and discuss the elements responsible for your response.

Poetry and Fine Art

The readings in this section—poems and works of art—offer unique opportunities to make connections and reflect on the different ways meaning can be conveyed using different media. All of these pieces of art can be "read", or considered alongside, a poem or story, either reprinted in this section or elsewhere in this anthology. In several instances, a painting or poem is paired with the work that inspired it. In every case, drawing these connections will likely affect your responses to each individual poem or work of art.

As you read and enter into the dialogue between the selected works of art and poems, keep in mind the following questions: What is your response to each work considered separately? Considered side by side? Are the poems in this section successful (or even comprehensible) without reference to the paintings? How are the works alike or different? With paired works, why does the poet choose to emphasize certain details of a painting and ignore others? What accounts for the order in which the poet deals with the details of the painting? Is the poet attempting an accurate and neutral description of the painting, or making some judgment about it?

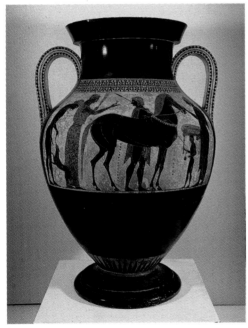

Achilles Painter, *The Departure of the Dioscuri (ca. fifth century B.C.)*
Black figure amphora. Museo Gregoriano Etrusco, Rome, Italy. Scala/Art Resource, New York.

FOR ANALYSIS
Examine the figures on the ancient Greek urn pictured here. What details are emphasized? What details are omitted? How would you describe the figures? Next, read John Keats's poem "Ode on a Grecian Urn" on p. 1265. Using as your model the scene Keats describes about another urn, write a description of the scene on this urn.

Pieter Brueghel the Elder, *Landscape with the Fall of Icarus* (ca. 1560)
Oil on panel (transferred to canvas.) 29 x 44 ⅛". Musées Royaux des Beaux-Arts, Brussels,
Belgium. Scala/Art Resource, New York.

FOR ANALYSIS

1. What do you notice about the size and placement of images in Brueghel's painting? For example, which images are in the foreground? Which are in the background? What effect do you think Brueghel is trying to achieve by placing the
images this way?

2. Read "Musée des Beaux Arts" by W. H. Auden (p. 1283). What accounts for the
order in which Auden deals with the details of the painting? For example, why
does he emphasize the plowman and the ship, and not mention the port city or the
mountains in the background?

3. Is Auden's poem successful without reference to the painting? Why or why not?
Does your reading of the poem change when you read it with the painting alongside it?

William Blake, *The Garden of Love* (1794)
from *Songs of Innocence and Experience*
Tinted engraving. The Huntington Library

FOR ANALYSIS

Read William Blake's poem "The Garden of Love" on p. 125. What information does it convey that the tinted engraving he created does not? What information does the engraving convey that the poem does not? How do the poem and engraving, taken together, interact to affect you as a reader?

Katsushika Hokusai, *The Great Wave at Kanagawa* (1831–33)
From the series "Thirty-six Views of Mount Fuji." Polychrome woodblock print. 10⅛ x 14¹⁵⁄₁₆".
The Metropolitan Museum of Art, The H. O. Havemeyer Collection. Bequest of Mrs. H. O.
Havemeyer, 1929. Photograph ©1991 The Metropolitan Museum of Art. (JP 1847)

FOR ANALYSIS

1. Examine the way Hokusai places things in the foreground or background of *The Great Wave at Kanagawa*. What is the effect of placing Mount Fuji in the deep background?

2. Is there anything in this picture that seems exaggerated or idealized? What effect does this have on you as a viewer?

3. What does "The Great Wave: Hokusai" suggest about the way a viewer responds to the Hokusai image? To art in general?

Donald Finkel (b. 1929)

The Great Wave: Hokusai 1959

But we will take the problem in its most obscure manifestation, and suppose that
our spectator is an average Englishman. A trained observer, carefully hidden
behind a screen, might notice a dilation in his eyes, even an intake of his breath,
perhaps a grunt.

—Herbert Read, *The Meaning of Art*

It is because the sea is blue,
Because Fuji is blue, because the bent blue
Men have white faces, like the snow
On Fuji, like the crest of the wave in the sky the color of their
Boats. It is because the air
Is full of writing, because the wave is still: that nothing
Will harm these frail strangers,
That high over Fuji in an earthcolored sky the fingers
Will not fall; and the blue men
Lean on the sea like snow, and the wave like a mountain leans   10
Against the sky.

           In the painter's sea
All fishermen are safe. All anger bends under his unity.
But the innocent bystander, he merely
'Walks round a corner, thinking of nothing': hidden
Behind a screen we hear his cry.
He stands half in and half out of the world; he is the men,
But he cannot see below Fuji
The shore the color of sky; he is the wave, he stretches
His claws against strangers. He is   20
Not safe, not even from himself. His world is flat.
He fishes a sea full of serpents, he rides his boat
Blindly from wave to wave toward Ararat.

Francisco de Goya, *The Third of May, 1808, Madrid* (1814)
Oil on canvas. 105½ x 136⅜". Museo del Prado, Madrid, Spain. Giraudon/Art
Resource, New York.

FOR ANALYSIS

1. What do you notice about the use of color and light in Goya's painting *The Third
of May*? How does he use them to direct the eye of the viewer? Next, read
Lawrence Ferlinghetti's poem "In Goya's Greatest Scenes" on p. 451. What images
does Ferlinghetti use to direct his readers?
2. What comparison does Ferlinghetti make between human suffering in Goya's art
and human suffering in the mid-twentieth century?

Paul Cézanne, *L'Estaque, View of the Gulf of Marseille* (1878–79).
Oil on canvas. Musée d'Orsay, Paris, France. Giraudon/Art Resource, New York.

Allen Ginsberg (1929–1997)

Cézanne's Ports 1961

In the foreground we see time and life
swept in a race
toward the left hand side of the picture
where shore meets shore.

But that meeting place
isn't represented;
it doesn't occur on the canvas.

For the other side of the bay
is Heaven and Eternity,
with a bleak white haze over its mountains.

And the immense water of L'Estaque is a go-between
for minute rowboats.

FOR ANALYSIS
1. What is your eye drawn to in Cézanne's painting? What parts of the picture get
the most emphasis? What is left out?
2. How does Allen Ginsberg's description of L'Estaque and Cézanne's painting of it
affect how you "read" this painting?

Vincent van Gogh, *The Starry Night* (1889)
Oil on canvas. 29 x 36¼". The Museum of Modern Art, New York. Acquired through the Lillie P. Bliss
Bequest. Photograph ©1997 The Museum of Modern Art.

Anne Sexton (1928–1974)

The Starry Night 1961

That does not keep me from having a terrible need of—shall I say the word—
religion. Then I go out at night to paint the stars.
—Vincent van Gogh in a letter to his brother

The town does not exist
except where one black-haired tree slips
up like a drowned woman into the hot sky.
The town is silent. The night boils with eleven stars
Oh starry starry night! This is how
I want to die

It moves. They are all alive.
Even the moon bulges in its orange irons
to push children, like a god from its eye.
The old unseen serpent swallows up the stars.   10
Oh starry starry night! This is how
I want to die:

into that rushing beast of the night,
sucked up by that great dragon, to split
from my life with no flag.
no belly,
no cry.

FOR ANALYSIS
1. Look at van Gogh's painting. How do the intense colors and the exaggerated
brush strokes affect you? What emotions are evoked?
2. Is Anne Sexton's interpretation of the painting defensible? Do you agree or disagree? Explain.

Edgar Degas, *The Dance Class* (1874)
Oil on canvas. 33 x 31¾". The Metropolitan Museum of Art. Bequest of Mrs. Harry Payne Bingham, 1986. Photograph ©1987 The Metropolitan Museum of Art. (1987.47.I.)

FOR ANALYSIS

Look carefully at the dancer at the center of *The Dance Class*. Next, read Richard Wilbur's "Museum Piece" on p. 453. How does Wilbur's description of the dancer in the third stanza capture the dancer in *The Dance Class*? What other evidence can you find in this painting of Degas' love of "Beauty joined to energy" (l. 13)?

W. D. Snodgrass (b. 1926)

Matisse: "The Red Studio" 1960

There is no one here.
But the objects: they are real. It is not
As if he had stepped out or moved away;
There is no other room and no
Returning. Your foot or finger would pass
Through, as into unreflecting water
Red with clay, or into fire.
Still, the objects: they are real. It is
As if he had stood
Still in the bare center of this floor,   10
His mind turned in in concentrated fury,
Till he sank
Like a great beast sinking into sands
Slowly, and did not look up.

Henri Matisse,
The Red Studio,
Issy-les-Moulineux (1911)
Oil on canvas. 71¼ x 86¼". The
Museum of Modern Art, New
York. Mrs. Simon Guggenheim
Fund. Photograph ©1997 The
Museum of Modern Art. ©1988
Succession H. Matisse, Paris/Artists
Rights Society (ARS), New York.

His own room drank him.
What else could generate this
Terra cotta raging through the floor and walls,
Through chests, chairs, the table and the clock,
Till all environments of living are
Transformed to energy—   20
Crude, definitive and gay.
And so gave birth to objects that are real.
How slowly they took shape, his children, here,
Grew solid and remain:
The crayons; these statues; the clear brandybowl;
The ashtray where a girl sleeps, curling among flowers;
This flask of tall glass, green, where a vine begins
Whose bines circle the other girl brown as a cypress knee.
Then, pictures, emerging on the walls:
Bathers; a landscape; a still life with a vase;   30
To the left, a golden blonde, lain in magentas with flowers scattering like stars;
Opposite, top right, these terra cotta women, living in their world of
          living's colors;
Between, but yearning toward them, the sailor on his red café chair, dark
          blue, self-absorbed.
These stay, exact,
Within the belly of these walls that burn,
That must hum like the domed electric web
Within which, at the carnival, small cars bump and turn,
Toward which, for strength, they reach their iron hands:
Like the heavens' walls of flame that the old magi could see;
Or those ethereal clouds of energy   40
From which all constellations form,
Within whose love they turn.
They stand here real and ultimate.
But there is no one here.

1363

Marcel Duchamp, *Nude Descending a Staircase, No. 2* (1912)
Oil on canvas. 58 x 35". Philadelphia Museum of
Art. The Louise and Walter Arensberg Collection.

X. J. Kennedy (b. 1929)

Nude Descending a Staircase 1960

Toe upon toe, a snowing flesh,
A gold of lemon, root and rind,
She sifts in sunlight down the stairs
With nothing on. Nor on her mind.

We spy beneath the banister
A constant thresh of thigh on thigh—
Her lips imprint the swinging air
That parts to let her parts go by.

One-woman waterfall, she wears
Her slow descent like a long cape   10
And pausing, on the final stair
Collects her motions into shape.

FOR ANALYSIS

1. What is the effect of repetition in the Duchamp painting? How well does the image of a figure descending a staircase come into focus for you? Is the painting confusing? What gaps does the painting call on you to fill?

2. How do you respond to X. J. Kennedy's telling of the story of the figure in *Nude Descending a Staircase, No. 2*? What is the effect of the poem's tone on your "reading" of the painting?

Thomas Hart Benton, *The Lord Is My Shepherd* (1926)
Tempera on canvas. 33¼ x 27⅞". Collection of the Whitney Museum of American Art,
New York. Purchase.

FOR ANALYSIS

1. Examine *The Lord Is My Shepherd* by Thomas Hart Benton. What type of people
do the man and woman in the painting appear to be? What details in the painting
serve as evidence to support your opinion?

2. Read "Good Country People" by Flannery O'Connor on p. 99. Does this couple
appear in any way similar to the characters in "Good Country People?" What evidence from the story and the painting would support the idea that the woman in
the painting is like Mrs. Freeman and that the man is like Mr. Freeman?

William Carlos Williams (1883–1963)

The Great Figure 1920

Among the rain
and lights
I saw the figure 5
in gold
on a red
fire truck
moving
tense
unheeded
to gong clangs
siren howls
and wheels rumbling
through the dark city

Charles Demuth, *I Saw the Figure 5 in Gold* (1928)
Oil on composition board. 36 x 29¾". The Metropolitan Museum
of Art, New York. The Alfred Stieglitz Collection, 1949.
Photograph ©1996 The Metropolitan Museum of Art. (49.59.1)

FOR ANALYSIS

1. Demuth's *I Saw the Figure 5 in Gold* was inspired by the poem by his friend
William Carlos Williams. Look closely at the painting, noting Demuth's use of text
and type. How do Demuth's references to Williams change how you view this
image?

2. How does the painting enhance the sense of motion conveyed by "The Great
Figure"?

<u>Nancy Sullivan</u> (b. 1929)

Number 1 by Jackson Pollock (1948) 1965

No name but a number.
Trickles and valleys of paint
Devise this maze
Into a game of Monopoly
Without any bank. Into
A linoleum on the floor
In a dream. Into
Murals inside of the mind.
No similes here. Nothing
But paint. Such purity   10
Taxes the poem that speaks
Still of something in a place
Or at a time.
How to realize his question
Let alone his answer?

FOR ANALYSIS

What do you find remarkable about the style of Pollock's *Number 1, 1948*? What,
if anything, do you see in the image? How does Nancy Sullivan's poem change
how you view Pollock's work?

Jackson Pollock, *Number 1, 1948* (1948)
Oil on canvas. 68 x 104". The Museum of Modern Art, New York.
Purchase. Photograph ©1997 The Museum of Modern Art.

Andy Warhol, *Gold Marilyn, 1962* (1962)
Silkscreen ink on synthetic polymer paint and oil on canvas. 83¼ x 57".
The Andy Warhol Foundation/Art Resource. ©The Andy Warhol Foundation.

FOR ANALYSIS

1. Read Charles Bukowski's poem "for marilyn m." on p. 453. In line 7, Bukowski writes "we will forget you, somewhat" regarding Marilyn Monroe. In lines 20–21, he writes "we forget, we remember, / we wait." Considering these lines in the context of the whole poem, what do you think the narrator of the poem is suggesting about the public's feelings about Marilyn Monroe?

2. Consider the size and placement of the image in this painting, as well as the use of color. Does Andy Warhol's painting suggest the same conflicts as Bukowski's poem? If so, how?

Glossary of Critical Approaches

INTRODUCTION

This glossary attempts to define, briefly and in general terms, some major critical approaches to literature. Because literary criticism has to do with the *value* of literature, not with its history, judgments tend to be subjective and disagreements frequent and even acrimonious. The truth of a work of art is, obviously, very different from the truth of a mathematical formula. Certainly one's attitudes toward war, religion, sex, and politics are irrelevant to the truth of a formula but quite relevant to one's judgment of a literary work.

Yet any examination of the broad range of literary criticism reveals that groups of critics (and all readers, ultimately, are critics) share certain assumptions about literature. These shared assumptions govern the way critics approach a work, the elements they tend to look for and emphasize, the details they find significant or insignificant, and, finally, the overall value they place on the work.

We do not suggest that one approach is more valid than another or that the lines dividing the various approaches are always clear and distinct. Readers will, perhaps, discover one approach more congenial to their temperament, more "true" to their sense of the world, than another. More likely, they will find themselves utilizing more than one approach in dealing with a single work. Many of the diverse approaches described here actually overlap, and even those critics who champion a single abstract theory often draw on a variety of useful approaches when they write about a particular work.

Formalist critics assume that a literary text remains independent of the writer who created it. The function of the critic, then, is to discover how the author has deployed language to create (or perhaps failed to create) a formal and aesthetically satisfying structure. The influential American formalists of the 1940s and 1950s (the New Critics) were fond of describing literary texts as "autonomous," meaning that political, historical, biographical, and other considerations were always secondary if not irrelevant to any discussion of the work's merits.

Further, formalist critics argue, the various elements of a "great" work interweave to create a seamless whole that embodies "universal" values. Unsurprisingly, the "universal" values formalist critics praise, upon close analysis, tend to parallel the moral, political, and cultural ideals of the critics' social class.

But the formalist point of view, cherishing the artwork's structure, spawned its own antithesis—a group of theorists called *deconstructionists*.

These writers argued that language itself was too shifty to support the expectations of formalist criticism. One reader might read a sentence literally, while another might read it ironically. Hence, their "understanding" of the text would be diametrically opposed.

The deconstructionists believe that intelligent readers cannot be expected to ignore those responses that interfere with some "correct" or "desirable" reading of the piece. Given what they see as the notoriously ambiguous and unstable nature of language, deconstructionist critics argue that a literary text can never have a fixed meaning.

While the formalists and deconstructionists wrestle over the philosophy of language and its implications for the nature of literary texts, other critics pursue quite different approaches. The literary critic Wayne Booth, in his book *The Company We Keep: An Ethics of Fiction* (1988), examines the meaning and relevance of "ethical criticism," which he characterizes as "this most important of all forms of criticism." The term *ethical criticism* describes a variety of approaches, all of which argue that literature, like any other human activity, connects to the real world and, consequently, influences real people.

Ethical criticism may range from a casual appraisal of a work's moral content to the more rigorous and systematic analysis driven by a coherent set of stated beliefs and assumptions. A *religious* critic (committed to certain moral positions) might attack a work—regardless of its artfulness or brilliance—because it does not condemn adultery. A *feminist* critic might focus on the way literary works devalue women, an *African American* critic on the way they stereotype blacks, a *Marxist* critic on the way they support class divisions, a *new historicist* critic on the way a dominant class interprets history to protect its own interests. But all of them agree that literary works invite ethical judgments. Most of them also agree that literary works must be judged as one of the means by which a society both defines and perpetuates its political institutions and cultural values. The feminist, the African American, and the Marxist critics would also agree that the political institutions and cultural values of most Western societies have been carefully designed to serve the interests of a dominant class: male, white, and wealthy.

Other critical approaches analyze literary works from yet other perspectives. *Reader-response* critics assert that a work of art is created as much by its audience as by the artist. For these critics, art has no significant abstract existence—a reader's experience of the work gives birth to it and contributes crucially to its power and value. Further, since each reader embodies a unique set of experiences and values, each reader's response to the work will in some respects be uniquely personal. *Psychoanalytic* criticism, similar to reader-response, is nevertheless distinctive in its application of psychoanalytic principles to works of art. Those principles, originally derived from the work of Sigmund Freud (1856–1939), now often reflect the views of more recent theorists such as Jacques Lacan (1901–1981) and others. There is, finally, the recently emergent approach called *new historical* criticism, which brings historical knowledge to bear on the analysis of literary works in new and sophisticated ways. The result is a sometimes dizzying proliferation of analyses that argue for the relationship between literature and life.

The glossary that follows reveals the widely diverse and often contradictory views expressed by professional theorists and critics.

Deconstruction   This approach grew out of the work of certain twentieth-century European philosophers, notably Jacques Derrida (b. 1930), whose study of language led to the conclusion that since we could only know through the medium of language and language is unstable and ambiguous, it is impossible to talk about truth and knowledge and meaning in any absolute sense. Verbal structures, these critics maintained, inevitably contained within themselves oppositions. Derrida asserted that in the Western world, language leads us to think in terms of opposites (for example, soul/body, man/woman, master/slave) that imply what he called "a violent hierarchy" with one of the terms (the first) always being superior to the other (the second). The aim of deconstruction is to show that this hierarchy of values cannot be permanent and absolute.

Readers therefore cannot be expected to ignore the oppositions and contradictions in a text just because they do not contribute to some "correct" or "desirable" reading of the piece which might uphold a particular political, social, or cultural view.

Formalism assures us that the successful artist is the master of language and that he or she consciously deploys all its resources to achieve a rich and unified work. Sensitive readers can aspire to a complete understanding of a work undistorted by their own idiosyncrasies, subjective states, or ideological biases.

Rejecting the formalist assumption about authorial control and conscious design, deconstruction attempts to show that by its very nature, language is constantly "saying" more than the writer can control or even know. Thus, a close study of any text (literary or otherwise) will reveal contradictory and irreconcilable elements.

Deconstructionist critics do not necessarily reject the validity of feminist, Marxist, formalist, and other critical approaches. In fact, they often draw upon the insights furnished by them. But the deconstructionist critic says that any discourse or critical approach that fails to recognize the inherently shifting and unstable nature of language is bound to produce only a partial if not misleading interpretation. For example, in his study *America the Scrivener: Deconstruction and the Subject of Literary Studies* (1990), Gregory S. Jay finds Emily Grierson, the protagonist of William Faulkner's story "A Rose for Emily" (p. 667), a "puzzle" and warns against simplistic interpretations:

As feminist subject, her story speaks of a revolutionary subversion of patriarchy; as herself, a figure of racial and class power, Emily also enacts the love affair of patriarchy with its own past, despite all the signs of decline and degradation. She is a split subject, crossed by rival discourses. What the text forces us to think, then, is the complex and ironic alliances between modes of possession and subjection, desire and ownership, identity and position.

Like Marxism and feminism, deconstruction defines itself both as a critical theory of literature and as a philosophy of human values. Hence, it is applicable not only to literature but also to an understanding of the power relations among humans and the societies they create. In insisting that we recognize the way language embodies and supports class, gender, and other biases, deconstruction challenges both the ethnocentrism of political structures and the idea of "universal values" in literary works.

Feminist Criticism   Feminist critics hold that literature is merely one of many expressions of a patriarchal society with a vested interest in keeping women subordinate to men. Thus literature, in the way it portrays gender roles, helps to condition women to accept as normal a society that directs them to become nurses rather than doctors, secretaries rather than attorneys or corporate executives, sex symbols rather than thinkers, elementary school teachers rather than university professors. Beyond this general critique of patriarchy, feminists differ in their detailed analyses. Some have re-examined history to show that a literary canon created by males has slighted and ignored female authors. Others, studying canonical works from a feminist perspective, have come up with fresh readings that challenge conventional interpretations, focusing on how women are empowered *in* literary texts or *through writing* literary texts. Some, believing that language itself allows men to impose their power, use literary analyses to expose the gender bias of language. Why, they ask, is the English language so rich in words to describe a quarrelsome, abusive woman ("shrew," "harridan," "termagant") but so lacking in comparable terms for men? Some feminists believe that the male bias of language, far deeper than mere words, is actually structural. The constellation of qualities connoted by "masculine" and "feminine," they say, reveals how deeply the positive (male) and negative (female) values are embedded in the language.

While a psychoanalytic critic might use Freud's Oedipal theories to explain Emily's relationship to Homer Barron in William Faulkner's "A Rose for Emily" (p. 667), the feminist critic Judith Fetterley maintains that the explanation is to be found in the fact that a patriarchal culture instills in us the notion "that men and women are made for each other" and that " 'masculinity' and 'femininity' are the natural reflection of that divinely ordained complement." In a society where there is "a massive differentiation of everything according to sex, one sees that in reality a sexist culture is one in which men and women are not simply incompatible but murderously so. . . . Emily murders Homer Barron because she must at any cost get a man" (*The Resisting Reader: A Feminist Approach to American Fiction,* 1978).

Formalist Criticism   Like deconstruction, formalism focuses on the ambiguous and multilayered nature of language but does so in order to achieve the precisely opposite effect. Formalism assures us that the successful artist is the master of language and consciously deploys all its resources to achieve a rich and unified work. Careful readers can aspire to a complete understanding of a work undistorted by their own idiosyncrasies or subjective states or ideological biases. The formalist rejects the central tenet of the reader-response critic, that a work comes into existence, so to speak, through the interaction of the reader with the work. For the formalist, the work exists independently of any particular reader. The work is a structured and formal aesthetic object comprising such elements as symbol, image, and sound patterns. Political, biographical, or historical considerations not embodied in the work itself are irrelevant.

The formalist sees literature as a sort of Platonic ideal form—immutable and objective. Works close to that ideal are praised for their aesthetic energy and their "universality" (a characteristic of the greatest literature). Works that do not exhibit this prized formal coherence are dispraised, and often dismissed as neither "universal" nor important. Because formalism focuses on the internal structure of literature above all else, it rejects didactic works—those intended to teach or convey moral observations. During the 1940s and 1950s, when the New Critics (as the formalists were called) dominated academic literary criticism, social protest writing was generally dismissed as subliterary because it lacked the "universality" of great literature. What was important in a work of art was not that it might change people's behavior, but that its parts coalesced into a beautiful whole. Consider the following comment by two formalist critics on Nathaniel Hawthorne's "Young Goodman Brown" (p. 61):

The dramatic impact [of "Young Goodman Brown"] would have been stronger if Hawthorne had let the incidents tell their own story: Goodman Brown's behavior to his neighbors and finally to his wife show us that he is a changed man. Since fiction is a kind of shorthand of human behavior and one moment may represent years in a man's life, we would have concluded that the change was to last his entire life. But Hawthorne's weakness for moralizing and his insufficient technical equipment betray him into the anticlimax of the last paragraph.

CAROLINE GORDON AND ALLEN TATE,
THE HOUSE OF FICTION (1950)

African American writers and critics, for example, especially complained that the criterion of universality was merely a way of protecting "white," conservative social and political dominance. The New Critics dismissed African American literature that sought to deal with racism and the struggle for equality as mere didacticism or agit-prop, not to be compared with the great "white" literary productions that achieved "universal" import. In a major work of New Criticism published in 1952, the influential critic R. P. Blackmur dismissed *Native Son,* a powerful and now classic novel about white racism, as "one of those books in which everything is undertaken with seriousness except the writing."

Marxist Criticism   The Marxist critic sees literature as one activity among many to be studied and judged in terms of a larger and all-encompassing ideology derived from the economic and political doctrines of Karl Marx (1818–1883). Marxism offers a comprehensive theory about the nature of humans and the way in which a few of them manage to seize control of the means of production and thereby exploit the masses of working people. But Marxism is about more than analysis. As Karl Marx himself said, "It is not enough to analyze society; we must also change it."

The Marxist critic analyzes literary works to show how, wittingly or unwittingly, they support the dominant social class, or how they, in some way, contribute to the struggle against oppression and exploitation. And since the Marxist critic views literature as just one among the variety of human activities that reflect power relations and class divisions, he or she is likely to be more interested in what a work says than in its formal structure.

The Marxist argues that one cannot properly understand a literary work unless one understands how it reflects the relationship between economic production and social class. Further, this relationship cannot be explored adequately without examining a range of questions that other critical approaches, notably formalism, deem irrelevant. How does the work relate to the profit-driven enterprise of publishing? What does the author's biography reveal about his or her class biases? Does the work accurately portray the class divisions of society? Does the work expose the economic bases of oppression and advance the cause of liberation?

And since Marxist critics see their duty—indeed, the duty of all responsible and humane people—as not merely to describe the world but to change it, they will judge literature by the contribution it makes to bringing about revolution or in some way enlightening its readers about oppression and the necessity for class struggle.

For example, a Marxist critic's analysis of Matthew Arnold's poem "Dover Beach" (p. 1006) might see it not as a brilliantly structured pattern of images and sounds but as the predictable end product of a dehumanizing capitalist economy in which a small class of oligarchs is willing, at whatever cost, to protect its wealth and power. The Marxist critic, as a materialist who believes that humans make their own history, would find Arnold's reference to "the eternal note of sadness" (line 14) a mystic evasion of the real sources of his alienation and pain: Arnold's misery can be clearly and unmystically explained by his fearful responses to the socioeconomic conditions of his time.

Arnold's refusal to face this fact leads him to the conclusion typical of a bourgeois artist-intellectual who cannot discern the truth. But the cure for Arnold's pain, the Marxist would argue, cannot be found in a love relationship, because relations between people are determined crucially by socioeconomic conditions. The cure for the pain he describes so well will be found in the world of action, in the struggle to create a society that is just and humane. "Dover Beach," the Marxist critic would conclude, is both a brilliant evocation of the alienation and misery caused by a capitalist economy and a testimony to the inability of a bourgeois intellectual to understand what is responsible for his feelings.

New Historical Criticism   There is nothing "new" about historians drawing upon literary works as significant documents to support and illuminate historical analysis; nor is there anything "new" about literary critics drawing upon history to illuminate literary works. For the historian, Sophocles' *Oedipus Rex* (p. 166) and *Antigonê* (p. 460) tell us much about the conflict between the old-time religion and the new secularism in fifth-century B.C. Athens. The literary critic of *Othello* (p. 1041) goes to the historian to understand the way in which Shakespeare and his contemporaries viewed black Africans. But until recently, the provinces of the historian and of the literary critics were pretty much mutually exclusive.

The new historians (influenced by modern theories of language and literature) began to question the very idea of history as it had been practiced. The historians of the past tended, for the most part, to think of history in terms of overarching themes and theses, and attempted to understand it in terms of some perceived "Geist" or "spirit" of the time. This kind of history was often linked to nationalism. Hence (for one example), nineteenth-century Americans created the idea of Manifest Destiny, and then used it to explain and justify the Western movement and its attendant atrocities. When the Nazis came to power in Germany, they developed the idea that "true" Germans were descended from a superior Aryan race, and then used that idea to deprive "inferior races" of civil rights, of property, and, finally, of life.

More abstractly, the purpose of writing history was to articulate and reinforce the values and beliefs that gave a culture unity. By that means, some new historians note, history became the story (and the ideas and beliefs and culture) of the rich, the powerful, the privileged, the victorious. The new historians see history not as the search for some grand, unifying thesis but as the articulation of the various kinds of discourse that compete with, contradict, overlap, and modify one another in the constant struggle for dominance. Indeed, the new historians, influenced by deconstructionist views of language, came to question the very idea of historical "truth."

The new historians also reject the traditional division between history and other disciplines, appropriating to historical studies many kinds of texts—including literary texts—that traditional historians left to others. These critics assert that without an understanding of the historical context that produced it, no work of literature could really be understood and, therefore, literature "belongs" as much to the historian as to the literary critic. Such critics aim at what they call a "thick" description of a literary work, one that brings to bear on a text as much information as can be gathered about every aspect of the author, his work, and his times.

Finally, it should be noted that new historicism has developed only recently and cannot be defined in detail. While its practitioners generally share the fundamental ideas outlined above, they can differ widely in the tools and methodologies they bring to bear on a literary text. That is to say, a new historian may also be a Marxist, feminist, or deconstructionist.

Psychoanalytic Criticism   Psychoanalytic criticism always proceeds from a set of principles that describes the inner life of all men and women. Though differing psychological theorists argue for diverse views, all analysts and all psychoanalytic critics assume that the development of the psyche is analogous to the development of the body. Doctors can provide charts indicating physical growth stages; analysts can supply similar charts indicating stages in the growth of the psyche. Sigmund Freud (1856–1939), for all practical purposes, invented psychoanalysis by creating a theoretical model for the human (mostly male) psyche.

The Oedipus complex is a significant element in that model. Freud contends that everyone moves through a childhood stage of erotic attachment to the parent of the opposite sex, and an accompanying hostility and aggression against the parent of the same sex, who is seen as a rival. Such feelings, part of the natural biography of the psyche, pass or are effectively controlled in most cases. But sometimes, the child grown to adulthood is still strongly gripped by the Oedipal mode, which then may result in neurotic or even psychotic behavior. Freud did not invent the Oedipus complex—he simply described it. It was always there, especially noticeable in the work of great literary artists who, in every era, demonstrate a special insight into the human condition.

Along with Oedipal feelings, the psyche inevitably embodies aggressive feelings— the urge to attack those who exercise authority, who deny us our primal desires. For the young, the authority figure is frequently a parent. Adults must deal with police, government officials, the boss at the office. As far back as the Hebrew Bible story of the Tower of Babel and the old Greek myths in which the giant Titans, led by Cronus, overthrow their father, Uranus, and Zeus and the Olympians subsequently overthrow Cronus, there appears evidence of the rebellion against the parent-authority figure. Freud views that aggressive hostility as another component of the developing psyche. But, in the interest of civilization, society has developed ways to control that aggressiveness.

Freud saw us as divided selves. An unconscious *id* struggles to gratify aggressive and erotic primal urges, while a *superego* (roughly what society calls "conscience"), by producing guilt feelings, struggles to control the id. The *ego* (the self) is defined by the struggle. Thus the Freudian psychoanalytic critic is constantly aware that authors and their characters suffer and re-suffer a primal tension that results from the conflict between psychic aggressions and social obligations.

Freud has been succeeded by a number of psychological theorists who present quite different models of the psyche—and recent literary theory has responded to these post-Freudian views. Among the most important are Carl Gustav Jung (1875–1961), who argued that there exists a collective (as well as a racial and individual) unconscious. Residing there are archetypes—original patterns—that emerge into our consciousness in the form of shadowy images that persistently appear and reappear in such literary themes as the search for the father, death and resurrection, the quest, and the double.

The psychoanalytic critic understands literature in terms of the psychic models that Freud and others defined. Originally, such critics tended to analyze literature in an attempt to identify the author's neuroses. More recently, psychoanalytic critics have argued that the patterns they discover in works allow us to tap into and, perhaps, resolve our own neuroses.

Reader-Response Criticism   Reader-response criticism (also called transactional theory) emerged in the 1970s as one of the many challenges to formalist principles. Reader-response critics focus on the interaction between the work and the reader, holding that, in a sense, a work exists only when it is experienced by the reader. If the work exists only in the mind of the reader, the reader becomes an active participant in the creative process rather than a passive receptacle for an "autonomous" work. The creation of a work thus becomes a dynamic enterprise between the reader and the text, each acting on the other. The study of the affective power of a work becomes not a "fallacy," as formalism holds, but the central focus of criticism. The task of the critic is to investigate this dynamic relationship between reader and text in order to discover how it works.

We know that various readers respond differently to the same text. In fact, the same reader might respond to the text quite differently at a different time. The reader-response critic wants to know why. In what ways do such conditions as age, gender, upbringing, and race account for differing responses? Does the reader's mood at the time of reading make a difference? If you accept the principles of reader-response criticism, the inevitable conclusion—*reductio ad absurdum,* its critics would say—is that there is no limit to the possible readings of any text. Consequently, many reader-response critics qualify the intense subjectivity of their approach by admitting that an "informed" or "educated" reader is likely to produce a more "valid" reading than an "uninformed" or "uneducated" one.

"Gaps" or "blanks" in literary texts provide particular opportunities to readers. Every narrative work omits, for example, periods of time that the reader must fill in. In Nathaniel Hawthorne's "Young Goodman Brown" (p. 61), the author omits all the years of Brown's life between his emergence from the forest and his death. The reader is free to imagine that history. In Sophocles' *Antigonê* (p. 460), we never see Antigonê and her betrothed, Haimon, together. The reader will supply the dynamics of that courtship. The filling in of these blanks enables readers to participate in "creating" a text, and reinforces the arguments of reader-response theorists.

Biographical Notes on the Authors

Chinua Achebe (b. 1930) Born in Ogidi, Nigeria, Achebe attended University College, Ibadan (1948–1953) and London University, where he earned a B.A. (1953). After spending some years working in broadcasting in his native country, Achebe began a distinguished academic career as professor of English at Anambra State University of Technology in Enugu. His acclaim as a writer led to many academic appointments and honors, including visiting professorships at the University of Massachussets–Amherst, the University of Connecticut, and the University of California, Los Angeles. His numerous literary awards include the Commonwealth Poetry Prize (1972) and a Booker Prize nomination for his novel *Anthills of the Savannah* (1988). Although Achebe's native language is Ibo, he writes in English, a language he learned in his youth. Achebe's novels include *Things Fall Apart* (1958) and *Arrow of God* (1964). He has also published volumes of poetry, short stories, and essays.

Woody Allen (b. 1935) After being dismissed from both City College of New York and New York University, this precocious and prototypical New Yorker became a television comedy writer at the age of eighteen. He wrote two successful Broadway plays; his first screenplay, *What's New Pussycat?*, appeared in 1965. A dozen years in show business gave him the confidence to set out on his own, and he began performing as a standup comic. Soon after, he embarked on the filmmaking—writing, performing, directing, and producing—career for which he is famous. His talents, and those of the actors and technical group he has brought together as a kind of filmmaking repertory company, account for his reputation as an innovative contributor to cinema history. (His 1977 film, *Annie Hall,* won four Academy Awards.) In his spare time, he plays the clarinet in a Dixieland jazz group at a New York nightspot, and continues to write occasional pieces such as *Death Knocks.*

Catherine Anderson (b. 1954) Born in Detroit, Michigan, Anderson is the author of *In the Mother Tongue* (1983), a book of poems published by Alice James Books of Cambridge, Massachusetts. She was the Cornelia Ward Fellow for Poetry at Syracuse University in 1976, where she received an M.A. in English and creative writing in 1979. She works as a community journalist and organizer in Boston's immigrant communities and has published in many journals, including *The American Voice, The Antioch Review,* and *The Harvard Review.*

Matthew Arnold (1822–1888) Born in Middlesex, England, Arnold attended Rugby School (where his father was headmaster) and studied classics at Oxford. Following his graduation in 1844, he became a fellow at Oxford, and a master at Rugby School. In 1851, he was appointed inspector of schools in England and was sent by the government to observe educational systems in Europe. He remained in that post for some thirty-five years. As a poet, Arnold took inspiration from Greek tragedies, Keats, and Wordsworth. His collections include *Empedocles on Etna and Other Poems* (1852). An eminent social and literary critic in his later years, Arnold lectured in America in 1883 and 1886. His essay "The Function of Criticism" sheds light on his transition from poet to critic. Much of his work is collected in *Complete Prose Works* (11 volumes, 1960–1977).

W. H. Auden (1907–1973)   A poet, playwright, translator, librettist, critic, and editor, Wystan Hugh Auden was born in York, England, son of a medical officer and a nurse. He attended Oxford from 1925 to 1928, then taught, traveled, and moved from faculty to faculty of several universities in the United States (where he became a naturalized citizen in 1946). He won the Pulitzer Prize in 1948 for his collection *The Age of Anxiety,* an expression he coined to describe the 1930s. While his early writing exhibited Marxist sympathies and reflected the excitement of new Freudian psychoanalytic thought, he later embraced Christianity and produced sharply honed verse in the rhyme and meter of traditional forms.

James Baldwin (1924–1987)   Born in New York City, the son of a Harlem minister, Baldwin began preaching as a young teenager. Some years later, he experienced a religious crisis, left the church, and moved to New York City's bohemian Greenwich Village, where he began his career as a writer, supporting himself with menial jobs and publishing occasional articles in journals such as the *Nation* and *Commentary.* By the end of the 1940s, Baldwin's anger over the treatment of African Americans led him into exile in France. There, Baldwin completed his acclaimed first novel, *Go Tell It on the Mountain* (1953), a work in which he drew heavily on his own childhood to depict the lives of members of a Harlem church, focusing on a minister's son. His next work, *Notes of a Native Son* (1955), a collection of personal, literary, and social essays, secured Baldwin's reputation as a major American writer. Two later collections of essays, *Nobody Knows My Name* (1961) and *The Fire Next Time* (1963), established Baldwin as one of the most powerful voices of the turbulent civil rights movement of the 1960s. But as riots, bombings, and other violence grew more frequent, Baldwin grew increasingly pessimistic over the prospect that white America could ever overcome its racism. That pessimism was deepened by two traumatic events: the 1964 bombing of the Sixteenth Avenue Baptist Church in Birmingham, Alabama, that killed four young girls attending a Sunday school class and the assassination of the Reverend Martin Luther King Jr. in 1968. Baldwin began making periodic trips to France, settling there permanently in 1974.

Toni Cade Bambara (1939–1995)   Born in New York City, Bambara was educated there and in Italy and Paris. Early in her career she worked as an investigator for the New York State Department of Social Welfare but later devoted herself for many years to teaching and writing. One of the best representatives of a group of African American writers who emerged in the 1960s, Bambara was a consistent civil rights activist, both politically and culturally involved in African American life. Much of her writing focuses on African American women, particularly as they confront experiences that force them to new awareness. She authored several collections of short stories, including *Gorilla, My Love* (1972) and *The Sea Birds Are Still Alive: Collected Stories* (1977), and two novels, *The Salt Eaters* (1980) and *If Blessing Comes* (1987). She also edited a groundbreaking collection of African American women's writing, *The Black Woman: An Anthology* (1970). *Deep Sightings and Rescue Missions: Fiction, Essays, and Conversations* was published in 1996.

Carol Bergé (b. 1928)   Bergé was first published at age eight while at The Fieldston School in New York City. In the fourth year of a degree program at New York University, she decided to study free-form the subjects that attracted her. Working days in publishing and advertising, at night she studied art history, literature, sociology, anthropology, comparative religion, copywriting, geology, the philosophy of politics, Shakespeare, and the stock market. In 1960, a divorced mother of a four-year-old son, she joined the Light Years Coffeehouse Readings in New York City and found support and encouragement to become a dedicated writer. Her poetry and fiction have appeared in numerous magazines and anthologies, and she has published five short-story collections, twelve books of poetry, and two novels. She has edited and published *Center,* a magazine for innovative fiction, and taught at several universities. She writes about people seeking love and self-respect, and her interest in the relationship between history and artifacts led her to become an anitques dealer in Santa Fe, New Mexico, where she now lives and continues to write, edit, and teach.

Elizabeth Bishop (1911–1979)   Bishop was born in Worcester, Massachusetts. Her father died before she was a year old; four years later, when her mother suffered a mental breakdown, Bishop was taken to live with her grandmother in Nova Scotia. Although her mother lived until 1934, Bishop saw her for the last time in 1916, a visit recalled in one of her rare autobiographical stories, "In the Village." Bishop planned to enter Cornell Medical School after graduating from Vassar, but was persuaded by poet Marianne Moore to become a writer. For the next fifteen years, she was a virtual nomad, traveling in Canada, Europe, and North and South America. In 1951, she finally settled in Rio de Janeiro, where she lived for almost twenty years. During the final decade of her life, Bishop continued to travel, but she resumed living in the United States and taught frequently at Harvard. She was an austere writer, publishing only four slim volumes of poetry: *North and South* (1946); *A Cold Spring* (1955), which won the Pulitzer Prize; *Questions of Travel* (1965); and *Geography III* (1976), which won the National Book Critics' Circle Award. *The Complete Poems, 1927–1979* (1984) was published after her death, as was a collection of her prose. Despite her modest output, she has earned an enduring place of respect among twentieth-century poets.

William Blake (1757–1827)   Born in London to an obscure family, Blake was educated at home until he was ten, then enrolled in a drawing school, advancing ultimately to a formal apprenticeship as an engraver. At an early age, Blake exhibited talent as both an artist and a poet, and throughout his life read widely among modern philosophers and poets. Throughout his life, he experienced mystical visions that provided him with the inspiration for many of his poems. Blake devised a process he called illuminated printing, which involved the preparation of drawings and decorative frames to complement his poems. He published *Songs of Innocence* (1789) and *Songs of Experience* (1794) in this fashion. These books, as well as the many subsequent works he wrote and illustrated, earned him a reputation as one of the most important artists of his day. Many of Blake's works assert his conviction that the established church and state hinder rather than nurture human freedom and the sense of divine love.

Bertolt Brecht (1898–1956) Born in Augsburg, Germany, Brecht studied medicine at Munich University but soon turned to writing. Following the First World War, he wrote his first play, *Baal* (1918). His second play, *Drums in the Night* (1922), earned him Germany's premier literary prize. During the following years, his reputation grew through his work in the radically staged epic theater. His collaboration with the composer Kurt Weill in 1928 produced *The Threepenny Opera,* still his most popular work. His works during this period were shaped by his Marxist beliefs and his conviction that drama should help advance the interests of the working class. The Nazi takeover of Germany in 1933 forced Brecht and his wife to flee to Scandinavia, where he wrote many poems and epic plays, among them *Mother Courage and Her Children* (1939), *The Life of Galileo* (1939), and *The Good Woman of Setzuan* (1940). In 1941, Brecht and his wife began a six-year stay in Hollywood, California, where he collaborated on several films and a volume of satirical songs, *Hollywood Elegies* (1942). By the late 1940s and early 1950s, Brecht's criticisms of American life and his well-known Marxism led to his being summoned to appear before the U.S. House of Representatives' Committee on Un-American Activities. Within days of that celebrated appearance, Brecht was back in Europe. He settled in East Berlin in 1949, where he remained until his death.

Edwin Brock (b. 1927) Born in London, Brock served two years in the Royal Navy. He was a police officer when he completed his first poetry collection, *An Attempt at Exorcism* (1959). Influenced by American confessional poets, Brock writes about family relationships, childhood memories, and sometimes shifts into the linguistic mode of an advertising copywriter (which he became in 1959). Suggesting that all poetry is to some extent autobiographical, Brock argues "that most activity is an attempt to define oneself in one way or another: for me poetry, and only poetry, has provided this self-defining act." His works include over a dozen poetry collections; a novel, *The Little White God* (1962); and an autobiography, *Here, Now, Always* (1977).

Robert Browning (1812–1889) Born in London, Browning attended a private school and was later tutored at home. After one year as a student of Greek at the University of London, he moved with his family to Hatcham, where he studied, wrote poetry, and practiced writing for the theater. In 1845, he began exchanging poems and letters with the already famous poet Elizabeth Barrett; they eloped in 1846. They moved to Italy, where Browning completed most of his work. When Elizabeth died in 1861, he returned to England and began to establish his own reputation. He is noted especially for his fine dramatic monologues in which a wide range of characters reveals the complexity of human belief and passion. His many volumes of poetry include *Dramatis Personae* (1864) and *The Ring and the Book* (1868–1869).

Charles Bukowski (1920–1994) Born in Germany and brought to the United States when he was two, Bukowski attended Los Angeles City College (1939–1941), then moved to New York to pursue a writing career. In 1946, he gave up writing and spent a decade traveling around the world. He returned to Los Angeles and began writing for the underground press, gaining popularity largely through word of mouth. His first volume of poetry, *Flower, Fist, and Bestial Wall* (1959), deals with the themes that were to occupy him throughout his career: the sense of a desolate, abandoned, and absurd world. His prolific output includes, besides journalism and essays, more than forty volumes of poems, novels, and stories. Collections of poems include *War All the Time: Poems 1981–1984* (1984) and *Days Run Away Like Wild Horses over the Hills* (1993). Among his novels and story collections are *Notes of a Dirty Old Man* (1973) and *The Most Beautiful Woman in Town, and Other Stories* (1983). Bukowski also wrote the screenplay for the film *Barfly* (1987).

Marianne Burke (b. 1957)   Born in Poughkeepsie, New York, Marianne Burke started writing poetry in her sophomore year at Vassar. She went on to Stanford University, where she earned an M.A. She won writing fellowships to both Yaddo (1991) and McDowell (1992), and has published her poems in various magazines, including the *Southern Poetry Review,* the *Threepenny Review,* and the *New Yorker.* Until recently she worked in the *New Yorker*'s editorial department. She lives in New York City. When asked to comment about her work she pointed out that "one of my earliest teachers, the poet William Heyen, used to say that it was possible to write too much. I'm just beginning to understand what he means. For instance, my poem 'Funeral Home' took two years to write. I needed that much time to write both feelingly and impersonally about my mother's death. Having lost both my parents at too early an age, death is one of my favorite subjects. I don't write poems to merely record my losses or to open old wounds, but to recover some of life's sweetness and mystery."

Robert Burns (1759–1796)   Born in Scotland to a family of poor tenant farmers, Burns was working in the fields with his father by age twelve. During these early years, the family moved often in fruitless attempts to improve its lot. Although Burns received formal education only intermittently, he read widely on his own. After the death of his father, Burns and his brother worked vainly to make their farm pay, an effort Burns was able to abandon when his first volume of poetry, *Poems, Chiefly in the Scottish Dialect* (1786) brought him overnight fame. One result of this fame was his appointment as an excise officer, a position that gave him some financial security while he continued to write poetry. Burns's humble origins instilled in him a lifelong sympathy for the poor and downtrodden, the rebels and iconoclasts, as well as a disdain for religion, particularly Calvinism and what he considered the hypocrisy of its "devout" ministers.

Robert Olen Butler Jr. (b. 1945)   Born in Granite City, Illinois, Butler attended Northwestern University as a theater major (B.S., 1967) and then switched to play-writing at the University of Iowa (M.A., 1969). He rose to the rank of sergeant in the Army Military Intelligence while serving in Vietnam (1969–1972). There he became a fluent speaker of the language and came to understand and honor Vietnamese culture. In 1972 he married the poet Marylin Geller—they have one child. After the usual collection of odd jobs, including steel mill labor, taxi driving, and substitute teaching in high schools, Butler joined Fairfield Publications and worked on such trade publications as *Electronic News*. He became editor-in-chief of *Energy User News* in 1975. Although his first published novel, *The Alleys of Eden* (1981), was rejected twenty-one times before it was finally published, it was well received and even nominated for a number of literary prizes. *Sun Dogs* (1982), as did his first novel, makes use of Butler's Vietnam experiences, and his collection of short stories, *A Good Scent from a Strange Mountain* (1992), reveals his remarkable ability to identify with the Vietnamese refugees trying to remake their lives in the United States. In a review of Butler's first novel, the writer praised Butler's "ability to catch tiny shifts of feeling, momentary estrangements, sudden dislocations of mood—a tool as valuable to the novelist as a scalpel to the surgeon." *A Good Scent from a Strange Mountain* was awarded the 1993 Pulitzer Prize for fiction.

George Gordon, Lord Byron (1788–1824)   Born in London of an aristocratic family, Byron was educated at the best grammar schools and at Cambridge. He early became a public figure, as much for the notoriety of his personal life as for the popularity of his irreverent, satiric poetry. Among his scandalous affairs, the one he was rumored to have had with his half-sister forced him into European exile in 1816. His political life was equally flamboyant: he began his career in the House of Lords with a speech defending the working classes and he met his death in Greece as the result of a fever he contracted while fighting for Greek independence. Byron published a volume of poetry while at Cambridge, but fame and popularity came with later volumes of poems, notably *Childe Harold's Pilgrimage* (1812–1818) and *Don Juan* (1819–1824). Despite Byron's acknowledged literary greatness and popularity, he was deemed morally unfit for burial in Westminster Abbey.

Thomas Campion (1567–1620)   Campion spent his early childhood in London, studied at Cambridge, then returned to London in 1586 to study law. It appears that Campion served, for a short time, as a soldier in France. In 1595, he published a collection of Latin poems, *Poemata*. After the publication of this volume, he apparently went abroad to study medicine and, later, music (though it is not known when or where). His first volume of English poems, *A Book of Ayres,* appeared in 1601; the other three volumes appeared between 1601 and 1617. Campion also wrote masques for presentation at court, often composing the music for his own lyrics. Toward the end of his life, he wrote a treatise on music that became a standard text.

Raymond Carver (1938–1988)   Carver was born in Clatskanie, Oregon, the son of a sawmill worker and a mother who did odd jobs. He graduated from high school at eighteen and was married and the father of two children before he was twenty. The following years were difficult as he struggled to develop a writing career while supporting a family. While at Chico State College (now California State University, Chico), Carver took a creative writing course that profoundly affected him. He went on to earn a B.A. degree (1963) from Humboldt State College in Eureka; he spent the following year studying writing at the University of Iowa. As he became known, he began to lecture on English and creative writing at various universities, including the University of Iowa Writer's Workshop. He taught at Goddard College in Vermont and was from 1980 to 1983 professor of English at Syracuse University. In 1983, he received the Mildred and Harold Strauss Living Award, which allowed him for the next five years to devote himself full-time to writing. His first collection of short stories, *Will You Please Be Quiet, Please* (1976), was nominated for the National Book Award. Other short story collections include *What We Talk about When We Talk* *about Love* (1981) and *Cathedral* (1984). He also published five volumes of poems, among them *Near Klamath* (1968), *Ultramarine* (1986), and *A New Path to the Waterfall* (1989), his last book. During the last ten years of his life, Carver lived with the poet and short story writer Tess Gallagher, whom he married shortly before his death.

Alice Childress (1920–1994)   Childress, born in Charleston, South Carolina, was taken to Harlem at age nine to live with her maternal grandmother after her parents separated. After completing her education in the public schools of New York, she began a career in the theater as actor, director, and playwright. Her plays include *Florence* (1949), *Wedding Band: A Love/Hate Story in Black and White* (1972), *Mojo: A Black Love Story* (1970), and *Moms: A Praise Play for a Black Comedienne* (1987). Besides plays, Childress has written a number of novels, among them *Those Other People* (1989) and *A Hero Ain't Nothin' but a Sandwich* (1973). She also wrote the screenplay for the 1978 film based on *A Hero Ain't Nothin' but a Sandwich*. She has received numerous awards and honors for her writings, among them the first Paul Robeson Award for Outstanding Contributions to the Performing Arts. Childress has described her writing as an attempt "to interpret the 'ordinary' because they are not ordinary. Each human is uniquely different. . . . I concentrate on portraying have-nots in a have society, those seldom singled out by mass media, except as source material for derogatory humor and/or condescending clinical, social analysis."

Kate Chopin (1851–1904)   Born Kate O'Flaherty in St. Louis, Missouri, Chopin was raised by her mother, grandmother, and great-grandmother, all widows, after her father's death when she was four. In 1870, following her graduation from Sacred Heart Convent, she married Oscar Chopin and moved to New Orleans, where she became a housewife and mother (she had six children). Upon her husband's death in 1882, she returned to her mother's home in St. Louis and began her career as a writer. Her first novel, *At Fault* (1890), and her stories, collected in *Bayou Folk* (1894) and *A Night In Acadie* (1897), gained her a reputation as a vivid chronicler of the lives of Creoles and Acadians ("Cajuns") in Louisiana. Many of these stories explore a female protagonist's attempts to achieve self-fulfillment. Her novel *The Awakening* (1899) is probably her most ambitious exploration of this theme. It is the story of a woman whose awakening to her passion and inner self leads her to adultery and suicide. The storm of controversy with which this work was met virtually ended Chopin's literary career.

Sandra Cisneros (b. 1954)   Cisneros, the daughter of a Mexican father and a Mexican American mother, grew up in poor neighborhoods of Chicago, where she attended public schools. The only daughter among seven children, Cisneros recalled that because her brothers attempted to control her and expected her to assume a traditional female role, she grew up feeling as if she had "seven fathers." The family's frequent moves, many of them between the United States and Mexico to visit a grandmother, left Cisneros feeling alone and displaced. She found refuge in reading widely and in writing poems and stories. In the late 1970s, Cisneros's writing talent earned her admission to the University of Iowa's Writers Workshop. There, Cisneros observed, "Everyone seemed to have some communal knowledge which I did not have. . . . My classmates were from the best schools in the country. They had been bred as fine hothouse flowers. I was a yellow weed among the city's cracks." This realization led Cisneros to focus her writing on the conflicts and yearnings of her own life and culture. Her writings include four volumes of poetry, *Bad Boys* (1980), *The Rodrigo Poems* (1985), *My Wicked, Wicked Ways* (1987), and *Loose Woman* (1994) and two volumes of fiction, *The House on Mango Street* (1983) and *Woman Hollering Creek and Other Stories* (1991). She is also the author of a bilingual children's book, *Hairs = Pelitos* (1994).

Lucille Clifton (b. 1936)   Born in Depew, New York, Clifton attended Howard University (1953–1955) and Fredonia State Teachers College. She worked as a claims clerk in the New York State Division of Employment, Buffalo (1958–1960), and as literature assistant in the Office of Education in Washington, D.C. (1960–1971). In 1969, she received the YM-YWHA Poetry Center Discovery Award, and her first collection, *Good Times*, was selected as one of the ten best books of 1969 by the *New York Times*. From 1971 to 1974 she was poet-in-residence at Coppin State College in Baltimore, and in 1979 she was named poet laureate of the state of Maryland. She has written many collections for children and a free-verse chronicle of five generations of her family, *Generations: A Memoir* (1976). Her most recent volume of poetry is *Quilting: Poems 1987–1990* (1991). Noted for celebrating ordinary people and everyday things, Clifton has said, "I am a black woman poet, and I sound like one."

Wendy Cope (b. 1945)   Cope was born in the south of England. Both parents held management positions with British companies. Cope earned a B.A. from Oxford (1966) and a diploma from the Westminster College of Education (1967). After teaching for several years at various junior schools in London, she became a free-lance writer and columnist. Her *Making Cocoa for Kingsley Amis* (1986) includes a number of literary jokes and parodies in the style of some of the most notable twentieth-century poets. Asked about her work, Cope asserted, "I dislike the term 'light verse' because it is used as a way of dismissing poets who allow humor into their work. I believe that a humorous poem can also be 'serious'—i.e., deeply felt and saying something that matters."

Stephen Crane (1871–1900)   Born in Newark, New Jesey, the fourteenth and youngest child of a Methodist minister who died when Stephen was nine years old, Crane was raised by his strong-minded mother. His brief college career, first at Lafayette College and then at Syracuse University, was dominated by his interest in baseball; he left college after two semesters, and moved on to a bohemian life in New York City. There he wandered through the slums, observing and developing a strong sympathy for the underclass of boozers and prostitutes that inhabited the Bowery. His first novel, *Maggie: A Girl of the Streets* (1893), described the inevitable consequences of grinding poverty—but no publisher would take a chance on Crane's bleak and biting vision. He published it at his own expense, but it found no audience. Without any military experience, and at the age of twenty-four, Crane produced *The Red Badge of Courage* (1895), a novel that made him famous and became an American classic. For the remainder of his life, he traveled about the world as a writer and war correspondent. He died of a tubercular infection in Badenweiler, Germany. Despite the brevity of his writing career, Crane left behind a substantial volume of work that includes a number of brilliant short stories and innovative poems.

Victor Hernández Cruz (b. 1949)   Cruz was born in Aguas Buenas, Puerto Rico, and came with his family to New York City in 1954. He recalls, "My family life was full of music, guitars and conga drums, maracas and songs. . . . Even when it was five below zero in New York [my mother] sang warm tropical ballads." By 1966, he had already completed a collection of verse, *Papa Got His Gun, and Other Poems,* and in 1969 published *Snaps.* He has edited *Umbra* magazine in New York, lectured at the University of California, Berkeley, and taught at San Francisco State University. Cruz says he writes in three languages: Spanish, English, and Bilingual. "From the mixture a totally new language emerges, an intense collison, not just of words, but of atti-tudes." His other works include *Mainland* (1973), *Tropicalizations* (1976), *Rhythm, Content, and Flavor: New and Selected Poems* (1989), and *Red Beans: Poems* (1991).

E. E. Cummings (1894–1962)   Born in Cambridge, Massachusetts, Edward Estlin Cummings attended Harvard (B.A., 1915; M.A., 1916), served as a volunteer ambu-lance driver in France during World War I, was imprisoned for three months in a French detention camp, served in the United States Army (1918–1919), then studied art and painting in Paris (1920–1924). His prose narrative *The Enormous Room* (1922), a recollection of his imprisonment, brought instant acclaim. Several volumes of poetry followed. His experiments with punctuation, line division, and capitaliza-tion make his work immediately recognizable. In a letter to young poets published in a high school newspaper, Cummings said, "[N]othing is quite so easy as using words like somebody else. We all of us do exactly this nearly all the time—and whenever we do it, we're not poets."

Emily Dickinson (1830–1886)   Dickinson, one of three children, was born in Amherst, Massachusetts. Her father was a prominent lawyer. Except for one year away at a nearby college and a trip with her sister to Washington, D.C., to visit her father when he was serving in Congress, she lived out her life, unmarried, in her parents' home. During her trip to Washington, she met the Reverend Charles Wadsworth, a married man, whom she came to characterize as her "dearest earthly friend." Little is known of this relationship except that Dickinson's feelings for Wadsworth were strong. In 1862 Wadsworth moved to San Francisco, an event that coincided with a period of Dickinson's intense poetic creativity. Also in that year, she initiated a literary correspondence with the critic T. W. Higginson, to whom she sent some of her poems for his reactions. Higginson, although he recognized her talent, was puzzled by her startling originality and urged her to write more conventionally. Unable to do so, she concluded, we may surmise, that she would never see her poems through the press. In fact, only seven of her poems were published while she was alive, none of them with her consent. After her death, the extraordinary rich-ness of her imaginative life came to light with the discovery of her more than one thousand lyrics.

Joan Didion (b. 1934)   A fifth-generation Californian, Didion was born in Sacra-mento and raised in the great central plain of California, an area she often describes nostalgically in her work. As an undergraduate English major at the University of California, Berkeley, she won an essay prize sponsored by *Vogue* magazine. As a result, *Vogue* hired her, and for eight years she lived in New York City, while she rose to associate features editor. She published her first novel, *Run River,* in 1963 and in the same year, married the writer John Gregory Dunne. In 1964 the couple returned to California, where they remained for twenty-five years. Although Didion wrote four more novels, her reputation rests on her essays collected as *Slouching toward Bethlehem* (1968) and *The White Album* (1979). In addition to her work as a columnist, essayist, and fiction writer, she has collaborated with her husband on a number of screenplays. She has focused her trenchant powers of observation in two documentary, book-length studies: *Salvador* (1983) and *Miami* (1987). Her most recent book is the novel *The Last Thing He Wanted* (1996). Her reputation as a prose stylist is reflected in a comment by one critic who asserts that "nobody writes better English prose than Joan Didion. Try to rearrange one of her sentences, and you've realized that the sentence was inevitable, a hologram." Didion characterizes herself as uneasy with abstractions: "I would try to think about the Great Dialectic and I would find myself thinking instead about how the light was falling through the window in an apartment I had on the North Side. How it was hitting the floor."

John Donne (1572–1631)   Born in London into a prosperous Roman Catholic family of tradespeople, at a time when England was staunchly anti-Catholic, Donne was forced to leave Oxford without a degree because of his religion. He studied law and, at the same time, read widely in theology in an attempt to decide whether the Roman or the Anglican Church was the true Catholic Church, a decision he was not able to make for many years. In the meantime, he became known as a witty man of the world and the author of original, often dense, erotic poems. Donne left his law studies, participated in two naval expeditions, and then became secretary to a powerful noble, a job he lost when he was briefly sent to prison for secretly marrying his patron's niece. In 1615, at the age of forty-two, Donne accepted ordination in the Anglican Church. He quickly earned a reputation as one of the greatest preachers of his time. He was Dean of St. Paul's from 1621 until his death. In his later years, Donne repudiated the poetry of his youth.

Paul Laurence Dunbar (1872–1906)   The son of former slaves, Dunbar was born in Dayton, Ohio, where he graduated from Dayton High School (1891) and worked for two years as an elevator operator. In 1894, he worked in Chicago at the World's Columbian Exhibition. His first verse collection, *Oak and Ivy,* was published in 1893. William Dean Howells, an eminent editor, author, and critic, encouraged him to write and had him join a Lecture Bureau in 1896. Dunbar read his own works in the United States and traveled to England in 1897. While Dunbar maintained that African American poetry was not much different from white (and wrote many poems in standard English), he often wrote poems in black dialect that seemed to cater to the racial stereotypes of his white audience. He died of tuberculosis in 1906. His complete works appear in *The Dunbar Reader* (1975).

Lars Eighner (b. 1948)   Born in Corpus Christi, Texas, Eighner was two when his parents divorced and he and his mother, a teacher of the deaf, moved to Houston. He became a student at the University of Texas in 1966 but dropped out after three years and took a job as a counselor in a drug-crisis center in Austin. In 1979, he was hired as an attendant at Austin State Hospital but lost his job after quarreling with his supervisor. Unable to support himself by writing stories, he was finally evicted from his Austin home and became a homeless itinerant. By 1990 Eighner, who has described himself as "a homosexual pornographer," had many stories published in obscure gay publications. In 1991, he became more widely known when the *Three-penny Review* published two of his essays on homelessness. The publication in 1993 of *Travels with Lizbeth,* an account of his three years of homelessness, was widely and enthusiastically reviewed. He is the author of two collections of stories, *Bayou Boy* and *B.M.O.C.* (both 1993), as well as *Pawn to Queen Four: A Novel* (1995). Eigner now lives with Lizbeth, his dog, in an apartment in Austin, Texas.

T. S. Eliot (1888–1965)   Thomas Stearns Eliot was born in St. Louis, Missouri. His father was president of the Hydraulic Press Brick Company, his mother a teacher, social worker, and writer. Educated in private academies, Eliot earned two philoso-phy degrees at Harvard (B.A., 1909; M.A., 1910). After graduate study in Paris and England, he worked for eight years as a clerk in Lloyd's Bank in London, and became a naturalized British citizen in 1927. He was editor, then director of Faber & Gwyer Publishers (later Faber & Faber) from 1925 to 1965, and spent time in the United States as a visiting lecturer and scholar. Admirers and detractors agree that Eliot was the most imposing and influential poet writing between the world wars. His poems "The Love Song of J. Alfred Prufrock" (1917) and *The Waste Land* (1922) are among his earliest and most famous. Acknowledging his dependence on a preexisting cul-tural tradition, Eliot explained: "The existing order is complete before the new work arrives; for order to persist after the supervention of novelty, the whole existing order must be altered." Eliot also wrote plays, including *Murder in the Cathedral* (1935) and *The Cocktail Party* (1950). The long-running Broadway musical *Cats* is based on his 1939 verse collection, *Old Possum's Book of Practical Cats.* He won the Nobel Prize for literature in 1948.

Harlan Ellison (b. 1934)   Born in Cleveland, Ohio, Ellison published his first story when he was thirteen. He left Ohio State University after two years and worked at a variety of odd jobs while establishing himself as a writer. In a career spanning over fifty years, he has written or edited fifty-eight books, more than twelve hundred stories, essays, reviews, articles, motion picture scripts, and teleplays. He has won the Hugo award eight and a half times, the Nebula three times, the Edgar Allan Poe award of the Mystery Writers of America twice, the Bram Stoker award of Horror Writers of America twice, the World Fantasy Award, the British Fantasy Award, and the Silver Pen award for journalism from P.E.N. He is the only scenarist in Hollywood ever to have won the Writers Guild of America award for Most Outstanding Teleplay four times for solo work. His recent books are *The Essential Ellison* (1986), a thirty-five-year retrospective of his work; *The Harlan Ellison Hornbook* (1990); and *The City on the Edge of Forever* (1995), the first book publication of his *Star Trek* script in its original (not aired) version. He lives with his wife, Susan, in the Lost Aztec Temple of Mars somewhere in the Los Angeles area.

Louise Erdrich (b. 1954)   Born in Little Falls, Minnesota, Erdrich grew up in Wa-hepton, North Dakota, a member of the Turtle Mountain Band of Chippewa. Her grandfather was for many years tribal chair of the reservation where her parents taught in the Bureau of Indian Affairs School. She attended Dartmouth College, earn-ing a degree in anthropology (1976) as well as prizes for fiction and poetry, includ-ing the American Academy of Poets Prize. She returned to North Dakota for a brief period of teaching before going on to study creative writing at Johns Hopkins University (M.A., 1979). The following year, she returned to Dartmouth as a writer-in-residence. Her works have appeared in the *New England Review* and *Redbook* as well as such anthologies of Native American writing as *Earth Power Coming* and *That's What She Said: Contemporary Poetry and Fiction by Native American Women.* She has published two collections of poems, *Jacklight* (1984) and *Baptism of Desire* (1989). Her novel *Love Medicine* (1984) won the National Book Critics Circle Award. *The Beet Queen* (1986), *Tracks* (1988), *The Bingo Palace* (1994), and *Tales of Burning Love* (1996) extend the histories of families dealt with in *Love Medicine.* In 1991, Erdrich and her then husband, Michael Dorris, a professor of Native American Studies at Dartmouth, published *The Crown of Columbus,* a collaborative novel about Christopher Columbus's discovery of America. They have pledged to donate a part of their royalties to American Indian charities.

William Faulkner (1897–1962)   Faulkner was born in New Albany, Mississippi, and lived most of his life in Oxford, the seat of the University of Mississippi. Although he did not graduate from high school, he did attend the university as a special student from 1919 to 1921. During this period, he also worked as a janitor, a bank clerk, and a postmaster. His southern forebears had held slaves, served during the Civil War, endured the indignities of Reconstruction, fought duels, even wrote the occasional romance of the old South. Faulkner mined these generous layers of history in his work. He created the mythical Yoknapatawpha County in northern Mississippi, and traced the destinies of its inhabitants from the colonial era to the middle of the twentieth century in such novels as *The Sound and the Fury* (1929), *Light in August* (1932), and *Absalom, Absalom!* (1936). Further, Faulkner described the decline of the pre–Civil War aristocratic families and the rise of mean-spirited money grubbers in a trilogy: *The Hamlet* (1940), *The Town* (1957), *The Mansion* (1959). Recognition came late, and Faulkner fought a constant battle to keep afloat financially. During the 1940s, he wrote screenplays in Hollywood. But, finally, his achievement brought him the Nobel Prize in 1950.

James Fenton (b. 1949)   Born in Lincoln, England, Fenton earned a B.A. (1970) from Magdalen College, Oxford University. His earliest volumes of verse appeared during his undergraduate years: *Our Western Furniture* (1968) and *Put Thou Thy Tears Into My Bottle* (1969). He wrote for the *New Statesman and Nation,* a leftist weekly magazine, and continued to publish relatively few but always finely crafted poems. Almost half of his collection *Children in Exile: Poems 1968–1984* is light verse, but often those poems move from whimsy to horror. He won the 1984 Geoffrey Faber Memorial Prize for his poetry. He translated the lyrics of Verdi's opera *Rigoletto,* controversially setting the action in the 1950s New York Mafia world. He accompanied Redmond O'Hanlon on a remarkable trip to Borneo that served as the source for O'Hanlon's comic travel book *Into the Heart of Borneo* (1984). *Children in Exile's* appearance in the United States (1985) generated an enthusiastic response to the relatively unknown British poet. More recently, Fenton has published a collection of essays, *The Snap Revolution* (1986) and a travel book with political overtones, *All the Wrong Places: Adrift in the Politics of the Pacific Rim* (1988). In 1994, he was appointed Professor of Poetry at Oxford University and published *Out of Danger,* a collection of poetry.

Lawrence Ferlinghetti (b. 1919)   Born Lawrence Ferling, this irreverent writer restored his original family name in 1954. He earned a B.A. in journalism from the University of North Carolina in 1941, served as lieutenant commander in the U.S. Naval Reserve during World War II, then received graduate degrees from Columbia and the University of Paris. He worked briefly as a translator of French before rising to prominence in the San Francisco–based "Beat" literary movement of the 1950s, comprised of a group of writers who felt strongly that art should be accessible to all, not just to a small group of intellectuals. Ferlinghetti received great praise from many readers and some critics for his attempts to incorporate American vernacular speech and the rhythms of modern jazz into his writings, while he was roundly attacked be defenders of the status quo. Ferlinghetti has been a prolific writer in all genres. In addition, he cofounded a San Francisco bookstore, City Lights, and two publishing enterprises, City Lights Books and the Pocket Book Series. He has published two novels, many plays, and over two dozen volumes of poetry. His early work, *A Coney Island of the Mind* (1958), remains his most popular and best-selling poetry collection.

Harvey Fierstein (b. 1954)   Fierstein was born in Brooklyn, New York. His father was a handkerchief manufacturer and his mother, a school librarian. He began his career in the theater at the age of eleven as a founding actor in the Gallery Players Community Theater in Brooklyn. He earned a B.F.A. from Pratt Institute in 1973, and added writing and producing to his early acting skills as he embarked on a remarkable career. He wrote the three one-act plays that constitute *Torch Song Trilogy* between 1976 and 1979—all were produced in small theaters. But when he starred in the production that opened in an off-off-Broadway house (1981), and later moved to Broadway, his considerable talents were widely recognized. In fact, he is the first person to win a Tony award for best actor and best play for the same production. Fierstein has characterized himself as the first "real live, out-of-the-closet queer on Broadway." He pointed out to one critic that Arnold, the homosexual central figure in the *Torch Song Trilogy,* is much like us all. "Everyone wants what Arnold wants— an apartment they can afford, a job they don't hate too much, a chance to go to the store once in a while and someone to share it all with." Fierstein wrote the book for the musical version of *La Cage aux Folles,* and a number of one-act and full-length plays and television dramas. His work has been recognized with numerous awards in addition to his Tonys. The original producer of *Torch Song Trilogy* illuminated the source of Fierstein's success when he pointed out that "what Harvey proved was that you could use a gay context and a gay experience and speak in universal truths."

Donald Finkel (b. 1929)   Donald Finkel was born in New York City, the son of an attorney. He earned a B.S. (1952) and an M.A. (1953) from Columbia University. In 1956 he married the writer Constance Urdang. Shortly thereafter, Finkel began a university teaching career at the University of Iowa, and, in 1960, moved to Washington University in St. Louis where he became poet in residence. His interest in Antarctica and exploration produced *Endurance: An Antarctic Idyll* and *Going Under* (1978). The first describes the shipwreck and rescue of Ernest Shackleton's 1914 expedition. The second examines two men who explored Kentucky's Mammoth Caves. His many books, including *Selected Shorter Poems* (1987) and *A Splintered Mirror: Chinese Poetry from the Democracy Movement* (1991), have earned him abundant awards and honors, among them a Guggenheim Fellowship (1967), nomination for a National Book Award (1970), and two nominations for the National Book Critics Circle Award (1975, 1981).

Carolyn Forché (b. 1950)   Born in Detroit, Forché earned a B.A. in international relations and creative writing at Michigan State University in 1972. After graduate study at Bowling Green State University in 1975, she taught at a number of universities, including the University of Arkansas, Vassar, and Columbia. She won the Yale Series of Younger Poets Award in 1976 for her first collection, *Gathering the Tribes.* Other honors include a Guggenheim Fellowship and the Lamont Award (1981). Forché was a journalist for Amnesty International in El Salvador in 1983 and Beirut correspondent for the National Public Radio program "All Things Considered." Her works include two collections of poetry, *The Country between Us* (1981) and *The Angel of History* (1994), both embodying her passionate preoccupation with the dehumanizing effects of political repression.

Robert Francis (1901–1987)   Born in Upland, Pennsylvania, Francis studied at Harvard (A.B., 1923; Ed.M., 1926). He taught at summer workshops and conferences and lectured at universities across the United States. His works include *Stand with Me Here* (1936); *Like Ghosts of Eagles: Poems 1966–1974* (1974); a novel, *We Fly Away* (1948); and an autobiography, *The Trouble with Francis* (1971). He won the Shelley Memorial Award in 1939.

Robert Frost (1874–1963)   Frost was born in San Francisco but from the age of ten lived in New England. He attended Dartmouth College briefly, then became a teacher, but soon decided to resume his formal training and enrolled at Harvard. He left Harvard after two years without a degree, and for several years supported himself and his growing family by tending a farm his grandfather bought for him. When he was not farming, he read and wrote intensively, though he received little recognition. Discouraged by his lack of success, he sold the farm and moved his family to England, where he published his first volumes of poetry, *A Boy's Will* (1913) and *North of Boston* (1914). After three years in England, Frost returned to America a recognized poet. Later volumes, notably *Mountain Interval* (1916), *New Hampshire* (1923), *West-Running Brook* (1928), and *A Further Range* (1936), won Frost numerous awards, including two Pulitzer Prizes, and a wide popularity. By the time he delivered his poem "The Gift Outright" at the inauguration of President John F. Kennedy in 1961, Frost had achieved the status of unofficial poet laureate of America, widely revered and beloved for his folksy manner and seemingly artless, accessible poems.

Athol Fugard (b. 1932)   Born in a remote village in South Africa, Fugard grew up in Port Elizabeth, the setting for most of his plays. He attended Cape Town University, spent two years as the only white seaman on a merchant ship in the Far East, then returned to South Africa. In 1958, he moved to Johannesburg where he worked as a court clerk, an experience that made him keenly aware of the injustices of apartheid, the theme of many of his plays. In that same year, he organized a multiracial theater for which he wrote, directed, and acted. Fugard's attacks on apartheid brought him into conflict with the South African government. After his play *Blood Knot* (1961) was produced in England, the government withdrew his passport for four years. His support in 1962 of an international boycott against the South African practice of segregating theater audiences led to further restrictions. The restrictions were relaxed somewhat in 1971, when he was allowed to travel to England to direct his play *Boesman and Lena* (1969). *A Lesson from Aloes* won the 1980 New York Drama Critics' Circle Award. *"Master Harold" . . . and the Boys* (1982) premiered at the Yale Repertory Theatre and then was taken to Broadway. He is also the author of *Cousins: A Memoir* (1997).

Willard Gaylin (b. 1925)   Gaylin was educated at Harvard University (A.B., 1947), Western Reserve (now Case Western Reserve) University (M.D., 1951), and Columbia University, where, after earning a certificate in psychoanalytic medicine, he served as a faculty member (1956). A practicing psychiatrist and psychoanalyst, he is also cofounder and president of the Hastings Center, which researches ethical issues in the life sciences. Among his publications are *In the Service of Their Country: War Resisters in Prison* (1970), *Feelings: Our Vital Signs* (1979), *The Killing of Bonnie Garland: A Question of Justice* (1982), *The Rage Within: Anger in Modern Life* (1984), *Adam and Eve and Pinocchio: On Being and Becoming Human* (1990), *The Male Ego* (1992), and *The Perversion of Autonomy: The Proper Uses of Coercion and Constraints in a Liberal Society* (1996).

Allen Ginsberg (1926–1997)   Ginsberg was born in Newark, New Jersey, earned an A.B. from Columbia in 1948, and became one of the most influential writers of the 1950s as the preeminent poet of the Beat generation. His long poem *Howl* (1956), formally influenced by Walt Whitman's work, cried out against a brutal, stifling society. Because of graphic sexual language in *Howl,* San Francisco police declared it obscene and arrested its publisher, Lawrence Ferlinghetti. In a well-publicized trial, Judge Clayton W. Horn ruled the work not obscene. A lifelong consciousness-raiser, Ginsberg helped create the "flower power" movement of the 1960s, cultivated meditation and mantra-chanting, and converted to Buddhism in 1972. While Ginsberg was largely ignored or attacked by the mainstream literary establishment in the 1950s and 1960s, in 1974 he won a National Book Award for *The Fall of America: Poems of These States 1965–1971* (1972). For all his literary ground breaking, Ginsberg considered himself a follower of Thoreau, Emerson, and Whitman, carrying "old-time American transcendentalist individualism . . . into the 20th century."

Nikki Giovanni (b. 1943)   Born Yolande Cornelia Giovanni Jr. in Knoxville, Tennessee, daughter of a probation officer and a social worker, Giovanni graduated with honors from Fisk University in 1967. She attended the University of Pennsylvania School of Social Work and Columbia School of the Arts, was assistant professor of black studies at Queens College (1968), and associate professor of English at Rutgers University (1968–1970). Giovanni's early work reflected her social activism as an African American college student in the 1960s, while her later works focused on the individual struggle for fulfillment rather than the collective struggle for black empowerment. Her books include *Black Feeling, Black Talk* (1970), *My House* (1972), and *The Women and the Men* (1975). She is also the author of a collection of essays, *Sacred Cows . . . and Other Edibles* (1988), as well as poetry and fiction for children. *The Selected Poems of Nikki Giovanni, 1968–1995* was published in 1996.

Susan Glaspell (1882–1948)   Born and raised in Davenport, Iowa, Glaspell began her career as a novelist and author of sentimental short stories for popular magazines. By 1915, she had turned her energies to the theater, becoming one of the founders of the Provincetown Players, a group devoted to experimental drama. In 1916, Glaspell moved with the company, now called the Playwright's Theatre, to Greenwich Village in New York, where for two seasons—as writer, director, and actor—she played an important role in a group that came to have a major influence on the development of American drama. *Trifles* was written to be performed with a group of one-act plays by Eugene O'Neill at the company's summer playhouse on Cape Cod. Also among her longer plays that embody a feminist perspective are *The Verge* (1921) and *Allison's House* (1931), a Pulitzer Prize–winning drama based upon the life of Emily Dickinson. Among more than forty short stories, some twenty plays, and ten novels, Glaspell's best works deal with the theme of the "new woman," presenting a protagonist who embodies the American pioneer spirit of independence and freedom.

Emma Goldman (1869–1940)   Socialist, anarchist, and feminist, Goldman was born in Russia and emigrated in 1885 to New York City, where she worked in clothing factories and began writing and lecturing on behalf of reform movements, including feminism and birth control. In 1893, she was arrested for inciting a riot after urging a group of unemployed workers to take food by force. In 1919, after serving time in prison for agitating against military conscription and U.S. involvement in World War I, she was deported to Russia, whose revolution in 1917 she had hailed as the dawn of a just society. After two years, she left Russia to travel in a number of countries, including Germany, England, and Canada. In two books, *My Disillusionment with Russia* (1923) and *My Further Disillusionment with Russia* (1924), Goldman announced her break with the Russian regime. She spent her final years in Canada, anxiously awaiting word on her request to end her exile. The request was denied. She died in Canada and is buried in Chicago. Other works include *Anarchism and Other Essays* (1911) and the autobiography *Living My Life* (1931).

Thom Gunn (b. 1929)   Gunn was born in Gravesend, England—both his parents were journalists. He earned a B.A. (1953) and an M.A. (1958) from Cambridge University. He lived in Paris (1950) and Rome (1953–1954), then moved to California where he has lived since 1954. He taught at the University of California, Berkeley, between 1958 and 1966 and has returned from time to time as a senior lecturer. His numerous awards and honors include a Guggenheim Fellowship (1971) and the Robert Kirsch Award for a body of work focused on the American West (1988). Writing in 1983 about his personal life, Gunn asserted "I am a completely anonymous person—my life contains no events, and I lack any visible personality." Others disagree. One critic argues, "Frank representations of violence, deviance, and the life of the counterculture based in San Francisco connect with 'yesterday and tomorrow' in Gunn's art."

Thomas Hardy (1840–1928)   Hardy was born near Dorchester, in southeastern England (on which he based the "Wessex" of many of his novels and poems). Hardy worked for the ecclesiastical architect John Hicks from 1856 to 1861. He then moved to London to practice architecture, and took evening classes at King's College for six years. In 1867, he gave up architecture to become a full-time writer, and after writing short stories and poems found success as a novelist. *The Mayor of Casterbridge* (1886) and *Tess of the d'Urbervilles* (1891) reveal Hardy's concern for victims of circumstance and his appeal to humanitarian sympathy in readers. After his novel *Jude the Obscure* (1896) was strongly criticized, Hardy set aside prose fiction and returned to poetry—a genre in which he was most prolific and successful after he reached the age of seventy.

Nathaniel Hawthorne (1804–1864)   The son of a merchant sea-captain who died in a distant port when Nathaniel was four, Hawthorne grew up in genteel poverty in Massachusetts and Maine. His earliest American ancestor, the magistrate William Hathorne, ordered the whipping of a Quaker woman in Salem. William's son John was one of the three judges at the Salem witch trials of 1692. Aware of his family's role in colonial America, Hawthorne returned to Salem after graduating from Bowdoin College (where future president Franklin Pierce was a friend and classmate), determined to be a writer. He recalled and destroyed copies of his first novel, the mediocre *Fanshawe* (1828). His short stories, often set in Puritan America, revealed a moral complexity that had not troubled his righteous ancestors William and John. His success as an author allowed him to marry Sophia Peabody in 1842 (after a four-year engagement). Though his stories were critically praised, they did not earn much money, and, in 1846, he used his political connections with the Democratic party to obtain a job at the Salem custom house. His dismissal in 1849 (when the Democrats lost) produced both anger and resolve. The result was a great American novel, *The Scarlet Letter* (1850), which made him famous and improved his fortune. Although he was friendly with Emerson and his circle of optimistic transcendentalists (some of whom established the utopian socialist community at Brook Farm), Hawthorne's vision of the human condition was considerably darker. Herman Melville dedicated *Moby Dick* to Hawthorne, and characterized him as a man who could say "No" in thunder.

Robert Hayden (1913–1980)   Born in Detroit, Hayden studied at Wayne State University and the University of Michigan (M.A., 1944). In 1946, he joined the faculty of Fisk University. He left Fisk in 1968 for a professorship at the University of Michigan, where he remained until his death. He produced some ten volumes of poetry but did not receive the acclaim many thought he deserved until late in life, with the publication of *Words in the Mourning Time: Poems* (1971). In the 1960s, he aroused some hostility from African Americans who wanted him to express more militancy. But Hayden did not want to be part of what he called a "kind of literary ghetto." He considered his own work "a form of prayer—a prayer for illumination, perfection."

Bessie Head (1937–1986)   Bessie Head was born in Pietermaritzburg, South Africa, the daughter of a racially mixed marriage. She was taken from her white mother and raised by foster parents until she was thirteen, and then placed in an orphanage; she overcame this difficult childhood and trained to be a primary-school teacher. After four years as a teacher, two years as a journalist, and a failed marriage in South Africa, she emigrated to Botswana where she lived for many years in deep poverty. She spent fifteen years in a refugee community at the Bamangwato Development Farm before winning Botswanian citizenship. At the development farm, she continued her distinguished career as a writer, though she had to plead for small advances from her publisher in order to buy paper to write on. Her writing brought her recognition and prominence, and she represented Botswana at international writers' conferences in the United States, Canada, Europe, and Australia. She died of hepatitis at age forty-nine. Along with several collections of short stories, she published three novels and two historical chronicles of African life. In an interview, Head acknowledged "that the regularity of her life in the refugee community brought her the peace of mind she sought: 'In South Africa, all my life I lived in shattered little bits. All those shattered bits began to grow together here. . . . I have a peace against which all the turmoil is worked out!' "

Seamus Heaney (b. 1939)   Heaney, the eldest of nine children, was born on his family's farm near Belfast in County Derry, Northern Ireland. He attended local schools, earned a degree in English with first-class honors from Queen's University, Belfast, and took a teacher's certificate in English at St. Joseph's College in Belfast. He published his first writings while a student at St. Joseph's and began a career as a teacher. His first volume of poetry, *Death of a Naturalist* (1966), won several prizes and launched Heaney's distinguished career as a poet. His many books include two volumes of essays, *The Government of the Tongue* (1988) and *The Redress of Poetry* (1995), as well as *Selected Poems: 1966–1987* (1990) and *The Spirit Level* (1996), his most recent volume of poetry. He has taught at Oxford University; University of California, Berkeley; and Harvard. An immensely popular poet, he enjoys the support of a host of "Heaneyboppers" who attend his readings. Several modern critics characterize him as "the most important Irish poet since Yeats." When asked "about his abiding interest in memorializing the people of his life, he replied, 'The elegiac Heaney? There's nothing else.' " In 1995, Heaney was awarded the Nobel Prize for literature.

Anthony Hecht (b. 1923)   Born in New York City, Hecht attended Bard College (B.A., 1944). After three years in the U.S. Army, serving in Europe and Japan, he continued his education at Columbia University (M.A., 1950). Hecht has taught at several universities, including the University of Rochester, where he was professor of poetry and rhetoric in 1967. He is presently a professor in the graduate school of Georgetown University. His awards include a 1951 Prix de Rome, and Guggenheim, Rockefeller, and Ford Foundation Fellowships, as well as the Bollingen Prize in Poetry. His first book of poetry, *A Summer of Stones* (1954), was followed by *Hard Hours* (1968), which won a Pulitzer Prize for poetry, *Millions of Strange Shadows* (1977), *Venetian Vespers* (1979), and *The Transparent Man* (1990). His most recent collection of poems is *Flight Among the Tombs* (1996). Hecht is also the author of a collection of critical essays, *Obbligati* (1986). Acclaimed for his technical expertise, Hecht was first devoted to traditional poetic forms, and his work was sometimes described as "baroque" and "courtly." More recently, his work has become less decorative.

Ernest Hemingway (1899–1961)   Born in Oak Park, Illinois, Hemingway became a cub reporter after high school. He was seriously wounded while serving as an ambulance driver in World War I. After the war, he lived in Paris, a member of a lively and productive expatriate community characterized by Gertrude Stein as "a lost generation." He lived an active life, not only as a writer, but as a war correspondent, big game hunter, and fisherman. In such novels as *The Sun Also Rises* (1926), *A Farewell to Arms* (1929), and *For Whom the Bell Tolls* (1940), his fictional characters exhibit a passion for courage and integrity, for grace under pressure. Hemingway's spare, unembellished style reinforced his central theme that one must confront danger and live honorably. He won the Nobel Prize in 1954. In 1961, unable to write because treatment for mental instability affected his memory, he killed himself with the shotgun he had so often used as a hunter.

Amy Hempel (b. 1951) Hempel was born in Chicago and spent her early years in California, where she attended Whittier College and San Francisco State College—"your basic non-linear education," she called it. She moved to New York to pursue a career in writing and was for a time a contributing editor at *Vanity Fair* magazine. Some of her unhappy experiences as a struggling writer in New York as well as the deaths of family members provide much of the material for *Reasons to Live* (1985), a collection of stories set in California, which grew out of a fiction workshop she attended at Columbia University in 1982. In many of these stories, her protagonists struggle against the alienating culture of California. Her collections of stories include *At the Gates of the Animal Kingdom* (1990) and *Tumble Home* (1997). She has edited, with Jim Shepard, *Unleashed: Poems by Writers' Dogs* (1995). "I am really interested in resilience," Hempel recently told an interviewer. "Dr. Christiaan Barnard said, 'Suffering isn't ennobling, recovery is.' If I have a motto for this particular bunch of stories, that's what it is."

Linda Hogan (b. 1947) A Chickasaw, Hogan was born in Denver, Colorado, and educated at the University of Colorado, where she received her M.A. in 1978. For a time, she supported herself with odd jobs and free-lance writing. By 1980, her success as a writer led to her appointment as writer-in-residence for the states of Colorado and Oklahoma. In 1982 she became an assistant professor in the TRIBES program at Colorado College, Colorado Springs. She is now associate professor of American Indian studies at the University of Minnesota. In 1980, her play, *A Piece of Moon,* won the Five Civilized Tribes Playwriting Award, and in 1983 she received the *Stand* magazine fiction award. Her writings include six volumes of poetry, *Calling Myself Home* (1979), *Daughters, I Love You* (1981), *Eclipse* (1983), *Seeing Through the Sun* (1985), *Savings* (1991), and *The Book of Medicines* (1993). Her fiction includes two volumes of short stories and two novels, *Mean Spirit* (1990) and *Solar Storms* (1995). Her collection of essays, *Dwellings: Reflections on the Natural World* (1995), describes her attempts to "relearn the tribal knowings of thousands of years."

M. Carl Holman (1919–1988) Holman was born in Minter City, Mississippi, and grew up in St. Louis, Missouri. He graduated magna cum laude from Lincoln University and earned a master's degree from the University of Chicago and a Master of Fine Arts from Yale, which he attended on a creative writing scholarship. He taught as an English professor at Hampton University, Lincoln University, and Clark College. For a while, he edited the Atlanta *Inquirer,* a weekly publication that reported on civil rights activities in the South. In 1962, he moved to Washington, D.C., to become an information officer at the U.S. Civil Rights Commission, becoming its deputy director in 1966. From 1971 to 1988, he served as director of the Urban Coalition, an organization formed after the riots of 1967 for the purpose of forging partnerships between industry and government to promote inner-city development.

Gerard Manley Hopkins (1844–1889) Raised in London, Hopkins won a scholarship to Balliol College, Oxford, where he studied classical literature. He converted to Roman Catholicism in 1866 and two years later entered the Jesuit Novitiate. In 1877, he was ordained as a Jesuit priest and served in missions in London, Liverpool, Oxford, and Glasgow until 1882. From 1884 to his death in 1889, he was professor of Greek at University College, Dublin. A technically innovative poet, Hopkins saw only three of his poems published during his lifetime, but gained posthumous recognition in 1918 when a friend (the Poet Laureate Robert Bridges) published his complete works. His early poems celebrate the beauty of God's world, but later works reflect his poor health and depression.

A. E. Housman (1859–1936) Born in Fockbury, England, and an outstanding student, Alfred Edward Housman nonetheless failed his final examinations at Oxford in 1881 (possibly as a result of emotional chaos caused by his love for a male classmate). Working as a clerk in the Patent Office in London, he pursued classical studies on his own, earned an M.A., and was appointed to the Chair of Latin at University College, London. In 1910, he became professor of Latin at Cambridge, where he remained until his death in 1936. As a poet, Housman was concerned primarily with the fleetingness of love and the decay of youth. After his first collection, *A Shropshire Lad,* was rejected by several publishers, Housman published it at his own expense in 1896. It gained popularity during World War I, and his 1922 collection, *Last Poems,* was well received. In his lecture "The Name and Nature of Poetry" (1933), Housman argued that poetry should appeal to emotions rather than intellect. *More Poems* (1936) was published posthumously.

Pam Houston (b. 1962) Houston grew up in New Jersey, the only child of an actress and an unsuccessful businessman. After graduating in English from Denison University in Ohio, she rode across Canada on a bicycle and then down to Colorado, where she worked at various odd jobs, among them bartender and flagwoman on a highway crew. Eventually, she entered a doctoral program at the University of Utah. Her first collection of short stories, *Cowboys Are My Weakness,* was published in 1992. Her stories have also appeared in *Mirabella, Mademoiselle,* and the *Mississippi Review,* and *Best American Short Stories* and her nonfiction has appeared in the *New York Times, Elle,* and *Vogue.* She recently edited *Women on Hunting: Essays, Fiction, and Poetry* (1994), and wrote the text for *Men Before Ten A.M.* (1997), a book of photographs by the French photographer Veronique Vial. A licensed river guide and accomplished horsewoman, Houston teaches at many writing conferences and programs in the United States and England. In explaining her pursuit of outdoor and often dangerous activities during her early twenties, she says: "You think I spent three summers leading hunters through Alaska because I like watching guys like David Duke shoot sheep? No. It was because if I didn't go with my boyfriend, somebody else would. I wanted to win."

Langston Hughes (1902–1967) Hughes was born in Joplin, Missouri. His father was a businessperson and lawyer, his mother a teacher. Hughes attended Columbia, graduated from Lincoln University in 1929, traveled throughout the world, and held many odd jobs as a young man. While Hughes had a long and prolific career as a writer in all genres, he is still remembered as the central figure of the Harlem

Renaissance of the 1920s, a movement which committed itself to the examination and celebration of black life in America and its African heritage. He was the Madrid correspondent for the Baltimore *Afro-American* (1937) and a columnist for the Chicago *Defender* (1943–1967) and the New York *Post* (1962–1967). His poems of racial affirmation and protest are often infused with the rhythms of blues and jazz music. He wrote over two dozen plays (many musicalized) and founded the Suitcase Theater (Harlem, 1938), the New Negro Theater (Los Angeles, 1939), and the Skyloft Players (Chicago, 1941). His works include *The Weary Blues* (1926), *Montage of a Dream Deferred* (1951), and *The Panther and the Lash: Poems of Our Times* (1969).

David Henry Hwang (b. 1957)   Born in Los Angeles to immigrants, his father a banker and his mother a professor of piano, Hwang graduated from Stanford University in 1979. But by 1978 he had already written his first play, *FOB* (Fresh Off the Boat), which won the 1981 Obie Award as the best new play of the season when Joseph Papp brought it to off-Broadway in New York. Hwang attended the famous Yale School of Drama during 1980 and 1981. Two more promising plays, *The Dance and the Railroad* and *Family Devotions,* based on the problems of immigrants— trying, sometimes, to assimilate and sometimes to avoid assimilation in a new culture—appeared in 1981. His 1985 marriage to Ophelia Y. M. Chong, an artist, ended in divorce. Hwang continued to write and direct during the 1980s, moving from the relatively narrow early material to "wider concerns of race, gender, and culture." His 1988 Broadway hit, *M. Butterfly,* won the Tony Award for best play, and established him as a major modern American playwright. A critic writing in *Time* argued that "the final scene of *M. Butterfly,* when the agony of one soul finally takes precedence over broad-ranging commentary, is among the most forceful in the history of the American theater. . . . If Hwang can again fuse politics and humanity, he has the potential to become the first important dramatist of American public life since Arthur Miller, and maybe the best of them all." His recent work includes *1,000 Airplanes on the Roof: A Science Fiction Music Drama* (1989), a collaboration with Philip Glass and Jerome Sirlin.

Henrik Ibsen (1828–1906)   Ibsen was born in Skien, Norway (a seaport about a hundred miles south of Oslo), the son of a wealthy merchant. When Ibsen was eight, his father's business failed, and at fifteen he was apprenticed to an apothecary in the tiny town of Grimstad. He hated this profession. To solace himself, he read poetry and theology and began to write. When he was twenty-two, he became a student in Christiania and published his first play. In 1851, his diligent, though unremarkable, writing earned him an appointment as "theater-poet" to a new theater in Bergen, where he remained until 1857, learning both the business and the art of drama. He wrote several plays based on Scandinavian folklore, held positions at two theaters in Christiania, and married. When he was thirty-six, he applied to the government for a poet's pension—a stipend that would have permitted him to devote himself to writing. The stipend was refused. Enraged, he left Norway, and, though he was granted the stipend two years later, spent the next twenty-seven years in Italy and Germany, where he wrote the realistic social dramas that established his reputation as the founder of modern theater. Such plays as *Ghosts* (1881), *An Enemy of the People* (1882), and *A Doll's House* (1878) inevitably generated controversy as Ibsen explored venereal disease, the stupidity and greed of the "compact majority," and the position of women in society. In 1891, he returned to live in Christiania, where he was recognized and honored as one of Norway's (and Europe's) finest writers.

Ben Jonson (1572–1637)   Jonson was born in Westminster, England, and, after leaving school, began earning his living (in the manner of his stepfather) as a bricklayer. Though he never attended university, he taught himself enough to be considered learned. He soon abandoned construction work and earned his reputation as one of the preeminent playwrights of his period. A contemporary of Shakespeare, he also wrote poetry and translations of classical Roman authors for his English Renaissance audience.

June Jordan (b. 1936)   Jordan was born in Harlem, New York, and attended Barnard College (1953–1955) and the University of Chicago (1955–1956). A poet, novelist, and writer of children's books, she has taught widely at university campuses, including the City College of the City University of New York (1966–1968) and Connecticut College (1969–1974), where she both taught English and served as director of Search for Education, Elevation and Knowledge (SEEK). She is currently Professor of English at the State University of New York, Stony Brook. In addition to many appointments as visiting professor, she has served as Chancellor's Distinguished Lecturer, University of California, Berkeley (1986). Her numerous honors include the Prix de Rome in Environmental Design (1970–1971), the Nancy Bloch Award (1971) for her reader *The Voice of the Children,* and the achievement award from the National Association of Black Journalists (1984). Her many books include *His Own Where* (1971), *Dry Victories* (1972), and *Kimako's Story* (1981), all for juvenile and young adult readers. Her collections of poetry include *Things That I Do in the Dark* (1977), *Living Room: New Poems, 1980–1984* (1985), *Naming Our Destiny: New and Selected Poems* (1989), *Poetic Justice* (1991), and *Haruko: Love Poems* (1994). Jordan is also the author of *On Call: New Political Essays, 1981–1985* (1985) and *Technical Difficulties: African-American Notes on the State of the Union* (1992).

James Joyce (1882–1941)   Though educated in Jesuit schools, Joyce came to reject Catholicism; though an expatriate living in Paris, Trieste, and Zurich for most of his adult life, he wrote almost exclusively about his native Dublin. Joyce's rebelliousness, which surfaced during his university career, generated a revolution in modern literature. His novels *Ulysses* (1922) and *Finnegans Wake* (1939) introduced radically new narrative techniques. "Araby," from his first collection of short stories, *Dubliners* (1914), is one of a series of sharply realized vignettes based on Joyce's experience in Ireland, the homeland he later characterized as "a sow that eats its own farrow." Joyce lived precariously on earnings as a language teacher and modest contributions from wealthy patrons. That support Joyce justified—he is certainly one of the most influential novelists of the twentieth century. Because *Ulysses* dealt frankly with sexuality and used coarse language, the U.S. Post Office charged that the novel was obscene, and forbade its importation. A celebrated 1933 court decision lifted the ban in the United States.

Lawrence Kearney (b. 1948)   Born in Oxford, England, Kearney grew up in Buffalo, New York. His first collection of poems is *Kingdom Come* (1980). He has published poems in the *Atlantic Monthly,* the *Chicago Review, Massachusetts Review, Michigan Quarterly Review, Paris Review,* and the *Virginia Quarterly Review.*

John Keats (1795–1821)   Keats was born in London, the eldest son of a stablekeeper who died in an accident in 1804. His mother died of tuberculosis shortly after re-marrying, and the grandmother who raised Keats and his siblings died in 1814. At eighteen, Keats wrote his first poem, "Imitation of Spenser," inspired by Edmund Spenser's long narrative poem *The Faerie Queene.* The thirty-three poems he wrote while training to be a surgeon were published in 1817, and Keats then gave up med-icine for writing. After more traumatic losses in 1818, including the departure of one brother for America and the death of his other brother of tuberculosis, Keats wrote his second collection, *Lamia, Isabella, The Eve of St. Agnes, and Other Poems* (1820). Ill with tuberculosis himself, Keats was sent to Rome to recover. He died at twenty-six, but despite his short career, he is a major figure of the romantic period.

X. J. Kennedy (b. 1929)   Born Joseph Charles Kennedy in Dover, New Jersey, Kennedy published his own science fiction magazine, *Terrifying Test-Tube Tales,* at age 12. He honed his writing skills at Seton Hall University and earned an M. A. degree from Columbia in 1951. From 1951 to 1955, he served in the U. S. Navy, at one time publishing a daily newssheet for the entertainment-starved crew of a destroyer at sea. Kennedy notes: "Nothing I have ever written since has been received so avidly." After further study, at the Sorbonne in Paris and the University of Michigan, Kennedy taught English at the University of North Carolina and moved to Tufts University in Massachusetts in 1963. His first poetry collection, *Nude Descending a Staircase* (1961), won the Lamont Award for that year. A free-lance writer since 1979, Kennedy prefers writing within the constraints of rhyme and metrical patterns. He is author of many collections of poetry for young people including *Talking Like the Rain: A First Book of Poems,* with Dorothy M. Kennedy (1992), as well as several textbooks.

Martin Luther King Jr. (1929–1968)   King was born in Atlanta, Georgia, where his father was pastor of the Ebenezer Baptist Church. He attended public schools (skip-ping the ninth and twelfth grades) and entered Morehouse College in Atlanta. He was ordained as a Baptist minister just before his graduation in 1948. He then enrolled in Crozer Theological Seminary in Pennsylvania and after earning a divinity degree there, attended graduate school at Boston University, where he earned a Ph.D. in theology in 1955. At Boston University, he met Coretta Scott; they were married in 1953. King's rise to national and international prominence began in Montgomery, Alabama, in 1955. In that year, Rosa Parks, an African American woman, was arrested for refusing to obey a city ordinance that required African Americans to sit or stand at the back of municipal buses. The African American citizens of the city (one of the most thoroughly segregated in the South) organized a bus boycott in protest and asked King to serve as their leader. Thousands boycotted the buses for more than a year, and despite segregationist violence against them, King grounded their protests on his deeply held belief in nonviolence. In 1956, the U.S. Supreme Court ordered Montgomery to provide integrated seating on public buses. In the following year, King and other African American ministers founded the Southern Christian Leadership Conference (SCLC) to carry forward the nonviolent struggle against segregation and legal discrimination. As protests grew, so did the unhappi-ness of King and his associates with the unwillingness of the president and Congress to support civil rights. The SCLC, therefore, organized massive demonstrations in

Montgomery (King wrote "Letter from Birmingham Jail" during these demonstrations). With the civil rights movement now in the headlines almost every day, President Kennedy proposed to Congress a far-reaching civil rights bill. On August 28, 1963, over 200,000 blacks and whites gathered at the Lincoln Memorial in Washington, D.C., where King delivered his now famous speech, "I Have a Dream." In the following year, Congress passed the Civil Rights Act of 1964, prohibiting racial discrimination in public places and calling for equal opportunity in education and employment. In that year, King received the Nobel Peace Prize. In 1965, King and others organized a march to protest the blatant denial of African Americans' voting rights in Selma, Alabama, where the march began. Before the protesters were able to reach Birmingham, the state capital, they were attacked by police with tear gas and clubs. This outrage, viewed live on national television, led President Johnson to ask Congress for a bill that would eliminate all barriers to voting rights. Congress responded by passing the landmark Voting Rights Act of 1965. King remained committed to nonviolence, but his conviction that economic inequality—not just race— was one of the root causes of injustice led him to begin organizing a Poor People's Campaign that would unite all poor people in the struggle for justice. These views also led him to criticize the role played by the United States in the Vietnam War. The Poor People's Campaign took King to Memphis, Tennessee, to support a strike of African American sanitation workers, where on April 4, 1968, he was shot and killed while standing on the balcony of his hotel room. Riots immediately erupted in scores of cities across the nation. A few months later, Congress enacted the Civil Rights Act of 1968, banning discrimination in the sale and rental of housing. King is the author of *Stride toward Freedom* (1958), dealing with the Montgomery bus boycott; *Strength to Love* (1953), a collection of sermons; and *Why We Can't Wait* (1964), a discussion of his general views on civil rights.

Carolyn Kizer (b. 1925)   Kizer was born in Spokane, Washington. Her father was a lawyer, her mother a biologist and professor. After graduating from Sarah Lawrence College in 1945, Kizer pursued graduate study at Columbia and the University of Washington. From 1959 to 1965, she was editor of *Poetry Northwest* (which she founded in 1959 in Seattle), and spent 1964 and 1965 as a State Department specialist in Pakistan, where she taught at a women's college and translated poems from Urdu into English. She chose to leave early after the U.S. decision to bomb North Vietnam in 1965. Later, she joined archaeological tours in Afghanistan and Iran. She has worked as director of literary programs for the National Endowment for the Arts in Washington, D.C., has taught at several universities, and was poet-in-residence at the University of North Carolina and Ohio University. Her volumes of poetry include *Yin* (1984), which won a Pulitzer Prize the following year, *Mermaids in the Basement: Poems for Women* (1984), *The Nearness of You* (1986), and *Harping On: Poems 1985–1995*. She has also published a collection of essays, *Proses: On Poems and Poets* (1993), and edited *100 Great Poems by Women: A Golden Ecco Anthology* (1995).

Etheridge Knight (1933–1991)   Knight was born in Corinth, Mississippi, attended two years of public high school in Kentucky, and served in the U.S. Army from 1948 to 1951. Convicted on a robbery charge and sentenced in 1960 to twenty years in Indiana State Prison, he discovered poetry; his first collection is entitled *Poems from*

Prison (1968). Knight was paroled after eight years. From 1968 to 1971 he was poet-in-residence at several universities. An important African American voice in the 1960s and 1970s, Knight rejected the American and European esthetic tradition, arguing that "the red of this esthetic rose got its color from the blood of black slaves, exterminated Indians, napalmed Vietnamese children." His collection *Belly Song and Other Poems* was nominated for the National Book Award and the Pulitzer Prize in 1973. His awards include National Endowment for the Arts and Guggenheim grants, and the 1987 American Book Award for *The Essential Etheridge Knight* (1986).

Maxine Kumin (b. 1925)   Born Maxine Winokur, Kumin attended Radcliffe College (B.A., 1946; M. A, 1948), and has lectured at many universities, including Princeton, Tufts, and Brandeis. She is the author of several collections of poetry, including *Up Country* (1972), for which she won a Pulitzer Prize, and, most recently, *Nurture* (1989), *Looking for Luck: Poems* (1992), and *Connecting the Dots: Poems* (1996). She has also published several novels, collections of essays and short stories, and more than twenty children's books, several of them in collaboration with the poet Anne Sexton.

Philip Larkin (1922–1985)   Born in Coventry, Larkin attended St. John's College, Oxford (B.A., 1943; M. A., 1947). He was appointed librarian at the University of Hull in 1955, wrote jazz feature articles for the London *Daily Telegraph* from 1961 to 1971, and won numerous poetry awards, including the Queens Gold Medal (1965) and the Benson Medal (1975). His first collection, *The North Ship* (1945), was not well received, but he gained recognition after publication of *The Less Deceived* (1960). Larkin once said, "Form holds little interest for me. Content is everything."

D. H. Lawrence (1885–1930)   David Herbert Lawrence grew up amidst the strife between his genteel and educated mother and his coarse miner father. As a youth in the Nottinghamshire mining village of Eastwood, Lawrence resented the rough ways of his drunken father, and adopted his mother's refined values as his own. Diligence brought him a scholarship to the local high school. Upon graduation, he worked as a clerk and as an elementary school teacher, and, in 1908, earned a teaching certificate from Nottingham University. He published a group of poems in 1909 and *The White Peacock,* his first novel, in 1911. He resigned his teaching position to devote himself to writing in 1912. That same year he ran away with Frieda von Richthofen Weekley (the sister of the World War I German ace fighter pilot), who left behind a husband and three children. They were married following her divorce in 1914. In 1915, his novel *The Rainbow* was declared indecent and suppressed in England. Angered by this event and by continual harassment for his outspoken opposition to World War I and his marriage to a prominent German, the Lawrences left England after the war. They traveled widely—in Europe, Australia, Mexico, and the American Southwest—seeking a community receptive to Lawrence's ideas and a climate to restore his failing health. His output was prodigious and included novels, short stories, poems, nonfiction, travel books, and letters. As a mature writer, Lawrence rejected the gentility his mother represented, and began to see his father's earthiness as a virtue. He died of tuberculosis in the south of France.

Ursula K. Le Guin (b. 1929)   The daughter of distinguished University of California, Berkeley, anthropologists, Le Guin graduated from Radcliffe and earned an M.A.

from Columbia University. She enjoyed early success writing for science fiction and fantasy magazines (a genre often stigmatized as subliterary popular fiction). But she quickly established a reputation that places her in the tradition of earlier writers who used fantastic circumstances to shape their understanding of the human condition, such as Jonathan Swift, Edgar Allan Poe, and H. G. Wells. A prolific writer of fantasy fiction, Le Guin's recent work, *Four Ways to Forgiveness* (1995), is a speculation on the future of humankind in space. *Wonderful Alexander and the Catwings* (1994) is the third in the Catwings series, which features flying cats. She is also the author of a collection of poems, *Going Out with Peacocks and Other Poems* (1994). Her most recent volume is *Unlocking the Air and Other Stories* (1996).

Li-Young Lee (b. 1957)   Lee was born in Jakarta, Indonesia, of Chinese parents. In 1959, after spending nineteen months in jail as a political prisoner, Lee's father fled Indonesia with his family. The family traveled through Hong Kong, Macau, and Japan before settling in the United States. Lee studied at several American universities, earning his B.A. at the University of Pittsburgh, and taught at various schools, including Northwestern University and the University of Iowa. During 1990, he traveled in Indonesia and China gathering material for an autobiographical prose work. His work has been honored with numerous prizes and awards, including a Guggenheim Fellowship in 1987. His second book of poems, *The City in Which I Love You* (1990), was the Lamont Poetry Selection of the Academy of American Poets. His most recent book is *The Winged Seed: A Remembrance* (1995).

Denise Levertov (b. 1923)   Born in Ilford, England, Levertov was raised in a literary household (her father was an Anglican priest) and educated privately. She was a nurse at a British hospital in Paris during World War II; after the war, she worked in an antique store and bookstore in London. Married to an American writer, she came to the United States in 1948, became a naturalized citizen in 1956, and taught at several universities, including M.I.T. and Tufts. Levertov began as what she called a "British romantic with almost Victorian background" and has become more politically active and feminist with time. She protested U.S. involvement in the Vietnam War and has also been involved in the antinuclear movement. Regarding angst-filled confessional poetry, Levertov once said, "I do not believe that a violent imitation of the horrors of our times is the concern of poetry. . . . I long for poems of an inner harmony in utter contrast to the chaos in which they exist." Her works include *The Double Image* (1946), *Relearning the Alphabet* (1970), *A Door in the Hive* (1989), and *Sands of the Well* (1996).

C. Day Lewis (1904–1972)   Born in Ireland, son of a minister, Cecil Day Lewis began writing poetry at age six. He attended Oxford, taught for seven years, served as editor for the Ministry of Information (1941–1946), was professor of poetry at Oxford (1951–1956), and visiting professor at Harvard (1964–1965). His early works *From Feathers to Iron* (1931) and *The Magnetic Mountain* (1933) reflect a politically radical ideology, but Lewis mellowed enough to be named poet laureate in 1968. From 1935 to 1964 he wrote nearly two dozen detective novels under the pseudonym Nicholas Blake. He commented, "In my young days, words were my antennae, my touch-stones, my causeway over a quaking bog of mistrust."

Liu Kexiang (b. 1957)   Kexiang was born in Taizhong in central Taiwan and received his B.A. in journalism from the Chinese Cultural University. His poetry has appeared in the *Anthology of Modern Chinese Poetry* (1992) edited by Michelle Yeh, and journals such as *eXchanges*. Recently, he served as assistant editor-in-chief of the literary supplement of the *China Times*.

Duane Locke (b. 1921)   Locke was born on a farm near Plains, Georgia, but because of the poverty of Depression years farm life, his parents brought their only child to Tampa, Florida, where he has lived ever since, except for stays in Europe. He attended the University of Tampa and earned a Ph.D. from the University of Florida. He spent his entire teaching career at the University of Tampa, and retired in 1989. He has published over a thousand pieces, mostly poetry, in over four hundred different magazines, and produced fourteen small press books of poems. By his own account, he now lives "unemployed with eight cats . . . and one wife in the slums of Tampa, Florida, where daily I experience the lower depths, although it has been about six weeks since I have seen a bleeding man dying in the streets."

Barry Holstun Lopez (b. 1945)   Born in Port Chester, New York, Lopez graduated from the University of Notre Dame in 1966 and earned a graduate degree there in 1968. He went on to further graduate study at the University of Oregon (1969–1970). His earliest book, *Desert Notes: Reflections in the Eye of a Raven* (1976), was the first of a trilogy which includes *River Notes: The Dance of Herons* (1979) and *Field Notes: The Grace Note of the Canyon Wren* (1994). Keenly interested in the traditions of the Northwest Indians, as well as natural history, he published a collection of Indian legends, *Giving Birth to Thunder, Sleeping with His Daughter* (1977), and a nonfiction study, *Of Wolves and Men* (1978). A collection of short stories, *Winter Count* (1981), reveals how deeply Lopez feels about the American Indian experience, as does his children's book based on Indian traditions, *Crow and Weasel* (1990). *Arctic Dreams: Imagination and Desire in a Northern Landscape* appeared in 1986. Lopez's skill as a photographer is evident in the illustrations included in several of his works. His essays are gathered together in *The Rediscovery of North America* (1991).

Audre Lorde (1934–1992)   Born to middle-class, West Indian immigrant parents in New York City, Lorde grew up in Harlem and attended the National University of Mexico (1954), Hunter College (B.A., 1959) and Columbia (M.L.S., 1961). Her marriage in 1962, which produced two children, ended in divorce in 1970. During these early years, she worked as a librarian, but in 1968 her growing reputation as a writer led to her appointment as lecturer in creative writing at City College in New York and, in the following year, lecturer in the education department at Herbert H. Lehman College. In 1970, she joined the English department at John Jay College of Criminal Justice and in 1980 returned to Hunter College as professor of English. Besides teaching, Lorde combined raising a son and a daughter in an interracial lesbian relationship with political organizing of other black feminists and lesbians, and in the early 1980s, helped to start Kitchen Table: Women of Color Press. In 1991, she was named New York State Poet. Lorde is probably best known for her prose writings, among them two collections of essays, *Sister Outsider* (1984) and *Burst of Light* (1988), and the autobiographical *Zami: The Cancer Journals* (1980), a chronicle of her struggle with the breast cancer that ultimately claimed her life. Her poetry publications include *The First Cities* (1968), *The Black Unicorn* (1978), and *Undersong: Chosen Poems Old and New* (1993). Near the end of her life, Lorde made her home on St. Croix, U.S. Virgin Islands, and adopted the African name Gamba Adisa ("Warrior—She Who Makes Her Meaning Known").

Amy Lowell (1874–1925)   Born to a prominent family in Brookline, Massachusetts, Lowell was privately educated. After the death of her parents, she inherited the family's ten-acre estate, including a staff of servants and a well-stocked library. Lowell wrote a great deal of undistinguished poetry that, unfortunately, prejudiced critics and readers against her better work. While traveling abroad, she became associated with the Imagists, a group of English and American poets in London who felt that sharply realized images gave poetry its power, and she gained recognition promoting their work in America after 1913. Her first collection of poems, *A Dome of Many-Coloured Glass,* appeared in 1912. Though her poetry never reached a wide audience, her criticism helped shape American poetic tastes of the time.

Kathryn Howd Machan (b. 1952)   Machan grew up in Woodbury, Connecticut, and Pleasantville, New York. She studied creative writing and literature at the College of Saint Rose and at the University of Iowa, taught college for five years, then returned to graduate school for a Ph.D. in Interpretation (Performance Studies) at Northwestern University. She is now on the faculty of the Writing Program of Ithaca College, New York. For eight years she coordinated the Ithaca Community Poets and directed the national Feminist Women's Writing Workshops. Her poems have appeared in numerous magazines (such as *Yankee, Nimrod, South Coast Poetry Journal, The Hollins Critic, Seneca Review,* and *Louisiana Literature*), in literature anthologies (such as *Early Ripening: American Women's Poetry Now, I Am Becoming the Woman I've Wanted, Writing Poems,* and *The Bedford Introduction to Literature*), and in numerous published collections.

Elaine Magarrell (b. 1928)   Born in Clinton, Iowa, of immigrant Jewish parents, she came of age in this small town during World War II. Her father owned a ladies' ready-to-wear shop where the whole family helped out. She was educated at the University of Iowa and Drake University. Although she wrote poetry from the age of ten, she burned the early work and did not write again until she was in her forties and teaching English in a public junior high school. In 1981, Magarrell quit her job as library clerk at the Washington Bureau of the *New York Times* to write full time. *On Hogback Mountain* (1985), her first book of poetry, won the Washington Writers' Publishing House Prize, and her subsequent book, *Blameless Lives* (1991), won the Word Works Prize. Her fiction and poetry appear in a number of literary journals, and she is a four-time recipient of grants in literature from the District of Columbia Commission on Arts and Humanities.

Bernard Malamud (1914–1986)   Born in Brooklyn, New York, and educated at the City College of New York and Columbia University, Malamud is one of a number of post–World War II writers whose works drew heavily on their urban New York, Jewish backgrounds. Malamud's works often dramatize the tension arising out of the clash between Jewish conscience and American energy and materialism or the difficulty of keeping alive the Jewish sense of community and humanism in American society. *A New Life* (1961); *The Fixer* (1966; winner of both a National Book Award and a Pulitzer Prize); and *Pictures of Fidelman* (1969) all have protagonists who struggle with these problems. Some of his other novels are *The Natural* (1952), *The Assistant* (1957), *The Tenants* (1971), and *God's Grace* (1982). His short stories are collected in *The Magic Barrel* (1958; winner of the National Book Award in 1959), *Idiots First* (1963), and *Rembrandt's Hat* (1973).

Christopher Marlowe (1564–1593)   Born in Canterbury, Marlowe was educated at Cambridge, where he embarked on a career of writing and political activity, eventually giving up his original intention of entering the priesthood. He was arrested in 1593 on a charge of atheism, but before he could be brought to trial he was murdered in a brawl apparently involving a wealthy family that had reason to want him silenced. Marlowe's literary reputation rests primarily on his plays, powerful in their own right and the most significant precursors of Shakespeare's poetic dramas. The most important are *Tamburlaine, Parts I and II* (ca. 1587–1588; published 1590), *The Jew of Malta* (1589; published 1633), and *The Tragical History of the Life and Death of Dr. Faustus* (1592; published 1604).

Andrew Marvell (1621–1678)   Born in Yorkshire and educated at Cambridge, Marvell received an inheritance upon his father's death that allowed him to spend four years traveling the Continent. Though not a Puritan himself, Marvell supported the Puritans' cause during the civil war and held a number of posts during the Puritan regime, including that of assistant to the blind John Milton, Cromwell's Latin Secretary. In 1659, a year before the Restoration, Marvell was elected to Parliament, where he served until his death. Soon after the Restoration, Marvell expressed strong disagreements with the government in a series of outspoken and anonymously printed satires. It was for these satires, rather than for his many love poems, that he was primarily known in his own day.

Katherine McAlpine (b. 1948)   Katherine McAlpine grew up in western New Jersey. She studied voice with Leon Kurzer of the Vienna Opera and worked for a number of years as a singer and voice teacher. She now lives in Downeast, Maine, where she works as a free-lance writer. Her poetry has appeared in a wide variety of magazines and in several anthologies. She was a 1992 winner of the *Nation*'s Discovery Award and the Judith's Room Award for emerging women poets.

Claude McKay (1890–1948)   Born in Sunny Ville, Jamaica, McKay had already completed two volumes of poetry before coming to the United States in 1912 at the age of twenty-three (the two volumes earned him awards, which paid his way). The racism he encountered as a black immigrant brought a militant tone to his writing. His popular poem "If We Must Die" (1919) helped to initiate the Harlem Renaissance of the 1920s. Between 1922 and 1934 he lived in Great Britain, Russia, Germany, France, Spain, and Morocco. His writings include four volumes of poems, many essays, an autobiography (*A Long Way from Home* [1937]), a novel (*Home to Harlem* [1928]), and a sociologial study of Harlem. His conversion to Roman Catholicism in the 1940s struck his audience as an ideological retreat. McKay wrote in a letter to a friend: "[T]o have a religion is very much like falling in love with a woman. You love her for her . . . beauty, which cannot be defined."

Bill McKibben (b. 1960)   Born in Palo Alto, California, McKibben graduated from Harvard University (B.A., 1982), and immediately was hired as an editor at the *New Yorker* magazine. At age twenty-six, dissatisfied with the frantic pace of urban life and work, he quit his job at the *New Yorker* and moved with his wife, writer Sue Halperin, to an isolated house (the nearest town is twelve miles away) in the Adirondack Mountains, in New York State. There, his concern over the growing threat to the earth's ecosystem posed by chemical pollution led him to the research and reflections described in his book *The End of Nature* (1989). Besides writing, McKibben spends much of his time hiking in the woods. He has said that he overcame a crisis in religious belief "to a greater or lesser degree by locating God in nature."

James Alan McPherson (b. 1943)   McPherson was born in Savannah, Georgia, attended Morgan State University (1963–1964), Morris Brown College (B.A., 1965), Harvard University (LL.B., 1968), and the University of Iowa, where he earned an M.F.A. (1969). Since 1981, he has been a professor of English at the University of Iowa. In 1965, he received first prize in the *Atlantic* short story contest. In 1969, his first collection of short stories, *Hue and Cry,* appeared. His many honors include the literature award of the National Institute of Arts and Letters (1970), and a Guggenheim Fellowship (1972–1973). In 1978, he received a Pulitzer Prize for his second collection of short stories, *Elbow Room.* His writing achievements earned him a MacArthur Fellowship in 1981. McPherson has been widely praised for his incisive depictions of ordinary people, mostly black, who attempt to cope with the indignities and desperations of everyday life.

Peter Meinke (b. 1932)   Born in Brooklyn, New York, son of a salesman, Meinke served in the U.S. Army from 1955 to 1957, attended Hamilton College (B.A. 1955), the University of Michigan (M.A., 1961), and earned his Ph.D. at the University of Minnesota (1965). He taught English at a New Jersey high school, Hamline University, and Presbyterian College (now Eckerd College) in Florida, where he began directing the writing workshop in 1972. His reviews, poems, and stories have appeared in periodicals such as the *Atlantic,* the *New Yorker,* and the *New Republic.* The latest of his three books in the Pitt Poetry Series is *Nightwatch on the Chesapeake* (1987). His collection of stories, *The Piano Tuner,* won the 1986 Flannery O'Connor Award. Also, he has been the recipient of an NEA Fellowship in Poetry.

Herman Melville (1819–1891)   The death of his merchant father when Melville was twelve shattered the economic security of his family. The financial panic of 1837 reduced the Melvilles to the edge of poverty, and, at age nineteen, Melville went to sea. Economic conditions upon his return were still grim, and after a frustrating stint as a country school teacher, he again went to sea—this time on a four-year whaling voyage. He deserted the whaler in the South Pacific, lived for some time with cannibals, made his way to Tahiti and Hawaii, and finally joined the navy for a return voyage. He mined his experiences for two successful South Sea adventure books, *Typee* (1846) and *Omoo* (1847). On the strength of these successes he married, but his next novel, *Mardi* (1849), was too heavy-handed an allegory to succeed. Driven by the obligation to support his growing family, Melville returned to sea adventure stories, with moderate success. But neither his masterpiece, *Moby Dick* (1851), nor his subsequent short stories and novels found much of an audience, and, in 1886, he accepted an appointment as customs inspector in Manhattan, a job he held until retirement. He continued to write, mostly poetry, and lived to see himself forgotten as an author. *Billy Budd,* found among his papers after his death and published in 1924, led to a revival of interest in Melville, now recognized as one of America's greatest writers.

James Merrill (1926–1995)   Born into a wealthy New York family (his father co-founded the Merrill Lynch stockbrokerage firm), Merrill was privately educated at home and then at Amherst College, where he received a B.A. degree in 1947. His first volume of poems, *First Poems* (1951), established his reputation as a writer of technical virtuosity, urbane eloquence, and wit. With the more personal and passionate poems of *Nights and Days* (1966) and *Mirabell: Books of Number* (1979), both recipients of the National Book Award, Merrill gained a wider and more enthusiastic audience. Merrill is probably most widely known as "The Ouija poet" for his narrative poems that record the Ouija board sessions he and a friend conducted with "spirits from another world." Merrill has also written plays (*The Immortal Husband* [1956] and *The Bait* [1960]) and novels (*The Seraglio* [1957] and *The (Diblos) Notebook* [1965]). In 1990, Merrill won the Bobbitt Prize from the Library of Congress.

Robert Mezey (b. 1935)   Born in Philadelphia, Mezey attended Kenyon College and served a troubled hitch in the U.S. Army before earning his B.A. from the University of Iowa in 1959. He worked as a probation officer, advertising copywriter, and social worker, did graduate study at Stanford, and began teaching English at Case Western Reserve University in 1963. After a year as poet-in-residence at Franklin and Marshall College, he joined the English department of California State University, Fresno, spent three years at the University of Utah, and settled in 1976 at Pomona College in Claremont, California. Winner in 1960 of the Lamont Award for *The Lovemaker,* he has published many poetry collections, coedited *Naked Poetry* (1969), and was one of several translators for *Poems from the Hebrew* (1973). *Evening Wind,* a book of poems, appeared in 1987.

Edna St. Vincent Millay (1892–1950)   Millay was born in Maine and educated at Vassar. By the time she graduated in 1917, she had already achieved considerable fame as a poet; in the same year, she moved to Greenwich Village in New York and published her first volume of poetry, *Renascence and Other Poems.* In Greenwich Village, she established her reputation as a poet and became notorious for her bohemian life and passionate love affairs. In 1923 she received a Pulitzer Prize for a collection of sonnets, *The Harp-Weaver,* that dealt wittily and flippantly with love. Her later works exhibit a more subdued and contemplative tone as well as a growing preoccupation with social and political affairs. Nevertheless, her best and most memorable verse deals with the bittersweet emotions of love and the brevity of life.

Arthur Miller (b. 1915)   Raised in New York City, the son of a school teacher and clothing manufacturer, Arthur Miller studied playwriting at the University of Michigan. Although he wrote radio scripts and plays, during World War II he made his living as a steam fitter. His first Broadway play in 1944 was a failure, but *All My Sons* (1947), about a corrupt defense contractor, was named best play of the year. The 1949 production of *Death of a Salesman* (which won the Pulitzer Prize) was an immense success and established Miller's reputation. The infamous loyalty hearings conducted by Senator Joseph McCarthy contributed to the substance of *The Crucible* (1953), an investigation into the Salem witchcraft trials. He was married to Marilyn Monroe from 1956–1961. In 1956, Miller was cited for contempt by the House Un-American Activities Committee when, after testifying fully about his own political activities, he refused to name others. His plays invariably turn on moral issues and continue to illustrate the comment he made to an interviewer after the success of *All My Sons:* "I don't see how you can write anything decent without using as your basis the question of right or wrong." His dedication to individual conscience and suspicion of government repression led him to adapt Ibsen's *An Enemy of the People* for the Broadway stage in 1951. His most recent play, *Broken Glass* (1994), focuses on the aftermath of Kristallnacht, the night in 1938 in Nazi Germany when thousands of Jewish shops and synagogues were destroyed. Miller is also the author of an autobiography, *Timebends* (1987), and a collection of stories, *Homely Girl, A Life: And Other Stories* (1995).

Jessica Mitford (1917–1996)   One of six sisters, Mitford was born in Gloucestershire, England, into an aristocratic and rather eccentric family. She was educated at home and early adopted political views that contrasted violently with those of her sister Diana, who married Sir Oswald Mosley, the pre–World War II leader of the British Fascist movement. Jessica, on the other hand, traveled to Loyalist Spain during its civil war, where she met her first husband. He was killed in action during World War II, and she later married a labor lawyer. They moved to California and joined the Communist party. They left the party in 1958, and Jessica embarked on a successful career as a muckraking journalist and writer. Her first work, *Lifeitselfmanship,* was privately published in 1956, but her attack on the funeral industry in *The American Way of Death* (1963) established her reputation as an incisive and witty enemy of social and economic pretentiousness. Her many books include *Kind and Usual Punishment: The Prison Business* (1973), the autobiographical *A Fine Old Conflict* (1979), and a collection of articles, *Poison Penmanship: The Gentle Art of Muckraking* (1979).

Felix Mnthali (b. 1933)   Mnthali was born and grew up in Malawi in south central Africa. He was educated at Malawi University and Cambridge University in England. He returned to Africa, and as a visitor at the University of Ibadan in Nigeria, he wrote and privately published *Echoes from Ibadan* (1961). Back in his homeland he became the head of the department of English at Malawi University. His published works include *When Sunset Comes to Saptiwa* (1980), a collection of poetry.

Bharati Mukherjee (b. 1940)   Born in Calcutta, India, Mukherjee attended the University of Calcutta (B.A., 1959), the University of Baroda (M.A., 1961), and the University of Iowa, where she took an M.F.A. (1963) and a Ph.D. (1969). In 1963 she married Clark Blaise, a Canadian writer and professor, and joined the faculty at McGill University in Montreal. In 1973, Mukherjee and her husband visited India and kept separate diaries of the trip, published as *Days and Nights in Calcutta* (1977). The diaries reveal marked differences in their responses: Mukherjee found her home environs, especially the status of women, worse than she remembered, while Blaise, after an initial revulsion at the squalor and poverty, found India a fascinating and attractive culture compared to the West. Mukherjee "left Canada after fifteen years due to the persistent effects of racial prejudice against people of my national origin," and joined the faculty in Skidmore College in New York. Later she moved to Queens College of the City University of New York. Her fiction frequently explores the tensions inevitable in intercultural relationships. Her first novel, *The Tiger's Daughter* (1972), deals with the disappointment of an expatriate's return to India. In her second novel, *Wife* (1975), a psychologically abused woman finally kills her husband. Her recent works include *The Middleman and Other Stories* (1988), which won the National Book Critics' Award, *The Holder of the World* (1993), and *Leave It to Me* (1997).

Susan Musgrave (b. 1951)   Musgrave draws on her experiences in public schools, psychiatric institutions, and maximum security penitentiaries across the country. She has published nineteen books; she is a poet, novelist, children's writer, essayist, book reviewer for the *Vancouver Sun,* and editor. She lives on Vancouver Island in British Columbia, Canada, with Stephen Reid and their two daughters. She travels widely, both in Canada and abroad, to give speeches, writing workshops, and poetry readings. Her most recent books are a poetry collection, *Forcing the Narcissus* (1994), and a book of personal essays, *Musgrave Landing* (1994). She has won numerous awards for her writing, culminating in the Presidential Writer in Residence Fellowship at the University of Toronto (1995).

Thomas Nashe (1567–1601)   Born in Lowestoft, England, the son of a minister, Nashe graduated from Cambridge, made a tour of France and Italy, and by 1588 was establishing himself in London as a professional writer. His hatred of Puritanism led him to join a group of pamphleteers who were defending the Anglican Church and its bishops against Puritan attacks. Nashe also wrote several plays and a picaresque prose narrative, *The Unfortunate Traveler* (1594), that inaugurated the novel of adventure in English literature.

Taslima Nasrin (b. 1962)   Born and educated in Mymensingh, Bangladesh, Nasrin began writing poetry in her childhood, her earliest works appearing in a literary journal edited by her eldest brother. Following in the footsteps of her doctor-father, she earned a degree in medicine from Mymensingh Medical College and for a few years practiced as a government doctor. Her study of modern science, Nasrin has written, "made me a rationalist." While practicing medicine, she continued her writing, publishing poems and novels. These works, along with the essays she wrote as a syndicated columnist in Bangladesh, earned her a number of important literary prizes in 1992 and 1993. However, her rationalism and her feminism, as well as her 1993 novel *Shame,* enraged Muslim fundamentalists. Forced into hiding by death threats, Nasrin fled to Europe in 1994, where she now lives in exile. In an essay titled "Women's Rights," Nasrin writes, "My poetry, my prose, my entire output expresses the deprivation of women who have been exploited for centuries. . . . My expression is loud and for that crime I am now out of my country. Though I have come to the West legally, with the government's permission, I do not know when I shall be able to return. . . . Even now the fundamentalists demand my death by hanging in public."

Barbara Neely (b. 1941)   Barbara Neely is a novelist and short-story writer who lives and writes in Jamaica Plain, Massachusetts. Her short fiction has appeared in many anthologies, including *Test Tube Women* (1984), *Things That Divide Us* (1985), *Angels of Power* (1986), and *Breaking Ice: An Anthology of Contemporary African American Fiction* (1990). She is the author of the award-winning Blanche White mystery novels *Blanche on the Lam* (1992) and *Blanche among the Talented Tenth* (1994), whose protagonist, a middle-aged black domestic, is reluctantly drawn into sleuthing.

Pablo Neruda (1904–1973)   Neruda was born in Parral, Chile, the son of a railroad worker. Shortly after leaving college, he joined the Chilean foreign service to begin a distinguished career as consul and ambassador at a variety of posts around the world, including Burma, Ceylon, Indonesia, Siam, Cambodia, Spain, France, and Mexico. He was elected to the Chilean senate as a communist. But when he published letters attacking the policies of Videla, the President of Chile, he was forced into exile. He returned to Chile after the victory of anti-Videla forces, and rejoined the foreign service. His vast literary output won many prizes and honors. And, although American readers found it difficult to separate his poetry from his politics, he was, at his prime, generally considered to be the greatest poet writing in Spanish. One critic pointed out that Neruda "never bothered his head about the state of poetry. He has just gone on exuding it as he draws breath." In an essay on impure poetry, Neruda wrote: "Let [this] be the poetry we search for: worn with the hand's obligations, as by acids, steeped in sweat and in smoke, smelling of lilies and urine, spattered diversely by the trades that we love by, inside the law or beyond it. A poetry impure as the clothing we wear, or our bodies, soup-stained, soiled with our shameful behavior, our wrinkles and vigils and dreams, observations and prophecies, declarations of loathing and love, idylls and beasts, the shocks of encounter, political loyalties, denials and doubts, affirmation and taxes." *Five Decades, a Selection: Poems, 1925–1970* appeared in 1974. He was awarded the Nobel Prize for literature in 1971.

Kathleen Norris (b. 1947)   Norris was born in Washington, D.C., and educated at Bennington College in Vermont (B.A., 1969). From 1969 to 1973, she worked for the Academy of American Poets in New York and was later affiliated with Leaves of Grass, Inc., in Lemmon, South Dakota, where she lives. Her awards include a Provincetown Fine Arts Center Fellowship (1972), and a Creative Artists Public Service Grant from the state of New York (1972–1973). Her works have appeared in many periodicals, including *Dragonfly, Lillabulero,* and the *New Yorker.* She is the author of two collections of poems, *Falling Off* (1971) and *The Middle of the World* (1981). Her most recent book is *The Cloister Walk* (1996).

Edna O'Brien (b. 1936)   O'Brien was born in a rural, Catholic village of about two hundred people in the west of Ireland and grew up on a farm. Educated at local schools and in a convent, she escaped rural life by briefly attending Pharmaceutical College in Dublin. Shortly after her marriage in 1952, she and her husband (Czech-Irish author Ernest Gebler) moved to London; they divorced after twelve years. O'Brien remained in London, where she raised her two sons alone. She has, since 1986, taught creative writing at City College of the City University of New York. Among her honors are the Kingsley Amis Award (1962) and the *Los Angeles Times* Book Prize (1990). O'Brien's prolific output includes *Johnny I Hardly Knew You* (1977), *The High Road* (1988), *The Country Girls Trilogy and Epilogue* (1989), *Time* *and Tide* (1990), and most recently the novel *Down by the River* (1997). Among her half-dozen collections of stories are *A Scandalous Woman* (1974), *A Fanatic Heart* (1984), and *Lantern Slides* (1990). She has also written stories for juveniles, stage plays, television plays, and screenplays, and has been a contributor to magazines such as the *New Yorker,* the *Ladies' Home Journal,* and *Cosmopolitan.* Of the connection between her writing and her life, O'Brien says, "It is as if the life lived has not been lived until it is set down in this unconscious sequence of words."

Tim O'Brien (b. 1946)   O'Brien was born in Austin, Minnesota, attended public schools, and received a B.A. summa cum laude from Macalester College. Immediately following graduation, he was drafted into the U.S. Army (1968–1970), earning a Purple Heart medal. On his return to civilian life, he pursued graduate work at Harvard University and worked as a national affairs reporter for the *Washington Post.* His first novel, *If I Die in a Combat Zone, Box Me Up and Ship Me Home* (1973), is a semifictionalized account of his own Vietnam experiences. All of O'Brien's novels are either set in Vietnam or focus on characters haunted by the war: *Northern Lights* (1975), *Going after Cacciato* (1978), which won a National Book Award, *The Nuclear Age* (1985), *The Things They Carried* (1990), and *In the Lake of the Woods* (1994). In an interview, O'Brien explained that his preoccupation with the Vietnam War was part of his need to write with "passion." Writing "good" stories, he went on to say, "requires a sense of passion, and my passion as a human being and as a writer intersect in Vietnam, not in the physical stuff but in the issues of Vietnam—of courage, rectitude, enlightenment, holiness, trying to do the right thing in the world."

Flannery O'Connor (1925–1964)   Afflicted with lupus erythematosus, O'Connor spent most of her tragically short life in Milledgeville, Georgia. She began writing while a student at Georgia State College for Women in her hometown and in 1947 earned an M.F.A. degree from the University of Iowa. Back in Milledgeville, she lived on a farm with her mother, raised peacocks, and endured the indignity of constant treatment for her progressive and incurable disease. She traveled and lectured when she could. She wrote two novels, *Wise Blood* (1952) and *The Violent Bear It Away* (1960), and two collections of stories, *A Good Man Is Hard to Find* (1955) and *Everything That Rises Must Converge* (1965). She was deeply religious, and wrote numerous book reviews for Catholic newspapers. Her southern gothic tales often force readers to confront physical deformity, spiritual depravity, and the violence they often engender.

Frank O'Connor (1903–1966)   Born Michael O'Donovan in Cork, Ireland, O'Connor later adopted his pen name to separate his civil-service career from his writing career. His family's poverty forced him to leave school at age fourteen. During the Irish struggle for independence, O'Connor served in the Irish Republican Army, and after the establishment of the Irish Free State, he worked as a librarian. Despite his lack of formal education, he became director of the Abbey Theatre in Dublin. He moved to America in the 1950s and taught at Harvard and Northwestern. A storyteller in the great Gaelic oral tradition, he appeared for a time on Sunday morning television. A perfectionist, O'Connor constantly polished and reworked his stories. He added to his stature with fine critical studies of the novel (*The Mirror in the Roadway* [1956]) and the short story (*The Lonely Voice* [1963]), and introduced Gaelic poetry to a wide audience through his English translations.

Sharon Olds (b. 1942)   Born in San Francisco, Olds attended Stanford (B.A., 1964) and Columbia University (Ph.D., 1972). She joined the faculty of Theodor Herzl Institute in 1976 and has given readings at many colleges. She is currently teaching at the Graduate Creative Writing Program at New York University. She won the Madeline Sadin Award from the *New York Quarterly* in 1978 for "The Death of Marilyn Monroe." Often compared to confessional poets Sylvia Plath and Anne Sexton, Olds published her first collection, *Satan Says,* in 1980, and won both the National Book Critics' Circle Award and the Lamont Award for *The Dead and the Living* in 1983. *The Gold Cell* was published in 1987, *The Father* appeared in 1992, and her most recent book of poems, *The Wellspring,* was published in 1996.

Mary Oliver (b. 1935)   Mary Oliver was born in Cleveland, Ohio. She spent one year at Ohio State University and a second year at Vassar. Her distinctive poetic talent led to an appointment as the chair of the writing department of the Fine Arts Workshop in Provincetown, Massachusetts (1972–1973). Though she never graduated from college, she was awarded the Mather Visiting Professorship at Case Western Reserve University for 1980 and 1982, and, among her many awards and honors, she received a National Endowment of the Arts Fellowship (1972–1973) and a Guggenheim Fellowship (1980–1981). The first of her several volumes of poems, *No Voyage and Other Poems,* appeared in 1963. Other books include *New and Selected Poems* (1992), *A Poetry Handbook* (1995), and *Blue Pastures* (1995), a collection of prose nature writing. One critic, commenting on her work, asserts that "her vision of nature is celebratory and religious in the deepest sense."

Eric Ormsby (b. 1941)   Eric Ormsby was born in Atlanta, Georgia, and grew up in Florida. He attended Columbia University and the University of Pennsylvania, where he graduated summa cum laude in Oriental Studies (1971). He went on to earn a masters degree in Library Science at Rutgers (1978), then attended Princeton, where he earned a doctorate (1981) in Near Eastern Studies, specializing in Islamic theology and Classical Arabic language and literature. Among other scholarly works, Ormsby is the author of *Theodicy in Islamic Thought* (1984). Ormsby began writing poetry as a young man and began publishing in 1985. He has written three poetry collections, *Bavarian Shrine and Other Poems* (1990), which won a Quebec prize for the best poetry of that year, *Coastlines* (1992), and *For a Modest God: New & Selected Poems* (1997). His poems have also been published in various Canadian and American journals. Ormsby resides in Montreal, where he is a professor at McGill's Institute of Islamic Studies.

George Orwell (1903–1950)   Born Eric Blair in India, the son of a minor British colonial officer, Orwell was raised in England. His education at good grammar schools, culminating with a stay at Eton, introduced him to what he later called the snobbish world of England's middle and upper classes. Denied a university scholarship, he joined the Indian Imperial Police in 1922 and served in Burma until he resigned in 1927, disgusted with the injustice of British imperialism in India and Burma. He was determined to be a writer and, living at the edge of poverty, deliberately mingled with social outcasts and impoverished laborers. These experiences produced *Down and Out in Paris and London* (1933). Although he was a socialist, his experiences while fighting alongside the leftists during the Spanish Civil War disillusioned him, and he embodied his distaste for any totalitarian system in *Animal Farm* (1945), a satirical attack on the leadership of the Soviet Union. In his pessimistic novel *1984* (1949), he imagined a social order shaped by a propagandistic perversion of language, in which the government, an extension of "Big Brother," uses two-way television to control the citizenry. Orwell succumbed to tuberculosis at the age of forty-seven, but not before he produced six novels, three documentary works, over seven hundred newspaper articles and reviews, and a volume of essays.

Wilfred Owen (1893–1918) Born in the Shropshire countryside of England, Owen had begun writing verse before he matriculated at London University, where he was known as a quiet and contemplative student. After some years of teaching English in France, Owen returned to England and joined the army. He was wounded in 1917 and killed in action leading an attack a few days before the armistice was declared in 1918. Owen's poems, published only after his death, along with his letters from the front to his mother, are perhaps the most powerful and vivid accounts of the horror of war to emerge from the First World War.

Dorothy Parker (1893–1967) Parker was born in West End, New Jersey, to a Scottish Presbyterian mother and a Jewish father as "a late unexpected arrival in a loveless family." She was educated in private schools and moved in 1911 to New York, where she lived in a boarding house and earned her living by playing piano at a dancing school. In 1915 one of the verses she had been sending around was accepted by *Vogue* magazine and the editor later hired her to write captions for fashion illustrations. Her native wit captivated the editor, and he persuaded her to join *Vanity Fair* as drama critic, although she was fired when she wrote unfavorable reviews of several plays. She became the first woman among the regulars of the Algonquin Round Table—a group of writers who met regularly at the Algonquin Hotel in New York City that included Alexander Woollcott, George S. Kaufman, Robert Benchley, and Edna Ferber (among others). A master of irony and scathing wit, Parker, despite a troubled personal life that led to suicide attempts, flourished as a humorist, poet, short-story writer, playwright, and screenwriter.

Paul (d. ca. A.D. 64) Paul was born in Tarsus of Cilicia (located near the Mediterranean Sea in south-central Turkey, near Syria). As an adult, he was an important Jerusalem Pharisee (his name then was Saul), and, according to accounts in the Acts of the Apostles, he vigorously attacked (both intellectually and physically) those who proclaimed the deity of Jesus. The same source (Chapter 9) provides an account of Paul's conversion, though Paul himself never mentions it. Traveling to Damascus to arrest followers of Jesus, he experienced an intense light that blinded him, and heard a voice that declared, "I am Jesus, whom you are persecuting." In Tarsus, his blindness was cured by Ananius, a follower of Jesus, and Paul became, arguably, the most important disciple of Jesus in the early Church—his letters (and those attributed to him) comprise a quarter of the New Testament. His attempts to preach the new Way in the synagogues of the region were rebuffed, sometimes violently, and Paul was frequently jailed. He became the apostle to the Gentiles, traveling throughout the Mediterranean region to establish churches. His epistles were addressed to those young and fragile congregations to help formulate the political, legal, and spiritual institutions of the early Church. His final arrest brought him to Rome to answer charges where, after two years of imprisonment, he died about A.D. 64.

Molly Peacock (b. 1947)   Born in Buffalo, New York, Peacock was educated at the State University of New York at Binghamton and at Johns Hopkins University, where she received an M.A. with honors in 1977. From 1970 to 1973, she was the director of academic advising at Binghamton. She was appointed honorary fellow at Johns Hopkins in 1977 and, in the following year, poet-in-residence at the Delaware State Arts Council in Wilmington. Since 1979, she has directed the Wilmington Writing Workshops. She has published in many magazines, including the *Southern Review,* the *Ohio Review,* and the *Massachusetts Review.* She has published four books of poems, *And Live Apart* (1980), *Raw Heaven* (1984), *Take Heart* (1989), the latter dealing with her father's alcoholism and the mental and physical abuse she endured while growing up, and, most recently, *Original Love* (1995). She was also co-editor of *Poetry in Motion: 100 Poems from the Subways and Buses* (1996), a collection of the popular poems displayed on placards in New York City's subways and buses.

Padraic Pearse (1879–1916)   Pearse, the son of an Irish mother and an English father, was born in Dublin and educated at the Christian Brothers' School. After graduating from the Royal University, he became a barrister. But he was an enthusiastic student of the Irish language and became a writer, writing in both English and Gaelic. Pearse envisioned a free Gaelic Ireland, and to encourage that end through education, he founded St. Enda's College, a school for boys. After visiting the United States, he joined the Irish Volunteers and later was commander-in-chief of the Irish rebel forces in the Easter Rebellion of 1916. Perceiving that the rebels' situation was hopeless, he ordered his troops to surrender to the British. He was arrested along with several other leaders (including his brother Willie) and shot by a firing squad on May 3, 1916.

Marge Piercy (b. 1936)   Born in Detroit, Marge Piercy was the first of her family to attend college. In 1957, she graduated from the University of Michigan (where she won prizes for poetry and fiction) and earned an M.A. from Northwestern University (1958). She was active in social and political causes and fought for equal treatment of women and minorities while opposing the Vietnam War. She supported herself with odd jobs in Chicago as she pursued a writing career, but her first novel was not published until after her 1969 move to Wellfleet, Massachusetts (where she still lives). She is an extraordinarily prolific writer. Among her more than a dozen novels are *He, She and It* (1991), *The Longings of Women* (1994), and *City of Darkness, City of Lights* (1996). Her many volumes of poetry include *My Mother's Body* (1985), *Available Light* (1988), *The Earth Shines Secretly: A Book of Days* (1990), and *Mars and Her Children* (1992). She has also written plays, several volumes of nonfiction, and has edited the anthology *Early Ripening: American Women's Poetry Now* (1987). Most recently, she has published a collection of poetry, *What Are Big Girls Made Of?* (1997). In the introduction to a volume of selected poems, *Circles on the Water* (1982), Piercy asserted that she wanted her poems to be "useful." "What I mean by useful is simply that readers will find poems that speak to and for them, will take those poems into their lives and say them to each other and put them up on the bathroom wall and remember bits and pieces of them in stressful or quiet moments. . . . To find ourselves spoken for in art gives dignity to our pain, our anger, our lust, our losses."

Luigi Pirandello (1867–1936)   Pirandello was born in Sicily, but moved to Rome when he was nineteen. He earned a degree in philosophy from the University of Bonn, and returned to Rome in 1897 to teach at a girl's high school. There he remained until 1923. He wrote poetry in his youth, but soon enjoyed considerable success for his novels and short stories. In 1912, a friend persuaded him to dramatize one of his own short stories, and that experience led to distinguished achievement in the theater. Pirandello's plays, particularly *Six Characters in Search of an Author* (1921), were performed and critically acclaimed throughout Europe and the United States. In 1920, he said: "My art is full of bitter compassion for all those who deceive themselves; but this compassion cannot fail to be followed by the ferocious derision of destiny which condemns man to deception." He won the Nobel Prize for literature in 1934.

Sylvia Plath (1932–1963)   Plath was born in Boston, Massachusetts, where her parents taught at Boston University. She graduated summa cum laude in English from Smith College (1955), earned an M.A. as a Fullbright scholar at Newnham College, Cambridge (1955–1957), and married British poet Ted Hughes (1956). Plath's poetry reveals the anger and anxiety that would eventually lead to her suicide. Her view that all relationships were in some way destructive and predatory surely darkened her life. Yet in 1963, during the month between the publication of her only novel, *The Bell Jar* (about a suicidal college student), and her death, Plath was extraordinarily productive; she produced finished poems every day. One critic suggests that for her, suicide was a positive act, a "refusal to collaborate" in a world she could not accept. Her *Collected Poems* was published in 1981.

Edgar Allan Poe (1809–1849)   Poe, the son of traveling actors, was born in Boston, Massachusetts. Within a year, his alcoholic father deserted his mother and three infant children. When his mother died of tuberculosis in Richmond, Virginia, three-year-old Edgar was adopted by John Allan and his wife. Allan, a prosperous businessperson, spent time in England, where Poe began his education at private schools. Back in the United States, Allan forced Poe to leave the University of Virginia in 1826, when Poe incurred gambling debts he could not pay. He served in the U.S. Army from 1827 to 1829, eventually attaining the rank of sergeant-major. Poe next attended West Point, hoping for further military advancement. Shortly thereafter, Mrs. Allan died of tuberculosis. Poe angrily confronted his foster father about his extra-marital affairs; for this candor he was disowned. Believing that Allan would never reinstate him as heir, Poe deliberately violated rules to provoke his dismissal from the Academy. In 1835, Poe began his career as editor, columnist, and reviewer, earning a living he could not make as a writer of stories and poems. He married his thirteen-year-old cousin, Virginia Clemm, in 1836, and lived with her and her mother during a period marked by illness and poverty. Virginia died of tuberculosis in 1847. Poe died, delirious, under mysterious circumstances, in 1849. He perfected the gothic horror story ("Fall of the House of Usher") and originated the modern detective story ("The Gold Bug," "The Murders in the Rue Morgue"). Poe's work fascinated the French poet Baudelaire, who translated it into French.

Sir Walter Ralegh (1552?–1618)   Born in Devonshire, England, into the landed gentry, Ralegh attended Oxford but dropped out after a year in order to fight for the

Huguenot cause in France. He returned to England, began the study of law, but again was drawn to a life of adventure and exploration. Through the influence of friends he came to the attention of Queen Elizabeth, and thenceforth his career flourished: he was knighted, given a number of lucrative commercial monopolies, made a member of Parliament and, in 1587, named captain of the Yeoman of the Guard. During these years, he invested in various colonies in North America, but all his settlements failed. He was briefly imprisoned in the Tower of London for offending the Queen but was soon back in favor and in command of an unsuccessful expedition to Guiana (now Venezuela) in 1595. In 1603, he was again imprisoned in the Tower, this time on a probably trumped-up charge of treason, where he remained until 1616, spending part of his time writing *A History of the World* (1614). After his release, he undertook still another expedition to Guiana but again returned empty-handed. As a consequence of more political intrigue, James I ordered him executed. Although Ralegh epitomized the great merchant adventurers of Elizabethan England, he was also a gifted poet.

Dudley Randall (b. 1914)   Born in Washington, D.C., Randall worked during the Depression in the foundry of the Ford Motor Company in Dearborn, Michigan, and then as a carrier and clerk for the U.S. Post Office in Detroit. He served in the U.S. Army Signal Corps (1942–1946), and graduated from Wayne State University (B.A., 1949) and the University of Michigan (M.A.L.S., 1951). He was a librarian at several universities, and founded the Broadside Press in 1965 "so black people could speak to and for their people." Randall told *Negro Digest*, "Precision and accuracy are necessary for both white and black writers. . . . 'A black aesthetic' should not be an excuse for sloppy writing." He urges African American writers to reject what was false in "white" poetry but not to forsake universal concerns in favor of a racial agenda. His works include *On Getting a Natural* (1969) and *A Litany of Friends: New and Selected Poems* (1981). He edited *The Black Poets* (1971), an extensive anthology of poetry, from slave songs to the present.

Henry Reed (1914–1986)   Reed was born in Birmingham, England, earned a B.A. from the University of Birmingham (1937), worked as a teacher and free-lance writer (1937–1941), and served in the British Army (1941–1942). His early poetry dealt with political events before and during World War II. "Naming of Parts" was based on his frustrating experience in cadet training. His collection of poetry, *A Map of Verona* (1946), revealed a formal, reverent, but also humorous and ironic voice. Another collection of poetry, *Lessons of War,* was published in 1970. Reed began writing radio plays in 1947 and has generated as many as four scripts a year. His best-known satirical work is the "Hilda Tablet" series, a 1960s BBC-Radio production that parodied British society of the 1930s.

Alastair Reid (b. 1926)   Born in Scotland, son of a minister, Reid graduated with honors from St. Andrews University after serving in the Royal Navy. He taught at Sarah Lawrence College (1951–1955) and, after his appointment as staff writer at the *New Yorker* in 1959, occasionally enjoyed visiting professorships across the United States and in England, teaching Latin American studies and literature. Acclaimed for his light, engaging style, Reid has been enthusiastically received as a poet, translator, essayist, and author of children's books, moving between genres as easily as he has moved between countries. Reid has lived in Spain, Latin America, Greece, and Morocco (to name a few places) and rejects the label "Scottish" writer. His deliberate rootlessness shows in his poetry, which is characterized by, in one critic's words, "natural irregularity."

Adrienne Rich (b. 1929)   Born to a middle-class family, Rich was educated by her parents until she entered public school in the fourth grade. She graduated Phi Beta Kappa from Radcliffe College in 1951, the same year her first book of poems, *A Change of World,* appeared. That volume, chosen by W. H. Auden for the Yale Series of Younger Poets Award, and her next, *The Diamond Cutters and Other Poems* (1955), earned her a reputation as an elegant, controlled stylist. In the 1960s, however, Rich began a dramatic shift away from her earlier mode as she took up political and feminist themes and stylistic experimentation in such works as *Snapshots of a Daughter-in-Law* (1963), *The Necessities of Life* (1966), *Leaflets* (1969), and *The Will to Change* (1971). In *Diving into the Wreck* (1973) and *The Dream of a Common Language* (1978), she continued to experiment with form and to deal with the experiences and aspirations of women from a feminist perspective. In addition to her poetry, Rich has published many essays on poetry, feminism, motherhood, and lesbianism. Her recent collections include *An Atlas of the Difficult World* (1991) and *Dark Fields of the Republic: Poems 1991–1995* (1995).

Edwin Arlington Robinson (1869–1935)   Robinson grew up in Gardiner, Maine, attended Harvard, returned to Gardiner as a free-lance writer, then settled in New York City in 1896. His various odd jobs included a one-year stint as subway-construction inspector. President Theodore Roosevelt, a fan of his poetry, had him appointed to the United States Customs House in New York, where he worked from 1905 to 1909. Robinson wrote about people, rather than nature, particularly New England characters remembered from his early years. Describing his first volume of poems, *The Torrent and the Night Before* (1896), he told a friend there was not "a single red-breasted robin in the whole collection." Popular throughout his career, Robinson won three Pulitzer Prizes (1921, 1924, 1927).

Theodore Roethke (1908–1963)   Born in Saginaw, Michigan, Roethke was the son of a greenhouse owner; greenhouses figure prominently in the imagery of his poems. He graduated magna cum laude from the University of Michigan in 1929, where he also earned an M.A. in 1936 after graduate study at Harvard. He taught at several universities, coached two varsity tennis teams, and settled at the University of Washington in 1947. Intensely introspective and demanding of himself, Roethke was renowned as a great teacher, though sometimes incapacitated by an ongoing manic-depressive condition. His collection *The Waking: Poems 1933–1953,* won the Pulitzer Prize in 1954. Other awards include Guggenheim Fellowships in 1945 and 1950, and a National Book Award and the Bollingen Prize in 1959 for *Words for the Wind* (1958).

Muriel Rukeyser (1913–1980)   Born in New York City, Rukeyser attended Vassar and Columbia, then spent a short time at Roosevelt Aviation School, which no doubt helped shape her first published volume of poetry, *Theory of Flight* (1935). In the early 1930s, she joined Elizabeth Bishop, Mary McCarthy, and Eleanor Clark in founding a literary magazine that challenged the policies of the *Vassar Review*. (The two magazines later merged.) A social activist, Rukeyser witnessed the Scottsboro trials (where she was one of the reporters arrested by authorities) in 1933. She visited suffering tunnel workers in West Virginia (1936) and went to Hanoi to protest U.S. involvement in the Vietnam War. She gave poetry readings across the United States and received several awards, including a Guggenheim Fellowship and the Copernicus Award. *Waterlily Fire: Poems 1935–1962* appeared in 1962, and later work was collected in *29 Poems* (1970). *The Collected Poems of Muriel Rukeyser* appeared in 1978. Her only novel, *The Orgy,* appeared in 1965.

Ira Sadoff (b. 1945)   Sadoff was born in Brooklyn, New York, the son of Russian Jewish immigrants. He earned a B.A. (1966) from Cornell University in industrial and labor relations and an M.F.A. (1968) from the University of Oregon. He has taught at several colleges and universities and is now the Dana Professor of Poetry at Colby College in Waterville, Maine. Among his volumes of poetry are *Settling Down* (1975), *Maine: Nine Poems* (1981), and *Emotional Traffic* (1989). He has also written a novel, *Uncoupling* (1982). An *Ira Sadoff Reader* was published in 1992. He has characterized himself as "one poet among a decreasing minority who is trying to resist the return to formalism, the sterile, conservative, aesthete academicism of the nineteen-fifties."

Sappho (ca. 610–ca. 580 B.C.)   Almost nothing certain is known of the finest woman lyric poet of the ancient world. She was born to an aristocratic family and had three brothers, one of whom was a court cupbearer (a position limited to the sons of good families). She is associated with the island of Lesbos, set in the Aegean Sea. She married and had a daughter. Until recently, her reputation depended on fragments of her work quoted by other ancient authors. However, in the late nineteenth century a cache of papyrus and vellum codices (dating from the second to the sixth centuries A.D.) containing authentic transcriptions of a few of her lyrical poems was discovered in Egypt. Unlike other ancient Greek poets, she wrote in ordinary Greek rather than an exalted literary dialect; her lyrics, despite their simple language, conveyed women's concerns with intense emotion.

William Saroyan (1908–1981)   Born and raised in Fresno, California, to Armenian immigrant parents, Saroyan's first success as a writer came with the publication in 1934 of his story "The Daring Young Man on the Flying Trapeze." He went on to become a prolific writer of fiction and plays, notable for their optimism and romantic celebrations of ordinary people pursuing the American dream. Among his best-known novels are *My Name is Aram* (1940) and *The Human Comedy* (1943), both dealing with children growing up in the San Joaquin Valley in California. His many plays include *My Heart's in the Highlands* and *The Time of Your Life* (both 1939). Saroyan refused the Pulitzer Prize for the latter play on the grounds that wealthy business people were incapable of judging art. His autobiographical works include *The Bicycle Rider in Beverly Hills* (1952), *Places Where I've Done Time* (1972), and *Obituaries* (1979). Five days before he died, he said to the Associated Press, "Everybody has got to die, but I have always believed an exception would be made in my case. Now what?"

May Sarton (1912–1995)   Born in Belgium, Sarton was brought to the United States in 1916 and became a naturalized citizen in 1924. She was educated at various private schools, including the Cambridge High and Latin School. In 1929, the year her first poems were published, she turned down a scholarship to Vassar College to become an apprentice with Eva Le Gallienne's Civic Repertory Theatre in New York. In 1936, when the Associated Actors Theatre, which she directed, disbanded, Sarton began to devote herself to writing. Her prolific output of poetry, fiction, and nonfiction brought her many honors, including appointment as a Guggenheim Fellow in poetry (1954–1955) and awards from the Poetry Society of America (1952), the Johns Hopkins University Poetry Festival (1961), the Before Columbus Foundation (1985), and the Women's Building/West Hollywood Conexxus Women's Crisis Center (1987). She has taught widely in American colleges and universities and is the recipient of numerous honorary doctorate degrees. She is the author of eighteen novels, among them *The Single Hound* (1938), *Mrs. Stevens Hears the Mermaids Singing* (1965), and *The Education of Harriet Hatfield* (1989). Her volumes of poetry include *Encounter in April* (1937), *Collected Poems: 1930–1973* (1974), *The Silence Now: New and Uncollected Earlier Poems* (1988), and *Coming into Eighty* (1994). In 1986, Sarton suffered a stroke. In describing her difficult recuperation, she remarked to an interviewer that since her illness, her poems explore "where I am now, as a woman . . . who has really faced growing old for the first time."

Richard Selzer (b. 1928)   The son of a family doctor, Selzer was born in Troy, New York. He attended Union College in Schenectady, New York, and earned an M.D. at Albany Medical College in 1953. He wrote *Rituals of Surgery* (1974), a collection of short stories, and he subsequently published numerous essays and stories in such magazines as *Redbook, Esquire,* and *Harper's.* These he collected in two volumes of essays, *Mortal Lessons* (1977) and *Confessions of a Knife* (1979), and a volume of essays and fiction, *Letters to a Young Doctor* (1982). In 1991, he contracted Legionnaire's disease but went on to document his recovery in *Raising the Dead: A Doctor's Encounter with His Own Mortality* (1994). In his writing, he draws upon his experience as a surgeon, and as one critic points out, he "forces physicians to think about the morality of medicine."

Anne Sexton (1928–1974)   Born in Newton, Massachusetts, Sexton attended Garland Junior College and Boston University, where she studied under Robert Lowell. She worked for a year as a fashion model in Boston and later wrote her first poetry collection, *To Bedlam and Part Way Back* (1960), while recovering from a nervous breakdown. Writing a poem almost every day was successful therapy for her. From 1961 to 1963, Sexton was a scholar at the Radcliffe Institute for Independent Study. A confessional poet, Sexton acknowledged her debt to W. D. Snodgrass, whose collection of poetry, *Heart's Needle* (1959), influenced her profoundly. Her second collection, *All My Pretty Ones* (1962), includes a quote from a letter by Franz Kafka that expresses her own literary philosophy: "A book should serve as the axe for the frozen sea within us." *Live or Die* (1967), her third collection of poems, won a Pulitzer Prize. She committed suicide in 1974.

William Shakespeare (1564–1616)   Shakespeare was born at Stratford-on-Avon in April 1564. His father became an important public figure, rising to the position of high bailiff (equivalent to mayor) of Stratford. Although we know practically nothing of his personal life, we may assume that Shakespeare received a decent grammar school education in literature, logic, and Latin (though not in mathematics or natural science). When he was eighteen, he married Anne Hathaway, eight years his senior; six months later their son was born. Two years later, Anne bore twins. We do not know how the young Shakespeare supported his family, and we do not hear of him again until 1592, when a rival London playwright sarcastically refers to him as an "upstart crow." Shakespeare seems to have prospered in the London theater world. He probably began as an actor, and earned enough as author and part owner of his company's theaters to acquire property. His sonnets, which were written during the 1590s, reveal rich and varied interests. Some are addressed to an attractive young man (whom the poet urges to marry); others to the mysterious dark lady; still others suggest a love triangle of two men and a woman. His dramas include historical plays based on English dynastic struggles; comedies, both festive and dark; romances such as *Pericles* (1608) and *Cymbeline* (1611) that cover decades in the lives of their characters; and the great tragedies: *Hamlet* (1602), *Othello* (1604), *King Lear* (1605), and *Macbeth* (1606). About 1611 (at age forty-seven), he retired to the second largest house in Stratford. He died in 1616, leaving behind a body of work that still stands as a pinnacle in world literature.

Irwin Shaw (1913–1984) Born and educated in New York City, where he received a B.A. from Brooklyn College in 1934, Shaw began his career as a scriptwriter for popular radio programs of the 1930s, then went to Hollywood to write for the movies. Disillusioned with the film industry, Shaw returned to New York. His first piece of serious writing, an antiwar play entitled *Bury the Dead,* was produced on Broadway in 1936. About this time, Shaw began contributing short stories to such magazines as the *New Yorker* and *Esquire.* His first collection of stories, *Sailor off the Bremen and Other Stories* (1939), earned him an immediate and lasting reputation as a writer of fiction. While continuing to write plays and stories, Shaw turned to the novel and published in 1948 *The Young Lions,* which won high critical praise as one of the most important novels to come out of World War II. The commercial success of the book and the movie adaptation brought Shaw financial independence and allowed him to devote the rest of his career to writing novels, among them *The Troubled Air* (1951), *Lucy Crown* (1956), *Rich Man, Poor Man* (1970), and *Acceptable Losses* (1982). Shaw's stories are collected in *Short Stories: Five Decades* (1978).

Percy Bysshe Shelley (1792–1822) Born near Horsham, England, Shelley was the son of a wealthy landowner who sat in Parliament. At University College, Oxford, he befriended Thomas Jefferson Hogg. Both became interested in radical philosophy and quickly became inseparable. After one year at Oxford they were expelled together for writing and circulating a pamphlet entitled "The Necessity of Atheism." Shelley married Harriet Westbrook soon after leaving Oxford. Though they had two children, the marriage was unsuccessful, and in 1814, Shelley left Harriet for Mary Wollstonecraft Godwin (author of *Frankenstein* [1818]). After Harriet's death (an apparent suicide), Shelley and Godwin were married. Escaping legal problems in England, he settled in Pisa, Italy, in 1820, and died in a sailing accident before his thirtieth birthday. A playwright and essayist as well as a romantic poet, Shelley is admired for his dramatic poem "Prometheus Unbound" (1820).

Stevie Smith (1902–1971)   Born Florence Margaret Smith in Hull, England, Stevie Smith was a secretary at Newnes Publishing Company in London from 1923 to 1953, and occasionally worked as a writer and broadcaster for the BBC. Though she began publishing verse, which she often illustrated herself, in the 1930s, Smith did not reach a wide audience until 1962—with the publication of *Selected Poems* and her appearance in the Penguin Modern Poets Series. She is noted for her eccentricity and mischievous humor, often involving an acerbic twist on nursery rhymes, common songs, or hymns. Force-fed with what she considered lifeless language in the New English Bible, she often aimed satirical barbs at religion. Smith won the Queen's Gold Medal for poetry in 1969, two years before her death. She published three novels in addition to her eight volumes of poetry.

W. D. Snodgrass (b. 1926)   Born in Pennsylvania, son of an accountant, William Dewitt Snodgrass attended Geneva College, earned three degrees from the University of Iowa (B.A., 1949; M.A., 1951; M.F.A., 1953), then taught at Cornell University, the University of Rochester, and Wayne State University. Acknowledged as one of the original confessional poets, he won the Pulitzer Prize in 1960 for his first collection, *Heart's Needle* (1959). His poems are deeply personal and often involve references to the wives and children from his three marriages. Surprising critics who had grown tired of his self-analytical style, Snodgrass distinguished himself again with his third collection, *The Führer Bunker: A Cycle of Poems in Progress* (1977), in which he explores the psyches of Hitler's senior officials during the month they shared his bunker in 1945. His more recent poetry collections include *Selected Poems, 1957–1987* (1987) and *The Fuehrer Bunker: The Complete Cycle* (1995).

Robert C. Solomon (b. 1942)   Solomon was born in Detroit. His father was a lawyer, his mother, an artist. After earning a B.A. (1963) at the University of Pennsylvania, he moved to the University of Michigan for an M.A. (1965) and Ph.D. (1967). He has held several teaching positions at such schools as Princeton University, the University of California, Los Angeles, and the University of Pittsburgh. In 1972, he moved to the University of Texas at Austin where he is now a professor of philosophy. His many books include *The Passions* (1976), *Love: Emotion, Myth, and Metaphor* (1981), *Above the Bottom Line: An Introduction to Business Ethics* (with Kristine R. Hansen) (1983), *A Passion for Justice* (1990), and the source of the essay reprinted in this text, *About Love: Reinventing Romance for Our Times* (1988). He is also a published songwriter. Responding to the standard questionnaire that asked him his religion, he wrote: "Peter Pantheist." As his avocations he listed "Travel, food, love, animals, life."

Sophocles (496?–406 B.C.)   Born into a wealthy family at Colonus, a village just outside Athens, Sophocles distinguished himself early in life as a performer, musician, and athlete. Our knowledge of him is based on a very few ancient laudatory notices, but he certainly had a brilliant career as one of the three great Greek classical tragedians (the other two are Aeschylus, an older contemporary, and Euripides, a younger contemporary). He won the drama competition associated with the Dionysian festival (entries consisted of a tragic trilogy and a farce) at least twenty times (far more often than his two principal rivals). However, *Oedipus Rex,* his most famous tragedy, and the three other plays it was grouped with, took second place (ca. 429 B.C.). He lived during the golden age of Athens, when architecture, philosophy, and the arts flourished under Pericles. In 440 B.C., Sophocles was elected as one of the ten *strategoi* (military commanders), an indication of his stature in Athens. But his long life ended in sadder times—when the Peloponnesian War (431–404 B.C.), between the Athenian empire and an alliance led by Sparta, darkened the region. Though Sophocles wrote some 123 plays, only 7 have survived; nonetheless, these few works establish him as the greatest of the ancient Western tragedians.

Helen Sorrells (b. 1908)   Born in Stafford, Kansas, the daughter of farmers, Sorrells earned a B.S. from Kansas State University in 1931. She married a technical writer, had two children and was approaching her seventh decade when she won the Borestone Award for her poem "Cry Summer." In 1968, she won the *Arizona Quarterly* Award for poetry and in 1973 received a creative writing grant from the National Endowment for the Arts, as well as the Poetry Society of America's Cecil Hemley Award for the poem "Tunnels." She has contributed to *Esquire* and *Reporter,* among others, and published a collection of poems, *Seeds as They Fall* (1971).

Gary Soto (b. 1952)   Gary Soto was born in Fresno, California, to working-class Mexican American parents. He grew up in the San Joaquin Valley, and worked as a migrant laborer in California's rich agricultural regions. Uncertain of his abilities, he began his academic career at Fresno City College, moving on to California State University, Fresno, and the University of California, Irvine, where he earned an M.F.A. degree (1976). In 1975, he married Carolyn Oda, a woman of Japanese ancestry. Although his work earned him recognition as early as 1975 (an Academy of American Poets Prize), his first book of poems, *The Elements of San Joaquin,* grim pictures of Mexican American life in California's central valley, appeared in 1977. In 1985, he joined the faculty at the University of California, Berkeley, where he taught in both the English and Chicano Studies departments. He stopped teaching in 1993 to become a full-time writer. His prolific output of poetry, memoirs, essays, and fiction continues unabated and has earned him numerous prizes, including an American Book Award from the Before Columbus Foundation for *Living up the Street* (1985). One critic points out that Soto has transcended the social commentary of his early work and shifted to "a more personal, less politically motivated poetry." Another argues that "Gary Soto has become not an important Chicano poet but an important American poet."

Art Spiegelman (b. 1948)   Spiegelman's parents, Anja and Vladek, were Polish Jews who survived imprisonment in the Nazi concentration camp at Auschwitz. Spiegelman was born in Stockholm, Sweden, and his family immigrated to the United States. He attended Harpur College (now State University of New York at Binghamton) from 1965 to 1968. His mother, Anja, committed suicide in 1968. In 1977 he married Françoise Mouly, a publisher. As a student, Spiegelman developed his talent for drawing and writing and became a creative consultant, designer, and writer for Topps Chewing Gum, Inc., where he produced novelty packaging and bubble gum cards. But he was fascinated by the provocative underground comics of the sixties, and began to create original and powerful comic book work addressed to an adult audience. *The Complete Mr. Infinity* appeared in 1970, succeeded by numerous other productions that culminated in *Maus: A Survivor's Tale* (1986). *Maus,* based on his father's experience as a Nazi concentration camp survivor, was nominated for a National Book Critics Circle Award, and won the Joel M. Cavior Award for Jewish Writing. In his "comic book," Spiegelman portrays the Nazis as cats and the Jews as their victim mice. He published the second volume of *Maus: A Survivor's Tale II: And Here My Troubles Began* in 1991. In 1980, Spiegelman and his wife founded *Raw*— an annual magazine that showcases the talents of avant-garde artist-writers of adult comics.

Elizabeth Spires (b. 1952)   Spires, born in Lancaster, Ohio, earned a B.A. from Vassar College (1974) and an M.A. from Johns Hopkins University (1979). From 1976–1977, she worked in publishing; from 1977 to 1981, she became a free-lance writer; and, thereafter, she taught at several colleges including Loyola College in Baltimore, Johns Hopkins University, and Goucher College in Towson, Maryland. In 1985 she married the novelist Madison Smartt Bell. She has won several awards and honors, including a National Endowment for the Arts Fellowship (1981). In addition to several volumes of poetry, including *Worldling* (1995), she has published a number of juvenile books. Commenting about her work, she has remarked, "I find myself . . . interested in writing about childhood experiences related to growing up Catholic."

Wallace Stevens (1879–1955)   Born in Reading, Pennsylvania, Stevens graduated from Harvard in 1900, worked for a year as a reporter for the New York *Herald Tribune*, graduated from New York University Law School in 1903, and practiced law in New York for twelve years. From 1916 to 1955, Stevens worked for the Hartford Accident and Indemnity Company, where he was appointed vice-president in 1934. He was in his forties when he published his first book of poetry, *Harmonium, Ideas of Order* (1923). Stevens argued that poetry is a "supreme fiction" that shapes chaos and provides order to both nature and human relationships. He illuminates his philosophy in *Ideas of Order* (1935) and *Notes toward a Supreme Fiction* (1942). His *Collected Poems* (1954) won the Pulitzer Prize and established him as a major American poet.

Nancy Sullivan (b. 1929)   Nancy Sullivan was born in Newport, Rhode Island, and earned a B.A. (1951) at Hunter College in New York City and a Ph.D. from the University of Connecticut (1963). After teaching and administrative work at Brown University (1953–1963), she joined the English Department at Rhode Island College. She has contributed poems and book reviews to numerous journals, including *Poetry, Ramparts, The Quarterly Review of Poetry,* and the *Massachusetts Review*. Her first book, *The History of the World as Pictures* (1965), won the first Annual Devins Memorial Award.

Jonathan Swift (1667–1745)   Born in Dublin, Ireland, of English parents, Swift moved to England following his graduation from Trinity College, Dublin. In 1695, he was ordained minister of the Anglican church of Ireland and five years later became a parish priest in Laracor, Ireland. The conduct of church business took Swift to England frequently, where his wit and skill in defense of Tory politics made him many influential friends. He was rewarded for his efforts in 1713, when Queen Anne appointed him dean of St. Patrick's Cathedral in Dublin. The accession of George I to the throne in the following year, followed by the Tory's loss of the government to Whig control, ended the political power of Swift and his friends. He spent the rest of his life as dean of St. Patrick's, writing during this period his most celebrated satirical narrative, *Gulliver's Travels* (1726), and his most savage essay, "A Modest Proposal" (1729). Among his many other works are *A Tale of a Tub* and *The Battle of the Books* (both 1704), and many poems.

Alfred, Lord Tennyson (1809–1892) Tennyson was born in Lincolnshire and attended Trinity College, Cambridge (1828–1831), where he won the Chancellor's Medal for Poetry in 1829. His 1842 collection, *Poems,* was not well received, but he gained prominence and the Queen's favor with the 1850 publication of *In Memoriam,* an elegy written over seventeen years and inspired by the untimely death of his friend Arthur Hallam in 1833. That same year he finally married Emily Sellwood, after a fourteen-year engagement. In 1850, he was named poet laureate of England after Wordsworth's death. His works include *Maud and Other Poems* (1855) and *Idylls of the King* (1859), based on the legendary exploits of King Arthur and the knights of the Round Table.

Dylan Thomas (1914–1953) Born in Swansea, Wales, Thomas decided to pursue a writing career directly after grammar school. At age twenty, he published his first collection, *Eighteen Poems* (1934), but his lack of a university degree deprived him of most opportunities to earn a living as a writer in England. Consequently, his early life (as well as the lives of his wife and children) was darkened by a poverty compounded by his free spending and heavy drinking. A self-proclaimed romanticist, Thomas called his poetry a "record of [his] struggle from darkness towards some measure of light." *The Map of Love* appeared in 1939 and *Deaths and Entrances* in 1946. Later, as a radio playwright and screenwriter, Thomas delighted in the sounds of words, sometimes at the expense of sense. *Under Milk Wood* (produced in 1953) is filled with his private, onomatopoetic language. He suffered from alcoholism and lung ailments, and died in a New York hospital in 1953. Earlier that year, he noted in his *Collected Poems:* "These poems, with all their crudities, doubts and confusions are written for the love of man and in Praise of God, and I'd be a damn fool if they weren't."

Lewis Thomas (1913–1993) Thomas was born in Flushing, New York. The son of a surgeon, he graduated from Princeton University and in 1937 earned an M.D. from Harvard. In his distinguished medical career, he combined an active practice with teaching and administration. He served as dean of the medical schools of Yale and New York Universities and was chief executive officer of the Sloan-Kettering Institute in New York City at the time of his death. His many scientific papers earned him membership in the National Academy of Sciences. But even as a medical student, Thomas displayed literary ambition and published a number of poems. In 1971, he began contributing a regular column, "Notes of a Biology Watcher," to the prestigious *New England Journal of Medicine.* Some of these essays he collected and published in 1974 as *The Lives of a Cell: Notes of a Biology Watcher.* These graceful essays found a sizable audience and won the National Book Award. Subsequent essay collections include *The Medusa and the Snail* (1979) and *Late Night Thoughts on Listening to Mahler's Ninth Symphony* (1983). *The Youngest Science: Notes of a Medicine Watcher* (1983) describes the making of a doctor.

James Thurber (1894–1961)   Born in Columbus, Ohio, Thurber went through the local public schools and graduated from Ohio State University. He began his writing career as a reporter, first for an Ohio newspaper, and later in Paris and New York City, before he became a staff member of the *New Yorker.* There he wrote the humorous satirical essays and fables (often illustrated with his whimsical drawings of people and animals) upon which his reputation rests—the most famous being "The Secret Life of Walter Mitty." In 1929, he and another *New Yorker* staffer, E. B. White, wrote *Is Sex Necessary? or, Why You Feel the Way You Do,* a spoof of the increasingly popular new psychological theories. In 1933, he published his humorous autobiography, *My Life and Hard Times.* With Elliott Nugent, he wrote *The Male Animal* (1940), a comic play that pleads for academic freedom, and, in 1959, he memorialized his associates at the *New Yorker* in *The Years with Ross.*

Leo Tolstoy (1828–1910)   Born in Russia into a family of aristocratic landowners, Tolstoy cut short his university education and joined the army, serving among the primitive Cossacks, who became the subject of his first novel, *The Cossacks* (1863). Tolstoy left the army and traveled abroad but was disappointed by Western material-ism and returned home. After a brief period in St. Petersburg, he became bored with the life of literary celebrity and returned to his family estate. There he wrote his two greatest novels, *War and Peace* (1869) and *Anna Karenina* (1877). Around 1876, Tolstoy experienced a kind of spiritual crisis that ultimately led him to reject his former beliefs, way of life, and literary works. Henceforth, he adopted the simple life of the Russian peasants, rejecting orthodoxy in favor of a rational Christianity that disavowed private property, class divisions, secular and institutional religious au-thority, as well as all art (including his own) that failed to teach the simple principles he espoused.

Su Tung-p'o (1036–1101)   Su Tung-p'o, one of the great poets of his time, was born and reared in Szechwan in western China and had a long career as a government bureaucrat. His sharp criticisms of government policy resulted in his twice being exiled by the emperor. As a government official, he upheld the Confucian ideals of public service and strived, according to contemporary accounts, to improve the lives of ordinary citizens. Like other great poets of his era, he often spoke out against gov-ernment abuse. He was also known as an essayist, calligrapher, and painter.

Mark Twain (1835–1910)   Born Samuel L. Clemens in Florida, Missouri, Twain grew up in Hannibal, Missouri, on the banks of the Mississippi River (*mark twain,* a phrase meaning "two fathoms deep," was used by Mississippi riverboat pilots in mak-ing soundings). Sometime after his father's death in 1847, Twain left school to become a printer's apprentice, worked as a journeyman printer and newspaper reporter in the East and Middle West, and became a steamboat pilot on the Missis-sippi River until the outbreak of the Civil War. In 1861, he departed for Nevada with his brother, spent a year prospecting for silver, then returned to newspaper work as a reporter. In 1867, a San Francisco newspaper sent him as correspondent on a cruise ship to Europe and the Holy Land. He used the dispatches he wrote about this voyage as the basis for his first, highly successful book, *The Innocents Abroad* (1869). His second book, *Roughing It* (1872), described his western years and added to his already considerable reputation as an irreverent humorist. No longer explicitly autobiographical but still drawing on his own life, Twain published his masterpieces, the novels *The Adventures of Tom Sawyer* (1876) and *The Adventures of Huckleberry Finn* (1884). Twain remained a prolific and important writer and by the time of his death had become something of a national institution, although he never again quite matched the achievements of these early works. Financial problems and personal tragedies contributed to his increasingly bleak view of the human condition, expressed most powerfully in such works as *A Connecticut Yankee in King Arthur's Court* (1889), *Pudd'nhead Wilson* (1894), *The Man That Corrupted Hadleyburg* (1900), and the posthumously published *The Mysterious Stranger* (1916).

Jill Tweedie (1936–1993)   A reviewer of Jill Tweedie's autobiography, *Eating Children: Young Dreams and Early Nightmares* (1993), reveals that she was born into an economically comfortable family of "impeccable rectitude," presided over by her father, "a Scottish patriarch pathologically incapable of affection." Tweedie was encouraged to become "feminine" and marriageable; she was given ballet lessons and sent to a Swiss finishing school, while her brother, and only sibling, was given an academic education. Her inevitable rebellion when she was eighteen years old precipitated a disastrous marriage (the first of three) to a jealous and abusive Hungarian count. After an acrimonious separation, she took her two children to a hippie commune in Wales where she discovered that, even there, women were burdened with "women's work" while the men, generally, did no work at all. She moved to London and lived in poverty while she struggled to support her household by writing—the only skill she commanded. Ultimately, she became the *Guardian*'s regular columnist on feminist issues. She has written several volumes on feminist themes, among them, *Letters from a Faint-hearted Feminist* (1982). Shortly before her death, when asked about the changes feminism had generated, she replied: "Assumptions about women are what has changed most radically. And a woman's whole psychic energy isn't wrapped up in men or nurturing the male ego. Young women don't appreciate that vast liberation."

Melvin I. Urofsky (b. 1939)   Melvin Urofsky was born and grew up in New York City, where he earned an A.B. (1961), M.A. (1962), and Ph.D. (1968) from Columbia University. He taught at Ohio State University, State University of New York at Albany, and is chair of the history department at Virginia Commonwealth University. In 1984, he earned a law degree from the University of Virginia. He has written and edited more than fifteen books, including a four-volume edition of the letters of Supreme Court Justice Louis D. Brandeis (with David W. Levy, 1971–1978). Urofsky has written and edited several books on the American Jewish experience, and was chair of the Zionist Academic Council (1976–1979). In *Letting Go: Death, Dying, and the Law* (1993), he examines the vexing relationships among dying patients, their physicians, their families, medical ethics, and the law. His most recent works are *The Supreme Court Justices: A Biographical Dictionary* (1994) and *Affirmative Action on Trial: Sex Discrimination in Johnson v. Santa Clara* (1997).

Stephanie Vaughn (b. 1943)   Vaughn was born in Millersburg, Ohio, into a military family that moved frequently from post to post. She grew up in Ohio, New York, Oklahoma, Texas, Italy, and the Philippine Islands. She earned a B.A. from Ohio State University and an M.F.A. from the University of Iowa. Her stories have appeared in the O. Henry and Pushcart Prize collections of best short stories, and her first book of stories, *Sweet Talk,* appeared in 1990. She is a professor in the English Department at Cornell University. One critic extolled the stories in *Sweet Talk:* "The tone is extraordinary, simple, clear, and defined like the ringing of a bell, and yet suggesting a world of the most difficult complexities—our world where there are no single, or even permanent, answers and where human beings veer toward and away from one another, never fully in reach."

Alice Walker (b. 1944)   Born in Eatonton, Georgia, the eighth child of sharecroppers, Walker was educated at Spelman College and Sarah Lawrence College. She has been deeply involved in the civil rights movement, working to register voters in Georgia and on behalf of welfare rights and Head Start in Mississippi. She also worked for the Welfare Department of New York City. She has taught at Wellesley and Yale and been an editor of *Ms.* Her nonfiction works include a biography for children, *Langston Hughes: American Poet* (1973); numerous contributions to anthologies about African American writers; and a collection of essays, *In Search of Our Mothers' Gardens: Womanist Prose* (1983). Her novels, all dealing with the African American experience in America, include *The Third Life of Grange Copeland* (1973), *Meridian* (1976), *The Color Purple* (1982), which won both the Pulitzer Prize and the National Book Award, *The Temple of My Familiar* (1989), and *Possessing the Secret of Joy* (1992). Her short stories are collected in two volumes, *In Love and Trouble: Stories of Black Women* (1973) and *You Can't Keep a Good Woman Down* (1981). Most recently, she has published *Her Blue Body Everything We Know: Earthling Poems, 1965–1990 Complete* (1991); *Warrior Marks: Female Genital Mutilation and the Sexual Blinding of Women* (with Pratibha Parmar), and *The Same River Twice: Honoring the Difficult: A Meditation on Life, Spirit, Art, and the Making of the Film, The Color Purple, Ten Years Later* (1996).

Edmund Waller (1606–1687)   Born in Hertfordshire, England, Waller was privately instructed as a young child, then sent to Eton and Cambridge. He served for several years as a member of Parliament, first as an opponent of the crown and later as a Royalist. His advocacy of the Royalist cause and his attempts to moderate between the crown and the Puritans in an increasingly revolutionary period led to his imprisonment and exile. He made his peace with Cromwell and returned to England in 1651. When the monarchy was restored in 1660, Waller regained his seat in Parliament. Waller was one of the earliest poets to use the heroic couplet, a form that was to dominate English poetry for over a century.

Walt Whitman (1819–1892)   One of nine children, Whitman was born in Huntington, Long Island, in New York, and grew up in Brooklyn, where his father worked as a carpenter. At age eleven, after five years of public school, Whitman took a job as a printer's assistant. He learned the printing trade and, before his twentieth birthday, became editor of the *Long Islander,* a Huntington newspaper. He edited several newspapers in the New York area and one in New Orleans before leaving the newspaper business in 1848. He then lived with his parents, worked as a part-time carpenter, and began writing *Leaves of Grass,* which he first published at his own expense in 1855. After the Civil War (during which he was a devoted volunteer, ministering to the wounded), Whitman was fired from his job in the Department of the Interior by

Secretary James Harlan, who considered *Leaves of Grass* obscene. Soon, however, he was rehired in the attorney general's office, where he remained until 1874. In 1881, after many editions, *Leaves of Grass* finally found a publisher willing to print it uncensored. Translations were enthusiastically received in Europe, but Whitman remained relatively unappreciated in America, where it was only after his death that a large audience would come to admire his original and innovative expression of American individualism.

Richard Wilbur (b. 1921)   Son of a portrait artist, Wilbur was born in New York City, graduated from Amherst College in 1942, became staff sergeant in the U.S. Army during World War II, then earned an M.A. from Harvard in 1947. He taught English at Harvard, Wellesley, and Wesleyan University, and was named writer-in-residence at Smith College in 1977. Former Poet Laureate of the United States and winner of the Pulitzer Prize, National Book Award, and the Bollingen Translation Prize, Wilbur has distinguished himself, in his several volumes of poetry, by using established poetic forms and meters, mining new insights from common, tangible images. A translator of French plays by Molière and Racine, Wilbur was colyricist (with Lillian Hellman) of *Candide,* the 1957 Broadway musical based on Voltaire's satirical novel. *New and Collected Poems* appeared in 1988, *More Opposites* in 1991, and most recently, *The Catbird's Song: Prose Pieces 1963–1995* in 1997.

Tennessee Williams (1911–1983)   Thomas Lanier Williams was born in Columbus, Mississippi, but grew up in St. Louis, Missouri. His "lonely and miserable" childhood, as he characterized it, was in large part due to an unsympathetic father and to schoolmates who often taunted him because of his small size and lack of physical prowess. A year before he was to graduate from the University of Missouri, his father removed him from college and got him a job with the International Shoe Company, where he worked by day and wrote by night. Three years later, he suffered a nervous breakdown and, while recovering at his grandparents' home in Memphis, Tennessee, wrote his first play. With his grandparents' financial help, he attended the University of Iowa, and earned a B.A. in 1938. In 1939, on the basis of a compilation of four one-act plays called *American Blues* (published in 1948), Williams won a playwriting grant and recognition as a promising playwright. The promise was fulfilled in 1945 with *The Glass Menagerie.* This was followed two years later with the equally successful *A Streetcar Named Desire* (for which he won a Pulitzer Prize in 1948). From then until his death, Williams's reputation as a premier American dramatist grew with such plays as *Cat on a Hot Tin Roof* (1955), *Suddenly Last Summer* (1958), and *The Night of the Iguana* (1961). Williams also published six volumes of prose and three volumes of poetry.

William Carlos Williams (1883–1963)   Born in Rutherford, New Jersey, Williams graduated from the University of Pennsylvania (M.D., 1906), interned at hospitals in New York City for two years, studied pediatrics in Leipzig, then returned to practice medicine in his hometown. As a general practitioner, Williams found ample poetic inspiration in his patients, and scribbled down lines between appointments and on the way to house calls. His early collections include *The Tempers* (1913), *Kora in Hell: Improvisations* (1920), and *Sour Grapes* (1921). A stroke in the mid-1950s forced him to retire from his medical practice, but gave him more time to write. His many honors include the National Book Award (1950) and the Pulitzer Prize (1963). *The Williams Reader* was published in 1966.

August Wilson (b. 1945)   Wilson was born in a Pittsburgh ghetto known as the Hill where he attended public schools. Disillusioned by the pervasive racism of several schools, he dropped out at age sixteen and worked at menial jobs. He nevertheless pursued a literary career, reading widely in the local library, where he discovered and was encouraged in his own literary aspirations by the writers of the Harlem Renaissance and other African American writers. Drawn to the theater and inspired by the civil rights movement, in 1968 Wilson founded the Black Horizons Theatre in St. Paul, Minnesota. Wilson's first two plays failed to gain much attention, but his third, *Ma Rainey's Black Bottom* (1982), about a group of black musicians discussing their experiences in racist America, won him wide recognition as an important new dramatist and interpreter of the African American experience. His subsequent plays have made him one of America's most celebrated dramatists and have earned him numerous prizes, among them the Tony Award (1985), the New York Drama Critics Circle Award (1985), and the Pulitzer Prize for drama (1990). His other plays include *Fences* (1985), *Joe Turner's Come and Gone* (1988), *The Piano Lesson* (1987), and *Two Trains Running* (1990).

Virginia Woolf (1882–1941)   Born in London, where she spent most of her life, Woolf, because of her frail health and her father's Victorian attitudes about the proper role of women, received little formal education (none at the university level). Nevertheless, the advantages of an upper-class family (her father, Sir Leslie Stephen, was a distinguished scholar and man of letters who hired tutors for her) and an extraordinarily powerful and inquiring mind allowed Woolf to educate herself. She began keeping a regular diary in her early teens. After moderate success with her first novels, the publication of *To the Lighthouse* (1927) and *Orlando* (1929) established her as a major novelist. While Woolf's reputation rests primarily on her novels, which helped revolutionize fictional technique, she was also a distinguished literary and social critic. A strong supporter of women's rights, she expressed her views on the subject in a series of lectures published as *A Room of One's Own* (1929) and in a collection of essays, *Three Guineas* (1938). Her reputation grew with the publication of her letters and diaries following her suicide by drowning.

William Wordsworth (1770–1850)   Born in Cockermouth in the Lake District of England, Wordsworth was educated at Cambridge. During a summer tour in France in 1790, Wordsworth had an affair with Annette Vallon that resulted in the birth of a daughter. The tour also made of Wordsworth an ardent defender of the French Revolution of 1789 and kindled his sympathies for the plight of the common person. Wordsworth's acquaintance with Samuel Taylor Coleridge in 1795 began a close friendship that led to the collaborative publication of *Lyrical Ballads* in 1798. Wordsworth supplied a celebrated preface to the second edition in 1800, in which he announced himself a nature poet of pantheistic leanings, committed to democratic equality and the language of common people. He finished *The Prelude* in 1805, but it was not published until after his death. As he grew older, Wordsworth grew increasingly conservative and, while he continued to write prolifically, little that he wrote during the last decades of his life attained the heights of his earlier work. In 1843, he was appointed poet laureate.

Richard Wright (1908–1960)   Wright grew up in Memphis, Tennessee, where his sharecropper father moved the family after he was forced off the farm near Natchez, Mississippi, where Wright was born. When Wright was six, his father abandoned the family, leaving his mother to support Wright and his younger brother with whatever jobs she could find. While their mother worked, the boys shifted for themselves. When he was eight, Wright's mother enrolled him in grammar school, but she fell ill and was unable to work. Consequently Wright and his brother were placed in an orphanage; reunited, the family lived with relatives, and Wright was able to resume his education, graduating from high school as valedictorian in 1925. Wright left the South for Chicago in 1927, hoping, as he said, that "gradually and slowly I might learn who I was, what I might be." After working at odd jobs, his efforts at writing paid off when he received a job as publicity agent for the Federal Negro Theater. Wright joined the Communist party in 1932 and was a member of the Federal Writers' Project from 1935 to 1937. He published his first collection, *Uncle Tom's Children,* in 1938. About the same time, he began a novel about a poor and angry ghetto youth who accidentally murders the daughter of his white, millionaire employer. The novel, *Native Son* (1940), was published to much critical and popular acclaim and remains his best-known work. Unable to accept party discipline, Wright quit the Communist party in 1944, and in the following year published *Black Boy,* an autobiography of his early years. Discouraged with the racism of America, Wright soon moved his family to France, where he spent the remainder of his life writing and supporting the cause of African independence. His later works include the novels *The Outsider* (1953) and *The Long Dream* (1958), and the nonfiction works *Black Power* (1954) and *White Man, Listen!* (1957).

William Butler Yeats (1865–1939)   Yeats was born in Ireland and educated in both Ireland and London. Much of his poetry and many of his plays reflect his fascination with the history of Ireland, particularly the myths and legends of its ancient, pagan past, as well as his interest in the occult. As Yeats matured, he turned increasingly to contemporary subjects, expressing his nationalism in poems about the Irish struggle for independence from England. In 1891, he became one of the founders of an Irish literary society in London (the Rhymers' Club) and of another in Dublin the following year. Already a recognized poet, Yeats helped to establish the Irish National Theater in 1899; its first production was his play *The Countess Cathleen* (written in 1892). His contribution to Irish cultural and political nationalism led to his appointment as a senator when the Irish Free State was formed in 1922. Yeats's preeminence as a poet was recognized in 1923, when he received the Nobel Prize for literature. Among his works are *The Wanderings of Oisin and Other Poems* (1889), *The Wind among the Reeds* (1899), *The Green Helmet and Other Poems* (1910), *Responsibilities: Poems and a Play* (1914), *The Tower* (1928), and *Last Poems and Two Plays* (1939).

Yevgeney Yevtushenko (b. 1933)   Son of two geologists, Yevtushenko was born in Siberia. He attended Gorky Literary Institute from 1951 to 1954, and worked on a geological expedition, at the same time establishing himself as an influential Soviet poet. During the 1950s, his books were published regularly and he was allowed to travel abroad. In 1960, he gave readings in Europe and the United States, but was criticized by Russians for linking them with anti-Semitism in his poem "Babi Yar," the name of a ravine near Kiev where 96,000 Jews were killed by Nazis during World

War II. Although considering himself a "loyal revolutionary Soviet citizen," he elicited official disapproval by opposing the 1968 occupation of Czechoslovakia (a performance of his play *Bratsk Power Station* [1967] was cancelled as a result) and for sending a telegram to then-Premier Brezhnev expressing concern for Aleksandr Solzhenitsyn after his arrest in 1974. His works include *A Precocious Autobiography* (1963), *From Desire to Desire* (1976), *Fatal Half Measures: The Culture of Democracy in the Soviet Union* (1991), an analysis of recent Russian history, and *Don't Die Before You're Dead* (1995), an autobiographical novel.

Glossary of Literary Terms

Abstract language Language that describes ideas, concepts, or qualities, rather than particular or specific persons, places, or things. *Beauty, courage, love* are abstract terms, as opposed to such concrete terms as *man, stone, woman.* George Washington, the Rosetta Stone, and Helen of Troy are particular concrete terms. Characteristically, literature uses *concrete* language to animate *abstract* ideas and principles. When Robert Frost, in "Provide, Provide" (p. 142), describes the pain of impoverished and lonely old age, he doesn't speak of an old, no longer beautiful female. He writes:

> The witch that came (the withered hag)
> To wash the steps with pail and rag,
> Was once the beauty Abishag.

Alexandrine In poetry, a line containing six iambic feet (iambic hexameter). Alexander Pope, in "An Essay on Criticism" (p. 14), reveals his distaste for the forms in a couplet: "A needless Alexandrine ends the song, / That like a wounded snake, drags its slow length along." *See* Meter.

Allegory A narrative in verse or prose, in which abstract qualities (*death, pride, greed,* for example) are personified as characters. In Bernard Malamud's story "Idiots First" (p. 1223) Ginzburg is the personification of death.

Alliteration The repetition of the same consonant sounds, usually at the beginning of words in close proximity. The *w* sounds in these lines from Robert Frost's "Provide, Provide" (p. 142) alliterate: "The witch that came (the withered hag) / To wash the steps with pail and rag, / Was once the beauty Abishag."

Allusion A reference in a literary work to something outside the work, usually to some famous person, place, thing, event, or other literary work.

Ambiguity A phrase, statement, or situation that may be understood in two or more ways. In literature, ambiguity is used to enrich meaning or achieve irony by forcing readers to consider alternative possibilities. When the duke in Robert Browning's "My Last Duchess" (p. 132) says that he "gave commands; / Then all smiles stopped together. There she stands / As if alive," the reader cannot know exactly what those commands were or whether the last words refer to the commands (as a result of which she is no longer alive) or merely refer to the skill of the painter (the painting is extraordinarily lifelike).

Analogy A comparison that uses a known thing or concept to explain something unfamiliar. *See* Metaphor; Simile.

Anapest A three-syllable metrical foot consisting of two unaccented syllables followed by an accented syllable. *See* Meter.

Antagonist A character in a story, play, or narrative poem who stands in opposition to the hero (*see* Protagonist). The conflict between antagonist and protagonist often generates the action or plot of the story.

Antistrophe *See* Strophe.

Apostrophe   A direct address to a person who is absent, or to an abstract or inanimate entity. In one of his Holy Sonnets (p. 1263), John Donne admonishes: "Death, be not proud!" And Wordsworth speaks to a river in Wales: "How oft, in spirit, have I turned to thee, / O sylvan Wye! thou wanderer through the woods" (p. 127).

Archaism   The literary use of obsolete language. When Keats, in "Ode on a Grecian Urn" (p. 1265), writes: "with brede / Of marble men and maidens overwrought," he uses an archaic word for *braid* and intends an obsolete definition, "worked all over" (that is, "ornamented"), for *overwrought.*

Archetype   Themes, images, and narrative patterns that are universal and thus embody some enduring aspects of human experience. Some of these themes are the death and rebirth of the hero, the underground journey, and the search for the father.

Assonance   The repetition of vowel sounds in a line, stanza, or sentence. By using assonance that occurs at the end of words—*my, pie*—or a combination of assonance and consonance (that is, the repetition of final consonant sounds—*fish, wish*—poets create rhyme. But some poets, particularly modern poets, often use assonantal and consonantal off rhymes (*see* Near rhyme). W. H. Auden, in "Five Songs" (p. 724), writes:

> That night when joy began
> Our narrowest veins to flush,
> We waited for the flash
> Of morning's levelled gun.

Flush and *gun* are assonantal, *flush* and *flash* are consonantal (and, of course, alliterative).

Atmosphere   *See* Tone.

Aubade   A love song or lyric to be performed at sunrise. Richard Wilbur's comic "A Late Aubade" (p. 1019) is a modern example. Philip Larkin's "Aubade" (p. 1286) uses the form ironically in a somber contemplation of mortality.

Ballad   A narrative poem, originally of folk origin, usually focusing upon a climactic episode and told without comment. The most common ballad form consists of quatrains of alternating four- and three-stress iambic lines, with the second and fourth lines rhyming. Often, the ballad will employ a *refrain*—that is, the last line of each stanza will be identical or similar. "Edward" (p. 1256) and "Bonny Barbara Allan" (p. 993) are traditional ballads. Dudley Randall's "Ballad of Birmingham" (p. 450) is a twentieth-century example of the ballad tradition.

Blank verse   Lines of unrhymed iambic pentameter. Shakespeare's dramatic poetry is written principally in blank verse. *See* Meter.

Cacophony   Language that sounds harsh and discordant, sometimes used to reinforce the sense of the words. Consider the plosive *b, p,* and *t* sounds in the following lines from Shakespeare's Sonnet 129 (p. 998): "and till action, lust / Is perjured, murderous, bloody, full of blame, / Savage, extreme, rude, cruel, not to trust." *Compare* Euphony.

Caesura   A strong pause within a line of poetry. Note the caesuras indicated by a double vertical line (∥) in these lines from Robert Browning's "My Last Duchess" (p. 132):

> That's my last Duchess painted on the wall,
> Looking as if she were alive, ‖ I call
> That piece a wonder, now: ‖ Frà Pandolf's hands
> Worked busily a day, ‖ and there she stands.

Carpe diem   Latin, meaning "seize the day." A work, usually a lyric poem, in which the speaker calls the attention of the auditor (often a young woman) to the shortness of youth, and life, and then urges the auditor to enjoy life while there is time. Andrew Marvell's "To His Coy Mistress" (p. 1002) is among the best of the *carpe diem* tradition in English. The opening stanza of a famous Robert Herrick poem nicely illustrates *carpe diem* principles.

> Gather ye rosebuds while ye may,
> Old Time is still a-flying
> And this same flower that smiles today,
> Tomorrow will be dying.

Catharsis   A key concept in the *Poetics* of Aristotle that attempts to explain why representations of suffering and death in drama paradoxically leave the audience feeling relieved rather than depressed. According to Aristotle, the fall of a tragic hero arouses in the viewer feelings of "pity" and "terror"—pity because the hero is an individual of great moral worth, and terror because the viewer identifies with and, consequently, feels vulnerable to the hero's tragic fate. Ideally, the circumstances within the drama allow viewers to experience a catharsis that purges those feelings of pity and terror and leaves them emotionally purified.

Central intelligence   *See* Point of view.

Character   A person in a literary work, sometimes classified as either *flat* (quickly describable) or *round* (more developed, complex). *See* Protagonist *and* Antagonist.

Chorus   Originally, a group of masked dancers who chanted lyric hymns at religious festivals in ancient Greece. In the plays of Sophocles, the chorus, while circling around the altar to Dionysius, chants the odes that separate the episodes. These odes, in some respects, represented an audience's reaction to, and comment on, the action in the episodes. In Elizabethan drama, and even, on occasion, in modern drama, the chorus appears, usually as a single person who comments on the action.

Comedy   In drama, the representation of situations that are designed to delight and amuse, and which end happily. Comedy often deals with ordinary people in their human condition, while tragedy deals with the ideal and heroic and, until recently, embodied only the high born as tragic heroes. *Compare* Tragedy.

Conceit   A figure of speech that establishes an elaborate parallel between unlike things. The *Petrarchan conceit* (named for the fourteenth-century Italian writer of love lyrics) was often imitated by Elizabethan sonneteers until the device became so hackneyed that Shakespeare mocked the tendency in Sonnet 130 (p. 998):

> My mistress' eyes are nothing like the sun;
> Coral is far more red than her lips' red;
> If snow be white, why then her breasts are dun;
> If hairs be wires, black wires grow on her head.

The *metaphysical conceit* employs strange, even bizarre, comparisons to heighten the wit of the poem. Perhaps the most famous metaphysical conceit is John Donne's elaborate and extended parallel of a drawing compass to the souls of the couple in "A Valediction: Forbidding Mourning" (p. 1033).

Concrete language *See* Abstract language.

Conflict The struggle of a protagonist, or main character, with forces that threaten to destroy him or her. The struggle creates suspense and is usually resolved at the end of the narrative. The force opposing the main character may be either another person—the antagonist—(as in Frank O'Connor's "My Oedipus Complex," p. 90), or society (as in Harlan Ellison's "'Repent, Harlequin!' Said the Ticktockman," (p. 395), or natural forces (as in Bernard Malamud's "Idiots First," p. 1223). A fourth type of conflict reflects the struggle of opposing tendencies within an individual (as in Tolstoy's "The Death of Iván Ilých," p. 1165).

Connotation The associative and suggestive meanings of a word, in contrast to its literal or *denotative* meaning. One might speak of an *elected official,* a relatively neutral term without connotative implications. Others might call the same person a *politician,* a more negative term; still others might call him or her a *statesman,* a more laudatory term. *Compare* Denotation.

Consonance Repetition of the final consonant sounds in stressed syllables. In the following verse from W. H. Auden's "Five Songs" (p. 724), lines one and four illustrate consonance, as do lines two and three.

> That night when joy began
> Our narrowest veins to flush,
> We waited for the flash
> Of morning's levelled gun.

Couplet A pair of rhymed lines—for example, these from A. E. Housman's "Terence, This is Stupid Stuff" (p. 137).

> Why, if 'tis dancing you would be,
> There's brisker pipes than poetry.

Dactyl A three-syllable metrical foot consisting of an accented syllable followed by two unaccented syllables. *See* Meter.

Denotation The literal dictionary definition of a word, without associative and suggestive meanings. *See* Connotation.

Denouement The final revelations that occur after the main conflict is resolved; literally, the "untying" of the plot following the climax.

Deus ex machina Latin for "god from a machine." Difficulties were sometimes resolved in ancient Greek and Roman plays by a god, who was lowered to the stage by means of machinery. The term is now used to indicate the use of unconvincing or improbable coincidences to advance or resolve a plot.

Dialect A variety of a language distinguished by its pronunciation, vocabulary, rhetoric, and grammar. When used in dialogue, dialect reveals a character's membership in certain groups or communities.

Dialogue The exchange of words between characters in a drama or narrative.

Diction The choice of words in a work of literature, and hence, an element of style crucial to the work's effectiveness. The diction of a story told from the point of view of an inner-city child (as in Toni Cade Bambara's "The Lesson," p. 115) will differ markedly from a similar story told from the point of view of a mature and educated adult, like the narrator of Frank O'Connor's "My Oedipus Complex" (p. 90).

Didactic A term applied to works with the primary and avowed purpose of persuading the reader that some philosophical, religious, or moral doctrine is true.

Dimeter A line of poetry consisting of two metrical feet. *See* Meter.

Distance   The property that separates an author or a narrator from the actions of the characters he or she creates, thus allowing a disinterested, or aloof, narration of events. Similarly, distance allows the reader or audience to view the characters and events in a narrative dispassionately.

Dramatic irony   *See* Irony.

Dramatic monologue   A type of poem in which the speaker addresses another person (or persons) whose presence is known only from the speaker's words. During the course of the monologue, the speaker (often unintentionally) reveals his or her own character. Such poems are dramatic because the speaker interacts with another character at a specific time and place; they are monologues because the entire poem is uttered by the speaker. Robert Browning's "My Last Duchess" (p. 132), Matthew Arnold's "Dover Beach" (p. 1006), and T. S. Eliot's "The Love Song of J. Alfred Prufrock" (p. 719) are dramatic monologues.

Elegy   Usually, a poem lamenting the death of a particular person, but often used to describe meditative poems on the subject of human mortality. A. E. Housman's "To an Athlete Dying Young" (p. 1269) and Theodore Roethke's "Elegy for Jane" (p. 1284) are elegies.

End-rhyme   *See* Rhyme.

End-stopped line   A line of verse that embodies a complete logical and grammatical unit. A line of verse that does not constitute a complete syntactic unit is called *run-on*. For example, in the opening lines of Robert Browning's "My Last Duchess" (p. 132): "That's my last Duchess painted on the wall, / Looking as if she were alive. I call / That piece a wonder, now: . . . ," The opening line is end-stopped, while the second line is run-on because the direct object of *call* runs on to the third line.

English sonnet   Also called *Shakespearean sonnet. See* Sonnet.

Enjambment   The use of run-on lines. *See* End-stopped line.

Epigraph   In literature, a short quotation or observation related to the theme and placed at the head of the work. T. S. Eliot's "The Love Song of J. Alfred Prufrock" (p. 719) has an epigraph, as does August Wilson's *Two Trains Running* (p. 565).

Epiphany   In literature, a showing forth, or sudden manifestation. James Joyce used the term to indicate a sudden illumination that enables a character (and, presumably, the reader) to understand his situation. The narrator of Joyce's "Araby" (p. 81) experiences an epiphany toward the end of the story, as does Iván Ilých" (p. 1165).

Epode   *See* Strophe.

Euphony   Language embodying sounds pleasing to the ear. *Compare* Cacophony.

Exposition   Information supplied to readers and audiences that enables them to understand narrative action. Often, exposition establishes what has occurred before the narrative begins or informs the audience about relationships among principal characters. The absence of exposition from some modern literature, particularly modern drama, contributes to the unsettling feelings sometimes experienced by the audience.

Farce   A type of comedy, usually satiric, that relies on exaggerated character types, ridiculous situations, and, often, horseplay.

Feminine rhyme   A two-syllable rhyme in which the second syllable is unstressed, as in the second and fourth lines of these verses from Edwin Arlington Robinson's "Miniver Cheevy" (p. 440):

> Miniver Cheevy, child of scorn,
> Grew lean while he assailed the seasons;
> He wept that he was ever born,
> And he had reasons.

Figurative language   A general term covering the many ways in which language is used nonliterally. *See* Hyperbole, Irony, Metaphor, Metonymy, Paradox, Simile, Symbol, Synecdoche, Understatement.

First-person narrator   *See* Point of view.

Foot   *See* Meter.

Free verse   Poetry, usually unrhymed, that does not adhere to the metrical regularity of traditional verse. Although free verse is not metrically regular, it is nonetheless clearly more rhythmic than prose and makes use of other aspects of poetic discourse to achieve its effects.

Heroic couplet   Iambic pentameter lines that rhyme *aa, bb, cc,* and so on. Usually, heroic couplets are *closed*—that is, the couplet's end coincides with a major syntactic unit so that the line is end-stopped. These lines from Alexander Pope's "Essay on Man" illustrate the form: "And, spite of pride, in erring reason's spite, / One truth is clear; Whatever IS, is RIGHT."

Hexameter   A line of verse consisting of six metrical feet. *See* Meter.

Hubris   In Greek tragedy, arrogance resulting from excessive pride. Oedipus, in Sophocles' *Oedipus Rex* (p. 166), is guilty of hubris.

Hyperbole   Figurative language that embodies overstatement or exaggeration. The boast of the speaker in Robert Burns's "A Red, Red Rose" (p. 1004) is hyperbolic: "And I will luve thee still, my dear, / Till a' the seas gang dry."

Iamb   A metrical foot consisting of an unstressed syllable followed by a stressed syllable. *See* Meter.

Imagery   Language that embodies an appeal to a physical sense, usually sight, although the words may invoke sound, smell, taste, and touch as well. The term is often applied to all figurative language. *Images* illustrate a concept, thing, or process by appealing to the senses.

Internal rhyme   *See* Rhyme.

Irony   Figurative language in which the intended meaning differs from the literal meaning. *Verbal irony* includes overstatement (hyperbole), understatement, and opposite statement. The following lines from Robert Burns's "A Red, Red Rose" (p. 1004) embody overstatement:

> As fair as thou, my bonnie lass,
> So deep in luve am I;
> And I will luve thee still, my dear,
> Till a' the seas gang dry.

These lines from Andrew Marvell's "To His Coy Mistress" (p. 1002) understate: "The grave's a fine and private place, / but none, I think, do there embrace." W. H. Auden's ironic conclusion to "The Unknown Citizen" (p. 448) reveals opposite statement: "Was he free? Was he happy? The question is absurd: / Had anything been wrong, we should certainly have heard." *Dramatic irony* occurs when a reader or audience knows things a character does not and, consequently, hears things differently. For example, in Shakespeare's *Othello* (p. 1041), the audience knows that Iago is Othello's enemy, but Othello doesn't. Hence, the audience's understanding of Iago's speeches to Othello differs markedly from Othello's.

Italian sonnet   Also called *Petrarchan sonnet. See* Sonnet.

Lyric   Originally, a song accompanied by lyre music. Now, a relatively short poem expressing the thought or feeling of a single speaker. Almost all the nondramatic poetry in this anthology is lyric poetry.

Metaphor   A figurative expression consisting of two elements in which one element is provided with special attributes by being equated with a second, unlike element. In Theodore Roethke's "Elegy for Jane" (p. 1284), for example, the speaker addresses his dead student: "If only I could nudge you from this sleep, / My maimed darling, my skittery pigeon." Here, Jane is characterized metaphorically as a "skittery pigeon," and all the reader's experience of a nervous pigeon's movement becomes attached to Jane. *See* Simile.

Meter   Refers to recurrent patterns of accented and unaccented syllables in verse. A metrical unit is called a *foot,* and there are four basic accented patterns. An *iamb,* or *iambic foot,* consists of an unaccented syllable followed by an accented syllable (bĕfóre, tŏdáy). A *trochee,* or *trochaic foot,* consists of an accented syllable followed by an unaccented syllable (fúnnў, phántŏm). An *anapest,* or *anapestic foot,* consists of two unaccented syllables followed by an accented syllable (in the line "If ĕv́ ‖ erўthĭng háp ‖ pn̆s thăt cán't ‖ bĕ dóne," the second and third metrical feet are anapests). A *dactyl,* or *dactyllic foot,* consists of a stressed syllable followed by two unstressed syllables (sýllăblĕ, métrĭcăl). One common variant, consisting of two stressed syllables, is called a *spondee,* or *spondaic foot* (dáybŕeak, moónshíne).

Lines are classified according to the number of metrical feet they contain.

one foot	monometer
two feet	dimeter
three feet	trimeter
four feet	tetrameter
five feet	pentameter
six feet	hexameter (An iambic hexameter line is an *Alexandrine.*)

Here are some examples of various metrical patterns:

Tŏ eách ‖ hĭs sŭff ‖ erĭngs: áll ‖ aře mén,	*iambic tetrameter*
Cŏndemńed ‖ ăl[ké ‖ tŏ groán;	*iambic trimeter*
Ońce ŭp ‖ ón ă ‖ mídnĭght ‖ dréarў, ‖ whíle Ĭ ‖	
póndeřed ‖ wéak ănd ‖ wéarў	*trochaic octameter*
Thĕ Ăssýr ‖ iăn came dówn ‖ likĕ ă wólf ‖ ŏn the fóld	*anapestic tetrameter*
Iš thís ‖ thĕ rég ‖ iŏn, thís ‖ thĕ soíl, ‖ thĕ clíme,	*iambic pentameter*
Fóllŏw ĭt ‖ úttĕrlў,	*dactyllic dimeter*
Hópe bĕ ‖ yónd hópe:	*dimeter line—trochee and spondee*

Metonymy   A figure of speech in which a word stands for a closely related idea. In the expression "The pen is mightier than the sword," *pen* and *sword* are metonyms for written ideas and physical force.

Monologue   A long, uninterrupted speech by a character.

Mood   The atmosphere or general feeling of a work.

Muses   Nine goddesses, the daughters of Zeus and Mnemosyne (memory), who preside over various humanities. Although there are some variations, generally they may be assigned as follows: Calliope, epic poetry; Clio, history; Erato, lyric poetry: Euterpe, music; Melpomene, tragedy; Polyhymnia, sacred poetry; Terpsichore, dance; Thalia, comedy; and Urania, astronomy.

Narrator   The speaker of the story, but not to be confused with the author. For kinds of narrators, *see* Point of view.

Near rhyme   Also called *off rhyme, slant rhyme,* or *oblique rhyme.* Usually the occurrence of consonance where rhyme is expected, as in *pearl, alcohol* or *heaven, given. See* Rhyme.

Octave   An eight-line stanza. More often, the opening eight-line section of an Italian sonnet, rhymed *abbaabba,* followed by the sestet that concludes the poem. *See* Sonnet.

Ode   Usually, a long, serious poem on exalted subjects, often in the form of an address. Keats's "Ode on a Grecian Urn" (p. 1265) is representative. In Greek dramatic poetry, odes consisting of three parts, the *strophe,* the *antistrophe,* and the *epode,* were sung by the chorus between the episodes of the play. *See* Strophe.

Off rhyme   *See* Near rhyme.

Omniscient narrator   *See* Point of view.

Onomatopoeia   Language that sounds like what it means. Words like *buzz, bark,* and *hiss* are onomatopoetic. Also, sound patterns that reinforce the meaning may be designated onomatopoetic. Alexander Pope illustrates such onomatopoeia in this passage from "An Essay on Criticism":

> 'Tis not enough no harshness gives offense,
> The sound must seem an echo to the sense:
> Soft is the strain when Zephyr gently blows,
> And the smooth stream in smoother numbers flows;
> But when loud surges lash the sounding shore,
> The hoarse, rough verse should like the torrent roar:
> When Ajax strives some rock's vast weight to throw,
> The line too labors, and the words move slow;
> Not so, when swift Camilla scours the plain,
> Flies o'er th' unbending corn, and skims along the main.

Opposite statement   *See* Irony.

Ottava rima   An eight-line, iambic pentameter stanza rhymed *abababcc.* Originating with the Italian poet Boccaccio, the form was made popular in English poetry by Milton, Keats, and Byron, among others.

Oxymoron   Literally, "acutely silly." A figure of speech in which contradictory ideas are combined to create a condensed paradox: *thunderous silence, sweet sorrow, wise fool.*

Paean   In classical Greek drama, a hymn of praise, usually honoring Apollo. Now, any lyric that joyously celebrates its subject.

Paradox   A statement that seems self-contradictory or absurd but is, somehow, valid. The conclusion of Donne's "Death, Be Not Proud" (p. 1263) illustrates: "One short sleep past, we wake eternally / And death shall be no more; Death, thou shalt die." In Holy Sonnet 14, Donne, speaking of his relationship with God, writes: "Take me to You, imprison me, for I, / Except You enthrall me, never shall be free, / Nor ever chaste, except You ravish me."

Parody An imitation of a work using the original's form or content as a model, meant to criticize or create a humorous effect.

Pastoral *Pastor* is Latin for "shepherd," and the pastoral is a poetic form invented by ancient Roman writers that deals with the complexities of the human condition as if they exist in a world peopled by idealized rustic shepherds. Pastoral poetry suggests that country life is superior to urban life. In the hands of such English poets as Marlowe and Milton, the pastoral embodies highly conventionalized and artificial language and situations. Christopher Marlowe's "The Passionate Shepherd to His Love" (p. 995) is a famous example, as is Sir Walter Ralegh's mocking response, "The Nymph's Reply to the Shepherd" (p. 996).

Pentameter A line containing five metrical feet. *See* Meter.

Persona Literally, "actor's mask." The term is applied to a first-person narrator in fiction or poetry. The persona's views may differ from the author's.

Personification The attribution of human qualities to nonhuman things, such as animals, aspects of nature, or even ideas and processes. When Donne exclaims in "Death, Be Not Proud" (p. 1263), "Death, thou shalt die," he uses personification, as does Edmund Waller when the speaker of "Go, Lovely Rose!" (p. 1002) says:

> Go, lovely rose!
> Tell her that wastes her time and me
>   That now she knows,
> When I resemble her to thee,
>   How sweet and fair she seems to be.

Petrarchan sonnet Also called *Italian sonnet. See* Sonnet.

Plot A series of actions in a story or drama that bear a significant relationship to each other. E. M. Forster illuminates the definition: "'The King died, and then the Queen died,' is a story. 'The King died, and then the Queen died of grief,' is a plot."

Poetic license Variation from standard word order to satisfy the demands of rhyme and meter.

Point of view The person or intelligence a writer of fiction creates to tell the story to the reader. The major techniques are:

First person, where the story is told by someone, often, though not necessarily, the principal character, who identifies himself or herself as "I" as in James Joyce's "Araby" (p. 81).

Third person, where the story is told by someone (not identified as "I") who is not a participant in the action and who refers to the characters by name or as "he," "she," and "they" as in Harlan Ellison's "'Repent, Harlequin!' Said the Ticktockman" (p. 395).

Omniscient, a variation on the third person, where the narrator knows everything about the characters and events, can move about in time and place as well as from character to character at will, and can, whenever he or she wishes, enter the mind of any character, as in Tolstoy's "The Death of Iván Ilých" (p. 1165).

Central intelligence, another variation on the third person, where narrative elements are limited to what a single character sees, thinks, and hears as in Edna O'Brien's "Sin," p. 967.

See also Unreliable narrator.

Prosody The study of the elements of versification, such as *rhyme, meter, stanzaic patterns,* and so on.

Protagonist Originally, the first actor in a Greek drama. In Greek, *agon* means "contest." Hence, the protagonist is the hero, the main character in a narrative, in conflict either with his or her situation or with another character. *See* Antagonist.

Quatrain A four-line stanza.

Refrain The repetition within a poem of a group of words, often at the end of ballad stanzas.

Rhyme The repetition of the final stressed vowel sound and any sounds following (*cat, rat; debate, relate; pelican, belly can*) produces perfect rhyme. When the last stressed syllable rhymes, the rhyme is called masculine (*cat, rat*). Two-syllable rhymes with unstressed last syllables are called feminine (*ending, bending*). When rhyming words appear at the end of lines, the poem is *end-rhymed*. When rhyming words appear within one line, the line contains *internal rhyme*. When the correspondence in sounds is imperfect (*heaven, given; began, gun*) *off rhyme, slant rhyme,* or *near rhyme* is produced.

Rhythm The quality created by the relationship between stressed and unstressed syllables. A regular pattern of alternation between stressed and unstressed syllables produces *meter.* Irregular alternation of stressed and unstressed syllables produces *free verse.* Compare the rhythm of the following verses from Robert Frost's "Stopping by Woods on a Snowy Evening" (p. 1275) and Walt Whitman's "Out of the Cradle Endlessly Rocking":

> Whose woods these are I think I know.
> His house is in the village though;
> He will not see me stopping here
> To watch his woods fill up with snow.

> Out of the cradle endlessly rocking,
> Out of the mocking-bird's throat, the musical shuttle,
> Out of the Ninth-month midnight,
> Over the sterile sands and the fields beyond, where the child leaving his bed
>   wander'd alone, bareheaded, barefoot,
> Down from the shower'd halo.

Run-on line *See* End-stopped line.

Satire Writing in a comic mode that holds a subject up to scorn and ridicule, often with the purpose of correcting human vice and folly. Harlan Ellison's "'Repent, Harlequin!' Said the Ticktockman" (p. 395) satirizes a society obsessed with time and order.

Scansion The analysis of patterns of stressed and unstressed syllables in order to establish the metrical or rhythmical pattern of a poem.

Sestet The six-line resolution of a Petrarchan sonnet. *See* Sonnet.

Setting The place where a story occurs. Often the setting contributes significantly to the story; for example, the tawdry gloom at the fair in James Joyce's "Araby" (p. 81) destroys the narrator's expectations.

Shakespearean sonnet Also called *English sonnet. See* Sonnet.

Simile Similar to metaphor, the simile is a comparison of unlike things introduced by the words *like* or *as.* Robert Burns, in "A Red, Red Rose" (p. 1004), for example, exclaims, "O My Luve's like a red, red rose," and Shakespeare mocks extravagant similes when he admits in Sonnet 130, "My mistress' eyes are nothing like the sun" (p. 998).

Slant rhyme   *See* Rhyme.

Soliloquy   A dramatic convention in which an actor, alone on the stage, speaks his or her thoughts aloud. Iago's speech that closes Act I of Shakespeare's *Othello* (p. 1041) is a soliloquy, as is Othello's speech in Act III, Scene 3, lines 258–78.

Sonnet   A lyric poem of fourteen lines, usually of iambic pentameter. The two major types are the Petrarchan (or Italian) and Shakespearean (or English). The Petrarchan sonnet is divided into an octave (the first eight lines, rhymed *abbaabba*) and sestet (the final six lines, usually rhymed *cdecde* or *cdcdcd*). The Shakespearean sonnet consists of three quatrains and a concluding couplet, rhymed *abab cdcd efef gg*. In general, the sonnet establishes some issue in the octave or three quatrains and then resolves it in the sestet or final couplet. Robert Frost's "Design" (p. 1276) is an Italian sonnet; several Shakespearean sonnets appear in the text.

Spondee   A metrical foot consisting of two stressed syllables, usually a variation within a metrical line. *See* Meter.

Stanza   The grouping of a fixed number of verse lines in a recurring metrical and rhyme pattern. Keats's "Ode on a Grecian Urn" (p. 1265), for example, employs ten-line stanzas rhymed *ababcdecde*.

Stream-of-consciousness technique   The narrative technique that attempts to reproduce the full and uninterrupted flow of a character's mental process, in which ideas, memories, and sense impressions may intermingle without logical transitions. Writers using this technique sometimes abandon conventional rules of syntax and punctuation.

Strophe   In Greek tragedy, the unit of verse the chorus chanted as it moved to the left in a dance rhythm. The chorus sang the *antistrophe* as it moved to the right and the *epode* while standing still.

Style   The way an author expresses his or her matter. Style embodies, and depends upon, all the choices an author makes—the diction, syntax, figurative language, and sound patterns of the piece.

Subplot   A second plot, usually involving minor characters. The subplot is subordinate to the principal plot, but often is resolved by events that figure in the main plot. For example, Iago's manipulation of Roderigo in Shakespeare's *Othello* (p. 1041) is a subplot that enters the main plot and figures prominently in the play's climax.

Symbol   An object, an action, or a person that represents more than itself. In Stephen Crane's "The Bride Comes to Yellow Sky" (p. 72), Scratchy represents the old mythic West made obsolete by the encroachment of Eastern values. The urn in Keats's "Ode on a Grecian Urn" (p. 1265) symbolizes the cold immortality of art. In both of these, the symbolism arises from the *context*. *Public* symbols, in contrast to these *contextual symbols,* are objects, actions, or persons that history, myth, or legend has invested with meaning—the cross, Helen of Troy, a national flag.

Synecdoche   A figure of speech in which a part is used to signify the whole. In "Elegy Written in a Country Churchyard," Gray writes of "Some heart once pregnant with celestial fire; / Hands that the rod of empire might have swayed." That heart, and those hands, of course, refer to whole persons who are figuratively represented by significant parts.

Synesthesia   An image that uses a second sensory impression to modify the primary sense impression. When one speaks of a "cool green," for example, the primary *vi-*

sual evocation of green is combined with the *tactile* sensation of coolness. Keats, in "Ode to a Nightingale," asks for a drink of wine "Tasting of Flora and the country green, / Dance, and Provençal song, and sunburnt mirth!" Here, the *taste* of wine is synesthetically extended to the sight of flowers and meadows, the movement of dance, the sound of song, and the heat of the sun.

Tetrameter   A verse line containing four metrical feet. *See* Meter.

Theme   The abstract moral proposition that a literary work advances through the concrete elements of character, action, and setting. The theme of Harlan Ellison's "'Repent, Harlequin!' Said the Ticktockman" (p. 395), in which an ordinary person defies an oppressive system, might be that to struggle against dehumanizing authority is obligatory.

Third-person narrator   A voice telling a story who refers to characters by name or as "he," "she," or "they." *See* Point of view.

Tone   The attitude embodied in the language a writer chooses. The tone of a work might be sad, joyful, ironic, solemn, playful. Compare, for example, the somber tone of Matthew Arnold's "Dover Beach" (p. 1006) with the comic tone of Anthony Hecht's "The Dover Bitch" (p. 1020).

Tragedy   The dramatic representation of serious and important actions that culminate in catastrophe for the protagonist, or chief actor, in the play. Aristotle saw tragedy as the fall of a noble figure from a high position and happiness to defeat and misery as a result of *hamartia,* some misjudgment or frailty of character. *Compare* Comedy.

Trimeter   A verse line consisting of three metrical feet. *See* Meter.

Triplet   A sequence of three verse lines that rhyme.

Trochee   A metrical foot consisting of a stressed syllable followed by an unstressed syllable. *See* Meter.

Understatement   A figure of speech that represents something as less important than it really is, hence, a form of irony. When in Robert Browning's "My Last Duchess" (p. 132) the duke asserts ". . . This grew; I gave commands; / Then all smiles stopped together . . . ," the words ironically understate what was likely an order for his wife's execution.

Unreliable narrator   The speaker or voice of a work who is not able to accurately or objectively report events, as in Stephanie Vaughn's "Other Women" (p. 979).

Verse   A term to describe a stanza of a poem or, more generally, used interchangeably with the term *poetry.*

Villanelle   A French verse form of nineteen lines (of any length) divided into six stanzas—five tercets and a final quatrain—employing two rhymes and two refrains. The refrains consist of lines one (repeated as lines six, twelve, and eighteen) and three (repeated as lines nine, fifteen, and nineteen). Dylan Thomas's "Do Not Go Gentle into That Good Night" (p. 1285) and Catherine Davis's response "After a Time" (p. 1288) are villanelles.

ACKNOWLEDGMENTS

Chinua Achebe. "Marriage is a Private Affair" from *Girls at War and Other Stories* by Chinua Achebe. Copyright © 1972, 1973 by Chinua Achebe. Used by permission of Doubleday, a division of Bantam Doubleday Dell Publishing Group, Inc.

Woody Allen. "Death Knocks" from *Getting Even* by Woody Allen. Copyright © 1968 by Woody Allen. Reprinted by permission of Random House, Inc.

Catherine Anderson. "Womanhood" from *Working Class* by Catherine Anderson. Reprinted with permission of the author.

Anonymous. "Edward," "Bonny Barbara Allan" from *The Earliest English Poems* translated by Michael Alexander. Copyright © 1966, 1977 Michael Alexander. Penguin Classics, Second edition, 1977. Reprinted by permission of Penguin Books Ltd.

W.H. Auden. "Five Songs," "Musée des Beaux Arts," and "The Unknown Citizen" from *W.H. Auden: Collected Poems by W.H. Auden,* edited by Edward Mendelson. Copyright © 1940; renewed 1968 by W.H. Auden. Reprinted by permission of Random House, Inc. and Faber and Faber Ltd.

James Baldwin. "Rage" from *Notes of a Native Son* by James Baldwin. Copyright © 1955, renewed 1983 by James Baldwin. Reprinted by permission of Beacon Press, Boston.

Toni Cade Bambara. "The Lesson" from *Gorilla, My Love* by Toni Cade Bambara. Copyright © 1972 by Toni Cade Bambara. Reprinted by permission of Random House, Inc.

Carol Berge. "Position." First appeared in *Yowl* magazine, edited by George Montgomery, in 1964; then in the book *Poems Made of Skin,* edited by Nelson Ball, Weed/Flower Press, Toronto, Canada, 1968. It was then included in the anthology *Mountain Moving Day,* edited by Elaine Gill, Crossing Press, Trumansburg, New York. Copyright © 1966 Carol Berge. Reprinted with permission of the author.

Richard Bernstein. "France Jails 2 in Odd Case of Espionage." *The New York Times,* May 11, 1986. Copyright © 1986 by The New York Times Co. Reprinted by permission.

Elizabeth Bishop. "One Art" from *The Complete Poems 1927–1979* by Elizabeth Bishop. Copyright © 1979, 1983 by Alice Helen Methfessel. Reprinted by permission of Farrar, Straus & Giroux, Inc.

Bertolt Brecht. "War has been given a bad name" from *Bertolt Brecht: Poems 1913–1956* by Bertolt Brecht and translated by John Willett (London: Methuen, 1976). Reprinted with permission of Routledge, Inc. and Random House UK Ltd.

Edwin Brock. "Five ways to kill a man." Copyright © Edwin Brock. Reprinted by permission of the author.

Charles Bukowski. "for marilyn m." from *Burning in Water Drowning in Flame: Selected Poems 1955–1973.* Copyright © 1974 by Charles Bukowski. Reprinted with the permission of Black Sparrow Press.

Marianne Burke, "Funeral Home" from *The New Yorker,* December 23, 1991. Reprinted with the permission of *The New Yorker*.

Robert Olen Butler. "Preparation" from *A Good Scent from a Strange Mountain* by Robert Olen Butler. Copyright © 1992 by Robert Olen Butler. Reprinted by permission of Henry Holt & Co., Inc.

Raymond Carver. "What We Talk About When We Talk About Love" from *What We Talk About When We Talk About Love* by Raymond Carver. Copyright © 1981 by Raymond Carver. Reprinted by permission of Alfred A. Knopf, Inc.

Alice Childress. "Wine in the Wilderness." Copyright © 1969 by Dramatists Play Service. Used by permission of Flora Roberts, Inc.

Kate Chopin. "The Storm" from *The Complete Works of Kate Chopin,* edited by Per Seyersted. Copyright © 1969 by Louisiana State University Press. Reprinted by permission of Louisiana State University Press.

Sandra Cisneros. "My Wicked Wicked Ways" from *My Wicked Wicked Ways.* Copyright © 1987 by Sandra Cisneros. Published by Third Woman Press and in hardcover by Alfred A. Knopf, Inc. Reprinted by permission of Third Woman Press and Susan Bergholz Literary Services, New York. All rights reserved. "The House on Mango Street," from *The House on Mango Street.* Copyright © 1984 by Sandra Cisneros. Published by Vintage Books, a division of Random House, Inc., New York and in hardcover by Alfred A. Knopf, Inc. in 1994. Reprinted by permission of Susan Bergholz Literary Services, New York. All rights reserved.

Lucille Clifton. "There is a girl inside." Now published in *good woman: poems and a memoir 1969–1980* by Boa Editions Ltd. Reprinted by permission of Curtis Brown, Ltd.

Wendy Cope. "Lonely Hearts" from *Making Cocoa for Kingsley Amis* by Wendy Cope. Reprinted by permission of Faber and Faber Ltd.

Victor Hernández Cruz. "Today Is a Day of Great Joy" from *Snaps* by Victor Hernández Cruz. Copyright © 1968, 1969 by Victor Hernández Cruz. Reprinted by permission of Random House, Inc.

E.E. Cummings. "when serpents bargain for the right to squirm," "If everything happens that can't be done," "nobody loses all the time," "the Cambridge ladies who live in furnished souls," and "Oh sweet spontaneous" from *Complete Poems: 1904–1962* by E.E. Cummings. Edited by George J. Firmage. Copyright 1923, 1925, 1926, 1931, 1935, 1938, 1939, 1940, 1944, 1945, 1946, 1947, 1948, 1949, 1950, 1951, 1952, 1953, 1954, © 1955, 1956, 1957, 1958, 1959, 1960, 1961, 1962, 1963, 1966, 1967, 1968, 1972, 1973, 1974, 1975, 1976, 1977, 1978, 1979, 1980, 1981, 1982, 1983, 1984, 1985, 1986, 1987, 1988, 1989, 1990, 1991 by the Trustees for the E.E. Cummings Trust. Copyright © 1973, 1976, 1978, 1979, 1981, 1983, 1985, 1991 by George James Firmage. Reprinted by permission of Liveright Publishing Corporation.

Catherine Davis. "After a Time." Reprinted by permission of the author.

Emily Dickinson. "I felt a Funeral, in my Brain," "Much Madness is divinest Sense," "She rose to His Requirement," "What Soft Cherubic Creatures," "Mine Enemy is growing old," "After great pain, a formal feeling comes," "I heard a Fly buzz—when I died," and "Apparently with no surprise" from *The Complete Poems of Emily Dickinson,* Thomas H. Johnson, ed., Cambridge, Mass.: The Belknap Press of Harvard University Press. Copyright © 1951, 1955, 1979, 1983 by the President and Fellows of Harvard College. Reprinted by permission of the publishers and the Trustees of Amherst College.

Joan Didion. "On Morality" from *Slouching Towards Bethlehem* by Joan Didion. Copyright © 1966, 1968 by Joan Didion. Reprinted by permission of Farrar, Straus & Giroux, Inc.

Lars Eighner. "On Dumpster Diving" from *Travels with Lizbeth: Three Years on the Road and on the Street* by Lars Eighner. Copyright © 1993 by Lars Eighner. Reprinted by permission of St. Martin's Press Incorporated.

T.S. Eliot. "The Love Song of J. Alfred Prufrock" from *Collected Poems: 1909–1962.* Reprinted by permission of Harcourt Brace & Co. and Faber and Faber Ltd.

Harlan Ellison. " 'Repent Harlequin!' said the Ticktockman." Copyright © 1965 by Harlan Ellison. Renewed copyright © 1993 by Harlan Ellison. Reprinted by arrangement with, and permission of, the Author and the Author's agent, Richard Curtis Associates, Inc., New York. All rights reserved.

Louise Erdrich. "The Red Convertible" from *Love Medicine: New and Expanded Version* by Louise Erdrich. Copyright © 1984, 1993 by Louise Erdrich. Reprinted by permission of Henry Holt & Co., Inc.

William Faulkner. "A Rose for Emily" from *Collected Stories of William Faulkner* by William Faulkner. Copyright © 1930; renewed 1958 by William Faulkner. Reprinted by permission of Random House, Inc.

James Fenton. "God, A Poem" from *Children in Exile: Poems 1968–1984* (1983). Copyright © James Fenton. Reprinted by permission of Sterling Lord Literistic, Inc.

Lawrence Ferlinghetti. "Constantly Risking Absurdity" and "In Goya's Greatest Scenes" from *A Coney Island of the Mind.* Copyright © 1958 by Lawrence Ferlinghetti. Reprinted by permission of New Directions Publishing Corp.

Harvey Fierstein. "On Tidy Endings" from *Safe Sex* by Harvey Fierstein. Copyright © 1987 by Harvey Fierstein. Reprinted with the permission of Scribner, a division of Simon & Schuster.

Donald Finkel. "The Great Wave" from *Selected Shorter Poems* by Donald Finkel. Copyright © 1987 by Donald Finkel. Used by permission of the author.

Carolyn Forché. "The Colonel" from *The Country Between Us* by Carolyn Forché. Copyright © 1981 by Carolyn Forché. Originally appeared in *Women's International Resource Exchange.* Reprinted by permission of HarperCollins Publishers Inc.

Robert Francis. "Pitcher" from *The Orb Weaver.* Copyright © 1960 by Robert Francis. Reprinted by permission of University Press of New England.

Robert Frost. "Departmental," "Nothing gold can stay," "The Silken Tent," "Fire and Ice," "Stopping by Woods On A Snowy Evening," "After Applepicking," "Provide, Provide," "Birches," "Out, Out," and "Design" from *The Poetry of Robert Frost* edited by Edward Connery Lathem. Copyright © 1942 by Robert Frost. Copyright © 1970 by Lesley Frost Ballantine. Copyright © 1969 by Henry Holt and Company, Inc. Reprinted by permission of Henry Holt and Company, Inc.

Athol Fugard. "Harold and the Boys" from *Master Harold . . . and the Boys* by Athol Fugard. Copyright © 1982 by Athol Fugard. Reprinted by permission of Alfred A. Knopf, Inc.

Williard Gaylin. "What's So Special About Being Human?" from *Adam and Eve and Pinocchio* by Willard Gaylin. Copyright © 1990 by Willard Gaylin. Used by permission of Viking Penguin, a division of Penguin Books USA Inc.

Allen Ginsberg. "To Aunt Rose" from *Collected Poems 1947–1980* by Allen Ginsberg. Copyright © 1958 by Allen Ginsberg, copyright renewed. Reprinted by permission of HarperCollins Publishers, Inc. "Cezanne's Ports" from *Collected Poems 1947–1980* by Allen Ginsberg. Copyright © 1984 by Allen Ginsberg. Reprinted by permission of HarperCollins Publishers, Inc.

Nikki Giovanni. "Dreams" from *The Women and the Men* by Nikki Giovanni. Copyright © 1970, 74, 75 by Nikki Giovanni. Reprinted by permission of William Morrow & Company, Inc.

Susan Glaspell. "Trifles" from *Plays* by Susan Glaspell. Copyright © 1951 by Walter H. Baker Company. Reprinted by permission of Baker's Plays, Boston, MA 02111.

Thom Gunn. "Memory Unsettled" from *The Man with Night Sweats* by Thom Gunn. Copyright © 1994 by Thom Gunn. Reprinted by permission of Farrar, Straus & Giroux, Inc. and Faber and Faber Ltd.

Robert Hayden. "Those Winter Sundays" from *Angle of Ascent: New and Selected Poems* by Robert Hayden. Copyright © 1966 by Robert Hayden. Reprinted by permission of Liveright Publishing Corporation.

Bessie Head. "Looking for a Rain God" from *The Collector of Treasures* by Bessie Head. First published in Heinemann's African Writers Series. Copyright © 1977 The Estate of Bessie Head. Reprinted by permission of John Johnson (Authors' Agent) Limited and Heinemann Publishers Oxford.

Seamus Heaney. "Mid-term Break" and "Valediction" from *Poems 1965–1975* by Seamus Heaney. Copyright © 1980 by Seamus Heaney. Reprinted by permission of Farrar, Straus & Giroux, Inc. and Faber and Faber Ltd.

Anthony Hecht. "More Light! More Light!" and "The Dover Bitch" from *The Hard Hours* by Anthony Hecht. Copyright © 1990 by Anthony E. Hecht. Reprinted by permission of Alfred A. Knopf, Inc.

Ernest Hemingway. "A Clean Well-Lighted Place" from *Winner Take Nothing* by Ernest Hemingway. Copyright © 1933 by Charles Scribner's Sons. Copyright renewed © 1961 by Mary Hemingway. Reprinted with permission of Scribner, a division of Simon & Schuster.

Amy Hempel. "In the Cemetery Where Al Jolson is Buried" from *Reasons to Live*. Copyright © 1985 by Amy Hempel. Reprinted by permission of Darhansof & Verrill Agency, New York.

Linda Hogan. "First Light" from *Savings* by Linda Hogan, Coffee House Press, 1988. Copyright © 1988 by Linda Hogan. Reprinted by permission of the publisher.

M. Carl Holman. "Mr. Z." Reprinted by permission of Mariella A. Holman.

A.E. Housman. "When I Was One-and-Twenty," "To an Athlete Dying Young," and "Terence, This Is Stupid Stuff" from *The Collected Poems of A.E. Housman* by A.E. Housman. Copyright © 1939, 1940, 1965 by Henry Holt and Company, Inc. Copyright © 1967 by Robert E. Symons. Reprinted by permission of Henry Holt and Company, Inc.

Pam Houston. "How to Talk to a Hunter" from *Cowboys Are My Weakness* by Pam Houston. Copyright © 1992 by Pam Houston. Reprinted by permission of W.W. Norton & Company, Inc.

Langston Hughes. "Dream Deferred" ("Harlem") from *The Panther and the Lash* by Langston Hughes. Copyright © 1951 by Langston Hughes. "Same in Blues," from *Collected Poems* by Langston Hughes. Copyright © 1994 by the Estate of Langston Hughes. Reprinted by permission of Alfred A. Knopf, Inc.

David Henry Hwang. "M. Butterfly." Copyright © David Henry Hwang. Copyright © 1985, 1987, 1988 by David Henry Hwang. Used by permission of Dutton Signet, a division of Penguin Books USA Inc.

June Jordan. "Memo." Copyright © June Jordan. Reprinted by permission of the author.

James Joyce. "Araby" from *Dubliners* by James Joyce. Copyright © 1916 by B.W. Huebsch. Definitive text copyright © 1967 by the Estate of James Joyce. Used by permission of Viking Penguin, a division of Penguin Books USA Inc.

Lawrence Kearney. "Father Answers His Adversaries" from *Kingdom Come*. Copyright © 1980 by Lawrence Kearney. Reprinted by permission of the University Press of New England.

X.J. Kennedy. "Nude Descending a Staircase." Copyright © 1960 by X.J. Kennedy. Originally published in *Nude Descending a Staircase*. Published by Doubleday & Co. "First Confession" and "Ars Poetica," from *Cross Ties* (1985) by X.J. Kennedy. Copyright © 1969 by X.J. Kennedy. Reprinted by permission of Curtis Brown Ltd. "A Visit from St. Sigmund," first published in *Light: A Magazine of Light Verse*. Copyright © 1993 by X.J. Kennedy. Reprinted by permission of the author.

Liu Kexiang. "Descendents of Myths" from *Anthology of Modern Chinese Poetry*, edited by Michelle Yeh. Published by Yale University Press, 1992. Reprinted by permission of the publisher.

Martin Luther King Jr. "Letter from Birmingham Jail" from *Why We Can't Wait* by Martin Luther King Jr. Reprinted by arrangement with The Heirs to the Estate of Martin Luther King Jr. c/o The Joan Daves Agency as agent for the proprietor. Copyright © 1963 by Martin Luther King Jr. Copyright © renewed 1991 by Coretta Scott King.

Carolyn Kizer. "Bitch" from *Mermaids in the Basement* by Carolyn Kizer. Copyright © 1984 by Carolyn Kizer. Reprinted by permission of Copper Canyon Press, PO Box 271, Port Townsend, WA 98368.

Etheridge Knight. "Hard Rock Returns to Prison from the Hospital for the Criminal Insane" from *The Essential Etheridge Knight* by Etheridge Knight. Copyright © 1986. Reprinted by permission of the University of Pittsburgh Press.

Maxine Kumin. "Woodchucks" from *Selected Poems 1960–1990* by Maxine Kumin. Copyright © 1972 by Maxine Kumin. Reprinted by permission of W.W. Norton & Company, Inc.

Philip Larkin. "Aubade" and "This be The Verse" from *Collected Poems* by Philip Larkin. Copyright © 1988, 1989 by the Estate of Philip Larkin. Reprinted by permission of Farrar, Straus & Giroux, Inc. and Faber and Faber, Inc.

D.H. Lawrence. "The Odour of Chrysanthemums" from *The Complete Short Stories of D.H. Lawrence* by D.H. Lawrence. Copyright © 1933 by the Estate of D.H. Lawrence. Renewed © 1961 by Angelo Ravagli and C.M. Weekley, Executors of the Estate of Frieda Lawrence. Used by permission of Viking Penguin, a division of Penguin Books USA Inc.

Ursula K. Le Guin. "The Ones Who Walk Away from Omelas." Copyright © 1973 by Ursula K. Le Guin. First appeared in *New Dimensions 3*. Reprinted by permission of the author and the author's agent, Virginia Kidd.

Denise Levertov. "The Mutes" from *Poems 1960–1967*. Copyright © 1966 by Denise Levertov. "Protesters" from *Evening Train*. Copyright © 1992 by Denise Levertov. Reprinted by permission of New Directions Publishing Corp.

C. Day-Lewis. "Come Live with me and be my love" from *Collected Poems* (1954). Copyright © C. Day-Lewis. Reprinted by permission on behalf of the Estate of C. Day-Lewis and Peters Fraser & Dunlop (Writers' Agents).

Li-Young Lee. "Between Seasons," from *Rose* by Li-Young Lee. Copyright © 1986 by Li-Young Lee. Reprinted with the permission of Boa Editions, Ltd. 260 East Ave., Brockport NY 14604.

Duane Locke. "Out in the Pasture." Copyright © 1995 by Duane Locke. Originally published in magazine Midwest Quarterly; reprinted in *Watching Wisteria*. Reprinted by permission of the author.

Barry Holstrun Lopez. "Winter Count 1973: Geese They Flew Over" from *Winter Count*. Copyright © 1981 by Barry Holstrun Lopez. Reprinted by permission of Sterling Lord Literistic, Inc.

Audre Lorde. "Power" from *The Black Unicorn, Poems* by Audre Lorde. Copyright © 1978 by Audre Lorde. Reprinted by permission of W.W. Norton & Company, Inc.

Katharyn Howd Machan. "Hazel Tells LaVerne" from *Light Year 1985*. Copyright © 1977 by Katharine Howd Machan. Reprinted by permission of the author.

Elaine Magarrell. "The Joy of Cooking" from *Sometime the Cow Kick Your Head, Light Year 88/89*. Reprinted by permission of the author.

Bernard Malamud. "Idiots First" from *Idiots First* by Bernard Malamud. Copyright © 1963 by Bernard Malamud. Copyright renewed © 1991 by Ann Malamud. Reprinted by permission of Farrar, Straus & Giroux, Inc.

Katherine McAlpine. "Plus C'est la Même Chose." First published in *The Nation*. Copyright © Katherine McAlpine. Reprinted by permission of the author.

Claude McKay. "If We Must Die" from *Selected Poems of Claude McKay*. Copyright © 1979. Reprinted by permission of The Archives of Claude McKay. Carl Cowl, Administrator.

William McKibben. "A Path of More Resistance" from *The End of Nature* by William McKibben. Copyright © 1989 by William McKibben. Reprinted by permission of Random House.

James Alan McPherson. "A Loaf of Bread" from *Elbow Room* by James Alan McPherson. Copyright © 1977 by James Alan McPherson. Reprinted by permission of Little, Brown and Company.

Peter Meinke. "Advice to My Son" from *Trying to Surprise God* by Peter Meinke. Copyright © 1981 by Peter Meinke. Reprinted by permission of the University of Pittsburgh Press.

James Merrill. "Casual Wear" from *Late Settings*, 1985. Reprinted by permission of the Estate of James Merrill.

Robert Mezey. "My Mother" from *The Door Standing Open* by Robert Mezey. Reprinted by permission of the author.

Edna St. Vincent Millay. "Sonnet XXX of Fatal Interview" by Edna St. Vincent Millay. From *Collected Poems*, HarperCollins. Copyright © 1931, 1956 by Edna St. Vincent Millay and Norma Millay Ellis. All rights reserved. Reprinted by permission of Elizabeth Barnett, literary executor.

Arthur Miller. Entire text of *Death of a Salesman.* Copyright © 1949; renewed © 1977 by Arthur Miller. Used by permission of Viking Penguin, a division of Penguin Books USA Inc.

Jessica Mitford. Excerpt from pages 15–21 in *The American Way of Death* by Jessica Mitford. Copyright © 1963, 1978 by Jessica Mitford. Reprinted by permission of Jessica Mitford. All rights reserved.

Felix Mnthali. "The Stranglehold of English Lit" from *Penguin Book of Modern African Poetry,* 3e. Copyright © Felix Mnthali. Reprinted by permission of Penguin Ltd. and the author.

Bharati Mukherjee. "Orbiting" from *The Middleman and Other Stories.* Copyright © 1988 by Bharati Mukherjee. Reprinted by permission of Grove/Atlantic, Inc. and Penguin Books Canada Limited.

Susan Musgrave. "Right through the Heart" from *Tarts and Muggers: Poems New and Selected* by Susan Musgrave. Copyright © 1982 by Susan Musgrave. Reprinted by permission of the author.

Taslima Nasrin. "Things Cheaply Had." *The New Yorker,* October 9, 1995. English translation copyright © 1995 by Carolyne Wright. Reprinted by permission.

Barbara Neely. "Spilled Salt" from *Breaking Ice: An Anthology of Contemporary African American Fiction,* edited by Terry McMillan. Viking Penguin 1990. Copyright © 1990 by Barbara Neely. No part of this material may be reproduced in whole or part without the express written permission of the author or her agent.

Pablo Neruda. "The Dead Woman" from *The Captain's Verses.* Copyright © 1972 by Pablo Neruda and Donald D. Walsh. Reprinted by permission of New Directions Publishing Corp.

Kathleen Norris. "The Ignominy of Living." *The New Yorker,* May 29, 1989. Copyright © 1989 by Kathleen Norris. Reprinted by permission of *The New Yorker.*

Edna O'Brien. "Sin." First published by *The New Yorker.* Copyright © 1994 by Edna O'Brien. Reprinted with the permission of The Wylie Agency, Inc.

Tim O'Brien. "On the Rainy River" from *The Things They Carried.* Copyright © 1990 by Tim O'Brien. Reprinted by permission of Houghton Mifflin Co./Seymour Lawrence. All rights reserved.

Flannery O'Connor. "Good Country People" from *A Good Man Is Hard to Find and Other Stories.* Copyright © 1955 by Flannery O'Connor; renewed 1983 by Regina O'Connor. Reprinted by permission of Harcourt Brace & Company.

Frank O'Connor. "My Oedipus Complex" from *Collected Stories* by Frank O'Connor. Copyright © 1950 by Frank O'Connor. Reprinted by permission of Alfred A. Knopf, Inc. and Writer's House, Inc. as agent for the proprietor.

Sharon Olds. "Sex Without Love" and "The Victims" from *The Dead and the Living* by Sharon Olds. Copyright © 1983 by Sharon Olds. Reprinted by permission of Alfred A. Knopf, Inc.

Mary Oliver. "The Black Walnut Tree" from *Twelve Moons* by Mary Oliver. Copyright © 1978 by Mary Oliver. First appeared in *The Ohio Review.* By permission of Little, Brown and Company. "When Death Comes" from *New and Selected Poems* by Mary Oliver. Copyright © 1992 by Mary Oliver. Used by permission of Beacon Press, Boston.

Eric Ormsby. "Address of a Grandmother." *The New Yorker,* November 16, 1992. Copyright © Eric Ormsby. Reprinted by permission of the author.

George Orwell. "Shooting an Elephant" from *Shooting an Elephant and Other Stories* by George Orwell. Copyright © 1950 by Sonia Brownell Orwell and renewed 1978 by Sonia Pitt-Rivers. Reprinted by permission of Harcourt Brace & Company. Copyright © Mark Hamilton as the literary executor of the estate of the late Sonia Brownell Orwell and Martin Secker and Warburg Ltd.

Wilfred Owen. "Dulce et decorum est" from *The Collected Poems of Wilfred Owen,* edited by C. Day Lewis. Copyright © 1963 by Chatto & Windus, Ltd. Published by New Directions Publishing Company and The Hogarth Press. Reprinted by permission of New Directions Publishing Corporation, the Estate of Wilfred Owen, and Random Century Limited.

Dorothy Parker. "One Perfect Rose" from *Portable Dorothy Parker* by Dorothy Parker. Copyright © 1929; renewed © 1957 by Dorothy Parker. Introduction by Brendan Gill. Used by permission of Viking Penguin, a division of Penguin Books USA Inc.

Molly Peacock. "Our Room" from *Raw Heaven* by Molly Peacock. Copyright © 1984 by Molly Peacock. "Say you love me" from *Take Heart* by Molly Peacock. Copyright © 1989 by Molly Peacock. Reprinted by permission of Random House, Inc.

Marge Piercy. "Cats like angels," "The low road," and "The long death" from *The Moon Is Always Female* by Marge Piercy. Copyright © 1980 by Marge Piercy. Reprinted by permission of Alfred A. Knopf, Inc.

Luigi Pirandello. "War" from *The Medal and Other Stories* by Luigi Pirandello. Reprinted by permission of the Pirandello Estate and Toby Cole, Agent.

Sylvia Plath. "Daddy" from *Ariel* by Sylvia Plath. Copyright © 1963 by Ted Hughes. Copyright renewed. Reprinted by permission of HarperCollins Publishers, Inc. and Faber & Faber, Ltd.

Dudley Randall. "Ballad of Birmingham." Reprinted by permission of Broadside Press.

Henry Reed. "Naming of Parts" from *Henry Reed's Collected Poems* edited by Jon Stallworthy (1991). Copyright © 1991 by The Executor of Henry Reed's Estate. Reprinted by permission of Oxford University Press.

Alistair Reid. "Curiosity" from *Weathering* (Dutton). Copyright © 1959 Alistair Reid. Originally published in *The New Yorker* magazine. Reprinted by permission of *The New Yorker*.

Otto Reinert. Notes on Shakespeare's *Othello*. Copyright © 1964. Reprinted by permission of the author.

Adrienne Rich. "Living in Sin" from *Collected Early Poems: 1950–1970* by Adrienne Rich. Copyright © 1993, 1955 by Adrienne Rich. Reprinted by permission of the author and W.W. Norton & Company, Inc.

Theodore Roethke. "Elegy for Jane." Copyright © 1950 by Theodore Roethke. "I Know a Woman." Copyright © 1954 by Theodore Roethke. "My Papa's Waltz." Copyright © 1942 by Hearst Magazines, Inc. From *The Collected Poems of Theodore Roethke* by Theodore Roethke. Used by permission of Doubleday, a division of Bantam Doubleday Dell Publishing Group, Inc.

Muriel Rukeyser. "Myth" from *Out of Silence.* Copyright © 1992 William L. Rukeyser. Triquarterly Books, Evanston, IL. Reprinted by permission of William L. Rukeyser.

Ira Sadoff. "Nazis" from *Emotional Traffic* by Ira Sadoff. Copyright © 1989 by Ira Sadoff. Reprinted by permission of David R. Godine, Publisher, Inc.

Sappho. "With his Venom." *Sappho: A New Translation* by Mary Barnard. Copyright © 1958 The Regents of the University of California. Copyright © renewed 1984 Mary Barnard. Reprinted by permission of the University of California Press.

William Saroyan. "Five Ripe Pears" from *The Saroyan Special* (1977) by William Saroyan. Permission granted by the Trustees of Leland Stanford University.

May Sarton. "AIDS" and "The Silence Now" from *Collected Poems 1930–1993* by May Sarton. Copyright © 1988 by May Sarton. Reprinted with permission of W.W. Norton & Company, Inc.

Anne Sexton. "The Farmer's Wife" from *To Bedlam and Part Way Back.* Copyright © 1960 by Anne Sexton, renewed © 1988 by Linda G. Sexton. "The Starry Night" from *All My Pretty Ones.* Copyright © 1962 by Anne Sexton; renewed © 1990 by Linda G. Sexton. "Cinderella" from *Transformations.* Copyright © 1971 by Anne Sexton. Reprinted by permission of Houghton Mifflin Company. All rights reserved.

Irwin Shaw. "The Girls in Their Summer Dresses" by Irwin Shaw. Reprinted by permission of The Irwin Shaw Literary Estate.

Stevie Smith. "Not Waving But Drowning," "To Carry the Child," and "The Frog Prince" from *Collected Poems of Stevie Smith.* Copyright © 1972 by Stevie Smith. Reprinted by permission of New Directions Publishing Corp.

W.D. Snodgrass. "April Inventory" from *Heart's Needle* by W.D. Snodgrass. Copyright © 1959 by William Snodgrass. Reprinted by permission of Alfred A. Knopf, Inc. "Matisse: The Red Studio" from *After Experience* by W.D. Snodgrass. Copyright © 1968 by W.D. Snodgrass. Reprinted by permission of the author.

Robert C. Solomon. Excerpt from pages 97–103, chapter titled "Love Stories," in *About Love* by Robert C. Solomon. Copyright © 1988 by Robert C. Solomon. Reprinted by permission of Melanie Jackson Agency.

Sophocles. "Antigone" from *Sophocles, The Oedipus Cycle: An English Version* by Dudley Fitts and Robert Fitzgerald. Copyright © 1939 by Harcourt Brace & Company and renewed 1967 by Dudley Fitts and Robert Fitzgerald. Reprinted by permission of the publisher. "Oedipus Rex" from *Sophocles, The Oedipus Cycle: An English Version* by Dudley Fitts and Robert Fitzgerald. Copyright © 1939 by Harcourt Brace & Company. Renewed 1977 by Cornelia Fitts and Robert Fitzgerald. Reprinted by permission of the publisher. Caution: All rights, including professional, amateur, motion picture, recitation, lecturing, performance, public reading, radio broadcasting, and television are strictly reserved. Inquiries on all rights should be addressed to Harcourt Brace & Company, Permissions Dept., Orlando, Fl. 32887-6777.

Helen Sorrells. "From a Correct Address in a Suburb of a Major City" from *Seeds as They Fall.* Published in 1971 by Vanderbilt University Press. Reprinted by permission of the publisher.

Gary Soto. "Oranges" from *New and Selected Poems* by Gary Soto. Copyright © 1995 by Gary Soto. Published by Chronicle Books, San Francisco. Reprinted by permission of the publisher and the author.

Art Spiegelman. "Prisoner on the Hell Planet" from *Maus: A Survivor's Tale* by Art Spiegelman. Copyright © 1973, 1980, 1981, 1982, 1983, 1984, 1985, 1986 by Art Spiegelman. Reprinted by permission of Pantheon Books, a division of Random House, Inc.

Elizabeth Spires. "Easter Sunday 1955" from *Worlding* by Elizabeth Spires. Copyright © 1995 by Elizabeth Spires. Reprinted by permission of the author and W.W. Norton & Company, Inc.

Wallace Stevens. "Sunday Morning" from *Collected Poems* by Wallace Stevens. Copyright © 1923 and renewed 1951 by Wallace Stevens. Reprinted by permission of Alfred A. Knopf, Inc.

Nancy Sullivan. "Number 1 by Jackson Pollock (1948)" from *The History of the World as Pictures* by Nancy Sullivan, University of Missouri Press. Copyright © 1965 by Nancy Sullivan. Reprinted by permission of the author.

Dylan Thomas. "Fern Hill," "Do Not Go Gentle Into That Good Night" from *The Poems of Dylan Thomas.* Copyright © 1952 by Dylan Thomas. Reprinted by permission of New Directions Publishing Corp. and David Higham Associates Ltd.

Lewis Thomas. "The Iks" from *The Lives of a Cell* by Lewis Thomas. Copyright © 1973 by The Massachusetts Medical Society. Used by permission of Viking Penguin, a division of Penguin Books USA Inc.

James Thurber. "The Greatest Man in the World" from *The Middle-Aged Man on The Flying Trapeze* (Harper & Row). Copyright © 1935 James Thurber. Copyright © 1963 Helen W. Thurber and Rosemary A. Thurber. Reprinted by permission of James Thurber Literary Properties.

Leo Tolstoy. "The Death of Ivan Ilych" from *The Death of Ivan Ilych and Other Stories* by Leo Tolstoy. Translated by Louise and Aylmer Maude. Copyright © 1925. Used by permission of Oxford University Press, Inc.

Su Tung-P'o. "On the birth of his son" from *Translations from the Chinese* by Arthur Waley. Copyright © 1919 and renewed 1947 by Arthur Waley. Reprinted by permission of Alfred A. Knopf Inc.

Jill Tweedie. "The Experience." Copyright © 1979 by Jill Tweedie. Reprinted by permission of Curtis Brown, Ltd.

Stephanie Vaughn. "Other Women" from *Sweet Talk* by Stephanie Vaughn. Copyright © 1978, 1981, 1990 by Stephanie Vaughn. Reprinted by permission of Georges Borchardt, Inc. for the author.

Alice Walker. "Everyday Use" from *In Love and Trouble: Stories of Black Women* by Alice Walker. Copyright © 1973 by Alice Walker. Reprinted by permission of Harcourt Brace & Company.

Richard Wilbur. "A Late Aubade" from *Walking to Sleep: New Poems and Translations.* Copyright © 1968 by Richard Wilbur. Originally appeared in *The New Yorker.* "Museum Piece" from *Ceremony and Other Poems.* Copyright © 1978 by Richard Wilbur. Reprinted by permission of Harcourt Brace & Company.

Tennessee Williams. *The Glass Menagerie.* Copyright © 1945 by Tennessee Williams and Edwina D. Williams. Renewed 1973 by Tennessee Williams. Reprinted by permission of Random House, Inc.

William Carlos Williams. "Tract" and "The Great Figure" from *Collected Poems: 1909–1939,* Volume I. Copyright © 1938 by New Directions Publishing Corp. Reprinted by permission of New Directions Publishing Corp.

August Wilson. "Two Trains Running" by August Wilson. Copyright © 1992 by August Wilson. Used by permission of Dutton Signet, a division of Penguin Books USA Inc.

Virginia Woolf. "Shakespeare's Sister" from *A Room of One's Own* by Virginia Woolf. Copyright © 1929 by Harcourt Brace & Company and renewed 1957 by Leonard Woolf. Reprinted by permission of the publisher.

Richard Wright. "The Man Who Lived Underground" from *Eight Men* by Richard Wright. Copyright © 1940, 1961 by Richard Wright. Copyright renewed 1989 by Ellen Wright. Reprinted by permission of HarperCollins Publishers, Inc. "Between the World and Me." By permission of Ellen Wright.

W.B. Yeats. "Easter 1916," "Leda and the Swan," and "Sailing into Byzantium" from *The Collected Works of W.B.Yeats, Volume 1: The Poems.* Revised and edited by Richard J. Finneran. Copyright © 1928 by Macmillan Publishing Company. Copyright renewed © 1956 by Georgie Yeats. Reprinted with the permission of Simon & Schuster.

Yevgeny Yevtushenko. "I Would Like" from *Yevgeny Yevtushenko: The Collected Poems 1952–1990*, edited by Albert C. Todd. Copyright © 1991 by Henry Holt and Company, Inc. Reprinted by permission of Henry Holt and Company, Inc. "People" from pages 85–86 from *Yevtushenko: Selected Poems* translated by Robin Milner-Gulland and Peter Levi (Penguin Books, 1962). Copyright © Robin Milner-Gulland and Peter Levi, 1962. Reprinted by permission of Penguin UK.

ART CREDITS

Pp. 19–21: *Hypothetical reconstruction of the interior of the Globe Theatre in the days of Shakespeare; A seventeenth-century French box stage;* and *The Dionysius Theatre in Athens* (photo by Norman Currie). Courtesy of the Bettmann Archive, Inc. *Interior of the Swan Theatre, London, 1596* (by DeWitt): Courtesy of Culver Pictures, Inc.

P. 58: *"Child in a Straw Hat,"* 1886 by Mary Cassatt, oil on canvas. Copyright © 1997 by the Board of Trustees, National Gallery of Art, Washington, Collection of Mr. and Mrs. Paul Mellon. Courtesy of the National Gallery of Art, Washington, D.C.

P. 310: *"Adam and Eve (Original Sin and the Fall from Terrestial Paradise),"* 1509–10 by Michelangelo Buonarroti. Sistine Chapel, Vatican Palace, Vatican State. Courtesy of Alinari/Art Resource, New York.

P. 664: *"At Connie's Inn,"* 1974 by Romare Bearden, collage and mixed media on Masonite. Brooklyn Museum of Art, John B. Woodward Memorial Fund. Courtesy of The Brooklyn Museum.

P. 994: *"Room in New York,"* 1932 by Edward Hopper. Oil on canvas. From the collection of the Sheldon Memorial Art Gallery, University of Nebraska–Lincoln, F.M. Hall Collection. Courtesy of the Sheldon Memorial Art Gallery.

P. 1150: *"The Dead Mother,"* 1895 by Edvard Munch. Kunsthalle, Bremen, Germany. Courtesy of Foto Marburg/Art Resource, New York.

Index of Authors and Titles